ADMINISTRATIVE LAW

THE AMERICAN PUBLIC LAW SYSTEM

CASES AND MATERIALS

Fifth Edition

By

Jerry L. Mashaw
Sterling Professor of Law
Yale University

Richard A. Merrill
Daniel Caplin Professor of Law
University of Virginia

Peter M. Shane
Joseph S. Platt-Porter, Wright, Morris and Arthur Professor of Law
The Ohio State University
Moritz College of Law

AMERICAN CASEBOOK SERIES®

Mat # 40109060

610 Opperman Drive
P.O. Box 64526
St. Paul, MN 55164–0526
1–800–328–9352

Printed in the United States of America

ISBN 0–314–14425–0

TEXT IS PRINTED ON 10% POST CONSUMER RECYCLED PAPER

For Jay and Mark,
for Patty and John,
and for Martha and Beth

*

Preface to the Fifth Edition

Neither teaching nor learning American administrative law is a straightforward enterprise. Doctrine is enunciated in general terms; yet, specific administrative programs operate within highly variable contexts. Doctrinal conceptualism without context is an arid exercise, but the examination of concrete questions of agency policy or procedure must be informed by an understanding of the broader issues of legality and institutional legitimation that the traditional doctrinal categories negotiate. These materials thus compromise between organization by doctrinal category and organization by case study of specific agency tasks or functions. The "compromise" is not so schizophrenic as it may sound. Case studies present doctrinal issues, and doctrinal analysis can often be pursued through judicial decisions reviewing the actions of a single agency.

Administrative programs are not the only "context" in play. Administrative law is intimately connected to legislative action. Administrative agencies operate in a world of statutes, whose creator, Congress, perceives administration to be largely an extension of the legislative formulation of policy. Nor is Congress the only political principal competing for agency attention. Presidents appoint agency heads and make them part of their administrations. Modern presidents have taken this relationship increasingly seriously and have created substantial executive infrastructure in an attempt to monitor and control the far-flung activities of federal officials. The institutional and legal instruments through which Congress and the President compete to direct administrative action and the shape of administrative law have become an essential part of the study of administrative law itself.

Administrative agencies are also subject to monitoring and direction by courts through a system of judicial review of administrative action whose decisions have long been the core of administrative law study. But traditional issues of remedy (encapsulated in doctrinal categories like standing, reviewability, governmental and official immunities, primary jurisdiction, and the like) are also linked to a broader remedial system that further defines the citizen's bundle of rights in the modern administrative state. Private rights and public law have many points of contact and continuous reciprocal influence, intersections that have largely been ignored by traditional texts. This is particularly true in modern federal administrative law, which has partially colonized domains formerly left to state common law, which relies on citizen enforcement of many regulatory norms, and which confides administration of many public programs to public and private entities outside the reach of traditional forms of judicial review.

The broader context of administrative action encompasses more than political and legal controls on agency action. Public oversight, complaint, and mobilization are potent factors in any agency's environment. Interest group and individual access to information about agency policies and processes is structured by a series of requirements for transparent operation and information revelation. Open government is facilitated by a free press and modern information technologies. But the almost ubiquitous availability of government information is in substantial part a function of legal requirements that, like the law regulating the government's compulsory access to privately held information, becomes a part of the legal environment within which the administrative lawyer works.

Finally, administrative law and agency action must be understood within their historical context. The form and function of administrative institutions in the United States have changed dramatically over the past two centuries. Social demands create constant experimentation with new forms of public action, which then give rise to anxieties about the legitimacy of those actions. These concerns press administrative law in new directions as it attempts to balance the need for governmental efficacy against the equally pressing need to maintain the rule of law and the protection of individual rights. These political and legal struggles influence and are influenced by the intellectual climate of the times, the visions of governance and legality that capture the legal and the political imagination.

Major changes have taken place in the arena of federal administrative law, for example, in just the three decades since the publication of the first edition of this book in 1975. The enthusiasm of the 1960s and early 1970s for federal regulation as a strategy of social management, with prescriptive administrative rulemaking as its primary legal technique, has waned. Command and control regulation finds itself in competition with demands for deregulation and for the use of conciliatory processes and market-like regulatory incentives. Central executive oversight has assumed increased importance as cost-benefit analysis has been institutionalized within agencies and made subject to the supervision of the Office of Management and Budget. The ambiguous proceduralist impulses of the U.S. Court of Appeals for the District of Columbia Circuit have been sharply constrained by the Supreme Court, which has shown reluctance either to "constitutionalize" administrative procedure or to exercise a creative interpretive role in its development. What to many seemed an emerging federal common law of remedies "implied" under federal regulatory statutes has yielded to renewed concern for primary administrative jurisdiction and for the prerogatives of both Congress and states. And separation of powers theory has experienced a reinvigoration few would have predicted in the early 1970s. This is a vital field subject to rapid change. Hence, the necessity to update once again.

The structure of this edition remains essentially unchanged from the third edition. We begin by introducing the basic building blocks of administrative law and the structure of administrative agencies, and put these foundational concepts in the context of the evolution of American administrative institutions and evolving ideas about the nature and function of administrative law. These are the tasks of Chapter 1.

We next (Chapters 2 and 3) consider the subject of political control, the legal principles governing the relationship of administrators to the elected branches–Congress and the President. This is an arena of constant action, considerable public interest, and sparse legal principle. Our interest is in the techniques of legal-institutional design that have been developed within the broad contours of legal doctrine.

Chapters 4 and 5 are devoted to the two primary formal avenues of agency lawmaking and implementation–adjudication and rulemaking. Regardless of current enthusiasms for deregulation and markets, these remain lively arenas of legal dispute, political conflict, and administrative experimentation. Many of the crucial battles for occupational safety and health, environmental protection, safe foods and drugs and fair treatment of claimants before bureaucracies of mass administrative justice are waged in terms of administrative law's demands for orderly, open, and reasoned processes of agency adjudication and rulemaking. Honoring these demands while enabling effective implementation of public policy remains the central challenge of American public administration.

Chapter 6 examines the issues raised by the reciprocal demands of government and private actors for information held by the other. Government was a public information economy long before the private sector became post-industrial. The legal principles here reflect both the long-standing tension between individual privacy and governmental efficacy and the contemporary reality that knowledge is indeed power.

Chapters 7 through 9 cover public law remedies. Standard forms of judicial review of agency action–once virtually synonymous with the whole of administrative law–are treated in Chapter 7. But modern public law litigants seek more from government and each other than traditional judicial review can provide. Chapter 8, therefore, looks at damage actions against the federal government and federal government officials. It is followed, in Chapter 9, by an exploration of beneficiary suits, premised on federal regulatory or benefits legislation, but prosecuted against private parties or state and local public entities. The chapter, and our study of the American administrative state, concludes with a look at the impact of federal public administrative law on pre-existing federal and state common law.

Our subject is large, varied, dynamic, and consequential. Administrative law structures much of what government does. And, as has been impressed on us once again as we prepared this fifth edition, American government does a lot.

JLM
RAM
PMS

New Haven
Charlottesville
Pittsburgh
May, 2003

*

Acknowledgements

The list of University of Virginia, Yale, Iowa, and Pittsburgh law students who assisted us during the life of this book is long. Many who have been exposed in class to earlier versions have contributed by calling our attention to errors of both substance and style, by supplying answers to questions that demand many minds to resolve, and by suggesting the issues that should be examined. Authors of any legal coursebook that goes through multiple editions also owe a considerable debt to generations of research assistants who have struggled with them through proofreading, cite-checking, and occasional periods of despair. Those who worked specifically on the Fifth Edition include Mary DeMing Fan, Dean Kawamoto, Jeffrey Manns, Jon Michaels, and Michael Shumsky, of Yale; Michael Brunet, Catherine DeRoever, and Kris Shepard, of the University of Virginia; and Beverly Betel and Jennifer Ray of the University of Pittsburgh. Our distinguished alumni of earlier editions include David Baker, Lynn Baker, Mark Barnes, Key Bartolo, Peter Benda, Victor Diaz, Roland DuBois, Vernon Dunbar, Daniel Esty, Kevin Gallagher, Mary Gilliberti, Rob Hawkins, Brent Heberlee, Kathy Hess, Christopher Kennedy, Alvin Lorman, Anne McClintock, Mac Norton, Janet Mahairas Pollan, James Ritter, Karen Rosenthal, Peter Swire, and Martin Wisott. We also thank numerous colleagues, at our own and other schools, who contributed to the preparation of these materials through criticism, suggestion, and classroom use. To all these we express our deep appreciation.

None of the foregoing friends and supporters, nor others unnamed, bear responsibility for any errors that remain in the final product or, of course, for its underlying concept. We acknowledge with appreciation the following authors, publishers, and journals which have generously granted permission to reprint excerpts from their publications:

American University Law Review: Harold H. Bruff, *On the Constitutional Status of the Administrative Agencies,* 36 Am.U.L.Rev. 491 (1987).

Arizona Law Review: Morton Rosenberg, *Presidential Control of Agency Rulemaking,* 23 Ariz.L.Rev. 1199 (1981); Peter M. Shane, *Presidential Regulatory Oversight and the Separation of Powers: The Legality of Executive Order No. 12,291,* 23 Ariz.L.Rev. 1235 (1981). Copyright © 1981 by The Arizona Board of Regents. Reprinted by permission.

Arkansas Law Review: Peter M. Shane, *Political Accountability in a System of Checks and Balances: The Case of Presidential Review of Rulemaking,* 48 Ark.L.Rev. 161 (1995).

Boston University Law Review: Jerry L. Mashaw, *Administrative Due Process: The Quest for a Dignitary Theory,* 61 Boston U.L.Rev. 885 (1981).

Brigham Young University Law Review: Gregory K. Orme, *Tucker Act Jurisdiction Over Breach of Trust Claims,* 1979 B.Y.U.L.Rev. 855.

The Brookings Institution: SHEP MELNICK, REGULATION AND THE COURTS (1983). Copyright © by the Brookings Institution, Washington, D.C.

California Law Review: Robert W. Hamilton, *Procedures for the Adoption of Rules of General Applicability: The Need for Procedural Innovation in Administrative Rulemaking,* 60 Cal.L.Rev. 1276 (1972). Copyright © 1972, California Law Review, Inc.

Carolina Academic Press: PETER M. SHANE & HAROLD H. BRUFF, THE LAW OF PRESIDENTIAL POWER (1988).

Catholic University Law Review: William S. Fields, *The Enigma of Bureaucratic Accountability*, 43 Cath.U.L.Rev. 505 (1994). © 1994 by The Catholic University of America and William S. Fields.

Chicago–Kent Law Review: Peter L. Strauss, *Presidential Rulemaking,* 72 Ch.-Kent L. Rev. 965, 984–86 (1997). © 1997 IIT Chi.–Kent College of Law.

Columbia Law Review: Peter L. Strauss, *Rules, Adjudications, and Other Sources of Law in an Executive Department: Reflections on the Interior Department's Administration of the Mining Law,* 74 Colum.L.Rev. 1231 (1974). Copyright © 1974 by the Directors for the Columbia Law Review Association, Inc. All rights reserved.

Cornell Law Review: Peter L. Strauss, *Formal and Functional Approaches to Separation-of-Powers Questions—A Foolish Inconsistency?,* 72 Corn.L.Rev. 488 (1987). Copyright © 1987 by Cornell University and reprinted by permission of Fred B. Rothman & Company. All rights reserved.

Duke Law Journal: Michael Asimow, *Nonlegislative Rulemaking and Regulatory Reform,* 1985 Duke L.J. 381; John Graham, *The Failure of Agency-forcing: The Regulation of Airborne Carcinogens under Section 112 of the Clean Air Act,* 1985 Duke L. J. 100. © 1985 by the Duke Law Journal and John D. Graham.

Ecology Law Quarterly: John Dwyer, *The Pathology of Symbolic Legislation,* 17 Ecology L.Q. 233 (1990).

Environmental Law: William P. Rodgers, *Judicial Review of Risk Assessments: The Role of Decision Theory in Unscrambling the Benzene Decision,* 11 Envtl.L. 301 (1981).

Environmental Law Reporter: Peter M. Shane, *Returning Separation of Powers Analysis to its Normative Roots: The Constitutionality* of Qui Tam *Actions and Other Private Suits to Enforce Civil Penalties*, 30 Env. L. Rep. 11,081 (2000). © 2000 Environmental Law Institute.

Federal Law Review: Glen O. Robinson, *Access to Government Information: The American Experience,* 14 Federal L.Rev. 35 (1983).

Georgetown Law Journal: Philip J. Harter, *Negotiating Regulations: A Cure for Malaise,* 71 Geo.L.J. 1 (1982). Reprinted with the permission of The Georgetown Law Journal Association; David B. Spence and Frank Cross, *A Public Choice Case for the Administrative State,* 89 Geo. L.J. 97 (2000). © 2000 by Georgetown Law Journal Association, David B. Spence, and Frank Cross.

George Washington Law Review: Harold M.Bruff, *Presidential Management of Agency Rulemaking,* 57 Geo.Wash.L.Rev. 533 (1989); Peter M. Shane, *Independent Policymaking and Presidential Power: A Constitutional Analysis,* 57 Geo.Wash.L.Rev. 596 (1989).

Harvard Law Review: Elana Kagan, Presidential Administration, 114 Harv. L. Rev. 2245, 2331–45 (2001). © 2001 by the Harvard Law Review Association; Thomas W. Merrill and Kathryn Tongue Watts, *Agency Rules with the Force of Law: The Original Convention,* 116 Harv. L. Rev. 467 (2002). © 2001 by the Harvard Law Review Association; Cass R. Sunstein, *Interpreting Statutes in the Regulatory State,* 103 Harv.L.Rev. 405 (1989) © 1979 by the Harvard Law Review Association; Kenneth E. Scott, *Standing in the Supreme Court—A Functional Analysis,* 86 Harv.L.Rev. 645 (1973). Copyright © 1973 by the Harvard Law Review Association.

Harvard University Press: JERRY MASHAW & DAVID HARFST, THE STRUGGLE FOR AUTO SAFETY (1990).

Journal of Law, Economics & Organization: Jerry L. Mashaw, *Pro–Delegation: Why Administrators Should Make Political Decisions,* 1 J.L. Econ. & Org. 81 (1985).

Michigan Law Review: Barry Boyer, *Alternatives to Administrative Trial–Type Hearings for Resolving Complex Scientific, Economic, and Social Issues,* 71 Mich.L.Rev. 111 (1972); Robert Burt, *Forcing Protection on Children and Their Parents: The Impact of* Wyman v. James, 69 Mich.L.Rev. 1259 (1971); Morton Rosenberg, *Beyond the Limits of Executive Power: Presidential Control of Agency Rulemaking Under Executive Order 12,291,* 80 Mich.L.Rev. 193 (1981).

Northwestern University Law Review: Ralph F. Fuchs, *Development and Diversification in Administrative Rule Making,* 72 Nw.U.L.Rev. 83 (1977). Reprinted by permission of the Northwestern University Law Review, Copyright © by Northwestern School of Law.

Regulation: Antonin Scalia, *The Freedom of Information Act Has No Clothes,* 6 Regulation 14 (Mar./Apr. 1982). Reprinted with permission of the American Enterprise Institute.

Supreme Court Review: Antonin Scalia, *Vermont Yankee: The APA, The D.C. Circuit, and The Supreme Court,* 1978 Sup.Ct.Rev. 345; Ralph Winter, *Judicial Review of Agency Decisions: The Labor Board and the Court,* 1968 Sup.Ct.Rev. 53. Reprinted with permission of the University of Chicago Press.

Tulane Law Review: Jerry L. Mashaw, *Constitutional Deregulation: Notes Toward a Public, Public Law,* 54 Tul.L.Rev. 849 (1980).

University of Chicago Law Review: Steven P. Croley, *White House Review of Agency Rulemaking: An Empirical Investigation,* 70 U. Chi. L.

Rev. ___ (2003). © 2003 University of Chicago; Kenneth Culp Davis, *The Liberalized Law of Standing,* 37 U.Chi.L.Rev. 450 (1970) © 1970 University of Chicago; Jerry L. Mashaw, *The Supreme Court's Due Process Calculus for Administrative Adjudication in Mathews v. Eldridge: Three Factors in Search of a Theory of Value,* 44 U.Chi.L.Rev. 28 (1976) © 1976 University of Chicago.

University of Colorado Law Review: David Engdahl, *Immunity and Accountability for Positive Governmental Wrongs,* 44 U.Colo.L.Rev. 1 (1972).

University of Florida Law Review: Jerry L. Mashaw, *Dignitary Process: A Political Psychology of Liberal Democratic Citizenship,* 39 U.Fla.L.Rev. 433 (1987). Reprinted with the permission of the University of Florida Law Review. Copyright © 1987.

University of Pennsylvania Law Review: Glen O. Robinson, *The Making of Administrative Policy: Another Look at Rulemaking and Adjudication and Administrative Procedure Reform,* 118 U.Pa.L.Rev. 485 (1970); Cass R. Sunstein, *Informational Regulation and Informational Standing:* Akins *and Beyond,* 147 U. Pa. L. Rev. 613, 645, 670–73 (1999). © 1999 University of Pennsylvania and Cass R. Sunstein.

University of Pittsburgh Law Review, Jerry L. Mashaw, *Reinventing Government and Regulatory Reform: Studies in the Neglect and Abuse of Administrative Law,* 57 U.Pitt.L.Rev. 405 (1996).

Virginia Law Review: Glen O. Robinson, *The Federal Communications Commission: An Essay on Regulatory Watchdogs,* 64 Va.L.Rev. 169 (1978).

The Washington Post: Robert G. Vaughn, *Our Government Stymies Open Government,* The Washington Post (July 1, 1984).

W. W. Norton and Company, Inc.: THEODORE LOWI, THE END OF LIBERALISM (1969).

Yale Journal on Regulation: Jerry L. Mashaw & David Harfst, *Regulation and Legal Culture: The Case of Motor Vehicle Safety,* 4 Yale J. on Reg. 258 (1987).

Yale Law Journal: Colin Diver, *The Optimal Precision of Administrative Rules,* 93 Yale L.J. 65 (1983); Morton C. Bernstein, *The NLRB's Adjudication–Rule Making Dilemma Under the Administrative Procedure Act,* 79 Yale L.J. 571 (1970); William Pedersen, *Formal Records and Informal Rulemaking,* 85 Yale L.J. 38 (1975). Reprinted by permission of The Yale Law Journal and Fred B. Rothman & Company.

Yale University Press: JERRY L. MASHAW, BUREAUCRATIC JUSTICE (1983).

Summary of Contents

Table of Contents

Table of Cases

The principal cases are in bold type. Cases cited or discussed in the text are roman type. References are to pages. Cases cited in principal cases and within other quoted materials are not included.

ADMINISTRATIVE LAW

THE AMERICAN PUBLIC LAW SYSTEM

CASES AND MATERIALS

Fifth Edition

*

Chapter 1

INTRODUCTION TO ADMINISTRATIVE LAW

A. WHAT (AND WHERE) IS ADMINISTRATIVE LAW?

Contemporary administrative law courses typically focus not only on the powers and decision making processes of federal (and sometimes state) administrative agencies, but also on the law governing those agencies' relationships to courts, legislatures, and elected executive officers. The reason for this expansive coverage is straightforward. To comprehend—and to participate effectively in—the nonjudicial law and policy making operations of government requires familiarity with more than agency procedures. One must also be aware of the tools available to legislatures and agencies in dealing with social and economic problems, the forces that give rise to legislative or administrative quiescence or vigor, and the full range of political and institutional relationships that shape the behavior of modern agencies.

What appears most salient to any observer of administrative law may depend on the role in which one expects to engage the public law system—as private counsel, agency lawyer or policymaker, public interest representative, legislator, judge, academic critic, or interested citizen. Whatever one's perspective, however, it is critical to understand the procedural norms governing agency decision making in an institutional context. In fulfilling their mandates, administrative agencies operate within a web of relationships with other governmental actors—other administrative bodies, legislatures, and courts—and with organized private and public interests, including, of course, the mass media. Only by considering the multiple forces operating on an agency in any particular policy making episode can one appreciate the significance that attaches to the procedural law governing the agency's decision making.

FIGURE 1. THE POLITICAL MILIEU OF THE ADMINISTRATIVE AGENCY

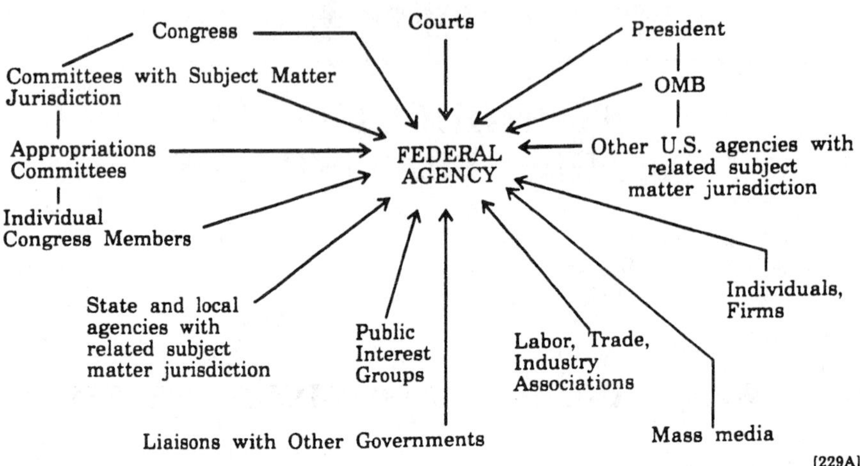

Except in our study of procedural due process, this book concentrates on the operation of federal agencies. We made this choice chiefly because the federal administrative system is the one with which virtually all users of this book will interact. This focus permits greater richness in our discussion of a single political culture within which to observe agency policy making. The disadvantage, of course, is that we cannot depict the rich variety in state administrative institutions and legal rules. Yet, students who master the vocabulary and policy debates surrounding the procedural law of federal agencies will find that these help in understanding the procedural law of the states, as well. This reflects both the common themes that converge whenever our legal system attempts to harmonize administrative efficiency with political accountability and the rule of law and the influence of federal law as a model for state law.

What may at first appear to be the bewildering diversity of federal administrative law is the result in part of the multiple relationships that agencies have with their dual political principals, Congress and the President; their ultimate legal overseers, the federal courts; other public entities, federal, state and local; their own employees; and the heterogenous world of non-governmental entities that they support, regulate, benefit and annoy. Administrative law is the law that structures these multiple relationships, determines the limits of political and legal controls on administrative action and specifies the participatory procedures and internal decision processes through which administrators may act. As might be imagined the sources of this law are also multiple. The legal requirements that govern agency life are rooted in:

- the U.S. Constitution and cases interpreting it;
- statutes that specify the organization and programs of particular agencies;

- annual measures authorizing the appropriation of agency funds, plus the annual appropriations statutes themselves;
- so-called generic statutes, such as the Administrative Procedure Act (APA), which apply to all bodies falling within the statutory definition of "agency";
- judicial opinions, either interpreting other sources of law or elaborating the federal common law of administration;
- opinions of the U.S. Attorney General;
- presidential executive orders and other directives; and
- agency law in the form of "circulars," directives, manuals, precedential adjudicative orders, or rules (as they may appear in the Federal Register or, as codified, in the Code of Federal Regulations).

The aim of this introductory chapter is to provide an institutional sense of administrative agencies by surveying, albeit with broad strokes, the history of U.S. public administration, the purposes, powers, structure, and organizational "location" of administrative agencies, the policy issues that tend to dominate debates over agency procedure, and contending theories regarding the forces that shape administration and administrative law.

B. U.S. PUBLIC ADMINISTRATION AND ADMINISTRATIVE LAW

Creating the Administrative State. Sound government administration was as important to political thinkers of our founding generation as it is today. The "true test of a good government," Alexander Hamilton wrote, "is its aptitude and tendency to produce a good administration." THE FEDERALIST, No. 68. Yet, what Hamilton's generation understood and experienced as administration was quite different from our own. Hamilton catalogued "the administration of government" that would fall "peculiarly within the province of the executive department" as follows:

> [t]he actual conduct of foreign negotiations, the preparatory plans of finance, the application and disbursement of the public moneys in conformity to the general appropriations of the legislature, the arrangement of the army and navy, the directions of the operations of war—* * * and other matters of a like nature.

THE FEDERALIST, No. 75. Hamilton could hardly have foreseen the modern state in which virtually no significant economic, social, or political activity is untouched by national administrative policy making. He would have had difficulty imagining even the present scope of state and local agencies—public school systems, zoning boards, departments of motor vehicles, public utility commissions, and professional licensing agencies, to name a few. To foresee such agencies as a Federal Aviation Administration or an Environmental Protection Agency would have entailed a technological and scientific prescience beyond even Benjamin Franklin.

Organizing the federal government was a critical legislative concern from the start. The First Congress created the Departments of War, of Foreign Affairs, and of the Treasury, as well as the Post Office and the Patent Office. It provided both for the collection of customs and for the administrative determination of pensions. It created the offices of the Attorney General and of the U.S. Attorneys, part-time employees who played a critical role in the execution of federal laws. See JENNINGS B. SANDERS, EVOLUTION OF EXECUTIVE DEPARTMENTS OF THE CONTINENTAL CONGRESS 1774–89, at 187–92 (1935); Gerhard Casper, *An Essay in Separation of Powers: Some Early Versions and Practices*, 30 Wm. & Mary L.Rev. 211 (1989).

As recounted in Chapter 3, the first Congress paid considerable attention to highly detailed issues of government structure and relationship, treating even relatively technical questions as having both constitutional importance and precedential significance. It was not until 1852, however, that Congress created the first regulatory apparatus charged with the supervision of economic activity for reasons of public safety and welfare. Throughout the first half of the nineteenth century, the nation experienced a rash of shipboard disasters caused by exploding steam boilers. Congress' 1852 bill followed the programmatic failure of legislation enacted in 1838—a year marked by 496 boiler-related deaths—which had authorized U.S. district court judges to appoint boiler inspectors, but dictated no specific inspection criteria. Act of July 7, 1838, Ch. 191, 5 Stat. 304. The 1852 legislation included precise standards for the design and manufacture of boilers, reauthorized the appointment of inspectors, and created a board of nine presidentially appointed supervising inspectors, organizationally "housed" within the Treasury Department. Act of Aug. 30, 1852, Ch. 106, 10 Stat. 61. These presidential appointees were charged not only to oversee the appointment of inspectors, but also, armed with subpoena power, to investigate accidents and possible infractions. The program helped produce a 65 percent drop in the loss of life on steamboats from all types of accidents in the next eight years. One commentator regards the enactment of this legislation and its apparent success as helping to legitimate the idea that a regime of private property could tolerate programs of government regulation to accomplish public welfare objectives. John D. Burke, *Bursting Boilers and the Federal Power*, 7 Technology and Culture 1 (1966).

It is common to trace the beginning of modern U.S. public administration to 1887, a year in which then-Professor Woodrow Wilson published an essay, "The Study of Administration," often credited with establishing public administration as a self-conscious field of Study, JOHN A. ROHR, TO RUN A CONSTITUTION: THE LEGITIMACY OF THE ADMINISTRATIVE STATE 55–75 (1986), and in which Congress created the Interstate Commerce Commission. The ICC was the first federal regulatory agency authorized to police broadly the detailed operations of a significant sector of the U.S. economy. In 1889, following the election of President Benjamin Harrison, a well-known railroad lawyer, Congress removed the ICC from its original home, the Interior Department, and reconstituted it as the first independent regulatory agency. JOSHUA BERNHARDT, THE INTERSTATE COMMERCE COMMISSION, ITS HISTORY, ACTIVITIES AND ORGANIZATION (1923); ROBERT E. CUSHMAN, THE INDEPENDENT REGULATORY COMMISSIONS (1972).

The creation of the ICC followed unsuccessful attempts by individual states to impose regulations against a host of notorious abuses by the railroads. Scholars differ, however, whether the impetus behind the ICC lay with shippers seeking to avoid railroad exploitation, railroads seeking to avoid a patchwork of inconsistent state regulation (and the burdens of unregulated competition), or more generalized popular demands for improvement in the efficiency of the nation's transportation network. JAMES M. LANDIS, THE ADMINISTRATIVE PROCESS (1938); GABRIEL KOLKO, RAILROADS AND REGULATION: 1877–1916 (1965); STEPHEN SKOWRONEK, BUILDING A NEW AMERICAN STATE: THE EXPANSION OF NATIONAL ADMINISTRATIVE CAPACITIES, 1877–1920 (1982). The Commission was important for our purposes because its regulatory activities generated a series of court decisions that provided the underpinnings for the development of a body of administrative law to insure the legality and procedural regularity of regulatory activity.

The creation of the ICC did not produce an immediate flood of new federal agencies on the same model. Indeed, the Progressive Era produced only one other major regulatory innovation between the Interstate Commerce Act and the Great Depression, the creation of the Federal Trade Commission. CUSHMAN, *supra*. The watershed period in the creation of new federal administrative agencies was the New Deal. (For an excellent general history, see WILLIAM LEUCHTENBERG, FRANKLIN D. ROOSEVELT AND THE NEW DEAL, 1932–1940 (1963).) Concerns of both practice and principle notwithstanding, the President and Congress created a host of new entities, often with broad and vaguely described authority, to respond to the national economic emergency. Not all were successes. The powers (and the abuses) of the National Industrial Recovery Administration provoked both widespread political opposition and the only decisions of the Supreme Court that have overturned federal statutes as unconstitutional because they delegated excessive power to administrators. Nonetheless, many other new agencies were created, and several, especially the Securities and Exchange Commission and the National Labor Relations Board, persisted and thrived, winning over time a series of judicial victories that significantly bolstered the policy making clout of the federal bureaucracy.

Although each agency has its own distinctive social and political history, agencies typically are responses not only to the perception of social problems warranting government response, but also to the perception that existing institutions are inadequate to the task. To return to our earlier examples, prior to the federal regulation of boiler safety, state common law and federal admiralty courts were available to impose liability on negligent owners and operators of steamships. State regulatory programs of considerable sophistication preceded the creation of the ICC, although diligent state regulation in some ways hastened rather than forestalled uniform federal legislation. The Federal Trade Commission was created in 1914 to prevent unfair competition partly in reaction to the perceived failure of prior federal efforts, namely, judicial enforcement of the Sherman Anti–Trust Act of 1890.

The most recent surge in the creation of new administrative agencies and programs occurred in the 1960s and 1970s. Congress created over 30 new agencies during this period alone, responding largely to increasing public demands that government eliminate race and sex discrimination, promote worker and consumer safety, protect individual and environmental health, and prevent consumer fraud. CHARLES SCHULTZE, THE PUBLIC USE OF PRIVATE INTEREST (1977); CASS SUNSTEIN, AFTER THE RIGHTS REVOLUTION: RECONCEIVING THE REGULATORY STATE (1990). These new agencies not only extended the regulatory reach of the federal government, but reflected in their structure and mandate critiques previously lodged against earlier agencies:

> The new agencies were to be different: their mandates more specific; their power more concentrated in a single administrator; their enforcement discretion more circumscribed; their processes more open to the participation of putative beneficiaries; and their powers more focused on the establishment of mandatory policy by general rule.

JERRY L. MASHAW & DAVID HARFST, THE STRUGGLE FOR AUTO SAFETY 5 (1990).

Students of public administration have proffered a variety of explanations for the extraordinary growth of bureaucratic government sketched here. Among them, the increase in government activity has been traced to the imperatives of modernization, the nature of public goods, the displacement to government of social welfare roles formerly played by families and private institutions, changes in public ideology, and the self-interested decisions of legislators and bureaucrats. Past national crises coinciding with the expansion of government include all major wars, the Depression, the civil rights movement, and the energy crisis of 1973–74. ROBERT HIGGS, CRISIS AND LEVIATHAN: CRITICAL EPISODES IN THE GROWTH OF AMERICAN GOVERNMENT (1987).

Whatever the causes, the growth of government activity over two centuries has been enormous. In 1800, the federal government employed approximately 3,000 civilian Employees. SOLOMON FABRICANT, TRENDS OF GOVERNMENT ACTIVITY IN THE UNITED STATES SINCE 1900, at 161–203 (1952). In 2000, the number was 2,708,101. U.S. BUREAU OF THE CENSUS STATISTICAL ABSTRACT OF THE UNITED STATES, 2001 at 319. Federal employees made up around 1.85 percent of the total employed and unemployed civilian labor market in 1900; in 2000 they represented about 1.9 percent. Calculated from U.S. BUREAU OF THE CENSUS, HISTORICAL STATISTICS OF THE UNITED STATES, COLONIAL TIMES TO 1970; U.S. BUREAU OF THE CENSUS, STATISTICAL ABSTRACT OF THE UNITED STATES, 2001. In the early years of this century, federal, state, and local government spending for goods and services accounted for roughly 8 percent of gross national product. Now, the figure hovers near 20 percent.

Interestingly, patterns of growth in federal expenditures and employment have not been parallel. Although federal budgets for the mid 1990s accounted for 4% more of GDP than those of the mid 1950s, federal civilian employment as a percentage of total civilian employment was lower under President Clinton than under President Eisenhower (2.47% versus 3.6%). Calculated from HISTORICAL STATISTICS and STATISTICAL ABSTRACT, *supra*. The re-engineering efforts of the Clinton–Gore White House, backed enthusiastically by a Republican Congress, had particularly dramatic effects. Federal civilian employment dropped 6.7% between 1990 and 1995, while by virtually any measure the responsibilities of federal administrative agencies grew substantially during the same period. For a skeptical view of the effects of downsizing the workforce while upgrading the demands placed upon it, see Jerry L. Mashaw, *Reinventing Government and Regulatory Reform: Studies in the Neglect and Abuse of Administrative Law*, 57 U.Pitt.L.Rev. 405 (1996).

Spending more while employing fewer has been accomplished in many ways, but especially by "contracting out" federal administration to states and localities, both through grant-in-aid programs for highways, sewage treatment plants, medical care for the indigent, and the like, and through the assignment of major regulatory enforcement tasks to the states in newer regulatory programs, such as environmental protection and occupational safety and health. When combined with contracting out to the private for-profit and non-profit sectors, such "cooperative federalism" produces a very large "shadow" federal work force that is funded by the federal government but managed by others. Estimating its size is tricky, but the shadow federal civilian work force may be as much as eight times as large as the formal numbers suggest. PAUL C. LIGHT, THE TRUE SIZE OF GOVERNMENT (1999).

The Changing Face of American Bureaucracy. Shifts in politics and ideology are conspicuous also in the history of the civil service. Given roughly 1000 jobs to fill in his first term, President Washington resisted the opportunity to create a patronage system: "His appointments were made with little regard to party loyalty, personal relations, or family Connections." SIDNEY M. MILKIS & MICHAEL NELSON, THE AMERICAN PRESIDENCY: ORIGINS AND DEVELOPMENT, 1776–1990, at 75 (1990). In eschewing partisanship, Washington was faithful to Article II's vision of a nonpartisan Presidency. RALPH KETCHAM, PRESIDENTS ABOVE PARTY, THE FIRST AMERICAN PRESIDENCY, 1789–1829 (1984).

Subsequent Presidents pursued that ideal, but with less success, in part because partisan caucuses within Congress had become an organizational reality by the late 1790s. Although Jefferson did not attempt a comprehensive anti-Federalist purge of the bureaucracy, there was a 50 percent turnover in federal civilian personnel during his first administration, and he appointed substantial numbers of his supporters to open positions. Yet, neither Jefferson nor his immediate Democratic–Republican successors, Madison, Monroe, and John Quincy Adams, relied on patronage to secure agreements from Congress or to build party organizations. Their view of patronage as an appropriate tool to build a personal following was more akin to the eighteenth century British practice of using patronage to enhance the individual standing of "Parliamentary notables." *Id.* at 152–153. In the United States, the post-appointment expectation of lifetime, nonpartisan bureaucratic service for all but the highest officers lasted until 1829, when Andrew Jackson introduced the democratic reform of the "spoils system." MILKIS & NELSON, *supra*, at 104; LEONARD D. WHITE, THE JEFFERSONIANS: A STUDY IN ADMINISTRATIVE HISTORY, 1801–1829 (1951); SAUL K. PADOVER, THE COMPLETE JEFFERSON (1943); PAUL C. VAN RIPER, HISTORY OF THE U.S. CIVIL SERVICE (1958). The change enhanced presidential power over administration, but also greatly strengthened local party organizations, which were influential in choosing lower-level officials and often successful in insisting that they contribute part of their salaries to the party in return. The postal system became the primary source of federal patronage for the party faithful. MILKIS & NELSON, *supra*, at 126–183.

The spoils system survived until 1883, when the Pendleton Act, discussed in greater detail in Chapter 3, established a competitive civil service for most of the federal civilian workforce. That act, strengthened by subsequent civil service reforms in this century and the Hatch Act prohibitions on government employee political activity, substantially depoliticized the civil service. Yet, the layers of political appointees atop the federal agencies—layers that have grown thicker during the past several decades—still permit considerably greater partisan influence than is evident, for example, in the French or British civil service.

Attempts to increase responsiveness to current administrations by increasing the number of political appointees have had very mixed effects. Recent presidents, even those with two terms, have been unable to come close to making appointments to all the offices nominally open to them. And appointees who stay about 30 months on average often leave little imprint on the policies or bureaus under their charge. Meanwhile the availability of so many political appointments has tended to undermine earlier reforms meant to reward and empower higher-level career officers in the Federal Executive Service.

The Rise [and Fall?] of Administrative Law. The history of administrative law is no less complex than the institutional history of public administration, although its major change points are less easily marked. Perhaps most remarkably, U.S. lawyers, like their British counterparts, were slow in conceptualizing administrative law as a distinct area of law. The first U.S. treatise and casebook on the subject appeared only in the early years of the 1900s. FRANK J. GOODNOW, PRINCIPLES OF THE ADMINISTRATIVE LAW OF THE UNITED STATES (1905); ERNST FREUND, CASES ON ADMINISTRATIVE LAW SELECTED FROM DECISIONS OF ENGLISH AND AMERICAN COURTS (1911). Throughout the nineteenth century, the common law writ system inherited from England was used to provide some measure of judicial control over federal officers. Administrative officers also remained liable for damages for common law torts that could not be justified as exercises of legal authority.

American lawyers seemed to share the view of their British counterparts that the failure to devise a system of controls for administration that would take account of the public character of administrative action was actually a virtue. The famed British jurisprude Alfred Dicey regarded the French creation of a distinctive set of executive courts for the control of administration to be a departure from the Rule of Law, which, in his formulation, demanded that all persons—including government officers—be subject to the same legal rules, enforced by the same authorities. ALFRED V. DICEY, INTRODUCTION TO THE STUDY OF THE LAW OF THE CONSTITUTION (1885).

The notion that the United States (and England) had no administrative law because they had no separate administrative courts was laid to rest by Frank Goodnow, who published a text on comparative administrative law in 1893 and PRINCIPLES OF ADMINISTRATIVE LAW IN THE UNITED STATES IN 1905. Goodnow's preoccupation, indeed the preoccupation of administrative law thinkers throughout the first third of this century, was the constitutional legitimacy of administration, in particular, to reconcile bureaucratic policy making with the constitutionally established institutions of representative democracy.

The New Deal put an end to the Diceyan tradition of eschewing the development of a distinct administrative law and confirmed the constitutional legitimacy of administrative agencies as well. Yet, critics of the agencies—including judges appointed during the 1920s—remained intensely skeptical of the activist administrative state and were unrelenting in their demands for further legal controls over agency decision making. President Roosevelt vetoed the 1940 Walter–Logan Act, Congress' first attempt to standardize agency decision making by ensuring formal procedures and by liberalizing the availability of judicial review of agency decisions. He was able to protect his veto, however, only because in 1939 he had established the Attorney General's Committee on Administrative Procedure to respond to the tide of criticism of agency performance. Two years later, that Committee issued a report that supported standardized procedures, so long as any statutory controls left agencies with significant flexibility to design their decision making processes and organizational structures. In 1946, Congress responded to the report and significant pressure from the organized bar by enacting the federal Administrative Procedure Act, now codified at 5 U.S.C. § 551 et seq. and explored in Chapters 4 through 7 of this text. MARTIN SHAPIRO, WHO GUARDS THE GUARDIANS? JUDICIAL CONTROL OF ADMINISTRATION 36–41 (1988).

The APA has been aptly termed "a catch-up statute trying to provide law to cover legitimate agency practices that were already growing up." *Id.* at 41. As such, the Act provided a fairly detailed code only for formal agency on-the-record hearings, through which many agencies enunciated policy as well as enforced the law until the 1960s. The APA says far less, however, about the requirements for the adoption of prospective rules—a gap that remains unfilled despite the profoundly greater importance of rulemaking today.

In several respects, U.S. administrative law entered a new stage in the 1960s and 1970s. First, scholarly attention was devoted for the first time to the immense quantity of informal agency activity that typically escapes judicial review, but that is critical to agency performance. See, e.g., KENNETH CULP DAVIS, DISCRETIONARY JUSTICE: A PRELIMINARY INQUIRY (1969). Second, judges displayed considerable optimism not only about the capacity of government agencies to respond to social problems, but also about the capacity of courts to contribute to the evolution of rational, accountable, effective policy making. The federal courts began to claim an active partnership with administrators in assuring the proper implementation of federal statutes, notably by interpreting the vague APA language on rulemaking in a way that afforded the courts significant powers of review and correction.

The Supreme Court's enthusiasm for active partnership began to ebb significantly in the 1970s, but without any revival of the 1920s' skepticism towards the legitimacy of administrative policy making. Indeed, two celebrated decisions, *Vermont Yankee Nuclear Power Corp. v. Natural Resources Defense Council*, 435 U.S. 519 (1978), and *Chevron, U.S.A. v. Natural Resources Defense Council*, 467 U.S. 837 (1984), signaled to many—including many lower court judges—the advent of a new era of judicial deference to administrative policy making. An attack on one aspect of the administrative apparatus that Congress erected during the New Deal—the array of independent agencies—was launched by Reagan Administration lawyers in both political and judicial forums. That campaign was largely rebuffed, however, in Supreme Court decisions excerpted in Chapter 3. And the Social Security Administration, which began its life as an independent agency in 1935, but became a subcabinet agency in 1939, returned full-circle to independent status in 1995.

Whether we are still in an era dominated by the legal understandings that were settled by legislative and judicial developments between 1946 and the 1960s or entering into a markedly new era is uncertain. The last quarter century witnessed important initiatives in deregulation, innovations in presidential oversight of administrative rulemaking, the greatly increased use of regulatory analysis as a policy making tool, an unprecedented congressional focus on the making of the national budget as critical policy making activity, and the reinvigoration of federalism. As discussed in Chapters 4 and 5, Congress in 1990 authorized the use of new, assertedly less formal procedures for both adjudication and rulemaking that could in theory alter the usual way of doing agency business.

In particular, the last decade's administrative law reforms suggest a decided shift in the focus of reform activity—from the courts, certainly the Supreme Court, to the Executive and Legislative branches. The authors contributing to the Administrative Law Review's 1996 issue commemorating the 50th anniversary of the Federal Administrative Procedure Act had surprisingly little to say about the core concerns of that statute, informal agency rulemaking, formal agency adjudication and judicial review. They concentrated instead on the impact of new congressional requirements for agency action and the multiple techniques for oversight and direction that have been developed both by Congress and the Executive Office of the President. 49 Admin. L. Rev. 1–198 (Winter, 1997). Political controls of the sorts canvassed in chapters 2 and 3 seem ascendent, legal controls via judicial review on the wane.

These shifts in emphasis were crystalized in the American public consciousness by Democratic President William Clinton's startling statement that "the era of big government is over". However hyperbolic, if measured by budgetary outlays, Clinton's aphorism certainly captures the tone that characterizes late 20th century and early 21st century policy discourse. Practitioners and theorists of public administration have begun to talk of the "new public administration," a set of theories and practices that emphasize downsizing, cost-control, contracting out, devolution, and managerial efficiency. While the principal focus of administrative law has been on administrative processes for deciding cases (adjudication) and promulgating binding policies (rulemaking), along with judicial review of administrative action, federal administrators now seem much more preoccupied with shifting functions to private or state and local actors, developing new techniques for contract management and creating flexible and cooperative legal regimes that promise to lower regulatory costs, generate "smarter" rules of conduct and improve compliance. The literature on these matters is vast and growing. See generally LESTER A. SALAMON, THE TOOLS OF GOVERNMENT (2002); DANIEL C. ESTY AND DAMIEN GERADIN, eds., REGULATORY COMPETITION AND ECONOMIC INTEGRATION (2001); JONATHON BOSTON, ET AL., PUBLIC ADMINISTRATION: THE NEW ZEALAND MODEL (1996); JOHN D. DONAHUE, THE PRIVATIZATION DECISION (1989).

These managerial and cooperative approaches to public administration, combined with devolution and contracting out pose extraordinary challenges for American administrative law, at least at the federal level. Private firms, non-profit organizations and non-federal public actors are not subject to the federal Administrative Procedure Act, including the Freedom of Information Act and a host of other federal statutes that have been developed to increase the transparency and legal accountability of public administration. Private actors generally evade constitutional constraints as well. For an introduction to these accountability issues, see, e.g., Jack M. Beermann, *Privatization and Political Accountability*, 28 Fordham Urb. L. J. 1507 (2001); William Peterson, *Contracting With the Regulated for Better Regulation*, 53 Admin. L. Rev. 1067 (2001); Matthew Diller, *The Revolution in Welfare Administration: Rules, Discretion and Entrepreneurial Government*, 75 N.Y.U. L. Rev. 1121 (2000); Jody Freeman, *The Private Role in Public Governance*, 75 N.Y.U. L. Rev. 543 (2000); Mark Seidenfeld, *An Apology for Administrative Law and the Contracting State*, 28 Fla. St. U. L. Rev. 215 (2000); Jody Freeman, *Collaborative Governance in the Administrative State*, 45 UCLA L. Rev. 1 (1997); David M. Lawrence, *The Private Exercise of Government Power*,

61 Ind. L. J. 647 (1986); Robert S. Moe and Ronald S. Gilmour, *Rediscovering Principles of Public Administration: The Neglected Foundations of Public Law*, 55 Pub. Admin. L. Rev. 135 (1995); Paul E. Peterson, *Devolution's Price*, 14 Yale L. & Pol'y Rev. 111 (1995); Ronald A. Cass, *Privatization: Politics, Law & Theory*, 71 Marquette L. Rev. 449 (1988). As the materials in Chapter 9 detail, the Supreme Court's recent jurisprudence has made it more rather than less difficult for the beneficiaries of federal policies to pursue non-federal actors whose implementation or compliance is crucial to the effectuation of federal law.

In addition to sources cited above, students interested in the history of U.S. public administration and administrative law would do well to consult DANIEL P. CARPENTER, THE FORGING OF BUREAUCRATIC AUTONOMY (2001); THOMAS L. MCCRAW, PROPHETS OF REGULATION (1984); THOMAS K. MCCRAW, ED., REGULATION IN PERSPECTIVE: HISTORICAL ESSAYS (1981); and Robert Rabin, *Federal Regulation in Historical Perspective*, 38 Stan. L.Rev. 1189 (1986).

C. THE ARCHITECTURE OF AN ADMINISTRATIVE AGENCY

The federal Administrative Procedure Act defines an "agency" as "each authority of the Government of the United States, whether or not it is within or subject to review by another agency." 5 U.S.C. § 551. The APA then excepts from this definition Congress and the courts of the United States, along with governments of territories or possessions, the government of the District of Columbia, certain elective and military bodies and a few others. Oddly, however, "authority" is not a defined term in the APA. In general, it would appear that virtually every entity, or indeed any individual, empowered to assist in the execution of federal law may be considered an "agency" of the United States and subject to the requirements of the APA. In terms of organizations and personnel, administrative agencies constitute most of what we identify as the governmental establishment of the United States.

1. THE LEGAL ORIGIN OF ADMINISTRATIVE AGENCIES

As the word "agency" suggests, the "authorities" that are the subject matter of administrative law are the *agents*—officers, boards, commissions, and the like—established by some *principal* to carry out that person's or body's purposes. Within the federal government, it is usually a statute that charters an agency to carry out public purposes. This common model would suggest that Congress is the principal and the administrative body is the agent whose existence, powers, purposes, and structure are within the control of the legislative branch.

The conception of most administrative agencies as agents of Congress is not misleading, provided it is hedged about with appropriate conditions. The most important is that, in this context, the relationship of principal and agent is extraordinarily complex. The idea that administrative agencies simply carry out the will of the legislative principal is at once normatively tempting and organizationally naive. Normatively, the accountability of administrative agents to the elected legislature is conventionally understood as helping to legitimate the actions of an unelected bureaucracy that affect the rights and duties of private persons. Yet, the rigor of such accountability is problematic because the statutes that charter an agency and its programs, and thus constitute the principal's instructions, are often phrased more in terms of broad collective aspirations than concrete policies. Moreover, time inexorably creates a gap, often substantial, between instructions and action; the principal that enacted agency legislation is usually not the Congress that currently sits. The agency's implementation of its statutory mandate inevitably reflects shifting social understandings and purposes, plus post-enactment changes in available information. Thus, the imagery of a faithful agency carrying out the directions of a single principal would be misleading even if we could plausibly treat Congress as the only available principal, and a collective agent, such as the Social Security Administration with its approximately 65,000 employees, as truly capable of acting in a unified fashion. Maintaining a coherent vision of agency accountability in the face of these complexities is much of what administrative law is about.

Not every federal agency originates in a statute. The astute reader may deduce that the APA's definition of "agency" on its face could encompass the President and Vice President of the United States. But the Supreme Court has denied that the President is subject to the APA, *Franklin v. Massachusetts*, 505 U.S. 788, 112 S.Ct. 2767 (1992), and would undoubtedly hold the same for the Vice–President. Because it does not provide for executive branch officers beyond these two, the U.S. Constitution establishes no "agencies" as that term is commonly used. By contrast, constitutional creation of administrative bodies is common in the states.

Agencies may also be chartered by other legal instruments. Presidential executive orders have created numerous federal agencies, including such important ones as the Environmental Protection Agency and the Army Corps of Engineers. Because agencies can be subparts of larger units, some are established by the issuance of orders or regulations by existing agencies.

We can, then, say this much about the legal origin of administrative agencies: They are bodies granted authority by some appropriate constitutional principal to exercise governmental functions in the name of the United States. Their origin can always be traced to some legal document (statute, executive order, constitution, charter, compact, rule, or order) which calls them to legal life and sets them in motion.

2. THE FORMS OF AGENCY–CREATING STATUTES

Because federal agencies engage in a vast array of activities, it is no surprise that they take many different forms. Nevertheless, it is possible to list a handful of topics that the legal instruments establishing federal administrative agencies generally address. These number but five: the agency's purposes, powers, and procedures, its structure, and its location within the federal establishment.

a. Purposes

Given the modern Supreme Court's expansive interpretation of Congress' powers under the Constitution, the purposes for which Congress may act to establish an administrative authority are limited in practice chiefly by congressional imagination. Even so, the purposes of most of the multitude of existing federal agencies can be categorized under a few headings.

The purposes of many federal agencies are *developmental*. Like the National Oceanographic and Atmospheric Administration or the Bureau of Labor Statistics, they gather and disseminate information to assist others, often private individuals and firms, in the pursuit of productive activities. Like the Department of Commerce or the National Science Foundation, they may promote learning and economic development. Like the Federal Highway Administration they may be concerned primarily with infrastructure development. Or, like the National Park Service, they may be concerned with the management of public property. In all these developmental activities, the government seeks to assist or to promote the growth of knowledge and of the citizenry's economic, recreational, or aesthetic well-being.

Another group of agencies have as their common purpose the provision of *social welfare* goods and services. Some, like the Social Security Administration, are primarily in the business of providing social insurance. Others, like the National Institutes of Health or the Family Support Administration seek in various ways to promote physical well-being and family stability. Yet others, like the Department of Veterans Affairs minister to the multiple health, employment, and social needs of a specific clientele.

A third group of agencies has been created to *regulate private economic activities*. These activities include macroeconomic "steering" of the national economy through the tax policies promoted by the Treasury Department and the monetary policies established by the Federal Reserve Board. At a somewhat more "micro" level, other agencies, such as the Controller of the Currency, the Federal Deposit Insurance Corporation, the Resolution Trust Corporation, the Securities and Exchange Commission, and the Commodity Futures Trading Commission, seek to maintain the integrity and smooth functioning of the principal financial intermediaries and markets that generate and allocate capital. At an even more specific level, agencies like the Federal Communications Commission, the Federal Power Commission, and the International Trade Commission, regulate significant economic aspects of particular industries.

Finally, a group of important, and in most cases, relatively new agencies is devoted to the *protection of health and safety*. These include bodies such as the Food and Drug Administration, the Occupational Safety and Health Administration, the Environmental Protection Agency, the National Highway Traffic Safety Administration, and parts of numerous other agencies and departments with additional missions, such as the Coast Guard and the Nuclear Regulatory Commission.

To be sure, some agencies have purposes that do not fit comfortably within the foregoing categories. The basic tax collection activities of the IRS, the proprietary activities of the General Services Administration and the far flung efforts of the Army, Navy, and Air Force encompass some developmental, social welfare, and regulatory purposes, but these labels fail to capture the essence of such agencies' goals. Nor do they fairly describe the purposes of the Immigration and Naturalization Service. We might even add some additional categories such as the *internal management* of the federal establishment—a task that might be said to occupy the Office of Personnel Management, the General Service Administration, and even the Office of Management and Budget. Indeed, we might have a simple category of *national defense*.

The basic point remains, however, that any statute chartering an agency can be expected, in its text or by reference to other documents, to set out the purposes that the agency is meant to further. Occasionally, these purposes must be inferred from other features of the legislation or background understandings captured in legislative history or prior practice. But most modern statutes contain a statement of an agency's mission, often including both positive statements of the agency's affirmative goals and limits on its jurisdiction. The affirmative statement will often be in ambitious language, such as, that the National Highway Traffic Safety Administration "meet the need for traffic safety." The stated purposes of administrative activity may thus both energize and frustrate. They tell the agency, and others, what the agency is meant to do; but they often state the goal in diffuse terms that render its achievement controversial.

b. Powers

The statement of purposes to guide agency action is usually accompanied—though often not matched—by the conferral of powers with which to accomplish the mission. As the statutory purposes describe what goals the agency is to seek, the powers sections define the legal tools with which it is empowered to pursue its goals. Administrative lawyers often describe agencies in terms of their primary legal tools—regulatory, prosecutorial, informational, and the like—although, in practice, what makes agencies effective is often the mix of direct and indirect methods afforded them to accomplish the statutory purposes.

Thus, for example, one may find certain developmental agencies described as grant and contract agencies. Their principal activities involve the funneling of funds, through grants or contracts, to others whose activities they are empowered to support. The National Science Foundation is a quintessential grant and contract agency. It does virtually nothing but support the activities, chiefly the research, of others. The same is also true of the Federal Highway Administration. Almost all road building is done by states and localities who are merely assisted by the FHWA, deploying the staggering financial resources generated by the federal government's fuel taxes.

Other agencies chiefly develop and report information. This is true of the National Oceanographic and Atmospheric Administration as well as the Bureau of Labor Statistics, and, less obviously, of even the U.S. Civil Rights Commission.

Grants, contracts, and information production are not the sorts of "administrative powers" conventionally thought to illustrate the authority of administrative agencies. Public attention focuses more commonly on agencies' coercive powers—the powers to search and seize, to order the cessation of illegal activity, to demand the recall of defective products, to assess penalties for the violation of administrative or statutory rules, to grant and revoke licenses, or to establish general rules that govern the activities of a whole industry, or perhaps of individuals and firms throughout the nation. Indeed, it is with reference to these more coercive powers that lawyers tend to classify agencies as primarily prosecutorial (e.g., the Federal Trade Commission) or standard setting (e.g., the Environmental Protection Agency), or licensing (e.g., the Federal Communications Commission) agencies.

Nevertheless, it should be noted that agencies of the grant and contract or information production variety often have ancillary coercive powers. They may act to terminate grants or contracts for malfeasance, or declare particular recipients or applicants ineligible for future awards because of prior poor performance. They may also have the power to engage in investigatory activity or to require reports from others in order to collect the information necessary for their own information dissemination activities.

By the same token prosecutorial agencies may have powers to require reports, engage in investigations, and issue rules that not only reinforce their prosecutorial powers, but sometimes supplant them. For example, to read the Food, Drug, and Cosmetic Act one would think the FDA was chiefly a prosecutorial or licensing agency, rather than an information disseminating or rulemaking agency. Yet, the Food and Drug Administration's implied power to warn the public about some adulterated food or drug often obviates any invocation of its formal seizure authority. FDA's adoption of general rules specifying the allowable ingredients of over-the-counter medications has made it virtually unnecessary for it to utilize its licensing or license revocation authority with respect to those same products. The interaction of an agency's "primary" and "secondary" statutory powers present many occasions for sophisticated strategic planning by agency attorneys and by private parties, as well.

c. *Procedures*

Closely connected to agency power is agency process. Indeed, whether an agency can effectively exercise a conferred power may depend on the procedures by which it must be exercised. For decades, therefore, agency procedure has been the central focus of U.S. administrative law. As post-New Deal courts approved virtually all public purposes as within the scope of the national government's legislative power, and as Congresses became more liberal in providing a full repertoire of administrative tools to the agencies they created, the principal legal restraint on agency action came to be judicially cognizable claims of procedural irregularity.

Accordingly, it is administrative procedure with which the Administrative Procedure Act, and most courses in administrative law, predominantly deal. The APA's definitional provisions identify two overarching processes for administrative decision making: rulemaking and adjudication (which includes licensing). To read the APA and much administrative law doctrine is to imagine (1) that agency activities fall neatly into these two categories and (2) that each type of proceeding has a relatively common form.

These are half-truths at best. A host of other procedures for the conduct of administrative business (including investigations, advice giving, negotiation, settlement, reporting routines, grant competitions, tests, elections, publicity, and so on)—are the true lifeblood of the administrative process. They are scarcely regulated by the general requirements of the APA. These "informal" processes go on within the shadow of more formal administrative processes, much as most private commercial dealings occur in the shadow of the private law and civil processes for lawmaking and dispute resolution.

In recent years, Congress has become more aware of the importance of informal procedure and has often sought to structure these "informal" processes in agency statutes. In addition, Congress has often modified the general forms of rulemaking and adjudication, as adumbrated by the APA, for specific agencies. Accordingly, while the unifying ambition of the 1946 Administrative Procedure Act is not yet a vanished dream, a subsequent half century has generated an astonishing variety of procedural approaches. Understanding any particular agency's procedures thus requires careful attention to the interaction of general principles, as enunciated in the text and judicial interpretations of the APA and the Constitution, with the increasingly detailed procedural requirements set forth in specific federal statutes and the agency's own procedural regulations.

d. *Internal Organization*

The internal organization of agencies is generally the product of judgments shaped both by the functional requirements of an agency's statutory mission, powers, and procedures, and by other general statutes or executive orders applicable to all federal agencies, whatever the peculiarities of their organic legislation. The organization charted below is imaginary—the chart represents no particular agency in the federal establishment. It would nevertheless appear authentic to most federal administrators. While there are many variations in internal organization there is a core of similarity induced by custom, common classification systems for executive personnel, and what we term "general framework" statutes.

FIGURE 2. THE XYZ AGENCY

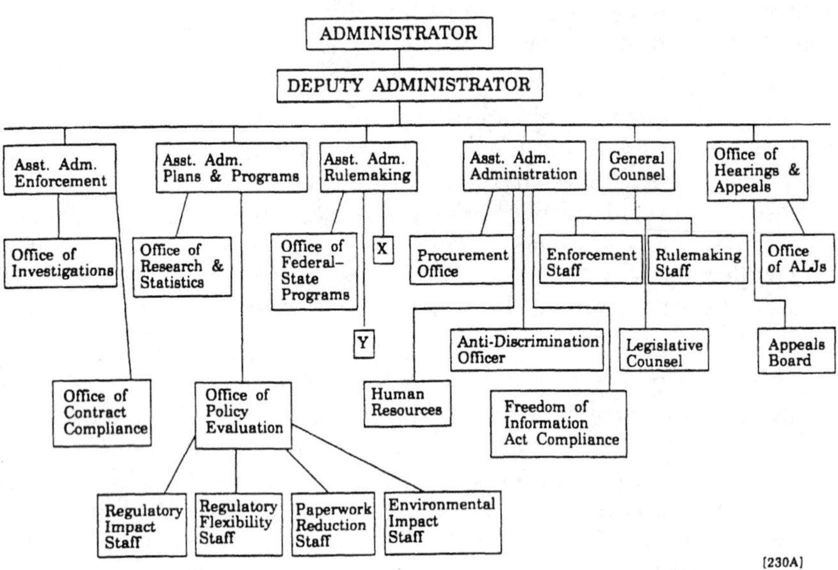

Hence, while a so-called independent commission, such as the FTC, would typically be headed by a set of commissioners rather than by a single administrator, and a department would have a Secretary at the top, in virtually all agencies, one finds a deputy secretary or deputy administrator or other chief operating officer at the second tier. Such officers may share some of the agency head's external functions, but their principal role usually is to unify the internal chain of command without allowing every problem from every major component to go directly to the top office.

Similarly, at the next—assistant administrator—level, one almost always finds a division by either function or subject matter. In our imagined agency, the division is functional with subject matter subdivisions falling under assistant administrators for various activities. If the chart were that of the National Highway Traffic Safety Administration, the boxes labeled X and Y under the Assistant Administrator for Rulemaking (whose jurisdiction is defined functionally) might be the "crash avoidance" staff and the "crashworthiness staff" respectively. In an agency like the Environmental Protection Agency (whose actual organization chart appears below) the function-subject matter division is in many instances reversed. In the EPA, one finds an Assistant Administrator for Solid Waste and Emergency Response and, under that office, an Office of Waste Programs Enforcement and an Office of Emergency and Remedial Response. Offices at this level might then break into further subdivisions by subject matter (or, in the case of enforcement, often by geographical region).

FIGURE 3. ENVIRONMENTAL PROTECTION AGENCY

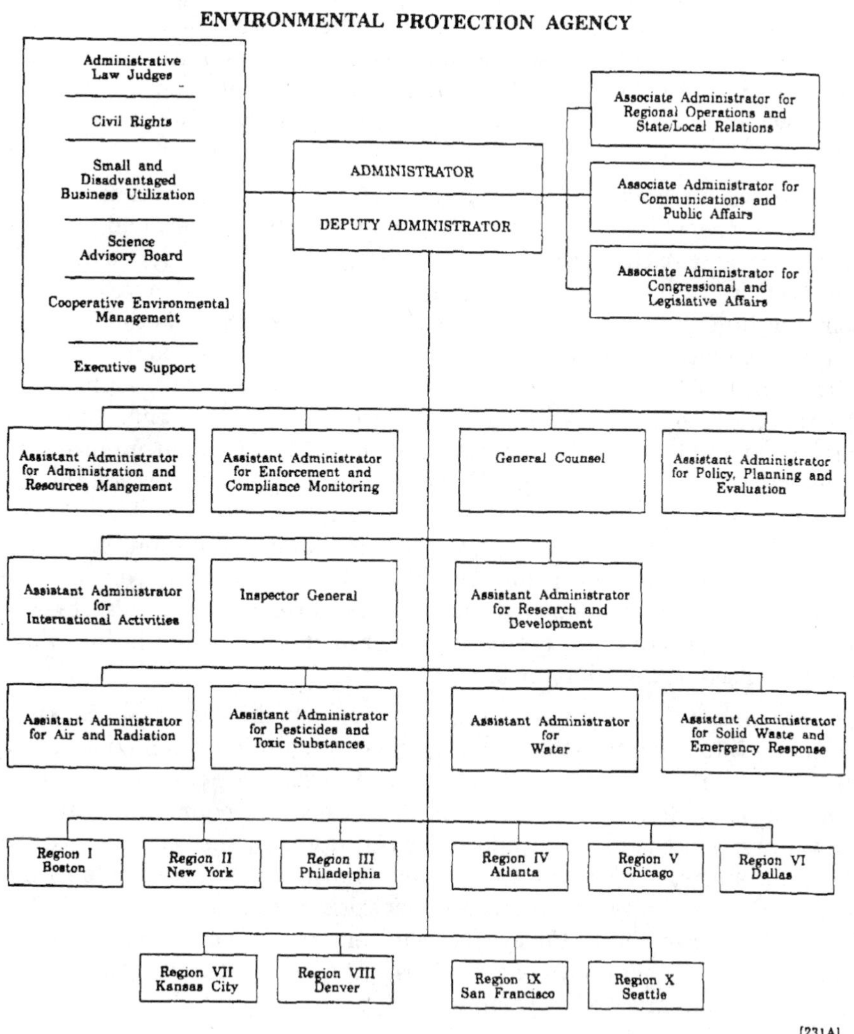

The functional differentiation chosen here highlights the influence of legal requirements on internal agency organization. The importance of administrative legality to agency operation is acknowledged by the location of the General Counsel's office. On our chart, as in the EPA, the General Counsel is at the same level as the line Assistant Administrators having major programmatic responsibilities. Otherwise the bureaucratic pecking order would routinely suppress considerations of legality when resolving issues of policy. That agencies commonly place the General Counsel's office at the assistant administrator level (or even above) suggests the importance of legal considerations in all of the activities of federal administrative agencies.

Similarly, the Office of Hearings and Appeals must be located, by virtue of the APA's requirements, to protect the independence of its Administrative Law Judges from agency officials who have enforcement responsibilities. While it is not technically necessary to have the Office at the same level as the Assistant Administrator for Enforcement, locating it elsewhere often creates sufficient awkwardness that it too is placed at a high level.

While a number of the boxes on the XYZ chart represent general functional considerations that are common aspects of federal administration, such as subject matter specialization, others are included to highlight the way certain general framework statutes or directives allocate common functions to federal agencies. A notable example is the Office of Policy Evaluation beneath the Assistant Administrator for Plans and Programs. Offices having similar titles are now common throughout the federal establishment. While policy evaluation is a function that one might imagine to be useful no matter what an agency's statute provides, such offices often serve primarily as internal implementors of the requirements of general federal statutes and executive orders. EPA's Assistant Administrator for Policy, Planning, and Evaluation, for example, has jurisdiction over an Office of Regulatory Management and Evaluation, which responds directly to requirements imposed by the presidential program of regulatory oversight administered by OMB, which is discussed in Chapter 3.

For illustrative purposes, the XYZ Agency divides these common functions into separate staffs, but the work might be combined within a single staff. However these functions are organized, the point is that many agencies must now satisfy executive orders requiring regulatory impact assessments of major policy decisions, and almost all must satisfy (1) statutory requirements for additional analysis made applicable by the Regulatory Flexibility Act and the Paperwork Reduction Act, and (2) the National Environmental Policy Act requirement of comprehensive evaluation of environmental impacts. These and other general framework statutes are summarized in Chapter 2.

Another way to think about this set of internal functions is to view them as the organizational embodiment of a group of "consciences" within every federal agency charged with major regulatory responsibilities. The job of these offices or staffs is to make certain that the agency, in carrying out its primary mission, has not forgotten that that mission is not the only goal of American governance. Similar general considerations explain other offices on the chart. Someone, like our hypothetical Office of Federal and State Programs, must assure that the agency does not run afoul of the Inter–Governmental Cooperation Act or of OMB directives to take account of the views of state and local governments. Someone else must monitor the agency's compliance with federal antidiscrimination statutes and executive orders. Someone must be responsible for compliance with the Freedom of Information Act's requirements for providing agency documents to persons who request them.

No organizational chart can capture the dynamics of agency policy development and action. Our imaginary chart suggests some things about agency priorities, but much remains mysterious. In our XYZ Agency, for example, the Office of Research and Statistics is not submerged in the Office of Policy Evaluation. This suggests that ORS may have a role in shaping the long term planning process allocated to the Assistant Administrator for Plans and Programs. On the other hand, because ORS is under a separate assistant administrator, one might wonder whether research activities have a strong impact on the agency's policy development. Investigation of a particular agency's internal environment might reveal a reality quite different from the one hypothesized by studying its organization chart.

Offices whose activities are backed by statutory command—that is, persons within an agency who can plausibly argue that failure to heed their counsel may be *illegal*, not just erroneous—will have considerable impact on agency behavior. While the Administrator may be persuaded to agree with the policy choices of the Assistant Administrator for Rulemaking when that officer is at odds with the professionals in the Office of Policy Evaluation and the General Counsel's office, the latter have external allies who may be important in leveraging their influence. An agency that has lost a number of cases in court can easily fall into a defensive posture that deemphasizes action. Hence, while general statutes that are intended to protect against tunnel vision have perfectly sound policy justifications, they are far from neutral in their impact on the aggressiveness of program implementation. As one thinks about the tradeoffs between "legality" and programmatic advance, it becomes clear that achieving the right balance in a particular agency is an extraordinarily subtle exercise in institutional design.

The specialized, hierarchical division of employees in federal agencies is intended to help maximize expertise and accountability. It does, however, pose an obvious problem for management, namely, the problem of coordination. The number of units an agency must consult on any major policy issue, the consensus building techniques that are characteristic of much agency decision making, the capacity in many agencies for any unit (or officer) with a role in formulating policy to veto aspects with which it disagrees—all are important factors in rendering bureaucratic policy making a cumbersome process. For an agency to take a full year to promulgate a significant rule on an important topic may represent a model of efficiency, and a decade from proposal to the adoption of a final rule is not unknown.

What roles do agency lawyers play in such policy making? An agency's General Counsel's office will look over any major proposal to see if it conforms to the agency's statutory authority. On especially controversial issues, the General Counsel may seek the legal imprimatur of the Attorney General, through the Justice Department's Office of Legal Counsel. The General Counsel may also play an "honest broker" role in negotiating among agency units. Lawyers may also work for individual offices and divisions, and may internally advocate the positions of their units against other units. Because whose legal advice the agency head ultimately depends upon is typically within that officer's discretion, various lawyers may compete to have their views put forward.

The legal issues latent in any proposed agency decision may of course be diffused in bureaucratic debate over a wide range of policy concerns. The legal issues may surface at different times and with varying strength, depending on the interests involved, the skill of the lawyers, and who has relevant information at important stages in the decision making process. In such an atmosphere, government lawyers regularly confront questions of professional responsibility: To whom does an agency lawyer owe his or her highest professional allegiance? How hard should one press for one's own legal views when the policy concerns are compelling, one's superiors take a contrary view, and no court will likely review the agency decision at hand? The appropriate responses to these questions may be affected by the breadth of policy discretion that Congress has vested in administrative agencies. The accuracy with which the United States claims to be a "government of laws" obviously depends on lawyers' conscientious attention to these issues.

e. Overall Structure and Location Within Government

A student of the federal administrative process must also be attentive to the choices Congress has made in structuring and locating particular agencies. The energy with which statutory objectives are pursued and the effectiveness of specific powers often depend on which cabinet department houses an agency or whether the agency operates outside any department. One should expect food and drug regulation to display a different ethos when performed under the aegis of the Department of Health and Human Services as compared to the Commerce Department.

An agency's specific location within a larger unit is also important. The vigor with which the National Highway Traffic Safety Administration seeks to regulate automobile safety, and the tools on which it relies, may vary depending upon whether it is housed within DOT's Federal Highway Administration or is a separate bureau with direct access to the Secretary. A major policy concern surrounding the creation in late 2002 of a new Department of Homeland Security was the potential impact on the important, but non-security-related, functions of the almost two dozen agencies, including, for example, the Coast Guard, that were combined into a new, security-focused agency.

Congresses that have been disappointed by agency performance or suspicious of a particular administration's designs on some aspect of public policy frequently attempt to "micro-manage" agency decision making through statutory prescription of internal structure or decision processes. Recent Congresses have prescribed such minutiae as the frequency of recipients' disability reexaminations by the Social Security Administration or who will write draft opinions for administrative law judges at the National Labor Relations Board. This tendency is likely to be reinforced when different political parties control the two elected branches, or when the incumbent President forcefully asserts his own management prerogatives, and thus limits an agency's ability to satisfy congressional oversight committees.

While statutes routinely designate the agency responsible for their administration, it is not always obvious what motives inspire Congress' choice. Surely the desire to take advantage of specialization and to promote coordination are influential. Thus, for example, most laws governing public lands are administered by the Secretary of the Interior, although this may also betray a congressional desire to sustain support from the constituencies served by the Interior Department. There are numerous exceptions, however, to the pattern of concentrating related laws and programs in a single department, which reflect other congressional policies. The U.S. Forest Service, which regulates public and private uses of national forests, has remained within the Department of Agriculture despite periodic suggestions for its removal to Interior, a department sometimes regarded as more "conservation minded." See, e.g., GLEN O. ROBINSON, THE FOREST SERVICE: A STUDY IN PUBLIC LAND MANAGEMENT 276 (1975). Agriculture has also retained authority over the marketing of all food containing meat and poultry in the face of vigorous proposals to combine this program with those of the FDA, which is responsible for regulating the rest of the food supply. V Study on Federal Regulation: Regulatory Organization, U.S. Senate Committee on Governmental Affairs, 95th Cong., 1st Sess. 113 et seq. (1977) [hereinafter, 1977 Study on Federal Regulatory Organization].

While one can generally discern from legislative history, text, or experience why Congress assigned authority to a specific agency, in recent years dispute has arisen over the implications of this choice for participation by officials elsewhere in government—specifically officials acting on behalf of the President. In Chapter 3 we consider whether Congress' delegation to a particular officer impliedly precludes presidential oversight, or even rejection, of that official's choices.

According to a 1977 study prepared for the Senate Committee on Governmental Affairs:

> It is our view that organizational structure is not neutral, that it is more than a game of moving boxes on an organizational chart, and that it is not devoid of policy implications. * * *
>
> Whether or not a given organizational structure for regulatory administration should be favored over all others will depend, in large part, on what political values are to be promoted. * * *

1977 Study on Federal Regulatory Organization, *supra*, at 21–22.

It is not only Congress that takes matters of agency structure and location seriously. Near the end of an illuminating essay on the need to strengthen presidential power over bureaucratic institutions, *Executive Reorganization and Presidential Power*, 1977 Sup.Ct.Rev. 1, 33–34, Professor Barry D. Karl observes that the "basic purpose" of periodic presidential efforts to reorganize the executive branch has been:

> to secure power over a bureaucracy whose real source of independence is congressional funding. Congress has reason to protect that independence, and the bureaucracy has reason to respect the loose political oversight Congress is able to provide. The president who seeks the power to reorganize must obtain it from a legislature that sees clear benefit in his not having the power. The grounds for compromise are narrow, therefore, and depend upon couching the issue in language that conceals the no-win game actually being played.

Until near the end of the 19th century, all administrative functions of the federal government were performed by officials within the executive branch under the supervision of some cabinet secretary or responsible to the President Directly. ROBERT RABIN, PERSPECTIVES ON THE ADMINISTRATIVE PROCESS 207 (1979). In the Interstate Commerce Commission, however, Congress fashioned a new regulatory entity that had both a distinctive location and structure: The ICC was considered to be outside and independent of the executive branch, yet not formally part of the legislature; and it was administered, not by a single head, but by a collegial body of five, ostensibly coequal, commissioners.

The 1977 Study on Federal Regulatory Organization, supra, at 26–36, describes the evolution in congressional perception of the "independent" status of the ICC and its numerous sister regulatory commissions:

> The vitality of the independent commission is also apparent in Congressional determination to distinguish those agencies from other forms of government organizations. In March 1977, in granting the President broad powers to reorganize the federal government, Congress expressly prohibited any reorganization plan that would abolish, consolidate or wholly transfer the functions of independent regulatory commissions. Significantly no previous reorganization authority, granted by Congress to every President from Truman through Nixon, contained that limitation.
>
> Several years ago Congress excepted the independent regulatory commissions from the requirement that all information-gathering forms first be cleared by the Office of Management and Budget, and instead transferred a more limited clearance authority for those agencies only to the Comptroller General. Further, there have been a series of attempts, some of which have been successful as to particular agencies, to exempt the independent commissions from general executive branch-wide requirements, concerning: standards and process for the selection of top level, noncareer agency staff members; clearance by the OMB of the agencies' budget requests,

legislative recommendations and testimony prior to submission to Congress; and the power to litigate in the courts independent of Justice Department supervision and control. * * *

Freedom from Presidential domination was within 20 years the principal justification voiced in Congress for the independent agency form. In 1910, debate on ICC amendments was filled with references to the agency's independent status, which very simply meant that it should not be subjected to control by an executive official. The ICC, it was reasoned, was exercising what were essentially legislative functions and was as such—an "arm of Congress," even a "committee of Congress." In short, the agency was legislative in character, and thereby enjoyed a special relationship to Congress. * * *

* * *

Yet the notion has not gone unchallenged. Certainly the most famous rebuttal in that regard was filed in 1937 by the Brownlow Commission, which declared that independent commissions

> * * * are in reality miniature independent governments set up to deal with the railroad problem, the banking problem, or the radio problem. They constitute a headless "fourth branch" of the Government, a haphazard deposit of irresponsible agencies and uncoordinated powers. They do violence to the basic theory of the American Constitution that there should be three branches of the Government and only three.[35]

* * *

Certainly the easiest way to identify an independent regulatory agency is when Congress, in the agency's organic act, labels it as such * * *.

The organizational situation does get rather confusing, and the structural location of an agency is not always a telling sign of its status. For instance, there is an independent regulatory agency that is fully within an executive department; conversely there are regulatory agencies, located outside such departments, which are not "independent" in the traditional sense of that term. * * *

Conversely, simply because an agency is located *outside* an executive department does not necessarily mean it is independent in the sense of being an "arm of Congress." * * * For example, the Environmental Protection Agency is regulatory in character, and is not within any other agency or department. It was created in 1970 by a reorganization plan submitted by the President to Congress, rather than by statute. In submitting the plan, then President

35. The President's Committee on Administrative Management, "Report of the Committee with Studies of Administrative Management in the Federal Government (1937)", as printed in, Subcommittee on Separation of Powers, Committee on the Judiciary, U.S. Senate, *Separation of Powers and the Independent Agencies: Cases and Selected Readings*, 91st Cong., 1st Sess., pp. 345–346 (1969).

Nixon did indicate that EPA was intended to be an independent agency, and it was repeatedly so characterized in Congress. * * *

But the EPA is by no means free of general direction by the President. As illustrated by this exchange at the [Administrator Russell] Train confirmation hearing, the EPA is not independent in that sense:

> Senator [Hugh] SCOTT: * * * I want to be absolutely fair and absolutely clear. It is my conception that you are 100 percent subject to the President. Is that your impression?
>
> Mr. TRAIN. I think legally that is probably entirely right. * * *
>
> I am fully assured that the President agrees with my interpretation and at such time, of course—I do not serve for a fixed term—that my conduct is not acceptable to the President, I can be removed forthwith. * * *

Service at the pleasure of the President is one critical difference between "independent agencies within the executive branch," such as the EPA, and other independent regulatory agencies. * * *

The size of the commission, the length of the terms, and the fact that they do not all lapse at one time are key elements of the independent structure. Because of those features, it was thought unlikely that any President would be able to influence the commissions, through the appointment power, in the same way as he could an executive department * * *. Congress placed other restrictions on the appointment power of the President. First no more than a simple majority of any commission's membership could come from a single political party; this would, it was thought, neutralize the number of commissioners selected from the President's party and assure bipartisan membership. In addition, Congress restricted the President's power to remove independent commissioners, by providing removal only for "inefficiency, neglect of duty, or malfeasance in office." * * *

All of the so-called "independent commissions" are collegial bodies, but collegial form may not be an expression primarily of Congress' desire to limit presidential influence over administrative policy. A major function of the first commissions involved the adjudication of individual cases—license applications, rate proposals, unfair trade or labor practice charges—for which a collegial tribunal may have seemed appropriate.

Criticism of collegial bodies has focused on their asserted inability to visualize the need for and to formulate general policies (i.e., to make rules) and on their deficiencies as administrators. See, e.g., MARVIN BERNSTEIN, REGULATING BUSINESS BY INDEPENDENT COMMISSION (1955): THE PRESIDENT'S ADVISORY COUNCIL ON EXECUTIVE ORGANIZATION: A NEW REGULATORY FRAMEWORK (1971) (the "Ash Council Report"). Yet no student of governmental organization has ever been able conclusively to link regulatory success or failure to the collegial or non-collegial form of an agency. See ROGER G. NOLL, REFORMING REGULATION: AN EVALUATION OF THE ASH COUNCIL PROPOSALS 102–03 (1971). See also Roger G. Noll, *The Economics and Politics of Regulation*, 57 Va.L.Rev. 1016 (1971).

When Congress creates a new agency to implement a new regulatory program, the reasons for its choice of delegate are likely to be subsumed in discussions of the powers and structure of the new entity. But Congress often delegates new authority to existing agencies, whose prior performance must surely be influential in its assignment of responsibility. The legislature may seek to influence performance by sheltering an agency from political oversight within the executive branch, e.g., FERC, or by precluding its subdelegation to officials who may lack political sensitivity.

Presidents likewise may take account of the influence of location and perspective on the exercise of delegated authority. The EPA was created by executive order in 1970, and given responsibility for administering environmental laws previously disbursed among the Departments of Agriculture, the Interior, and HEW. One motive for reassigning responsibilities was the expectation that EPA would pursue policies different from those adopted by the original delegates. See generally Alfred Marcus, *Environmental Protection Agency*, ch. 8, in JAMES Q. WILSON, THE POLITICS OF REGULATION (1980).

The rationale for the structure and location of agencies is nevertheless sometimes elusive. The return of the Social Security Administration to its pre–1939, independent status ("independent agency within the executive branch") is illustrative. Social Security Independence and Program Improvements Act of 1994, 108 Stat. 1464. The move had been brewing since at least 1983, and seems to have started in reaction to a perception of excessive political direction in the Reagan administration. This idea is voiced in the Report on the 1994 Legislation, House Report No. 103–506, U.S. Code Cong. & Admin. News, 103d Cong. 2d Sess., Vol. 4 at 1494 (1994). But the implementing device chosen in the House bill, authority vested in a three-member, bi-partisan Board, was rejected by the Senate. The Senate's structure, a single Commissioner with a fixed term, removable by the President only for cause, was finally adopted—apparently with full recognition that the Justice Department considered any limitation on the President's removal power as raising a "significant constitutional question." Statement by President William J. Clinton upon signing H.R. 4277 (Aug. 15, 1994). Id. at 1624.

The other purpose stated by the House was to improve service to the public. The President's signing statement emphasized instead bolstering public confidence in the Social Security program. The bearing of "independence" on either of these purposes is, to say the least, indirect.

In deciding where to locate an agency or regulatory program, the modern Congress confronts two strong traditions of presidential control of the administrative establishment. One is embodied in the Office of Management and Budget, which in addition to its increasingly important function as the President's policy-making coordinator, has, for over half a century, played a central role in managing the executive's budgetary affairs. As the title suggests—and its original name, Bureau of the Budget, made clear—OMB was established to provide the President a means of controlling legislative initiatives and budgetary demands. OMB has continued to perform the two main functions assumed by the old Bureau of the Budget, *viz.*, reviewing proposals for new legislation from, and annual budget requests by, all non-Congressional agencies. Although Congress has generally acquiesced in this role, albeit not without objection, it has occasionally enacted legislation specifically directing that an agency shall not be required to submit its budget requests to OMB or other Presidential officials. E.g., 15 U.S.C. § 2076(k)(1), (2) (CPSC); 7 U.S.C. § 4a(h)(1), (2) (CFTC).

The other, even older tradition makes the Attorney General, often historically a close confidant of the President, responsible for most of the government's litigation. By statute, 28 U.S.C. § 516, Pub. L. No. 89–554, § 4(c), 80 Stat. 613 (1966), only the Attorney General may ordinarily represent the United States in court. While the Department of Justice lacks the staff to handle all of the cases to which the United States or some agency is a party, it nominally decides which cases shall be brought, defended, and appealed, and determines what arguments will be advanced on the government's behalf.

The foregoing illustrations of congressional concern for agency structure, location, and relationships reveal a recurrent theme: the desire to limit the President's influence over the development and implementation of administrative policy. Often this desire is accompanied by an expectation that an agency insulated against presidential influence will be more susceptible to congressional overtures, e.g., from oversight and budget committees. Statutory specifications of structure or process may, however, have other important policy objectives.

Congress has frequently, either initially or in the light of experience, attempted to separate governmental functions that it regarded as incompatible. The APA itself prohibits the commingling of prosecutorial and adjudicatory functions, save by the individuals who constitute the agency itself. See 5 U.S.C. § 554(d). This provision reflects a judgment that such a combination impairs the fairness of agency adjudications. An analogous perception is reflected in laws that assign the roles of policymaker, prosecutor, and judge to two separate agencies. The 1970 Occupational Safety and Health Act, 29 U.S.C. § 651, assigned to OSHA responsibility for promulgating and enforcing workplace health and safety standards, 29 U.S.C. § 659, but created, also within the Department of Labor, an independent tribunal for determining guilt and assessing penalties, the Occupational Safety and Health Review Commission. 29 U.S.C. § 661.

Pursuing a different concern about the commingling of incompatible functions, Congress in 1974 disassembled the old Atomic Energy Commission, which had been responsible both for supporting development of civilian nuclear power and for assuring the safety of new generating facilities. 1977 Study on Federal Regulatory Organization, *supra*, at 102–

105. Congress made a similar judgment in 1958 when it removed responsibility for regulating the safety of commercial aviation equipment and facilities from the Civil Aeronautics Board and reassigned it to a new executive agency, the Federal Aviation Administration, which is now part of the Department of Transportation. See Louis J. Hector, *Problems of the CAB and the Independent Regulatory Commissions*, 69 Yale L.J. 931 (1960).

It would be a mistake to assume that any specific statute reflects a single coherent programmatic vision. Legislation typically embodies diverse, sometimes even conflicting conceptions of desirable public policy, with individual provisions reflecting the demands of changing political coalitions and compromise between the President and Congress. Indeed, it has been argued that modern delegations to administrators do not enunciate national policy but rather shift the debate over its content to another arena. E.g., Earl Latham, *The Group Basis of Politics: Notes for a Theory*, 46 Am.Pol.Sci.Rev. 376 (1952). In *Welcome to the Marketplace that is Washington, Mr. President*, Wash. Post, Jan. 20, 1981, at Z28, William Greider wrote:

> Congress, after all, does not really enact laws in most areas * * *. It declares worthy intentions. Let us end poverty. Let there be literacy. Let there be clean meat. * * *
>
> The legislative process has become a reflexive exercise in wishful thinking. Congress concludes that too many workers are killed and maimed every year in American industry. To general applause, it enacts a law that says industrial deaths and injuries are a grave national affliction and unsafe working conditions ought to be eliminated.
>
> Then the whole mess is turned over to an agency of the executive branch with vague instructions to work out the details. * * *

D. CRITIQUE AND REFORM OF ADMINISTRATIVE GOVERNMENT

The creation of an agency implicitly reflects two distinct sets of legislative judgments. One is that some problem requires a government response. This response is often labeled government "intervention," although the choice of rhetoric here—as throughout administrative and regulatory law—is ideologically weighted. The second is that an adequate response cannot be provided by our regulatory bodies of oldest vintage, the courts.

Administrative agencies offer an appealing alternative to courts for the implementation of policy for a variety of reasons. Most obviously, agencies can employ a variety of decision making processes and administrative tools and can be "pro-active" in defining their agendas. Additionally, an agency has a sustained, not intermittent relationship with the parties it regulates and the problems put in its charge. It can secure for itself, subject, of course, to resource constraints and privacy considerations, whatever knowledge, analysis, or analytic capacity it thinks appropriate. An "expert" agency, unlike a "generalist" court, is not dependent for what it knows about the world on the parties to particular disputes. Finally, an agency can legitimately be linked through political oversight to elected officials to a degree that would be highly inappropriate in the judicial management of litigation.

Which administrative tools and decision making processes best fit a particular government objective is, however, often far from obvious, and debate over administrative reform in the United States has proceeded unabated since the 1930s. In 1964, Congress even created a body—the Administrative Conference of the United States (ACUS)—with virtually the exclusive task of recommending improvements in administrative procedure to the other agencies of the federal government. Even in the face of substantial evidence that the ACUS was providing useful counsel and increasing understanding of administrative performance, it fell victim to the budget reduction enthusiasm of the 1990s. Exiting the administrative scene, the ACUS became yet another counter example to the conventional wisdom that agencies, once created, never die.

At the risk of oversimplification, it is a fair statement that most debates over procedural choice or reform involve the debaters' hopes to achieve some conception of one of a few common values widely associated with sound administrative process.

- Consistency with the rule of law.
- Process fairness.
- Instrumental rationality.
- Cost-effectiveness.
- Political accountability.
- Interest representation.
- Consistency with general public values (nondiscrimination, efficiency, environmental sensitivity, etc.).

Of course, one's allegiance to these values may vary in intensity, but it is rare to find commentators or, indeed, advocates, wholly indifferent to any of them. What makes reform debates interesting is not only disagreement over which of these values are most critical and over which conceptions of them are most compelling, but the realization that, in designing any decision making process, it is usually impossible to optimize all these values at once. Decisions may be responsive to the wishes of elected officials, but irrational; solicitous of the views of affected groups, but costly; responsive to public values, but outside the agency's limited legislative mandate.

In evaluating both positive and negative assessments of administrative performance, skepticism is essential. Praise or criticism of agency action inevitably emphasizes particular value priorities and may also be premised largely on sympathy or hostility towards an agency's substantive mission. Here, as elsewhere, it is rare to find a process critic who favors an agency's substantive decision, and *vice versa*.

Borrowing a page from Karl Llewellyn's famous critique of the canons of statutory interpretation, *Remarks on the Theory of Appellate Decision and the Rules or Canons About How Statutes Are to be Construed*, 3 Vand.L.Rev. 395 (1950), critiques of administrative structure, authority, procedure, or actions often march in matched pairs:

THRUST	BUT	PARRY
1. Agencies have vague mandates that make them politically and legally unaccountable.		Agencies should be permitted to avoid adherence to the strict or literal terms of their mandates where the statute would require unreasonable results.
2. Agencies are unresponsive to the concerns of affected interests.		Agencies are captured by the interests they serve or regulate.
3. Agencies flit from issue to issue with the political winds and address ephemeral, and often unimportant, public concerns.		Agencies are lumbering behemoths that cannot change direction with changing times.
4. Agencies combine legislative, executive and judicial powers in tyrannical forms.		Agencies are so bogged down in the minutiae of procedural fairness that they get nothing done.
5. Agencies spend too much time on inefficient case-by-case adjudication.		Agencies create massive inefficiencies through overgeneral regulations.
6. Agencies are bloated bureaucracies that waste public funds.		Agencies lack the resources to do their jobs and their failures to implement the law make much legislation purely "aspirational."
7. Agencies are beset by "tunnel vision" and pursue their mandates with little attention to broader public values.		Agencies are required to analyze everything and, therefore, end up doing nothing.
8. Agency regulation protects vested interests and stifles innovation.		Agencies cripple industries by demanding actions that are technologically and economically infeasible.

The reader can surely add to this list of thrusts and parries by merely consulting this morning's newspaper.

Whether these criticisms are sound—either generally or in the context of any single agency—involves matters of the deepest debate. The familiarity of these critiques, however, is part of the political milieu in which federal agencies operate. As readers form their own opinions of their merits, it is also important to consider what reform strategies are possible. A crucial question is which of the foregoing problems, even if genuine, might be mitigated through the redesign of agency mandates, powers, process, or structures of accountability—without making some other problem worse.

The difficulties of administrative reform can be highlighted by considering recent legislative and executive reform efforts—efforts that at least one of us has found less than reformative:

JERRY L. MASHAW, REINVENTING GOVERNMENT AND REGULATORY REFORM: STUDIES IN THE NEGLECT AND ABUSE OF ADMINISTRATIVE LAW

57 U.Pitt.L.Rev. 405 (1996).

I. Introduction

* * * The thesis of this article is straightforward: Reform of the administrative state is on everyone's agenda. The executive branch is busily "reinventing government" to make it more effective. Congress is proposing major "regulatory reform" legislation to promote more efficient and responsive regulation. Both initiatives are deeply problematic. The reinvention effort, by analogizing public to private action, confuses managing with governing. It therefore ignores the crucial legitimating role of public, particularly administrative, law. The congressional "regulatory reform" initiative, by contrast, exalts and exploits legal process. But the proposed "reforms" seem designed largely to skew, delay or thwart, rather than improve, administrative policy choice. Moreover, these independently destructive executive and legislative reform programs have a potential negative synergy. They may thus simultaneously undermine important legal norms while making government less effective.

II. Myopic Managerialism: The Reinvention Initiative

Presidents and Congresses have always competed for the allegiance of implementing officials. Such, for good and ill, is our constitutional design. * * *

At least since the Brownlee Committee created the idea of the chief executive virtually from whole cloth, the President's main claims have sounded in managerial efficiency. Franklin Roosevelt said as much in seeking an end to government by "independent commission" and the authority to reorganize the executive branch. He got the latter, but the power to reorganize is not the power to direct. As Harry Truman famously remarked, "He'll sit here and he'll say, 'Do this! Do that!' and nothing will happen. Poor Ike—it won't be a bit like the Army." But Presidents have continued to seek control through managerial initiatives. Richard Nixon resuscitated FDR's reorganization authority and gained legislative approval for a vastly expanded Executive Office of the President. If the President was not to have direct authority to control every federal administrative appointee (Roosevelt's lament), he would at least have a staff—perhaps sufficient—to evaluate, coordinate and monitor the far-flung executive establishment.

More recently, Ronald Reagan, as chief executive officer ("CEO"), pioneered the use of the Vice President as chief operating officer ("COO"), giving George Bush a domestic portfolio of regulatory relief activities designed to tame a fractious regulatory bureaucracy. Al Gore is the current inheritor of this mantle, passed down from Bush through his Vice President Dan Quayle. * * **

[I]t is safe to say that none of our "Chief Executives," or their COO, has been immune to the management fraternities' panaceas *du jour*. Roosevelt's demands for straight lines of executive authority reflected Taylorist visions of hierarchical control. Nixon staffed up in response to a decade or more of academic emphasis on analytic capacity as the key to rational decision making in organizations. Today, Taylor has been turned on his head: devolution is in; hierarchy is out. Similarly, the staff-heavy, policy-analytic bureaus that were the legacy of the 1960s and 1970s are now viewed as bloated at best, dysfunctional on average. Management theory has taken a new tack, and Al Gore has become the guru of government reengineering, the primary publicist for the new management paradigm of lean, flat, "customer-driven" public organizations.

The Vice President's first National Performance Review ("NPR 1") began with a report issued in September 1993 that promised nothing less than a revolutionary reshaping of the federal government. Streamlining, downsizing, and the empowering of line officials were the watchwords of the NPR's proposals. The NPR thus borrowed directly from the contemporary "customer-centered" and "empowerment-oriented" managerial philosophies that have spread rapidly throughout the private sector.

The 1993 NPR also promised $108 billion in savings. A substantial part of that savings was to come from eliminating jobs for approximately one-quarter-million government employees. With the Federal Workforce Restructuring Act of 1994, Congress quickly signed on to the downsizing goals outlined in the NPR. * * *

* Al Gore, From Red Tape to results: Creating a Government That Works Better and Costs Less; Report of the National Performance Review (1993) [hereinafter NPR I]; Reinventing the Federal Government—Phase II, in Budget of the United States Government, Fiscal Year 1996, at 141–57 (1995) [hereinafter NPR II]. The NPR is actually an ongoing process of reports, recommendations, legislative proposals, executive orders, and other activities now celebrated (sorry, reported) on its own Web Page.

But much of NPR I has little to do with simple cost savings. The Report urges downsizing from a particular perspective. Government bureaus are to be reconfigured to give better service by empowering line personnel to respond to "customer" demands. "Empowerment" here is essentially a form of internal deregulation. By executive order, President Clinton directed all agencies to jettison at least fifty percent of their internal "red tape." Thus, many of the jobs to be eliminated are those of middle managers who developed and oversaw agency systems and processes, audited compliance with internal agency policies, and evaluated personnel. They will not be needed once the regulations that they developed and policed—the "red tape" presumably strangling the line bureaucracy—have been discarded. * * *

III. Some Realism About Managerialism

It is difficult, indeed impossible, to oppose the broad goals of NPR I. Better government service at lower cost is not controversial. The problem is that these ambitious ideas concerning cutting "red tape," focusing on customers first, empowering employees, and getting back to basics seem to miss the point of the activities of most federal public agencies. * * *

When giving out Social Security disability benefits, for example, are the customers the claimants, the general working public that pays FICA taxes to support the program, or the public that politically supports the program? Surely "all of the above" is correct. These "customers," however, have differing interests. Whose demands are to be met? In making benefits determinations, at what point do procedural due process and administrative safeguards which ensure the integrity of the program become "red tape" that should be jettisoned in the interest of quicker service?

To return to the more general point, talk about doing better for less fundamentally misunderstands the purpose of most federal administrative activity. To be sure, there is some relatively straightforward service delivery at the federal level—defense and the administration of public lands loom large in this regard. The postal service and Amtrak do, as well, although both have been already partially "privatized." But most federal agencies develop general norms and adjudicate cases. They are in the governance business, not the service provision business. Their purpose is to pursue the common good, not to cater to the preferences of individual customers.

This category mistake—confusing citizens with customers—has major political and legal consequences. So conceived, NPR I has a reform agenda that conflicts with some central understandings about the political and legal control of administrative governance in the United States. On the political side, for example, NPR I seems committed to a "Greyhound theory" of congressional legislation and oversight. "Just tell us the destination and leave the driving to the front line administrators," seems to be the message to Congress. Indeed, it is hard to see how moving authority down that hierarchy could fail to lessen congressional control of public policy. * * *

[More] importantly for this discussion, it is possible that the enthusiasm for managerial reinvention has obscured the ways in which radical decentralization affects legal, as well as political, control. The long-term commitment of American administrative law has been to assure that administrative discretion is structured checked, and balanced. Administrative efficacy must be weighed against demands for liberty and legality, as well as political accountability.

When pursuing this project, American administrative law tends to presuppose clear lines of authority, hierarchical control, and responsibility focused on the top level management of agencies. For example, lawsuits claiming an improper denial of Social Security disability benefits are nominally against the Secretary of Health and Human Services. Is it to be a defense in such a proceeding for the Secretary to point out that, in the process of agency reinvention, authority to make disability decisions has been devolved to lower levels of administration that are now effectively outside of her control? Are lower level bureaucrats to be made individually responsible in damages for errors in administration? * * *

While these questions may seem fanciful, they suggest the logical implications of NPR I's management philosophy. We really cannot have the cake of dispersed administrative discretion and ingest significant legal control of it as well. * * *

The simple fact of the matter is that legal control is wonderfully bureaucratizing. Nothing focuses an administrator's mind more keenly on record keeping, turning square procedural corners, elaborate justificatory analysis, and a host of other red-tape-producing activities than the prospect of judicial review. * * *

The point is plain enough: NPR I's basic managerial presuppositions are on a collision course with administrative law's contemporary understanding of legality in administration. * * *

IV. Ensuring Regulatory Rigor Mortis: Congress Pursues Regulatory Reform

* * * [C]urrent regulatory reform proposals in Congress head in precisely the opposite direction. Seizing on administrative law's capacity to incapacitate administration, Congress is proposing to impose additional layers of legal constraint on bureaucracies that are now struggling to meet minimal performance expectations.

Prior Congresses have hardly been pikers when it comes to imposing generalized procedural or analytic requirements on agency decision making. The National Environmental Policy Act of 1969 ("NEPA"), the Paperwork Reduction Act of 1980, the Regulatory Flexibility Act, indeed the Administrative Procedure Act ("APA") itself, all impose information-gathering and analysis requirements on federal agencies. Only the first and the last, however, permitted judicial review of compliance. * * *

[M]any commentators find existing analytic requirements * * * sufficient to disable regulatory agencies. But, that is apparently not sufficient procedural protection for contemporary "regulatory reformers."

Title II of the Unfunded Mandates Reform Act of 1995 * * * codifies many of the analytic requirements that were contained in presidential executive orders from Carter through Clinton. The statute, however, makes a number of these requirements considerably more burdensome. In particular, it requires coordination and consultation with state, local, or tribal governments which might be affected by regulation and the inclusion of a summary of their comments in the rationale for any proposed or final rule. In addition, the agency must identify and consider a reasonable number of regulatory alternatives and "select the least costly, most cost-effective or least burdensome alternative."

Yet more analytic requirements were appended to the reauthorization of the Paperwork Reduction Act of 1995. * * * [T]he Congress struck another blow for analytic excess in the Small Business Regulatory Enforcement Fairness Act of 1996 and is considering a major increase in risk-benefit analysis requirements for virtually all agencies in the bipartisan Regulatory Improvement Act of 1997. (S. 981) Although it is hard to be against careful analysis truth in packaging would require that this bill be titled "The Administrative Gridlock, and Lawyers and Economists Relief Act of 199[7]."

* * * The basic idea * * * is not hard to grasp. While arguably reinforcing the accountability, reasonableness, and procedural fairness of administrative policymaking, these "regulatory reform[s]" are designed to stall and derail many rulemaking efforts. They take some of the unfortunate tendencies of contemporary American administrative law to their logical conclusions* * *. [A]dministrative legality [is] in no danger, but effective administrative governance may warrant listing in the catalogue of endangered species.

V. Conclusion

[T]he executive and legislative branches of the federal government have remarkably different ideas about what is needed to make administrative governance more responsive to the will of the people. The executive exalts efficacy seemingly heedless of its effect on legality. The Congress exalts legality precisely to destroy efficacy. That the two institutions are at cross purposes is not surprising* * *. [T]his results not only from partisan ideological differences, but because of a long-standing institutional competition built into our constitutional structure.

* * * The current executive neglect and congressional abuse of administrative law seem to have a negative form of synergy. Apparently agreeing only that government should be smaller, the combined activities of the political branches seem designed to ensure even higher levels of

incompetence and illegality. Congress is bent on adding "red tape" at least as fast as the executive purports to eliminate it. Moreover, the new "red tape" is backed by enforceable legal demands for compliance. But, with a radically downsized labor force, particularly in the staff positions necessary to meet the new regulatory reform requirements, agencies are unlikely to be able to act either effectively or legally.

Administrative Law has always seemed to walk a fine line between impertinence and irrelevance. Impertinence because it risked delaying, deflecting, or derailing needed public action. Irrelevance because notwithstanding its claims to ensure legality, administrative discretion remained ubiquitous. Striking the proper balance between legality and efficacy has never been easy. It has motivated administrative law's constant reform efforts over at least the last six decades. While arguably within that continuing reform tradition, current movements in Congress and the Executive Branch do not, in my judgment, promise much assistance in the serious task of ensuring effective governance under law.

E. UNDERSTANDING LEGISLATION, ADMINISTRATION, AND ADMINISTRATIVE LAW

Before confronting administrative law's primary materials—statutes, regulations, and cases—it is useful to think about how this field of law has emerged and what gives it distinctive shape. No single explanation will be totally satisfying, but unless we have some hypotheses about what motivates and structures this domain of U.S. law we may have little to motivate and structure our own thinking about it. As you will see, administrative law is filled with issues of institutional design—questions such as how Congress should draft the statutes that supposedly guide the activities of administrators; what role the President should have in shaping agency policies; how much deference courts should give to agency judgments; whether particular parties or groups should have greater or lesser rights to be heard in administrative proceedings or to challenge agency actions in court; and whether private parties should be able to enforce public law directly instead of federal authorities, or indirectly by seeking damages from derelict officials. How you approach these questions will depend importantly on how you think public legislative, administrative, and judicial processes *really* work and how they ought, if possible, to be made to work.

Not surprisingly, there are competing explanations of the nature of American regulatory statutes, of the behavior of bureaucrats, and of the purposes of administrative law. For present purposes we will divide the world roughly into two camps—idealists and realists. Idealists embrace a belief in the public interest and see the function of administrative law as structuring institutions and organizing agents in ways that best further public aims. Realists by contrast are skeptical that a "public interest" exists and doubt the desire of agents, public or private, to serve aims other than their own. We begin with the vision of "legal idealists"—scholars, judges, legislators, and administrative practitioners—as reflected in the conventional discourse of public law. Their explanatory rhetoric still dominates judicial opinions, legislative committee reports, and regulatory analyses, and inhabits scholarly literature.

1. THE WORLD OF THE LEGAL IDEALISTS

During the crucial middle decades of the 20th century, when the modern American state was taking its current form, the vision of government that dominated legal consciousness was one of a well-ordered input/output machine. Into the machine went social problems and political values; out came legislative programs that would translate social ideals into social reality. The new activist state was purposeful and pragmatic. Collective purposes were defined through electoral and legislative debates. Realization of those purposes was achieved through the application of expertise by administrators to whom Congress assigned specific policy domains.

During this period dramatic changes took place in society's conception of which public problems were most pressing and which institutional devices were best suited to address them. New Deal problems of infrastructure disorganization, economic distortion, and worker insecurity gave way to the Great Society's focus on civil rights and on threats to health and the environment and gaps in the welfare state. The conventional image of expert administration in the progressive and New Deal eras—an independent commission operating as a specialized tribunal—was replaced by the image of a technocratically or scientifically expert bureau, acting through prescriptive rules. Whatever the institutional details, our political and legal rhetoric celebrated the progressive translation of widely approved public ideas into concrete government programs. Failures to realize public purposes were viewed as failures of conception—either poor understanding of problems or a choice of the wrong institution to solve them. See generally STEPHEN BREYER, REGULATION AND ITS REFORM (1982).

This idealist vision of government encompassed an idealist administrative law. From this perspective, legal controls over administration—*administrative law*—should effectuate basic liberal or pluralist democratic values while simultaneously creating a flexible legal regime that accommodated great variety in programmatic designs. Flexibility was indeed crucial in a conception of government programs as exercises in pragmatic problem-solving.[1] Rigid delimitation of legislative and execu-

1. Indeed, the shift toward "pragmatism" was the great triumph of the New Deal's administrative lawyers. Beset by vigorous, sometimes vicious, attacks from conservative lawyers (see *Report of the Special Committee*, 62 Am.BarAssoc.Rev. 7819 (1937)), and even leading academic theorists (Roscoe Pound, *The Future of Law*, 47 Yale L.J. 1 (1937)), they responded by burying the critics in facts. See, e.g., James M. Landis, *Crucial Issues in Administrative Law*, 53 Harv.L.Rev. 1077–102 (1940); Louis Jaffe, *Invective and Investigation in Administrative Law*, 52 Harv.L.Rev., 1201–45 (1939); and CHARLES WOLTZ, ED., ADMINISTRATIVE PROCEDURE IN GOVERNMENT AGENCIES (1968).

tive functions was rejected. Wholesale delegations of policy discretion from Congress to administrators were sanctioned in the interests of programmatic efficacy.[2] Separation of powers allowed statutory restraints on presidential control over officers whose independence might be compromised by political interference. See *Humphrey's Executor v. United States*, 295 U.S. 602 (1935).

But administrative law was not all flexible accommodation. It embodied constraints on Congress and the executive as well. Judicial review had a recognized role in confining administrators within their jurisdictions and harnessing them to the purposes expressed in legislation. See LOUIS L. JAFFE, JUDICIAL CONTROL OF ADMINISTRATIVE ACTION (1965). Moreover, judicial enforcement of procedural safeguards reinforced the conception of citizens as rights holders in the new administrative state, and supported their participation in ongoing processes of administration. Richard B. Stewart, *The Reformation of American Administrative Law*, 88 Harv.L.Rev. 1667 (1975).

The central concern of administrative law was to mediate the tension between the ideals of governmental efficacy and participatory governance. Resolving this tension was hardly easy, but the construction of an effective legal regime for the pursuit of public purposes clearly motivated and guided the enterprise. The activist system that emerged over this period, was a pastiche of liberal and pluralist political programs. A closer look at how these two normative visions differ, and yet can be combined, will provide a sharper picture of contemporary idealist legal consciousness and its implications for administrative process.

Liberal democratic ideals of limited government and citizen rights, which initially had justified opposition to the rise of the administrative state,[3] provided inspiration for many features of modern administrative government aimed at preserving individual rights through the maintenance of the "rule of law."[4] A fundamental element of this essentially

2. As is generally well-known, the Supreme Court has invalidated a delegation of authority as too broad in only two cases in its history: *Panama Refining Co. v. Ryan*, 293 U.S. 388 (1935); and *A.L.A. Schechter Poultry Corp. v. United States*, 295 U.S. 495 (1935). Although the Supreme Court's statements concerning the vitality of the nondelegation principle both before and since 1935 suggest a vigorous constitutional restraint, see, e.g., *Field v. Clark*, 143 U.S. 649 (1892), the doctrine is in fact very nearly an empty formalism. See *Yakus v. United States*, 321 U.S. 414 (1944); *Arizona v. California*, 373 U.S. 546 (1963).

3. JAMES T. PATTERSON, CONGRESSIONAL CONSERVATION AND THE NEW DEAL: THE GROWTH OF THE CONSERVATIVE COALITION IN CONGRESS, 1933–1939 (1967). Indeed, this opposition had arisen during the progressive era and had been expressed by the leaders of the bar (Frank J. Goodnow, *Private Rights and Administrative Discretion*, 41 Am.BarAssoc.Rev. 408 (1916); Elihu Root, *Presidential Address*, 41 Am.BarAssoc.Rev. 355 (1916)). This opposition was not just opposition to a progressive social program. It included a liberal legal ideology that focused as much on procedure and remedies as on the substance of programs. ARNOLD M. PAUL, CONSERVATIVE CRISIS AND THE RULE OF LAW: ATTITUDES OF THE BAR AND BENCH, 1887–1895 (1960); see also JAMES M. BECK, OUR WONDERLAND OF BUREAUCRACY (1932); WILLIAM C. CHASE, THE AMERICAN LAW SCHOOL AND THE RISE OF ADMINISTRATIVE GOVERNMENT (1982); BARON GORDON HEWART, THE NEW DESPOTISM (1929).

4. New Dealers themselves admitted that the law must maintain protection for individual freedom notwithstanding the need for collective governmental action. Felix Frankfurter, *The Task of Administrative Law*, 75 U.Pa.L.Rev. 614 (1927).

Madisonian program is policy making anchored in a constrained legislative process—that is, a process accountable to the electorate, subject to the checks of bicameralism and the presidential veto, and confined by the constitutional limits on federal power.

Limited, accountable policy making cannot, however, avoid all conflict between state power and individual rights, nor are these structural limits self-implementing. Liberal democratic ideals demanded further that government decisions affecting individual rights be made in accordance with due process of law, e.g., *Joint Anti-Fascist Refugee Committee v. McGrath*, 341 U.S. 123 (1951), and that there be an opportunity for judicial review of the legality of decisions altering those rights, *American School of Magnetic Healing v. McAnnulty*, 187 U.S. 94 (1902). Implementing these requisites of procedural regularity and substantive legality dictates many of the subsidiary demands of U.S. administrative process—including at least (a) process transparency (published norms, open proceedings, and reason-giving), and (b) decision rationality (adequate fact-finding and justification of decisions in terms of the relevant statutory norms and evidentiary record(s)). The linchpin of the entire enterprise is judicial review to assure the protection of both substantive and procedural rights. See JAFFE, *supra*, at 320–94.

According to the now standard story, as New Deal state activism triumphed in the post-World War years over laissez-faire constitutionalism, the ideals of liberal legality in administrative law beat a hasty retreat. The law's ostensible demand for a tight connection between legislative policy and administrative action, expressed in statutory standards, collapsed. So, too, did the notion that "due process" entails judicial, or at least formal adjudicatory, process. Sanford H. Kadish, *Methodology and Criteria in Due Process Adjudication—A Survey and Criticism*, 66 Yale L.J. 319 (1957); JERRY L. MASHAW, DUE PROCESS IN THE ADMINISTRATIVE STATE (1985). In the hands of progressive judges, the notion of individual rights became as much a shield for administrative discretion as a protection for private interests. G. Edward White, *Allocating Power Between Agencies and Courts: The Legacy of Justice Brandeis*, 1974 Duke L.J. 195. Judicial search for solid evidentiary support and cogent rationalization of decisions surrendered to claims of deference to expertise and the conversion of legal issues (for courts) into questions of fact (for administrators). See, e.g., *NLRB v. Hearst Publications*, 322 U.S. 111 (1944).

Yet this apparent relaxation of legal constraints on administrative decision making did not discard liberal democratic ideas or abandon constitutional presuppositions against unconstrained administrative discretion. The appropriate techniques for defending private interests against administrative power, however, came to be understood in terms of a new political conception of democracy—normative pluralism. THEODORE LOWI, THE END OF LIBERALISM: IDEOLOGY, POLICY, AND THE CRISIS OF PUBLIC AUTHORITY (1969).

While the demand that the legislature must provide standards might be more formal than real, administrative legality still implied nonarbitrariness—that is, the rationalization of discrete decisions in terms of general norms or policies. Where were those policies to be found if not in statutes? The answer scholars and later courts provided was in *administrative* rules, KENNETH CULP DAVIS, ADMINISTRATIVE LAW TREATISE § 3:15 (1978), and prior *administrative* adjudications, HENRY FRIENDLY, THE FEDERAL ADMINISTRATIVE AGENCIES: THE NEED FOR BETTER DEFINITION OF STANDARDS (1962). Administrators could be expected, and should be required, to generate their own substantive standards, and then be held accountable to them. However, this process of administrative law making could not be wholly self-referential if accountability was to be more than a fiction. There thus emerged a complex idea of process rationality comprising several elements. One strand focused on substantive rights, not as impediments to the implementation of state policy, as "vested rights" had been in the pre–1937 Supreme Court, but as claims to procedural protections against errors in the application of policy. These substantive rights were themselves the creations of regulatory and social welfare regimes—such as business licenses and disability benefits. Sound administration thus entailed the procedural inclusion of claimants whose legal interests were artifacts of the administrative state.[5] Claimants might only have the substantive "rights" that the legislature accorded them, but courts, in policing administrative decisions, could insure that they were accompanied by procedural safeguards necessary to make those rights meaningful.[6]

As significant as they might have been, process rights in individual adjudications nevertheless could have left policy development through general rulemaking wholly to administration discretion. To fill that void the courts experimented with a host of techniques. The Administrative Procedure Act was reinterpreted to recognize new "rights" to judicial review that evaded the old rights-based limitations on standing, *Association of Data Processing Service Organizations, Inc. v. Camp*, 397 U.S. 150 (1970), ripeness, *Abbott Laboratories v. Gardner*, 387 U.S. 136 (1967), and reviewability, *Citizens to Preserve Overton Park, Inc. v. Volpe*, 401 U.S. 402 (1971). Judges "proceduralized" rulemaking by aligning the processes of fact-gathering and reason-giving in administrative policy formation more with the formal techniques of agency adjudication. Stephen F. Williams, *"Hybrid Rulemaking" Under the Administrative Procedure Act: A Legal and Empirical Analysis*, 42 U.Chi.L.Rev. 401 (1975). Courts guaranteed broad access to policy making processes by rigorous demands for notice of proposed administrative action and concurrent justification for policy choices reached in the face of vigorous

5. Charles Reich, *The New Property*, 73 Yale L.J. 733 (1964); *Individual Rights and Social Welfare: The Emerging Legal Issues*, 74 Yale L.J. 1245 (1965). These ideas were relied upon explicitly by the Supreme Court in *Goldberg v. Kelly*, 397 U.S. 254, 262 n. 8 (1970).

6. Henry Friendly, "*Some Kind of Hearing*," 123 U.Pa.L.Rev. 1267 (1975); Douglas Rendleman, *The New Due Process: Rights and Remedies*, 63 Ky.L.J. 531 (1974–75).

objection. Jerry Mashaw and David Harfst, *Regulation and Legal Culture: The Case of Motor Vehicle Safety*, 4 Yale J. on Reg. 257 (1987). Putative beneficiaries of agency protection were accorded increasing power to force action by lethargic administrators. See Chapter 9.

These developments can be described in a terminology reminiscent of liberal legality—as attempts to limit discretion by holding administrators accountable to substantive statutory criteria and to the procedural requirements of the constitution and APA. But, the form of control employed (call it "proceduralism") has other normative bases. The proceduralist conception of administrative law is the micro-political analogue of John Hart Ely's vision of constitutional adjudication. DEMOCRACY AND DISTRUST: A THEORY OF JUDICIAL REVIEW (1980). In this view, judicial review is justified by the necessity to maintain access for all groups to a political process whose democratic legitimacy consists precisely in its potential responsiveness to the wishes of those groups. Similarly, a pluralist vision of administrative process sees both procedural design and judicial policing of those designs primarily as devices for providing access to policymakers for all relevant interests. Administrative legality connotes policy making that accommodates these interests by giving them serious consideration in the development of substantive norms.

The shift from liberal to pluralist ideals required little refurbishing of administrative law's doctrinal rhetoric. Demands for process transparency and decision rationality can be used both to protect individual rights and limit government (liberalism) and to assure access for appropriate accommodation of interest groups (pluralism). The capaciousness of legal idealist categories does not, however, prevent us from distinguishing liberal or pluralist normative commitments, and their procedural analogues, from radically different ones. Secret and coercive state processes—without minimal notice, opportunity to participate, or reason giving—could hardly be part of either a liberal or a pluralist law of administration.

One of the distinctive features of the conventional administrative law discourse that we have been discussing is its presumption that norms are efficacious. Legal idealists may quarrel over whether the law ought to be protecting individual rights or facilitating interest group bargaining, but they will rarely ask whether the structures of law that they favor will really have the effects claimed. It is in this sense that the conventional rhetoric of administrative law, indeed most areas of law, reflects an idealist orientation.

To be sure, one can construct an implicit behavioral theory that follows almost necessarily from idealist talk. When judges, legislators, or administrators devise administrative procedures, or structural and review checks on administrative action they are contributing to the construction of an operationally effective and symbolically appropriate normative regime. That is administrative law's purpose and its explanation.

2. REALIST EXPLANATIONS OF ADMINISTRATIVE LAW

Realist perspectives on administrative law begin with those questions of efficacy and behavioral motivation that idealists tend to assume away. They put at center stage the question whether the normative structures that are constructed can be efficacious and they view as deeply problematic any behavioral predictions that assume altruistic behavior or ideological commitment. It is to two such theories that we now turn. One should notice as we explore them, however, that they are mirror images of the idealist vision. As idealist views about behavioral questions emerge only implicitly, so realist assumptions about normative goodness can only be inferred from the behavioral stories that they tell.

Critical Theory. "Critical realists"[7] describe administrative law using much the same rhetorical repertoire as legal idealists. Their analysis works from within the theoretical structure of legal regimes to expose the ways in which that structure fails to legitimate itself. Moreover, the critical approach recognizes that legality has a relationship both to the concrete exercise of state power and to the intellectual stories that describe the way in which power is structured, checked, and controlled. Much that the standard discourse treats as "neutral" or "natural" is revealed by critical analysis to be both biased and socially constructed.

The critical realists' story of U.S. administrative law is relatively straightforward. A law to govern administration confronts a basic conflict between individual freedom and bureaucratic control. Gerald Frug, *The Ideology of Bureaucracy in U.S. Law*, 97 Harv.L.Rev. 1276 (1984). The law's function is to maintain freedom within an apparently necessary bureaucratization of social, and particularly economic and political life. This story is highly reminiscent of the conventional lawyers' and legal academics' account of administrative process. In the idealists' vision of legality, bureaucratic domination is avoided through constraints that rely on either decisional impersonality or rational consent. *Id.* JERRY L. MASHAW, DUE PROCESS IN THE ADMINISTRATIVE STATE (1985).

For our purposes the crucial claim of critical analysis is that none of the structures or stories that purport to explain the legitimacy of administrative power suffice. Although the norms of administrative law attempt to check and structure bureaucratic power so that human freedom is maintained, they all fail for the same reason: the impossibility of separating objective and subjective spheres of decision making and, therefore, of confining bureaucratic discretion to objective judgments that preserve citizens' freedom.

The plausibility of this critique can be appreciated by a single example. One way of maintaining objectivity in administration is

7. We use this term to refer to analysts who both dissent from the dominant normative regime or ideology and who seek to unmask it as a cover for material interests. The major practitioners in the U.S. have been loosely allied in the school of Critical Legal Studies which, broadly described, promotes a methodology of "total criticism" long associated with continental social theory and deconstructive literary criticism. Critical race theory and some aspects of feminist jurisprudence also fit the mold we have in mind.

through a "formalist" explanation of the exercise of administrative power. In this view, bureaucratic implementation is a form of instrumental rationality. The goals of administration are prespecified in statutes. Those goals are objective in the sense that they are specified through a process of democratic choice. The task of administration then is itself liberating. It allows us to pursue our predetermined goals efficiently, while preserving social resources for the pursuit of other social ends. The coerciveness of any exercise of bureaucratic power is but an act of self-paternalism; it imposes on us decisions that we have already made.

To state the formalist theory in this way is virtually to reveal its defects. No selection of statutory goals can perfectly represent our collective desires even if the underlying legislative process was itself an exercise in ideal democratic choice. Not only are there gaps and "unprovided for cases," the purposes stated in any single piece of legislation are likely to conflict with those articulated in others. Bureaucratic coordination and gap-filling will, at the very least, provide occasions for exercises of discretion which are in no strong sense "controlled" by statutory language, that is, by democratic choice.

The doctrinal articulation of this formalist approach to legitimation, the "nondelegation doctrine," which ostensibly prohibits the delegation of legislative policy choice to administrators, itself contains contradictions that recognize the impossibility of formalist legality. After all, one of the purposes that we may choose by legislation is to delegate flexible authority to administrators. Our hope is that the administrators' subsequent and better understanding of the problems giving rise to collective action can produce wiser policies than we could have constructed at the time of legislating. Hence, the notion that legislators may not delegate too much legislative—that is, policy making—authority to administrators must also contain within it the idea that they *may* (and *should*) delegate *some* legislative power to administrators. Nondelegation must permit delegation. Furthermore, in order to accommodate both ideas, the nondelegation doctrine must be conceptualized as a set of standards that are sufficiently abstract to permit the continuing dialectic of constraint and flexibility in the actual practice of administrative judgment.

This is, of course, to say that the legal "rule" that maintains formalist legality, the nondelegation doctrine, is inadequate to the task of maintaining formalist legality. It contains contradictions that can be managed only through the exercise of a decisional competence that cannot be explained by, or controlled by, the Janus-faced legal rule.

Much critical scholarship has been devoted to exposing the contradictions and inefficacy of the doctrinal categories that structure contemporary liberal democratic legal discourse. The focus is on ideology, not institutions. Hence, the critical literature does not offer a comprehensive story that connects legislation and public administration with administrative law. Nonetheless, there is in the critical realists' account the continuous suggestion that legislative and bureaucratic action constitute forms of oppression. This implication is almost a foregone conclusion within the context of a theory that presumes, like the liberal or pluralist legality that it criticizes, that the exercise of state power must be constrained by law in order to preserve the liberty of the citizenry. If the realist critique is correct, that the norms that have been generated to control government oppression are contradictory or vacuous, and therefore inefficacious, it must follow that the essence of legislative and bureaucratic action is the imposition of the will of certain elites—legislators, bureaucrats, and their supporters—on everyone else.

Although Critical Legal Studies does not necessarily specify who is likely to be the dominant elite, a significant strand of CLS scholarship embraces class analysis to argue that liberal ideology works hand-in-hand with domination by the interests of capital. See generally MORTON J. HOROWITZ, THE TRANSFORMATION OF AMERICAN LAW, 1780–1860 (1977); MORTON J. HOROWITZ, THE TRANSFORMATION OF AMERICAN LAW, 1870–1960: THE CRISIS OF LEGAL ORTHODOXY (1992). Two other schools of critical thought, a strand of feminist theory and critical race studies, treat gender and race domination, respectively, as equally central features of social organization. Scholars working in these traditions—who share with CLS and with each other significant methodological, as well as analytical commitments—have produced large bodies of work in other areas of law. Yet, we have only recently begun to see work within these traditions on bureaucracy and the state that might eventually point the way to larger attacks on conventional administrative law analysis. DERRICK BELL, AND WE ARE NOT SAVED: THE ELUSIVE QUEST FOR RACIAL JUSTICE (2d ed. 1989); CATHERINE MACKINNON, TOWARD A FEMINIST THEORY OF THE STATE (1989); KATHY E. FERGUSON, THE FEMINIST CASE AGAINST BUREAUCRACY (1984); LINDA GORDON, PITIED BUT NOT ENTITLED (1994); THEDA SKOCPOL, PROTECTING SOLDIERS AND MOTHERS: THE POLITICAL ORIGINS OF SOCIAL POLICY IN THE UNITED STATES (1992); Cynthia Farina, *Conceiving Due Process*, 3 Yale J.L. & Feminism 189 (1991); Cynthia R. Farina, *Getting From Here to There*, 1991 Duke L. J. 689; Cynthia R. Farina, *Faith, Hope and Rationality, or Public Choice and the Perils of Occam's Razor*, 28 Fla. St. U. L. Rev. 109 (2000); Lucie White, *Subordination, Rhetorical Survival Skills, and Sunday Shoes: Notes on the Hearing of Mrs. G.*, 38 Buff. L.Rev. 1 (1990).

The material importance of such realist accounts is obvious. The justificatory task of administrative law looks radically different if one's background beliefs and experiences are of systematic oppression or disadvantage rather than of respect and opportunity. And, it is hardly surprising that the work of feminist and critical race theorists who have focused on public administration often relates to the welfare or social services bureaucracy—those aspects of the modern state directly involved with the support and regulation of women, particularly women of color.

"Public Choice" or "Positive Political Theory". Our second, "realist" vision of modern government, "positive political theory," makes the notion that public law pursues particular, not general interests explicit by building the process of law-creation from the ground up, from citizen

voting to administrative implementation. Although really a family of related theories, the unifying thread in positive political theory is the assumption that all actors in political life—voters, interest groups, representatives, legislative committees, bureaucrats—behave rationally to maximize or optimize some objective function (wealth, status, power). Governmental institutions and activities are thus to be explained as the outcome of the rational pursuit of individual or group ends. Because this approach emphasizes the self-interested motivations of political actors, it shares fundamental behavioral premises with microeconomics, and it is sometimes described as the application of economic analysis to politics. See generally JERRY L. MASHAW, GREED, CHAOS, AND GOVERNANCE: USING PUBLIC CHOICE TO IMPROVE PUBLIC LAW (1997).

This body of theory is "positive" in the sense that it aspires to make predictions about the form that institutions or collective action will take or the expected outputs of collective action given certain organizational forms. Positive analysts do not explicitly assert that rational persons would value only wealth, or anything else. The underlying presupposition of rational actors pursuing their own "self interest," however, may easily be interpreted as suggesting that the normative rhetoric of much political action—and of conventional administrative law discourse—is only so much window-dressing obscuring the underlying pursuit of private satisfaction. Positive political theory thus has a "realist" flavor similar to the explanations of various critical realists, but without engaging questions of ideology or the dominance of particular social groups.

To see the "unmasking" side of positive political theory in stark relief we might contrast it with an idealized version of the democratic-bureaucratic process. A naive idealistic vision of lawmaking in the U.S. democratic system might say something like this: Under conditions of majority rule statutes express the desires of a majority of citizens. Bureaucratic organizations are designed to assure that administrators carry out the citizens' desires as expressed in statutes. Administrative law is that body of law that protects the citizenry against the failure of administrators to carry out the statutory policies put in their charge and against unfairness in the treatment of any person or group in further specifying or applying those policies.

Now, almost everyone would immediately object that U.S. democracy is "representative democracy" and that therefore the laws passed by representative assemblies should not be imagined to reflect perfectly the desires of the citizenry. Nevertheless, in the idealist account this "defect" is assumed to be ameliorated by the dynamics of the system. Over time the voters can replace legislators whose preferences do not reflect those of their constituents. Similarly, everyone recognizes some slack in the system of statutory instructions for bureaucrats. But, here again, congressional oversight, congressional budgetary authority, and the opportunity for statutory amendment, together with judicial policing of particular actions for irrationality and lack of authority, combine in the idealist account to keep bureaucratic organizations within the pathways marked out by the people's representatives.

The basic implication of much of positive political theory is that the benign governmental process just described does not exist and is impossible to construct. The notion that voters' preferences control legislative action or that legislative action controls bureaucratic decision making is, in this view, a fundamental misdescription of U.S. government. In fact, positive political theory seems to say, there is no demonstrable relationship between voter or even representative preferences and the outcomes of the legislative process. Rather, the most plausible view of both representative assemblies and bureaucracies is that they satisfy the demands of certain special interest groups, including the interests of legislators and bureaucrats themselves.

In the positivists' account the initial and fundamental difficulty with the story of majority rule is the presupposition that citizens pay attention to governance. In one of the foundational texts of positive political theory, THE CALCULUS OF CONSENT, LOGICAL FOUNDATIONS OF CONSTITUTIONAL DEMOCRACY (1962), James Buchanan and Gordon Tullock present a strong argument instead for rational voter apathy. Any citizen who calculated the likelihood that his or her vote would be determinative in the election of a legislative representative, discounted by the probability that the representative would in fact correctly express the citizen's preferences with respect to legislation that came before the assembly, would conclude that voting is useless. The expected value from casting a vote is dwarfed by the combined costs of obtaining sufficient information to determine how to vote and of voting itself. Moreover, even if we were to assume that voters were conscientious and well informed about the actions of their representatives—or could exclude representatives entirely by choosing policy directly—we could have no confidence that the policies chosen actually represented the preferences of the electorate. That at least is the implication of another foundational text, Kenneth Arrow's famous SOCIAL CHOICE AND INDIVIDUAL VALUES (1963).

Moreover, since Arrow's initial article on the subject in 1950, he and others have demonstrated that this "paradox of voting" may apply to a large number of the run-of-the-mill issues that come before electorates or assemblies. See generally DENNIS MUELLER, PUBLIC CHOICE (1979); WILLIAM RIKER, LIBERALISM AGAINST POPULISM: A CONFRONTATION BETWEEN THE THEORY OF DEMOCRACY AND THE THEORY OF SOCIAL CHOICE (1982); AMARTYA SEN, COLLECTIVE CHOICE AND SOCIAL WELFARE (1970); Amartya Sen, *Social Choice Theory: A Re-Examination*, 45 Econometrica 53 (1977).

Although interesting in its own right and suggestive concerning certain features of institutional design, the voting theory branch of positive political theory need not detain us. Our interest is primarily in bureaucratic institutions. Moreover, however useless it may be, many voters do vote. And, however unknowable the relationship between majority rule outcomes and the underlying preferences of the electorate, people do engage in political action *as though* their demands might influence what public policies are chosen. How are we to understand the political behavior that we observe?

This strand of positive political theory owes much to another important text: Mancur Olson's THE LOGIC OF COLLECTIVE ACTION (1965). Observing that people do engage in politics, particularly as members of pressure groups demanding particular policies or statutes, Olson asked what the determinants of political mobilization would be for rational political actors. The unsurprising answer is that people will engage in politics when the expected returns from that effort exceed its cost. And, while this might rarely be true for any single act of voting, where politics permit individuals or groups to demand specific policies, they may find that the benefits of convincing legislators to take favorable action exceed the costs of political mobilization.

Olson, however, recognized another problem with political mobilization. If A and B both want and will benefit from the same policy, each has a strong incentive to shift the costs of political mobilization to the other. Since most policies that favor a group do so in a way that makes it impossible to prevent the benefits from accruing to all members, including those who remained on the sidelines during the (sometimes expensive) campaign for their enactment, all potential political action groups are beset by a "free rider" problem. The crucially important question then is, "Which groups will form and engage in political action?" Or to put it in other terms, "How can the free rider problem be solved for groups who would be better off if they could all act together to pursue policies that benefit the group?"

Olson predicts that solutions will emerge in two basic situations. In one sort of case groups need not actually form to lobby for a policy because benefits to a single member more than offset the full costs of the political action necessary to secure its adoption. This "group member" might be a quasi-monopolistic producer or even a politician who hopes to make a career out of a particular issue. In the other prototypical situation, groups solve their organizational difficulties through some device for penalizing members who fail to pay their fair share of the costs of political action. The most straightforward situation is one in which the group already provides selective benefits in forms such as technical information, professional prestige, group health benefits, or the like. Receipt of these goods and services can often be "tied" to support of lobbying activity in ways such as dues, that prevent members from receiving the first without contributing to the second.

The clear implication of Olson's work is that group formation and hence political activity, will be dominated by interest groups which either need not organize or which can solve the "free rider" problem by the selective provision of benefits. Large groups, those whose members will normally have similar small stakes in a particular issue, will find it difficult to overcome the impediments to effective political action. By contrast, monopolistic or quasi-monopolistic enterprises that can capture most of the benefits from particular public actions, or producer and professional groups that have already formed for other purposes, have a major advantage in pluralist politics.[8]

Olson's analysis describes only the "demand" side of the legislative equation. Why should legislators respond to attempts by special interests to feather their nests at the expense of the general public? To answer this question positive political theory must identify an "objective function" for legislators. According to DAVID MAYHEW, CONGRESS: THE ELECTORAL CONNECTION (1974), and MORRIS FIORINA, CONGRESS: KEYSTONE OF THE WASHINGTON ESTABLISHMENT (2d ed. 1979), the legislator's objective function is reelection. He or she responds to interest group demands based on the expected benefits of that response in retaining office. Legislators will supply legislation to interest groups which demand it when doing so helps the legislator—or a majority of them—gain or stay in office.

The trick in predicting what legislation will emerge is to be able to describe how interest group demand matches up with legislative supply. Michael Hayes, in LOBBYISTS AND LEGISLATORS: A THEORY OF POLITICAL MARKETS (1981), develops a general "transactional model" of the legislative process. In doing so he draws on a taxonomy of legislative politics first developed by James Q. Wilson in his work, POLITICAL ORGANIZATIONS (1973).

The results of Hayes' transactional analysis are not very encouraging. It tells us to expect that policies having widely distributed benefits and costs will not be adopted even if they would substantially improve general welfare. No one will organize to demand or supply them. By contrast, where policies offer concentrated benefits whose costs can be distributed to an unorganized and apathetic public, the political exchange markets should generate a large number of transactions. Perhaps even more depressing, where broad public benefits are achievable through the imposition of costs on a small number of enterprises or individuals we should expect that the legislature will either fail to act or will delegate the imposition of these costs to an administrative agency. And by later denying the agency the necessary resources to get the job done, legislators may protect well-organized interests from most of the costs and simultaneously blame the bureaucrats for failing to carry out the ringing mandate embodied in the statute. Similar behavior should be expected where benefits and costs are both concentrated.

It is at this point in the positive account of lawmaking that administrators finally make an appearance. But, they have not been overlooked elsewhere in positive political theory. In particular, William Niskanen has developed a theory of bureaucratic action that does for agencies what Mayhew and Fiorina did for legislators, that is, describes an objective function for bureaus and explains how that objective function might be used to predict administrative behavior. WILLIAM NISKANEN, BUREAUCRACY AND REPRESENTATIVE GOVERNMENT (1971).

8. For an empirical analysis partially confirming but partially disconfirming Olson's predictions, see KAYE SCHLOZMAN & JON TIERNEY, ORGANIZED INTERESTS AND AMERICAN DEMOCRACY (1986).

In Niskanen's models, agencies have a straightforward goal: to maximize the size of their budgets. These budgets are obtained from a Congress which has sole possession of the keys to the federal treasury. Nevertheless, agencies are not without weapons. In particular, they may have a virtual monopoly over information about the effects of particular policies or over the relationship between bureaucratic inputs and policy outcomes. The result, according to Niskanen, is a process of monopsonistic bargaining between Congress (or the relevant committees) and the agencies concerning the size of the bureaucratic budget. The outcome of this bargaining is predictable—the steady growth of agency budgets over time. Not only are agencies themselves well-organized interest groups which can provide favors to legislators in return for increases in appropriations, legislators are not by inclination budget cutters. Because the existence of administrative agencies is explicable, in positive political theory, in terms of their electoral advantages for legislators, and because appropriations subcommittees can be expected to be made up of members most benefitted by the activities of agencies whose budgets they oversee, administrators will be bargaining with highly sympathetic legislators.

Positive political theory acknowledges some difficulties with this depiction of compliant legislators and accommodating agencies, supported, of course, by demanding interest groups—the so-called "iron triangle." The agencies' monopoly over information may mean that it is difficult for legislators to determine whether the agencies' activities are actually beneficial to their reelection. Monitoring agency activities and penalizing them for poor performance is costly for legislators, and it gives rise to a problem of "agency costs," an issue that has been extensively developed in the literature on private firms. To put the matter concretely, the problem is to discover how principals can, at least cost, insure that their agents are serving the principal's interests rather than pursuing interests of their own.

The answer offered by one group of positive political theorists speaks directly to the question of what explains the structure of administrative law. According to Matthew McCubbins, Roger Noll and Barry Weingast, legislators attempt to solve their agency cost problems by the construction of administrative procedures, or more generally, administrative law. *Administrative Procedures as Instruments of Political Control*, 3 J.L.Econ. & Org. 243 (1987); *Structure and Process, Politics and Policy: Administrative Arrangements and the Political Control of Agencies*, 75 Va.L.Rev. 431 (1989). Although complexly argued, the "McNoll-Gast" thesis is straightforward. Legislators who vote to create programs, at least hypothetically, want administrators to carry out the statutory instructions. Because monitoring of administrators is costly, legislators may empower others (citizens, firms and courts) to monitor administrators for them. Their desire to empower others to monitor administrators to protect original legislative bargains, according to this view, explains many of administrative law's demands for transparency, open and regular procedures, and judicial review.

Legislatures define administrative procedure, that is they define specific beneficiary rights, prescribe processes through which those rights may be defended, and set up external institutions—particularly judicial review—to protect beneficiary-monitors' interests. In so doing legislators protect their own interests in maintaining the bargains they have struck and maintain the political support of those with whom they have transacted. From this perspective, the normative emphasis in conventional legal discourse on the protection of individual rights or the pluralistic values of participation in administrative processes is translated into the positive political vocabulary of monitoring, agency costs, and sanctioning techniques. Rather than the elaboration of some fundamental commitment to liberal or pluralist democracy, as in the idealists' story, the hallmark features of U.S. administrative process are explicable as the creations of legislators bent on controlling their agents at the least cost to themselves.

As this discussion suggests, positive political theory is composed of a nested set of interrelated hypotheses. While no theorist claims to offer a complete, positive view of governance in all its many guises, the insights of different theorists fit together to provide an overall picture. Yet, the resulting portrait is one that many find unpersuasive. Indeed, positive political theory has been attacked root and branch, perhaps stem, leaf, and tendril.[9]

At the most fundamental level critics object that the positivists have completely misunderstood what politics and political action are about. Rather than the aggregate attempts by individuals to maximize previously determined private values, neo-republican theorists argue that politics is primarily about the collective definition of public values.[10] From this perspective the activities that positive political theorists classify as costs—becoming informed about public issues, organizing groups to act on the basis of collective beliefs and the like—are really benefits that people seek by engaging in political action.[11]

Other critics argue that the predictions of positive political theory are falsified more often than proved, and they adduce impressive evidence for this claim. Categories of statutes that are not supposed to exist, e.g., health and safety regulatory regimes providing diffuse benefits

9. Two excellent general critiques are Daniel Farber and Philip Frickey, *The Jurisprudence of Public Choice*, 65 Tex.L.Rev. 873 (1987); and William H. Panning, *Formal Legislative Processes*, in J. Loewenberg, S. Patterson and M. Jewell Eds., Handbook of Legislative Research 669–97 (1985). Although influential in the U.S., the U.K., Australia and New Zealand, many European scholars discount public choice or positive political theory as "normatively impoverished and analytically incomplete." Gregory S. Alexander, *New Theories of the Regulatory State: Playing With Fire*, 87 Corn. L. Rev. 449, 451 (2002).

10. See, e.g., A. Maass, Congress and the Common Good (1983); Cass Sunstein, *Interest Groups in American Public Law*, 38 Stan.L.Rev. 29 (1985); *Legal Interference With Private Preferences*, 53 U.Chi.L.Rev. 1129 (1986).

11. See, e.g., Michael C. Dorf & Charles F. Sabel, *A Constitution of Democratic Experimentation*, 98 Colum. L. Rev. 267 (1998). For a more skeptical view of the possibility of modern governance in this form, see Frank Michelman, *The Supreme Court, 1985 Term—Forward: Traces of Self-Government*, 100 Harv.L.Rev. 4 (1986).

and imposing concentrated costs, proliferate. And, empirical investigations of the voting behavior of legislators find that ideology—a legislator's value commitments—explains as much as, or more than, the material interests of those whose support is needed for reelection. See generally Joseph P. Kalt and Mark A. Zupan, *The Apparent Ideological Behavior of Legislatures: Testing for Principal–Agent Slack in Political Institutions*, 33 J.L. & Econ. 103 (1990), and authorities there cited.

At another level, positive political theory is faulted for its scientific pretensions and its addiction to the *post hoc ergo propter hoc* fallacy. See, e.g., DONALD GREEN & IAN SHAPIRO, PATHOLOGIES OF RATIONAL CHOICE THEORY (1994); Mark Kelman, *On Democracy Bashing: A Skeptical Look at the Theoretical and Empirical Practice of the Public Choice Movement*, 74 Va.L.Rev. 199 (1988). Predictive incompetence is not a happy feature for an approach claiming to have only "positive" implications. Worse yet, these modern realists are found to be naive about electioneering and the political organization of the Congress. They appear to have missed the fact that legislators may solidify electoral support through false favors that have no effect on legislative output. Morris Fiorina and Roger Noll, *Voters, Legislators, and Bureaucracy: Institutional Design in the Public Sector*, 68 Am.Econ.Rev. 256 (1978). And, the presumption that committee membership will be unrepresentative of the Congress is argued not only to be false, but a violation of what a more sophisticated rationale choice perspective on congressional organization should predict. KEITH KREHBIEL, INFORMATION AND LEGISLATIVE ORGANIZATION (1991). Some public choice scholars even propose that the public choice perspective supports the current structure of the administrative state as a plausible device for pursuing something like the "public interest". See David D. Spence and Frank Cross, *A Public Choice Case for the Administrative State*, 89 Geo. L. J. 97 (2000); David B. Spence, *Public Choice Progressivism, Continued*, 87 Corn. L. Rev. 397 (2002).

Indeed, the circumstance that positive political theory has been developed in fits and starts by many minds with many interests provides fertile opportunity for pointing out that positive theorist B has forgotten about the findings of positive theorist A. Interest group theorists, for example, often seem to forget the serious monitoring cost problems that are the principal preoccupations of agency theorists. See Jerry L. Mashaw, *Pro-Delegation: Why Administrators Should Make Political Decisions*, 1 J.L.Econ. & Org. 81 (1985). Meanwhile the latter may be so preoccupied with ferreting out how politicians solve the "agency" problem that they forget to ask whether they would want it solved in any event. Jerry L. Mashaw, *The Economics of Politics and the Understanding of Public Law*, 65 Chi.-Kent L.Rev. 123 (1989). And if strategic rationality is tough for armchair theorists, how difficult must it be for politicians in the legislative hot seat? It could even drive frustrated legislators to vote their consciences and to support administrative process reforms that promoted fairness and rationality.

3. A PERSPECTIVE ON PERSPECTIVES

An attempt to place the competition between idealist and realist accounts of legislation, administration, and administrative law into historical perspective would see it as part of an ongoing conversation. The conventional normative rhetoric of the idealist account is perhaps the quintessential expression of the "legal process school" of U.S. jurisprudence. Reacting to a formalist common law ideology that rejected the possibility of the modern administrative state, the pragmatic realists of the 1920s and 1930s exposed the implicit normative commitments of U.S. private law and debunked the idea that a commitment to legality entailed a commitment to the status quo. THURMAN ARNOLD, THE FOLKLORE OF CAPITALISM (1937). Nevertheless, the realists failed to generate a comprehensive explanation of the bases for legal legitimacy. That task remained for the legal process school, which connected the pluralists' vision of an "open" democracy with a set of institutional understandings that legitimated the exercise of governmental power.[12] For the legal process school the key idea was that legitimacy—what they termed "the principle of institutional settlement"—flowed from the appropriateness of the processes and institutional structures for legal decision making, not from substantive agreement with all decisional results. For them, the duly arrived at result of properly established procedures ought to be accepted as binding upon all of society unless and until they are duly changed.

Contemporary non-academic discourse in administrative law adheres very closely to this model. Debate is constant about where authority should properly be allocated and by what processes agencies ought to make the decisions properly put in their charge. This legal process approach to law generally and to administrative law in particular is as conventional today as legal formalism was a century earlier. But the academic literature is much more "realist" in tone, and academic scribblers have had influence before.

The contemporary realist critique of the legal process view in some sense repeats the critique that the original realists made of legal formalism in the 1920s. See, e.g., Jan Deutsch, *Neutrality, Legitimacy and the Supreme Court: Some Intersections Between Laws and Political Science*, 20 Stan.L.Rev. 169 (1968). From the perspective of critical legal studies, for example, the normative structure of administrative law is contradictory or vacuous. Thus, the institutional roles and process characteristics that are employed to legitimate state power should have no greater standing than the formalist legal doctrine exploded two generations earlier. But, like their legal realist forbears, the critical legal scholars offer no normative program to put in the place of the legal process school's commitment to institutional and procedural appropriateness.

12. The foundational texts here are LON FULLER, THE LAW IN QUEST OF ITSELF (1940), and HENRY HART & ALBERT SACKS, THE LEGAL PROCESS: BASIC PROBLEMS IN THE MAKING AND APPLICATION OF LAW (Tent. ed. 1958).

Positive political theory may represent an even more devastating attack, if its "findings" are to be believed. And even some of its strongest opponents believe that "public choice" now sets the scholarly agenda. Cynthia Farina, *Getting From Here to There*, 1991 Duke L.J. 689. Yet, it too lacks explicit normative underpinnings. People may act principally on the basis of rational calculations of their own self-interest,[13] but that does not suggest what the structure of legal control over public institutions ought to look like. Positive theory may properly instruct us not to forget the teachings of a much earlier generation of practical political scientists—those who wrote the Constitution and the Federalist Papers—but having pointed out that ordinary humans do not put on the mantle of sainthood by ascending to public office, they do not tell us how we should want to structure our collective institutions or control the activities through administrative law.

Of course if the exercise of state power is but a mask for the pursuit of private interest, dismantling public programs and public institutions might well be the implicit normative program of positive political theory. Allocative and distributive decisions should be returned to the market or to the control of social norms. If some public action is necessary, institutional designers should rely on "market-mimicking" forms of regulation and cost-effectiveness analysis to discover "least/worse" means of governance. Thomas Merrill has argued that, "Those who have thoroughly assimilated public choice analysis tend to be libertarians." *Capture Theory and the Courts, 1967–1983*, 72 Chi.-Kent L. Rev. 1039, 1070 (1997). Perhaps, but this is not a *necessary* implication of the positive analysis of public institutions.

The normative emptiness of realist positions has begun to be filled by a new group, recently given the name of "New Public Law Scholars," see *Symposium: The New Public Law*, 89 Mich.L.Rev. 707 (1991), who seek to rebuild a vision of normative legality by attending to those things that are underdeveloped in the legal process perspective. Informed by the two realist critiques we have discussed, these theorists emphasize the purposive and forward-looking nature of legal rules and legal institutions, the substantive as well as the procedural aspects of justice, the need to reconnect majority rule with a greater sense of self-governance and equal participation in public life, and the ways in which public values are created as part of or through the processes of governance. As of yet this new "school" is an eclectic collection of ideas held together more by tone and style than by fully articulated theory. These scholars nevertheless take even more seriously than their legal process forbears the notions that in law the "is" and the "ought" are intimately and complexly linked, that principles of legality must be grounded in normative ideals, and that those ideals are constantly evolving through a dialogic process in which values are sharply contested. See JERRY L. MASHAW, GREED, CHAOS AND GOVERNANCE; USING PUBLIC CHOICE TO IMPROVE PUBLIC LAW 1–49 (1997).

13. For a concise exploration of the analytic difficulties with this position, see JON ELSTER, SOUR GRAPES: STUDIES IN THE SUBVERSION OF RATIONALITY (1983).

Feminist theory is likewise contributing to the evolving debates about the normative underpinnings of the administrative state. Historically, American notions of administrative legitimacy are tightly bound to ideas of liberal legality. The latter emphasize norms of universality and impartiality, along with the practical utility (if not necessity) of organizational hierarchy. Feminist approaches to the sociology of organizations, and to the understanding of moral justification for the exercise of power, challenge the basic moral premises of administrative law as conventionally understood. See generally ALBERT J. MILLS AND PETA TANCRED, EDS., GENDERING ORGANIZATIONAL ANALYSIS (1992); Alison M. Jagger, *Caring as a Feminist Practice of Moral Reason, in* VIRGINIA HELD, ED., JUSTICE AND CARE: ESSENTIAL READINGS IN FEMINIST ETHICS 179–202 (1995); Sara Ruddick, *Remarks on the Sexual Politics of Reason*, in EVA KITTAY AND DIANA T. MEYERS, EDS., BEYOND MORAL THEORY 237–260 (1987).

These theoretical debates, of course, also have complex connections with ongoing political activities outside the academy and, indeed, outside the legal profession. Idealist visions seem congenial to periods in which many groups or movements seem destined to convince an activist state that their programs—whether of social insurance, regulation of monopolies, civil rights, or environmental protection, to name but a few prominent examples—embody "the public interest." Realist accounts voice disappointment with the degree to which public programs fail to achieve their public interest ideals, and seek to explain that underachievement observed either in terms of the hidden agendas of dominant elites or through a deep skepticism concerning the possibility of distinguishing the "public interest" from interest group special pleading. They seem congenial in a world perceived as hopelessly incapable of discovering common ends and mired in conflict over the means for achieving even agreed upon aims.

Yet to say that the optimistic period of the mid-century "fits" the idealists' account, while post–1960s realism responds better to our contemporary sense of the possibilities for effective collective action, would itself prejudge the direction of causation between ideas and events. Events clearly mold our beliefs and beliefs our interpretations of events. Actions and ideas together generate a legal culture[14] that we must seek to understand, even as we subtly shift it by the understandings we create. In that important sense learning is action. For as we attempt to understand administrative law, we cannot help but make it as well.

It is in that sense, too, that intellectual commitments shape and are shaped by political commitments and actions. Legal idealists often share an activist faith in the power of government to do good. Realist critics have often either been radicalized by the limitations of the collective "goods" they have seen produced or have turned back toward the

14. Indeed, yet another approach to administrative law would study the field explicitly in terms of cultural analysis. See, e.g., JERRY L. MASHAW & DAVID L. HARFST, THE STRUGGLE FOR AUTO SAFETY (1990); Errol Meidinger, *Regulatory Culture: A Theoretical Outline*, 9 L. & Pol. 355 (1987); Richard Pildes, *The Unintended Cultural Consequences of Public Policy: A Comment on the Symposium*, 89 Mich.L.Rev. 936 (1991).

continuing alternative vision that inhabits U.S. politics—an emphasis on private property and market allocation. The "privatization" and "deregulation" efforts of post-Vietnam American governance are ample evidence of the strength of these sentiments.

This is not an argument that differing explanations of administrative law should be reduced to some set of political beliefs that they support. Each of the explanatory approaches we have discussed deserves evaluation in its own terms for rigor, coherence, predictive or explanatory utility, and normative attractiveness. The point is merely that, in making such assessments, to ignore the political dimension of alternative claims would be an exercise in naivete, not virtue. Moreover, the close connection of theoretical concerns in administrative law with *both* current events and political commitments provides added zest to the search for truths that will remain both contestable and contested.

4. BACK TO THE FUTURE

American administrative law has been around even less than the "four score and seven years" that marked the distance between our founding and the Gettysburg Address. Although the federal government took on major developmental (and certain other administrative) responsibilities during the Nineteenth Century, substantial federal regulatory and entitlement programs began with the New Deal. Virtually no case or statute passed prior to the Administrative Procedure Act of 1946 is today viewed as significant for contemporary understanding of administrative legality. (*Marbury v. Madison* is perhaps the exception that proves the rule.)

Rapid as these developments have been, many would describe American administrative law as currently out of touch with administrative, much less economic, social, and political, reality. On this view, administrative legality has been built on a vision of centralized administration and accountability through hierarchical control that is no longer either feasible or desirable. Large manufacturing enterprises are giving way to smaller and more specialized firms and to a dominant services sector. The administrative and regulatory behemoths in the public sector that mimicked private industrial organization—both to support and to regulate it—seem increasingly anachronistic. Locked into legal paradigms of rule-bound administration and ubiquitous legal accountability, these organizations arguably lack the flexibility, knowledge, and legal instruments to implement existing statutory requirements.

Against this backdrop, our steady diet of efforts to reform administrative law and administrative organization is not surprising. Major regulatory agencies like the Interstate Commerce Commission and the Civil Aeronautics Board have disappeared. As we have noted, the federal administrative establishment has for some time been embarked on a thoroughgoing attempt to streamline its operations and downsize its presence. Large areas of federal responsibility have devolved to states or have been "contracted out" to private for-profit or nonprofit enterprises.

One alternative future of administrative law thus might be to increase its efficacy by marginalizing its relevance. The more the government deregulates, privatizes, and "contracts out," the less administration there is and the less administrative law.

Yet it is hard to imagine the abandonment of the economic security goals that dominated New Deal activism or the attempts to tame the externalities of super-abundance that inspired the important regulatory and entitlements legislation of the last three decades of the 20th century. And, if that is true, then a return to the legal structure of American capitalism in the 19th and early 20th centuries seems highly unlikely. The obvious need for continued state involvement in the direction of economic and social life thus confronts the looming incapacity of government in its current form to play an effective role in a radically changed and still rapidly changing economic and social environment. What are we to do with an administrative law understood to be simultaneously necessary and incompetent?

International events are likely to make these questions appear only more pressing on both a national and global basis. The accelerating integration of the European Union, accompanied by corresponding advances in the exercise of policymaking authority by transnational governance structures, has aroused the deepest possible interest among academics, politicians, and the broader publics of Europe regarding questions of democratic legitimacy and the role of accountable administrative government in responding to social needs. The governments involved, and the new transnational institutions they are evolving, are paying explicit attention to "reinventing government" initiatives in the United States, while spawning reform efforts of arguably even more ambitious scope. However improbably, American administrators have begun to repay these attentions of others. A 2002 OMB report to Congress on the costs and benefits of regulation sought explicitly to put recent administrative reforms in the United States in the context of recommendations by the OECD and other international organizations—a rather amazing rhetorical move in an administration hardly known for its internationalist perspective on domestic policy making. OMB OFFICE OF INFORMATION AND REGULATORY AFFAIRS, STIMULATING SMARTER REGULATION: 2002 REPORT TO CONGRESS ON THE COSTS AND BENEFITS OF REGULATIONS AND UNFUNDED MANDATES ON STATE, LOCAL AND TRIBAL ENTITIES 64–69 (2002).

Indeed, the European Union has found it far easier not only to imagine, but actually to implement an activist transnational executive apparatus, than it has a genuinely representative and responsive continental legislature. It thus hardly seems coincidental that the advance of administrative governance abroad has helped motivate global interest in normative theories of democracy that do not rest exclusively on the accountability of elected representatives to vigilant voters to explain democracy's legitimating force. Instead, theories of so-called "deliberative democracy" find such legitimating force chiefly in structures of reasoned discourse among free and equal citizens jointly ascertaining what the public interest requires in the face of society's innumerable challenges. See James Bohman, *Introduction*, in JAMES BOHMAN AND WILLIAM REHG, DELIBERATIVE DEMOCRACY: ESSAYS ON REASON AND POLITICS (1997).[15] "Deliberation," in such theories, is a special form of rational communication operating in formal arenas and under specified norms (which, pursuant to deliberation, may become further specified). The fact that new information and communications technologies—the Internet, most notably–now exist to facilitate low-cost information sharing, deliberation, and opinion aggregation on an international basis has seemed to lend at least some plausibility to the institutionalization of such a model of democracy.

Given Americans' oft-expressed discontents with the force of our own special interests and ideological factions, as well as an apparently deepening sentiment that the voices of "ordinary" citizens go unheard in the halls of power, American academics have also shown interest in a view of democracy that embraces the capacity of deliberating citizens to act in publicly motivated ways. Some see in the administrative law model of notice-and-comment rulemaking, followed by judicial review, the plausible seeds of a more genuine spirit of public deliberation. For others, reenvisioning public administration and public law to make it adequate to the needs of the Twenty–First Century entails far more thoroughgoing change. See, e.g., Michael C. Dorf and Charles F. Sabel, *A Constitution of Democratic Experimentalism*, 98 Colum.L.Rev. 267 (1998). The basic idea of these more ambitious theorists is to make law as decentralized, flexible, and dynamic as the society it seeks to structure and govern—without at the same time reverting to the "expertise" model of administrative law that beguiled the early 20th Century progressive movement. Indeed, something like this idea has been a persistent strain in the "law and society" literature over the past several decades. See, e.g., PHILLIP SELZNICK, LAW AND SOCIETY IN TRANSITION: TOWARD RESPONSIVE LAW (1978); Gunther Teubner, *Substantive and Reflexive Elements in Modern Law*, 17 L. and Soc'y Rev. (1983).

These intellectual efforts are, for now, at relatively giddy heights of abstraction. And, as one commentator has remarked, "Faced with having to envision a new decisionmaking regime, erect the legal structures necessary to support it, and defend its constitutionality, it is easier to insist that nothing really new is going on." Jody Freedman, *Collaborative Governance and the Administrative State*, 45 UCLA L.Rev. 1, 98 (1997). That is, after all, the usual path of legal development, as the chapters that follow will often demonstrate.

15. The seminal modern text on deliberative democratic theory is JÜRGEN HABERMAS, BETWEEN FACTS AND NORMS: CONTRIBUTIONS TO A DISCOURSE THEORY OF LAW AND DEMOCRACY (1996) (William Rehg, trans.), which appeared in German in 1992. For American scholars, however, the theme of deliberation is a conspicuous feature of constitutional thought as early as THE FEDERALIST (Clinton Rossiter, ed. 1961), whose authors advocated the new constitutional structure devised at the Philadelphia convention of 1787, in part based on the spirit of deliberation it would likely foster.

Chapter 2

THE LEGISLATIVE CONNECTION

Virtually all agency action begins with a statute. More importantly for purposes of administrative law, statutes provide the legitimating standard for much of agency decision making. The agent—the administrative agency—has only those powers provided by its principal—the legislature. Legislative specification of agency jurisdiction, purposes, and powers thus is thought to provide both democratic legitimation for the exercise of administrative authority and an instrumental conception of administration as essentially the task of implementing policy choices made in the political process.

It is hardly surprising, therefore, that one of the concerns of U.S. administrative law should be to regulate the linkage between legislative and administrative action. But, legal doctrine confronts a world wonderfully more complex than the one our simplistic principal-agent analogy suggests. In that world, agencies may appear to behave more like independent entrepreneurs seeking funding from the Congress for projects of their own than like well-instructed agents implementing their principal's orders. Whether administrative law should seek to provide a structure within which this and other sorts of legislative-administrative connections can flourish, or should seek to reinforce the principal-agent model, is but one of the issues that these pages pursue.

A. STATUTORY VAGUENESS AND ITS ANTIDOTES

1. THE "NONDELEGATION" DOCTRINE

Article I, section 1 of the United States Constitution provides: "All legislative Powers herein granted shall be vested in a Congress of the United States, which shall consist of a Senate and House of Representatives." Similar provisions appear in virtually every state constitution. For at least 150 years the Supreme Court's decisions were replete with categorical statements suggesting that Congress may not relinquish any of its power to enact legislation through grants of policy making power to administrators. The following statement by the first Justice Harlan in *Field v. Clark*, 143 U.S. 649 (1892), is typical:

> That Congress cannot delegate legislative power to the President is a principle universally recognized as vital to the integrity and maintenance of the system of government ordained by the constitution.

Yet in that case the Court upheld a provision of the Tariff Act of 1890 which authorized the President to suspend favorable tariff treatment for nations that imposed on American products "any duties or other exactions * * * which * * * [he] may deem to be reciprocally unequal and unreasonable." The Court theorized that the Act simply accorded the President the authority to make the factual determination requisite for implementation of the policy prescribed by Congress. "He was the mere agent of the law-making department to ascertain and declare the event upon which * * * [the legislature's] expressed will was to take effect."

In decisions both before and after *Field v. Clark* the Supreme Court upheld, against attack as invalid delegations of legislative power, statutes that accorded the President, or occasionally other executive officers, a large role in formulating as well as implementing national policy. Many of these laws dealt with foreign affairs, a field in which Congress might have believed the President should have wide discretion in effectuating legislative judgment. The Court offered a variety of rationales for upholding such loose delegations of authority. Some laws were said merely to accord the President authority to determine the "contingency"—e.g., violation of the nation's neutrality rights by a foreign power—that brought congressional policy into force. E.g., *The Brig Aurora*, 11 U.S. (7 Cranch) 382 (1813). In other statutes, the Court suggested Congress had firmly established the general contours of public policy and simply left the President to "fill up the details" of regulation, even though such "filling up" might involve the power to declare conduct criminal. E.g., *United States v. Grimaud*, 220 U.S. 506 (1911).

Perhaps the most widely quoted formulation of the "old" nondelegation doctrine appears in *J.W. Hampton, Jr. & Co. v. United States*, 276 U.S. 394 (1928). The Court there upheld the Tariff Act of 1922, part of which set precise duties to be imposed on designated classes of imported goods. Section 312(a) of the Act, however, commanded:

> whenever the President, upon investigation of the differences in costs of production of articles wholly or in part the growth or product of the United States and of like or similar articles wholly or in part the growth or product of competing foreign countries, shall find * * * that the duties fixed in this Act do not equalize the said differences in costs of production in the United States and the principal competing country he shall * * * ascertain said differences and determine and proclaim the changes in classifications or increases or decreases in any rate of duty provided in the Act shown by said ascertained differences in such costs of production necessary to equalize the same.

Any increased duties proclaimed by the President pursuant to this section would go into effect thirty days later.

The Court acknowledged that Congress could not feasibly prescribe in detail the rules governing every facet of federally regulated activity. Chief Justice Taft concluded from his reading of *Field v. Clark* and *Grimaud*: "If Congress shall lay down by legislative act an *intelligible principle* to which the person or body authorized to fix * * * rates is directed to conform, such legislative action is not a forbidden delegation of legislative power" (emphasis added).

In all these early decisions, the Court kept insisting that the Constitution forbade abdication of Congress' monopoly of legislative power. But not once did it invalidate any delegation Congress saw fit to make, and it upheld phrases such as "just and reasonable rates" for railroad regulation and "public interest, convenience, or necessity" for the issuance of broadcast licenses as establishing "meaningful standards" for agencies to apply. It therefore is not surprising that by the early 1930s, the "nondelegation doctrine" was thought to have become an empty formalism. Louis L. Jaffe, Judicial Control of Administrative Action 51–62 (1965).

However, in 1935, the Court for the first—and last—time struck down congressional enactments as unlawful delegations of legislative power. The Court did so in two cases dealing with separate sections of the National Industrial Recovery Act, an early piece of New Deal legislation that soon fell into disfavor with most elements of the Roosevelt constituency.

In *Panama Refining Co. v. Ryan*, 293 U.S. 388 (1935), the provision at issue was section 9(c) of the National Industrial Recovery Act.* That section authorized the President to exclude from interstate commerce oil products "produced or withdrawn from storage in excess of the amount permitted to be produced or withdrawn from storage by any state law or valid regulation. * * * " Disobedience to an exclusion order was made a crime punishable by fine and imprisonment. Section 9(c) provided no criteria on which the President was to base his action, and the Court refused to find the requisite guiding principles in the Act's declaration of policy, which listed many competing objectives apparently without preference.** Nor did the Act require the President "to ascertain and

* The Petroleum Code of Fair Competition, promulgated under the NIRA, was also challenged in this suit. The Court did not pass on the validity of the Petroleum Code, however, because the offending section had been amended out of existence, unknown to the prosecuting authorities and the lower courts. This embarrassing event led to the enactment of the Federal Register Act of 1935, 44 U.S.C. §§ 1501–11. See Louis L. Jaffe, Judicial Control of Administrative Action 61–62 (1965).

** The declaration of policy, set out in section 1 of Title I of the Act, provided in part:

> It is hereby declared to be the policy of Congress to remove obstructions to the free flow of interstate and foreign commerce which tend to diminish the amount thereof; and to provide for the general welfare by promoting the organization of industry for the purpose of cooperative action among trade groups, to induce and maintain united action of labor and management under adequate governmental sanctions and supervision, to eliminate unfair competitive practices, to promote the fullest possible utilization of the present productive capacity of industries, to avoid undue restriction of production (except as may be temporarily required), to increase the consumption of industrial and agricultural products by increasing purchasing power, to reduce and relieve

proclaim the conditions prevailing in the industry which made the prohibition necessary." Canvassing its previous precedents, the Court declared:

> Thus, in every case in which the question has been raised, the Court has recognized that there are limits of delegation which there is no constitutional authority to transcend. We think that § 9(c) goes beyond those limits. As to the transportation of oil production in excess of state permission, the Congress has declared no policy, has established no standard, has laid down no rule. There is no requirement, no definition of circumstances and conditions in which the transportation is to be allowed or prohibited.
>
> If § 9(c) were held valid, it would be idle to pretend that anything would be left of limitations upon the power of the Congress to delegate its law-making function. The reasoning of the many decisions we have reviewed would be made vacuous and their distinctions nugatory. Instead of performing its law-making function, the Congress could at will and as to such subjects as it chose transfer that function to the President or other officer or to an administrative body. The question is not of the intrinsic importance of the particular statute before us, but of the constitutional processes of legislation which are an essential part of our system of government.

With but a single dissent, the Court thus struck down the "hot oil" provisions of the NIRA.

Four months after the *Panama Refining* decision, in *A.L.A. Schechter Poultry Corp. v. United States*, 295 U.S. 495 (1935), the Court invalidated section 3 of the same Act, which empowered the President to approve industry codes of "fair competition" upon submission by trade associations or business groups. The only conditions limiting the President's power were that the groups submitting codes for approval had to be "truly representative" of the industry and could impose no "inequitable restrictions on admission to membership," and that no code could "be designed to promote monopolies or to eliminate or oppress small enterprises * * * [or] operate to discriminate against them. * * *" Upon adoption a code became the standard of fair competition for an industry, and violation became a criminal misdemeanor, carrying a fine of up to $500. The Schechter brothers had been prosecuted under the Act for violating the code approved by the President for their industry. Again the Supreme Court, this time without dissent, found the statements of congressional policy in section 1 of Title I wholly insufficient as criteria for the President's exercise of his wide authority. The Court specifically noted that the Act, unlike other statutes upheld as valid delegations of legislative authority, provided no procedural safeguards—

unemployment, to improve standards of labor, and otherwise to rehabilitate industry and to conserve natural resources.

such as notice, hearing, and findings based on evidence—for the adoption of codes of fair competition.

Justice Cardozo, who had been the lone dissenter in *Panama Refining*, joined the majority in *Schechter*. "The delegated power of legislation which has found expression in this Code," he declared, "is not canalized within banks that keep it from overflowing. It is unconfined and vagrant. * * * "

Since the *Schechter* case the Supreme Court has not invalidated a single statute on the basis of excessive delegation. This result—not surprising, of course, given the history of the doctrine—cannot be explained by improvements since 1935 in the drafting of statutes.

The first post-New Deal nondelegation challenge to reach the Supreme Court signaled the Supreme Court's reversion to form. In *Yakus v. United States*, 321 U.S. 414 (1944), it upheld Congress' World War II delegation of authority to control prices, which was implemented by the Office of Price Administration (OPA). The Court said:

> Congress enacted the Emergency Price Control Act in pursuance of a defined policy and required that the prices fixed by the Administrator should further that policy and conform to standards prescribed by the Act. The boundaries of the field of the Administrator's permissible action are marked by the statute. It directs that the prices fixed shall effectuate the declared policy of the Act to stabilize commodity prices so as to prevent war-time inflation and its enumerated disruptive causes and effects. In addition the prices established must be fair and equitable, and in fixing them the Administrator is directed to give due consideration, so far as practicable, to prevailing prices during the designated base period, with prescribed administrative adjustments to compensate for enumerated disturbing factors affecting prices. In short the purposes of the Act specified in § 1 denote the objective to be sought by the Administrator in fixing prices—the prevention of inflation and its enumerated consequences. The standards set out in § 2 define the boundaries within which prices having that purpose must be fixed. It is enough to satisfy the statutory requirements that the Administrator finds that the prices fixed will tend to achieve that objective and will conform to those standards, and that the courts in an appropriate proceeding can see that substantial basis for those findings is not wanting.
>
> The Act is unlike the National Industrial Recovery Act considered in *Schechter Poultry Corp. v. United States*, which proclaimed in the broadest terms its purpose "to rehabilitate industry and to conserve natural resources." It prescribed no method of attaining that end save by the establishment of codes of fair competition, the nature of whose permissible provisions was left undefined. It provided no standards to which those codes were to conform. The function of formulating the codes was delegated, not to a public official

responsible to Congress or the Executive, but to private individuals engaged in the industries to be regulated. * * *

Acting within its constitutional power to fix prices it is for Congress to say whether the data on the basis of which prices are to be fixed are to be confined within a narrow or a broad range. In either case the only concern of courts is to ascertain whether the will of Congress has been obeyed. This depends not upon the breadth of the definition of the facts or conditions which the administrative officer is to find but upon the determination whether the definition sufficiently marks the field within which the Administrator is to act so that it may be known whether he has kept within it in compliance with the legislative will. * * * Only if we could say that there is an absence of standards for the guidance of the Administrator's action, so that it would be impossible in a proper proceeding to ascertain whether the will of Congress has been obeyed, would we be justified in overriding its choice of means for effecting its declared purpose of preventing inflation. The standards prescribed by the present Act, with the aid of the "statement of the considerations" required to be made by the Administrator, are sufficiently definite and precise to enable Congress, the courts and the public to ascertain whether the Administrator, in fixing the designated prices, has conformed to those standards. * * *

As the following pages reveal, the Supreme Court has since upheld many other grants of administrative authority in the face of plausible charges that they were no more specific than the two found wanting in 1935. Even statutes of major political and economic significance, containing provisions of great detail and complexity, often exhibit vagueness precisely at the point of critical policy choice. One can, therefore, see the *Schechter* and *Panama Refining* cases as "sports," better explainable in terms of the politics of the justices of the Supreme Court in 1935 than in terms of legal doctrine. This explanation, however, does not give sufficient weight to other factors at work in those cases, nor does it, even if substantially accurate, necessarily detract from the importance of the nondelegation doctrine. That doctrine is admittedly political, for it deals explicitly with the fundamental political organization of the state. The Court's reiteration of the nondelegation principle, coupled with its very sparing use to strike down legislation, illustrates a continuing judicial effort to harmonize the modern administrative state with traditional notions of representative government and the rule of law. It testifies also to a judicial sense, illustrated in the following famous case, that legal techniques short of declaring statutes invalid are generally preferable means for accommodating the necessities of public policy with effective control of administrative discretion.

The apparent futility of nondelegation challenges to regulatory legislation since *Schechter* has not stifled all claims that Congress has unconstitutionally surrendered its authority—and responsibility—to set governmental policy. An attack on legislation enacted during the Nixon administration to address concerns about price and wage inflation elicited the following famous response by Judge Harold Leventhal, who for his two decades on the bench enjoyed a reputation as one of the nation's leading administrative law scholars.

AMALGAMATED MEAT CUTTERS v. CONNALLY

United States District Court, District of Columbia, 1971.
337 F.Supp. 737.

LEVENTHAL, CIRCUIT JUDGE.

In this litigation Plaintiff Union, the Amalgamated Meat Cutters suing on its own behalf and on behalf of its affiliated local unions, attacks the constitutionality of the Economic Stabilization Act of 1970.

Two different actions are consolidated in the complaint. Count II seeks to require the major meat packing companies to perform their obligations, under their 1970 collective bargaining agreements with the Union, to grant a general wage increase of twenty-five cents an hour effective September 6, 1971. * * * The employers respond that the implementation of the wage increase obligation would violate Executive Order 11615, promulgated by President Nixon August 15, 1971 * * *. This Executive Order, Stabilization of Prices, Rents, Wages and Salaries, establishes a 90–day price-wage freeze, a requirement that "prices, rents, wages and salaries shall be stabilized for a period of 90 days" at levels no greater than the highest rates pertaining to a substantial volume of actual transactions by the seller of commodities or services involved in a specified base period preceding August 15. The Union's position is that this defense is insufficient as a matter of law because the Act is unconstitutional and the Executive Order invalid.

The broader aspect of the controversy before us appears in Count I of the Complaint, an action brought against John B. Connally, who as Secretary of the Treasury is Chairman of the Cost of Living Council, and the other officials constituting the Council. In Executive Order 11615 President Nixon established the Cost of Living Council "which shall act as an agency of the United States," specified that it shall be composed of certain designated officials as members and "delegated to the Council all of the powers conferred on the President by the Economic Stabilization Act of 1970."

In Count I the Union seeks a declaratory judgment that the Act and Executive Order 11615 are illegal and unconstitutional, and also an injunction against the officials named as defendants, individually and as members of the Council, restraining and enjoining them from administering or giving any force or effect to the Executive Order and the Act. * * *

The Union's position is that the Act's broad authority to the President "to issue such orders and regulations as he may deem appropriate to stabilize prices, rents, wages and salaries" vests "unbridled legislative power in the President," a "naked grant of authority" to determine whether they "will be controlled, and the scope, manner and timing of those controls."

* * *

The matter has been argued to us on principle and precedent* * *. The Government cites numerous authorities but relies most heavily on *Yakus v. United States* sustaining the grant in the Emergency Price Control Act of 1942 of broad price-fixing authority. The Union particularly invokes the 1935 decisions in *Schechter Corp. v. United States* and *Panama Refining Co. v. Ryan*, holding invalid provisions of the National Industrial Recovery Act.

We are of the view that the *Yakus* ruling and principles there applied provide the more meaningful guidance for the novel problem at hand, and that this constitutional assault cannot be sustained. * * *

* * * There is no analytical difference, no difference in kind, between the legislative function—of prescribing rules for the future—that is exercised by the legislature or by the agency implementing the authority conferred by the legislature. The problem is one of limits.

An agency assigned to a task has its freedom of action circumscribed not only by the constitutional limitations that bind Congress but by the perimeters described by the legislature as hedgerows defining areas open to the agency. The question is the extent to which the Constitution limits a legislature that may think it proper and needful to give the agency broad flexibility to cope with the conditions it encounters.

* * *

Concepts of control and accountability define the constitutional requirement. The principle permitting a delegation of legislative power, if there has been sufficient demarcation of the field to permit a judgment whether the agency has kept within the legislative will, establishes a principle of accountability under which compatibility with the legislative design may be ascertained not only by Congress but by the courts and the public. That principle was conjoined in *Yakus* with a recognition that the burden is on the party who assails the legislature's choice of means for effecting its purpose, a burden that is met "[o]nly if we could say that there is an absence of standards for the guidance of the Administrator's action, so that it would be impossible in a proper proceeding to ascertain whether the will of Congress has been obeyed."

* * * [T]he broadest delegation yet sustained and the one closest to the case before us came in *Yakus*, for the ultimate standard in the 1942 statute was only that the maximum prices be "generally fair and equitable."

Under these governing concepts we cannot say that in the Act before us there is such an absence of standards that it would be impossible to ascertain whether the will of Congress has been obeyed.

In some respects, indeed, Congress has been precise in its limitations. The President is given an authority to stabilize prices and wages by § 202(a) of the Act, but not at levels less than those prevailing on May 25, 1970.

Moreover the legislation is not as vulnerable as it would have been prior to the amendment adopted earlier in 1971, under which the President is precluded by § 202(b) from singling out "a particular industry or sector of the economy upon which to impose controls" unless he makes a specific finding that wages or prices in that industry or sector have increased at a rate disproportionate to the rate for the economy as a whole. * * *

The limitation on the President's power to take action in particular industries or sectors made this authority more narrow than the authority over prices in the 1942 legislation.[14] It also clarified the will of Congress. Congress gave the President broad authority to stabilize prices, rents, wages and salaries, but in effect it contemplated that controls to achieve broad stabilization would begin with a regulation applicable to the entire economy. * * * The House Banking and Currency Committee Report specifically envisaged a 3–month "freeze" to get "a handle on inflation."

This ascertainment of the contours of the power to "stabilize" is fortified by explicit legislative history. But even the text of the law, the starting point of analysis, must not be taken in a vacuum. In rejecting claims of invalid delegation of legislative power the Court has made clear that the standards of a statute are not to be tested in isolation and derive "meaningful content from the purposes of the Act, its factual background, and the statutory context."

The historical context of the 1970 law is emphasized in the Government's submission:

> "In enacting the legislation in question here, Congress was, of course, acting against a background of wage and price controls in both wars. The administrative practice under both of those Acts was the subject of extensive judicial interpretation and review. This substantial background of prior law and practice provides a further framework for assessing whether the Executive has stayed within the bounds authorized by Congress and provides more than adequate standards for the exercise of authority granted by the Act."

We think this contention is sound. The context of the 1970 stabilization law includes the stabilization statutes passed in 1942, and the stabilization provisions in Title IV of the Defense Production Act of 1950, and the "common lore" of anti-inflationary controls established by the agency approaches and court decisions, including the probing analy-

14. That Act * * * permitted the administrator to set maximum prices in a particular industry where prices, in his judgment, "have risen or threaten to rise to an extent or in a manner inconsistent with the purposes of this Act." The administrator issued maximum price regulations for particular industries until the General Maximum Price Regulation, issued April 30, 1942, 7 F.R. 3153, forbade the sale of most commodities at prices in excess of the highest price charged by the seller during March 1942.

ses of the Emergency Court of Appeals. We do not suggest that the 1970 law was intended as or constitutes a duplicate of the earlier laws. But those laws and their implementation do provide a validating context as against the charge that the later statute stands without any indication to the agencies and officials of legislative contours and contemplation.

* * *

An undeniably prominent feature of the earlier stabilization programs was the adoption thereunder of across-the-board wage and price controls, typically with "freeze" and "hold-the-line" approaches, subject to relaxation for hardships and inequities under implementing standards. There can be no doubt that in its broad outlines the general freeze ordered by the President conforms to the legislative intention. * * *

The Union challenges the thesis that the 1970 Act can be sustained by reference to the earlier stabilization laws and rulings thereunder, complaining that unlike the earlier statutes the present law is "shorthand legislation," devoid of any statement of policy or objectives, or of conditions under which action is to be taken, or findings of Congressional intent.

The Act is obviously different in its structure from the law upheld in *Yakus*, which was replete with just such statements of policy, objectives and findings. The difference is largely one of drafting style, ascribable perhaps to the circumstance that the 1942 law was proposed by the Executive, and introduced on that basis after scrutiny by the legislature's drafting staffs. * * *

The purposes of the 1970 law, to a considerable extent inherent in the very authority to "stabilize," are set forth more explicitly in the Report of the House Committee on Banking and Currency which inserted these provisions into the legislative process. H.R.Rep. No. 91–1330 (hereafter cited as House Report). * * *

Whether legislative purposes are to be obtained from committee reports, or are set forth in a separate section of the text of the law, is largely a matter of drafting style. Plainly the 1970 legislative purpose set forth in the House Report does not differ in material degree from the statement of legislative purpose in the 1942 legislation upheld in *Yakus*. This purpose was reiterated in debate on the 1970 Act.

We see no merit in the contention that the Act is constitutionally defective because the timing of the imposition of controls was delegated to the President. * * *

The House Report clarifies that this delegation was not an abdication by Congress, but the product of a reasoned analysis that only such delegation as to timing would further the legislative purpose of stabilization. * * *

The issue whether the delegation before us is excessive must be considered in the light of the unique situation, with the President not in accord with the conclusion of Congress as to the need or desirability of the power entrusted to him. Thus the Speaker, supporting the law, put it that the President and his advisers "are prescribing the wrong medicine for the particular inflationary virus now affecting the Nation," that restrictive fiscal and monetary policies are appropriate for combating traditional "demand-pull inflation" but the country was now beset by "cost-push inflation" for which direct controls were needed. It is not our place to review the merits of these differences. But the physician-virus metaphor is revealing. Viewing the President as a physician in charge, Congress could advise but not mandate his diagnosis. It sought in the national interest to have the right remedy available on a standby basis, if the President should wish to adopt that prescription, following his further reflection and taking into account future developments and experience.

* * *

Finally the House Report takes cognizance, in support of delegation of "timing" to the President, that Congress might not be in session when action was requisite.

* * *

The need felt by Congress to delegate broadly to the President is not undercut by the circumstance that the country was not experiencing and Congress did not contemplate a sudden or dramatic price rise, such as sometimes accompanies a war or shooting emergency, but only a "creeping" inflation. * * * Congress had reason to authorize the President to begin prompt treatment with direct controls whenever he concluded this was the proper course and regardless of the prior rate of spread of the disease. * * *

This is a suitable juncture to refer to the undoubted and substantial significance of the interrelation between the domestic wage and price controls and the actions taken by the President on August 15, 1971, in the field of international trade and monetary adjustments. The President's message identifies the existence of such an interrelation though not its exact nature. The House Report's recount of legislative policy includes its recital that the current inflation malady is significantly responsible for the balance-of-payments crisis and liquidity squeeze. This was a 1970 problem and a legislative objective not known at the time of the 1942 and 1950 legislation. The consequence for international trade, liquidity and monetary relationships, enhances the range of power Congress may permissibly delegate to the President. * * * And it particularly substantiates the legitimacy of delegating to the President the authority as to the timing for the blending of actions with international consequences.

It is also material, though not dispositive, to note the limited time frame established by Congress for the stabilization authority delegated to the President. The Act as enacted on August 15, 1970 expired February 28, 1971, establishing a lifespan of about six months. Two subsequent extensions provided even shorter durations. When the current expiration date of April 30, 1972, was set on May 18, 1971, Congress rejected the administration request for a two-year extension. Thus, in the words of the Government's memorandum, Congress established a "close control." It conjoined flexibility in the President to act promptly with an obligation in Congress to undertake an affirmative review without prolonged delay, without the option of acquiescence by inaction.

* * *

The Union says that during this period the President has been given a "blank check" for internal affairs which is intolerable in our constitutional system. The Union notes that the order exempted from controls the prices charged for raw agricultural products without statutory authority for the exemption. It claims that the failure of Congress to require, as in the 1942 and 1950 legislation that ongoing regulations be "fair and equitable" is tantamount to a delegation to the President of the power to be unfair and inequitable. The Union complains that there was a failure to provide a system for testing these orders, administratively and by judicial review, as in the earlier legislation.

The net result, charges the Union, is a legislative initiation of control by bare executive fiat, with completely unlimited authority put at the disposal of the President.

This is a formidable fusillade, devastating verbally and not without force analytically. When the smoke clears away, however, we conclude that the Rule of Law has been beleaguered but not breached. * * *

If the Act gives the President authority to be unfair and inequitable, as the Union claims, this legislative vessel may indeed founder on a constitutional rock. But we do not reach this constitutional issue because we do not think the Act can be given the extremist interpretation offered by the Union.

We take this view not only because of the doctrine that statutes are to be construed so as to avoid serious constitutional questions, but more directly because we do not think it can sensibly or fairly be said that this extremist approach was what was intended by the legislature. * * *

* * * The ultimate standard for follow-on controls replacing the freeze is a standard of fairness and equity. This standard of removal of "gross inequities" is voiced as an authority of the President in § 202 of the Act. We think there is fairly implicit in the Act the duty to take whatever action is required in the interest of broad fairness and avoidance of gross inequity, although presumably his range of discretion means there may be inequities that a President may remove that he is not compelled by law to remove. * * *

Another feature that blunts the "blank check" rhetoric is the requirement that any action taken by the Executive under the law, subsequent to the freeze, must be in accordance with further standards as developed by the Executive. This requirement, inherent in the Rule of Law and implicit in the Act, means that however broad the discretion of the Executive at the outset, the standards once developed limit the latitude of subsequent executive action. * * *

The requirement of subsidiary administrative policy, enabling Congress, the courts and the public to assess the Executive's adherence to the ultimate legislative standards, is in furtherance of the purpose of the constitutional objective of accountability. This 1970 Act gives broadest latitude to the Executive. Certainly there is no requirement of formal findings. But there is an on-going requirement of intelligible administrative policy that is corollary to and implementing of the legislature's ultimate standard and objective. This requirement is underscored by the consideration that the exercise of wide discretion will probably call for "imaginative interpretation," leaving the courts to see whether the Executive, using its experience, "has fairly exercised its discretion within the vaguish, penumbral bounds" of the broad statutory standard. * * *

The claim of undue delegation of legislative power broadly raises the challenge of undue power in the Executive and thus naturally involves consideration of the interrelated questions of the availability of appropriate restraints through provisions for administrative procedure and judicial review. These components of fairness are themselves elements of statutory and constitutional rights but it is appropriate to discuss them in present context because they bear on the issue whether there has been undue delegation to the Executive.

The safeguarding of meaningful judicial review is one of the primary functions of the doctrine prohibiting undue delegation of legislative powers. * * *

The Government concedes and we agree that the Executive's actions under the 1970 Act are not immune from judicial review. * * *

The Government's position rests on the proposition that since the Act provides for enforcement either by way of fine (§ 204) or by way of injunction restraining violations (§ 205), and the person charged with violation is able to obtain judicial review by inserting a defense to either type of enforcement proceeding, this provides ample judicial review for constitutional purposes.

We need not consider whether under conditions of modern life the Constitution permits a restriction to enforcement proceedings of judicial review of Executive discretion as broad in range and significant in impact as that provided by this law, requiring citizens with substantial doubts concerning the validity of the exercise of such broad discretion to run the risk of criminal proceedings. * * *

It is our conclusion that in addition to the judicial reviews noted by the Government, challenges may be made under the provisions for judicial review in the Administrative Procedure Act, 5 U.S.C. §§ 701–706. These provisions contemplate an action for declaratory judgment or injunction, assuming pertinent requirements for these forms of action are met, as well as a defense in civil or criminal proceedings, see 5 U.S.C. § 703. They provide that a person suffering legal wrong because of agency action is entitled to review thereof, 5 U.S.C. § 702. Judicial review is provided for final agency action for which there is no other adequate remedy in court, 5 U.S.C. § 704.

When the impact of regulations is direct and immediate, so that the controversy is "ripe" for judicial resolution, these provisions of 5 U.S.C. §§ 701–706, permit pre-enforcement judicial review. * * *

The leading students of the APA, whose analyses are often cited by the Supreme Court, * * * seem to be in agreement that the term "agency" in the APA included the President—a conclusion fortified by the care taken to make express exclusion of "Congress" and "the courts."

But we need not consider whether an action for judicial review can be brought against the President *eo nomine*. Certainly such actions can be brought against the official who exercises functions vested by Congress in the President and delegated by the President * * *. The Cost of Living Council is an "authority" of the United States and Executive Order 11615 was only recording the incontrovertible when it specified that the Council "shall act as an agency of the United States." * * * The applicability of the Administrative Procedure Act cannot be doubted.

By the same token actions under this 1970 Act are subject to the administrative procedure provisions of the Administrative Procedure Act, 5 U.S.C. § 551 ff. It may well be that the applicability of these provisions will have no practical consequence. The rule-making provisions of 5 U.S.C. § 553, requiring notice and opportunity for participation by interested persons, are subject to the provision in subsection (b) removing those requirements "(B) when the agency for good cause finds (and incorporates the finding and a brief statement of reasons therefor in the rules issued) that notice and public procedure thereon are impracticable, unnecessary, or contrary to the public interest." The adjudication provisions of 5 U.S.C. § 554 are applicable only when an agency hearing is required by the statute, or by compulsion of general law. * * * And *Yakus* upheld the validity of the failure to provide for such hearings in the 1942 maximum price law.

* * *

We turn finally to precedents cited by the Union. They remind us that Separation of Powers is a doctrine with vitality. It is the force that motivated *Youngstown Sheet & Tube Co. v. Sawyer*, 343 U.S. 579 (1952)—where however the executive order seizing the nation's steel mills was without any authorization in legislation. Given a legislative enactment, there have not been any Supreme Court rulings holding statutes unconstitutional for excessive delegation of legislative power since the *Panama Refining* and *Schechter* cases invalidated provisions of the National Industrial Recovery Act of 1933.

These cases express a principle that has validity—reserved for the extremist instance. These precedents were referred to in *Fahey v. Mallonee*, 332 U.S. 245, 249 (1947):

> Both cited cases dealt with delegation of a power to make federal crimes of acts that never had been such before and to devise novel rules of law in a field in which there had been no settled law or custom.

They are without vigor for a case like the one before us, where the delegation is in a context of historical experience with anti-inflation legislation.

The particular application of the delegation principle in *Panama Refining* was colored, as students of the Court's decisions have noted, by the circumstance that the regulation in that case was not generally available and had been inadvertently amended out of effect—a circumstance that led to the creation of the Federal Register.

In *Schechter*, which held invalid the provisions of the National Industrial Recovery Act that authorized the fixing of codes of fair conduct, the "function of formulating the codes was delegated, not to a public official responsible to Congress or the Executive, but to private individuals engaged in the industries to be regulated." * * * The "corporate state" aspects of the Blue Eagle codes that emerged in practice were made possible and reinforced by a legal context of authority to prescribe "codes of fair competition" that covered the entire range of economic life, going beyond even the broad subject matter before us.

* * *

* * * Our view of the applicable law makes it clear that plaintiff's motion for injunctive relief must be denied.

So ordered.

ECONOMIC STABILIZATION ACT OF 1970

P.L. 91–379, 84 Stat. 799 (1970).

* * *

§ 202. Presidential authority

(a) The President is authorized to issue such orders and regulations as he may deem appropriate to stabilize prices, rents, wages, and salaries at levels not less than those prevailing on May 25, 1970. Such orders and regulations may provide for the making of such adjustments as may be necessary to prevent gross inequities.

(b) The authority conferred on the President by this section shall not be exercised with respect to a particular industry or segment of the economy unless the President determines, after taking into account the seasonal nature of employment, the rate of employment or underemployment, and other mitigating factors, that prices or wages in that industry or segment of the economy have increased at a rate which is grossly disproportionate to the rate at which prices or wages have increased in the economy generally.

§ 203. Delegation

The President may delegate the performance of any function under this title to such officers, departments, and agencies of the United States as he may deem appropriate.

§ 204. Penalty

Whoever willfully violates any order or regulation under this title shall be fined not more than $5,000.

§ 205. Injunctions

Whenever it appears to any agency of the United States, authorized by the President to exercise the authority contained in this section to enforce orders and regulations issued under this title, that any person has engaged, is engaged or is about to engage in any acts or practices constituting a violation of any regulation or order under this title, it may in its discretion bring an action, in the proper district court of the United States or the proper United States court of any territory or other place subject to the jurisdiction of the United States to enjoin such acts or practices, and upon a proper showing a permanent or temporary injunction or restraining order shall be granted without bond. Upon application of the agency, any such court may also issue mandatory injunctions commanding any person to comply with any regulation or order under this title.

§ 206. Expiration

The authority to issue and enforce orders and regulations under this title expires at midnight April 30, 1972, but such expiration shall not affect any proceeding under section 204 for a violation of any such order or regulation, or for the punishment for contempt committed in the violation of any injunction under section 205, committed prior to May 1, 1972.

Notes

1. *Indicia of "Control and Accountability."* One of the healthy impediments to "delegation run riot" that Judge Leventhal found in the *Amalgamated Meat Cutters (AMC)* case was the shortness of the period for which presidential authority was conferred. This provided some assurance that executive action would not continue long without congressional review of performance that presumably would accompany a decision whether to extend the Act. Indeed, within two months of the *AMC* decision Congress again extended and amended the 1970 legislation. The amendments included a detailed statement of national policy, extensive congressional findings to justify wage and price controls, and more detailed standards to be followed in administering the Act. Among these standards was the explicit duty to be "generally fair and equitable." The amendments also established specific administrative procedures and, as Judge Leventhal had already held, expressly stipulated that the rulemaking provisions of the Administrative

Procedure Act (APA) applied to administration of the Act. Congress also provided for judicial review of wage and price orders, including appellate review of district court decisions by a Temporary Emergency Court of Appeals. See generally Harold Leventhal, *Principled Fairness and Regulatory Urgency*, 25 Case W.Res.L.Rev. 66 (1974).

In addition, Judge Leventhal found safeguards against administrative arbitrariness (1) in the requirement that power be exercised generally rather than by singling out particular industries, (2) in the availability of judicial review, (3) in the prior history of wage-price controls, (4) in the procedural safeguards of the APA, and (5) in the notion that the administration of the Act would be self-confining as policy was developed and expressed in regulatory form. The court thus shifted the focus of discussion away from debate over whether the power conferred was "legislative" to the issue of whether the legal order could, consistent with the rule of law, accommodate the legislative judgment that the choice of anti-inflation strategy and the timing of its application should, for reasons both of coordination and expedition, reside largely with the executive branch.

2. *Judge Leventhal's Optimism.* In evaluating Judge Leventhal's reasons for believing that the authority conferred by the Economic Stabilization Act would be subject to effective legal control, consider the following:

Judicial Review. Courts can exercise effective control over specific administrative acts only where there are relatively clear standards against which to measure administrative performance. To be sure, it is not essential that those standards appear in legislation—they can be promulgated in regulations or emerge from the pattern of agency decisions. But there was no guarantee that either basis for judicial review would develop quickly under the Economic Stabilization Act. The program of emergency wage-price controls might be over before a firm basis for review emerged in the "common law" generated by agency activity.

Nor was it clear that there was only limited room for individualized judgment under the statute. The basic action before the court was general—a ninety-day freeze on wages and prices—but its implementation required many specific decisions interpreting exactly what was frozen and when. The President conferred on the Cost of Living Council (CLC) the power to define any terms in the freeze order, to make exceptions and exemptions, and to issue any other appropriate order. 3 C.F.R. § 199 (1971). Thus, even if controls were general, individualized action was clearly possible by way of interpretation, exemption, or other "appropriate" action. During the ninety days of the freeze the CLC received 50,000 complaints of violations, 6,000 formal requests for exceptions, and 750,000 requests for interpretations. See generally ROBERT A. KAGAN, REGULATORY JUSTICE: IMPLEMENTING A WAGE-PRICE FREEZE (1978). Is it conceivable that all, or even a small share, of these individual determinations could be reviewed in court? And, for those that were challenged, how were the courts to decide whether an agency action was lawful?

The answer of the few cases that reached the Temporary Emergency Court of Appeals seems to have been, "on the basis of the desire of the Congress to give the executive broad discretion." For example, a landlord who contended that the Cost of Living Council had misconstrued the

President's freeze order was rebuffed in part by the remarkable statement that his argument ignored the fact that the order had delegated to the Council all the power of the President under the act—including presumably the power to change the meaning of the order. *United States v. Lieb*, 462 F.2d 1161 (Temp.Emer.Ct.App.1972). And, when the University of Southern California appealed an order that required it to refund an increase in the price of 1971 season football tickets (although the tickets had been sold prior to August 17, 1971) on the theory that the "transaction" occurred with the post-freeze playing of the football games, it was met with the response that the court must give great weight to the interpretations of the agency charged with administrative responsibility, particularly where, as here, "the broadest possible delegation of power was given." *University of Southern Cal. v. Cost of Living Council*, 472 F.2d 1065 (Temp.Emer.Ct.App.1972), *cert. denied*, 410 U.S. 928 (1973). In the latter case, the court was discomfited by the fact that the Council had previously decided that universities could charge higher tuition and dormitory prices scheduled, but not collected, before August 17 and had apparently decided the "date of transaction" question both ways with respect to teachers' salaries. See *United States v. Jefferson Parish School Board*, 333 F.Supp. 418 (E.D.La.1971). However, recognizing that the Council was faced with a "gargantuan task," the court of appeals found "any inconsistencies in interpretation—[to be] reasonable." 472 F.2d at 1072.

The Constraint of History. Nowhere in the judicial decisions under the 1970 act does one find serious reference to the earlier OPA experience as a source of limiting standards for administrative action. Indeed, one wonders whether that prior experience, with "demand-pull" inflation in wartime, should be made concretely applicable to decisions directed at "cost-push" inflation in peacetime.

In other contexts, however, judicial reliance on prior experience has been influential. In *Kent v. Dulles*, 357 U.S. 116 (1958), for example, a wholly open-ended delegation of power to the Secretary of State to issue or deny passports was, in response to an improper delegation challenge, judicially confined to a determination of whether the applicant was a citizen or owed allegiance to the United States and was engaged in lawful conduct. The Supreme Court found these standards for the exercise of the Secretary's discretion in the historic practice of the Department of State, implicitly approved by the Congress. Given these precise limits, it rejected the power assumed by the Secretary—to refuse issuance of passports to Communists—and the constitutional question of improper delegation thus was "not reached." But cf. *Haig v. Agee*, 453 U.S. 280 (1981).

The courts' familiarity with historically operative standards has often helped sustain legislative delegations. Regulation of common carriers on the basis of "public interest, convenience, and necessity" is a common, well-understood, and judicially accepted administrative function, although the statutory formula appears vacuous. Here and elsewhere a long history of governmental regulation, or a common-law heritage, may both sustain a delegation and provide a reasonably firm basis for judicial review. See, e.g., *Department of Health v. Owens–Corning Fiberglas Corp.*, 100 N.J.Super. 366, 242 A.2d 21 (1968), *affirmed*, 53 N.J. 248, 250 A.2d 11 (1969), which upholds a delegation of authority to regulate "air pollution" where that term is defined to correspond roughly with the common-law definition of nuisance.

Procedural Safeguards. Judge Leventhal's assurance that the 1970 Economic Stabilization Act fits within a well-defined system of administrative law making rests mainly on the APA. Yet again, as he obliquely concedes, the APA's procedural safeguards lacked force in the *AMC* context. The APA's exceptions from required public rulemaking procedures (described in Chapter 5, *infra*) probably covered most CLC regulations, and the Economic Stabilization Act did not mandate formal adjudication for any executive decisions, including individual exemptions or orders. Indeed, the CLC was later accused of employing highly secretive procedures that impeded both effective participation by affected parties and judicial review. See Note, *The Administration of Economic Controls: The Economic Stabilization Act of 1970*, 29 Case W.Res.L.Rev. 458 (1979).

Moreover, even if strict procedural formalities had been mandated and followed, procedures may not be a total substitute for substantive standards. The opportunity to present evidence, cross-examine witnesses, and make oral argument can be effective only to the extent that the bases for an eventual decision are reasonably well understood. Before contestants can exercise their procedural rights sensibly they must know what facts are relevant, what portions of opposing testimony are crucial, and what issues of policy or precedent are important.

3. *Delegation to Prescribe Criminal Standards.* The structural concern underlying the nondelegation doctrine is often expressed as an anxiety about a legislative abdication of power. Abdications to the executive, however, not only threaten to disable the legislative branch, but also to expand executive branch functions inappropriately. Broad delegations of authority to define the elements of criminal offenses, for example, combine in the executive the powers to prescribe criminal law and to prosecute its violation. For this reason, it is a fair question whether courts should be more stringent in policing the delegation of authority to define criminal offenses.

In *Touby v. United States*, 500 U.S. 160 (1991), the Court acknowledged: "Our cases are not entirely clear as to whether or not more specific guidance is in fact required" when Congress "authorizes another Branch to promulgate regulations that contemplate criminal sanctions." At issue was a 1984 amendment to the Controlled Substances Act, 21 U.S.C. § 811, permitting the Attorney General to "schedule" a drug as a controlled substance temporarily if "necessary to avoid an imminent hazard to the public safety." In implementing this authority, the Attorney General may follow an expedited procedure, dispensing with notice-and-comment rulemaking and avoiding immediate judicial review.

The Court unanimously concluded that, even if the nondelegation doctrine should apply more stringently in the criminal law context, the 1984 Amendments would pass such a test. The statute prescribes several specific standards by which to assess the Attorney General's exercise of delegated authority, for example, whether temporary scheduling is "necessary to avoid an imminent hazard to the public safety," 21 U.S.C. § 811(h)(1), and "does not preclude an individual facing criminal charges from bringing a challenge to a temporary scheduling order as a defense to prosecution." Under such a circumstance, the Court said, the statute's failure to provide for preenforcement judicial review as a means of policing the Attorney General's exercise of discretion was not fatal.

Justices Marshall and Blackmun concurred separately, concluding that "an opportunity to challenge a delegated lawmaker's compliance with congressional directives is a constitutional necessity when administrative standards are enforced by criminal law." They voted to uphold the Controlled Substances Act amendment because the statute did permit that opportunity by way of a defense to a criminal charge.

The Court also responded to a challenge against combining both criminal law-prescribing and prosecutorial functions in a single officer, the Attorney General. The Court concluded that—assuming the permissibility of delegating temporary scheduling authority to *any* executive official—Congress' choice of the Attorney General as its agent did not implicate separation of powers concerns: "The principle of separation of powers * * * does not speak to the manner in which authority is parceled out within a single Branch."

This assertion is surely controversial. As Judge Leventhal's *AMC* opinion suggests, separation of powers theory in the nondelegation context merges with concerns for impartiality in law enforcement that would have implications for the appropriateness of the delegate chosen to "fill in the details" of the law. Taken together, these considerations might well be thought to impose some limits on Congress' ability to combine prosecutorial and lawmaking functions in a single official. See Paul R. Verkuil, *Separation of Powers, the Rule of Law and the Idea of Independence*, 30 Wm. & Mary L.Rev. 301 (1989). We consider this problem in greater detail in our discussion of administrative hearing rights in Chapter 4.

In the following case, the only principal case decided by a state court in the casebook, the Oregon Supreme Court, faced with a vague (but hardly unique) delegation of authority to a state agency, saw the challenge for the legal system in somewhat narrower terms than Judge Leventhal.

SUN RAY DRIVE–IN DAIRY, INC. v. OREGON LIQUOR CONTROL COMMISSION

Court of Appeals of Oregon, 1973.
16 Or.App. 63, 517 P.2d 289.

TANZER, JUDGE.

Petitioner appeals from an order of the Oregon Liquor Control Commission denying its application for a Class B Package Store liquor license for its store in Ontario, Oregon. The commission based its refusal on ORS 471.295(1) which provides that the Commission may refuse to license an applicant if it has reasonable ground to believe that there are "sufficient licensed premises in the locality" or that the granting of the license is "not demanded by public interest or convenience." * * *

Various persons employed by the licensing division of the commission testified at the hearing on petitioner's application. Mr. William Alexander, a liquor control officer, * * * initially testified that he recommended refusal of petitioner's application because of (1) objections of area residents; (2) the large number of existing outlets; and (3) the fact that petitioner's store did not have a broad inventory of groceries. However, he subsequently abandoned the last ground. He testified that even if the petitioner's store had been a Safeway, he would have recommended refusal because of the number of outlets already in the area. * * *

Mr. Alexander's * * * direct superior, Mr. Charles Miller, * * * testified that he reviewed Mr. Alexander's report and agreed that the application should be denied. Mr. Miller's reasons * * * [were the same as] Mr. Alexander's. * * * Mr. Miller testified that he had no "yard-stick" to go by and that his recommendation was based on his "past experience and judgment."

Mr. Miller's recommendation was * * * passed on to Mr. Don Church, the commission's director of licensing. Mr. Church testified that the number of other licensees in a particular area was not a factor in deciding whether to issue a license. * * * Mr. Church stated that if a store is deemed by the Commission to be a "legitimate grocery store," the commission's policy is to grant the store a Class B Package Store license, regardless of how many other licensees are in the immediate area. The reason for his recommendation of denial to the Commission, Mr. Church said, was that petitioner's store had been represented to him in the reports from his subordinates as a "gasoline station with dairy products." Mr. Church concluded from the evidence he heard at the hearing that petitioner's store more closely approximated a "legitimate grocery store" than he had supposed, but that there would have to be still greater expansion of the scope of petitioner's inventory and the number of items of each type before he would recommend approval. Mr. Church expressed concern, for example, that the store's inventory listed only three packages of Birdseye creamed peas.

Petitioner gave evidence that several similar businesses in the Ontario area and neighboring cities, some with significantly smaller grocery inventories and one that appears to be an ordinary gas station, had package licenses.

The commission then made the following findings of fact and ultimate facts upon which the denial of license is based:

"FINDINGS OF FACT

"Sun Ray Drive–In Dairy, Inc., * * * factually demonstrated that * * * their Sun Ray Dairy store in Ontario during the month of January, 1973, made gross sales of $15,797.25 plus sales of dairy and food items of $8,909.18; that theirs is a 'convenient convenience' store with inventory running about 6 to $7,000.00 which inventories are refilled weekly. There were local objectors to the issuance of PB license to the applicants. There are fifteen licensed outlets for beer sales in Ontario, with five outlets within four blocks of the applicant. The listed inventory was not sufficient for a grocery store. The Commission particularly noted applicant's inventory listed one can of beef stew, three twelve-ounce packages of weiners (sic), two cans of chili, three cans of pork and beans and one Quaker Oats together with other groceries and dairy products.

"ULTIMATE FACTS

"There are sufficient licensed premises in the locality of the application. There were local objections to the issuance of Package Store Class B license to the applicant. The applicant's inventory is not sufficient for a grocery store."

Petitioner asks that we reverse the findings of fact, contending that the proof of each ultimate fact was otherwise. We are unable to review for substantial evidence because we are unable to ascertain the issues or the standards against which the evidence is to be measured. How many licensed premises are "sufficient" in the "locality?" Is sufficiency to be measured by population density, supply and demand, geographical area to be covered, other factors, or a combination of factors? How are public objections to be weighed? What ratio of acceptability should be required? Within what area of the license applicant? Finally, are all grocery stores entitled to a package license? If so, how is "grocery store" defined?

The legislature has not answered these questions by statute. * * *

The commission has not published rules or regulations establishing standards by which the statutory grounds for refusal for "sufficient licensed premises in the locality" or that the license "is not demanded by public interest or convenience," are to be applied. Instead, the licensing personnel of the commission testified at the hearing as to the "policy" of the commission. Those policies * * * have the quality of folklore in that unwritten rules are passed on orally by culture carriers from one generation of employees to another, from one level of employees to another, without the stabilizing effect of the written word.

A legislative delegation of power in broad statutory language such as the phrase "demanded by public interest or convenience" places upon the administrative agency a responsibility to establish standards by which that law is to be applied. The legislature has provided for such rule making in the [Oregon] Administrative Procedures Act.

* * * Unwritten standards and policies are no better than no standards and policies at all. Without written, published standards, the entire system of administrative law loses its keystone. The ramifications affect every party and every procedure involved in the fulfillment of the agency's responsibility under the law, *e.g.*, the public, the applicant, agency personnel, the participants in the hearing, the commission, the legislature and the judiciary.

The policies of an agency in a democratic society must be subject to public scrutiny. Published standards are essential to inform the public. Further, they help assure public confidence that the agency acts by rules and not from whim or corrupt motivation. In addition, interested parties and the general public are entitled to be heard in the process of rule adoption under the Administrative Procedures Act.

An applicant for a license should be able to know the standards by which his application will be judged before going to the expense in time, investment and legal fees necessary to make application. Thereafter, he is entitled to even treatment by rule of law and reasonable confidence that he has received such treatment. This cannot be achieved without published rules.

* * * In this case, as an example of what occurs in the absence of rules, the field investigator and his supervisor each recommended against approval because of the number of licensees already in the area, but the director of licensing who was in charge of their activities testified that the number of pre-existing outlets was not significant. He recommended disapproval because applicant was not a grocery store. The order of the commission, however, adopts both reasons as grounds for its denial. An administrative agency cannot properly perform its duty under the law unless employees at all levels work toward the same objectives under a clear direction of policy from the head of that agency, in this case the commission. * * *

Written standards enable the decision making body, in this case the commission, to make its decisions by rule of law rather than for subjective or ad hominem reasons. In this case, for example, the applicant introduced evidence of several similar businesses in the area which had package licenses. There is no way for him or for us to know whether he was singled out for discriminatory treatment or whether he was subjected to the same policy standards which were employed when the other comparable outlets were licensed and renewed. We recognize the wide discretion vested in the commission by its enabling legislation, but that discretion is not unbridled. It is discretion to make policies for even application, not discretion to treat each case on an ad hoc basis.* * *

The legislature is entitled to know whether or not the policies and practices of the agency are consistent with the legislative policies upon which the delegation of legislative power to the agency is based. In the absence of published rules, members of the legislature must form their judgments instead upon rumor, individual cases, isolated news reports and other fragmentary, impressionistic and often unreliable sources of information.* * *

Finally, and most directly applicable to this case, the parties to a contested case are entitled to judicial review. Judicial review is among the safeguards which serve to legitimatize broad legislative delegations of power to administrative agencies. In the absence of standards, however, the courts are unable to perform that task of judicial review. We cannot determine whether substantial evidence supported the findings because we cannot know what was in issue at the hearing. * * * Until the commission adopts appropriate rules, we cannot perform our judicial function.

Notes

1. *Fairness vs. Accountability*. The promulgation of administrative standards by the Oregon Liquor Control Commission (or any agency) might enhance the fairness and coherence of the agency's work in a number of ways. The Oregon court's approach, however, does little to address the ostensible aim of federal nondelegation doctrine, namely, the preservation of legislative accountability for significant policy choice. Should courts worry less about "blank check" legislative delegations of authority if the agency promulgates its own standards or takes other steps to avoid arbitrariness in implementing the law?

The Supreme Court wrestled with this issue in the New Deal nondelegation cases. Recall that, in *Schechter Poultry,* the Court concluded that the NIRA provided insufficient statutory guidance to direct the President in his approval or disapproval of proposed industry codes of fair competition. Yet, the Court had previously upheld very loose delegations of authority to agencies such as the Interstate Commerce Commission, Federal Trade Commission, and Federal Radio Commission. Congress had charged the ICC to permit one carrier to acquire control of another only if the acquisition were "in the public interest." Congress had charged the FTC to prevent "unfair methods of competition." Congress authorized the FRC (later the FCC) to issue broadcast licenses if "the public interest, convenience and necessity would be served."

The *Schechter* majority distinguished these precedents on the ground that these agencies were required to follow formal adjudicatory procedures in implementing their broad mandates. They were constituted as quasi-judicial bodies, gave notice of intended actions, held hearings, and assembled records for decision. Justice Cardozo agreed that the NIRA fair competition provisions amounted to "delegation running riot," but distinguished the ICC, FTC, and FRC precedents on the somewhat different ground that the delegations upheld in those cases were no broader than Congress could reasonably have designed given the missions of the agencies involved.

2. *Does Due Process Demand Standards*? Like the *Sun Ray* decision, some federal courts have gone beyond Judge Leventhal's gentle suggestion in *AMC* that agency standards might ultimately substitute for legislative standards, by insisting, in reliance upon procedural due process rather than the nondelegation doctrine, that agencies develop policies and criteria for making particularized judgments. See, e.g., *Holmes v. New York City Housing Authority*, 398 F.2d 262 (2d Cir.1968); *Hornsby v. Allen*, 326 F.2d 605 (5th Cir.1964). In *Hornsby,* the district court was instructed to enjoin the denial of liquor licenses by the City of Atlanta unless and until "ascertainable standards" for such denials had been established by the Board of Aldermen. In *Holmes* the court held that a complaint alleging that the Housing Authority had established no standards governing the selection of nonpreference applicants for public housing in New York City stated a cause of action under the due process clause. See Note, *Judicial Review of Public Housing Admissions*, 1971 Urban L.Ann. 228.

WHITMAN v. AMERICAN TRUCKING ASSOCIATIONS, INC.

Supreme Court of the United States, 2001.
531 U.S. 457, 121 S.Ct. 903, 149 L.Ed.2d 1.

JUSTICE SCALIA delivered the opinion of the Court.

These cases present the following questions: (1) Whether § 109(b)(1) of the Clean Air Act (CAA) delegates legislative power to the Administrator of the Environmental Protection Agency (EPA). (2) Whether the Administrator may consider the costs of implementation in setting national ambient air quality standards (NAAQS) under § 109(b)(1). * * *

I

Section 109(a) of the CAA requires the Administrator of the EPA to promulgate NAAQS for each air pollutant for which "air quality criteria" have been issued under § 108. Once a NAAQS has been promulgated, the Administrator must review the standard (and the criteria on which it is based) "at five-year intervals" and make "such revisions * * * as may be appropriate." These cases arose when, on July 18, 1997, the Administrator revised the NAAQS for particulate matter (PM) and ozone. American Trucking Associations, Inc., and its co-respondents which include, in addition to other private companies, the States of Michigan, Ohio, and West Virginia—challenged the new standards in the Court of Appeals for the District of Columbia Circuit.

The District of Columbia Circuit accepted some of the challenges and rejected others. It agreed with the * * * respondents that § 109(b)(1) delegated legislative power to the Administrator in contravention of the United States Constitution, Art. I, § 1, because it found that the EPA had interpreted the statute to provide no "intelligible principle" to guide the agency's exercise of authority. 175 F.3d 1027, 1034 (1999). The court thought, however, that the EPA could perhaps avoid the unconstitutional delegation by adopting a restrictive construction of § 109(b)(1), so instead of declaring the section unconstitutional the court remanded the NAAQS to the agency. On the second issue that the Court of Appeals addressed, it unanimously rejected respondents' argument that the court should depart from the rule of *Lead Industries Assn., Inc. v. EPA*, 647 F.2d 1130, 1148 (C.A.D.C.1980), that the EPA may not consider the cost of implementing a NAAQS in setting the initial standard. * * *

II

In *Lead Industries Assn., Inc.* v. *EPA*, the District of Columbia Circuit held that "economic considerations [may] play no part in the promulgation of ambient air quality standards under Section 109" of the CAA. In the present cases, the court adhered to that holding, as it had done on many other occasions. Respondents argue that these decisions are incorrect. We disagree; and since the first step in assessing whether a statute delegates legislative power is to determine what authority the statute confers, we address that issue of interpretation first and reach respondents' constitutional arguments in Part III, *infra*.

Section 109(b)(1) instructs the EPA to set primary ambient air quality standards "the attainment and maintenance of which * * * are requisite to protect the public health" with "an adequate margin of safety." Were it not for the hundreds of pages of briefing respondents have submitted on the issue, one would have thought it fairly clear that this text does not permit the EPA to consider costs in setting the standards. The language, as one scholar has noted, "is absolute." D. Currie, Air Pollution: Federal Law and Analysis 4–15 (1981). The EPA, "based on" the information about health effects contained in the technical "criteria" documents compiled under § 108(a)(2), is to identify the maximum airborne concentration of a pollutant that the public health can tolerate, decrease the concentration to provide an "adequate" margin of safety, and set the standard at that level. Nowhere are the costs of achieving such a standard made part of that initial calculation.

* * * Accordingly, to prevail in their present challenge, respondents must show a textual commitment of authority to the EPA to consider costs in setting NAAQS under § 109(b)(1). And because § 109(b)(1) and the NAAQS for which it provides are the engine that drives nearly all of Title I of the CAA, that textual commitment must be a clear one. Congress, we have held, does not alter the fundamental details of a regulatory scheme in vague terms or ancillary provisions—it does not, one might say, hide elephants in mouseholes. Respondents' textual arguments ultimately founder upon this principle.

* * * It should be clear from what we have said that the canon requiring texts to be so construed as to avoid serious constitutional problems has no application here. No matter how severe the constitutional doubt, courts may choose only between reasonably available interpretations of a text. The text of § 109(b), interpreted in its statutory and historical context and with appreciation for its importance to the CAA as a whole, unambiguously bars cost considerations from the NAAQS-setting process, and thus ends the matter for us as well as the EPA.[4] We therefore affirm the judgment of the Court of Appeals on this point.

III

Section 109(b)(1) of the CAA instructs the EPA to set "ambient air quality standards the attainment and maintenance of which in the judgment of the Administrator, based on [the] criteria [documents of § 108] and allowing an adequate margin of safety, are requisite to

4. Respondents' speculation that the EPA is secretly considering the costs of attainment without telling anyone is irrelevant to our interpretive inquiry. If such an allegation could be proved, it would be grounds for vacating the NAAQS, because the Administrator had not followed the law. It would not, however, be grounds for this Court's changing the law.

protect the public health." The Court of Appeals held that this section as interpreted by the Administrator did not provide an "intelligible principle" to guide the EPA's exercise of authority in setting NAAQS. "[The] EPA," it said, "lack[ed] any determinate criteria for drawing lines. It has failed to state intelligibly how much is too much." The court hence found that the EPA's interpretation (but not the statute itself) violated the nondelegation doctrine. We disagree.

In a delegation challenge, the constitutional question is whether the statute has delegated legislative power to the agency. * * * We have never suggested that an agency can cure an unlawful delegation of legislative power by adopting in its discretion a limiting construction of the statute. Both *Fahey v. Mallonee*, 332 U.S. 245 (1947), and *Lichter v. United States*, 334 U.S. 742 (1948), mention agency regulations in the course of their nondelegation discussions, but *Lichter* did so because a subsequent Congress had incorporated the regulations into a revised version of the statute, and *Fahey* because the customary practices in the area, implicitly incorporated into the statute, were reflected in the regulations. The idea that an agency can cure an unconstitutionally standardless delegation of power by declining to exercise some of that power seems to us internally contradictory. The very choice of which portion of the power to exercise—that is to say, the prescription of the standard that Congress had omitted—would *itself* be an exercise of the forbidden legislative authority. Whether the statute delegates legislative power is a question for the courts, and an agency's voluntary self-denial has no bearing upon the answer.

We agree with the Solicitor General that the text of § 109(b)(1) of the CAA at a minimum requires that "[f]or a discrete set of pollutants and based on published air quality criteria that reflect the latest scientific knowledge, [the] EPA must establish uniform national standards at a level that is requisite to protect public health from the adverse effects of the pollutant in the ambient air." Requisite, in turn, "mean[s] sufficient, but not more than necessary." These limits on the EPA's discretion are strikingly similar to the ones we approved in *Touby v. United States*, 500 U.S. 160 (1991), which permitted the Attorney General to designate a drug as a controlled substance for purposes of criminal drug enforcement if doing so was " 'necessary to avoid an imminent hazard to the public safety.' " They also resemble the Occupational Safety and Health Act provision requiring the agency to " 'set the standard which most adequately assures, to the extent feasible, on the basis of the best available evidence, that no employee will suffer any impairment of health' "—which the Court upheld in *Industrial Union Dept., AFL–CIO v. American Petroleum Institute*, 448 U.S. 607 (1980), and which even then-JUSTICE REHNQUIST, who alone in that case thought the statute violated the nondelegation doctrine, would have upheld if, like the statute here, it did not permit economic costs to be considered. See *American Textile Mfrs. Institute, Inc. v. Donovan*, 452 U.S. 490 (1981) (REHNQUIST, J., dissenting).

The scope of discretion § 109(b)(1) allows is in fact well within the outer limits of our nondelegation precedents. * * *

It is true enough that the degree of agency discretion that is acceptable varies according to the scope of the power congressionally conferred. While Congress need not provide any direction to the EPA regarding the manner in which it is to define "country elevators," which are to be exempt from new-stationary-source regulations governing grain elevators, it must provide substantial guidance on setting air standards that affect the entire national economy. But even in sweeping regulatory schemes we have never demanded, as the Court of Appeals did here, that statutes provide a "determinate criterion" for saying "how much [of the regulated harm] is too much." * * *

We therefore reverse the judgment of the Court of Appeals remanding for a reinterpretation that would avoid a supposed delegation of legislative power. It will remain for the Court of Appeals—on the remand that we direct for other reasons—to dispose of any other preserved challenge to the NAAQS under the judicial-review provisions contained in 42 U.S.C. § 607(d)(9).

* * *

Justice Stevens, with whom Justice Souter joins, concurring in part and concurring in the judgment.

Section 109(b)(1) delegates to the Administrator of the Environmental Protection Agency (EPA) the authority to promulgate national ambient air quality standards (NAAQS). In Part III of its opinion, the Court convincingly explains why the Court of Appeals erred when it concluded that § 109 effected "an unconstitutional delegation of legislative power." I wholeheartedly endorse the Court's result and endorse its explanation of its reasons, albeit with the following caveat.

The Court has two choices. We could choose to articulate our ultimate disposition of this issue by frankly acknowledging that the power delegated to the EPA is "legislative" but nevertheless conclude that the delegation is constitutional because adequately limited by the terms of the authorizing statute. Alternatively, we could pretend, as the Court does, that the authority delegated to the EPA is somehow not "legislative power." Despite the fact that there is language in our opinions that supports the Court's articulation of our holding, I am persuaded that it would be both wiser and more faithful to what we have actually done in delegation cases to admit that agency rulemaking authority is "legislative power."

The proper characterization of governmental power should generally depend on the nature of the power, not on the identity of the person exercising it. * * * If the NAAQS that the EPA promulgated had been prescribed by Congress, everyone would agree that those rules would be the product of an exercise of "legislative power." The same characterization is appropriate when an agency exercises rulemaking authority pursuant to a permissible delegation from Congress.

My view is not only more faithful to normal English usage, but is also fully consistent with the text of the Constitution. In Article I, the

Framers vested "All legislative Powers" in the Congress, Art. I., § 1, just as in Article II they vested the "executive Power" in the President, Art. II, § 1. Those provisions do not purport to limit the authority of either recipient of power to delegate authority to others. * * * Surely the authority granted to members of the Cabinet and federal law enforcement agents is properly characterized as "Executive" even though not exercised by the President.

It seems clear that an executive agency's exercise of rulemaking authority pursuant to a valid delegation from Congress is "legislative." As long as the delegation provides a sufficiently intelligible principle, there is nothing inherently unconstitutional about it. * * *

Notes

1. *Agency Power to Legitimate Overbroad Delegation*. Justice Scalia's emphatic dismissal of the D.C. Circuit's suggestion that the loose language of Section 110 of the Clean Air Act might be cured if the EPA were to adopt a narrowing construction does not necessarily reflect lack of concern for the problem addressed by the Oregon Supreme Court in *Sun Ray Drive–In*. Scalia (and the other Justices) clearly saw the nondelegation attack on Section 110 as raising an issue of legislative accountability for a policy that placed exclusive weight on health and—at least within the parameters of that provision—ignored cost and technological feasibility. The *Sun Ray* court, by contrast, was concerned primarily with the potential the legislature's delegation created for invidious, corrupt, or even whimsical administration.

In the context of the Clean Air Act's Section 110, the latter possibility seems remote. The EPA has set NAAQS for only six conventional air pollutants, in each case through a lengthy and very public process that provides some confidence that the same criteria are being applied. This does not mean that the statutory scheme as a whole does not create opportunities for invidious or biased decisions downstream as states—on which primary responsibility for controlling pollution to achieve the NAAQS rests—develop plans that impose specific control obligations on different types of pollution sources. But Congress was, and is, clearly aware of this possibility and, indeed, can be said to accept it as a byproduct of reposing in the states ultimate responsibility for determining which sources have the capability and the resources to control air pollution.

In the fulfillment of this responsibility the states are entitled, indeed expected, to take into account factors—cost and technical feasibility—that, according to Justice Scalia, Congress in Section 110 directed the EPA to ignore. Hence, it is possible to read the Clean Air Act as a whole as providing for consideration of all of the factors that the respondents in *American Trucking* insisted that Congress should have identified but did not. In a real sense, then, the respondents were challenging, not a failure to specify whether such factors should or may be considered in fashioning pollution controls, but a clear decision by Congress that cost and feasibility were more appropriately weighed at the state level.

2. *Nondelegable Functions*. Even if toothless in most contexts, the nondelegation doctrine may limit the delegation of particular functions. In THE FEDERALIST, for example, Madison opined that the President could not delegate his pardon power. By analogy, perhaps Congress is forbidden to delegate its impeachment power, JAMES O. FREEDMAN, CRISIS AND LEGITIMACY: THE ADMINISTRATIVE PROCESS AND AMERICAN GOVERNMENT 86–88 (1978), or to establish the "United States Appropriations Agency." See generally SOTIRIOS A. BARBER, THE CONSTITUTION AND THE DELEGATION OF CONGRESSIONAL POWER (1975) (arguing that constitutional supremacy necessarily implies that Congress may not abdicate powers intended by the Constitution to be lodged in Congress). For a suggestion that a delegation of "taxing power" would at least present a "constitutional problem," see *National Cable Television Ass'n v. United States*, 415 U.S. 336 (1974) (invalidating as unauthorized certain assessments that the FCC imposed on cable systems). But see *Touby v. United States*, 500 U.S. 160 (1991), *supra* p. 85.

Delegation, Representation, and Good Government

In THE END OF LIBERALISM: IDEOLOGY, POLICY, AND THE CRISIS OF PUBLIC AUTHORITY 125, 126, 148–49, 155 (1969), Theodore J. Lowi argues that modern toleration of broad statutory delegations of policy making authority to administrators is part of a political tradition that is antithetical to *law* (that is, to rules or standards as distinguished from procedures) and that the legislature's failure to prescribe policy inevitably results in a failure of government to develop coherent policy and ultimately in the replacement of law by ad hoc bargaining. In particular, Professor Lowi contends that broad delegations will generally result, not in administrative rulemaking to determine policy, but in policy remaining permanently indeterminate. This is true, he argues, because in individual cases it will be too costly for affected parties to insist upon a clear statement of policy:

> Interest-group liberalism has little place for law because laws interfere with the political process. * * *
>
> In brief, law, in the liberal view, is too authoritative a use of authority. Authority has to be tentative and accessible to be acceptable. If authority is to be accommodated to the liberal myth that it is "not power at all," it must emerge out of individual bargains.
>
> * * * Delegation of power provides the legal basis for rendering a statute tentative enough to keep the political process in good working order all the way down from Congress to the hearing examiner, the meat inspector, the community action supervisor, and the individual clients with which they deal. Everyone can feel that he is part of one big policy-making family. * * *
>
> *Wages and Hours Regional*: Mr. Employer, we find that you owe your ten employees a total of $10,000 in back wages, plus fines, for having them take telephone messages while having lunch on the premises.

Employer: I object. You interrogated my employees without my knowledge, and did not interrogate me at all. And, besides, where do you get off saying my boys were "on call" because they heard the phone ring? Talk to my lawyer.

Regional: How about $5,000 in back pay and no fines?

Employer: Good God, now I'm really disgusted. I want in writing your official interpretation governing such a case: And aren't there rules about notice and hearings?

Regional: How about $2,500 in back pay?

Employer: Well, hell, I * * *

Regional: How about an exchange of memoranda indicating future compliance?

Employer: Mmm * * * [aside: Lawyers' fees * * * trips to testify * * * obligations to that damned congressman of ours * * *]

Official memo from Regional, weeks later: You are hereby directed to cease * * *

Posted in employees' toilet: You are hereby directed to eat lunch off the premises.

This drama could have taken place in one long-distance call or in half a dozen letters strung out over many weeks. However, the demoralizing part is not what one might expect. It isn't "bureaucracy." * * * Disgust, disappointment, and distrust would arise in such a case because the agency appears "gutless." Its effort to avoid enunciating a rule may be rationalized as flexibility, but to most intelligent people directly involved in such a problem it can end in reduced respect—for the agency and for government. And meanwhile, no rule. * * *

* * * Admittedly the complexity of modern life forces Congress into vagueness and generality in drafting its statutes. Admittedly the political pressure of social unrest forces Congress and the President into premature formulations that make delegation of power inevitable. But to take these causes and effects as natural and good, and then to build the system around them, is to doom the system to remaining always locked into the original causes and effects.

Professor Lowi is by no means alone in believing that the practice of broad delegation is a formula for bad government. In DEMOCRACY AND DISTRUST: A THEORY OF JUDICIAL REVIEW (1980), John Hart Ely views the failure of the "legislature [i.e., Congress] to legislate [i.e., decide policy questions]" as one of the major obstacles to a truly representative democracy. "There can be little point in worrying about the distribution of the franchise and other personal political rights unless the important policy choices are being made by elected officials." In Ely's view, restricting legislative delegations will not produce perfect, only democratic, governance. "I'm not saying we may not still end up with a fair number of clowns as representatives, but at least then it will be because clowns are what we deserve."

Similar sentiments seem to underlie the dissenting opinions by Justice Rehnquist and Chief Justice Burger in *Industrial Union Department, AFL–CIO v. American Petroleum Institute*, 448 U.S. 607, 671 (1980), and *American Textile Manufacturers Institute, Inc. v. Donovan*, 452 U.S. 490, 543 (1981). Both would apparently send section 6(b)(5) of the Occupational Safety and Health Act, 29 U.S.C. § 655(b)(5), back to Congress for further specification of the criteria by which the Occupational Safety and Health Administration should balance the objectives of protecting worker health and maintaining a healthy economy. The pertinent language of section 6(b)(5) directs OSHA, in regulating worker exposure to toxic chemicals, to prescribe the standard that "most adequately assures, to the extent feasible * * * that no employee will suffer material impairment of health or functional capacity even if such employee has regular exposure to the hazard * * * for the period of his working life." Union representatives claimed that this instruction obliged OSHA to mandate the use of whatever available technology an industry could afford to install without bankrupting itself, while employer groups insisted that the agency was required to weigh the costs of controls against health benefits in deciding what standard is "feasible." Adoption of the first interpretation could in some instances force employers to spend hundreds of millions of dollars, while acceptance of the latter version would substantially reduce protection for workers in industries where control technology was expensive.

According to Justice Rehnquist in *Industrial Union Dept.*:

> In drafting § 6(b)(5), Congress was faced with a clear, if difficult, choice between balancing statistical lives and industrial resources or authorizing the Secretary to elevate human life above all concerns save massive dislocation. * * * That Congress chose * * * to pass this difficult choice on to the Secretary is evident from the spectral quality of the standard it selected.

448 U.S. at 685. In *Donovan*, Rehnquist, joined by the Chief Justice, suggested that the "spectral" language of section 6(b)(5) masked a policy disagreement so profound that had Congress been required to resolve it "there would have been no bill for the President to sign."

The Lowi–Ely–Rehnquist critique dramatizes an apparently serious flaw in American government—a legislature fleeing from choice on critical issues, not by postponing action but by adopting ambiguous statutes conferring policy making power on administrators who will themselves be deeply compromised by their lack of clear statutory authority. Thus, it is suggested, we blunder our way into an administrative state that has traded its democratic values for little or no increase in effective governance.

Yet before accepting this depressing vision, and embracing the judicial insistence on statutory specificity that it apparently entails, consider some critical questions. First, are you convinced that Congress should decide all basic policy issues *by statute* when it launches any public program? For example, are you as confident as Justice Rehnquist that there should be no OSHA program absent an initial congressional decision firmly establishing priorities between health and economic well-being? Do you agree with Professor Lowi that the lack of a clear rule for making such tradeoffs in specific industries will be demoralizing? Is it clear, as Professor Ely would seem to suggest, that this sort of ambiguity about basic values is "unrepresentative" of the electorate, or otherwise interferes with republican government? See generally GUIDO CALABRESI & PHILIP BOBBITT, TRAGIC CHOICES (1978).

Even if we were to agree that Congress *should* determine the basic social values that are to be implemented by public programs, to what extent can statutory language realistically control subsequent events? When statutory criteria are specific, the administrator charged with implementation still will possess considerable discretion to determine the place of a statute and its enforcement in the overall agency agenda, the timetable according to which regulations will be promulgated, the vigor with which regulations will be enforced, and a host of other matters that determine as much as the statute the day-to-day operational significance of Congress' policy command.

A further argument can be made that broad delegations actually enhance the democratic responsiveness of government by empowering Presidents to respond to changing voter preferences:

> Strangely enough it may make sense to imagine the delegation of political authority to administrators as a device for improving the responsiveness of government to the desires of the electorate. This argument can be made even if we accept many of the insights of the political and economic literature that premises its predictions of congressional and voter behavior on a direct linkage between benefits transferred to constituents and the election or reelection of representatives. All we need do is not forget there are also presidential elections and that, as the Supreme Court reminds us in *Chevron* [*v. Natural Resources Defense Council*, 467 U.S. 837 (1984)], Presidents are heads of administrations.
>
> Assume then that voters view the election of representatives to Congress through the lens of the most cynical interpretation of the modern political science literature on congressional behavior. In short, the voter chooses a representative for that representative's effectiveness in supplying governmental goods and services to the local district, including the voter. The representative is a good representative or a bad representative based upon his or her ability to provide the district with at least its fair share of governmental largesse. In this view, the Congressperson's position on various issues is of modest, if any, importance.
>
> The voter's vision of presidential electoral politics is arguably quite different. The President has no particular constituency to

which he or she has special responsibility to deliver benefits. Presidents are hardly cut off from pork-barrel politics. Yet issues of national scope and the candidates' positions on those issues are the essence of presidential politics. Citizens vote for a president based almost wholly on a perception of the difference that one or another candidate might make to general governmental policies.

If this description of voting in national elections is reasonably plausible, then the utilization of vague delegations to administrative agencies takes on significance as a device for facilitating responsiveness to voter preferences expressed in presidential elections. The high transactions costs of legislating specifically suggests that legislative activity directed to the modification of administration mandates will be infrequent. Agencies will thus persist with their statutory empowering provisions relatively intact over substantial periods of time. Voter preferences on the direction and intensity of governmental activities however, are not likely to be so stable. Indeed, one can reasonably expect that a President will be able to affect policy in a four-year term only because being elected President entails acquiring the power to exercise, direct, or influence policy discretion. The group of executive officers we commonly call "the Administration" matters only because of the relative malleability of the directives that administrators have in their charge. If congressional statutes were truly specific with respect to the actions that administrators were to take, presidential politics would be a mere beauty contest. For, in the absence of a parliamentary system or a system of strict party loyalty, specific statutes would mean that Presidents and administrations could respond to voter preferences only if they were able to convince the legislature to make specific changes in the existing set of specific statutes. Arguments for specific statutory provisions constraining administrative discretion may reflect therefore a desire merely for conservative, not responsive, governance.

Of course, the vision of a President or an administration having to negotiate with the Congress for changes in policy is not one that is without its own attractiveness. Surely, we desire some limits on the degree to which a President can view a national election as a referendum approving all the President's (or the President's colleagues') pet projects, whether disclosed or undisclosed during the campaign. Those who abhor the policies of the Reagan administration, for example, might surely be attracted to a system that would have required that particular President to act almost exclusively through proposals for legislative change. Yet it seems likely that the flexibility that is currently built into the processes of administrative governance by relatively broad delegations of statutory authority permits a more appropriate degree of administrative, or administration, responsiveness to the voter's will than would a strict nondelegation doctrine.

Jerry L. Mashaw, *Pro–Delegation: Why Administrators Should Make Political Decisions*, 1 J.L., Econ. & Org. 81 (1985).

In *A Public Choice Case for the Administrative State*, 89 Geo. L.J. 97 (2000), David B. Spence and Frank Cross offer negative justifications for not simply tolerating, but preferring, vague delegations to agencies:

> One must consider why Congress does not currently enact highly specific legislation, as it plainly has the power to do. There are two obvious reasons, one involving transaction costs and the other involving political expediency.
>
> The transaction cost explanation involves the need for information. The costs of legislating with specificity are quite high, as evidenced by the very magnitude of the federal bureaucracy that has arisen to fill in the interstices of prevailing vague statutory commands. The primary cost of specificity is the cost of information regarding the need for action and the proper action to be taken. * * * It would place an enormous burden on Congress to evaluate all the data supplied in a typical notice-and-comment rulemaking process before an agency. The frequency of legislative hearings and the size of legislative staff would have to multiply many times over. Additionally, there is little that could be done to provide Congress with the engineering expertise of OSHA or EPA. * * *
>
> An even more serious shortcoming of legislative specificity arises in the context of modifying legal requirements. Wise regulatory commands should be flexible enough to adapt to changes in circumstances and the growth of scientific knowledge. Congress is a very bad choice of institutions if the goal is any sort of flexible regulatory policy. * * * For Congress, there are also considerable opportunity costs to taking such action. Unlike a single-mission agency, Congress must deal with all the public demands in all areas of government. For example, if the public is particularly concerned about crime, Congress may lack the time to act upon an environmental policy, even if it were universally considered a desirable action, simply because it would have a lower priority. * * *
>
> Nor is legislative specificity an answer to those who fear rent-seeking agency capture. The most specific legislative enactments are among the most objectionable features to be found in contemporary government action. An example of legislative specificity is the breaks inserted into tax laws for a category of taxpayers of that has only one (unnamed) member. Another infamous classic of legislative specificity is the Smoot–Hawley tariff law, in which Congress wrote specific tariffs for particular products, in response to industry demands.

Spence and Cross then consider how Congress might respond to a revitalized non-delegation doctrine:

> * * * [T]here is ample reason to consider the possibility that Congress would react to a nondelegation rule by continuing to pass vague, symbolic legislation without delegating interpretive authority to agencies. This is in fact by far the most likely outcome of a nondelegation doctrine, one that is implied by historical experience.

> * * * [W]hen Congress passes vague legislation without delegating discretionary authority to implementing agencies, the authority for interstitial discretionary interpretation inevitably devolves to the courts. * * * The courts have virtually all of the alleged disadvantages of bureaucratic agencies, with none of the counteracting benefits that agencies offer. The courts lack democratic accountability and are far more difficult for Congress and the President to check and correct than are agencies. Judges do not possess the technical expertise that justify agency delegations, and courts are the poorest of all government institutions when it comes to independent information-gathering capabilities. * * *
>
> The delegation of authority to the courts also provides greater opportunities for special interest rent-seeking than does delegation to agencies. While courts may not be directly captured by special interests, they can be readily manipulated by those interests. Courts are reactive and have their agenda set by litigants, who typically represent special factional interests. Doctrines such as standing preclude the public from being a party to litigation and having a voice before the courts. Through strategic selection of cases for litigation, the special interest groups can control the path of precedent. This ability to manipulate courts explains why special interest groups are insistent about expanding their opportunities for judicial review of delegated agency decisions.

Whether one favors clearer legislative directions depends also, of course, on one's perceptions of the legislative process. As materials in Chapter 1 suggest, there is a lively debate whether explicit legislative choice among competing policies would actually result in decisions more likely to be socially beneficial or representative of majoritarian preferences than choices arrived at by administrative agencies. For further discussion, see Peter Aranson, Ernest Gellhorn, & Glen Robinson, *A Theory of Legislative Delegation*, 68 Corn.L.Rev. 1 (1982); see generally ROBERT ABRAMS, FOUNDATIONS OF POLITICAL ANALYSIS: AN INTRODUCTION TO THE THEORY OF COLLECTIVE CHOICE (1980); DAVID SCHOENBROD, POWER WITHOUT RESPONSIBILITY: HOW CONGRESS ABUSES THE PEOPLE THROUGH DELEGATION (1993); Symposium, *The Phoenix Rises Again: The Nondelegation Doctrine From Constitutional and Policy Perspectives*, 20 Cardozo L. Rev. 731 (1999).

2. THE "LEGISLATIVE VETO"

Defenders of broad delegations of policy making authority to administrators can, of course, point to Congress' power to repeal legislation or to proscribe by subsequent amendments any administrative initiatives it does not approve. The enactment of legislation, however, is usually both time-and energy-consuming, and pressing crises can drive specific regulatory issues far down on Congress's agenda. Moreover, repeal of a statute or enactment of a law nullifying an administrative initiative requires the President's approval, unless Congress can muster the super-majority sufficient to override the veto. Accordingly, Congress has continually sought more efficient mechanisms to check agency action. For several decades following World War II a popular procedural innovation was the "legislative veto," a shorthand phrase covering a variety of mechanisms short of enacting new legislation to prevent administrative initiatives disagreeable to Congress from having legal effect.

IMMIGRATION AND NATURALIZATION SERVICE v. CHADHA

Supreme Court of the United States, 1983.
462 U.S. 919, 103 S.Ct. 2764, 77 L.Ed.2d 317.

CHIEF JUSTICE BURGER delivered the opinion of the Court.

* * *

Chadha is an East Indian who was born in Kenya and holds a British passport. He was lawfully admitted to the United States in 1966 on a nonimmigrant student visa. His visa expired on June 30, 1972. On October 11, 1973, the District Director of the Immigration and Naturalization Service ordered Chadha to show cause why he should not be deported for having "remained in the United States for a longer time than permitted." Pursuant to § 242(b) of the Immigration and Nationality Act (Act), 8 U.S.C. § 1254(b), a deportation hearing was held before an immigration judge on January 11, 1974. Chadha conceded that he was deportable for overstaying his visa and the hearing was adjourned to enable him to file an application for suspension of deportation under § 244(a)(1) of the Act. Section 244(a)(1) provides:

> "(a) As hereinafter prescribed in this section, the Attorney General may, in his discretion, suspend deportation and adjust the status to that of an alien lawfully admitted for permanent residence, in the case of an alien who applies to the Attorney General for suspension of deportation and—
>
> "(1) is deportable under any law of the United States except the provisions specified in paragraph (2) of this subsection; has been physically present in the United States for a continuous period of not less than seven years immediately preceding the date of such application, and proves that during all of such period he was and is a person of good moral character; and is a person whose deportation would, in the opinion of the Attorney General, result in extreme hardship to the alien or to his spouse, parent, or child, who is a citizen of the United States or an alien lawfully admitted for permanent residence."

* * *

Pursuant to § 244(c)(1) of the Act, the immigration judge suspended Chadha's deportation and a report of the suspension was transmitted to Congress. Section 244(c)(1) provides:

> "Upon application by any alien who is found by the Attorney General to meet the requirements of subsection (a) of this section

the Attorney General may in his discretion suspend deportation of such alien. If the deportation of any alien is suspended under the provisions of this subsection, a complete and detailed statement of the facts and pertinent provisions of law in the case shall be reported to the Congress with the reasons for such suspension. Such reports shall be submitted on the first day of each calendar month in which Congress is in session."

Once the Attorney General's recommendation for suspension of Chadha's deportation was conveyed to Congress, Congress had the power under § 244(c)(2) of the Act to veto[2] the Attorney General's determination that Chadha should not be deported. Section 244(c)(2) provides:

> "(2) In the case of an alien specified in paragraph (1) of subsection (a) of this subsection—if during the session of the Congress at which a case is reported, or prior to the close of the session of the Congress next following the session at which a case is reported, either the Senate or the House of Representatives passes a resolution stating in substance that it does not favor the suspension of such deportation, the Attorney General shall thereupon deport such alien or authorize the alien's voluntary departure in the manner provided by law. If, within the time above specified, neither the Senate nor the House of Representatives shall pass such a resolution, the Attorney General shall cancel deportation proceedings."

* * *

On December 12, 1975, Representative Eilberg, Chairman of the Judiciary Subcommittee on Immigration, Citizenship, and International Law, introduced a resolution opposing "the granting of permanent residence in the United States to [six] aliens," including Chadha. The resolution was referred to the House Committee on the Judiciary. On December 16, 1975, the resolution was discharged from further consideration by the House Committee on the Judiciary and submitted to the House of Representatives for a vote. The resolution had not been printed and was not made available to other Members of the House prior to or at the time it was voted on. So far as the record before us shows, the House consideration of the resolution was based on Representative Eilberg's statement from the floor that

> "[i]t was the feeling of the committee, after reviewing 340 cases, that the aliens contained in the resolution [Chadha and five others] did not meet these statutory requirements, particularly as it relates to hardship; and it is the opinion of the committee that their deportation should not be suspended."

2. In constitutional terms, "veto" is used to describe the President's power under Art. I, § 7 of the Constitution. See BLACK'S LAW DICTIONARY 1403 (5th ed. 1979). It appears, however, that Congressional devices of the type authorized by § 244(c)(2) have come to be commonly referred to as a "veto." * * * We refer to the Congressional "resolution" authorized by § 244(c)(2) as a "one-House veto" of the Attorney General's decision to allow a particular deportable alien to remain in the United States.

The resolution was passed without debate or recorded vote. Since the House action was pursuant to § 244(c)(2), the resolution was not treated as an Article I legislative act; it was not submitted to the Senate or presented to the President for his action. * * *

Pursuant to § 106(a) of the Act, Chadha filed a petition for review of the deportation order in the United States Court of Appeals for the Ninth Circuit. The Immigration and Naturalization Service agreed with Chadha's position before the Court of Appeals and joined him in arguing that § 244(c)(2) is unconstitutional. In light of the importance of the question, the Court of Appeals invited both the Senate and the House of Representatives to file briefs *amici curiae*. * * *

Explicit and unambiguous provisions of the Constitution prescribe and define the respective functions of the Congress and of the Executive in the legislative process. Since the precise terms of those familiar provisions are critical to the resolution of this case, we set them out verbatim. Art. I provides:

> "All legislative Powers herein granted shall be vested in a Congress of the United States, which shall consist of a Senate *and* a House of Representatives." Art. I, § 1. (Emphasis added).
>
> "Every Bill which shall have passed the House of Representatives *and* the Senate, *shall*, before it become a Law, be presented to the President of the United States; * * *" Art. I, § 7, cl. 2. (Emphasis added).
>
> "*Every* Order, Resolution, or Vote to which the Concurrence of the Senate and House of Representatives may be necessary (except on a question of Adjournment) *shall* be presented to the President of the United States; and before the Same shall take Effect, *shall be* approved by him, or being disapproved by him, *shall be* repassed by two thirds of the Senate and House of Representatives, according to the Rules and Limitations prescribed in the Case of a Bill." Art. I, § 7, cl. 3. (Emphasis added).

* * *

THE PRESENTMENT CLAUSES

The records of the Constitutional Convention reveal that the requirement that all legislation be presented to the President before becoming law was uniformly accepted by the Framers. Presentment to the President and the Presidential veto were considered so imperative that the draftsmen took special pains to assure that these requirements could not be circumvented. During the final debate on Art. I, § 7, cl. 2, James Madison expressed concern that it might easily be evaded by the simple expedient of calling a proposed law a "resolution" or "vote" rather than a "bill." As a consequence, Art. I, § 7, cl. 3 was added.

The decision to provide the President with a limited and qualified power to nullify proposed legislation by veto was based on the profound conviction of the Framers that the powers conferred on Congress were the powers to be most carefully circumscribed. * * *

The President's role in the lawmaking process also reflects the Framers' careful efforts to check whatever propensity a particular Congress might have to enact oppressive, improvident, or ill-considered measures. The President's veto role in the legislative process was described later during public debate on ratification:

> "It establishes a salutary check upon the legislative body, calculated to guard the community against the effects of faction, precipitancy, or of any impulse unfriendly to the public good which may happen to influence a majority of that body. * * * The primary inducement to conferring the power in question upon the Executive is to enable him to defend himself: the secondary one is to increase the chances in favor of the community against the passing of bad laws through haste, inadvertence, or design." The Federalist No. 73 at 458 (A. Hamilton).

The Court also has observed that the Presentment Clauses serve the important purposes of assuring that a "national" perspective is grafted on the legislative process:

> "The President is a representative of the people just as the members of the Senate and of the House are, and it may be, at some times, on some subjects, that the President elected by all the people is rather more representative of them all than are the members of either body of the Legislature whose constituencies are local and not country-wide. * * *" *Myers v. United States*, 272 U.S. 52, 123 (1926).

BICAMERALISM

The bicameral requirement of Art. I, §§ 1, 7 was of scarcely less concern to the Framers than was the Presidential veto and indeed the two concepts are interdependent. By providing that no law could take effect without the concurrence of the prescribed majority of the Members of both Houses, the Framers reemphasized their belief, already remarked upon in connection with the Presentment Clauses, that legislation should not be enacted unless it has been carefully and fully considered by the Nation's elected officials. * * *

This view was rooted in a general skepticism regarding the fallibility of human nature later commented on by Joseph Story:

> "Public bodies, like private persons, are occasionally under the dominion of strong passions and excitements: impatient, irritable, and impetuous. * * * If [a legislature] feels no check but its own will, it rarely has the firmness to insist upon holding a question long enough under its own view, to see and mark it in all its bearings and relations to society." * * *

However familiar, it is useful to recall that apart from their fear that special interests could be favored at the expense of public needs, the Framers were also concerned, although not of one mind, over the apprehensions of the smaller states. Those states feared a commonality of interest among the larger states would work to their disadvantage; representatives of the larger states, on the other hand, were skeptical of a legislature that could pass laws favoring a minority of the people. It need hardly be repeated here that the Great Compromise, under which one House was viewed as representing the people and the other states, allayed the fears of both the large and small states.

We see therefore that the Framers were acutely conscious that the bicameral requirement and the Presentment Clauses would serve essential constitutional functions. * * * It emerges clearly that the prescription for legislative action in Art. I, §§ 1, 7 represents the Framers' decision that the legislative power of the Federal government be exercised in accord with a single, finely wrought and exhaustively considered, procedure.

* * * [We] must nevertheless establish that the challenged action under § 244(c)(2) is of the kind to which the procedural requirements of Art. I, § 7 apply. Not every action taken by either House is subject to the bicameralism and presentment requirements of Art. I. Whether actions taken by either House are, in law and fact, an exercise of legislative power depends not on their form but upon "whether they contain matter which is properly to be regarded as legislative in its character and effect."

Examination of the action taken here by one House pursuant to § 244(c)(2) reveals that it was essentially legislative in purpose and effect. In purporting to exercise power defined in Art. I, § 8, cl. 4 to "establish an uniform Rule of Naturalization," the House took action that had the purposes and effect of altering the legal rights, duties and relations of persons, including the Attorney General, Executive Branch officials and Chadha, all outside the legislative branch. Section 244(c)(2) purports to authorize one House of Congress to require the Attorney General to deport an individual alien whose deportation otherwise would be cancelled under § 244. The one-House veto operated in this case to overrule the Attorney General and mandate Chadha's deportation; absent the House action, Chadha would remain in the United States. Congress has *acted* and its action has altered Chadha's status.

The legislative character of the one-House veto in this case is confirmed by the character of the Congressional action it supplants. Neither the House of Representatives nor the Senate contends that, absent the veto provision in § 244(c)(2), either of them, or both of them acting together, could effectively require the Attorney General to deport an alien once the Attorney General, in the exercise of legislatively delegated authority,[16] had determined the alien should remain in the

16. Congress protests that affirming the Court of Appeals in this case will sanction "lawmaking by the Attorney General. * * * Why is the Attorney General exempt from submitting his proposed changes in the law to the full bicameral process?" Brief of the United States House of Representatives 40. To be sure, some administrative agency action—rule making, for example—may resemble "lawmaking." See 5 U.S.C.

United States. Without the challenged provision in § 244(c)(2), this could have been achieved, if at all, only by legislation requiring deportation. * * *

Finally, we see that when the Framers intended to authorize either House of Congress to act alone and outside of its prescribed bicameral legislative role, they narrowly and precisely defined the procedure for such action. There are but four provisions in the Constitution, explicit and unambiguous, by which one House may act alone with the unreviewable force of law, not subject to the President's veto:

(a) The House of Representatives alone was given the power to initiate impeachments. Art. I, § 2, cl. 6;

(b) The Senate alone was given the power to conduct trials following impeachment on charges initiated by the House and to convict following trial. Art. I, § 3, cl. 5;

(c) The Senate alone was given final unreviewable power to approve or disapprove presidential appointments. Art. II, § 2, cl. 2;

(d) The Senate alone was given unreviewable power to ratify treaties negotiated by the President. Art. II, § 2, cl. 2.

Clearly, when the Draftsmen sought to confer special powers on one House, independent of the other House, or of the President, they did so in explicit, unambiguous terms. * * *

Since it is clear that the action by the House under § 244(c)(2) was not within any of the express constitutional exceptions authorizing one House to act alone, and equally clear that it was an exercise of legislative

§ 551(4), which defines an agency's "rule" as "the whole or part of an agency statement of general or particular applicability and future effect designed to implement, interpret, or prescribe *law* or policy." * * * This Court has referred to agency activity as being "quasi-legislative" in character. *Humphrey's Executor v. United States*, 295 U.S. 602, 628 (1935). Clearly, however, "[i]n the framework of our Constitution, the President's power to see that the laws are faithfully executed refutes the idea that he is to be a lawmaker." *Youngstown Sheet & Tube Co. v. Sawyer*, 343 U.S. 579, 587 (1952). When the Attorney General performs his duties pursuant to § 244, he does not exercise "legislative" power. The bicameral process is not necessary as a check on the Executive's administration of the laws because his administrative activity cannot reach beyond the limits of the statute that created it—a statute duly enacted pursuant to Art. I, §§ 1, 7. The constitutionality of the Attorney General's execution of the authority delegated to him by § 244 involves only a question of delegation doctrine. The courts, when a case or controversy arises, can always "ascertain whether the will of Congress has been obeyed." *Yakus v. United States*, 321 U.S. 414, 425 (1944), and can enforce adherence to statutory standards. It is clear, therefore, that the Attorney General acts in his presumptively Art. II capacity when he administers the Immigration and Nationality Act. Executive action under legislatively delegated authority that might resemble "legislative" action in some respects is not subject to the approval of both Houses of Congress and the President for the reason that the Constitution does not so require. That kind of Executive action is always subject to check by the terms of the legislation that authorized it; and if that authority is exceeded it is open to judicial review as well as the power of Congress to modify or revoke the authority entirely. A one-House veto is clearly legislative in both character and effect and is not so checked; the need for the check provided by Art. I, §§ 1, 7 is therefore clear. Congress' authority to delegate portions of its power to administrative agencies provided no support for the argument that Congress can constitutionally control administration of the laws by way of a Congressional veto.

power, that action was subject to the standards prescribed in Article I. * * * To accomplish what has been attempted by one House of Congress in this case requires action in conformity with the express procedures of the Constitution's prescription for legislative action: passage by a majority of both Houses and presentment to the President. * * *

Affirmed.

Justice Powell, concurring in the judgment.

The Court's decision, based on the Presentment Clauses, Art. I, § 7, cl. 2 and 3, apparently will invalidate every use of the legislative veto. The breadth of this holding gives one pause. Congress has included the veto in literally hundreds of statutes, dating back to the 1930s. Congress clearly views this procedure as essential to controlling the delegation of power to administrative agencies. One reasonably may disagree with Congress' assessment of the veto's utility, but the respect due its judgment as a coordinate branch of Government cautions that our holding should be no more extensive than necessary to decide this case. In my view, the case may be decided on a narrower ground. When Congress finds that a particular person does not satisfy the statutory criteria for permanent residence in this country it has assumed a judicial function in violation of the principle of separation of powers. Accordingly, I concur in the judgment.

Justice White, dissenting. * * *

The prominence of the legislative veto mechanism in our contemporary political system and its importance to Congress can hardly be overstated. It has become a central means by which Congress secures the accountability of executive and independent agencies. Without the legislative veto, Congress is faced with a Hobson's choice: either to refrain from delegating the necessary authority, leaving itself with a hopeless task of writing laws with the requisite specificity to cover endless special circumstances across the entire policy landscape, or in the alternative, to abdicate its law-making function to the executive branch and independent agencies. To choose the former leaves major national problems unresolved; to opt for the latter risks unaccountable policymaking by those not elected to fill that role. Accordingly, over the past five decades, the legislative veto has been placed in nearly 200 statutes. The device is known in every field of governmental concern: reorganization, budgets, foreign affairs, war powers, and regulation of trade, safety, energy, the environment and the economy. * * *

The history of the legislative veto also makes clear that it has not been a sword with which Congress has struck out to aggrandize itself at the expense of the other branches—the concerns of Madison and Hamilton. Rather, the veto has been a means of defense, a reservation of ultimate authority necessary if Congress is to fulfill its designated role under Article I as the nation's lawmaker. While the President has often objected to particular legislative vetoes, generally those left in the hands of congressional committees, the Executive has more often agreed to legislative review as the price for a broad delegation of authority. To be sure, the President may have preferred unrestricted power, but that could be precisely why Congress thought it essential to retain a check on the exercise of delegated authority.

For all these reasons, the apparent sweep of the Court's decision today is regrettable. The Court's Article I analysis appears to invalidate all legislative vetoes irrespective of form or subject. Because the legislative veto is commonly found as a check upon rulemaking by administrative agencies and upon broadbased policy decisions of the Executive Branch, it is particularly unfortunate that the Court reaches its decision in a case involving the exercise of a veto over deportation decisions regarding particular individuals. * * *

* * * The power to exercise a legislative veto is not the power to write new law without bicameral approval or presidential consideration. The veto must be authorized by statute and may only negative what an Executive department or independent agency has proposed. On its face, the legislative veto no more allows one House of Congress to make law than does the presidential veto confer such power upon the President.

The terms of the Presentment Clauses suggest only that bills and their equivalent are subject to the requirements of bicameral passage and presentment to the President. Article I, § 7, cl. 2, stipulates only that "Every Bill which shall have passed the House of Representatives and the Senate, shall before it becomes a Law, be presented to the President" for approval or disapproval, his disapproval then subject to being overridden by a two-thirds vote of both houses. Section 7, cl. 3 goes further:

> Every Order, Resolution, or Vote to which the Concurrence of the Senate and House of Representatives may be necessary (except on a question of Adjournment) shall be presented to the President of the United States: and before the same shall take Effect, shall be approved by him, or being disapproved by him, shall be repassed by two-thirds of the Senate and House of Representatives, according to the Rules and Limitations prescribed in the Case of a Bill.

Although the Clause does not specify the actions for which the concurrence of both Houses is "necessary," the proceedings at the Philadelphia Convention suggest its purpose was to prevent Congress from circumventing the presentation requirement in the making of new legislation. * * * This reading is consistent with the historical background of the Presentation Clause itself which reveals only that the Framers were concerned with limiting the methods for enacting new legislation. The Framers were aware of the experience in Pennsylvania where the legislature had evaded the requirements attached to the passing of legislation by the use of "resolves," and the criticisms directed at this practice by the Council of Censors. There is no record that the Convention contemplated, let alone intended, that these Article I requirements would someday be invoked to restrain the scope of Congressional authority pursuant to duly-enacted law.

When the Convention did turn its attention to the scope of Congress' lawmaking power, the Framers were expansive. The Necessary and Proper Clause, Art. I, § 8, cl. 18, vests Congress with the power "to make all laws which shall be necessary and proper for carrying into Execution the foregoing Powers [the enumerated powers of § 8], and all other Powers vested by this Constitution in the government of the United States, or in any Department or Officer thereof." It is long-settled that Congress may "exercise its best judgment in the selection of measures, to carry into execution the constitutional powers of the government," and "avail itself of experience, to exercise its reason, and to accommodate its legislation to circumstances." *McCulloch v. Maryland*, 4 Wheat. 316, 415–416, 420 (1819).

The Court heeded this counsel in approving the modern administrative state. The Court's holding today that all legislative-type action must be enacted through the lawmaking process ignores that legislative authority is routinely delegated to the Executive branch, to the independent regulatory agencies, and to private individuals and groups. * * *

This Court's decisions sanctioning such delegations make clear that Article I does not require all action with the effect of legislation to be passed as a law. * * *

If Congress may delegate lawmaking power to independent and executive agencies, it is most difficult to understand Article I as forbidding Congress from also reserving a check on legislative power for itself. Absent the veto, the agencies receiving delegations of legislative or quasi-legislative power may issue regulations having the force of law without bicameral approval and without the President's signature. It is thus not apparent why the reservation of a veto over the exercise of that legislative power must be subject to a more exacting test. In both cases, it is enough that the initial statutory authorizations comply with the Article I requirements.

Nor are there strict limits on the agents that may receive such delegations of legislative authority so that it might be said that the legislature can delegate authority to others but not to itself. While most authority to issue rules and regulations is given to the executive branch and the independent regulatory agencies, statutory delegations to private persons have also passed this Court's scrutiny. In *Currin v. Wallace*, 306 U.S. 1 (1939), the statute provided that restrictions upon the production or marketing of agricultural commodities was to become effective only upon the favorable vote by a prescribed majority of the affected farmers. *United States v. Rock Royal Co-operative*, 307 U.S. 533, 577 (1939), upheld an act which gave producers of specified commodities the right to veto marketing orders issued by the Secretary of Agriculture. Assuming *Currin* and *Rock Royal Co-operative* remain sound law, the Court's decision today suggests that Congress may place a "veto" power over suspensions of deportation in private hands or in the hands of an independent agency, but is forbidden from reserving such authority for itself. Perhaps this odd result could be justified on other constitutional grounds, such as the separation of powers, but certainly it cannot be defended as consistent with the Court's view of the Article I presentment and bicameralism commands. * * *

The central concern of the presentation and bicameralism requirements of Article I is that when a departure from the legal status quo is undertaken, it is done with the approval of the President and both Houses of Congress—or, in the event of a presidential veto, a two-thirds majority in both Houses. This interest is fully satisfied by the operation of § 244(c)(2). The President's approval is found in the Attorney General's action in recommending to Congress that the deportation order for a given alien be suspended. The House and the Senate indicate their approval of the Executive's action by not passing a resolution of disapproval within the statutory period. Thus, a change in the legal status quo—the deportability of the alien—is consummated only with the approval of each of the three relevant actors. The disagreement of any one of the three maintains the alien's pre-existing status: the Executive may choose not to recommend suspension; the House and Senate may each veto the recommendation. The effect on the rights and obligations of the affected individuals and upon the legislative system is precisely the same as if a private bill were introduced but failed to receive the necessary approval. * * *

Thus understood, § 244(c)(2) fully effectuates the purposes of the bicameralism and presentation requirements. I now briefly consider possible objections to the analysis.

First, it may be asserted that Chadha's status before legislative disapproval is one of nondeportation and that the exercise of the veto, unlike the failure of a private bill, works a change in the status quo. This position plainly ignores the statutory language. At no place in § 244 has Congress delegated to the Attorney General any final power to determine which aliens shall be allowed to remain in the United States. Congress has retained the ultimate power to pass on such changes in deportable status. By its own terms, § 244(a) states that whatever power the Attorney General has been delegated to suspend deportation and adjust status is to be exercisable only "as hereinafter prescribed in this section." Subsection (c) is part of that section. A grant of "suspension" does not cancel the alien's deportation or adjust the alien's status to that of a permanent resident alien. A suspension order is merely a "deferment of deportation," which can mature into a cancellation of deportation and adjustment of status only upon the approval of Congress—by way of silence—under § 244(c)(2). Only then does the statute authorize the Attorney General to "cancel deportation proceedings" § 244(c)(2), and "record the alien's lawful admission for permanent residence * * *" § 244(d). The Immigration and Naturalization Service's action, on behalf of the Attorney General, "cannot become effective without ratification by Congress." Until that ratification occurs, the executive's action is simply a recommendation that Congress finalize the suspension—in itself, it works no legal change.

Second, it may be said that this approach leads to the incongruity that the two-House veto is more suspect than its one-House brother. Although the idea may be initially counter-intuitive, on close analysis, it is not at all unusual that the one-House veto is of more certain constitutionality than the two-House version. If the Attorney General's action is a proposal for legislation, then the disapproval of but a single House is all that is required to prevent its passage. Because approval is indicated by the failure to veto, the one-House veto satisfies the requirement of bicameral approval. The two-House version may present a different question. The concept that "neither branch of Congress, when acting separately, can lawfully exercise more power than is conferred by the Constitution on the whole body," is fully observed. * * *

The Court of Appeals struck § 244(c)(2) as violative of the constitutional principle of separation of powers. * * *

* * * *Nixon v. Administrator of Gen. Servs.*, 433 U.S. 425 (1977), * * * in rejecting a separation of powers objection to a law requiring that the Administrator take custody of certain presidential papers, set forth a framework for evaluating such claims:

> [I]n determining whether the Act disrupts the proper balance between the coordinate branches, the proper inquiry focuses on the extent to which it prevents the Executive Branch from accomplishing its constitutionally assigned functions. Only where the potential for disruption is present must we then determine whether that impact is justified by an overriding need to promote objectives within the constitutional authority of Congress.

Section 244(c)(2) survives this test. The legislative veto provision does not "prevent the Executive Branch from accomplishing its constitutionally assigned functions." First, it is clear that the Executive Branch has no "constitutionally assigned" function of suspending the deportation of aliens. * * * Here, § 244 grants the executive only a qualified suspension authority and it is only that authority which the President is constitutionally authorized to execute. * * *

Nor does § 244 infringe on the judicial power, as Justice Powell would hold. Section 244 makes clear that Congress has reserved its own judgment as part of the statutory process. Congressional action does not substitute for judicial review of the Attorney General's decisions. The Act provides for judicial review of the refusal of the Attorney General to suspend a deportation and to transmit a recommendation to Congress. * * *

I regret that I am in disagreement with my colleagues on the fundamental questions that this case presents. But even more I regret the destructive scope of the Court's holding. It reflects a profoundly different conception of the Constitution than that held by the Courts which sanctioned the modern administrative state. Today's decision strikes down in one fell swoop provisions in more laws enacted by Congress than the Court has cumulatively invalidated in its history. I fear it will now be more difficult "to insure that the fundamental policy decisions in our society will be made not by an appointed official but by the body immediately responsible to the people." I must dissent.

Notes

1. *Vetoes of Agency Rules.* While *Chadha* was pending in the Supreme Court, the D.C. Circuit upheld two challenges to legislative vetoes of agency regulations. In *Consumer Energy Council of America v. Federal Energy Regulatory Commission*, 673 F.2d 425 (D.C.Cir.1982), petitioners challenged the constitutionality of a provision of the Natural Gas Policy Act of 1978 which authorized either House of Congress to veto a rule, mandated by the Act, extending "incremental pricing" of natural gas to new classes of industrial users. In *Consumers Union of U.S., Inc. v. Federal Trade Commission*, 691 F.2d 575 (D.C.Cir.1982) (en banc), the court invalidated a provision of the Federal Trade Commission Improvements Act of 1980 that obligated the FTC to submit trade regulation rules for congressional review, and allowed a rule to become effective after 90 days unless previously disapproved by both Houses of Congress.

On July 6, 1983, with Justice Powell not participating, the Court summarily affirmed the judgments in *Consumer Energy Council* and the *Consumers Union* case, without any elaboration of *Chadha*'s reasoning. While unsurprised by the result, Justice White commented:

> Where the veto is placed as a check upon the actions of the independent regulatory agencies, the Article I analysis relied upon in *Chadha* has a particularly hollow ring. * * *
>
> The President's authority to control independent agency lawmaking, which on a day-to-day basis is nonexistent, could not be affected by the existence or exercise of the legislative veto. To invalidate the device, which allows Congress to maintain some control over the lawmaking process, merely guarantees that the independent agencies, once created, for all practical purposes are a fourth branch of the government not subject to the direct control of either Congress or the executive branch. I cannot believe that the Constitution commands such a result.

Process Gas Consumers Group v. Consumer Energy Council of America, 463 U.S. 1216, 1217–19 (1983).

2. *Distinguishing Among Legislative Vetoes.* In *A Political Context for Legislative Vetoes*, 93 Pol.Sci.Q. 241 (1978), political scientist Louis Fisher described four categories of veto, which he argued raised very different constitutional implications.

The first is the explicit *quid pro quo*, where Congress gives the President, subject to "veto," a power that it otherwise would not confer. Authority to reorganize executive branch departments is a principal example. Because reorganization plans are few in number, are subjected to careful congressional scrutiny, and begin only by presidential initiative, Fisher viewed them as impairing neither the legislative function of the Congress nor the presentment clause protection of presidential power. The Second Circuit, however, has since interpreted *Chadha* as invalidating the veto provisions of the 1977 Reorganization Act, and with them the statute itself.

EEOC v. CBS, Inc., 743 F.2d 969 (2d Cir.1984). Compare *Muller Optical Co. v. EEOC*, 743 F.2d 380 (6th Cir.1984).

A second category includes several compromise solutions to problems in the perennial borderlands of congressional and presidential power. Fisher viewed the legislative veto included in the Impoundment Control Act of 1974, Pub.L.No. 93–344, 88 Stat. 297 (codified at 31 U.S.C. §§ 665, 1400–1407), and the War Powers Resolution of 1973, Pub.L.No. 93–148, 87 Stat. 555 (codified at 50 U.S.C. §§ 1541–1548), for example, not as provisions for legislative nullification but as "a procedural link between two rival interpretations" of constitutional authority. Because each interpretation is both plausible and useful, the veto serves the beneficial function of maintaining these mutually contradictory perspectives.

A more problematic category is exemplified by congressional retention of a veto over administrative rulemaking. Rulemaking initiatives do not imply presidential involvement, nor is a *quid pro quo* so obvious. Moreover, the possibility of constant revision of "legislative intent" via veto resolutions tends to undermine the distinction between legislative action and legislative oversight. Fisher argued that this blurring of distinct functions could compromise both legislative and administrative processes and should usually be regarded as impermissible.

Finally, Fisher viewed the *Chadha* case itself as involving a unconstitutional form of legislative veto. The section 244(c) procedure was, in his opinion, a legislative incursion into a specific adjudicatory function without any semblance of adjudicatory due process.

Both *Chadha* and the summary affirmance in *Process Gas Consumers Group*, *supra*, conspicuously declined to draw the sorts of distinctions Fisher emphasized.

One lower court has entertained the suggestion that *Chadha* may not invalidate veto provisions in statutes ostensibly authorized by a provision of the Constitution other than article I, which establishes the bicameral and presentment requirements that Chief Justice Burger held had been ignored. *National Wildlife Federation v. Watt*, 571 F.Supp. 1145 (D.D.C.1983), *National Wildlife Federation v. Clark*, 577 F.Supp. 825 (D.D.C.1984) (*Chadha* might not apply to committee veto over public lands authority vested in the Interior Secretary pursuant to article IV, section 3, which gives Congress—without reference to the President—"power to dispose of and make all needful rules and regulations respecting the Territory or other Property belonging to the United States"). Commentary on this possibility is divided. Compare Roger M. Sullivan, Jr., *The Power of Congress Under the Property Clause: A Potential Check on the Effect of the* Chadha *Decision on Public Land Legislation*, 6 Pub.Land.L.Rev. 65 (1985), with Robert L. Glicksman, *Severability and the Realignment of the Balance of Power Over the Public Lands: The Federal Land Policy and Management Act of 1976 After the Legislative Veto Decisions*, 36 Hastings L.J. 1 (1984).

3. *The Influence of Congressional Committees*. The primary defense of the legislative veto was its supposed utility in checking administrative discretion under broad delegations of authority. But precisely who exercised power under legislative veto arrangements is not altogether clear. Professors Bruff and Gellhorn argued that several vetoes empowered specific congres-

sional subcommittees (and, perhaps more to the point, their staffs) to exercise significant pressure over the agencies they oversee. Such influence by subunits of one House of Congress might be difficult to reconcile with democratic theory or with a balanced perspective on the public interest, Harold Bruff & Ernest Gellhorn, *Congressional Control of Administrative Regulation: A Study of Legislative Vetoes*, 90 Harv.L.Rev. 1369 (1977), unless, of course, one believes that committees and subcommittees are representative of the views of Congress as a whole. KEITH KREHBIEL, INFORMATION AND LEGISLATIVE ORGANIZATION (1991).

4. *Encroachment on Judicial Authority*. Although the Supreme Court discussed the legislative veto in *Chadha* as an intrusion into the President's constitutional veto power, the Ninth Circuit opinion in *Chadha* (authored by now-Justice Kennedy) concluded that the veto device encroached also into the power of the judiciary. "The duty of the Judiciary under this and numerous other statutory schemes," the court said, "is to determine, at the conclusion of administrative proceedings, whether the Executive Branch has correctly applied the statute that establishes its authority." *Chadha v. Immigration and Naturalization Service*, 634 F.2d 408, 430 (9th Cir.1980). In Kennedy's view, Congress could undermine a judicial decision to remand an administrative decision on legal grounds by simply vetoing any outcome of the remand inconsistent with Congress's view of the underlying statute. Such authority, in this view, had the capacity to render judicial interpretations of statutes "impermissible advisory opinions."

5. *Severability of Veto Provisions*. Of great concern after *Chadha* was—and is—the severability of now vulnerable veto provisions found in over 200 laws, which underpin literally thousands of administrative rules and presidential actions. In *Chadha* the Court found that a severability clause in the act itself created a conclusive presumption that the Attorney General's authority survived invalidation of Congress' veto, a conclusion with which Justices Power and White disagreed.

The Supreme Court clarified its position concerning the severability of legislative veto provisions in *Alaska Airlines, Inc. v. Brock*, 480 U.S. 678 (1987). At issue was section 43 of the Airline Deregulation Act of 1976, which established an employee protection program and authorized the Secretary of Labor, subject to a one-house legislative veto, to issue regulations for the administration of that program. The district court held the legislative veto provision unconstitutional and not severable, and therefore invalidated the entire employee protection program. The D.C. Circuit Court of Appeals reversed on the issue of severability and the Supreme Court affirmed.

In its unanimous opinion, authored by Justice Blackmun, the Court stated.

> The * * * relevant inquiry in evaluating severability is whether the statute will function in a *manner* consistent with the intent of Congress. In considering this question in the context of a legislative veto, it is necessary to recognize that the absence of the veto necessarily alters the balance of powers between the Legislative and Executive Branches of the Federal Government. Thus, it is not only appropriate to evaluate the importance of the veto in the original legislative bargain, but also to

consider the nature of the delegated authority that Congress made subject to a veto. Some delegations of power to the Executive or to an independent agency may have been so controversial or so broad that Congress would have been unwilling to make the delegation without a strong oversight mechanism. The final test, for legislative vetoes as well as for other provisions, is the traditional one: the unconstitutional provision must be severed unless the statute created in its absence is legislation that Congress would not have enacted.

In finding that the authority delegated to the Secretary of Labor was not notably broad the Court was influenced by the fact that the employee protection provisions imposed direct responsibilities on employers without any exercise of authority by the Secretary of Labor. Indeed, the Secretary's regulatory authority was, in the Court's phrase, "obviously designed merely to facilitate the obligation to hire imposed upon certain carriers. * * *" Moreover, because employers had a responsibility to hire even in the absence of regulations by the Secretary of Labor, the Court thought it unlikely that the Congress itself would want the functioning of the employee protection program as a whole to hinge on the continued vitality of the opportunity for one house to veto the Secretary's regulations.

Nor had the section 43 regulatory authority been controversial. Examining the legislative history of the employee protection program the Court discerned very modest attention by Congress to the veto provision. The legislative veto was mentioned in only one sentence of the Senate Report on the bill, and during floor debates it was alluded to only by Representative Elliott Levitas, for whom legislative veto provisions had become something of a personal crusade.

The D.C. Circuit's ruling in *City of New Haven v. United States*, 809 F.2d 900 (D.C.Cir.1987), that the Impoundment Control Act of 1974, Pub. L.No. 93–344, 88 Stat. 332, would not have been enacted save for its authorization of a one-house veto of Presidential impoundment orders, prompted Congress to amend the statute to eliminate the offending provision. Balanced Budget and Emergency Deficit Control Reaffirmation Act of 1987, Pub.L.No. 100–119, 101 Stat. 785. The amended statute narrows the circumstances in which the President may order deferral of the expenditure of appropriated funds and reaffirms the Comptroller General's authority to bring suit for the release of improperly deferred funds. See Irwin R. Kramer, *The Impoundment Control Act of 1974: An Unconstitutional Solution to a Constitutional Problem*, 58 U.M.K.C.L.Rev. 157 (1990). For further discussion of severability issues, see Note, *The Aftermath of* Chadha: *The Impact of the Severability Doctrine on the Management of Intragovernmental Relations*, 71 Va.L.Rev. 1211 (1985).

6. *Congressional Responses to* Chadha. Many members of Congress greeted the Supreme Court's ruling with dismay, characterizing the invalidation of the legislative veto as undermining not only the prerogatives of Congress but the liberties of American citizens. They advanced a variety of proposals to restore some effective legislative role in controlling decisions—particularly new regulations—by administrators. One proposal was to require, either through general legislation or amendment of individual statutes, that agency rules be approved by joint resolution (involving the

concurrence of both houses *and* the President) before they could become effective. Proponents conceded that this device might have to be confined to "major" rules, if only to spare Congress the burden of reviewing the thousands of new rules promulgated each year. This device was incorporated in the 1984 amendments to the since expired Reorganization Act, pp. 187–188 *infra*, effectively forcing Congress to legislate twice before administrative action could become effective.

Another proposal was to require agencies to submit their rules to Congress before they become effective—"report and wait"—and thus be subject to disapproval through joint resolution. Under this arrangement, Congress would have to legislate a second time to *prevent* the adoption of a rule it did not like. Proposals to implement such a requirement often prescribed a timetable, *e.g.*, submission of rules at least 30 days before their effective date, with additional time allowed if either House, or in other versions a committee of either House, votes a resolution of disapproval. For a discussion of these devices, see Michael J. Horan, *Of Train Wrecks, Time Bombs, and Skinned Cats: The Congressional Response to the Fall of the Legislative Veto*, 13 J. Legis. 22 (1986).

7. *The Congressional Review Act*. On March 29, 1996, President Clinton signed Public Law 104–121, the Contract with America Advance Act of 1996, whose Title II (labeled the Small Business Regulatory Enforcement Fairness Act) added a new chapter 8 (hereafter the Congressional Review Act or CRA) to Title 5 of the U.S. Code. The Congressional Review Act provides a generic procedure for congressional review of agency regulations. Under the Act (reprinted in Appendix G), all federal agencies, including independent agencies, must submit each final and interim rule for analysis by the General Accounting Office and review by Congress before it is scheduled to take effect. An agency's submission must include a copy of any cost-benefit analysis of the rule, information concerning the agency's compliance with the Regulatory Flexibility Act and the Unfunded Mandates Reform Act, and information relevant to its compliance with other laws or any Executive Order. "Major rules" may not take effect until at least 60 days have elapsed or the process for review has concluded.

The Act provides a formal procedure by which members may propose and each house may consider, under expedited procedures, a joint resolution of disapproval. A joint resolution requires the concurrence of the President, or adoption over the President's veto. The Act specifies that Congress' failure to take up or adopt a resolution of disapproval shall not be considered by any reviewing court. And, significantly, it prohibits an agency from promulgating in substantially the same form a rule that has been disapproved unless "specifically" authorized by a law enacted *after* the adoption of the joint resolution of disapproval.

This CRA drew both strong support and sharp criticism upon its adoption. Daniel Cohen and Peter Strauss offer this skeptical analysis:

> * * * The great volume of regulatory actions that Congress will theoretically be called upon to consider means, in most cases, that Congress will fail to provide useful guidance on agency implementation of statutes. * * * The inevitable reliance on staff, as well as the limited debate that will result from hearing so many possible targets for action,

opens the door for individual members of Congress, or lobbyists interested in opposing particular regulatory actions, to persuade the Congress as a whole to adopt a joint resolution of disapproval without the full consideration that would be likely if Congress reviewed only the relatively few "major" rules. * * *

In at least two important respects, the Act fails to secure the enhanced congressional responsibility for the outcomes of rulemaking that seems to be among its principal justifications. * * * Of course Congress may amend statutes. Under this procedure, however, a simple and unelaborated "No!" withdraws from agencies a range of substantive authority that cannot be determined without subsequent litigation. This uncertainty is in effect a delegation to the courts, without intelligible principle, of power to narrow agency authority. * * *

The second failure of responsibility represented by this statute arises from the provision that courts interpreting the statute are to attach no importance to Congress's failure to act* * *. One might have hoped that the submission of a controversial, high-consequence rule for congressional review might enable a court to draw some sort of conclusion from Congress's action or inaction with respect to that rulemaking. In particular, any active congressional review process could bear importantly on "hard-look" review for arbitrariness or capriciousness of agency judgment. Hard-look review, widely criticized for its contributions to rulemaking ossification, is defended as a kind of substitute for adequate political controls. A regular process for congressional review of the policy aspects of rulemaking could have provided the basis for some judicial retreat from the current intensity of fact-and-policy review* * *.

The statute's impact will be to raise further the costs of rulemaking. Particularly at a time when the government's budget is being severely curtailed, one can expect agencies to look for alternative means of accomplishing their business.

Daniel Cohen and Peter Strauss, *Congressional Review of Agency Regulations*, 49 Admin.L.Rev. 95 (1997).

Fears that the Congressional Review Act would either bring administrative rulemaking to a halt or drown Congress in paper have not yet been confirmed. According to Representative Mary Sue Kelly, roughly one year after the Act's passage 4,574 non-major and 72 major rules had been submitted to the GAO and to Congress. These figures were close to the recent historical average for each category. During this period not a single resolution of disapproval had been considered by the House of Representatives. 143 Cong.Rec. E1031–02 (May 22, 1997).

To date Congress has used the CRA to revoke just one rule. This occurred shortly after President George W. Bush was inaugurated in January 2001. In November 2000, the Occupational Safety and Health Administration (OSHA) had completed a ten-year effort to establish ergonomics standards to reduce the number and severity of musculoskeletal disorders (MSDs) experienced by U.S. workers. The agency estimated that its regulations would cost $4.5 billion to implement, but would save $9 billion a year in preventing workplace injuries. The regulations' effective date was January 16, 2002, four days before President Clinton left office. Under the terms of the CRA, however, Congress had 56 additional days in which to act on a resolution of disapproval.

Seeing an opportunity, opponents of OSHA's new standards—including the U.S. Chamber of Commerce and the National Association of Manufacturers—mobilized their political allies. They stressed that the standards were vague and complex, and, disputing OSHA's estimate, charged that their cost to employers could reach $100 billion annually. On March 1, Senator Don Nickles (R. Okla.), then Assistant Majority leader, introduced Senate Joint Resolution 6 to revoke the ergonomics regulations. Republican leaders bypassed routine committee procedures and brought the resolution directly to the Senate floor, limiting debate to ten hours. On March 6, a majority of six Democrats and fifty Republicans passed the resolution. The next day, after just one hour of debate, the House approved the resolution by a 223–206 vote. President Bush signed the resolution of disapproval on March 20, declaring that this was "a good and proper use of the [Congressional Review] Act because the different branches of our Government need to be held accountable." The President's statement emphasized that "a bureaucratic one-size-fits-all solution" was "not good government at work." Statement by the President Upon Signing S.J.Res. 6, March 20, 2001. No other agency rule has been the subject of challenge under the CRA.

Professor Robert Percival has argued that this single use of the CRA is the exception that proves the rule. "The circumstances surrounding the repeal of OSHA's ergonomics regulation—occurring in the early days of a new administration to repeal a rule issued by the outgoing administration of a president from a different political party—probably reflects the already high degree of presidential control over rulemaking." *Presidential Management of the Administrative State: The Not–So–Unitary Executive*, 51 Duke L.J. 963, 1002 (2001).

Even if the CRA is rarely used, however, it may still have a significant impact on agency behavior. Legislative vetoes that had no obvious effects on agency jurisdiction still "generate[d] strong anticipatory reactions by agency officials," including ex parte contacts between these officials and members of Congress or their staff. Peter H. Schuck, *Delegation and Democracy: Comments on David Schoenbrod*, 20 Cardozo L. Rev. 775, 786 (1999).

8. *Other Mechanisms of Legislative Control*. Congress has also sought to discipline agency discretion through mechanisms that do not entail Congress's retrospective assessment of the agency's work product:

More Specific Statutes. One obvious alternative is to take greater pains in chartering programs to define standards for administrative decision making—the very response the nondelegation doctrine was intended to provoke. This is what occurred when Congress adopted amendments to the Impoundment Control Act of 1974, p. 109 *supra*, which narrow the circumstances under which the President may lawfully defer the expenditure of appropriated funds.

Since *Chadha*, as for most of the period following Richard Nixon's election in 1968, Democrats and Republicans have divided control of the national government. During the Reagan and Bush-41 presidencies, a Democratic Congress showed itself increasingly inclined to specify the details of governmental policy in the text of legislation. One study of environmental legislation during the 1980s documented a clear trend in the direction of tightened statutory control over the content and timetable of administrative implementation. See Sidney A. Shapiro and Robert L. Glicksman, *Congress, the Supreme Court, and the Quiet Revolution in Administrative Law*, 1988 Duke L.J. 819. A notable, if extreme illustration is provided by the 1990 amendments to the Clean Air Act, which specify precisely the amount of pollutant reduction that each of several hundred named sources of carbon dioxide emissions must achieve. It would not be far-fetched to claim that the statute *constitutes* EPA's regulations. When the Republicans gained control of Congress with President Clinton in the White House the pattern resumed.

Sunset Laws. So-called "sunset laws" have been enacted in a number of states, which force periodic legislative reexamination of the performance of government programs. No general federal sunset law has ever been enacted, but Congress has often limited the life of regulatory statutes, including the major environmental laws and the Consumer Product Safety Act. The scheduled expiration of such authorizing legislation forces Congress, or at least its relevant committees, to review program performance and consider changes in the agency's mandate. The 1990 Clean Air Act Amendments were in a formal sense indispensible to the continued operation of the federal air pollution program. One difficulty with short-term authorizations, however, is that inability to agree on what statutory changes are needed, coupled with a general, even if grudging, consensus that the program *must* continue in *some* form, frequently leads Congress to charter successive years' operations through appropriations measures. But the need to renew such resolutions at least means that the agency program in question remains under scrutiny, and sometimes it can result in fundamental changes in statutory mandate. See, e.g., Consumer Product Safety Amendments of 1981, 95 Stat. 7224 (amending 15 U.S.C. § 2051 to modify the CPSC's rulemaking authority, reform its procedures, and subject its decisions to external scientific review). See also Elliot Klayman, *Standard Setting Under the Consumer Product Safety Amendments of 1981: A Shift in Regulatory Philosophy*, 51 Geo. Wash.L.Rev. 96 (1982).

Appropriations Riders. Finally, Congress has continued to employ a technique that provokes controversy, and whose constitutional boundaries have not been determined. This is the enactment of substantive limits on agency activity as part of appropriations legislation. The usual approach is to specify that no part of any agency's budgeted funds may be expended to carry out a specific program, or more commonly to implement an objectionable regulation.

In a controversial example, Congress voted in 1987 to prohibit the use of appropriations for implementing or enforcing a particular form through which federal employees promised to comply with stringent procedures to prevent their unauthorized disclosure of confidential government information. Omnibus Continuing Resolution for Fiscal Year 1988, § 630, Pub.L.No. 100–202, 101 Stat. 1329 (1987). The U.S. District Court for the District of Columbia held that the appropriations rider unconstitutionally restricted "the President's power to fulfill obligations imposed upon him by his express constitutional powers and the role of the executive in foreign relations." *National Federation of Federal Employees v. United States*, 688 F.Supp. 671 (D.D.C.1988). On direct appeal, the Supreme Court vacated the district court judgment for possible mootness without expressing a view on the separation of powers conclusion that Judge Gasch reached. *American Foreign Service Association v. Garfinkel*, 490 U.S. 153 (1989). On remand, the district court concluded that revised confidentiality agreements promulgated subsequent to its prior decision did not run afoul of the 1989 reenactment of the disputed appropriations rider, thus rendering any constitutional adjudication unnecessary. 732 F.Supp. 13 (D.D.C.1990). For supportive and antagonistic views, respectively, of congressional authority to circumscribe executive branch activity through appropriations riders, see Kate Stith, *Congress' Power of the Purse*, 97 Yale L.J. 1343 (1988), and J. Gregory Sidak, *The President's Power of the Purse*, 1989 Duke L.J. 1162 (1989). It is clear, however, that Congress may not confer a similar power to the President vis a line-item veto. *Clinton v. New York*, 524 U.S. 417 (1998).

3. DELEGATIONS OF ADJUDICATORY AUTHORITY

Even casual students of modern American government quickly recognize that administrative agencies have been delegated a broad range of functions in addition to that of formulating substantive governmental policy—the role that has triggered charges of unconstitutional delegations of legislative power. Prominent among these other functions is the responsibility to decide specific disputes, i.e., to function like a court. Assignment of adjudicatory power to executive officers dates from the very first Congress. See Richard J. Fallon, *Of Legislative Courts, Administrative Agencies, and Article III*, 101 Harv.L.Rev. 916, 919 (1988). Indeed, adjudication is a primary function of many contemporary agencies, such as the Social Security Administration and the National Labor Relations Board. The number of cases decided by administrative tribunals—both state and federal—dwarfs the caseload of all of the courts in the country.

This mixing of ostensibly separate powers has engendered less controversy than delegations of law-formulating power. Indeed, as we have seen, the Court in *Schechter Poultry* argued that broad delegations of such authority were *less* troubling if the mechanism for formulating law was to be a formal evidentiary hearing. Yet Article III of the Constitution specifies that "the judicial Power of the United States shall be vested in one Supreme Court and in such inferior Courts as the Congress may from time to time ordain and establish." The next sentence provides that the judges of both "supreme and inferior" courts shall enjoy life tenure and that their salaries shall not be diminished. "[T]he most plausible construction of this language," according to Professor Fallon, "would hold that if Congress creates any adjudicative bodies at all, it must grant them the protections of judicial independence that are contemplated by Article III."

Despite the appeal of this argument, for many decades there were relatively few challenges to the constitutionality of congressional delegations of adjudicative power to decision makers outside the federal courts who lack the protections of independence accorded federal judges. *Crowell v. Benson*, 285 U.S. 22 (1932), represented the controlling precedent on congressional delegation of adjudication to administrative agencies. In *Crowell* the Court upheld a statute assigning responsibility for deciding cases under the Longshoremen's and Harbor Workers Compensation Act to an administrative agency, the United States Employees' Compensation Commission. The Court pointed to the accepted view that Congress, under Article I, could create courts to decide cases arising in federal territories and federal enclaves, including the District of Columbia (whose judges even now do not enjoy full Article III protection), or in the armed forces. *Crowell* enunciated a distinction between public rights, creations of federal statute, and private rights, involving "the liability of one individual to another under the [common] law as defined." Disputes involving so-called public rights, typically between an individual and the government, could be assigned by Congress exclusively to administrative tribunals. For disputes involving private rights, however, access to an Article III court had to be afforded. The *Crowell* Court viewed the subject of its underlying dispute as one involving private rights, but it upheld the statute on the theory that the commission was responsible for deciding facts, in the same fashion as a special master, while its decisions on questions of law were subject to (presumably plenary) review in an Article III court. With this reasoning "*Crowell* permitted significant inroads into traditional conceptions of the necessary role of Article III courts. Most notably, *Crowell* found Article III to be satisfied by a review of the agency's fact finding only upon the administrative record." Fallon, *supra* at 924.

Crowell v. Benson was thought to legitimate a wide range of schemes for administrative adjudication of disputes between citizens and the government and most statutes conferring power on administrative tribunals to decide cases between private citizens—subject to the losing litigant's right to seek review in a district or circuit court. Within four years in the mid–1980s, however, the Supreme Court decided three cases that have been read as disturbing this settled, if not wholly convincing, understanding of Congress' power to delegate judicial power beyond Article III courts.

COMMODITY FUTURES TRADING COMMISSION v. SCHOR

Supreme Court of the United States, 1986.
478 U.S. 833, 106 S.Ct. 3245, 92 L.Ed.2d 675.

JUSTICE O'CONNOR delivered the opinion of the Court.

The question presented is whether the Commodity Exchange Act (CEA or Act), 7 U.S.C. § 1 *et seq.*, empowers the Commodity Futures Trading Commission (CFTC or Commission) to entertain state law counterclaims in reparation proceedings and, if so, whether that grant of authority violates Article III of the Constitution.

I

The CEA broadly prohibits fraudulent and manipulative conduct in connection with commodity futures transactions. In 1974, Congress "overhaul[ed]" the Act in order to institute a more "comprehensive regulatory structure to oversee the volatile and esoteric futures trading complex." H.R.Rep.No. 93–975, p. 1 (1974). Congress also determined that the broad regulatory powers of the CEA were most appropriately vested in an agency which would be relatively immune from the "political winds that sweep Washington." It therefore created an independent agency, the CFTC, and entrusted to it sweeping authority to implement the CEA.

Among the duties assigned to the CFTC was the administration of a reparations procedure through which disgruntled customers of professional commodity brokers could seek redress for the brokers' violations of the Act or CFTC regulations. Thus, § 14 of the CEA provides that any person injured by such violations may apply to the Commission for an order directing the offender to pay reparations to the complainant and may enforce that order in federal district court. Congress intended this administrative procedure to be an "inexpensive and expeditious" alternative to existing fora available to aggrieved customers, namely, the courts and arbitration. S.Rep.No. 95–850, p. 11 (1978).

In conformance with the congressional goal of promoting efficient dispute resolution, the CFTC promulgated a regulation in 1976 which allows it to adjudicate counterclaims "aris[ing] out of the transaction or occurrence or series of transactions or occurrences set forth in the complaint." This permissive counterclaim rule leaves the respondent in a reparations proceeding free to seek relief against the reparations complaint in other fora.

The instant dispute arose in February 1980, when respondents Schor and Mortgage Services of American invoked the CFTC's reparations jurisdiction by filing complaints against petitioner ContiCommodity Services, Inc. (Conti), a commodity futures broker, and Richard L. Sandor, a Conti employee. Schor had an account with Conti which contained a debit balance because Schor's net futures trading losses and expenses, such as commissions, exceeded the funds deposited in the account. Schor alleged that this debit balance was the result of Conti's numerous violations of the CEA.

Before receiving notice that Schor had commenced the reparations proceeding, Conti had filed a diversity action in Federal District Court to recover the debit balance. Schor counterclaimed in this action, reiterating his charges that the debit balance was due to Conti's violations of the CEA. Schor also moved on two separate occasions to dismiss or stay the district court action, arguing that the continuation of the federal action would be a waste of judicial resources and an undue burden on the litigants in view of the fact that "[t]he reparations proceedings * * * will fully * * * resolve and adjudicate all the rights of the parties to this action with respect to the transactions which are the subject matter of this action."

Although the District Court declined to stay or dismiss the suit, Conti voluntarily dismissed the federal court action and presented its debit balance claim by way of a counterclaim in the CFTC reparations proceeding. * * *

After discovery, briefing and a hearing, the Administrative Law Judge (ALJ) in Schor's reparations proceeding ruled in Conti's favor on both Schor's claims and Conti's counterclaims. After this ruling, Schor for the first time challenged the CFTC's statutory authority to adjudicate Conti's counterclaim. The ALJ rejected Schor's challenge, stating himself "bound by agency regulations and published agency policies." The Commission declined to review the decision and allowed it to become final, at which point Schor filed a petition for review with the Court of Appeals for the District of Columbia Circuit. Prior to oral argument, the Court of Appeals, *sua sponte*, raised the question of whether CFTC could constitutionally adjudicate Conti's counterclaims in light of *Northern Pipeline Construction Co. v. Marathon Pipe Line Co.*, 458 U.S. 50 (1982) (*Northern Pipeline*). * * *

* * * [T]he Court of Appeals upheld the CFTC's decision on Schor's claim in most respects, but ordered the dismissal of Conti's counterclaims on the ground that "the CFTC lacks authority (subject matter competence) to adjudicate" common law counterclaims. In support of this latter ruling, the Court of Appeals reasoned that the CFTC's exercise of jurisdiction over Conti's common law counterclaim gave rise to "[s]erious constitutional problems" under *Northern Pipeline*. * * *

* * * The Court of Appeals therefore "adopt[ed] the construction of the Act that avoids significant constitutional questions," reading the CEA to authorize the CFTC to adjudicate only those counterclaims alleging violations of the Act or CFTC regulations. * * *

* * * This Court granted the CFTC's petition for certiorari, vacated the Court of Appeals' judgment, and remanded the case for further consideration in light of *Thomas* [*v. Union Carbide Agricultural Products Co.*, 473 U.S. 568 (1985)]. * * *

On remand, the Court of Appeals reinstated its prior judgment. * * *

II

* * * [T]he court below did not seriously contest that Congress intended to authorize the CFTC to adjudicate *some* counterclaims in reparations proceedings. Rather, the court read into the facially unqualified reference to counterclaim jurisdiction a distinction between counterclaims arising under the Act or CFTC regulations and all other counterclaims. While the court's reading permitted it to avoid a potential Article III problem, it did so only by doing violence to the CEA. * * *

* * * [T]he instant controversy illustrates the crippling effect that the Court of Appeals' restrictive reading of the CFTC's counterclaim jurisdiction would have on the efficacy of the reparations remedy. The dispute between Schor and Conti is typical of the disputes adjudicated in reparations proceedings: a customer and a professional commodities

broker agree that there is a debit balance in the customer's account, but the customer attributes the deficit to the broker's alleged CEA violations and the broker attributes it to the customer's lack of success in the market. The customer brings a reparations claim; the broker counterclaims for the amount of the debit balance. In the usual case, then, the counterclaim "arises out of precisely the same course of events" as the principal claim and requires resolution of many of the same disputed factual issues.

Under the Court of Appeals' approach, the entire dispute may not be resolved in the administrative forum. Consequently, the entire dispute will typically end up in court, for when the broker files suit to recover the debit balance, the customer will normally be compelled either by compulsory counterclaim rules or by the expense and inconvenience of litigating the same issues in two fora to forgo his reparations remedy and to litigate his claim in court. * * *

* * * [T]he CFTC's long held position that it has the power to take jurisdiction over counterclaims such as Conti's is eminently reasonable and well within the scope of its delegated authority. Accordingly, as the CFTC's contemporaneous interpretation of the statute it is entrusted to administer, considerable weight must be accorded the CFTC's position.

Such deference is especially warranted here, for Congress has twice amended the CEA since the CFTC declared by regulation that it would exercise jurisdiction over counterclaims arising out of the same transaction as the principal reparations dispute but has not overruled the CFTC's assertion of jurisdiction. * * *

In view of the abundant evidence that Congress both contemplated and authorized the CFTC's assertion of jurisdiction over Conti's common law counterclaim, we conclude that the Court of Appeals' analysis is untenable. * * * We therefore are squarely faced with the question of whether the CFTC's assumption of jurisdiction over common law counterclaims violates Article III of the Constitution.

III

* * *

Although our precedents in this area do not admit of easy synthesis, they do establish that the resolution of claims such as Schor's cannot turn on conclusory reference to the language of Article III. Rather, the constitutionality of a given congressional delegation of adjudicative functions to a non-Article III body must be assessed by reference to the purposes underlying the requirements of Article III. This inquiry, in turn, is guided by the principle that "practical attention to substance rather than doctrinaire reliance on formal categories should inform application of Article III." *Thomas, supra. See also Crowell v. Benson.*

Article III, § 1 serves both to protect "the role of the independent judiciary within the constitutional scheme of tripartite government," and to safeguard litigants' "right to have claims decided before judges who are free from potential domination by other branches of government." *United States v. Will*, 449 U.S. 200 (1980). Although our cases have provided us with little occasion to discuss the nature or significance of this latter safeguard, our prior discussions of Article III, § 1's guarantee of an independent and impartial adjudication by the federal judiciary of matters within the judicial power of the United States intimated that this guarantee serves to protect primarily personal, rather than structural, interests. * * *

Our precedents also demonstrate, however, that Article III does not confer on litigants an absolute right to the plenary consideration of every nature of claim by an Article III court. Moreover, as a personal right, Article III's guarantee of an impartial and independent federal adjudication is subject to waiver, just as are other personal constitutional rights that dictate the procedures by which civil and criminal matters must be tried. * * *

* * * Schor indisputably waived any right he may have possessed to the full trial of Conti's counterclaim before an Article III court. Schor expressly demanded that Conti proceed on its counterclaim in the reparations proceeding rather than before the District Court, and was content to have the entire dispute settled in the forum he had selected until the ALJ ruled against him on all counts. * * *

* * * Schor had the option of having the common law counterclaim against him adjudicated in a federal Article III court, but, with full knowledge that the CFTC would exercise jurisdiction over that claim, chose to avail himself of the quicker and less expensive procedure Congress had provided him. In such circumstances, it is clear that Schor effectively agreed to an adjudication by the CFTC of the entire controversy by seeking relief in this alternative forum.

As noted above, our precedents establish that Article III, § 1 * * * also serves as "an inseparable element of the constitutional system of checks and balances." Article III, § 1 safeguards the role of the Judicial Branch in our tripartite system by barring congressional attempts "to transfer jurisdiction [to non-Article III tribunals] for the purpose of emasculating" constitutional courts, and thereby preventing "the encroachment or aggrandizement of one branch at the expense of the other." *Buckley v. Valeo*, 424 U.S. 1, 122 (1976) (*per curiam*). To the extent that this structural principle is implicated in a given case, the parties cannot by consent cure the constitutional difficulty for the same reason that the parties by consent cannot confer on federal courts subject matter jurisdiction beyond the limitations imposed by Article III, § 2. * * *

In determining the extent to which a given congressional decision to authorize the adjudication of Article III business in a non-Article III tribunal impermissibly threatens the institutional integrity of the Judicial Branch, the Court has declined to adopt formalistic and unbending rules. Although such rules might lend a greater degree of coherence to this area of the law, they might also unduly constrict Congress' ability to take needed and innovative action pursuant to its Article I powers. Thus, in reviewing Article III challenges, we have weighted a number of factors, none of which has been deemed determinative, with an eye to the practical effect that the congressional action will have on the constitutionally assigned role of the federal judiciary. Among the factors upon which we have focused are the extent to which the "essential attributes of judicial power" are reserved to Article III courts, and, conversely, the extent to which the non-Article III forum exercises the range of jurisdiction and powers normally vested only in Article III courts, the origins and importance of the right to be adjudicated, and the concerns that drove Congress to depart from the requirements of Article III.

An examination of the relative allocation of powers between the CFTC and Article III courts * * * demonstrates that the congressional scheme does not impermissibly intrude on the province of the judiciary. The CFTC's adjudicatory powers depart from the traditional agency model in just one respect: the CFTC's jurisdiction over common law counterclaims. While wholesale importation of concepts of pendent or ancillary jurisdiction into the agency context may create greater constitutional difficulties, we decline to endorse an absolute prohibition on such jurisdiction out of fear of where some hypothetical "slippery slope" may deposit us. Indeed, the CFTC's exercise of this type of jurisdiction is not without precedent. * * *

In the instant case, we are likewise persuaded that there is little practical reason to find that this single deviation from the agency model is fatal to the congressional scheme. * * *

The CFTC, like the agency in *Crowell*, deals only with a "particularized area of law," whereas the jurisdiction of the bankruptcy courts found unconstitutional in *Northern Pipeline*, extended to broadly "all civil proceedings arising under title 11 or arising in or *related to* cases under title 11." CFTC orders, like those of the agency in *Crowell*, but unlike those of the bankruptcy courts under the 1978 Act, are enforceable only by order of the District Court. CFTC orders are also reviewed under the same "weight of the evidence" standard sustained in *Crowell*, rather than the more deferential standard found lacking in *Northern Pipeline*. The legal rulings of the CFTC, like the legal determinations of the agency in *Crowell*, are subject to *de novo* review. Finally, the CFTC, unlike the bankruptcy courts under the 1978 Act, does not exercise "all ordinary powers of district courts," and thus may not, for instance, preside over jury trials or issue writs of habeas corpus.

Of course, the nature of the claim has significance in our Article III analysis quite apart from the method prescribed for its adjudication. The counterclaim asserted in this case is a "private" right for which state law provides the rule of decision. It is therefore a claim of the kind assumed to be at the "core" of matters normally reserved to Article III courts. Yet this conclusion does not end our inquiry; just as this Court has rejected any attempt to make determinative for Article III purposes the distinction between public rights and private rights, there is no reason inherent in separation of powers principles to accord the state law character of a claim talismanic power in Article III inquiries.

We have explained that "the public rights doctrine reflects simply a pragmatic understanding that when Congress selects a quasi-judicial method of resolving matters that 'could be conclusively determined by the Executive and Legislative Branches,' the danger of encroaching on the judicial powers" is less than when private rights, which are normally within the purview of the judiciary, are relegated as an initial matter to administrative adjudication. * * * The risk that Congress may improperly have encroached on the federal judiciary is obviously magnified when Congress "withdraw[s] from judicial cognizance any matter which, from its nature, is the subject of a suit at the common law, or in equity, or admiralty" and which therefore has traditionally been tried in Article III courts, and allocates the decision of those matters to a non-Article III forum of its own creation. Accordingly, where private, common law rights are at stake, our examination of the congressional attempt to control the manner in which those rights are adjudicated has been searching. In this case, however, "[l]ooking beyond form to the substance of what" Congress has done, we are persuaded that the congressional authorization of limited CFTC jurisdiction over a narrow class of common law claims as an incident to the CFTC's primary, and unchallenged, adjudicative function does not create a substantial threat to the separation of powers.

It is clear that Congress has not attempted to "withdraw from judicial cognizance" the determination of Conti's right to the sum represented by the debit balance in Schor's account. Congress gave the CFTC the authority to adjudicate such matters, but the decision to invoke this forum is left entirely to the parties and the power of the federal judiciary to take jurisdiction of these matters is unaffected. In such circumstances, separation of powers concerns are diminished, for it seems self-evident that just as Congress may encourage parties to settle a dispute out of court or resort to arbitration without impermissible incursions on the separation of powers, Congress may make available a quasi-judicial mechanism through which willing parties may, at their option, elect to resolve their differences. * * *

When Congress authorized the CFTC to adjudicate counterclaims, its primary focus was on making effective a specific and limited federal regulatory scheme, not on allocating jurisdiction among federal tribunals. Congress intended to create an inexpensive and expeditious alternative forum through which customers could enforce the provisions of the CEA against professional brokers. Its decision to endow the CFTC with jurisdiction over such reparations claims is readily understandable given the perception that the CFTC was relatively immune from political pressures, and the obvious expertise that the Commission possesses in applying the CEA and its own regulations. This reparations scheme itself is of unquestioned constitutional validity. It was only to ensure the effectiveness of this scheme that Congress authorized the CFTC to assert jurisdiction over common law counterclaims. Indeed, as was explained above, absent the CFTC's exercise of that authority, the purposes of the reparations procedure would have been confounded.

It also bears emphasis that the CFTC's assertion of counterclaim jurisdiction is limited to that which is necessary to make the reparations procedure workable. The CFTC adjudication of common law counterclaims is incidental to, and completely dependent upon, adjudication of reparations claims created by federal law, and in actual fact is limited to claims arising out of the same transaction or occurrence as the reparations claim. * * *

Nor does our decision in *Bowsher v. Synar*, 478 U.S. 714 (1986) [decided the same day], require a contrary result. Unlike *Bowsher*, this case raises no question of the aggrandizement of congressional power at the expense of a coordinate branch. Instead, the separation of powers question presented in this case is whether Congress impermissibly undermined, without appreciable expansion of its own power, the role of the Judicial Branch. In any case, we have, consistent with *Bowsher*, looked to a number of factors in evaluating the extent to which the congressional scheme endangers separation of powers principles under the circumstances presented, but have found no genuine threat to those principles to be present in this case. * * *

JUSTICE BRENNAN, with whom JUSTICE MARSHALL joins, dissenting.

On its face, Article III, § 1, seems to prohibit the vesting of judicial functions in either the Legislative or the Executive Branches. The Court has, however, recognized three narrow exceptions to the otherwise absolute mandate of Article III: territorial courts; courts martial; and courts that adjudicate certain disputes concerning public rights. * * *

The Framers * * * understood that a principal benefit of the separation of the judicial power from the legislative and executive powers would be the protection of individual litigants from decisionmakers susceptible to majoritarian pressures. * * *

These important functions of Article III are too central to our constitutional scheme to risk their incremental erosion. The exceptions we have recognized for territorial courts, courts martial, and administrative courts were each based on "certain exceptional powers bestowed upon Congress by the Constitution or by historical consensus." Here, however, there is no equally forceful reason to extend further these exceptions to situations that are distinguishable from existing precedents. * * *

* * * Article III's prophylactic protections were intended to prevent just this sort of abdication to claims of legislative convenience. The Court requires that the legislative interest in convenience and efficiency be weighed against the competing interest in judicial independence. In doing so, the Court pits an interest the benefits of which are immediate, concrete, and easily understood against one, the benefits of which are almost entirely prophylactic, and thus often seem remote and not worth

the cost in any single case. Thus, while this balancing creates the illusion of objectivity and ineluctability, in fact the result was foreordained, because the balance is weighted against judicial independence. The danger of the Court's balancing approach is, of course, that as individual cases accumulate in which the Court finds that the short-term benefits of efficiency outweigh the long-term benefits of judicial independence, the protections of Article III will be eviscerated. * * *

It is impossible to reconcile the radically different approaches the Court takes to separation powers in this case and in *Bowsher*. The Framers established *three* coequal branches of government and intended to preserve *each* from encroachment by either of the others. The Constitution did not grant Congress the general authority to bypass the judiciary whenever Congress deems it advisable, any more than it granted Congress the authority to arrogate to itself executive functions.

According to the Court, the intrusion into the province of the federal judiciary caused by the CFTC's authority to adjudicate state-law counterclaims is insignificant, both because the CFTC *shares* in, rather than displaces, federal district court jurisdiction over these claims and because only a very narrow class of state-law issues are involved. * * * If the administrative reparations proceeding is so much more convenient and efficient than litigation in federal district court that abrogation of Article III's commands is warranted, it seems to me that complainants would rarely, if ever, choose to go to district court in the first instance. Thus, any "sharing" of jurisdiction is more illusory than real.

* * * The decision today may authorize the administrative adjudication only of state-law claims that stem from the same transaction or set of facts that allow the customer of a professional commodity broker to initiate reparations proceedings before the CFTC, but the *reasoning* of this decision strongly suggests that, given "legislative necessity" and party consent, any federal agency may decide state-law issues that are ancillary to federal issues within the agency's jurisdiction. Thus, while in this case "the magnitude of intrusion on the judicial branch" may conceivably be characterized as "*de minimis*," the potential impact of the Court's decision on federal court jurisdiction is substantial. * * *

In my view, the structural and individual interests served by Article III are inseparable. The potential exists for individual litigants to be deprived of impartial decisionmakers only where federal officials who exercise judicial power are susceptible to congressional and executive pressure. That is, individual litigants may be harmed by the assignment of judicial power to non-Article III federal tribunals only where the Legislative or Executive Branches have encroached upon judicial authority and have thus threatened the separation of powers. * * * Because the individual and structural interests served by Article III are coextensive, I do not believe that a litigant may ever waive his right to an Article III tribunal where one is constitutionally required. In other words, consent is irrelevant to Article III analysis. * * *

Notes

1. *Distinguishing "Private" from "Public Rights."* In *Northern Pipeline Construction Co. v. Marathon Pipe Line Co.*, 458 U.S. 50 (1982), Northern had initiated a reorganization proceeding in U.S. Bankruptcy Court and then sued Marathon in that court on contract claims arising out of state law. Marathon moved to dismiss the action on the ground that the 1978 Bankruptcy Act conferral of jurisdiction over such claims on bankruptcy judges, who lacked lifetime tenure and salary protection, violated article III. Under the statute bankruptcy judges possessed most of the powers enjoyed by article III courts, save for the power to enjoin another court or to punish criminal contempt committed outside their presence. Their judgments, reaching potentially all matters in bankruptcy proceedings including disputes otherwise triable in state courts, would be final if unchallenged, but were subject to review by article III courts.

Writing for a plurality, Justice Brennan found this scheme unconstitutional. He relied on the distinction drawn in *Crowell v. Benson* between public rights, which "must at a minimum arise 'between the government and others,'" and private rights, whose resolution had to be confined to article III courts. He rejected the characterization of bankruptcy judges as merely "adjunct" to the district courts; they exercised so much authority that it could not be said that the district courts, in performing their review role, "retained 'the essential attributes of the judicial power.'" Justice Rehnquist, joined by Justice O'Connor, concurred separately, stressing that Marathon was being forced to submit to bankruptcy court resolution of a claim it could ordinarily prosecute in state courts.

Justice White, joined by Chief Justice Burger and Justice Powell, dissented. Acknowledging that the plurality's approach had some logic as a matter of constitutional history, White still found it untenable as a contemporary response to the question "what limits article III places on Congress' ability to create adjudicative institutions designed to carry out federal policy established pursuant to the substantive authority given Congress elsewhere in the Constitution." *Id.* at 94. Rejection of the 1978 Bankruptcy Act, he suggested, would require overruling a host of precedents upholding the conferral of adjudicatory power on a variety of article I courts and invalidation of the statutes creating most administrative agencies. For Justice White, the availability of article III court review of the decisions of bankruptcy judges helped save the congressional scheme.

Northern Pipeline prompted Congress to amend the Bankruptcy Act in several respects. First, Bankruptcy Court jurisdiction over any case requires an affirmative referral from the district court in which the case is filed—a now universal practice. Second, although a bankruptcy judge may still determine core bankruptcy issues, related claims of the sort raised in *Northern Pipeline* are subject only to the bankruptcy judge's proposed decision, which, in turn, is reviewable de novo in district court. 28 U.S.C. §§ 157–58. Congress provided, however, that a bankruptcy judge may nonetheless finally determine such related issues if all parties to a bankruptcy proceeding consent. As a matter of practice, this consent is likely always to be given both in the interest of expediency and in the interest of preserving good relations with the bankruptcy judge. Finally, as if to underscore its intent not to compromise the authority of Article III judges, Congress removed the appointment power over bankruptcy judges from the President and vested that power instead in the Courts of Appeals. 28 U.S.C. § 152.

2. *Relaxing the Private/Public Rights Distinction*. Three years later, in *Thomas v. Union Carbide Agricultural Products Co.*, 473 U.S. 568 (1985), the Court returned again to the question of Congress' power to delegate adjudicative power to other than Article III courts. The case involved a recent amendment to the Federal Insecticide, Fungicide, and Rodenticide Act (FIFRA), which empowered EPA to rely on the test data submitted by the first manufacturer (registrant) of a pesticide in evaluating and approving later marketing applications from competitors. The statute required a later registrant to offer compensation to the originator of the data, and provided for binding arbitration of any disagreement over the amount of compensation. The arbitrator's decision was subject to judicial review only for "fraud, misrepresentation or other misconduct." This allocation of essentially final authority to decide disputes about the value of the test data was claimed unconstitutionally to withdraw jurisdiction from Article III courts.

Writing for five Justices, Justice O'Connor upheld the congressional scheme. She found that no state law claim was involved; by submitting the data to EPA, the original registrant had surrendered any claim that the data were protected by state trade secret law. Whatever legal protection existed against uncompensated use or disclosure by EPA was the product of federal statute. While she rejected *Northern Pipeline's* distinction between public and private rights as determinative, Justice O'Connor acknowledged that the right to compensation created by FIFRA was a right between two private parties, but stressed that it also "bears many of the characteristics of a 'public' right." She thought that Congress, in fashioning a complex regulatory scheme, had authority to fix the terms on which marketing approval for new pesticides should be available. The scheme did not in any significant way threaten the role of the independent judiciary. Moreover, its provision for judicial review, while limited, satisfied whatever requirements due process might impose:

> Our holding is limited to the proposition that Congress, acting for a valid legislative purpose pursuant to its constitutional powers under Article I, may create a seemingly "private" right that is so closely integrated into a public regulatory scheme as to be a matter appropriate for agency resolution with limited involvement by the Article III judiciary.

3. *The Private/Public Rights Distinction Reconfirmed*? The two *Schor* dissenters, two members of the *Schor* majority, and two new Justices combined in 1989 to reconfirm the legal salience of the distinction between private and public rights. In *Granfinanciera, S.A. v. Nordberg*, 492 U.S. 33 (1989), the Court considered whether the defendant corporation was entitled to a jury trial in a bankruptcy trustee's suit to recover allegedly fraudulent payments made to the defendant by the bankrupt's corporate predecessor. Justice Brennan, writing also for the Chief Justice, and Justices Marshall, Stevens, Scalia, and Kennedy, concluded that such claims should be regarded as legal and not equitable for purposes of Seventh Amendment analysis, and

that a bankruptcy trustee's action to recover a fraudulent conveyance to a private third party asserted a "private" right. In reaching the latter conclusion, the majority emphasized the resemblance between the trustee's federal statutory action and a state common law contract action to increase the size of a bankruptcy estate.

Then, for the same group minus Justice Scalia, Justice Brennan concluded that Congress may not deny a jury trial in an action at law if the statutory right asserted is a private right:

> If a statutory right is not closely intertwined with a federal regulatory program Congress has power to enact, and if that right neither belongs to nor exists against the Federal Government, then it must be adjudicated by an Article III court. If the right is legal in nature, then it carries with it the Seventh Amendment's guarantee of a jury trial.

Justice Scalia wrote separately to express the view that a case should not be deemed to involve "public rights" for Article III or Seventh Amendment purposes unless the federal government is a party, no matter what the relationship between the right asserted and a regulatory statute. He characterized *Thomas* as a decision with "no constitutional basis," and criticized the Court for "reconfirm[ing] our error" in *Schor*.

Justice White dissented because the historical evidence was unclear whether a trustee's claim to recover a fraudulent conveyance should be deemed an action at law. He would have deferred to Congress' determination that such claims were integrally related to equitable bankruptcy proceedings. Agreeing that the historical evidence is inconclusive, Justices Blackmun and O'Connor would presume a right to jury trial in such cases. In this case, however, they believed that the presumption was overcome by Congress' reasonable determination that the statutory right to recover the conveyance was so integral a part of its pervasive statutory scheme as to be a "public right" assignable to an Article I forum.

4. *The Court's Uncertain Path*. Critics of this series of decisions dealing with Congress' power to delegate adjudicatory power to administrative tribunals have had difficulty discerning clear governing principles.

> * * * [I]n *Northern Pipeline Construction Co. v. Marathon Pipe Line Co.* a plurality of the Justices sought to revitalize a modified form of Article III literalism: unless historical practice has entrenched an exception to the norm, the plurality declared, the only permissible federal adjudicative bodies are Article III courts whose judges enjoy life tenure. * * * But the perceived doctrinal shift threatened the settled functions of administrative agencies, and the Court [in *Union Carbide* and in *Schor*] was quick to revise its course. Expressing doubts about the utility of statements of general principle, the Court now has endorsed an ad hoc balancing test that is almost wholly open-ended and amorphous. The chief attraction of the Court's form of balancing seems to be that it avoids almost all of the most basic questions, or at least appears to do so. Uncertainty continues rife. Prediction is often impossible.

Fallon, *supra,* at 917; see also Martin H. Redish, *Legislative Courts, Administrative Agencies, and the* Northern Pipeline *Decision*, 1983 Duke L.J. 197;

Ralph U. Whitten, *Consent, Caseload, and Other Justifications for Non-Article III Courts and Judges: A Comment on* Commodity Futures Trading Commission v. Schor, 20 Creighton L.Rev. 11 (1986).

Professor Fallon's criticism of the Court's current analysis of statutory delegations of adjudicatory power to administrative bodies has been echoed by other scholars. E.g., Richard B. Saphire & Michael E. Solimine, *Shoring Up Article III: Legislative Court Doctrine in the Post* CFTC v. Schor *Era*, 68 B.U.L.Rev. 85 (1988) ("The mandate of Article III is only satisfied when Congress, in creating a non-Article III tribunal, makes available article III review of that tribunal's factual and legal determinations"); Gordon G. Young, *Public Rights and the Federal Judicial Power: From* Murray's Lessee *Through* Crowell *to* Schor, 35 Buff.L.Rev. 765 (1986).

5. *Arbitration and Delegated Power.* If delegations of adjudicatory authority to Article I tribunals are thought to raise constitutional doubts, then delegations of such authority to private arbitrators would seem doubly problematic. Yet, Congress in 1990 broadly authorized parties to federal agency adjudicatory proceedings to select private arbitrators to assist in the resolution of disputes. Administrative Dispute Resolution Act, Pub.L.No. 101–552, 104 Stat. 2736 (1990), discussed in Chapter 4. Congress sought to avoid any impermissible delegation of adjudicatory authority to nongovernmental actors by vesting, in any agency using an arbitrator, plenary authority to terminate the arbitration proceeding or to vacate any award before it becomes final. The constitutional issues surrounding administrative arbitration schemes are extensively analyzed in Harold H. Bruff, *Public Programs, Private Deciders: The Constitutionality of Arbitration in Federal Programs*, 67 Tex.L.Rev. 441 (1989).

B. STATUTORY PRECISION AND ITS CONSEQUENCES

The previous part, which explored the constitutional and political problems posed by legislative decisions to confer broad discretion on agencies, highlighted the implications of statutory vagueness. However, as the following materials illustrate, Congress can and frequently does enact very detailed laws that mandate specific decisions. Statutory precision can present administrative problems and, according to a cluster of now-dated Supreme Court opinions, may raise constitutional issues as well. A decision by Congress that specific consequences should always attach to particular facts or circumstances has two effects. The first is that the implementing agency may not forthrightly exempt any case that exhibits the specified features from the prescribed consequences, even if those consequences seem wholly unreasonable or inappropriate in the circumstances. The second is that the agency cannot, without congressional revision of the law, respond to new knowledge or changed political circumstances to modify the policies embodied in ill-fitting or outdated statutory instructions.

1. IRREBUTTABLE PRESUMPTIONS

UNITED STATES DEPARTMENT OF AGRICULTURE v. MURRY

Supreme Court of the United States, 1973.
413 U.S. 508, 93 S.Ct. 2832, 37 L.Ed.2d 767.

JUSTICE DOUGLAS delivered the opinion of the Court.

* * *

Appellee Murry has two sons and ten grandchildren in her household. Her monthly income is $57.50, which comes from her ex-husband as support for her sons. Her expenses far exceed her monthly income. By payment, however, of $11 she received $128 in food stamps. But she has now been denied food stamps because her ex-husband (who has remarried) had claimed her two sons and one grandchild as tax dependents in his 1971 income tax return. That claim, plus the fact that her eldest son is 19 years old, disqualified her household for food stamps under § 5(b) of the [Food Stamp] Act.[1] * * *

* * * Section 5(b) makes the entire household of which a "tax dependent" was a member ineligible for food stamps for two years: (1) during the tax year for which the dependency was claimed and (2) during the next 12 months. During these two periods of time § 5(b) creates a conclusive presumption that the "tax dependent's" household is not needy and has access to nutritional adequacy.

* * *

The tax dependency provision was generated by congressional concern about nonneedy households participating in the Food Stamp program. The legislative history reflects a concern about abuses of the program by "college students, children of wealthy parents." But, as the District Court said, the Act goes far beyond that goal and its operation is inflexible. "Households containing no college student, that had established clear eligibility for Food Stamps and which still remain in dire need and otherwise eligible are now denied stamps if it appears that a household member 18 years or older is claimed by someone as a tax dependent."

Tax dependency in a prior year seems to have no relation to the "need" of the dependent in the following year. It doubtless is much easier from the administrative point of view to have a simple tax "dependency" test that will automatically—without hearing, without witnesses, without findings of fact—terminate a household's claim for eligibility of food stamps. Yet, as we recently stated in *Stanley v. Illinois*:

1. Section 5(b) of the Act provides in part: "Any household which includes a member who has reached his eighteenth birthday and *who is claimed as a dependent child for Federal income tax purposes by a taxpayer who is not a member of an eligible household*, shall be ineligible to participate in any food stamp program established pursuant to this chapter during the tax period such dependency is claimed and for a period of one year after expiration of such tax period. * * * " (Emphasis added.) * * *

"[I]t may be argued that unmarried fathers are so seldom fit that Illinois need not undergo the administrative inconvenience of inquiry in any case, including Stanley's. The establishment of prompt efficacious procedures to achieve legitimate state ends is a proper state interest worthy of cognizance in constitutional adjudication. But the Constitution recognizes higher values than speed and efficiency. Indeed, one might fairly say of the Bill of Rights in general, and the Due Process Clause in particular, that they were designed to protect the fragile values of a vulnerable citizenry from the overbearing concern for efficiency and efficacy that may characterize praiseworthy government officials no less, and perhaps more, than mediocre ones."

We have difficulty in concluding that it is rational to assume that a child is not indigent this year because the parent declared the child as a dependent in his tax return for the prior year. But even on that assumption our problem is not at an end. Under the Act the issue is not the indigency of the child but the indigency of a different household with which the child happens to be living. Members of the different household are denied Food Stamps if one of its present members was used as a tax deduction in the past year by his parents even though the remaining members have no relation to the parent who used the tax deduction, even though they are completely destitute and even though they are one, or 10 or 20 in number. We conclude that the deduction taken for the benefit of the parent in the prior year is not a rational measure of the need of a different household with which the child of the tax-deducting parent lives and rests on an irrebuttable presumption often contrary to fact. It therefore lacks critical ingredients of due process found wanting in *Vlandis v. Kline*, 412 U.S. 441, 452 (1973); *Stanley v. Illinois*, 405 U.S. 645 (1972); and *Bell v. Burson*, 402 U.S. 535 (1971).

[Justice Stewart's concurring opinion is omitted.]

JUSTICE MARSHALL, concurring.

* * * One aspect of fundamental fairness, guaranteed by the Due Process Clause of the Fifth Amendment, is that individuals similarly situated must receive the same treatment by the Government. * * * It is a corollary of this requirement that, in order to determine whether persons are indeed similarly situated, "such procedural protections as the particular situation demands" must be provided. Specifically, we must decide whether, considering the private interest affected and the governmental interest sought to be advanced, a hearing must be provided to one who claims that the application of some general provision of the law aimed at certain abuses will not in fact lower the incidence of those abuses but will instead needlessly harm him. In short, where the private interests affected are very important and the governmental interest can be promoted without much difficulty by a well-designed hearing procedure, the Due Process Clause requires the Government to act on an individualized basis, with general propositions serving only as

rebuttable presumptions or other burden-shifting devices. That, I think, is the import of *Stanley v. Illinois*.

Is this, then, such a case? Appellants argue that Congress could rationally have thought that persons claimed as tax dependents by a taxpayer himself not a member of an eligible household in one year could, during that year and the succeeding one, probably receive sufficient funds from the taxpayer to offset their need for food stamps. If those persons received food stamps, they would be denying to the truly needy some of the limited benefits Congress has chosen to make available. The statute, on this view, is aimed at preventing abuse of the program by persons who do not need the benefits Congress has provided. Even if, as appellants urge, the statute is interpreted to make ineligible for food stamps only those persons validly claimed as tax dependents, I do not think that Congress adopted a method for preventing abuse that is reasonably calculated to eliminate only those who abuse the program. In particular, it could not be fairly concluded that, because one member of the household had received half his support from a parent, the *entire* household's need for assistance in purchasing food could be offset by outside contributions.

It is, of course, quite simple for Congress to provide an administrative mechanism to guarantee that abusers of the program were eliminated from it. All that is needed is some way for a person whose household would otherwise be ineligible for food stamps because of this statute to show that the support presently available from the person claiming a member of the household as a tax dependent does not in fact offset the loss of benefits. Reasonable rules stating what a claimant must show before receiving a hearing on the question could easily be devised. We deal here with a general rule that may seriously affect the ability of persons genuinely in need to provide an adequate diet for their households. In the face of readily available alternatives that might prevent abuse of the program, Congress did not choose a method of reducing abuses that was "fairly related to the object of the regulation," by enacting the statute challenged in this case.

This analysis, of course, combines elements traditionally invoked in what are usually treated as distinct classes of cases, involving due process and equal protection. But the elements of fairness should not be so rigidly cabined. Sometimes fairness will require a hearing to determine whether a statutory classification will advance the legislature's purposes in a particular case so that the classification can properly be used only as a burden-shifting device, while at other times the fact that a litigant falls within the classification will be enough to justify its application. There is no reason, I believe, to categorize inflexibly the rudiments of fairness. Instead, I believe that we must assess the public and private interests affected by a statutory classification and then decide in each instance whether individualized determination is required or categorical treatment is permitted by the Constitution.

[Justice Blackmun's dissenting opinion is omitted.]

JUSTICE REHNQUIST, with whom THE CHIEF JUSTICE and JUSTICE POWELL concur, dissenting. * * *

Notions that in dispensing public funds to the needy Congress may not impose limitations which "go beyond the goal" of Congress, or may not be "inflexible," have not heretofore been thought to be embodied in the Constitution. In *Dandridge v. Williams*, 397 U.S. 471 (1970), the Court rejected this approach in an area of welfare legislation that is indistinguishable from the food stamp program here involved: * * *

> "In the area of economics and social welfare, a state does not violate the Equal Protection Clause merely because the classifications made by its laws are imperfect. If the classification has some 'reasonable basis,' it does not offend the Constitution simply because the classification 'is not made with mathematical nicety or because in practice it results in some inequality.' "

In placing the limitations on the availability of food stamps which are involved in this case, Congress has not in any reasoned sense of that word employed a conclusive presumption as stated by the majority; it has simply made a legislative decision that certain abuses which it conceived to exist in the program as previously administered were of sufficient seriousness to warrant the substantive limitation which it enacted.* * *

Thus, we deal not with the law of evidence, but with the extent to which the Fifth Amendment permits this Court to invalidate such a determination by Congress. In *Williamson v. Lee Optical*, 348 U.S. 483, 487–488 (1955), the Court said:

> "But the law need not be in every respect logically consistent with its aims to be constitutional. It is enough that there is an evil at hand for correction, and that it might be thought that the particular legislative measure was a rational way to correct it."

The majority concludes that a "deduction taken for the benefit of the parent in the prior year is not a rational measure of the need of a different household with which the child of the tax-deducting parent lives." But judged by the standards of the foregoing cases, the challenged provision of the Food Stamp Act has a legitimate purpose and cannot be said to lack any rational basis. * * * [I]n order to disqualify a household for food stamps, the taxpayer claiming one of its members as a dependent must both provide over half of the dependent's support and must himself be a member of a household with an income large enough to disqualify that household for food stamps. These characteristics indicate that the taxpayer is both willing and able to provide his dependent with a significant amount of support. To be sure, there may be no perfect correlation between the fact that the taxpayer is part of a household which has income exceeding food stamp eligibility standards and his provision of enough support to raise his dependent's household above such standards. But there is some correlation, and the provision is, therefore, not irrational. * * *

Notes

1. *The Fleeting Renaissance of Irrebuttable Presumption Doctrine*. The Supreme Court's analysis in *Murry* had some precedent in cases from the early 20th Century in which the Court invalidated several tax statutes on the ground that they embodied inaccurate irrebuttable presumptions: "Yet these cases seemed inextricably tied to disfavored intervention based on notions of substantive due process, and hence were largely ignored by the Court after 1937." Note, *The Irrebuttable Presumption Doctrine in the Supreme Court*, 87 Harv.L.Rev. 1534, 1539 (1974).

The early 1970s saw a resurgence of the doctrine. *Bell v. Burson*, 402 U.S. 535 (1971), invalidated a Georgia statute providing for the automatic suspension, pending a determination of liability, of the license of any uninsured motorist who was involved in an accident that resulted in damages. The Court viewed the statute, in part, as impermissibly presuming that all uninsured motorists in accidents were at fault.

Stanley v. Illinois, 405 U.S. 645 (1972), invalidated an Illinois statute that made any child who had no surviving parent a ward of the state. The statute permitted Illinois to assert custody of a child over the objections of a "parent" only if the parent were judged unfit. The statute, however, included within the definition of "parents," in addition to the mother and father of a child born in wedlock, only the mother of a child born to unmarried parents. Stanley, the unmarried biological father of several children whose mother had died, had not been adjudged unfit in fact, but Illinois nonetheless instituted proceedings seeking custody of his children. The Supreme Court concluded that the statute amounted to an impermissible presumption of the parental unfitness of unmarried fathers, and held that Stanley was entitled to a hearing on the issue of his fitness.

In *Vlandis v. Kline*, 412 U.S. 441 (1973), the Court invalidated a Connecticut statute that classified individuals, for state university tuition purposes, as permanent nonresidents of Connecticut if (1) they were married and resided outside Connecticut at the time of their application to the university or (2) they were unmarried and resided outside Connecticut in the 12 months prior to application. The Court held that individualized hearings were required to determine the bona fide domicile of any student seeking the lower tuition afforded in-state residents.

Finally, in *Cleveland Board of Education v. LaFleur*, 414 U.S. 632 (1974), the Court invalidated school board regulations that mandated disability leave for teachers after the fourth month of pregnancy without any inquiry into actual disability.

The Harvard Law Review note cited above remarked the conceptual difficulty inherent in characterizing statutory classifications as impermissible presumptions because they are overinclusive:

> Once a court determines the purpose toward which a classification is directed, it can always rephrase the statute as an irrebuttable presumption. And since nearly all classifications contain some measure of inaccuracy, very few acts of legislation could survive the test of "necessarily or universally true in fact" promulgated by the irrebuttable

> presumption cases. Thus, this new basis for judicial intervention appears to have remarkably wide-ranging applicability.

87 Harv.L.Rev. at 1549.

Even during the flurry of irrebuttable presumption cases in the early 1970s the Court did not apply the doctrine wholesale. And after *LaFleur* the Court quietly abandoned the irrebuttable presumption language in cases not raising issues that the challenged statute itself characterized as evidentiary. See, e.g., *Leary v. United States*, 395 U.S. 6, 29–53 (1969).

One of us has criticized both the Court's use and its silent abandonment of irrebuttable presumption analysis.

> * * * [The irrebuttable presumption] cases make hash of the prior procedural due process jurisprudence. It had been (indeed still is) thought obvious that there was no need for a hearing where there was nothing to talk about. And since the driver in *Bell* and the father in *Stanley* admitted that they fell squarely within the legislative disqualifications, "hearing" talk seems misplaced—substance and procedure have somehow been conflated.
>
> * * * [T]he irrebuttable presumption doctrine has a voracious appetite for statutes. Left long at large it will gnaw its way through substantial portions of the codes of the fifty states and the U.S. Code as well. If the validity of some of our most ubiquitous legal rules—the fifty-five mile per hour speed limit, twenty-one years as the age of majority, statutes of limitations, formal requirements for testamentary disposition, for example—is to be tested by asking whether the general principle or purpose that underlies the rule (safety, knowing consent, etc.) is furthered *in every instance* of its application, then rules are no longer possible.
>
> Because such a state of affairs is insupportable we need some way of avoiding this particular proceduralist perspective. But in the irrebuttable presumption cases the Court does not (and indeed cannot) tell us when an attack on legislative over-generality should be perceived for what it is—a substantive rationality claim that under current doctrine is a sure loser—and when it may be translated into a "right-to-hearing"/"irrebuttable presumption" claim that is a sure winner. Confronted with an extremely important question (When is it permissible to generalize by rule rather than particularize by reference to a principle or standard?) the Court, having barred itself from considering the substantive rationality of legislative judgments, had nothing to say.

Jerry L. Mashaw, *Constitutional Deregulation: Notes Toward a Public, Public Law*, 54 Tul.L.Rev. 849, 863–64 (1980).

2. *Irrebuttable Presumptions and Rationality Review*. A statutory classification may be invalidated under the equal protection clause or perhaps even as a violation of "substantive due process" if a court concludes that it is not closely enough tied to a sufficiently weighty government purpose. There appears to be no analytic difference between such a finding and a decision invalidating an overinclusive statutory classification as an impermissible "irrebuttable presumption." Under each of these approaches, the judicial conclusion is that the government lacks sufficient reason for not guarding

against the overinclusiveness of its policy, either through a better-drawn classification or through inquiry into individual circumstances.

Should irrebuttable presumption analysis be reserved for statutes that touch interests—like the interests in avoiding race or sex discrimination—that would ordinarily trigger heightened constitutional scrutiny? This is the implication of the plurality opinion in *Michael H. and Victoria D. v. Gerald D.*, 491 U.S. 110 (1989). Michael H. was almost certainly the biological father of Victoria D., whose mother, Carole D., was married to her current husband, Gerald D., at the time of Victoria's birth. Gerald had always held himself out as Victoria's father. When Michael sued for visitation rights, Gerald successfully sought summary judgment, in part on the ground that, under California law, "the issue of a wife cohabiting with her husband, who is not impotent or sterile, is conclusively presumed to be a child of the marriage." Michael challenged the evidentiary rule as an impermissible irrebuttable presumption.

Writing for a plurality, Justice Scalia refused to scrutinize more than minimally the policy embodied in California's "conclusive" presumption. The Constitution did not entitle Michael H. to an individualized hearing on actual paternity because the Constitution did not protect the category of relationship Michael H. was asserting.

Justice Stevens provided the fifth vote to make a majority, but only because he did not interpret the evidentiary presumption of paternity as having any conclusive consequence for a biological father's legal rights. In particular, Justice Stevens interpreted California law as allowing an individualized hearing on application by a person in Michael's position to obtain visitation rights based on a "best interests of the child" standard.

Justice Stevens' opinion illustrates the institutional implications of rejecting overbroad, but clear and determinate statutory standards. He would translate the sharp categories of father/non-father into the broad question whether visitation serves "the best interests of the child." This opens up a vast arena of potentially relevant facts and enormously expands the official discretion conferred on the decider. While the decider in *Michael H.* would be a judge, in other contexts, such as *Murry*, *Vlandis*, and *LaFleur*, judgment would often fall to an administrator. The "irrebuttable presumption" doctrine might then be relabled the "pro-delegation" doctrine.

2. EXPLICIT STATUTORY INSTRUCTIONS

a. The Decisive Delaney Clause

As the previous section reveals, Congress is capable of formulating its instructions in terms that allow little administrative discretion, terms that imply unequivocal judgments about appropriate policy outcomes. A famous illustration is the so-called Delaney Clause in the Federal Food, Drug, and Cosmetic Act, 21 U.S.C. § 321 *et seq.* The clause appears in the provision of the Act that empowers the Food and Drug Administration (FDA) to approve or disapprove "food additives," a category that includes most ingredients in processed food. Added to the law in 1958, the Food Additives Amendment directs the FDA to refuse approval of any *food additive* not shown to be safe. To this general instruction the Delaney Clause adds the proviso that

> no additive shall be deemed to be safe if it is found to induce cancer when ingested by man or animal, or if it is found, after tests which are appropriate for the evaluation of the safety of food additives, to induce cancer in man or animals.

For nearly twenty years this proviso had little influence on the FDA's actions. Only a tiny handful of food additives had been shown to cause cancer in animal experiments—the primary means of assessing safety. On March 9, 1977, however, the FDA announced that it would initiate proceedings to ban the use of the artificial sweetener saccharin in all food products marketed in the United States. This action was to be based on a finding, supported by earlier experiments and confirmed in a recent Canadian study, that saccharin induced cancer in test animals. Because at the time no other nonnutritive sweetener was approved for use in the United States—aspartame ("Nutrasweet") was not approved until 1980—the FDA announcement threatened the marketing of all artificially sweetened foods and beverages and, consequently, precipitated intense public controversy.

SACCHARIN BAN MORATORIUM

House Report 95–658.

95th Congress, 1st Session (October 3, 1977).

* * * [A]ccording to FDA officials, the Delaney clause authorizes the agency to exercise scientific judgment in determining whether a test is an appropriate one. * * *

* * * Once the agency has exercised scientific judgment with respect to the appropriateness of the test, however, the Delaney clause does not permit the agency to make further inquiry. It may not, for example, establish a maximum level of safe use[7] or authorize further use of an additive based on a judgment that the benefits of continued use outweigh the risks involved. * * *

It * * * became clear during the hearing that there is a paucity of direct evidence linking bladder cancer in humans to the use of saccharin. Several epidemiological studies were cited, including studies on diabetic populations, which showed no correlation between saccharin usage and bladder cancer. However, * * * because of the population sizes used in the epidemiological studies, an increase in the incidence of bladder cancer of less than 30 to 40 percent would have been undetectable. By way of contrast, extrapolation of the Canadian rat data to humans would result in an increase in the incidence of bladder cancer of only around 7 percent, an increase which would be unlikely to have been detected in a small scale epidemiological study.

7. It is the position of the FDA and the National Cancer Institute—and most scientists—that a safe threshold level for a cancer-producing substance has not been established.

It was further argued during the hearings by representatives of health organizations (as the American Heart Association, the Juvenile Diabetes Foundation, and the American Diabetes Association) that saccharin provides an enormous benefit to persons, such as diabetics, and the obese, who must restrict their intake of sugar. It was contended that while saccharin is not essential to such individuals, it nevertheless has enabled them to enjoy the same quality of life as individuals who need not restrict their intake of sugar, and that this is a benefit which outweighs what is, at worst, a relatively low risk of bladder cancer. * * *

This report was a product of a hearing before a subcommittee of the House Committee on Interstate and Foreign Commerce, at which Congressman Henry Waxman of California quizzed the FDA Commissioner, Dr. Donald Kennedy.

HEARING BEFORE THE SUBCOMMITTEE ON HEALTH AND ENVIRONMENT OF THE HOUSE COMMITTEE ON INTERSTATE AND FOREIGN COMMERCE

95th Congress, 1st Session.

(June 27, 1977).

MR. WAXMAN. Dr. Kennedy * * * [t]his ban brought more protests to Members of Congress than any issue since Nixon's Saturday night massacre. It resulted in House of Representatives' action last week forbidding the use of any of the funds in the appropriation bill for enforcement of this ban * * *.

All of this indicates that the public is furious over the idea saccharin is going to be taken away from them. * * *

MR. [DAVID] SATTERFIELD [D.Va.]. Given all the facts, and let's assume we take them all for granted, why wouldn't it be a wise thing to do to just inform the public * * * of what the risks are and let them make their own decision as to whether or not they want to use saccharin?

DR. KENNEDY. I think the question you are really asking, Mr. Satterfield, is why don't the food additive laws allow the balancing of risks and benefits? I think Congress had in mind, when they put in the provisions of the food safety laws, that it is not easy for all members of the public to determine what is in their foods. * * *

* * * Many of the people who consume diet soft drinks are youngsters who may not have the same access to understanding as other members of the public. I worry about making it freely available to them, and I wonder if their freedom of choice is as informed as you and I would like to see it be. * * *

MR. SATTERFIELD. You don't feel their parents have the capability of making it; the government can make a better decision than parents? * * *

DR. KENNEDY. * * * I think my Agency's responsibility is to carry out its statutory mandate and our statutory mandate does not allow us to consider those issues—

MR. SATTERFIELD. I would like to see us rescind that mandate.

At the conclusion of these hearings, the House Commerce Committee observed:

> While * * * there appears to be an increasingly strong circumstantial case being mounted against the safety of saccharin, it is, at worst, a mild carcinogen. The Committee further notes that there is still much disagreement among experts as to the actual risk to the human population due to the consumption of saccharin and whether or not the benefits from its use outweigh the risks.

In the face of these uncertainties the committee recommended that the House amend law but without revising either the general safety standard for food additives or the Delaney Clause. Thus, H.R. 8518, which became Pub.L.No. 95–203, 91 Stat. 1451, prohibited FDA for two years from restricting the sale of saccharin "based on its potential carcinogenicity as demonstrated by any previously reported study," required warning labels on saccharin-sweetened foods, and directed that a study be conducted by the National Academy of Sciences "to evaluate the data on saccharin's carcinogenicity and health benefits, if any, and to recommend reforms in the existing food safety law." Thereafter, for over two decades, Congress repeatedly reenacted the moratorium.

On its face, the Delaney Clause reflects a legislative policy of unusual clarity. The clause makes a single fact—the capacity of a food additive to cause cancer in experimental animals—determinative of policy outcome: no such additive shall be approved for human food use. So far as Congress was concerned, it appears, whether a particular animal carcinogen presents a risk for humans, how large such a risk might be, or the possibility that any risk may be accompanied by offsetting benefits is irrelevant.

The Delaney Clause was the inspiration of Representative James J. Delaney, who in 1950 chaired a new House Select Committee to Investigate the Use of Chemicals in Foods and Cosmetics. The Department of Health, Education and Welfare (now Health and Human Services, or HHS), the FDA's parent, at first opposed singling out carcinogens, but, confronted by Delaney's continued pressure for an explicit ban, it ultimately agreed to the language that appears in the statute. The clause was not the focus of debate in the House; it was not mentioned during the Senate debates; and the Senate Report endorsed its inclusion with the statement that "we believe the bill reads and means the same with or without the inclusion of the clause." See Charles H. Blank, *The Delaney Clause: Technical Naivete and Scientific Advocacy in the Formulation of Public Health Policies*, 62 Calif.L.Rev. 1084 (1974).

For nearly twenty years, the FDA espoused the view that the Delaney Clause was redundant because the statute's requirement that food additives be proved "safe" precluded approval of any food additive that has been shown to induce cancer in laboratory animals. The agency's traditional position was squarely set forth in its 1977 proposal to ban saccharin:

> FDA has previously prohibited the use in food of ingredients found to cause cancer in laboratory animals to which the Delaney Clause was not applicable. * * *
>
> It is of course true that the present law would afford the Commissioner no choice but to prohibit the marketing of saccharin as an ingredient in foods even if he were not persuaded that the scientific evidence independently warranted such action. * * *

Saccharin and Its Salts: Proposed Rulemaking, 42 Fed.Reg. 19996, 20002 (April 15, 1977).

This account was incomplete, however. Although the FDA had indeed banned other food ingredients as carcinogens, its more common response to evidence that a substance might be carcinogenic had been to find some means to avoid a ban if it presented only slight risks or offered substantial benefits. See Richard A. Merrill, *FDA's Implementation of the Delaney Clause: Repudiation of Congressional Choice or Reasoned Adaptation to Scientific Progress?*, 5 Yale J. on Reg. 1 (1988). As the agency often pointed out, the law expressly allows it to decide whether tests for carcinogenicity were appropriate (e.g., was the right compound administered?) as well as whether the results demonstrate induction of cancer (e.g., were the lesions observed malignant tumors or something else?). And, the FDA has sometimes concluded that a substance is not a "food additive," and, therefore, not subject to the Delaney Clause, even though it occurs in food, arguably through human agency. For example, the agency has resolutely refused to brand fish contaminated by PCBs, corn and nuts contaminated by the potent carcinogen, aflatoxin.

Thus by the mid–1980s the FDA had effectively narrowed the application of the Delaney Clause to direct food additives. However, the agency had never been willing to argue that a carcinogenic substance added directly to processed food could under any circumstances escape the clause. Further scientific developments forced FDA to reassess that position as the following case illustrates.

In addition to the ban on carcinogenic food additives, the FD & C Act contains two other near-identical anticancer clauses. One, enacted just two years after the original Delaney Clause, applies to color additives, 21 U.S.C. § 376(B), which can be used to color food, drugs, or cosmetics. This anti-cancer clause is not automatically triggered by a finding that a color induces cancer in laboratory animals if the color is not approved for ingested use. The FDA Commissioner must first find that the study is "appropriate" for evaluating the color's safety. Once this finding is made, however, the 1960 version of the Delaney Clause appears to dictate the result the agency must reach.

PUBLIC CITIZEN v. YOUNG

United States Court of Appeals, District of Columbia Circuit, 1987.
831 F.2d 1108.

WILLIAMS, CIRCUIT JUDGE:

The Color Additive Amendments of 1960 * * * establish an elaborate system for regulation of color additives in the interests of safety. A color additive may be used only after the Food and Drug Administration ("FDA") has published a regulation listing the additive for such uses as are safe. Such listing may occur only if the color additive in question satisfies (among other things) the requirements of the applicable "Delaney Clause." * * *

The FDA listed Orange No. 17 and Red No. 19 for use in externally applied cosmetics on August 7, 1986. In the listing notices, it carefully explained the testing processes for both dyes and praised the processes as "current state-of-the-art toxicological testing." In both notices it specifically rejected industry arguments that the Delaney Clause did not apply because the tests were inappropriate for evaluation of the dyes. It thus concluded that the studies established that the substances caused cancer in the test animals.

The notices then went on to describe two quantitative risk assessments of the dyes, one by the Cosmetic, Toiletry and Fragrance Association ("CTFA," an intervenor here and the industry proponent of both dyes) and one by a special scientific review panel made up of Public Health Service scientists.[2] * * *

The assessments considered the risk to humans from the substances when used in various cosmetics—lipsticks, face powders and rouges, hair cosmetics, nail products, bathwater products, and wash-off products. The scientific review panel found the lifetime cancer risks of the substances extremely small: for Orange No. 17, it calculated them as one in 19 billion at worst, and for Red No. 19 one in nine million at worst. The FDA * * * characterized the risks as "so trivial as to be effectively no risk." It concluded that the two dyes were safe.

The FDA * * * acknowledged that "[a] strictly literal application of the Delaney Clause would prohibit FDA from finding [both dyes] safe, and therefore, prohibit FDA from permanently listing [them]. * * * "

2. Agencies have used quantitative risk assessments in a variety of regulatory contexts. For example, the Occupational Safety and Health Administration is under a mandate to establish standards "reasonably necessary or appropriate to provide safe or healthful * * * places of employment," 29 U.S.C. § 652(8) (1982), which was construed in *Industrial Union Dep't v. American Petroleum Institute*, 448 U.S. 607, 639–40 (1980), to call for promulgation of standards only where appropriate to remedy a "significant risk of material health impairment." In fulfillment of this mandate, OSHA used quantitative risk assessment in promulgating a rule on exposure limits to airborne inorganic arsenic. 48 Fed.Reg. 1864 (1983). *See also* Environmental Protection Agency, "Proposed Guidelines for Carcinogen Risk Assessment," 49 Fed.Reg. 46,294 (1984). The FDA itself has used the technique in evaluating safety where the Delaney Clause did not apply. See 47 Fed. Reg. 14,138 (1982) (Green No. 6). * * *

Because the risks presented by these dyes were so small, however, the agency declared that it had "inherent authority" under the de minimis doctrine to list them for use in spite of this language. It indicated that as a general matter any risk lower than a one-in-one-million lifetime risk would meet the requirements for a de minimis exception to the Delaney Clause.

Assuming that the quantitative risk assessments are accurate, as we do for these purposes, it seems altogether correct to characterize these risks as trivial. * * *

* * * The natural—almost inescapable—reading of [the Delaney Clause] is that if the Secretary finds the additive to "induce" cancer in animals, he must deny listing. Here, of course, the agency made precisely the finding that Orange No. 17 and Red No. 19 "induce[ ] cancer when tested in laboratory animals."

The setting of the clause supports this strict reading. Adjacent to it is a section governing safety generally and directing the FDA to consider a variety of factors, including probable exposure, cumulative effects, and detection difficulties. The contrast in approach seems to us significant. For all safety hazards other than carcinogens, Congress made safety the issue, and authorized the agency to pursue a multifaceted inquiry in arriving at an evaluation. For carcinogens, however, it framed the issue in the simple form, "If A [finding that cancer is induced in man or animals], then B [no listing]." There is language inviting administrative discretion, but it relates only to the process leading to the finding of carcinogenicity: "appropriate" tests or "other relevant exposure," and the agency's "evaluation" of such data. Once the finding is made, the dye "shall be deemed unsafe, and shall not be listed."

Courts (and agencies) are not, of course, helpless slaves to literalism. One escape hatch, invoked by the government and CTFA here, is the de minimis doctrine, shorthand for de minimis non curat lex ("the law does not concern itself with trifles"). The doctrine—articulated in recent times in a series of decisions by Judge Leventhal—serves a number of purposes. One is to spare agency resources for more important matters. See *Alabama Power Co. v. Costle*, 636 F.2d 323, 360 (D.C.Cir.1979). But that is a goal of dubious relevance here. The finding of trivial risk necessarily followed not only the elaborate animal testing, but also the quantitative risk assessment process itself; indeed, application of the doctrine required additional expenditure of agency resources.

More relevant is the concept that "notwithstanding the 'plain meaning' of a statute, a court must look beyond the words to the purpose of the act where its literal terms lead to 'absurd or futile results.'" Imposition of pointless burdens on regulated entities is obviously to be avoided if possible, especially as burdens on them almost invariably entail losses for their customers: here, obviously, loss of access to the colors made possible by a broad range of dyes. * * *

Assuming as always the validity of the risk assessments, we believe that the risks posed by the two dyes would have to be characterized as "acceptable." Accordingly, if the statute were to permit a de minimis exception, this would appear to be a case for its application. * * *

Judge Leventhal articulated the standard for application of de minimis as virtually a presumption in its favor. * * * But the doctrine obviously is not available to thwart a statutory command; it must be interpreted with a view to "implementing the legislative design." Nor is an agency to apply it on a finding merely that regulatory costs exceed regulatory benefits.

Here, we cannot find that exemption of exceedingly small (but measurable) risks tends to implement the legislative design of the color additive Delaney Clause. The language itself is rigid; the context—an alternative design admitting administrative discretion for all risks other than carcinogens—tends to confirm that rigidity. * * *

The [1960] Delaney Clause arose in the House bill and was, indeed, what principally distinguished the House from the Senate bill. The House included it in H.R. 7624, and the Senate accepted the language without debate. The House committee gave considerable attention to the degree of discretion permitted under the provision. The discussion points powerfully against any de minimis exception, and is not contradicted either by consideration on the House floor or by a post-enactment colloquy in the Senate. * * *

Moreover, our reading of the legislative history suggests some possible explanations for Congress's apparent rigidity. One is that Congress, and the nation in general (at least as perceived by Congress), appear to have been truly alarmed about the risks of cancer. * * * This concern resulted in a close focus on substances increasing cancer threats and a willingness to take extreme steps to lessen even small risks. Congress hoped to reduce the incidence of cancer by banning carcinogenic dyes, and may also have hoped to lessen public fears by demonstrating strong resolve.

A second possible explanation for Congress' failure to authorize greater administrative discretion is that it perceived color additives as lacking any great value. * * *

Finally, as we have already noted, the House committee (or its amanuenses) considered the possibility that its no-threshold assumption might prove false and contemplated a solution: renewed consideration by Congress. * * *

The CTFA also argues that in a number of respects scientific advance has rendered obsolete any inference of congressional insistence on rigidity. CTFA notes that while in 1958 (date of enactment of the food additive Delaney Clause) there were only four known human carcinogens, by 1978 there were 37 substances known to produce cancer in humans and over 500 in animals. They identify an impressive array of food ingredients now found to be animal carcinogens and that appear in a large number of food products. These include many items normally viewed as essential ingredients in a healthy diet, such as vitamins C and

D, calcium, protein, and amino acids. If the color additive Delaney Clause has no de minimis exception, it follows (they suggest) that the food additive one must be equally rigid. The upshot would be to deny the American people access to a healthy food supply.

As a historical matter, the argument is overdrawn: the House committee was clearly on notice that certain common foods and nutrients were suspected carcinogens.

Beyond that, it is not clear that an interpretation of the food additive Delaney Clause identical with our interpretation of the color additive clause would entail the feared consequences. The food additive definition contains an exception for substances "generally recognized" as safe (known as the "GRAS" exception), an exception that has no parallel in the color additive definition, 21 U.S.C. § 321(t)(1). That definition may permit a de minimis exception at a stage that logically precedes the FDA's ever reaching the food additive Delaney Clause. * * *

Finally, even a court decision construing the food additive provisions to require a ban on dietary essentials would not, in fact, bring about such a ban. * * * [T]he FDA could bring critical new discoveries to Congress' attention. If the present law would lead to the consequences predicted, we suppose that the FDA would do so, and that Congress would respond. * * *

* * *

In sum, we hold that the Delaney Clause of the Color Additive Amendments does not contain an implicit de minimis exception for carcinogenic dyes with trivial risks to humans. We based this decision on our understanding that Congress adopted an "extraordinarily rigid" position, denying the FDA authority to list a dye once it found it to "induce cancer in * * * animals" in the conventional sense of the term. We believe that, in the color additive context, Congress intended that if this rule produced unexpected or undesirable consequences, the agency should come to it for relief. That moment may well have arrived, but we cannot provide the desired escape. * * *

Notes

1. *Responsibility to Correct Legislative Rigidity*. Accept, for purposes of argument, that literal application of the Delaney Clause would sometimes produce wrong outcomes—outcomes that almost certainly a majority of the 1958 Congress did not anticipate and that their contemporary colleagues would deplore. Whose responsibility should it be to correct such legal malfunctions? Should the FDA simply proceed to apply the statute's rigid instructions until Congress itself steps in to correct the agency's, or its own, mistakes? Or should the agency assume that though it has implicit authority to moderate the consequences of literal application of the law?

Professor Cass Sunstein criticized the D.C. Circuit for failing to uphold FDA's *de minimis* exception:

> The Delaney Clause was enacted at a time when carcinogenic substances were difficult to detect and all detectable carcinogens were extremely dangerous. These facts, however, no longer hold true, and under current conditions the Delaney Clause almost undoubtedly increases health risks by keeping relatively safe substances off the market and by forcing consumers to resort either to noncarcinogenic substances that pose other risks or to substances that were approved by earlier administrators using the cruder technology of their day. * * *
>
> * * * [R]egulatory statutes should ordinarily be understood to contain de minimis exceptions. In such cases, the costs of regulation outweigh the benefits, which are by hypothesis insubstantial. * * * Administrators should be allowed to refuse to impose costly regulations for highly speculative or minimal gains. * * * Indeed, courts should probably require such exceptions in the absence of an explicit statutory text or plausible substantive justifications to the contrary. * * *
>
> * * * Because Congress did not focus on the question of de minimis risks in its original enactment, a de minimis exception would not have defeated Congress' will. The factual background against which the Delaney Clause was enacted was so different from the present circumstances that the statutory terms "induce cancer" must be treated as ambiguous. * * * In these circumstances, interpretation of the clause to permit such exceptions seems consistent with permissible understandings of statutory construction, and quite sensible to boot.

Cass R. Sunstein, *Interpreting Statutes in the Regulatory State*, 103 Harv. L.Rev. 405 (1989). *Cf.* Cass R. Sunstein, *Avoiding Absurdity? A New Canon in Regulatory Law*, 32 ELR 11126 (2002).

Professor John Dwyer takes a similar view of administrative authority and judicial responsibility, but his argument focuses on the institutional deficiencies of the legislature rather than on changes in the original factual predicate for legislation. He lumps the Delaney Clause with other environmental laws under the heading "symbolic legislation." In *The Pathology of Symbolic Legislation*, 17 Ecology L.Q. 233 (1990),* Dwyer offers this account of the political genesis of such laws and the consequences of their adoption:

> By enacting this type of statute, legislators reap the political benefits of voting for "health and the environment" and against "trading lives for dollars," and successfully sidestep the difficult policy choices that must be made in regulating public health and the environment. Thus, while the statute, literally read, promises a risk-free environment, the hard issues involved in defining acceptable risk are passed on to the regulatory agency or to the courts.
>
> Believing that it would be irresponsible and politically mad to interpret and implement symbolic statutory provisions literally, the agency's usual response is to resist implementation. Although an agency may experiment with interpretations that moderate the stringent statutory standard-setting criteria, it will implement its reformulation slowly in order to delay judicial review.

The most significant problem with symbolic legislation, however, is not delay; it is the resulting distortions in the regulatory process. Symbolic legislation hobbles the regulatory process by polarizing public discussion in agency proceedings and legislative hearings. Environmental groups take the legislation's promise of a risk-free environment at face value and tend to refuse to compromise the "rights" inherent in such promises. Industry fears that regulators will implement the statute literally and, consequently, vigorously opposes the regulatory process at every stage. By making promises that cannot be kept, and by leaving no middle ground for accommodation, the legislature makes it more difficult to reach a political compromise (either in the agency or the legislature) that would produce a functional regulatory program. * * *

The argument for agency revision is based on a number of considerations. First, Congress occasionally enacts regulatory laws that cannot be implemented because of economic or political constraints. * * * Agency revision bridges the gap between congressional goals and economic, technological, and political reality.

Second, the regulatory agency is deeply and continuously involved in lawmaking. This involvement stems partly from the legislative delegation inherent in ambiguous statutory language and partly from the agency's enforcement responsibilities. But the agency is also deeply involved as a result of its relationship and interactions with Congress. Not only is the agency an important source of policy initiatives—in many cases it is intimately involved in drafting and amending statutes—it often shares with Congress the responsibility of determining statutory meaning.

Third, regulatory agencies are responsive to majoritarian preferences. A regulatory agency—especially EPA—typically operates in a politically charged atmosphere, in which competing groups fight for the agency's attention and seek to persuade or compel it to adopt or change certain policies. The openness of agency proceedings and policymaking and the broad opportunities for interest groups to seek congressional and judicial review have made agencies sensitive to shifting majoritarian preferences. * * *

Judicial review, however, threatens to undermine the process of agency revision. Courts should defer to the agency's interpretation under an expanded or alternate doctrine of deference to "reasonable" agency interpretations of regulatory statutes.

2. *The Fate of Saccharin.* In addition to forbidding FDA to ban saccharin based on the Canadian rat study, Congress in 1977 directed the Department of HEW to seek the advice of the National Academy of Sciences. The Academy panel confirmed FDA's conclusion that saccharin was a carcinogen, albeit a weak one, in laboratory animals. With respect to saccharin's supposed benefits, the NAS panel's chair had this to say: "There are no scientific studies that can be accepted as credible studies that prove a health benefit. * * * [A]ppropriate studies could be done. * * * [but] they would be very difficult, expensive, and they would not offer answers in the immediate future." Hearing before the Subcomm. on Health and the Envi-

ronment of the House Comm. on Interstate and Foreign Commerce, 96th Cong., 1st Sess. (April 11, 1979).

The 1977 legislation amended the FD & C Act to require a warning on all foods containing saccharin and similar notices at all retail establishments and on all vending machines offering such foods. The original read: "USE OF THIS PRODUCT MAY BE HAZARDOUS TO YOUR HEALTH. THIS PRODUCT CONTAINS SACCHARIN WHICH HAS BEEN DETERMINED TO CAUSE CANCER IN LABORATORY ANIMALS." Thereafter the moratorium on any ban of saccharin was reenacted seven times, six times for two years each, a seventh (in 1996) for five years.

During this period concern that saccharin might cause cancer in humans declined as questions about the relevance of the original animals studies were raised and research into the experience of long-time saccharin users failed to uncover a heightened cancer risk. In supporting the 1996 extension of the moratorium, Senator Orrin Hatch declared to his colleagues:

> Frankly, Congress long ago recognized, based on the established science on the issue, that the benefits of saccharin exceed the risk. * * * Because * * * no evidence has come to light that the risk of saccharin is greater than previously thought, I see no more reason to ban this product today than existed in 1977. In fact, I understand that more recent studies indicate saccharin does not pose the cancer risk in animals that it was thought to pose 20 years ago.

142 Cong. Rec. S8608 (July 24, 1996).

Within a few years, additional doubts were raised about saccharin's carcinogenicity. In 1997, the National Toxicology Program, whose duties include the biennial publication of a "report on carcinogens," announced that its scientific advisers would be reviewing the status of saccharin, 62 Fed. Reg. 51674 (Oct. 2, 1997), and the following spring invited public comments on whether saccharin should continue to be listed as a suspect carcinogen. 63 Fed. Reg. 13418 (Mar. 19, 1998). In May 2000 the NTP released its ninth list of potential human carcinogens, from which saccharin had been deleted. While the agency acknowledged that "there is evidence for the carcinogenicity in rats, * * * [the] factors thought to contribute to tumor induction * * * in rats would not be expected to occur in humans." Appendix b, *Ninth Report on Carcinogens*, at http://ehp.niehs.nih.gov/roc/ninth/append/appb.pdf (last visited Sept. 28, 2002). According to one article, "the American Medical Association, the American Cancer Society, and the American Dietetic Association, agree that saccharin use in acceptable." John Henkel, *Sugar Substitutes: Americans Opt for Sweetness and Lite,* at http://www.fda.gov/fdac/features/1999/699_suggr.html (last visited Sept. 29, 2002).

A few months later, Congress enacted the Saccharin Warning Elimination Via Environmental Testing Employing Science and Technology Act, dubbed the S.W.E.E.T.E.S.T. Act, which repealed the warning requirements for saccharin and saccharin sweetened foods, effectively affirming—at least as a legal matter—the safety of saccharin as a food additive.

3. *Reform Proposals*. A recent FDA Commissioner, Dr. David Kessler, acknowledged in testimony before Congress that the Delaney Clause pro-

vides "no real public health protection." How then should the instructions given to the FDA be revised?

The NAS panel commissioned by the Saccharin Ban Moratorium legislation thought that the law should be amended to allow FDA to rank additives in three risk categories: those so serious as to merit banning, those so trivial as to warrant no regulatory action, and those whose acceptability should depend on an assessment of benefits and other means of control.

In 1979 the Carter Administration put forward a proposal which would have allowed FDA to sanction the use or presence in food of an animal carcinogen if the estimated human cancer risk was "insignificant," and would have allowed the agency to take a substance's benefits into account in limited circumstances. This proposal made little progress as memories of the furor over saccharin dimmed. Congress' failure to act may confirm FDA Commissioner Kessler's observation that "what [the Delaney Clause] provides is symbolic protection, and there clearly is a real political problem in attempting to move away from it."

Formulating statutory standards for setting health-protecting limits on any economic activity is not an easy exercise. In THE STRATEGY OF SOCIAL REGULATION: DECISION FRAMEWORKS FOR POLICY (1981), Professor Lester B. Lave has outlined several possible statutory frameworks. One possibility would be to forbid any risky additive so long as it was technologically feasible to do so. This is essentially how the law now regulates water pollutants, but the formula does not fit genuine food additives very well because refusing or ending their use faces no technological impediments.

A "risk-risk" standard would instruct the FDA to ask whether the cancer risk posed by a carcinogenic (or indeed any) additive exceeds the health risk of doing without it. Lave offers the classic illustration of sodium nitrite, a probable animal carcinogen, which is used to cure meat products to prevent the growth of botulism, and the usually fatal poisonings that would accompany the sale of untreated products. The law could mandate a wider-ranging inquiry into risks. What about the risk of injury to farmworkers that is reduced by allowing the use of DES in livestock feed to increase the growth rate of cattle and sheep (and reduce the time they need to be cared for)?

Suggestions that the FDA should be empowered to consider "benefits"—cheaper beef, not merely safer cowhands, or less expensive pesticide-treated fruits and vegetables—have been recurrent from the time the Food Additives Amendment was passed. The idea that the FDA should be allowed to consider an additive's benefits, however, got nowhere when the Amendment was adopted in 1958. Industry representatives made clear that they did not want any government agency in the business of deciding whether an additive provided any "benefits"; they insisted that this judgment should be left to the marketplace. See Richard M. Cooper, *The Role of Regulatory Agencies in Risk–Benefit Decision–Making*, 33 Food Drug Cosm.L.J. 755 (1978).

Professor Lave reminds us that statutes that allow consideration of a wide range of factors not only expand the scope of administrative inquiry; they raise the cost of decisions by encouraging the decision maker to obtain, and requiring or permitting private parties to supply, evidence about the diverse effects of differential levels of regulatory control. They also inevitably accord the responsible agency freedom to reach decisions that fit *its* sense of the appropriate balance of competing values.

4. *Reform Achieved.* In 1996, nearly forty years after the enactment of the Delaney Clause, Congress sharply but indirectly restricted its impact. The Food Quality Protection Act, P.L. 104–170, 110 Stat. 1489, changes the terms on which EPA is to set "tolerances" for pesticide residues in food, a function EPA took over from FDA in 1970. EPA's authority (like FDA's) derived from §§ 408 and 409 of the FD & C Act, the latter containing the law's flat prohibition of food additives that induced cancer.

Because of the complex interaction between these provisions, the EPA rarely faced the need to apply the Delaney Clause to any pesticide before the 1990s. By then, however, the EPA confronted a series of difficult decisions resulting from scientific developments similar to those that FDA had experienced. Modern animal studies of many older (and in some cases valuable) pesticides revealed that several caused cancer, and advances in chemical analysis revealed that some of these remained in field-treated foods after they were processed—thereby falling into the FD & C Act's definition of "food additive." Because the levels of such "additives" were low, in most cases the risks for consumers of the processed foods were calculated to be small, in some instances extremely small.

EPA was soon petitioned to implement the Delaney Clause by revoking tolerances for four such widely used pesticides. The agency's initial response was a reprise of the FDA's unsuccessful defense of its de minimis policy in *Public Citizen v. Young, supra.* EPA claimed that it had authority to ignore carcinogenic residues that posed a risk to consumers no greater than 1 in 1,000,000. This argument did not convince the Ninth Circuit which, in *Les v. Reilly*, 968 F.2d 985 (9th Cir.1992), held that pesticide residues in processed food were food additives subject to the Delaney Clause which allowed no de minimis exception. On the heels of this ruling, the petitioners reversed their demand that EPA revoke the tolerances for the four pesticides. But, as soon as EPA initiated the revocation process, the manufacturers of two of the pesticides demanded an evidentiary hearing on the issues of carcinogenicity and concentration—and *they* took the agency to court when it refused.

The Food Quality Protection Act was Congress' response to what appeared to be becoming a litigation as well as a policy quagmire. The Act made major changes in the statutory framework for regulating food-use pesticides. Allison D. Carpenter, *The Impact of the Food Quality Protection Act of 1996*, 3 Envtl.Law. 479, 480–96 (1997); Scott Douglas Bauer, *The Food Quality Protection Act of 1996: Replacing Old Impracticalities with New Uncertainties in Pesticide Regulation*, 75 N.C.L.Rev. 1369, 1372–90 (1997).

Press accounts incorrectly reported that the FQPA "amended" the Delaney Clause; in fact, the Act left the language of the Clause untouched. Instead, so that supporters would not have to explain why they had voted to "weaken" the Delaney Clause, the legislation simply excluded pesticide residues from the statutory definition of "food additive." It then prescribed, in considerable detail, the standards EPA must apply in deciding whether to approve or maintain a tolerance for any pesticide residue:

(A) General rule

(I) Standard

The Administrator may establish or leave in effect a tolerance for a pesticide chemical residues in or on a food only if the Administrator determines that the tolerance is safe * * *

(II) Determination of safety

As used in this section, the term "safe," * * * means that the Administrator has determined that there is a reasonable certainty that no harm will result from aggregate exposure to pesticide chemical residue, including all anticipated dietary exposures and all other exposures for which there is reliable information.

The amended statute then proceeds to address how EPA may determine that a tolerance for a pesticide shown to cause cancer is nonetheless "safe:"

(B) Tolerances for eligible pesticide chemical residues

(I) Definition

As used in this subparagraph, the term "eligible pesticide chemical residue" means a pesticide chemical as to which—

(I) the Administrator is not able to identify a level of exposure to the residue at which the residue will not cause or contribute to known or anticipated harm to human health (referred to in this section as a "nonthreshold effect");

(II) the lifetime risk of experiencing the nonthreshold effect is appropriately assessed by quantitative risk assessment; and

(III) with regard to any known or anticipated harm to human health for which the Administrator is able to identify a level at which the residue will not cause such harm (referred to in this section as a "threshold effect"), the Administrator determines that the level of aggregate exposure is safe.

The legislative history of the FQPA elaborates the statutory definition of "safe," drawing a distinction, suggested in the statutory language just quoted, between pesticides that have been shown to cause non-threshold effects (such as cancer) and those that only produce toxicity at doses above an identifiable threshold. In determining whether the residue of a non-threshold pesticide is "safe," EPA is authorized to use quantitative risk assessment—the methodology on which the FDA relied in *Public Citizen v. Young*. The congressional drafters in the end did not accept a suggestion that the law specify the risk level that EPA may consider "safe," but the legislative history reflects an assumption that the agency will ordinarily apply a 1 in 1,000,000 standard. In determining whether the residue of a pesticide that causes threshold-limited toxicity is "safe," EPA is clearly expected to apply a conventional 100–fold safety factor (i.e., dividing the dose shown to be without adverse effects in animals by 100 to arrive at a presumed threshold for humans). H.R.Rep.No. 104–669, 104th. Cong., 2d Sess., Pt. 2, at 41 (1996).

Congress added a proviso to this last instruction which many now consider to be one of the important achievements of the Delaney proponents in Congress. The law directs EPA, in setting any tolerance, to take account of the potential risks faced by infants and children, whose small size, dietary habits, and developing physiology may make them specially vulnerable to toxic insults. To protect infants and children, the agency is under instructions at least to consider, and, some argue, to insist upon, an additional safety factor of ten, i.e., 1,000–fold. Because children generally consume the same pesticide-treated foods as adults, this directive is likely to result in sharp reductions in overall dietary exposure to pesticides—and perhaps require application limits that will nullify the value of pesticide use.

The new standard for tolerance approval makes no reference to the benefits of pesticide use. Elsewhere, the FQPA significantly narrows the circumstances under which EPA may take benefits into account. It forbids EPA to consider the putative benefits of a pesticide in establishing any new tolerance. The agency may, however, take benefits into account in maintaining an existing tolerance for a non-threshold pesticide that would not otherwise meet the "safe" standard—but only under carefully defined conditions. The estimated annual risk allowed by a benefits-justified tolerance may not exceed 10 times the risk that would be considered "safe," and the estimated lifetime risk cannot exceed 2 times the lifetime risk that would be considered "safe." The Act also mandates phase-out periods for benefits-supported tolerances: 14 years for any tolerance that allows a risk of 1 in 100,000, and 70 years for any tolerance that allows a risk of 2 in 1,000,000.

b. Section 112 of the 1970 Clear Air Act

The main focus of Professor Dwyer's attack on "symbolic legislation," quoted earlier, is a famous provision of the most important federal environmental statute, the Clean Air Act (CAA). The history of Section 112, which contains Congress' instructions for curbing levels of so-called toxic air pollutants, exposes many of the same problems with statutory specificity that are revealed in the history of the Delaney Clause.

The Supreme Court's opinion in *American Trucking*, p. 83 *supra*, describes the CAA's basic structure for controlling so-called conventional air pollutants. The EPA is directed to establish nationally applicable health-based ambient air quality standards for each of a half dozen pollutants, leaving it to the states to enforce controls on air pollution sources sufficiently rigorous to achieve those standards. In assigning responsibility for limiting pollution, however, the states could—invariably did—consider costs as well as technological feasibility. For toxic pollutants, by contrasts, Congress in Section 112 made the EPA responsible not only for identifying the substances to be regulated and determining what ambient levels could be allowed, but also for establishing the limits sources of such pollutants much achieve. (Confusingly, the statute used the same word to describe the end-product of the EPA's role under the two statutory provisions. The national air quality "standards" the EPA is to set for conventional pollutants describe the condition that the air must achieve or maintain; the standards that the EPA is to prescribe for toxic pollutants specify the performance that individual pollution sources must meet).

From the beginning it was understood that some of the substances to be regulated under Section 112 would be carcinogens, which may partly explain the language Congress chose to describe the EPA's responsibility: Once the agency determined that a pollutant should be regulated under 112—a decision reflected by "listing" the pollutant—EPA was instructed, within 180 days, to set emission standards (which could vary by type of source) "at the level which in [the Administrator's] judgment provides an ample margin of safety to protect the public health." The statute was silent with respect to other factors that could, in theory, be relevant, including the availability of control technologies and the costs of installing them.

Unlike the Delaney Clause, whose policy imperfections did not become manifest for several years, it was almost immediately recognized that Section 112 posed serious difficulties for the EPA, at least when applied to toxic pollutants recognized as carcinogens—such as vinyl chloride and benzene. The EPA's dilemma was described by John O. Graham, then a Harvard assistant professor and most recently Director of the OMB Office of Information and Regulatory Affairs:

> A basic problem with section 112 is the unworkable statutory test for setting emissions standards for nonthreshold pollutants, such as airborne carcinogens* * *. [T]he scientific community has not established a safe or "no-effect" level of exposure for any known carcinogen. A significant segment of the scientific community believe * * * that any human exposure to a carcinogen, however small, poses some incremental risk of cancer. Under these conditions it is impossible for the EPA to establish nonzero emission limits for carcinogens that protect public health, let alone provide an ample margin of safety. The EPA has acknowledged that a literal interpretation of the Act might require that zero emission limits be established for all non-threshold pollutants.

The Failure of Agency Forcing: The Regulation of Airborne Carcinogens under Section 112 of the Clean Air Act, 1985 Duke L.J. 100.

The realization that the statute might require a total ban of some pollutants, which could in some instances mean a complete shut-down of pollution sources, caused the EPA to proceed slowly. It listed very few pollutants, notwithstanding convincing evidence of their toxicity, and adopted emission standards for fewer than half a dozen in 15 years. The agency spent most of the time trying to fashion an interpretation of Section 112 that would allow it to consider factors that good sense impelled it to consider—the capabilities and cost of pollution control measures.

By the late 1970s the EPA had come up with an interpretation that many observers, including Professor Graham, found appealing as policy but implausible as law:

> The EPA's legal defense of the technology-based approach to standard setting is a remarkable exercise in statutory (re)interpretation. The Agency begins with the premise that members of Congress did not have nonthreshold pollutants in mind when section 112 was written. * * * If * * * zero exposure is the only safe level, then the

ample-margin-of-safety formula cannot be applied. Because Congress did not explicitly indicate its intent to create the economic disaster that zero-emission standard [sic] would bring about, and because a zero-emission standard renders the margin-of-safety concept meaningless, the EPA infers that zero-emission standards for non-threshold pollutants were not intended by Congress. From this point, the EPA proceeds to advocate a technology-based approach to setting emission standards, which calls for zero emissions only where an unreasonable risk persists after the best control technologies have been installed by polluters. Residual cancer risks are "unreasonable" if the EPA determines that the costs of further emission control are not grossly disproportionate to the marginal health benefits.

The EPA followed this problematic interpretation in setting emissions standards for vinyl chloride, which presented the D.C. Circuit with two opportunities to grapple with the meaning of Section 112. An environmental group's challenge to the EPA's standards was initially heard by a panel consisting of Judges Harry Edwards, J. Skelly Wright, and Robert Bork, who wrote the majority opinion upholding the agency's reading of Congress's instructions. *Natural Resources Defense Council v. U.S. EPA*, 804 F.2d 710 (D.C.Cir.1986). Judge Wright's indignant dissent led to a rehearing en banc and a rather different opinion—surprisingly, also written by Judge Bork. *Natural Resources Defense Council v. U.S. EPA*, 824 F.2d 1146 (D.C.Cir.1987).

The unanimous(!) en banc court set aside the EPA's finite emissions standards, concluding that it had misinterpreted Section 112. The court began by rejecting NRDC's claim that safety was the only factor the EPA could consider in setting emission standards, pointing out that the statutory language did not preclude consideration of other factors. But the court was even more emphatic in rejecting the EPA claim that Congress, in amending the Clean Air Act in 1977, had effectively ratified the agency's position that it must give substantial weight to cost and technological feasibility. It then offered its own, authoritative, interpretation of the EPA's responsibilities:

> We find that the congressional mandate to provide "an ample margin of safety" to "protect the public health" requires the Administrator to make an initial determination of what is "safe." This determination must be based exclusively upon the Administrator's determination of the risk to health at a particular emission level* * *. We do wish to note, however, that the Administrator's decision does not require a finding that "safe" means "risk-free," or a finding that the determination of free from uncertainty. Instead, we find only that the Administrator's decision must be based upon an expert judgment with regard to the level of emission that will result in an "acceptable" risk to health* * *. The Administrator cannot under any circumstances consider cost and technology at this stage of the analysis.

Judge Bork went on to address Section 112's ample margin of "safety" instruction, which he said allowed the EPA to require emissions limits even more stringent than needed to assure that exposures would be "safe." And he added that it was at this stage—the stage of deciding how much added protection for health a standard should provide—that the EPA could take technological feasibility into account. The implication, however, was that if available technology could not assure the safety of those exposed to a pollutant, the EPA might have to prohibit emissions altogether.

The D.C. Circuit's opinion forced the EPA to reassess not only its interpretation of Section 112 but its entire strategy for regulating toxic air pollutants. It subsequently published an advance notice of proposed rulemaking in which it invited comments on a cluster of different ways of determining what theoretical level of risk could nonetheless satisfy the agency's duty to assure that exposure to emissions would be "safe." 53 Fed. Reg. 28,946 (1988). Before the agency could complete its rulemaking, however, Congress acted.

In 1990, as part of omnibus revisions to the Clean Air Act, Congress gave the EPA new instructions for controlling emissions of toxic air pollutants—including nonthreshold carcinogens. Revised Section 112 directs the EPA to establish emissions standards, for each of a statutorily prescribed list of pollutants, that require installation of the "maximum achievable control technology" (MACT). The legislation made clear that the EPA was not to consider the cost (or health benefits) of installing MACT. Nor, at what was planned to be just the first decision making stage, was the EPA told to confirm that MACT would assure the safety of those exposed to controlled emissions. This inquiry was postponed until several years after the adoption of initial technology-based emissions standards. Eight years after MACT is installed, the EPA is to determine whether additional controls are necessary to provide the "ample margin of safety" that the original Section 112 mandated. For carcinogens, the amended statute requires the EPA to control residual risks if the "most exposed individual" faces a lifetime cancer risk of greater than one in 1,000,000.

Thus, in its 1990 amendments, Congress essentially turned original Section 112 upside down. Instead of focusing initially on health, the EPA is directed to consider only what technology can achieve in the way of emissions control—which is assumed to be a simpler and accordingly a quicker inquiry. The presumably more complex assessment of the health risks posed by different levels of exposure is postponed—and possibly obviated.

c. *NHTSA and Statutory Specificity*

Legislative specificity, or decisiveness, comes in a number of different forms. The examples just discussed generally involve legislative provisions that are far from specific but that, nevertheless, strongly control the exercise of agency discretion. The Delaney Clause is a generic requirement; it applies to all food additives. Section 112 of the Clean Air Act has a similar form. But, Congress may limit or foreclose agency discretion in a host of other ways. Indeed, much congressional "fine tuning" of statutes involves micro-management of agency decisionmaking which respect to highly specific issues. That, of course, was the purpose of attaching a legislative veto to particular exercises of agency jurisdiction and is also a common feature of so-called "appropriations riders" that prevent agencies from expending any appropriated funds on some specific segment of their general jurisdiction. (Appropriations riders are discussed in more detail in the next section.)

Where Congress intervenes to micro-manage specific agency decisions, it often does so in order to substitute political for expert judgment, without simultaneously changing the agency's basic decisionmaking criteria. These interventions produce decisions that are not only at odds with an agency's best judgment; they may be decisions that an agency could not justify in a way that would satisfy a court that it had not behaved in a fashion that is, as loosely described by the Administrative Procedure Act, "arbitrary" or "capricious." We will encounter precisely such a case in Chapter 5, *National Tire Dealers and Retreaders Assoc., Inc. v. Brinegar*, where the reviewing court strikes down as arbitrary most parts of a rule issued by the National Highway Traffic Safety Administration, but sustains two parts exclusively on the ground that the Congress mandated them. As the *Brinegar* court said, "No administrative procedure test applies to an act of Congress."

Nor was this the only occasion on which the Congress sought to micro-manage NHTSA decisionmaking. Congress has outlawed NHTSA's use of a technologically sound and economically sensible device to increase seat belt use (an ignition interlock) that it found politically offensive. And, it has required the agency to adopt rules concerning school bus safety that have no safety engineering basis—indeed that may create new safety hazards—but that satisfy particular constituencies. Nor have these congressional incursions into agency jurisdiction had only modest effects on the accomplishment of NHTSA's overall mission. A huge proportion of the agency's energy and resources over the last decade has been spent on two problems—deaths and injuries from air bag inflation and tire safety and rollover problems involving sport utility vehicles. In both cases the agency's agenda and its approach to regulation have been dictated by congressional politics, not safety engineering. For a more detailed discussion of these matters see JERRY L. MASHAW AND DAVID L. HARFST, THE STRUGGLE FOR AUTO SAFETY (1990); Jerry L. Mashaw, *Law and Engineering: In Search of the Law of Science Problem*, 66 Law and Contemp. Prob. 137 (2003).

The NHTSA experience is hardly unique. The appropriate location of decisional discretion—in a general political body like the Congress or in a jurisdictionally limited, professional body like an administrative agency—can hardly be made in the abstract. Context matters, and scientifically bizarre congressional judgments often have counterparts in politically naive bureaucratic decisions. The point is simply this—a call for more specific, and presumably more democratically accountable, congressional policy making should not be confused with a call for more sensible or informed public policy.

C. PERVASIVE TECHNIQUES OF LEGISLATIVE CONTROL

1. THE STATUTORY ENVIRONMENT OF FEDERAL ADMINISTRATION

The examples examined so far all focus on statutes that create or govern a specific agency or program. Such organic or program laws, however, by no means exhaust the statutory guidance that modern agencies receive from Congress. In reality, the substance and procedures of administrative decision making are subject to multiple sets of congressional instructions. An agency's own organic or program statute is, therefore, only the starting place for exploring issues of legislative control of administrative action. The numerous general laws that constitute the current framework of federal administration, moreover, illustrate many of the dominant themes of contemporary American administrative law.

At the beginning of this century, however, there was no extensive body of federal administrative law—judicial or statutory. To be sure, beginning with *Marbury v. Madison*, the federal courts had enunciated and sometimes enforced principles establishing the legal accountability of federal officers (*e.g.*, Henry P. Monaghan, Marbury *and the Administrative State*, 83 Colum.L.Rev. 1 (1983)), and a smattering of federal statutes, such as the Interstate Commerce Act, the 1906 Food and Drugs Act, and the Meat Inspection Act, created what we would recognize as regulatory programs. But there were no general laws limiting the powers or defining the procedures of federal administrators. During the next forty years, the number of new federal programs grew rapidly, especially during the 1930s as the nation struggled to escape from the Depression. By the time World War II broke out, the U.S. Code was full of authorizing statutes, accompanied by a relatively small number of laws applicable to administrators generally. Most of the latter addressed prosaic matters, such as the appointment and pay of civil servants and the acquisition and use of property.

By the 1980s the shape of this legal terrain had changed dramatically. The accretion of new government programs had not slowed. The 1970s produced a flowering of new statutes addressed to health, civil rights, the environment, and public welfare, which expanded and substantially reoriented federal social regulation. But more importantly, commencing with the Administrative Procedure Act in 1946, 5 U.S.C. §§ 551 *et seq.*, Congress has enacted a series of general statutes that speak to, and restrict the discretion of, most federal agencies. Accordingly, if one attempts to describe the legal context in which any federal agency now operates—even one created to administer a new statutory program—one must discuss a long list of statutes that make no reference whatever to that program, yet by their terms embrace and limit it.

a. *Statutes Promoting Procedural Fairness and Openness*

Administrative Procedure Act. Without doubt, the Administrative Procedure Act (APA) remains the most important of these statutes. From one vantage point, this influential law bears a resemblance to the Federal Rules of Civil Procedure, since it purports to establish uniform procedures for certain formal actions—rulemaking and adjudication—by any federal administrative tribunal or official. But this analogy both overstates the APA's achievement in unifying agency procedures and ignores the many quasi-substantive obligations the Act imposes.

The APA was the product of over a decade of efforts within Congress and the private bar to systematize the procedures employed by federal agencies whose number had grown so rapidly during the New Deal and, equally important, to curtail perceived abuses such as the commingling of prosecutorial and judging functions within the same organization. See Jerry Williams, *Fifty Years of the Law of the Federal Administrative Agencies—And Beyond*, 29 Fed.Bar J. 267, 268 (1970). Its goals are to subject all federal administrators to a common set of minimum procedural standards and to assure that those subject to regulation have an opportunity for court review of agency compliance with substantive and procedural limits on agency authority.

From the beginning the APA was recognized as interstitial legislation; it supplied the procedures an agency was obliged to follow if its own statute did not provide different (and typically more demanding) instructions. Thus Congress always could, and with increasing frequency it did, supplement or supplant the APA's requirements with more explicit directives for particular agencies or programs. Most environmental statutes, for example, contain detailed instructions that generally go beyond the procedural demands of the APA.

The APA's basic structure is easily summarized. Section 2 defines terms, including the term "agency" which determines the law's coverage. Section 3 prescribes an agency's obligations to make public information about its organization, procedures, and substantive requirements. Section 4 mandates minimum basic procedures for administrative rulemaking. Sections 5 through 8 speak to the procedures an agency is obligated to follow in formal, usually case-by-case, decision making, such as the imposition of penalties or the issuance of licenses or permits. Finally, section 10 outlines the general conditions for judicial review of the decisions of federal administrators. (These section references are to the sections of the APA in its Public Law and Statutes at Large form, and, even today, continue to find their way into judicial opinions and legal scholarship. The APA has been codified, however, in various sections of Title 5 of the U.S. Code, beginning with 5 U.S.C. § 551, and most judicial opinions and secondary commentaries refer to its provisions by their U.S. Code nomenclature, as does the version that we have reproduced in Appendix C.)

The APA's original text has been remarkably durable; most parts of sections 4 through 10 have remained largely unchanged, though judicial interpretations have significantly altered the obligations that these sections impose. (The APA's specific requirements are the focus of later chapters.) Congress has not since attempted a comprehensive recodification of federal administrative procedure. See *Panel Discussion, Time for a New APA?*, 32 Admin. L.Rev. 357, 371 (1980). It has, however, shown strong continuing interest in agency procedures in a variety of other ways, including the enactment in 1990 of the Administrative Dispute Resolution Act, Pub.L.No. 101–552, 104 Stat. 2736 (1990), and the Negotiated Rulemaking Act, Pub.L.No. 101–648, 104 Stat. 4949 (1990), intended to remedy supposed shortcomings in administrative adjudication and informal rulemaking, respectively, as those processes have evolved in recent decades. Congress has made a number of important additions to certain sections of the APA, amplifying its instructions to the entire administrative apparatus. One notable example is a 1976 amendment to section 10, which eliminated sovereign immunity as a barrier to suits seeking declaratory or injunctive relief against the government. Pub.L.No. 94–574, 90 Stat. 2721. Other notable examples are the Freedom of Information Act, enacted in 1966 as a comprehensive rewriting of section 2 of the APA, 5 U.S.C. § 552, and the Government in the Sunshine Act, Pub.L.No. 94–409, 90 Stat. 1241 (1976), 5 U.S.C. § 552b. These and certain other statutes not only apply to all agencies covered by the APA; they also are rarely modified by the specific terms of program statutes.

The fiftieth anniversary of the enactment of the Administrative Procedure Act produced several journal symposia, including *The Future of the American Administrative Process*, 49 Admin.L.Rev. 149–98 (1997); *The Fiftieth Anniversary of the Administrative Procedure Act: Past and Prologue*, 32 Tulsa L.J. 185–353 (1996); *The Administrative State at a Crossroads: The APA at Fifty*, 63 U.Chi.L.Rev. 1375–1571 (1996). The American Bar Association Section of Administrative Law and Regulatory Practice set out to mark the occasion with an attempt to draft a new version of the Administrative Procedure Act that would take into account the intervening decades' legal developments. What emerged instead was an attempt to "restate," rather than reform the current law of administrative procedure. The Section's work product largely tracks the structure of the APA, while addressing some matters of constitutional law and others covered by other statutes. Section of Administrative Law and Regulatory Practice of the American Bar Association, *A Blackletter Statement of Federal Administrative Law,* 54 Admin. L. Rev. 17 (2002).

Federal Register Act. The Federal Register Act, enacted in 1935, 49 Stat. 500, 44 U.S.C. §§ 1501 *et seq.*, was the first general statute addressed to the public procedures of federal agencies. The Act's requirement that agencies publish their rules and its provisions for their codification in the Code of Federal Regulations have become such well-engrained parts of agency behavior that the law now rarely attracts notice. See generally Note, *The Federal Register and the Code of Federal Regulations—A Reappraisal*, 80 Harv.L.Rev. 439, 451 (1966); Laurence F. Schmeckebier & Roy B. Eastin, Government Publications And Their Use 300–29 (2d rev.ed.1969).

Freedom of Information Act. The FOIA, Pub.L.No. 89–487, 80 Stat. 250 (codified at 5 U.S.C. § 552), examined in depth in Chapter 6, has become one of the most prominent features of the statutory landscape in which federal administrators function. Passed in 1966 and amended several times since, the FOIA's obligations touch most activities of federal administrators and facilitate the work of the many organizations and individuals who report on or give advice about federal decision making.

The FOIA's basic thrust is straightforward. Notably, the Act requires an agency, in response to a request from any member of the public, to make available for examination (i.e., to copy and release) any "agency record" that does not fall within any of ten specified exempt categories. An agency also *may* release exempt documents unless some other law prohibits it from doing so or it would be "arbitrary" to do so. The FOIA thus embodies a strong presumption in favor of disclosure. The Act imposes no requirement that the person seeking access to a record have a good, or indeed any announced, reason for requesting it.

The FOIA was adopted in response to claims that many important documents and other information underlying important agency decisions were not available to the public, thereby impairing the rights of citizens to monitor government performance and impeding the functions of the Press. See Note, *The Freedom of Information Act: A Seven-year Assessment*, 74 Colum.L.Rev. 895 (1974); Project, *Government Information and the Rights of Citizens*, 73 Mich.L.Rev. 971 (1975).

Government in the Sunshine Act. The Sunshine Act, Pub.L.No. 94–409, 90 Stat. 1241 (codified as amended at 5 U.S.C. § 552b), parallels the "open meetings" laws of many states and is similarly designed to prevent secrecy in government. Its reach and impact are more limited than the FOIA's. The Sunshine Act applies to agencies headed by collegial bodies, such as the FTC, the SEC, and the CPSC. It obligates such agencies to provide advance notice of meetings at which agency business is to be conducted, and to meet in public unless the members, by majority vote, decide that the subject matter falls within one of nine statutory exemptions. These exemptions parallel those in the FOIA, except for the "inter-and intra-agency memoranda" exemption, which has no obvious application to oral discussions. But Congress recognized the legitimacy of protecting oral deliberations on issues whose resolution could be undermined by premature disclosure and thus section 9(B) of the Sunshine Act permits closure if discussion would

> disclose information the premature disclosure of which would * * * be likely to significantly frustrate implementation of a proposed agency action * * * but [this exception] shall not apply in any

> instance where the agency has already disclosed to the public the content or nature of its proposed action, or * * * is required by law to make such disclosure on its own initiative prior to taking final agency action on such proposal.

The narrow terms of this exception make closure of meetings problematic in most cases.

Suits to enforce the Sunshine Act have been far less frequent than claims under the FOIA because they generally require knowledge of a pending meeting far enough in advance to prepare court papers. Agencies also sometimes neglect to provide advance notice of their meetings. Most covered agencies, however, have followed the Act reasonably conscientiously—even sacrificing opportunities for private discussion of controversial issues. See, e.g., Richard A. Merrill, *CPSC Regulation of Cancer Risks in Consumer Products: 1972–1981*, 67 Va.L.Rev. 1261 (1981); Stuart M. Statler, *Let the Sunshine In?*, 67 A.B.A.J. 573 (1981); Thomas H. Tucker, *Sunshine—The Dubious New God*, 32 Admin.L.Rev. 537 (1980); David M. Welborn, *Implementation and Effects of the Federal Government in the Sunshine Act*, Report to the U.S. Administrative Conference (Sept. 1983). Congress amended the Act in 1995 to require each covered agency to report every year on its compliance with the Act and complaints or litigation relating to its implementation. P.L. 104–66, 109 Stat. 734.

The same year, as one of its final acts, the Administrative Conference of the United States formed a special committee to assess the impact and effectiveness of the Sunshine Act. Among other findings, the special committee reported that many observers, including some sitting or former members of multi-member agencies, charged that the act's requirements had had a " 'chilling effect' on the willingness and ability of agency members to engage in collegial deliberations." The committee's report observed:

> * * * [T]he Committee has received extensive and credible testimony that the restrictions imposed by the Act have had the effect of not only diminishing discussions on the merits of issues before agencies, but also preventing debate concerning agency priorities and the establishment of agency agendas, even though such discussions of a preliminary nature do not technically constitute a "meeting" otherwise required to be held in public under the Act.

Based on its investigations, the ACUS committee concluded that "generally, true collective decision making does not occur at agency public meetings" and that the Act "promotes inefficient practices within agencies which themselves contribute to the erosion of collegial decision making and, correspondingly, to a decline in the quality of agency decisions that the public receives." One practice that the committee questioned was increasing reliance on so-called "notation voting," described as "voting on an item by circulation based on a memorandum without discussion in a public meeting."

> [I]t must be remembered that the principal reason that Congress established multi-member agencies in the first place is because Congress has made the judgment that, for the matters subject to the agency's jurisdiction, there is a benefit from a collegial decision making process that brings to bear * * * the diverse viewpoints of agency members who have different philosophies, experiences, and expertise.

The ACUS committee ended by recommending that Congress establish a time-limited pilot program that would allow agencies more leeway to have private meetings, subject to appropriate memorialization. See Administrative Conference of the United States, *Report & Recommendation by the Special Committee to Review the Government in the Sunshine Act*, 49 Admin. L. Rev. 421 (1997).

Federal Advisory Committee Act. The FACA, 5 U.S.C.app. 2, was enacted in 1972, Pub.L.No. 92–463, 86 Stat. 770, and amended in 1976 to incorporate the Sunshine Act standards for requiring open meetings, Pub.L.No. 94–409, 90 Stat. 1240 (1976). The Act has several purposes. It establishes requirements that agencies must follow when consulting groups of individuals who are not federal employees, and it prescribes how such groups—perforce "advisory committees"—shall proceed in rendering their service to the agency. The main requirements for the creation of an advisory committee are issuance of a charter, which must be approved by the General Services Administration; selection of members to assure diverse views on the issues to be considered; and mandatory expiration, or rechartering, after two years. The main obligations of established committees are to publish advance notice of their meetings and to deliberate in public, subject to the Sunshine Act exceptions permitting closure. See Henry H. Perritt and James A. Wilkinson, *Open Advisory Committees and the Political Process: The Federal Advisory Committee Act After Two Years*, 63 Geo.L.J. 725 (1975).

The FACA clearly seeks to facilitate public awareness of the advice agencies receive and to inhibit preferential access by favored private individuals or entities. A less obvious purpose of the original Act, authored by Senator Metcalf of Montana, was to discourage agency reliance on outside "experts" by making it difficult to create advisory committees. 118 Cong.Rec. S3529 (daily ed. Sept. 15, 1972). Metcalf's investigations persuaded him that few committees performed essential functions and that most were expensive to maintain. Most new administrations have seized upon FACA's rechartering requirement to shrink the government's total number of advisory committees and, thereby, to justify claims that the total number of federal "agencies" had been reduced. Michael H. Cardozo, *The Federal Advisory Committee Act in Operation*, 33 Admin.L.Rev. 1, 5 (1981). The Act's requirements significantly affect agencies, like the FDA, the EPA, and the National Institutes of Health, whose responsibilities require access to scientific expertise that may not exist within government. See NATIONAL RESEARCH COUNCIL, RISK ASSESSMENT IN THE FEDERAL GOVERNMENT: MANAGING THE PROCESS (1983).

For an excellent comprehensive analysis of the history and operation of the FACA, see Steven P. Croley & William F. Funk, *The Federal Advisory Committee Act and Good Government*, 14 Yale J. on Reg. 451 (1997).

Privacy Act. The 1974 Privacy Act, Pub.L.No. 93–579, 88 Stat. 1896 (codified as amended at 5 U.S.C. § 552a), is intended to provide individuals access to personal information in the government's possession, and to improve the management and security of such records. The FOIA excepts from mandatory disclosure records whose release would constitute an "unwarranted invasion of personal privacy." The Privacy Act makes this exemption mandatory and guarantees individuals—though not firms or associations—access to any records about them in an agency's possession that are retrievable by name or some identifying number or symbol. It also provides a procedure by which an individual may correct or supplement personal information in government files. For useful discussions of the Act, see Note, *The Privacy Act of 1974: An Overview*, 1976 Duke L.J. 301; Jerome J. Hanus and Harold C. Relyea, *A Policy Assessment of the Privacy Act of 1974*, 25 Am.U.L.Rev. 555 (1976).

b. Procedural Statutes With Substantive Goals

The APA was intended to unify the procedures that federal agencies follow in formulating rules and adjudicating cases. The FOIA, the Federal Register Act, and the Sunshine Act were intended to enhance public awareness of federal agency decision making and to provide opportunities for affected individuals and organizations to participate in the process. While these laws have affected the content of administrative decisions by bringing new information and views to the attention of administrators and, more subtly, through exposure and sometimes delay, Congress was not primarily seeking through their enactment to effect specific substantive policies. Other statutes addressed to federal administrators generally, however, do have clear substantive objectives, though they often employ ostensibly "procedural" means.

National Environmental Policy Act. The National Environmental Policy Act of 1969 (NEPA), Pub.L.No. 91–190, 83 Stat. 852 (1970) (codified at 42 U.S.C. §§ 4321 *et seq.*), is perhaps the best known of these statutes. The Act enunciates a national concern for the environment and sets forth procedural requisites to assure agency consideration of environmental values in the formulation and implementation of policy. See Roger O. Cramton and Richard Berg, *On Leading a Horse to Water: NEPA and the Federal Bureaucracy*, 71 Mich.L.Rev. 511 (1973). Its core is the requirement that, before taking any "major action" that may significantly affect "the quality of the human environment," an agency must prepare an environmental impact statement (EIS) identifying those effects, assaying their significance, and evaluating alternatives. NEPA does not direct that all actions harmful to the environment must be avoided, and it expressly applies only to the extent not inconsistent with an agency's organic law. But it clearly was intended to increase awareness of the environmental consequences of governmental actions and prompt rethinking of those whose effects seem disproportionate.

Most of the voluminous continuing litigation under NEPA concerns the circumstances under which an EIS must be prepared and, somewhat less frequently, the adequacy of those that are prepared. See generally FREDERICK R. ANDERSON, NEPA IN THE COURTS: A LEGAL ANALYSIS OF THE NATIONAL ENVIRONMENTAL POLICY ACT (1973). There is still substantial doubt whether a reviewing court can set aside an agency's action, taken after ventilation of its environmental effects, on the ground that these effects are excessive. See *Strycker's Bay Neighborhood Council, Inc. v. Karlen*, 444 U.S. 223 (1980). NEPA authorizes the Council on Environmental Quality to coordinate the environmental consideration among federal agencies and, with presidential support, the Council has periodically issued guidelines for the preparation of environmental impact statements. See Note, *Implementation of the Environmental Impact Statement*, 88 Yale L.J. 596 (1979).

NEPA has served as a model for other statutes and, indeed, for presidential orders that seek to broaden the range of values and the types of information administrators weigh in making decisions. This is so despite considerable controversy as to the scope and desirability of the impacts that EIS's have had on government decision making. See Eugene Bardach and Lucian Pugliaresi, *The Environmental Impact Statement vs. The Real World*, The Public Interest, Fall 1977, 22–38; Joseph Sax, *The (Unhappy) Truth about NEPA*, 26 Okla.L.Rev. 239, 245–46 (1973).

In 1997 the Council on Environmental Quality, a body situated in the Executive Office of the President, which is responsible for overseeing implementation of NEPA government-wide, commissioned a report of the statute's effectiveness. THE NATIONAL ENVIRONMENTAL POLICY ACT: A STUDY OF ITS EFFECTIVENESS AFTER TWENTY-FIVE YEARS. CEQ concluded that NEPA "has made agencies take a hard look at the potential environmental consequences of their actions, and it has brought the public into the agency decision making process like no other statute." Id. at iii. However, the CEQ study also questioned the statute's substantive impact. Some agencies, it reported, "act as if the detailed statement called for [by NEPA] is an end in itself, rather than a tool to enhance and improve decision-making." Agencies are inclined to seek litigation-proof documents rather than explore all of the plausible alternatives to the course of action initially selected. The study also found delays in the EIS process and excessive details in the resulting analyses. In response, CEQ announced that it would "reinvent the NEPA process" and promised to take steps "to strengthen planning, public information and input, interagency, coordination, interdisciplinary and place-based decision making and science-based and flexible management approaches." See ROBERT V. PERCIVAL, ET AL., ENVIRONMENTAL REGULATION: LAW, SCIENCE, AND POLICY 900 following (5th ed., 2000).

Regulatory Flexibility Act. The Regulatory Flexibility Act (RFA), Pub.L.No. 96–354, 94 Stat. 1164 (1980) (codified as amended at 5 U.S.C. § 601 *et seq.*), was a product of mounting congressional concern about the impact of regulation—particularly environmental and health regulation—on economic growth generally and on small businesses specifically. Proponents of the RFA argued that "regulations tend to be uniform in design, permit little discretion in their implementation and implicitly assume that all those subject to them are basically alike." 126 Cong.Rec. S10935 (August 6, 1980).

The focus of the RFA is ostensibly procedural; it does not alter, or require any agency to alter, substantive regulations. Rather, it compels each agency to gather information about, and make findings concerning, the impact of regulatory requirements on small business. This obligation applies both in the issuance of new regulations and in the review, which the Act mandates, of existing regulations.

The RFA requires all federal agencies to modify their rulemaking procedures and to consider regulatory alternatives to rules "likely to have a significant economic impact on a substantial number of small entities." 5 U.S.C. §§ 602, 603, and 604. Before initiating rulemaking an agency must assess the economic impact of a contemplated rule and, if it can not certify that it will *not* significantly affect a substantial number of small businesses, include the initiative on its biennial "regulatory flexibility agenda"—a public listing designed to elicit information from small businesses about the impact of, and alternatives to, new agency rules. Before issuing a proposal, the agency has to prepare an "initial regulatory flexibility analysis" that estimates the proposed rule's impact on small entities and explores alternatives that would accomplish the same objectives. A final "flexibility analysis" is required to be part of the record of the agency's published rule.

Congress left unclear how compliance with the RFA was to be assured. The original Act specified that an agency's failure to prepare a "regulatory flexibility analysis" for a rule not certified as exempt shall void the rule. But it went on to provide that agency determinations of the Act's applicability as well as their analyses "shall not be subject to judicial review." At the same time, any analysis prepared for a rule whose validity was challenged "shall constitute part of the whole record of agency action in connection with the review." This latter requirement means that a reviewing court will have before it any RFA analysis that an agency has conducted, which the court may weigh in determining whether the agency's ultimate action is arbitrary or capricious under the APA. See, e.g., *Small Refiner Lead Phase–Down Task Force v. U.S. EPA*, 705 F.2d 506 (D.C.Cir.1983); *Transmission Access Policy Study Group v. F.E.R.C.*, 225 F.3d 667 (D.C.Cir.2000).

Useful analyses of the original RFA include Richard Stewart, *The New Regulatory Flexibility Act*, 67 A.B.A.J. 66 (January 1981), and Paul R. Verkuil, *A Critical Guide to the Regulatory Flexibility Act*, 1982 Duke L.J. 213. See also Jeffrey L. Davis, *Regulatory Reform and Congressional*

Control of Regulation, 17 New Eng.L.Rev. 1199 (1982); Peter L. Strauss, *Regulatory Reform in a Time of Transformation*, 15 Suffolk U.L.Rev. 903 (1981).

In the spring of 1996 Congress "overwhelmingly passed" a major overhaul of the Regulatory Flexibility Act, entitled the Small Business Regulatory Enforcement Fairness Act, P.L. 104–121, 110 Stat. 857 (to be codified in scattered sections of Titles 5, 15, and 28 of the U.S. Code). See Thomas O. Sargentich, *The Small Business Regulatory Enforcement Fairness Act*, 49 Admin.L.Rev. 123 (1997). Probably the most significant feature of SBREFA is the provision allowing judicial review of the contents of an agency's final RFA analysis, of the agency's certification that a rule will not have significant impact on small entities, of any delay in its completion of a RFA analysis, and of the agency's fulfillment of its obligation to review existing rules to see if they should be amended or rescinded in order to minimize significant economic impacts on small entities. The 1996 legislation also prescribed additional steps certain agencies, notably EPA and OSHA, must take to elicit the views of small business entities, and requires agencies generally to publish guides for small business on how to comply with agency rules. SBREFA creates a Small Business and Agriculture Regulatory Enforcement Ombudsman in the Small Business Administration, one of whose tasks is to provide a forum for small business entities to register—on a confidential basis—complaints about agency audits and inspections. Finally, the statute amends the Equal Access to Justice Act to allow small entities to recover attorneys' fees and costs attributable to substantially excessive and unreasonable demands by an agency in a regulatory enforcement context.

Claims that an agency has failed to comply with the RFA have now become a standard feature of suits challenging agency rules, but its no means clear that Congress's 1996 authorization of judicial review has had a significant impact on judicial attitudes—or on agency behavior for that matter. The judicial inquiry into whether an agency has been arbitrary has conventionally encompassed assessment of the agency's treatment of claims that proposed requirements are too costly, too burdensome, or impractical. Compare *U.S. Air Tour Ass'n v. F.A.A.*, 298 F.3d 997 (D.C.Cir.2002), with *National Tire Dealers & Retreaders Ass'n v. Brinegar*, 491 F.2d 31 (D.C.Cir.1974), reproduced in Chapter 5. Many suits challenge agency failures to prepare an RFA analysis and so far the courts of appeals, at least, display little inclination to second-guess agency determinations that an action will not significantly burden small businesses. Further, the cases make clear that an agency need only consider the impacts on small businesses that are directly subject to its rule, and not possible second-order effects, whatever their scope or magnitude. See *American Trucking Ass'ns v. E.P.A.* 175 F.3d 1027 (D.C.Cir.1999) (holding that EPA was not required to assess the possible impact on small businesses of revised national standards for ozone and particulates because small businesses would only be affected when states adopted plans to control point source polluters).

In *Cement Kiln Recycling Coalition v. EPA*, 255 F.3d 855 (D.C.Cir. 2001), a suit challenging EPA emission standards for hazardous waste combusters, the D.C. Circuit offered this analysis of the influence of the RFA:

> Failure to comply with the RFA "may be, but does not have to be, grounds for overturning a rule." * * * An agency may dispense with the regulatory analysis if it certifies "that the rule will not, if promulgated, have a significant economic impact on a substantial number of small entities." * * * [T]his court has consistently rejected the contention that the RFA applies to small businesses indirectly affected by the regulation of other entities. * * * The statute requires that the agency conduct the relevant analysis or certify "no impact" for those small businesses that are "subject to" the regulation, that is, those to which the regulation "will apply." * * * [T]o require an agency to assess the impact on all of the nation's small businesses possibly affected by a rule would be to convert every rulemaking process into a massive exercise in economic modeling, an approach we have already rejected.

Paperwork Reduction Act. The Paperwork Reduction Act, Pub.L.No. 96–511, 94 Stat. 2812 (1980) (codified as amended at 44 U.S.C. §§ 3501 et seq.), was one of the last pieces of legislation signed by President Carter, and reflected concerns about the impact of regulation similar to those that inspired the original RFA. See OMB, PAPERWORK AND RED TAPE (Sept. 1979). Unlike the RFA, however, the Paperwork Reduction Act from the outset included provisions that assured it would have immediate impact on the policies of administrative agencies.

The Paperwork Act amends the Federal Reports Act of 1942, which was itself intended to systemize government information gathering activities and to minimize the burden of official record keeping and reporting requirements. The 1942 Act, however, had been construed as inapplicable to three-quarters of all federal information demands on the private sector. See S.Rep.No. 96–930, 96th Cong., 2d Sess. 75 (1980). The 1980 legislation retains the basic format of the 1942 law, which purported to require central approval for agency information demands on businesses and individuals, but it eliminates virtually all agency exemptions and centralizes control in OMB.

Any agency that desires to impose any new demand for information on the private sector, whether in a proposed rule or independently, must first convince OMB that the information sought "is necessary for the proper performance of the functions of the agency, including whether the information will have practical utility." OMB's refusal to approve a request is final, unless the request comes from an independent agency and a majority of its members vote to override the "veto." OMB may not veto a proposal to obtain information that is demanded by an agency's program statute, but it nonetheless must be given an opportunity to review such proposals. The Act's clear thrust is to discourage new information demands and reduce the "paperwork burden" created by existing agency requirements for records and reports.

Congress updated and, in the words of one author, "strengthened" the Paperwork Reduction Act in 1995. P.L. 104–13, 109 Stat. 163. See Jeffery S. Lubbers, *Paperwork Redux: The (Stronger) Paperwork Reduction Act of 1995*, 49 Admin.L.Rev. 111 (1997) Among the changes, Congress broadened the coverage of the act embodied in the definition of "collection of information." As Mr. Lubbers recounts:

> [T]he Act's coverage is quite broad, providing that a "collection of information" includes
>
> > the obtaining, causing to be obtained, soliciting, or requiring the disclosure to third parties or the public, of facts or opinions by or for an agency, regardless of format, calling for either answers to identical questions posed to or identical reporting or record keeping requirements on ten or more persons, other than agencies, instrumentalities, or employees of the United States.
>
> * * * Literally speaking, the requirement of a cockpit recorder in an airplane is covered because it is [sic] an oral statement of fact or opinion being imposed on ten or more persons. Warning placards or signs may also be covered, unless the wording is specifically dictated by the government. Purely voluntary surveys, even if used to determine whether regulated parties have problems with existing regulations, are covered, as are focus groups used to determine whether a regulation is clear or is burdensome, if more than ten persons are involved in the group.

49 Admin.L.Rev. at 117–19. The controversy over whether, and to what extent, the Act may be succeeding is reviewed in Chapter 6.

Like suits alleging violations of the Regulatory Flexibility Act, claims under the Paperwork Reduction Act are increasingly common, although they rarely constitute the sole or central ground for a challenging to agency action. No doubt this is because some courts have interpreted the Paperwork Act as failing to provide for court challenges to the OMB's approval of or failure to act on an agency's information collection request, and extended this reasoning to preclude challenges to an agency's failure to follow prescribed procedures for securing OMB approval. See *Tozzi v. EPA*, 148 F.Supp. 2d 35 (D.D.C.2001); see also *Sutton v. Providence St. Joseph Medical Center*, 192 F.3d 826 (9th Cir.1999) (Paperwork Act provides no private right of action for its alleged violation).

As amended in 1995, however, the Act does contain what is termed a public protection provision, which provides:

> (a) Notwithstanding any other provision of law, no person shall be subject to any penalty for failure to comply with a collection of information that is subject to this chapter if (1) the collection of information does not display a valid control number assigned by the Director [of OMB] in accordance with this chapter. * * *

> (b) The protection provided by this section may be raised in the form of a complete defense, bar, or otherwise at any time during the agency administrative process or judicial action applicable thereto.

In a much-cited case, *Saco River Cellular v. FCC*, 133 F.3d 25 (D.C.Cir. 1998), the D.C. Circuit upheld the FCC's revocation of the award of a broadcast license to the petitioners. The Commission had previously disqualified a competing applicant based on its failure to provide the formal documentation of financial support that the agency's rules mandated. When it was shown that OMB approval for this "information collection" had not been secured, the Commission reversed field, reinstated the disqualified applicant, and revoked the license awarded to petitioners. The court of appeals rejected the petitioners' argument that the Commission's error was harmless because it had belatedly secured OMB approval for its demand.

> Northeast's argument loses sight of the Congress' purpose in enacting the PRA to "minimize the paperwork burden for individuals, small businesses, educational and non-profit institutions, Federal contractors, State, local and tribal governments, and other persons." In order to fulfill that purpose, the PRA must protect a member of the public when the agency imposes the paperwork burden upon it, not merely when the agency relies upon the paperwork in making a decision, which (as this case illustrates) can be years later. Therefore, an agency may not, having belatedly gotten OMB approval of an information collection requirement, punish a respondent for its faulty compliance while the collection was still unauthorized. Because § 22.917(b) lacked a control number when the Commission required that PortCell submit information about its financial commitment, the Commission could not punish PortCell for failing to submit the information it required.

The Unfunded Mandates Reform Act. By votes of 91 to 9 and 394 to 28, the Senate and House, respectively, passed the Unfunded Mandates Reform Act of 1995. The Act imposes procedural requirements on Congress that are supposed to make it more difficult to enact legislation that imposes costly new regulations on state and local governmental bodies without providing additional funding. And it seeks to force administrative agencies to take account of the implications of the mandates they impose on state and local entities. First, agencies are obligated to seek information from and consult with state and local officials about the impact of new regulatory requirements. Second, agencies must prepare an analysis of local government impacts, for any proposed or final rule that "may result in the expenditure by State, local, and tribal governments, in the aggregate, or by the private sector, of $100 million or more * * * in any one year." This analysis becomes part of the rulemaking record and may be considered by a reviewing court in determining whether the agency's final action was arbitrary or capricious. Third, the Act requires an agency to "identify and consider a reasonable number of regulatory alternatives, and from those alternatives select the least costly, most cost-effective or least burdensome alternative that achieves the objectives of the rule * * *" unless it explains why another choice is superior or is dictated by law. Compliance with the last requirement is said not to be reviewable in court. See Daniel E. Troy, *The Unfunded Mandates Reform Act of 1995*, 49 Admin.L.Rev. 139 (1997). The D.C. Circuit in *American Trucking Ass'ns v. EPA*, 175 F.3d 1027 (1999), agreed that review of an agency's compliance with the UMRA was precluded by the statute itself, but it acknowledged that the requirement that any agency's regulatory analysis be made part of the record could open the door to limited judicial scrutiny under the APA's arbitrariness standard. However, in this case, the court continued:

> No information in an RIS * * * could lead us to conclude that the EPA improperly set the PM and ozone NAAQS; the only information that such a statement would add to the rulemaking record for a NAAQS would pertain to the costs of implementation, and the EPA is precluded from considering those costs in setting a NAAQS. Accordingly, the failure to prepare a RIS does not render the NAAQS arbitrary and capricious.

See also *Allied Local and Regional Manufacturers Caucus v. U.S. EPA*, 215 F.3d 61 (D.C.Cir.2000).

Congress amended the UMRA in 1999 with the State Flexibility Clarification Act (SFCA). 106 Pub. L. 141, 113 Stat. 1699. The SFCA will have little effect on regulatory agencies. The law's aim is to increase the amount of information about unfunded mandates required in congressional reports supporting legislation and force supporters to acknowledge when a bill would reduce federal spending on state-administered entitlement programs and address the options open to state authorities in responding to the reduction.

Data Quality Act. In 2000, Congress enacted Section 515 of Public Law 106–554, the Treasury and General Government Appropriations Act for fiscal 2001, which directed the Director of the Office of Management and Budget to issue guidelines designed to ensure and maximize "the quality, objectivity, utility, and integrity of information * * * disseminated by" any federal agency. As part of its guidelines, OMB was directed to require each agency subject to the Paperwork Reduction Act to establish, by October 1, 2002, its own guidelines for assuring the quality of information that it disseminated. In addition to establishing standards for information quality, OMB was instructed to require agencies to "establish administrative mechanisms allowing affected persons to seek and obtain correction of information maintained and disseminated by the agency that does not comply with the guidelines."

OMB promptly commenced a proceeding, which included opportunity for public comment, for the issuance of its own guidelines, which were published in the Federal Register on January 3, 2002. Publication of the OMB guidelines triggered the obligation of all departments and regulatory agencies to develop and adopt their own guidelines, a task that most had completed by the October 1, 2002, deadline.

The apparent aim of what is now known as the Data Quality Act, enacted as a rider to general appropriation legislation without hearings in either house and unaccompanied by traditional legislative history, is two-fold. One objective is to curb the supposed inclination of some agencies—EPA and its Toxics Release Inventory are often featured in commentary of proponents of the law—to "regulate" by releasing information that has not been verified. The second goal is to provide a means by which private parties can challenge the accuracy and relevance of information that agencies disseminate in ways that do not result in formal public proceedings in which the information can be contested.

As noted, the data quality law has only very recently become effective and it is too early to judge its effects. Defenders predict that it will improve the reliability of information disseminated by the government. Critics fear that it will serve as yet another ground for challenging actions of regulatory agencies and burden agencies with complaints about a vast range of public communication activities. The statute does not provide for, but neither does it rule out, judicial review of an agency's compliance with its own internal procedures or standards, or its refusal to correct or withdraw information that is claimed to be unreliable. An open question is how the Data Quality Act's requirements should mesh with the requirements an agency must follow under the APA when engaged in rulemaking. May a private party who disputes the supposed facts on which an agency relies in proposing a rule invoke the Act's correction remedy before the rulemaking proceeding has run its course? Should the Act be construed as imposing a higher standard of factual reliability than the APA's "arbitrary or capricious" test? These and other questions will doubtless be explored in challenges expected to reach the federal courts as early as 2003. For an early assessment of the Data Quality Act's impact, see Frederick R. Anderson, *The Potential Impact on Agencies and Data Sources: Challenges are Available to Any 'Affected Person,'* National Journal, October 14, 2002, at B9.

c. *Statutes Safeguarding the Integrity of Agency Decision Makers*

Executive officials and employees of independent commissions function within a framework of legal restrictions designed both to assure competence and protect integrity. The very concept of a "civil service" implies a rejection of partisan affiliation as a criterion for public employment. The Pendleton (or the Civil Service) Act, now codified at 5 U.S.C. §§ 1101–1105, an early victory for the Progressive Movement, was a response to perceived abuses in the hiring and removal of federal employees under Presidents Grant and Hayes. The original Act created the U.S. Civil Service Commission, which for more than 80 years oversaw the employment practices of the entire federal civilian establishment—except for the courts and Congress.

This apparatus underwent major changes in 1978, when President Carter persuaded Congress to enact the Civil Service Reform Act, Pub. L.No. 95–454, 92 Stat. 1111. The new law's chief objectives were to foster conditions that rewarded able and conscientious civil servants and made it easier for dedicated managers to discipline or remove employees who performed poorly. The 1978 Act created a new Senior Executive Service (SES), which staffs executive positions throughout government, and gives supervisors substantial flexibility to adjust pay and reassign duties. 5 U.S.C. § 1101.

The various civil service laws have been designed to stifle partisan influence in the appointment and removal of federal employees, save those at the upper tiers of government who must enjoy the Administration's confidence. In recent years attention has shifted from political favoritism to the potential influence of private personal investment or the expectation of future private-sector employment. The U.S. Code has long prohibited federal employees from participating in the disposition of any "particular matter" in which they have a financial interest, and barred former employees from representing private interests in any "particular matter" in which they were personally involved in government. 18 U.S.C. §§ 205, 207. These well-established statutory prohibitions have been augmented by a blizzard of administrative regulations and new legislation.

Well-publicized controversies surrounding the behavior of current and former White House officials, as well as members of Congress, in their dealing with parties who have ongoing relations with the government echo a recurrent question: Can administrators be trusted to separate the government's business from their own? President George H.W. Bush responded to accusations about his predecessor's administration by issuing Executive Order No. 12,674, 54 Fed.Reg. 15159 (1989), as amended, which required employees to "endeavor to avoid any actions *creating the appearance* that they are violating the law or the ethical standards promulgated pursuant to" the President's order. (Emphasis added.) President Clinton, for his part, required senior appointees in all executive agencies to sign detailed ethics commitments, Executive Order No. 12834, 58 Fed. Reg. 5911 (1993), a system he revoked at the end of his second Administration, whether to relieve members of the Administration leaving government to seek new positions unencumbered by those restrictions or to permit his successor to handle the matter as he preferred. Executive Order No. 13184, 66 Fed. Reg. 697 (2000).

Ethics in Government Act. The Ethics in Government Act of 1978, 5 U.S.C.app. §§ 401–405 imposed two new obligations on current employees. It broadened the requirement that management-level employees annually file statements of their financial holdings and, more controversially, those of close family members. 5 U.S.C.app. §§ 202, 402. These statements were to help guide both employees and, in questionable cases, the Office of Government Ethics to identify decisions, or classes of decisions, in which employees should not participate. A more controversial innovation was a provision making these financial statements available for public inspection. 5 U.S.C.app. § 402(b)(3). This disclosure requirement provoked cries of invaded privacy and caused some part-time government employees, mostly academics serving on advisory committees, to terminate their government service.

The Ethics in Government Act also erected new barriers to protect agency decisions from self-interested influence by former employees. It imposes a lifetime ban on an employee's formal or informal appearance in any "particular matter" in which he or she was "personally and substantially" involved while in the government. This category embraces any adjudicated dispute, grant, or contract. A proceeding to establish a rule, however, is not considered a "particular matter." 18 U.S.C. § 207(a)(1). Congress continued these strictures and added others in 1989 and 1990. As amended, the Act imposes a two-year ban on such appearances in connection with any "particular matter" pending within the former employee's area of official responsibility, even if he or she had not participated personally. 18 U.S.C. § 207(a)(2). The Act forbids a former high-level employee for one year from approaching his or her old agency on any matter, including rulemaking, whether or not the matter was pending during his or her government employment. 18 U.S.C. § 207(c). For the highest executive officers, such as department heads, the law precludes such contacts with any agency, 18 U.S.C. § 207(d). These provisions are enforceable through criminal prosecution (a rare event), civil suit, or disciplinary action by the agency to which an unlawful application is made. 18 U.S.C. § 216.

Another innovation of the 1989 Ethics Reform Act was the extension of parallel financial disclosure requirements and some restrictions on post-employment lobbying for the first time to members of Congress and their legislative staff members. See *Pay–Raise Bill Also Spells Out New Ethics, Lobbying Rules*, Cong. Q., Weekly Rpt. Dec. 2, 1989, at 3327.

The statutory restrictions on conflict of interest in government service and post-employment conduct of former employees are intended to insulate government decisions from improper private influence and personal self-dealing. Other laws betray congressional concern about excessive deference of executive employees to the wishes of the President and his appointees. The appointment of Archibald Cox as Special Watergate Prosecutor revived congressional interest in an institution that had enjoyed popularity at the state level. In 1978 Congress passed legislation to institutionalize this method for enforcing limits on the conduct of executive officers, whom the Department of Justice may be unwilling to pursue. See *Morrison v. Olson*, excerpted in Chapter 3. (The Independent Counsel Act was substantially revised and reauthorized in 1994. P.L. 103–270, §§ 3(j), (k), 4, 108 Stat. 735.) The Act was allowed to lapse shortly after President Clinton's impeachment, although Independent Counsels appointed prior to the expiration date and still in operation were allowed to continue and complete their investigations.

In the 1978 Act, Congress for the first time accorded statutory sanction for another hallowed Washington practice—"whistleblowing," a term that embraces almost any effort by federal employees to expose the mistakes or malfeasance of their superiors. "Whistleblowing" by civil servants enjoys special popularity in Congress, particularly during periods of divided government when members welcome its potential to embarrass the incumbent administration. The practice also enjoys popularity among members of the press. See Keith Richburg, *Do We Really Want Britain's Secrecy Laws?*, Wash. Post, Jan. 29, 1984, at D1, D5.

Statutory protection for "whistleblowing," in the form of prohibiting disciplinary action against employees who seek to expose mistakes and wrongdoing, became a precondition for many members' support of the Civil Service Reform Act of 1978. Congress significantly strengthened those protections in the Whistleblower Protection Act of 1989, Pub.L.No. 101–12, 103 Stat. 16, which, among other things, bolstered the independence and authority of the Special Counsel charged with protecting federal employees from prohibited personnel practices.

Inspector General Act. Another statute designed to protect the integrity of agency decisions, as well as protect the U.S. treasury against waste and fraud, is the Inspector General Act of 1978, Pub.L.No. 95–452, 92 Stat. 1101 (1978), reprinted in 5 U.S.C. app. 3. The IGA was enacted in the same era, and with most of the same supporters, as the Ethics in Government Act. It extended to all cabinet departments (and since to almost all executive branch agencies) an oversight mechanism originally attached to just two departments—Energy and Health, Education, and Welfare (later Health and Human Services). The Act provides for presidential appointment and Senate confirmation of an Inspector General, whose duties include oversight of all audit and internal investigations, review of proposed and existing regulations for their impact on "fraud, abuse, and waste," recommendation of preventative policies, and investigation and prosecution of persons within the agency and outside for fraud and abuse. Each IG is directed to make regular reports of his or her activities to the agency head and to Congress.

This last feature—the requirement to report to Congress—originally led the Department of Justice in the Carter Administration, to oppose extension of the IG structure beyond Energy and HEW, but the bracketing of this initiative with civil service and ethics reforms ultimately caused the administration to withdraw its opposition to what was from the outset a legislative initiative. IG's can be removed by the President, but the statute impedes close presidential supervision. The IG is entitled to report directly to the agency or department head, rather than to any subordinate and is also expected to provide semi-annual reports to Congress—without clearance by the White House. See generally Margaret J. Gates and Marjorie Fine Knowles, *The Inspector General Act in the Federal Government: A New Approach to Accountability*, 36 Ala. L. Rev. 473 (1985); see also PAUL C. LIGHT, MONITORING GOVERNMENT: INSPECTORS GENERAL AND THE SEARCH FOR ACCOUNTABILITY (Brookings 1992).

The quasi-independence of Inspector Generals has been a continuing source of controversy. The Department of Justice, in particular, has been jealous of its near-exclusive authority to control the government's enforcement of criminal laws. In 1989 then-HHS Secretary Louis Sullivan, under pressure by a House oversight committee, delegated to the HHS IG jurisdiction to investigate criminal violations of the Federal Food, Drug, and Cosmetic Act, an action that was challenged as infringing FDA's, and the Justice Department's, historical enforcement responsibility. This delegation was rescinded several months later, ostensibly because the need had passed, but also after Secretary Sullivan's attention was drawn to a Department of Justice ruling that the Labor Department IG lacked authority to investigate regulatory violations and was limited to investigating charges of waste or fraud by department employees, contractors, and recipients of federal funds. See William S. Fields, *The Enigma of Bureaucratic Accountability*, 43 Catholic U.L. Rev. 505 (1994).

> The Office of Legal Counsel opinion was not issued in a vacuum, but came after the Inspectors General had, for over a decade, successfully been conducting the types of investigations which it sought to prohibit. Many of those investigations had been conducted at the request of other Justice Department components, particularly the Criminal Division and the offices of the United States Attorneys. * * * With the issuance of the opinion, however, the Inspectors General thought that Justice was now sending them mixed signals.
>
> * * *
>
> * * * Republican administrations were firmly on record as being against government waste, fraud, and abuse, but they also had made other vague promises, such as "getting government off the backs of the people," which the conservative theoreticians at the Office of Legal Counsel also had to consider. While it might be all right to let the Inspectors General beat up upon hapless bureaucrats for the amusement of the electorate, it was a different matter when they started harassing private citizens—especially key Republican constituencies, like doctors and businessmen.

Id. at 513–514. See also, James R. Richards and William S. Fields, *The Inspector General Act: Are Its Investigative Provisions Adequate to Meet Current Needs?*, 12 Geo. Mason L. Rev. 227 (1990).

The Office of Legal Counsel position—that the Inspectors General presumptively lacked authority to investigate or prosecute alleged regulatory violations by private citizens—received partial support from the Fifth Circuit in *Burlington Northern Railroad v. Office of Inspector General, Railroad Retirement Board*, 983 F.2d 631 (5th Cir.1993). The court there declined to enforce a subpoena issued by the Railroad Retirement Board IG pursuant to the IG's investigation of the railroad's possible failure to pay tax contributions under the Railroad Retirement Act. The RRBIG contended that its investigation was detecting deficiencies in the Board's own procedures for collecting and accounting for railroad contributions. The district court, however, found that the IG's investigation was from the outset essentially an audit of Burlington Northern's compliance with its tax obligations. The court of appeals accepted this characterization as supported by the record and concluded that the IG's inquiry exceeded the authority of his office:

> We hold that an Inspector General lacks statutory authority to conduct, as part of a long-term, continuing plan, regulatory compliance investigations or audits. * * * Thus, as a general rule, when a regulatory statute makes a federal agency responsible for ensuring compliance with its provisions, the Inspector General of that agency will lack the authority to make investigations or conduct audits which are designed to carry out that function directly.

2. LEGISLATIVE OVERSIGHT, CASEWORK, AND INFLUENCE

The enactment of authorizing legislation does not end the dialogue between Congress and its delegates. Rather, relations assume a variety of new forms, which expose administrative performance to episodic legislative observation—and influence—with irregular frequency and variable effect. Congress is called upon each year to appropriate funds to sustain, enlarge, or curtail agency programs. Legislative committees, through oversight hearings, monitor specific agency activities and, far less frequently, undertake comprehensive reviews of agency performance. Individual members of both houses inquire about the status of cases or contemplated rules, often at the initiative of constituents or financial backers. And the Senate participates with the President in the appointment of many top managers through its confirmation power. In performing these various functions, members of Congress can call upon a substantial staff—whose rate of growth since 1970 has substantially outpaced that of government generally—and several congressionally chartered agencies, such as the General Accounting Office and the Congressional Research Service of the Library of Congress.

Political scientists have examined these diverse channels for the expression of congressional preferences about agency performance in a vast literature; their complex conclusions do not lend themselves to easy summary. Their recurrent themes, however, raise doubt whether existing connections between Congress and administrative bodies are effective means for accomplishing any of several plausible objectives, including assuring fidelity to congressional intent, preserving the political responsiveness of administration, or dispassionately assessing the strengths and weaknesses of regulatory programs. Traditional scholarship suggests that oversight and casework, for example, may be even less predictable instruments of congressional control than the organizational choices made in organic laws. One notable assessment of the impact of oversight concludes:

> Unless [the oversight activity] reveals a scandalous situation with possibilities for favorable publicity for the legislator, the work is considered dull and potentially troublesome * * *. For elected officials, the incentives favor looking ahead, not back. Responding to current concerns and working on legislation desired by influential groups have more direct bearing on future elections—and political survival is paramount.

Bernard Rosen, Holding Government Bureaucracies Accountable 21 (1982). And studies of particular agencies tend to agree: "Oversight and ad hoc monitoring activities seldom influence [FTC] activities, although they do cause the Commission to expend valuable resources in responding to them." Kenneth W. Clarkson & Timothy J. Muris, The Federal Trade Commission Since 1970: Economic Regulation And Bureaucratic Behavior 34 (1981).

Although Congress since 1947 has assigned broad oversight responsibilities to legislative and appropriations committees, established special committees on government operations in both houses, and increased its staff nearly ten-fold, oversight of administrative agency activity occupies only a small part of the agenda of committee hearings and meetings. Joel Aberbach, *Changes in Congressional Oversight*, 22 Am.Behav. Scientist 493, 502 (1979). A congressionally-funded (and staff-authored) study concludes:

> The legislative committees have a formidable array of oversight tools. * * * But unlike the appropriations committees other committees do not systematically conduct oversight. Indeed, one of the most notable features of oversight by nonappropriating committees is its sporadic, unsystematic functioning.
>
> This *ad hoc* approach to oversight is particularly evident in the regulatory area. Only those agencies with a periodic authorization are actually guaranteed review by a legislative committee. Between authorization periods, there may or may not be regular oversight hearings called. While the appropriations committees respond to a set agenda, other committees rarely do. The wide range of techniques available to legislative committees are seldom marshalled for an annual review. An oversight hearing may be held every six months, but a careful analysis of the entire agency's operation may never occur. * * *
>
> * * * The oversight effort is usually initiated not in accordance with any preplanned set of priorities, but rather in response to a newspaper article, a complaint from a constituent or special interest group, or information from a disgruntled agency employee. * * *
>
> The *ad hoc* approach to oversight is illustrated by committee treatment of agency regulations. Very few committees or committee staff members systematically review the regulations issued by agencies under their jurisdiction. Issues of the *Federal Register* containing proposed agency rules are not regularly scrutinized. One committee staff member explained that he did not have time to review all of the regulations issued by "his" agency. Only when complaints were registered about a particular rule did he inquire about it. * * *

U.S. Senate Committee on Government Operations, II Study on Federal Regulation: Congressional Oversight of Regulatory Agencies 66–67 (1977).

So-called "casework" occupies a larger segment of legislative-agency interactions. As one member of Congress is said to have lamented, "I thought I was going to be Daniel Webster, but I found out that most of my work was personal work for constituents." CHARLES CLAPP, THE CONGRESSMAN: HIS WORK AS HE SEES IT 51 (1963). Officials of agencies such as the Social Security Administration, which receives 100,000 congressional inquiries each year, would surely agree. Yet casework seldom seems to have relevance for general agency policy. An empirical study of its impact concluded:

> The quantity and variety of complaints received by congressional offices provide a rich source of information upon which to base legislative reform of agencies. Although many congressional offices believe that casework already serves this function, in fact, individual cases handled by congressional offices rarely stimulate investigation and correction of administrative problems. Offices only infrequently perceive and almost never act upon the larger agency problems implied in citizens' allegations.

Robert Klonoff, *The Congressman as Mediator Between Citizens and Government Agencies: Problems and Prospects*, 16 Harv.J.Legis. 701, 712–13 (1979).

Some scholars have begun to question the conventional wisdom that agencies are largely unaffected by informal overtures by members of Congress. For example, in their study of the Federal Trade Commission during the decade of the 1970s, Mark Moran and Barry Weingast conclude that the FTC "is remarkably sensitive to even small changes in composition of preferences represented on the [oversight] subcommittee and its subcommittee chairman." *Congress as a Source of Regulatory Decisions: The Case of the Federal Trade Commission*, 72 AEA Papers and Proceedings 109, 111 (1982). Moreover, they maintain this finding is true of both the FTC's general policy initiatives and its enforcement activities. See also Barry Weingast and Mark Moran, *Bureaucratic Discretion or Congressional Control? Regulatory Policymaking at the Federal Trade Commission*, 91 J.Pol.Econ. 765 (1983). The authors, who employ statistical techniques for associating changes in agency policy with changes in the voting profiles of oversight subcommittee members, do not question the prevalent findings that congressional-agency contacts are infrequent, sporadic, and superficial. But they contend those findings are nonetheless consistent with substantial congressional influence over regulatory policy. Weingast and Moran argue "that the mechanics of congressional influence are both subtle and indirect, so much so that even careful observers may not perceive their operation." *The Myth of the Runaway Bureaucracy—the Case of the FTC*, 6 Regulation 33 (May/June 1982). And, of course, the more obvious sanctions of critical hearings and threatened appropriations may have much to do with an agency's responsiveness to the "subtle and indirect" signals it receives about the preferences of the members of Congress who sit on relevant subcommittees. John Ferejohn & Charles Shipan, *Congressional Influence on Bureaucracy*, 6 J.L. & Econ. & Org. 1 (1990) (special issue).

Should the Weingast and Moran thesis prove correct for most agencies over the long term, Congress' propensity for broad delegations, even with the loss of the legislative veto, might seem less troublesome to those concerned about agencies' "democratic deficit." Neither would signal the demise of electoral accountability—so long as we can presume that "the Congress" is adequately represented by its committees and subcommittees. On that matter there is a continuing controversy. Compare Kenneth A. Shepsley and Barry R. Weingast, *The Institutional Foundations of Committee Power*, 81 Am.Pol.Sci.Rev. 85 (1987), and Barry R. Weingast & William J. Marshall, *The Industrial Organization of Congress; or, Why Legislators, Like Firms, Are Not Organized As Markets*, 96 J.Pol.Econ. 132 (1988), with KEITH KREHBIEL, INFORMATION AND LEGISLATIVE ORGANIZATION (1991).

The most obvious reason to question the "representativeness" of congressional subunits is that they include only a small percentage of the membership of either house. Moreover, the sheer number of standing subcommittees—well over 100 in the House of Representatives—in practice means that only the chair and ranking minority member can remain informed about what an agency is doing. The process for selecting chairs still gives weight to seniority as well as to constituent interest, neither of which may contribute to a balanced perspective of an agency's role or its performance. Performance as chair of a committee or subcommittee apparently has little impact on a member's reelection prospects. At the very least, committee chairs turn over whenever there is a change in party control, and retirements of one or two senior members can produce a series of leadership changes, regardless of constituent satisfaction with the performance of incumbents. The personalized character of committee management in both houses—the chair usually chooses the committee's staff, dictates its agenda, and, to the extent any elected official does so, directs its investigations—undermines any notion that committees are microcosms of the whole body, much less reliable amplifiers of current popular sentiment on matters within a committee's jurisdiction. Most expressions of purported "committee" interest—just like those of individual members—are unencumbered by any of the constraints of genuinely collegial decision making. This does not mean, of course, that an agency will not be interested in, or even subservient to, the wishes of the chairs of the committees in whose jurisdictions it falls, but simply that its inclination to be responsive will have little to do with its perception that the chairs are reliable expositors of original legislative intent or current congressional sentiment.

Yet we must remember that committee chairs can exercise nearly as much autonomous influence over the drafting and passage of program legislation. Powerful chairs can prevent, or at least substantially delay, votes on bills that would command broad support were they to reach the floor. They can largely determine whether hearings will be scheduled on a bill, or a markup session held. The chair's staff will determine who writes the important legislative history, sometimes even the history of legislation the chair dislikes but declines to oppose. Thus, final statutory language as well as the ostensibly authentic sources of legislative history, such as committee reports, can reflect the decisive influence of a very few powerful individuals. Nonetheless, the necessity to secure a majority—within the committee, on the floor, and among the conferees—gives many members the opportunity to affect what "Congress" says in legislation. More informal expressions of attitude or preference, reflected in letters, questions, even reports of hearings, are not subject to the same collegial constraints.

Congressional inquiries can reach the entire range of an agency's activities, from decisions about budgetary choices, to the employment and assignment of personnel, to the relocation of branch offices. Most decisions of these sorts are not the product of formal agency proceedings nor required by law to be based on any administrative record. But many visible, and thus controversial, decisions of administrators are the product of procedures structured to nullify or expose certain kinds of overtures. Members of Congress and their staffs, however, have frequently displayed indifference towards such distinctions.

For their part, the federal courts have responded cautiously to demands that they intervene to protect the integrity of the administrative process from congressional intrusion. *Pillsbury Co. v. FTC*, 354 F.2d 952, 963–65 (5th Cir.1966), is exemplary. In an interlocutory administrative ruling the Commission had taken the position—rejecting the argument of its prosecutorial staff—that the acquisition of active competitors by Pillsbury, a company with a substantial share of the milling market, was not a *per se* violation of the Clayton Act. The Commission had, however, reversed the trial examiner's finding that no prima facie case of monopolization had been made out and remanded the case for further hearings on whether Pillsbury's acquisitions had in fact substantially lessened competition. Ultimately, it resolved that issue against the company, and ordered divestiture.

While the case was back before the trial examiner, Commission Chairman Howrey and several staff members were called to testify before Senator Estes Kefauver's Antitrust and Monopoly Subcommittee and its counterpart in the House. At the Senate hearings the FTC witnesses were subjected to prolonged hostile questioning concerning the Commission's initial rejection of the *per se* theory. The case was referred to more than 100 times during the several sessions and Chairman Howrey thereafter disqualified himself from further participation in it. He later explained this action:

> I wrote the [interlocutory] opinion. It is still a pending adjudication; and because of some of the penetrating questions over on the Senate side, I felt compelled to withdraw from the case because I did not think I could be judicial any more when I had been such an advocate of [the Commission's] views in answering questions.

On appeal from the Commission's divestiture order, the court of appeals determined that the persistent questioning during the congressional hearings had so intruded into the Commission's decision processes that other commissioners who participated in the final decision should also be disqualified:

> [C]ommon justice to a litigant requires that we invalidate the order entered by a quasi-judicial tribunal that was importuned by members of the United States Senate, however innocent they intended their conduct to be, to arrive at the ultimate conclusion which they did reach. * * *
>
> We are sensible of the fact that, pursuant to its quasi-legislative function, it frequently becomes necessary for a commission to set forth policy statements or interpretative rules * * * in order to inform interested parties of its official position on various matters. This is as it should be.
>
> At times similar statements of official position are elicited in Congressional hearings. In this context, the agencies are sometimes called to task for failing to adhere to the "intent of Congress" in supplying meaning to the often broad statutory standards from which the agencies derive their authority * * *. Although such investigatory methods raise serious policy questions as to the *de facto* "independence" of the federal regulatory agencies, it seems doubtful that they raise any constitutional issues. However, when such an investigation focuses directly and substantially upon the mental decisional processes of a commission *in a case which is pending before it*, Congress is no longer intervening in the agency's *legislative* function, but rather, in its *judicial* function. At this latter point, we become concerned with the right of private litigants to a fair trial and, equally important, with their right to the appearance of impartiality, which cannot be maintained unless those who exercise the judicial function are free from powerful external influences. * * *
>
> * * * [But] we are convinced that the Commission is not permanently disqualified to decide this case. * * * [T]he passage of time, coupled with the changes in personnel on the Commission, sufficiently insulate the present members from any outward effect from what occurred in 1955.

Pressure by one or a few members of Congress may also jeopardize agency action that is not "quasi-judicial" in character, as *D.C. Federation of Civic Associations v. Volpe*, 459 F.2d 1231, 1245–49 (D.C.Cir. 1971), indicates. That case was a challenge to a decision by the Secretary of Transportation to proceed with the (later abandoned) "Three Sisters Bridge" project as a part of the interstate highway system in the District of Columbia. In the process of ordering a remand for further fact-finding by the trial court, Judge Bazelon had this to say about congressional influence in highway planning:

> As the District Court pointed out,
>
>> [t]here is no question that the evidence indicates that strong political pressure was applied by certain members of congress in

> order to secure approval of the bridge project. Congressman Natcher stated publicly and made no secret of the fact that he would do everything that he could to withhold Congressional appropriations for the District of Columbia rapid transit system, the need for which is universally recognized in the Washington metropolitan area, until the District complied with the 1968 Act.

When funds for the subway were, in fact, blocked, Representative Natcher:

> made his position perfectly clear, stating that "as soon as the freeway project gets under way beyond recall then we will come back to the House and recommend that construction funds for rapid transit be approved." * * *

* * * [T]he underlying problem cannot be illuminated by a simplistic effort to force the Secretary's action into a purely judicial or purely legislative mold. His decision was not "judicial" in that he was not required to base it solely on a formal record established at a public hearing. At the same time, it was not purely "legislative" since Congress had already established the boundaries within which his discretion could operate. But even though his action fell between these two conceptual extremes, it is still governed by principles that we had thought elementary and beyond dispute. If, in the course of reaching his decision, Secretary Volpe took into account "considerations that Congress could not have intended to make relevant," his action proceeded from an erroneous premise and his decision cannot stand. The error would be more flagrant, of course, if the Secretary had based his decision solely on the pressures generated by Representative Natcher. But it should be clear that his action would not be immunized merely because he also considered some relevant factors. * * *

To avoid any misconceptions about the nature of our holding, we emphasize that we have not found—nor, for that matter, have we sought—any suggestion of impropriety or illegality in the actions of Representative Natcher and others who strongly advocate the bridge. They are surely entitled to their own views on the need for the Three Sisters Bridge, and we indicate no opinion on their authority to exert pressure on Secretary Volpe. Nor do we mean to suggest that Secretary Volpe acted in bad faith or in deliberate disregard of his statutory responsibilities. He was placed, through the action of others, in an extremely treacherous position. Our holding is designed, if not to extricate him from that position, at least to enhance his ability to obey the statutory command notwithstanding the difficult position in which he was placed.

Outside the adjudicatory contexts, however, the mere possibility of bias or prejudgment due to congressional influence apparently has never led to judicial invalidation. See *Sierra Club v. Costle*, reproduced in Chapter 5. *American Public Gas Association v. Federal Power Commis-*

sion, 567 F.2d 1016, 1067–70 (D.C.Cir.1977), reviewing a national proceeding to set rates for natural gas, is suggestive. Certain gas producers sought to upset the resulting rate order because of allegedly improper congressional pressure, described by the court of appeals as follows:

> The factual basis for the producers' position, in brief, is that while the rehearing was pending the members of the Commission were summoned before an Oversight Subcommittee of the House Committee on Interstate and Foreign Commerce and were subjected, particularly Chairman Dunham, to an intensive examination by Subcommittee Chairman Moss and Subcommittee Counsel Atkisson. Congressman Moss and three other Subcommittee members were parties to the proceedings before the Commission and as such had an interest in the Commission's decision on rehearing. At the Subcommittee hearing, particularly during the examination by Congressman Moss and Subcommittee Counsel Atkisson, the rationale of several important decisions underlying the rates established by Opinion No. 770 came under attack. These decisions were among those subject to reconsideration by the Commission, and this occurred notwithstanding warnings that the issues were pending before the Commission on the rehearing, and despite objections from other Subcommittee members. The questioning was not confined to explication of "what the Opinion means and what its implications are." Chairman Moss went further, stating:
>
> > I am most committed as an adversary. I find that I am outraged by Order 770. I find it very difficult to comprehend any standard of just (sic) and reasonableness in the decision and I would not want the record to be ambiguous on that point for one moment.

Referring to the prior case law the court continued:

> We doubt the proper utility of classifying the ratemaking undertaken in the present proceedings by the Power Commission as entirely a judicial or a legislative function, or a combination of the two, for in any event the need for an impartial decision is obvious. Congressional intervention which occurs during the still-pending decisional process of an agency endangers, and may undermine, the integrity of the ensuing decision, which Congress has required be made by an impartial agency charged with responsibility for resolving controversies within its jurisdiction. Congress as well as the courts has responsibility to protect the decisional integrity of such an agency.
>
> Nevertheless, upon consideration of the whole setting in which the producers now present their claim of disqualification, we are led under settled principles to deny the producers the relief they seek. When Opinion No. 770 was pending on rehearing they concededly had knowledge of all the facts which they now assert had disqualified the Commission, except of course such changes as were made on the rehearing and stated in Opinion No. 770–A. Fully aware of the

facts which are the only basis upon which the claim of disqualification can stand, the producers failed to call upon the Commission to disqualify itself. * * *

Our denial of relief at the instance of the producers does not dispose fully of the problem. Independent of the status of the parties seeking relief we think it is obvious that within the equitable relationship between the reviewing court and the agency there resides—there inheres—judicial jurisdiction, and responsibility in the public interest, to decide whether there occurred here such an inroad upon the integrity of the decisional function of the independent agency as to require the court sua sponte to set aside the whole or any part of Opinion No. 770–A. This necessitates our consideration of: the character and scope of the interference alleged; the fact that the parties who raise the disqualification question seem not to have deemed what occurred to impair the impartiality of the Commission itself independent of the result it reached; the fact that in one important respect, and indeed the issue that was most vehemently examined by the Congressmen, namely the correctness of the Commission's decision respecting the income tax component, the Commission left standing the disposition criticized at the Subcommittee hearing; the fact that there is nothing to lead the court to find that actual influence affected Opinion No. 770–A; and the fact that insofar as any actions of the Commissioners themselves are concerned no appearance of partiality is evident. In these circumstances we decline to set aside any part of Opinion No. 770–A sua sponte by reason of what occurred before the congressional Subcommittee.

In concluding as above we recognize the possibility, but not the probability, that what occurred may have influenced the Commission. We consider the intervention through the Subcommittee regrettable and quite inconsistent with that due regard for the independence of the Commission which Congress and the courts must maintain. Nevertheless, when weighed in the context of the record as a whole, the possibility of influence upon the Commission is too intangible and hypothetical a basis for this court of its own motion to nullify Opinion No. 770–A. * * *

Chapter 3

EXECUTIVE SUPERVISION OF ADMINISTRATIVE ACTION

The U.S. Constitution is more than usually delphic in describing the structure and the powers of the executive branch. Article II concerns itself primarily with the election, compensation, and removal of the President and Vice President. Other executive branch officials are mentioned in two contexts: (1) The President is empowered, with the advice and consent of two-thirds of the Senate, to appoint and "commission" "officers of the United States"; and (2) the President is authorized to demand "the opinion, in writing, of the principal officer in each of the executive departments, upon any subject relating to the duties of their respective offices." The chief domestic power of the President is stated as a responsibility—"he shall take care that the laws be faithfully executed"—and is listed, almost as an afterthought, following instructions that the President make reports and recommendations to the Congress and "receive Ambassadors and other Public Ministers."

From these meager textual underpinnings the modern executive branch, with its multiple departments, hundreds of bureaus, and millions of employees, has gradually emerged. Yet the growth of administrative governance and power over these more than two hundred years has left undecided (if "decision" implies judicial interpretation) most of the constitutional questions that could have been asked in 1787. What is an "office" to which the President is authorized to appoint? How are "officers" who are not subject to impeachment to be removed? What is a "department?" How are they to be created, staffed, and managed? What techniques are available to the President, beyond demanding reports in writing, to "execute" the laws? In responding to these questions, as one author puts it, "appellate adjudications are, for the most part, replete with examples of issue-avoidance, purposeful equivocation, ambiguity and indecision." John Burkoff, *Appointment and Removal Under the Federal Constitution: The Impact of Buckley v. Valeo*, 22 Wayne L.Rev. 1335 (1976).

This gap in our constitutional jurisprudence does not reflect continuous harmonious adjustment. Ambiguity or vagueness concerning the powers of the executive almost always suggests the *possibility* of legislative power. The brevity of Article II thus leads not to a power vacuum but to a power struggle. The battle began in the first Congress (see I ANNALS OF CONGRESS 473–608 (1789)) concerning the removal power (see Burkoff, *supra*, at 1379–83), and has been raging ever since, as the *Chadha* case in Chapter 2 attests. This is a political war with many truces but no possibility of a comprehensive, stable peace treaty. For neither the President nor the Congress is a political lightweight; the political stakes are often high; and each has regular opportunities to encroach on domains claimed by the other.

Consider, for example, the techniques available to the modern President to shape administrative policy. First, the President possesses powers to appoint, and to remove, agency officials. These powers are amplified by the authority to issue executive orders, directives, or simple statements of policy. The President can also explore possibilities for agency organization and reorganization, impose requirements for interagency coordination, and demand central clearance of budget requests and legislative proposals. Lying behind these various carrots and sticks are others, ranging from the Attorney General's control over agency litigation to the President's unique access to the media.

Congress, however, has powers to check and balance the President. Appointments can be blocked and removals prohibited or conditioned by statute on "cause." Congress may delegate authority to appoint and remove to officials other than the President. Agencies can be set up as "independent" or outside the Executive branch; agency budgets can be cut or expanded; statutory administrative powers can be altered, deleted, or withheld. Presidential ambitions for new legislation may be held hostage to congressional desires for administrative changes of direction. Congressional oversight hearings may be structured to embarrass the President politically. Even impeachment, while rare, is not unknown.

To be sure, not all the things the President and the Congress *might* do as they contend for political control of administration are necessarily constitutional. Indeed, because virtually every technique available to one contestant has implications for the reserved powers of the other, each thrust and parry necessarily raises an issue of separation of powers. Moreover, certain forms of interbranch competition for control of the federal bureaucracy may affect the constitutional, statutory, or common law rights of third parties. Thus some (and, with the decline of traditional barriers to justiciability, an increasing number of) disputes bearing on executive control of administrative action make their way into the courts.

Section A focuses on a set of cases in which the Supreme Court has addressed the President's supervisory authority over administrators, in the context of Congress' attempts either (1) to reserve a role for itself in choosing or removing administrators (other than through impeachment), or (2) to limit the President's power to remove administrators at will. Section B examines the President's power to formulate policy independently and to direct the policy making activities of other administrators. The cases in these sections raise obvious issues of constitutional interpretation, but our primary interest concerns the likely implications of different separation of powers approaches for administrative decision making. Against the constitutional background, Section C portrays recent presidential efforts to assert greater central control over regulatory decision making. It focuses on the evolving role of the Office of Management and Budget in coordinating administrative policy making.

A. THE PRESIDENT'S POWER TO APPOINT AND REMOVE ADMINISTRATORS

1. ADMINISTRATIVE ORGANIZATION AND THE SHIFTING BALANCE OF CONGRESSIONAL AND PRESIDENTIAL POWER

Any attempt to portray accurately the distribution of powers between Congress and the President regarding administration must underscore the highly unstable quality of the political relationship between the two elected branches. That relationship did not emerge against the backdrop of any late eighteenth century consensus as to the detailed institutional or organizational implications of separation of powers Principles. GERHARD CASPER, SEPARATING POWER: ESSAYS ON THE FOUNDING PERIOD (1997); William Gwyn, *The Indeterminacy of the Separation of Powers and the Federal Courts*, 57 Geo.Wash.L.Rev. 474 (1989). Moreover, it is a relationship in which the balance of power has shifted repeatedly. One context in which to observe these shifts is the changing locus of authority over one of the most basic aspects of policy making control, namely, the power to organize the administrative apparatus of government.

On this question constitutional text provides little guidance. The Constitution explicitly envisions the existence of government "Departments," yet is silent regarding details of administrative organization below the level of President and Vice–President. The Constitution gives Congress the power "To make all Laws which shall be necessary and proper for carrying into Execution * * * all Powers vested by this Constitution in the Government of the United States, or in any Department thereof," U.S. Const., art. I, § 8, ¶ 18—presumably including laws for the organization and control of the bureaucracy. Yet Congress, as we have already seen in Chapter 2, may (and does) delegate its powers to organize and control. Indeed, compared to the overtly substantive policy making delegations discussed in Chapter 2, Congress' delegations of authority to manage the bureaucracy would seem less likely to represent abdications of the legislative role, and more consistent with what, in the modern mind, is the President's "chief executive" role as top administrator in the executive branch.

It would be a mistake, however, to equate the President's modern role with conceptions of the presidency prevailing at the time of the Constitution's ratification. Willoughby's authoritative constitutional law text said:

> It was undoubtedly intended that the President be little more than a political chief; that is to say, one whose function should, in the main consist in the performance of those political duties which are not subject to judicial control. It was quite clear that it was intended that he should not, except as to these political matters, be the administrative head of the government, with general power of directing and controlling the acts of subordinate federal administrative agents.

3 Westel Woodward Willoughby, Constitutional Law 1479–80 (2d ed. 1929). See also 1 Frank J. Goodnow, Comparative Administrative Law 52–62 (1893).

Early statutes establishing various departments of the government seem to recognize this intention, at least with respect to domestic functions as distinguished from presidential power with respect to foreign affairs and military matters. When establishing the departments of Foreign Affairs (Act of July 27, 1789, ch. 4, § 1, 1 Stat. 28), War (Act of August 7, 1789, ch. 7, § 1, 1 Stat. 49), and Navy (Act of April 30, 1798, ch. 35, § 1, 1 Stat. 553), legislation explicitly gave the President a power of direction. For example, the acts creating the departments of Foreign Affairs and War stipulated that the Secretaries "perform and execute such duties as shall from time to time be enjoined on or intrusted to [them] by the President" and "conduct the business of said department in such manner as the President * * * shall from time to time order or instruct." Act of July 22, 1789, ch. 4, § 1 (1 Stat. 29); Act of August 7, 1789, ch. 7, § 1 (1 Stat. 50). The Act establishing the Department of the Navy placed the Secretary even more firmly under direct control and supervision, instructing him simply "to execute such orders as he shall receive from the President." Act of April 30, 1798, ch. 35, § 1 (1 Stat. 553).

This power of direction was not included, however, in establishments such as the Treasury Department (Act of September 2, 1789, ch. 12, § 1, 1 Stat. 65 (1789)), the Post Office (Act of May 8, 1794, ch. 23, § 3, 1 Stat. 357), or the Interior Department (Act of March 3, 1849, ch. 108, § 1, 9 Stat. 395). The Treasury Department statute did not even mention the President, required the Secretary to make reports to Congress, and said that the Secretary of the Treasury should "generally * * * perform all those services relative to the finances, as he shall be directed to perform." Act of September 2, 1789, ch. 12, § 2, 1 Stat. 66 (1789). In the context of the statute, apparently, any "directions" were expected to come from Congress. During the early years of the republic, secretaries of departments seem to have been viewed as independent political actors often competing with each other, sometimes at odds with the President politically, and dependent upon the Congress for much of their power. See Leonard D. White, The Federalists 44–49, 68–87, 94–96, 218–252 (1948).

This vision of the non-managerial presidency was not unanimous. Alexander Hamilton had strong views on the need for centralized administration (although, during his own tenure as Secretary of the Treasury, he willingly served Congress, in essence, as the equivalent of a modern-day chair of the House Ways and Means Committee). The Jackson presidency certainly emphasized the political accountability of office holders to the President. See Leonard D. White, The Jacksonians 23–28, 33–44, 50–124, 300–346, 552–567 (1954). It was not, however, until the vast increases in federal bureaucratic operations after the Civil War that administrative management became a significant issue for those concerned about federal government organization. See generally Barry D. Karl, *Executive Reorganization and Presidential Power*, 1977 Sup.Ct.Rev. 1, 11–28. Interest in "managerial" questions increased steadily in response to increases in the scale of the private and public organizations in the late nineteenth and early twentieth centuries.

In the early New Deal, the management of the executive branch was recognized as a critical problem. President Roosevelt set up a Committee on Administrative Management to report to him on the organization and effectiveness of the executive branch. It is fair to say that the committee was appalled by the state of federal administrative organization. It urgently recommended, and the Congress enacted, legislation reorganizing and strengthening the role of the Bureau of the Budget and providing other central staff to assist the President in developing and coordinating the organization and financing of the government's administrative functions. Report of President's Committee on Administrative Management 5–6, 16–25, 33–38, 51–53 (Washington, U.S. GPO 1937). Moreover, the Committee's report suggested that the operative constitutional conception of the chief executive had been radically transformed. The Committee referred quite unselfconsciously to "our constitutional ideal of a fully coordinated executive branch responsible to the president." *Id.* at 41. Moreover, the Report viewed with alarm the growth of the so-called independent regulatory commissions. In the Committee's words, "They constitute a headless fourth branch of the government, a haphazard deposit of irresponsible agencies and uncoordinated powers. They do violence to the basic theory of the American Constitution that there should be three major branches of the government and only three. The Congress has found no effective way of supervising them, they cannot be controlled by the President, and they are answerable to the courts only in respect to the legality of their activities. * * * " *Id.* at 40.

From the New Deal Deal through the Carter Administration, there was no lack of commissions, task forces, and reports on the organization of the executive branch, including the independent regulatory commissions. Some of the more important were the Commission on Organization of the Executive Branch of Government (the Hoover Commission) (1947–1949); the United States Commission on Organization of the

Executive Branch of the Government (Second Hoover Commission) (1953–1955); James M. Landis' Report on the Regulatory Agencies to the President-elect (Senate Committee on the Judiciary, 86th Cong., 2d Sess. (Comm. Print, 1960)); the President's Advisory Council on Executive Organization (the Ash Council Report, 1971); and ABA COMMISSION ON LAW AND THE ECONOMY, FEDERAL REGULATION: ROADS TO REFORM (1979). Virtually all such task forces or reports were critical of independent regulatory agencies and expressed concern about the incapacity of the President to supervise and direct their activities. A defense of independent regulatory structure, however, appeared in V Study on Federal Regulation, Senate Comm. on Governmental Affairs, 95th Cong., 1st Sess. 6–7, 67–81 (1977).

The reports of these commissions, task forces, and individuals likewise generated their own secondary literature, both critical and supportive. See, e.g., Louis J. Hector, *Problems of the CAB and the Independent Regulatory Commissions*, 69 Yale L.J. 931 (1960); Carl A. Auerbach, *Some Thoughts on the Hector Memorandum,* 1960 Wis.L.Rev. 183; Philip Elman, *A Modest Proposal for Radical Reform*, 56 A.B.A. J. 1045 (1970); *Symposium on Federal Regulatory Agencies: A Response to the Ash Report*, 57 Va.L.Rev. 925 (1971); Emmette S. Redford, *The President and the Regulatory Commissions*, 44 Texas L.Rev. 288 (1965); HENRY FRIENDLY, THE FEDERAL ADMINISTRATIVE AGENCIES (1962); Carl McFarland, *Landis' Report: The Voice of One Crying in the Wilderness*, 47 Va.L.Rev. 373 (1961).

In response to the various reports, Congress began in the late 1930s to authorize presidents—subject to legislative veto—to implement "reorganization plans" for redistributing the functions of executive agencies and overhauling their structure. From the close of the second World War until April 1, 1973, Congress—with occasional lapses, none of which lasted more than two years—consistently renewed the reorganization authority, and between 1939 and 1973 it accepted 83 of the 105 reorganization plans submitted to it by six presidents. JAMES L. SUNDQUIST, THE DECLINE AND RESURGENCE OF CONGRESS 54 (1981). The Carter Administration continued the pattern of enthusiasm for presidential reorganization. After successfully urging Congress in 1977 to renew reauthorization authority for a three-year period, President Carter prepared 10 reorganization plans that gained Congress' acquiescence.

Many of these 93 reorganization plans were designed to strengthen the internal structure of agencies without adding much to the President's power of supervision, direction, or control. Yet the aim of presidential proposals was often also to alter the substantive agenda of agencies by giving certain functions a higher institutional profile, by submerging functions through the combining of offices, or by changing the policy making process through the institutionalization of some new pattern of management. Congress did not always go along. President Carter was unsuccessful, for example, in proposing to establish a Department of Natural Resources that would have absorbed the Interior

Department and included the Forest Service from the Agriculture Department and the National Oceanic and Atmospheric Administration from the Commerce Department. A likely policy consequence of the plan would have been to subject the ordinarily pro-development Forest Service to a different ethos of policy making in the ordinarily pro-preservation Interior Department. The impact would have been to upgrade conservationist tendencies in forest administration, just as creation of the EPA and the reassignment of the USDA's pesticide program added vigor to the control of toxics.

By the 1980s, commentators had begun to ask whether the reorganization authority process really served the interests of either elected branch. See, e.g., Louis Fisher and Ronald C. Moe, *Presidential Reorganization Authority: Is It Worth the Cost?*, 96 Pol.Sci.Q. 301 (Winter 1981–82). Congress reenacted reorganization authority only twice more, including a one-year reauthorization in 1980, and an even briefer reauthorization in late 1984. Reorganization Act Amendments of 1984, § 3(a), Pub.L.No. 98–614, 98 Stat. 3192, codified at 5 U.S.C. § 906.

The change in attitudes toward reorganization reflected at least three factors. First, in any post–1980 reenactment, Congress would have had to deal with *Chadha*'s invalidation of legislative vetoes. The 1984 Amendments authorized the President only to propose a reorganization plan that Congress, if it chose, could implement by statute under a fast-track procedure. The new act thus gave the President no opportunity to short-cut the legislative process to accomplish reorganization, and President Reagan never sought to use this authority. There would be little incentive for future presidents to seek it.

Second, during the Reagan presidency, Congress reclaimed the initiative over government organization. President Reagan had promised in 1980 to reduce the cabinet by eliminating two departments, Energy and Education. Not only did both survive his time in office, but the cabinet grew larger when Congress, with Reagan's explicit blessing, elevated the Veterans Administration to cabinet level status as the Department of Veterans Affairs.

Third, as all post-Carter administrations have discovered, there are far more direct ways to accomplish regulatory reform than the redistribution of regulatory functions among agencies. The Reagan and first Bush Administrations pioneered yet more ambitious attempts at presidential regulatory management, which are discussed in Section B, *infra*. The Clinton Administration proposed a thorough program of agency "reengineering" at the managerial level, much of which could be accomplished without additional legislative authority. AL GORE, FROM RED TAPE TO RESULTS: CREATING A GOVERNMENT THAT WORKS BETTER AND COSTS LESS—REPORT OF THE NATIONAL PERFORMANCE REVIEW (1993).

This does not mean that reorganization has ceased to be an important form of political response to perceived national needs. The attempt of President George W. Bush, in the wake of the September 11, 2001, attacks on New York City and Washington, D.C., to coordinate homeland security by executive order, Exec. Order No. 13228, 66 Fed. Reg. 51812 (Oct. 8, 2001), revealed just how weak a reed presidential command may be when not backed by congressional authority. Pursuant to the Bush order, Governor Tom Ridge was given authority to exhort, cajole, and perhaps beg for cooperation, but nothing more. Thus, after months of negotiation, Congress and President Bush finally agreed on a Homeland Security Act of 2002, Pub. L. No.107–296, 116 Stat. 2140, creating a new cabinet level domestic security department The new Department of Homeland Security would "have the mission of preventing terrorist attacks within the United States, reducing the United States' vulnerability to terrorism, minimizing the damages from attacks, and assisting in recovery from any attacks, should they occur." Homeland Security Act of 2002, H.R. Rept. No. 609 (Pt. I), 107th Cong., 2d Sess. 63 (2002). Toward these ends, Congress consolidated within the new department roughly 170,000 employees from 22 agencies that previously existed either independently or within larger administrative entities. The newly consolidated agencies include the Federal Emergency Management Agency (FEMA); the U.S. Secret Service; the U.S. Customs Service; the U.S. Coast Guard; the enforcement functions of the Immigration and Naturalization Service (INS); the Transportation Security Administration of the Department of Transportation; the Federal Protective Service (FPS) and the Federal Computer Incident Response Center of the General Services Administration (GSA); the National Infrastructure Protection Center, the National Domestic Preparedness Office, the Office for Domestic Preparedness, and the Domestic Emergency Support Teams of the Department of Justice (DOJ); the Critical Infrastructure Assurance Office of the Department of Commerce; and the National Communications System of the Department of Defense. Specific programs of the Departments of Agriculture, Energy, and Health and Human Services have also been absorbed into the new department.

So massive an undertaking plainly posed serious questions: Would the prospect of improved effectiveness through tighter coordination offset the costs to productivity from forcing so many units to reacclimate to new bureaucratic conditions and physical locations? (It is questionable, for example, whether those agencies long ago consolidated into the Departments of Transportation and of Energy have yet fully to overcome their identity conflicts.) Would shifting the emphasis of multi-function units towards homeland security diminish their effectiveness in fulfilling other functions. (Consider, in this respect, the boating safety, as opposed to security, functions of the Coast Guard.) Could even this degree of organizational consolidation produce well organized antiterrorist strategies given that key agencies—most notably, the Federal Bureau of Investigation and the intelligence agencies—remain under separate and historically turf-conscious management?

2. CONTROLLING CONGRESSIONAL ATTEMPTS TO APPOINT AND REMOVE ADMINISTRATORS

BUCKLEY v. VALEO

Supreme Court of the United States, 1976.
424 U.S. 1, 96 S.Ct. 612, 46 L.Ed.2d 659.

PER CURIAM.

These appeals present constitutional challenges to the key provisions of the Federal Election Campaign Act of 1971 (Act), and related provisions of the Internal Revenue Code of 1954, all as amended in 1974. * * *

* * * The statutes at issue summarized in broad terms, contain the following provisions: (a) individual political contributions are limited to $1,000 to any single candidate per election, with an overall annual limitation of $25,000 by any contributor; independent expenditures by individuals and groups "relative to a clearly identified candidate" are limited to $1,000 a year; campaign spending by candidates for various federal offices and spending for national conventions by political parties are subject to prescribed limits; (b) contributions and expenditures above certain threshold levels must be reported and publicly disclosed; (c) a system for public funding of Presidential campaign activities is established by Subtitle H of the Internal Revenue Code; and (d) a Federal Election Commission is established to administer and enforce the legislation.

* * *

The 1974 amendments to the Act create an eight-member Federal Election Commission (Commission) and vest in it primary and substantial responsibility for administering and enforcing the Act. The question * * * is whether, in view of the manner in which a majority of its members are appointed, the Commission may under the Constitution exercise the powers conferred upon it. We find it unnecessary to parse the complex statutory provisions in order to sketch the full sweep of the Commission's authority. It will suffice for present purposes to describe what appear to be representative examples of its various powers.

Chapter 14 of Title 2 makes the Commission the principal repository of the numerous reports and statements which are required by that chapter to be filed by those engaging in the regulated political activities. Its duties under § 438(a) with respect to these reports and statements include filing and indexing, making them available for public inspection, preservation, and auditing and field investigations. It is directed to "serve as a national clearinghouse for information in respect to the administration of elections."

Beyond these recordkeeping, disclosure, and investigative functions, however, the Commission is given extensive rulemaking and adjudicative powers. Its duty under § 438(a)(10) is "to prescribe suitable rules and regulations to carry out the provisions of * * * chapter [14]." Under § 437(d)(8) the Commission is empowered to make such rules "as are necessary to carry out the provisions of this Act." Section 437d(a)(9) authorizes it to "formulate general policy with respect to the administration of this Act" and enumerated sections of Title 18's Criminal Code, as to all of which provisions the Commission "has primary jurisdiction with respect to [their] civil enforcement." § 437c(b). The Commission is authorized under § 437f(a) to render advisory opinions with respect to activities possibly violating the Act, the Title 18 sections, or the campaign funding provisions of Title 26, the effect of which is that "[n]otwithstanding any other provision of law, any person with respect to whom an advisory opinion is rendered * * * who acts in good faith in accordance with the provisions and findings [thereof] shall be presumed to be in compliance with the [statutory provision] with respect to which such advisory opinion is rendered." In the course of administering the provisions for Presidential campaign financing, the Commission may authorize convention expenditures which exceed the statutory limits.

The Commission's enforcement power is both direct and wide ranging. It may institute a civil action for (i) injunctive or other relief against "any acts or practices which constitute or will constitute a violation of this Act"; (ii) declaratory or injunctive relief "as may be appropriate to implement or con[s]true any provisions" of Chapter 95 of Title 26, governing administration of funds for Presidential election campaigns and national party conventions; and (iii) "such injunctive relief as is appropriate to implement any provision" of Chapter 96 of Title 26, governing the payment of matching funds for Presidential primary campaigns. If after the Commission's post-disbursement audit of candidates receiving payments under Chapter 95 or 96 it finds an overpayment, it is empowered to seek repayment of all funds due the Secretary of the Treasury. In no respect do the foregoing civil actions require the concurrence of or participation by the Attorney General: conversely, the decision not to seek judicial relief in the above respects would appear to rest solely with the Commission. With respect to the referenced Title 18 sections, § 437g(a)(7) provides that if, after notice and opportunity for a hearing before it, the Commission finds an actual or threatened criminal violation, the Attorney General "upon request by the Commission * * * shall institute a civil action for relief." Finally, as "[a]dditional enforcement authority," § 456(a) authorizes the Commission, after notice and opportunity for hearing, to make "a finding that a person * * * while a candidate for Federal office, failed to file" a required report of contributions or expenditures. If that finding is made within the applicable limitations period for prosecutions, the candidate is thereby "disqualified from becoming a candidate in any future election for Federal office for a period of time beginning on the date of such finding and ending one year after the expiration of the term of the Federal office for which such person was a candidate."

The body in which this authority is reposed consists of eight members. The Secretary of the Senate and the Clerk of the House of

Representatives are *ex officio* members of the Commission without the right to vote. Two members are appointed by the President *pro tempore* of the Senate "upon the recommendations of the majority leader of the Senate and the minority leader of the Senate." Two more are to be appointed by the Speaker of the House of Representatives, likewise upon the recommendations of its respective majority and minority leaders. The remaining two members are appointed by the President. Each of the six voting members of the Commission must be confirmed by the majority of both Houses of Congress, and each of the three appointing authorities is forbidden to choose both of their appointees from the same political party.

* * *

The principle of separation of powers was not simply an abstract generalization in the minds of the Framers: it was woven into the document that they drafted in Philadelphia in the summer of 1787. Article I, § 1, declares: "All legislative Powers herein granted shall be vested in a Congress of the United States." Article II, § 1, vests the executive power "in a President of the United States of America," and Art. III, § 1, declares that "The judicial Power of the United States, shall be vested in one supreme Court, and in such inferior Courts as the Congress may from time to time ordain and establish." The further concern of the Framers of the Constitution with maintenance of the separation of powers is found in the so-called "Ineligibility" and "Incompatibility" Clauses contained in Art. I, § 6:

> "No Senator or Representative shall, during the Time for which he was elected, be appointed to any civil Office under the Authority of the United States, which shall have been created, or the Emoluments whereof shall have been increased during such time; and no Person holding any Office under the United States, shall be a Member of either House during his Continuance in Office."

It is in the context of these cognate provisions of the document that we must examine the language of Art. II, § 2, cl. 2. * * *

> "[The President] shall nominate, and by and with the Advice and Consent of the Senate, shall appoint Ambassadors, other public Ministers and Consuls, Judges of the Supreme Court, and all other Officers of the United States, whose Appointments are not herein otherwise provided for, and which shall be established by Law: but the Congress may by Law vest the Appointment of such inferior Officers, as they think proper, in the President alone, in the Courts of Law, or in the Heads of Departments."

* * * We think [the] fair import [of this language] is that any appointee exercising significant authority pursuant to the laws of the United States is an "Officer of the United States," and must, therefore, be appointed in the manner prescribed by § 2, cl. 2, of the Article. * * * [I]t is difficult to see how the members of the Commission may escape inclusion. If a postmaster first class, *Myers v. United States*,

and the clerk of a district court, *Ex parte Hennen*, 38 U.S. 230, 13 Pet. 230 (1839), are inferior officers of the United States within the meaning of the Appointments Clause, as they are, surely the Commissioners before us are at the very least such "inferior Officers" within the meaning of that Clause.[162]

Although two members of the Commission are initially selected by the President, his nominations are subject to confirmation not merely by the Senate, but by the House of Representatives as well. The remaining four voting members of the Commission are appointed by the President *pro tempore* of the Senate and by the Speaker of the House. While the second part of the Clause authorizes Congress to vest the appointment of the officers described in that part in "the Courts of Law, or in the Heads of Departments," neither the Speaker of the House nor the President *pro tempore* of the Senate comes within this language.

* * *

The Appointments Clause specifies the method of appointment only for "Officers of the United States" whose appointment is not "otherwise provided for" in the Constitution. But there is no provision of the Constitution remotely providing any alternative means for the selection of the members of the Commission or for anybody like them. Appellee Commission has argued, and the Court of Appeals agreed, that the Appointments Clause of Art. II should not be read to exclude the "inherent power of Congress" to appoint its own officers to perform functions necessary to that body as an institution. But there is no need to read the Appointments Clause contrary to its plain language in order to reach the result sought by the Court of Appeals. Article I, § 3, cl. 5, expressly authorizes the selection of the President *pro tempore* of the Senate, and § 2, cl. 5, of that Article provides for the selection of the Speaker of the House. Ranking nonmembers, such as the Clerk of the House of Representatives, are elected under the internal rules of each House and are designated by statute as "officers of the Congress." There is no occasion for us to decide whether any of these member officers are "Officers of the United States" whose "appointment" is otherwise provided for within the meaning of the Appointments Clause, since even if they were such officers their appointees would not be. Contrary to the fears expressed by the majority of the Court of Appeals, nothing in our holding with respect to Art. II, § 2, cl. 2, will deny to Congress "all power to appoint its own inferior officers to carry out appropriate legislative functions."

162. "*Officers of the United States*" does not include all employees of the United States, but there is no claim made that the Commissioners are employees of the United States rather than officers. Employees are lesser functionaries subordinate to officers of the United States, see *Auffmordt v. Hedden*, 137 U.S. 310, 327 (1890); *United States v. Germaine*, 99 U.S. 508 (1879), whereas the Commissioners, appointed for a statutory term, are not subject to the control or direction of any other executive, judicial, or legislative authority.

* * *

The trilogy of cases from this Court dealing with the constitutional authority of Congress to circumscribe the President's power to *remove* officers of the United States is entirely consistent with this conclusion. In *Myers v. United States*, the Court held that Congress could not by statute divest the President of the power to remove an officer in the Executive Branch whom he was initially authorized to appoint. In explaining its reasoning in that case, the Court said:

> "The vesting of the executive power in the President was essentially a grant of the power to execute the laws. But the President alone and unaided could not execute the laws. He must execute them by the assistance of subordinates. * * * As he is charged specifically to take care that they be faithfully executed, the reasonable implication, even in the absence of express words, was that as part of his executive power he should select those who were to act for him under his direction in the execution of the laws.
>
> * * *
>
> "Our conclusion on the merits, sustained by the arguments before stated, is that Article II grants to the President the executive power of the Government, i.e., the general administrative control of those executing the laws, including the power of appointment and removal of executive officers—a conclusion confirmed by his obligation to take care that the laws be faithfully executed. * * *"

In the later case of *Humphrey's Executor*, where it was held that Congress could circumscribe the President's power to remove members of independent regulatory agencies, the Court was careful to note that it was dealing with an agency intended to be independent of executive authority "*except in its selection*," 295 U.S., at 625 (emphasis in original). *Wiener v. United States*, 357 U.S. 349 (1958), which applied the holding in *Humphrey's Executor* to a member of the War Claims Commission, did not question in any respect that members of independent agencies are not independent of the Executive with respect to their appointments.

Thus, on the assumption that all of the powers granted in the statute may be exercised by an agency whose members have been appointed in accordance with the Appointments Clause, the ultimate question is which, if any, of those powers may be exercised by the present voting Commissioners, none of whom was appointed as provided by that Clause. Our previous description of the statutory provisions disclosed that the Commission's powers fall generally into three categories: functions relating to the flow of necessary information—receipt, dissemination, and investigation; functions with respect to the Commission's task of fleshing out the statute—rulemaking and advisory opinions; and functions necessary to ensure compliance with the statute and rules—informal procedures, administrative determinations and hearings, and civil suits.

Insofar as the powers confided in the Commission are essentially of an investigative and informative nature, falling in the same general category as those powers which Congress might delegate to one of its own committees, there can be no question that the Commission as presently constituted may exercise them. * * *

But when we go beyond this type of authority to the more substantial powers exercised by the Commission, we reach a different result. The Commission's enforcement power, exemplified by its discretionary power to seek judicial relief, is authority that cannot possibly be regarded as merely in aid of the legislative function of Congress. A lawsuit is the ultimate remedy for a breach of the law, and it is to the President, and not to the Congress, that the Constitution entrusts the responsibility to "take Care that the Laws be faithfully executed." Art. II, § 3.

Congress may undoubtedly under the Necessary and Proper Clause create "offices" in the generic sense and provide such method of appointment to those "offices" as it chooses. But Congress' power under that Clause is inevitably bounded by the express language of Art. II, § 2, cl. 2, and unless the method it provides comports with the latter, the holders of those offices will not be "Officers of the United States." They may, therefore, properly perform duties only in aid of those functions that Congress may carry out by itself, or in an area sufficiently removed from the administration and enforcement of the public law as to permit their being performed by persons not "Officers of the United States." * * *

We hold that these provisions of the Act, vesting in the Commission primary responsibility for conducting civil litigation in the courts of the United States for vindicating public rights, violate Art. II, § 2, cl. 2, of the Constitution. Such functions may be discharged only by persons who are "Officers of the United States" within the language of that section.

All aspects of the Act are brought within the Commission's broad administrative powers: rulemaking, advisory opinions, and determinations of eligibility for funds and even for federal elective office itself. These functions, exercised free from day-to-day supervision of either Congress or the Executive Branch, are more legislative and judicial in nature than are the Commission's enforcement powers, and are of kinds usually performed by independent regulatory agencies or by some department in the Executive Branch under the direction of an Act of Congress. Congress viewed these broad powers as essential to effective and impartial administration of the entire substantive framework of the Act. Yet each of these functions also represents the performance of a significant governmental duty exercised pursuant to a public law. While the President may not insist that such functions be delegated to an appointee of his removable at will, *Humphrey's Executor v. United States*, none of them operates merely in aid of congressional authority to legislate or is sufficiently removed from the administration and enforcement of public law to allow it to be performed by the present Commission. These administrative functions may therefore be exercised only by persons who are "Officers of the United States." * * *

Note

And We Mean *It!* Congress' post-*Buckley* repair of the Federal Election Commission provided for the appointment by the House and Senate of two nonvoting members. The D.C. Circuit held these appointments also intruded congressional influence impermissibly into the administrative process. *Federal Election Commission v. NRA Political Victory Fund*, 6 F.3d 821 (D.C.Cir. 1993), *petition for cert. dismissed for lack of jurisdiction*, 513 U.S. 88 (1994).

General Statutes Constraining Executive Control Over Personnel

Congress' attempts, as in the original Federal Election Campaign Act, to vest administrative appointment powers in itself by no means exhaust the range of legislation that impinges, directly or indirectly, on the President's power of appointment. Even with respect to the heads of departments—as to whom the President enjoys explicit constitutional powers of selection—the range of available candidates will likely be narrowed by the salary scale that Congress enacts, 5 U.S.C. § 5301 et seq., by statutory requirements for financial disclosure by federal officials, 5 U.S.C. app. 4 § 101 et seq., and by ethics legislation, discussed in Chapter 2, that limits the post-termination economic activities of former government employees, 18 U.S.C. § 207. A more direct set of limitations arises from statutes that dictate the qualifications or characteristics of particular appointees, including provisions that limit the number of agency members who may belong to the same political party, e.g., 15 U.S.C. § 41 (no more than three FTC members may belong to the same party).

The Supreme Court has at least hinted that, at some point, statutes constraining executive discretion in appointments even indirectly could unconstitutionally abridge the President's authority regarding appointments. For example, in *Public Citizen v. U.S. Department of Justice*, 491 U.S. 440 (1989), a Ralph Nader-led public interest group sought access under the Federal Advisory Committee Act (FACA), 5 U.S.C. app. 2 § 1 et seq., to deliberations of the American Bar Association Standing Committee on the Federal Judiciary. That committee provides advice to the Justice Department on potential judicial nominees—including presidential nominees to the Supreme Court. The Act, if applicable, would have required most committee meetings and records to be open to the public.

The majority avoided a separation of powers controversy by holding that the FACA did not apply to the ABA committee. To sustain its conclusion, the majority had to resort to legislative history to avoid the strong contrary implications of the FACA's categorical language, which covers

> any committee * * * utilized by one or more agencies, in the interest of obtaining advice or recommendations for the President or one or more agencies or officers of the federal Government. * * *

§ 3(2)(C). Although the legislative history was fairly persuasive that the language of the Act did not fairly convey Congress' intent, the Court also stressed the importance of construing the FACA to avoid "formidable constitutional difficulties." Such difficulties would have arisen had the Court found that Congress indeed had attempted to control the processes by which the President secures advice concerning the exercise of constitutionally vested appointments powers.

Justice Kennedy, writing also for Chief Justice Rehnquist and Justice O'Connor, would have held that the Act, by its plain terms, did apply and, accordingly, unconstitutionally abridged the President's power to nominate federal judges. The Constitution, according to Justice Kennedy, "commits the power (of judicial nomination) to the exclusive control of the President," and any "direct and real interference" by Congress "with the President's exclusive responsibility" is categorically impermissible. Public Citizen, he noted, failed to contest district court findings that

> at minimum, * * * the application of FACA to the ABA would potentially inhibit the President's freedom to investigate, to be informed, to evaluate, and to consult during the nomination process.

Because the Constitution explicitly commits the appointment power to the President, Justice Kennedy would not have entertained any balancing test to determine if such an intrusion was outweighed by the Act's vindication of some purpose within Congress' power to pursue. Justice Scalia did not participate in the case.

Association of American Physicians and Surgeons v. Clinton, 997 F.2d 898 (D.C.Cir.1993), was a similar suit challenging the confidential deliberations of President Clinton's Task Force on National Health Care Reform. The plaintiffs' central claim was that the Task Force was subject to the open meeting requirements of the Federal Advisory Committee Act (FACA) because one of its leading participants was Hillary Rodham Clinton, who was not a federal employee. Writing for two members of the Court of Appeals, Judge Silberman expressed sympathy for the Government's argument that the President's spouse was widely recognized, including by Congress, as an official assistant to the President and thus should be considered a "full-time officer or employee" under FACA. But he was not entirely convinced:

> Indeed, the government is uncomfortable at having to choose whether Mrs. Clinton should be thought of as an officer or employee. * * * Mrs. Clinton has not in any sense been appointed or elected to office, and, assuming she is an officer under Title I, due to the duties delegated to her under 3 U.S.C. § 105(e), how, one might ask, could she be removed?

Ultimately, however, Silberman was persuaded to accept the Government's argument in order to avoid a construction that would raise serious doubts about the constitutionality of the FACA. Were the Act interpreted to preclude private consultations between the President and the President's spouse, or convert any gathering of employees the spouse joined into an open advisory committee, it could be thought to interfere with the President's constitutionally conferred executive functions. Judge Buckley concurred in the judgment, though he found the majority's construction of the FACA indefensible. He would have held the Act unconstitutional as applied.

By far the greatest constraint that Congress places on the executive branch's capacity to use the appointment process as a vehicle for the coordination of administrative policy making, however, is the complex of statutes that establish the civil service system. Indeed, not only do federal civil service laws limit the executive's appointment power, but they create a workforce now comprising millions of employees who, by statute, may be removed only for "such cause as will promote the efficiency of the service," 5 U.S.C. § 7513(a).

The constitutionality of such a system apparently rests on a distinction recognized by the Supreme Court between "Officers of the United States," whose appointment is governed by Article II, and "employees," whom Congress may regulate:

> "Officers of the United States" does not include all employees of the United States. * * * Employees are lesser functionaries subordinate to officers of the United States, see *Auffmordt v. Hedden*, 137 U.S. 310 (1890); *United States v. Germaine*, 99 U.S. 508 (1879). * * *

Buckley v. Valeo, 424 U.S. at 126 n.162. The Court, unfortunately, has neither articulated the theory behind this distinction, nor offered much guidance on the distinction between those "lesser functionaries" who are "employees" and those who retain the constitutional status of "inferior officers."

The Pendleton (or Civil Service) Act of 1883, 22 Stat. 403, now codified at 5 U.S.C. §§ 1101–1105, was an early victory for the Progressive Movement. It initiated the development of a complex framework of legal restrictions designed both to assure the competence and protect the integrity of executive branch officials and employees of the independent commissions. Conceived as a response to perceived abuses, this landmark legislation enshrined the basic principles of merit selection and relative security of tenure for subordinate government officials. The Act also created the U.S. Civil Service Commission, which for more than 80 years oversaw the employment practices of the federal civilian establishment. For general historical background on the events leading up to the passage of the Pendleton Act, see STEPHEN SKOWRONEK, BUILDING A NEW AMERICAN STATE 47–68 (1982), and sources cited therein. On the appointment and removal policies of presidents up to 1829, see DAVID H. ROSENBLOOM, FEDERAL SERVICE AND THE CONSTITUTION 19–46 (1971).

The relatively limited protection initially afforded subordinate government officials by the terms of the Pendleton Act is understandable when viewed in light of the apparently widespread contemporary concern that the attempt (via introduction of the new merit system) to place limitations or conditions upon the appointment power amounted to a congressional intrusion upon executive authority. Indeed, although subsequently driven underground, constitutional doubts about the CSC's role were never decisively laid to rest. The theory that sustains the constitutionality of those civil service laws bearing on the selection process seems to be that while "the officer to whom the appointing power is given retains the discretion which it was intended he should exercise in making appointments, * * * as an aid to his exercise of that power, another body may be given the power to determine the qualifications necessary for the position under consideration." Oliver Field, as quoted in Paul P. Van Riper, History of the United States Civil Service 107 (1958). In any event, owing much no doubt to these constitutional scruples, Congress determined not to go too far in making the provisions of the Pendleton Act mandatory upon the President. The original act placed only ten per cent of the 140,000–odd positions in the federal public service under the merit system to form the classified civil service, the remaining "unclassified" positions to be brought under the new regime by executive order when and if the President saw fit.

The Pendleton Act's compromise on the power to remove reflected even greater solicitude for the basic principles laid down in the "decision of 1789." Indeed, as one historian has noted, "That the removal power of the President was left largely untouched was the outstanding difference between pre-Civil War attempts at [civil service] reform and the Act of 1883." *Id.* at 102. To be sure, the reformers were no less concerned than previously to restrain abuses in the exercise of the removal power, but the constitutional crisis precipitated by the Tenure of Office Act of 1867 (the violation of which provided one ground for President Andrew Johnson's impeachment) counseled against any further attempts to assert direct legislative control over presidential authority in this context. Hence, while provisions prohibiting removals of classified civil servants for failure to contribute money or to render service for political purposes were eventually included in the Pendleton Act, principal emphasis was placed on the regulation of the selection process. Presumably, if appointments had to be made on a merit basis, the temptation for improper removals would be correspondingly diminished.

Though the Pendleton Act was effective for a time in preventing widespread removals from merit positions—during the first sixteen months of the Cleveland Administration, the turnover rate for the 5,000–odd classified positions stood at 6.5 per cent, as against 68 per cent for unclassified positions and 90 per cent for "presidential offices" (i.e. those whose appointments were subject to the Senate's advice and consent)—events were soon to disclose the limitations of the original system in preventing arbitrary dismissals. While the CSC had been directed to prepare rules to implement the various prohibitions against the political manipulation and/or removal of competitive employees, the failure of the Act to attach criminal penalties for their violation (with the exception of the provisions prohibiting political assessments), and the fact that prosecution of the offenders was left to the discretion of the chief executive, left the Commission all but powerless with respect to enforcement. By the mid–1890s, as evidence accumulated that neither purely arbitrary removals nor dismissals on the basis of an individual civil servant's political and religious opinions or affiliations had really been stymied, reform leader Carl Schurz and others disowned their initial "sanguine expectation" that the abusive practices of the past would cease with the introduction of the competitive system. ROSENBLOOM, *supra*, at 88. Calls for corrective action, specifically for the introduction of procedural safeguards, were issued with increasing regularity.

These calls were first answered when, on July 27, 1897, President McKinley provided by executive order that "no removal shall be made from any position subject to competitive examination except for just cause and upon written charges filed with the head of the Department, or other appointing officer, and of which the accused shall have full notice and an opportunity to make a defense." 18 CSC Annual Report 282 (1901). This rule went through several modifications in the years that followed, but in essence, it was incorporated into law by the Lloyd–LaFollette Act of August 24, 1912 (37 Stat. 555), at which time the current locution, "except for such cause as will promote the efficiency of the service," was adopted. ("Efficiency of the service," while somewhat vague, was given more determinate meaning by the law's provision for rating efficiency. See 37 Stat. 413 (August 23, 1912).)

Beginning with the administration of President Theodore Roosevelt (himself a former Civil Service Commissioner), the substantive supervisory authority of the Commission in dealing with merit employees was fortified by a series of executive orders, and steps were taken to ensure that the CSC would have adequate institutional resources to enforce a host of new rules (especially those having to do with "neutrality") regulating the nonpartisan realm of the civil service. The efforts of Presidents Roosevelt and Taft to build a strong, stable, and professional arm of civil administration under executive control nevertheless provoked considerable controversy, because the adoption of the Lloyd–LaFollette Act had been prompted by Congress' desire to assert its role "as an equal and alternative ear for all administrative interests." On the political struggles in this context during the period 1900–1920, see SKOWRONEK, *supra*, at 177–211.

Civil service coverage was greatly expanded, albeit in halting and uneven fashion, by executive order as presidents exercised the discretionary authority granted them under the Pendleton Act. By 1920, over 70 per cent of the executive civil service (then totalling roughly 560,000) was under the merit system. *Id.* at 210. Since 1947, by which time the civil service numbered some two million, the figure has been over 80 per cent. ROSENBLOOM, *supra*, at 83. The removal provisions of the Lloyd–LaFollette Act remained in effect throughout this period, and the protections accorded classified individuals against arbitrary dismissal were augmented by additional procedural safeguards, including rights to a hearing and representation. These provisions were enforced through an elaborate system operated by the CSC for adjudicating disciplinary actions against civil servants who had completed probationary service.

See, e.g., Richard A. Merrill, *Procedures for Adverse Action Against Federal Employees*, 59 Va.L.Rev. 196 (1973).

If by mid-century the principle of protection against arbitrary removal for classified civil servants was firmly in place, traditional concerns about political manipulation of the civil service as a whole had by no means been laid to rest. The basic issues of presidential and congressional authority for public personnel administration which were left unsettled by the Pendleton Act had never been resolved. In the midst of continuing debate about what central authority, if any, should govern the system as a whole and over how responsibility for protecting it from political partisanship should be organized, the civil service remained "a precarious idea in an ambiguous organizational structure." Hugh Heclo, A Government of Strangers 23 (1977).

After four decades of truncated efforts at reform, far-reaching changes in the apparatus inherited from the nineteenth century were introduced in 1978, when President Carter persuaded Congress to enact the Civil Service Reform Act, Pub.L.No. 95–454, 92 Stat. 1111. The 1978 Act divided the CSC into two units, a presidential agency to oversee civil service policies, the Office of Personnel Management, 5 U.S.C. §§ 1101–1105, and a separate unit to police the civil service rules, the independent Merit Systems Protection Board, 5 U.S.C. §§ 1201–1205.

One of the law's chief objectives was also to make it easier for dedicated managers to remove employees who performed poorly. Under the new ground rules, an agency need sustain an employee's removal for incompetence only by "substantial evidence," rather than a preponderance. 5 U.S.C. § 7701(c)(1). The Act further created a separate classification scheme (the Senior Executive Service, or "SES") for high-level "employees" and low-level "officers" that facilitates both personnel transfers and the use of financial incentives to encourage performance. However, while the legislation generally strengthened the hand of government managers, it also afforded, as had the Ethics in Government Act, Pub.L.No. 95–521, 92 Stat. 1824 (1978) (codified at 5 U.S.C. app. 4), of the same year special protection for civil servants who report improprieties by their supervisors or agencies—"whistleblowers" in the Washington vernacular. 5 U.S.C. § 2301(b)(9). The Act's broad language prohibits a supervisor from taking, or failing to take, personnel action, i.e., disciplining or failing to reward, against an employee who discloses—to the press, Congress, or others—unclassified information which the employee "reasonably believes evidences a violation of law, rule, or regulation or mismanagement, a gross waste of funds, an abuse of authority, or a substantial and specific danger to public health and safety. * * * " For a sympathetic analysis of this legislation, see Robert G. Vaughn, *Statutory Protection of Whistleblowers in the Federal Executive Branch*, 1982 U.Ill.L.Rev. 615. The opposing view—that the Act is unlikely to protect the righteous and is subject to abuse by the self-righteous—is advanced in Bruce D. Fisher, *The Whistleblower Protection Act of 1989: A False Hope for Whistleblowers*, 43 Rutgers L.Rev. 355 (1991).

The tension between management flexibility and workers' rights was a major issue in the debate over the Homeland Security Act of 2002, discussed above. Section 841 of the Homeland Security Act, to be codified at 5 U.S.C. § 9701, authorizes the Secretary of Homeland Security, in concert with the Director of the Office of Personnel Management, to "establish" and "adjust" a "human resources management system for some or all of the organizational units" of the Department that is to be "flexible" and "contemporary," while holding in place certain of the protections ordinarily extended to classified workers under the civil service system. Congressional dissenters charged that the "flexibility" would essentially authorize the Secretary to limit the rights Department employees enjoyed in the units that employed them prior to consolidation. Among the rights at stake were a guarantee against pay reduction, the right to appeal disciplinary actions to the Merit Systems Protection Board (MSPB), and the protections of the employee classification system and statutory provisions regarding salary. The Act also expanded the President's authority to waive employees' collective bargaining rights in the new Department. Supporters insisted that the potential expansion of managerial control over the civil service was essential to the effective discharge of the new department's functions. Critics asserted that the changes were but the leading edge of a general campaign to undermine longstanding protections against supervisory abuses.

BOWSHER v. SYNAR

Supreme Court of the United States, 1986.
478 U.S. 714, 106 S.Ct. 3181, 92 L.Ed.2d 583.

CHIEF JUSTICE BURGER delivered the opinion of the Court.

The question presented by these appeals is whether the assignment by Congress to the Comptroller General of the United States of certain functions under the Balanced Budget and Emergency Deficit Control Act of 1985 violates the doctrine of separation of powers.

I

On December 12, 1985, the President signed into law the Balanced Budget and Emergency Deficit Control Act of 1985, popularly known as the "Gramm–Rudman–Hollings Act." The purpose of the Act is to eliminate the federal budget deficit. To that end, the Act sets a "maximum deficit amount" for federal spending for each of fiscal years 1986 through 1991. * * * If in any fiscal year the federal budget deficit exceeds the maximum deficit amount by more than a specified sum, the Act requires across-the-board cuts in federal spending to reach the targeted deficit level, with half of the cuts made to defense programs and the other half made to non-defense programs. The Act exempts certain priority programs from these cuts.

These "automatic" reductions are accomplished through a rather complicated procedure, spelled out in § 251, the so-called "reporting provisions" of the Act. Each year, the Directors of the Office of Management and Budget (OMB) and the Congressional Budget Office (CBO) independently estimate the amount of the federal budget deficit for the upcoming fiscal year. If that deficit exceeds the maximum targeted deficit amount for that fiscal year by more than a specified amount, the Directors of OMB and CBO independently calculate, on a program-by-program basis, the budget reductions necessary to ensure that the deficit does not exceed the maximum deficit amount. The Act then requires the Directors to report jointly their deficit estimates and budget reduction calculations to the Comptroller General.

The Comptroller General, after reviewing the Directors' reports, then reports his conclusions to the President. The President in turn must issue a "sequestration" order mandating the spending reductions specified by the Comptroller General. There follows a period during which Congress may by legislation reduce spending to obviate, in whole or in part, the need for the sequestration order. If such reductions are not enacted, the sequestration order becomes effective and the spending reductions included in that order are made.

Anticipating constitutional challenge to these procedures, the Act also contains a "fallback" deficit reduction process to take effect "[i]n the event that any of the reporting procedures described in section 251 are invalidated." Under these provisions, the report prepared by the Directors of OMB and the CBO is submitted directly to a specially-created Temporary Joint Committee on Deficit Reduction, which must report in five days to both Houses a joint resolution setting forth the content of the Directors' report. Congress then must vote on the resolution under special rules, which render amendments out of order. If the resolution is passed and signed by the President, it then serves as the basis for a Presidential sequestration order.

Within hours of the President's signing of the Act,[1] Congressman Synar, who had voted against the Act, filed a complaint seeking declaratory relief that the Act was unconstitutional. Eleven other Members later joined Congressman Synar's suit. A virtually identical lawsuit was also filed by the National Treasury Employees Union. The Union alleged that its members had been injured as a result of the Act's automatic spending reduction provisions, which have suspended certain cost-of-living benefit increases to the Union's members.

A three-judge District Court, appointed pursuant to 2 U.S.C. § 992(a)(5) (Supp.1986), invalidated the reporting provisions. *Synar v. United States*, 626 F.Supp. 1374 (D.D.C.1986) (Scalia, Johnson, Gasch, JJ.). * * *

Although the District Court concluded that the Act survived a delegation doctrine challenge, it held that the role of the Comptroller General in the deficit reduction process violated the constitutionally imposed separation of powers. * * *

1. In his signing statement, the President expressed his view that the Act was constitutionally defective because of the Comptroller General's ability to exercise supervisory authority over the President.

We affirm.

[Part II of the majority opinion finds, in one paragraph, that the union plaintiffs clearly have standing and that the standing of the other litigants need not, therefore, be resolved.]

III

* * *

The Constitution does not contemplate an active role for Congress in the supervision of officers charged with the execution of the laws it enacts. The President appoints "Officers of the United States" with the "Advice and Consent of the Senate. * * * " Article II, § 2. Once the appointment has been made and confirmed, however, the Constitution explicitly provides for removal of Officers of the United States by Congress only upon impeachment by the House of Representatives and conviction by the Senate. An impeachment by the House and trial by the Senate can rest only on "Treason, Bribery or other high Crimes and Misdemeanors." Article II, § 4. A direct congressional role in the removal of officers charged with the execution of the laws beyond this limited one is inconsistent with separation of powers. * * *

[W]e conclude that Congress cannot reserve for itself the power of removal of an officer charged with the execution of the laws except by impeachment.[4] To permit the execution of the laws to be vested in an officer answerable only to Congress would, in practical terms, reserve in Congress control over the execution of the laws. As the District Court observed, "Once an officer is appointed, it is only the authority that can remove him, and not the authority that appointed him, that he must fear and, in the performance of his functions, obey." 626 F.Supp., at 1401. The structure of the Constitution does not permit Congress to execute the laws; it follows that Congress cannot grant to an officer under its control what it does not possess.

Our decision in *INS v. Chadha*, 462 U.S. 919 (1983), supports this conclusion. * * *

To permit an officer controlled by Congress to execute the laws would be, in essence, to permit a congressional veto. Congress could simply remove, or threaten to remove, an officer for executing the laws in any fashion found to be unsatisfactory to Congress. This kind of

4. Appellants therefore are wide of the mark in arguing that an affirmance in this case requires casting doubt on the status of "independent" agencies because no issues involving such agencies are presented here. The statutes establishing independent agencies typically specify either that the agency members are removable by the President for specified causes, see, e.g., 15 U.S.C. § 41 (members of the Federal Trade Commission may be removed by the President "for inefficiency, neglect of duty, or malfeasance in office"), or else do not specify a removal procedure, see, e.g., 2 U.S.C. § 437c (Federal Election Commission). This case involves nothing like these statutes, but rather a statute that provides for direct Congressional involvement over the decision to remove the Comptroller General. Appellants have referred us to no independent agency whose members are removable by the Congress for certain causes short of impeachable offenses, as is the Comptroller General.

congressional control over the execution of the laws, *Chadha* makes clear, is constitutionally impermissible.

The dangers of congressional usurpation of Executive Branch functions have long been recognized. "[T]he debates of the Constitutional Convention, and the Federalist Papers, are replete with expressions of fear that the Legislative Branch of the National Government will aggrandize itself at the expense of the other two branches." *Buckley v. Valeo*, 424 U.S. 1, 129 (1976). Indeed, we also have observed only recently that "[t]he hydraulic pressure inherent within each of the separate Branches to exceed the outer limits of its power, even to accomplish desirable objectives, must be resisted." *Chadha*, 462 U.S., at 951. With these principles in mind, we turn to consideration of whether the Comptroller General is controlled by Congress.

IV

Appellants urge that the Comptroller General performs his duties independently and is not subservient to Congress. We agree with the District Court that this contention does not bear close scrutiny.

The critical factor lies in the provisions of the statute defining the Comptroller General's office relating to removability.[5] Although the Comptroller General is nominated by the President from a list of three individuals recommended by the Speaker of the House of Representatives and the President pro tempore of the Senate, see 31 U.S.C. § 703(a)(2),[6] and confirmed by the Senate, he is removable only at the initiative of Congress. He may be removed not only by impeachment but also by Joint Resolution of Congress "at any time" resting on any one of the following bases:

"(i) permanent disability;

"(ii) inefficiency;

"(iii) neglect of duty;

"(iv) malfeasance; or

"(v) a felony or conduct involving moral turpitude."

31 U.S.C. § 703(e)(1).[7]

5. We reject appellants' argument that consideration of the effect of a removal provision is not "ripe" until that provision is actually used. As the District Court concluded, "it is the Comptroller General's presumed desire to avoid removal by pleasing Congress, which creates the here-and-now subservience to another branch that raises separation-of-powers problems." The Impeachment Clause of the Constitution can hardly be thought to be undermined because of non-use.

6. Congress adopted this provision in 1980 because of "the special interest of both Houses in the choice of an individual whose primary function is to provide assistance to Congress." S.Rep. 96–570, 96th Cong., 2d Sess., 10 (1980).

7. Although the President could veto such a joint resolution, the veto could be overridden by a two-thirds vote of both Houses of Congress. Thus, the Comptroller General could be removed in the face of Presidential opposition. Like the District Court, we therefore read the removal provision as authorizing removal by Congress alone.

This provision was included, as one Congressman explained in urging passage of the Act, because Congress "felt that [the Comptroller General] should be brought under the sole control of Congress, so that Congress at the moment when it found he was inefficient and was not carrying on the duties of his office as he should and as the Congress expected, could remove him without the long, tedious process of a trial by impeachment." * * *

* * * [T]he dissent's assessment of the statute fails to recognize the breadth of the grounds for removal. The statute permits removal for "inefficiency," "neglect of duty," or "malfeasance." These terms are very broad and, as interpreted by Congress, could sustain removal of a Comptroller General for any number of actual or perceived transgressions of the legislative will. * * *

We need not decide whether that "inefficiency" or "malfeasance" are terms as broad as "maladministration" in order to reject the dissent's position that removing the Comptroller General requires "a feat of bipartisanship more difficult than that required to impeach and convict." Surely no one would seriously suggest that judicial independence would be strengthened by allowing removal of federal judges only by a joint resolution finding "inefficiency," "neglect of duty," or "malfeasance."

Justice White, however, assures us that "[r]ealistic consideration" of the "practical result of the removal provision" reveals that the Comptroller General is unlikely to be removed by Congress. The separated powers of our government can not be permitted to turn on judicial assessment of whether an officer exercising executive power is on good terms with Congress. The Framers recognized that, in the long term, structural protections against abuse of power were critical to preserving liberty. In constitutional terms, the removal powers over the Comptroller General's office dictate that he will be subservient to Congress.

This much said, we must also add that the dissent is simply in error to suggest that the political realities reveal that the Comptroller General is free from influence by Congress. The Comptroller General heads the General Accounting Office, "an instrumentality of the United States Government independent of the executive departments," 31 U.S.C. § 702(a), which was created by Congress in 1921 as part of the Budget and Accounting Act of 1921. Congress created the office because it believed that it "needed an officer, responsible to it alone, to check upon the application of public funds in accordance with appropriations." H. Mansfield, The Comptroller General: A Study in the Law and Practice of Financial Administration 65 (1939). * * *

V

The primary responsibility of the Comptroller General under the instant Act is the preparation of a "report." This report must contain detailed estimates of projected federal revenues and expenditures. The report must also specify the reductions, if any, necessary to reduce the deficit to the target for the appropriate fiscal year. The reductions must be set forth on a program-by-program basis.

In preparing the report, the Comptroller General is to have "due regard" for the estimates and reductions set forth in a joint report submitted to him by the Director of CBO and the Director of OMB, the President's fiscal and budgetary advisor. However, the Act plainly contemplates that the Comptroller General will exercise his independent judgment and evaluation with respect to those estimates. The Act also provides that the Comptroller General's report "shall explain fully any differences between the contents of such report and the report of the Directors." § 251(b)(2).

Appellants suggest that the duties assigned to the Comptroller General in the Act are essentially ministerial and mechanical so that their performance does not constitute "execution of the law" in a meaningful sense. On the contrary, we view these functions as plainly entailing execution of the law in constitutional terms. Interpreting a law enacted by Congress to implement the legislative mandate is the very essence of "execution" of the law. Under § 251, the Comptroller General must exercise judgment concerning facts that affect the application of the Act. He must also interpret the provisions of the Act to determine precisely what budgetary calculations are required. Decisions of that kind are typically made by officers charged with executing a statute.

The executive nature of the Comptroller General's functions under the Act is revealed in § 252(a)(3) which gives the Comptroller General the ultimate authority to determine the budget cuts to be made. Indeed, the Comptroller General commands the President himself to carry out, without the slightest variation (with exceptions not relevant to the constitutional issues presented), the directive of the Comptroller General as to the budget reductions:

> "The [presidential] order *must provide* for reductions in the manner specified in section 251(a)(3), *must incorporate* the provisions of the [Comptroller General's] report submitted under section 251(b), and *must be consistent with such report in all respects*. The President *may not modify or recalculate any of the estimates, determinations, specifications, bases, amounts, or percentages* set forth in the report submitted under section 251(b) in determining the reductions to be specified in the order with respect to programs, projects, and activities, or with respect to budget activities, within an account. * * *" § 252(a)(3) (emphasis added).

See also § 251(d)(3)(A).

Congress of course initially determined the content of the Balanced Budget and Emergency Deficit Control Act; and undoubtedly the content of the Act determines the nature of the executive duty. However, as *Chadha* makes clear, once Congress makes its choice in enacting legislation, its participation ends. Congress can thereafter control the execution of its enactment only indirectly—by passing new legislation. *Chadha*, 462 U.S., at 958. By placing the responsibility for execution of the

Balanced Budget and Emergency Deficit Control Act in the hands of an officer who is subject to removal only by itself, Congress in effect has retained control over the execution of the Act and has intruded into the executive function. The Constitution does not permit such intrusion. * * *

Our judgment is stayed for a period not to exceed 60 days to permit Congress to implement the fallback provisions.

JUSTICE STEVENS, with whom JUSTICE MARSHALL joins, concurring in the judgment.

* * * I agree with the Court that the "Gramm–Rudman–Hollings" Act contains a constitutional infirmity so severe that the flawed provision may not stand. * * * I am convinced that the Comptroller General must be characterized as an agent of Congress because of his longstanding statutory responsibilities; that the powers assigned to him under the Gramm–Rudman–Hollings Act require him to make policy that will bind the Nation; and that, when Congress, or a component or an agent of Congress, seeks to make policy that will bind the Nation, it must follow the procedures mandated by Article I of the Constitution—through passage by both Houses and presentment to the President. * * *

I

The fact that Congress retained for itself the power to remove the Comptroller General is important evidence supporting the conclusion that he is a member of the Legislative Branch of the Government. Unlike the Court, however, I am not persuaded that the congressional removal power is either a necessary, or a sufficient, basis for concluding that his statutory assignment is invalid.

As Justice White explains, Congress does not have the power to remove the Comptroller General at will, or because of disagreement with any policy determination that he may be required to make in the administration of this, or any other, Act. * * *

The notion that the removal power at issue here automatically creates some kind of "here-and-now subservience" of the Comptroller General to Congress is belied by history. There is no evidence that Congress has ever removed, or threatened to remove, the Comptroller General for reasons of policy. Moreover, the President has long possessed a comparable power to remove members of the Federal Trade Commission, yet it is universally accepted that they are independent of, rather than subservient to, the President in performing their official duties. * * *

II

In assessing the role of the Comptroller General, it is appropriate to consider his already existing statutory responsibilities. Those responsibilities leave little doubt that one of the identifying characteristics of the Comptroller General is his statutorily required relationship to the Legislative Branch. * * *

The Comptroller General's current statutory responsibilities on behalf of Congress are fully consistent with the historic conception of the Comptroller General's office. The statute that created the Comptroller General's office—the Budget and Accounting Act of 1921—provided that four of the five statutory responsibilities given to the Comptroller General be exercised on behalf of Congress, three of them exclusively so. On at least three occasions since 1921, moreover, in considering the structure of government, Congress has defined the Comptroller General as being a part of the Legislative Branch. In the Reorganization Act of 1945, Congress specified that the Comptroller General and the General Accounting Office "are a part of the legislative branch of the government." In the Reorganization Act of 1949, Congress again confirmed that the Comptroller General and the General Accounting Office "are a part of the legislative branch of the Government." Finally, in the Budget and Accounting Procedures Act of 1950, Congress required the "auditing for the Government, conducted by the Comptroller General of the United States as an agent of the Congress." Like the already existing statutory responsibilities, then, the history of the Comptroller General statute confirms that the Comptroller General should be viewed as an agent of the Congress.

This is not to say, of course, that the Comptroller General has no obligations to the Executive Branch, or that he is an agent of the Congress in quite so clear a manner as the Doorkeeper of the House. * * *

Obligations to two Branches are not, however, impermissible and the presence of such dual obligations does not prevent the characterization of the official with the dual obligations as part of one branch. It is at least clear that, in most, if not all, of his statutory responsibilities, the Comptroller General is properly characterized as an agent of the Congress.[11]

III

* * *

The Court concludes that the Gramm–Rudman–Hollings Act impermissibly assigns the Comptroller General "executive powers." The dissent agrees that "the powers exercised by the Comptroller under the Act may be characterized as 'executive' in that they involve the interpretation and carrying out of the Act's mandate." This conclusion is not only far from obvious but also rests on the unstated and unsound premise

11. Despite the suggestions of the dissents, it is quite obvious that the Comptroller General, and the General Accounting Office, have a fundamentally different relationship with Congress than do independent agencies like the Federal Trade Commission. Rather than an independent agency, the Comptroller General and the GAO are functionally equivalent to congressional agents such as the Congressional Budget Office, the Office of Technology Assessment, and the Library of Congress' Congressional Research Service. As the statutory responsibilities make clear, like those congressional agents, the Comptroller General and the General Accounting Office function virtually as a permanent staff for Congress. * * *

that there is a definite line that distinguishes executive power from legislative power. * * *

One reason that the exercise of legislative, executive, and judicial powers cannot be categorically distributed among three mutually exclusive branches of government is that governmental power cannot always be readily characterized with only one of those three labels. On the contrary, as our cases demonstrate, a particular function, like a chameleon, will often take on the aspect of the office to which it is assigned. * * *

The powers delegated to the Comptroller General by § 251 of the Act before us today have a similar chameleon-like quality. The District Court persuasively explained why they may be appropriately characterized as executive powers. But, when that delegation is held invalid, the "fallback provision" provides that the report that would otherwise be issued by the Comptroller General shall be issued by Congress itself. In the event that the resolution is enacted, the congressional report will have the same legal consequences as if it had been issued by the Comptroller General. In that event, moreover, surely no one would suggest that Congress had acted in any capacity other than "legislative." * * *

Despite the statement in Article I of the Constitution that "All legislative Powers herein granted shall be vested in a Congress of the United States," it is far from novel to acknowledge that independent agencies do indeed exercise legislative powers. * * *

Thus, I do not agree that the Comptroller General's responsibilities under the Gramm–Rudman–Hollings Act must be termed "executive powers," or even that our inquiry is much advanced by using that term. For, whatever the label given the functions to be performed by the Comptroller General under § 251—or by the Congress under § 274—the District Court had no difficulty in concluding that Congress could delegate the performance of those functions to another branch of the Government. If the delegation to a stranger is permissible, why may not Congress delegate the same responsibilities to one of its own agents? That is the central question before us today.

IV

* * *

The Gramm–Rudman–Hollings Act assigns to the Comptroller General the duty to make policy decisions that have the force of law. The Comptroller General's report is, in the current statute, the engine that gives life to the ambitious budget reduction process. * * *

If Congress were free to delegate its policymaking authority to one of its components, or to one of its agents, it would be able to evade "the carefully crafted restraints spelled out in the Constitution." That danger—congressional action that evades constitutional restraints—is not present when Congress delegates lawmaking power to the executive or to an independent agency. * * *

In my opinion, Congress itself could not exercise the Gramm–Rudman–Hollings functions through a concurrent resolution. The fact that the fallback provision in § 274 requires a joint resolution rather than a concurrent resolution indicates that Congress endorsed this view.[21] I think it equally clear that Congress may not simply delegate those functions to an agent such as the Congressional Budget Office. Since I am persuaded that the Comptroller General is also fairly deemed to be an agent of Congress, he too cannot exercise such functions. * * *

I concur in the judgment.

JUSTICE WHITE, dissenting.

* * * [T]he Court's decision rests on a feature of the legislative scheme that is of minimal practical significance and that presents no substantial threat to the basic scheme of separation of powers. * * *

I

* * *

Before examining the merits of the Court's argument, I wish to emphasize what it is that the Court quite pointedly and correctly does *not* hold: namely, that "executive" powers of the sort granted the Comptroller by the Act may only be exercised by officers removable at will by the President. The Court's apparent unwillingness to accept this argument, which has been tendered in this Court by the Solicitor General,[2] is fully consistent with the Court's longstanding recognition that it is within the power of Congress under the "Necessary and Proper" Clause, Art. I, § 8, to vest authority that falls within the Court's definition of executive power in officers who are not subject to removal at will by the President and are therefore not under the President's direct control. See, e.g., *Humphrey's Executor v. United States*, 295 U.S. 602 (1935); *Wiener v. United States*, 357 U.S. 349 (1958). * * *

It is evident (and nothing in the Court's opinion is to the contrary) that the powers exercised by the Comptroller General under the Gramm–Rudman Act are not such that vesting them in an officer not subject to removal at will by the President would in itself improperly interfere with Presidential powers. Determining the level of spending by the Federal Government is not by nature a function central either to the

21. The fact that Congress specified a joint resolution as the fallback provision has another significance as well. For it reveals the congressional intent that, if the Comptroller General could not exercise the prescribed functions, Congress wished to perform them itself, rather than delegating them, for instance, to an independent agency or to an Executive Branch official. This choice shows that Congress intended that the important functions of the Act be no further from itself than the Comptroller General.

2. The Solicitor General appeared on behalf of the "United States," or, more properly, the Executive departments, which intervened to attack the constitutionality of the statute that the Chief Executive had earlier endorsed and signed into law.

exercise of the President's enumerated powers or to his general duty to ensure execution of the laws; rather, appropriating funds is a peculiarly legislative function, and one expressly committed to Congress by Art. I, § 9, which provides that "[n]o Money shall be drawn from the Treasury, but in Consequence of Appropriations made by Law." * * * Delegating the execution of this legislation—that is, the power to apply the Act's criteria and make the required calculation—to an officer independent of the President's will does not deprive the President of any power that he would otherwise have or that is essential to the performance of the duties of his office. Rather, the result of such a delegation, from the standpoint of the President, is no different from the result of more traditional forms of appropriation: under either system, the level of funds available to the Executive Branch to carry out its duties is not within the President's discretionary control. To be sure, if the budget-cutting mechanism required the responsible officer to exercise a great deal of policymaking discretion, one might argue that having created such broad discretion Congress had some obligation based upon Art. II to vest it in the Chief Executive or his agents. In Gramm–Rudman, however, Congress has done no such thing; instead, it has created a precise and articulated set of criteria designed to minimize the degree of policy choice exercised by the officer executing the statute and to ensure that the relative spending priorities established by Congress in the appropriations it passes into law remain unaltered.[5] * * *

II

If, as the Court seems to agree, the assignment of "executive" powers under Gramm–Rudman to an officer not removable at will by the President would not in itself represent a violation of the constitutional scheme of separated powers, the question remains whether, as the Court concludes, the fact that the officer to whom Congress has delegated the authority to implement the Act is removable by a joint resolution of Congress should require invalidation of the Act. * * *

The deficiencies in the Court's reasoning are apparent. First, the Court badly mischaracterizes the removal provision when it suggests that it allows Congress to remove the Comptroller for "executing the laws in any fashion found to be unsatisfactory"; in fact, Congress may remove the Comptroller only for one or more of five specified reasons, which "although not so narrow as to deny Congress any leeway, circumscribe Congress' power to some extent by providing a basis for judicial review of congressional removal." Second, and more to the point, the

5. That the statute provides, to the greatest extent possible, precise guidelines for the officer assigned to carry out the required budget cuts not only indicates that vesting budget-cutting authority in an officer independent of the President does not in any sense deprive the President of a significant amount of discretionary authority that should rightfully be vested in him or an officer accountable to him, but also answers the claim that the Act represents an excessive and hence unlawful delegation of legislative authority. Because the majority does not address the delegation argument, I shall not discuss it at any length, other than to refer the reader to the District Court's persuasive demonstration that the statute is not void under the nondelegation doctrine.

Court overlooks or deliberately ignores the decisive difference between the congressional removal provision and the legislative veto struck down in *Chadha*: under the Budget and Accounting Act, Congress may remove the Comptroller only through a joint resolution, which by definition must be passed by both Houses and signed by the President. In other words, a removal of the Comptroller under the statute *satisfies the requirements of bicameralism and presentment laid down in Chadha*. The majority's citation of *Chadha* for the proposition that Congress may only control the acts of officers of the United States "by passing new legislation," in no sense casts doubt on the legitimacy of the removal provision, for that provision allows Congress to effect removal only through action that constitutes legislation as defined in *Chadha*. * * *

That a joint resolution removing the Comptroller General would satisfy the requirements for legitimate legislative action laid down in *Chadha* does not fully answer the separation of powers argument, for it is apparent that even the results of the constitutional legislative process may be unconstitutional if those results are in fact destructive of the scheme of separation of powers. The question to be answered is whether the threat of removal of the Comptroller General for cause through joint resolution as authorized by the Budget and Accounting Act renders the Comptroller sufficiently subservient to Congress that investing him with "executive" power can be realistically equated with the unlawful retention of such power by Congress itself; more generally, the question is whether there is a genuine threat of "encroachment or aggrandizement of one branch at the expense of the other," *Buckley v. Valeo*, 424 U.S., at 122. Common sense indicates that the existence of the removal provision poses no such threat to the principle of separation of powers.

The statute does not permit anyone to remove the Comptroller at will; removal is permitted only for specified cause, with the existence of cause to be determined by Congress following a hearing. Any removal under the statute would presumably be subject to post-termination judicial review to ensure that a hearing had in fact been held and that the finding of cause for removal was not arbitrary. These procedural and substantive limitations on the removal power militate strongly against the characterization of the Comptroller as a mere agent of Congress by virtue of the removal authority. * * *

Congress' substantively limited removal power will undoubtedly be less of a spur to subservience than Congress' unquestionable and unqualified power to enact legislation reducing the Comptroller's salary, cutting the funds available to his department, reducing his personnel, limiting or expanding his duties, or even abolishing his position altogether.

More importantly, the substantial role played by the President in the process of removal through joint resolution reduces to utter insignificance the possibility that the threat of removal will induce subservience to the Congress. * * *

The majority's contrary conclusion rests on the rigid dogma that, outside of the impeachment process, any "direct congressional role in the removal of officers charged with the execution of the laws * * * is inconsistent with separation of powers." Reliance on such an unyielding principle to strike down a statute posing no real danger of aggrandizement of congressional power is extremely misguided and insensitive to our constitutional role. * * * [T]he role of this Court should be limited to determining whether the Act so alters the balance of authority among the branches of government as to pose a genuine threat to the basic division between the lawmaking power and the power to execute the law. Because I see no such threat, I cannot join the Court in striking down the Act.

I dissent.

JUSTICE BLACKMUN, dissenting.

* * * The only relief sought in this case is nullification of the automatic budget-reduction provisions of the Deficit Control Act, and that relief should not be awarded even if the Court is correct that those provisions are constitutionally incompatible with Congress' authority to remove the Comptroller General by joint resolution. Any incompatibility, I feel, should be cured by refusing to allow congressional removal—if it ever is attempted—and not by striking down the central provisions of the Deficit Control Act. * * *

In the absence of express statutory direction, I think it is plain that, as both Houses urge, invalidating the Comptroller General's functions under the Deficit Control Act would frustrate congressional objectives far more seriously than would refusing to allow Congress to exercise its removal authority under the 1921 law.

Notes

1. *The Problem of "Aggrandizement."* Justice White's dissent, like his dissent in *Chadha,* complains that the Court is too formalistic in assessing the legality of an innovation in government administration and correspondingly oblivious to actual administrative practice. *Bowsher* was decided the same day, however, as *Commodity Futures Trading Commission v. Schor,* excerpted in Chapter 2, which distinguished *Bowsher* as follows:

> Unlike *Bowsher*, this case raises no question of the aggrandizement of congressional power at the expense of a coordinate branch. Instead, the separation of powers question presented in this case is whether Congress impermissibly undermined, without appreciable expansion of its own power, the role of the Judicial Branch. * * * [W]e have also been faithful to our Article III precedents, which counsel that bright line rules cannot effectively be employed to yield broad principles applicable in all Article III inquiries.

478 U.S. at 856–57. The Court seems in this passage to imply that, contrary to Justice White's call for some real-world empiricism in assessing how administration works, strong categorical rules are necessary to prevent congressional "aggrandizement."

Dean Harold H. Bruff, in *On the Constitutional Status of the Administrative Agencies*, 36 Am.U.L.Rev. 491, 493–94 (1987), has argued that the Court's hard line against aggrandizement is necessary, if perhaps not sufficient to preserve political accountability in administration:

> The Supreme Court's recent separation of powers cases have clarified political responsibility for administration. The Court has consistently rejected schemes that would have given Congress power to share in administrative decisions without full political responsibility for doing so. If *Buckley* had allowed both presidential and congressional appointments to regulatory agencies, neither branch would answer for the agencies' decisions. If *Chadha* had upheld the legislative veto, neither branch would be solely responsible for regulation that did take effect. If *Bowsher* had upheld the role of the Government Accounting Office (GAO) in the Gramm–Rudman Act, it would be difficult to identify the branch that was determining whether sequestration was needed.
>
> Thus the Court's formalism may rest on a value judgment that accountability for administration should be centered in the executive branch. Such a judgment does not necessarily answer *where* in the executive authority should lie, but it does create an essentially unitary executive with regard to Congress. * * *
>
> Congressional partisans might respond that under the rejected schemes, both branches would be responsible, with the necessary cooperation between them providing an *increase* in political accountability. I think that the Court has been silently rejecting such a notion, and properly so. Congress was not required to endorse executive policy in a way that carried clear responsibility. The presence of some congressional appointees on a commission would not tie its every action to Congress. Failure to pass a legislative veto resolution, it was often asserted in Congress, would not endorse an executive action, but would only indicate that it was not wholly unacceptable. Under the Gramm–Rudman Act, three differently composed entities were to generate estimates; it would be difficult to place the final product at anyone's door. Still, it could be argued that congressional accountability was increased under these schemes even if it was divided with the executive. Yet any gains for Congress were offset by losses for the executive as the ultimate responsibility for decisions became blurred. Each branch could point to the other as the author of defective policy.
>
> Perhaps hopes for clarity in political accountability are dashed by the practical interdependence that permeates modern government. Surely the Court is aware that Congress retains many avenues of informal influence even when the formal sharing of power is forbidden. * * *
>
> Nevertheless, a scheme of independent authority that is open to influence is fundamentally different from one with shared responsibility. A branch possessing formal authority is politically accountable for a decision no matter how vigorous outside pressure may be. Such clarity does not exist when the power to decide is shared.

2. *The Problem of Analytic Style*. Although Professor Peter L. Strauss generally agrees with Dean Bruff that the practical impact of congressional interventions in administration should count in assessing their constitution-

ality, he does not believe it helpful in analyzing such issues to visualize the government as a tripartite structure in which every agency is located firmly within one of the branches:

> The Constitution does not define the administrative, as distinct from the political, organs of the federal government; it leaves that *entirely* to Congress. What the Constitution describes instead are three generalized national institutions (Congress, President, and Supreme Court) which, together with the states, serve as the principal heads of political and legal authority. Each of these three generalist institutions serves as the ultimate authority for a distinctive governmental authority-type (legislative, executive, or judicial). * * *
>
> Although these heads of government serve distinct functions, employing distinctive procedures, * * * the same cannot be said of the administrative level of government. Virtually every part of the government Congress has created—the Department of Agriculture as well as the Securities and Exchange Commission—exercises *all three* of the governmental functions the Constitution so carefully allocates among Congress, President, and Court. These agencies adopt rules having the shape and impact of statutes, mold governmental policy through enforcement decisions and other initiatives, and decide cases in ways that determine the rights of private parties. If in 1787 such a merger of function was unthinkable, in 1987 it is unavoidable given Congress' need to delegate at some level the making of policy for a complex and interdependent economy, and the equal incapacity (and undesirability) of the courts to resolve all matters appropriately characterized as involving "adjudication." A formal theory of separation of powers that says these functions cannot be joined is unworkable; that being so, a theory that locates each agency "in" one or another of the three conventional "branches" of American government, according to its activities, fares no better. * * *
>
> Rather than describe agencies in terms of branches, * * * one could examine their relationships with each of the three named heads of government, to see whether those relationships undermine the intended distribution of authority *among those three.* * * * [T]his analysis of separation-of-powers issues proposes examining the quality of relationships between an agency and each of the three named heads of government. It is not necessary to insist that there be particular relationships between an agency and any of the named constitutional actors (beyond the few specified in the constitutional text) in order to require relationships of a certain overall character or quality. * * *
>
> [Regarding *Bowsher*, it] is not simply that Congress chose a particular mechanism for protecting the "independence" and "objectivity" of the Comptroller General. * * * The Comptroller General's relationships with the President, from the proposing of his appointment onward, are strikingly weaker than those that characterize other agencies; the President and the courts both are utterly divorced from participating in the control of the particular functions under review; and the relationship between Congress and the Comptroller General is far more embracive and proprietary than the relationships that characterize the rest of

government. Here one could fairly describe Congress as having appropriated to itself the President's characteristic functions (and made nugatory those of the courts). Functionalist and formalist could be equally concerned with these outcomes; that the Court chose a formalist analysis speaks to possible rhetorical advantages, but not to outcome.

Viewing "aggrandizement" in terms of the full set of relationships among agency, Congress, President, and courts rather than in terms of a single "talismanic" feature of one of those relationships is, of course, precisely what the *Bowsher* Court failed to do. * * * If the right question is whether the arrangements under challenge threaten to aggrandize one of the three named constitutional actors at the expense of another, thus imperiling the balance of American government and the performance of core functions by the weakened actor, then that question requires a broader view.

Note that the question asks nothing directly about the agency empowered to act—the GAO or the CFTC—but rather asks about the impact of the challenged arrangements on the three named heads of constitutional government and the relationships among them. Although one can easily agree with the *Schor* majority that empowering the CFTC to entertain counterclaims under state common law entails no such consequences, the equation in *Bowsher* is not as clear. In *Bowsher*, aggrandizement *is* present: what the President loses in the way of ordinary controls over the tenure of government officials, Congress has asserted for itself. * * * Congress could be excused much in its own relationship with the GAO if it recognized conventional presidential and judicial relationships with that agency. Its insistence on an exclusive relationship, a device which if successful could indeed propel Congress into a general position of dominance over the national government, is the differentiating feature. * * *

Peter L. Strauss, *Formal and Functional Approaches to Separation-of-Powers Questions—A Foolish Inconsistency?*, 72 Corn.L.Rev. 488, 492–94, 519–21 (1987).

3. *The Perils of Functionalism.* The pleas of Justice White and Professor Strauss for functional assessment of government organization are likely to have strong appeal to administrative lawyers. Yet, their writings may also suggest why the majority opinions in the "aggrandizement" cases eschew any attempt to assess the practical impact of various congressional innovations.

Once the permissibility of a congressional intrusion into appointments or removals is made to depend on its practical effects, the Court would have to determine which effects "count" in the constitutional assessment and how they are to be weighed. In a case like *Bowsher*, Professor Strauss would pay attention to any disturbance of the "parity" between Congress and the President in influencing administration. Yet, there is no obvious reason to regard "parity" over administration as a constitutional command. The history of interbranch relations reflects a tidal ebb and flow of power rather than a stable "parity." As for weighing effects, Professor Strauss would apparently join the majority in *Bowsher* because he regards the Comptroller

General statute as failing to respect parity; Justice White strongly implies a contrary judgment on just this point.

The Court's hard line against congressional aggrandizement may, as Professor Bruff suggests, incidentally facilitate sound administration. But the Court may have concluded that it cannot reason definitively in terms of administrative practicality, and prefer bright-line, text-based constitutional analysis for this reason alone. To put the point another way, a majority of the Justices may regard adherence to text and avoidance of balancing as the best contribution the Court can make to the sound working of government.

4. *The Problem of Indirect "Aggrandizement."* In *Metropolitan Washington Airports Authority v. Citizens for Abatement of Aircraft Noise, Inc.*, 501 U.S. 252 (1991), the Supreme Court overturned what it took to be an impermissible, if novel extension of congressional power over administration—one not inspired by the competition between President and Congress that lies at the core of earlier cases. In 1986, Congress authorized the transfer of federal control over National (now Reagan National) and Dulles Airports near the District of Columbia to the Metropolitan Washington Airport Authority, a regional authority established by Virginia–D.C. compact. Congress subjected the transfer, however, to an unusual condition. To assume control of the airports, the MWAA Board of Directors would have to create a nine-member Board of Review with the power to veto certain actions of the Directors. The nine members of the Board of Review were required to be members of Congress, "serving in their individual capacities, as representatives of the users of the Metropolitan Washington Airports." The MWAA Board of Directors was required further to select eight of the nine Board of Review members from the membership of designated congressional committees having jurisdiction over transportation. One of the first matters subjected to the Board of Review's potential veto was a "master plan" providing for the enhanced usage of National Airport, an airport especially convenient to Capitol Hill and already the target of citizen complaints about aircraft noise. If upheld, this scheme would have assured that the views of members of Congress were raised in the course of MWAA policy making and discouraged the adoption of policies that might reduce the convenience of National. Indeed, Congress hit upon this special arrangement only after *Chadha* nullified its preferred mechanism, the legislative veto.

Six members of the Court held that the Board of Review's power to veto decisions by the MWAA Directors represented federal action taken on behalf of Congress. If considered legislative, the majority reasoned, the Board's functions would run afoul of *Chadha*, If considered executive action, they were impermissibly vested in members of Congress, contrary to *Bowsher*. The majority regarded the challenged Act as "a blueprint for extensive expansion of the legislative power. * * * " It said Congress could use similar structures "to enable its Members or its agents to retain control, outside the ordinary legislative process, of the activities of state grant recipients charged with executing virtually every aspect of national policy." Justice White vigorously dissented, joined by the Chief Justice and by Justice Marshall. He argued that separation of powers analysis was inapplicable to the functions of members of Congress serving in their individual capacities on a body created under state law. In any event, it was implausible to regard Board of Review members as agents of Congress when (a) Congress did not appoint them, (b) continuity in Congress or on any committee was not a condition for completion of service on the Board, (c) Congress could not remove Board members, and (d) Board members had no legal obligations to Congress.

5. *Fiscal Responsibility and the Spectre of Congressional Abdication: The Line–Item Veto.* It is not surprising, as *Bowsher v. Synar* illustrates, that budget politics should have provided the backdrop for Congress's institutional experimentation in the 1980s. The decade was marked by stunning growth in the federal deficit, a problem that neither elected branch displayed much appetite for confronting. Given the difficult political choices available, it is easy enough to understand the appeal to members of Congress of the save-us-from-ourselves approach of Gramm–Rudman–Hollings.

When the major parties' control of the respective political branches switched hands in the 1990s, Congress enacted another budget-driven innovation, a presidential "line-item veto." Line Item Veto Act, P.L. 104–130, codified at 2 U.S.C. § 691 *et seq.* The Act provided:

> [T]he President may, with respect to any bill or joint resolution that has been signed into law pursuant to Article I, section 7, of the Constitution of the United States, cancel in whole—
>
> (1) any dollar amount of discretionary budget authority;
>
> (2) any item of new direct spending; or
>
> (3) any limited tax benefit;
>
> if the President—
>
> (A) determines that such cancellation will—
>
> (i) reduce the Federal budget deficit;
>
> (ii) not impair any essential Government functions; and
>
> (iii) not harm the national interest; and
>
> (B) notifies the Congress of such cancellation by transmitting a special message * * * within five calendar days (excluding Sundays) after the enactment of the law providing the dollar amount of discretionary budget authority, item of new direct spending, or limited tax benefit that was canceled.

2 U.S.C. § 691.

Unlike Gramm–Rudman–Hollings, however, the Line–Item Veto Act seemed to many, including a number of determined congressional opponents, to be an unconstitutional abdication of legislative authority. Under the standards-oriented approach to nondelegation highlighted in Chapter 2, *supra*, the statute seems unobjectionable. The language quoted above compares favorably in terms of its clarity and specificity to many statutory provisions that have been upheld. The Supreme Court nonetheless overturned the line-item veto, in a highly formalistic opinion reminiscent of its condemnation of the line-item veto in the *Chadha* case, discussed in Chapter Two. The Court concluded that the Act empowered the President, in effect, to repeal or amend existing law without following the constitutionally prescribed process for legislating. *Clinton v. City of New York*, 524 U.S. 417 (1998). The re-emergence of deficit politics as a hot-button issue may yet again provoke creative attempts by the elected branches to strap themselves to the mast of budget restraint. Like *Chadha*, however, *Bowsher v. Synar* and *Clinton v. City of New York* provide strong cautions against apparent departures from ordinary legislative processes. Whether Congress seeks to augment its authority, as in *Chadha* and *Bowsher*, or to abridge its powers, as in *Clinton v. City of New York*, the Court appears determined to resist congressional innovations in the process of legislating that threaten to short-circuit the prescribed formalities of Article I.

3. CONGRESS' POWER TO REGULATE THE PRESIDENT'S RELATIONSHIP WITH ADMINISTRATORS

HUMPHREY'S EXECUTOR v. UNITED STATES

Supreme Court of the United States, 1935.
295 U.S. 602, 55 S.Ct. 869, 79 L.Ed. 1611.

JUSTICE SUTHERLAND delivered the opinion of the Court.

Plaintiff brought suit in the Court of Claims against the United States to recover a sum of money alleged to be due the deceased for salary as a Federal Trade Commissioner from October 8, 1933, when the President undertook to remove him from office, to the time of his death on February 14, 1934. The court below has certified to this court two questions in respect of the power of the President to make the removal. The material facts which give rise to the questions are as follows:

William E. Humphrey, the decedent, on December 10, 1931, was nominated by President Hoover to succeed himself as a member of the Federal Trade Commission, and was confirmed by the United States Senate. He was duly commissioned for a term of seven years expiring September 25, 1938; and, after taking the required oath of office, entered upon his duties. On July 25, 1933, President Roosevelt addressed a letter to the commissioner asking for his resignation, on the ground "that the aims and purposes of the Administration with respect to the work of the Commission can be carried out most effectively with personnel of my own selection," but disclaiming any reflection upon the commissioner personally or upon his services. The commissioner replied, asking time to consult his friends. After some further correspondence upon the subject, the President on August 31, 1933, wrote the commissioner expressing the hope that the resignation would be forthcoming and saying: "You will, I know, realize that I do not feel that your mind and my mind go along together on either the policies or the administering of the Federal Trade Commission, and, frankly, I think it is best for the people of this country that I should have a full confidence."

The commissioner declined to resign; and on October 7, 1933, the President wrote him: "Effective as of this date you are hereby removed from the office of Commissioner of the Federal Trade Commission."

Humphrey never acquiesced in this action, but continued thereafter to insist that he was still a member of the commission, entitled to perform its duties and receive the compensation provided by law at the rate of $10,000 per annum. Upon these and other facts set forth in the certificate, which we deem it unnecessary to recite, the following questions are certified:

"1. Do the provisions of section 1 of the Federal Trade Commission Act, stating that 'any commissioner may be removed by the President for inefficiency, neglect of duty, or malfeasance in office,' restrict or limit the power of the President to remove a commissioner except under one or more of the causes named?

"If the foregoing question is answered in the affirmative, then—

"2. If the power of the President to remove a commissioner is restricted or limited as shown by the foregoing interrogatory and the answer made thereto, is such a restriction or limitation valid under the Constitution of the United States?"

The Federal Trade Commission Act, at 15 U.S.C. §§ 41, 42, creates a commission of five members to be appointed by the President by and with the advice and consent of the Senate, and § 1 provides: "Not more than three of the commissioners shall be members of the same political party. The first commissioners appointed shall continue in office for terms of three, four, five, six, and seven years, respectively, from the date of the taking effect of this Act, the term of each to be designated by the President, but their successors shall be appointed for terms of seven years, except that any person chosen to fill a vacancy shall be appointed only for the unexpired term of the commissioner whom he shall succeed. The commission shall choose a chairman from its own membership. No commissioner shall engage in any other business, vocation, or employment. Any commissioner may be removed by the President for inefficiency, neglect of duty, or malfeasance in office." * * *

First. The question first to be considered is whether, by the provisions of § 1 of the Federal Trade Commission Act already quoted, the President's power is limited to removal for the specific causes enumerated therein. * * *

* * * [T]he fixing of a definite term subject to removal for cause, unless there be some countervailing provision or circumstance indicating the contrary, which here we are unable to find, is enough to establish the legislative intent that the term is not to be curtailed in the absence of such cause. But if the intention of Congress that no removal should be made during the specified term except for one or more of the enumerated causes were not clear upon the face of the statute, as we think it is, it would be made clear by a consideration of the character of the commission and the legislative history which accompanied and preceded the passage of the act.

The commission is to be non-partisan; and it must, from the very nature of its duties, act with entire impartiality. It is charged with the enforcement of no policy except the policy of the law. Its duties are neither political nor executive, but predominantly quasi-judicial and quasi-legislative. Like the Interstate Commerce Commission, its members are called upon to exercise the trained judgment of a body of experts "appointed by law and informed by experience."

The legislative reports in both houses of Congress clearly reflect the view that a fixed term was necessary to the effective and fair administration of the law. * * *

The debates in both houses demonstrate that the prevailing view was that the commission was not to be "subject to anybody in the government but * * * only to the people of the United States"; free from "political domination or control" or the "probability or possibility of such a thing"; to be "separate and apart from any existing department of the government—not subject to the orders of the President." * * *

Thus, the language of the act, the legislative reports, and the general purposes of the legislation as reflected by the debates, all combine to demonstrate the Congressional intent to create a body of experts who shall gain experience by length of service—a body which shall be independent of executive authority, *except in its selection*, and free to exercise its judgment without the leave or hindrance of any other official or any department of the government. To the accomplishment of these purposes, it is clear that Congress was of the opinion that length and certainty of tenure would vitally contribute. And to hold that, nevertheless, the members of the commission continue in office at the mere will of the President, might be to thwart, in large measure, the very ends which Congress sought to realize by definitely fixing the term of office.

We conclude that the intent of the act is to limit the executive power of removal to the causes enumerated, the existence of none of which is claimed here; and we pass to the second question.

Second. To support its contention that the removal provision of § 1, as we have just construed it, is an unconstitutional interference with the executive power of the President, the government's chief reliance is on *Myers v. United States*, 272 U.S. 52 [1926]. That case has been so recently decided, and the prevailing and dissenting opinions so fully review the general subject of the power of executive removal, that further discussion would add little of value to the wealth of material there collected. These opinions examine at length the historical, legislative and judicial data bearing upon the question, beginning with what is called "the decision of 1789" in the first Congress and coming down almost to the day when the opinions were delivered. They occupy 243 pages of the volume in which they are printed. Nevertheless, the narrow point actually decided was only that the President had power to remove a postmaster of the first class, without the advice and consent of the Senate as required by act of Congress. In the course of the opinion of the court, expressions occur which tend to sustain the government's contention, but these are beyond the point involved and, therefore, do not come within the rule of *stare decisis*. In so far as they are out of harmony with the views here set forth, these expressions are disapproved. * * *

The office of a postmaster is so essentially unlike the office now involved that the decision in the *Myers* case cannot be accepted as controlling our decision here. A postmaster is an executive officer restricted to the performance of executive functions. He is charged with no duty at all related to either the legislative or judicial power. The actual decision in the *Myers* case finds support in the theory that such an officer is merely one of the units in the executive department and, hence, inherently subject to the exclusive and illimitable power of removal by the Chief Executive, whose subordinate and aid he is. Putting aside *dicta*, which may be followed if sufficiently persuasive but which are not controlling, the necessary reach of the decision goes far enough to include all purely executive officers. It goes no farther;—much less does it include an officer who occupies no place in the executive department and who exercises no part of the executive power vested by the Constitution in the President.

The Federal Trade Commission is an administrative body created by Congress to carry into effect legislative policies embodied in the statute in accordance with the legislative standard therein prescribed, and to perform other specified duties as a legislative or as a judicial aid. Such a body cannot in any proper sense be characterized as an arm or an eye of the executive. Its duties are performed without executive leave and, in the contemplation of the statute, must be free from executive control. In administering the provisions of the statute in respect of "unfair methods of competition"—that is to say in filling in and administering the details embodied by that general standard—the commission acts in part quasi-legislatively and in part quasi-judicially. In making investigations and reports thereon for the information of Congress under § 6, in aid of the legislative power, it acts as a legislative agency. Under § 7, which authorizes the commission to act as a master in chancery under rules prescribed by the court, it acts as an agency of the judiciary. To the extent that it exercises any executive function—as distinguished from executive power in the constitutional sense—it does so in the discharge and effectuation of its quasi-legislative or quasi-judicial powers, or as an agency of the legislative or judicial departments of the government.[1]

If Congress is without authority to prescribe causes for removal of members of the trade commission and limit executive power of removal accordingly, that power at once becomes practically all-inclusive in respect of civil officers with the exception of the judiciary provided for by the Constitution. The Solicitor General, at the bar, apparently recognizing this to be true, with commendable candor, agreed that his view in respect of the removability of members of the Federal Trade Commission necessitated a like view in respect of the Interstate Commerce Commission and the Court of Claims. We are thus confronted with the serious question whether not only the members of these quasi-legislative and

1. The provision of § 6(d) of the [FTC] act which authorizes the President to direct an investigation and report by the commission in relation to alleged violations of the anti-trust acts, is so obviously, collateral to the main design of the act as not to detract from the force of this general statement as to the character of that body.

quasi-judicial bodies, but the judges of the legislative Court of Claims, exercising judicial power, continue in office only at the pleasure of the President.

We think it plain under the Constitution that illimitable power of removal is not possessed by the President in respect of officers of the character of those just named. The authority of Congress, in creating quasi-legislative or quasi-judicial agencies, to require them to act in discharge of their duties independently of executive control cannot well be doubted; and that authority includes, as an appropriate incident, power to fix the period during which they shall continue in office, and to forbid their removal except for cause in the meantime. For it is quite evident that one who holds his office only during the pleasure of another, cannot be depended upon to maintain an attitude of independence against the latter's will.

The fundamental necessity of maintaining each of the three general departments of government entirely free from the control or coercive influence, direct or indirect, of either of the others, has often been stressed and is hardly open to serious question. So much is implied in the very fact of the separation of the powers of these departments by the Constitution; and in the rule which recognizes their essential co-equality. * * *

The result of what we now have said is this: Whether the power of the President to remove an officer shall prevail over the authority of Congress to condition the power by fixing a definite term and precluding a removal except for cause, will depend upon the character of the office; the *Myers* decision, affirming the power of the President alone to make the removal, is confined to purely executive officers; and as to officers of the kind here under consideration, we hold that no removal can be made during the prescribed term for which the officer is appointed, except for one or more of the causes named in the applicable statute.

To the extent that, between the decision in the *Myers* case, which sustains the unrestrictable power of the President to remove purely executive officers, and our present decision that such power does not extend to an office such as that here involved, there shall remain a field of doubt, we leave such cases as may fall within it for future consideration and determination as they may arise. * * *

Notes

1. *Congress' Role in Administrative Design.* Unlike *Bowsher* and *Buckley, Humphrey's Executor* involves a claimed usurpation of executive power that did not directly augment the powers of Congress. Yet, weakening presidential influence over administration presumably promotes the effectiveness of congressional influence, and, unsurprisingly, all these cases share common concerns regarding the relationships among President, Congress, and administrative agencies. Even so, the decisions necessarily leave the contours of both Congress' powers to restrict and channel administration

and the President's power to control it incompletely defined. Many established practices remain questionable without ever being challenged, and the few judicial opinions available for interpretation leave many puzzles unresolved.

For example, standing alone, *Bowsher* and *Buckley* are susceptible to at least two quite distinct readings. They could be read as recognizing a constitutionally mandated role for the President in the supervision of government administration. Proponents of this reading claim the two cases protect not only the President's authority to appoint officers of the United States, but also his right to supervise their exercise of discretion. Under the broadest such reading of *Bowsher* and *Buckley*, there would be no such creature as an "independent agency," constitutionally speaking. See, e.g., Geoffrey P. Miller, *Independent Agencies*, 1986 Sup.Ct.Rev. 41. An alternative reading interprets *Bowsher* and *Buckley* only as enforcing narrow formal constraints on Congress' ability to aggrandize its powers. Peter M. Shane, *Conventionalism in Constitutional Interpretation and the Place of Administrative Agencies*, 36 Am.U.L.Rev. 573 (1987). Under this reading, the decisions go no further than recognizing two exceptional, albeit explicit limits on Congress' otherwise broad authority to structure government administration.

On its face, the result in *Humphrey's Executor* is more consistent with the latter view, under which Congress has fairly broad authority to determine the degree of independence from direct presidential supervision that even presidentially appointed administrators enjoy. *Humphrey's Executor* articulates a sharp distinction between "executive" officers, removable at the President's will, and independent agency officers, removable by the President only on such terms as Congress prescribes. Because the power to remove is often thought to include the power to control, *Humphrey's Executor* is cited as the case that legitimated the so-called "independent agency" as a constitutional matter.

2. *"Executive" v. "Independent" Agencies. Humphrey's Executor* does not use the term "independent agency," but instead distinguishes between agencies that are "purely executive" and those established to "exercise * * * judgment without the leave or hindrance of any other official or any department of the government." The latter, it suggests, comprise officers "who occup[y] no place in the executive department and who exercise[ ] no part of the executive power vested by the Constitution in the President."

The idea that "executive" and "independent" agencies occupy different boxes on the constitutional organization chart is puzzling. After all, the Constitution charges the President to "take care that the Laws be faithfully executed." It is thus difficult to perceive how any agency engaged in implementing federal statutes can be regarded as exercising "no part of the executive power vested by the Constitution in the President." Moreover, if the functions of certain agencies were to take them wholly outside the executive branch, the possibility would exist that our separation of powers not only permits, but mandates certain limits on the President's capacity to direct domestic administration. Otherwise, the President would seemingly have the power to direct administrative activity outside the executive domain.

One of us has proposed a different understanding of "independent agencies":

> Federal agencies do not come in two discrete models, one "executive" and one "independent," that are recognizable by clearly distinguishable characteristics. * * * The general reason why some agencies are informally denominated "independent agencies" is that certain of their features are designed to mitigate the degree to which [presidential] politics can dominate their decisionmaking. Not all of these structural features are controversial. Well-accepted accoutrements of independence include the adoption of collegial decisionmaking, staggered terms for the agency's prime decisionmakers, terms of office that are longer than the four-year presidential term, and quotas on the number of agency members who may belong to either of the major parties. * * *
>
> The one aspect of some agencies' independence that has attracted current challengers is the supposed immunity from removal of certain agency heads who refuse to follow the policy directives of the President. Although these "independent" administrators are apparently removable "for cause," it is conventionally understood that it would not be cause for removal that such an administrator declined to follow the President's policy preferences in favor of policy initiatives that the administrator prefers and which are also within the administrator's lawful discretion. This insulation from direct presidential policy supervision is the aspect of agency design that is most provocatively independent, and it may be most helpful to refer to such insulation as "policy independence."

Peter M. Shane, *Independent Policymaking and Presidential Power: A Constitutional Analysis*, 57 Geo.Wash.L.Rev. 596, 608–09 (1989). Under this view, "executive" and "independent" agencies are both "in" the executive branch. What distinguishes the two sets of agencies would be the degree to which Congress has exercised its constitutional discretion to limit the President's influence—without directly expanding its own—over agency policy making. Thus, to call the FTC "independent" and the EPA "executive" is only to recognize the statutory differences in presidential removal power, not a difference in location on a constitutional "organization chart."

This interpretation would help resolve any ambiguity in the purview of the faithful execution clause. The substantive scope of that clause is debatable. Advocates of more centralized executive control over administration argue that the clause vests in the President significant policy making authority in the implementation of domestic legislation. Others, perhaps with greater historical warrant, would treat the clause as empowering the President only to assure that statutes are not effectively suspended in their operation through maladministration or willful nonenforcement. *Id.* at 611; Peter M. Shane, *The Separation of Powers and the Rule of Law: The Virtues of "Seeing the Trees,"* 30 Wm. & Mary L.Rev. 375, 380 (1989). The "laws" to be faithfully executed would seem necessarily to include all federal statutes, however, regardless of who administers them.

3. *Identifying Independent Agencies—Removal Provisions. Humphrey's Executor* does not indicate exactly how the "independence" of an agency is to be determined or precisely what that classification implies. Professor Shane

suggests that "it is conventionally understood" that presidents may not lawfully discharge independent administrators based on policy disagreements. But Congress has never stated explicitly whether policy disagreement *should* count as cause for dismissing an administrator whose tenure in office is protected by a "for cause" removal provision, and identifying "independent agencies" according to the removal provisions in various statutes is, therefore, to draw an inference about congressional intent based more on customary practice than on explicit discussion.

The removability-independence nexus is problematic because statutory provisions for the removal of officers are hardly uniform. Although many statutes provide that commissioners may be removed only for "cause," that cause is variously articulated. "Inefficiency, neglect of duty, or malfeasance in office" is a common formulation. But there is seldom any provision for determining whether a presidential removal on one of these grounds is in fact justified. The National Labor Relations Act may be unique in providing that in removing a member of the Board the President shall act "upon notice and hearing." Presumably the disappointed office holder removed under other statutes would test out the propriety of the removal in a suit for back pay. The efficacy of the remedy in curbing presidential power is perhaps suggested, however, by the identity of the party that brought Humphrey's claim.

Not all appointees to independent commissions enjoy statutory "for cause" limitations on their removal. During the time between the *Myers* case and *Humphrey's Executor*, Congress created the Securities and Exchange Commission, the Federal Communications Commission and the Federal Power Commission. In each case, presumably on the basis of the *Myers* holding, Congress provided no restrictions on the President's power of removal. Does this mean, following *Humphrey's*, that the President's power of removal with respect to these commissioners is in fact unrestricted?

Some statutes seem to recognize a division between (1) policy formation and prosecutorial functions and (2) licensing and adjudicatory functions, both in the structure of agencies and in the provisions for the removal of officers. The Energy Reorganization Act of 1974, for example, replaced the Atomic Energy Commission with two agencies: one, the Energy Research and Development Administration, is described in the statute as "an independent executive agency," whatever that means, 42 U.S.C. § 5811; the other, the Nuclear Regulatory Commission, is styled "an independent regulatory commission." 42 U.S.C. § 5841. The ERDA, which has responsibility for military and production activities and for basic research, is headed by an Administrator who is appointed by the President, with the advice and consent of the Senate, for an indefinite term. There is no mention of the removal of the Administrator in the statute. The five NRC commissioners, on the other hand, are appointed by the President with the advice and consent of the Senate, for five-year terms and are made removable by the President for "inefficiency, neglect of duty, or malfeasance in office."

If an administrator's refusal to follow a specific presidential directive could constitute legal cause for removal under the statutory language, the constitutional debate over independent agencies would arguably be moot. Although the President could not insist on controlling the overall policy disposition of a particular individual, the President (or OMB minions) could monitor agency proceedings and dictate to administrators, in each case, the policies to be implemented. Geoffrey P. Miller, *Independent Agencies*, 1986 Sup.Ct.Rev. 41. And presumably, the President could generally expect his orders to be followed if he were willing to exercise the power of removal any time one was not.

On the other hand, it is not always conceded that the President has plenary removal authority over even nominally "executive" officials. For example, President Reagan set off a political tempest in 1983 when he removed three members of the Civil Rights Commission, which by statute was an executive agency. 42 U.S.C. § 1975(a) (1982). After several months of widely publicized debate, a compromise was reached that retained two of the three commissioners. A new enabling statute was enacted, expanding the number of commissioners from six to eight, and making the Commission independent. Pub.L.No. 98–183, 97 Stat. 1301 (1983). The clear language in the original act—"there is created in the executive branch"—obviously did not prevent claims by civil rights groups and some members of Congress that the Commission should be considered operationally independent, and that the removals were improper. Nor did this language convince the U.S. District Court for the District of Columbia, which issued a preliminary injunction blocking the removals. *Berry v. Reagan*, 32 Empl.Prac.Dec. (CCH) ¶ 31,304, *vacated as moot*, 732 F.2d 949 (D.C.Cir.1983). Indeed, the Civil Rights Commission had previously been held, in *Hannah v. Larche*, 363 U.S. 420 (1960), to be exercising a purely legislative investigatory function and therefore to be bound to provide only those procedures (arguably none) demanded of *legislative* bodies by the due process clause. Does that mean that the Commission's members could have been appointed by Congress? Congress clearly thought so because half the membership of the newly formed Civil Rights Commission is chosen by Congress.

4. *Identifying Independent Agencies—Agency Functions*. Twenty years after *Humphrey's Executor,* in *Wiener v. United States*, 357 U.S. 349 (1958), the Court embraced a functional approach to the determination whether an agency was "independent," and its members subject to plenary removal. This also was a suit for back pay, by a member of the War Claims Commission, a temporary body established to hear claims, "according to law," arising out of enemy activity during World War II. Wiener was removed by President Eisenhower six months prior to the expiration of the Commission's mandate for reasons virtually identical to those President Roosevelt offered Humphrey. The statute creating the War Claims Commission did not mention removal. Justice Frankfurter, for the Court, concluded:

> When Congress has for distribution among American claimants funds derived from foreign sources, it may proceed in different ways. Congress may appropriate directly; it may utilize the Executive; it may resort to the adjudicatory process. For Congress itself to have made appropriations for the claims with which it dealt under the War Claims Act was not practical in view of the large number of claimants and the diversity in the specific circumstances giving rise to the claims. The House bill in effect put the distribution of the narrow class of claims that it acknowledged into Executive hands, by vesting the procedure in the Federal Security Administrator. The final form of the legislation, as

we have seen, left the widened range of claims to be determined by adjudication. Congress could, of course, have given jurisdiction over these claims to the District Courts or to the Court of Claims. The fact that it chose to establish a Commission to "adjudicate according to law" the classes of claims defined in the statute did not alter the intrinsic judicial character of the task with which the Commission was charged. The claims were to be "adjudicated according to law," that is, on the merits of each claim supported by evidence and governing legal considerations, by a body that was "entirely free from the control or coercive influence, direct or indirect," *Humphrey's Executor v. United States*, of either the Executive or the Congress. If, as one must take for granted, the War Claims Act precluded the President from influencing the Commission in passing on a particular claim, *a fortiori* must it be inferred that Congress did not wish to have hang over the Commission the Damocles' sword of removal by the President for no reason other than that he preferred to have on that Commission men of his own choosing.

For such is this case. We have not a removal for cause involving the rectitude of a member of an adjudicatory body, nor even a suspensory removal until the Senate could act upon it by confirming the appointment of a new Commissioner or otherwise dealing with the matter. Judging the matter in all the nakedness in which it is presented, namely, the claim that the President could remove a member of an adjudicatory body like the War Claims Commission merely because he wanted his own appointees on such a Commission, we are compelled to conclude that no such power is given to the President directly by the Constitution, and none is impliedly conferred upon by statute simply because Congress said nothing about it. The philosophy of *Humphrey's Executor*, in its explicit language as well as its implications, precludes such a claim.

5. *Identifying Independent Agencies—Congressional Labeling.* Congress has, on one occasion, itemized the agencies it considers to be "independent regulatory commissions." Paperwork Reduction Act of 1980, 44 U.S.C. § 3502(10). The operational consequence of being labeled "independent" in § 3502(10), is that an agency is not bound by OMB disapproval, under the Paperwork Reduction Act, of its use of particular methods for the collection of information from private parties. 44 U.S.C. § 3507(c). The statute does not indicate, however, any other way in which the agency is to be deemed exempt from the President's direct policy influence.

In any event, Congress' use of the label "independent" presumably cannot be conclusive as to all questions regarding the President's relationship with that agency. If that were so, Congress could limit the President's control over constitutionally based powers that he exercises personally by purporting to lodge such powers with an agency and denominating it "independent."

6. *Statutory Independence and Political Reality.* Limits on the removability of administrators may not be a reliable measure of an agency's effective political independence from the President. The President often need not remove officers in order ultimately to control the membership of inde-

pendent agencies. Members of independent boards and commissions rarely serve their full terms. One study examined the history from 1945 to 1970 of seven important agencies, whose members were statutorily granted terms of office ranging from five to seven years. During this period the President had only once needed more than three years to name an actual majority of the Commissioners, and the average time from inauguration to appointment of a majority was 21 months. When the Presidency changed parties, the average time for the President to gain a *partisan* majority on a Commission was but 7 months. These figures illustrate that, even with limited removal authority, the President retains substantial power to shape the membership, and thus presumably the policies, of the independent agencies. Charles T. Goodsell & Ceferina C. Gayo, *Appointive Control of Federal Regulatory Commissions*, 23 Admin. L. Rev. 291 (1971). For skeptical assessments whether agency structural independence is a reliable predictor of agency cooperation with the President's policy agenda, see *Symposium: The Independence of Independent Agencies*, 1988 Duke L.J. 215 (1988).

It would be hard to argue, for example, that President Reagan was more successful in implementing his environmental policies through the "executive" Environmental Protection Agency than he was in promoting his economic philosophy through the "independent" Federal Trade Commission. In 1981, the President appointed new heads to both agencies—EPA Administrator Anne Gorsuch and FTC Chair James C. Miller III—who were entirely sympathetic to the Administration's economic and regulatory philosophies. Gorsuch, however, was forced to resign after one of her key appointees, Rita Lavelle, was charged with mismanagement of the Superfund program for the cleanup of toxic waste and convicted of lying to Congress about the program. To restore the agency's credibility, Reagan appointed former EPA head William Ruckelshaus, a moderate who enjoyed respect in the environmental community and who quickly became a proponent of vigorous enforcement. Ruckelshaus' stature and the Administration's vulnerability on environmental issues after the Gorsuch debacle gave EPA substantial room to pursue its own policies, its "purely executive" status notwithstanding. By contrast, the FTC chair, soon joined by other Reagan appointees, led the "independent" commission to embrace the Reagan Administration's deregulatory philosophy, which Dr. Miller had helped formulate.

In similar fashion, the Federal Communications Commission, chaired during most of the Clinton Administration by attorney Reed E. Hundt, a close associate of then-Vice President Gore, likewise implemented a regulatory policy conspicuously in tune with the Administration's public policy agenda. Mr. Hundt's insightful and entertaining account of his FCC tenure provides clear evidence of the special nuance that must attend any realistic understanding of agency "independence." Reed E. Hundt, You Say You Want a Revolution: A Story of Information Age Politics (2000). (Of course, following the strictures of the Administrative Procedure Act, as explored in Chapter 4, the FCC presumably did not allow the Commissioners' political ties to influence judgments in on-the-record adjudicatory proceedings, *e.g.*, in license revocations or comparative hearings. On the other hand, the APA applies to such on-the-record proceedings, whether or not the adjudicating agency is politically "independent.")

Yet more recently, the FCC has provided the George W. Bush Administration—as well as Congress—a dramatic example of the unpredictability that agency "independence" may bring. In February, 2003, the Republican-controlled agency seemed poised under chairman Michael Powell to adopt rules significantly deregulating various aspects of the telephone and broadcast industries. A series of proposed changes in rules that the FCC adopted after Congress enacted the Telecommunications Act of 1996 were especially important to the regional Bell operating companies (also known as "incumbent local exchange carriers" or ILECs) that have dominated local telephone service since the breakup of A.T.&T. in the 1980s. These rule changes would have entitled the telephone companies to enter profitable new lines of business without leasing their local residential voice lines to new local competitors—a condition imposed by the 1996 Act and its implementing regulations.

Unfortunately for Chairman Powell, a fellow Republican commissioner, Kevin Martin, was unpersuaded of Powell's approach, which he thought left too little discretion to state public utilities commissioners with regard to the regulation of local telephone service. Instead of backing the Chairman's position, Martin decided to negotiate a compromise with the two Democratic FCC commissioners. Congressional supporters of the ILECs were furious—and stymied. Rep. Billy Tauzin (R–LA), chair of House Energy and Commerce Committee, reportedly threatened to thwart White House initiatives on a variety of issues if the White House, in effect, did not whip Commissioner Martin into line. Bill McConnell, *Latest Prime Suspect in FCC Coup: Powell,* Broadcasting & Cable, Mar. 3, 2002, at 1. Except that Martin's spouse is employed as a press aide to Vice President Cheney and that Martin might conceivably find Rep. Tauzin's enmity an impediment to some unannounced political ambitions, it is not clear what leverage either branch would have over him. Certainly, basing particular votes on such considerations would be hard to square with the model of impartial rationality imposed on agency rulemaking through judicial review, a subject to be explored in Chapters 5 and 7.

MORRISON v. OLSON

Supreme Court of the United States, 1988.
487 U.S. 654, 108 S.Ct. 2597, 101 L.Ed.2d 569.

CHIEF JUSTICE REHNQUIST delivered the opinion of the Court.

This case presents us with a challenge to the independent counsel provisions of the Ethics in Government Act of 1978, 28 U.S.C. §§ 49, 591 *et seq.* (Supp.1988). We hold today that these provisions of the Act do not violate the Appointments Clause of the Constitution, Art. II, § 2, cl. 2, or the limitations of Article III, nor do they impermissibly interfere with the President's authority under Article II in violation of the constitutional principle of separation of powers.

I

Briefly stated, Title VI of the Ethics in Government Act allows for the appointment of an "independent counsel" to investigate and, if appropriate, prosecute certain high ranking government officials for violations of federal criminal laws. The Act requires the Attorney General, upon receipt of information that he determines is "sufficient to constitute grounds to investigate whether any person [covered by the Act] may have violated any Federal criminal law," to conduct a preliminary investigation of the matter. When the Attorney General has completed this investigation, or 90 days has elapsed, he is required to report to a special court (the Special Division) created by the Act "for the purpose of appointing independent counsels." If the Attorney General determines that "there are no reasonable grounds to believe that further investigation is warranted," then he must notify the Special Division of this result. In such a case, "the division of the court shall have no power to appoint an independent counsel." If, however, the Attorney General has determined that there are "reasonable grounds to believe that further investigation or prosecution is warranted," then he "shall apply to the division of the court for the appointment of an independent counsel."[2] The Attorney General's application to the court "shall contain sufficient information to assist the [court] in selecting an independent counsel and in defining that independent counsel's prosecutorial jurisdiction." Upon receiving this application, the Special Division "shall appoint an appropriate independent counsel and shall define that independent counsel's prosecutorial jurisdiction."

With respect to all matters within the independent counsel's jurisdiction, the Act grants the counsel "full power and independent authority to exercise all investigative and prosecutorial functions and powers of the Department of Justice, the Attorney General, and any other officer or employee of the Department of Justice." § 594(a).[6] The functions of the independent counsel include conducting grand jury proceedings and other investigations, participating in civil and criminal court proceedings and litigation, and appealing any decision in any case in which the counsel participates in an official capacity. Under § 594(a)(9), the counsel's powers include "initiating and conducting prosecutions in any court of competent jurisdiction, framing and signing indictments, filing informations, and handling all aspects of any case, in the name of the United States." * * * In addition, whenever a matter has been referred to an independent counsel under the Act, the Attorney General and the Justice Department are required to suspend all investigations and proceedings regarding the matter. * * *

Two statutory provisions govern the length of an independent counsel's tenure in office. The first defines the procedure for removing an independent counsel. Section 596(a)(1) provides:

2. The Act also requires the Attorney General to apply for the appointment of an independent counsel if 90 days elapse from the receipt of the information triggering the preliminary investigation without a determination by the Attorney General that there are no reasonable grounds to believe that further investigation or prosecution is warranted. Pursuant to § 592(f), the Attorney General's decision to apply to the Special Division for the appointment of an independent counsel is not reviewable "in any court."

6. The Attorney General, however, retains "direction or control as to those matters that specifically require the Attorney General's personal action under section 2516 of title 18."

> "An independent counsel appointed under this chapter may be removed from office, other than by impeachment and conviction, only by the personal action of the Attorney General and only for good cause, physical disability, mental incapacity, or any other condition that substantially impairs the performance of such independent counsel's duties."

If an independent counsel is removed pursuant to this section, the Attorney General is required to submit a report to both the Special Division and the Judiciary Committees of the Senate and the House "specifying the facts found and the ultimate grounds for such removal." Under the current version of the Act, an independent counsel can obtain judicial review of the Attorney General's action by filing a civil action in the United States District Court for the District of Columbia. Members of the Special Division "may not hear or determine any such civil action or any appeal of a decision in any such civil action." The reviewing court is authorized to grant reinstatement or "other appropriate relief." § 596(a)(3).

The other provision governing the tenure of the independent counsel defines the procedures for "terminating" the counsel's office. Under § 596(b)(1), the office of an independent counsel terminates when he notifies the Attorney General that he has completed or substantially completed any investigations or prosecutions undertaken pursuant to the Act. In addition, the Special Division, acting either on its own or on the suggestion of the Attorney General, may terminate the office of an independent counsel at any time if it finds that "the investigation of all matters within the prosecutorial jurisdiction of each independent counsel * * * have been completed or so substantially completed that it would be appropriate for the Department of Justice to complete such investigations and prosecutions."

Finally, the Act provides for Congressional oversight of the activities of independent counsels. An independent counsel may from time to time send Congress statements or reports on his activities. The "appropriate committees of the Congress" are given oversight jurisdiction in regard to the official conduct of an independent counsel, and the counsel is required by the Act to cooperate with Congress in the exercise of this jurisdiction. The counsel is required to inform the House of Representatives of "substantial and credible information which [the counsel] receives * * * that may constitute grounds for an impeachment." In addition, the Act gives certain Congressional Committee Members the power to "request in writing that the Attorney General apply for the appointment of an independent counsel." The Attorney General is required to respond to this request within a specified time but is not required to accede to the request.

The proceedings in this case provide an example of how the Act works in practice. In 1982, two subcommittees of the House of Representatives issued subpoenas directing the Environmental Protection Agency (EPA) to produce certain documents relating to the efforts of the EPA and the Land and Natural Resources Division of the Justice Department to enforce the "Superfund Law." At that time, appellee Olson was the Assistant Attorney General for the Office of Legal Counsel (OLC), appellee Schmults was Deputy Attorney General, and appellee Dinkins was the Assistant Attorney General for the Land and Natural Resources Division. Acting on the advice of the Justice Department, the President ordered the Administrator of EPA to invoke executive privilege to withhold certain of the documents on the ground that they contained "enforcement sensitive information." The Administrator obeyed this order and withheld the documents. In response, the House voted to hold the Administrator in contempt, after which the Administrator and the United States together filed a lawsuit against the House. The conflict abated in March 1983, when the Administration agreed to give the House committees limited access to the documents.

The following year, the House Judiciary Committee began an investigation into the Justice Department's role in the controversy over the EPA documents. During this investigation, appellee Olson testified before a House subcommittee on March 10, 1983. * * * In 1985, the majority members of the Judiciary Committee published a lengthy report on the Committee's investigation. The report not only criticized various officials in the Department of Justice for their role in the EPA executive privilege dispute, but it also suggested that appellee Olson had given false and misleading testimony to the subcommittee on March 10, 1983, and that appellees Schmults and Dinkins had wrongfully withheld certain documents from the Committee, thus obstructing the Committee's investigation. The Chairman of the Judiciary Committee forwarded a copy of the report to the Attorney General with a request, pursuant to 28 U.S.C. § 592(c), that he seek the appointment of an independent counsel to investigate the allegations against Olson, Schmults, and Dinkins.

The Attorney General directed the Public Integrity Section of the Criminal Division to conduct a preliminary investigation. The Section's report concluded that the appointment of an independent counsel was warranted to investigate the Committee's allegations with respect to all three appellees. After consulting with other Department officials, however, the Attorney General chose to apply to the Special Division for the appointment of an independent counsel solely with respect to appellee Olson. * * *

On April 23, 1986, the Special Division appointed James C. McKay as independent counsel to investigate "whether the testimony of * * * Olson and his revision of such testimony on March 10, 1983, violated either 18 U.S.C. § 1505 or § 1001, or any other provision of federal law." The court also ordered that the independent counsel

> "shall have jurisdiction to investigate any other allegation of evidence of violation of any Federal criminal law by Theodore Olson developed during investigations, by the Independent Counsel, referred to above, and connected with or arising out of that investiga-

tion, and Independent Counsel shall have jurisdiction to prosecute for any such violation."

McKay later resigned as independent counsel, and on May 29, 1986, the Division appointed appellant Morrison as his replacement, with the same jurisdiction. * * *

* * * [I]n May and June 1987, appellant caused a grand jury to issue and serve subpoenas *ad testificandum* and *duces tecum* on appellees. All three appellees moved to quash the subpoenas, claiming, among other things, that the independent counsel provisions of the Act were unconstitutional and that appellant accordingly had no authority to proceed. On July 20, 1987, the District Court upheld the constitutionality of the Act and denied the motions to quash. * * *

A divided Court of Appeals reversed. *In re Sealed Case*, 838 F.2d 476 (1988). The majority ruled first that an independent counsel is not an "inferior Officer" of the United States for purposes of the Appointments Clause. Accordingly, the court found the Act invalid because it does not provide for the independent counsel to be nominated by the President and confirmed by the Senate, as the Clause requires for "principal" officers. * * * In the majority's view, the Act also violates the Appointments Clause insofar as it empowers a court of law to appoint an "inferior" officer who performs core executive functions; the Act's delegation of various powers to the Special Division violates the limitations of Article III; the Act's restrictions on the Attorney General's power to remove an independent counsel violate the separation of powers; and finally, the Act interferes with the Executive Branch's prerogative to "take care that the Laws be faithfully executed," Art. II, § 3. * * *

[Part II of the majority opinion rejected appellant's contention that the constitutional issues could not be presented in an appeal from a contempt judgment on the ground that that question had not been timely raised in the district court proceeding.]

III

The Appointments Clause of Article II reads as follows:

"[The President] shall nominate, and by and with the Advice and Consent of the Senate, shall appoint Ambassadors, other public Ministers and Consuls, Judges of the Supreme Court, and all other Officers of the United States, whose Appointments are not herein otherwise provided for, and which shall be established by Law: but the Congress may by Law vest the Appointment of such inferior Officers, as they think proper, in the President alone, in the Courts of Law, or in the Heads of Departments." U.S. Const. Art. II, § 2, cl. 2.

The parties do not dispute that "[t]he Constitution for purposes of appointment * * * divides all its officers into two classes." * * * The initial question is, accordingly, whether appellant is an "inferior" or a "principal" officer.[12] If she is the latter, as the Court of Appeals concluded, then the Act is in violation of the Appointments Clause.

The line between "inferior" and "principal" officers is one that is far from clear, and the Framers provided little guidance into where it should be drawn. * * * We need not attempt here to decide exactly where the line falls between the two types of officers, because in our view appellant clearly falls on the "inferior officer" side of that line. Several factors lead to this conclusion.

First, appellant is subject to removal by a higher Executive Branch official. Although appellant may not be "subordinate" to the Attorney General (and the President) insofar as she possesses a degree of independent discretion to exercise the powers delegated to her under the Act, the fact that she can be removed by the Attorney General indicates that she is to some degree "inferior" in rank and authority. Second, appellant is empowered by the Act to perform only certain, limited duties. An independent counsel's role is restricted primarily to investigation and, if appropriate, prosecution for certain federal crimes. Admittedly, the Act delegates to appellant "full power and independent authority to exercise all investigative and prosecutorial functions and powers of the Department of Justice," but this grant of authority does not include any authority to formulate policy for the Government or the Executive Branch, nor does it give appellant any administrative duties outside of those necessary to operate her office. The Act specifically provides that in policy matters appellant is to comply to the extent possible with the policies of the Department.

Third, appellant's office is limited in jurisdiction. Not only is the Act itself restricted in applicability to certain federal officials suspected of certain serious federal crimes, but an independent counsel can only act within the scope of the jurisdiction that has been granted by the Special Division pursuant to a request by the Attorney General. Finally, appellant's office is limited in tenure. There is concededly no time limit on the appointment of a particular counsel. Nonetheless, the office of independent counsel is "temporary" in the sense that an independent counsel is appointed essentially to accomplish a single task, and when that task is over the office is terminated, either by the counsel herself or by action of the Special Division. Unlike other prosecutors, appellant has no ongoing responsibilities that extend beyond the accomplishment of the mission that she was appointed for and authorized by the Special Division to undertake. * * *

This does not, however, end our inquiry under the Appointments Clause. Appellees argue that even if appellant is an "inferior" officer, the Clause does not empower Congress to place the power to appoint such an officer outside the Executive Branch. They contend that the Clause does not contemplate congressional authorization of "interbranch appoint-

12. It is clear that appellant is an "officer" of the United States, not an "employee."

ments," in which an officer of one branch is appointed by officers of another branch. * * * On its face, the language of this "excepting clause" admits of no limitation on interbranch appointments. Indeed, the inclusion of "as they think proper" seems clearly to give Congress significant discretion to determine whether it is "proper" to vest the appointment of, for example, executive officials in the "courts of Law." We recognized as much in one of our few decisions in this area, *Ex parte Siebold*, [100 U.S. (10 Otto) 371, 397–98 (1879)], where we stated:

> It is no doubt usual and proper to vest the appointment of inferior officers in that department of the government, executive or judicial, or in that particular executive department to which the duties of such officers appertain. But there is no absolute requirement to this effect in the Constitution; and, if there were, it would be difficult in many cases to determine to which department an office properly belonged. * * *

We also note that the history of the clause provides no support for appellees' position. * * *

We do not mean to say that Congress' power to provide for interbranch appointments of "inferior officers" is unlimited. In addition to separation of powers concerns, which would arise if such provisions for appointment had the potential to impair the constitutional functions assigned to one of the branches, *Siebold* itself suggested that Congress' decision to vest the appointment power in the courts would be improper if there was some "incongruity" between the functions normally performed by the courts and the performance of their duty to appoint. * * * In this case, however, we do not think it impermissible for Congress to vest the power to appoint independent counsels in a specially created federal court. We thus disagree with the Court of Appeals' conclusion that there is an inherent incongruity about a court having the power to appoint prosecutorial officers.[13] * * * Congress of course was concerned when it created the office of independent counsel with the conflicts of interest that could arise in situations when the Executive Branch is called upon to investigate its own high-ranking officers. If it were to remove the appointing authority from the Executive Branch, the most logical place to put it was in the Judicial Branch. In the light of the Act's provision making the judges of the Special Division ineligible to participate in any matters relating to an independent counsel they have appointed, 28 U.S.C. § 49(f), we do not think that appointment of the independent counsels by the court runs afoul of the constitutional limitation on "incongruous" interbranch appointments.

13. Indeed, in light of judicial experience with prosecutors in criminal cases, it could be said that courts are especially well qualified to appoint prosecutors. This is not a case in which judges are given power to appoint an officer in an area in which they have no special knowledge or expertise, as in, for example, a statute authorizing the courts to appoint officials in the Department of Agriculture or the Federal Energy Regulatory Commission.

IV

Appellees next contend that the powers vested in the Special Division by the Act conflict with Article III of the Constitution. We have long recognized that by the express provision of Article III, the judicial power of the United States is limited to "Cases" and "Controversies." As a general rule, we have broadly stated that "executive or administrative duties of a nonjudicial nature may not be imposed on judges holding office under Art. III of the Constitution." *Buckley*, 424 U.S., at 123. * * *

Most importantly, the Act vests in the Special Division the power to choose who will serve as independent counsel and the power to define his or her jurisdiction. Clearly, once it is accepted that the Appointments Clause gives Congress the power to vest the appointment of officials such as the independent counsel in the "courts of Law," there can be no Article III objection to the Special Division's exercise of that power, as the power itself derives from the Appointments Clause, a source of authority for judicial action that is independent of Article III. Appellees contend, however, that the Division's Appointments Clause powers do not encompass the power to define the independent counsel's jurisdiction. We disagree. In our view, Congress' power under the Clause to vest the "Appointment" of inferior officers in the courts may, in certain circumstances, allow Congress to give the courts some discretion in defining the nature and scope of the appointed official's authority. Particularly when, as here, Congress creates a temporary "office" the nature and duties of which will by necessity vary with the factual circumstances giving rise to the need for an appointment in the first place, it may vest the power to define the scope of the office in the court as an incident to the appointment of the officer pursuant to the Appointments Clause. This said, we do not think that Congress may give the Division *unlimited* discretion to determine the independent counsel's jurisdiction. In order for the Division's definition of the counsel's jurisdiction to be truly "incidental" to its power to appoint, the jurisdiction that the court decides upon must be demonstrably related to the factual circumstances that gave rise to the Attorney General's investigation and request for the appointment of the independent counsel in the particular case.[17]

The Act also vests in the Special Division various powers and duties in relation to the independent counsel that, because they do not involve appointing the counsel or defining her jurisdiction, cannot be said to derive from the Division's Appointments Clause authority. * * *

Leaving aside for the moment the Division's power to terminate an independent counsel, we do not think that Article III absolutely prevents Congress from vesting these other miscellaneous powers in the Special Division pursuant to the Act. * * * In this case, the miscellaneous

17. Our conclusion that the power to define the counsel's jurisdiction is incidental to the power to appoint also applies to the Division's authority to expand the jurisdiction of the counsel upon request of the Attorney General under § 593(c)(2).

powers described above do not impermissibly trespass upon the authority of the Executive Branch. Some of these allegedly "supervisory" powers conferred on the court are passive: the Division merely "receives" reports from the counsel or the Attorney General, it is not entitled to act on them or to specifically approve or disapprove of their contents. Other provisions of the Act do require the court to exercise some judgment and discretion,[19] but the powers granted by these provisions are themselves essentially ministerial. The Act simply does not give the Division the power to "supervise" the independent counsel in the exercise of her investigative or prosecutorial authority. * * *[20]

We are more doubtful about the Special Division's power to terminate the office of the independent counsel pursuant to § 596(b)(2). As appellees suggest, the power to terminate, especially when exercised by the Division on its own motion, is "administrative" to the extent that it requires the Special Division to monitor the progress of proceedings of the independent counsel and come to a decision as to whether the counsel's job is "completed." * * *

We think that the Court of Appeals overstated the matter when it described the power to terminate as a "broadsword and * * * rapier" that enables the court to "control the pace and depth of the independent counsel's activities." The provision has not been tested in practice, and we do not mean to say that an adventurous special court could not reasonably construe the provision as did the Court of Appeals; but it is the duty of federal courts to construe a statute in order to save it from constitutional infirmities, and to that end we think a narrow construction is appropriate here. The termination provisions of the Act do not give the Special Division anything approaching the power to *remove* the counsel while an investigation or court proceeding is still underway—this power is vested solely in the Attorney General. As we see it, "termination" may occur only when the duties of the counsel are truly "completed" or "so substantially completed" that there remains no need for any continuing action by the independent counsel. It is basically a device for removing from the public payroll an independent counsel who

19. The Special Division must determine whether the Attorney General has shown "good cause" for his request for an extension of the time limit on his preliminary investigation, § 592(a)(3); the court must decide whether and to what extent it should release to the public the counsel's final report or the Attorney General's removal report, §§ 596(a)(2), (b)(2); and the court may consider the propriety of a request for attorney's fees, § 593(f).

20. By way of comparison, we also note that federal courts and judges have long performed a variety of functions that, like the functions involved here, do not necessarily or directly involve adversarial proceedings within a trial or appellate court. For example, federal courts have traditionally supervised grand juries and assisted in their "investigative function" by, if necessary, compelling the testimony of witnesses. Federal courts also participate in the issuance of search warrants and review applications for wiretaps, both of which may require a court to consider the nature and scope of criminal investigations on the basis of evidence or affidavits submitted in an *ex parte* proceeding. In *Young v. United States ex rel. Vuitton et Fils S.A.*, 481 U.S. 787, 793 (1987), we recognized that federal courts possess inherent authority to initiate contempt proceedings for disobedience to their orders, and this authority necessarily includes the ability to appoint a private attorney to prosecute the contempt.

has served her purpose, but is unwilling to acknowledge the fact. So construed, the Special Division's power to terminate does not pose a sufficient threat of judicial intrusion into matters that are more properly within the Executive's authority to require that the Act be invalidated as inconsistent with Article III. * * *

V

We now turn to consider whether the Act is invalid under the constitutional principle of separation of powers. Two related issues must be addressed: The first is whether the provision of the Act restricting the Attorney General's power to remove the independent counsel to only those instances in which he can show "good cause," taken by itself, impermissibly interferes with the President's exercise of his constitutionally appointed functions. The second is whether, taken as a whole, the Act violates the separation of powers by reducing the President's ability to control the prosecutorial powers wielded by the independent counsel. * * *

Unlike both *Bowsher* and *Myers*, this case does not involve an attempt by Congress itself to gain a role in the removal of executive officials other than its established powers of impeachment and conviction. The Act instead puts the removal power squarely in the hands of the Executive Branch; an independent counsel may be removed from office, "only by the personal action of the Attorney General, and only for good cause." There is no requirement of congressional approval of the Attorney General's removal decision, though the decision is subject to judicial review. In our view, the removal provisions of the Act make this case more analogous to *Humphrey's Executor v. United States*, 295 U.S. 602 (1935), and *Wiener v. United States*, 357 U.S. 349 (1958), than to *Myers* or *Bowsher*. * * *

Appellees contend that *Humphrey's Executor* and *Wiener* are distinguishable from this case because they did not involve officials who performed a "core executive function." They argue that our decision in *Humphrey's Executor* rests on a distinction between "purely executive" officials and officials who exercise "quasi-legislative" and "quasi-judicial" powers. In their view, when a "purely executive" official is involved, the governing precedent is *Myers*, not *Humphrey's Executor*. * * * [26]

We undoubtedly did rely on the terms "quasi-legislative" and "quasi-judicial" to distinguish the officials involved in *Humphrey's Executor* and *Wiener* from those in *Myers*, but our present considered view is that the determination of whether the Constitution allows Congress to impose a "good cause"—type restriction on the President's power to remove an official cannot be made to turn on whether or not that official

26. This same argument was raised by the Solicitor General in *Bowsher v. Synar*, 478 U.S. 714 (1986), although as Justice White noted in dissent in that case, the argument was clearly not accepted by the Court at that time. *Id.*, at 738–739, and nn. 1–3.

is classified as "purely executive."[27] The analysis contained in our removal cases is designed not to define rigid categories of those officials who may or may not be removed at will by the President, but to ensure that Congress does not interfere with the President's exercise of the "executive power" and his constitutionally appointed duty to "take care that the laws be faithfully executed" under Article II. *Myers* was undoubtedly correct in its holding, and in its broader suggestion that there are some "purely executive" officials who must be removable by the President at will if he is to be able to accomplish his constitutional role.[29] * * *

At the other end of the spectrum from *Myers*, the characterization of the agencies in *Humphrey's Executor* and *Wiener* as "quasi-legislative" or "quasi-judicial" in large part reflected our judgment that it was not essential to the President's proper execution of his Article II powers that these agencies be headed up by individuals who were removable at will.[30] We do not mean to suggest that an analysis of the functions served by the officials at issue is irrelevant. But the real question is whether the removal restrictions are of such a nature that they impede the President's ability to perform his constitutional duty, and the functions of the officials in question must be analyzed in that light.

Considering for the moment the "good cause" removal provision in isolation from the other parts of the Act at issue in this case, we cannot say that the imposition of a "good cause" standard for removal by itself unduly trammels on executive authority. There is no real dispute that the functions performed by the independent counsel are "executive" in the sense that they are law enforcement functions that typically have been undertaken by officials within the Executive Branch. As we noted above, however, the independent counsel is an inferior officer under the Appointments Clause, with limited jurisdiction and tenure and lacking policymaking or significant administrative authority. Although the counsel exercises no small amount of discretion and judgment in deciding

27. Indeed, this Court has never held that the Constitution prevents Congress from imposing limitations on the President's power to remove *all* executive officials simply because they wield "executive" power. *Myers* itself expressly distinguished cases in which Congress had chosen to vest the appointment of "inferior" executive officials in the head of a department. In such a situation, we saw no specific constitutional impediment to congressionally imposed restrictions on the President's removal powers. * * *

29. The dissent says that the language of Article II vesting the executive power of the United States in the President requires that every officer of the United States exercising any part of that power must serve at the pleasure of the President and be removable by him at will. This rigid demarcation—a demarcation incapable of being altered by law in the slightest degree, and applicable to tens of thousands of holders of offices neither known nor foreseen by the framers—depends upon an extrapolation from general constitutional language which we think is more than the text will bear. It is also contrary to our holding in *United States v. Perkins*, 116 U.S. 483 (1886), decided more than a century ago.

30. The terms also may be used to describe the circumstances in which Congress might be more inclined to find that a degree of independence from the Executive, such as that afforded by a "good cause" removal standard, is necessary to the proper functioning of the agency or official. It is not difficult to imagine situations in which Congress might desire that an official performing "quasi-judicial" functions, for example, would be free of executive or political control.

how to carry out her duties under the Act, we simply do not see how the President's need to control the exercise of that discretion is so central to the functioning of the Executive Branch as to require as a matter of constitutional law that the counsel be terminable at will by the President.[31]

Nor do we think that the "good cause" removal provision at issue here impermissibly burdens the President's power to control or supervise the independent counsel, as an executive official, in the execution of her duties under the Act. This is not a case in which the power to remove an executive official has been completely stripped from the President, thus providing no means for the President to ensure the "faithful execution" of the laws. Rather, because the independent counsel may be terminated for "good cause," the Executive, through the Attorney General, retains ample authority to assure that the counsel is competently performing her statutory responsibilities in a manner that comports with the provisions of the Act. Although we need not decide in this case exactly what is encompassed within the term "good cause" under the Act, the legislative history of the removal provision also makes clear that the Attorney General may remove an independent counsel for "misconduct." Here, as with the provision of the Act conferring the appointment authority of the independent counsel on the special court, the congressional determination to limit the removal power of the Attorney General was essential, in the view of Congress, to establish the necessary independence of the office. We do not think that this limitation as it presently stands sufficiently deprives the President of control over the independent counsel to interfere impermissibly with his constitutional obligation to ensure the faithful execution of the laws.

The final question to be addressed is whether the Act, taken as a whole, violates the principle of separation of powers by unduly interfering with the role of the Executive Branch. * * *

We observe first that this case does not involve an attempt by Congress to increase its own powers at the expense of the Executive Branch. Unlike some of our previous cases, most recently *Bowsher v. Synar*, this case simply does not pose a "dange[r] of congressional usurpation of Executive Branch functions." Indeed, with the exception of the power of impeachment—which applies to all officers of the United States—Congress retained for itself no powers of control or supervision over an independent counsel. The Act does empower certain members of Congress to request the Attorney General to apply for the appointment of an independent counsel, but the Attorney General has no duty to comply with the request, although he must respond within a certain time limit. Other than that, Congress' role under the Act is limited to receiving reports or other information and oversight of the independent counsel's activities, functions that we have recognized generally as being incidental to the legislative function of Congress.

31. We note by way of comparison that various federal agencies whose officers are covered by "good cause" removal restrictions exercise civil enforcement powers that are analogous to the prosecutorial powers wielded by an independent counsel. * * *

Similarly, we do not think that the Act works any *judicial* usurpation of properly executive functions. As should be apparent from our discussion of the Appointments Clause above, the power to appoint inferior officers such as independent counsels is not in itself an "executive" function in the constitutional sense, at least when Congress has exercised its power to vest the appointment of an inferior office in the "courts of Law." We note nonetheless that under the Act the Special Division has no power to appoint an independent counsel *sua sponte*; it may only do so upon the specific request of the Attorney General, and the courts are specifically prevented from reviewing the Attorney General's decision not to seek appointment. In addition, once the court has appointed a counsel and defined her jurisdiction, it has no power to supervise or control the activities of the counsel. * * *

Finally, we do not think that the Act "impermissibly undermine[s]" the powers of the Executive Branch or "disrupts the proper balance between the coordinate branches [by] prevent[ing] the Executive Branch from accomplishing its constitutionally assigned functions." It is undeniable that the Act reduces the amount of control or supervision that the Attorney General and, through him, the President exercises over the investigation and prosecution of a certain class of alleged criminal activity. The Attorney General is not allowed to appoint the individual of his choice; he does not determine the counsel's jurisdiction; and his power to remove a counsel is limited.[34] Nonetheless, the Act does give the Attorney General several means of supervising or controlling the prosecutorial powers that may be wielded by an independent counsel. Most importantly, the Attorney General retains the power to remove the counsel for "good cause," a power that we have already concluded provides the Executive with substantial ability to ensure that the laws are "faithfully executed" by an independent counsel. No independent counsel may be appointed without a specific request by the Attorney General, and the Attorney General's decision not to request appointment if he finds "no reasonable grounds to believe that further investigation is warranted" is committed to his unreviewable discretion. The Act thus gives the Executive a degree of control over the power to initiate an investigation by the independent counsel. In addition, the jurisdiction of the independent counsel is defined with reference to the facts submitted by the Attorney General, and once a counsel is appointed, the Act requires that the counsel abide by Justice Department policy unless it is not "possible" to do so. Notwithstanding the fact that the counsel is to some degree "independent" and free from Executive supervision to a greater extent than other federal prosecutors, in our view these features of the Act give the Executive Branch sufficient control over the independent counsel to ensure that the President is able to perform his constitutionally assigned duties.

34. With these provisions, the degree of control exercised by the Executive Branch over an independent counsel is clearly diminished in relation to that exercised over other prosecutors, such as the United States Attorneys, who are appointed by the President and subject to termination at will.

VI

In sum, we conclude today that it does not violate the Appointments Clause for Congress to vest the appointment of independent counsels in the Special Division; that the powers exercised by the Special Division under the Act do not violate Article III; and that the Act does not violate the separation of powers principle by impermissibly interfering with the functions of the Executive Branch. The decision of the Court of Appeals is therefore

Reversed.

JUSTICE SCALIA, dissenting. * * *

I

* * * [B]y the application of this statute in the present case, Congress has effectively compelled a criminal investigation of a high-level appointee of the President in connection with his actions arising out of a bitter power dispute between the President and the Legislative Branch. Mr. Olson may or may not be guilty of a crime; we do not know. But we do know that the investigation of him has been commenced, not necessarily because the President or his authorized subordinates believe it is in the interest of the United States, in the sense that it warrants the diversion of resources from other efforts, and is worth the cost in money and in possible damage to other governmental interests; and not even, leaving aside those normally considered factors, because the President or his authorized subordinates necessarily believe that an investigation is likely to unearth a violation worth prosecuting; but only because the Attorney General cannot affirm, as Congress demands, that there are *no reasonable grounds to believe* that further investigation is warranted. The decisions regarding the scope of that further investigation, its duration, and, finally, whether or not prosecution should ensue, are likewise beyond the control of the President and his subordinates.

II

If to describe this case is not to decide it, the concept of a government of separate and coordinate powers no longer has meaning. The Court devotes most of its attention to such relatively technical details as the Appointments Clause and the removal power, addressing briefly and only at the end of its opinion the separation of powers. * * * I think that has it backwards. * * *

* * * Art. II, § 1, cl. 1 of the Constitution provides:

> "The executive Power shall be vested in a President of the United States."

As I described at the outset of this opinion, this does not mean *some of* the executive power, but *all of* the executive power. It seems to me, therefore, that the decision of the Court of Appeals invalidating the present statute must be upheld on fundamental separation-of-powers principles if the following two questions are answered affirmatively: (1)

Is the conduct of a criminal prosecution (and of an investigation to decide whether to prosecute) the exercise of purely executive power? (2) Does the statute deprive the President of the United States of exclusive control over the exercise of that power? Surprising to say, the Court appears to concede an affirmative answer to both questions, but seeks to avoid the inevitable conclusion that, since the statute vests some purely executive power in a person who is not the President of the United States, it is void.

The Court concedes that "[t]here is no real dispute that the functions performed by the independent counsel are 'executive,' " though it qualifies that concession by adding "in the sense that they are 'law enforcement' functions that typically have been undertaken by officials within the Executive Branch." The qualifier adds nothing but atmosphere. In what *other* sense can one identify "the executive Power" that is supposed to be vested in the President (unless it includes everything the Executive Branch is given to do) *except* by reference to what has always and everywhere—if conducted by Government at all—been conducted never by the legislature, never by the courts, and always by the executive. There is no possible doubt that the independent counsel's functions fit this description. * * *

As for the second question, whether the statute before us deprives the President of exclusive control over that quintessentially executive activity: The Court does not, and could not possibly, assert that it does not. That is indeed the whole object of the statute. Instead, the Court points out that the President, through his Attorney General, has at least *some* control. That concession is alone enough to invalidate the statute, but I cannot refrain from pointing out that the Court greatly exaggerates the extent of that "some" presidential control. "Most importan[t]" among these controls, the Court asserts, is the Attorney General's "power to remove the counsel for 'good cause.' " This is somewhat like referring to shackles as an effective means of locomotion. As we recognized in *Humphrey's Executor v. United States*, 295 U.S. 602 (1935)—indeed, what *Humphrey's Executor* was all about—limiting removal power to "good cause" is an impediment to, not an effective grant of, presidential control. * * * What we in *Humphrey's Executor* found to be a means of eliminating presidential control, the Court today considers the "most importan[t]" means of assuring presidential control. Congress, of course, operated under no such illusion when it enacted this statute, describing the "good cause" limitation as "protecting the independent counsel's ability to act independently of the President's direct control" since it permits removal only for "misconduct." * * *

[I]t is ultimately irrelevant *how much* the statute reduces presidential control. The case is over when the Court acknowledges, as it must, that "[i]t is undeniable that the Act reduces the amount of control or supervision that the Attorney General and, through him, the President exercises over the investigation and prosecution of a certain class of alleged criminal activity." * * *

Is it unthinkable that the President should have such exclusive power, even when alleged crimes by him or his close associates are at issue? No more so than that Congress should have the exclusive power of legislation, even when what is at issue is its own exemption from the burdens of certain laws. See Civil Rights Act of 1964, Title VII, 42 U.S.C. § 2000e *et seq.* (prohibiting "employers," not defined to include the United States, from discriminating on the basis of race, color, religion, sex or national origin). No more so than that this Court should have the exclusive power to pronounce the final decision on justiciable cases and controversies, even those pertaining to the constitutionality of a statute reducing the salaries of the Justices. See *United States v. Will*, 449 U.S. 200, 211–217 (1980). A system of separate and coordinate powers necessarily involves an acceptance of exclusive power that can theoretically be abused. * * * While the separation of powers may prevent us from righting every wrong, it does so in order to ensure that we do not lose liberty. The checks against any Branch's abuse of its exclusive powers are twofold: First, retaliation by one of the other Branch's use of *its* exclusive powers: Congress, for example, can impeach the Executive who willfully fails to enforce the laws; the Executive can decline to prosecute under unconstitutional statutes; and the courts can dismiss malicious prosecutions. Second, and ultimately, there is the political check that the people will replace those in the political branches (the branches more "dangerous to the political rights of the Constitution," Federalist No. 78, p. 465) who are guilty of abuse. * * *

In my view, moreover, even as an ad hoc, standardless judgment the Court's conclusion must be wrong. Before this statute was passed, the President, in taking action disagreeable to the Congress, or an executive officer giving advice to the President or testifying before Congress concerning one of those many matters on which the two branches are from time to time at odds, could be assured that his acts and motives would be adjudged—insofar as the decision whether to conduct a criminal investigation and to prosecute is concerned—in the Executive Branch, that is, in a forum attuned to the interests and the policies of the Presidency. That was one of the natural advantages the Constitution gave to the Presidency, just as it gave Members of Congress (and their staffs) the advantage of not being prosecutable for anything said or done in their legislative capacities. It is the very object of this legislation to eliminate that assurance of a sympathetic forum. * * * Perhaps the boldness of the President himself will not be affected—though I am not even sure of that. * * * But as for the President's high-level assistants, who typically have no political base of support, it is as utterly unrealistic to think that * * * their advice to him and their advocacy of his interests before a hostile Congress will not be affected, as it would be to think that the Members of Congress and their staffs would be unaffected by replacing the Speech or Debate Clause with a similar provision. It deeply wounds the President, by substantially reducing the President's ability to protect himself and his staff. That is the whole object of the law, of course, and I cannot imagine why the Court believes it does not succeed.

Besides weakening the Presidency by reducing the zeal of his staff, it must also be obvious that the institution of the independent counsel enfeebles him more directly in his constant confrontations with Congress, by eroding his public support. Nothing is so politically effective as the ability to charge that one's opponent and his associates are not merely wrong-headed, naive, ineffective, but, in all probability, "crooks." And nothing so effectively gives an appearance of validity to such charges as a Justice Department investigation and, even better, prosecution. * * *

[In Part III, Justice Scalia argues that the majority characterization of the independent counsel as an "inferior officer" is incorrect, and that, therefore, she could be appointed only by the President, with the Senate's advice and consent. He first disputes the majority's reliance on Morrison's removability, her statutorily constrained powers, and her limited tenure and jurisdiction. He then urges, "more fundamentally," that Morrison cannot be considered an "inferior officer" because she is not subordinate to any other official, including the President, in exercising whatever discretion she enjoys in implementing her statutory powers: "To be sure, it is not a sufficient condition for 'inferior officer' status that one be subordinate to a principal officer. * * * But surely it is a necessary condition."]

IV

I will not discuss at any length why the restrictions upon the removal of the independent counsel also violate our established precedent dealing with that specific subject. * * * I cannot avoid commenting, however, about the essence of what the Court has done to our removal jurisprudence today. * * *

Since our 1935 decision in *Humphrey's Executor v. United States*—which was considered by many at the time the product of an activist, anti-New Deal court bent on reducing the power of President Franklin Roosevelt—it has been established that the line of permissible restriction upon removal of principal officers lies at the point at which the powers exercised by those officers are no longer purely executive. * * * It has often been observed, correctly in my view, that the line between "purely executive" functions and "quasi-legislative" or "quasi-judicial" functions is not a clear one or even a rational one. But at least it permitted the identification of certain officers, and certain agencies, whose functions were entirely within the control of the President. Congress had to be aware of that restriction in its legislation. Today, however, *Humphrey's Executor* is swept into the dustbin of repudiated constitutional principles. * * *

* * * "[O]ur present considered view" is simply that *any* Executive officer's removal can be restricted, so long as the President remains "able to accomplish his constitutional role." There are now no lines. If

the removal of a prosecutor, the virtual embodiment of the power to "take care that the laws be faithfully executed," can be restricted, what officer's removal cannot? This is an open invitation for Congress to experiment. What about a special Assistant Secretary of State, with responsibility for one very narrow area of foreign policy, who would not only have to be confirmed by the Senate but could also be removed only pursuant to certain carefully designed restrictions? Could this possibly render the President "[un]able to accomplish his constitutional role?" Or a special Assistant Secretary of Defense for Procurement? The possibilities are endless, and the Court does not understand what the separation of powers, what "[a]mbition * * * counteract[ing] ambition," is all about, if it does not expect Congress to try them. As far as I can discern from the Court's opinion, it is now open season upon the President's removal power for all executive powers, with not even the superficially principled restriction of *Humphrey's Executor* as cover. The Court essentially says to the President "Trust us. We will make sure that you are able to accomplish your constitutional role." I think the Constitution gives the President—and the people—more protection than that.

V

* * * Under our system of government, the primary check against prosecutorial abuse is a political one. The prosecutors who exercise this awesome discretion are selected and can be removed by a President, whom the people have trusted enough to elect. Moreover, when crimes are not investigated and prosecuted fairly, nonselectively, with a reasonable sense of proportion, the President pays the cost in political damage to his administration. * * *

* * * [A]n additional advantage of the unitary Executive that it can achieve a more uniform application of the law. Perhaps that is not always achieved, but the mechanism to achieve it is there. The mini-Executive that is the independent counsel, however, operating in an area where so little is law and so much is discretion, is intentionally cut off from the unifying influence of the Justice Department, and from the perspective that multiple responsibilities provide. What would normally be regarded as a technical violation (there are no rules defining such things), may in her small world assume the proportions of an indictable offense. What would normally be regarded as an investigation that has reached the level of pursuing such picayune matters that it should be concluded, may to her be an investigation that ought to go on for another year. How frightening it must be to have your own independent counsel and staff appointed, with nothing else to do but to investigate you until investigation is no longer worthwhile—with whether it is worthwhile not depending upon what such judgments usually hinge on, competing responsibilities. And to have that counsel and staff decide, with no basis for comparison, whether what you have done is bad enough, willful enough, and provable enough, to warrant an indictment. How admirable the constitutional system that provides the means to

avoid such a distortion. And how unfortunate the judicial decision that has permitted it. * * *

Notes

1. *Independence v. Executive Accountability*. The independent counsel (originally "special prosecutor") provisions of the Ethics in Government Act represented a conspicuous attempt at compromise between independence and executive control. Note, for example, despite the Act's rationale, that Congress gave a prominent role to the Attorney General, who will ordinarily be a close political ally of the President.

Two sets of amendments to the original act illustrate Congress' attempts to fine-tune the balance between presidential control and prosecutorial independence:

> Congress' 1982 reauthorization of the special prosecutor statute included several changes from the original act. These included (a) changing the name of the "special prosecutor" to "independent counsel"; (b) changing the standard that triggers a preliminary investigation of covered officials to allow the Attorney General to consider the credibility of the accuser and the specificity of the information received; and (c) permitting the Attorney General to remove independent counsel for "good cause," instead of only for "extraordinary impropriety" or mental and physical disability. The 1982 amendments further required the appointment of independent counsel only when the Attorney General "finds reasonable grounds to believe that further investigation or prosecution is warranted." This language replaced a more stringent earlier standard, which required a special prosecutor unless the information received "is so unsubstantiated that no further investigation is warranted." A final change of considerable importance was permitting the Attorney General, in determining whether reasonable grounds exist to warrant further investigation or prosecution, to "comply with the written or other established policies of the Department of Justice with respect to the enforcement of criminal law." Under this last provision, for example, the Attorney General could forbear from appointing an independent counsel in an undisputed case of illicit drug possession by a high level executive branch official, if the Department of Justice has a preexisting policy not to prosecute possession offenses unless the quantity of substance involved is greater than present in the particular case. * * *
>
> Despite constitutional misgivings, President Reagan, in December, 1987, signed another five-year reauthorization of the special prosecutor process. Congress moved this time to restrict the Attorney General's discretion and to buttress the autonomy of the independent counsel. The reauthorization, for example, requires a preliminary investigation "whenever the Attorney General receives information sufficient to constitute grounds to investigate whether any person [covered by the act] *may have* committed a violation of any Federal criminal law other than a petty offense." The earlier acts triggered investigations only when the information received suggested that a person covered by the Act "has

> committed" a serious criminal violation. Further, the reauthorization would forbid the Attorney General to rely "upon a determination that [a] person lacked the state of mind required for the violation of criminal law" as a reason for not having a preliminary investigation or not applying for the appointment of an independent counsel.

PETER M. SHANE & HAROLD H. BRUFF, THE LAW OF PRESIDENTIAL POWER 455–56 (1988).

Congress reauthorized the Act for five years in 1994, Independent Counsel Reauthorization Act of 1994, Pub.L. 103–270, 108 Stat.732, but allowed it to lapse in the wake of Special Counsel Kenneth Starr's investigation of the Whitewater and Monica Lewinsky episodes and the impeachment and acquittal of President Clinton. Given the problems the Act ultimately posed for Presidents of both parties, its demise was little mourned. Starr's critics found in Justice Scalia's *Morrison* dissent a fairly prescient description of what they perceived to be abuses in the prosecutorial process. The episode spawned an enormous literature debating whether abuses of the sort alleged were unavoidable under any special counsel mechanism or the result of circumstances peculiar to the Starr investigation. A good sampling appears at Symposium, *The Independent Counsel Statute: Reform or Repeal?*, 62 Law & Contemp. Probs. 1 (1999). A helpful bibliography can be found in Judith Roof, *Investigating the Special: the Symbolic Function of the Independent Counsel*, 77 Ind. L.J. 277, 277 n.2 (2002). For a comprehensive historical treatment of the Act and the prosecutions under it, see GERALD S. GREENBERG, ED., HISTORICAL ENCYCLOPEDIA OF U.S. INDEPENDENT COUNSEL INVESTIGATIONS (2000). A defense of the act by a controversial special counsel who would have preferred amendment rather than repeal is Lawrence E. Walsh, *Kenneth Starr and the Independent Counsel Act*, N.Y.Rev. of Books, Mar. 5, 1998, at 4.

2. *Historical Practice.* The central premise of Justice Scalia's dissent is that the vesting clause of Article II gives the President exclusive control over all exercises of executive power, including all functions typically performed by members of the executive branch. Neither he nor the majority takes account of historical evidence concerning the vesting of executive power in the President. The record of state criminal prosecution in the 18th and 19th centuries strongly suggests, in fact, that there was no common understanding that the direction of criminal prosecution in a government of separated powers would be an inherently executive function. William Gwyn, *The Indeterminacy of the Separation of Powers and the Federal Courts*, 57 Geo.Wash.L.Rev. 474 (1989); Note, *Is Prosecution a Core Executive Function?* Morrison v. Olson *and the Framers' Intent*, 99 Yale L.J. 1069 (1990); Shane, *Independent Policymaking*, *supra* page 226, at 603–06.

3. Morrison, Mistretta, *and Independent Agencies. Morrison* is read by many as removing any doubt about the constitutionality of protecting "independent agency" heads through "for cause" limitations on their removability. See *Securities and Exchange Commission v. Blinder, Robinson & Co. Inc.*, 855 F.2d 677 (10th Cir.1988) (upholding SEC enforcement power).

That conclusion was buttressed by the Court's decision the following term in *Mistretta v. United States*, 488 U.S. 361 (1989), which upheld the structure of the United States Sentencing Commission (USSC), created under the Sentencing Reform Act of 1984, as amended, 18 U.S.C. § 3551 et seq., and 28 U.S.C. §§ 991–998. Congress created the USSC to promulgate guidelines to constrain the sentencing discretion of federal judges and produce greater consistency. The Act provided that the USSC was to be an "independent commission in the judicial branch of the United States," 28 U.S.C. § 991(a), consisting of seven members, at least three of whom would be federal judges. The President was empowered to appoint all seven members, subject to Senate advice and consent, but no member could be removed except for good cause.

Mistretta, a drug offender sentenced under USSC guidelines, mounted a series of separation of powers arguments against the agency's structure and governmental locus:

> Mistretta * * * argues that Congress, in constituting the Commission as it did, effected an unconstitutional accumulation of power within the Judicial Branch while at the same time undermining the Judiciary's independence and integrity. Specifically, petitioner claims that in delegating to an independent agency within the Judicial Branch the power to promulgate sentencing guidelines, Congress unconstitutionally has required the Branch, and individual Article III judges, to exercise not only their judicial authority, but legislative authority—the making of sentencing policy—as well. Such rulemaking authority, petitioner contends, may be exercised by Congress, or delegated by Congress to the Executive, but may not be delegated to or exercised by the Judiciary.
>
> At the same time, petitioner asserts, Congress unconstitutionally eroded the integrity and independence of the Judiciary by requiring Article III judges to sit on the Commission, by requiring that those judges share their rulemaking authority with nonjudges, and by subjecting the Commission's members to appointment and removal by the President. According to petitioner, Congress, consistent with the separation of powers, may not upset the balance among the Branches by co-opting federal judges into the quintessentially political work of establishing sentencing guidelines, by subjecting those judges to the political whims of the Chief Executive, and by forcing judges to share their power with nonjudges.

The Court, over Justice Scalia's lone dissent, rejected each of these contentions. The Court rejected the argument that placing the USSC within the judicial branch marked a constitutional impairment of the executive:

> In the field of sentencing, the Executive Branch never has exercised the kind of authority that Congress has vested in the Commission. Moreover, since Congress has empowered the President to appoint and remove Commission members, the President's relationship to the Commission is functionally no different from what it would have been had Congress not located the Commission in the Judicial Branch. Indeed, since the Act grants ex officio membership on the Commission to the Attorney General or his designee, the Executive Branch's involvement in the Commission is greater than in other independent agencies, such as the Securities and Exchange Commission, not located in the Judicial Branch.

Nor did the Court regard the USSC as impermissibly compromising the powers of the judiciary. Authorizing the President to appoint judges to the USSC and to remove judge-commissioners for good cause did not, in the majority's view, realistically threaten the independence of the judiciary or the reality or appearance of impartiality in the execution of the judiciary's ordinary functions.

Among other grounds for dissent, Justice Scalia denied that Congress could constitutionally determine to locate an administrative agency outside the executive:

> I am sure that Congress can divide up the government any way it wishes, and employ whatever terminology it desires, for nonconstitutional purposes—for example, perhaps the statutory designation that the Commission is "within the Judicial Branch" places it outside the coverage of certain laws which say they are inapplicable to that Branch, such as the Freedom of Information Act. For such statutory purposes, Congress can define the term as it pleases. But since our subject here is the Constitution, to admit that that congressional designation "has [no] meaning for separation-of-powers analysis" is to admit that the Court must therefore decide for itself where the Commission is located for purposes of separation-of-powers analysis.
>
> It would seem logical to decide the question of which Branch an agency belongs to on the basis of who controls its actions. * * * In *Humphrey's Executor v. United States*, we approved the concept of an agency that was controlled by (and thus within) none of the Branches. * * * Over the years, however, *Humphrey's Executor* has come in general contemplation to stand for something quite different—not an "independent agency" in the sense of an agency independent of all three Branches, but an "independent agency" in the sense of an agency within the Executive Branch (and thus authorized to exercise executive powers) independent of the control of the President.
>
> We approved that concept last Term in *Morrison*. I dissented in that case, essentially because I thought that concept illogical and destructive of the structure of the Constitution. I must admit, however, that today's next step—recognition of an independent agency in the Judicial Branch—makes *Morrison* seem, by comparison, rigorously logical. "The Commission," we are told, "is an independent agency in every relevant sense." There are several problems with this. First, once it is acknowledged that an "independent agency" may be within any of the three Branches, and not merely within the Executive, then there really is no basis for determining what Branch such an agency belongs to, and thus what governmental powers it may constitutionally be given, except (what the Court today uses) Congress' say-so. More importantly, however, the concept of an "independent agency" simply does not translate into the legislative or judicial spheres. * * * For unlike executive power, judicial and legislative powers have never been thought delegable. * * * Thus, however well established may be the "independent agencies" of the Executive Branch, here we have an anomaly beyond equal: an independent agency exercising governmental power on behalf of a

Branch where all governmental power is supposed to be exercised personally by the judges of courts. * * *

For an overall analysis of the performance of the USSC as an administrative agency, see Ronald F. Wright, *Sentencers, Bureaucrats, and the Administrative Law Perspective on the Federal Sentencing Commission*, 79 Cal.L.Rev. 1 (1991).

4. *Did the Independent Counsel's Focused Mandate Promote Overprosecution?* In *Morrison*, Justice Scalia worries that the enthusiasms of the independent counsel, as compared to her Justice Department counterparts, will be uncurbed by any other administrative agenda for which she is responsible. The two most famous special counsel investigations of the post-Watergate period—the investigation of the Iran–Contra affair by Lawrence E. Walsh and the investigation of the Whitewater and Lewinsky affairs by Kenneth Starr—appeared to many of their respective critics to exemplify such prosecutorial overzealousness. Is there an objective way to measure this? For example, in a 21–year period between 1976 and 1997, eight investigations referred to independent counsels concluded without indictment. Does this suggest the investigations ought not to have been launched at all, or do such non-prosecutions rebut the contention that special counsels will pursue their targets relentless, regardless of the merits? Unlike the Clinton investigation, the Iran–Contra prosecutions produced convictions of high-level administration officials, although two were overturned on appeal because insufficient steps were taken to prevent the inculpatory use of immunized congressional testimony. *United States v. North*, 910 F.2d 843 (D.C.Cir.), *modified*, 920 F.2d 940 (D.C.Cir.1990) (en banc); *United States v. Poindexter*, 951 F.2d 369 (D.C.Cir.1991).

5. *Federalism and Executive Law Enforcement Authority.* In *Printz v. United States*, 521 U.S. 898 (1997), the Supreme Court invalidated provisions of the Brady Handgun Control Act that would have required state and local law enforcement officers to run background checks on would-be gun purchasers pending the completion of a federal system for such investigations. The Court held that the Tenth Amendment barred Congress from relying on the commerce clause to "commandeer" state law enforcement apparatus for the implementation of a federal regulatory program. In dicta, the majority, speaking through Justice Scalia and without mentioning *Morrison*, also said that such commandeering was a violation of the separation of powers:

> We have thus far discussed the effect that federal control of state officers would have upon the first element of the "double security" alluded to by Madison: the division of power between State and Federal Governments. It would also have an effect upon the second element: the separation and equilibration of powers between the three branches of the Federal Government itself. The Constitution does not leave to speculation who is to administer the laws enacted by Congress; the President, it says, "shall take Care that the Laws be faithfully executed," Art. II, § 3, personally and through officers whom he appoints (save for such inferior officers as Congress may authorize to be appointed by the "Courts of Law" or by "the Heads of Departments" who are themselves presidential appointees), Art. II, § 2. The Brady Act effec-

> tively transfers this responsibility to thousands of CLEOs ["chief law enforcement officers"] in the 50 States, who are left to implement the program without meaningful Presidential control (if indeed meaningful Presidential control is possible without the power to appoint and remove). The insistence of the Framers upon unity in the Federal Executive—to insure both vigor and accountability—is well known. See The Federalist No. 70 (A. Hamilton); 2 Documentary History of the Ratification of the Constitution 495 (M. Jensen ed. 1976) (statement of James Wilson); *see also* Calabresi & Prakash, *The President's Power to Execute the Laws*, 104 Yale L.J. 541 (1994). That unity would be shattered, and the power of the President would be subject to reduction, if Congress could act as effectively without the President as with him, by simply requiring state officers to execute its laws.

If this reasoning is followed for all it is worth, it would seem to cast doubt on the constitutionality also of federal regulatory schemes in which states undertake federal law enforcement responsibilities in exchange for federal funding of various programs. The financial quid pro quo has long been thought to eliminate any taint of Tenth Amendment overreaching by the national government, see, e.g., *South Dakota v. Dole*, 483 U.S. 203 (1987). Eliminating Tenth Amendment concerns, however, would not address the problem of achieving unitary presidential control over the implementation of federal law. It may be that *Printz* is virtually unique in presenting this problem. In typical "cooperative federalism" statutes, the federal government retains the power, through an executive branch decision, to return implementation authority to the federal government by declaring a state to be out of compliance or by canceling a contract for non-performance. Perhaps this federal fall-back authority constitutes sufficient executive control to satisfy separation of powers requirements. On the other hand, it seems odd, to say the least, that the President's capacity to discharge his constitutional role is compromised more by local law enforcement officers checking the criminal records of putative gun purchasers (even without federal fall-back authority) than by judicially appointed prosecutors investigating the President or his top aides. That, of course, may be Justice Scalia's point in inserting this separation of powers dictum into an opinion dominated by other concerns.

6. *Constitutionality of Private Enforcement Actions.* Since *Morrison*, lower courts have held that Congress does not impermissibly undermine executive authority over prosecutions by authorizing *qui tam* actions, that is, prosecutions for violations of public statutes brought by private persons, even in cases when the executive has decided not to prosecute. *Riley v. St. Luke's Episcopal Hospital*, 252 F.3d 749 (5th Cir.2001) (en banc) (upholding *qui tam* provisions of the False Claims Act); *United States ex rel. Stillwell v. Hughes Helicopters, Inc.*, 714 F.Supp. 1084 (C.D.Cal.1989) (same); *United States ex rel. Truong v. Northrop Corp.*, 728 F.Supp. 615 (C.D.Cal.1989) (same). See generally Note, *The False Claims Act,* Qui Tam *Relators, and the Government, Which is the Real Party to the Action?*, 43 Stan.L.Rev. 1061 (1991). Likewise, no court has invalidated on Article II grounds any of the many provisions, most notably in federal environmental laws, authorizing so-called "citizen suits" to enforce compliance with regulatory standards. These issues are explored further in Chapter 9.

7. *What Is a "Department?"* In *Freytag v. CIR*, 501 U.S. 868 (1991), the Court unanimously upheld the authority of the Chief Judge of the United States Tax Court, an Article I tribunal, to appoint special trial judges. Although the latter are indubitably "inferior officers," the Court split five to four as to whether their appointment was permissible because the Chief Judge is the head of a "Department" within the meaning of Article II, or instead, because the Tax Court is a "court of law." The majority took the latter approach, concluding that the appointments clause reference to "Courts of Law" was not limited to Article III courts, and that "a holding that every organ in the Executive Branch is a department would multiply indefinitely the actors eligible to appoint." Those concurring separately found it implausible to regard Article I tribunals as "Courts of Law" for constitutional purposes, and thought the reference to "Heads of Departments" logically and historically must include "the heads of all agencies immediately below the President in the organizational structure of the Executive Branch."

B. EXECUTIVE AUTHORITY TO DIRECT AGENCY POLICY

Although patronage is not unimportant in political life or in constitutional theory, the powers to appoint and to remove government officers represent only a portion of the stakes in the elected branches' political competition. The degree to which the President may influence or even dictate the decisions made pursuant to authority delegated by statute to others is, in many contexts, much more critical.

1. THE PRESIDENT'S POWER OF POLICY INITIATION

a. The Youngstown *Framework*

The conventional starting point for analyzing the scope of presidential authority to initiate policy is *Youngstown Sheet & Tube Co. v. Sawyer*, 343 U.S. 579 (1952). *Youngstown* invalidated a 1952 executive order in which President Truman ordered his Secretary of Commerce to take control of most U.S. steel mills, which faced an impending strike, to insure continued production during the Korean War. Although the six Justices who made up the majority differed in their rationales, all of the opinions—including the dissent—started from a common premise, that the Secretary's power to seize the steel mills under presidential order must have its source in a grant of power to the President either from the Constitution or from a constitutionally enacted statute.

The majority Justices agreed—and the dissent did not dispute—that the President's constitutional role as commander-in-chief did not encompass power to seize the steel mills. Writing for the Court, Justice Black, with Justice Douglas in close agreement, accordingly held that the President was without power to act as he did. Absent independent constitutional authority, the President could lawfully seize the steel mills only if authorized, explicitly or by fair implication, by statute. Because no statute authorized the President to take the action he undertook, it was unlawful.

Justices Clark and Burton took a different tack. Each agreed that the President, in an emergency, might have sufficient Article II power to take affirmative steps to protect the public interest in ways not expressly authorized by Congress. Congress, however, had expressly contemplated the possibility that labor disputes would threaten the national interest, including the national defense, and had responded by enacting a number of statutes. None, however, conferred the power that the President claimed.

The Defense Production Act of 1950 authorized mediation, which President Truman had unsuccessfully pursued in an effort to head off the steel strike. The Labor Management Relations Act (Taft–Hartley) authorized the President to seek injunctive relief for a period of 80 days against a threatened work stoppage, but Truman had declined to invoke that authority. The Selective Service Act would have authorized a seizure of any plant that failed within a reasonable period prescribed by the President to fill specific orders for supplies required by the armed services. But Truman had also failed to employ this procedure. By providing the President several tools to respond to the very sort of emergency Truman confronted, Congress, in the judgment of Justices Clark and Burton, had preempted the field, leaving the President no residual authority to respond independently.

In the most celebrated opinion in the case, Justice Jackson analyzed the dispute against a "somewhat oversimplified" tripartite "grouping of practical situations in which a President may doubt, or others may challenge, his powers." Jackson noted first that Presidents sometimes act pursuant to express or implied statutory authority, where their authority is at its utmost. The President's action would be upheld in these situations if the Constitution vested either power in the President to act as he had or power in Congress to authorize the challenged initiative through delegated authority.

Conversely, presidential action could contradict Congress' express or implied policy. In such a circumstance, the President's claim of authority would be most dubious. The action would be lawful only if based on a constitutional grant of exclusive power to the President that was beyond Congress' power to limit or regulate.

Finally, Jackson observed, there is a middle ground in which the President may act "in absence of either a congressional grant or denial of authority." The President in such a case

> can only rely upon his own independent powers, but there is a zone of twilight in which he and Congress may have concurrent authority, or in which its distribution is uncertain. Therefore, congressional inertia, indifference or quiescence may sometimes, at least as a practical matter, enable, if not invite, measures on independent presidential responsibility.

In Jackson's view, President Truman's seizure of the steel mills was an action in derogation of congressional will. This was not a situation of legislative quiescence because Congress *had* legislated on the subject of Korea-like emergencies. Moreover, in debating the Taft–Hartley Act, Congress had expressly considered and rejected granting the President precisely the sort of authority that Truman sought to invoke. The President thus had to be judged as acting in a manner "incompatible with the expressed or implied will of Congress," but had no plausible grant of exclusive constitutional authority on which to rely.

Justice Frankfurter, the sixth member of the majority, offered an additional nuance. He laid special emphasis upon Congress' rejection of presidential seizure authority in its consideration of the Taft–Hartley Act. He took note, however, that the history of presidential practice could properly color the Court's interpretation of the extent to which Congress' failure to authorize a presidential initiative actually deprived the President of authority to act:

> [A] systematic, unbroken executive practice, long pursued to the knowledge of the Congress and never before questioned, engaged in by Presidents who have also sworn to uphold the Constitution, making as it were such exercise of power part of the structure of our government, may be treated as a gloss on "executive Power" vested in the President by § 1 of Art. II.

Under the opinions of Justices Clark, Burton, and Jackson—and under this suggestion by Justice Frankfurter—there would be at least some emergency occasions in which the President would be deemed to have constitutional authority to create new legal obligations in the public interest, even absent express or implied congressional authority.

That conclusion provided the starting point for the dissent by Chief Justice Vinson and Justices Reed and Minton. In summary, their view was that Congress had not expressly prohibited the sort of seizure Truman undertook; his initiative was a reasonable way of securing the general objectives that underlay a number of statutes Congress passed to support military procurement and national defense; and a history of prior presidential seizures of domestic plants for defense purposes supported the argument that emergency seizures were within executive power when not expressly proscribed by Congress.

Perhaps the key "lesson" of *Youngstown* lies in its discussion of the intricate interplay of statutory and constitutional law in determining the scope of presidential power to direct subordinate officials. Although Article II may confer some independent law making power on the President in the fields of military and foreign affairs, a judge's conviction that the President is or is not acting contrary to congressional policy is likely to be decisive in evaluating the legality of domestic initiatives. Yet, the very ambiguity of Article II and varying judicial assessments of the separation of powers consequences of extending presidential authority are likely to color a judge's understanding of the content of statutory expressions. Both the majority and the dissenters in *Youngstown* advanced plausible grounds for very different interpretations of the several relevant statutes. The majority relied variously on the absence of explicit authority for Truman's action, the existence of alternative statutory procedures, Congress' failure on a recent occasion to enact the authority Truman purported to exercise, and a sense that historical precedent for the President's initiative was lacking. The dissenters, on the other hand, stressed that no statute forbade the President's initiative, and that the President's initiative could be regarded as vindicating at least the general purposes of several statutory programs. In their view, other Presidents, in other emergencies, had effected industrial seizures without congressional challenge.

The interpretive stance adopted by each "side" seems clearly to reflect its assessment of the constitutional implications of deciding one way or the other. The majority was explicitly concerned about the consequences of permitting the President to seize private property under the circumstances presented. Approval of such a course of action seemed to these Justices to have adverse consequences both for constitutionally protected civil liberties and for the overall workings of government. The dissenters, on the other hand, disputed the legitimacy of these very concerns. They voiced a deeper apprehension that, if the President is denied the authority to respond to national emergencies, the constitutional order might collapse before Congress could act.

b. *Presidential Exercise of Inherent Constitutional Power*

Prior to *Youngstown*, the Supreme Court had decided three key cases on inherent executive authority to respond to domestic emergencies that would seem to have augured a different result. Their holdings can nevertheless be reconciled with the Jackson framework. Because the "executive power" they analyze is constitutionally vested in the President (even if exercised, in two of these cases, by subordinates), the decisions provide further implicit guidance on the President's capacity to rely on Article II as a source of independent policy making power.

In re Neagle, 135 U.S. 1 (1890), was a habeas corpus action brought by a deputy U.S. Marshal to contest his prosecution by California on a charge of homicide. No summary can do justice to the melodramatic facts of the case, but, in short, the victim was David S. Terry, the husband of one Sarah Althea Hill. Hill had claimed a previous marriage to a William Sharon, who, in turn, had sued successfully in Nevada to have her purported marriage contract involving him declared fraudulent and void. After Sharon's death, and subsequent to Hill's refusal to surrender her contract for its formal cancellation, Sharon's son sued Hill and Terry in federal court to have the Nevada decree revived in California, where they resided. Following a raucous court proceeding that Neagle witnessed, Justice Stephen Field, riding circuit, granted judgment for Sharon. Terry and Hill repaid Field with a year of repeated vituperative public denunciations, including threats on his life. Responding to a request from the Attorney General to deal with these threats, a local U.S. Marshal assigned Neagle to guard Field during a subsequent trip out West. When Neagle, Field, Terry, and Hill found themselves together on a train dining car, a confrontation ensued and Neagle shot Terry, mistakenly thinking Terry was about to draw a knife on the Justice, as he had previously done in court.

Neagle argued that the state could not constitutionally prosecute him for an act authorized by federal "law," even though no statute then authorized the executive branch to direct U.S. Marshals to serve as bodyguards to Supreme Court justices. The Court upheld Neagle's defense. Neagle was described as acting pursuant to inherent executive authority, specifically, the President's authority to take care that the laws be faithfully executed. This embraced, the Court said, the enforcement of all "rights, duties and obligations growing out of the Constitution itself, our international relations, and all the protection implied by the nature of the government under the Constitution."

In *In re Debs*, 158 U.S. 564 (1895), Eugene Debs, later a Socialist candidate for President, challenged the constitutionality of an injunction, granted on the petition of the Justice Department, which had enjoined him from communicating with railway employees during the Pullman Strike of 1894. No statute had authorized the Attorney General to seek such relief in labor disputes. In expansive dicta, the Court stated: "[W]henever the wrongs complained of are such as affect the public at large, and are in respect of matters which by the Constitution are entrusted to the care of the Nation, and concerning which the Nation owes the duty to all citizens of securing to them their common rights," the executive branch has standing to seek judicial relief against unlawful and forcible interference with those interests. The executive, acting here through the Attorney General, had inherent authority to seek judicial relief because the strike threatened interstate commerce—even though Congress, to which the Constitution grants the power to regulate that commerce, had not authorized the injunction.

Finally, in *United States v. Midwest Oil Co.*, 236 U.S. 459 (1915), the Court upheld the President's 1910 order withdrawing certain federal lands from oil exploration despite an express statutory declaration that the specific tracts would be open to exploration. The President had acted to prevent the depletion of oil reserves during a period of international tension and before Congress had an opportunity to reconsider its policy.

It is easy enough to imagine how President Truman's lawyers characterized the seizure of the steel mills as falling within the broad descriptions of presidential authority uttered by the Court in *Neagle* and in *Debs*. Truman surely seemed on stronger ground than had President Taft in *Midwest Oil*.

Yet, it is also understandable why a Justice taking Jackson's view of the institutional and civil liberties implications of *Youngstown* would distinguish the earlier cases. Although, in *Neagle* and *Debs*, the executive could not point to express authority for its acts, Congress had not rejected either initiative. Neither initiative seemed to threaten the institutional authority of Congress or of the courts, or to jeopardize any individual's right to due process of law.[1] In contrast, Jackson was alarmed at the implications of upholding Truman's initiative based only on a claim of "inherent authority," augmented by a rational assertion of national need: "[N]o doctrine that the Court could promulgate," Jackson wrote, "would seem to me more sinister or alarming than that a President whose conduct of foreign affairs is so largely uncontrolled, and often even is unknown, can vastly enlarge his mastery over the internal affairs of the country by his own commitment of the Nation's armed forced forces to some foreign venture."

Midwest Oil is harder to explain because there the President seemed to violate a statutory command. But, as Justice Frankfurter later noted, Congress had enacted the relevant statute against a long, consistent history of presidential orders of the kind upheld in *Midwest Oil*. The decision went no further in practice than acknowledging a presidential role, implicitly approved by Congress, as Congress' land-agent-in-chief, who might occasionally feel compelled to contradict his principal's express directions in order to preserve the principal's interest in the property involved.

This analysis further suggests that the persuasiveness of the President's justification for an independent initiative, and the Court's perceptions of its consequences, are highly dependent on historical context. Consider, for example, *Dames & Moore v. Regan*, 453 U.S. 654 (1981), in which the petitioner challenged President Carter's executive order establishing a claims settlement procedure with Iran in order to secure the release of U.S. hostages. Among other steps, the order required the suspension of any lawsuit that had been filed in United States courts against an Iranian national, and directed that such claims be pursued exclusively in a claims settlement tribunal created in the Hague. Although the International Emergency Economic Powers Act supported other measures directed by the order, no statute authorized this particular bargain with the Iranians.

The Court concluded that the order was lawful because Congress' treatment of other international claims settlements displayed a longstanding expectation that the President would use his executive order power to settle claims as a means of furthering U.S. foreign relations. The settlement was consistent with a congressional policy of seeking the peaceful release of international hostages. Further, Congress had not attempted to block the President's orders through subsequent legislation. The majority reserved the question whether Dames & Moore, or similar claimants, might have "just compensation" claims against the government if the international claims settlement tribunal afforded significantly less relief than they might have obtained in U.S. courts.

1. This is debatable in the *Debs* case because the availability of an injunction meant that Debs could be held in contempt without a jury trial. A criminal conviction for his strike activities would have been harder to obtain. (Indeed, the criminal prosecution of Debs for his Pullman strike activities ended in a mistrial after a juror became ill and the prosecution declined to empanel another jury.)

The majority hinted, however, that it thought the President's order left the individual claimants in a better, not worse, position against Iran.

c. *Implementation of Statutory Authority*

Presidents do not often undertake administrative initiatives in domestic affairs without some congressional authorization. Whether the President may direct subordinates to perform duties that Congress has vested in the President personally, and whether, or to what extent, the President may direct how subordinates exercise functions vested specifically by statute in them are questions of greater day-to-day practical importance than the scope of presidential authority vested directly by Article II.

The first question is easily answered because Congress has recognized the practical necessity for subdelegation. 3 U.S.C. § 301 expressly permits the President to delegate to executive officials who are subject to Senate confirmation any function that Congress has vested in the President by statute, as well as any function that such officials are authorized by statute to perform subject to presidential "approval, ratification, or other action." Recall, for example, that, when Congress in 1970 vested wage and price control authority in President Nixon, he re-delegated that authority to the Cost of Living Council. See *Amalgamated Meat Cutters v. Connally*, in Chapter 2. Under the language of § 301, Nixon could have delegated final say over wage-price control decisions to the Council, even if Congress had authorized the Council to make wage and price control decisions "subject to review and approval by the President."

The foundational statement about the President's authority when Congress has vested statutory functions in a subordinate official is *Marbury v. Madison*, 5 U.S. (1 Cranch) 137 (1803). William Marbury sought to challenge the Secretary of State's refusal, under President Jefferson's instructions, to deliver his commission to the statutory office of Justice of the Peace in the District of Columbia—a commission which President Adams had signed and then-Secretary of State John Marshall had duly sealed. In assessing the decision to withhold Marbury's commission, Chief Justice John Marshall—in remarks that were technically dicta—constitutionalized the traditional common law distinction between judicially reviewable "ministerial" acts and nonreviewable "political" acts for which accountability lies with an executive officer's "conscience." In writing about the President's "political" powers—by which he meant "discretionary" powers—Marshall referred specifically to powers invested in the President "by the Constitution of the United States." Ministerial powers, by contrast, are powers that "the legislature proceeds to impose on [an executive] officer * * *; when he is directed peremptorily to perform certain acts; when the rights of individuals are dependent on the performance of those acts. * * * " The consequence of this distinction was to import an "extraordinary writ" of English law, designed originally for the control of the King and his officers, as a mechanism for judicial control of the U.S. executive. In Marshall's analysis, mandamus would have been the appropriate remedy because Madison's refusal to deliver Marbury's commission amounted to a failure to perform a compulsory ministerial duty, which the President no authority to control.

Marshall reinforced the role of Congress in limiting the President's administrative discretion a year later in *Little v. Barreme*, 6 U.S. (2 Cranch) 170 (1804). The Court unanimously upheld a damages award against a ship's captain who, on the President's orders, seized a vessel sailing from France to the United States. The Court concluded that the President's powers of seizure had been delimited by a statute, the Nonintercourse Act, and because the challenged seizure failed to conform to that Act, held it unlawful. *Little* foreshadows *Youngstown* in signalling the interplay of constitutional and statutory powers: The Court acknowledged that the President's foreign affairs authority might have justified his action had Congress not acted pursuant to its express powers over foreign trade to forbid the seizure. Congress' exercise of its explicit legislative power, in short, effectively preempted any presidential reliance on a less well-defined executive power.

The first case to result in the issuance of mandamus against a federal officer was *Kendall v. United States ex rel. Stokes*, 37 U.S. (12 Pet.) 524 (1838), a suit for money due pursuant to an accounting by the Solicitor of the Treasury. The Postmaster General defended his refusal to pay by invoking an express direction from the President. The important issue was whether a court could direct the action of an executive official under these circumstances. The Postmaster General argued that it could not. His actions, he claimed, were discretionary and only the President could direct him to exercise his discretion in a particular way. The Court disagreed:

> The executive power is vested in a President; and as far as his powers are derived from the constitution, he is beyond the reach of any other department, except in the mode prescribed by the constitution through the impeaching power. But it by no means follows, that every officer in every branch of that department is under the exclusive direction of the President. Such a principle, we apprehend, is not, and certainly cannot be claimed by the President.
>
> There are certain political duties imposed upon many officers in the executive department, the discharge of which is under the direction of the President. But it would be an alarming doctrine, that Congress cannot impose upon any executive officer any duty they may think proper, which is not repugnant to any rights secured and protected by the constitution; and in such cases, the duty and responsibility grow out of and are subject to the control of the law, and not to the direction of the President. And this is emphatically the case, where the duty enjoined is of a mere ministerial character. * * *
>
> It was urged at the bar, that the postmaster general was alone subject to the direction and control of the President, with respect to

> the execution of the duty imposed upon him by this law, and this right of the President is claimed, as growing out of the obligation imposed upon him by the constitution, to take care that the laws be faithfully executed. This is a doctrine that cannot receive the sanction of this court. It would be vesting in the President a dispensing power, which has no countenance for its support in any part of the constitution; and is asserting a principle, which, if carried out in its results, to all cases falling within it, would be clothing the President with a power entirely to control the legislation of Congress, and paralyze the administration of justice.
>
> To contend that the obligation imposed on the President to see the laws faithfully executed, implies a power to forbid their execution, is a novel construction of the constitution, and entirely inadmissible.

Taken together, these early cases are generally read to stand for two propositions: (1) If Congress, within its constitutional powers, directs the executive to implement a particular action, the President has no lawful right to suspend the law. (2) If Congress, within its constitutional powers, prohibits the executive from implementing a particular action, the President has no lawful right to authorize the action.

These propositions, however, leave the President and subordinate administrators with a critical and potentially large area of ambiguity. Statutes that prescribe administrative duties always leave some room for discretion in their implementation. This discretion may be relatively trivial. A statute directing the Secretary of State to seal and deliver a presidential commission might leave the Secretary a choice of sealing wax colors or whether to transmit the commission personally or by mail. On the other hand, as the nondelegation materials revealed, the scope of discretion lawfully conferred by statute may be very great. For example, the authorization to the FCC to grant broadcast licenses based on a showing of "public interest, convenience, and necessity" obviously leaves the agency a lot of room for deciding what these terms mean.

Kendall can be understood as prohibiting the President from ordering a subordinate to choose an implementation strategy outside the zone of discretion delimited by statute in a case where that zone was well-defined. Presumably, the same principle would apply, even if less susceptible to easy implementation, where the administrator's zone of discretion is more capacious or ambiguous. Thus, for example, if Congress were to direct the Department of Education to order federally funded school districts to implement "programs of bilingual education that are maximally efficacious, irrespective of cost," the President could not order the Department to order the implementation of "programs of bilingual education that are maximally cost-effective, irrespective of educational impact," even if the President could argue that his was the better policy in some public welfare sense. The President's command, in other words, could not render lawful an *ultra vires* act.

The far more likely circumstance is that the President and an administrator may disagree on the scope of discretion conferred by statute, or though agreeing on the zone of discretion, disagree about which lawful implementation strategy is preferable as a matter of policy. In the latter situation, the administrator could conceivably fashion a reasoned statement to sustain either choice, and assemble a record sufficient to support the chosen policy. Following our earlier example, the administrator could provide sufficient reasons on educational grounds—because social scientists are so divided on the issue—either to prefer bilingual programs that immerse non-native English speakers immediately in English or those that would effect a more gradual transition.

In such a case, the President's political position is more complex than in *Marbury* or *Kendall*. If Congress has vested decision making responsibility in a subordinate administrator, it is not likely that the administrator's policy explanation, "The President made me do it," would suffice to sustain the policy. On the other hand, nothing in *Marbury* or *Kendall* prohibits the President from trying to "persuade" a subordinate to implement the President's preferred policy if it can be defended. No court has adjudicated whether a statutory prohibition on such presidential persuasion (or command) would be constitutional, and Congress has never tried to limit the President so bluntly. The D.C. Circuit, however, has said that, at least absent a statute restricting policy supervision, pressure on an administrator to conform decisions to the President's agenda is both expected and proper. *Sierra Club v. Costle*, 657 F.2d 298, 405–06 (D.C.Cir.1981), excerpted in Chapter 5, *infra*. After all, the press and public routinely assign political responsibility for subordinates' actions whether or not the Executive Office of the President had any substantial role in their decisions. Accepting and exercising that responsibility arguable promotes democratic accountability. See Elana Kagan, *Presidential Administration*, 114 Harv. L. Rev. 2245 (2001), excerpted *infra*.

For Congress, the issue is how far it may go in regulating or curtailing the President's power to influence subordinates' exercise of delegated power. The drafters of legislation—or members of Congress who represent the beneficiaries of legislation—may be sharply at odds with a President regarding both the scope of authority delegated by a statute and the factors that should guide its implementation. For Presidents, the issue is how much direction or guidance to subordinate administrators is permissible given Congress' decisions to vest particular decisional powers in those administrators, rather than in the President directly.

2. THE INSTRUMENTS OF PRESIDENTIAL COMMAND: EXECUTIVE ORDERS

Executive orders constitute an important, and institutionally the most formal, species of communication through which the President issues commands to the executive branch. Yet however ancient their usage, there is no official definition of what properly constitutes an executive order, nor a well-settled jurisprudence governing the extent of the President's power to act in this fashion. Executive Order No. 10,006, which establishes procedures for the issuance of executive orders, does not define the term. (Thus, for example, President Bush's order providing for the military detention and trial of certain non-citizens in the wake of the World Trade Center attack is captioned merely a "Notice." Detention, Treatment, and Trial of Certain Non–Citizens in the War Against Terrorism, 66 Fed. Reg. 57833 (Nov. 13, 2001).) Executive orders were not numbered until 1907 when the Department of State, in order to organize its files of presidential documents, began to give numbers to those that it could locate. Executive Order No. 1 was assigned to President Lincoln's order of October 20, 1862, establishing a provisional court to function during the military occupation of Louisiana. (Lincoln's most celebrated unilateral lawmaking effort was styled a "proclamation." Emancipation Proclamation, Jan. 1, 1863, 12 Stat. 1268.) Executive orders were then numbered chronologically from that date, although some were later discovered and had to be inserted out of order. Various estimates put the total of unnumbered executive orders at between fifteen and twenty thousand.

The Federal Register Act contributed to regularity by requiring that all official executive documents including "any presidential proclamation or executive order and any order * * * issued * * * by a federal agency" be published in the Federal Register. That statute also defined "federal agency" in a way that included the President of the United States. In Executive Order No. 7,298 President Roosevelt, in 1936, first established a procedure for the issuance of executive orders and proclamations. The basic procedure remains unchanged. Proposed executive orders are first submitted to and analyzed by the Office of Management and Budget. They may originate with any federal agency. If, after analysis, OMB approves an executive order, it is then submitted to the Department of Justice (Assistant Attorney General, Office of Legal Counsel) for consideration both as to its form and its legality. If the order clears these two hurdles, and is signed by the President, it is then published in the Federal Register.

Over the years executive orders have had an enormous range of uses. Most have been documents that can fairly be described as "internal" to the federal executive establishment. They are directions to the whole or a part of the bureaucracy concerning the organization and conduct of their business. Many concern personnel and budgetary matters and the use of public lands.

Yet from the beginning executive orders have used language suggesting effects on private parties. George Washington, for example, issued a "proclamation" in 1793 for the purpose "of preventing interference of the citizens of the United States in the war between France and Great Britain." Charles M. Thomas, American Neutrality in 1793, at 26 (1931). That proclamation enjoined United States citizens "from all acts and proceedings whatsoever, which * * * tend to contravene such disposition * * * [of] a conduct friendly and impartial toward the belligerent powers. * * * " The proclamation indicated that the sanction for failure to abide by its terms was prosecution. Since Congress passed the first Neutrality Act in the following year, the President's power to issue a binding declaration of neutrality was never tested. Washington's proclamation nevertheless precipitated a dispute between Hamilton and Madison in the press, with Hamilton supporting its constitutionality and Madison opposing. See EDWARD S. CORWIN, THE PRESIDENT, OFFICE AND POWERS, 1787–1984, at 179 (5th ed. 1984).

Executive orders have often been used in wartime to create necessary public agencies. During World War I, for example, the War Trade Board, the Committee For Public Information, the Food Administration and the Grain Corporation were all established by executive order. As might be imagined, Franklin Roosevelt used the device extensively during the 1930s. In the three years 1933, 1934, and 1935, Roosevelt issued nearly fifteen hundred executive orders. By contrast, in the years 1953–56, a mere two hundred fifty executive orders were issued. (Perhaps interest in the executive order form was dampened by President Truman's experience in the *Youngstown Sheet & Tube* case.)

It seems clear, however, that the executive order has frequently been used over the last half century in circumstances where legislation would have been equally appropriate. In 1953, for example, President Truman ordered the heads of all federal contracting agencies to incorporate, and enforce, nondiscrimination clauses in all government contracts. Executive Order No. 10,479, 18 Fed.Reg. 4899 (1953). President Kennedy issued a far-reaching executive order in 1962 on nondiscrimination in housing owned, operated, or financed by the federal government. Executive Order No. 11,063, 27 Fed.Reg. 11527 (1962). Subsequent Presidents have revised the nondiscrimination requirements from time to time, for example, to include gender among the grounds on which federal contractors may not discriminate. Executive Order No. 11,375, 32 Fed.Reg. 14303 (1967). President Carter used executive orders to implement his agreement with the government of Iran for the release of American hostages. These orders appear as Executive Orders Nos. 12,276–12,285, 46 Fed.Reg. 7913–32 (1981).

As we noted in Chapter 2, the executive order has also been used as a device to institute wage and price controls through the government's power of procurement and its use of publicity. The courts' receptivity has been mixed, however, with regard to the presidential use of broadly defined procurement powers to implement social policy through executive orders. Compare *Contractors Association of Eastern Pennsylvania v. Secretary of Labor*, 442 F.2d 159 (3d Cir.), *cert. denied*, 404 U.S. 854 (1971) (upholding executive order imposing affirmative action requirements on federal contractors), with *Chamber of Commerce of the United States of America v. Reich*, 83 F.3d 439 (D.C.Cir.1996) (invalidating Executive Order authorizing Secretary of Labor to disqualify from certain federal contracts employers who hire permanent replacement workers during a lawful strike).

Like many statutes, the President's directives to federal agencies, if followed, would often work to the benefit of particular private parties. For example, the careful preparation of a cost-benefit analysis pursuant to the executive orders on regulatory oversight, see Section C of this chapter, might produce environmental regulations more favorable, depending on the case, to industry or to conservationists. Yet, courts are reluctant to find that an executive order "confers" a private right of action to secure an agency's compliance with the order's obligations. See, e.g., *Manhattan–Bronx Postal Union v. Gronouski*, 350 F.2d 451 (D.C.Cir.1965), *cert. denied*, 382 U.S. 978 (1966); *Stevens v. Carey*, 483 F.2d 188 (7th Cir.1973). The rationale behind this reluctance varies. In some cases, a court may resist enforcing an order because the order explicitly disavows private enforceability. See, e.g., *Louisiana ex rel. Guste v. Verity*, 853 F.2d 322 (5th Cir.1988) (holding Executive Order No. 12,291 requirement for regulatory analysis not judicially enforceable). Probably the most comprehensive and detailed presidential disavowal of enforceability appears in Executive Order 12,778, § 6, 56 Fed.Reg. 55,195, 55,200 (1991), requiring federal litigators to act in a variety of ways to reduce the "burdens and costs" imposed by civil litigation in which the government is involved. In other cases, courts have determined that—irrespective of presidential intent—the President lacks inherent power to create judicially enforceable government obligations without congressional authorization. See *In re Surface Mining Regulation Litigation*, 627 F.2d 1346 (D.C.Cir.1980) (holding Executive Order No. 11,821, requiring inflation impact analysis, not judicially enforceable).

Some executive orders demanding regulatory analysis have sought a middle position on private enforceability. Although disavowing the creation of private rights, an order may provide that the analytic documents prepared pursuant to the executive order shall be part of the record on judicial review of the rule to which they pertain. See, e.g., Executive Order No. 12,291, § 9, 46 Fed.Reg. 13,193 (1981). President Clinton did not include such a provision in his revision of the executive order on presidential regulatory oversight, see Executive Order No. 12,866, 58 Fed. Reg. 51735 (1993), although some of the regulatory analyses prepared pursuant to that order will become part of the record for judicial review because they also fulfill statutory requirements for cost-benefit analysis. See, e.g., 2 U.S.C. § 1571 (Unfunded Mandates Reform Act); 5 U.S.C. § 611 (Regulatory Flexibility Act).

On the subject of executive orders generally, see KENNETH R. MAYER, WITH THE STROKE OF A PEN: EXECUTIVE ORDERS AND PRESIDENTIAL POWER (2001); Peter Raven–Hansen, *Making Agencies Follow Orders: Judicial Review of Agency Violations of Executive Order 12,291*, 1983 Duke L.J. 285; Note, *Presidential Power: Use and Enforcement of Executive Orders*, 39 Notre Dame Law. 44 (1963); House Comm. on Government Operations, Executive Orders and Proclamations: A Study of a Use of Presidential Powers, 85th Cong., 1st Sess. (Comm.Print 1957).

C. PRESIDENTIAL OVERSIGHT OF REGULATORY POLICY

Recent decades have witnessed an intensified debate concerning the President's powers over administration, largely because of a significant series of institutional developments within the executive branch itself. In particular, each President since Nixon has not only asserted presidential authority to guide the exercise of administrative discretion, but has attempted, with increasing ambition, to systematize the President's capacity to oversee and coordinate policy making within the executive branch. President Nixon's initial effort in this respect was the creation of a so-called "Quality of Life Review" process in OMB, requiring informal interagency discussions of proposed environmental regulations. See generally John Quarles, Cleaning up America: An Insider's View of the Environmental Protection Agency (1976). President Ford, responding to rising inflation during the 1970s, required executive agencies generally to prepare Inflation Impact Statements in connection with "major proposals" for legislation or regulation. Executive Order No. 11,821, 3 C.F.R. 926 (1971–75 compilation).

President Carter went further. He revoked Executive Order No. 11,821 and replaced it with a far more detailed order requiring, among other things, that executive agencies prepare analyses of major proposed regulations to help assure simplicity, clarity, and cost-effectiveness. Executive Order No. 12,044, 3 C.F.R. 152 (1979). These regulatory analyses, available to the public in both proposed and final form, were to indicate alternative regulatory approaches that the agency considered, the anticipated economic impacts of each, and "a detailed explanation of the reasons for choosing one alternative over the others." Executive Order No. 12,044 also imposed obligations on agencies to review existing regulations for possible improvement, but left to each agency the task of developing a review process.

President Reagan was even more ambitious. Less than a month after his first inaugural, Reagan issued Executive Order No. 12,291, which imposed detailed responsibilities on OMB for managing the process of producing and reviewing regulatory impact analyses, articulated a set of overarching executive branch policy mandates with respect to administrative rule-making, and, unlike earlier orders, required executive agency heads, to the extent permitted by statute, to be guided by both the order's stated policy goals and its procedural requirements in the exercise of administrative discretion.

At the start of his second term, Reagan supplemented Executive Order No. 12,291 with Executive Order No. 12,498. That order sought to buttress central executive review of individual regulations with a more comprehensive agenda-setting program that would permit OMB and the heads of individual agencies to oversee a wide range of agency regulatory activity.

President George H.W. Bush left the 12,291/12,498 process in OMB formally intact. As Vice President, he had chaired a Task Force on Regulatory Relief created by Executive Order No. 12,291 to oversee its implementation. As President, however, Bush vested the Task Force role in the President's Council on Competitiveness, chaired by Vice President Quayle. Although composed of the Administration's major economic advisers, the Council functioned chiefly through the Vice President's staff as a source of pressure on OMB and other agencies, especially EPA, to take account of economic impacts in the course of regulatory policy making. See Kirk Victor, *Quayle's Quiet Coup*, Nat'l J., July 6, 1991, at 1676. Throughout the Presidential election campaign of 1992, Candidate Clinton was strongly critical of the Reagan–Bush approach to regulation. As President, however, he implemented a redesign of regulatory oversight that owed a great deal to his predecessors. And intriguingly, despite obvious differences regarding substantive regulatory policy, Clinton's successor, George W. Bush, amended the Clinton executive order very little, chiefly to vest functions that Clinton vested in the Vice President instead in the President's Chief of Staff or in the Director of the Office of Management and Budget (OMB). Exec. Order No. 13,258, 67 Fed. Reg. 9385 (2002).

All presidential regulatory oversight programs since the Carter Administration have vested a key managerial role in OMB, an agency within a larger agency called the Executive Office of the President. As its name implies, OMB is a bureaucracy atop the bureaucracy, whose role is to help the President to budget and manage the executive branch. The director of OMB, in turn, uses a component of OMB, the Office of Information and Regulatory Affairs (OIRA), to coordinate implementation of presidential regulatory oversight. Congress created OIRA to implement the Paperwork Reduction Act of 1980, and the OMB Director determined that the programs had enough common elements to make their joint administration sensible. Assessing the Reagan regulatory oversight program, Dean Bruff offered this brief observation about the use of OMB and OIRA for a regulatory oversight role:

> Recast from the old Bureau of the Budget, OMB consists of a few hundred civil servants (most of them budget officers) and a growing cadre of political appointees at the top. Since the 1970s, OMB staffing has become increasingly political, with a sharp upsurge from nine to twenty-five Schedule C political appointees in the first Reagan term alone. * * *
>
> Budget functions have long dominated OMB, to the dismay of some political scientists who yearn for more attention to management. In budgeting, OMB's classic stance has been the skeptical reviewer of requests from agencies that are always wanting "too much." Indeed, a famous theory of bureaucratic behavior holds that the principal endeavor of agencies is to expand their budgets, in search of the power and perquisites that more money can buy. Whether or not this theory fits reality, to the extent that it is accepted within OMB, it affects OMB's behavior.

Attitudes born of the budget process probably carry over to supervision of rulemaking by OIRA. * * * Although the direct tradeoffs between scarce federal dollars that characterize the budget process do not occur in the oversight of regulation, the perspective of anyone working in OMB is determined by its placement at the apex of the executive branch. An office that sees the full scope of federal regulation must be impressed by its net burdens, and is likely to doubt that any particular rule is indispensable to national welfare. Analogies to budgeting, however, can ignore the principal differences between these functions: unlike regulatory review, budget requests are not confined by preexisting statutory standards, and they lead to automatic legislative resolution of policy issues.

For similar reasons of perspective, agency personnel are likely to view OMB as institutionally overcautious about regulation. Focusing on the statutory missions committed to them, bureaucrats lack any incentive to view their own regulations in competition with other claims for scarce national resources. Therefore, any system for central oversight of regulation will produce conflict between the regulators and their overseers, regardless of the politics of the administration in power.

Harold H. Bruff, *Presidential Management of Agency Rulemaking*, 57 Geo.Wash.L.Rev. 533, 552–53 (1989).

Presidential regulatory oversight raises questions of both law and policy. The legal issues are addressed in a Justice Department memorandum for former OMB Director David Stockman, which outlines the legal premises upon which President Reagan relied in adopting Executive Order No. 12,291.

UNITED STATES DEPARTMENT OF JUSTICE MEMORANDUM FOR HONORABLE DAVID STOCKMAN

Director

Office of Management and Budget

Re: Proposed Executive Order on Federal Regulation

* * *

I. Legal Authority: Executive Branch Agencies

The President's authority to issue the proposed Executive Order derives from his constitutional power to "take Care that the Laws be faithfully executed." U.S. Const., Art. II, § 3. It is well established that this provision authorizes the President, as head of the Executive Branch, to "supervise and guide" Executive officers in "their construction of the statutes under which they act in order to secure that unitary and uniform execution of the laws which Article II of the Constitution evidently contemplated in vesting general executive power in the President alone." *Myers v. United States*, 272 U.S. 52, 135 (1926).[1]

The supervisory authority recognized in *Myers* is based on the distinctive constitutional role of the President. The "take Care" clause charges the President with the function of coordinating the execution of many statutes simultaneously: "Unlike an administrative commission confined to the enforcement of the statute under which it was created * * * the President is a constitutional officer charged with taking care that a 'mass of legislation' be executed," *Youngstown Sheet & Tube Co. v. Sawyer*, 343 U.S. 579, 702 (1952) (Vinson, C.J., dissenting). Moreover, because the President is the only elected official who has a national constituency, he is uniquely situated to design and execute a uniform method for undertaking regulatory initiatives that responds to the will of the public as a whole. In fulfillment of the President's constitutional responsibility, the proposed Order promotes a coordinated system of regulation, ensuring a measure of uniformity in the interpretation and execution of a number of diverse statutes. If no such guidance were permitted, confusion and inconsistency could result as agencies interpreted open-ended statutes in differing ways.

Nevertheless, it is clear that the President's exercise of supervisory powers must conform to legislation enacted by Congress.[3] In issuing directives to govern the Executive Branch, the President may not, as a general proposition, require or permit agencies to transgress boundaries set by Congress. It is with these basic precepts in mind that the proposed Order must be approached.

We believe that an inquiry into congressional intent in enacting statutes delegating rulemaking authority will usually support the legality of presidential supervision of rulemaking by Executive Branch agencies. When Congress delegates legislative power to Executive Branch agencies, it is aware that those agencies perform their functions subject to presidential supervision on matters of both substance and procedure. This is not to say that Congress never intends in a specific case to restrict presidential supervision of an Executive agency; but it should not be presumed to have done so whenever it delegates rulemaking power directly to a subordinate Executive Branch official rather than the President. Indeed, after *Myers* it is unclear to what extent Congress may insulate Executive Branch agencies from presidential supervision. Congress is also aware of the comparative insulation given to the independent regulatory agencies, and it has delegated rulemaking authority to such agencies when it has sought to minimize presidential interference.

1. In *Buckley v. Valeo*, 424 U.S. 1, 140–41 (1976), the Supreme Court held that any "significant governmental duty exercised pursuant to a public law" must be performed by an "Officer of the United States," appointed by the President or the Head of a Department pursuant to Art. II, § 2, cl. 2. We believe that this holding recognizes the importance of preserving the President's supervisory powers over those exercising statutory duties, subject of course to the power of Congress to confine presidential supervision by appropriate legislation.

3. In certain circumstances, statutes could invade or intrude impermissibly upon the President's "inherent" powers, but that issue does not arise here.

By contrast, the heads of non-independent agencies hold their positions at the pleasure of the President, who may remove them from office for any reason. It would be anomalous to attribute to Congress an intention to immunize from presidential supervision those who are, by force of Art. II, subject to removal when their performance in exercising their statutory duties displeases the President. * * *

Procedurally, [the Order] would direct agencies to prepare an RIA assessing the costs and benefits of major rules. We discern no plausible legal objection to this requirement, which like most procedural requisites is at most an indirect constraint on the exercise of statutory discretion. * * *

Substantively, the Order would require agencies to exercise their discretion, within statutory limits, in accordance with the principles of cost-benefit analysis. More complex legal questions are raised by this requirement. Some statutes may prohibit agencies from basing a regulatory decision on an assessment of the costs and benefits of the proposed action. See, e.g., *EPA v. National Crushed Stone Ass'n*, 101 S.Ct. 295 (1980). The Order, however, expressly recognizes this possibility by requiring agency adherence to principles of cost-benefit analysis only "to the extent permitted by law." The issue is thus whether, when cost-benefit analysis is a statutorily authorized basis for decision, the President may require Executive agencies to be guided by principles of cost-benefit analysis even when an agency, acting without presidential guidance, might choose not to do so. We believe that such a requirement is permissible. First, there can be little doubt that, when a statute does not expressly or implicitly preclude it, an agency may take into account the costs and benefits of proposed action. * * *

Second, the requirement would not exceed the President's powers of "supervision." It leaves a considerable amount of decisionmaking discretion to the agency. Under the proposed Order, the agency head, and not the President, would be required to calculate potential costs and benefits and to determine whether the benefits justify the costs. * * *

We believe that the President would not exceed any limitations on his authority by authorizing * * * the Director to supervise agency rulemaking as the Order would provide. The Order does not empower the Director * * * to displace the relevant agencies in discharging their statutory functions or in assessing and weighing the costs and benefits of proposed actions. The function of * * * the Director would * * * include such tasks as the supplementation of factual data, the development and implementation of uniform systems of methodology, the identification of incorrect statements of fact, and the placement in the administrative record of a statement disapproving agency conclusions that do not appear to conform to the principles expressed in the President's Order. Procedurally, the Director * * * would be authorized to require an agency to defer rulemaking while it responded to their statements of disapproval of proposed agency action. This power of consultation would not, however, include authority to reject an agency's ultimate judgment, delegated to it by law, that potential benefits outweigh costs, that priorities under the statute compel a particular course of action, or that adequate information is available to justify regulation. * * *

II. Independent Regulatory Commissions

We now consider whether the proposed Order may legally be applied to the independent regulatory commissions in certain respects. Principally, the Order would require independent agencies to prepare RIA's and would authorize the Director or the Task Force to exercise limited supervision over the RIA's. For reasons stated below, we believe that, under the best view of the law, these and some other requirements of the Order can be imposed on the independent agencies. We would emphasize, however, that an attempt to exercise supervision of these agencies through techniques such as those in the proposed Order would be lawful only if the Supreme Court is prepared to repudiate certain expansive dicta in the leading case on the subject, and that an attempt to infringe the autonomy of the independent agencies is very likely to produce a confrontation with Congress, which has historically been jealous of its prerogatives with regard to them. * * *

The holding of *Humphrey's Executor* is that Congress may constitutionally require cause for the removal of an FTC Commissioner; the Court's opinion, however, contains broad dicta endorsing a perceived congressional purpose to insulate the FTC almost entirely from Presidential supervision:

> The commission is to be non-partisan; and it must, from the very nature of its duties, act with entire impartiality. It is charged with the enforcement of no policy except the policy of the law. Its duties are neither political nor executive, but predominately quasi-judicial and quasi-legislative. Like the Interstate Commerce Commission, its members are called upon to exercise the trained judgment of a body of experts "appointed by law and informed by experience."

295 U.S. at 624 (quoting *Illinois Cent. Ry. v. ICC*, 206 U.S. 441 (1906)). The Court continued:

> Thus, * * * the Congressional intent to create a body of experts who shall gain experience by length of service—a body which shall be independent of executive authority *except in its selection*, and free to exercise its judgment without the leave or hindrance of any other official or any department of the government. * * * And to hold that, nevertheless, the members of the commission continue in office at the mere will of the President, might be to thwart, in large measure, the very ends which Congress sought to realize by definitely fixing the term of office.

If the dicta of *Humphrey's Executor* are taken at face value, the President's constitutional power to supervise the independent agencies is limited to his power of appointment, and none of the proposed Order's requirements may legally be applied to the independent agencies. We believe, however, that there are several reasons to conclude that the Supreme Court would today retreat from these dicta. First, the Court in *Humphrey's Executor* and *Wiener* focused primarily on the inappropriateness of Presidential interference in agency adjudication, a concern not pertinent to supervision of rulemaking. Second, insofar as the Court was concerned about rulemaking, it did not take account of the fact that Executive Branch and independent agencies engage in rulemaking in a functionally indistinguishable fashion. Third, the Court espoused what is now an outmoded view about the "apolitical" nature of regulation. It is now recognized that rulemaking may legitimately reflect political influences of certain kinds from a number of sources, including Congress and the affected public. Fourth, the President has today a number of statutory powers over the independent agencies, which recognize the legitimacy of his influence in their activities. * * *

It seems clear that Congress intends the independent agencies to be free of Presidential supervision on matters of substantive policy. * * * We believe that the holding of *Humphrey's Executor*, shorn of the Court's broad dicta that these agencies are independent "except in [their] selection," fully supports the view that Congress may remove some rulemaking from Presidential supervision of the sort that would be appropriate in the absence of such a provision. It remains necessary, then, to reconcile the holding of *Humphrey's Executor* with the President's duty under Article II, § 3, to "take Care that the Laws be faithfully executed." Certainly provisions requiring cause for removal must be read as expressing congressional intent to minimize Presidential supervision of these agencies. Accordingly, a frequent formulation of the President's power over the independent agencies has been that he may supervise them as necessary to ensure that they are faithfully executing the laws, although he may not displace their substantive discretion to decide particular adjudicative or rulemaking matters.[14] Such a formulation would allow for many types of procedural supervision.

In addition to his constitutional powers, the President has been given some statutory powers that extend to independent as well as Executive Branch agencies. These powers include reorganization authority, OMB's budgetary and legislative request processes, the deferral or rescission of appropriations, and the selection of agency chairmen. We do not interpret these statutes to imply broad authority for presidential supervision of the independent agencies, because of the clear congressional intent to minimize presidential supervision that is expressed in

14. See, e.g., James M. Landis, *Report on Regulatory Agencies to the President-Elect* 33 (1960):

> The congestion of the dockets of the agencies, the delays incident to the disposition of cases, the failure to evolve policies pursuant to basic statutory requirements are all a part of the President's constitutional concern to see that the laws are faithfully executed. The outcome of any particular adjudicatory matter is, however, as much beyond his concern, except where he has a statutory responsibility to intervene, as the outcome of any cause pending in the courts and his approach to such matters before the agencies should be exactly the same as his approach to matters pending before the courts.

removal restrictions. Nevertheless, we do believe that these statutes recognize the legitimacy of some presidential influence in the activities of independent agencies, especially when it consists of a coordinating role with only an indirect effect on substantive policymaking.

We believe that the foregoing constitutional and statutory analysis supports the application to the independent agencies of those portions of the Order that would be extended to them. The principal requirement is that independent agencies prepare RIA's. These analyses would have only an indirect effect on substantive discretion, since the identification of costs and benefits and the particular balance struck would be for the agency to make. It should also be possible for OMB to prescribe criteria for independent agencies to follow in preparing their RIA's, to consult with them in the process, and to disagree with an independent agency's analysis on the administrative record. None of these actions would directly displace the agencies' ultimate discretion to decide what rule best fulfills their statutory responsibilities. * * *

Notes

1. *Exemption of Independent Agencies*. The Justice Department Office of Legal Counsel memorandum advised that at least some provisions of Executive Order No. 12,291 could be extended to independent agencies, but the White House originally chose not to go that far. President Reagan's lawyers may have disagreed with the Justice Department's legal view, but, more likely, the President's advisers simply deemed it prudent to avoid a "turf fight" with Congress over independent agencies. President Clinton took up that challenge in Executive Order No. 12,866, reprinted as Appendix F, *infra*. But, although the Clinton order imposed substantive requirements on agencies other than independent agencies, it imposed on the independent agencies purely procedural requirements only.

2. *Constitutionality of the Reagan Orders*. A report prepared soon after Executive Order No. 12,291 was promulgated, authored by Morton Rosenberg, a specialist in American public law at the Congressional Research Service, for the House Committee on Energy and Commerce, observed:

> The scheme of [Executive Order No. 12,291], in scope and substance, is a marked departure from previous Presidential efforts to control administrative lawmaking. It does not appear to draw its authority from any specific congressional enactment. Indeed, the order itself refers only to "the authority vested in me as President by the Constitution and laws of the United States of America." * * *
>
> * * * [T]he question raised is whether the President in promulgating Executive Order 12,291 has engaged in an exercise of Executive lawmaking without either constitutional or statutory authority and thereby violated the separation of powers doctrine.

Morton Rosenberg, *Presidential Control of Agency Rulemaking: An Analysis of Constitutional Issues That May Be Raised By Executive Order 12,291*, 23 Ariz.L.Rev. 1199 (1981). Relying on familiar authority—*Youngstown, Humphrey's Executor*, and *Wiener*—Rosenberg answered this question in the affirmative. He rejected the notion that the President was ever intended to be an administrative manager sitting atop a centralized executive branch. Officers, in his view, receive their authority to act from legislation; they are congressional delegates, not executive subordinates.

In a follow-up article, Rosenberg also challenged the notion that the central clearance functions of OMB suggest congressional acquiescence in the form of presidential direction to agencies contemplated by Executive Order No. 12,291. Rosenberg offered the following portrayal of the relevant history:

> Since early in this century, the President, with Congress's blessing, has wielded a great deal of authority over the agency budget process. Through his budget office, the President has been authorized to present a unified annual budget on behalf of federal agencies, clear agency information requests, and even decide which legislative proposals urged by the agencies should receive congressional attention. * * *
>
> Presidential authority in the agency budget process began with the enactment of the Budget and Accounting Act of 1921, which allowed the President to formulate a national budget with the assistance of a newly created Bureau of the Budget (BOB). Previously, each agency had submitted its annual budget request directly to Congress. Finding this process inefficient and unwieldy, Congress created the BOB to review the morass of agency budgetary information and to approve agency budget requests. By 1970, the BOB possessed an impressive array of legal authorities for supervision of nearly all departments and agencies. In addition to reviewing and approving agency budget requests, the Bureau was authorized to study agency organization, to clear agency proposals for legislation or agency comments on proposed legislation, and to control agencies' requests for information.
>
> In granting these powers to the President, Congress intended—at least in part—that he would play a policy-neutral role; the President was to coordinate the vast tangle of administrative agencies. Through his authority to study agency organization and review budget requests, the President could identify overlapping efforts, eliminate needless duplication, and resolve interagency conflicts. One must recognize, however, that the powers that enabled the President to carry out his managerial responsibilities also gave him the capacity to influence administrative policy. In the threat of budget reductions, the President possesses a powerful tool that he can use to enforce his own policy designs. The President could, moreover, use his clearance powers to focus congressional attention on agency proposals or comments agreeable to him. Yet the BOB, notwithstanding its significant policy-influencing potential, maintained an image of bipartisan neutrality, and its Director was seen as a personal technical adviser on fiscal and organizational matters. Although, in principle, the President has long been able to influence substantively the policies formulated by administrative agencies, until recently the power was relatively dormant.
>
> In 1970, however, President Nixon reconstituted the BOB as the OMB and sought to expand its role. Departing from the history of policy-neutrality, President Nixon began to use the OMB, together with

his self-proclaimed impoundment powers, to alter or end established programs. As the OMB began to be viewed as a political instrument of the President, Congress's response to President Nixon's unprecedented efforts was far-reaching; the legislature severely limited the OMB's autonomy and forcefully asserted its own desire to control administrative policy-making. For the first time, Congress required Senate confirmation of the OMB's Director and Deputy Director. The OMB's monopoly on the processing of agency budget requests was ended as Congress created its own central budget evaluator, the Congressional Budget Office (CBO). Congress has, on a selective basis, either eliminated the requirement that the OMB clear agency budget requests or mandated that the requests be concurrently submitted to the CBO. Equally significant was the enactment of the Budget Impoundment and Control Act of 1974, which greatly limited the President's putative authority to impound agency funds and his concomitant power to shape policy. Finally, Congress countered the institutional development of the OMB by enhancing the authority of its watchdog audit agency, the General Accounting Office, with program evaluation functions and a special oversight role in preventing presidential impoundments. The spate of legislation following the politicization of the OMB conclusively demonstrates that Congress, rather than acquiescing to presidential policy-making, desired to maintain control over administrative agencies. Congress has empowered the President to act in the interests of coordination and organizational efficiency, but has carefully restrained such action, lest it assume substantive policy dimensions.

Congressional limitations on the President's reorganizational powers reiterate the theme that the President's managerial role does not encompass control of administrative policy-making. Congress has several times delegated to the President extensive powers of governmental reorganization. The policy-making potential stemming from these powers was great: The President typically could transfer, consolidate, or abolish agency functions, including rulemaking. In principle, the President could have transferred rulemaking programs from one agency to another possessing a fundamentally different mission. Hesitant to confer power with such potential substantive impact, Congress has imposed several conditions on the President's reorganizational authority. First, all of the reorganization acts have been of limited duration, none being effective for more than four years. Second, some of the acts specifically restricted reorganizational power. Illustratively, the most recent reorganization act, which lapsed on April 7, 1981, expressly prohibited the President from abolishing "any enforcement or statutory program," creating any new executive departments, or consolidating two or more departments. Third, with two short-lived exceptions, all of the reorganization acts adopted since 1932 have included provisions authorizing a legislative veto. Each of these restrictions, and particularly the provisions for a legislative veto, reflect Congress's intent to cabin even the potential for presidential control of administratively formulated policy.

Morton Rosenberg, *Beyond the Limits of Executive Power: Presidential Control of Agency Rulemaking Under Executive Order 12,291*, 80 Mich. L.Rev. 193, 221–225 (1981).

Professor Shane, who, as an OMB lawyer, assisted in counseling those drafting the executive order, disputed Mr. Rosenberg's assertion that Congress had rigorously limited its acquiescence to policy-neutral presidential management of administrative agencies:

> [T]here is simply no telling across-the-board conclusion concerning Congress' desires for the working of the administrative process to be drawn from its decisions, standing alone, to vest certain administrative decisionmaking authority in Presidential subordinates rather than in the President directly. Congress has also chosen, for example, to preserve those subordinates' vulnerability to discretionary Presidential removal, to forego procedural restrictions on *ex parte* White House contacts with those subordinates in the informal rulemaking process, and to subject those subordinates expressly to a major degree of budget and policy coordination by the Executive Office of the President. The picture that emerges from all these decisions is hardly a considered legislative intention to fractionalize Executive power.

Peter M. Shane, *Presidential Regulatory Oversight and the Separation of Powers: The Legality of Executive Order No. 12,291*, 23 Ariz.L.Rev. 1235 (1981). Shane did not believe that *Youngstown* cast doubt on the legality of Executive Order No. 12,291:

> By its very terms, the order avoids facial conflict with any statute. Its substantive principles apply, and the Director is authorized to exercise his managerial role, only "to the extent permitted by law."
>
> * * *
>
> Similarly, although the Director's review power with respect to proposed rules and RIA's undeniably creates the potential for regulatory delay, the order expressly provides that the vesting of review power in the Director "shall (not) be construed as displacing the agencies' responsibilities delegated by law."
>
> * * * [T]he Rosenberg Report purports to find serious legal problems on the face of Executive Order No. 12,291 because of the order's supposed conflict with policies underlying Congress' decision to vest certain administrative decisionmaking authority in subordinate executive officers, and because the order assertedly impairs the administrative flexibility that Congress intended to achieve through the APA.
>
> * * * [T]here exists no justification for treating broad, unstated policy concerns, at most implicit in the enactments of Congress, as binding expressions of legislative will limiting the President's powers of administrative supervision.
>
> In the current situation, Congress' will, if such a thing exists, has not been recently stated in the express rejection of the power for which the President contends. To the extent Congress was aware, when it enacted the APA in 1946, of arguments for and against presidential oversight of the regulatory process, it did not consider those arguments against the background of an administrative bureaucracy as large, complex, and varied as the one that currently exists. Nor, in exercising powers of supervision and guidance is the President, as a general matter, asserting doubtful Executive powers. To the extent Congress is

> concerned with preserving its policy prerogatives in the regulatory process, it is institutionally capable of doing so through an oversight system more extensive than the President's, through annual appropriations and authorization battles and through new substantive legislation. Indeed, the risk of Executive usurpation seems all the slighter in this context because the courts are available also, as they might not be in military or foreign affairs disputes, to police fully Executive compliance with Congress' commands.

Since the promulgation of Executive Order No. 12,291, Congress has enacted several statutes that either demand cost-benefit analyses of certain categories of rules, or that provide, in the case of the Congressional Review of Agency Rulemaking Act, 5 U.S.C. § 801, that any cost-benefit analyses prepared with regard to a rule be made available to Congress. Do such provisions, especially the latter, provide whatever congressional ratification that *Youngstown*-minded Justices might have needed in order to uphold the initiatives of the Carter through Bush-43 Administrations with regard to presidential regulatory oversight?

* * *

As the documents above suggest, not only the legality of presidential regulatory review but its effectiveness is likely to depend critically on the details of how that review is conducted. The different executive orders under which OMB has been implementing its review process have differed in a variety of especially important details. This appears not to be a purely partisan matter. The Reagan and George H. W. Bush Administrations functioned under an order promulgated by President Reagan in the early months of his first Administration. President Clinton replaced that order with one of his own, but, with fairly minor amendments, President George W. Bush has kept the Clinton order in place. The following excerpt analyzes the structure of both orders, as well their differences and common elements.

PETER M. SHANE, POLITICAL ACCOUNTABILITY IN A SYSTEM OF CHECKS AND BALANCES: THE CASE OF PRESIDENTIAL REVIEW OF RULEMAKING

48 Ark. L. Rev. 161, 174–92 (1995).

[B]oth the structure and strategy of President Clinton's Executive Order No. 12,866 have obvious links to President Reagan's Executive Order No. 12,291,[68] under which OIRA conducted regulatory oversight even through the [George H. W.] Bush Administration. Both orders commence with statements of overall presidential goals and with principles of regulatory policy that the orders directly impose on the agencies within their purview. Both orders coordinate centralized regulatory review through the Office of the Vice President and the Office of Management and Budget. Each contemplates both a general regulatory planning process for individual agencies, plus separate regulatory impact analyses as a tool for managing the oversight process for certain signifi-

68. Exec. Order No. 12,291, 3 C.F.R. 127 (1982).

cant regulations. Neither order purports to deprive any agency of decision making power that Congress has vested in the agency.

Within this common framework, however, there exist truly significant differences. These differences render the Clinton regulatory review process—at least on paper—less biased against regulation, more consultative, more accessible, and more deferential to policy making by individual agencies. On its face, the resulting system is more susceptible to "checking and balancing" by Congress and the courts.

A. Presidential Objectives

President Reagan stated the objectives underlying Executive Order No. 12,291 in succinct and, with one exception, generally nonsubstantive terms:

> to reduce the burdens of existing and future regulations, increase agency accountability for regulatory actions, provide for presidential oversight of the regulatory process, minimize duplication and conflict of regulations, and insure well-reasoned regulations.[69]

The only hint of genuinely substantive regulatory policy in this preamble is the desire to reduce regulatory "burdens," which foreshadows the subsequent RB [Reagan–Bush] deregulatory emphasis on cost-benefit analysis.

Executive Order No. 12,866 reaffirms the value commitments of the 12,291 preamble, but adds others. * * *[70] Conspicuous in [the new order] is acceptance of a positive case for regulation. It is conceived that a regulatory system can "protect[] and improve[] * * * health, safety, environment, and well-being and improve[] the performance of the economy * * * " Undue burdens are decried as in 12,291; there should be no "unacceptable or unreasonable costs on society." But costs are, by implication, not unreasonable if a regulation efficiently facilitates an important social goal.

There are additional ways in which the Clinton preamble plainly seeks to distance itself from a philosophy it tacitly imputes to RB regulatory review * * * The apparent negative implications of the [preamble's rhetoric] are that earlier Administrations had (1) compromised the decision making primacy of federal agencies, (2) jeopardized the integrity and legitimacy of regulatory review, and (3) cloaked regulatory oversight in too much secrecy. Reasserting the primacy of individual agencies and opening regulatory policy making to public scrutiny are two strategies, which, if implemented, could significantly diffuse effective power over regulatory decision making within the executive branch.

B. Mandatory Principles of Regulation

Both the Reagan and Clinton orders move beyond a hortatory preamble statement of general goals to specific principles that the

69. *Id.*, Preamble, at 127.

70. Exec. Order No. 12,866, Preamble, 3 C.F.R. 638, 638 (1994).

respective Presidents would require agencies to follow to the extent otherwise permitted by law. The essential commands of the Reagan order are easily summarized: to regulate only where regulatory benefits outweigh costs, and to choose regulatory means that minimize the net cost of the administrative initiative.[71] There is little elaboration in the order as to how such decisions shall be made.

The Clinton Order focuses on a similar mandate, but describes it with greater nuance. The section on "regulatory philosophy" purportedly limits the occasions for regulation, but does so in a way that rhetorically acknowledges the frequent legitimacy of regulation. * * * Although echoing the earlier Order's call for cost sensitivity, the Clinton Order cautions against an overreliance on "hard variables." * * * The order [also] explicitly articulates a number of regulatory benefits that are not readily monetizable. * * *

The Clinton Order gives additional guidance on the analytic process by which its philosophy is to be implemented. Prior to issuing any new regulations, agencies are instructed to consider whether administrative objectives may be accomplished through alternatives to new regulation, including the modification of existing schemes.[72] Yet, even this direction to seek cost-effectiveness is modified by an analysis facially more complex than straightforward bottom-line analysis:

> In [designing regulations in the most cost-effective manner], each agency shall consider incentives for innovation, consistency, predictability, the costs of enforcement and compliance (to the government, regulated entities, and the public), flexibility, distributive impacts, and equity.[77]

There are also specific requirements for agencies "to the extent feasible, [to] specify performance objectives, rather than specifying the behavior or manner of compliance that regulated entities must adopt,"[78] and "[w]herever feasible, [to] seek views of appropriate State, local, and tribal officials before imposing regulatory requirements that might significantly or uniquely affect those governmental entities."[79]

Institutionally, these directives have significance beyond the obvious substitution of a conservative Republican regime with an Administration of moderate-to-liberal Democrats. * * * [T]he more eclectic set of presidentially approved regulatory concerns—including "public health and safety, and other advantages; distributive impacts; and equity"—creates a value structure more readily aligned with the policies underlying a host of regulatory statutes, none of which necessarily embodies the procrustean cost-benefit orientation of the RB approach. The broader framework that the order endorses for assessing a regulation's appropriateness would additionally support a broader-based, less bounded consultation

71. Exec. Order No. 12,291, § 2, 3 C.F.R. 127, 128 (1982).

72. *Id.*, § 6(a)(3)(C)(iii), at 646.

77. *Id.*, § (1)(b)(5), at 639.

78. *Id.*, § (1)(b)(8), at 639.

79. *Id.*, § (1)(b)(9), at 640.

both within and outside the Administration as to the justification for any particular regulatory initiative.

C. General Regulatory Planning

Both the Reagan and Clinton orders envision a general regulatory planning process. Executive Order 12,291 mandated only a portion of that process, which President Reagan later amplified in Executive Order No. 12,498.[80] The key planning tool under 12,291 was the "regulatory agenda," earlier mandated by President Carter. * * * Executive Order No. 12,498 * * * required [each agency] to develop and submit in draft to OMB an annual "Regulatory Program." The order empowered the OMB director to review the draft programs for consistency with Administration policies, and to identify further "regulatory or deregulatory actions as may, in his view, be necessary in order to achieve such consistency."[83] * * *

Executive Order No. 12,866 substitutes for both of these Reagan orders a planning process that is in various ways more fluid and more elaborate. The threshold difference, however, lies in the very range of agencies required to participate. The Reagan orders applied to every agency covered by the fairly comprehensive definition of "agency" in the Paperwork Reduction Act, excluding those listed in that Act as "independent regulatory agencies."[87] The regulatory analysis provisions of the Clinton order have the identical purview,[88] but the general planning system extends further, embracing the independent agencies, whom the Reagan Administration had only invited to participate voluntarily in the 12,291 regulatory review process.[89]

The Clinton planning process is prefaced by a general allocation of authority to those whom the Order treats as the key "players" in regulatory planning and review. First, the agencies themselves are described as "responsible for developing regulations and assuring that the regulations are consistent with applicable law, the President's priorities, and the principles set forth in [the Clinton executive] order."[90] OMB is charged with the "coordinated review of agency rulemaking," both to help insure, as do the agencies, that regulations are consistent with both law and the President's policies, but also to see "that decisions made by one agency do not conflict with the policies or actions taken or planned by another agency."[91] The Vice President is designated "the principal advisor to the President on" regulatory matters, and is ordered to "coordinate the development and presentation of recommendations concerning, regulatory policy, planning, and review."[92]

80. Exec. Order No. 12,498, 3 C.F.R. 323 (1986).

83. Exec. Order No. 12,498, § 3(a), 3 C.F.R. 323, 324 (1986).

87. Exec. Order No. 12,291, § 1(d), 3 C.F.R. 127, 128 (1982).

88. Exec. Order No. 12,866, § 3(b), 3 C.F.R. 638, 641 (1994).

89. *Id.* § 4(b), at 642.

90. *Id.* § 2(a), at 640.

91. *Id.* § 2(b), at 640.

92. *Id.* § 2(c), at 640. [In early 2002, President George W. Bush amended the Clinton Order for the sole purpose of eliminating the Vice Presidential role that Executive Order 12,866 originally contemplated.

Within this framework, the Clinton Order envisions an annual "planning cycle," early in which the Vice President shall convene a meeting of the so-called "Advisors,"[93] together with the heads of agencies. The purpose of the meeting is "to seek a common understanding of priorities and to coordinate regulatory efforts to be accomplished in the upcoming year."[94] As under the Reagan system, each agency is required during the planning cycle to prepare both a "Unified Regulatory Agenda," and a "Regulatory Plan," with contents similar to those mandated in the earlier orders.[95]

Upon receiving an agency's Regulatory Plan, however, the Clinton order neither envisions an indefinite period for unilateral OMB review, nor bestows discretion over the Plan's interagency circulation to the Director. Instead, each agency is ordered to forward its annual plan by June 1 to OMB's Office of Information and Regulatory Affairs (OIRA), which, in turn, is required in all cases to "circulate it to other affected agencies, the Advisors, and the Vice President."[96] The intended result is presumably a significant diffusion of official authority to raise issues about a Plan, and a consequent reduction in OMB's exclusive power to second-guess agencies. The Order permits "any agency head who believes that a planned regulatory action of another agency may conflict with its own policy or action taken or planned" to raise that issue with the issuing agency, the Advisors, and the Vice President.[97] The Administrator of OIRA is likewise authorized to alert that same group if she "believes that a planned regulatory action of an agency may be inconsistent with the President's priorities or the principles set forth in [the] Executive order or may be in conflict with any policy or action taken or planned by another agency."[98]

It is noteworthy that the circulation of the plan presumably leaves the initiating agency an opportunity to mobilize it allies, as well as to arouse its opponents, among other agencies. Moreover, the Order directs that "[t]he Plans *developed by the issuing agency* shall be published annually in the October publication of the Unified Regulatory Agenda."[99] The italicized language and the absence of any reference in the order to the submission of a "draft plan," strongly suggests that OMB does not have authority to preclear or to stop publication of a plan that an agency is prepared to publish.[100]

Responsibilities that President Clinton vested in then-Vice President Gore now repose in the Director of OMB or the Chief of Staff to the President. Executive Order 13258, 67 Fed. Reg. 9385 (Feb. 26, 2002).]

93. § 3(a), at 641. [As amended by President George W. Bush, the meeting is now convened by the Director of OMB, and not by the Vice President. Exec. Order. No. 13258, § 4, 67 Fed. Reg. 9385 (Feb. 26, 2002).]

94. *Id.* § 4(b), at 642.

95. *Id.* § 4(b)–(c), at 642–43.

96. *Id.* § 4(c)(2) and (3), at 643.

97. *Id.* § 4(c)(4), at 643.

98. *Id.* § 4(c)(5), at 643.

99. *Id.* § 4(c)(7), at 643 (emphasis added).

100. This inference is buttressed by Section 8 of the Clinton order, concerning the publication or issuance of regulatory actions. *Id.*, § 8, at 648–49. In brief, that section requires agencies to delay the publication of "any regulatory *action* that is subject to review under Section 6" of the Order. (Emphasis added.) Because regulatory *plans* are subject to review under Section 4,

* * *

In designing its planning process, the drafters of the Clinton order apparently inferred an additional lesson from their predecessors. Executive Order 12,291 did no more about old regulations than (1) require agencies, in general terms, to "initiate reviews of currently effective rules in accordance with the purposes of this Order,"[104] and (2) empower the OMB director to designate certain existing rules for regulatory analysis.[105] In contrast, the new order requires each agency to submit to OIRA:

> a program, consistent with its resources and regulatory priorities, under which the agency will periodically review its existing significant regulations to determine whether any such regulations should be modified or eliminated so as to make the agency's regulatory program more effective in achieving the regulatory objectives, less burdensome, or in greater alignment with the President's priorities and the principles set forth in [the] Executive order.[106]

Moreover, the RWG, and state, local, and tribal governments are asked to participate in the process of identifying outmoded regulations or rules otherwise in need of reform.[107] * * * The obvious aim of this effort is to avoid subjecting to extensive review only new regulations that, of necessity, are most likely to reflect the most up-to-date information and policy thinking, while leaving untouched regulations that, equally of necessity, do not reflect current information or policy consultation.

D. Regulatory Review

Most of the remainder of both the Reagan and Clinton orders is devoted to their respective review processes for individual regulations. The Orders adopt virtually identical definitions for the "regulations" they cover.[109] The Clinton order additionally covers "regulatory actions," defined as:

> any substantive action by an agency (normally published in the Federal Register) that promulgates or is expected to lead to the promulgation of a final rule or regulation, including notices of inquiry, advance notices of proposed rulemaking, and notices of proposed rulemaking.[110]

not Section 6, the negative implication of this provision is that agencies need not stay the publication of their plans pending OMB review or approval.

104. Exec. Order No. 12,291, § 3(i), 3 C.F.R. 127, 130 (1982).

105. *Id.*

106. Exec. Order No. 12,866, § 5(a), 3 C.F.R. 638, 644 (1994).

107. *Id.*, § 5(b), at 644.

109. The only obvious difference is that both exclude from their coverage "[r]egulations or rules that pertain to a military or foreign affairs function of the United States," except that the Clinton order carves out of this exception "procurement regulations and regulations involving the import or export of non-defense articles and services," which are made subject to the Order. *Compare* Exec. Order No. 12,291, § 1(a), 3 C.F.R. 127, 128 (1982), *with* Exec. Order No. 12,866, § 3(d)(2), 3 C.F.R. 638, 641 (1994).

110. Exec. Order No. 12,866, § 3(e), 3 C.F.R. 638, 641 (1994).

From this universe of administrative activity, each order then seeks to focus regulatory review only on regulations or regulatory actions that are "major" or "significant."[111]

Here, the Orders articulate a significant substantive difference. The Reagan Order measured the significance of a regulation entirely in cost terms. * * *[112] Any rule falling within this Reagan order definition would be deemed "significant" under the Clinton order as well.[113] But a regulation or regulatory action under the new order will also be deemed significant, and hence potentially subject to centralized review, if it could * * * significantly hurt the environment, public health, or safety, or diminish the rights of individuals receiving governments entitlements, grants, or loans.[114] Excessive cost, in other words, is not the only "red flag" to arouse OMB's attention.

Beyond differences in the regulatory actions covered, the orders employ similar, but not identical in their strategy for review. The key review mechanism under the Reagan order was the "regulatory impact analysis" (RIA), which each agency was required to perform "in connection with every major rule."[115] In the ordinary case * * * each agency would prepare a preliminary RIA to accompany each NPRM and submit both to OMB at least 60 days prior to publication.[117] A final RIA would accompany a final rule, both of which would be submitted to OMB 30 days prior to publication.[118] The RIA would include, in essence, an assessment of a major rule's expected costs and benefits, and a description of alternative approaches that might be more cost-effective, but were not chosen.[119]

Although not using the RIA terminology, the Clinton order requires a similar analysis for all "significant regulatory actions," unless OIRA waives the requirement.[120] OMB's capacity to use regulatory review for the indefinite delay of a regulatory action appears, however, to be substantially curtailed. * * * Absent from [the Reagan Order] was a deadline for OMB either to complete its review of a proposed RIA or to submit its comments for a final rulemaking. The impact one might have predicted, a lengthy extension of the rulemaking process for any regulation opposed by OMB, seems to have occurred.[124]

111. Exec. Order No. 12,291, § 1(b), 3 C.F.R. 127, 127–28 (1982); Exec. Order No. 12,866, § 3(f), 3 C.F.R. 638, 641–42 (1994). [Although the Reagan Order imposed more extensive analytic requirements for major than for non-major rules, the order required that all rules be transmitted for OMB review. In contrast, the Clinton Order requires OMB review only for "significant regulatory actions." Although the universe of "regulatory actions" is broader, by definition, than "regulations," the targeting of OMB review only to "significant" actions has dramatically reduced the number of proposed rules that OIRA analyzes.]

112. Exec. Order No. 12,291, § 1(b), 3 C.F.R. 127, 127–28 (1982).

113. Exec. Order No. 12,866, § 3(f), 3 C.F.R. 638, 641–42 (1994).

114. *Id.*

115. Exec. Order No. 12,291, § 3(a), 3 C.F.R. 127, 128 (1982).

117. *Id.*, § 3(c)(2), at 129.

118. *Id.*

119. *Id.*, § 3(d), at 129.

120. Exec. Order No. 12,866, § 6(a)(3)(B) and (C), 3 C.F.R. 638, 645–46 (1994).

124. Bruff, *supra* note 32, at 565–68; Percival, *supra* note 7, at 156–61.

The Clinton order, in contrast, includes a tight timetable within which a review process is to proceed. OMB is subject to strict deadlines at each stage of review, and is permitted in reviewing any proposed or final regulatory action to extend its process only "once by no more than 30 calendar days upon the written approval of the Director."[125] Moreover:

> [f]or each regulatory action that the Administrator of OIRA returns to an agency for further consideration of some or all of its provisions, the Administrator of OIRA [is required to] provide the issuing agency a written explanation for such return, setting forth the pertinent provision of this Executive order on which OIRA is relying.[126]

The requirement that OIRA focus its concerns in writing is a potentially significant mechanism for avoiding undue delay in regulatory review. The exercise of putting objections in writing may discipline OMB in lodging objections because it requires some precision of scope and explanation; when an objection is lodged, the agency will presumably also be better off by having clear notice where its analytical energies must be focused in order to satisfy OMB.

The intent to prevent undue OMB-induced postponements of regulatory action is reinforced by the Clinton order's provisions concerning the publication of regulatory actions. As under Executive Order No. 12,291, agencies are not to publish regulatory actions subject to OIRA review until "the Administrator of OIRA notifies the agency that OIRA has waived its review of the action or has completed its review without any requests for further consideration."[127] However, unlike Executive Order No. 12,291, the new order provides that extended OIRA silence is tantamount to authorizing the agency to publish; agencies are entitled to go forward if "the applicable time period * * * expires without OIRA having notified the agency that it is returning the regulatory action for further consideration."[128] The intended consequence of these provisions is to render OMB more accountable in the discharge of its functions and to restore a more even balance of power between the agency and OMB in fine-tuning agency regulations.

E. Sunshine Provisions

Yet another respect in which the Clinton order differs markedly from Executive Order No. 12,291 is in its codification of disclosure provisions and protections against ex parte contacts. Both orders require agencies to make their regulatory analyses available to the public once the relevant regulatory action is published.[129] The Clinton order, however, codifies certain disclosure measures voluntarily adopted by OMB

125. *Id.*, § 6(b)(2)(C), at 647.

126. Exec. Order No. 12,866, § 6(b)(3), 3 C.F.R. 638, 647 (1994).

127. *Id.*, § 8, at 648.

128. *Id.*

129. Exec. Order No. 12,291, § 3(h), 3 C.F.R. 127, 130 (1982); Exec. Order No. 12,866, § 6(a)(3)(E)(i), 3 C.F.R. 638, 646 (1994).

during the Reagan Administrations,[130] though not required to do so by Executive Order No. 12,291. Moreover, Executive Order 12,866 adopts the sunshine measures mentioned earlier that were urged upon, but resisted by the [first] Bush Administration in a fight that led to Congress's refusal to reauthorize OIRA when its statutory mandate expired in 1990.[131]

First, the Clinton order contains significant protections to insure that agencies are not subject to pressures from OMB based on outside communications of which the agencies were never informed. * * * Moreover, the public is entitled to significant information about the review process, even while it is ongoing. * * * This is a dramatic change of policy, given the scope of RB resistance to the disclosure of documents revealing the deliberative processes entailed in regulatory policy making. * * *

Note

The Institutional Impetus for Presidential Regulatory Oversight. The routinization of presidential regulatory oversight has been, by most accounts, the most important federal administrative law development of the last quarter of the twentieth century. At least four forces converged to produce this innovation, although the order of their significance is surely a matter of debate. First, the '60s and '70s witnessed both a growth in the number of federal regulatory agencies and a pronounced turn towards the promulgation of general, mandatory administrative rules as the preferred method of statutory implementation. As a consequence, there was a rise in the amount of regulatory activity that would touch most Americans—and which, if unattended, could have significant political repercussions for a sitting President.

Second, most regulatory legislation since the late 1960s is the product of a Congress controlled in one or both Houses by the party not in the White House. Between 1969 and 2002, the President's party controlled both Houses of Congress for only 6 years—from 1977–1981 and from 1993–1995. As a consequence, recent legislation has been both drafted and implemented in an atmosphere of intense partisan, as well as institutional, competition. Increased attention to the exercise of administrative discretion may enable a President to accomplish through bureaucratic supervision at least some of what could not be accomplished through negotiations over the drafting or redrafting of legislation. As noted in Chapter 2, the broader the delegation, the greater the potential presidential policy making role.

Third, recessions in the '70s and '80s, together with an unprecedented rate of inflation in the late '70s, engendered bipartisan caution about imposing regulatory costs on businesses. Every President, Republican or

130. OMB agreed in 1986 to disclose draft notices of proposed rulemaking and final rules submitted for OMB review, together with any related correspondence between agency heads and OIRA. Bruff, *supra* note 32, at 582. See Exec. Order No. 12,866, § 6(a)(3)(E) and (b)(4)(D), 3 C.F.R. 638, 646, 658 (1994).

131. See text at notes 31–34, *supra*. OMB's current "logging" requirements appear at Exec. Order No. 12,866, § 6(b)(4)(C), 3 C.F.R. 638, 647 (1994).

Democrat, has an obvious political stake in appearing to respond vigorously to economic problems, and regulations, unlike other economic forces, are at least susceptible to direct control.

Finally, Presidents have repeatedly expressed frustration over the perceived tendency of agencies to develop core loyalties to their own programs and constituencies. The multiplication of specialized agencies, attended by the recruitment of expert staffs personally committed to their narrow regulatory objectives, has, from a presidential perspective, resulted in a pro-regulatory bureaucratic outlook often at odds with the Administration's announced agenda. The expectation of bureaucratic resistance was so great that President Reagan required Executive Order No. 12,291 to be drafted largely in secret, to avoid the "watering down" of his oversight program that might have occurred had news of it leaked or had the draft been subject to consultation throughout the executive establishment.

ENVIRONMENTAL DEFENSE FUND v. THOMAS

United States District Court, District of Columbia, 1986.
627 F.Supp. 566.

FLANNERY, DISTRICT JUDGE.

* * *

In November of 1984, Congress enacted the Hazardous and Solid Waste Amendments of 1984 ("1984 Amendments"), which amended the Resource Conservation and Recovery Act ("RCRA"), 42 U.S.C. § 6924. RCRA is a comprehensive statute designed to regulate the management of hazardous and solid wastes. One of the new amendments, Section 3004(w) of RCRA, provides that "(n)ot later than March 1, 1985, the (Environmental Protection Agency or 'EPA') Administrator shall promulgate final permitting standards under this section for underground tanks that cannot be entered for inspection."

This deadline was not met. Plaintiffs contend that EPA's ability to promulgate the regulations was further prevented by the unlawful interference of the Office of Management and Budget ("OMB"). * * * Plaintiffs seek an order that EPA must promulgate the regulations by April 25, 1986. Plaintiffs also seek injunctive relief against OMB to prevent similar interference in the future. * * *

Plaintiffs contend that OMB's interference with the promulgation of the EPA regulations unlawfully delayed their promulgation, in violation of both the RCRA amendments and the Administrative Procedure Act ("APA"), 5 U.S.C. § 706. Plaintiffs argue that under 28 U.S.C. § 1331 and § 1361, this court may exercise inherent equitable powers to grant injunctive relief preventing further OMB interference.

Defendants respond that ordering OMB to refrain from reviewing any proposed regulations under RCRA whenever such review would delay promulgation of the regulation beyond a statutory deadline is an unjustifiable and inappropriate use of this court's power. As defendants see it, neither the RCRA nor the APA gives this court jurisdiction over

OMB in this matter. Further, there is no jurisdiction to enforce any constraints found within the Executive Order itself.

There is no doubt that this court has jurisdiction over both plaintiffs' RCRA and APA claims against the Administrator of EPA. In compelling EPA to perform non-discretionary duties, however, it is also appropriate to fashion equitable relief to ensure that such duties are performed without the interference of other officials acting outside the scope of their authority in contravention of federal law. Though injunctive relief is not appropriate in these circumstances, as discussed below, there can be no doubt that an executive agency or agencies can be enjoined by this court from failing to execute laws enacted by Congress.

Congress set March 1, 1985, as the deadline for promulgating the regulations. OMB commenced its review of the proposed permitting standards on March 4, 1985. Since these were not "major rules" under the meaning of EO 12291, EPA anticipated that OMB would complete its review within 10 days. On March 15, 1985, EPA staff briefed OMB staff on the proposed regulations. OMB refused to clear the regulations and on March 25, 1985, notified EPA that it was extending its review of the proposed regulations. OMB apparently wanted EPA to gather additional information prior to promulgating the regulations even though it would delay the process. By April 10, 1985, EPA had still not received any formal comments from OMB.

By April 12, 1985, it was clear that OMB had serious differences with EPA over what regulations to propose. At a meeting of April 16, 1985 between OMB and EPA staff members, OMB sought significant changes in the proposed regulations in four areas. The idea, apparently, was to shift the goal of the regulations away from EPA's philosophy of containing all leaks of waste disposal to OMB's philosophy of preventing only leaks of waste that can be demonstrated by risk analysis to threaten harm to human health.

Internal disagreement within OMB further delayed OMB's consideration of the regulations. Some OMB staff members apparently felt that OMB should not be dictating substantive policy decisions to EPA while others felt the precedent being set an important one for OMB review of other RCRA regulations.

After this suit was filed on May 30, 1985, OMB continued to seek specific changes in EPA's proposed regulations as well as changes not previously discussed. After various negotiations regarding the substance of the regulations, OMB completed its review and cleared the proposed regulations on June 12, 1985. The EPA Administrator signed them June 14, 1985 and the proposed regulations were published in the Federal Register on June 26, 1985, 50 Fed.Reg. 26444, after OMB approved some last-minute stylistic changes made by EPA staff.

A. The Final Date for Promulgating the Regulations

The parties agree and this court finds that the Administrator of EPA has failed to comply with his nondiscretionary duties under

§ 3004(w) of the RCRA. There is disagreement, however, about when the final regulations should be ordered promulgated. Plaintiffs contend that a reasonable time is April 25, 1986 while defendants prefer a deadline of one year from the date the regulations were proposed (i.e. June 30, 1986). * * *

Promulgation of regulations 16 months after a Congressional deadline is highly irresponsible. Congress was aware of the complexity of these hazardous waste regulations and yet decided that quick promulgation was of paramount importance. Now that the damage is done, however, this court must fashion an equitable remedy that best achieves the Congressional purpose. * * * After reviewing the proposed schedule set forth by EPA in this case, it appears that the June 30, 1986 deadline is reasonable. This date is only two months later than the date sought by plaintiffs. Therefore, it is ordered that the regulations be promulgated by that time. Failure to do so would be capricious and would merit stronger equitable treatment.

B. OMB's Interference With the Promulgation Process

From the discussion above, it seems clear that OMB did contribute to the delay in the promulgation of the regulations by insisting on certain substantive changes. * * *

A certain degree of deference must be given to the authority of the President to control and supervise executive policymaking. *Sierra Club v. Costle*, 657 F.2d 298, 405 (D.C.Cir.1981) [excerpted in chapter 5, *infra*]. * * * Yet, the use of EO 12291 to create delays and to impose substantive changes raises some constitutional concerns. Congress enacts environmental legislation after years of study and deliberation, and then delegates to the expert judgment of the EPA Administrator the authority to issue regulations carrying out the aims of law. Under EO 12291, if used improperly, OMB could withhold approval until the acceptance of certain content in the promulgation of any new EPA regulation, thereby encroaching upon the independence and expertise of EPA. Further, unsuccessful executive lobbying on Capitol Hill can still be pursued administratively by delaying the enactment of regulations beyond the date of a statutory deadline. This is incompatible with the will of Congress and cannot be sustained as a valid exercise of the President's Article II powers. * * *

This court has previously found that in certain egregious situations, statutory delay caused by OMB review is in contravention to applicable law under Section 8(a)(2) of EO 12291 and therefore that no further OMB review could occur. *NRDC v. Ruckelshaus*, 14 ELR 20817, 20818 (D.D.C.1984). In *Ruckelshaus*, however, by the time the court order issued, EPA was six years past the deadline set by Congress. In the case at bar, enjoining OMB from interacting at all with EPA simply because OMB *might* cause delay past the new judicial deadline is premature and an unwarranted intrusion into discretionary executive consultations.

There is, however, some credence in plaintiffs' fear that the regulations due June 30, 1986, may still be delayed by OMB. While defendants claim that OMB review of the final regulations in May of 1986 will be concurrent with EPA senior level review, such concurrent review of the proposed regulations in the spring of 1985 resulted in considerable delay. Concurrent review does not eliminate delay, since any changes sought by OMB must then be reviewed by senior level EPA officials. This court declares therefore that further review by OMB which creates any delay in meeting the June 30, 1986 deadline is unreasonable and unacceptable. EPA is obligated to promulgate the regulations by that date and may not use the excuse of OMB review to refrain from doing so.

Plaintiffs also protest that OMB routinely reviews other EPA regulations subject to statutory deadlines even if such review will delay promulgation beyond the deadline. Unless this court declares that OMB has no authority to delay promulgation of all EPA regulations beyond statutory deadlines, OMB will continue to do so both for the Section 3004(w) standards and for other RCRA regulations subject to statutory deadlines in the 1984 amendments. Through answers to interrogatories, plaintiffs show that EPA submitted 169 regulations to OMB which were subject to statutory or judicial deadlines, and on 86 occasions OMB extended its review beyond the time periods outlined in EO 12291. OMB's propensity to extend review has become so great that EPA keeps a running record of the number of its rulemaking actions under extended review by OMB and the resulting delays. The average delay per regulation is 91 days; total delays were more than 311 weeks. Apparently Section 8(a)(2) of EO 12291 is simply ignored.

Congress clearly is concerned with OMB's use of EO 12291 with regard to the deadlines set within the 1984 Amendments. The House Committee report that accompanied the 1984 Amendments states:

> The Committee is extremely concerned that EPA has not been able to comply with past statutory mandates and timetables, not just for RCRA, but for virtually all its programs. * * * The Administrator's ability to meet this deadline (for publishing a schedule for land disposal ban decisions) as with all other deadlines in this bill, shall not be impaired in any way whatsoever by Executive Order 12291.

Hazardous Waste Control and Enforcement Act of 1983, Report of House Comm. on Energy and Commerce, 98th Cong., 1st Sess., May 17, 1983, at 34, 35.

The Hazardous and Solid Waste Amendments of 1984 added at least 44 new deadlines to RCRA, 29 of which must be satisfied within the next 20 months.

This court declares that OMB has no authority to use its regulatory review under EO 12291 to delay promulgation of EPA regulations arising from the 1984 Amendments of the RCRA beyond the date of a statutory deadline. Thus, if a deadline already has expired, OMB has no authority to delay regulations subject to the deadline in order to review them under the executive order. If the deadline is about to expire, OMB may review the regulations only until the time at which OMB review will result in the deadline being missed. * * *

While this may be an intrusion into the degree of flexibility the executive agencies have in taking their time about promulgating these regulations, this is simply a judicial recognition of law as passed by Congress and of the method for dealing with deadlines laid down by the President himself. * * * Indeed, OMB itself admits that it cannot prevent an agency from complying with statutory requirements. Yet declaratory relief is necessary to ensure compliance with the clearly expressed will of Congress. This is not an inappropriate interference with the interaction of executive agencies; all such interaction may continue absent a "conflict with deadlines imposed by statute or by judicial order." Sec. 8, EO 12291.

Notes

1. *Curbing OMB Review of Specific Programs.* Since the issuance of the Reagan executive order on regulatory oversight, Congress has occasionally stipulated that a particular rulemaking is not to be cleared by OMB, see, e.g., Marine Mammals Protection Act of 1972 Amendments, § 4(d)(2), Pub. L.No. 97–58, 95 Stat. 984 (1981). More frequently, Congress sets deadlines for regulatory actions with perhaps the tacit hope of curtailing any major OMB oversight role. An example is the Nutrition Labeling and Education Act of 1990, Pub.L.No. 101–535, 104 Stat. 2361. The Act not only set time limits for the adoption of several regulations, but provided that, should the limits expire prior to the promulgation of final regulations, the proposed regulations would become effective automatically. See, e.g., § 3(b)(2), *id.* at 2364. Such provisions are intended to alter the balance of power between OMB and the FDA in negotiating the administration's final position under the Act.

Congress, of course, may seek to limit the President's capacity to consult off the record on a particular rulemaking because of partisan or other policy differences, fears that presidential influence can frustrate judicial review (or congressional oversight) by rendering the public rulemaking record an incomplete account of the agency's decision making, or concerns that OMB will act as a "conduit" to the agency of views or information from vested interests who are unwilling to place them squarely before the public. We consider the procedural implications of these possibilities in Chapter 5.

2. *Statutory Silence and the Legality of Presidential Oversight.* Note from the *Thomas* opinion that no statute provided guidance concerning Congress' understanding of the appropriate level or nature of presidential supervision of EPA. Indeed, analysis of the legality of OMB's influential role and of its procedures for exercising influence has generally been obscured by statutory imprecision. Virtually all statutes conveying rulemaking power to executive (as well as "independent") agencies are silent on such questions as whether the agency head may consult with the President or his agents and, if so, on what basis. Most were passed before President Reagan, or President Carter for that matter, prescribed White House review of regulation.

Nor do generic statutes on presidential management advance the analysis. Congress has expressly authorized presidential oversight of agency budgeting, 31 U.S.C. § 1101 *et seq.*, and information collection, 44 U.S.C. § 3507, even with respect to independent agencies. These statutes have no obvious implications, however, regarding Congress' intent concerning other forms of presidential supervision.

3. *Information Policy and OMB Regulatory Oversight.* Command-and-control regulation, of course, is not the only tool through which administrative agencies seek to affect economic and social behavior. The collection and dissemination of information—whether to promote publicity, responsible self-monitoring, the promulgation of voluntary standards, or as the predicate for future regulatory action—is a significant instrument of public policy. As the government's role in collecting and disseminating information for public purposes has expanded, Congress has reposed significant authority in OMB for monitoring other agencies' information policies.

Two statutes are of critical importance. The first, the Paperwork Reduction Act, 44 U.S.C. § 3501 *et seq.*, authorizes OMB to approve "information collection requests" by executive agencies. The Act then defines "information collection requests" to include any "written report form, application form, schedule, questionnaire, reporting or recordkeeping requirement, collection of information requirement, or other similar method calling for the collection of information." 44 U.S.C. § 3502(11). OMB may also review "information collection requests" by independent regulatory agencies, as enumerated in 44 U.S.C.§ 3502(5), except that such agencies may, by majority vote, reject OMB's disapprovals of their collection initiatives. 44 U.S.C. § 3507(f).

The second is the Data Quality Act, contained in Sec. 515 of the Treasury and General Government Appropriations Act for Fiscal Year 2001, Pub. L. No. 106–554. That Act directed OMB to issue, by September 30, 2001, "policy and procedural guidance" to those federal agencies subject to the Paperwork Reduction Act that would require such agencies (1) to issue data quality guidelines "ensuring and maximizing the quality, objectivity, utility, and integrity of information (including statistical information) disseminated" by the agency "in fulfillment of the purposes and provisions" of that act and (2) to establish "administrative mechanisms allowing affected persons to seek and obtain correction of information maintained and disseminated by the agency that does not comply with the guidelines." Covered agencies, in turn, were given a year to adopt agency-specific guidelines and procedures in compliance with OMB's government-wide guidelines. OMB then reviewed each agency's submission to insure consistency with OMB's published requirements.

This initial process was completed by October, 2002. See Memorandum from John D. Graham, Administrator, OIRA, for the President's Management Council Re: Executive Branch Implementation of the Information Quality Law (Oct. 4, 2002). Covered agencies are henceforth to report annually to OMB "the number and nature of complaints received by the agency regarding the accuracy of information disseminated by the agency; and how such complaints were handled by the agency." Moreover, OMB has directed the agencies to provide significant information on an ongoing basis regarding significant complaints, in contemplation of providing "the agencies with clarifying guidance and assistance on applying the OMB guidelines." OIRA Administrator Graham expressed his intention to "discuss with agencies the issues * * * raised [in administrative complaints] regarding the case-specific application of the OMB Information Quality Guidelines and [the agencies'] own guidelines." Private parties will almost certainly seek to transform these processes for objecting to the quality of agency information into a potent weapon for delaying agency enforcement activity, whether formal or informal. OMB's role in interpreting and implementing the DQA will have a great deal to do with the ultimate effectiveness of such strategies.

Towards Presidential Control of Rulemaking?

White House regulatory oversight has now become sufficiently entrenched that a number of commentators—some happily, some critically—have observed a subtle shift in the President's role vis-a-vis the regulatory agencies. To understand the shift, it is important to recall three foundational legal principles upon which all relevant actors agree. First, agencies empowered by Congress to regulate may do so only if consistent with their underlying statutory mandates. Second, absent the most extraordinary circumstances, the President may not order an agency to violate its mandate. Third, assuming an agency could fulfill its statutory duties through a variety of approaches, the President is entitled to push the agency towards the particular approach the Administration most favors as a matter of policy or politics. Presumably—and we will discuss the extent of this presumption further in Chapter 5—this is permissible even if the factors leading the President to favor one lawful approach over another are not, technically speaking, among the factors that Congress directed the agency to consider in deciding how or whether to regulate. Unless the President orders the agency to make a decision based on forbidden grounds, he is within his discretion to influence a choice among plausibly lawful alternatives.

When the Nixon Administration launched presidential oversight of environmental rulemaking, and even when the Reagan Administration systematized the regulatory oversight functions of OMB, it was commonly understood that the center of gravity in agency rulemaking still rested with the agency. Conventional legal wisdom held that Congress' delegations of authority to agency heads were intended to vest those officials with primary decision making power, and that presidential influence was to be something of a marginal nudge. Conventional political wisdom was that Presidents would not want to appear publicly as making every significant regulatory decision themselves, lest they be held accountable for every controversial rule.

The first Bush Administration took this "hidden-hand" model of presidential influence about as far as it could go. In addition to structuring OMB review of individual regulatory proposals, the original Reagan Executive Order No. 12,291 established a "Presidential Task Force on Regulatory Relief" to oversee the regulatory review process. By memorandum, in June, 1990, President George H.W. Bush assigned that body's tasks to the President's Council on Competitiveness, chaired by Vice President Quayle.

The Council on Competitiveness sought to impose the Administration's regulatory philosophy through a more focused strategy. Rather than reacting to all agency proposals, the Council early identified certain controversial areas of regulatory activity—most notably, clean air—on which to focus sustained attention. It followed no regular procedures. It had no formal or informal agreement with Congress over legislative access to the documentation of its deliberative contributions. It did not establish any controls on the degree or nature of its substantive contacts with outside interests. It functioned chiefly not through its members—all presidential advisers, cabinet members, or designated representatives from particular agencies—but through the personal staff of the Vice President. In short, it tried to exercise as much presidential influence as possible without creating any clear record of the nature of that influence.

The Council's secrecy proved a lightning rod for critics. A year after the Council commenced its regulatory oversight, its activities prompted Senator Glenn to propose a bill to regulate any "entity" established by the President for regulatory review. S. 1942, 102d Cong., 1st Sess. (1991). The Glenn proposal would not only have assured public access to such entities' written communications, but would also have imposed a tight across-the-board time limit on all such review processes. Moreover, delays in issuing regulations under the 1990 Clean Air Act prompted eight states and two environmental groups to challenge the authority of the Competitiveness Council to screen legally mandated regulations. *New York v. Reilly*, No. 92–0493 (N.D.N.Y. filed Apr. 13, 1992).

The design of the Regulatory Working Group established by Executive Order No. 12,866, was intended to comfort critics of the Competitiveness Council approach. But an unexpected thing happened. In the words of Dean Elana Kagan, former Deputy Assistant to President Clinton for Domestic Policy and Deputy Director of the Domestic Policy Council: "President Clinton treated the sphere of regulation as his own, and in doing so made it his own, in a way no other modern President had done. Clinton came to view administration as perhaps the single most critical—in part because the single most available—vehicle to achieve his domestic policy goals." Elana Kagan, *Presidential Administration*, 114 Harv. L. Rev. 2245, 2281–82 (2001). Dean Kagan cites the Clinton Administration's efforts with regard to tobacco regulation and paid family leave as two notable examples of a President claiming regulatory decision making to be his own.

Professor Peter Strauss was among the first academic commentators to note this trend and to be wary of it:

> [T]he President is simply in error and disserves the democracy he leads when he behaves as if rulemakings were his rulemakings. The delegations of authority that permit rulemaking are ordinarily made to others, not him—to agency heads whose limited field of action and embeddedness in a multi-voiced framework of legislature,

President, and court are the very tokens of their acceptability in a culture of law. Where Congress has placed the statutory duty in the Administrator of the EPA, or the Secretary of Labor, one could say it has delegated rulemaking power to the President only if that were the necessary constitutional consequence of its choice. That proposition does not live in the cases or in the Constitution's ambiguous text. In the text both of the Constitution and of Congress's statutes, it is the heads of departments who have legal duties vis a vis regulatory law. The President can ask about those duties and see that they are faithfully performed, but he and his department heads are to understand that the duties themselves are theirs—if not "ministerial," in Marshall's sense, they are emphatically not matters "only politically examinable." Indeed, even the President's political controls will be shaped by that allocation of duty, and by his consequent knowledge that however free he may seem to be to remove an incumbent and appoint a substitute officer more willing to do his bidding, that result will turn on his ability to get his new nominee confirmed.

The President's public behavior suggesting that agency rules are his rules threatens to make us forget just this middle ground. It invites us to give up the constraints of law in favor of those of politics. While, from a political perspective, one can applaud a President who goes out of his way to take responsibility as well as credit for the policy judgments of his administration, this seems a high price to pay. To be sure, agency process, perhaps particularly rulemaking process, is increasingly seen as political rather than expert; that perception, in its way, has animated the recent apparent revival of interest in "delegation," and other respects in which political elements of the Constitution's structural arrangements have become prominent. And for those to whom the Constitution itself requires that any power granted by Congress to the Executive branch be directly exercisable by the President himself, direct presidential rulemaking may seem even a constitutional necessity. Yet, as seen, the text of the Constitution settles no more than that the President is to be the overseer of executive government, and—as * * * struggles over even the milder presidential roles staked out to date must suggest—the contours and extent of present-day government make a stronger reading unacceptably hazardous to the public health. If we accept that rulemaking is irreducibly political in some respects, we imagine components of expertise as well; otherwise we would not be fighting as hard as we do over proper elements of risk analysis—the best means for identifying and managing uncertainties about complex technical facts, and so forth. The issue is mediating between politics and law—recognizing the strengths and weaknesses of each and finding ways of promoting their proper contribution—rather than pretending to locate the practice at either pole.

One kind of presidential response, perhaps implicit in paper trails that track the laws' assignments of responsibility, is that, in acting as he has been, President Clinton has in fact not been displacing the apparatus of government but simply voicing its results—that of course an air bags rule will be the product of the informed analysis of the NHTSA's staff or a tobacco rule of the FDA's—but that in associating himself with these outcomes he simply acknowledges the responsibility the people would hold him to in any event. These are his bureaucrats, and it is politically useful to both government morale and citizen appreciation for the President to associate himself with regulatory outcomes in this way. Yet this argument, in my judgment, really does put us into the thick of the law/politics problem. It elides Congress's constitutional prerogatives in structuring government, the duties it may confer on Heads of Departments who are not the President although they operate within the framework of the President's responsibility to see to it that the laws are faithfully executed. For him to make the bureaucrats believe that they are his is precisely to tear down the structures of law and regularity Congress has built up in relation to the presidency. It is Congress that gets to say how many people work in the White House, how many in the Department of Labor, how many in political offices, how many in the Senior Executive Service. In the current brouhaha about political fund-raising and use of the White House, we see both the importance of formal lines (i.e., the proposition that the White House may not be used as the site of political fund-raising) and the erosive effects of their repeated testing. The lines that are the focus of this commentary are of equal, and not unrelated, consequence.

This is, of course, a formal argument. It accepts the variety of political ways in which the President and those immediately around him chivvy in rulemaking, from the formal apparatus of Executive Order 12,866 to the informal checking and massaging that inevitably occur. The President in this respect is not too different from individual members of Congress and committees who may equally attempt to impress on administrative actors their views and the importance of respecting them in their discretionary activities. He is, to be sure, our chief executive, the one our Constitution has invested with executive power; but he wields that power, in these respects, within the constraints of law that Congress has established. No more than he could assign to the Secretary of the Interior responsibilities Congress had placed in the hands of the Secretary of Agriculture but he thought could be more capably met on F Street, can he depart from Congress's other assignments of responsibility. The bureaucrat or political appointee confronted by presidential chivvying can perhaps more easily see in this perspective the tension between duty and advice, grasp the limits on the President's capacity to understand and act on what may be quite complex technical matters with a sparse and largely political staff. The stakes for the psychology of government, for the extent to which civil servants and political appointees imagine themselves acting within a culture of law, are rather high.

Peter L. Strauss, *Presidential Rulemaking*, 72 Chi.–Kent L. Rev. 965, 984–86 (1997).

Consider, in light of Professor Strauss's concerns, Dean Elana Kagan's more sanguine assessment:

ELANA KAGAN, PRESIDENTIAL ADMINISTRATION

114 Harv. L. Rev. 2245, 2331–45 (2001).

Presidential administration promotes accountability in two principal and related ways. First, presidential leadership enhances transparency, enabling the public to comprehend more accurately the sources and nature of bureaucratic power. Second, presidential leadership establishes an electoral link between the public and the bureaucracy, increasing the latter's responsiveness to the former. Modern attributes of the relationship between the President and the public make these claims stronger than ever before. * * *

[T]he bureaucratic form—in its proportions, its reach, and its distance—is impervious to full public understanding, much less control. But for this very reason, the need for transparency, as an aid to holding governmental decisionmakers to account, here reaches its apex. To the extent possible, consistent with congressional command and other policy objectives, there is good reason to impose clear lines of command and to simplify and personalize the processes of bureaucratic governance.

Gauged by this standard, the President has natural and growing advantages over any institution in competition with him to control the bureaucracy. The Presidency's unitary power structure, its visibility, and its "personality" all render the office peculiarly apt to exercise power in ways that the public can identify and evaluate. The new strategies of presidential leadership, focused as they are on intensifying the direct connection between the President and public, enhance these aspects of the office and the transparency they generate; so too does the increased media coverage of the President, which is at once a cause and a result of these strategies. * * * presidentializing of the bureaucracy is to at least some extent the publicizing of the bureaucracy, with respect alike to outcomes and processes.

Consider now the related issue of which control mechanism best promotes responsiveness to the policy preferences of the general public. * * * [A] President has won a national election. More, this election, exactly because it was national in scope, probably focused on broad policy questions, conveying at least some information to the public about the future President's attitude toward regulation. * * * Because the President has a national constituency, he is likely to consider, in setting the direction of administrative policy on an ongoing basis, the preferences of the general public, rather than merely parochial interests. A prudent President, once elected, works to expand his base of support among the public. In his first term, the desire for reelection alone provides a reason to do so, including through the adoption of policies favored by a majority of the voting public. And even in his second term, a President retains strong incentives to consider carefully the public's views as to all manner of issues—incentives here related to his ambition for achievement, and beyond that for a chosen successor or historical legacy. The sum and general direction of the President's policy decisions, after all, may well affect his standing with his national constituency, and it is by now a truism of presidential scholarship that a President's standing among the general public critically affects his ability to achieve his policy and political agenda (which, in an endless feedback loop, in turn affects his public standing).

* * * This argument, however, needs * * * refinement, relating * * * to the openness of presidential involvement in administration (and thus drawing the connection between transparency and responsiveness). To the extent that presidential supervision of agencies remains hidden from public scrutiny, the President will have greater freedom to play to parochial interests. * * * It is when presidential control of administrative action is most visible that it most will reflect presidential reliance on and responsiveness to broad public sentiment. * * *

Assuming that enhanced presidential control of administration serves democratic norms, it still must meet another and sometimes conflicting standard—that of regulatory effectiveness. In using this broad term, I mean to include a number of so-called technocratic values: cost-effectiveness, consistency, and rational priority-setting. I also and even more firmly intend to refer to a certain kind of dynamism or energy in administration, which entails both the capacity and the willingness to adopt, modify, or revoke regulations, with a fair degree of expedition, to solve perceived national problems. * * *

Because the public holds Presidents, and often Presidents alone, responsible for so many aspects of governmental performance, Presidents have a large stake in ensuring an administration that works, at least in the eyes of the public. * * * Presidents want a bureaucracy that responds to them and provides them with the tools they need to be, and be perceived as, successful leaders. * * * [A]mong those tools is a high level of administrative effectiveness as commonly understood: the capacity to achieve set objectives, without undue cost, in an expeditious and coherent manner. Moreover, a President, by virtue of the attributes of his office, stands in a relatively good position to achieve these operational goals. Because he is a unitary actor, he can act without the indecision and inefficiency that so often characterize the behavior of collective entities. And because his "jurisdiction" extends throughout the administrative state (or at least, the executive branch), he can synchronize and apply general principles to agency action in a way that congressional committees, special interest groups, and bureaucratic experts cannot. * * *

There remains, of course, a question whether to count this presidential capacity for leadership over administration as virtue or vice, as a promise or a danger. * * * The argument against this kind of activism in government has an august lineage in this country. The system of checks and balances established in the Constitution is in no small measure based upon it: James Madison's famed prescription of "[a]mbition * * * counteract[ing] ambition" was designed to generate a kind of friction that would make governmental deliberation extensive and governmental action difficult to accomplish. From this perspective, now as then, institutional arrangements promoting dynamic government, such as the presidential control of bureaucracy, pose a risk of both tyranny and instability that should not be tolerated. * * *

Throughout American history, however, a countertradition has flourished that calls for enhanced governmental, and in particular executive, vigor. At its core is Hamilton's vision of a strong and efficacious government, with leadership provided by a chief executive operating with "[d]ecision" and "dispatch." The system of separation of powers, as distinguished from its moderating system of checks and balances, was partly meant to attain this objective by creating and then concentrating certain powers in an executive capable of resolute action. From this perspective, now as then, institutional arrangements promoting dynamic government, such as presidential control of administration, play a critical role in a well-functioning political system. * * * The argument extols governmental activism and innovation, making it equally ironic that in today's debate, those committed to what one scholar calls the "legacy of the New Deal" are the President's principal opponents.

In recent years, a number of political scientists and lawyers alike have argued that modern political developments, including most notably the demise of single-party control of the political branches, have tipped the balance in this historic argument toward the recognition of a greater need for energy in government. * * * With the advent of divided government in the mid-twentieth century, combined with the still more recent development of polarization between the congressional parties, this capacity for concerted action to meet national needs declined: partisan differences were superimposed on institutional differences, and the system increasingly succumbed to the phenomenon (and, indeed, by now the cliché) of gridlock. These new circumstances create a need for institutional reforms that will strengthen the President's ability to provide energetic leadership in an inhospitable political environment.

This argument becomes yet more powerful when the focus is narrowed from the surrounding political context to the administrative process. This is because political gridlock has had a counterpart in administrative ossification, emerging and intensifying at roughly the same time. In part, this increased rigidity in the administrative system was a natural part of its lifecycle; as earlier discussed, large-scale organizations, left to their own devices, exhibit over time a diminished capacity to innovate and a correspondingly greater tendency to do what they always have done even in the face of dramatic changes in needs, circumstances, and priorities. In part, too, this ossification arose because of the increased demands that courts made on agencies to include interest groups in their rulemaking processes; the resulting proliferation of procedural requirements, as noted earlier, made agencies unwilling to depart from even outmoded or otherwise undesirable administrative policies. The combination has made torpor a defining feature of administrative agencies, resulting both in inadequate and in overzealous regulatory efforts. The need for an injection of energy and leadership thus again becomes apparent, lest an inert bureaucracy encased in an inert political system grind inflexibly, in the face of new opportunities and challenges, toward (at best) irrelevance or (at worst) real harm.

Both Reagan and Clinton used their methods of administrative control to drive a resistant bureaucracy and political system. * * * Both Presidents, however well- or ill-advised their substantive policies, thus countered the dominant contemporary forces of bureaucratic and political lethargy through their practices of influencing agency decisions. If it is more important that government have some capacity for action and reaction than that it never make an error, then the resulting energy should count as a significant point in favor of presidential administration.

Notes

1. *Presidential Regulatory Oversight During Transitional Periods.* Any outgoing President, especially one who is aware that his successor belongs to a different political party, will seek in the concluding months of the outgoing Administration to put as many regulatory projects into final form as possible. This will entrench, at least temporarily, the policy preferences of the outgoing White House. Just as President Reagan intensified White House regulatory oversight generally, however, he also initiated a practice—emulated by each succeeding President—of imposing a moratorium designed to keep a previous Administration's last-minute regulatory initiatives from going into effect without approval of the new Administration. (Not that President Reagan acted wholly without historical precedent. His moratorium was the regulatory analogue of President Jefferson's instruction to Madison to hold up the appointments of Marbury and other Federalist judges.)

Most recently, on the day of President George W. Bush's inauguration, his chief of staff, Andrew Card, Jr., issued a memorandum to the heads and acting heads of executive departments and agencies, directing them to withdraw any regulations sent to the Office of the Federal Register (OFR) but not yet published, to postpone temporarily the effective dates of published regulations not yet in effect, and to delay sending to the OFR any proposed or final regulations not approved by the current Administration. Comment, *Taking Care that Presidential Oversight of the Regulatory Process is Faithfully Executed: A Review of Rule Withdrawals and Rule Suspensions under the Bush Administration's Card Memorandum*, 54 Admin. L. Rev. 1479, 1480 (2002) (William M. Jack). Although the last of these directives would appear relatively uncontroversial, unresolved legal questions exist about the legality of the first two measures as applied to particular rules.

Perhaps the most serious is whether agencies may postpone the effective dates of published final rules without following notice-and-comment rule-making, a matter not yet definitively addressed by the courts. Id. at 1498–1511.

Among the criticisms levied at the Card Memorandum was the Bush Administration's subsequent failure to track systematically all the rules that were affected by it. There is thus no definitive record how many rules were delayed or otherwise affected by the memorandum; the only evidence came from an informal poll conducted by OMB following a GAO request. For future administrations, should Congress regulate the transitional review process in order to insure the transparency essential to the accountability benefits that Dean Kagan touts?

2. *Presidential "Ownership" of Administration v. Checks and Balances—Further Reading.* Recent decades have witnessed an unprecedented outpouring of academic literature on the proper constitutional understanding of the Presidency and of the President's relationship to administration. Major articles, from a variety of perspectives, that would support the kind of executive vigor for which Dean Kagan contends include Steven G. Calabresi & Saikrishna B. Prakash, *The President's Power to Execute the Laws*, 104 Yale L.J. 541 (1994); Lawrence Lessig & Cass R. Sunstein, *The President and the Administration,* 94 Colum. L. Rev. 1 (1994); and Geoffrey P. Miller, *Independent Agencies*, 1986 Sup. Ct. Rev. 41. In addition to Professor Strauss's article excerpted above, contending works that seek to extend the "checks and balances" perspective in a manner that is far more cautionary on the virtues of presidential "ownership" of regulation include Cynthia R. Farina, *Undoing the New Deal Through the New Presidentialism*, 22 Harv. J.L. & Pub. Pol'y 227, 227 (1998); Martin S. Flaherty, *The Most Dangerous Branch*, 105 Yale L.J. 1725 (1996); Abner S. Greene, *Checks and Balances in an Era of Presidential Lawmaking*, 61 U. Chi. L. Rev. 123, 128 (1994); Thomas O. Sargentich, *The Administrative Process in Crisis—The Example of Presidential Oversight of Agency Rulemaking*, 6 Admin. L.J. 710, 716 (1993); Peter M. Shane, *Political Accountability in a System of Checks and Balances: The Case of Presidential Review of Rulemaking,* 48 Ark. L. Rev. 161, 174 (1995). A thoughtful, if unconventional, reading of the Constitution as requiring "parity" between the elected branches in controlling administration is Peter L. Strauss, *The Place of Agencies in Government: Separation of Powers and the Fourth Branch*, 84 Colum. L. Rev. 573, 649–50 (1984).

3. *Other Systems.* Often, the implications of U.S. government organization for regulatory oversight and the quality of administration stand out in sharper relief when compared to even a rough view of how other nations handle public administration. England and France, for example, each of which shares with the United States some key features of administrative law, nevertheless differ markedly from the United States and from one another in their organization of executive power. An illuminating brief treatment of U.K. public administration is Anthony H. Birch, The British System of Government (10th ed. 1998). For details on the French executive, see William Safran, The French Polity (5th ed. 1997); Malcolm Anderson, Government in France (1970); L. Neville Brown & J. F. Garner, French Administrative Law (3d ed. 1983); Henry W. Ehrmann, Politics in France (5th

ed. 1998); and F. F. Ridley & Jean Blondel, Public Administration in France (2d ed. 1969).

Presidential Administration and Open Government

As Dean Kagan argues, the appeal of more intense presidential involvement in regulatory oversight partly depends on whether such involvement would make the process more transparent. It is surely true that increasing White House involvement in regulatory review has predictably heightened demands for public access to information concerning the form and impact of that involvement. Yet, the more deeply the President becomes personally involved in such oversight, the more likely it is that intrabranch deliberations concerning regulatory policy will fall within the purview of some version of executive privilege.

For example, the plaintiffs in *Wolfe v. Department of Health and Human Services*, 839 F.2d 768 (D.C.Cir.1988) (en banc), sought access under the Freedom of Information Act to HHS records indicating what proposed and final regulations FDA had sent forward and the dates of their transmittal either to the Secretary of HHS or to OMB. The district court held these records were not deliberative communications exempted from mandatory disclosure by exemption 5 of the FOIA (discussed further in chapter 6), and a divided Court of Appeals panel affirmed. On reconsideration en banc, a seven–judge majority reversed, in an opinion by Judge Robert Bork. The majority concluded that such information was integral to the deliberative process because it would (a) indicate the various administrators' tentative approval or disapproval of the regulatory proposals at issue, and (b) identify the offices or officers delaying a regulation's issuance, which could invite targeted campaigns by outside groups that might alter the decision making process. The dissenters did not believe that the requested disclosures threatened to reveal any developing policies prematurely or, indeed, the substance of any regulatory proposal. They therefore concluded that the information had to be disclosed.

Notwithstanding *Wolfe*, U.S. District Court Judge June Hens Green refused to grant the White House summary judgment in an FOIA suit seeking from the now-defunct Task Force on Regulatory Relief all documents concerning "its review of or involvement in regulations that were or still are under consideration" by the EPA, FDA, or OSHA. In an opinion with obvious implications for Vice President Quayle's Competitiveness Council, Judge Green held (1) that the Task Force was an "agency" for FOIA purposes because its functions went beyond merely providing the President with advice and personal assistance, and (2) that the deliberative status of the documents that OMB identified as responsive did not relieve the White House of the obligation to release any segregable factual portions of those documents. *Meyer v. Bush*, 1991 WL 212215 (D.D.C.1991).

The sunshine provisions of the Clinton Order, described on pages 286–287, *supra*, sought to respond to the complaints of insufficient public access to information about regulatory oversight by OMB. See

Executive Order No. 12,866, § 6(b). At the current moment, however, it is a fair statement that the executive branch is not wholly of one mind on the subject of executive branch openness.

On one hand, and quite remarkably, it is possible through the Bush Administration's OMB web site to track meeting records, oral communication records, and public comment on all regulations subject to review. The site includes a list of regulations, updated daily, under Executive Order 12866 review, as well as reviews completed with the last 30 days; lists and statistics regarding concluded Executive Order reviews; the text of all OIRA letters either returning proposals for further analysis or seeking to instigate regulatory action ("prompt letters"), as well as of all post-review letters. Plainly, much of this information would be regarded, under *Wolfe*, *supra*, as protected from mandatory public disclosure, at least presumptively, by executive privilege.

On the other hand, critics have charged that, in a variety of contexts, the Bush-43 Administration has "vastly expanded the zone of secrecy that surrounds the White House and most of the federal government." Gary D. Bass and Sean Moulton, *The Bush Administration's Secrecy Policy* (OMB Watch Working Paper Oct. 2002), available at http://www.ombwatch.org/rtk/secrecy.pdf. In part, this is undoubtedly a reaction to the 2001 terrorist attacks. But the Administration's efforts have also included advancing arguments for executive privilege that are arguably more ambitious in both scope and significance than any articulated by any president since before the Watergate scandal during the Nixon Administration. For example, President Bush issued, on November 1, 2001, Executive Order No. 13,233, "Further Implementation of the Presidential Records Act," which purported to authorize executive privilege claims not only by former Presidents, but also by former vice presidents and, in cases of incapacity, by the legal representatives of former Presidents. The manifest aim of the executive order was to permit executive privilege claims to be lodged on behalf of the Reagan Administration, whose records were about to be disclosed under the Presidential Records Act.

In perhaps its most celebrated campaign for secrecy in ordinary domestic policy making, the Bush-43 Administration has sought to obviate the need for a formal claim of executive privilege by invoking other defenses against the mandatory disclosure of certain records. In particular, both public interest groups and the General Accounting Office have sought to compel the Bush Administration to release records concerning the so-called National Energy Policy Development Group ("NEPDG"), created by President Bush shortly after his 2001 inauguration "to develop a national energy policy designed to help the private sector, and as necessary and appropriate Federal, State, and local governments, promote dependable, affordable, and environmentally sound protection and distribution of energy." *Walker v. Cheney*, 230 F.Supp.2d 51, 54 (D.D.C.2002). In particular, two members of Congress asked the Comptroller General, who is head of the Government Accounting Office, to investigate allegations that NEPDG meetings had "included exclusive groups of non-governmental participants—including political contributors—to discuss specific policies, rules, regulations, and legislation." Judicial Watch and other private plaintiffs sought disclosure of much the same material under the Federal Advisory Committee and Freedom of Information Acts. The Administration was initially successful in persuading one federal district judge that the Comptroller General lacked constitutional standing to sue the Vice President for release of the information in question. Meanwhile, another district judge held that requiring the Vice President and other members of the NEPDG to comply with discovery requests aimed at the same documents did not by itself impose an unconstitutional burden on the Executive. *Judicial Watch, Inc. v. National Energy Policy Development Group*, 230 F.Supp.2d 12 (D.D.C.2002).

Whatever the outcome of these struggles, the practices challenged bear on contemporary debates about the value of "presidential administration." The context for the Bush Administration's resistance to disclosure, in this instance, was the formulation of an overall policy, not the review of a particular regulation vested in a statutorily designated agency decision maker. Nonetheless, the Administration's resistance, in this context, to disclosing with whom it consulted in making policy might well be thought in tension with Dean Kagan's argument that presidential regulatory initiative increases government transparency.

Assessments of OMB's Regulatory Oversight Role

The long-term appeal of yet more intense presidential involvement in regulatory oversight presumably depends not only on constitutional values, but also on the actual performance of the White House in conducting regulatory review. Yet, the quality of that review has proved notoriously difficult to assess. After 20 years, for example, it has yet to be shown with genuine rigor either that OMB review has led to regulatory policies more socially beneficial than would likely have been the case without such review (as its champions would claim) or that presidential involvement has prompted agencies to subordinate their rule-of-law fidelity to White House politics (as critics have feared). According to one assessment, the "clearest impact" of the program during the 1980s was simply to delay rulemaking. NATIONAL ACADEMY OF PUBLIC ADMINISTRATION, PRESIDENTIAL MANAGEMENT OF RULEMAKING IN REGULATORY AGENCIES 7, 47 (1987).

Among the most critical accounts of OMB's early impact was a report prepared for the Senate Committee on Environment and Public Works, Office of Management and Budget Influence on Agency Regulations, 99th Cong., 2d Sess. (1986). This report, which highlighted several examples of assertedly excessive or illegitimate oversight, most of them involving EPA regulations, offered the following assessment:

> While both Executive orders contain language constraining their effect "to the extent permitted by statute," * * * the collective strength of these authorities, combined with OMB's budget review

> powers, has supported OMB recommendations which conflict with agency statutory mandates, impede the EPA Administrator's use of his discretionary authority, and delay EPA promulgation of regulations. Most critics of OMB's role in review of agency regulations would support a coordinating and advisory role for Presidential oversight of Federal regulations. What causes concern is the delay, secrecy, lack of accountability (to the public or Congress), and potential for displacement of agency expertise and agency administrative and policy authorities created by current OMB practices.

In a similar vein are Erik D. Olson, *The Quiet Shift of Power: Office of Management & Budget Supervision of Environmental Protection Agency Rulemaking Under Executive Order 12,291*, 4 Va.J.Nat.Res.L. 1 (1984), and Note, *Executive Orders 12,291 and 12,498: Usurpation of Legislative Power or Blueprint for Legislative Reform?*, 54 Geo.Wash.L.Rev. 512, 527 (1986). As noted above, the Clinton Administration's redesign of the oversight process, later followed as well by the Bush-43 Administration, was intended precisely to remedy "delay, secrecy, [and] lack of accountability."

Both the Clinton and Bush-43 Administrations have claimed a variety of significant successes in regulatory improvement attributable to the OMB review process. In early 1995 testimony to a House subcommittee, OIRA Director Sally Katzen described several improvements in new regulations, which she attributed to the success of the Executive Order analytic process:

> For example, the Department of Transportation's National Highway Traffic Safety Administration rule making on side impact protection for light trucks was accompanied by a first-rate regulatory analysis that led the agency to delete a significant, expensive component of the proposed rule and instead request comment on a less costly but more effective safety feature. In designing its rules under the Mammography Quality Standards Act, the Food and Drug Administration made the standards less burdensome on mammography facilities, which are nearly all small businesses, by incorporating existing industry standards to the maximum extent possible. The Coast Guard, in promulgating rules to alert crews about the likelihood of unanticipated oil spills, proposed allowing the use of lower cost signaling devices (i.e., overfill stick gauges) rather than more costly and sophisticated alarm systems.

Statement of Sally Katzen, Administrator, OIRA, before the House Committee on Government Reform and Oversight, Subcommittee on National Economic Growth, 104th Cong., 1st Sess. (Jan. 19, 1995).

The Bush-43 Administration—perhaps surprisingly for an administration overtly sympathetic to deregulation—has claimed successes in urging agencies, through so-called OIRA "prompt letters," to "address potential opportunities to save lives and improve health through cost-effective regulation." According to OIRA Administrator John Graham:

> One OMB letter has accelerated FDA's deliberations on a rule that would require labeling of foods for their trans-fatty acid content, an important risk factor for coronary heart disease. Another OMB letter to OSHA has stimulated a national information program to promote workplace use of automatic defibrillators, a technology that saves lives from sudden cardiac arrest and is already found in airports and federal buildings. A recent letter to NHTSA requires that priority be given to a rulemaking to test cars and light trucks in offset crash tests, an approach that may reduce the frequency and severity of lower extremity injuries in car crashes.

John D. Graham, Speech to the National Press Club on "Presidential Management of the Regulatory State," Dec. 17, 2001.

Although we lack a comprehensive analysis of the overall costs and benefits of the OMB review process, some data do exist on the operation of the review process itself. A recent study described the overall volume as follows:

> For the twenty-year period from 1981 to 2000, the White House reviewed a grand total of 34,386 rules (proposed and final combined). Of these, 1,693 were economically major or economically significant, and 32,693 were otherwise major or significant. Among economically major/significant rules, as defined by the Reagan and Clinton orders rules from the EPA, The Department of Health and Human Services ("HHS"), the DOT, and the Department of Agriculture ("USDA") made up the lion's share, with a combined total of 1,155, or in other words sixty-eight percent of all economically major/significant rules. The next tier, by quantity of rules submitted, was occupied by the Department of Commerce ("DOC"), The Interior Department ("DOI"), and the Department of Labor ("DOL").

Steven P. Croley, *White House Review of Agency Rulemaking: An Empirical Investigation*, 70 U. Chi. L. Rev. ___ (2003). The aggregate data somewhat mute the special role of environmental regulation in this process. Not only did EPA issue more economically significant proposed rules during the Clinton years than any other agency, but its rules were disproportionately likely to be the subject of OIRA consultative meetings and disproportionately likely to be the target of OIRA changes.

Moreover, as Professor Croley explains, the overall numbers disguise a major shift from the Reagan and Bush I Administrations to the Clinton and Bush II Administrations. In particular, starting in 1994, the Clinton Administration began to focus OIRA attention on a far narrower set of rules. As a result, the average number of rules reviewed from 1981 to 1993 was 2329, while the average from 1994 through 2001 was 605. Office of Information and Regulatory Affairs, Stimulating Smarter Regulation: 2002 Report to Congress on the Costs and Benefits of Federal Regulations and Unfunded Mandates on State, Local, and Tribal Entities 14 (December 2002).

Not surprisingly, OIRA's tighter focus has resulted in quicker processing of proposed rules. As of late 2001, OIRA claimed to have reduced to nearly zero the total number of regulatory reviews taking over 90 days. At the same time, while the Reagan and Bush-41 Administrations, on an annual basis, changed a larger absolute number of rules during the course of OIRA review than have Clinton and Bush-43, Professor Croley found that the percentage of rules changed under the Clinton Administration was significantly higher. Indeed, between 1995 and 2000, OIRA review resulted in changes to more rules than were approved without change.

Because of skeptics' concerns that presidential regulatory review might provide special interests with an extra forum for influencing regulatory outcomes, Professor Croley paid special attention to the degree to which, during the Clinton Administration,* OIRA-induced rule changes correlated with meetings about the rules with "outsiders." There was a definite correlation between such meetings and the likelihood of change, although, as Professor Croley reviewed the data, he doubted that outside interventions were themselves the cause of rule change: "More than eighty-five percent of the rules the subject of OIRA meetings were changed during the OIRA review process, as compared with less than sixty percent of all rules reviewed during the same period, though it seems doubtful that meetings themselves were the direct cause of change, as opposed to reflections of underlying political dynamics that prompted a change." That finding is based, in part, on Professor Croley's conclusion that the likelihood of an OMB-induced rule change did not depend on the kinds of outsider interests represented at the meetings in question—that is, whether they were narrow or broad-based interests. Instead, rules that were inherently controversial—disproportionately, rules proposed by the EPA—were the most likely to be changed as a consequence of OMB's intervention.

Based on his study, Professor Croley believes there exist data to support both the sanguine and skeptical views of presidential regulatory oversight, although, on balance, he thinks the development a positive one:

> A defender of the strong regulatory president can point to several * * * is, or can be, benign. First of all, the White House seems to concentrate on a manageable amount of rules—manageable given its institutional resources—numbering in the several hundreds. * * * [T]he White House has the institutional capacity to undertake meaningful review of agency rules.
>
> Second, judging from the institutional resources that the White House commits to rule review, White House review at least appears

* Data were not available for a comparable study of the influence of outsider meetings during the Reagan and Bush I Administrations, so that it cannot be known whether the patterns observed by Professor Croley were distinctive to the Clinton Administration. Because the George W. Bush Administration is keeping the Clinton order's logging system in place, a cross-Administration comparison will eventually be possible.

to be technocratic. Rules are reviewed in part as a check on agencies' cost-benefit analyses. * * * Of course, there is room for the White House to put values on regulatory costs or benefits in such as way as to advance its own political agenda, as critics of White House review (and of cost-benefit analysis more generally) often point out, but that task would not be as easy as critics suggest, for doing so in a crude political way would require corruption of OIRA's civil service. * * *

Some of the OIRA meetings data provide further support for this conclusion. First, the fact that agencies typically attend OIRA meetings suggests that the White House has kept good on Executive Order 12866's instruction for agency personnel to be informed of criticisms to their rules by outside groups, and further that there is at least some level of give-and-take between the White House and rulemaking agencies, as opposed to utterly hierarchical control over agency rules once they reach the White House. * * * Furthermore, the fact that White House representation from offices other than OIRA does not predict a change in a rule suggests that the White House does not change rules whenever political considerations might dictate. * * *

Third, with respect to OIRA meetings, defenders of White House oversight could point to the fact that OIRA will hold meetings to discuss rules under review with any outside party who requests a meeting. Furthermore, while narrowly focused interest groups make more requests than do other groups, still about forty percent of OIRA meetings were attended either only by broad-based groups or by broad-based groups as well as narrow interest groups. More importantly still, the type of interest group in attendance at an OIRA meetings does not predict whether the rule the subject of that meeting will be changed during the review process, perhaps surprisingly to some. If the White House used the review process to deliver regulatory benefits to powerful interests, one might have expected the presence of narrow interest groups to predict a change in rules. For that matter, if the White House used the review process to deliver regulatory benefits to interests it favored, such as environmental groups, whether or not they were politically powerful, then again one might have predicted the presence of broad-based groups to predict a change in rules. But interest group type predicts nothing. The fact that the economic significance of a rule is no predictor of change casts further doubt on the idea that the White House uses the review process as a cover to benefit politically powerful groups. * * *

On the other hand, there are arguments to be made against the strong regulatory president, which find at least some support from the above findings. First of all, the data suggest that White House review is not simply a review for major rulemaking mistakes or inconsistencies. Rather the White House has inserted itself into the rulemaking process in a thoroughgoing way. * * * [T]o the extent defenders of White House oversight have argued that such oversight simply serves an inter-agency coordination role to avoid regulatory redundancy and inconsistency, White House review has become much more.

Second, critics of expanded White House oversight find some of their fears about uneven interest-group pressures and political favoritism realized by the finding that narrow interest groups outnumber all other types during the OIRA meeting process. Although almost half of the rules the subject of OIRA meetings led to broad-based pluralistic meetings, still more than half led to meetings attended only by narrow interest groups. * * *

More generally, if the existence of an OIRA meeting can be taken as an indicator of political controversy surrounding a rule, then the OIRA meetings data suggest that politically controversial rules are usually changed through the White House review process. That conclusion challenges the view of OIRA review as purely technocratic. * * *

The fact that agency presence at OIRA meetings is positively correlated with changes to rules the subject of those meetings might also provide support for worries that White House review inappropriately interferes with agency autonomy. That is, although the White House solicits agencies' views about rules under review and invites agencies to OIRA meetings, both as required by Executive Order 12866 and its implementing directives, it appears that agencies do not usually succeed in persuading White House reviewers that their rules would be best unchanged. * * *

Finally, although Executive Order 12866 sought to make White House review more transparent, in fact the process is merely translucent. OIRA does keep a log of meetings, but again only a small percentage of rules under review are ever the subject of meetings—an unusually important set, to be sure, but a small minority of rules nonetheless. Because there is no way to observe communications between other offices within the White House and OIRA for rules not the subject of an OIRA meeting, it is impossible to know how often and with what effect other offices within the White House make their views known to OIRA reviewers—facts that would be important to any final assessment of the political dimensions of the White House's influence on rulemaking.

On balance, however, White House review of agency rulemaking is a welcome development in administrative governance. Ultimately, the debate over expanded White House oversight might be settled by the allocation of the burden of persuasion, for proving that White House oversight promotes good government is at least as difficult as proving that it does not. To the extent critics believe that White House oversight is unwelcome no matter how transparent and evenhanded—unwelcome because, in principle, such oversight constitutes an unwarranted interference with agency autonomy and congressional will—there is probably little to be said to refute that conviction. On the other hand, to the extent critics do not object to expanded White House oversight as a matter of principle, then data about how that oversight is exercised might challenge many of the common particular criticisms made of presidential involvement in rulemaking. Most of the data above go farther to assuage fears about presidential involvement in rulemaking than they do to accentuate those fears. * * *

[W]hile it is true that examining available data concerning OIRA rulemaking review to some extent constitutes a case of "looking where the light happens to be"—but only to some extent, as none of the data presented above is publicized much less discussed—the point remains that it is unlikely a great deal of regulatory favoritism takes place in total darkness: Given the institutional position and importance of OIRA to the White House's oversight of agencies, it is hard to imagine that White—House favoritism is pervasive completely outside of the OIRA. Granted, behind-the-scenes rent-seeking is by its very nature hard to rule out, but for the same reason is hard to confirm as well. Undoubtedly, some amount of regulatory function by the White House takes place. Even so, it would be much too glib to dismiss the above findings that OIRA review appears to be evenhanded and technocratic as misleading or irrelevant to the question about the nature of White House review.

Moreover, if regulatory favoritism by the White House independent of the OIRA review process is common, that fact probably argues in favor of a greater, not a lesser, role for OIRA in rulemaking review. In other words, now OIRA review becomes an antidote to behind-the-scenes influence on agency rulemaking from other parts of the White House. The greater OIRA's relevance and influence, the more difficult it should be for other arms of the White House to affect the final form of agency rules. * * *

[T]he question about the White House's proper role with respect to agency rulemaking should focus, as always, on the marginal effects of White House review. In other words, the real question asks whether White House review of agency rulemaking is desirable given all of the other features of the rulemaking process and all other influences on agency rulemaking. * * * Several of the above findings—that OIRA evaluates agency rules with respect to established criteria, that OIRA apparently possesses the human and organizational resources to understand agency rules, that rulemaking agencies are consulted during the review process, that the presence of narrow interest groups at OIRA meetings does not affect the likelihood that a rule will be changed, that White House presence at an OIRA meetings similarly does not affect the probability that a rule will be changed, and that in recent years the propensity of the White House to require changes in rules reflects as much as anything the Administration's regulatory priorities (such as its focus on environmental regulation)—support such a conclusion.

Steven P. Croley, *White House Review of Agency Rulemaking: An Empirical Investigation*, 70 U. Chi. L. Rev. ___ (2003).

Chapter 4

ADMINISTRATIVE ADJUDICATION

A. INTRODUCTION

Many administrative decisions are the product of procedures similar to civil trials. Formal adjudication in a courtroom setting is surely familiar to students who have been through a basic course in civil procedure—indeed, to anyone exposed to American theater, television, or motion pictures. The courtroom trial is a ubiquitous part of our culture; a constant source of social fascination, dramatic inspiration, and political as well as legal commentary. But what of administrative adjudication? The very term, administrative adjudication, threatens to dampen interest—until one recalls a few highly visible examples. The adjudication of Dr. Robert Oppenheimer's claim to a security clearance provides a classic illustration. The FDA's decision concerning the safety of silicone breast implants is a more recent example. Moreover, notoriety is a poor measure of social importance. Administrative adjudicators make thousands of decisions everyday concerning the crucial interests of ordinary people—whether to grant a disability pension, provide Medicaid benefits, allow continued residence in the United States or issue a professional licence—to name but a few arenas of high-volume, low-visibility, mass administrative justice.

As these instances illustrate, the contexts in which administrative tribunals function are astonishingly diverse. Moreover, because administrative adjudications represent a governmental exercise vaster by far than the caseload of all civil and criminal courts, it seems obvious that the elaborate judicial trial model could not be replicated in all administrative adjudications or even in all cases involving substantial or valuable interests. Indeed, as the extraordinarily high rates of settlement in civil cases and of plea bargains in criminal ones suggests, the judicial trial model cannot be applied routinely anywhere in U.S. law. Although administrative processes, like civil and criminal processes, sometimes provide a routine right to adversary trial that can be avoided at the parties' option, administrative law has also sought in many instances to construct unique adjudicatory processes tailored to the needs of particular administrative programs.

A central concern of this chapter, therefore, is the appropriate extent of departures from the civil or criminal adjudication model in the administrative context. The responses to this question by U.S. courts—and legislatures and administrators—have been varied. Administrative adjudication plays numerous roles in the history and the contemporary functioning of our government, and the sources of administrative hearing rights are multiple. The lawyer who would perform successfully within this ostensibly familiar legal environment must see adjudication performed by administrators not simply in a new light, but as bathed simultaneously in several new lights.

First, administrative adjudication is a concept of enormous breadth and one that receives rather odd treatment under the federal Administrative Procedure Act. According to that statute, "adjudication" means an "agency process for the formulation of an order." An "order" includes any final disposition by an agency in a matter that is not "rulemaking." The latter is then tautologically defined as an "agency process for formulating, amending, or appealing a rule." In short, the APA definition of adjudication seems to encompass any decision by an agency having any legal effect unless that decision can be characterized as a rule—whatever that is (a subject to which we turn in Chapter 5). Presumably anything from a Social Security clerk's authorization to begin paying retirement benefits on a particular Social Security account, to a local Forest Service employee's decision to close an access road temporarily because of an avalanche, to an Occupational Safety and Health Administration inspector's determination that a fire extinguisher is improperly located in a workshop, to a Federal Trade Commission determination that a proposed merger is anticompetitive, to a Food and Drug Administration determination that AZT may be marketed for the treatment of HIV infection, qualifies as an adjudication. Can all of these decisions be subject to the same process requirements?

"No" is the expected and implicit answer of the Administrative Procedure Act. Indeed, the APA makes very little depend on the classification of a decision as an adjudication. To be sure, adjudications are definitionally excluded from the provisions of section 553 on "rulemaking." Beyond that clear exclusion, however, the APA contents itself with supplying process requirements for proceedings that administrative lawyers customarily call "formal hearings." But, in the language of the Administrative Procedure Act, an adjudication, like a rulemaking proceeding, is subject to these formal hearing requirements only to the extent that it is an "adjudication required by statute to be determined on the record after opportunity for agency hearing." In short, the APA supplies a generic form of formal hearing process, but only for those instances in which some other statute requires that formal process be employed. Administrative adjudicatory processes may range across a spectrum of formality from the internal mental operations of a single individual to protracted judicial-style proceedings before multimember commissions with all the accoutrements of an adversary trial. But, on the question of the requisite characteristics of any adjudicatory process short of a proceeding required by some other statute to be "on the record after a hearing" the APA stands virtually mute. (But see 5 U.S.C. § 558 on licensing). And even with respect to formal processes, the APA's provisions may be superseded by the specific provisions of an agency's organic statute.

In an important sense, this picture of administrative adjudication as following a set of particularistic requirements emanating from multiple statutes is accurate. Most debate and conflict about administrative hearing rights at the federal level goes on within a statutory framework or frameworks (that is, the APA plus some more specific statute). Legal argument tends to focus on issues of statutory interpretation. One must never forget, however, a second perspective on administrative adjudication: the perspective of constitutional due process. To be sure, the Constitution's two Due Process Clauses speak with even less precision than does the Administrative Procedure Act. Administrative processes, whether of federal or state origin, must provide affected parties with "due process." But what process is due? That is a difficult and fascinating question to which we will shortly turn. For now we need only point out that, within our particular constitutional tradition, the fact that a decision is an adjudication, that is, that it focuses on individual situations and makes the facts of individual cases legally relevant, makes a significant difference.

Although the Constitution subjects our government to few procedural constraints in adopting legislative rules of general applicability, government decision making that applies general rules to individual cases often demands an individualized inquiry into specific facts and circumstances. In a case often cited as exemplifying this tradition, *Londoner v. Denver*, 210 U.S. 373 (1908), the Supreme Court reviewed a tax "assessed under the provisions of the charter of the city of Denver, which confer[red] upon the city the power to make local improvements and to assess the cost upon property specially benefitted." The city had levied taxes on several property owners for municipal improvements without affording an opportunity to challenge either their inclusion in the levy or their relative shares of the tax. The Court held that the property owners were entitled to individualized hearings. In contrast, in *Bi–Metallic Investment Co. v. State Board of Equalization*, 239 U.S. 441, 445 (1915), the Court rebuffed a taxpayer's demand for an individual hearing before the defendant state agency could revalue *all* taxable property in Denver by forty per cent. The government decision, because general rather than individualized in nature, did not require an adjudicatory proceeding.

That the taxpayers in *Londoner* were entitled to some kind of individualized hearing does not, of course, inform us what kind of hearing they should have. Moreover, because virtually all federal administrative processes are routinely organized to fall comfortably within constitutional due process minima, much of the contemporary jurisprudence on constitutional due process involves state or local programs, as *Londoner* and *Bi–Metallic* again illustrate. Constitutional due process might thus be viewed as a curiosity having little relevance to federal administrative adjudication. As we shall see, however, when we look at the interpretation of specific statutory hearing provisions, due process ideas about adjudicatory structure and process exercise significant influence. Here as elsewhere, in cases of doubt, courts fall back on what they perceive to be the legal system's fundamental understandings and commitments. And, because no statute can avoid leaving "unprovided-for cases," these background constitutional ideas are important even when the constitutional text is not obviously implicated. Indeed, because the Constitution is often not mentioned, much judicial "interpretation" of statutory hearing provisions might as easily be characterized as administrative common law.

Finally, structuring administrative adjudication confronts a crucial competition between bureaucratic management and individualized justice. This contest is manifest on the face of the constitutional controversies with which the chapter begins. But, if anything, the conflict is more profound and more pervasive than even these cases portray it. Individualized adjudicatory justice, particularly if it entails all the trappings of formal adversary procedure, is wonderfully anti-bureaucratic. Were adjudication to be conducted in administrative agencies essentially on the common law model of civil or criminal trial, administrators would be hard pressed to run coherent, much less efficient, administrative operations. As in the courts, an impossible docket would force resort to settlement, and the negotiating leverage provided to private parties by the threat to demand a full trial-type proceeding would distort agency policy. Agencies can be expected to resist formal hearing processes, therefore, almost as fiercely as individual claimants will clamor for their inclusion in administrative schemes. The stage is thus set for continuous trench warfare between ideas of managerial competence and individual fairness, or perhaps we should say, between the partisans of these two quite divergent visions of how administrative adjudication ought to be organized. These battles are a ubiquitous feature of administrative legal life and are waged on a host of procedural fronts.

In this chapter, we explore these differing perspectives on administrative adjudication in a slightly different order than they are discussed above. We begin with constitutional questions, move on to issues of statutory hearing rights, and conclude with an exploration of administrative adjudication in contexts that highlight the multiple tensions between administrative efficacy and the procedural protection of individual interests.

B. ADJUDICATORY DUE PROCESS

1. TIMING AND ELEMENTS OF A DUE PROCESS HEARING

In a celebrated article, the late Judge Henry Friendly identified eleven features that might in a particular case be regarded as essential to a fair hearing:

1. An unbiased tribunal;
2. Notice of the proposed action and the grounds asserted for it;
3. An opportunity to present reasons why proposed action should not be taken;
4. The right to call witnesses;
5. The right to know the evidence against oneself;
6. The right to have a decision based exclusively on the evidence presented;
7. The right to counsel;
8. The making of a record;
9. The availability of a statement of reasons for the decision;
10. Public attendance; and
11. Judicial review.

Henry Friendly, *"Some Kind of Hearing,"* 123 U.Pa. L. Rev. 1267 (1975). One should add to this list another critical variable, the timing of the required hearing—need it occur before the government's decision takes effect, or will "post-deprivation" procedures satisfy the demands of due process?

The Supreme Court has not developed discrete lines of analyses for each of these elements. ("Notice" requirements are a prominent exception, *see Dusenbery v. United States*, 534 U.S. 161 (2002).) Instead, current constitutional doctrine tends to proceed in two steps, one "qualitative"—"Is this the type of government decision for which the Constitution guarantees certain minimum procedures?"; and the second "quantitative"—"How much process is due, given the need to "balance" the importance of the private party's interest, the government's need for expedition and informality, and the likelihood of erroneous decisions absent the procedural protections sought?" The breadth of these inquiries obviously invites continuous dispute concerning what due process demands. The only undisputed proposition may be that, whatever the content of "due process" the Supreme Court has interpreted the Fifth and Fourteenth Amendments to impose identical requirements on federal, state, and local agencies.

Trenchant due process criteria have never been easy to discern. In a seminal essay, *Methodology and Criteria in Due Process Adjudication—A Survey and Criticism*, 66 Yale L.J. 319 (1957), Sanford Kadish reviewed the Supreme Court's due process jurisprudence with a sense of frustration. One strain of the case law seemed reasonably coherent: it simply relied upon tradition. Processes that had close analogues in wide use, or that were historically sanctioned, were deemed legitimate; other processes—relatively uncommon—were deemed illegitimate. Yet, as Kadish discovered, the tradition-based approach hardly exhausted the courts' repertoire of due process analysis. Other cases spoke in terms of such concepts as "fundamental fairness" or "governmental necessity." In the end Kadish could only suggest that beyond tradition-sanctioned procedures, the federal courts recognized a concept of "flexible due process" which lacked any apparent principle of similar generality.

Viewed from a more contemporary perspective, due process doctrine does not display much more coherence. It is now possible, however, to suggest that due process jurisprudence consists principally of variations on three central themes, which we can term "tradition," "natural rights," and "interest balancing." Each theme is complex and richly embellished in the cases. Each has its adherents and detractors. See generally JERRY L. MASHAW, DUE PROCESS IN THE ADMINISTRATIVE STATE (1985). Here we can only introduce the core ideas and suggest their limitations.

Tradition. A tradition-based approach to due process analysis asks whether the procedures at issue conform to the customary processes of law. As an historical matter this way of putting the due process question has much to recommend it. The original understanding of the due process constraint may have been that it provided protection against oppressive governmental acts enforced through "special" proceedings. The Due Process Clause is thus the constitutional heir of English concerns with Star Chamber proceedings and revolutionary resistance to an arbitrary colonial magistracy.

But tradition has serious limitations as a decisional guide. As a jurisprudential technique, its weakness lies in the difficulty of identifying a single appropriate tradition. When, for example, the Supreme Court in *Goldberg v. Kelly*, 397 U.S. 254 (1970), *infra* p. 322, confronted the distinctly twentieth century question of an appropriate process for terminating welfare benefits, it was required to choose from among competing traditions. The long tradition of nonenforcement of gratuitous promises, including promises of continuous income support, suggested that there was no legal interest involved sufficient to actuate due process concern. The tradition of commercial law remedies suggested that the welfare recipient (creditor) should have post-termination recourse to ordinary civil process to determine the legality of the government's (debtor) failure to perform. The tradition of governmental cancellation of other valuable privileges, such as common carrier certificates or professional licenses, suggested that, absent emergency, some form of pretermination proceeding was necessary. By what jurisprudential technique does a court decide which tradition is most relevant?

The value presuppositions of a tradition-focused approach to due process protection are also troublesome. If tradition implies adherence to the original understanding of "life, liberty, or property," then many governmental activities that encroach on modern notions of humane values evade constitutional constraint. And, on one "original" understanding of due process—meaning the processes of the ordinary courts or of the legislature—much of the regulatory apparatus of the administrative state applicable to property interests would be unconstitutional (the national labor relations laws, all federal environmental legislation, most safety legislation, the anti-fraud activities of the Federal Trade and Securities and Exchange Commissions, to name a few). By modern standards the process constraints of such a traditional approach to due process (a choice limited to representative assemblies and judicial trials) are as overprotective as the traditional view's substantive values (protection only against death, incarceration, or invasion of common-law property) are underinclusive.

Natural Rights. A natural rights analysis takes a quite different view of the due process problem. It begins, not with the historical contingencies of tradition, but with a basic moral premise concerning individual autonomy. Each citizen is an end, not merely a means for the attainment of collective ends. The government cannot, therefore, pursue its purposes through processes that ignore the independent status and purposes of the individual. From the natural rights perspective this dignitary principle is what the Due Process Clause, like other portions of the Bill of Rights, protects. A conception of human dignity thus informs the historic demand for "fundamental fairness."

While this secular formulation of the natural rights approach has substantial support in liberal political theory (see, e.g., MASHAW, *supra*; Edmund L. Pincoffs, *Due Process, Fraternity, and a Kantian Injunction*, *in* DUE PROCESS: NOMOS XVIII 172 (J.R. Pennock & J. Chapman, eds. 1977)), and clear connections with the individualistic ethos of ordinary political discourse (see, e.g., EMMETTE S. REDFORD, DEMOCRACY IN THE ADMINISTRATIVE STATE (1969)), it also raises problems of application. The set of procedural rights necessary to preserve individual dignity seems infinitely expansive. See, e.g., Richard B. Saphire, *Specifying Due Process Values: Toward a More Responsive Approach to Procedural Protection*, 127 U.Pa. L. Rev. 111 (1978); Mark Tushnet, *The Newer Property: Suggestions for the Revival of Substantive Due Process*, 1975 Sup.Ct.Rev. 261. Any governmentally imposed disappointment provides an occasion for invocation of the principle. Moreover, autonomy implies that due process should be defined as those procedures freely accepted by the individuals affected. Because such a principle forecloses governance, limitations must be imposed. But, what are the principles of limitation? Where is the objective set of *truly important* human values and *sufficiently dignified* procedures for making collective decisions about them?

The judicial dilemma is apparent. Questions of value are crucial to the application of the Due Process Clause. The constitutional text requires that human interests be characterized as "life, liberty, or property"—concerns that either have or do not have sufficient status to trigger due process protection. And, substantive stakes in decisional outcomes aside, it is surely not irrelevant whether governmental processes do or do not respect individual interests in autonomy. Yet, in an increasingly secular and scientific society, confronting questions of moral value directly, and in an authoritative context, can be embarrassing. Because they have no attachment to revealed truth and no empirical underpinning, moral pronouncements *cum* constitutional interpretations appear radically subjective. Decisions based on "fundamental fairness" seem to measure justice, as in the old saw, by the length of the Chancellor's foot.

Interest Balancing. The dominant contemporary mode of due process analysis promises the functional criteria so conspicuously absent from natural rights propositions. Under the prevailing Supreme Court formulation, the assessment of process adequacy requires consideration of (1) the magnitude of the interests of private parties, (2) the governmental interest in procedural efficiency, and (3) the likely contribution of various procedural ingredients to the correct resolution of disputes. See *Mathews v. Eldridge*, 424 U.S. 319 (1976), *infra* p. 337. In short, the Court performs a social welfare calculation to determine whether society will be better or worse off if it honors the claim to more formalized procedure.

The great advantages of the interest balancing approach are its adaptability to virtually any question of procedural adequacy and its recognition that judgments about process adequacy necessarily involve trade-offs between collective and individual ends. But, as a constitutional theory this brand of utilitarianism has the defects of its virtues. For one thing, interest balancing suggests that, given a good enough reason, the government can use whatever process it pleases. The Bill of Rights is, however, not meant only to facilitate adaptation of constitutional constraints to changing governmental forms; its most obvious function is to protect against official encroachments on individual liberty. The interest balancing methodology thus seems to contradict the basic libertarian presuppositions of the text that it would implement. Moreover, the information requirements of a rigorous utilitarian calculus are very substantial, perhaps excessive. Jerry L. Mashaw, *Administrative Due Process As Social–Cost Accounting*, 9 Hofstra L.Rev. 1423 (1981). Can the dignitary costs of individuals and the administrative costs of government, for example, be measured in the same currency? Is it really possible to predict the effect of any discrete changes in the decision process on the accuracy of decisions?

Given even this sketchy introduction to the strengths and weaknesses of the dominant due process methodologies, it is hardly surprising that the Supreme Court has never chosen a single approach and adhered to it. The interest-balancing approach is clearly ascendent, but many cases—without any *de novo* cost-benefit analysis—still rely upon prior authorities (tradition) that are themselves predicated on ideas of fundamental fairness (natural rights). Nor, when operating ostensibly under the dominant interest-balancing mode has the Court achieved consistency. This vagueness and vacillation combine with—some might say induce—a continuing high level of suits against government agencies claiming rights to some aspect of trial type process. This level of conflict over administrative procedure has been variously characterized as a "process explosion" or a "due process revolution." See, e.g., Henry Friendly, *"Some Kind of Hearing,"* 123 U.Pa. L. Rev. 1267, 1268 (1975); Doug Rendleman, *The New Due Process: Rights and Remedies*, 63 Ky. L. J. 532 (1975).

While "explosions" and "revolutions" are presumably a cause for concern, if not alarm, the continuing flow of due process claims should be kept in perspective. The emergence of due process cases as an important category of constitutional litigation seems to be directly related to the relative activism of government. Between 1787 and 1866 only one due process case was decided by the Supreme Court. And, for the next sixty-five years, until the New Deal, virtually all of the Supreme Court's due process jurisprudence was concerned with the activities of state government. Why? Because, prior to 1933, governmental activity directly affecting individual citizens and enterprises was carried on primarily by states and localities. And before the ratification of the Civil War amendments such state and local activity was not subject to due process review under the federal Constitution. Following the adoption of the Fourteenth Amendment, such review was increasingly sought with respect to these relatively "activist" levels of government.

Indeed, in the mid–1870s the Supreme Court complained about its due process case load in terms that might well have been used a century later. In *Davidson v. New Orleans*, 96 U.S. (6 Otto) 97, 103–04 (1877), the Court lamented:

> It is not a little remarkable, that while [the Due Process Clause] has been in the Constitution of the United States, as a restraint upon the authority of the Federal government, for nearly a century * * * this special limitation upon its powers has rarely been invoked in the judicial forum * * *. But while it has been a part of the Constitution, as a restraint upon the power of the States, only a very few years, the docket of this court is crowded with cases in which we are asked to hold that State courts and State legislatures have deprived their own citizens of life, liberty, or property without due process of law. There is here abundant evidence that there exists some strange misconception of the scope of this provision as found in the Fourteenth Amendment. In fact, it would seem, from the character of many of the cases before us, and the arguments made in them, that the clause under consideration is looked upon as a means of bringing to the test of the decision of this court the abstract opinions of every unsuccessful litigant in a State court of the justice of the decision against him, and of the merits of the legislation on which such a decision may be founded.

The New Deal reversed the balance of federal and state governmental activity. Where four of every five due process claims that reached the Supreme Court between 1866 and 1933 concerned state action, from the New Deal to the Great Society four out of five involved the federal government. Thereafter, the proportions are again reversed. In part this reflects the greater attention given to procedural matters in federal statutes. It also reflects changes in the mode of federal implementation. While new federal regulatory and subsidy programs were still being generated in abundance in the post–1965 period, those programs increasingly were implemented by state and local officials. And it is at the level of implementation that demands for procedural protection customarily arise.

The explanation for the historic association between due process litigation and governmental activism seems relatively straightforward. As government acts in new areas, or expands activity in older ones, it adopts new forms. While tradition has a strong hold on the legal imagination, legislation is an empiric business—experimentation is constant. Within the lifetime of many still living, for example, there has been a shift in the paradigmatic legal techniques of social control. Legislative rules of conduct, enforceable by criminal sanction in the courts, have been replaced by the more flexible techniques of regulatory commissions. *Post hoc* regulation of primary conduct through liability rules has given way to *ex ante* intervention, either to regulate harmful activities or to subsidize useful ones. *Laissez faire* has been replaced by an administrative state. Much of the citizen's wealth and security have come to be held, not in the currency of physical capital and familial attachment, but in the coin of government contract, license, regulation or subsidy. Legislative grants of individual licenses, charters or subsidies were replaced by legislative programs administered by specialized agencies.

These profound changes in our forms of governance generated two predictable legal responses: attacks on the constitutional legitimacy of change by those whose interests lay with the old regime and attempts to regularize and reinforce the legal relationships that reconstituted the citizen's portfolio of welfare state entitlements. Both responses are portentous for the evolution of adjudicatory rights. The enticing vagueness of the Due Process Clause permits virtually any lament of "what sort of government is this anyway?" to be reformulated as a justiciable claim to process protection. Moreover, when cast in procedural terms, such claims invite the courts to interpose constraints on governmental action without confronting directly the substantive powers of the legislature. Process fairness can be zealously protected without exciting much alarm concerning the judiciary's constitutional mandate—or at least less than when "substantive due process" is seen to be involved.

Given our peculiar governmental and constitutional history, procedural due process claims thus provide many of the occasions for our ongoing conversation concerning the appropriate structure of an increasingly administrative state. Yet the central place of due process adjudication in any discussion of constitutional history, interpretive method, or administrative law cannot be fully portrayed here even through rigorous analysis and an historical and institutional contextualization of the most important of the Supreme Court's due process decisions. Most of the great political issues of post-Civil War America—immigration, economic regulation, feared communist subversion, welfare rights, the status of public employees, the treatment of prisoners and patients, to name but a few—have converged on the federal courts with due process claims leading the charge. Within only the last two decades the Supreme Court has heard procedural challenges to the actions of administrators who implement programs of public assistance, unemployment insurance, medical insurance, and disability insurance; who license nursing homes, automobile drivers and nuclear reactors; who oversee institutions for public education, and for the custody and rehabilitation of the emotionally disturbed, mentally incompetent or socially deviant; who control access to alcoholic beverages, immigration, public employment, parole, and electrical service; who regulate railroad rates; and who enforce public safety ordinances. From this diverse and politically charged caseload—itself not fully representative of judicial activity—we can select only an illustrative sample, from the field in which the dominant balancing test was most cogently formulated.

GOLDBERG v. KELLY

Supreme Court of the United States, 1970.
397 U.S. 254, 90 S.Ct. 1011, 25 L.Ed.2d 287.

JUSTICE BRENNAN delivered the opinion of the Court.

* * *

This action was brought in the District Court for the Southern District of New York by residents of New York City receiving financial aid under the federally assisted program of Aid to Families with Dependent Children (AFDC) or under New York State's general Home Relief program. Their complaint alleged that the New York State and New York City officials administering these programs terminated, or were about to terminate, such aid without prior notice and hearing, thereby denying them due process of law. At the time the suits were filed there was no requirement of prior notice or hearing of any kind before termination of financial aid. However, the State and city adopted procedures for notice and hearing after the suits were brought, and the plaintiffs, appellees here, then challenged the constitutional adequacy of those procedures.

* * *

* * * A caseworker who has doubts about the recipient's continued eligibility must first discuss them with the recipient. If the caseworker concludes that the recipient is no longer eligible, he recommends termination of aid to a unit supervisor. If the latter concurs, he sends the recipient a letter stating the reasons for proposing to terminate aid and notifying him that within seven days he may request that a higher official review the record, and may support the request with a written statement prepared personally or with the aid of an attorney or other person. If the reviewing official affirms the determination of ineligibility, aid is stopped immediately and the recipient is informed by letter of the reasons for the action. Appellees' challenge to this procedure emphasizes the absence of any provisions for the personal appearance of the recipient before the reviewing official, for oral presentation of evidence, and for confrontation and cross-examination of adverse witnesses. However, the letter does inform the recipient that he may request a post-termi-

nation "fair hearing." This is a proceeding before an independent state hearing officer at which the recipient may appear personally, offer oral evidence, confront and cross-examine the witnesses against him, and have a record made of the hearing. If the recipient prevails at the "fair hearing" he is paid all funds erroneously withheld. A recipient whose aid is not restored by a "fair hearing" decision may have judicial review.

The constitutional issue to be decided, therefore, is the narrow one whether the Due Process Clause requires that the recipient be afforded an evidentiary hearing *before* the termination of benefits. * * *

Appellant does not contend that procedural due process is not applicable to the termination of welfare benefits. Such benefits are a matter of statutory entitlement for persons qualified to receive them.[8] Their termination involves state action that adjudicates important rights. The constitutional challenge cannot be answered by an argument that public assistance benefits are "a 'privilege' and not a 'right.'" *Shapiro v. Thompson*, 394 U.S. 618, 627 n. 6 (1969). Relevant constitutional restraints apply as much to the withdrawal of public assistance benefits as to disqualification for unemployment compensation, *Sherbert v. Verner*, 374 U.S. 398 (1963); or to denial of a tax exemption, *Speiser v. Randall*, 357 U.S. 513 (1958); or to discharge from public employment, *Slochower v. Board of Higher Education*, 350 U.S. 551 (1956). The extent to which procedural due process must be afforded the recipient is influenced by the extent to which he may be "condemned to suffer grievous loss," *Joint Anti–Fascist Refugee Committee v. McGrath*, 341 U.S. 123, 168 (1951) (Frankfurter, J., concurring), and depends upon whether the recipient's interest in avoiding that loss outweighs the governmental interest in summary adjudication. Accordingly, as we said in *Cafeteria & Restaurant Workers Union v. McElroy*, 367 U.S. 886, 895 (1961), "consideration of what procedures due process may require under any given set of circumstances must begin with a determination of the precise nature of the government function involved as well as of the private interest that has been affected by governmental action."

It is true, of course, that some governmental benefits may be administratively terminated without affording the recipient a pretermin-

8. It may be realistic today to regard welfare entitlements as more like "property" than a "gratuity." Much of the existing wealth in this country takes the form of rights that do not fall within traditional common-law concepts of property. It has been aptly noted that

> "[s]ociety today is built around entitlement. The automobile dealer has his franchise, the doctor and lawyer their professional licenses, the worker his union membership, contract, and pension rights, the executive his contract and stock options; all are devices to aid security and independence. Many of the most important of these entitlements now flow from government: subsidies to farmers and businessmen, routes for airlines and channels for television stations; long term contracts for defense, space, and education; social security pensions for individuals. Such sources of security, whether private or public, are no longer regarded as luxuries or gratuities; to the recipients they are essentials, fully deserved, and in no sense a form of charity. It is only the poor whose entitlements, although recognized by public policy, have not been effectively enforced."

Reich, *Individual Rights and Social Welfare: The Emerging Legal Issues*, 74 Yale L.J. 1245, 1255 (1965). *See also* Reich, *The New Property*, 73 Yale L.J. 733 (1964).

ation evidentiary hearing. But we agree with the District Court that when welfare is discontinued, only a pretermination evidentiary hearing provides the recipient with procedural due process. For qualified recipients, welfare provides the means to obtain essential food, clothing, housing, and medical care. Thus, the crucial factor in this context—a factor not present in the case of the blacklisted government contractor, the discharged government employee, the taxpayer denied a tax exemption, or virtually anyone else whose governmental entitlements are ended—is that termination of aid pending resolution of a controversy over eligibility may deprive an *eligible* recipient of the very means by which to live while he waits. Since he lacks independent resources, his situation becomes immediately desperate. His need to concentrate upon finding the means for daily subsistence, in turn, adversely affects his ability to seek redress from the welfare bureaucracy.[12]

Moreover, important governmental interests are promoted by affording recipients a pre-termination evidentiary hearing. From its founding the Nation's basic commitment has been to foster the dignity and well-being of all persons within its borders. We have come to recognize that forces not within the control of the poor contribute to their poverty. This perception, against the background of our traditions, has significantly influenced the development of the contemporary public assistance system. Welfare, by meeting the basic demands of subsistence, can help bring within the reach of the poor the same opportunities that are available to others to participate meaningfully in the life of the community. At the same time, welfare guards against the societal malaise that may flow from a widespread sense of unjustified frustration and insecurity. Public assistance, then, is not mere charity, but a means to "promote the general Welfare, and secure the Blessings of Liberty to ourselves and our Posterity." The same governmental interests that counsel the provisions of welfare, counsel as well its uninterrupted provision to those eligible to receive it; pre-termination evidentiary hearings are indispensable to that end.

Appellant does not challenge the force of these considerations but argues that they are outweighed by countervailing governmental interests in conserving fiscal and administrative resources. These interests, the argument goes, justify the delay of any evidentiary hearing until after discontinuance of the grants. Summary adjudication protects the public fisc by stopping payments promptly upon discovery of reason to believe that a recipient is no longer eligible. Since most terminations are accepted without challenge, summary adjudication also conserves both the fisc and administrative time and energy by reducing the number of evidentiary hearings actually held.

We agree with the District Court, however, that these governmental interests are not overriding in the welfare context. The requirement of a

12. His impaired adversary position is particularly telling in light of the welfare bureaucracy's difficulties in reaching correct decisions on eligibility. See Comment, *Due Process and the Right to a Prior Hearing in Welfare Cases*, 37 Ford. L. Rev. 604, 610–611 (1969).

prior hearing doubtless involves some greater expense, and the benefits paid to ineligible recipients pending decision at the hearing probably cannot be recouped, since these recipients are likely to be judgment-proof. But the State is not without weapons to minimize these increased costs. Much of the drain on fiscal and administrative resources can be reduced by developing procedures for prompt pre-termination hearings and by skillful use of personnel, and facilities. * * * As the District Court correctly concluded: "[t]he stakes are simply too high for the welfare recipient, and the possibility for honest error or irritable misjudgment too great, to allow termination of aid without giving the recipient a chance, if he so desires, to be fully informed of the case against him so that he may contest its basis and produce evidence in rebuttal."

We also agree with the District Court, however, that the pre-termination hearing need not take the form of a judicial or quasi-judicial trial. We bear in mind that the statutory "fair hearing" will provide the recipient with a full administrative review.[14] Accordingly, the pre-termination hearing has one function only: to produce an initial determination of the validity of the welfare department's grounds for discontinuance of payments in order to protect a recipient against an erroneous termination of his benefits. Thus, a complete record and a comprehensive opinion, which would serve primarily to facilitate judicial review and to guide future decisions, need not be provided at the pre-termination stage. We recognize, too, that both welfare authorities and recipients have an interest in relatively speedy resolution of questions of eligibility, that they are used to dealing with one another informally, and that some welfare departments have very burdensome caseloads. These considerations justify the limitation of the pre-termination hearing to minimum procedural safeguards, adapted to the particular characteristics of welfare recipients, and to the limited nature of the controversies to be resolved. We wish to add that we, no less than the dissenters, recognize the importance of not imposing upon the States or the Federal Government in this developing field of law any procedural requirements beyond those demanded by rudimentary due process.

"The fundamental requisite of due process of law is the opportunity to be heard." *Grannis v. Ordean*, 234 U.S. 385, 394 (1914). The hearing must be "at a meaningful time and in a meaningful manner." *Armstrong v. Manzo*, 380 U.S. 545, 552 (1965). In the present context these principles require that a recipient have timely and adequate notice detailing the reasons for a proposed termination, and an effective opportunity to defend by confronting any adverse witnesses and by presenting his own arguments and evidence orally. These rights are important in cases such as those before us, where recipients have challenged proposed

14. Due process does not, of course, require two hearings. If, for example, a State simply wishes to continue benefits until after a "fair" hearing there will be no need for a preliminary hearing.

terminations as resting on incorrect or misleading factual premises or on misapplication of rules or policies to the facts of particular cases.[15]

We are not prepared to say that the seven-day notice currently provided by New York City is constitutionally insufficient *per se*, although there may be cases where fairness would require that a longer time be given. Nor do we see any constitutional deficiency in the content or form of the notice. New York employs both a letter and a personal conference with a caseworker to inform a recipient of the precise questions raised about his continued eligibility. Evidently the recipient is told the legal and factual bases for the Department's doubts. This combination is probably the most effective method of communicating with recipients.

The city's procedures presently do not permit recipients to appear personally with or without counsel before the official who finally determines continued eligibility. Thus a recipient is not permitted to present evidence to that official orally, or to confront or cross-examine adverse witnesses. These omissions are fatal to the constitutional adequacy of the procedures.

The opportunity to be heard must be tailored to the capacities and circumstances of those who are to be heard. It is not enough that a welfare recipient may present his position to the decision maker in writing or secondhand through his caseworker. Written submissions are an unrealistic option for most recipients, who lack the educational attainment necessary to write effectively and who cannot obtain professional assistance. Moreover, written submissions do not afford the flexibility of oral presentations; they do not permit the recipient to mold his argument to the issues the decision maker appears to regard as important. Particularly where credibility and veracity are at issue, as they must be in many termination proceedings, written submissions are a wholly unsatisfactory basis for decision. The secondhand presentation to the decision maker by the caseworker has its own deficiencies; since the caseworker usually gathers the facts upon which the charge of ineligibility rests, the presentation of the recipient's side of the controversy cannot safely be left to him. Therefore a recipient must be allowed to state his position orally. Informal procedures will suffice; in this context due process does not require a particular order of proof or mode of offering evidence.

In almost every setting where important decisions turn on questions of fact, due process requires an opportunity to confront and cross-examine adverse witnesses. What we said in *Greene v. McElroy*, 360 U.S. 474, 496–497 (1959), is particularly pertinent here:

15. This case presents no question requiring our determination whether due process requires only an opportunity for written submission, or an opportunity both for written submission and oral argument, where there are no factual issues in dispute or where the application of the rule of law is not intertwined with factual issues. See *FCC v. WJR*, 337 U.S. 265, 275–77 (1949).

> "Certain principles have remained relatively immutable in our jurisprudence. One of these is that where governmental action seriously injures an individual, and the reasonableness of the action depends on fact findings, the evidence used to prove the Government's case must be disclosed to the individual so that he has an opportunity to show that it is untrue. While this is important in the case of documentary evidence, it is even more important where the evidence consists of the testimony of individuals whose memory might be faulty or who, in fact, might be perjurers or persons motivated by malice, vindictiveness, intolerance, prejudice, or jealousy. We have formalized these protections in the requirements of confrontation and cross-examination. They have ancient roots. They find expression in the Sixth Amendment * * *. This Court has been zealous to protect these rights from erosion. It has spoken out not only in criminal cases, * * * but also in all types of cases where administrative * * * actions were under scrutiny."

Welfare recipients must therefore be given an opportunity to confront and cross-examine the witnesses relied on by the department.

"The right to be heard would be, in many cases, of little avail if it did not comprehend the right to be heard by counsel." *Powell v. Alabama*, 287 U.S. 45, 68–69 (1932). We do not say that counsel must be provided at the pre-termination hearing, but only that the recipient must be allowed to retain an attorney if he so desires. Counsel can help delineate the issues, present the factual contentions in an orderly manner, conduct cross-examination, and generally safeguard the interests of the recipient. We do not anticipate that this assistance will unduly prolong or otherwise encumber the hearing. * * *

Finally, the decision maker's conclusion as to a recipient's eligibility must rest solely on the legal rules and evidence adduced at the hearing. To demonstrate compliance with this elementary requirement, the decision maker should state the reasons for his determination and indicate the evidence he relied on, though his statement need not amount to a full opinion or even formal findings of fact and conclusions of law. And, of course, an impartial decision maker is essential. We agree with the District Court that prior involvement in some aspects of a case will not necessarily bar a welfare official from acting as a decision maker. He should not, however, have participated in making the determination under review.

Affirmed.

JUSTICE BLACK, dissenting.

In the last half century the United States, along with many, perhaps most, other nations of the world, has moved far toward becoming a welfare state, that is, a nation that for one reason or another taxes its most affluent people to help support, feed, clothe, and shelter its less fortunate citizens. The result is that today more than nine million men, women, and children in the United States receive some kind of state or federally financed public assistance in the form of allowances or gratuities, generally paid them periodically, usually by the week, month, or quarter. Since these gratuities are paid on the basis of need, the list of recipients is not static, and some people go off the lists and others are added from time to time. These ever-changing lists put a constant administrative burden on government and it certainly could not have reasonably anticipated that this burden would include the additional procedural expense imposed by the Court today.

* * *

The more than a million names on the relief rolls in New York, and the more than nine million names on the rolls of all the 50 States were not put there at random. The names are there because state welfare officials believed that those people were eligible for assistance. Probably in the officials' haste to make out the lists many names were put there erroneously in order to alleviate immediate suffering, and undoubtedly some people are drawing relief who are not entitled under the law to do so. Doubtless some draw relief checks from time to time who know they are not eligible, either because they are not actually in need or for some other reason. Many of those who thus draw undeserved gratuities are without sufficient property to enable the government to collect back from them any money they wrongfully receive. * * * In other words, although some recipients might be on the lists for payment wholly because of deliberate fraud on their part, the Court holds that the government is helpless and must continue, until after an evidentiary hearing, to pay money that it does not owe, never has owed, and never could owe. I do not believe there is any provision in our Constitution that should thus paralyze the government's efforts to protect itself against making payments to people who are not entitled to them. * * * The Court, however, relies upon the Fourteenth Amendment and in effect says that failure of the government to pay a promised charitable instalment to an individual deprives that individual of *his own property*, in violation of the Due Process Clause of the Fourteenth Amendment. It somewhat strains credulity to say that the government's promise of charity to an individual is property belonging to that individual when the government denies that the individual is honestly entitled to receive such a payment.

* * * Although the majority attempts to bolster its decision with limited quotations from prior cases, it is obvious that today's result does not depend on the language of the Constitution itself or the principles of other decisions, but solely on the collective judgment of the majority as to what would be a fair and humane procedure in this case.

* * *

* * * Reduced to its simplest terms, the problem in this case is similar to that frequently encountered when two parties have an ongoing legal relationship that requires one party to make periodic payments to the other. Often the situation arises where the party "owing" the money stops paying it and justifies his conduct by arguing that the recipient is

not legally entitled to payment. The recipient can, of course, disagree and go to court to compel payment. But I know of no situation in our legal system in which the person alleged to owe money to another is required by law to continue making payments to a judgment-proof claimant without the benefit of any security or bond to insure that these payments can be recovered if he wins his legal argument. Yet today's decision in no way obligates the welfare recipient to pay back any benefits wrongfully received during the pre-termination evidentiary hearings or post any bond, and in all "fairness" it could not do so. These recipients are by definition too poor to post a bond or to repay the benefits that, as the majority assumes, must be spent as received to insure survival.

The Court apparently feels that this decision will benefit the poor and needy. In my judgment the eventual result will be just the opposite. While today's decision requires only an administrative, evidentiary hearing, the inevitable logic of the approach taken will lead to constitutionally imposed, time-consuming delays of a full adversary process of administrative and judicial review. In the next case the welfare recipients are bound to argue that cutting off benefits before judicial review of the agency's decision is also a denial of due process. Since, by hypothesis, termination of aid at that point may still "deprive an *eligible* recipient of the very means by which to live while he waits," I would be surprised if the weighing process did not compel the conclusion that termination without full judicial review would be unconscionable. After all, at each step, as the majority seems to feel, the issue is only one of weighing the government's pocketbook against the actual survival of the recipient, and surely that balance must always tip in favor of the individual. Similarly today's decision requires only the opportunity to have the benefit of counsel at the administrative hearing, but it is difficult to believe that the same reasoning process would not require the appointment of counsel, for otherwise the right to counsel is a meaningless one since these people are too poor to hire their own advocates. Thus the end result of today's decision may well be that the government, once it decides to give welfare benefits, cannot reverse that decision until the recipient has had the benefits of full administrative and judicial review, including, of course, the opportunity to present his case to this Court. Since this process will usually entail a delay of several years, the inevitable result of such a constitutionally imposed burden will be that the government will not put a claimant on the rolls initially until it has made an exhaustive investigation to determine his eligibility. While this Court will perhaps have insured that no needy person will be taken off the rolls without a full "due process" proceeding, it will also have insured that many will never get on the rolls, or at least that they will remain destitute during the lengthy proceedings followed to determine initial eligibility.

* * *

CHIEF JUSTICE BURGER, with whom JUSTICE BLACK joins, dissenting.
* * *

The procedures for review of administrative action in the "welfare" area are in a relatively early stage of development: HEW has already taken the initiative by promulgating regulations requiring that AFDC payments be continued until a final decision after a "fair hearing" is held. The net effect would be to provide a hearing prior to a termination of benefits. Indeed, the HEW administrative regulations go far beyond the result reached today since they require that recipients be given the right to appointed counsel, a position expressly rejected by the majority. As the majority notes, these regulations are scheduled to take effect in July 1970.* Against this background I am baffled as to why we should engage in "legislating" via constitutional fiat when an apparently reasonable result has been accomplished administratively. * * *

The Court's action today seems another manifestation of the now familiar constitutionalizing syndrome: once some presumed flaw is observed, the Court then eagerly accepts the invitation to find a constitutionally "rooted" remedy. If no provision is explicit on the point, it is then seen as "implicit" or commanded by the vague and nebulous concept of "fairness." * * *

I would not suggest that the procedures of administering the Nation's complex welfare programs are beyond the reach of courts, but I would wait until more is known about the problems before fashioning solutions in the rigidity of a constitutional holding.

By allowing the administrators to deal with these problems we leave room for adjustments if, for example, it is found that a particular hearing process is too costly. The history of the complexity of the administrative process followed by judicial review as we have seen it for the past 30 years should suggest the possibility that new layers of procedural protection may become an intolerable drain on the very funds earmarked for food, clothing, and other living essentials.[3]

Aside from the administrative morass that today's decision could well create, the Court should also be cognizant of the legal precedent it may be setting. The majority holding raises intriguing possibilities concerning the right to a hearing at other stages in the welfare process which affect the total sum of assistance, even though the action taken might fall short of complete termination. For example, does the Court's holding embrace welfare reductions or denial of increases as opposed to terminations, or decisions concerning initial applications or requests for special assistance? The Court supplies no distinguishable considerations and leaves these crucial questions unanswered.

* [The proposed regulations were withdrawn before they took effect and were redrafted to take account of the *Goldberg* decision; among other changes, the right to appointed counsel was eliminated. Eds.]

3. We are told, for example, that Los Angeles County alone employs 12,500 welfare workers to process grants to 500,000 people under various welfare programs. The record does not reveal how many more employees will be required to give this newly discovered "due process" to every welfare recipient whose payments are terminated for fraud or other factors of ineligibility or those whose initial applications are denied.

[Justice Stewart also dissented in a cryptic paragraph which merely described the question, for him, as "a close one." In a companion case, *Wheeler v. Montgomery*, 397 U.S. 280 (1970), the Court invalidated California's procedure for terminating old age assistance benefits because it failed to afford the recipient "an evidentiary hearing at which he may personally appear to offer oral evidence and confront and cross-examine the witnesses against him."]

Hearings and Administration: What Was At Stake in Goldberg

1. *The Claimant's Stake.* The Supreme Court in *Goldberg* speaks rather abstractly about the "brutal need" of welfare claimants. The District Court's description, *sub nom. Kelly v. Wyman*, 294 F.Supp. 893, 899–900 (S.D.N.Y.1968), is more graphic:

> * * * The case of Angela Velez * * * makes the point starkly. She was terminated on March 11, 1968, because her husband allegedly visited her home every night. She requested the post-termination state fair hearing in mid-March. The hearing was held in June, and, pursuant to the request of this court for expedition, the decision issued on July 10. The State Commissioner found that the information that caused suspension of benefits came from Mrs. Velez's landlady, that the information was untrue, that the husband does not live with his wife, that she had obtained a court order in 1966 to prevent his night visits, that he is allowed to visit the four small children only on Wednesday, and that at that time he brings his support money of $30 a week, but no more, in accordance with an agreement worked out in Family Court. Accordingly, the State Commissioner directed the local agency to reinstate assistance. However, in the four months between termination of AFDC benefits and the decision reversing the local agency, Mrs. Velez and her four children, ages one to six, were evicted from her apartment for non-payment of rent and went to live with her sister, who has nine children and is on relief. Mrs. Velez and three children have been sleeping in two single beds in a small room, and the youngest sleeps in a crib in the same room. Thirteen children and two adults have been living in one apartment, and Mrs. Velez states that she has been unable to feed her children adequately, so that they have lost weight and have been ill.
>
> The case of Mrs. Esther Lett * * * is also instructive. According to the affidavits of plaintiff Lett and her Legal Aid Society attorney: She and her four dependents, aged three months to fifteen years, were abruptly terminated for public assistance on February 1, 1968. The purported ground was that she had concealed her current employment by the Board of Education. In fact, she had worked for Operation Head Start in July and August 1967, but had not been employed by the Board of Education after August 20, 1967. Since that date and up to February 1968, she had worked at Day Care Centers on twenty-six different days, earning a total of $300, with the knowledge of the local welfare agency. As a result of termination of assistance, she and her dependents were forced to live on the handouts of neighbors. On February 18, she and her family had to go to the hospital for severe diarrhea, apparently brought on by the only means they had had that day—spoiled chicken

and rice donated by a neighbor. She applied for emergency aid and a post-termination state "fair hearing" but the aid was refused and the fair hearing was not scheduled. Through the herculean efforts of The Legal Aid Society, including numerous telephone calls and three personal trips to local agencies, it was learned that the Board of Education had apparently made an error. However, the Board would not so inform the welfare agency until it requested a new verification. On Tuesday, February 27, Mrs. Lett went to a local center to seek emergency aid. Because she had not eaten all day, she fainted in the center, but when she awoke she was told that she could not get money for food immediately because it had not yet been authorized. Finally, after waiting eight hours, she was given $15 to feed herself and four dependents and told to return on Friday. After suit was brought, her assistance was apparently temporarily reinstated without prejudice.

Poignant though they are, these facts should not be taken as demonstrating the lack of concern of the welfare bureaucracy for accurate and fair determinations of eligibility for public assistance. Welfare law in the United States is often complex and involves highly discretionary judgments. The complexity results from our historic and only partially successful attempt to provide assistance to the "deserving poor" without trenching too heavily on the work incentives that are thought critical to the well-being of a market economy and on the public support politically necessary to continue public assistance. Discretion is the result of the attempt to tailor money payments and other social services to fit the needs of individuals or families. As a consequence, the often underpaid and undertrained welfare eligibility technician may be faced with regulations which could fill a bookshelf four feet wide and yet, under the programs at issue in *Goldberg*, also with the necessity of deciding such ineffable questions as whether an individual is "essential to the well-being" of a dependent child and therefore eligible to have his or her needs included in determining the need of the "family budget unit." See generally JOINT ECONOMIC COMMITTEE OF THE CONGRESS, STUDIES IN PUBLIC WELFARE, PAPER NO. 5 (PART 1), *Issues in Welfare Administration: Welfare, An Administrative Nightmare*, 92d Cong. (1972). Of course not all "errors" in eligibility determinations are the result of complexity and work load. See Jerry L. Mashaw, *Welfare Reform and Local Administration of Aid to Families with Dependent Children in Virginia*, 57 Va. L. Rev. 818 (1971).

2. *Hearings and Accurate Decision Making*. Assume that errors in the welfare system may be the product of two factors—agency recalcitrance and simple inefficiency. How will the hearing rights prescribed in *Goldberg* help prevent errors traceable to these causes? Consider, for example, the prospects for consistent protection of claimants' rights through hearings where denials, limitations, reductions or terminations of assistance are a consequence of agency disagreement with state or federal policy. The right to a prior hearing is likely to be effective in this context only to the extent that claimants are aware of their rights, are aggressive, and have legal assistance readily available. For public assistance claimants none of these conditions is likely to exist. First, in a system that baffles the bureaucrat, the applicant's or recipient's knowledge is almost certain to be too general to provide a basis for recognizing that a departmental decision is open to question. Second, persons who are chronically or even temporarily dependent should not be

expected to be aggressive in asserting their rights. Appeals are not likely to be forthcoming from those who remain attached to the welfare system except when the limitation or reduction of assistance is very substantial. It is not sensible to challenge the decisions of administrators who make continuous highly discretionary judgments about one's basic necessities (e.g., whether to grant funds for a new mattress, a telephone, or an additional heating allowance) unless the issue is serious and the prospects for success are high. See generally Joel F. Handler, *Controlling Official Behavior in Welfare Administration*, 54 CALIF. L. REV. 479 (1966); Joel F. Handler & Ellen Jane Hollingsworth, *Reforming Welfare: The Constraints of the Bureaucracy and the Clients*, 118 U.PA. L. REV. 1167 (1970).

Third, we should also recognize that the incentive to appeal resulting from the continuation of benefits under the prior-hearing requirement of *Goldberg* will not operate in the context of disputes raising only issues of policy or law. A hearing prior to termination is required only where there is a disputed issue of fact or of application of law to fact.

Finally, the recalcitrant welfare agency has virtually complete control over the factors that make a hearing meaningful—adequate notice, access to evidence, aid in preparing an appeal, and convenient scheduling of hearings. Ultimately a very detailed court order and vigilant monitoring for contempt may be necessary to realize the full benefits of a right to hearing in the face of a strong disapproval by local officials of the bases for an appellant's claim. Judicial enforcement, of course, requires the availability of free legal service—a commodity that is always in short supply.

Administrative hearing requirements might produce greater benefits where the usual disputes involve claims of bureaucratic error rather than issues of official lawlessness. Appeals are less threatening in this context. Issues should often involve factual disputes or disputes over the application of policy to fact rather than policy disagreements and thus should often require a prior hearing with its attendant incentive for appeal. And an intention to thwart effective exercise of hearing rights should not be presumed. It must be recognized, however, that the same overworked and under-trained bureaucracy that makes initial determinations is also heavily involved in the appeals process. If initial decisions cannot be made correctly, there is reason to doubt that the hearing process will be run effectively. These doubts were in part confirmed by an evaluation of the hearing process in New York City soon after *Goldberg*. See D. Kirchheimer, *Community Evaluation of Fair Hearing Procedures Available to Public Assistance Recipients* (mimeo, New York City Human Resources Administration, May 1973). Based on a random sample of appeals decided in October of 1972, the evaluation found: (1) 5 percent of appellants had received no notice of a proposed adverse action; (2) 25 percent did not receive timely notice; (3) 63 percent of all notices failed to contain an adequate statement of what action was proposed to be taken and what the factual and policy bases for the action were; (4) in 12 percent of the cases aid had not been continued as required pending appeal; (5) only 25 percent of the appellants who requested access to relevant agency files prior to appeal were given such access; and (6) in only 7 percent of the cases was an opportunity for cross-examination afforded by having opposing witnesses present.

No matter what the causes of underlying errors, hearings are not a major protection unless they are utilized. Even in the post-*Goldberg*, prior-hearing era, hearings have been requested sparingly. Only two to three percent of the potentially appealable determinations are appealed, and over 50 percent of all appeals reported in some periods are attributable to two or three states. Appellants win about 20 percent of the reported appeals.

Of course, even if 20 percent is considered a relatively low success rate by appellants, those who get errors corrected derive tangible benefits, and even those who fail to obtain relief may develop a greater sense of fairness and therefore acceptance of results. There is also the possibility that hearings will clarify policies, and their proper application, so that other decisions will be made correctly in the first instance. However, in an administrative system that is overburdened, or staffed by recalcitrant officials, these latter benefits seem highly speculative.

3. *The Costs of Due Process*. The cost side of the equation is no less difficult to assess. Obviously, there are the costs of the hearings themselves and the costs of continuing aid pending their completion. The State of Michigan estimated its *"Goldberg"* payments at $450,000 in 1971, and in 92 percent of the Michigan appeals the hearing confirmed the initial decision. In short, a very high percentage of the payments made between the notice of proposed action and the final decision after opportunity for hearing are made to ineligible persons. *Problems in Administration of Public Welfare Programs: Hearings before the Subcommittee on Fiscal Policy of the Joint Economic Committee,* 687, 92d Cong. (1972) [hereinafter *Hearings*]. Its spotty compliance with *Goldberg*'s demands notwithstanding, in June of 1972, New York City's payments for cases noticed for reduction of termination had reached a rate of $5,000,000 per month. Peter Kihss, *Mayor Assails Relief Rule*, Wall St.J., Aug. 14, 1972, at 3.

This may seem a small price to pay for basic fairness, but one should ask whether welfare claimants themselves have not been paying the price. State appropriations for welfare payments are generally made in a lump sum. If money runs short the state agency usually has the power to reduce the percentage of need covered by public assistance payments in order to make the books balance. Hence, an unexpectedly high number of pre-termination appeals may simply result in a reduction of welfare benefits to eligible recipients by the amount paid out to appellants who are determined not to have been entitled to benefits. Moreover, because welfare departments are required to continue payments pending hearings, the number of ineligibles on the rolls at any given time is increased. And the more numerous such ineligibles ("welfare cheaters" in the political vernacular), the greater general disaffection with the welfare system is likely to be. Such disaffection is at least as likely to manifest itself in reduced or static appropriations as in progressive welfare reform.

There is also the question of the effects of hearings on the ability of the welfare bureaucracy to provide benefits to which people are entitled. The head of the Fulton County Department of Family and Children Services in Atlanta testified that while fair hearings were good "in themselves," they "drastically and negatively" affected services to other recipients because of the very large drain on staff time when hearings are properly prepared and conducted. *Hearings, supra,* at 1042.

The difficulty of balancing the costs and benefits of procedural safeguards does not necessarily suggest that the courts should refrain from imposing procedural due process protections in the way that they have retreated from policing rationality via substantive due process. What may be needed is an approach to due process that recognizes both the peculiarities of particular administrative systems and that techniques for assuring accuracy and fairness other than trial-type hearings might also be a part of due process of law. See generally Jerry L. Mashaw, *The Management Side of Due Process: Some Theoretical and Litigation Notes on the Assurance of Accuracy, Fairness, and Timeliness in the Adjudication of Social Welfare Claims*, 59 Corn. L.Rev. 772 (1974).

4. *Other Institutional Impacts of* Goldberg. As the Fulton County administrator suggested, the *Goldberg* ruling presented welfare administrators with a significant problem. First, if a substantial percentage of the recipients noticed for termination exercised their appeal rights, the welfare departments would simply be unable to process the cases without a large infusion of funds for administration. Because of the complexity of welfare decision making, adequate preparation of cases to prove the correctness of termination decisions was likely to be quite costly. But the alternative would be even more expensive—leaving substantial numbers of persons believed to be ineligible on the rolls. These administrative difficulties fed into and reinforced a political difficulty. Welfare rolls were already increasing rapidly. State legislators were simply unwilling to provide more funds either for well-constructed hearings or for welfare benefits themselves. As Justice Black's dissent seems to recognize, a strategy was needed that would preserve fiscal integrity and produce defensible decisions.

Indeed the incremental changes that followed *Goldberg* went far beyond his speculation that welfare officials were likely to tighten up and slow down the initial eligibility determination process. In addition many welfare departments moved to generalize and objectify their substantive eligibility criteria so that messy subjective judgments about individual cases would not have to be made and defended. This in turn led to the realization that well-trained or professionalized social welfare workers were no longer needed. Costs could then be reduced further by reducing the quality of the staff and by depersonalizing staff-claimant encounters. If these reactions were not sufficient to restore fiscal balance, then payment levels could be reduced or allowed to remain stable in the face of rising prices. A tougher stance was also taken with respect to work requirements and prosecution of absent parents. Moreover, because hearings presumably protected the claimants' interests, internal audit procedures were skewed to ignore nonpayment and underpayment problems and to concentrate on preventing overpayments and payments to ineligibles. See generally DANIEL J. BAUM, THE WELFARE FAMILY AND MASS ADMINISTRATIVE JUSTICE (1974); JOEL HANDLER, PROTECTING THE SOCIAL SERVICE CLIENT: LEGAL AND STRUCTURAL CONTROLS ON OFFICIAL DISCRETION (1979); William H. Simon, *Legality, Bureaucracy, and Class in the Welfare System*, 92 Yale L.J. 1198 (1983).

5. *The New World of TANF.* All change, of course, is not incremental. The AFDC program that was most prominently at issue in *Goldberg* has now been replaced by the program of Temporary Assistance for Needy Families (TANF), part of the Personal Responsibility and Work Opportunity Reconciliation Act of 1996, Pub. L. No. 104–109, 110 Stat. 2105 (codified at 42 U.S.C. §§ 601–619 (2000)) (PRWORA), which gives block grants to states for the support of state public assistance programs. PRWORA makes very substantial changes in the framework within which states and localities develop the rules, practices and culture of welfare administration.

The new federal program eliminates previous federal eligibility criteria for public assistance, enjoining states simply to use their block grants in any manner "reasonably calculated to accomplish the purpose of the act." That purpose, as the title of the statute signals, is to develop the personal responsibility and work opportunities of former welfare recipients, not to provide them any continuous entitlement to income support. Indeed, while the statute requires that state programs "set forth objective criteria for the delivery of benefits and the determination of eligibility and for fair and equitable treatment", the statute also, in TANFs first provision, states that "this part shall not be interpreted to entitle any individual * * * to assistance under any state program." While state statutes and regulations may provide legal interests that are subject to due process protection, a subject to which we will return shortly, PRWORA signals that the "legal-bureaucratic" regime that characterized welfare administration in the post-*Goldberg* era has been rejected.

States have responded by instituting radical changes in administration. In some sense the new style of welfare administration is a return to the pre–1970s social work paradigm. In the social work model, determinations of eligibility for assistance were combined with social services, both under the control of highly-trained professionals. These workers were given broad discretion to decide which potential recipients were "worthy" of assistance because assistance was merely one tool, among others, to be used to effect positive changes in individual behavior.

The social work model's critics argued that broad discretion in the hands of welfare administrators left recipients at the mercy of caseworkers and produced radically divergent treatment of similarly situated persons. Nor was discrimination random. In her classic 1965 study, AID TO DEPENDENT CHILDREN, Winifred Bell demonstrated how states used broad and vague eligibility rules to exclude black families from the AFDC program. *Goldberg* may represent the high water mark of the critics' legal triumphs. Under both legal and fiscal pressure state welfare departments transformed the AFDC program into a rule-bound, deprofessionalized program in which income eligibility was detached from social services and "regularized" through objective criteria.

In PRWORA caseworker discretion makes a major comeback. The work requirements embodied in the federal statute and in all state regimes call for a series of judgments about whether a recipient can work, what type of work is appropriate for them, whether the recipient has access to suitable child care and, when work attempts fail, whether recipients were justified in leaving their jobs.

In a number of states caseworkers are also authorized to "divert" recipients away from the program by providing one time lump sum payments in lieu of ongoing assistance. Case workers can determine which recipients or potential recipients are offered these grants and in some cases the amount of payments. Caseworkers may determine the nature of recipients' job search efforts and disqualify them for inadequate performance. They also oversee such matters as whether recipients are providing appropriate assistance in child support collection, whether they are providing their children with appropriate care, including medical immunizations, and what sort of training recipients may engage in or rehabilitation programs they should enter.

Recipient obligations may be further specified or expanded in "personal responsibility agreements" that constitute a contract between the recipient and the agency. All of these obligations, both regulatory and contractual, are backed by sanctions of various levels that can be applied or not at the discretion of the recipient's caseworker.

Because temporary assistance, services, work effort, responsibilities for behavioral modification, and sanctions for failure or misbehavior are all part of an overall plan to move recipients toward self-support, these activities tend to be put under the control of a single caseworker. Rather than dealing with a number of administrators, each of whom had a narrow role, TANF recipients are more likely to deal with a single individual who makes all important decisions concerning their case. The bureaucracy now has a human face, a face that represents both help and a source of very substantial discretionary authority.

Whereas caseworkers in the old "social work" paradigm were thought to be constrained by professional norms, and late 20th century welfare administrators by rules, welfare administration under PRWORA is being regulated through a combination of economic incentives and attempts to shift the "institutional culture." Numerous provisions of PRWORA emphasize case load reduction and reward states with federal dollars for meeting or exceeding performance measures. These economic incentives are recast in state programs as fiscal incentives to cities or counties with superior case load reduction performance and by tying caseworkers' advancement and salary to outcome measures, such as case load reductions. States and localities have also engaged in vigorous retraining programs to bring home the message that work is now the primary objective of caseworker activity, not entitlements determinations. The role for law in this new regime is presumptively deemphasized. On welfare administration under TANF, see generally, Matthew Diller, *The Revolution in Welfare Administration: Rules, Discretion and Entrepreneurial Government*, 75 N.Y.U. L. Rev. 1121 (2000); Christine M. Cimini, *Welfare Entitlements in the Area of Devolution*, 9 Geo. J. on Poverty L. & Pol'y 89 (2002); Christine M. Cimini, *The New Contract: Welfare Reform, Devolution and Due Process,* 61 Md. L. Rev. 246 (2002).

MATHEWS v. ELDRIDGE

Supreme Court of the United States, 1976.

424 U.S. 319, 96 S.Ct. 893, 47 L.Ed.2d 18.

JUSTICE POWELL delivered the opinion of the Court.

The issue in this case is whether the Due Process Clause of the Fifth Amendment requires that prior to the termination of Social Security disability benefit payments the recipient be afforded an opportunity for an evidentiary hearing.

Cash benefits are provided to workers during periods in which they are completely disabled under the disability insurance benefits program created by the 1956 amendments to Title II of the Social Security Act, 42 U.S.C. § 423. Respondent Eldridge was first awarded benefits in June 1968. In March 1972, he received a questionnaire from the state agency charged with monitoring his medical condition. Eldridge completed the questionnaire, indicating that his condition had not improved and identifying the medical sources, including physicians, from whom he had received treatment recently. The state agency then obtained reports from his physician and a psychiatric consultant. After considering these reports and other information in his file the agency informed Eldridge by letter that it had made a tentative determination that his disability had ceased in May 1972. The letter included a statement of reasons for the proposed termination of benefits, and advised Eldridge that he might request reasonable time in which to obtain and submit additional information pertaining to his condition.

In his written response, Eldridge disputed one characterization of his medical condition and indicated that the agency already had enough evidence to establish his disability.[2] The state agency then made its final determination that he had ceased to be disabled in May 1972. This determination was accepted by the Social Security Administration (SSA), which notified Eldridge in July that his benefits would terminate after that month. The notification also advised him of his right to seek reconsideration by the state agency of this initial determination within six months.

Instead of requesting reconsideration Eldridge commenced this action challenging the constitutional validity of the administrative procedures established by the Secretary of Health, Education, and Welfare for assessing whether there exists a continuing disability. He sought an immediate reinstatement of benefits pending a hearing on the issue of his disability. The Secretary moved to dismiss on the grounds that Eldridge's benefits had been terminated in accordance with valid administrative regulations and procedures and that he had failed to exhaust available remedies. In support of his contention that due process requires a pretermination hearing, Eldridge relied exclusively upon this Court's decision in *Goldberg v. Kelly*, which established a right to an "evidentiary hearing" prior to termination of welfare benefits. The

2. Eldridge originally was disabled due to chronic anxiety and back strain. He subsequently was found to have diabetes. The tentative determination letter indicated that aid would be terminated because available medical evidence indicated that his diabetes was under control, that there existed no limitations on his back movements which would impose severe functional restrictions, and that he no longer suffered emotional problems that would preclude him from all work for which he was qualified. In his reply letter he claimed to have arthritis of the spine rather than a strained back.

Secretary contended that *Goldberg* was not controlling since eligibility for disability benefits, unlike eligibility for welfare benefits, is not based on financial need and since issues of credibility and veracity do not play a significant role in the disability entitlement decision, which turns primarily on medical evidence.

The District Court concluded that the administrative procedures pursuant to which the Secretary had terminated Eldridge's benefits abridged his right to procedural due process. The court viewed the interest of the disability recipient in uninterrupted benefits as indistinguishable from that of the welfare recipient in *Goldberg*. * * * Reasoning that disability determinations may involve subjective judgments based on conflicting medical and nonmedical evidence, the District Court held that prior to termination of benefits Eldridge had to be afforded an evidentiary hearing of the type required for welfare beneficiaries under Title IV of the Social Security Act. Relying entirely upon the District Court's opinion, the Court of Appeals for the Fourth Circuit affirmed the injunction barring termination of Eldridge's benefits prior to an evidentiary hearing. We reverse.

* * *

Procedural due process imposes constraints on governmental decisions which deprive individuals of "liberty" or "property" interests within the meaning of the Due Process Clause of the Fifth or Fourteenth Amendment. The Secretary does not contend that procedural due process is inapplicable to terminations of Social Security disability benefits. He recognizes, as has been implicit in our prior decisions, that the interest of an individual in continued receipt of these benefits is a statutorily created "property" interest protected by the Fifth Amendment. Rather, the Secretary contends that the existing administrative procedures, detailed below, provide all the process that is constitutionally due before a recipient can be deprived of that interest.

This Court consistently has held that some form of hearing is required before an individual is finally deprived of a property interest. * * * Eldridge agrees that the review procedures available to a claimant before the initial determination of ineligibility becomes final would be adequate if disability benefits were not terminated until after the evidentiary hearing stage of the administrative process. The dispute centers upon what process is due prior to the initial termination of benefits, pending review.

In recent years this Court increasingly has had occasion to consider the extent to which due process requires an evidentiary hearing prior to the deprivation of some type of property interest even if such a hearing is provided thereafter. In only one case, *Goldberg v. Kelly*, has the Court held that a hearing closely approximating a judicial trial is necessary. In other cases requiring some type of pretermination hearing as a matter of constitutional right the Court has spoken sparingly about the requisite procedures.

* * *

These decisions underscore the truism that " '[d]ue process,' unlike some legal rules, is not a technical conception with a fixed content unrelated to time, place and circumstances." * * * Accordingly, resolution of the issue whether the administrative procedures provided here are constitutionally sufficient requires analysis of the governmental and private interests that are affected. More precisely, our prior decisions indicate that identification of the specific dictates of due process generally require consideration of three distinct factors: First, the private interest that will be affected by the official action; second, the risk of an erroneous deprivation of such interest through the procedures used, and the probable value, if any, of additional or substitute procedural safeguards; and finally, the Government's interest, including the function involved and the fiscal and administrative burdens that the additional or substitute procedural requirement would entail.

We turn first to a description of the procedures for the termination of Social Security disability benefits and thereafter consider the factors bearing upon the constitutional adequacy of these procedures.

* * *

In order to establish initial and continued entitlement to disability benefits a worker must demonstrate that he is unable

> "to engage in any substantial gainful activity by reason of any medically determinable physical or mental impairment which can be expected to result in death or which has lasted or can be expected to last for a continuous period of not less than 12 months * * *." 42 U.S.C. § 423(d)(1)(A).

To satisfy this test the worker bears a continuing burden of showing, by means of "medically acceptable clinical and laboratory diagnostic techniques," § 423(d)(3), that he has a physical or mental impairment of such severity that

> "he is not only unable to do his previous work but cannot, considering his age, education, and work experience, engage in any other kind of substantial gainful work with which exists in the national economy, regardless of whether such work exists in the immediate area in which he lives, or whether a specific job vacancy exists for him, or whether he would be hired if he applied for work." § 423(d)(2)(A).

The principal reasons for benefits terminations are that the worker is no longer disabled or has returned to work. As Eldridge's benefits were terminated because he was determined to be no longer disabled, we consider only the sufficiency of the procedures involved in such cases.

The continuing-eligibility investigation is made by a state agency acting through a "team" consisting of a physician and a nonmedical person trained in disability evaluation. The agency periodically communicates with the disabled worker, usually by mail—in which case he is sent a detailed questionnaire—or by telephone, and requests information concerning his present condition, including current medical restrictions and sources of treatment, and any additional information that he considers relevant to his continued entitlement to benefits.

Information regarding the recipient's current condition is also obtained from his sources of medical treatment. If there is a conflict between the information provided by the beneficiary and that obtained from medical sources such as his physician, or between two sources of treatment, the agency may arrange for an examination by an independent consulting physician. Whenever the agency's tentative assessment of the beneficiary's condition differs from his own assessment, the beneficiary is informed that benefits may be terminated, provided a summary of the evidence upon which the proposed determination to terminate is based, and afforded an opportunity to review the medical reports and other evidence in his case file.[18] He also may respond in writing and submit additional evidence.

The state agency then makes its final determination, which is reviewed by an examiner in the SSA Bureau of Disability Insurance. If, as is usually the case, the SSA accepts the agency determination it notifies the recipient in writing, informing him of the reasons for the decision, and of his right to seek *de novo* reconsideration by the state agency. Upon acceptance by the SSA, benefits are terminated effective two months after the month in which medical recovery is found to have occurred.

If the recipient seeks reconsideration by the state agency and the determination is adverse, the SSA reviews the reconsideration determination and notifies the recipient of the decision. He then has a right to an evidentiary hearing before an SSA administrative law judge. The hearing is nonadversary, and the SSA is not represented by counsel. As at all prior and subsequent stages of the administrative process, however, the claimant may be represented by counsel or other spokesmen. If this hearing results in an adverse decision, the claimant is entitled to request discretionary review by the SSA Appeals Council, and finally may obtain judicial review.

Should it be determined at any point after termination of benefits, that the claimant's disability extended beyond the date of cessation initially established, the worker is entitled to retroactive payments. If, on the other hand, a beneficiary receives any payments to which he is later determined not to be entitled, the statute authorizes the Secretary to attempt to recoup these funds in specified circumstances.

Despite the elaborate character of the administrative procedures provided by the Secretary, the courts below held them to be constitution-

18. The disability recipient is not permitted personally to examine the medical reports contained in his file. This restriction is not significant since he is entitled to have any representative of his choice, including a lay friend or family member, examine all medical evidence. The Secretary informs us that this curious limitation is currently under review.

ally inadequate, concluding that due process requires an evidentiary hearing prior to termination. In light of the private and governmental interests at stake here and the nature of the existing procedures, we think this was error.

Since a recipient whose benefits are terminated is awarded full retroactive relief if he ultimately prevails, his sole interest is in the uninterrupted receipt of this source of income pending final administrative decision on his claim. His potential injury is thus similar in nature to that of the welfare recipient in *Goldberg*, the nonprobationary federal employee in *Arnett v. Kennedy*, 416 U.S. 134 (1974), and the wage earner in *Sniadach v. Family Finance Corp.*, 395 U.S. 337 (1969).

Only in *Goldberg* has the Court held that due process requires an evidentiary hearing prior to a temporary deprivation. It was emphasized there that welfare assistance is given to persons on the very margin of subsistence. * * *

Eligibility for disability benefits, in contrast, is not based upon financial need.[24] Indeed, it is wholly unrelated to the worker's income or support from many other sources, such as earnings of other family members, workmen's compensation awards, tort claims awards, savings, private insurance, public or private pensions, veterans' benefits, food stamps, public assistance, or the "many other important programs, both public and private, which contain provisions for disability payments affecting a substantial portion of the work force * * *."

As *Goldberg* illustrates, the degree of potential deprivation that may be created by a particular decision is a factor to be considered in assessing the validity of any administrative decision-making process. The potential deprivation here is generally likely to be less than in *Goldberg*, although the degree of difference can be overstated. As the District Court emphasized, to remain eligible for benefits a recipient must be "unable to engage in substantial gainful activity." Thus, in contrast to the discharged federal employee in *Arnett*, there is little possibility that the terminated recipient will be able to find even temporary employment to ameliorate the interim loss.

As we recognized last Term in *Fusari v. Steinberg*, 419 U.S. 379, 389 (1975), "the possible length of wrongful deprivation of * * * benefits [also] is an important factor in assessing the impact of official action on the private interests." * * * [T]he delay between the actual cutoff of benefits and final decision after a hearing exceeds one year.

In view of the torpidity of this administrative review process, and the typically modest resources of the family unit of the physically disabled worker,[26] the hardship imposed upon the erroneously terminat-

24. The level of benefits is determined by the worker's average monthly earnings during the period prior to disability, his age, and other factors not directly related to financial need, specified in 42 U.S.C. § 415 (1970 ed., Supp. III). See § 423(a)(2).

26. *Amici* cite statistics compiled by the Secretary which indicate that in 1965 the mean income of the family unit of a disabled worker was $3,803, while the median income for the unit was $2,836. The mean liquid assets—i.e., cash, stocks, bonds—of

ed disability recipient may be significant. Still, the disabled worker's need is likely to be less than that of a welfare recipient. In addition to the possibility of access to private resources, other forms of government assistance will become available where the termination of disability benefits places a worker or his family below the subsistence level.[27] In view of these potential sources of temporary income, there is less reason here than in *Goldberg* to depart from the ordinary principle, established by our decisions, that something less than an evidentiary hearing is sufficient prior to adverse administrative action.

An additional factor to be considered here is the fairness and reliability of the existing pretermination procedures, and the probable value, if any, of additional procedural safeguards. Central to the evaluation of any administrative process is the nature of the relevant inquiry. In order to remain eligible for benefits the disabled worker must demonstrate by means of "medically acceptable clinical and laboratory diagnostic techniques," that he is unable "to engage in any substantial gainful activity by reason of any *medically determinable* physical or mental impairment. * * *" In short, a medical assessment of the worker's physical or mental condition is required. This is a more sharply focused and easily documented decision than the typical determination of welfare entitlement. In the latter case, a wide variety of information may be deemed relevant, and issues of witness credibility and veracity often are critical to the decision-making process.

* * *

By contrast, the decision whether to discontinue disability benefits will turn, in most cases, upon "routine, standard, and unbiased medical reports by physician specialists," *Richardson v. Perales*, 402 U.S. at 404, concerning a subject whom they have personally examined.[28] In *Richard-*

these family units was $4,862; the median was $940. These statistics do not take into account the family unit's nonliquid assets—i.e., automobile, real estate, and the like. Brief for AFL–CIO et al. as *Amici Curiae* App. 4a.

27. *Amici* emphasize that because an identical definition of disability is employed in both the Title II Social Security Program and in the companion welfare system for the disabled, Supplemental Security Income (SSI), the terminated disability-benefits recipient will be ineligible for the SSI Program. There exist, however, state and local welfare programs which may supplement the worker's income. In addition, the worker's household unit can qualify for food stamps if it meets the financial need requirements. Finally, in 1974, 480,000 of the approximately 2,000,000 disabled workers receiving Social Security benefits also received SSI benefits. Since financial need is a criterion for eligibility under the SSI program, those disabled workers who are most in need will in the majority of cases be receiving SSI benefits when disability insurance aid is terminated. And, under the SSI program, a pretermination evidentiary hearing is provided, if requested.

28. The decision is not purely a question of the accuracy of a medical diagnosis since the ultimate issue which the state agency must resolve is whether in light of the particular worker's "age, education, and work experience," he cannot "engage in any * * * substantial gainful work which exists in the national economy. * * *" Yet information concerning each of these worker characteristics is amenable to effective written presentation. The value of an evidentiary hearing, or even a limited oral presentation, to an accurate presentation of those factors to the decision maker does not appear substantial. Similarly, resolution of the inquiry as to the types of employment opportunities that exist in the national economy for a physically impaired worker with a particular set of skills would not

son the Court recognized the "reliability and probative worth of written medical reports," emphasizing that while there may be "professional disagreement with the medical conclusions" the "spectre of questionable credibility and veracity is not present." To be sure, credibility and veracity may be a factor in the ultimate disability assessment in some cases. But procedural due process rules are shaped by the risk of error inherent in the truth-finding process as applied to the generality of cases, not the rare exceptions. The potential value of an evidentiary hearing, or even oral presentation to the decision maker, is substantially less in this context than in *Goldberg*.

The decision in *Goldberg* also was based on the Court's conclusion that written submissions were an inadequate substitute for oral presentation because they did not provide an effective means for the recipient to communicate his case to the decision maker. Written submissions were viewed as an unrealistic option, for most recipients lacked the "educational attainment necessary to write effectively" and could not afford professional assistance. In addition, such submissions would not provide the "flexibility or oral presentations" or "permit the recipient to mold his argument to the issues the decision maker appears to regard as important." In the context of the disability-benefits-entitlement assessment the administrative procedures under review here fully answer these objections.

The detailed questionnaire which the state agency periodically sends the recipient identifies with particularity the information relevant to the entitlement decision, and the recipient is invited to obtain assistance from the local SSA office in completing the questionnaire. More important, the information critical to the entitlement decision usually is derived from medical sources, such as the treating physician. Such sources are likely to be able to communicate more effectively through written documents than are welfare recipients or the lay witnesses supporting their cause. The conclusions of physicians often are supported by X-rays and the results of clinical or laboratory tests, information typically more amenable to written than to oral presentation.

A further safeguard against mistake is the policy of allowing the disability recipient's representative full access to all information relied upon by the state agency. In addition, prior to the cutoff of benefits the agency informs the recipient of its tentative assessment, the reasons therefor, and provides a summary of the evidence that it considers most relevant. Opportunity is then afforded the recipient to submit additional evidence or arguments, enabling him to challenge directly the accuracy of information in his file as well as the correctness of the agency's tentative conclusions. These procedures, again as contrasted with those before the Court in *Goldberg*, enable the recipient to "mold" his argument to respond to the precise issues which the decision maker regards as crucial.

necessarily be advanced by an evidentiary hearing. The statistical information relevant to this judgment is more amenable to written than to oral presentation.

Despite these carefully structured procedures, *amici* point to the significant reversal rate for appealed cases as clear evidence that the current process is inadequate. Depending upon the base selected and the line of analysis followed, the relevant reversal rates urged by the contending parties vary from a high of 58.6% for appealed reconsideration decisions to an overall reversal rate of only 3.3%.[29] Bare statistics rarely provide a satisfactory measure of the fairness of a decision making process. Their adequacy is especially suspect here since the administrative review system is operated on an open-file basis. A recipient may always submit new evidence, and such submissions may result in additional medical examinations. Such fresh examinations were held in approximately 30% to 40% of the appealed cases, in fiscal 1973, either at the reconsideration or evidentiary hearing stage of the administrative process. In this context, the value of reversal rate statistics as one means of evaluating the adequacy of the pretermination process is diminished. Thus, although we view such information as relevant, it is certainly not controlling in this case.

In striking the appropriate due process balance the final factor to be assessed is the public interest. This includes the administrative burden and other societal costs that would be associated with requiring, as a matter of constitutional right, an evidentiary hearing upon demand in all cases prior to the termination of disability benefits. The most visible burden would be the incremental cost resulting from the increased number of hearings and the expense of providing benefits to ineligible recipients pending decision. No one can predict the extent of the increase, but the fact that full benefits would continue until after such hearings would assure the exhaustion in most cases of this attractive option. Nor would the theoretical right of the Secretary to recover undeserved benefits result, as a practical matter, in any substantial offset to the added outlay of public funds. The parties submit widely varying estimates of the probable additional financial cost. We only need say that experience with the constitutionalizing of government procedures suggests that the ultimate additional cost in terms of money and administrative burden would not be insubstantial.

Financial cost alone is not a controlling weight in determining whether due process requires a particular procedural safeguard prior to some administrative decision. But the Government's interest, and hence that of the public, in conserving scarce fiscal and administrative resources is a factor that must be weighed. At some point the benefit of an additional safeguard to the individual affected by the administrative

29. By focusing solely on the reversal rate for appealed reconsideration determinations *amici* overstate the relevant reversal rate. [I]n order fully to assess the reliability and fairness of a system of procedure, one must also consider the overall rate of error for all denials of benefits. Here that overall rate is 12.2%. Moreover, about 75% of these reversals occur at the reconsideration stage of the administrative process. Since the median period between a request for reconsideration review and decision is only two months, the deprivation is significantly less than that concomitant to the lengthier delay before an evidentiary hearing. Netting out these reconsideration reversals, the overall reversal rate falls to 3.3%.

action and to society in terms of increased assurance that the action is just, may be outweighed by the cost. Significantly, the cost of protecting those whom the preliminary administrative process has identified as likely to be found undeserving may in the end come out of the pockets of the deserving since resources available for any particular program of social welfare are not unlimited.

But more is implicated in cases of this type than ad hoc weighing of fiscal and administrative burdens against the interests of a particular category of claimants. The ultimate balance involves a determination as to when, under our constitutional system, judicial-type procedures must be imposed upon administrative action to assure fairness. * * * The judicial model of an evidentiary hearing is neither a required, nor even the most effective, method of decision-making in all circumstances. * * * All that is necessary is that the procedures be tailored, in light of the decision to be made, to "the capacities and circumstances of those who are to be heard," *Goldberg v. Kelly*, 397 U.S., at 268–269 (footnote omitted), to insure that they are given a meaningful opportunity to present their case. In assessing what process is due in this case, substantial weight must be given to the good-faith judgments of the individuals charged by Congress with the administration of social welfare programs that the procedures they have provided assure fair consideration of the entitlement claims of individuals. This is especially so where, as here, the prescribed procedures not only provide the claimant with an effective process for asserting his claim prior to any administrative action, but also assure a right to an evidentiary hearing, as well as to subsequent judicial review, before the denial of his claim becomes final.

We conclude that an evidentiary hearing is not required prior to the termination of disability benefits and that the present administrative procedures fully comport with due process.

The judgment of the Court of Appeals is reversed.

* * *

JUSTICE BRENNAN, with whom JUSTICE MARSHALL concurs, dissenting.

For the reasons stated in my dissenting opinion in *Richardson v. Wright*, 405 U.S. 208, 212 (1972), I agree with the District Court and the Court of Appeals that, prior to termination of benefits, Eldridge must be afforded an evidentiary hearing of the type required for welfare beneficiaries under Title IV of the Social Security Act * * *. I would add that the Court's consideration that a discontinuance of disability benefits may cause the recipient to suffer only a limited deprivation is no argument. It is speculative. Moreover, the very legislative determination to provide disability benefits, without any prerequisite determination of need in fact, presumes a need by the recipient which is not this Court's function to denigrate. Indeed, in the present case, it is indicated that because disability benefits were terminated there was a foreclosure upon the Eldridge home and the family's furniture was repossessed, forcing Eldridge, his wife, and their children to sleep in one bed. Finally, it is also no argument that a worker, who has been placed in the untenable position of having been denied disability benefits, may still seek other forms of public assistance.

Notes

1. *In Search of Social Welfare*. Justice Powell's careful formulation and application of the "three factor" test in *Eldridge* suggests an attempt to integrate and unify the Court's approach to the administrative due process questions that had been brought to it in increasing numbers since *Goldberg*. The generality of the *Eldridge* test seems to have been designed to lend consistency and principle to the Court's approach while permitting review of differing administrative functions in the light of their particular circumstances. Yet, the *Eldridge* formulation was immediately criticized as flawed in principle and incapable of coherent application. Jerry L. Mashaw, *The Supreme Court's Due Process Calculus for Administrative Adjudication in Mathews v. Eldridge: Three Factors in Search of a Theory of Value*, 44 U. Chi. L.Rev. 28, 47–49 (1976):

> * * * [T]he three-factor analysis enunciated in *Eldridge* appears to be a type of utilitarian, social welfare function. That function first takes into account the social value at stake in a legitimate private claim; it discounts that value by the probability that it will be preserved through the available administrative procedures, and it then subtracts from that discounted value the social cost of introducing additional procedures. When combined with the institutional posture of judicial self-restraint, utility theory can be said to yield the following plausible decision-rule: "Void procedures for lack of due process only when alternative procedures would so substantially increase social welfare that their rejection seems irrational."
>
> The utilitarian calculus is not, however, without difficulties. The *Eldridge* Court conceives of the values of procedure too narrowly: it views the sole purpose of procedural protections as enhancing accuracy, and thus limits its calculus to the benefits or costs that flow from correct or incorrect decisions. No attention is paid to "process values" that might inhere in oral proceedings or to the demoralization costs that may result from the grant-withdrawal-grant-withdrawal sequence to which claimants like Eldridge are subjected. Perhaps more important, as the Court seeks to make sense of a calculus in which accuracy is the sole goal of procedure, it tends erroneously to characterize disability hearings as concerned almost exclusively with medical impairment and thus concludes that such hearings involve only medical evidence, whose reliability would be little enhanced by oral procedure. As applied by the *Eldridge* Court the utilitarian calculus tends, as cost-benefit analyses typically do, to "dwarf soft variables" and to ignore complexities and ambiguities.
>
> The problem with a utilitarian calculus is not merely that the Court may define the relevant costs and benefits too narrowly. However broadly conceived, the calculus asks unanswerable questions. For example, what is the social value, and the social cost, of continuing disability

> payments until after an oral hearing for persons initially determined to be ineligible? Answers to those questions require some technique for measuring the social value and social costs of government income transfers, but no such technique exists. Even if such formidable tasks of social accounting could be accomplished, the effectiveness of oral hearings in forestalling the losses that result from erroneous terminations would remain uncertain. In the face of these pervasive indeterminacies the *Eldridge* Court was forced to retreat to a presumption of constitutionality.
>
> Finally, it is not clear that the utilitarian balancing analysis asks the constitutionally relevant questions. The Due Process Clause is one of those Bill of Rights protections meant to insure individual liberty in the face of contrary collective action. Therefore, a collective legislative or administrative decision about procedure, one arguably reflecting the intensity of the contending social values and representing an optimum position from the contemporary social perspective, cannot answer the constitutional question of whether due process has been accorded. A balancing analysis that would have the Court merely redetermine the question of social utility is similarly inadequate. There is no reason to believe that the Court has superior competence or legitimacy as a utilitarian balancer except as it performs its peculiar institutional role of insuring that libertarian values are considered in the calculus of decision.

See also Jerry L. Mashaw, *Administrative Due Process as Social–Cost Accounting*, 9 Hofstra L.Rev. 1423 (1981), for a more elaborate development of the information demands of the *Eldridge* approach and of techniques for managing the imponderables of a social welfare calculus.

2. *The Inconsistent Application of* Eldridge. Doctrinal consistency (beyond repeated enunciation of the *Eldridge* test) has not characterized the post-*Eldridge* Supreme Court jurisprudence. To be sure, assessing the consistency of the application of a formulation as open-textured as the *Eldridge* criteria, especially to practices and claims as varied as those raised in administrative due process cases, is a problematic enterprise. However, some oscillations in the Court's approach are virtually impossible to reconcile on any persuasive ground.

Consider *Memphis Light, Gas and Water Division v. Craft,* 436 U.S. 1 (1978), a case involving the adequacy of a municipal utility's procedure for resolving disputes with customers. Craft complained that the utility had failed to notify him of the availability of the company's pre-termination review procedure when threatening him with termination of services for nonpayment. The company admitted its failure to notify, but argued that the available common-law remedies—pre-termination injunction, post-termination damages and a post-payment action for refund—made a pre-termination conference superfluous. The utility's argument rested on the decision, only one term earlier, in *Ingraham v. Wright*, 430 U.S. 651 (1977). There the Court had held that there was no need for "pre-paddling" hearings in a school system employing corporal punishment precisely because, "the available civil and criminal sanctions for abuse * * * afford significant protection against unjustified corporal punishment." Indeed, the Memphis utility seemed to have an *a fortiori* case. The holding in *Ingraham* emerged from a context in which (a) any common law remedy would have been available only for "abuse," not error; (b) no pre-punishment common law remedy was thought to exist; and (c) no court in the affected state had ever recognized a remedy against a teacher for corporal punishment. The utility must certainly have been surprised, therefore, to learn that common law remedies were not "an adequate substitute for a pre-termination review of the disputed bill with a designated employee."

Lujan v. G & G Fire Sprinklers, Inc., 532 U.S. 189 (2001), seems to return to the *Ingraham* position. The Court held there that the existence of a post-deprivation common law remedy satisfies due process, and eliminates the necessity for any form of administrative hearing, whether pre-or post-deprivation, when a state assesses a penalty for non-compliance with contract terms. The unanimous opinion in *G & G Fire Sprinklers* mentions neither *Ingraham* nor *Memphis Light,* or for that matter any other case dealing with the adequacy of common law remedies as a substitute for administrative hearings.

Of course, the problem here may be that the *Memphis Light* case should not be described as a case involving the adequacy of post-deprivation common law remedies. In *City of West Covina v. Perkins*, 525 U.S. 234 (1999), the Court considered whether authorities who had seized property pursuant to a search warrant were required by due process to notify the owner of the seizure and of the procedures through which the property could be reclaimed. Seven members of the Court thought that the first type of notice was required, but none thought that the second was a requirement of due process. In the course of the majority opinion the *Memphis Light* case was distinguished as a case in which the utilities' constitutional error lay in its failure to give adequate notice of informal procedures that were available for resolving billing disputes, but not published and accessible to customers. Because the procedures for the return of seized property were in the California Penal Code, the property owners in *West Covina* were deemed to have sufficient notice of available remedies. *Memphis Light* may thus illustrate, not an inconsistency in the Court's jurisprudence on the role of available common law remedies in due process analysis, but instead the difficulties of characterizing multi-dimensional cases decided under a broad balancing test. This problem, plagues all doctrinal analysis, but it seems particularly acute in the field of constitutional due process.

A brace of cases involving psychiatric assessment, and a similar pair relating to decisions based on character, intelligence, and good faith, further illustrate the difficulties of "lining up" the Due Process jurisprudence, even when decisions are almost simultaneous. Consider first *Parham v. J.R.*, 442 U.S. 584 (1979), and *Vitek v. Jones*, 445 U.S. 480 (1980).

In *Parham* the issue was whether a minor was entitled to a hearing prior to commitment to an institution for treatment of mental illness. The Court thought not, in substantial part because a hearing would provide little additional protection from error: "Common human experience and scholarly opinions suggest that the supposed protections of an adversary hearing to determine the appropriateness of medical decisions for the commitment and treatment of mental and emotional illness may well be more illusory than real." This sentiment seems quite consistent with the Court's view of medical evidence in *Eldridge*. Yet in *Vitek*, where the question was whether a prisoner should have a hearing prior to being transferred to a mental hospital, the suggestion that psychiatric judgment was involved elicited the following judicial response: "The medical nature of the inquiry * * * does not justify dispensing with due process requirements. *It is precisely '[t]he subtleties and nuances of psychiatric diagnoses' that justify the requirement of adversary hearings*." 445 U.S. at 495 (quoting *Addington v. Texas*, 441 U.S. 418, 430 (1979)) (emphasis supplied).

Greenholtz v. Inmates, 442 U.S. 1 (1979), and *Califano v. Yamasaki*, 442 U.S. 682 (1979), are no less baffling. *Greenholtz* holds that a face-to-face, oral hearing is *not* required in parole decisions based on an assessment of the offender's personality, readiness to undertake responsibilities, intelligence, training, "mental and physical makeup," attitude toward law and authority, and any other factors the parole board deems relevant. Accuracy, the Court ruled, could be achieved by a review of the prisoner's files. Yet *Yamasaki* requires an oral hearing (at least a conversation) before the Secretary of HHS declines to waive recoupment of overpaid disability benefits because the waiver standard, lack of fault, rests "on an evaluation of all 'pertinent circumstances' including the recipient's intelligence * * * and physical and mental condition as well as his good faith." 442 U.S. at 696–97 (quoting from 10 C.F.R. § 404.507).

The difficulties of applying *Eldridge* across cases are mirrored in the Justices' differing assessments of how to apply the analysis in the same case, particularly where the issue is how to read the scales when determining the "balance" between state and individual interests. *Brock v. Roadway Express, Inc.*, 481 U.S. 252 (1987) is illustrative. Pursuant to section 405 of the Surface Transportation Assistance Act of 1982 the Secretary of Labor had ordered reinstatement of one of the appellant's drivers after an ex parte investigation found reasonable cause to believe that the driver had been discharged for reporting safety violations by Roadway to the Department of Transportation. During the Labor Department investigation, Roadway was given an explanation of the substance of the complaint against it and invited to respond; but its requests for an identification of the witnesses who were providing information, for specific testimony provided by those witnesses, and for procedures in which it could confront and cross-examine adverse witnesses, were denied. The question for the Court was whether the section 405 procedure was constitutional given that the Labor Department's "preliminary" administrative order included reinstatement of the employee with back pay and that the post-reinstatement evidentiary hearing to which the employer was entitled might be delayed for many months.

A plurality (Justices Marshall, Blackmun, Powell, and O'Connor) found the procedures used sufficient to pass constitutional muster, save for the Secretary's failure to provide Roadway with the relevant evidence that supported the employee's complaint. Balancing the interests in protecting whistleblowers' employment rights against the employer's right to remove employees for cause, the plurality believed that assured confrontation and cross-examination at the preliminary reinstatement stage would not provide sufficient additional guarantees of the reasonableness of such decisions to justify their cost—at least not where the employer had had an opportunity to respond with full knowledge of the evidence that had been turned up in the Secretary's investigation.

Justice Brennan agreed that the employer was entitled to more process than the Secretary's procedures had provided, but thought that the plurality had failed to get the balance right. In his view, confrontation and cross-examination of witnesses were essential where the Secretary's order affected a serious interest of the employer and might be continued indefinitely pending a formal hearing.

Justices White and Scalia and Chief Justice Rehnquist believed that the statute itself had struck the appropriate balance. Given the purpose of section 405, protecting whistleblowers from employer retaliation, they had no difficulty in imagining situations in which the government might have excellent reason to withhold the names of witnesses and specific identifying evidence from an employer against which a preliminary reinstatement order might run.

Finally, Justice Stevens reiterated his increasing skepticism of the open-ended balancing methodology that his colleagues employed:

> The Court's willingness to sacrifice due process to the Government's obscure suggestion of necessity reveals the serious flaws in its due process analysis. It is wrong to approach the due process analysis in each case by asking anew what procedures seem worthwhile and not too costly. Unless a case falls within a recognized exception, we should adhere to the strongest presumption that the Government may not take away life, liberty or property before making a meaningful hearing available. * * * Such a hearing necessarily includes the creation of a public record developed in a proceeding in which hostile witnesses are confronted and cross examined.

2. THE INTERESTS PROTECTED BY DUE PROCESS HEARING RIGHTS

a. *The Right/Privilege Distinction and Its "Demise"*

The Fifth and Fourteenth Amendments provide identically that due process of law is a prerequisite to any denial of "life, liberty, or property." This is a conspicuously ambiguous text. One could read "life, liberty, or property" as an elegant way of encompassing everything that people hold important. So read, the Due Process Clause would be applicable to all government decisions that affect individuals in important ways—or, given *Londoner v. Denver, supra* p. 314, at least all such decisions that are "adjudicatory" in nature. Alternatively, one could read "life, liberty, or property" as historically fixed categories with specific common law referents.

Until the 1950s, the latter, narrow reading prevailed—or, perhaps more accurately, was presumed. The relevant cases, often without serious discussion, invoked a distinction between common law property rights, protected by due process, and mere privileges or government largesse, whose disposition was subject only to those procedures that the government chose to provide. Although uttered in a First, rather than a

Fifth Amendment context, Justice Holmes' remark that a person may have the right to talk politics but not to be a police officer is the pithiest expression of the right/privilege distinction. *McAuliffe v. Mayor of New Bedford*, 155 Mass. 216, 220, 29 N.E. 517 (1892).

This narrow reading of the interests protected by due process is well illustrated by *Bailey v. Richardson*, 182 F.2d 46 (D.C.Cir.1950), *affirmed by an equally divided court*, 341 U.S. 918 (1951). Bailey had been dismissed as a training officer with the former Federal Security Agency based on a determination by the Loyalty Review Board of the Civil Service Commission that there were "reasonable grounds" to regard her as disloyal to the United States. Although invited to present a defense (both written and oral, and through counsel), "she was not told the names of the informants against her. She was not permitted to face or to cross-examine those informants. She was not given the dates or places at which she was alleged to have been active in the named alleged subversive organizations." The court of appeals concluded that Bailey was not entitled to specific charges, to confrontation and cross-examination of witnesses, or to a hearing upon evidence openly submitted, because "the Due Process Clause does not apply to the holding of a Government office." A vigorous dissent insisted that the government was obligated to provide "all the safeguards of a judicial trial" before it could injure an employee's reputation and employability by dismissing her for suspected disloyalty.

Within ten years, however, the Supreme Court—in a factually similar case—wrote very differently about the applicability of due process. In *Cafeteria & Restaurant Workers Union v. McElroy*, 367 U.S. 886 (1961), the Court reviewed the dismissal on loyalty grounds of a short-order cook at a cafeteria operated on the premises of a naval gun factory. The plaintiff had been treated even more summarily than Ms. Bailey:

> On November 15, 1956, Mrs. Brawner was required to turn in her identification badge because of Lieutenant Commander Williams' determination that she had failed to meet the security requirements of the installation. The Security Officer's determination was subsequently approved by Admiral Tyree * * *. At the request of the petitioner Union, which represented the employees at the cafeteria, [the restaurant operator] sought to arrange a meeting with officials of the Gun Factory "for the purpose of a hearing regarding the denial of admittance to the Naval Gun Factory of Rachel Brawner." This request was denied by Admiral Tyree on the ground that such a meeting would "serve no useful purpose."

Although the Court, by a five to four majority, upheld Brawner's dismissal, it followed a longer path than had the D.C.Circuit in *Bailey*. First, the Court rejected *Bailey*'s major premise:

> This question cannot be answered by easy assertion that, because she had no constitutional right to be there in the first place, she was not deprived of liberty or property by the Superintendent's action. "One may not have a constitutional right to go to Baghdad, but the

Government may not prohibit one from going there unless by means consonant with due process of law." *Homer v. Richmond*, 292 F.2d 719, 722.

Instead, the Court said:

> [C]onsideration of what procedures due process may require under any given set of circumstances must begin with a determination of the precise nature of the government function involved as well as of the private interest that has been affected by governmental action.

Turning to these factors, the majority concluded that a balancing of interests justified the Navy's summary procedure. With respect to the government function involved, the Court said:

> [T]he governmental function operating here was * * * the power * * *, as proprietor, to manage the internal operation of an important federal military establishment. In that proprietary military capacity, the Federal Government, as has been pointed out, has traditionally exercised unfettered control.

As for the private interest involved:

> It most assuredly was not the right to follow a chosen trade or profession. Rachel Brawner remained entirely free to obtain employment as a short-order cook or to get any other job, either with M & M or with any other employer. All that was denied her was the opportunity to work at one isolated and specific military installation. * * * [T]his is not a case where government action has operated to bestow a badge of disloyalty or infamy, with an attendant foreclosure from other employment opportunity. All this record shows is that, in the opinion of the Security Officer of the Gun Factory, concurred in by the Superintendent, Rachel Brawner failed to meet the particular security requirements of that specific military installation. There is nothing to indicate that this determination would in any way impair Rachel Brawner's employment opportunities anywhere else.

In *Cafeteria Workers*, the Court also took note of its recent ruling in another security case, *Greene v. McElroy*, 360 U.S. 474 (1959), which held that the Defense Department had wrongfully revoked the security clearance of an aeronautical engineer, resulting in his discharge by his government contractor employer. The case turned on the Court's determination that neither the President nor Congress had delegated authority to the Defense Department to terminate contractor security clearances without a hearing. The Court took special note, however, of the impact of the government's decision on Mr. Greene: "[P]etitioner's work opportunities have been severely limited on the basis of a fact determination rendered after a hearing which failed to comply with our traditional ideas of fair procedure."

Cafeteria Workers and *Greene*, it turned out, foreshadowed a dramatic liberalization in the availability of due process hearings following *Goldberg v. Kelly*, excerpted above. Strictly speaking, the applicability of due process to the welfare claimants in *Goldberg* was not at issue because the government conceded as much. Yet, the Court in *Goldberg* was expressly influenced (see footnote 8) by a widely cited academic article, Charles Reich's *The New Property*, 73 Yale L. J. 733 (1964). Professor Reich argued that the assurance of individual liberty in the modern state requires some legal protection for economic interests and relationships that are critically important to individuals but that do not fit within traditional private law definitions of property. The Court's approving citation of Reich's work was widely thought to signal the interment of the "right/privilege distinction."

b. The Return to the Search for "Entitlements": The Case of Public Employment

BOARD OF REGENTS OF STATE COLLEGES v. ROTH

Supreme Court of the United States, 1972.
408 U.S. 564, 92 S.Ct. 2701, 33 L.Ed.2d 548.

JUSTICE STEWART delivered the opinion of the Court.

In 1968 the respondent, David Roth, was hired for his first teaching job as assistant professor of political science at Wisconsin State University–Oshkosh. He was hired for a fixed term of one academic year. The notice of his faculty appointment specified that his employment would begin on September 1, 1968, and would end on June 30, 1969. The respondent completed that term. But he was informed that he would not be rehired for the next academic year.

The respondent had no tenure rights to continued employment. Under Wisconsin statutory law a state university teacher can acquire tenure as a "permanent" employee only after four years of year-to-year employment. Having acquired tenure, a teacher is entitled to continued employment "during efficiency and good behavior." A relatively new teacher without tenure, however, is under Wisconsin law entitled to nothing beyond his one-year appointment. There are no statutory or administrative standards defining eligibility for re-employment. State law thus clearly leaves the decision whether to rehire a nontenured teacher for another year to the unfettered discretion of university officials.

The procedural protection afforded a Wisconsin State University teacher before he is separated from the University corresponds to his job security. As a matter of statutory law, a tenured teacher cannot be "discharged except for cause upon written charges" and pursuant to certain procedures. A nontenured teacher, similarly, is protected to some extent during his one-year term. Rules promulgated by the Board of Regents provide that a nontenured teacher "dismissed" before the end of the year may have some opportunity for review of the "dismissal." But the Rules provide no real protection for a nontenured teacher who simply is not re-employed for the next year. He must be informed by February 1 "concerning retention or non-retention for the ensuing

year." But "no reason for non-retention need be given. No review or appeal is provided in such case."

In conformance with these Rules, the President of Wisconsin State University–Oshkosh informed the respondent before February 1, 1969, that he would not be rehired for the 1969–1970 academic year. He gave the respondent no reason for the decision and no opportunity to challenge it at any sort of hearing.

The respondent then brought this action in Federal District Court alleging that the decision not to rehire him for the next year infringed his Fourteenth Amendment rights. * * * First, he alleged that the true reason for the decision was to punish him for certain statements critical of the University administration, and that it therefore violated his right to freedom of speech. Second, he alleged that the failure of University officials to give him notice of any reason for nonretention and an opportunity for a hearing violated his right to procedural due process of law. * * *

I

The requirements of procedural due process apply only to the deprivation of interests encompassed by the Fourteenth Amendment's protection of liberty and property. When protected interests are implicated, the right to some kind of prior hearing is paramount. But the range of interests protected by procedural due process is not infinite.

The District Court decided that procedural due process guarantees apply in this case by assessing and balancing the weights of the particular interests involved. It concluded that the respondent's interest in re-employment at Wisconsin State University–Oshkosh outweighed the University's interest in denying him re-employment summarily. Undeniably, the respondent's re-employment prospects were of major concern to him—concern that we surely cannot say was insignificant. And a weighing process has long been a part of any determination of the form of hearing required in particular situations by procedural due process. But, to determine whether due process requirements apply in the first place, we must look not to the "weight" but to the nature of the interest at stake. We must look to see if the interest is within the Fourteenth Amendment's protection of liberty and property.

"Liberty" and "property" are broad and majestic terms. They are among the "[g]reat [constitutional] concepts * * * purposely left to gather meaning from experience. * * * [T]hey relate to the whole domain of social and economic fact, and the statesmen who founded this Nation knew too well that only a stagnant society remains unchanged." *National Mutual Ins. Co. v. Tidewater Transfer Co.*, 337 U.S. 582, 646 (Frankfurter, J., dissenting). For that reason, the Court has fully and finally rejected the wooden distinction between "rights" and "privileges" that once seemed to govern the applicability of procedural due process rights. The Court has also made clear that the property interests protected by procedural due process extend well beyond actual ownership of real estate, chattels, or money. By the same token, the Court has required due process protection for deprivations of liberty beyond the sort of formal constraints imposed by the criminal process.

Yet, while the Court has eschewed rigid or formalistic limitations on the protection of procedural due process, it has at the same time observed certain boundaries. For the words "liberty" and "property" in the Due Process Clause of the Fourteenth Amendment must be given some meaning.

II

"While this Court has not attempted to define with exactness the liberty * * * guaranteed [by the Fourteenth Amendment], the term has received much consideration and some of the included things have been definitely stated. Without doubt, it denotes not merely freedom from bodily restraint but also the right of the individual to contract, to engage in any of the common occupations of life, to acquire useful knowledge, to marry, establish a home and bring up children, to worship God according to the dictates of his own conscience, and generally to enjoy those privileges long recognized * * * as essential to the orderly pursuit of happiness by free men." *Meyer v. Nebraska*, 262 U.S. 390, 399. In a Constitution for a free people, there can be no doubt that the meaning of "liberty" must be broad indeed.

There might be cases in which a State refused to reemploy a person under such circumstances that interests in liberty would be implicated. But this is not such a case.

The State, in declining to rehire the respondent, did not make any charge against him that might seriously damage his standing and associations in his community. It did not base the nonrenewal of his contract on a charge, for example, that he had been guilty of dishonesty, or immorality. Had it done so, this would be a different case. For "[w]here a person's good name, reputation, honor, or integrity is at stake because of what the government is doing to him, notice and an opportunity to be heard are essential." *Wisconsin v. Constantineau*, 400 U.S. 433, 437. In such a case, due process would accord an opportunity to refute the charge before University officials.[12] In the present case, however, there is no suggestion whatever that the respondent's "good name, reputation, honor, or integrity" is at stake.

Similarly, there is no suggestion that the State, in declining to reemploy the respondent, imposed on him a stigma or other disability that foreclosed his freedom to take advantage of other employment opportunities. The State, for example, did not invoke any regulations to bar the respondent from all other public employment in state universities. Had it done so, this, again, would be a different case. * * * It stretches the concept too far to suggest that a person is deprived of "liberty" when he

12. The purpose of such notice and hearing is to provide the person an opportunity to clear his name. Once a person has cleared his name at a hearing, his employer, of course, may remain free to deny him future employment for other reasons.

simply is not rehired in one job but remains as free as before to seek another.

III

The Fourteenth Amendment's procedural protection of property is a safeguard of the security of interests that a person has already acquired in specific benefits. These interests—property interests—may take many forms. * * *

To have a property interest in a benefit, a person clearly must have more than an abstract need or desire for it. He must have more than a unilateral expectation of it. He must, instead, have a legitimate claim of entitlement to it. It is a purpose of the ancient institution of property to protect those claims upon which people rely in their daily lives, reliance that must not be arbitrarily undermined. It is a purpose of the constitutional right to a hearing to provide an opportunity for a person to vindicate those claims.

Property interests, of course, are not created by the Constitution. Rather, they are created and their dimensions are defined by existing rules or understandings that stem from an independent source such as state law—rules or understandings that secure certain benefits and that support claims of entitlement to those benefits. Thus, the welfare recipients in *Goldberg v. Kelly*, had a claim of entitlement to welfare payments that was grounded in the statute defining eligibility for them. The recipients had not yet shown that they were, in fact, within the statutory terms of eligibility. But we held that they had a right to a hearing at which they might attempt to do so.

Just as the welfare recipients' "property" interest in welfare payments was created and defined by statutory terms, so the respondent's "property" interest in employment at Wisconsin State University–Oshkosh was created and defined by the terms of his appointment. Those terms secured his interest in employment up to June 30, 1969. But the important fact in this case is that they specifically provided that the respondent's employment was to terminate on June 30. They did not provide for contract renewal absent "sufficient cause." Indeed, they made no provision for renewal whatsoever.

Thus, the terms of the respondent's appointment secured absolutely no interest in re-employment for the next year. They supported absolutely no possible claim of entitlement to re-employment. Nor, significantly, was there any state statute or University rule or policy that secured his interest in re-employment or that created any legitimate claim to it.[16] In these circumstances, the respondent surely had an abstract concern in being rehired, but he did not have a property interest sufficient to

16. To be sure, the respondent does suggest that most teachers hired on a year-to-year basis by Wisconsin State University–Oshkosh are, in fact, rehired. But the District Court has not found that there is anything approaching a "common law" of re-employment, see *Perry v. Sindermann*, so strong as to require University officials to give the respondent a statement of reasons and a hearing on their decision not to rehire him.

require the University authorities to give him a hearing when they declined to renew his contract of employment.

JUSTICE POWELL took no part in the decision of this case.

JUSTICE DOUGLAS, dissenting.

Respondent Roth, like Sindermann in the companion case, has no tenure under Wisconsin law and, unlike Sindermann, he had had only one year of teaching at Wisconsin State University–Oshkosh—where during 1968–1969 he had been Assistant Professor of Political Science and International Studies. Though Roth was rated by the faculty as an excellent teacher, he had publicly criticized the administration for suspending an entire group of 94 black students without determining individual guilt. He also criticized the university's regime as being authoritarian and autocratic. He used his classroom to discuss what was being done about the black episode; and one day, instead of meeting his class, he went to the meeting of the Board of Regents. * * *

No more direct assault on academic freedom can be imagined than for the school authorities to be allowed to discharge a teacher because of his or her philosophical, political, or ideological beliefs * * *. When a violation of First Amendment rights is alleged, the reasons for dismissal or for nonrenewal of an employment contract must be examined to see if the reasons given are only a cloak for activity or attitudes protected by the Constitution.

In the case of teachers whose contracts are not renewed, tenure is not the critical issue. * * * [W]hen a State proposes to deny a privilege to one who it alleges has engaged in unprotected speech, Due Process requires that the State bear the burden of proving that the speech was not protected. "[T]he 'protection of the individual against arbitrary action' * * * [is] the very essence of due process," *Slochower v. Board of Education*, 350 U.S. 551, 559, but where the State is allowed to act secretly behind closed doors and without any notice to those who are affected by its actions, there is no check against the possibility of such "arbitrary action."

Moreover, where "important interests" of the citizen are implicated they are not to be denied or taken away without due process. *Bell v. Burson* involved a driver's license. But also included are disqualification for unemployment compensation, discharge from public employment, denial of tax exemption, and withdrawal of welfare benefits. We should now add that nonrenewal of a teacher's contract, whether or not he has tenure, is an entitlement of the same importance and dignity. * * *

JUSTICE MARSHALL, dissenting.

* * * While I agree with Part I of the Court's opinion, setting forth the proper framework for consideration of the issue presented, and also with those portions of Parts II and III of the Court's opinion that assert that a public employee is entitled to procedural due process whenever a State stigmatizes him by denying employment, or injures his future employment prospects severely, or whenever the State deprives him of a

property interest, I would go further than the Court does in defining the terms "liberty" and "property."

The prior decisions of this Court, discussed at length in the opinion of the Court, establish a principle that is as obvious as it is compelling—i.e., federal and state governments and governmental agencies are restrained by the Constitution from acting arbitrarily with respect to employment opportunities that they either offer or control. Hence, it is now firmly established that whether or not a private employer is free to act capriciously or unreasonably with respect to employment practices, at least absent statutory or contractual controls, a government employer is different. The government may only act fairly and reasonably. * * *

In my view, every citizen who applies for a government job is entitled to it unless the government can establish some reason for denying the employment. This is the "property" right that I believe is protected by the Fourteenth Amendment and that cannot be denied "without due process of law." And it is also liberty—liberty to work—which is the "very essence of the personal freedom and opportunity" secured by the Fourteenth Amendment.

This Court has often had occasion to note that the denial of public employment is a serious blow to any citizen. Thus, when an application for public employment is denied or the contract of a government employee is not renewed, the government must say why, for it is only when the reasons underlying government action are known that citizens feel secure and protected against arbitrary government action. * * *

When something as valuable as the opportunity to work is at stake, the government may not reward some citizens and not others without demonstrating that its actions are fair and equitable. And it is procedural due process that is our fundamental guarantee of fairness, our protection against arbitrary, capricious, and unreasonable government action. * * *

It may be argued that to provide procedural due process to all public employees or prospective employees would place an intolerable burden on the machinery of government. The short answer to that argument is that it is not burdensome to give reasons when reasons exist. Whenever an application for employment is denied, an employee is discharged, or a decision not to rehire an employee is made, there should be some reason for the decision. It can scarcely be argued that government would be crippled by a requirement that the reason be communicated to the person most directly affected by the government's action.

Where there are numerous applicants for jobs, it is likely that few will choose to demand reasons for not being hired. But, if the demand for reasons is exceptionally great, summary procedures can be devised that would provide fair and adequate information to all persons. As long as the government has a good reason for its actions it need not fear disclosure. It is only where the government acts improperly that procedural due process is truly burdensome. And that is precisely when it is most necessary.

It might also be argued that to require a hearing and a statement of reasons is to require a useless act, because a government bent on denying employment to one or more persons will do so regardless of the procedural hurdles that are placed in its path. Perhaps this is so, but a requirement of procedural regularity at least renders arbitrary action more difficult. Moreover, proper procedures will surely eliminate some of the arbitrariness that results, not from malice, but from innocent error. * * * When the government knows it may have to justify its decisions with sound reasons, its conduct is likely to be more cautious, careful, and correct. * * *

Accordingly, I dissent.

PERRY v. SINDERMANN

Supreme Court of the United States, 1972.
408 U.S. 593, 92 S.Ct. 2694, 33 L.Ed.2d 570.

JUSTICE STEWART delivered the opinion of the Court.

From 1959 to 1969 the respondent, Robert Sindermann, was a teacher in the state college system of the State of Texas. After teaching for two years at the University of Texas and for four years at San Antonio Junior College, he became a professor of Government and Social Science at Odessa Junior College in 1965. He was employed at the college for four successive years, under a series of one-year contracts. He was successful enough to be appointed, for a time, the cochairman of his department.

During the 1968–1969 academic year, however, controversy arose between the respondent and the college administration. The respondent was elected president of the Texas Junior College Teachers Association. In this capacity, he left his teaching duties on several occasions to testify before committees of the Texas Legislature, and he became involved in public disagreements with the policies of the college's Board of Regents. In particular, he aligned himself with a group advocating the elevation of the college to four-year status—a change opposed by the Regents. And, on one occasion, a newspaper advertisement appeared over his name that was highly critical of the Regents.

Finally, in May 1969, the respondent's one-year employment contract terminated and the Board of Regents voted not to offer him a new contract for the next academic year. The Regents issued a press release setting forth allegations of the respondent's insubordination.[1] But they provided him no official statement of the reasons for the nonrenewal of his contract. And they allowed him no opportunity for a hearing to challenge the basis of the nonrenewal.

The respondent then brought this action in Federal District Court. He alleged primarily that the Regents' decision not to rehire him was

1. The press release stated, for example, that the respondent had defied his superiors by attending legislative committee meetings when college officials had specifically refused to permit him to leave his classes for that purpose.

based on his public criticism of the policies of the college administration and thus infringed his right to freedom of speech. He also alleged that their failure to provide him an opportunity for a hearing violated the Fourteenth Amendment's guarantee of procedural due process. The petitioners—members of the Board of Regents and the president of the college—denied that their decision was made in retaliation for the respondent's public criticism and argued that they had no obligation to provide a hearing. * * *

The Court of Appeals * * * held that, despite the respondent's lack of tenure, the nonrenewal of his contract would violate the Fourteenth Amendment if it in fact was based on his protected free speech. Since the actual reason for the Regents' decision was "in total dispute" in the pleadings, the court remanded the case for a full hearing on this contested issue of fact. Second, the Court of Appeals held that, despite the respondent's lack of tenure, the failure to allow him an opportunity for a hearing would violate the constitutional guarantee of procedural due process if the respondent could show that he had an "expectancy" of re-employment. It, therefore, ordered that this issue of fact also be aired upon remand. We granted a writ of certiorari, and we have considered this case along with *Board of Regents v. Roth*.

I

The first question presented is whether the respondent's lack of a contractual or tenure right to re-employment, taken alone, defeats his claim that the nonrenewal of his contract violated the First and Fourteenth Amendments. We hold that it does not.

For at least a quarter-century, this Court has made clear that even though a person has no "right" to a valuable governmental benefit and even though the government may deny him the benefit for any number of reasons, there are some reasons upon which the government may not rely. It may not deny a benefit to a person on a basis that infringes his constitutionally protected interests—especially, his interest in freedom of speech. For if the government could deny a benefit to a person because of his constitutionally protected speech or associations, his exercise of those freedoms would in effect be penalized and inhibited. This would allow the government to "produce a result which [it] could not command directly." Such interference with constitutional rights is impermissible.

We have applied this general principle to denials of tax exemptions, unemployment benefits, and welfare payments. But, most often, we have applied the principle to denials of public employment. We have applied the principle regardless of the public employee's contractual or other claim to a job. Thus, the respondent's lack of a contractual or tenure "right" to re-employment for the 1969–1970 academic year is immaterial to his free speech claim. * * * [W]e agree with the Court of Appeals that there is a genuine dispute as to "whether the college refused to renew the teaching contract on an impermissible basis—as a reprisal for the exercise of constitutionally protected rights." * * *

For this reason we hold that the grant of summary judgment against the respondent, without full exploration of this issue, was improper.

II

The respondent's lack of formal contractual or tenure security in continued employment at Odessa Junior College, though irrelevant to his free speech claim, is highly relevant to his procedural due process claim. But it may not be entirely dispositive.

* * * [T]he respondent here has yet to show that he has been deprived of an interest that could invoke procedural due process protection. As in *Roth*, the mere showing that he was not rehired in one particular job, without more, did not amount to a showing of a loss of liberty. Nor did it amount to a showing of a loss of property.

But the respondent's allegations—which we must construe most favorably to the respondent at this stage of the litigation—do raise a genuine issue as to his interest in continued employment at Odessa Junior College. He alleged that this interest, though not secured by a formal contractual tenure provision, was secured by a no less binding understanding fostered by the college administration. In particular, the respondent alleged that the college had a de facto tenure program, and that he had tenure under that program. He claimed that he and others legitimately relied upon an unusual provision that had been in the college's official Faculty Guide for many years:

> "Teacher Tenure: Odessa College has no tenure system. The Administration of the College wishes the faculty member to feel that he has permanent tenure as long as his teaching services are satisfactory and as long as he displays a cooperative attitude toward his co-workers and his superiors, and as long as he is happy in his work."

Moreover, the respondent claimed legitimate reliance upon guidelines promulgated by the Coordinating Board of the Texas College and University System that provided that a person, like himself, who had been employed as a teacher in the state college and university system for seven years or more has some form of job tenure. Thus, the respondent offered to prove that a teacher with his long period of service at this particular State College had no less a "property" interest in continued employment than a formally tenured teacher at other colleges, and had no less a procedural due process right to a statement of reasons and a hearing before college officials upon their decision not to retain him.

We have made clear in *Roth* that "property" interests subject to procedural due process protection are not limited by a few rigid, technical forms. Rather, "property" denotes a broad range of interests that are secured by "existing rules or understandings." A person's interest in a benefit is a "property" interest for due process purposes if there are such rules or mutually explicit understandings that support his claim of entitlement to the benefit and that he may invoke at a hearing.

A written contract with an explicit tenure provision clearly is evidence of a formal understanding that supports a teacher's claim of entitlement to continued employment unless sufficient "cause" is shown. Yet absence of such an explicit contractual provision may not always foreclose the possibility that a teacher has a "property" interest in re-employment. For example, the law of contracts in most, if not all, jurisdictions long has employed a process by which agreements, though not formalized in writing, may be "implied." Explicit contractual provisions may be supplemented by other agreements implied from "the promisor's words and conduct in the light of the surrounding circumstances." And, "[t]he meaning of [the promisor's] words and acts is found by relating them to the usage of the past."

A teacher, like the respondent, who has held his position for a number of years, might be able to show from the circumstances of this service—and from other relevant facts—that he has a legitimate claim of entitlement to job tenure. Just as this Court has found there to be a "common law of a particular industry or of a particular plant" that may supplement a collective-bargaining agreement, so there may be an unwritten "common law" in a particular university that certain employees shall have the equivalent of tenure. This is particularly likely in a college or university, like Odessa Junior College, that has no explicit tenure system even for senior members of its faculty, but that nonetheless may have created such a system in practice.

In this case, the respondent has alleged the existence of rules and understandings, promulgated and fostered by state officials, that may justify his legitimate claim of entitlement to continued employment absent "sufficient cause." We disagree with the Court of Appeals insofar as it held that a mere subjective "expectancy" is protected by procedural due process, but we agree that the respondent must be given an opportunity to prove the legitimacy of his claim of such entitlement in light of "the policies and practices of the institution." Proof of such a property interest would not, of course, entitle him to reinstatement. But such proof would obligate college officials to grant a hearing at his request, where he could be informed of the grounds for his nonretention and challenge their sufficiency.

Therefore, while we do not wholly agree with the opinion of the Court of Appeals, its judgment remanding this case to the District Court is Affirmed.

Justice Powell took no part in the decision of this case.

[The concurring opinion of Chief Justice Burger is omitted.]

Justice Brennan, with whom Justice Douglas joins, dissenting in *Roth* and dissenting in part in *Perry*.

Although I agree with Part I of the Court's opinion in [*Roth*], I also agree with my Brother Marshall that "respondent[s] [were] denied due process when [their] contract[s] [were] not renewed and [they were] not informed of the reasons and given an opportunity to respond." Since respondents were entitled to summary judgment on that issue, I would affirm the judgment of the Court of Appeals in [*Roth*], and, to the extent indicated by my Brother Marshall, I would modify the judgment of the Court of Appeals in [*Perry*].

JUSTICE MARSHALL, dissenting in part.

* * * [F]or the reasons stated in my dissenting opinion in *Board of Regents v. Roth*, I would modify the judgment of the Court of Appeals to direct the District Court to enter summary judgment for respondent entitling him to a statement of reasons why his contract was not renewed and a hearing on disputed issues of fact.

Notes

1. *The* Roth–Perry *Two-Step. Roth* and *Perry* are emphatic that the question whether due process "applies" must be distinguished from, and answered prior to, the question of what process is due if due process is triggered. They also insist that interest balancing is not part of this threshold determination. The appeal of this analytic approach, however, is far from self-evident. In *Cafeteria & Restaurant Workers Union v. McElroy*, *supra* p. 323, the Court seemed to presume the applicability of due process to Rachel Brawner's employment claim and move directly to the question of to what sort of "hearing" she was entitled. Although the answer in that case was "none," the Court's analysis was rooted entirely in its assessment of the competing interests involved. Are there reasons to prefer the more categorical approach of *Roth–Perry*?

2. *Substantive Constitutional Rights as Procedurally Protected Interests*. Professor Roth attributed the non-renewal of his contract to retaliation by his employer against Roth's public criticism of university administrators. Some such government employee criticism is, indeed, protected by the First Amendment, *Pickering v. Board of Education*, 391 U.S. 563 (1968), and the Supreme Court has recognized a constitutional right not to be fired for the exercise of First Amendment rights, e.g., *Branti v. Finkel*, 445 U.S. 507 n. 3 (1980) ("[P]laintiffs' constitutional right * * * is the right not to be dismissed from public employment upon the sole ground of their political beliefs."). Protection of First Amendment interests extends to independent contractors as well. *Board of County Commissioners v. Umbehr*, 518 U.S. 668 (1996); *O'Hare Truck Service v. Northlake*, 518 U.S. 712 (1996).

If Roth's claim is at least colorable, why is the First Amendment right he asserts not a liberty interest that can support a procedural claim for a due process hearing? Would an administrative hearing on his non-renewal have served any value, given the availability of a judicial forum in which to test Roth's claim?

3. *"Property" and Statutory Construction. Roth* and *Perry* insist that "property" is entirely the creation of a state's legal regime. They instruct courts to examine the terms of statutes and other regulatory instruments to determine whether the substantive discretion of government decision makers has been limited. If a statute expressly confines an administrator by establishing criteria for decision, could the legislature, perhaps through

legislative history, still nullify the inference that it created "property?" Could it do so by specifying in the statute itself: "Nothing in the preceding section is intended to create a property interest under the Fourteenth Amendment?"

The preceding question is, of course, not purely hypothetical. We earlier noted the "no entitlement" language in PRWORA, and certain state and local statutes have taken a similar approach. Courts that have considered the effects of this language have not been willing to view it as determinative. Indeed, they have been skeptical that such disclaimers should have any independent weight.

In *Washington Legal Clinic for the Homeless v. Barry*, 107 F.3rd 32 (D.C.Cir.1997), plaintiffs alleged that the District of Columbia's documentation policies for verifying eligibility for emergency shelter assistance violated the Due Process Clause. The District of Columbia Circuit dismissed the city's argument that the question was answered by the D.C. Code section which stated expressly that nothing in the code created an entitlement to shelter. In its view the question under *Roth* was whether statutes or regulations limited official discretion by explicit, mandatory language. But, the appeals court's dismissal of the city code's "no entitlement" language is arguably pure dictum. Applying the *Roth* standard, the court could find no mandatory, discretion confining language in the applicable laws concerning the allocation of the District's limited temporary shelter space.

The Colorado Court of Appeals addressed the property issue in the PRWORA context in *Weston v. Cassata*, 37 P. 3rd 469 (Colo.Ct.App.2001). *Weston* involved a class action challenge by welfare recipients to sanction notices issued to them by the Adams County Welfare authorities. The complaint alleged that these notices contained inadequate or inaccurate information about the sanction and appeals process and consequently violated the recipients' due process rights. The county countered by urging that welfare recipients had no property interests in the continued receipt of welfare for purposes of the Due Process Clause. The argument relied not only on the provisions of PRWORA, but also on a similar section in the Colorado Works Program Act. Section 26–2–704(1), C.R.S. (2000).

Reading the statute as a whole, the Colorado Court of Appeals rejected the county's defense. The court noted that, not only did the Colorado statute provide that "a participant shall receive a basic assistance grant," it also protected those rights by mandating that "a participant shall continue to receive a basic cash assistance grant during pendency of an appeal," and "an applicant is entitled to receive prior written notice of any agency action affecting his/her eligibility." The court concluded from these provisions that, if a participant met the criteria set forth by the statutes, there was no discretion to deny welfare benefits.

The Colorado Court of Appeals interpreted the federal statute's "no entitlement" language as speaking to the availability of block grants to the states. Those grants are always conditional upon the availability of federal funds. To the extent that PRWORA was meant to say anything about individual entitlements, the court read it as merely eliminating any notion that there was some unconditional entitlement to welfare benefits which might have been thought to have existed under the prior AFDC program.

Relying on PRWORA's demand that states implementing TANF programs set forth "objective criteria for the delivery of benefits and the determination of eligibility and for fair and equitable treatment," the Colorado Court of Appeals concluded that "despite the forcefulness and apparent specificity of the 'no entitlement' language, the construction of the remainder of the welfare statutory scheme illustrates that the federal government did not, and constitutionally could not, eliminate all forms of entitlement to welfare benefits."

The *Weston* court cited and explicitly adopted Professor Cynthia Farina's analysis in *On Misusing "Revolution" and "Reform": Procedural Due Process in the New Welfare Act*, 50 Admin. L. Rev. 591 (1998). There Professor Farina distinguishes between three types of entitlements: The *King v. Smith* (392 U.S. 309 (1968)) entitlement (discussed *infra* at Chapter 9), which "provides a right of action for welfare recipients to enforce against the states the beneficiary-favoring conditions of the Social Security Act;" a Reichian entitlement of the sort elaborated in Charles Reich's famous "New Property" article, "a very robust conception with substantive as well as procedural dimensions, which has never been more than an unrealized ideal;" and the *Roth* entitlement which "defines the new property as the presence of discretion constraining regulatory standards and then constitutionalizes the procedure by which procedures applying those standards are made." In Farina's view, and that of the Colorado Court of Appeals, the legislature has control over whether or not to provide mandatory, discretion-constraining standards. But "the question of whether a statute, once enacted, has created a constitutionally protected interest is surely for the judiciary."

4. *Procedural Indicia of Property*. A legislature that empowers an adjudicator to act through summary procedure might well be construed as intending not to create a protected interest, regardless of the substantive criteria for decision. Authorizing decisions to be made without any formal process is, after all, one way of articulating the breadth of an administrator's discretion. Conversely, a statutory prescription of formal decision making procedure might suggest an intention to create a protected interest.

In *Arnett v. Kennedy*, 416 U.S. 134 (1974), the Supreme Court attempted to address the interrelationship of substantive and procedural rights in divining the existence and scope of property interests.

Kennedy had been removed from his federal employment at the Office of Economic Opportunity's Chicago Regional Office by his supervisor, Mr. Verduin, for possibly alleging that Verduin had made an offer of a $100,000 community action grant as a "bribe" to a local community action representative. As a non-probationary civil servant protected by the Lloyd–LaFollette Act, Kennedy could only be removed for "such cause as will promote the efficiency of the service." That same statute provided only an informal appeal to the employer's supervisor prior to taking any "adverse action," but it assured a formal post-removal hearing before either the employing agency or the Civil Service Commission. Kennedy challenged the limited pre-removal procedures as a denial of due process. In denying that claim Justice Rehnquist had this to say about that interrelationship of Kennedy's substantive and procedural rights:

> * * * [T]he very section of the statute which granted him that right * * * expressly provided also for the procedure by which "cause" was to be determined, and expressly omitted the procedural guarantees which appellee insists are mandated by the Constitution. Only by bifurcating the very sentence of the Act of Congress which conferred upon appellee the right not to be removed save for cause could it be said that he had an expectancy of that substantive right without the procedural limitations which Congress attached to it. * * * Congress was obviously intent on according a measure of statutory job security to governmental employees which they had not previously enjoyed, but was likewise intent on excluding more elaborate procedural requirements which it felt would make the operation of the new scheme unnecessarily burdensome in practice. Where the focus of legislation was this strongly on the procedural mechanism for enforcing the substantive right which was simultaneously conferred, we decline to conclude that the substantive right may be viewed wholly apart from the procedure provided for its enforcement. The employee's statutorily defined right is not a guarantee against removal without cause in the abstract, but such a guarantee as enforced by the procedures which Congress has designated for the determination of cause. * * *

Rehnquist's opinion went on to remind Kennedy that he had to "take the [statutory] bitter with the sweet."

Though Justice Powell and Justice Blackmun concurred in the result, they objected strongly to the plurality's analysis, as did the four dissenters. In Powell's words:

> The plurality opinion evidently reasons that the nature of appellee's interest in continued federal employment is necessarily defined and limited by the statutory procedures for discharge and that the constitutional guarantee of procedural due process accords to appellee no procedural protections against arbitrary or erroneous discharge other than those expressly provided in the statute. * * * This view misconceives the origin of the right to procedural due process. That right is conferred not by legislative grace, but by constitutional guarantee. While the legislature may elect not to confer a property interest in federal employment, it may not constitutionally authorize the deprivation of such an interest, once conferred, without appropriate procedural safeguards. * * *

While Justice Rehnquist's "bittersweet" theory never garnered the votes of five Justices, it was nevertheless influential in the courts of appeals, which led to the following ruling:

CLEVELAND BD. OF EDUCATION v. LOUDERMILL

Supreme Court of the United States, 1985.
470 U.S. 532, 105 S.Ct. 1487, 84 L.Ed.2d 494.

JUSTICE WHITE delivered the opinion of the Court.

In these cases we consider what pretermination process must be accorded a public employee who can be discharged only for cause.

I

In 1979 the Cleveland Board of Education. * * * hired respondent James Loudermill as a security guard. On his job application, Loudermill stated that he had never been convicted of a felony. Eleven months later, as part of a routine examination of his employment records, the Board discovered that in fact Loudermill had been convicted of grand larceny in 1968. By letter dated November 3, 1980, the Board's Business Manager informed Loudermill that he had been dismissed because of his dishonesty in filling out the employment application. Loudermill was not afforded an opportunity to respond to the charge of dishonesty or to challenge his dismissal. On November 13, the Board adopted a resolution officially approving the discharge.

Under Ohio law, Loudermill was a "classified civil servant." Ohio Rev. Code Ann. § 124.11 (1984). Such employees can be terminated only for cause, and may obtain administrative review if discharged. § 124.34 (1984). Pursuant to this provision, Loudermill filed an appeal with the Cleveland Civil Service Commission on November 12. * * * On July 20, 1981, the full Commission heard argument and orally announced that it would uphold the dismissal. * * *

Although the Commission's decision was subject to judicial review in the state courts, Loudermill instead brought the present suit in the Federal District Court for the Northern District of Ohio. The complaint alleged that § 124.34 was unconstitutional on its face because it did not provide the employee an opportunity to respond to the charges against him prior to removal. As a result, discharged employees were deprived of liberty and property without due process. * * *

Before a responsive pleading was filed, the District Court dismissed for failure to state a claim on which relief could be granted. See Fed.Rule Civ.Proc. 12(b)(6). It held that because the very statute that created the property right in continued employment also specified the procedures for discharge, and because those procedures were followed, Loudermill was, by definition, afforded all the process due. The post-termination hearing also adequately protected Loudermill's liberty interests. * * *

The other case before us arises on similar facts and followed a similar course. Respondent Richard Donnelly was a bus mechanic for the Parma Board of Education. In August 1977, Donnelly was fired because he had failed an eye examination. He was offered a chance to retake the examination but did not do so. Like Loudermill, Donnelly appealed to the Civil Service Commission. After a year of wrangling about the timeliness of his appeal, the Commission heard the case. It ordered Donnelly reinstated, though without backpay. In a complaint essentially identical to Loudermill's, Donnelly challenged the constitutionality of the dismissal procedures. The District Court dismissed for failure to state a claim, relying on its opinion in Loudermill.

* * * A divided panel of the Court of Appeals for the Sixth Circuit reversed in part and remanded. 721 F.2d 550 (1983). * * * [T]he Court of Appeals found that both respondents had been deprived of due

process. It disagreed with the District Court's original rationale. Instead, it concluded that the compelling private interest in retaining employment, combined with the value of presenting evidence prior to dismissal, outweighed the added administrative burden of a pretermination hearing. * * *

II

Respondents' federal constitutional claim depends on their having had a property right in continued employment. If they did, the State could not deprive them of this property without due process. * * *

The Ohio statute plainly creates such an interest. Respondents were "classified civil service employees," Ohio Rev.Code Ann. § 124.11 (1984), entitled to retain their positions "during good behavior and efficient service," who could not be dismissed "except * * * for * * * misfeasance, malfeasance, or nonfeasance in office," * * *.

* * * The Ohio statute plainly supports the conclusion, reached by both lower courts, that respondents possessed property rights in continued employment. Indeed, this question does not seem to have been disputed below.

The Parma Board argues, however, that the property right is defined by, and conditioned on, the legislature's choice of procedures for its deprivation. The Board stresses that in addition to specifying the grounds for termination, the statute sets out procedures by which termination may take place.[6] The procedures were adhered to in these cases. According to petitioner, "[t]o require additional procedures would in effect expand the scope of the property interest itself."

This argument, which was accepted by the District Court, has its genesis in the plurality opinion in *Arnett v. Kennedy*, 416 U.S. 134 (1974). * * *

This view garnered three votes in *Arnett*, but was specifically rejected by the other six Justices. Since then, this theory has at times seemed to gather some additional support. See *Bishop v. Wood*, 426 U.S. 341 (1976) (White, J., dissenting); *Goss v. Lopez*, 419 U.S., at 586–587 (Powell, J., joined by Burger, C.J., and Blackmun and Rehnquist, JJ., dissenting). More recently, however, the Court has clearly rejected it. In *Vitek v. Jones*, 445 U.S. 480 (1980), we pointed out that "minimum [procedural] requirements [are] a matter of federal law, they are not diminished by the fact that the State may have specified its own

6. After providing for dismissal only for cause, § 124.34 states that the dismissed employee is to be provided with a copy of the order of removal giving the reasons therefor. Within 10 days of the filing of the order with the Director of Administrative Services, the employee may file a written appeal with the State Personnel Board of Review or the Commission. "In the event such an appeal is filed, the board or commission shall forthwith notify the appointing authority and shall hear, or appoint a trial board to hear, such appeal within thirty days from and after its filing with the board or commission, and it may affirm, disaffirm, or modify the judgment of the appointing authority." Either side may obtain review of the Commission's decision in the State Court of Common Pleas.

procedures that it may deem adequate for determining the preconditions to adverse official action." This conclusion was reiterated in *Logan v. Zimmerman Brush Co.*, 455 U.S. 422 (1982), where we reversed the lower court's holding that because the entitlement arose from a state statute, the legislature had the prerogative to define the procedures to be followed to protect that entitlement.

In light of these holdings, it is settled that the "bitter with the sweet" approach misconceives the constitutional guarantee. If a clearer holding is needed, we provide it today. The point is straightforward: the Due Process Clause provides that certain substantive rights—life, liberty, and property—cannot be deprived except pursuant to constitutionally adequate procedures. The categories of substance and procedure are distinct. Were the rule otherwise, the Clause would be reduced to a mere tautology. "Property" cannot be defined by the procedures provided for its deprivation any more than can life or liberty. The right to due process "is conferred, not by legislative grace, but by constitutional guarantee. While the legislature may elect not to confer a property interest in [public] employment, it may not constitutionally authorize the deprivation of such an interest, once conferred, without appropriate procedural safeguards."

In short, once it is determined that the Due Process Clause applies, "the question remains what process is due." The answer to that question is not to be found in the Ohio statute.

III

An essential principle of due process is that a deprivation of life, liberty, or property "be preceded by notice and opportunity for hearing appropriate to the nature of the case." *Mullane v. Central Hanover Bank & Trust Co.*, 339 U.S. 306 (1950).[7] * * * This principle requires "some kind of a hearing" prior to the discharge of an employee who has a constitutionally protected property interest in his employment. * * * Even decisions finding no constitutional violation in termination procedures have relied on the existence of some pretermination opportunity to respond. For example, in *Arnett* six Justices found constitutional minima satisfied where the employee had access to the material upon which the charge was based and could respond orally and in writing and present rebuttal affidavits. * * *

The need for some form of pretermination hearing, recognized in these cases, is evident from a balancing of the competing interests at stake. These are the private interests in retaining employment, the governmental interest in the expeditious removal of unsatisfactory employees and the avoidance of administrative burdens, and the risk of an erroneous termination. See *Mathews v. Eldridge*, 424 U.S. 319 (1976).

7. There are, of course, some situations in which a post-deprivation hearing will satisfy due process requirements. See *Ewing v. Mytinger & Casselberry, Inc.*, 339 U.S. 594 (1950).

First, the significance of the private interest in retaining employment cannot be gainsaid. We have frequently recognized the severity of depriving a person of the means of livelihood. While a fired worker may find employment elsewhere, doing so will take some time and is likely to be burdened by the questionable circumstances under which he left his previous job.

Second, some opportunity for the employee to present his side of the case is recurringly of obvious value in reaching an accurate decision. Dismissals for cause will often involve factual disputes. Even where the facts are clear, the appropriateness or necessity of the discharge may not be; in such cases, the only meaningful opportunity to invoke the discretion of the decisionmaker is likely to be before the termination takes effect.

The cases before us illustrate these considerations. Both respondents had plausible arguments to make that might have prevented their discharge. The fact that the Commission saw fit to reinstate Donnelly suggests that an error might have been avoided had he been provided an opportunity to make his case to the Board. As for Loudermill, given the Commission's ruling we cannot say that the discharge was mistaken. Nonetheless, in light of the referee's recommendation, neither can we say that a fully informed decisionmaker might not have exercised its discretion and decided not to dismiss him, notwithstanding its authority to do so. In any event, the termination involved arguable issues,[9] and the right to a hearing does not depend on a demonstration of certain success.

The governmental interest in immediate termination does not outweigh these interests. As we shall explain, affording the employee an opportunity to respond prior to termination would impose neither a significant administrative burden nor intolerable delays. Furthermore, the employer shares the employee's interest in avoiding disruption and erroneous decisions; and until the matter is settled, the employer would continue to receive the benefit of the employee's labors. It is preferable to keep a qualified employee on than to train a new one. A governmental employer also has an interest in keeping citizens usefully employed rather than taking the possibly erroneous and counter-productive step of forcing its employees onto the welfare rolls. Finally, in those situations where the employer perceives a significant hazard in keeping the employee on the job, it can avoid the problem by suspending with pay.

IV

The foregoing considerations indicate that the pretermination "hearing," though necessary, need not be elaborate. We have pointed out that "[t]he formality and procedural requisites for the hearing can vary, depending upon the importance of the interests involved and the nature

9. Loudermill's dismissal turned not on the objective fact that he was an ex-felon or the inaccuracy of his statement to the contrary, but on the subjective question whether he had lied on his application form. His explanation for the false statement is plausible in light of the fact that he received only a suspended 6–month sentence and a fine on the grand larceny conviction.

of the subsequent proceedings." *Boddie v. Connecticut*, 401 U.S., 371, 378 (1971). In general, "something less" than a full evidentiary hearing is sufficient prior to adverse administrative action. Under state law, respondents were later entitled to a full administrative hearing and judicial review. The only question is what steps were required before the termination took effect.

In only one case, *Goldberg v. Kelly*, has the Court required a full adversarial evidentiary hearing prior to adverse governmental action. However, as the *Goldberg* Court itself pointed out, that case presented significantly different considerations than are present in the context of public employment. Here, the pretermination hearing need not definitively resolve the propriety of the discharge. It should be an initial check against mistaken decisions—essentially, a determination of whether there are reasonable grounds to believe that the charges against the employee are true and support the proposed action.

The essential requirements of due process, and all that respondents seek or the Court of Appeals required, are notice and an opportunity to respond. The opportunity to present reasons, either in person or in writing, why proposed action should not be taken is a fundamental due process requirement. See Friendly, *Some Kind of Hearing*, 123 U.Pa. L. Rev. 1267, 1281 (1975). The tenured public employee is entitled to oral or written notice of the charges against him, an explanation of the employer's evidence, and an opportunity to present his side of the story. To require more than this prior to termination would intrude to an unwarranted extent on the government's interest in quickly removing an unsatisfactory employee.

V

Our holding rests in part on the provisions in Ohio law for a full post-termination hearing. In his cross-petition Loudermill asserts, as a separate constitutional violation, that his administrative proceedings took too long. The Court of Appeals held otherwise, and we agree.[11] A 9–month adjudication is not, of course, unconstitutionally lengthy *per se*. Yet Loudermill offers no indication that his wait was unreasonably prolonged other than the fact that it took nine months. The chronology of the proceedings set out in the complaint, coupled with the assertion that nine months is too long to wait, does not state a claim of a constitutional deprivation.

VI

We conclude that all the process that is due is provided by a pretermination opportunity to respond, coupled with post-termination administrative procedures as provided by the Ohio statute. Because respondents allege in their complaints that they had no chance to

11. It might be argued that once we find a due process violation in the denial of a pretermination hearing we need not and should not consider whether the post-termination procedures were adequate. * * *

respond, the District Court erred in dismissing for failure to state a claim. * * *

[Justice Marshall concurred specially to emphasize his view that the limited hearing right provided by the majority was a function of the claims presented by the parties before the Court. They had been given all they asked for, but in Marshall's opinion were also entitled to confront and advise cross-examination witnesses and to present supporting witnesses.

Justice Brennan agreed with Marshall that further process would be required where an employee's removal rested on contested issues of fact, and he interpreted the majority opinion as not deciding that question. Brennan then dissented from the "undue delay" portion of the Court's opinion because, in his view, the record was inadequate to permit "the careful multifaceted analysis of the facts we consistently have employed in the past."]

JUSTICE REHNQUIST, dissenting.

In *Arnett v. Kennedy*, six Members of this Court agreed that a public employee could be dismissed for misconduct without a full hearing prior to termination. A plurality of Justices agreed that the employee was entitled to exactly what Congress gave him, and no more. * * *

* * * In these cases, the relevant Ohio statute provides in its first paragraph that

> "[t]he tenure of every officer or employee in the classified service of the state and the counties, civil service townships, cities, city health districts, general health districts, and city school districts thereof, holding a position under this chapter of the Revised Code, shall be during good behavior and efficient service and no such officer or employee shall be reduced in pay or position, suspended, or removed, except * * * for incompetency, inefficiency, dishonesty, drunkenness, immoral conduct, insubordination, discourteous treatment of the public, neglect of duty, violation of such sections or the rules of the director of administrative services or the commission, or any other failure of good behavior, or any other acts of misfeasance, malfeasance, or nonfeasance in office." Ohio Rev. Code Ann. § 124.34 (1984).

The very next paragraph of this section of the Ohio Revised Code provides that in the event of suspension of more than three days or removal the appointing authority shall furnish the employee with the stated reasons for his removal. The next paragraph provides that within 10 days following the receipt of such a statement, the employee may appeal in writing to the State Personnel Board of Review or the Commission, such appeal shall be heard within 30 days from the time of its filing, and the Board may affirm, disaffirm, or modify the judgment of the appointing authority.

Thus in one legislative breath Ohio has conferred upon civil service employees such as respondents in these cases a limited form of tenure during good behavior, and prescribed the procedures by which that tenure may be terminated. * * *

We ought to recognize the totality of the State's definition of the property right in question, and not merely seize upon one of several paragraphs in a unitary statute to proclaim that in that paragraph the State has inexorably conferred upon a civil service employee something which it is powerless under the United States Constitution to qualify in the next paragraph of the statute. This practice ignores our duty under *Roth* to rely on state law as the source of property interests for purposes of applying the Due Process Clause of the Fourteenth Amendment. While it does not impose a federal definition of property, the Court departs from the full breadth of the holding in *Roth* by its selective choice from among the sentences the Ohio Legislature chooses to use in establishing and qualifying a right.

Having concluded by this somewhat tortured reasoning that Ohio has created a property right in the respondents in these cases, the Court naturally proceeds to inquire what process is "due" before the respondents may be divested of that right. This customary "balancing" inquiry conducted by the Court in these cases reaches a result that is quite unobjectionable, but it seems to me that it is devoid of any principles which will either instruct or endure. The balance is simply an ad hoc weighing which depends to a great extent upon how the Court subjectively views the underlying interests at stake. * * * The lack of any principled standards in this area means that these procedural due process cases will recur time and again. Every different set of facts will present a new issue on what process was due and when. One way to avoid this subjective and varying interpretation of the Due Process Clause in cases such as these is to hold that one who avails himself of government entitlements accepts the grant of tenure along with its inherent limitations. * * *

Notes

1. *Can Procedure and Substance Be Separated?* The *Loudermill* majority restates the general rubric of *Board of Regents v. Roth*—"[P]roperty interests are not created by the Constitution, 'they are created and their dimensions are defined by existing rules or understandings that stem from an independent source such as state law. * * * ' " The Court then finds that the procedural dimensions of the right to discharge only for cause under the Ohio statute are defined, not by state law, but by the Court's view of the requirements of constitutional procedural due process.

Do you agree with Justice Rehnquist, in dissent, when he says that the Court has taken back with one hand what it gave with the other? The Court seems to be reading state statutes as if they establish rights that have independent content quite apart from the procedural safeguards that accompany their deprivation. Rehnquist claims, at least implicitly, that the latter would make sense only if those "rights" acquired, by their simple statement in state law, a constitutional substance independent of their definition under state law. But if that were true, then the constitutional definition of the right would be different from the state positive law definition of the right. And that is precisely what the Court denies.

To appreciate the difficulty of the distinction that the Court is trying to draw between substantive and procedural rights, consider a hypothetical Ohio statute designed to respond to the *Loudermill* case itself. As a substitute for Ohio Revised Code Annotated § 124.34, the statute might read simply: "A discharged civil service employee has a right to appeal his or her dismissal and to reinstatement unless the state employer demonstrates that the discharge was effected for good cause." Here the right itself is stated in procedural terms, but its contours are precisely the same as those of the statute that was at issue in *Loudermill*.

What should a court confronted with such a statute do? It could of course interpret it as providing, first, a substantive right—discharge only for cause—with, second, a right of an appeal as a procedural protection for that substantive right. If a court should interpret the statute in this bifurcated fashion, however, it will hardly have been faithful to the intentions of the Ohio legislature. In this context, belief in the *Roth* proposition that substantive rights are the creation of state law rather than federal constitutional law is stretched very thin. Yet, if the court interprets the statute as creating a procedural right only, thus apparently not activating the further protections of the Due Process Clause that *Loudermill* finds essential, it will have made the procedural protections of the Due Process Clause turn entirely on the formal, and possibly calculated, language of the state statute that is being tested. And that, of course, is the same as saying that the plaintiff's right to constitutional due process is defined by state law—a statement that the *Loudermill* majority takes special pains to reject, but that seems to be borne out by many lower court cases. See, e.g., *Fried v. Hinson*, 78 F.3d 688 (D.C.Cir.1996) (no property interest in license renewal because statute allowed non-renewal for any reason); *Miller v. Crystal Lake Park Dist.*, 47 F.3d 865 (7th Cir.1995) ("just cause" provision in personnel handbook provides no property interest where handbook disclaims that it is "contractual").

Commenting on this dilemma in *Dignitary Process: A Political Psychology of Liberal Democratic Citizenship*, 39 U.Fla. L. Rev. 433, 436–438 (1987), Professor Mashaw argues:

> If it can be assumed * * * that the Court means what it says in *Loudermill*, when reaffirming *Roth*, the maintenance of state discretion to define positive law rights becomes a mere formality. It is a function of the way state statutes are drafted. Recognizing this, *Loudermill* will ultimately lend no more assistance to lower courts than has the Court's prior jurisprudence. Formal distinctions are notoriously unstable. As lower courts struggle with meaningless distinctions between procedure and substance, form and result, they inevitably will produce a perplexing and inconsistent jurisprudence. The Supreme Court's attempt at clarity in *Loudermill* [seems] doomed to failure * * *.
>
> The problems with the *Loudermill–Roth* position are deeper yet. This positivist approach to defining interests cognizable under the Due Process Clause produces bizarre constitutional valuations of claims. A

prisoner's hobby kit, for example, is "property," raising due process concern,[12] while a patient's removal from a nursing home, with its risks of physical and mental decline, does not rise to the level of constitutional notice.[13] Having one's picture circulated to local merchants as an active shoplifter by the police department infringes no property or liberty interest,[14] but failure to inform a ratepayer of the municipal utility company's procedures for pre-termination review of disputed bills invades the ratepayer's property interests.[15] * * *

Finally, this focus on positive law triggers for due process concern leads to more than jurisprudential incoherence and bizarre assignments of constitutional value to citizens' interests. Such an approach is functionally inadequate to ... the problems of governmental or bureaucratic discretion that the Due Process Clause was meant to address. The positive law trigger approach gives legal protection, or at least due process attention, where some legal protection already exists, while excluding due process concern where a legal regime seems to permit official arbitrariness. Although many have a taste for irony, few would choose Kafka or Ionesco as constitutional draftsmen.

Consider, for example, the situation in *Holmes v. New York City Housing Authority*.[16] There, a public housing agency had no established standards for processing non-preference applications for public housing. The Second Circuit Court of Appeals, relying on *Hornsby v. Allen*,[18] held that this violated due process. In *Hornsby*, a local liquor commission was ordered to grant all applications for liquor licenses until it established standards on which to base denial. Both *Holmes* and *Hornsby* are widely cited for the proposition that unconstrained administrative discretion violates due process. Both cases seem correctly decided. Protection against Kafkaesque, unlimited discretion of officials is the underlying goal of the Due Process Clause.

Despite their widespread citation, *Holmes* and *Hornsby* are virtually moribund authorities. A few liquor licensing decisions in the Fifth Circuit have followed *Hornsby*,[21] and *Holmes* has found application in a small number of cases dealing with other forms of welfare benefits.[22] The reason for the limited effect of these cases is easily discernable. Where no standards exist for the exercise of administrative discretion, even broad and loose ones such as the "cause" standard in *Loudermill*, positive law grants no substantive "rights." If there is no right, there is no life, liberty, or property interest that would trigger the Due Process Clause. The Supreme Court, indeed, has made this position clear. In *Leis v. Flynt*[, 439 U.S. 438 (1979),] the Court reversed a lower court decision ordering the promulgation of standards, because the need for

12. *Parratt v. Taylor,* 451 U.S. 527 (1981).

13. *O'Bannon v. Town Court Nursing Center*, 447 U.S. 773 (1980).

14. *Paul v. Davis,* 424 U.S. 693 (1976).

15. *Memphis Light, Gas and Water Division v. Craft*, 436 U.S. 1 (1978).

16. 398 F.2d 262 (2d Cir.1968).

18. 326 F.2d 605 (5th Cir.1964).

21. See *Block v. Thompson*, 472 F.2d 587 (5th Cir.1973); *Atlanta Bowling Center v. Allen*, 389 F.2d 713 (5th Cir.1968); *Johnson v. Brown*, 584 F.Supp. 510 (M.D.Ga. 1984).

22. See, e.g., *Carey v. Quern*, 588 F.2d 230, 232 (7th Cir.1978).

standards indicated a lack of entitlement. In short, the Court's entitlement analysis, grounded in positive law prescriptions, causes due process protection to drop out of the Constitution when needed most. Discretion bounded by standards requires due process; but absolute discretion—discretion carrying the greatest danger of political oppression—escapes constitutional notice under the current analysis.

Independently considered, these three objections to the positive law trigger requirement are serious. Collectively, they make an overwhelming case for abandonment.

2. *Uncoupling Liberty Interests From State Law: Prison Cases*. There is some evidence that the Supreme Court has begun to rethink its strong delegation of rights creation to state law. In *Sandin v. Conner*, 515 U.S. 472 (1995), a five member-majority held that a prisoner was not deprived of a liberty interest when subjected to 30 days of solitary confinement on the basis of a determination that he had engaged in "high misconduct." In so doing, the majority abandoned the methodology of a substantial line of cases in which the Court had held that virtually any interest governed by established prison rules created a "protected liberty interest" for purposes of the application of the Due Process Clause. Concluding that those decisions had both enabled prisoners to convert thousands of trivial disputes into constitutional cases and had discouraged prison officials from issuing rules applicable to many aspects of prison life, the *Sandin* majority enunciated a new standard for the determination of liberty interests. Hereafter a prisoner would be considered to be deprived of such an interest only where prison authorities impose "atypical and significant hardship on the inmate in relation to the normal incidents of prison life."

This new standard for the recognition of protected liberty interests in prison cases is clearly not one created by state law. It is an interpretation of the meaning of "liberty" in the Fourteenth Amendment or an aspect of constitutional common law, which may be much the same thing. Moreover, the emphasis on the significance of the interest invaded harks back to notions of "fundamental fairness" that have been a significant aspect of criminal due process at least since *Hurtado v. California*, 110 U.S. 516 (1884). The *Sandin* approach thus threatens to lead the Court into a controversial evaluation of the importance of human interests and the procedural requisites for their protection, unaided by the dictates of positive law. For all its faults, the positivist approach at least avoided that horn of the judicial dilemma.

For additional discussion of this quandary, see Jerry L. Mashaw, *Administrative Due Process: The Quest for a Dignitary Theory*, 61 B.U.L.Rev. 885 (1981); Frank Michelman, *Formal and Associational Aims in Procedural Due Process*, *in* DUE PROCESS: NOMOS XVIII 126 (J.R. Pennock & J. Chapman, eds. 1977); Henry P. Monaghan, *Of "Liberty" and "Property"*, 62 Corn. L.Rev. 405 (1977); Mark Tushnet, *The Newer Property: Suggestion for the Revival of Substantive Due Process*, 1975 Sup.Ct.Rev. 261; William Van Alstyne, *Cracks in "The New Property": Adjudicative Due Process in the Administrative State*, 62 Corn. L.Rev. 445 (1977).

3. *Timing Again*. Although the Court was motivated to hear *Loudermill* by the opportunity it presented to deal with the *Arnett* issue, its decision

also addresses the "second step" of the due process analysis: what process is due? In particular, the majority reiterates the presumption that some hearing should occur prior to the government's deprivation of one's life, liberty, or property. The Court indicates, however, that the formality required for the pre-deprivation hearing will depend on the promptness and fullness of any post-deprivation hearing that may be available to the claimant.

The Court has repeatedly held that in an emergency, deprivations of constitutionally protected interests may occur without any pre-deprivation hearing. For example, *North American Cold Storage Co. v. Chicago*, 211 U.S. 306 (1908), upheld the seizure of unsafe food without a prior hearing on a rationale of exigent circumstances. Cf. *Goss v. Lopez*, 419 U.S. 565 (1975) (approving in dicta the summary disciplinary suspension of public school students where an immediate threat to safety is presented). "Emergencies" sufficient to justify summary procedures need not be as pressing as *North American* suggests, however, to satisfy the Court. In *Bowles v. Willingham*, 321 U.S. 503 (1944), the Court upheld the Office of Price Administration's power to fix rents without prior hearings because of exigent wartime circumstances and the extraordinary burden that would be posed by prior hearings. See also *Mackey v. Montrym*, 443 U.S. 1 (1979) (upholding the summary 90–day suspension of a driver's license of any person refusing to take a breath analysis test); *Ewing v. Mytinger & Casselberry, Inc.*, 339 U.S. 594 (1950) (upholding summary seizures of apparently misbranded, but otherwise harmless drugs).

Moreover, the Supreme Court has retrenched on *Loudermill's* apparent requirement that a government employer not suspend an employee without pay without providing some sort of pre-suspension hearing. Reversing a circuit court decision that enunciated precisely that rule, the Court in *Gilbert v. Homar*, 520 U.S. 924 (1997), reemphasized the flexibility of due process analysis and the necessity of weighing governmental interests against the risk of baseless or unwarranted actions when assessing the necessity for a pre-termination hearing of any sort.

Gilbert v. Homar involved the suspension without pay of a university police officer who had been arrested and charged with a felony. In rejecting the necessity for a pre-suspension hearing, the Supreme Court distinguished *Loudermill* both on the basis of the severity of the effect on the employee (Loudermill had been terminated, not suspended) and the importance of the state interest in *Homar* (maintaining public confidence in the university police force). The Court also noted that the purpose of a pre-suspension hearing—to determine whether there were reasonable grounds to believe charges against the employee—had been satisfied by the arrest and filing of charges. The Court recognized that an arrest and a charge were not as persuasive as a grand jury indictment, such as the one that had justified the avoidance of pre-suspension proceedings in *FDIC v. Mallen*, 486 U.S. 230 (1988). Nevertheless, it concluded that arrest and formal charge by an independent party provided assurance that the suspension was not arbitrary.

In addition, the *Homar* court rejected the argument that the employee was entitled to a pre-suspension hearing in order to have an opportunity to persuade the university of his innocence, or at least to exercise its discretion not to suspend him without pay. Here again the distinction turned on the difference between suspension and termination. For, although *Loudermill* recognized that in a termination situation the only meaningful opportunity to invoke the decisionmaker's discretion was likely to be before termination took effect, in a suspension case there is opportunity to invoke that discretion later before ultimate disposition of case.

American Manufacturers Mutual Insurance Company v. Sullivan, 526 U.S. 40 (1999), puts an entirely different spin on the timing question by merging it with the question of whether the complaining parties have a property interest. *Sullivan* involved a suit by workers covered under the Pennsylvania worker's compensation system. Pennsylvania statutes permit worker's compensation insurers to withhold payment for disputed medical treatments pending an independent "utilization review" conducted by a state agency. Utilization review seeks to determine whether the medical treatments for which compensation is sought are "reasonable and necessary" within the terms of the worker's compensation policy.

The complaining parties urged that the Pennsylvania procedures violated due process because beneficiaries had no right to submit any information prior to the utilization review decision concerning the reasonableness or necessity for the medical treatments that they had received. Although they were entitled to a post-determination process to contest the utilization review decision, respondents argued that this was insufficient to protect their interest in prompt payment of their medical claims.

The Third Circuit Court of Appeals agreed and the petitioners sought Supreme Court review. However, rather than formulating the issue as one of the adequacy of a post-deprivation hearing to protect the respondent's interests, petitioners claimed that the respondents had no property interest in medical payments under the worker's compensation statute until a determination had been made that the medical treatments received were in fact reasonable and necessary. In a confusing and fractured opinion the Supreme Court reversed. The Court, or most of its members, seem to have viewed the respondents as asserting an essentially substantive due process claim—that they were entitled as a matter of federal constitutional law to medical payments under the Pennsylvania statute with no determination of whether they were reasonable or necessary. Construing the Pennsylvania law, the Court held that there was no property interest in unreasonable or unnecessary medical treatment and, therefore, to the extent that the claimants had a property interest at all, it would arise only after a favorable utilization review determination. But, of course, if that were true, it would seem to follow that a negative decision by the utilization review agency would cut off their property rights and make it unnecessary for the State of Pennsylvania to provide any proceeding by which to contest the determination after the fact.

Only Justice Stevens seemed to perceive that this construction of the Pennsylvania statutes would produce an extremely peculiar worker's compensation law. Workers would have bargained away their tort recoveries against employers for the promise of payment of their medical expenses (and other compensable items) only if the insurer voluntarily decided that it should pay. Justice Stevens concurred separately on the ground that changes in the Pennsylvania procedures, made subsequent to the Third Circuit's opinion and providing some opportunity for claimants to submit information to the utilization review agency, justified the delay of a full hearing on the matter to a latter time.

c. *Contextual Coherence in the Analysis of Entitlements?*

The difficulty of discovering underlying principles in the Court's "liberty" and "property" jurisprudence may tempt readers to abandon the search for coherence in due process law prematurely. The decisions may seem more coherent, or at least more explicable, if the cases are grouped to emphasize the kinds of programs or interests involved, or to highlight other important institutional concerns that may influence judgment notwithstanding their technical irrelevance to the Court's announced due process calculus. When one notices, for example, that, jurisprudential difficulties aside, the Court consistently treats licenses as protected property, a contextual approach to modern due process cases seems inviting. See, e.g., *Bell v. Burson*, 402 U.S. 535 (1971) (driver's license); *Gibson v. Berryhill*, 411 U.S. 564 (1973) (optometrist's license); *Barry v. Barchi*, 443 U.S. 55 (1979) (horse trainer's license).

The Court's due process decisions also resonate with some fairly consistent themes in cases involving public schooling. The Court's rulings have been generous in recognizing protected interests, while, at the same time, displaying considerable deference to educational administrators' choice of decision making procedures. This deference is undergirded both by the Court's apparent faith in the expertise of educators and by its desire to preserve what it takes to be the properly nonadversarial environment of educational institutions.

A leading example is *Goss v. Lopez*, 419 U.S. 565 (1975), in which several high school students successfully claimed that they had a protected property interest in avoiding even a 10–day or less suspension. Because this interest was more than *de minimis*, the Court agreed the students were entitled to a "hearing." It then reasoned that the nature of the hearing could reflect not only the modest sanction threatened, but also the essentially non-adversarial and communal nature of the educational setting and the school's legitimate interests in maintaining discipline. Specifically, *Goss* elaborates a model of what might be considered "minimal due process" before the imposition of a non-trivial loss on an individual: notice plus a "hearing" (which may be contemporaneous) that includes an explanation of the evidence on which the school authorities are relying, and an informal opportunity for rebuttal. These procedures, the Court said are "if anything, less than a fair-minded principal would [voluntarily] impose."

Goss is of special interest because it casts doubt on the comprehensiveness of *Eldridge*'s balancing approach. *Goss* requires a hearing, however minimal, even when the adjudicator was a witness to the events prompting the decision to suspend. The values served by permitting the student to "characterize his conduct and put it in what he deems the proper context" presumably deal with the possibilities of pleading excuse or mitigation, values not accounted for in *Eldridge*'s discussion of decision making accuracy.

The Court's vision of the school setting as non-adversarial and communal also played a decisive part in *Ingraham v. Wright*, 430 U.S. 651 (1977), which held that due process does not require prior notice and an opportunity to be heard before the infliction of corporal punishment on a public school student. Strictly speaking, *Ingraham* was not a dispute over entitlements; the state conceded the existence of a constitutionally based liberty interest in freedom from the arbitrary infliction of physical punishment. The Court concluded, however, that Florida adequately protected that interest by allowing a tort action against a teacher for assault. Under *Eldridge*, this conclusion was puzzling because it appeared that proof a teacher acted in good faith would be a complete defense, even if the student had in fact been punished mistakenly. Florida thus offered no procedural protection at all against administrative error. The Court, however, expressed concern that required hearing procedures might disrupt the ability of school authorities to preserve order. The "openness of the school"—that is, the students' daily contact with their families and the community's continual scrutiny of its schools—provided additional protection against any but occasional and aberrant instances of arbitrary treatment.

In cases involving institutions of higher education, the Court has offered a further reason for deference to academic judgment. The subtlety and expertise supposedly involved in academic decision making may substitute for adversarial hearings as a protection against arbitrariness. In *Board of Curators v. Horowitz*, 435 U.S. 78 (1978), the Court upheld a state medical school's decision without a prior hearing to expel a student on academic grounds. The student's performance had been considered repeatedly by other students, faculty, outside physicians, and the dean. Justice Rehnquist's majority opinion suggested no hearing at all was necessary, and the Court was unanimous in holding that the evaluative procedures afforded the expelled student would have satisfied the *Eldridge* calculus in any event.

The majority said no adversarial hearing was required because the expulsion was based on academic performance, not conduct, and the assessment of academic performance depends on largely subjective standards and expert review. The Court also thought the state had an interest in preserving a non-adversarial atmosphere in the school. The ultimate reach of the reasoning is unclear. It seems improbable that the shortcomings attributed to Ms. Horowitz would have justified summary expulsion. Yet, the attitude of deference is pronounced. Horowitz's alleged weaknesses included poor attendance, poor personal hygiene, and poor clinical performance—charges entirely susceptible to exploration at a hearing. See also *Regents of the University of Michigan v. Ewing*, 474 U.S. 214 (1985) (courts should not overturn academic decision unless "it is such a substantial departure from accepted academic norms as to demonstrate that the person or committee responsible did not actually exercise professional judgment").

By contrast, the Court's premises seem much less certain in cases involving state-authored damage to individual reputation. In *Roth*, the Court accepted both the general proposition that the Constitution itself recognizes and protects fundamental liberty interests and the specific proposition that such interests include one's "standing and associations in the community." The Court seemed already to have held as much in *Wisconsin v. Constantineau*, 400 U.S. 433 (1971).[1] Under Wisconsin law, local officials were authorized to post summarily the name of any person who, because of "excessive drinking," exhibited particular traits. The consequence of such posting was to render it unlawful for anyone to give or sell the "posted" person intoxicating liquor. The *Constantineau* opinion explicitly treats state-imposed disgrace as a sufficient legal harm to warrant a hearing, and approvingly quotes the lower court's assertion that the reputational harm was more serious than the denial of access to liquor.

Yet, in *Paul v. Davis*, 424 U.S. 693 (1976), the Court found no due process violation in the Louisville Police Department's erroneous inclusion of the petitioner on a poster identifying "Active Shoplifters," which it circulated to 800 local merchants. When distinguishing *Constantineau* the majority insisted that the constitutional injury recognized there was not the "defamatory character of the posting" of the plaintiff as a habitual drunk, but rather the alteration of "her status as a matter of state law," namely, the denial of her right to purchase liquor.

However tortured the majority's argument, the result in *Paul* may be comprehensible on at least two grounds. First, the Court may consider administrative hearings as unnecessary to protect against unusual, nonrecurring defamatory actions that are not part of an ongoing administrative program. Constantineau's name was posted pursuant to a legislatively sanctioned scheme of law enforcement; the Louisville Police Department's Christmas bulletin was an experiment, if not a frolic. Had the police been required to conduct hearings prior to distributing such information, it seems likely that they would forego such initiatives altogether—a policy decision that the Court might have been unwilling

1. Indeed, the constitutionally protected status of reputational interests was implicit even in pre-*Goldberg* jurisprudence. In *Hannah v. Larche*, 363 U.S. 420 (1960), the Court rejected a claim that witnesses subpoenaed to testify before the U.S. Civil Rights Commission concerning alleged voting discrimination in Louisiana were entitled to confront and cross-examine others who had furnished evidence to the Commission. The Court regarded it as speculative whether the hearings would cause the petitioner witnesses to suffer public opprobrium, job loss, or prosecution, but, more importantly, said it would not impose the requested procedural safeguards where the alleged harms would merely represent the collateral consequences of a government investigation without any adjudicatory findings. In *Jenkins v. McKeithen*, 395 U.S. 411 (1969), a 3–Justice plurality of the then 8–member Court distinguished *Hannah* in a challenge to a state commission charged with identifying specific persons who had violated state criminal laws relating to labor relations. Because the commission "exercise[d] a function very much akin to making an official adjudication of criminal culpability," a potential witness was entitled to procedural due process; although the commission did not itself impose sanctions, it did threaten injury to the witness's "reputation and * * * economic well-being." The plurality was joined by Justices Douglas and Black, who would have upheld the witnesses' claim for additional safeguards in *Hannah*.

to force. Nothing the Court says in *Paul*, however, relies on the ad hoc character of the particular program at issue.

Paul may also be comprehensible as an attempt to avoid constitutionalizing common law torts—in this case, defamation—inflicted on private persons by state employees. Recall that the Court declined to require pre-punishment hearings in *Ingraham v. Wright*, in part because a wrongfully beaten child could pursue common law relief. The Court has similarly held that the false imprisonment of a suspect's twin brother did not implicate the Due Process Clause. *Baker v. McCollan*, 443 U.S. 137 (1979).

Before one concludes that the existence of state law remedies is the decisive factor in the Court's thinking, however, it bears noting that most cases in which the Court has resisted constitutionalizing tort law involve prison administration. The animating force behind such decisions may have less to do with tort law than a fear of undermining the ability of public authorities to control a disputatious and sometimes dangerous subpopulation with more than occasional grievances and the time and incentive to litigate many of them.[2] It was in prison cases that the Court denied that *negligent* action resulting in bodily injury amounts to a "deprivation" of liberty in constitutional terms. See *Daniels v. Williams*, 474 U.S. 327 (1986) (prisoner injured after tripping on pillow negligently left on stairs by prison guard); *Davidson v. Cannon*, 474 U.S. 344 (1986) (prison authorities allegedly negligent in failing to protect prisoner from attack by other prisoners). It was also in prison cases that the Court held procedural due process inapplicable to the tortious destruction of property by a government employee, whether *negligent* or

2. No subspecialty in this area is more complex than the due process claims of prisoners. Given the Constitution's explicit protection of "liberty," virtually every administrative decision connected with conditions of confinement could plausibly trigger due process requirements. In *Meachum v. Fano*, 427 U.S. 215 (1976), however, the Court held that a prisoner incarcerated pursuant to a lawfully obtained conviction forfeits his or her constitutionally based interests in liberty during the period of confinement in prison. Thus, the search for liberty interests in a prison case necessarily focuses upon state or federal rules outside the Constitution. Indeed, from the early 1980s until the mid–90s, the search became more positivist in prison liberty cases than in property cases generally because, according to the Court, state-created liberty interests must be found in explicit rules, and, unlike property interests, may not be inferred from custom and practice. *Connecticut Board of Pardons v. Dumschat*, 452 U.S. 458 (1981). The Court changed its stance again, however, in *Sandin v. Conner*, 515 U.S. 472 (1995), as discussed in note 2, *supra* p. 347.

Besides *Meachum*, which deals with inter-prison transfers, some other leading cases in this area involve:

(1) the revocation of "good time credits," *Wolff v. McDonnell*, 418 U.S. 539 (1974);

(2) the grant, *Greenholtz v. Inmates of Nebraska Penal and Correctional Complex*, 442 U.S. 1 (1979); *Board of Pardons v. Allen*, 482 U.S. 369 (1987), or revocation of parole, *Morrissey v. Brewer*, 408 U.S. 471 (1972);

(3) the imposition of solitary confinement, *Hewitt v. Helms*, 459 U.S. 460 (1983);

(4) visiting privileges, *Kentucky Department of Corrections v. Thompson*, 490 U.S. 454 (1989);

(5) involuntary transfers from prison to mental hospitals, *Vitek v. Jones*, 445 U.S. 480 (1980); and

(6) the involuntary administration of antipsychotic drugs, *Washington v. Harper*, 494 U.S. 210 (1990).

intentional, if such destruction results from a "random and unauthorized" act, rather than from an authorized practice or policy. *Parratt v. Taylor*, 451 U.S. 527 (1981) (negligent destruction of a prisoner's hobby kit); *Hudson v. Palmer*, 468 U.S. 517 (1984) (intentional destruction of prisoner's noncontraband property). In such contexts, the state is obviously unable to afford a pre-deprivation hearing. Its post-deprivation obligation is only to provide an adequate tort remedy. *Cf. Logan v. Zimmerman Brush Co.*, 455 U.S. 422 (1982) (invalidating state *policy* denying judicial hearing to claimant based solely on state agency's negligence in failing to hold timely administrative hearing required by statute in order to obtain judicial review).

As the reputational harms and prison cases suggest, context is hardly self-defining. *Paul* and *Constantineau* look inconsistent as reputation cases, but the inconsistency is tempered if we imagine that *Paul* poses a torts/federalism issue while *Constantineau* responds more to the jurisprudence of licensing. But, how are we to tell which categorization will dominate? Or more precisely, what determines when considerations beyond the standard due process criteria will provoke a retreat from or expansion of previously established due process doctrines?

For example, recall that in *Arnett v. Kennedy* the Court recognized a constitutionally protected property interest in a federal civil service statute that permitted discharge only "for such cause as will promote the efficiency of the service." Yet, in *Bishop v. Wood*, 426 U.S. 341 (1976), the Court found no such interest created by the following city ordinance:

> Dismissal. A permanent employee whose work is not satisfactory over a period of time shall be notified in what way his work is deficient and what he must do if his work is to be satisfactory. If a permanent employee fails to perform work up to the standard of the classification held, or continues to be negligent, inefficient, or unfit to perform his duties, he may be dismissed by the City Manager. Any discharged employee shall be given written notice of his discharge setting forth the effective date and reasons for his discharge if he shall request such a notice.

Accordingly, the Court upheld a police officer's summary dismissal for alleged misconduct that he vigorously disputed.

That so apparently discretion-confining an ordinance would not, after *Arnett*, give rise to a property right suggests doctrinal incoherence. Yet, the majority's explanation indicates that other factors were at work. The Court first emphasized deference to state law as well as deference to lower court construction of that law:

> We do not have any authoritative interpretation of this ordinance by a North Carolina state court. We do, however, have the opinion of the United States District Judge who, of course, sits in North Carolina and practiced law there for many years. Based on his understanding of state law, he concluded that petitioner "held his position at the will and pleasure of the city." This construction of North Carolina law was upheld by the Court of Appeals for the

Fourth Circuit, albeit by an equally divided court. In comparable circumstances, this Court has accepted the interpretation of state law in which the District Court and the Court of Appeals have concurred even if an examination of the state-law issue without such guidance might have justified a different conclusion.

Moreover, while both *Arnett* and *Bishop* are "employment cases," the *Bishop* majority provided further institutional reasons for divining property interests less readily from state and local law than from federal sources:

> The federal court is not the appropriate forum in which to review the multitude of personnel decisions that are made daily by public agencies. We must accept the harsh fact that numerous individual mistakes are inevitable in the day-to-day administration of our affairs. The United States Constitution cannot feasibly be construed to require federal judicial review for every such error. * * * [W]e must presume that official action was regular and, if erroneous, can best be corrected in other ways. The Due Process Clause of the Fourteenth Amendment is not a guarantee against incorrect or ill-advised personnel decisions.

Indeed, a number of observers believe that the Supreme Court will ultimately withdraw from the oversight of public employee contract disputes. An evenly divided Court upheld a divided panel of the Seventh Circuit in *Board of Education of Paris Union School District v. Vail*, 466 U.S. 377 (1984), *aff'g*, 706 F.2d 1435 (7th Cir.1983). There a school board had voted not to renew the contract of the football coach for a second year. The coach's contract had covered only one year, but the Board had allegedly promised a second year contract prior to the coach's entering into his one-year agreement. A majority of the Seventh Circuit panel held that the board had violated a "property" interest of the coach in failing to renew the contract without any type of hearing. But, even the majority objected to what it believed was demanded of it by the *Roth* and *Sindermann* jurisprudence. Judge Posner, in dissent, suggested that the Court had at least three exits from the public employee/due process jurisprudence: It could hold that the interest created by a contract for a short fixed term was not property; it could hold that a simple breach of contract does not deprive an employee of a property right; or, it could simply hold that, given the availability of contract remedies at common law, leaving the disappointed employee to those remedies was not a denial of due process. For arguments that the Court should take one or more of these roads out of the public employee due process business, see Stephen F. Williams, *Liberty and Property: The Problem of Government Benefits*, 12 J. Legal Stud. 3 (1983); Leonard Kreynin, Note, *Breach of Contract as a Due Process Violation*, 90 Colum. L. Rev. 1098 (1990); and Richard J. Pierce, *The Due Process Counter-revolution of the 1990s?*, 96 Colum. L. Rev. 1973 (1996).

The attempt to cluster due process decisions by context advances analysis somewhat beyond the conclusion that every case provides its own, unique context. Moreover, grouping by context or subject matter has the advantage of pursuing due process in the way that responds to the interests of most litigants and most commentators. Of the 390 articles in the WestLaw data base that have "due process" in the title and a date between 1/01/1997 and 10/17/2002, virtually all are concerned with particular statutes or subject matter areas not with due process in general. Here, as elsewhere, litigants look for authorities that have a similar fact pattern. Electronic search engines balk at providing all the cases that have cited *Mathews v. Eldridge* and no law firm would assign even its summer interns to try to read them.

But, if by "progress" we mean advances in the predictability of outcomes, sorting due process cases by context seems to provide modest gains. The literally unretrievable number of cases litigating due process issues, and 390 law review articles with due process in the title in less than six years, suggest that the due process jurisprudence is hardly settled, however much the Supreme Court might like to retreat from some parts of it.

Professor Farina has suggested that the inherent flexibility of due process analysis provides opportunities as well as grounds for criticism. Exalting rather than decrying particularity, she favors a mode of inquiry yet more consciously open-ended and particularized than the Court's recent decisions—an approach that would embrace "fluidity and sensitivity to context," and authorize judges to inquire in detail whether the state has "fashion[ed] administrative environments that concentrate on inducing officials to be their best, rather than on trying to block them from being their worst." Cynthia Farina, *Conceiving Due Process*, 3 Yale J.L. & Feminism 189, 268, 275 (1991). On its face Professor Farina's suggestion might seem either utopian or excessively activist, perhaps both. But, considering how deeply enmeshed the courts are in resolving due process claims already, it is hardly obvious that her suggestions would add much to their burdens or provide them with decisional criteria that are more unruly than the ones they currently wield.

C. FEDERAL STATUTORY HEARING RIGHTS

1. FINDING A HEARING RIGHT

Statutes provide the primary starting point for determining the nature and existence of hearing rights in federal programs. There are two reasons: First, Congress almost always provides for hearings when authorizing programs of adjudicatory decision making that implicate constitutionally protected "liberty" or "property." Second, when Congress creates hearing rights, it generally prescribes their features in sufficient detail to meet any plausible due process minimum.

Even so, divining the existence and nature of statutory hearing rights turns out to be a complex enterprise. One complicating factor is that, although the Court interprets due process as guaranteeing a hearing only in adjudicatory contexts, Congress is not so limited. It may—and has—prescribed hearings for rulemaking. A second complication is the interplay of program statutes with the Administrative Procedure Act. The APA provides a detailed description of a formal hearing when *some other statute*—that is, the statute that an agency is implementing—requires a decision "to be determined on the record after opportunity for an agency hearing." 5 U.S.C. §§ 553(c), 554(a) (1994). The procedures described chiefly in 5 U.S.C. §§ 556 and 557, are applicable in "formal" rulemaking and in "formal" adjudication. Although these APA sections raise their own issues of interpretation, it is easy enough to confirm their applicability when another statute refers to them expressly or incorporates the precise triggering language just quoted. Often, however, an agency statute requires a "hearing" but fails to say whether this amounts to a requirement that decisions "be determined on the record after opportunity for an agency hearing."

Additionally, Congress may confer a right to a hearing in language that would trigger the APA but specify in the same statute different or additional procedures. In such a circumstance, the APA does not provide a comprehensive guide to the applicable procedural requirements, but instead supplies a backdrop that fills in the procedural details that Congress did not specifically cover.

Accordingly, to determine the elements of any hearing based on a federal statute, it is necessary to ask at least the following questions: Does the statute authorizing the agency's decision require any hearing? If so, does it require that the decision "be determined on the record after opportunity for an agency hearing" within the meaning of the APA? If so, does the agency's statute modify or add to the procedural elements that the APA prescribes? And, if a hearing is required, but APA requirements are not triggered, what sort of hearing?

UNITED STATES v. FLORIDA EAST COAST RAILWAY CO.

Supreme Court of the United States, 1973.
410 U.S. 224, 93 S.Ct. 810, 35 L.Ed.2d 223.

JUSTICE REHNQUIST delivered the opinion of the Court.

Appellees, two railroad companies, brought this action in the District Court for the Middle District of Florida to set aside the incentive per diem rates established by appellant Interstate Commerce Commission in a rulemaking proceeding. The District Court sustained appellees' position that the Commission had failed to comply with the applicable provisions of the Administrative Procedure Act, and therefore set aside the order. * * * The District Court held that the language of § 1(14)(a)[1]

1. Section 1(14)(a) provides:

"The Commission may, after hearing, on a complaint or upon its own initiative without complaint, establish reasonable rules, regulations, and practices with respect to car service by common carriers by railroad subject to this chapter, including the compensation to be paid and other terms of contract, agreement, or arrangement for the use of any locomo-

of the Interstate Commerce Act required the Commission in a proceeding such as this to act in accordance with the Administrative Procedure Act, 5 U.S.C. § 556(d) and that the Commission's determination to receive submissions from the appellees only in written form was a violation of that section because the appellees were "prejudiced" by that determination within the meaning of that section. * * *

I.

This case arises from the factual background of a chronic freight-car shortage on the Nation's railroads. * * * Congressional concern for the problem was manifested in the enactment in 1966 of an amendment to § 1(14)(a) of the Interstate Commerce Act, enlarging the Commission's authority to prescribe per diem charges for the use by one railroad of freight cars owned by another. * * *

The Commission in 1966 commenced an investigation "to determine whether information presently available warranted the establishment of an incentive element increase, on an interim basis, to apply pending further study and investigation." * * *

In December 1967, the Commission initiated the rulemaking procedure giving rise to the order that appellees here challenge. It directed Class I and Class II line-haul railroads to compile and report detailed information with respect to freight-car demand and supply at numerous sample stations for selected days of the week during 12 four-week periods, beginning January 29, 1968.

Some of the affected railroads voiced questions about the proposed study or requested modification in the study procedures outlined by the Commission in its notice of proposed rulemaking. In response to petitions setting forth these carriers' views, the Commission staff held an informal conference in April 1968, at which the objections and proposed modifications were discussed. Twenty railroads, including appellee Seaboard, were represented at this conference, at which the Commission's staff sought to answer questions about reporting methods to accommodate individual circumstances of particular railroads. The conference adjourned on a note that undoubtedly left the impression that hearings

tive, car, or other vehicle not owned by the carrier using it (and whether or not owned by another carrier), and the penalties or other sanctions for nonobservance of such rules, regulations, or practices. In fixing such compensation to be paid for the use of any type of freight car, the Commission shall give consideration to the national level of ownership of such type of freight car and to other factors affecting the adequacy of the national freight car supply, and shall, on the basis of such consideration, determine whether compensation should be computed solely on the basis of elements of ownership expense involved in owning and maintaining such type of freight car, including a fair return on value, or whether such compensation should be increased by such incentive element or elements of compensation as in the Commission's judgment will provide just and reasonable compensation to freight car owners, contribute to sound car service practices (including efficient utilization and distribution of cars), and encourage the acquisition and maintenance of a car supply adequate to meet the needs of commerce and the national defense. * * * "

would be held at some future date. A detailed report of the conference was sent to all parties to the proceeding before the Commission.

The results of the information thus collected were analyzed and presented to Congress by the Commission during a hearing before the Subcommittee on Surface Transportation of the Senate Committee on Commerce in May 1969. Members of the Subcommittee expressed dissatisfaction with the Commission's slow pace in exercising the authority that had been conferred upon it by the 1966 Amendments to the Interstate Commerce Act. * * *

The Commission, now apparently imbued with a new sense of mission, issued in December 1969 an interim report announcing its tentative decision to adopt incentive per diem charges on standard boxcars based on the information compiled by the railroads. * * * Embodied in the report was a proposed rule adopting the Commission's tentative conclusions and a notice to the railroads to file statements of position within 60 days, couched in the following language:

> "That verified statements of facts, briefs, and statements of position respecting the tentative conclusions reached in the said interim report, the rules and regulations proposed in the appendix to this order, and any other pertinent matter, are hereby invited to be submitted pursuant to the filing schedule set forth below by an interested person whether or not such person is already a party to this proceeding.
>
> * * *
>
> "That any party requesting oral hearing shall set forth with specificity the need therefor and the evidence to be adduced."

Both appellee railroads filed statements objecting to the Commission's proposal and requesting an oral hearing, as did numerous other railroads. In April 1970, the Commission, without having held further "hearings," issued a supplemental report making some modifications in the tentative conclusions earlier reached, but overruling *in toto* the requests of appellees. * * *

II.

In *United States v. Allegheny–Ludlum Steel Corp.*, [406 U.S. 742 (1972)] we held that the language of § 1(14)(a) * * * authorizing the Commission to act "after hearing" was not the equivalent of a requirement that a rule be made "on the record after opportunity for an agency hearing" as the latter term is used in § 553(c) of the Administrative Procedure Act. Since the 1966 amendment to § 1(14)(a), under which the Commission was here proceeding, does not by its terms add to the hearing requirement contained in the earlier language, the same result should obtain here unless that amendment contains language that is tantamount to such a requirement. Appellees contend that such language is found in the provisions of that Act requiring that:

> "[T]he Commission shall give consideration to the national level of ownership of such type of freight car and to other factors affecting the adequacy of the national freight car supply, and shall, on the basis of such consideration, determine whether compensation should be computed. * * * "

While this language is undoubtedly a mandate to the Commission to consider the factors there set forth in reaching any conclusion as to imposition of per diem incentive charges, it adds to the hearing requirements of the section neither expressly nor by implication. We know of no reason to think that an administrative agency in reaching a decision cannot accord consideration to factors such as those set forth in the 1966 amendment by means other than a trial-type hearing or the presentation of oral argument by the affected parties. Congress by that amendment specified necessary components of the ultimate decision, but it did not specify the method by which the Commission should acquire information about those components.

* * *

* * * The District Court observed that it was "rather hard to believe that the last sentence of § 553(c) was directed only to the few legislative spots where the words 'on the record' or their equivalent had found their way into the statute book." This is, however, the language which Congress used, and since there are statutes on the books that do use these very words, see, e.g., the Fulbright Amendment to the Walsh–Healey Act, 41 U.S.C. § 43a, and 21 U.S.C.A. § 371(e)(3), the regulations provision of the Food and Drug Act, adherence to that language cannot be said to render the provision nugatory or ineffectual. We recognized in *Allegheny–Ludlum* that the actual words "on the record" and "after * * * hearing" used in § 553 were not words of art, and that other statutory language having the same meaning could trigger the provisions of §§ 556 and 557 in rulemaking proceedings. But we adhere to our conclusion, expressed in that case, that the phrase "after hearing" in § 1(14)(a) * * * does not have such an effect.

III.

Inextricably intertwined with the hearing requirement of the Administrative Procedure Act in this case is the meaning to be given to the language "after hearing" in § 1(14)(a) * * *. Appellees, both here and in the court below, contend that the Commission procedure here fell short of that mandated by the "hearing" requirement of § 1(14)(a), even though it may have satisfied § 553 of the Administrative Procedure Act. * * *

The term "hearing" in its legal context undoubtedly has a host of meanings. Its meaning undoubtedly will vary depending on whether it is used in the context of a rulemaking-type proceeding or in the context of a proceeding devoted to the adjudication of particular disputed facts. It is by no means apparent what the drafters of the Esch Car Service Act of 1917, which became the first part of § 1(14)(a), * * * meant by the term. * * * What is apparent, though, is that the term was used in granting authority to the Commission to make rules and regulations of a prospective nature.

* * *

Under these circumstances, confronted with a grant of substantive authority made after the Administrative Procedure Act was enacted, we think that reference to that Act, in which Congress devoted itself exclusively to questions such as the nature and scope of hearings, is a satisfactory basis for determining what is meant by the term "hearing" used in another statute. Turning to that Act, we are convinced that the term "hearing" as used therein does not necessarily embrace either the right to present evidence orally and to cross-examine opposing witnesses, or the right to present oral argument to the agency's decisionmaker.

Section 553 excepts from its requirements rulemaking devoted to "interpretative rules, general statements of policy, or rules of agency organization, procedure, or practice," and rulemaking "when the agency for good cause finds * * * that notice and public procedure thereon are impracticable, unnecessary, or contrary to the public interest." This exception does not apply, however, "when notice or hearing is required by statute"; in those cases, even though interpretative rulemaking be involved, the requirements of § 553 apply. But since these requirements themselves do not mandate any oral presentation, it cannot be doubted that a statute that requires a "hearing" prior to rulemaking may in some circumstances be satisfied by procedures that meet only the standards of § 553. * * *

Similarly, even where the statute requires that the rulemaking procedure take place "on the record after opportunity for an agency hearing," thus triggering the applicability of § 556, subsection (d) provides that the agency may proceed by the submission of all or part of the evidence in written form if a party will not be "prejudiced thereby." Again, the Act makes it plain that a specific statutory mandate that the proceedings take place on the record after hearing may be satisfied in some circumstances by evidentiary submission in written form only.

We think this treatment of the term "hearing" in the Administrative Procedure Act affords a sufficient basis for concluding that the requirement of a "hearing" contained in § 1(14)(a) * * * did not by its own force require the Commission either to hear oral testimony, to permit cross-examination of Commission witnesses, or to hear oral argument. Here, the Commission promulgated a tentative draft of an order, and accorded all interested parties 60 days in which to file statements of position, submissions of evidence, and other relevant observations. The parties had fair notice of exactly what the Commission proposed to do, and were given an opportunity to comment, to object, or to make some other form of written submission. The final order of the Commission indicates that it gave consideration to the statements of the two appellees here. Given the "open-ended" nature of the proceedings, and the Commission's announced willingness to consider proposals for modification after operating experience had been acquired, we think the hearing requirement of § 1(14)(a) of the Act was met.

Appellee railroads cite a number of our previous decisions dealing in some manner with the right to a hearing in an administrative proceeding. Although appellees have asserted no claim of constitutional deprivation in this proceeding, some of the cases they rely upon expressly speak in constitutional terms, while others are less than clear as to whether they depend upon the Due Process Clause of the Fifth and Fourteenth Amendments to the Constitution or upon generalized principles of administrative law formulated prior to the adoption of the Administrative Procedure Act. * * *

The basic distinction between rulemaking and adjudication is illustrated by this Court's treatment of two related cases under the Due Process Clause of the Fourteenth Amendment. In *Londoner v. Denver*, the Court held that due process had not been accorded a landowner who objected to the amount assessed against his land as its share of the benefit resulting from the paving of a street. Local procedure had accorded him the right to file a written complaint and objection, but not to be heard orally. This Court held that due process of law required that he "have the right to support his allegations by argument however brief, and if need be, by proof, however informal." But in the later case of *Bi–Metallic Investment Co. v. State Board of Equalization*, the Court held that no hearing at all was constitutionally required prior to a decision by state tax officers in Colorado to increase the valuation of all taxable property in Denver by a substantial percentage. The Court distinguished *Londoner* by stating that there a small number of persons "were exceptionally affected, in each case upon individual grounds."

Later decisions have continued to observe the distinction adverted to in *Bi–Metallic Investment Co.* * * * While the line dividing them may not always be a bright one, these decisions represent a recognized distinction in administrative law between proceedings for the purpose of promulgating policy-type rules or standards, on the one hand, and proceedings designed to adjudicate disputed facts in particular cases on the other.

Here, the incentive payments proposed by the Commission in its tentative order, and later adopted in its final order, were applicable across the board to all of the common carriers by railroad subject to the Interstate Commerce Act. No effort was made to single out any particular railroad for special consideration based on its own peculiar circumstances. Indeed, one of the objections of appellee Florida East Coast was that it and other terminating carriers should have been treated differently from the generality of the railroads. But the fact that the order may in its effects have been thought more disadvantageous by some railroads than by others does not change its generalized nature. Though the Commission obviously relied on factual inferences as a basis for its order, the source of these factual inferences was apparent to anyone who read the order of December 1969. The factual inferences were used in the formulation of a basically legislative-type judgment, for prospective application only, rather than in adjudicating a particular set of disputed facts.

* * *

Justice Douglas, with whom Justice Stewart concurs, dissenting.

* * * Seaboard argued that it had been damaged by what it alleged to be the Commission's sudden change in emphasis from specialty to unequipped boxcars and that it would lose some $1.8 million as the result of the Commission's allegedly hasty and experimental action. Florida East Coast raised significant challenges to the statistical validity of the Commission's data, and also contended that its status as a terminating railroad left it with a surfeit of standard boxcars which should exempt it from the requirement to pay incentive charges. * * *

Section 1(14)(a) of the Interstate Commerce Act bestows upon the Commission broad discretionary power to determine incentive rates. These rates may have devastating effects on a particular line. According to the brief of one of the appellees, the amount of incentive compensation paid by debtor lines amounts to millions of dollars each six-month period. Nevertheless, the courts must defer to the Commission as long as its findings are supported by substantial evidence and it has not abused its discretion. "All the more insistent is the need, when power has been bestowed so freely, that the 'inexorable safeguard' * * * of a fair and open hearing be maintained in its integrity."

Accordingly, I would hold that appellees were not afforded the hearing guaranteed by § 1(14)(a) of the Interstate Commerce Act and 5 U.S.C. §§ 553, 556 and 557, and would affirm the decision of the District Court.

Notes

Distinguishing Rulemaking from Adjudication. In interpreting the nature of the "hearing" required by the Interstate Commerce Act, Justice Rehnquist adverts to the distinction drawn in *Londoner* and *Bi–Metallic* discussed in the Introduction to this chapter, which is described as a distinction between "essentially" *adjudicatory* decisions (which may entail due process hearing rights) and "essentially" *legislative* decisions (which never do). In interpreting statutory hearing requirements, this distinction is not dispositive—as it may be in due process cases—because Congress may, if it chooses, prescribe a hearing for legislative-type decisions. Under Justice Rehnquist's analysis, the distinction is deployed essentially to create a presumption: when Congress authorizes an agency to make decisions that are legislative in character, it is presumed to have authorized informal, legislative-style procedures, unless greater formality is clearly mandated.

How, then, do we distinguish adjudicatory from legislative decisions?

1. *Numbers Affected.* In *Bi–Metallic*, Justice Holmes implied a distinction based on numbers of persons affected: "Where a rule of conduct applies to more than a few people it is impracticable that everyone should have a

direct voice in its adoption." Yet, Congress enacts "private legislation" affecting individual persons, and courts decide class actions. Numbers affected may be relevant, but cannot be dispositive.

2. *Prospectivity*. Should it make a difference that legislative judgments are often forward-looking, seeking to establish future policy, while adjudicatory judgments are retrospective, seeking to assess prior conduct under a preexisting rule? Of course, legislatures may enact measures that unsettle past arrangements and private expectations built upon them. And, courts often order wholly prospective relief, and the adjudicatory orders of both courts and agencies are often intended to have precedential value. But where administrative agencies are concerned the Supreme Court has not been inclined to find that Congress has authorized agencies to adopt rules with retrospective effect. Indeed, Justice Scalia would go further to hold that "retroactive rules" are never permitted given the definition of "rule" in the APA as an agency statement having "future effect." See *Bowen v. Georgetown University Hosp.*, 488 U.S. 204 (1988).

3. *Factual Bases*. In his influential treatise, Professor Kenneth Culp Davis argues that the true distinction is between decisions based on "legislative" facts and those based on "adjudicative" facts:

> Adjudicative facts are the facts about the parties and their activities, businesses, and properties. Adjudicative facts usually answer the questions of who did what, where, when, how, why, with what motive or intent; adjudicative facts are roughly the kind of facts that go to a jury in a jury case. Legislative facts do not usually concern the immediate parties but are general facts which help the tribunal decide questions of law and policy and discretion.
>
> Facts pertaining to the parties and their businesses and activities, that is, adjudicative facts, are intrinsically the kind of facts that ordinarily ought not to be determined without giving the parties a chance to know and to meet any evidence that may be unfavorable to them, that is, without providing the parties an opportunity for trial. The reason is that parties know more about the facts concerning themselves and their activities than anyone else is likely to know, and the parties are therefore in an especially good position to rebut or explain evidence that bears upon adjudicative facts. Yet people who are not necessarily parties, frequently the agencies and their staffs, may often be the masters of legislative facts. Because the parties may often have little or nothing to contribute to the development of legislative facts, the method of trial often is not required for the determination of disputed issues about legislative facts.

KENNETH CULP DAVIS, ADMINISTRATIVE LAW TEXT 160 (1959). Should it follow that adjudicatory hearings ought never be required to establish legislative facts? Isn't the failure to take specific circumstance into account the crux of the railroads' complaints?

CALIFANO v. YAMASAKI

Supreme Court of the United States, 1979.
442 U.S. 682, 99 S.Ct. 2545, 61 L.Ed.2d 176.

JUSTICE BLACKMUN delivered the opinion of the Court.

[Under section 204(a)(1) of the Social Security Act, recoupment of overpayments of disability benefits was to be accomplished by deductions from future payments. However, Section 204(b) precludes recoupment where the Secretary finds that the recipient is without fault and adjustments or recovery would *either* "defeat the purposes" of the Act *or* "be against equity and good conscience."]

The Secretary has undertaken to define the terms employed in § 204(b). Under his regulations, "without fault" means that the recipient neither knew nor should have known that the overpayment or the information on which it was based was incorrect. * * *

The regulations say that to "defeat the purpose of the subchapter" is to "deprive a person of income required for ordinary and necessary living expenses." * * * Recoupment is "against equity and good conscience" when the recipient "because of a notice that such payment would be made or by reason of the incorrect payment, relinquished a valuable right * * * or changed his position for the worse." * * *

The Secretary's practice is to make an ex parte determination under § 204(a) that an overpayment has been made, to notify the recipient of that determination, and then to shift to the recipient the burden of either (i) seeking reconsideration to contest the accuracy of that determination, or (ii) asking the Secretary to forgive the debt and waive recovery in accordance with § 204(b). If a recipient files a written request for reconsideration or waiver, recoupment is deferred pending action on that request. * * * The papers are sent to one of the seven regional offices where the request is reviewed.

If the regional office decision goes against the recipient, recoupment begins. The recipient's monthly benefits are reduced or terminated[3] until the overpayment has been recouped. Only if the recipient continues to object is he given an opportunity to present his story in person to someone with authority to decide his case. That opportunity takes the form of an on-the-record *de novo* evidential hearing before an independent hearing examiner. The recipient may seek subsequent review by the Appeals Council, and finally by a federal court. If it is decided that the Secretary's initial determination was in error, the amounts wrongfully recouped are repaid.

3. The Secretary has altered his procedures in several respects since the initiation of this litigation, including: (i) rather than terminate all benefits until recoupment is completed, the Secretary now in nonfraud cases usually reduces the recipient's monthly payments by only 25%, see Claims Manual § 5515 (January 1979); and (ii) recipients who report excessive earnings and are found to have been overpaid now receive notice before, rather than after, recoupment begins. See *Elliott v. Weinberger*, 564 F.2d 1219, 1223 (C.A.9 1977). Neither party contends that these changes moot this case.

[After describing the lower court judgments finding the procedures constitutionally defective and requiring an oral hearing prior to recoupment the Court continued.]

A court presented with both statutory and constitutional grounds to support the relief requested usually should pass on the statutory claim before considering the constitutional question.

The District Courts and Court of Appeals in the cases now before us gave these principles somewhat short shrift in declining to pass expressly on respondents' contention that § 204 itself requires a pre-recoupment oral hearing. We turn to the statute first, and find that it fairly may be read to require a pre-recoupment decision by the Secretary. With respect to § 204(a) reconsideration as to whether overpayment occurred, we agree that the statute does not require that the decision involve a prior oral hearing, and we reject respondents' contention that the Constitution does so. With respect to § 204(b) waiver of the Secretary's right to recoup, however, because the nature of the statutory standards makes a hearing essential, we find it unnecessary to determine whether the Constitution would require a similar result.

On its face, § 204 requires that the Secretary make a pre-recoupment waiver decision, and that the decision, like that concerning the fact of the overpayment, be accurate. In the imperative voice,[9] it says "there shall be no adjustment of payments to, or recovery by the United States from, any person" who qualifies for waiver. Echoing this requirement, § 204(a) says that only "proper" adjustments or recoveries are to be made. The implication is that recoupment from a person qualifying under § 204(a) would not be "proper."

Insofar as § 204 is read to require a pre-recoupment decision, the reading is in accord with the manner in which the Secretary presently administers the statute. No recoupment is made until a preliminary

9. A number of statutes authorizing the recovery of federal payments make an exception for cases that are "against equity and good conscience." Most are entirely permissive. They provide that recovery "is not required," e.g., 10 U.S.C. §§ 1442, 1453 (serviceman's family annuity and survivors' benefit); or that an agency "may waive" recovery if a proper showing is made, 5 U.S.C. § 4108(c) (civil service training expenses), 5 U.S.C. § 5922(b)(2) (foreign station allowances); or that the agency head "shall make such provision as he finds appropriate," 42 U.S.C. § 1383(b) (supplemental security income); or simply that recovery "may be waived," 10 U.S.C. § 2774(a) (military pay).

In contrast, § 204 is mandatory in form. It says "there shall be no" recovery when waiver is proper. In this regard it resembles the "equity and good conscience" waiver provisions found in only four other statutes: 38 U.S.C. § 3102(a) (veterans benefits); 42 U.S.C. § 1395gg(c) (Medicare); 45 U.S.C. § 231i(c) (Railroad Retirement Act); 45 U.S.C. § 231i(c) (Railroad Retirement Act of 1974); 45 U.S.C.A. § 352(d) (Railroad Unemployment Insurance Act). Even those statutes are not identical to § 204 in all material respects. While the use of the word "shall," particularly with reference to an equitable decision, does not eliminate all discretion, see *Hecht Co. v. Bowles,* 321 U.S. 321, 327–331 (1944), it at least imposes on the Secretary a duty to decide. And here where the provision for recovery, § 204(a), and the provision for waiver, § 204(b), are phrased in equally mandatory terms, it is reasonable to infer that in this particular statute Congress did not intend to exalt recovery over waiver.

The legislative history of § 204(b) indicates merely that Congress intended to make recovery more equitable by authorizing waiver.

waiver or reconsideration decision has taken place, either by default after the recipient has received proper notice, or by review of a written request. Claims Manual §§ 5503.2(c), 5503.4(b). This interpretation is also reinforced by a comparison with other sections of the Social Security Act. Section 204 is strikingly unlike § 225,[10] which expressly permits suspension of disability benefits before eligibility is finally decided. On the other hand, an analogy may be drawn between § 204 and § 303(a)(1), 42 U.S.C. § (a)(1), which this Court in *California Human Resources Dept. v. Java*, 402 U.S. 121 (1971), interpreted to require payment of unemployment benefits pending a final determination of eligibility.[11] Neither § 204 nor § 303(a)(1) expressly addresses the timing of a hearing, but both speak in mandatory terms and imply that the mandated act—here waiver of recoupment, there payment of benefits—is to precede other action.

The heart of the present dispute concerns not whether a pre-recoupment decision should be made, but whether making the decision by regional office review of the written waiver request is sufficient to protect the recipient's right not to be subjected to an improper recoupment.

In this regard, requests for reconsideration under § 204(a), as to whether overpayment occurred, may be distinguished from requests for waiver of the Secretary's right to recoup under § 204(b). * * * [R]equests under § 204(a) for reconsideration involve relatively straightforward matters of computation for which written review is ordinarily an adequate means to correct prior mistakes. Many of the named respondents were found to have been overpaid based on earnings reports they themselves had submitted. But unlike the Court of Appeals in this case, we do not think that the rare instance in which a credibility dispute is relevant to a § 204(a) claim is sufficient to require the Secretary to sift through all requests for reconsideration and grant a hearing to the few that involve credibility. The statute authorizes only "proper" recoupment, but some leeway for practical administration must be allowed. Nor do the standards of the Due Process Clause, more tolerant than the strict language here in issue, require that pre-recoupment oral hearings be afforded in § 204(a) cases. The nature of a due process hearing is shaped by the "risk of error inherent in the truthfinding process as applied to the generality of cases, not the rare exceptions." *Mathews v. Eldridge*. It would be inconsistent with that principle to require a

10. Section 225 provides:

"If the Secretary, on the basis of information obtained by or submitted to him, believes that an individual entitled to [disability benefits] * * * may have ceased to be under a disability, the Secretary may suspend the payment of benefits * * * until it is determined * * * whether or not such individual's disability has ceased or until the Secretary believes that such disability has not ceased."

11. Section 303(a) provides:

"The Secretary of Labor shall make no certification for payment to any State unless he finds that the law of such state * * * includes provisions for—

"(1) Such methods of administration * * * as are found by the Secretary of Labor to be reasonably calculated to insure full payment of unemployment compensation when due."

hearing under § 204(a) when review of a beneficiary's written submission is an adequate means of resolving all but a few § 204(a) disputes.

By contrast, written review hardly seems sufficient to discharge the Secretary's statutory duty to make an accurate determination of waiver under § 204(b). Under that subsection, the Secretary must assess the absence of "fault" and determine whether or not recoupment would be "against equity and good conscience." These standards do not apply under § 204(a). The Court previously has noted that a "broad 'fault' standard is inherently subject to factual determination and adversarial input." *Mitchell v. W.T. Grant Co.*, 416 U.S. 600, 617 (1974). As the Secretary's regulations make clear, "fault" depends on an evaluation of "all pertinent circumstances" including the recipient's "intelligence * * * and physical and mental condition" as well as his "good faith." 20 C.F.R. § 404.507 (1978). We do not see how these can be evaluated absent personal contact between the recipient and the person who decides his case. Evaluating fault, like judging detrimental reliance, usually requires an assessment of the recipient's credibility, and written submissions are a particularly inappropriate way to distinguish a genuine hard luck story from a fabricated tall tale.

The consequences of the injunctions entered by the District Courts confirm the reasonableness of interpreting § 204(b) to require a pre-recoupment oral hearing. In compliance with those orders, the Secretary, beginning with calendar year 1977, has granted what respondents term "a short personal conference with an impartial employee of the Social Security Administration at which time the recipient presents testimony and evidence and cross-examines witnesses, and the administrative employee questions the recipient." Of the approximately 2,000 conferences held between January 1977 and October 1978, 30% resulted in a reversal of the Secretary's decision. This rate of reversal confirms the view that, without an oral hearing, the Secretary may misjudge a number of cases that he otherwise would be able to assess properly, and that the hearing requirement imposed by the Court of Appeals significantly furthers the statutory goal that "there shall be no" recoupment when waiver is appropriate. We therefore agree with the Court of Appeals that an opportunity for a pre-recoupment oral hearing is required when a recipient requests waiver under § 204(b).

Notes

1. *The Puzzles of* Yamasaki. Although the Court in *Yamasaki* purports to rely on the Social Security Act to find a right to a hearing in connection with requests for pre-recoupment waivers, it does not rely either on that Act or on the APA to define the procedures of the required hearing. This is not surprising given the lack of any Social Security Act language providing a pre-recoupment hearing or triggering the APA. The odd result is that under *Yamasaki*, recoupment of overpaid disability benefits through reductions in future payments is accompanied by greater procedural safeguards than *Eldridge* demanded for the complete termination of those same benefits.

2. *Formalizing Informal Adjudication.* The Court's creativity in defining the Secretary's procedural obligations in *Yamasaki* seems in tension with a more recent decision also authored by Justice Blackmun. In *Pension Benefit Guaranty Corp. v. LTV Corporation*, 496 U.S. 633 (1990), the Court held that judges lack the authority to go beyond statutory procedural requirements in imposing adjudicatory procedural obligations on federal agencies.

PGBC is a government-owned corporation that insures private sector pension plans that meet the criteria of the Employee Retirement Income Security Act of 1974 (ERISA), Pub. L. No. 93–406, 88 Stat. 829 (1974). PGBC's insurance responsibility comes into play when a pension plan is terminated without sufficient assets to meet its pension obligations. An employer may terminate a plan under specified conditions of financial distress, unless the termination would violate a collective bargaining agreement. The PGBC may also terminate any plan without the employer's consent, for example, if the plan fails to meet minimum funding standards or would be unable to meet its benefit obligations when due. The PGBC may also restore a terminated plan to its pretermination status if it "determines such action to be appropriate and consistent with its duties under" the relevant provisions of ERISA. 29 U.S.C. § 1347.

This case arose after PGBC terminated three LTV plans, two negotiated in collective bargaining, after LTV filed a petition for Chapter 11 reorganization. LTV and a union subsequently concluded a new collective bargaining agreement, in which LTV agreed to fund a new pension arrangement which would assure workers receiving the same level of benefits as the old plan. LTV accomplished this level of funding by combining the proceeds of PGBC insurance with additional LTV contributions. The PGBC considers such arrangements improper "follow-on plans," which seek to secure PGBC subsidies for ongoing private pension systems. LTV nonetheless ignored PGBC objections and obtained the Bankruptcy Court's permission to fund its new arrangement.

PGBC subsequently reviewed the improving financial condition of the steel industry and determined that the previously terminated LTV plans should be restored. It issued a notice of proposed restoration, pointing to both the industry's improved economic condition and LTV's "abuse" of ERISA. When LTV refused to comply with the restoration decision, PGBC filed an enforcement action, which the district court dismissed as exceeding PGBC's authority. The Second Circuit affirmed, concluding, among other things, that the restoration decision followed an informal adjudicative process that lacked adequate procedural safeguards: PGBC had provided LTV no explanation of the record on which it was basing its decision, no opportunity to rebut, and no detailed opinion explaining its reasons for restoration.

The Supreme Court reversed, concluding that judges lacked authority to create procedural rights in adjudication that could not be traced to constitutional requirements or to a statute. Because the Court could not discern any right of LTV to notice, rebuttal, or a statement of reasons in the APA or ERISA, it held that the lower courts were precluded from demanding added procedures. The sole dissenter, Justice Stevens, did not address the procedural issues, resting entirely on his conclusion that PGBC lacked substantive authority under ERISA to use its restoration powers to prohibit "follow-on" pension plans.

It is hard to see, however, why the case for a hearing right under ERISA was less compelling than the analysis Justice Blackmun proffers in *Yamasaki*. In *LTV*, the Court could well have echoed *Yamasaki*'s determination that "the nature of the statutory standards makes a hearing essential," especially if the Court accepted PGBC's conclusion that a restoration decision may be based on a fault-based standard of abuse. LTV did not challenge the PGBC's procedural informality on due process grounds, but, just as *Yamasaki* interprets the Social Security Act to imply hearing requirements where the absence of such procedures might raise a plausible due process concern, the same canon of construction could have been invoked in *LTV*.

Where an agency is required by statute to follow the APA's detailed formal adjudicatory procedures, no judge would likely be tempted to engraft additional procedures. Yet, the *LTV* decision is potentially applicable to the wide range of agency decision making that the APA leaves wholly unaddressed, namely, "informal adjudication"—any adjudicatory decision making under procedures more summary than those outlined in 5 U.S.C. §§ 554, 556, and 557. *Yamasaki* does not suggest that judges may go beyond statutes or the Due Process Clause to impose procedural requirements on agencies, but it represents an approach to statutory interpretation that gives judges far greater discretion to impose their views of appropriate agency procedures than *LTV*, or most subsequent cases, suggest.

3. Statutes, Constitutions and the Chevron *Doctrine*. The restrained, *LTV* interpretive style probably better represents current doctrine. As we shall see in Chapter 5, the Supreme Court has been impatient with judicial creativity concerning rulemaking procedures and the *Florida East Coast* opinion seems to demand strong evidence of a congressional desire to impose formal procedures, at least where the action seems "quasi-legislative".

Restraint on judicial elaboration of statutory hearing rights, even where the decision in question is clearly adjudicatory, has also gained considerable support from *Chevron U.S.A. v. Natural Resources Defense Council*, 467 U.S. 837 (1984). Broadly speaking, *Chevron* requires that formal agency interpretations (those made when exercising an agency's lawmaking power via either rulemaking or adjudication) of ambiguous statutory terms be upheld unless the agency's interpretation is unreasonable. (For an extended consideration of the *Chevron* doctrine, see *infra*, Chapter 7.) Because silence, as in *Yamasaki* and *LTV*, or the mere requirement of a "hearing," as in *Florida East Coast*, is hardly a clear statement of congressional intent (although the problem is really "vagueness" rather than "ambiguity"), one would expect that agencies are entitled to have their procedural regulations interpreting such statutes respected—unless, of course, they are unreasonable. (It is possible, of course, that a facially silent or vague statute could so clearly presume a formal adjudicatory hearing that it would be "unambiguous" under *Chevron*, but no such cases seem to have arisen.)

Indeed, *Chevron* deference may have multiple effects on the analysis of statutory hearing rights: first, it tends to foreclose *Yamasaki*-like independent judicial interpretation of what the statute requires. Second, it tends to separate the question of the interpretive reasonableness of an agency's procedural choices from the question of the procedure's constitutional legitimacy.

Chemical Waste Management, Inc. v. U.S. Environmental Protection Agency, 873 F.2d 1477 (D.C.Cir.1989), is a good example. There plaintiffs argued that an informal hearing was inadequate to determine whether they should be subjected to an order to take corrective action to prevent or mitigate the release of hazardous waste into the environment under the Resource Conservation and Recovery Act (RCRA) as amended. The procedural claim was based both on RCRA and the U.S. Constitution. The statutory claim relied on a rule of the DC Circuit enunciated in *Union of Concerned Scientists v. U.S. N.R.C.*, 735 F.2d 1437 (D.C.Cir.1984), that, when a statute calls for a hearing with respect to an adjudication, that hearing is presumptively governed by the "on the record" procedures of the Administrative Procedure Act. RCRA required that the plaintiffs be given a "hearing" and an order to take corrective action was clearly adjudicative. Writing for a unanimous court, Judge Ginsberg held that the *UCS* presumption had been foreclosed by *Chevron*.[12] The simple statutory requirement that an agency is required to hold a "hearing" could hardly, by itself, make the failure to hold a formal trial type hearing *presumptively* unreasonable. The court then reviewed the agency's rationale for using informal processes in the light of the language, structure, legislative history and functioning of RCRA, and concluded that the agency's position was entirely reasonable.

The court separately considered whether the process employed was constitutionally reasonable under the standards enunciated in *Mathews v. Eldridge*. When pursuing this analysis the court used the *Eldridge* balancing test, not an inquiry focused on the congruence of the agency's interpretation with statutory text or congressional intent. Once again the agency prevailed. To be sure there is overlap between arguments for the reasonableness (or unreasonableness) of the agency's procedural policy choice when analyzing the statutory claim and the discussion of the likely impact of formal adjudicatory procedures on accuracy when applying the *Eldridge* formula. But a *Chevron*-based analytic approach avoids the virtual conflation of constitutional principles and statutory demands that are a hallmark of cases like *Florida East Coast,* which cites constitutional precedent as an aid in interpreting the statutory hearing requirement.

One might wonder, however, whether these two questions can be made to remain distinct. A court *could* find that an agency's construction of its statute was a reasonable rendering of congressional intent, yet an unreasonable process judged by the standards of the Due Process Clause. But this may be only a conceptual possibility. Judicial reluctance to find that Congress intended an unconstitutional result when a constitutional construction can be put on the statute seems to press reviewing courts in the direction of finding that unconstitutional constructions of ambiguous or vague statutory language are not reasonable constructions of congressional intent.

12. Judge Ginsberg used a special rule of the D.C. Circuit which permits a panel to overturn a prior *en banc* position where its ruling is first circulated to and approved by the entire court.

Chevron deference to procedural judgments, like that exhibited in *Chemical Waste Management*, might also affect constitutional adjudication. Most agencies have authority to specify implementing procedures. Where they have done so by rule (which was not true in *Yamasaki*), giving *Chevron* deference to the agency's statutory interpretation seems likely to lend even greater force to the *Eldridge* majority's injunction that courts defer to "the good-faith judgments of the individuals charged by Congress with the administration of [government] programs that the procedures they have provided assure fair[ness]."

Third-Party Hearing Rights

Our discussion of statutory hearing rights has so far proceeded on the assumption that the party invoking the hearing right is the subject of the adjudicatory action in question. There are, however, at least two categories of disputes in which other parties may be able to force an agency to conduct an on-the-record proceeding.

Comparative Hearings. One such category is illustrated by *Ashbacker Radio Corp. v. Federal Communications Commission*, 326 U.S. 327 (1945). Ashbacker had applied to the FCC to change to a different frequency for its broadcasts from Muskegon, Michigan. Under § 309(e) of the Federal Communications Act, 47 U.S.C. § 309(e) (1994), the FCC was required to afford Ashbacker a hearing if it was not prepared to grant the petition summarily.

At the same time, the FCC had before it an application from Fetzer Broadcasting for a construction permit that the Act required for the building of a new broadcast station on the same frequency in Grand Rapids, Michigan. Under FCC regulations, stations in Muskegon and Grand Rapids would be too close geographically to be permitted to broadcast on the same frequency. The FCC responded by summarily granting Fetzer's application and then, at Ashbacker's hearing, simply applying its geographic proximity rule as a conclusive bar to Ashbacker's petition.

The Supreme Court reversed and remanded to the agency for a comparative hearing on the two applications. The Court said:

> We do not think it is enough to say that the power of the Commission to issue a license on a finding of public interest, convenience or necessity supports its grant of one of two mutually exclusive applications without a hearing of the other. For if the grant of one effectively precludes the other, the statutory right to a hearing which Congress has accorded applicants before denial of their applications becomes an empty thing. We think that is the case here.
>
> The Commission in its notice of hearing on petitioner's application stated that the application "will not be granted by the Commission unless the issues listed above are determined in favor of the applicant on the basis of a record duly and properly made by means of a formal hearing." One of the issues listed was the determination of "the extent of any interference which would result from the

simultaneous operation" of petitioner's proposed station and Fetzer's station. Since the Commission itself stated that simultaneous operation of the two stations would result in "intolerable interference" to both, it is apparent that petitioner carries a burden which cannot be met. To place that burden on it is in effect to make its hearing a rehearing on the grant of the competitor's license rather than a hearing on the merits of its own application. That may satisfy the strict letter of the law but certainly not its spirit or intent.

The result in *Ashbacker* was to require the FCC to hold the on-the-record proceeding on the Fetzer application that the agency had sought to avoid. *Ashbacker*, however, did not tell the agency what kind of hearing to conduct. In fact, in co-channel cases like *Ashbacker* involving different communities, the FCC hearing does not now involve a full-blown comparison of the competing broadcasters, but only of the service needs of the respective communities. The FCC holds comparative hearings regarding broadcaster merits only for same-community applications. (Moreover, the FCC's experience with comparative hearings as a licensing device proved so frustrating over the decades that they are not now used for commercial broadcast licenses or construction permits, but only for more limited classes of applicants, such as public broadcast stations and other noncommercial educational broadcasters. Otherwise, when the FCC accepts mutually exclusive applications for initial license or construction permits, then, most often, the Commission is now directed by statute to grant the license or permit to one of the competing qualified applicants through a system of competitive bidding. 47 U.S.C. § 309(j).)

Ashbacker also does not dictate when applications for government approval are "mutually exclusive." At a technological level this issue is unlikely to cause confusion at the FCC, because the agency has set fixed, quantitative measures of acceptable electrical interference, and has allocated FM and TV frequencies geographically by rule. (Note, however, that what makes applications for broadcast licenses mutually exclusive is precisely the agency's own policy, albeit one driven by technology.) But what if two stations wish to serve the same area on different frequencies but in a context suggesting that only one station can be economically viable?

ANR Pipeline Company v. FERC, 205 F.3rd 403 (D.C.Cir.2000) considered this question in the context of competing applications to construct natural gas pipelines. The FERC had granted both applications and ANR appealed arguing that only one project was economically viable and that FERC should have held a comparative hearing to grant only one license. The D.C. circuit disagreed. While "the short term difficulty of competing with an incumbent pipeline makes two pipelines in some sense exclusive * * * FERC seems at least implicitly to have concluded that this kind of economic disadvantage is different from a situation in which economic factors make it possible to grant only one license, so that *Ashbacker* does not apply here. We think its judgment was reasonable." The Ninth Circuit has given a similar response in a case, *Western Radio Services Co. v. Glickman*, 113 F.3rd 966 (9th Cir.1997), where physical exclusivity was at issue. Although the court recognized that the granting of a special use permit for a telephone tower in a national forest was in one sense an exclusive right (only one applicant could construct a tower at the approved site), physical exclusivity did not prevent the accommodation of both telephone companies' desires to use the tower for cellular transmission. Indeed, both parties had agreed that if granted a special use permit, their tower could accommodate the competing applicant's transmission needs.

Third–Party Intervention. A second category of cases in which parties not directly regulated by an agency may nonetheless be positioned to compel or expand an on-the-record hearing involves public interest intervenors.

The leading case on third-party hearing rights is *Office of Communication of the United Church of Christ v. Federal Communications Commission*, 359 F.2d 994 (D.C.Cir.1966). At issue was an FCC license renewal proceeding involving a Mississippi television station, WLBT. WLBT had defied a then-existing regulatory obligation to broadcast multiple points of view on significant questions of public policy by refusing to broadcast any programming in support of racial desegregation. It had broadcast programs supporting segregation and, in one instance, cut off a national network broadcast that would have included a statement by the general counsel of the NAACP. A local church and two individual civil rights activists (pleading also that they were television viewers, who had unsuccessfully urged WLBT to give air time to viewpoints supportive of civil rights) complained to the FCC that, on WLBT, "Negro individuals and institutions are given very much less television exposure than others are given and that programs are generally disrespectful toward Negroes." The agency also received reports of anti-Catholic bias by the station.

In reviewing a license application, the FCC is obligated to determine whether the broadcaster is serving the "public interest, convenience, and necessity." 47 U.S.C. § 309(a). If the FCC is, "for any reason * * * unable to make the [required] finding," it is required to designate the license application for a hearing. In the WLBT matter, the FCC determined that the allegations brought to its attention precluded a public interest finding without a hearing that would sustain the renewal of WLBT's license for a full term. The Commission nonetheless, without a hearing, offered WLBT a one-year probationary renewal, which the station accepted.

The petitioners protested that, because they were "parties in interest" within the meaning of 47 U.S.C. § 309(d)(1), the FCC had denied *their* rights by proceeding without a formal hearing to grant WLBT any broadcast authority. The D.C. Circuit agreed. The Court acknowledged that the FCC had authority to establish and apply "rules for * * * public participation [in hearings], including rules for determining which community representatives are to be allowed to participate and how many are reasonably required to give the Commission the assistance it needs in vindicating the public interest." Noting, however, that the FCC had already determined that the petitioners were responsible representatives of WLBT's listening public, the Court held that the FCC was compelled to give some or all of them an opportunity to substantiate their allegations in an on-the-record proceeding. It made no difference, in the Court's view, that the petitioners were not broadcasters and would suffer no adverse economic consequence as a result of WLBT's license renewal.

The *United Church of Christ* decision is the seminal modern case on public interest intervention. Its broadening of intervention rights reflects the thesis articulated by Professor Richard Stewart that the representation of affected interests in administrative proceedings is a key to the legitimacy of the modern administrative state. Richard Stewart, *The Reformation of American Administrative Law*, 88 Harv. L. Rev. 1669 (1975). Agencies have, in some instances, gone even further to encourage public participation by offering to subsidize public involvement in formal agency proceedings. Carl W. Tobias, *Of Public Funds and Public Participation: Resolving the Issue of Agency Authority to Reimburse Public Participants in Administrative Proceedings*, 82 Colum. L. Rev. 906 (1982). Although states typically do not subsidize public intervenors, public utility commissions often have public panel-type representation, with similar aims.

To be sure, the *United Church of Christ* litigation arrived at the D.C. Circuit in an unusual posture. Because the FCC conceded that it could not make a "public interest" finding to justify the full renewal of the broadcaster's license, it could not avoid a hearing on the ground that no material issue of qualifications existed. A hearing was thus avoidable only by denying "party in interest" status to the United Church of Christ. In most cases, the FCC will review a petition for intervention and (1) deny a hearing on the merits, putting aside any standing question or (2) schedule a hearing on its own initiative, which reduces the incentive to exclude intervenors.

Moreover, both the agency and the court characterized the issue posed in *Church of Christ* as one of "standing," using a term also associated with a party's capacity, discussed in Chapter 7, to invoke judicial review of a defendant's behavior. Indeed, the D.C. Circuit analyzed the petitioners' right to protest WLBT's license before the Commission as though it were assessing its standing to seek judicial review of the FCC's licensing decision.

"Standing" need not, however, have the same implications in the two contexts. Article III courts, the Supreme Court has determined, are constitutionally limited to hearing only those disputes that fall within categories that Article III denominates "cases" and "controversies." The Article III-based standing inquiries, whether a would-be plaintiff has suffered the requisite injury and sought meaningful judicial relief, aim to preserve the proper constitutional role of judges.

Whether particular parties ought to be able to present their views in agency adjudication, however, poses a different set of questions: Does

Congress intend that a particular class of parties have such access? Could an agency's grant (or denial) of access be defended as consistent with the legislative goals reasonably imputed to a particular statute? It would not be irrational, for example, for Congress (1) to permit organized groups with obvious expertise to participate in adjudicatory proceedings that do not involve any question of redressing injury to those groups, or (2) in the name of efficiency, to limit the involvement at the agency level of parties whose access to judicial review may be sufficient to protect their interests.

Because the FCC mandate is so broad, the D.C. Circuit may have inferred that the cause of rational policy making would be well served by broad audience participation at the agency level. In such a circumstance, standing to participate should be at least as broad as it would be in federal court because no constitutional limits on standing apply to administrative proceedings. On the other hand, if the agency's discretion were confined narrowly by statute, intervention at the agency level might threaten unproductive delay, especially when aggrieved parties could seek post-decision judicial review. If an agency is inclined to regard intervention as a burden, broad intervention rights may provide a further incentive to avoid formal adjudication or to limit its scope through rulemaking, topics discussed below. For analyses of the cost-benefit issues that attend public interest representation in agency decision making, see Earnest Gellhorn, *Public Participation in Administrative Proceedings*, 81 Yale L.J. 359 (1972), and Tobias, *supra*.

Due Process Revisited. Cases involving statutory third-party hearing rights are analogous to disputes in which third-parties seek to trigger the procedural due process rights of another. In *O'Bannon v. Town Court Nursing Center*, 447 U.S. 773 (1980), the Court held that the elderly residents of a nursing home were not constitutionally entitled to a hearing before a state or federal agency could revoke the home's authority to provide them nursing care at government expense. (The nursing home itself did have a cognizable property interest in its certification, but was regarded as adequately protected by a post-revocation hearing.) The majority opinion turned on the absence of any language in the relevant statute conferring a right on Medicaid recipients to continued residence in nursing homes of their choice. In his separate concurrence, Justice Blackmun concluded that the patients did enjoy a protected property interest in their residency, but argued, given the competing interests involved, that their interest was adequately protected by the formal post-termination hearing procedures provided to the nursing home. The implication of either the majority or Justice Blackmun's approach would seem to be that, if a statutory decision making scheme does not envision hearing rights on behalf of persons affected indirectly by adjudicatory decisions, the Court is unlikely to find such rights in the Constitution.

Circuit courts have struggled with the due process rights of indirectly affected parties in a number of contexts. In *Ridder v. Office of Thrift Supervision*, 146 F.3rd 1035 (D.C.Cir.1998), bank officers brought suit to enjoin enforcement of a temporary order prohibiting a bank holding company from paying their legal expenses. The plaintiffs argued that the temporary order deprived them of their right to receive fees and costs without notice and hearing. But, because they were not the subjects of the temporary order, the D.C. Circuit rejected the appellants due process claim. In its view "any harm the appellants have suffered from the issuance of the order was a consequential result of the lawful action OTS directed toward the holding company and therefore was no due process violation." *Id.* at 1041.

G & G Fire Sprinklers v. Bradshaw, 156 F.3d 893 (9th Cir.1998) (the appeals court decision reviewed on other grounds in *Lujan v. G & G Fire Sprinklers, Inc., supra* at p. 349 reached a different result on arguably distinguishable facts. Appellant was a subcontractor on a California state construction project. The California Department of Labor issued withholding notices to the prime contractor based upon the appellant's alleged violation of certain California labor regulations. When G & G filed suit challenging this action, which had prompted the prime contractor to withhold its payments from G & G, the state interposed an argument based on *O'Bannon*. The Ninth Circuit rejected the state's defense. Although G & G was not the subject of the withholding order it was clearly its target. The affects on G & G were not an incidental consequence of actions against someone else. In the circuit court's view when the government acts against one person for the purpose of punishing or restraining another, it intends to affect that second party's interests in ways that give it an independent claim to procedural due process.

2. ON–THE–RECORD ADJUDICATORY PROCESS

A Roadmap of "On-the-Record" Adjudication Under the APA

Because Congress' specific directives frequently diverge from or add to the APA procedures, and because agency regulations typically embroider on the APA model in any event, it is not possible to describe a "typical" agency hearing. Counsel's procedural expectations will not be the same, for example, (a) in seeking to avoid the SSA's cutoff of a client's disability payments; (b) in seeking DOT approval of an overseas route for a client airline, and (c) in seeking to avoid FTC sanction for a client's alleged unfair trade practice. Nonetheless, thoughtful reading of the APA highlights a host of issues on which Congress or an agency will always have to focus in designing a formal hearing procedure.

Initiation. Under the APA, to commence a formal hearing, an agency must notify parties of the time, place, and nature of the hearing, and of the legal authority under which it is to be held. If the hearing is adjudicatory, the notice must indicate "the matters of fact and law" asserted by the agency, § 554(b)(3), including, in most license revocation or suspension proceedings, notice of the facts or conduct that assertedly warrants such action. § 558(c). When "private persons are the moving parties" in an adjudication, then other parties to the proceeding must be given notice of controverted issues of fact and law. *Id.* All other pleading rules in a formal proceeding are prescribed by the individual agency.

Informal settlement. After a formal adjudicatory hearing is announced, an agency is still required—"when time, the nature of the proceeding, and the public interest permit"—to give parties the opportunity to propose offers of settlement or other resolutions of the issues that may obviate the need for a hearing. § 554(b).

Initial Decision Maker. Unless some other statute designates the initial decision maker in a formal hearing, an agency may decide to leave the taking of evidence to the agency itself,[1] to one or more members of the body that constitutes the agency, or to an administrative law judge. § 556(b). The last option is by far the most common.

The presiding officer at a formal hearing has several powers to assure the smooth conduct of the proceedings—powers that resemble those of judges in civil trials. These include the authority to administer oaths, to issue subpoenas (if the agency has subpoena authority), and to make evidentiary and procedural rulings. § 556(c).

The agency may determine that the presiding officer's role shall be limited to compiling the formal record, which must be certified to the agency for final decision. § 557(b). Far more commonly, in an adjudicatory hearing, the person or persons presiding at the hearing will be responsible for rendering an initial decision.

Exclusivity of Record; Ex Parte Contacts. The transcript of testimony, the exhibits, and all other formally filed papers constitute "the exclusive record for decision" in a formal APA hearing. § 556(e). The exclusivity of the record is protected by several means.

In any on-the-record proceeding, once the hearing is "noticed," there may be no ex parte communication "relevant to the merits of the proceeding" between "any interested person outside the agency" and any "member of the body comprising the agency, administrative law judge, or other employee who is or may reasonably be expected to be involved in the decisional process of the proceeding." § 557(d)(1)(A), (B). If the hearing is adjudicatory and not for the purpose of determining an initial licensing application, the presiding officer is forbidden to "consult" any "person or party"—presumably, whether or not the person is "interested" or outside the agency—"on a fact in issue, unless on notice and opportunity for all parties to participate." § 554(d).

There are two notable exceptions to the bar against ex parte contacts. There is no statutory prohibition against ex parte contacts

1. At this point, among others, there is an ambiguity in the APA's use of the word "agency." Most often, the word denotes an institution of the sort that falls within the statutory definition of "agency," typically, a department or commission. On some occasions, however, the word makes sense only if understood to mean the person who heads the institution. It would be absurd to regard the APA's authorization for "the agency" to preside at the taking of evidence as contemplating that the entire institution would preside. Similarly, exempting "the agency" from the APA's separation of functions provision would obliterate that provision if "the agency" means the institution, rather than merely its head.

between the persons constituting the agency and the presiding officer at a formal hearing, § 554(d), or against persons other than the presiding officer giving information ex parte to Congress about the merits of a proceeding. § 557(d)(2).

If an impermissible contact does occur, it must, once discovered, be made part of the public record, § 557(d)(1)(C), and the agency, ALJ, or other official presiding at a hearing may impose sanctions, including the dismissal of a claim. § 557(d)(1)(D). If ex parte contacts are not unearthed before the final decision, the agency will not necessarily be required to redo the proceeding. In procedural terms, the agency's decision becomes "voidable," but not "void," and a reviewing court will assess such factors as the substance of the communication, the likelihood that it tainted the outcome, and whether the party responsible for improper contacts benefited from them. For an example of how extensive ex parte contacts can be *without* voiding a proceeding, see *PATCO v. Federal Labor Relations Authority*, 685 F.2d 547 (D.C.Cir.1982).

These limitations do not mean that agency adjudicators cannot use staff or expert panels to assist in analyzing complex data, but post-hearing analysis may not add critical facts that were not made a part of the record. The First Circuit Court of Appeals put the matter this way in *Seacoast Anti–Pollution League v. Costle*, 572 F.2d 872, *cert. denied* 439 U.S. 824 (1978):

> Petitioners object to the Administrator's use of a panel of EPA scientists to assist him in reviewing the Regional Administrator's initial decision. The objection is two-fold: first, that the Administrator should not have sought such help at all; and, second, that the panel's report (the Report) to the Administrator included information not in the administrative record.
>
> Petitioners point out that by the EPA's own regulations "[the] Administrator shall decide the matters under review on the basis of the record presented and any other consideration he deems relevant." It is true that when a decision is committed to a particular individual that individual must be the one who reviews the evidence on which the decision is to be based. But it does not follow that all other individuals are shut out of the decision process. That conclusion runs counter to the purposes of the administrative agencies which exist, in part, to enable government to focus broad ranges of talent on particular multi-dimensional problems. The Administrator is charged with making highly technical decisions in fields far beyond his individual expertise. "The strength [of the administrative process] lies in staff work organized in such a way that the appropriate specialization is brought to bear upon each aspect of a single decision, the synthesis being provided by the men at the top." 2 K. Davis, Administrative Law Treatise 84 (1958). Therefore, "[evidence] * * * may be sifted and analyzed by competent subordinates." *Morgan v. United States*, *supra*. *Cf.* 5 U.S.C. § 557(d) (forbidding ex parte communications only with persons outside the

agency). The decision ultimately reached is no less the Administrator's simply because agency experts helped him to reach it.

A different question is presented, however, if the agency experts do not merely sift and analyze but also add to the evidence properly before the Administrator. The regulation quoted above cannot allow the Administrator to consider evidence barred from consideration by the APA, 5 U.S.C. § 556(e) * * * To the extent the technical review panel's Report included information not in the record on which the Administrator relied, § 556(e) was violated. In effect the agency's staff would have made up for PSCO's failure to carry its burden of proof.

Our review of the Report indicates that such violations did occur. The most serious instance is on page 19 of the Report where the technical panel rebuts the Regional Administrator's finding that PSCO had failed to supply enough data on species' thermal tolerances by saying:

> "There is little information in the record on the thermal tolerances of marine organisms exposed to the specific temperature fluctuation associated with the Seabrook operation. However, the scientific literature does contain many references to the thermal sensitivity of members of the local biota."

Whether or not these references do exist and whether or not they support the conclusions the panel goes on to draw does not concern us here. What is important is that the record did not support the conclusion until supplemented by the panel. The panel's work found its way directly into the Administrator's decision * * *.

Separation of Functions. In an adjudicatory hearing, the agency employee who takes evidence may not be subject to the supervision of anyone in the agency (other than the agency heads themselves) who is responsible for the agency's investigative or prosecutorial functions. Likewise, no employee involved in the agency's investigative or prosecutorial functions—except the agency members themselves—may participate or advise at any stage in the agency's decisional process in a formal adjudication. § 554(d).

Appearance of Parties and Other Interested Persons. A party to a formal hearing is entitled to appear personally or through counsel. Any person compelled to appear at an agency hearing may be accompanied and represented by counsel. Other interested persons may appear before the agency "so far as the orderly conduct of agency business permits," but have no apparent right to counsel, if not appearing under compulsion. § 555(b).

Discovery. On this critical issue of procedure, the APA is all but silent, indicating generally that subpoenas, required reports, inspections, and other investigative measures may be pursued only "as authorized by law." § 555(c). The APA's omission of any rule comparable to Fed.R.Civ. Proc., Rule 26, which allows generous discovery, has resulted in great variation in agency discovery practice. In 1962, the U.S. Administrative Conference recommended that all agencies promulgate explicit discovery rules, and, in 1970, following the failure of all but a few agencies to respond, it offered extensive recommendations for discovery in agency adjudication. 1 C.F.R. § 305.70–4 (1970). Despite this effort, comprehensive discovery rules are available only in a "handful of agencies." BERNARD A. SCHWARTZ, ADMINISTRATIVE LAW (3d ed. 1991).

The APA does offer a minor gesture in the direction of equalizing the position of parties to a formal hearing, requiring that "[a]gency subpoenas authorized by law shall be issued to a party on request." § 555(d). Equality, however, is illusory because agencies typically have methods to elicit information about private parties—through required reports, for example—that private parties cannot duplicate. Some agencies, such as the Food and Drug Administration, lack subpoena power, and thus offer no subpoena capacity to responding parties at all. And, § 555(d)'s language notwithstanding, agencies have discretion to deny subpoenas where they conclude that they are not reasonably necessary to develop relevant evidence. See, e.g., *Calvin v. Chater*, 73 F.3d 87, 88 (6th Cir.1996) (denying subpoena for physician who had submitted adverse medical report in SSI disability case). One consequence of the current situation is that the Freedom of Information Act, (discussed in Chapter 6), which provides public access to a great many agency records, is often the most important discovery tool at a party's disposal.

Evidence and Rules on Proof. Parties to formal APA hearings are entitled to present their case by oral or documentary evidence, to submit rebuttal evidence, and to cross-examine witnesses. § 556(d). The APA, however, also grants agencies broad power to determine the varieties of oral or documentary evidence to be admitted at formal hearings, and, in connection with formal rulemaking or initial license applications, the agency may limit the parties to written presentations "when a party will not be prejudiced thereby."

The APA states in delphic terms: "Except as otherwise provided by statute, the proponent of a rule or order has the burden of proof." It does not specify, however, who is to be considered the "proponent of an order," or whether the "burden" referred to encompasses the burdens both of production and of persuasion. As a consequence, allocation of these burdens may vary in different agency proceedings.

For example, although an agency will probably always be deemed the "proponent of an order" imposing some sanction, a would-be licensee seeking a hearing to overcome agency objections to its application may be deemed the "proponent of an order" granting its license. And, even if the agency is the proponent of a sanction, it may, depending on the statute being implemented, shift to a private respondent the burden of persuasion on particular defenses.

The APA is silent on the standard of proof that must be met by the party with the burden of persuasion. The Supreme Court has held that, in the absence of special circumstances, the standard of proof that the proponent shoulders at an agency hearing is "preponderance of the evidence." Compare *Steadman v. SEC*, 450 U.S. 91 (1981) (applying preponderance standard to anti-securities fraud hearing), with *Woodby v. INS*, 385 U.S. 276 (1966) (requiring "clear and convincing" evidence for deportation proceedings).

The Supreme Court is nevertheless clear that agencies may not shift the ultimate burden of proof where "burden of proof" refers to the "burden of persuasion" not the burden of coming forward with some evidence. In *Director, Office of Workers' Compensation Programs, Department of Labor v. Greenwich Collieries*, 512 U.S. 267 (1994), the Court overturned 50 years of Labor Department practice under the Long Shore and Harbor Workers' Compensation Act, and nearly two decades of practice under the Black Lung Benefits Act. In proceedings under both statutes the Labor Board had by rule specified that where the evidence was equally probative of the existence or nonexistence of a compensable disability, the claimant would be determined to have carried his or her own burden of proof and benefits would be awarded. This so-called "true doubt" rule, meaning "in case of true doubt the claimant gets the benefit of the doubt," reversed the usual resolution of claims in evidentiary equipoise, which the Supreme Court read § 556(d)of the APA as confirming. The Court did not deny that specific statutes could provide this advantage to proponents of a rule or order, but it did not find sufficiently explicit language in either the Long Shore and Harbor Workers Compensation Act or the Black Lung Benefits Act to overcome the APA formulation.

Justices Souter, Blackmun and Stevens dissented, arguing that the Court's decision overturned not only 50 years of practice, but the original understanding of the Administrative Procedure Act and several of the Court's prior precedents.

The Product of the Hearing. Unless an agency itself presides at the formal hearing, and thus makes all relevant decisions itself in the first instance, it has two options regarding the form of the ultimate decision to result from that hearing. It can treat the outcome of the hearing as the agency's "initial decision," which becomes final unless a party seeks to have the agency change it. § 557(b). Alternatively, it can provide that the decision shall constitute only a tentative decision or recommendation, which must be formally adopted by the agency in order to be implemented. *Id.*

Any decision—whether initial, tentative, recommended, or final—must include statements of findings and conclusions on all material issues of fact, law, and discretion, and must contain the rule, order, sanction, relief, or denial thereof that is the consequence of the hearing. § 557(c).

Administrative Appeals. When the agency permits other officials to preside at a hearing and make the initial decision, the agency may still provide for administrative review. Such review may be an appeal as of right or at the agency's discretion. § 557(b). Some agencies set up internal boards to hear appeals, reserving certiorari-like discretionary review to themselves. In reviewing a subordinate's decision, the agency "has all the powers which it would have in making the initial decision except as it may limit the issues on notice or by rule." *Id.*

In an adjudication other than an initial licensing, the presiding officer at the hearing—if it is not the agency itself—must render a recommended decision. In initial licensing, as in formal rulemaking proceedings discussed in Chapter 5, the agency or another of its employees may be assigned the responsibility for issuing a tentative decision or, in cases of unavoidable necessity, the agency may forego the recommended decision stage altogether.

RICHARDSON v. PERALES

Supreme Court of the United States, 1971.
402 U.S. 389, 91 S.Ct. 1420, 28 L.Ed.2d 842.

JUSTICE BLACKMUN delivered the opinion of the Court.

In 1966 Pedro Perales, a San Antonio truck driver, then aged 34, height 5′11″, weight about 220 pounds, filed a claim for disability insurance benefits under the Social Security Act. Sections 216(I)(1) and 223(d)(1) of that Act both provide that the term "disability" means "inability to engage in any substantial gainful activity by reason of any medically determinable physical or mental impairment which * * *." Section 205(g), 42 U.S.C. § 405(g), relating to judicial review, states, "The findings of the Secretary as to any fact, if supported by substantial evidence, shall be conclusive. * * * "

The issue here is whether physicians' written reports of medical examinations they have made of a disability claimant may constitute "substantial evidence" supportive of a finding of nondisability, within the § 205(g) standard, when the claimant objects to the admissibility of those reports and when the only live testimony is presented by his side and is contrary to the reports.

I

In his claim Perales asserted that on September 29, 1965, he became disabled as a result of an injury to his back sustained in lifting an object at work. He was seen by a neurosurgeon, Dr. Ralph A. Munslow, who first recommended conservative treatment. When this provided no relief, myelography was performed and surgery * * * was advised. * * * On recurrence of pain, however, he consented to the recommended procedure. Dr. Munslow operated on November 23. * * * No disc protrusion or other definitive pathology was identified at surgery. The post-operative diagnosis was: "Nerve root compression syndrome, left." The patient was discharged from Dr. Munslow's care on January 25, 1966, with a final diagnosis of "Neuritis, lumbar, mild."

Mr. Perales continued to complain, but Dr. Munslow and Dr. Morris H. Lampert, a neurologist called in consultation, were still unable to find any objective neurological explanation for his complaints. Dr. Munslow advised that he return to work.

In April 1966 Perales consulted Dr. Max Morales, Jr., a general practitioner of San Antonio. Dr. Morales hospitalized the patient from April 15 to May 2. His final discharge diagnosis was: "Back sprain, lumbo-sacral spine."

Perales then filed his claim. As required by § 221 of the Act, the claim was referred to the state agency for determination. The agency obtained the hospital records and a report from Dr. Morales. The report set forth no physical findings or laboratory studies, but the doctor again gave as his diagnosis: "Back sprain—lumbo-sacral spine," this time "moderately severe," with "Ruptured disk not ruled out." The agency arranged for a medical examination, at no cost to the patient, by Dr. John H. Langston, an orthopedic surgeon. * * *

Dr. Langston's ensuing report to the Division of Disability Determination was devastating from the claimant's standpoint. The doctor referred to Perales' being "on crutches or cane" since his injury. He noted a slightly edematous condition in the legs, attributed to "inactivity and sitting around"; slight tenderness in some of the muscles of the dorsal spine, thought to be due to poor posture; and "a very mild sprain [of those muscles] which would resolve were he actually to get a little exercise and move." Apart from this, * * * Dr. Langston found no abnormalities of the lumbar spine. Otherwise, he described Perales as a "big physical healthy specimen * * * obviously holding back and limiting all of his motions, intentionally * * *." * * *

The state agency denied the claim. Perales requested reconsideration. Dr. Morales submitted a further report to the agency and an opinion to the claimant's attorney. This outlined the surgery and hospitalizations and his own conservative and continuing treatment of the patient, the medicines prescribed, the administration of ultrasound therapy, and the patient's constant complaints. The doctor concluded that the patient had not made a complete recovery from his surgery, that he was not malingering, that his injury was permanent, and that he was totally and permanently disabled. He recommended against any further surgery.

The state agency then arranged for an examination by Dr. James M. Bailey, a board-certified psychiatrist with a subspecialty in neurology. Dr. Bailey's report to the agency on August 30, 1966, concluded with the following diagnosis:

> "Paranoid personality, manifested by hostility, feelings of persecution and long history of strained interpersonal relationships.
>
> "I do not feel that this patient has a separate psychiatric illness at this time. It appears that his personality is conducive to anger, frustrations, etc."

The agency again reviewed the file. The Bureau of Disability Insurance of the Social Security Administration made its independent review.

The report and opinion of Dr. Morales, as the claimant's attending physician, were considered, as were those of the other examining physicians. The claim was again denied.

Perales requested a hearing before a hearing examiner. The agency then referred the claimant to Dr. Langston and to Dr. Richard H. Mattson for electromyography studies. Dr. Mattson's notes referred to "some chronic or past disturbance of function in the nerve supply" to the left and right anterior tibialis muscles and right extensor digitorium brevis muscles that was "strongly suggestive of lack of maximal effort" and was "the kind of finding that is typically associated with a functional or psychogenic component to weakness." There was no evidence of "any active process effecting [sic] the nerves at present." Dr. Langston advised the agency that Dr. Mattson's finding of "very poor effort" verified what Dr. Langston had found on the earlier physical examination.

The requested hearing was set for January 12, 1967, in San Antonio. * * * The hearing took place at the time designated. A supplemental hearing was held March 31. The claimant appeared at the first hearing with his attorney and with Dr. Morales. * * * The reports of Dr. Morales and of Dr. Munslow were then submitted by the claimant's counsel and admitted.

At the two hearings oral testimony was submitted by claimant Perales, by Dr. Morales, by a former fellow employee of the claimant, by a vocational expert, and by Dr. Lewis A. Leavitt, a physician board-certified in physical medicine and rehabilitation, and chief of, and professor in, the Department of Physical Medicine at Baylor University College of Medicine. Dr. Leavitt was called by the hearing examiner as an independent "medical adviser," that is, as an expert who does not examine the claimant but who hears and reviews the medical evidence and who may offer an opinion. The adviser is paid a fee by the Government. The claimant, through his counsel, objected to any testimony by Dr. Leavitt not based upon examination or upon a hypothetical. Dr. Leavitt testified over this objection and was cross-examined by the claimant's attorney. He stated that the consensus of the various medical reports was that Perales had a mild low-back syndrome of musculotendinous origin.

The hearing examiner, in reliance upon the several medical reports and the testimony of Dr. Leavitt, observed in his written decision, "There is objective medical evidence of impairment which the heavy preponderance of the evidence indicates to be of mild severity. * * * Taken altogether, the Hearing Examiner is of the conclusion that the claimant has not met the burden of proof." * * * The hearing examiner's decision, * * * was that the claimant was not entitled to a period of disability or to disability insurance benefits.

It is to be noted at this point that § 205(d) of the Act, provides that the Secretary has power to issue subpoenas requiring the attendance and testimony of witnesses and the production of evidence and that the

Secretary's regulations, authorized by § 205(a), provide that a claimant may request the issuance of subpoenas. Perales, however, who was represented by counsel, did not request subpoenas for either of the two hearings. * * * The Appeals Council ruled that the decision of the hearing examiner was correct.

Upon this adverse ruling the claimant instituted the present action for review pursuant to § 205(g). * * * On appeal the Fifth Circuit noted the absence of any request by the claimant for subpoenas and held that, having this right and not exercising it, he was not in a position to complain that he had been denied the rights of confrontation and of cross-examination. It held that the hearsay evidence in the case was admissible under the Act; that, specifically, the written reports of the physicians were admissible in the administrative hearing; that Dr. Leavitt's testimony also was admissible; but that all this evidence together did not constitute substantial evidence when it was objected to and when it was contradicted by evidence from the only live witnesses. * * *

III

* * * Congress has provided that the Secretary

> "shall have full power and authority to make rules and regulations and to establish procedures * * * necessary or appropriate to carry out such provisions, and shall adopt reasonable and proper rules and regulations to regulate and provide for the nature and extent of the proofs and evidence and the method of taking and furnishing the same in order to establish the right to benefits hereunder."

§ 205(a).

Section 205(b) directs the Secretary to make findings and decisions; on request to give reasonable notice and opportunity for a hearing; and in the course of any hearing to receive evidence. It then provides:

> "Evidence may be received at any hearing before the Secretary even though inadmissible under rules of evidence applicable to court procedure."

In carrying out these statutory duties the Secretary has adopted regulations that state, among other things:

> "The hearing examiner shall inquire fully into the matters at issue and shall receive in evidence the testimony of witnesses and any documents which are relevant and material to such matters. * * * The * * * procedure at the hearing generally * * * shall be in the discretion of the hearing examiner and of such nature as to afford the parties a reasonable opportunity for a fair hearing."

20 CFR § 404.927.

From this it is apparent that (a) the Congress granted the Secretary the power by regulation to establish hearing procedures; (b) strict rules of evidence, applicable in the courtroom, are not to operate at social security hearings so as to bar the admission of evidence otherwise pertinent; and (c) the conduct of the hearing rests generally in the examiner's discretion. There emerges an emphasis upon the informal rather than the formal. This, we think, is as it should be, for this administrative procedure, and these hearings, should be understandable to the layman claimant, should not necessarily be stiff and comfortable only for the trained attorney, and should be liberal and not strict in tone and operation. This is the obvious intent of Congress so long as the procedures are fundamentally fair. * * *

V

* * * The question * * * is as to what procedural due process requires with respect to examining physicians' reports in a social security disability claim hearing.

We conclude that a written report by a licensed physician who has examined the claimant and who sets forth in his report his medical findings in his area of competence may be received as evidence in a disability hearing and, despite its hearsay character and an absence of cross-examination, and despite the presence of opposing direct medical testimony and testimony by the claimant himself, may constitute substantial evidence supportive of a finding by the hearing examiner adverse to the claimant, when the claimant has not exercised his right to subpoena the reporting physician and thereby provide himself with the opportunity for cross-examination of the physician.

We are prompted to this conclusion by a number of factors that, we feel, assure underlying reliability and probative value:

1. The identity of the five reporting physicians is significant. Each report presented here was prepared by a practicing physician who had examined the claimant. A majority * * * were called into the case by the state agency. Although each received a fee, that fee is recompense for his time and talent otherwise devoted to private practice or other professional assignment. We cannot, and do not, ascribe bias to the work of these independent physicians, or any interest on their part in the outcome of the administrative proceeding beyond the professional curiosity a dedicated medical man possesses.

2. The vast workings of the social security administrative system make for reliability and impartiality in the consultant reports. We bear in mind that the agency operates essentially, and is intended so to do, as an adjudicator and not as an advocate or adversary. * * *

3. * * * The particular reports of the physicians who examined claimant Perales were based on personal consultation and personal examination and rested on accepted medical procedures and tests. * * *

These are routine, standard, and unbiased medical reports by physician specialists concerning a subject whom they had seen. That the reports were adverse to Perales' claim is not in itself bias or an indication of nonprobative character.

4. The reports present the impressive range of examination to which Perales was subjected. * * * It is fair to say that the claimant received professional examination and opinion on a scale beyond the reach of most persons and that this case reveals a patient and careful endeavor by the state agency and the examiner to ascertain the truth.

5. So far as we can detect, there is no inconsistency whatsoever in the reports of the five specialists. Yet each result was reached by independent examination in the writer's field of specialized training.

6. Although the claimant complains of the lack of opportunity to cross-examine the reporting physicians, he did not take advantage of the opportunity afforded him under 20 CFR § 404.926 to request subpoenas for the physicians. * * * This inaction on the claimant's part supports the Court of Appeals' view that the claimant as a consequence is to be precluded from now complaining that he was denied the rights of confrontation and cross-examination.

7. Courts have recognized the reliability and probative worth of written medical reports even in formal trials and, while acknowledging their hearsay character, have admitted them as an exception to the hearsay rule. * * *

9. There is an additional and pragmatic factor which, although not controlling, deserves mention. This is what Chief Judge Brown has described as "[t]he sheer magnitude of that administrative burden," and the resulting necessity for written reports without "elaboration through the traditional facility of oral testimony." With over 20,000 disability claim hearings annually, the cost of providing live medical testimony at those hearings, where need has not been demonstrated by a request for a subpoena, over and above the cost of the examinations requested by hearing examiners, would be a substantial drain on the trust fund and on the energy of physicians already in short supply.

VI

1. Perales relies heavily on the Court's holding and statements in *Goldberg v. Kelly* * * *.

The Perales proceeding is not the same. We are not concerned with termination of disability benefits once granted. Neither are we concerned with a change of status without notice. Notice was given to claimant Perales. The physicians' reports were on file and available for inspection by the claimant and his counsel. And the authors of those reports were known and were subject to subpoena and to the very cross-examination that the claimant asserts he has not enjoyed. Further, the specter of questionable credibility and veracity is not present; there is professional disagreement with the medical conclusions, to be sure, but there is no attack here upon the doctors' credibility or veracity. * * *

3. The claimant, the District Court, and the Court of Appeals also criticize the use of Dr. Leavitt as a medical adviser. Inasmuch as medical advisers are used in approximately 13% of disability claim hearings,

comment as to this practice is indicated. We see nothing "reprehensible" in the practice, as the claimant would describe it. The trial examiner is a layman; the medical adviser is a board-certified specialist. He is used primarily in complex cases for explanation of medical problems in terms understandable to the layman-examiner. He is a neutral adviser. This particular record discloses that Dr. Leavitt explained the technique and significance of electromyography. He did offer his own opinion on the claimant's condition. That opinion, however, did not differ from the medical reports. Dr. Leavitt did not vouch for the accuracy of the facts assumed in the reports. No one understood otherwise. We see nothing unconstitutional or improper in the medical adviser concept and in the presence of Dr. Leavitt in this administrative hearing.

4. Finally, the claimant complains of the system of processing disability claims. He suggests, and is joined in this by the briefs of amici, that the Administrative Procedure Act, rather than the Social Security Act, governs the processing of claims and specifically provides for cross-examination. The claimant goes on to assert that in any event the hearing procedure is invalid on due process grounds. He says that the hearing examiner has the responsibility for gathering the evidence and "to make the Government's case as strong as possible"; that naturally he leans toward a decision in favor of the evidence he has gathered; that justice must satisfy the appearance of justice; and that an "independent hearing examiner such as in the" Longshoremen's and Harbor Workers' Compensation Act should be provided.

We need not decide whether the APA has general application to social security disability claims, for the social security administrative procedure does not vary from that prescribed by the APA. Indeed, the latter is modeled upon the Social Security Act. The cited § 556(d) provides that any documentary evidence "may be received" subject to the exclusion of the irrelevant, the immaterial, and the unduly repetitious. It further provides that a "party is entitled to present his case or defense by oral or documentary evidence * * * and to conduct such cross-examination as may be required for a full and true disclosure of the facts" and in "determining claims for money or benefits * * * an agency may, when a party will not be prejudiced thereby, adopt procedures for the submission of all or part of the evidence in written form."

These provisions conform, and are consistent with, rather than differ from or supersede, the authority given the Secretary by the Social Security Act's §§ 205(a) and (b) "to establish procedures," and "to regulate and provide for the nature and extent of the proofs and evidence and the method of taking and furnishing the same in order to establish the right to benefits," and to receive evidence "even though inadmissible under rules of evidence applicable to court procedure." Hearsay, under either Act, is thus admissible up to the point of relevancy.

The matter comes down to the question of the procedure's integrity and fundamental fairness. We see nothing that works in derogation of that integrity and of that fairness in the admission of consultants' reports, subject as they are to being material and to the use of the subpoena and consequent cross-examination. This precisely fits the statutorily prescribed "cross-examination as may be required for a full and true disclosure of the facts." * * *

We therefore reverse and remand for further proceedings. We intimate no view as to the merits. It is for the District Court now to determine whether the Secretary's findings, in the light of all material proffered and admissible, are supported by "substantial evidence" within the command of § 205(g).

It is so ordered.

JUSTICE DOUGLAS, with whom JUSTICE BLACK and JUSTICE BRENNAN concur, dissenting.

* * * [H]earsay may be received, as the Administrative Procedure Act provides that "[a]ny oral or documentary evidence may be received." But * * * hearsay evidence cannot by itself be the basis for an adverse ruling. The same section of the Act states that "[a] party is entitled * * * to conduct such cross-examination as may be required for a full and true disclosure of the facts." * * *

Cross-examination of doctors in these physical injury cases is, I think, essential to a full and fair disclosure of the facts. * * *

One doctor whose word cast this claimant into limbo never saw him, never examined him, never took his vital statistics or saw him try to walk or bend or lift weights.

He was a "medical adviser" to HEW. The use of circuit-riding doctors who never see or examine claimants to defeat their claims should be beneath the dignity of a great nation. Three other doctors who were not subject to cross-examination were experts retained and paid by the Government. Some, we are told, who were subject to no cross-examination were employed by the workmen's compensation insurance company to defeat respondent's claim. * * *

The use by HEW of its stable of defense doctors without submitting them to cross-examination is the cutting of corners—a practice in which certainly the Government should not indulge. The practice is barred by the rules which Congress has provided; and we should enforce them in the spirit in which they were written.

I would affirm this judgment.

Notes

1. *Hearsay in Administrative Adjudication.* *Perales* follows a modern trend in apparently rejecting the so-called residuum rule. Under the residuum rule, a court could not uphold an agency order under the test of "substantial evidence" unless the record contained at least a "residuum" of non-hearsay support for the underlying factfinding. The rule, still followed in some states, was articulated in *Carroll v. Knickerbocker Ice Co.*, 218 N.Y.

435, 113 N.E. 507 (1916). *Carroll* overturned a grant of worker's compensation to a deceased worker solely on the basis of his reported statements that a 300–pound block of ice fell on him while he was working. His body was unbruised, and three professed eyewitnesses testified that no such accident occurred.

Perales may be read to imply that agency reliance solely upon hearsay would deny due process if that hearsay lacked sufficient indicia of reliability. Courts weighing hearsay in light of such factors as the available contradictory direct testimony, internal evidence of reliability, the form of hearsay, the reputation of its source, and the availability of corroboration may well come to results no different in most cases from those that the residuum rule would dictate. See, e.g., *Commonwealth Unemployment Compensation Board of Review v. Ceja*, 493 Pa. 588, 427 A.2d 631 (1981) (decision denying unemployment benefits voided because of unreliability of hearsay evidence).

2. *Subpoenas*? It is easy to read the court's opinion in *Richardson v. Perales* as suggesting that the disability claimant would have been issued subpoenas for cross-examination of the consulting physicians had he but requested them. But Social Security Administration regulations have never provided an absolute right to subpoenas. Rather, 20 C.F.R. § 404.950(d)(1) (2002) tracks the language of the Administrative Procedure Act in providing that subpoenas will be issued "when it is reasonably necessary for the full presentation of a case. * * * "

Although it is settled law at the federal level that an administrative determination may be based on reliable hearsay evidence, rights to cross-examine witnesses are not conterminous with the demands of "substantial evidence". Due process may also be involved. In the context of Social Security disability claims numerous denied applicants have argued that cross-examination of opposing witnesses is an absolute right guaranteed by the Due Process Clause. Refusals to issue subpoenas for such witnesses are, therefore, unconstitutional. The circuit courts have split on this issue, with the 5th and 8th circuits granting a right to a subpoena whenever the claimant seeks one, *Lidy v. Sullivan*, 911 F.2d 1075 (5th Cir.1990); *Coffin v. Sullivan*, 895 F.2d 1206 (8th Cir.1990); and the 2nd, 6th and 7th circuits holding that the grant of a subpoena is within the sound discretion of administrative law judges. *Yancey v. Apfel*, 145 F.3rd 106 (2d Cir. 1998); *Flatford v. Chater*, 93 F.3rd 1296 (6th Cir.1996); *Butera v. Apfel*, 173 F.3rd 1049 (7th Cir.1999).

Given the balancing test enunciated in *Mathews v. Eldridge*, the "sound discretion" circuits would seem to have the better of the argument. Where evidence is cumulative and circumstantially reliable, as it was in *Richardson v. Perales*, the contribution of cross-examination to accurate factfinding seems modest. Moreover, the Social Security Administration has plausible administrative grounds for rejecting an absolute right to subpoena consultative physicians. Payments for doing consultative examinations are modest and physicians are somewhat reluctant to provide them. Such consultations are for evidentiary purposes only. The physician is not the claimant's treating physician, and is unlikely to see the claimant again. Busy physicians, which means most with good reputations, prefer to spend their time treating patients, not providing evidence for the Social Security Administration. Were they subject to subpoena in every case in which they gave a consultative opinion, the Social Security Administration fears that most board-certified specialists would decline to provide consultants' reports in disability claims. Because such reports are sought in a substantial number of cases, indeed in virtually all that go to hearing, SSA may rightly fear that routine issuance of subpoenas for consulting physicians would result in its incapacity to make sound decisions in disability cases.

On the other hand, it is surely difficult to predict whether cross-examination is reasonably necessary for a full presentation of a case in the absence of the knowledge of what cross-examination might disclose. And, if one is suspicious, as Justice Douglas clearly was in *Richardson v. Perales*, that some percentage of consultative physicians are repeat players who are biased toward limiting government payments, the good sense, if not the necessity, for cross-examination of consulting physicians takes on a quite different light.

3. *Advisors*. Note further that there was another physician called to advise the administrative law judge in *Richardson v. Perales*. That physician advisor gave no evidence, but instead explained the technical evidence to the ALJ. Because physician advisors give no evidence, they are obviously not subject to cross-examination. And the *Perales* Court follows the well-established view that administrative adjudicators are entitled to consult with staff or others as a means of fully understanding technical materials. The substantial number of medical personnel who may be involved in a disability determination, and yet not be subject to confrontation and cross-examination by claimants or their attorneys, may have contributed to the rule in a number of federal circuits that a claimant's treating physician's evidence is entitled to special weight. By contrast, other circuits have emphasized the potential conservative bias of treating physicians and their possible propensity "to quickly find disability." *Stephens v. Heckler*, 766 F.2d 284, 289 (7th Cir.1985). Caught between warring circuits the Social Security Administration has by regulation sought to structure ALJs' consideration of the reliability of treating physician evidence by specifying six factors to be considered by ALJs when weighing the value of a physician's opinion. 20 C.F.R. §§ 404.1527(d), 416.927(d) (2002). The first factor, "the nature and extent of the treatment relationship," tilts in favor of treating physicians. Factor number six, "the specialization of the physician," gives the edge to consultants.

4. *Three Hats or Two?* Although the *Perales* majority endorsed the inquisitorial approach of Social Security hearings in which administrative law judges arguably represent the interests of the claimant, of the government and of impartial adjudication, changing times may have altered the dynamics of that process. When *Perales* was decided relatively few disability claimants were represented by counsel in administrative hearings. Now the vast majority have legal representation. With the claimant represented and the government not, many observers have wondered whether administrative law judges might be pressed toward a more adversarial role that would conflict with impartial decisionmaking. The Social Security Administration has toyed with the idea of having someone represent the government's interest in hearings where the claimant was also represented. A demonstra-

tion project to test this initiative was shelved when a district court found SSA's program impermissible.

Adjudicative Consistency: Stare Decisis, Res Judicata, Estoppel

Stare Decisis. The APA provides no direct guidance on the future-binding impact of formal agency adjudication, and most courts acknowledge that the doctrine of stare decisis has less force in the administrative than in the judicial context, e.g., *International Business Machines Corp. v. United States*, 170 Ct.Cl. 357, 343 F.2d 914 (1965), *cert. denied*, 382 U.S. 1028 (1966). Many decisions make clear, however, that an agency's departure from prior law must be explained, expressly invoking APA § 706. KENNETH CULP DAVIS, ADMINISTRATIVE LAW TEXT § 17.07, at 352 (1972).

In the agency context the requirement of reasoned decisionmaking supports respect for prior decisions in somewhat the same fashion that *stare decisis* promotes adherence to judicial precedent. For example, in *Bush–Quayle, '92 Primary Committee v. Federal Election Commission*, 104 F.3d 448 (D.C.Cir.1997), the court overturned an FEC order requiring the Bush–Quayle campaign to repay certain public funds that it found to have been expended in violation of the Presidential Primary Matching Payment Account Act, 26 U.S.C. § 9031–9042 (1974). The FEC's rationale was that a number of the Bush–Quayle expenditures, although technically prior to the nomination, looked toward the general election and were therefore not "in connection with" the Bush–Quayle primary campaign.

The Bush–Quayle Primary Committee claimed that their treatment inexplicably departed from the treatment the Commission had afforded the Reagan–Bush campaign in 1984 when it had established a "bright line" standard that any expenditures prior to the nomination were primary expenditures. The FEC decision denied that it had adopted a bright line test. In its words the Reagan–Bush precedent "supports examining all of the particular facts surrounding an expenditure to determine whether it was 'in connection with' the primary election."

The D.C. Circuit was not satisfied. In its view the FEC discussion merely glossed over the precedent with a "bare assertion that the two cases are different. Without adequate elucidation, this Court has no way of ascertaining whether the cases are indeed distinguishable, whether the Commission has a principled reason for distinguishing them, or whether the Commission is refusing to treat like cases alike." Reciting language from a previous opinion that the court clearly cherished, it said "while here the agency's error was not complete inattention to its prior policies, its discussion is so perplexing as to sow doubt whether this is a process of reasoned policy making, with a change in direction put in effect for a navigational objective, or the confusion of an agency that is rudderless and adrift." *Public Service Commission for the State of New York v. Federal Power Commission*, 511 F.2d 338, 353 (D.C.Cir.1975).

Res Judicata. Agency success when invoking or seeking to avoid res judicata seems to depend on reviewing courts' assessments of whether res judicata advances the purposes of the statute the agency is implementing. A private party will not be permitted to relitigate issues already decided in administrative proceedings where ordinary considerations supporting adjudicatory finality predominate. *United States v. Utah Construction & Mining Co.*, 384 U.S. 394 (1966) (refusing to permit government contractor to relitigate administratively determined lack of entitlement to additional compensation under contract).

On the other hand, notions of substantive justice may trump res judicata in a regime such as an SSA disability adjudication. For example, in *Thompson v. Schweiker*, 665 F.2d 936 (9th Cir.1982), the SSA was required to afford a hearing to a disability claimant although his application presented no new facts as compared to earlier applications that had been denied without a hearing. The court thought the administrative record inadequate to support the denial of benefits, and concluded: "Fairness in the administrative process is more important than finality of administrative judgments". Whether fairness or finality will prevail in a particular case is not necessarily easy to predict. Compare *Hirschey v. FERC*, 701 F.2d 215 (D.C.Cir.1983) (FERC not permitted to reopen licensing proceeding for comparative review after granting construction license for power plant construction and statutory time for review had passed).

Res judicata similarly limits agencies' ability to relitigate identical administrative claims involving the same parties. But courts are less willing to apply collateral estoppel to prevent agencies from relitigating the same issues, with different parties. Thus, for example, in *United States v. Mendoza*, 464 U.S. 154 (1984), a naturalization applicant argued that the government could not deny his application based on legal arguments that had been rejected by a different district court just a few years earlier in a proceeding to which he had not been a party. The Court unanimously permitted the Government to relitigate its position. A contrary holding would have constrained the government to follow the decision of a single local district court as setting a national rule, unless it could win on appeal or successfully invoke certiorari. As Chapter 7's discussion of agency "nonacquiescence" in judicial review reveals, agencies often decline to follow the rulings of even circuit courts where they believe reviewing courts have erred on matters of importance to the agencies' overall program.

Estoppel. While agencies may be bound by prior adjudications or barred from unexplained abandonment of precedent, the government is not bound, under principles of equitable estoppel, by informal statements of agency personnel with respect to either law or policy. *Office of Personnel Management v. Richmond*, 496 U.S. 414 (1990), provided an important statement of current estoppel doctrine. There, a welder, not wishing to exceed a statutory limit on earnings that would jeopardize his disability annuity, sought advice from a federal employee. Relying on the erroneous response, he proceeded to earn more than permitted by the statutory eligibility requirements and lost six months of benefits. The Supreme Court declined to adopt the Solicitor General's broad argument that the government could never be estopped by an unauthorized statement of its employee, but held, nevertheless, that money claims against the government could not be based on such misstatements:

> Extended to its logical conclusion, operation of estoppel against the Government in the context of payment of money from the Treasury could in fact render the Appropriations Clause a nullity. If agents of the Executive were able, by their unauthorized oral or written statements to citizens, to obligate the Treasury for the payment of funds, the control over public funds that the Clause reposes in Congress in effect could be transferred to the Executive. If, for example, the President or Executive Branch officials were displeased with a new restriction on benefits imposed by Congress to ease burdens on the fisc (such as the restriction imposed by the statutory change in this case) and sought to evade them, agency officials could advise citizens that the restrictions were inapplicable. Estoppel would give this advice the practical force of law, in violation of the Constitution.

Although *Richmond's* grounding in the Appropriations Clause limits its scope to some degree, most estoppel issues arise in the context of claims for money relief. Hence while individuals and firms routinely rely on informal (and overwhelmingly accurate) advice from government officials, the government is likely to be bound by those statements only when made by officials with clear authority to make policy or decide cases, and then only if no payment from government funds is required.

3. FORMAL ADJUDICATION AND BUREAUCRATIC DECISION MAKING

a. *Administration v. Adjudication*

The procedural elements of administrative adjudication—whether governed by the "minimum safeguards" of due process or the elaborate formality of the APA—have clear analogies to the processes by which the courts conduct their business. Two peculiarities of administration, however, render problematic the wholesale incorporation of the formal judicial model of decision making.

The first is the mass character of modern government. One of the great strengths of administrative organization is its capacity—through the combination of specialization and coordination—to utilize the talent, knowledge, and energy of many persons to achieve a common goal. The customary routines of bureaucratic decision making thus emphasize particularized expertise and dispersed responsibility, unified ultimately through hierarchical control.

Second, most bureaucracies exist primarily to pursue positive programs, not to resolve individualized disputes. The role of the bureaucratic enterprise is, in Weber's words, "to exercise power on the basis of knowledge." Adjudication in this context is a means of implementation, a device for achieving general goals in particular cases. Moreover, implementation of a continuing national program extends across space and through time. Each adjudicatory decision, therefore, is but a part of an overall scheme whose ultimate, aggregate success provides the agency's *raison d'être*.

The superimposition of trial-type procedures on the process of bureaucratic implementation produces some discordant notes, for the techniques of trial are borrowed from a different institutional context. Courts have no institutional responsibility to seek out crimes, torts, or breaches of contract or to "implement" bodies of law governing these categories of activity; nor do they possess armies of specialists who can pursue the technical facts germane to legal disputes. Courts decide disputes within a particularistic microcosm of fact and law, developed and presented by outsiders, shaped to suit those parties' particular purposes, and related primarily to their past conduct. Many of the key features of conventional trial process—party initiative, exclusionary rules, pleading requirements, confinement to "record" evidence—may do more to preserve the privacy of litigants than to inform the decision maker.

In his study of the administration of the social security disability program Professor Mashaw suggests that "administration" and "adjudication"—in his terms "bureaucratic rationality" and "moral judgment"—have distinct goals, decisional techniques, legitimating values, and organizational presuppositions. The core of these two different approaches or "models" of legal decision making may be captured in the following terms.

JERRY L. MASHAW, BUREAUCRATIC JUSTICE

(Yale 1983).

BUREAUCRATIC RATIONALITY

Given the democratically (legislatively) approved task—to pay disability benefits to eligible persons—the administrative goal in the ideal conception of bureaucratic rationality is to develop, at the least possible cost, a system for distinguishing between true and false claims. Adjudication should be both accurate (the legislatively specified goal) and cost-effective. This approach can be stated more broadly by introducing trade-offs between error, administrative, and other "process" costs such that the goal becomes "minimize the sum of error and other associated costs."

A system focused on correctness defines the questions presented to it by implementing decisions in essentially factual and technocratic terms. Individual adjudicators must be concerned about the facts in the real world that relate to the truth or falsity of the claimed disability. At a managerial level the question becomes technocratic: What is the least-cost methodology for collecting and combining those facts about claims that will reveal the proper decision? To illustrate by contrast, this model would exclude questions of value or preference as obviously irrelevant to the administrative task, and it would view reliance on nonreplicable, nonreviewable *judgment* or *intuition* as a singularly unattractive methodology for decision. The legislature should have previously decided the value questions; and decision on the basis of intuition would cause authority to devolve from the bureau to individuals, thereby preventing a supervisory determination of whether any adjudicative action taken corresponded to a true state of the world.

The general decisional technique, then, is information retrieval and processing. * * * And, of course, this application of knowledge must in any large-scale program be structured through the usual bureaucratic routines: selection and training of personnel, detailed specification of administrative tasks, specialization and division of labor, coordination via rules and hierarchical lines of authority, and hierarchical review of the accuracy and efficiency of decisionmaking. In the disability program, for example, decisionmaking goes on not in one head but, initially, in the heads of thousands of state agency examiners.

From the perspective of bureaucratic rationality, administrative justice is accurate decisionmaking carried on through processes appropriately rationalized to take account of costs. The legitimating force of this conception flows both from its claim to correct implementation of otherwise legitimate social decisions and from its attempt to realize society's preestablished goals in some particular substantive domain while conserving social resources for the pursuit of other valuable ends. No program, after all, exhausts our conception of good government, much less of a good society or a good life. * * *

Moral Judgment

The traditional goal of the adjudicatory process is to resolve disputes about rights, about the allocation of benefits and burdens. The paradigm adjudicatory situations are those of civil and criminal trial. In civil cases, the contest generally concerns competing claims to property or the mutual responsibilities of the litigants. Property claims of "It has been in my family for generations" confront counterclaims of "I bought it from a dealer" or "I have made productive use of it"; "The smell of your turkey farm is driving me mad" confronts "I was here first." In the [criminal trial context], accused murderers claim self-defense or diminished responsibility. The goal in individual adjudications is to decide who deserves what.

To some degree these traditional notions of justice in adjudicatory process imply merely getting the facts right in order to apply existing legal rules. So conceived, the goal of a moral judgment model of justice is the same as that of a bureaucratic rationality model—factually correct realization of previously validated legal norms. If this conception exhausted the notion of adjudicatory fairness, moral judgment's competition with bureaucratic rationality would entail merely a technical dispute about the most efficient way to find facts. But there is more to the competition than that.

The moral judgment model views decisionmaking as value defining. The turkey farmer's neighbor makes a valid appeal not to be burdened by "noisome" smells, *provided* his conduct in locating nearby is "reasonable" and he is not being "overly sensitive." The turkey farmer also has a valid claim to carry on a legitimate business, *provided* he does so in ways that will not unreasonably burden his neighbors. The question is not just who did what, but who is to be preferred, all things considered, when interests and the values to which they can be relevantly connected conflict. Similarly, the criminal trial seeks to establish not just whether a harmful and proscribed act took place but also whether or to what extent the actor is culpable.

This entitlement-awarding goal of the moral judgment model gives an obvious and distinctive cast to the basic issue for adjudicatory resolution. The issue is the deservingness of some or all of the parties in the context of certain events, transactions, or relationships that give rise to a claim. This issue, in turn, seems to imply certain things about a just process of proof and decision. For example, fair disposition of charges of culpability or lack of desert requires that claims be specifically stated and that any affected party be given an opportunity to rebut or explain allegations. And in order for this contextualized exploration of individual deservingness to be meaningful the decisionmaker must be neutral—that is, not previously connected with the relevant parties or events in ways that would impair the exercise of independent judgment on the evidence and arguments presented.

Moreover, given the generally threatening nature of an inquiry into moral desert, parties should be able to exclude from the decisional context information not directly related to the entitlements issue that gives rise to the disputed claim. This power of exclusion may take the form of pleading rules, of notions of standing or proper parties, and, more importantly, may permit total exclusion of directive judgment where claims are abandoned or disputants come to some mutually satisfactory agreement concerning the relevant allocation. The goal is limited: to resolve particular claims of entitlement in a way that fairly allocates certain benefits and burdens, not to allocate benefits and burdens in general in accordance with the relative deservingness of individuals or groups. The decider is to a degree passive. The parties control how much of their lives or relationships is put at issue and what factual and normative arguments are brought to bear on the resolution of the dispute.

While the traditional examples of entitlements-oriented individualized adjudication involve adversary process, this feature is not critical. Claims to publicly provided benefits via nonadversary hearing processes may also conform to the model. Indeed, the Supreme Court has come very close to saying that such processes must involve a traditional oral hearing where substantive standards are so open-textured that each decision both defines the nature of the entitlement and awards or denies it to a particular party. [See *Califano v. Yamasaki*]

* * * The important point is that the "justice" of this model inheres in its promise of a full and equal opportunity to obtain one's entitlements. Its authority rests on the neutral development and application of common moral principles within the contexts giving rise to entitlement claims.

COMPARISON

As we have described them, each justice model is composed of distinctive goals, specific approaches to framing the questions for administrative determination, basic techniques for resolving those questions, and subsidiary decision processes and routines that functionally describe the model. The distinctive features of the * * * models are outlined in the accompanying chart. These features are, of course, meant to indicate the central tendencies, not to suggest that features, and whole models, do not shade one into another at the margins.

		Legitimating Values	*Primary Goal*	*Structure or Organization*	*Cognitive Technique*
Model of Decision	**Bureaucratic Rationality**	Accuracy & Efficiency	Program Implementation	Hierarchical	Information Processing
Making	**Moral Judgment**	Fairness	Conflict Resolution	Independent	Contextual Interpretation

These contrasts cannot be pressed too far. Some "agencies" might as easily be viewed as courts, and modern public law litigation has thrust federal trial courts into managerial and political tasks that are traditionally the domain of administration. See, e.g., Abraham Chayes, *The Role of the Judge in Public Law Litigation*, 89 Harv. L. Rev. 1281 (1976); *Forward: Public Law Litigation and the Burger Court*, 96 Harv. L. Rev. 4 (1982); Colin Diver, *The Judge as Political Power Broker: Superintending Structural Change in Public Institutions*, 65 Va. L. Rev. 43 (1979); Owen Fiss, *Forward: The Forms of Justice*, 93 Harv. L. Rev. 1 (1979). Compare Theodore Eisenberg and Steven Yeazell, *The Ordinary and the Extraordinary in Institutional Litigation*, 93 Harv. L. Rev. 465 (1980); Steven Yeazell, *From Group Litigation to Class Action—Part I: The Industrialization of Group Litigation*, 27 U.C.L.A. L. Rev. 514 (1980); *Part II: Interest, Class, and Representation*, 27 U.C.L.A. L. Rev. 1067 (1980). Yet the central tendencies of judicial and administrative functions are sufficiently distinct to provide a basis for predicting that the use of trial process in administrative contexts will often render certain features of that process problematic. This recognition, of course, informs the Supreme Court's obvious reluctance to impose trial-type process on many administrative functions *via* the Due Process Clause. But the difficulties of accommodating bureaucratic organization and adjudicatory formality do not disappear when the right to formal adjudicatory process is provided by statute.

Hierarchy v. Personal Judgment

A classic illustration is provided by the famous *Morgan* cases. There the complaining parties alleged that the Secretary of Agriculture had issued a commodity rate order, which was required to be made on the record after formal hearing, without personally reviewing the evidence presented or having read the briefs or heard oral argument. They further alleged that the Secretary's decision was based solely on ex parte consultations with employees of the Department of Agriculture who were familiar with the case. The Supreme Court held that proof of these allegations would establish a denial of an adequate hearing, *Morgan v. United States*, 298 U.S. 468 (1936), and, in oft-quoted language, it said, "The one who decides must hear."

Yet, in the same opinion the Court also said, "Evidence may be taken by an examiner. Evidence thus taken may be sifted and analyzed by competent subordinates." Obviously, the Court was not using "hear" literally. Indeed, the second time the case came before it, the Court specifically approved the manner in which the Secretary proceeded, that is, by reading the briefs of the parties and the transcript of oral argument and by discussing the issues with several subordinates. The Secretary did not read the bulky record, but "dipped into it * * * to get its drift"; and he described the decision as his "independent reactions to the findings of the men in the Bureau of Animal Industry." On this basis the Court was convinced that the Secretary had "considered the evidence before signing the order." *Morgan v. United States*, 304 U.S. 1, 17–18 (1938). Yet the Court simultaneously decided that the parties had not received a full and fair hearing because they had not been given notice of the proposed findings and conclusions submitted to the Secretary by subordinates and ultimately adopted by him virtually verbatim. This practice was said to have deprived the complainants of a reasonable opportunity "to know the claims thus presented and to meet them."

The complainants managed to return to the Supreme Court two more times. And in its fourth *Morgan* opinion the Court, perhaps perceiving the implications of the process of review on which it had embarked, stated categorically that once the Secretary had been shown to have considered the evidence, the extent to which he considered it and how he went about arriving at a decision could not be inquired into any more than one could attack a judicial decision on the ground that the judge had not thought about it hard or long enough. *United States v. Morgan*, 313 U.S. 409 (1941). In the end the Court in the *Morgan* cases seems to have given a very wide latitude to an ultimate decision maker, who has *some* exposure to evidence and argument, to use the assistance of subordinates in arriving at a decision and to hear or read the raw evidentiary record developed by others, if at all, only to the extent that he believes necessary for conscientious decision making. The Court thus placed its imprimatur on what has come to be called the "institutional decision"—that is, a decision that is the product of many hands and minds but that is the final responsibility of those at the top of the agency hierarchy. Yet, and crucially, it did so in litigation that repeatedly reversed the Secretary of Agriculture's decisions in the interest of providing a personal hearing that was meaningful to the ultimate exercise of judgment.

Factual Context v. Policy Implementation

This ambivalence about the linkage between hearing rights and bureaucratic decision making is also implicit in two provisions of the APA. Section 557(b) provides that an agency reviewing an examiner's initial decision has "all the powers it would have had in making the initial decision." But section 557(c) provides that all decisions, including recommended, tentative, or initial decisions, are a part of the record of an agency proceeding. The problem thus posed is this: Suppose a reviewing court is convinced that there is not substantial evidence in the whole record for an agency decision because the hearing examiner (whose initial decision is a part of the record) made convincing findings of fact that are contrary to those made by the agency. Assume further that, absent the hearing officer's initial decision, the court would have been willing to find that the agency decision was based on substantial evidence. Should the court reverse, thereby denying to the agency the power it would have had had it made the initial decision; or should it affirm on the basis of evidence which it considers insubstantial in the light of the hearing officer's evaluation?

This was precisely the situation presented to the Supreme Court in *Universal Camera Corp. v. NLRB*, 340 U.S. 474, 493, 496–97 (1951). The hearing examiner in that case had found that a particular employee had been discharged because of insubordination, not, as charged in an unfair labor practices complaint, because he had been a witness in a previous NLRB proceeding. The testimony at the hearing had been sharply conflicting and the decision may have turned in the final analysis on who was to be believed. The Board independently examined the record and reversed the hearing examiner's ruling. The Board's decision was upheld by the court of appeals on the ground that it could not say that the Board had committed a clear error of law in reversing the examiner, and that therefore it was constrained to treat the fact that the examiner had made a contrary finding as irrelevant. *NLRB v. Universal Camera Corp.*, 179 F.2d 749 (2d Cir.1950). The Court rejected the court of appeals' approach:

> We are aware that to give the examiner's findings less finality than a master's and yet entitled them to consideration in striking the account, is to introduce another and an unruly factor into the judgmatical process of review. But we ought not to fashion an exclusionary rule merely to reduce the number of imponderables to be considered by reviewing courts. * * *
>
> We do not require that the examiner's findings be given more weight than in reason and in the light of judicial experience they deserve. The "substantial evidence" standard is not modified in any way when the Board and its examiner disagree. We intend only to

> recognize that evidence supporting a conclusion may be less substantial when an impartial, experienced examiner who has observed the witnesses and lived with the case has drawn conclusions different from the Board's than when he has reached the same conclusion. The findings of the examiner are to be considered along with the consistency and inherent probability of testimony. The significance of his report, of course, depends largely on the importance of credibility in the particular case. To give it this significance does not seem to us materially more difficult than to heed the other factors which in sum determine whether evidence is "substantial."

This approach seems sensible, but the Court correctly anticipated the unruliness of the consideration introduced into judicial review by *Universal Camera*. Certainly, in the next case that raised a similar issue. *NLRB v. James Thompson & Co.*, 208 F.2d 743, 746 (2d Cir.1953), Judge Hand stated the principle much too broadly when he said:

> We do not see any rational escape from accepting a finding [of the examiner] unless we can say that the corroboration of this lost [demeanor] evidence could not have been enough to satisfy any doubts raised by the words; and it must be owned that few findings will not survive such a test.

The issue upon which the Board and its examiner had disagreed in *James Thompson & Co.* was whether an employer had unlawfully refused to deal with a union. The examiner believed the employer when he said that he was justifiably uncertain about whether the union had obtained enough employees' authorizations to act as their representative. The Board thought that the undisputed acts of the employer, both before and after the principal instance of his refusal to deal, indicated a pattern of hostility toward the formation of a union which was unlawful under the Act. The court of appeals thus seemed to be saying that the Board could not rely on circumstantial evidence in the record as a whole to rebut a fact found by the examiner on the basis of direct testimony.

The Supreme Court in *FCC v. Allentown Broadcasting Corp.*, 349 U.S. 358, 364 (1955), sought to redress the balance between agencies and their hearing officers. Although the case was resolvable, and perhaps resolved, on other grounds, the Court had this to say about the court of appeals' emphasis on the conflict between the FCC's findings and its examiner's:

> The Court of Appeals' conclusion of error as to evasiveness relies largely on its understanding that the Examiner's findings based on demeanor of a witness are not to be overruled by a Board without a "very substantial preponderance in the testimony as recorded," citing *National Labor Relations Board v. Universal Camera Corp.* We think this attitude goes too far. It seems to adopt for examiners of administrative agencies the "clearly erroneous" rule of the Fed.Rules Civ.Proc., 52(a), applicable to courts. In *Universal Camera Corp. v. Labor Board*, we said, as to the Labor Management Relations Act hearings:

> "Section 10(c) of the Labor Management Relations Act provides that 'If upon the preponderance of the testimony taken the Board shall be of the opinion that any person named in the complaint has engaged in or is engaging in any such unfair labor practice, then the Board shall state its findings of fact * * *.' The responsibility for decision thus placed on the Board is wholly inconsistent with the notion that it has power to reverse an examiner's findings only when they are 'clearly erroneous.' Such a limitation would make so drastic a departure from prior administrative practice that explicitness would be required."

That comment is here applicable.

The uncertain weight to be accorded an administrative law judge's decision when the agency disagrees is hardly limited to Labor Board cases or to federal administrative law. Obviously concerned that agency policy preferences were overwhelming adjudicatory fairness, North Carolina amended its Administrative Procedure Act in 2001 to require that an agency make special findings when rejecting an administrative law judge's findings of fact, and to prohibit agencies from rejecting ALJ fact finding unless those findings are clearly contrary to the preponderance of the evidence. The North Carolina amendments then provide that in any case where an agency has rejected an ALJ's finding, the scope of judicial review of the agency's final determination will be *de novo*, that is, the court should give the agency no deference when reviewing its determination. See generally Charles E. Daye, *Power of Administrative Law Judges, Agencies and Courts: An Analytical and Empirical Assessment*, 79 N.C. L. Rev. 1571 (2001).

The conflict between adjudicatory fairness and effective decision making appears most sharply in agencies that develop policy primarily through formal adjudication. The tension is evident in *Universal Camera*. Justice in the individual case seems to demand broad discretion for the hearing examiner (now ALJ) to allocate fault in accordance with his or her contextualized judgment of what actually occurred. Protection of the Board's policy making role, on the other hand, may argue for resolving doubts in a way that provides the most complete possible protection to witnesses in Board proceedings. While in *Universal Camera* the conflict emerges in a debate about the substantial evidence test, similar differences concerning the appropriate perspective from which to view adjudication have often also been embedded in arguments concerning the separation or combination of functions within agencies.

Neutrality v. Institutional Intelligence

That the persons who constitute an agency—FTC Commissioners, NLRB Board Members, the FDA Commissioner—may be ultimately responsible for investigation, prosecution, and final decision in the same case without impairing fundamental fairness is now a well-entrenched feature of American administrative law. Such "combinations of functions," however, inspired intense opposition to administrative regulation in the New Deal era and in the years leading up to the adoption of the APA in 1946. Administrative agencies were chastised as "that hybrid thing beloved by tyrants and abhorred by free men," and the ABA Special Committee on Administrative Law in 1934 strongly argued that the adjudicatory functions of agencies be transferred to an administrative court or courts. Partisans on the other side inflamed the debate by advocating that independent regulatory commissions be absorbed into the executive branch to make them more responsive to governmental policy. See generally ADMINISTRATIVE PROCEDURE IN GOVERNMENT AGENCIES *vi* (Charles K. Woltz, ed., 1968).

The general approach to separation of functions that has prevailed at the federal level, however, is that recommended by the Attorney General's Committee on Administrative Procedure and embodied in the APA—an internal separation of personnel within agencies for purposes of formal adjudication, which results in clear divisions of responsibility at the lower levels of adjudication and an insulation of even top administrators from investigative and prosecutorial staff, save on the public record.

ATTORNEY GENERAL'S COMMITTEE ON ADMINISTRATIVE PROCEDURE, ADMINISTRATIVE PROCEDURE IN GOVERNMENT AGENCIES

Senate Document No. 8, 77th Cong., 55–59 (1941).

The recommendations made in the preceding sections of this report looking toward the creation of the office of hearing commissioners [subsequently called "hearing examiners" in the APA and now "administrative law judges"] to hear and initially to decide cases which go to formal proceedings, together with the recommendations looking toward a greater delegation of administrative functions within the agencies, would insure internal but nevertheless real and actual separation of the adjudicating and the prosecuting or investigating functions. The person who heard and weighed the evidence, who made the initial findings of fact and the initial order in each case, would be entirely different from those persons who had investigated the case and presented it in formal proceedings. He would have had no connection with the initiation or prosecution of the case. * * *

But current discussions of the administrative process raise the question whether separation of function ought not to go further than this. Specifically, it has been urged that possession of the deciding functions of a "judge" is inconsistent with possession of the "prosecutor's" functions of investigation, initiation of action, and advocacy. The proposal is accordingly made that the deciding powers of Federal administrative agencies should be vested in separate tribunals which are independent of the bodies charged with the functions of prosecution and perhaps other functions of administration.

Two points are important to put the problem in a just perspective. The first is that * * * an administrative agency is not one man or a few men but many. It is important, the Committee believes, not to make the mistake of conceiving of an agency as a collective person and concluding that, because the agency initiates action and renders decision thereafter, the same person is doing both. In an agency's organization there are varied possibilities of internal separation of function to the end that the same individuals who do the judging do not do the "prosecuting." Such internal separation by no means eliminates the problem of combination of functions; but it alters, or if wisely done may alter, its entire set and cast. The second major point is that the functions of so-called prosecution belonging to administrative agencies are actually of varying types. It is important to distinguish among these types not only because agencies differ in the functions which they possess but because different questions, in relation to the function of judging, arise with respect to different types of functions.

Two characteristic tasks of a prosecutor are those of investigation and advocacy. It is clear that when a controversy reaches the stage of hearing and formal adjudication the persons who did the actual work of investigating and building up the case should play no part in the decision. * * * [Likewise] the advocate—the agency's attorney who upheld a definite position adverse to the private parties at the hearing—cannot be permitted to participate after the hearing in the making of the decision. * * *

These types of commingling of functions of investigation or advocacy with the function of deciding are thus plainly undesirable. But they are also avoidable and should be avoided by appropriate internal division of labor. For the disqualifications produced by investigation or advocacy are personal psychological ones which result from engaging in those types of activity; and the problem is simply one of isolating those who engage in the activity. Creation of independent hearing commissioners insulated from all phases of a case other than hearing and deciding will, the Committee believes, go far toward solving this problem at the level of the initial hearing provided the proper safeguards are established to assure the insulation. A similar result can be achieved at the level of final decision on review by the agency heads by permitting the views of the investigators and advocates to be presented only in open hearing where they can be known and met by those who may be adversely affected by them.

A distinctive function, which may be regarded as one of prosecution, is that of making preliminary decisions to issue a complaint or to proceed to formal hearing in cases which later the agency heads will decide. Before a complaint is issued * * * or before an application raising doubtful questions is set down for formal hearing, a determination must be made that the action is proper. The Committee has heretofore recommended * * * that authority to make such preliminary determinations should be delegated as far as possible to appropriate officers. Where this is done, no question can arise that the ultimate deciding officers have been biased through having made, ex parte, a preliminary determination in a case which they have later to decide. Yet such delegation, of course, cannot be complete; novel and difficult questions must from time to time be presented to the heads of the agency. The question must be faced, therefore, whether the making of such a preliminary determination in itself works unfairness in the final decision. Assuming that the agency heads simply pass on the sufficiency of material developed and presented to them by others, the Committee is satisfied that no such unfairness results. * * * The ultimate judgment of the agency heads need be no more influenced by the preliminary authorization to proceed than is the ultimate judgment of a court by the issuance of a temporary restraining order pending a formal hearing for a permanent injunction.

What remains to be discussed is the heart of the problem. * * * [S]o far as the agency is empowered to initiate action at all, the agency heads do have the responsibility of determining the general policy according to which action is taken. They have at least residual powers to control, supervise, and direct all the activities of the agency, including the various preliminary and deciding phases of the process of disposing of particular cases. The question is whether there are dangers in the possession of these powers such as to make advisable a total separation.

An answer to this question requires first of all a counting of the costs which such a separation would entail. These costs include substantial dangers both to private and to public interests. Most obvious are the disadvantages of sheer multiplication of separate governmental organizations. If the proposal were rigorously carried out, two agencies would grow in each case where one grew before.

Particularly in cases where adjudicatory functions are not a principal part of the agency's work or are closely interrelated with other activities, whatever gains might result from separation would be plainly outweighed by the loss in consistency of action as a whole. * * * The Civil Aeronautics Board, the Securities and Exchange Commission, and other agencies * * * act through exercise of a number of interrelated powers. These powers must be exercised consistently and, therefore, by the same body, not only to realize the public purposes which the statutes are designed to further but also to avoid confusion of private interests.

There are, however, some agencies such as the Federal Trade Commission and the National Labor Relations Board whose principal duty is the enforcement, by decision of cases, of certain statutory prohibitions. In the case of such agencies, the practical objection which has just been noted to isolating the adjudicatory function and handing it over to some independent body would not exist to the same extent. It would be theoretically possible to assign to one agency the task of investigating charges and filing complaints of statutory violations, and to another agency the task of deciding the controversies thus arising. * * *

Further practical objections, however, have to be taken into account in relation to these as well as other agencies. Of prime importance among these objections is the danger of friction and of a break-down of responsibility as between the two complementary agencies. * * * At present the added responsibility of deciding exercises a restraining influence which limits the activities of the agency as a whole. If only to save itself time and expense an agency will not prosecute cases which it knows are defective on the facts or on the law—which it knows, in short, it will dismiss after hearing. The situation is likely to be different where the function of prosecuting is separated out. First, a body devoted solely to prosecuting often is intent upon "making a record." It has no responsibility for deciding and its express job is simply to prosecute as often and successfully as possible. Second, it must guess what the deciding branch will think. It can explore the periphery; it can try everything; and meanwhile the individual citizen must spend time and money before some curb can be exercised by the deciding branch. And, it should be noted, a separation of functions would seriously militate against what this Committee has already noted as being, numerically and otherwise, the lifeblood of the administrative process—negotiations and informal settlements. * * *

These factors are thrown into clear relief if it is recalled that the statutory prohibitions which administrative agencies are commonly called upon to enforce are not and cannot be as clear and precise as a promissory note or bill of sale. * * * It is and must be left to the administrative agencies to apply these general prohibitions to a great variety of conduct. As this is done, it is expected that the general terms will take on concreteness and that subsidiary principles may be worked out by which certain types of conduct will be known as improper and others as permissible. To do this involves the investigation of many informal complaints and the settlement by agreement of many situations where the practices may have been innocently or inadvertently or not consistently engaged in. To divorce entirely the investigating and enforcing arm from the deciding arm may well impart additional confusion to this process. * * *

Moreover, when one examines the specific criticisms of specific agencies, one is struck by the fact that a mere splitting up of functions would not itself cure the criticisms which appear most common. Insofar as predispositions may exist in the more highly charged fields in which administrative agencies operate, they are mainly the product of many factors of mind and experience, and have comparatively little relation to the administrative machinery. There is no simple way of eliminating them by mere change in the administrative structure. They can only be exercised by wise and self-controlled men.

Notes

1. *Due Process and Separation of Functions*. The Supreme Court has addressed this issue under the Due Process Clause. *Withrow v. Larkin*, 421 U.S. 35, 39, 51–52 (1975), involved investigation and decertification by a state professional licensing board. In this instance the focus of the investigation by the Wisconsin Medical Examining Board was a Michigan physician

who also had obtained licensure in Wisconsin through a reciprocity agreement between the states. His practice in Wisconsin consisted of performing abortions in a Milwaukee office. He sought to enjoin the board's proceedings after it initiated an investigation and hearing to determine whether he had "engaged in practices that are inimical to the public health, whether he ha[d] engaged in conduct unbecoming a person licensed to practice medicine, and whether he ha[d] engaged in conduct detrimental to the best interests of the public."

In vacating a lower court injunction premised on a general antipathy to such "combinations of functions" the Court, through Justice White, said:

> * * * The issue is substantial, it is not new, and legislators and others concerned with the operations of administrative agencies have given much attention to whether and to what extent distinctive administrative functions should be performed by the same persons. No single answer has been reached. Indeed, the growth, variety, and complexity of the administrative process have made any one solution highly unlikely. Within the Federal Government itself, Congress has addressed the issue in several different ways, providing for varying degrees of separation from complete separation of functions to virtually none at all. * * *
>
> * * * Similarly, our cases, although they reflect the substance of the problem, offer no support for the bald proposition applied in this case by the District Court that agency members who participate in an investigation are disqualified from adjudicating * * *.

See also *Friedman v. Rogers*, 440 U.S. 1 (1979); *Gibson v. Berryhill*, 411 U.S. 564 (1973); *FTC v. Cement Institute*, 333 U.S. 683 (1948).

2. *Impartial Decision Makers.* The "separation of functions" issue is but part of a larger constitutional concern with the impartiality of government decision making. The Supreme Court has long held that due process requires an unbiased adjudicator, and the APA explicitly incorporates that requirement as well. 5 U.S.C. § 556(b).

The source of a decision maker's livelihood may be sufficient to demonstrate bias. The Court invalidated a decision by the Alabama State Board of Optometrists to revoke the licenses of all optometrists in the state—nearly half the total number—who were employed in business corporations. The Court concluded that the Board, composed solely of self-employed optometrists, had so direct a pecuniary stake in their determination as to violate the dictates of basic fairness. *Gibson v. Berryhill*, 411 U.S. 564 (1973).

The Court has not been so ready, however, to detect impermissible "institutional" bias. In *Marshall v. Jerrico, Inc.*, 446 U.S. 238 (1980), the Court unanimously upheld the Employment Standards Administration's procedures for collecting fines for violations of the Fair Labor Standards Act, even though the fines were returned to the agency's budget. In *Schweiker v. McClure*, 456 U.S. 188 (1982), the Court unanimously upheld a practice of reimbursing private insurers for reviewing Medicare claims as agents of the U.S. Department of Health and Human Services, using hearing officers who were employees of the private carriers. Because the private carriers did not ultimately pay the cost of Medicare claims, the Court was unpersuaded that the hearing officers were unduly motivated to conserve the insurers' funds.

Nor did the Court find inappropriate pressure by HHS on the insurers to hold down to overutilization of medical services.

The Court has further held that a decision maker's personal knowledge of the disputed facts will not always be disqualifying. *See Goss v. Lopez*, 419 U.S. 565, 584 (1975) (permitting school disciplinarian who had witnessed misconduct to conduct a hearing on possible short-term suspension).

3. *Impartiality Under the APA.* The APA's provision for an impartial decision maker does not specify any precise standard for disqualification. The D.C. Circuit, however, has crafted a stringent standard for assessing the impartiality of a decision maker in a formal adjudicatory setting. In *American Cyanamid v. FTC*, 363 F.2d 757, 767–78 (6th Cir.1966), the Commission had found that American Cyanamid and others had entered into a complex series of agreements by which they monopolized the market in the sale of the "wonder drug" tetracycline. The company sought judicial review of the decision on the ground that Chairman Dixon had prejudged the case while serving as Chief Counsel and Staff Director of the Senate Subcommittee on Antitrust and Monopoly. Undisputed evidence revealed that prior to his appointment to the Commission, but after the complaint against Cyanamid had been issued, Dixon had directed an intensive inquiry into the pharmaceutical industry and particularly into the marketing of tetracycline. At the conclusion of that inquiry the subcommittee issued a report, of which Dixon was reputedly primary author, that detailed the machinations of the companies producing tetracycline and concluded that, "With the consummation of these arrangements, the *orderly and controlled* marketing of tetracycline was an inevitable and expected result."

The court of appeals reversed the FTC's order, stating in part:

> It is to be emphasized that the Commission is a factfinding body. As Chairman, Mr. Dixon sat with the other members as triers of the facts and joined in making the factual determination upon which the order of the Commission is based. As counsel for the Senate Subcommittee, he had investigated and developed many of these same facts.
>
> The result of the participation of Chairman Dixon in the decision of the Commission is not altered by the fact that his vote was not necessary for a majority. "Litigants are entitled to an impartial tribunal whether it consists of one man or twenty and there is no way which we may know of whereby the influence of one upon the others can be quantitatively measured."
>
> We therefore must vacate the order and decision of the Federal Trade Commission and remand the case for a de novo consideration of the record without the participation of Chairman Dixon. We reject the argument of the Commission that such a holding "would create an unworkable concept of administrative bias." Our decision on this issue goes no further than to hold that disqualification is required when, as in the present case, the legislative committee investigation involved the same facts and issues concerning the same parties named as respondents before the administrative agency, and to the extent here presented. * * * Our decision is based upon the depth of the investigation and the questions and comments by Mr. Dixon as counsel. * * *

On March 15, 1968, the ubiquitous Chairman Dixon made a speech before the Government Relations Workshop of the National Newspaper Association concerning press responsibility for policing consumer frauds. In it he said:

> How about ethics on the business side of running a paper? What standards are maintained on advertising acceptance? * * * What about carrying ads that offer college educations in five weeks, fortunes by raising mushrooms in the basement, getting rid of pimples with a magic lotion, or becoming an airline's hostess by attending a charm school? * * * Without belaboring the point I'm sure you're aware that advertising acceptance standards could stand more tightening by many newspapers. Granted that newspapers are not in the advertising policing business, their advertising managers are savvy enough to smell deception when the odor is strong enough. * * *

At the time Dixon spoke the Commission had pending before it a case charging false advertising by the Cinderella Career and Finishing Schools, Inc. The agency's complaint charged that Cinderella's advertisements had deceptively promised the equivalent of a college course in five weeks and that its graduates might be qualified for jobs as airline hostesses. The company subsequently appealed an adverse Commission ruling on the ground, *inter alia*, that Chairman Dixon's statements prejudged the case. The indignant court of appeals agreed:

> It requires no superior olfactory powers to recognize that the danger of unfairness through prejudgment is not diminished by a cloak of self-righteousness. * * *
>
> We indicated in our earlier opinion in this case that "there is in fact and law authority in the Commission, acting in the public interest, to alert the public to *suspected violations* of the law by *factual press releases* whenever the Commission shall have reason to believe that a respondent is engaged in activities made unlawful by the Act. * * *" This does not give individual Commissioners license to prejudge cases or to make speeches which give the appearance that the case has been prejudged. Conduct such as this may have the effect of entrenching a Commissioner in a position which he has publicly stated, making it difficult, if not impossible, for him to reach a different conclusion in the event he deems it necessary to do so after consideration of the record. There is a marked difference between the issuance of a press release which states that the Commission has filed a complaint because it has "reason to believe" that there have been violations, and statements by a Commissioner after an appeal has been filed which gave the appearance that he has already prejudged the case and that the ultimate determination of the merits will move in predestined grooves. * * *
>
> We find it hard to believe that former Chairman Dixon is so indifferent to the dictates of the Court of Appeals that he has chosen once again to put his personal determination of what the law requires ahead of what the courts have time and again told him the law requires. * * * [W]e will spell out for him once again, avoiding tired cliche and weary generalization, in no uncertain terms, exactly what those require-

ments are, in the fervent hope that this will be the last time we have to travel this wearisome road.

> The test for disqualification * * * [is] whether "a disinterested observer may conclude that [the agency] has in some measure adjudged the facts as well as the law of a particular case in advance of hearing it." * * *

TEST

Cinderella Career and Finishing Schools, Inc. v. FTC, 425 F.2d 583, 590–91 (D.C.Cir.1970).

Notwithstanding the generally well-worn grooves within which bias, prejudgment, and separation of function cases run, unfairness claims of these types continue to be well-represented in the lower courts. As the late Professor Bernard Schwartz put it in his 1996 annual review of administrative law cases:

> The cases on bias and administrative decisionmaking continue to present interesting fact patterns. Among them are cases involving claims of bias because of pre-judgment, a commissioner's previous participation in the case as a general counsel, the wife of an agency member's part time employment by a party, an agency member who testified in the case, an agency member's pecuniary interest, an agency member who had been a defendant in the lawsuit by a party whose case is being heard, a deciding officer who had investigated prior charges and appointed the hearing officer or authored the draft decision, and even a 'cranky' and 'overly abrupt and intimidating' hearing officer.

Bernard Schwartz, *Administrative Law Cases During 1996*, 49 ADMIN. L. REV. 519, 525–26 (1997).

b. Managing Adjudicatory Personnel

The need to harness formal adjudicatory activity to administrative policy presents different issues for an agency like the Social Security Administration, which does not attempt to make policy in the course of adjudication. Rather, it seeks to prevent the disposition of individual cases from altering its policies or (which is much the same thing) from implicitly generating policies that agency managers view as undesirable. Both of these latter activities involve attempts to control or direct the decisions made by the SSA staff of over 1,000 administrative law judges. This administrative "control" or "direction" may, of course, impair the ALJs' independence. It, therefore, raises questions concerning the adequacy of the formal hearings prescribed by the Social Security Act and governed by the requirements of 5 U.S.C. §§ 554, 556, and 557.

The "ALJ independence problem" at the SSA chiefly involves the disability program, which we encountered earlier in *Mathews v. Eldridge* and *Richardson v. Perales*. Pursuant to that program persons insured under the Social Security Act are entitled to early retirement if they are unable "to engage in any substantial gainful activity by reason of any medically determinable physical or mental impairment" which may last for at least one year or result in death. Benefits are also available to needy persons under Title XVI of the Social Security Act, but in both cases:

> * * * an individual shall be determined to be under a disability only if his physical or mental impairment or impairments are of such severity that he is not only unable to do his previous work but cannot, considering his age, education and work experience, engage in any other kind of substantial gainful work which exists in the national economy, regardless of whether such work exists in the immediate area in which he lives, or whether a specific job vacancy exists for him, or whether he would be hired if he applied for work. For purposes of the preceding sentences (with respect to any individual), "work which exists in the national economy" means work which exists in significant numbers either in the region where such individual lives or in several regions of the country.

The SSA disability insurance program supports approximately 5 million American workers and their dependants at an annual cost of over $50 billion. SSA receives about 1.3 million applications per year for disability benefits. Disappointed applicants, or, as in *Eldridge*, terminated recipients, request hundreds of thousands of hearings per year before the agency's administrative law judges. As the Court in *Eldridge* noted, one problem with this process is its "torpidity." Applicants typically receive a judgment from the initial, informal level of adjudication within 30 to 45 days of application. But ALJ hearing decisions require months from request to disposition. This is, of course, extremely swift by comparison with civil court trials involving similar amounts but nonetheless distressingly slow for persons who are ill, lack alternative means of support, and may be unable to obtain cash or medical benefits unless found eligible.

There is also concern that the hearing process is both profligate and arbitrary. Over time the ALJs have accounted for an increasing share of disability awards. In 1964, 97.5 per cent of all recipients received these awards at the pre-hearing levels of decision; ALJ awards thus accounted for a negligible 2.5 per cent. By 1996, however, nearly 30 per cent of all recipients were receiving benefits pursuant to an administrative law judge's award. Moreover, ALJ award and denial patterns are far from uniform. Indeed, the histogram that follows (adapted from JERRY L. MASHAW, ET AL., SOCIAL SECURITY HEARINGS AND APPEALS 21 (1978)) suggests that the likelihood of an award is largely a function of which ALJ hears a particular case. It deserves emphasis that *no* systematic differences in the caseloads of different SSA ALJs have been discovered that might explain this variance.

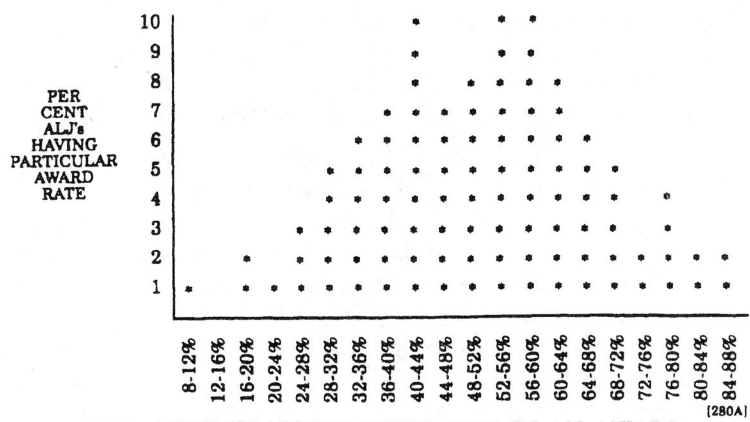

PER CENT HEARINGS RESULTING IN AN AWARD

[Each asterisk represents approximately 1% of observations. Data is from 1976.]

The SSA has addressed the problems of timeliness, increasing award levels, and inconsistency in a variety of ways. United States General Accounting Office, Social Security Disability: SSA Must Hold Itself Accountable For Improvement In Decision-Making (Aug., 1997). Hierarchical control through the enunciation of precedents has been largely unsuccessful. Although SSA has a centralized Appeals Council, that body decides tens of thousands of cases per year. Claimants, their attorneys (should they be represented), and ALJs can hardly be expected to retrieve and follow a decisional output of this magnitude—even if the Appeals Council were capable of unifying its own jurisprudence through carefully crafted opinions. Indeed, the fact-based, highly contextual decision making involved in the disability program simply cannot be structured through precedent. Variation among ALJs is something like the variance that one would expect from one-person juries applying the "reasonable person" standard. And, of course, precedential decisions would do nothing about the problem of delay.

The inaccessibility or irrelevance of precedent as a corrective leaves the SSA with two other techniques: managerial supervision and attempts to constrain ALJ discretion through substantive rulemaking. It has used both; and both have been challenged as incompatible with the independence of SSA ALJs and with the rights of claimants to an individualized hearing on eligibility.

NASH v. CALIFANO

United States Court of Appeals, Second Circuit, 1980.

613 F.2d 10.

Irving R. Kaufman, Chief Judge.

* * *

The appellant, Simon Nash, is an Administrative Law Judge (ALJ) of 22 years' experience in the Social Security Administration's Bureau of Hearings and Appeals. * * *

The Bureau's corps of approximately 650 ALJs is divided among 145 field offices, each one headed by an Administrative Law Judge in Charge (ALJIC), who has managerial and administrative authority over all personnel assigned to his or her field office, in addition to responsibility for the same caseload as other ALJs. ALJICs receive the same salaries as other ALJs. Each ALJIC reports to one of the ten Regional Chief Administrative Law Judges who, in turn, are under the managerial authority of the Director of the Bureau of Hearings and Appeals and his chief assistant, the Chief Administrative Law Judge. While Administrative Law Judges are civil service employees, the Director of the Bureau is appointed by, and serves at the pleasure of, the Commissioner of the Social Security Administration.

In December of 1967, Judge Nash became ALJIC for the Buffalo field office. During his tenure in that position, he, along with numerous other ALJICs, urged adoption of a number of administrative reforms—including the hiring of staff attorneys and the use of summary opinions in appropriate cases—to cope with the mounting backlog of cases before the Bureau of Hearings and Appeals. Those pleas for reform went unheeded until 1975, when appellee Robert Trachtenberg was appointed Director of the Bureau. Facing a record backlog of 113,000 cases,[6] Director Trachtenberg instituted many of the reforms long advocated by Nash and his colleagues.

Trachtenberg's goal of eliminating unconscionable delays in processing appeals is, of course, commendable. Appellant, however, alleges that appellees and their staff employees have interfered with the decisional independence of the administrative law judges in violation of the Administrative Procedure Act, the Social Security Act and the Due Process Clause of the Fifth Amendment. * * *

The first practice challenged in the complaint is the Bureau's "Regional Office Peer Review Program." According to Nash, Trachtenberg, Brown and Tannenbaum, as well as non-ALJ members of their staffs, known as "Development Center Analysts" and "Program Operation Officers," review the work of ALJs outside the normal appellate process. In conjunction with this ongoing review, the appellees or their staffs give plaintiff and all other ALJs detailed, purportedly mandatory instructions concerning the proper length of hearings and opinions, the amount of evidence required in specific cases, and the proper use of expert witnesses. Through the Peer Review Program, the Bureau has

6. Several courts have found that the long delays in processing appeals from denials of Social Security benefits have denied claimants the right to a hearing within the reasonable time called for by 42 U.S.C.A. § 405(b). In *White v. Mathews,* 559 F.2d 852 (2d Cir.1977), *cert. denied,* 435 U.S. 908 (1978), this court affirmed an order granting prospective benefits to claimants who had not received administrative adjudication of their claims within specified time periods. * * *

allegedly arrogated to itself the power to control the conduct of hearings vested in ALJs by the Administrative Procedure Act.

Nash also avers that an arbitrary monthly production quota has been established for him and all his colleagues. Unless an ALJ renders a specified number of decisions per month, the agency, appellant claims, threatens to file incompetence charges against him with the Civil Service Commission. In his view, the agency's production quota constitutes a performance rating forbidden by the Administrative Procedure Act, 5 U.S.C. § 4301(2)(E) and 5 C.F.R. § 930.211.

An additional threat to the ALJs statutory independence is allegedly posed by the so-called "Quality Assurance Program," which attempts to control the number of decisions denying Social Security Benefits. The agency has "let it be known" that the average 50 per cent "reversal rate" for all ALJs is an "acceptable" one. Appellant further claims in his amended complaint that the reversal rates of all ALJs are monitored, and those who deviate from the mean are counseled and admonished to bring their rates in line with the national average. This attempt to influence the ALJs' decisionmaking process, it is urged, violates 5 U.S.C. §§ 556 & 3105 and the Fifth Amendment to the Constitution.

Nash's fourth claim centers upon plans that call for the national implementation (in whole or in part) of an "Employee Pool System" developed at the White Plains, New York field office with the knowledge and approval of the Director. Under this program, many of the ALJs' judicial responsibilities—including the writing of decisions—are vested in clerical and managerial personnel. The use of such "mass production" techniques, it is charged, violates 5 U.S.C. §§ 556(c) & 3105.

The amended complaint goes on to contest the authority of the Secretary of HEW to delegate the power to hold hearings to members of the Appeals Council. Although no members of the Council are alleged to have held hearings in that capacity, Nash asserts that such power may be vested only in an ALJ. Finally, he contends, the Chief ALJ and the 10 Regional Chief ALJs improperly combine judicial and managerial duties in violation of 5 U.S.C. § 3105.

* * * Without addressing Nash's claims separately, but after considering affidavits and submitted documents, Judge Elfvin, apparently treating the motion as one for summary judgment, dismissed the amended complaint for lack of standing in a colloquial statement delivered after argument, since he found "nothing right here and now that lands on * * * Judge Nash." No written opinion was filed by the district judge. Judgment dismissing the complaint was entered on July 10, 1979 and this appeal, *pro se*, followed.

Article III limits federal judicial power to the adjudication of "cases or controversies." Thus, a threshold question in every suit is whether plaintiff has alleged that he has in fact suffered (or is imminently subject to suffering) a cognizable injury. * * * The gravamen of appellant's complaint is that rights conferred upon him and all other ALJs by statute, regulation and prior agency practice are being continuously infringed by the appellees' actions. Accordingly, we must turn to the sources of the right asserted to assess appellant's claim of injury.

* * *

As originally enacted in 1946, the Administrative Procedure Act (APA) vested hearing examiners (as ALJs were then called) with a limited independence from the agencies they served. The hearing examiners had previously been on a par with other agency employees, their compensation and promotion dependent upon agency ratings. The expanding scope of agency activity during the 1930s and early 1940s led to increasingly heavy criticism, however, because the hearing examiners came to be perceived as "mere tools of the agency concerned." *Ramspeck v. Trial Examiners Conference*, 345 U.S. 128, 131 (1953). In response, Congress enacted § 11 of the APA, removing control over the hearing examiners' tenure and compensation from the agencies and vesting it, to a large degree, in the Civil Service Commission.

The APA provides that ALJs "are entitled to pay prescribed by the Office of Personnel Management independently of agency recommendations or ratings." 5 U.S.C. § 5372. In addition, section 4301 and its implementing regulation (5 C.F.R. § 930.211) exempts ALJs from the performance ratings prescribed for other civil service employees. ALJ tenure, moreover, is specially safeguarded by 5 U.S.C. § 554, which provides that ALJs, unlike other civil servants, may not be removed without a formal adjudication.

* * *

It is clear that these provisions confer a qualified right of decisional independence upon ALJs. First recognized by the Supreme Court in *Ramspeck v. Trial Examiners Conference*, this special status is a creation of statute, rather than the Constitution. And as their role has expanded, the ALJs' functional comparability to judges has gained recognition. For example, in *Butz v. Economou*, 438 U.S. 478 (1978), the Supreme Court held that ALJs enjoy absolute immunity from liability in damages for actions taken in their quasi-judicial capacity.

The Social Security Administration has, moreover, recognized the limitations upon its power over the ALJs' decisionmaking process. The position description for ALJs issued by the Administration's Bureau of Hearings and Appeals states that ALJs possess "full and complete individual independence of action and decision * * * without review [and] full responsibility and authority" for the conduct of hearings and the disposition of cases. "The Social Security and Administrative Procedure Acts," the description continues, "prohibit substantive review and supervision of the [ALJ] in the performance of his quasi-judicial functions. His decisions may not be reviewed before publication, and after publication only by the Appeals Council in certain prescribed circumstances. He is subject only to such administrative supervision as may be required in the course of general office management."

It is not insignificant that when Director Trachtenberg instituted the extraordinary review and counseling practices challenged in Nash's complaint, he recognized their potential dangers. In a memorandum dated February 7, 1977 to the Regional Chief ALJs setting forth the Regional Office Peer Review Program, he wrote:

> "You can readily discern from this memorandum my concern and, indeed, my resolve that none of these programs, including this new regional technical review effort, should denigrate or undermine the ALJs' substantive independence. While these programs can serve a needed, valued public service, in the wrong hands, with the wrong attitude, and without constant vigilance, they could cause a serious setback to the system of administrative justice of which we all rightly should be proud. * * * "

Director Trachtenberg apparently entertained similar doubts as to the propriety of instituting special programs for low-producing and high- and low-reversing ALJs. In a letter dated November 1, 1977, he solicited the comments of the Executive Director of the U.S. Civil Service Commission on possible conflicts between the Quality Assurance System and the Administrative Procedure Act or Civil Service Commission regulations. The Executive Director was of the opinion that the system, as outlined to him, would not violate the APA but qualified his statement appropriately: "Agency programs which seek to enhance the efficiency and quality of an adjudicatory program are in the public interest *so long as they do not impinge upon the decisional independence of Administrative Law Judges*." (emphasis supplied).

The APA creates a comprehensive bulwark to protect ALJs from agency interference. The independence granted to ALJs is designed to maintain public confidence in the essential fairness of the process through which Social Security benefits are allocated by ensuring impartial decisionmaking. Since that independence is expressed in terms of such personal rights as compensation, tenure and freedom from performance evaluations and extraordinary review, we cannot say that ALJs are so disinterested as to lack even standing to safeguard their own independence.

The scrutiny and affirmative direction alleged by Nash reaches virtually every aspect of an ALJ's daily role. Under the Quality Assurance System and the Peer Review Program, the number of reversals, the number of dispositions, and the manner of trying and deciding each case are recorded and measured against prescribed standards. ALJ Nash and his colleagues allegedly receive mandatory, unlawful instructions regarding every detail of their judicial role. Nash, therefore, has "the personal stake and interest that impart the concrete adverseness required by Article III." * * *

* * *

Finally, we reiterate that our discussion of Nash's standing to sue in no way reflects upon the merits of his claims. We merely note that premature dismissal for want of standing may deprive litigants of the "focused and careful decision on the merits to which they are clearly entitled." The current explosion of claims and appeals within the Social Security system has posed an awesome challenge to effective administration, and our holding is not intended to undermine the Bureau's good faith attempts to meet this challenge. By providing an authoritative delineation of the respective rights and powers of the parties to this litigation, and by recognizing that good administration must not encroach upon adjudicative independence, the district court on remand will have the opportunity to advance the principal goal of judicial and quasi-judicial administration: reduction of delay without compromise to the demands of due process, of which judicial independence is but one, important part.

Notes

1. *Bellmon Review.* The same year *Nash* was decided, Congress amended the Social Security Act to require, among other things, that the SSA conduct a continuing disability investigation (CDI) of every SSDI recipient with a non-permanent disability at least once every three years, beginning in January, 1982. 42 U.S.C. § 421 (2000). Concerned with the quality control implications of so potentially great an increase in the SSA workload, Senator Bellmon successfully introduced a further amendment requiring the Secretary to "implement a program of reviewing, on his own motion" ALJ disability determinations. Social Security Disability Amendments of 1980, Pub. L. No. 96–265, § 304(g), 94 Stat. 456 (1980).

The "Bellmon Review" program instituted pursuant to these amendments continued the Quality Assurance Program challenged in *Nash.* Indeed, HHS provoked a significant furor in Congress, the courts, the states, and the disability bar by (1) advancing the starting date for CDI's to March, 1981, resulting in a much faster upturn in the volume of disability reviews, (2) announcing that the Bellmon Review would focus initially only on those ALJs with above-average rates of claim allowance, and (3) refusing to "acquiesce" in the rulings of numerous district and circuit courts that regarded the standards for the reviewing cases in the CDI program as inconsistent with the Social Security Act. For a review of the political history of disability adjudication in the 1980–85 period, see Jerry L. Mashaw, *Disability Insurance in an Age of Retrenchment: The Politics of Implementing Rights, in* Social Security: Beyond the Rhetoric of Crisis (Theodore R. Marmor & Jerry L. Mashaw, eds., 1988). See also Subcomm. on Oversight of Government Management of the Senate Comm. on Governmental Affairs, The Role of the Administrative Law Judge in the Title II Social Security Disability Insurance Program, 98th Cong., 1st Sess. (Comm. Print 1983).

Following implementation of this program, the Association of Administrative Law Judges challenged Bellmon Review on *Nash*-like grounds. *Association of Administrative Law Judges, Inc. v. Heckler*, 594 F.Supp. 1132 (D.D.C.1984). The district court agreed with the ALJs that HHS's "unremitting focus on allowance rates in the individual ALJ portion of the Bellmon Review Program created an atmosphere of tension and unfairness, which violated the spirit of the APA, if no specific provision thereof." While it lamented HHS's "insensitivity to the decisional independence" of ALJs, the court withheld any injunctive relief following a decision by the SSA to abandon any selection of individual ALJs for review based on their allowance rate.

2. *Management Techniques and Decisional Fairness*. Does it appear to you that all of the practices challenged by Judge Nash and his colleagues threaten equally to undermine ALJ decisional independence? To what extent would you expect Director Trachtenberg's initiatives to benefit or harm disability claimants? Would a quota or target for claim allowances, e.g., 50 per cent, be unconstitutional? Do any other challenges to SSA's managerial initiatives suggest due process problems? For additional insight into these questions see JERRY L. MASHAW, ET. AL., SOCIAL SECURITY HEARINGS AND APPEALS 101–24 (1978); Deborah A. Chassman and Howard Rolston, *Social Security Disability Hearings: A Case Study in Quality Assurance and Due Process*, 65 Cornell L.Rev. 801 (1980); Jerry L. Mashaw, *How Much of What Quality: A Comment on Conscientious Procedural Design*, 65 Cornell L.Rev. 823 (1980); Antonin Scalia, *The ALJ Fiasco—A Reprise*, 47 U.Chi. L. Rev. 56 (1979).

3. *The Status of ALJs*. The *Nash* and *AALJ* cases represent part of a continuing effort by ALJs generally to augment their status and independence. For a detailed history of their controversial campaign, see Victor G. Rosenblum, *The Administrative Law Judge in the Administrative Process: Interrelations of Case Law with Statutory and Pragmatic Factors in Determining ALJ Roles*, printed in Subcommittee on Social Security, House Committee on Ways and Means, Recent Studies Relevant to the Disability Hearings and Appeals Crisis 171 (1975); Daniel T. Gifford, *Federal Administrative Law Judges: The Relevance of Past Choices to Future Directions*, 49 ADMIN. L. REV. 1 (1997). See also Memorandum by Floyd Lewis, American Law Division, Congressional Research Service, on The Administrative Law Judge System (Sept. 15, 1982). Almost every Congress sees the reintroduction of legislation proposing to remove all ALJs from line agencies and establish them as a separate, independent corps of administrative law judges. On the 1992 version, see Joseph J. Simeone, *The Function, Flexibility, and Future of United States Judges of the Executive Department*, 44 Admin. L. Rev. 159 (1992). And litigants continue, unsuccessfully, to attack the impartiality of ALJ's based on their location within the agencies whose cases they hear. E.g., *Harline v. Drug Enforcement Administration*, 148 F.3d 1199 (10th Cir.1998). This organization is not only controversial, it is a unique compromise between adjudicatory independence and managerial responsibility born of the peculiar history of administrative governance in the United States. Michael Asimow, *The Administrative Judiciary: ALJs in Historical Perspective*, 20 J. Nat'l A. Admin. L. Judges 157 (2000).

Trench warfare between administrative law judges and policy makers at the Social Security Administration has continued unabated. A 1997 internal memorandum from Shirley S. Chater, Commissioner of the Social Security Administration, to her executive staff (prepared by the SSA general counsel) codifies the continuing terms of the conflict. The memorandum laments the "confusion" that exists in various parts of the Agency concerning the meaning of "decisional independence" and the way in which independence limits the authority of the agency to manage ALJ performance. From the standpoint of the agency's ALJ corps two sentences in this memorandum were both revealing and pernicious. "In a judicial system, the quality of the decision and the quality of justice depend on the quality of the judge. A bureaucratic system depends on the quality of supervision and internal bureaucratic review." Counter attack was swift. Wendell Fennell and Fred Young, writing in the Journal of the National Association of Administrative Law Judges said: "[I]t is of great concern to all of us who believe in the idea of impartiality and fairness that * * * judicial independence is under such intense attack. The attacks emanating from those within the leadership roles of the administrative bureaucracy include the Agency's leaders and the government attorneys (Office of the General Counsel) in the * * * Social Security Administration (SSA)." *Judicial Independence Under Siege*, 17 J. Nat'l Ass'n Admin. Judges 211 (1997).

The controversy in SSA has taken on all the hallmarks of a protracted labor management dispute in which any concession might be construed as capitulation and no utterance is free from quotation out of context. Three decades after *Richardson v. Perales*, for example, SSA is unwilling to concede the point that the decision left open, i.e., whether SSA is required by the Administrative Procedure Act to use administrative law judges to hear Social Security claims. This notwithstanding the agency's uninterrupted, half-century-long practice of using only APA qualified ALJs in its hearings.

It was, of course, the wholly symbolic nature of this question that convinced the Supreme Court that it need not resolve it in *Perales*. But symbols are potent. Commissioner Chater's successor, Kenneth Apfel, attempted to reassure the administrative law judges of the agency's support of their decisional independence at their annual meeting in Washington in July, 2000. In the discussion period following the Commissioner's remarks he was met with the demand that he put his commitment to the independence of SSA ALJs under the Administrative Procedure Act in writing. Somewhat nonplussed the Commissioner replied that he would have to seek counsel. "I don't know if there's a wrinkle in here that I am unaware of." For an account of this and a host of other skirmishes in the long-simmering ALJ controversy at the Social Security Administration, see Jeffrey Scott Wolfe, *Are you Willing to Make the Commitment in Writing? The APA, ALJs and SSA,* 55 Okla. L. Rev. 203 (2002) (the author is himself an administrative law judge with the Social Security Administration).

4. *Non–APA Hearing Officers*. There are many more non-APA hearing officers in federal agencies than there are APA-qualified administrative law judges. In his 1992 survey, Paul R. Verkuil, *Reflections Upon the Federal Administrative Judiciary*, 39 U.C.L.A. L. Rev. 1341 (1992), found that there were twice as many "administrative judges" as ALJs. They were deciding 350,000 cases a year outside of APA formal adjudication requirements. The largest group are "immigration judges" who hear and decide cases for the Immigration and Naturalization Service in the Department of Justice. These non-ALJ administrative judges have less decisional independence, lower pay and benefits, and less job security than ALJs. Their selection and appointment are controlled by the agencies by whom they are employed. While many find it anomalous that the judges making crucial, sometimes life-determining, decisions with respect to deportation and asylum have less decisional independence than an ALJ deciding a reparations claim under the

Commodities Futures Trading Act, fiscal constraints, if nothing more, seem destined to prevent congressional action to reenforce the independence of non-ALJ administrative hearer-deciders. Bernard Schwartz, *Adjudication and the Administrative Procedure Act*, 32 Tulsa L.Rev. 203, 217–18 (1996). See also Jeffrey S. Lubbers, *APA–Adjudication: Is the Quest for Uniformity Faltering?*, 10 Admin. L. J. 65 (1996).

c. *Controlling Adjudication Through Rulemaking*

HECKLER v. CAMPBELL

Supreme Court of the United States, 1983.
461 U.S. 458, 103 S.Ct. 1952, 76 L.Ed.2d 66.

JUSTICE POWELL delivered the opinion of the court.

The issue is whether the Secretary of Health and Human Services may rely on published medical-vocational guidelines to determine a claimant's right to Social Security disability benefits. * * *

In 1978, the Secretary of Health and Human Services promulgated regulations implementing [the statutory definition of disability]. See 43 Fed.Reg. 55349 (1978). The regulations recognize that certain impairments are so severe that they prevent a person from pursuing any gainful work. A claimant who establishes that he suffers from one of these impairments will be considered disabled without further inquiry. If a claimant suffers from a less severe impairment, the Secretary must determine whether the claimant retains the ability to perform either his former work or some less demanding employment. If a claimant can pursue his former occupation, he is not entitled to disability benefits. If he cannot, the Secretary must determine whether the claimant retains the capacity to pursue less demanding work.

The regulations divide this last inquiry into two stages. First, the Secretary must assess each claimant's present job qualifications. The regulations direct the Secretary to consider the factors Congress has identified as relevant: physical ability, age, education and work experience. * * *

Prior to 1978, the Secretary relied on vocational experts to establish the existence of suitable jobs in the national economy. After a claimant's limitations and abilities had been determined at a hearing, a vocational expert ordinarily would testify whether work existed that the claimant could perform. Although this testimony often was based on standardized guides, see 43 Fed.Reg. 9286 (1978), vocational experts frequently were criticized for their inconsistent treatment of similarly situated claimants. To improve both the uniformity and efficiency of this determination, the Secretary promulgated medical-vocational guidelines as part of the 1978 regulations.

These guidelines relieve the Secretary of the need to rely on vocational experts by establishing through rulemaking the types and numbers of jobs that exist in the national economy. They consist of a matrix of the four factors identified by Congress—physical ability, age, education, and work experience[3]—and set forth rules that identify whether jobs requiring specific combinations of these factors exist in significant numbers in the national economy. Where a claimant's qualifications correspond to the job requirements identified by a rule,[5] the guidelines direct a conclusion as to whether work exists that the claimant could perform. If such work exists, the claimant is not considered disabled.

In 1979, Carmen Campbell applied for disability benefits because a back condition and hypertension prevented her from continuing her work as a hotel maid. After her application was denied, she requested a hearing *de novo* before an Administrative Law Judge. He determined that her back problem was not severe enough to find her disabled without further inquiry, and accordingly considered whether she retained the ability to perform either her past work or some less strenuous job. He concluded that even though Campbell's back condition prevented her from returning to her work as a maid, she retained the physical capacity to do light work. In accordance with the regulations, he found that Campbell was 52–years old, that her previous employment consisted of unskilled jobs and that she had a limited education. He noted that Campbell, who had been born in Panama, experienced difficulty in speaking and writing English. She was able, however, to understand and read English fairly well. Relying on the medical-vocational guidelines, the Administrative Law Judge found that a significant number of jobs existed that a person of Campbell's qualifications could perform. Accordingly, he concluded that she was not disabled.

This determination was upheld by both the Social Security Appeals Council, and the District Court for the Eastern District of New York. The Court of Appeals for the Second Circuit reversed. *Campbell v. Secretary of HHS*, 665 F.2d 48 (C.A.2 1981). It accepted the Administrative Law Judge's determination that Campbell retained the ability to do light work. And it did not suggest that he had classified Campbell's age, education, or work experience incorrectly. The court noted, however, that it

3. Each of these four factors is divided into defined categories. A person's ability to perform physical tasks, for example, is categorized according to the physical exertion requirements necessary to perform varying classes of jobs—i.e., whether a claimant can perform sedentary, light, medium, heavy, or very heavy work. 20 CFR § 404.1567. Each of these work categories is defined in terms of the physical demands it places on a worker, such as the weight of objects he must lift and whether extensive movement or use of arm and leg controls is required.

5. The regulations recognize that the rules only describe "major functional and vocational patterns." 20 CFR pt. 404, subpt. P, app. 2, § 200.00(a). If an individual's capabilities are not described accurately by a rule, the regulations make clear that the individual's particular limitations must be considered. See app. 2, §§ 200.00(a), (d). Additionally, the regulations declare that the Administrative Law Judge will not apply the age categories "mechanically in a borderline situation," 20 CFR § 404.1563(a), and recognize that some claimants may possess limitations that are not factored into the guidelines, see app. 2, § 200.00(e). Thus, the regulations provide that the rules will be applied only when they describe a claimant's abilities and limitations accurately.

> "has consistently required that 'the Secretary identify specific alternative occupations available in the national economy that would be suitable for the claimant' and that 'these jobs be supported by "a job description clarifying the nature of the job, [and] demonstrating that the job does not require" exertion or skills not possessed by the claimant.' " *Id.* at 53 (quoting *Decker v. Harris*, 647 F.2d 291, 298 (C.A.2 1981)).

The court found that the medical-vocational guidelines did not provide the specific evidence that it previously had required. It explained that in the absence of such a showing, "the claimant is deprived of any real chance to present evidence showing that she cannot in fact perform the types of jobs that are administratively noticed by the guidelines." The court concluded that because the Secretary had failed to introduce evidence that specific alternative jobs existed, the determination that Campbell was not disabled was not supported by substantial evidence. * * *

The Secretary argues that the Court of Appeals' holding effectively prevents the use of the medical-vocational guidelines. By requiring her to identify specific alternative jobs in every disability hearing, the court has rendered the guidelines useless. * * *

The Social Security Act directs the Secretary to "adopt reasonable and proper rules and regulations to regulate and provide for the nature and extent of the proofs and evidence and the method of taking and furnishing the same" in disability cases. * * * Where, as here, the statute expressly entrusts the Secretary with the responsibility for implementing a provision by regulation, our review is limited to determining whether the regulations promulgated exceeded the Secretary's statutory authority and whether they are arbitrary and capricious.

We do not think that the Secretary's reliance on medical-vocational guidelines is inconsistent with the Social Security Act. It is true that the statutory scheme contemplates that disability hearings will be individualized determinations based on evidence adduced at a hearing. But this does not bar the Secretary from relying on rulemaking to resolve certain classes of issues. The Court has recognized that even where an agency's enabling statute expressly requires it to hold a hearing, the agency may rely on its rulemaking authority to determine issues that do not require case-by-case consideration. See *FPC v. Texaco, Inc.*, 377 U.S. 33, 41–44 (1964); *United States v. Storer Broadcasting Co.*, 351 U.S. 192, 205 (1956). A contrary holding would require the agency continually to relitigate issues that may be established fairly and efficiently in a single rulemaking proceeding.

The Secretary's decision to rely on medical-vocational guidelines is consistent with *Texaco* and *Storer*. As noted above, in determining whether a claimant can perform less strenuous work, the Secretary must make two determinations. She must assess each claimant's individual abilities and then determine whether jobs exist that a person having the claimant's qualifications could perform. The first inquiry involves a determination of historic facts, and the regulations properly require the Secretary to make these findings on the basis of evidence adduced at a hearing. We note that the regulations afford claimants ample opportunity both to present evidence, relating to their own abilities and to offer evidence that the guidelines do not apply to them.[11] The second inquiry requires the Secretary to determine an issue that is not unique to each claimant—the types and numbers of jobs that exist in the national economy. This type of general factual issue may be resolved as fairly through rulemaking as by introducing the testimony of vocational experts at each disability hearing.

As the Secretary has argued, the use of published guidelines brings with it a uniformity that previously had been perceived as lacking. To require the Secretary to relitigate the existence of jobs in the national economy at each hearing would hinder needlessly an already overburdened agency. We conclude that the Secretary's use of medical-vocational guidelines does not conflict with the statute, nor can we say on the record before us that they are arbitrary and capricious.

We now consider Campbell's argument that the Court of Appeals properly required the Secretary to specify alternative available jobs. Campbell contends that such a showing informs claimants of the type of issues to be established at the hearing and is required by both the Secretary's regulation, 20 CFR § 404.944 (1980), and the Due Process Clause.

By referring to notice and an opportunity to respond, the decision below invites the interpretation given it by respondent. But we do not think that the decision fairly can be said to present the issues she raises. * * * Rather the court's reference to notice and an opportunity to respond appears to be based on a principle of administrative law—that when an agency takes official or administrative notice of facts, a litigant must be given an adequate opportunity to respond.

This principle is inapplicable, however, when the agency has promulgated valid regulations. Its purpose is to provide a procedural safeguard: to ensure the accuracy of the facts of which an agency takes notice. But when the accuracy of those facts already has been tested fairly during rulemaking, the rulemaking proceeding itself provides sufficient procedural protection.

The Court of Appeals' decision would require the Secretary to introduce evidence of specific available jobs that respondent could perform. It would limit severely her ability to rely on the medical-vocational guidelines. We think the Secretary reasonably could choose to rely on these guidelines in appropriate cases rather than on the testimony of

11. Both *FPC v. Texaco, Inc.* and *United States v. Storer Broadcasting Co.* were careful to note that the statutory scheme at issue allowed an individual applicant to show that the rule promulgated should not be applied to him. The regulations here provide a claimant with equal or greater protection since they state that an Administrative Law Judge will not apply the rules contained in the guidelines when they fail to describe a claimant's particular limitations.

avocational expert in each case. Accordingly, the judgment of the Court of Appeals is

Reversed.

[Justice Brennan concurred, while pointing out that the record contained very little evidence concerning Campbell's capacity to do "light work." Justice Marshall dissented essentially on the same ground.]

Notes

1. *The SSA's "Residual Functional Capacity" Grid.* The so-called "grid regulations" at issue in *Heckler* are set out in the form of four tables—one for each classification of work—sedentary, light, medium, and heavy work. Each table then breaks down into a series of age classifications (55 and over, 50–54, 45–49, 18–44), educational qualifications (high school or more, limited high school or less, illiterate or unable to communicate in English), and skill categories (skilled or semi-skilled, skills transferable; skilled or semi-skilled, skills non-transferable; unskilled or none). Having found that a claimant, such as Ms. Campbell, can do light work, is between 50–54, has a limited education, and has previously done unskilled work, the ALJ can go to the line in the "light work" table presenting these characteristics and read out the appropriate conclusion—"not disabled." The tabular conclusion is based upon a determination by the Secretary that there are substantial numbers of jobs in the national economy that can be performed by persons fitting this categorical description. The Secretary's determination in the rulemaking proceeding that produced the grid regulations was again premised largely on Labor Department descriptions of job classifications and their requirements in the *Dictionary of Occupational Titles*, a compendium of thousands of job descriptions assembled over many years of collecting data on the national labor market.

While the residual functional capacity grid has remained the backbone of the vocational factors evaluation in deciding Social Security disability claims, claimants and reviewing courts remain skeptical of its accuracy when deciding particular cases. The regulations themselves provide a number of avenues for escape. As the Supreme Court noted in *Heckler v. Campbell*, the grid applies only to exertional restrictions and many claimants have both exertional and non-exertional disabilities. And, once an administrative law judge accepts as a fact that the claimant has a non-exertional limitation, the use of the grid becomes problematic.

For example, in an important opinion, *Sykes v. Apfel*, 228 F.3rd 259 (3d Cir. 2000), the SSA's finding of non-disability was overturned for lack of substantial evidence. The claimant had both exertional limits and a loss of binocular vision caused by blindness in one eye. The administrative law judge determined that the claimant was capable of doing light work, given his exertional limits, and that the exclusion of all jobs classified as light work and requiring binocular vision would not significantly compromise the claimant's ability to do a substantial number of jobs available in the national economy. The Third Circuit found that the administrative law judge's analysis was insufficient. Non-exertional limitations are not included in the grid regulations and there was no evidence in the record concerning the number of jobs in the light work category that could be performed with only monocular vision. The reviewing court, after exhaustive analysis of decisions in other circuits, held that SSA must produce evidence on this point, either by the testimony of a vocational expert or by the introduction of expert literature. The claimant would then have an opportunity to rebut or refute the evidence offered.

The grid regulations' reliance on age categories is also often sharply disputed. Indeed, the Social Security Administration's regulations provide that these categories should not be "mechanically" applied. This leaves open the possibility that any applicant who is near the upper end of an age category may contest whether he or she should be assigned to the next higher age group—an assignment that often tips the balance under the grid between disability and non-disability. Moreover, it is unclear what evidence is pertinent concerning whether a person on the cusp of an age group should be assigned "mechanically" or non-mechanically. Because the claimant's residual functional capacity has already been taken into account, the Social Security Administration takes the position that that evidence does not bear on whether a 54 year old should really be considered 55 or over. To do so, in the administration's view, would be to double count the residual functional capacity determination. But, if that evidence is excluded, what evidence would bear on the issue? For discussion, see *Daniels v. Apfel*, 154 F.3rd 1129 (10th Cir.1998).

2. *"Severity" By Rule.* The Supreme Court revisited the Social Security Administration's process for evaluating disability claims in *Bowen v. Yuckert*, 482 U.S. 137 (1987). At issue was the validity of the agency's "severity regulation," which the majority opinion explained as follows:

> The Secretary has established a five-step sequential evaluation process for determining whether a person is disabled. Step one determines whether the claimant is engaged in "substantial gainful activity." If he is, disability benefits are denied. If he is not, the decisionmaker proceeds to step two, that determines whether the claimant has a medically severe impairment or combination of impairments. That determination is governed by the "severity regulation" at issue in this case. The severity regulation provides:
>
> > "If you do not have any impairment or combination of impairments which significantly limits your physical or mental ability to do basic work activities, we will find that you do not have a severe impairment and are, therefore, not disabled. We will not consider your age, education, and work experience."
>
> The ability to do basic work activities is defined as "the abilities and aptitudes necessary to do most jobs." Such abilities and aptitudes include "[p]hysical functions such as walking, standing, sitting, lifting, pushing, pulling, reaching, carrying, or handling"; "[c]apacities for seeing, hearing, and speaking"; "[u]nderstanding, carrying out, and remembering simple instructions"; "[u]se of judgment"; "[r]esponding appropriately to supervision, co-workers, and usual work situations"; and "[d]ealing with changes in a routine work setting."

> If the claimant does not have a severe impairment or combination of impairments, the disability claim is denied. If the impairment is severe, the evaluation proceeds to the third step, that determines whether the impairment is equivalent to one of a number of listed impairments that the Secretary acknowledges are so severe as to preclude substantial gainful activity. If the impairment meets or equals one of the listed impairments, the claimant is conclusively presumed to be disabled. If the impairment is not one that is conclusively presumed to be disabling, the evaluation proceeds to the fourth step, that determines whether the impairment prevents the claimant from performing work he has performed in the past. If the claimant is able to perform his previous work, he is not disabled. If the claimant cannot perform this work, the fifth and final step of the process determines whether he is able to perform other work in the national economy in view of his age, education, and work experience. The claimant is entitled to disability benefits only if he is not able to perform other work.

Yuckert contended that the severity regulation prevented the Secretary from ever reaching the question of whether she was disabled in light of the combination of her medical impairments and her age, education and work experience. Having determined that her medical impairments were not "severe," the sequential determination process ended after the second step. According to Yuckert, this was contrary to the Social Security Act's requirement that the Secretary consider each claim individually and after considering both medical impairment and the so-called "vocational factors" of age, education and work experience.

A majority of the Court was unmoved by this argument. On its face, the regulation is not inconsistent with the statutory definition of disability. The Act "defines 'disability' in terms of the effect a physical or mental impairment has on a person's ability to function in the workplace." The regulation adopts precisely this functional approach to determining the effects of medical impairments. If the impairments are not severe enough to limit significantly the claimant's ability to perform most jobs, by definition the impairment does not prevent the claimant from engaging in any substantial gainful activity. The Secretary, moreover, has express statutory authority to place the burden of showing a medically determinable impairment on the claimant. The Act provides that "[a]n individual shall not be considered to be under a disability unless he furnishes such medical and other evidence of the existence thereof as the Secretary may require." § 423(d)(5)(A).

The Court found this facial, textual consistency supported by the legislative history of the initial 1954 disability legislation and specifically confirmed by both the language and the legislative history of the Social Security Disability Benefits Reform Act of 1984. Pub. L. No. 98–460, 98 Stat. 1794 (1984). The Court was also convinced that the regulations were essential to the proper functioning of the disability decision process.

> We have recognized that other aspects of the Secretary's sequential evaluation process contribute to the uniformity and efficiency for disability determinations. *Heckler v. Campbell.* The need for such an evaluation process is particularly acute because the Secretary decides more than 2 million claims for disability benefits each year, of which

more than 200,000 are reviewed by administrative law judges. The severity regulation increases the efficiency and reliability of the evaluation process by identifying at an early stage those claimants whose medical impairments are so slight that it is unlikely they would be found to be disabled even if their age, education, and experience were taken into account. Similarly, step three streamlines the decision process by identifying those claimants whose medical impairments are so severe that it is likely they would be found disabled regardless of their vocational background.

Although the majority had little difficulty sustaining the facial validity of the Secretary's regulation, Justices O'Connor's concurrence, joined by Justice Stevens, recognized the potentially radical disjunction between the reasonableness of a regulation on its face and its application by widely dispersed decision makers in hundreds of thousands of adjudications.

> * * * I have no doubt that the Act authorizes the Secretary to weed out at an early stage of the administrative process those individuals who cannot possibly meet the statutory definition of disability. Accordingly, I concur in the Court's opinion and judgment that the regulation is not facially invalid, and that the case must be remanded so that the lower courts may determine whether or not the Secretary's conclusion that Janet Yuckert is not suffering from a sufficiently severe impairment is supported by substantial evidence.
>
> I write separately, however, to discuss the contention of respondent and various *amici* (including 29 States and 5 major cities) that this facially valid regulation has been applied systematically to deny benefits to claimants who *do* meet the statutory definition of disability. Respondent directs our attention to the chorus of judicial criticism concerning the step 2 regulation, as well as to substantially unrefuted statistical evidence. Despite the heavy deference ordinarily paid to the Secretary's promulgation and application of his regulations, all 11 regional Federal Courts of Appeals have either enjoined the Secretary's use of the step 2 regulations or imposed a narrowing construction upon it. * * *
>
> Empirical evidence cited by respondent and the *amici* further supports the inference that the regulation has been used in a manner inconsistent with the statutory definition of disability. Before the step 2 regulations were promulgated approximately 8 per cent of all claimants were denied benefits at the "not severe" stage of the administrative process; afterwards approximately 40 per cent of all claims were denied at this stage. As the lower federal courts have enjoined use of step 2 and imposed narrowing constructions, the step 2 denial rate has fallen to about 25 per cent. Allowance rates in social security disability cases have increased substantially when federal courts have demanded that the step 2 regulation not be used to disqualify those who are statutorily eligible. * * *
>
> To be sure the Secretary faces an administrative task of staggering proportions in applying the disability benefits provisions of the Social Security Act. Perfection in processing millions of such claims annually is impossible. But respondent's evidence suggests that step 2 has been applied systematically in a manner inconsistent with the statute. Indeed,

the Secretary himself has recently acknowledged a need to "clarify" step 2 in light of this criticism and has attempted to do so by issuing new interpretative guidelines. See Social Security Ruling 85–28.

In my view, step 2 may not be used to disqualify those who meet the statutory definition of disability. The statute does not permit the Secretary to deny benefits to a claimant who may fit within the statutory definition without determining whether the impairment prevents the claimant from engaging in either his prior work or substantial gainful employment that, in light of the claimant's age, education, and experience, is available to him in the national economy. Only those claimants with slight abnormalities that do not significantly limit any "basic work activity" can be denied benefits without undertaking this vocational analysis. As the Secretary has recently admonished in his new guideline:

> "Great care should be exercised in applying the not severe impairment concept. If an adjudicator is unable to determine clearly the effect of an impairment or combination of impairments on the individual's ability to do basic work activities, the sequential evaluation process should not end with the not severe evaluation step. Rather, it should be continued. In such a circumstance, if the impairment does not meet or equal the severity level of the relevant medical listing, sequential evaluation requires that the adjudicator evaluate the individual's ability to do past work, or to do other work based on the consideration of age, education, and prior work experience." Social Security Ruling 85–28.

Applied in this manner, step 2, I believe, can produce results consistent with the statute in the vast majority of cases and still facilitate the expeditious and just settlement of claims.

3. *Official Notice*. The Second Circuit actually treated the Secretary's rulemaking in *Heckler v. Campbell* as an impermissible form of "official notice." "Official notice" is the evidentiary analogue in administrative proceedings of "judicial notice" in court proceedings. Under Rule 201 of the Federal Rules of Evidence, however, judicial notice of a fact is permissible only if the fact is not subject to reasonable dispute because it is a matter of general knowledge or susceptible of determination by recourse to sources whose accuracy cannot reasonably be questioned. These are not prerequisites to official notice. Indeed, official notice is probably most often used when an agency, having successfully defended the accuracy of specific data in one proceeding, seeks to have the data accepted as accurate in a later proceeding. The data may well concern disputed issues that are not matters of common knowledge.

The APA expressly contemplates the possibility of taking official notice in a federal agency proceeding. "When an agency decision rests on official notice of a material fact not appearing in the evidence in the record, a party is entitled, on timely request, to an opportunity to show the contrary." 5 U.S.C. § 556(e). The obvious implication of this rule is that an agency may not take official notice without so informing the parties to the proceeding. The rule responds to the Supreme Court's earlier holding, in the context of a state ratemaking proceeding, that an agency's recourse to official notice without informing the parties involved could be tantamount to the denial of a legally required hearing. *Ohio Bell Telephone Co. v. Public Utilities Commission of Ohio*, 301 U.S. 292 (1937). But the rule is not always followed. See *Gonzalez v. INS*, 77 F.3d 1015, 1024 (7th Cir.1996) (INS may officially notice changed political circumstances in Nicaragua without giving the applicant an opportunity for rebuttal). *Contra*, *Gonzalez v. INS*, 82 F.3d 903, 910 (9th Cir.1996).

Is it always likely to be clear to a decision maker, however, that he or she is taking "official notice?" An Administrative Law Judge could hardly give notice to the parties of all the beliefs that the ALJ has developed in his or her field of expertise because of experience presiding in other cases. Note also that the APA seems to permit the agency members to consult ex parte with disinterested persons outside the agency regarding agency proceedings. See § 554(d), 557(d)(1). Thus, to take a perhaps far-fetched example, in adjudicating an alleged "deceptive trade practice," a member of the Federal Trade Commission—without violating ex parte contact rules—could call up his or her favorite social psychologist for an off-the-record briefing on the likely communicative impact of a contested advertisement. Is such a practice consistent with § 556(e)?

d. Avoiding Adjudication Through Rulemaking

The SSA disputes reviewed above involved agency efforts to lighten the burdens of formal adjudication by narrowing the issues to be explored in formal hearings and simplifying their resolution. The following case deals with an agency's use of rulemaking to eliminate a class of hearings altogether.

AIR LINE PILOTS ASSOCIATION v. QUESADA

United States Court of Appeals, Second Circuit, 1960.
276 F.2d 892, *cert. denied*, 366 U.S. 962, 81 S.Ct. 1923, 6 L.Ed.2d 1254 (1961).

Before LUMBARD, CHIEF JUDGE, HAND and HINCKS, CIRCUIT JUDGES.

LUMBARD, CHIEF JUDGE:

On December 1, 1959 the defendant, Elwood R. Quesada, Administrator of the Federal Aviation Agency, promulgated a regulation which provides:

> "No individual who has reached his 60th birthday shall be utilized or serve as a pilot on any aircraft while engaged in air carrier operations."

This regulation took effect on March 15, 1960.

The regulation does not apply to private or other pilots not engaged in carrying passengers, mail, or freight for hire.

The plaintiffs, thirty-five individual pilots, their collective bargaining representative, Air Line Pilots Association, and its president, brought the suit in January 1960 for a declaratory judgment that the regulation was null and void and for an injunction against its threatened application. The complaint alleged—and the plaintiffs contend on this appeal—that the regulation is invalid because it was issued without the holding of adjudicatory hearings required by the Administrative Procedure Act, and by § 609 of the Federal Aviation Act of 1958, 49 U.S.C. § 1429, before an airman's license may be amended, modified, suspended or revoked, and because it was arbitrary, discriminatory and without reasonable relation to the standards set forth in § 601 of the Act, 49 U.S.C. § 1421, under which it was issued. The plaintiffs also claim that the regulation, by terminating their right to pilot planes in commercial service after age sixty, deprives them of property in their pilots' licenses without due process of law. The district court, after submission of lengthy affidavits, denied the plaintiffs' motion for a preliminary injunction but reserved judgment on the Administrator's cross motion for summary judgment. * * * We affirm the order.

The Federal Aviation Act was passed by Congress for the purpose of centralizing in a single authority—indeed, in one administrator—the power to frame rules for the safe and efficient use of the nation's airspace. The Administrator was given the authority, theretofore divided between the Civil Aeronautics Board and the Civil Aeronautics Authority:

> "* * * To promote safety of flight of civil aircraft in air commerce by prescribing and revising from time to time:
>
> * * *
>
> (5) Reasonable rules and regulations governing, in the interest of safety, the maximum hours or periods of service of airmen, and other employees, of air carriers; and
>
> (6) Such reasonable rules and regulations, or minimum standards, governing other practices, methods, and procedure as the Administrator may find necessary to provide adequately for national security and safety in air commerce."[3]

Pursuant to this statutory authority the Administrator and his medical staff in the fall of 1958 began a study concerning the aging process and the diseases and physiological deterioration that accompany it in an effort to determine whether a maximum age should be set for service by commercial pilots. The Administrator took counsel with various experts in aviation medicine and safety and, among other things, determined the practices followed by five foreign air lines with respect to a mandatory retirement age. Finally, in June 1959 the Administrator published a proposed regulation in substance the same as that ultimately prescribed. In accordance with the rule-making requirements of § 4 of the Administrative Procedure Act, opportunity was afforded for the

3. Federal Aviation Act of 1958, § 601(a), 49 U.S.C. § 1421(a). Section 601(b) goes on to state in part:

"In prescribing standards, rules, and regulations * * * the Administrator shall give full consideration to the duty resting upon air carriers to perform their services with the highest possible degree of safety in the public interest. * * * The Administrator shall exercise and perform his powers and duties under this chapter in such manner as will best tend to reduce or eliminate the possibility of, or recurrence of, accidents in air transportation. * * *"

submission of written data and briefs. About one hundred comments, including those of the plaintiff association, were received. A large majority favored the regulation. No hearing was held since the Administrator determined, as he was entitled to under the rule-making provisions of the Administrative Procedure Act, that a hearing would not "serve a useful purpose" and that it was not "necessary in the public interest."

Plaintiffs assert that since the certificates of all commercial pilots are in effect modified by the regulation, and in the case of pilots already sixty, terminated, promulgation of the regulation was not rule-making within the meaning of the Administrative Procedure Act, but that the Administrator was obliged to proceed by holding an adjudicative hearing for each airman affected and by the entry of an "order." Alternatively, they say that whether one labels the issuance of the regulation rule-making or not, § 609 of the Federal Aviation Act, requires the Administrator to hold a hearing and permit each pilot affected to submit evidence as to the fairness of the regulation before his certificate can be amended.

Section 2 of the Administrative Procedure Act, 5 U.S.C. § 1001, defines a "rule" as "any agency statement of general or particular applicability and future effect designed to implement, interpret, or prescribe law or policy * * *" The regulation before us is just such a statement. It is directed to all the commercial airlines and to the more than 18,000 licensed commercial pilots. It looks to the future. It has the character of legislative enactment carried out on an administrative level. Adjudication, on the other hand, whether administrative or judicial, is the application of a statute or other legal standard to a given fact situation involving particular individuals. Promulgation of the age sixty limitation by the Administrator was the very antithesis of adjudication; it was the formulation of a general rule to be applied to individual pilots at a subsequent time. We think the directive was properly issued in accordance with the rule-making requirements of § 4 of the Administrative Procedure Act.

The Administrator's action does not lose the character of rule-making because it modifies the plaintiff pilots' claimed property rights in their licenses and their contractual rights under collective bargaining agreements to pilot planes beyond age sixty. Nor does the regulation violate due process because it modifies pilots' rights without affording each certificate holder a hearing. Administrative regulations often limit in the public interest the use that persons may make of their property without affording each one affected an opportunity to present evidence upon the fairness of the regulation. Bowles v. Willingham, 321 U.S. 503, 519–520 (1944). Obviously, unless the incidental limitations upon the use of airmen's certificates were subject to modification by general rules, the conduct of the Administrator's business would be subject to intolerable burdens which might well render it impossible for him effectively to discharge his duties. All changes in certificates would be subject to adjudicative hearings, including appeals to the courts, and each pilot whose license was affected—here some 18,000—might demand to be heard individually. When met with a similar challenge, Justice Holmes stated:

> "Where a rule of conduct applies to more than a few people it is impracticable that everyone should have a direct voice in its adoption. The Constitution does not require all public acts to be done in town meeting or an assembly of the whole. General statutes within the state power are passed that affect the person or property of individuals, sometimes to the point of ruin, without giving him a chance to be heard."

Bi–Metallic Investment Co. v. State Board of Equalization, 239 U.S. 441, 445 (1915).

All private property and privileges are held subject to limitations that may reasonably be imposed upon them in the public interest. Only when the limitations are too stringent in relation to the public interest to be served are they invalid. The limitations here are entirely reasonable. * * *

The plaintiffs strenuously urge that, however things may be under the Administrative Procedure Act, the statutory scheme of the Federal Aviation Act shows that Congress intended to afford airmen the greater protection of an individual hearing before their certificates may be modified. We disagree. * * * The immediate impetus to the legislation was a series of major air crashes culminating in the midair collision of two large air-lines over the Grand Canyon in 1956 with the loss of 128 lives. Congress believed there was a need for a more streamlined and efficient means for safety rule-making in place of the system of divided duties and responsibilities existing under the Civil Aeronautics Act. * * * [E]laborate procedural requirements * * * are patently incompatible with the expedition with which Congress intended that the Administrator should act in the promulgation of safety rules. The clear public interest in the speedy adoption of rules relating to air safety far outweighs any possible advantage in a multitude of piecemeal and time-consuming hearings brought by each contesting airman * * *.[10]

Plaintiffs assert that the age sixty limitation is arbitrary and discriminatory and without relation to any requirements of safety. For purposes of judicial review, such an argument must mean that the Administrator had no reasonable basis for his exercise of judgment. Surely this is not the fact in the case before us as there is considerable support for the Administrator's action. The Administrator found that the number of commercial pilots over sixty years of age has until recent years been very few but is increasing rapidly; that older pilots because of their seniority under collective bargaining agreements often fly the newest, largest, and fastest planes; that available medical studies show that sudden incapacitation due to heart attacks or strokes become more

10. * * * [W]e doubt that the Administrator is required by the statute to afford anyone an opportunity to apply for an exemption from any requirement of the regulations, [but] we think it is probable that the present statute and regulations do afford just such an opportunity. * * *

frequent as men approach age sixty and present medical knowledge is such that it is impossible to predict with accuracy those individuals most likely to suffer attacks; that a number of foreign air carriers contacted had mandatory retirement ages of sixty or less; and that numerous aviation safety experts advocated establishing a maximum age of sixty or younger. In spite of these considerations, plaintiffs ask us to weigh other arguments against the establishment of a maximum age and to hold that the Administrator's action was unreasonable. It is not the business of courts to substitute their untutored judgment for the expert knowledge of those who are given authority to implement the general directives of Congress. The Administrator is an expert in his field; this is the very reason he was given the responsibility for the issuance of air safety regulations. We can only ask whether the regulation is reasonable in relation to the standards prescribed in the statute and the facts before the Administrator. Of that there can be no doubt in this case.

Nor is the regulation discriminatory because it applies only to the piloting of commercial aircraft, and does not restrict pilots with respect to other planes. The Administrator did not act unreasonably in placing greater limitations on the certificates of pilots flying planes carrying large numbers of passengers who have no opportunity to select a pilot of their own choice. The Federal Aviation Act contemplates just such distinctions between the regulations governing "air commerce" and those governing other air transportation.

The preliminary injunction was properly denied. The order is affirmed.

Notes

1. *Shooting Down the Pilots—Again and Again.* Later suits seeking to keep sexagenarian pilots aloft have been no more successful than *Quesada.* Various pilots sought to circumvent the rule through an exceptions process, and courts of appeals warned that a refusal to consider the impact of advances in medical technology on the reasonableness of denying exemptions might result in the invalidity of the rule. See, e.g., *Starr v. FAA*, 589 F.2d 307, 314 (7th Cir.1978). In 1988, the Seventh Circuit remanded to the FAA 28 unsuccessful applications for exemption that the court determined warranted more fully reasoned responses. *Aman v. FAA*, 856 F.2d 946 (7th Cir.1988). The agency had not responded to the petitions based on individualized hearings; it based its denials instead on information gleaned from a panel of experts and from public comment regarding the possibility of preserving a high level of safety without the imposition of an inflexible age rule. In particular, it concluded (a) no battery of available psychological and physical tests, administered to 60–year-old pilots, could reduce all incremental safety risks associated with the aging process, and (b) the flight experience of certain older pilots would not offset any increased risk of accident due to sudden incapacitation or skill deterioration. Although the court regarded the first conclusion as adequately justified, the latter was not. On reconsideration, the FAA reaffirmed its position, granting no exemptions. The Seventh Circuit, grudgingly finding support by "substantial, albeit

certainly not compelling, evidence,'' upheld the agency policy. *Baker v. FAA*, 917 F.2d 318, 322 (7th Cir.1990).

The pilots' battle with the FAA seems to have entered the trench warfare stage. In *Professional Pilots Federation v. FAA*, 118 F.3d 758 (D.C.Cir.1997), the court once again upheld the FAA's decision not to amend the age restriction at issue in *Quesada*, notwithstanding further information that suggested some weakening of the factual predicate for the rule. The Professional Pilot's Federation, a group devoted to abolishing the age 60 rule, responded by beefing up the scientific basis for allowing exemptions from the rule. In an attempt to satisfy the FAA's regulatory requirement that any petition for exemption contain a proposed technique that would assess an individual pilot's abilities and risks of subtle and sudden incapacitation, the Federation employed a panel of eight renowned physicians in multiple fields—their so-called ''age 60 exemption panel''. The panel developed an extensive set of medical/neuro-psychological tests, administered them to 69 commercial airline pilots in their mid-to late-fifties and declared them all competent to continue flying. The 69 pilots then requested an exemption. When it was summarily denied the petitioners went to court. The FAA, perhaps sensing that an unreasoned summary denial did not put it in the most favorable litigating position, requested and received a remand to reconsider. After receiving further comments from interested parties, the FAA issued an extensive opinion finding flaws in all the pilots' submissions. The pilots went back to court.

In *Yetman v. Garvey*, 261 F.3rd 664 (7th Cir.2001) Chief Judge Flaum issued an opinion which bristles with barely-controlled exasperation. In its 1990 decision in *Baker* the Seventh Circuit had recognized that the pilots were in a catch-22 situation. They cannot get exemptions until they can show that they can fly large passenger aircraft safely, but they cannot show that they can fly such planes safely until they get exemptions. Notwithstanding that recognition, the court affirmed the FAA's refusal to grant exemptions without precise data demonstrating that flying after age 60 would not compromise air safety. After exhaustively canvassing the pilots arguments, many of which he clearly viewed as recycled from other losing cases, Judge Flaum concluded:

> We recognize that the FAA's requirements for granting exemptions to the Age Sixty Rule are so demanding that if the agency had initially chosen an age fifty cutoff, pilots above that age would have difficulty meeting those standards. Yet, the rigorous nature of the FAA's exemption requirements is not pertinent at this juncture. Our inquiry is limited to examining whether the FAA has appropriately considered the evidence, and provided sufficient justifications for its decisions. We cannot say that the FAA has failed to take into account new advances in medical technology. * * * Yet given the fact that the FAA has nevertheless denied every petition for exemption, an argument could be made that the FAA has examined these studies and protocols only to satisfy the burden which we have placed on the agency. However, that would require that we delve into the motivations of the agency, an inappropriate inquiry under our deferential standard of review. While our review of the evidence submitted by the petitioners might lead us to conclude that a strict age sixty cutoff, without exceptions, is a rule better suited

> to 1959 than to 2001, this court is not an expert in aerospace medicine, and Congress did not endow this court with the duty to make such a policy judgment. The FAA has the discretionary power to establish a rigid policy. * * * [I]t may adhere inflexibly to a rule whose validity has been upheld by the courts and reevaluated by Congress, so long as it continues to consider, as we are satisfied it has done here, new advances in medical technology.

2. *Are Exceptions Necessary?* In *Campbell*, the Supreme Court upheld HHS's "grid" regulations on residual functional capacity, in part because "the regulations afford claimants ample opportunity * * * to offer evidence that the guidelines do not apply to them." The concurrence in *Yuckert* by Justices O'Connor and Stevens (whose votes were necessary for the majority) emphasized that the Secretary's categorical exclusion of claimants with only insignificant impairments would not exclude from full consideration any "claimant who *may* fit within the statutory definition of disability * * *" (emphasis added). Thus, in both cases, HHS's efforts to limit the scope its formal hearings on disability were upheld ostensibly because the rules, on their face, did not deny individual claimants an opportunity to demonstrate the exceptional character of their situation. Thus viewed, the rules worked less to exclude certain cases from on-the-record inquiry than as a device to shift the burden of proof.

In emphasizing the rights of claimants under the grid regulations, the majority in *Campbell* cites *United States v. Storer Broadcasting Co.*, 351 U.S. 192 (1956), and *FPC v. Texaco, Inc.*, 377 U.S. 33 (1964). In *Storer*, the Court upheld an FCC rule setting fixed limits on the number of FM radio and television stations one person could own. The FCC proposed to reject, without a hearing, applications from persons who already owned the maximum number of stations authorized by its station ownership regulation. In sustaining this approach, the Supreme Court observed:

> We agree with the contention of the Commission that a full hearing, such as is required by [§ 309 of the FCC's Act], would not be necessary on all such applications. As the Commission has promulgated its Rules after extensive administrative hearings, it is necessary for the accompanying papers to set forth reasons, sufficient if true, to justify a change or waiver of the Rules. We do not think Congress intended the Commission to waste time on applications that do not state a valid basis for a hearing. * * *

In *Texaco*, the Court upheld a FPC regulation similarly restricting the opportunity for a hearing on applications by natural gas companies for certificates approving the sale of gas to interstate pipelines. The agency's regulation provided for summary rejection of contracts containing pricing provisions other than those it specifically identified as "permissible." Like the Communications Act, the Natural Gas Act required the FPC to set "for hearing" all producer applications for permission to supply natural gas.

The Court concluded, on the authority of *Storer*, that the FPC's approach was permissible:

> [T]he statutory requirement for a hearing under § 7 does not preclude the Commission from particularizing statutory standards through the rule making process and barring at the threshold those who neither

measure up to them nor show reasons why in the public interest the rule should be waived.

In both *Storer* and *Texaco* the Court called attention to language in the agencies' regulations permitting an applicant to seek a waiver from their terms, and implied that such restrictions on the availability of statutorily mandated hearings might present a more difficult issue if they purported to prevent the agency from changing its mind when confronted by special circumstances. These judicial suggestions have generally prompted agencies to include some form of waiver process or "escape clause" in their so-called "bright line" rules, and courts occasionally find that these waiver provisions have been applied arbitrarily. See, e.g., *Matlovich v. Secretary of the Air Force*, 591 F.2d 852, 857 (D.C.Cir.1978); *WAIT Radio v. FCC*, 418 F.2d 1153, 1157–59 (D.C.Cir.1969). See generally Alfred Aman, *Administrative Equity: An Analysis of Exceptions to Administrative Rules*, 1982 Duke L.J. 277.

3. *Rules Without Exceptions*. Yet, experience clearly suggests that the FAA rule upheld in *Quesada* and subsequent suits does not permit exceptions. Can Congress' decision to confer formal hearing rights be squared with substantive rulemaking that effectively precludes certain classes of claimants from asserting their exceptional status?

The Supreme Court certainly treats it as settled law that "even if a statutory scheme requires individualized determinations, the decision maker has the authority to rely on rulemaking to resolve certain issues of general applicability unless Congress clearly expresses an intent to withhold that authority." *American Hospital Ass'n v. NLRB*, 499 U.S. 606, 612 (1991). But, in most cases where that standard is enunciated, either the rule in question has a provision for waiver (as the NLRB rule contested in *American Hospital Ass'n*. did for "exceptional circumstances") or the statutory scheme contains no obligatory individual hearing requirement. See, e.g., *Lopez v. Davis*, 531 U.S. 230 (2001) (upholding a Bureau of Prisons regulations categorically denying early release to prisoners convicted of a felony attended by the carrying, possession, or use of a firearm).

The Court upheld a hearing-limiting rule that permitted no exceptions in *FCC v. WNCN Listeners Guild*, 450 U.S. 582 (1981). The FCC determined through informal rulemaking that a broadcaster's change in its entertainment format would in no event be a ground for refusing to find that the "public interest, convenience, and necessity" warranted license renewal. (The FCC concluded that its regulation of entertainment format did not advance the public interest, which was better served by market forces.) As a consequence, listener objections to license renewal applications, if based on entertainment format changes, would never trigger a formal hearing. A majority held that the FCC's conclusive treatment of the entertainment format issue was consistent with Congress' policies underlying the Communications Act. The opinion does not, however, address the question whether the FCC might be found to have abused its discretion were it to deny all possibility that the rule might be waived in extraordinary circumstances.

4. *Limiting Hearings Through Evidentiary Rules*. Most cases upholding agency attempts to avoid formal hearings through rules involve redefinition of the substantive standards for decision. But, agencies may pursue similar ends through procedural rules. The FDA's implementation of the

1962 Drug Amendments is a prominent example, as well as an example of the thin line between procedure and substance. Arguably, the FDA sought to implement a major substantive change in the standards of drug testing through a revision of its procedures for summary judgment.

The FDA regulates the marketing of therapeutic drugs under the much-amended Federal Food, Drug and Cosmetic Act, 21 U.S.C. §§ 301–397 (2000). The original 1938 Act created a scheme for drug licensing, requiring pre-marketing administrative review for safety. Congress amended the Act in 1962 to require premarketing proof of effectiveness, as well. The FDA was directed to refuse, or withdraw approval of a new drug if, after notice and opportunity for a hearing, it found "there is a lack of substantial evidence that the drug will have the effect it purports or is represented to have * * *." Congress simultaneously instructed the FDA, after a two-year grace period, to withdraw approved drugs for which "substantial evidence" was lacking. This latter assignment presented an enormous task. Between 1938 and 1962, some 7,000 drug formulations had been approved as safe, and approximately 4,000 of these remained on the market. Accordingly, in June, 1986, the FDA signed a contract with the National Academy of Sciences to undertake a retrospective review of all previously licensed drugs.

When the NAS, some three years later, completed its review of pre–1962 licensed drugs, it concluded that some 15 per cent were lacking substantial evidence of effectiveness, and that another 35 per cent were only "possibly effective." It then fell to the FDA to implement these conclusions.

Early in the process, the FDA turned its attention to the Upjohn Company's drug, Panalba, whose annual sales in 1968 exceeded $20 million. The agency concurred in the NAS finding that Panalba was ineffective and gave notice of its intent to withdraw the drug's approval after affording Upjohn thirty days to submit additional data. Testimonial letters supporting Panalba poured in from doctors all around the country. Concluding that these testimonials did not qualify as "substantial evidence," the FDA in May, 1969, published an order declaring its intention to withdraw approval of the drug and providing that anyone adversely affected could submit objections which, if supported by reasonable grounds, could necessitate a hearing. But the order stipulated that any demand for a hearing would have to identify the adequate and well-controlled studies that supported Panalba's efficacy.

Upjohn promptly requested a hearing and proffered some fifty clinical studies of Panalba. When the FDA delayed ruling on its request, Upjohn brought suit contending that it was entitled to a hearing as a matter of right. In a confusing opinion, *Upjohn Co. v. Finch*, 303 F.Supp. 241 (W.D.Mich. 1969), the district court ruled for the company. Almost simultaneously, the FDA lost a similar suit brought by the manufacturer of another drug the NAS had rated ineffective. *American Home Products Corp. v. Finch*, 303 F.Supp. 448 (D.Del.1969).

Thus, in mid-summer of 1969, the FDA saw its efforts to implement the 1962 efficacy studies stalled. Manufacturers had shown little inclination to cease marketing commercially successful drugs that the NAS panels had rated less than effective. One court had intimated that a showing of the kind made for Panalba—consisting of favorable endorsements in the medical literature and a record of long use among practicing physicians—ought to suffice to obtain a hearing. And in such a hearing the agency would likely be unable to avoid protracted inquiry into the reliability and import of all the data submitted by manufacturers, which had strong incentives for delay. Congressional pressure, however, was building on the agency to speed up its long-delayed implementation of the NAS evaluations.

Following the *Upjohn* decision, the FDA ruled that the company's objections did not demonstrate the "reasonable grounds" expressly required by the Act for an evidentiary hearing on the withdrawal of an antibiotic. And on September 19, 1969, it issued a final order denying a hearing and ordering Panalba withdrawn. Simultaneously, it published new regulations, effective immediately, requiring a showing of "reasonable grounds" to obtain a hearing on the withdrawal of any drug and specifying in detail the "adequate and well-controlled [clinical] investigations" that would have to be presented to establish such grounds.

The new regulations were promptly challenged by the Pharmaceutical Manufacturers Association, makers of more than 90 percent of all prescription drugs marketed in the U.S. In *Pharmaceutical Manufacturers Association v. Finch*, 307 F.Supp. 858 (D.Del.1970), the court ruled that the FDA had promulgated its criteria for clinical studies without notice and opportunity for public comment in violation of APA § 553. Within a few weeks, the agency republished its "adequate and well-controlled studies" regulations as a proposal, and, following the receipt of public comments, it promulgated final regulations which closely resembled the original version. Commissioner's Order, 35 Fed.Reg. 7250 (May 8, 1970). These regulations were promptly upheld against substantive challenge. *Pharmaceutical Manufacturers Association v. Richardson*, 318 F.Supp. 301 (D.Del.1970).

Once its criteria for "adequate and well-controlled clinical investigations" were upheld, the FDA began proceedings to withdraw approval of many of the drugs rated "ineffective" by the NAS review panels. When a manufacturer sought an evidentiary hearing, the agency generally found that its supporting evidence failed to satisfy the regulations and summarily withdrew marketing approval.

Not surprisingly, FDA decisions to withdraw marketing approval by awarding itself summary judgment against a manufacturer produced further litigation. Following lower court setbacks for the FDA, however, the Supreme Court, in *Weinberger v. Hynson, Westcott and Dunning, Inc.*, 412 U.S. 609 (1973), upheld the agency's summary judgment procedure. The Court concluded first that the FDA Commissioner's rigorous standards governing the kind of evidence needed to sustain a showing of effectiveness reflected "well-established principles of scientific investigation" and consistent with congressional intent. Citing *Storer* and *Texaco*, the Court further held that the FD & C Act's provision for an evidentiary hearing did not preclude summary disposition when it was obvious, from the manufacturer's own submissions, that it had not furnished evidence meeting the regulation's criteria for evidence from "adequate and well-controlled investigations."

5. *Leveling the Playing Field By Restricting Proof.* While the Social Security Administration has been concerned about maintaining the flow of medical evidence into its disability proceedings, the Labor Department when

adjudicating claims under the Black Lung Benefits Act has had almost the reverse problem. Black Lung Benefits proceedings are adversarial, pitting miners claims of pneumoconiosis against mine operator's defenses, either that the condition does not exist or that it was caused by something other than coal mining. Although other factors are also at work, the astonishingly low success rate in Black Lung claims, 7.6 per cent, is attributable in substantial part to the financial incapacity of claimants to match coal companies' development of medical evidence. Miners' evidence of disability from a treating physician, and, perhaps, an x-ray reading by a consultant, is often countered by multiple, sometimes dozens, of opinions from company expert witnesses. Labor Department ALJs who have compiled a hearing record with evidence massively weighted in the companies' favor find it difficult to grant a claim in a form that will withstand judicial review. And review of awards is routinely sought.

Recognizing the potential injustice of this system, the Labor Department published new rules filling nearly 200 pages of the Federal Register. Regulations Implementing the Federal Coal Mine Health and Safety Act of 1969, as amended, 65 Fed. Reg. 79,920 (Dec. 20, 2000). The new rules limit each party in its affirmative case to two chest x-ray interpretations, the results of two pulmonary function tests, two arterial blood gas studies, and two medical reports. Rebuttal evidence is limited to one interpretation of each document submitted in the opponent's affirmative case, and responses to rebuttal evidence are required to come only from the physician whose report or interpretation was the subject of rebuttal. The rules allow administrative law judges to permit parties to exceed these limitations on a showing of good cause.

Noting that the Administrative Procedure Act itself, 5 U.S.C. § 556(d) empowers agencies to "exclude * * * irrelevant, immaterial, or unduly repetitious evidence," the District of Columbia Court of Appeals gave short shrift to the National Mining Association's claim that the new rules were impermissible. Although *Heckler v. Campbell* was all over the litigant's briefs, the D.C. Circuit felt no necessity to cite any authority to uphold a rule that the Secretary justified largely on the ground that it would permit administrative law judges to focus their attention on the quality of the medical evidence rather than its quantity and to avoid having their time wasted with excessive production of medical testimony. *National Min. Ass'n. v. Department of Labor*, 292 F.3rd 849 (D.C.Cir.2002). For a fuller discussion see Brian C. Murchison, *Due Process, Black Lung, and the Shaping of Administrative Justice*, 54 Admin. L. Rev. 1025 (2002).

e. *Informal Alternatives to Formal Adjudication*

Our survey of on-the-record decision making hardly portrays the full universe of agency adjudicatory processes. The APA mandate that parties be given the opportunity to settle disputes, § 554(c)(2), barely hints at the wide range of informal mechanisms that agencies have long used to implement general policies in individual cases. For example, the FDA's ostensibly formal new drug approval procedure has evolved into an informal, consensual and largely closed process, in part because of the proprietary nature of much of the information involved. Typically, it involves many exchanges of correspondence and several meetings between FDA staff and the manufacturer, in which the two sides exchange information and negotiate over the design and pace of clinical studies, the interpretation of their results, and the language of final labeling. Since 1962, the agency has held only three formal hearings on refusals to approve a drug.

Similarly, prosecutorial agencies, like the FTC, routinely seek settlements in a manner akin to civil litigation. An unusual feature of the FTC process is that its "consent orders" are subject by statute to public notice and comment. Other agency devices to avert formal hearings include jawboning, rendering advisory opinions, the use or threat of publicity as an informal sanction, and "voluntary" product recalls.

Just as concerns about judicial caseloads have increased interest in alternative means of dispute resolution, observers of administrative adjudication have urged agencies to employ ADR techniques to reduce backlogs and expedite the resolution of adjudicatory disputes. Experiments in the early 1980s included a program of arbitrating appeals before the Merit Systems Protection Board, the EPA's use of mediation to resolve pollution disputes, and the use of mini-trials by the Army Corps of Engineers and the Navy to resolve contract disputes. Charles Pou, Jr., *Federal Agency Use of "ADR": The Experience to Date*, reprinted in Administrative Conference of the United States, Sourcebook: Federal Agency Use of Alternative Means of Dispute Resolution (1987); William F. Smith, *Alternative Means Of Dispute Resolution: Practices and Possibilities in the Federal Government*, 1984 Mo.J.Disp.Res. 9 (1984). The Administrative Conference regarded the experiments as sufficiently promising to recommend in 1986 that agencies generally adopt ADR techniques, where legally permissible, and that Congress authorize voluntary arbitration as a general alternative to formal APA adjudication. ACUS Recommendation 86–3, *Agencies' Use of Alternative Means Of Dispute Resolution*, 1 C.F.R. § 305.86.3 (1987). See also Philip J. Harter, *Points on a Continuum: Dispute Resolution Procedures and the Administrative Process*, 1 Admin. L. J. 141 (1987).

In 1990, Congress responded to the ACUS recommendation by enacting the Administrative Dispute Resolution Act, Pub. L. No. 101–552, 104 Stat. 2736 (1991) (reprinted in Appendix E to this volume). The Act amends 5 U.S.C. § 556(c)(6) to authorize the presiding officer at an agency hearing to hold conferences for the settlement or simplification of issues "by the use of alternative means of dispute resolution" as provided elsewhere in the Act. Section 556(c) is amended further to authorize the presiding officer to inform the parties of the availability of ADR and to require party representatives to attend any settlement conference.

Subchapter IV of the Act details the ADR proceedings now authorized by Congress. In general, an agency may use ADR if the parties agree, the dispute is deemed by the agency to lack precedential or policy development significance, the dispute does not significantly affect unrepresented parties, a full public record of the proceeding is not important, and the agency does not anticipate a need for its own continuing jurisdiction over the matter in controversy. To facilitate ADR, the agency and other parties may consent to the use of a neutral conciliator, facilitator, or mediator, or to the use of an arbitrator.

Under the Act, a final arbitration award, even against the United States, is judicially enforceable. An agency head, however, has discretion at any time up to 30 days after service of the arbitrator's final order to terminate the arbitration proceeding or vacate the award. Should the agency exercise such authority, it may be required to reimburse other parties for the expenses of arbitration. Congress presumably gave the agency this power, however, to avoid any charge that it had impermissibly delegated governmental decision making power to a private individual. Section 5 of the Act authorizes district courts to set aside arbitration awards "if the use of arbitration or the award is clearly inconsistent with the factors" precluding the use of ADR under the new statute. A suit to set aside an award may be brought by "a person, other than a party to the arbitration, who is adversely affected or aggrieved by the award."

Although the new charter for ADR is intended to enhance agency flexibility and discretion, it is questionable whether needed flexibility can be codified. What may be happening is in part the application of new labels to old techniques. Moreover, the Administrative Dispute Resolution Act enumerates specific grounds for collateral attack on the ADR it authorizes, with the potential over time to erode the flexibility it hoped to foster.

The ACUS also recommended that agencies employ "case management" techniques to expedite agency adjudication and facilitate participation by non-buyers. Administrative Conference of the United States, Case Management as a Tool for Improving Agency Adjudication, 1 C.F.R. § 305.86–7 (1991). President Clinton ordered all agencies to follow this advice "to the extent reasonable and practicable" and when "not in conflict with other sections" of his Executive Order 12988—Civil Justice Reform, 61 Fed. Reg. 4729 (Feb. 5, 1996). In addition to ordering agencies to be quick, user friendly and unbiased, President Clinton urged that fact-finders and deciders be given additional discretion to facilitate early settlement of claims. But in "*The Adolescence of Administrative ADR,*" 21 Admin. & Reg.L.News 20 (1996), Phillip J. Harter, Administrative ADR's putative father, questions whether other executive branch policies so limit the capacity to use ADR techniques that the Executive Order in an empty exhortation.

The general impulse to promote relatively unchecked agency discretion in the interest of informality and expedition raises larger issues of agency accountability. Just a generation ago, such discretion was widely regarded as a problem, not a solution. See, e.g., KENNETH CULP DAVIS, DISCRETIONARY JUSTICE: A PRELIMINARY INQUIRY (1969). It is also not obvious that individuals can hope to use ADR as successfully as corporate or other organizational entities, whose resources for negotiation more closely match those of the bureaucracy.

Yet, reliance on negotiated decisions, which has long been a feature of administrative government, illustrates a persistent need for informal methods to implement statutory programs. Just as courts could not long function without civil settlements and criminal plea bargains, administrative government has always depended on "alternative dispute resolution," however labeled. This fact, coupled with the continuing expansion of issues within regulatory purview, may assure increasing use of ADR.

Chapter 5

ADMINISTRATIVE RULEMAKING

Administrators make law both by adjudication and through the adoption of general rules of conduct. Administrative lawmaking through rulemaking poses special problems—both of political and legal accountability and of process fairness. What are the appropriate substantive checks on administrators' rulemaking discretion? What procedures should be required for administrative action in legislative, or quasi-legislative, form?

Answers to these questions are not to be found in the jurisprudence governing judicial review of legislation. The judiciary is notoriously deferential to procedural errors by the legislature. A famous 19th century case, *Field v. Clark*, 143 U.S. 649 (1892), enunciates the "enrolled bill" rule. The courts will not entertain a claim that the Constitution's procedures for the passage of bills were not observed unless proof of the defect is on the face of the statute ("enrolled bill") filed with the Secretary of State. This doctrine has no counterpart in the jurisprudence on judicial review of agency rulemaking procedure, where scrutiny for procedural error is commonplace and often intense. Similarly, in contrast with their customary deference to legislative policy choices, e.g., *Williamson v. Lee Optical*, 348 U.S. 483 (1955), courts demand some evidentiary support for, and a reasoned explanation of, rules adopted by administrators.

This markedly different judicial posture is in part the product of the Administrative Procedure Act, which establishes general minimum procedures for federal agency rulemaking and expressly contemplates some degree of judicial review of the substantive decisions reached by administrators. But, more fundamentally, the judicial posture toward agency "legislation" reflects a continuing ambivalence about the political legitimacy of administrative policy making. Attenuated political accountability has promoted legal demands for process transparency and substantive rationality. Administrators may exercise a delegated power to legislate, but the legal controls on this "quasi-legislation" are far more intrusive than judicial review of legislative action by legislators.

A. AGENCY AUTHORITY TO MAKE LEGISLATIVE RULES

NATIONAL PETROLEUM REFINERS ASSOCIATION v. FEDERAL TRADE COMMISSION

United States Court of Appeals, District of Columbia Circuit, 1973.
482 F.2d 672, *cert. denied*, 415 U.S. 951, 94 S.Ct. 1475, 39 L.Ed.2d 567 (1974).

J. SKELLY WRIGHT, CIRCUIT JUDGE.

This case presents an important question concerning the powers and procedures of the Federal Trade Commission. We are asked to determine whether the Commission, under its governing statute, the Trade Commission Act and specifically 15 U.S.C. § 46(g), is empowered to promulgate substantive rules of business conduct or, as it terms them, "Trade Regulation Rules." The effect of these rules would be to give greater specificity and clarity to the broad standard of illegality—"unfair methods of competition in commerce, and unfair or deceptive acts or practices in commerce"—which the agency is empowered to prevent. Once promulgated, the rules would be used by the agency in adjudicatory proceedings aimed at producing cease and desist orders against violations of the statutory standard. The central question in such adjudicatory proceedings would be whether the particular defendant's conduct violated the rule in question.

The case is here on appeal from a District Court ruling that the Commission lacks authority under its governing statute to issue rules of this sort. * * * Specifically at issue in the District Court was the Commission's rule declaring that failure to post octane rating numbers on gasoline pumps at service stations was an unfair method of competition and an unfair or deceptive act or practice.[1] The plaintiffs in the District Court, appellees here, are two trade associations and 34 gasoline refining companies. Plaintiffs attacked the rule on several grounds, but the District Court disposed of the case solely on the question of the

1. The rule provides:

"In connection with the sale or consignment of motor gasoline for general automotive use, in commerce as 'commerce' is defined in the Federal Trade Commission Act, it constitutes an unfair method of competition and an unfair or deceptive act or practice for refiners or others who sell to retailers, when such refiners or other distributors own or lease the pumps through which motor gasoline is dispensed to the consuming public, to fail to disclose clearly and conspicuously in a permanent manner on the pumps the minimum octane number or numbers of the motor gasoline being dispensed. In the case of those refiners or other distributors who lease pumps, the disclosure required by this section should be made as soon as it is legally practical; for example, not later than the end of the current lease period. Nothing in this section should be construed as applying to gasoline sold for aviation purposes.

"NOTE: For the purposes of this section, 'octane number' shall mean the octane number derived from the sum of research (R) and motor (M) octane numbers divided by 2; (R + M)/2. The research octane (R) and motor octane number (M) shall be as described in the American Society for Testing and Materials (ASTM) 'Standard Specifications for Gasoline' D 439–70, and subsequent revisions, and ASTM Test Methods D 2699 and D 2600."

36 Fed.Reg. 23871 (1971).

Commission's statutory authority to issue such rules. That is the only question presented for our consideration on appeal. * * *

I

* * *

As always, we must begin with the words of the statute creating the Commission and delineating its powers. Section 5 directs the Commission to "prevent persons, partnerships, or corporations * * * from using unfair methods of competition in commerce and unfair or deceptive acts or practices in commerce." Section 5(b) of the Trade Commission Act specifies that the Commission is to accomplish this goal by means of issuance of a complaint, a hearing, findings as to the facts, and issuance of a cease and desist order. * * *

Appellees argue that since Section 5 mentions only adjudication as the means of enforcing the statutory standard, any supplemental means of putting flesh on that standard such as rule-making, is contrary to the overt legislative design. But Section 5(b) does not use limiting language suggesting that adjudication alone is the only proper means of elaborating the statutory standard. * * * Nor are we persuaded by appellees' argument that, despite the absence of limiting language in Section 5 regarding the role of adjudication in defining the meaning of the statutory standard, we should apply the maxim of statutory construction *expressio unius est exclusio alterius*. * * * For the Trade Commission Act includes a provision which specifically provides for rule-making * * *. Section 6(g) of the Act, 15 U.S.C. § 46(g), states that the Commission may "[f]rom time to time * * * classify corporations and * * * make rules and regulations for the purpose of carrying out the provisions of sections 41 to 46 and 47 to 58 of this title."[7]

* * *

Of course, it is at least arguable that * * * [Section 6(g) only empowers the Commission] to promulgate procedural, as opposed to substantive, rules for administration of the Section 5 adjudication and enforcement powers. But we see no reason to import such a restriction on the "rules and regulations" permitted by Section 6(g). * * * The substantive rule here unquestionably implements the statutory plan. Section 5 adjudications—trial type proceedings—will still be necessary to obtain cease and desist orders against offenders, but Section 5 enforcement through adjudication will be expedited, simplified, and thus "carried out" by use of this substantive rule. And the overt language of both Section 5 and Section 6, read together, supports its use in Section 5 proceedings.

II

Our belief that "rules and regulations" in Section 6(g) should be construed to permit the Commission to promulgate binding substantive

7. 15 U.S.C. § 45 is § 5 of the Trade Commission Act.

rules as well as rules of procedure is reinforced by the construction courts have given similar provisions in the authorizing statutes of other administrative agencies. * * * In *National Broadcasting Co. v. United States*, 319 U.S. 190 (1943), for example, the Supreme Court upheld the Federal Communications Commission's chain broadcasting rules regulating programming arrangements between networks and affiliates, in part on the basis of the FCC's generalized rule-making authority in 47 U.S.C. § 303(r) (1962). It rejected arguments similar to those made here, ruling that this authority extended beyond specification technical and financial qualifications to be used as guides in the administration of the Commission's license-granting power. It permitted the FCC to use rule-making to elaborate the terms of its mandate to pursue the "public convenience, interest, or necessity," by framing rules carrying out public policy objectives like affiliate independence and avoidance of undue network control over programming in the hope that listeners would be ensured a diversity of program offerings.

United States v. Storer Broadcasting Co., 351 U.S. 192 (1956), took the FCC's rule-making power a step further, holding that applicants for licenses could be rejected before receiving a hearing specified by statute in the event they did not comply with the Commission's rule limiting networks' power to own stock in affiliates and did not give sufficient reasons why the rule should be waived. * * *

Storer and its successors are, of course, closely related to the question we face here. For a major component of appellees' complaint is the abridgement of their interest in having the Trade Commission Act's standard of illegality elaborated only in an adjudicatory context. In our view, this argument was adequately answered in *Storer*, at least to the extent the FTC's rule serves the "purpose of shortening and simplifying the adjudicative process and of clarifying the law in advance," and thus, in *Storer's* language, aids the Commission in the "orderly conduct of its business."

* * *

Just as there has been little question of allowing substantive rule-making to intrude on asserted rights to a full hearing before an agency for a determination of a party's rights and liabilities, there has been a similar lack of hesitation in construing broad grants of rule-making power to permit promulgation of rules with the force of law as a means of agency regulation of otherwise private conduct. * * * Indeed, the general rule courts have adopted toward agencies' use of rule-making power to define standards of conduct by regulated parties, where a general rule-making provision is in the agency statute, was stated succinctly and definitively for this court by Judge Fahy in *Public Service Comm'n of State of New York v. FPC*, 327 F.2d 893, 897 (1964):

> "All authority of the Commission need not be found in explicit language. Section 16 [the general rule-making provision] demonstrates a realization by Congress that the Commission would be confronted with unforeseen problems of administration in regulating

this huge industry and should have a basis for coping with such confrontation. While the action of the Commission must conform with the terms, policies and purposes of the Act, it may use means which are not in all respects spelled out in detail. * * * "

* * *

Thus there is little question that the availability of substantive rule-making gives any agency an invaluable resource-saving flexibility in carrying out its task of regulating parties subject to its statutory mandate. More than merely expediting the agency's job, use of substantive rule-making is increasingly felt to yield significant benefits to those the agency regulates. Increasingly, courts are recognizing that use of rule-making to make innovations in agency policy may actually be fairer to regulated parties than total reliance on case-by-case adjudication.

* * *

* * * [U]tilizing rule-making procedures opens up the process of agency innovation to a broad range of criticism, advice and data that is ordinarily less likely to be forthcoming in adjudication. Moreover, the availability of notice before promulgation and wide public participation in rule-making avoids the problem of singling out a single defendant among a group of competitors for initial imposition of a new and inevitably costly legal obligation.

* * *

III

Appellees contend, however, that these cases and the general practice of agencies and courts in underwriting the broad use of rule-making are irrelevant to the FTC. They argue that the Trade Commission is somehow *Sui generis*, that it is best characterized as a prosecuting rather than a regulatory agency, and that substantive rule-making power should be less readily implied from a general grant of rule-making authority where the agency does not stand astride an industry with pervasive license-granting, rate-setting, or clearance functions. * * *

Given the expanse of the Commission's power to define proper business practices, we believe it is but a quibble to differentiate between the potential pervasiveness of the FTC's power and that of the other regulatory agencies merely on the basis of its prosecutorial and adjudicatory mode of proceeding. Like other agencies, wholly apart from the question of rule-making power it exerts a powerfully regulatory effect on those business practices subject to its supervision. * * *

IV

* * * The opinion of the District Court argues forcefully that, in spite of the clear and unlimited language of Section 6(g) granting rule-making authority to the Commission, the Congress that enacted Section 5 and Section 6(g) gave clear indications of its intent to reject substan-

tive rule-making, that the FTC's own behavior in the years since that time supports a narrow interpretation of its mandate to promulgate "rules and regulations," and that where Congress desired to give the FTC substantive rule-making authority in discrete areas it did so in subsequent years in unambiguous terms. Our own conclusion, based on an independent review of this history, is different. We believe that, while the legislative history of Section 5 and Section 6(g) is ambiguous, it certainly does not compel the conclusion that the Commission was not meant to exercise the power to make substantive rules with binding effect in Section 5(a) adjudications. * * *

Moreover, while we believe the historical evidence is indecisive of the question before us, we are convinced that the broad, undisputed policies which clearly motivated the framers of the Federal Trade Commission Act of 1914 would indeed be furthered by our view as to the proper scope of the Commission's rule-making authority. * * *

* * * Without the rule, the Commission might well be obliged to prove and argue that the absence of the rating markers in each particular case was likely to have injurious and unfair effects on consumers or competition. Since this laborious process might well have to be repeated every time the Commission chose to proceed subsequently against another defendant on the same ground, the difference in administrative efficiency between the two kinds of proceedings is obvious. Furthermore, rules, as contrasted with the holdings reached by case-by-case adjudication, are more specific as to their scope, and industry compliance is more likely simply because each company is on clearer notice whether or not specific rules apply to it.

Moreover, when delay in agency proceedings is minimized by using rules, those violating the statutory standard lose an opportunity to turn litigation into a profitable and lengthy game of postponing the effect of the rule on their current practice. As a result, substantive rules will protect the companies which willingly comply with the law against what amounts to the unfair competition of those who would profit from delayed enforcement as to them. This, too, will minimize useless litigation and is likely to assist the Commission in more effectively allocating its resources. * * *

V

* * *

Any fears that the agency could successfully use rule-making power as a means of oppressive or unreasonable regulation seem exaggerated in view of courts' general practice in reviewing rules to scrutinize their statement of basis and purpose to see whether the major issues of policy pro and con raised in the submissions to the agency were given sufficient consideration. *Automotive Parts & Accessories Ass'n v. Boyd*, 407 F.2d 330 (1968). The Commission is hardly free to write its own law of consumer protection and antitrust since the statutory standard which the rules may define with greater particularity is a legal standard.

Although the Commission's conclusions as to the standard's reach are ordinarily shown deference, the standard must "get [its] final meaning from judicial construction." * * *

VI

Our conclusion as to the scope of Section 6(g) is not disturbed by the fact that the agency itself did not assert the power to promulgate substantive rules until 1962 and indeed indicated intermittently before that time that it lacked such power. * * * The various statements made by Commission representatives questioning its authority to promulgate rules which are to be used with binding effect on subsequent adjudications are not determinative of the question before us. True, the accustomed judicial practice is to give "great weight" to an agency's construction of its own enabling legislation, particularly when such a construction stretches back, as here, to a time close to the agency's origin. The argument for judicial deference is not so strong where, as here, the question does not require special agency competence or expertise, requiring the agency, for example, to make a complex judgment involving its areas of expertise, competition and impact of business practices on consumer behavior. Here, the question is simply one of statutory interpretation concerning the procedures and setting in which the Commission may elaborate its statutory standard. Since this sort of question calls largely for the exercise of historical analysis and logical and analogical reasoning, it is the everyday staple of judges as well as agencies. Thus we feel confident in making our own judgment as to the proper construction of Section 6(g). We are, of course, reassured by the fact that the Commission itself, as distinguished from its former spokesman, has come to the same conclusion.

* * *

A more troubling obstacle to the Commission's position here is the argument that Congress was made fully aware of the formerly restrictive view of the Commission's power and passed a series of laws granting limited substantive rule-making authority to the Commission in discrete areas allegedly on the premise that the 1914 debate withheld such authority. * * *

* * * The view that the Commission lacked substantive rule-making power has been clearly brought to the attention of Congress and, rather than simply failing to act on the question, Congress, in expanding the agency's powers in several discrete areas of marketing regulation, affirmatively enacted limited grants of substantive rule-making authority in the Wool Products Act of 1939, the Fur Products Labeling Act of 1951, the Flammable Fabrics Act of 1953, as amended in 1967, the Textile Fiber Products Identification Act of 1958 and the Fair Packaging and Labeling Act of 1967. Thus it is argued that Congress would not have granted the agency such powers unless it had felt that otherwise the agency lacked rule-making authority.

Conceding the greater force of this argument than one premised on congressional inaction, we believe it must not be accepted blindly. In such circumstances, it is equally possible that Congress granted the power out of uncertainty, understandable caution, and a desire to avoid litigation. * * * For there is ample evidence that, while some of the limited rule-making legislation may well have been influenced by the belief that the 1914 Act did not grant the Commission substantive rule-making power, at least during the passage of the Packaging and Labeling Act of 1967, this assumption was not accepted and was thought by many congressmen to be an open question, despite the protestations of the Commission's chairman that the agency was powerless under the 1914 Act. The report of the House Committee on Interstate and Foreign Commerce, while pointing out that the agency lacked "*specific* authority" (emphasis added) to issue regulations prescribing standards for package labeling, suggested that the question of the agency's general authority under Section 6(g) to do so was open. The report noted that the "authority of the Commission to issue trade regulation rules * * * has never been passed on in the courts." H.R.Rep.No. 2076, 89th Cong., 2d Sess., 22 (1966). * * * Where there is solid reason, as there plainly is here, to believe that Congress, in fact, has not wholeheartedly accepted the agency's viewpoint and instead enacted legislation out of caution and to eliminate the kind of disputes that invariably attend statutory ambiguity, we believe that relying on the *de facto* ratification argument is unwise. In such circumstances, we must perform our customary task of coming to an independent judgment as to the statute's meaning, confident that if Congress believes that its creature, the Commission, thus exercises too much power, it will repeal the grant.[40]

VII

* * * We rely, therefore, on the plain language of Section 6(g) which gives the Commission the authority to "make rules and regulations for the purpose of carrying out the provisions of [Section 5]." We hold that under the terms of its governing statute, and under Section 6(g) in particular, the Federal Trade Commission is authorized to promulgate rules defining the meaning of the statutory standards of the illegality the Commission is empowered to prevent. Thus we must reverse the District Court's judgment and remand this case for further proceedings.

It is so ordered.

Notes

1. *Legislative Rules and Agency Leverage*. The petroleum companies' claim was unequivocal that the FTC had no authority to adopt legislative rules. Yet the success of that claim would have had the same effect on the

40. We are aware, of course, that in both the just concluded 92nd Congress and the current 93rd Congress legislation granting the FTC limited substantive rule-making power in the area of "unfair and deceptive practices" has been under consideration * * *.

FTC as would the success of the pilots' claims in *Quesada*: to force the agency to explore and resolve the issues addressed and purportedly resolved by its rule in potentially repetitive formal adjudicatory proceedings.

Thus, while Judge Wright portrays rulemaking in much the same way that courts concerned about broad delegations have viewed it—as a means for cabining agency discretion and thereby protecting individual interests—the petroleum dealers viewed the Commission's asserted authority as threatening their interests. Judge Wright clearly appreciates how the latter may be true, but to grasp the significance of the companies' position it is useful to consider the formal adjudicatory alternative open to the agency.

The Commission was free, without adopting a formal rule, to bring charges against individual gasoline sellers who failed to post octane ratings, relying on precisely the same legal theory as embodied in its rule, viz., that the failure to provide this information was "unfair" or "deceptive" under section 5(a). And unquestionably it could have announced publicly its plan to institute such proceedings. Moreover, as Judge Wright's opinion makes clear, confirmation of the FTC's power to adopt the rule did not relieve the agency of the burden of enforcing it through individual cease-and-desist proceedings.

Assuming all of the foregoing is true, why were the petroleum refiners so opposed to recognition of the FTC's power to make legislative rules?

Any attempt to answer this question requires a more thorough understanding of the FTC's traditional mode of enforcing section 5. Traditionally, when the FTC encountered a business practice it considered deceptive, it issued a complaint against the responsible party. If the respondent was not prepared to change its practices, the matter was sent for a trial-type hearing at which the Commission bore the burden of showing that the respondent's practices had deceived, or were likely to deceive, a substantial number of purchasers. Counsel assigned to prosecute the complaint customarily had to introduce evidence sufficient to support the Commission's theory of deception. In the *Petroleum Refiners* context, this would have meant that they would attempt to show the wide range of octane levels among marketed gasolines, general consumer ignorance of the ratings of specific brands, the waste of purchasing more octane than one's car engine requires, and, probably, the tendency of consumers, in the absence of information, to purchase fuel octane higher than their cars required. On each of these issues the respondent would be entitled to present evidence and cross-examine the agency's witnesses. Following the evidentiary hearing an administrative law judge, and ultimately the Commission, would have had to decide whether the facts proved demonstrated a violation of the Act. If the Commission concluded that they did, its decision would have been subject to judicial review. The most important features of this process from the respondent's viewpoint were probably the assurance of an opportunity to present its own evidence and the right to cross-examine adverse witnesses on the central factual issues in the case.

What procedure could the Commission follow after adopting its octane-posting rule? The basic procedural steps would remain unchanged, but the issues to be litigated in enforcement proceedings would be narrowed significantly. If any gasoline distributor failed to comply with the rule, the Commission would have to initiate the complaint, hearing, decision, and judicial review process previously outlined against each one. However, assuming its rule was valid and binding, the Commission would have to show only that a respondent had failed to comply with the rule—not that its omission of octane ratings was deceptive under section 5. The Commission would have established the necessary factual predicate for its judgment that such omission was deceptive in the original rulemaking proceeding. A respondent could of course present evidence and cross-examine on the issue of whether the required postings were made, but it would not be able to relitigate the factual premises of the rule.

Suppose that the FTC lacked authority to adopt binding rules but decided nonetheless to announce its conclusion that any gasoline distributor who failed to post octane ratings was guilty of violating section 5? This interpretation by the expert agency responsible for the Act's enforcement would elicit *some* deference from the courts and probably engender voluntary compliance from *some* gasoline distributors, but in litigated cases the Commission could not rely on its policy to sustain its burden of proof or foreclose the introduction of contrary evidence by respondents.

The very fact that the octane posting rule would ease the Commission's burden of proof and narrow the issues to be adjudicated could also reduce litigation. Probably few gasoline distributors would be prepared to expend the resources necessary to defend a proceeding in which the central issue was the easily resolved: "Did you or did you not display the octane ratings required by the Commission's rule?" And though the FTC Act did not in 1974 provide penalties for past failure to comply with a Commission rule—by contrast with failure to comply with a cease-and-desist order—blatant defiance of so clear a directive would have little appeal for most companies.

2. *Rulemaking Authority and Political Accountability*. The issue of rulemaking authority in *Petroleum Refiners* was not, however, merely a matter of litigating leverage. The central question was whether Congress had meant to confer authority on the FTC to adopt the sort of rules that the agency was threatening to apply to sellers of gasoline, i.e., a substantive standard of conduct. And while the language of the 1914 statute on which the Commission relied was facially broad enough to support its claim of authority, the issue raised by the refiners was surely not a spurious one given (a) the agency's failure to exploit this apparent authority during the first 60 years of its existence, and (b) its efforts during the 1950s and 1960s to secure enactment of legislation explicitly conveying power to promulgate trade regulation rules.

Remember also that the FTC's power to restrain "unfair" and "deceptive" commercial practices applies to all businesses operating in interstate commerce, a jurisdiction vaster by far than that exercised by the FAA, the FCC, or the FERC. Should the scope of the power claimed by the FTC, combined with the vague generality of section 5's prohibitions, have raised a genuine issue of "unconstitutional delegation?" The majority opinion in *Schechter* distinguished the power granted by section 5 from the invalid authority to prescribe industry codes of "fair competition" precisely on the ground that the FTC was required to exercise its power through quasi-judicial proceedings. 295 U.S. at 532, 533.

The very generality of the FTC Act's conferral of power to adopt rules was, arguably, another weakness in the Commission's case. In modern statutes, Congress usually stipulates with some care the subjects and scope of agency power to adopt legislative rules. And, as we shall see, it is common for Congress, in the same or a nearby provision, to specify the procedures that the agency is to follow in adopting rules. Yet, the FTC Act's rulemaking provision must mean *something*, and, if not a general grant of authority to promulgate trade regulation rules, then what? One possibility, apparently the one embraced by the Commission itself for its first several decades, was that this was a grant of housekeeping and management authority, i.e., authority to adopt rules specifying internal agency procedures and setting requirements for the submission of reports, the form of pleadings, and the conduct of otherwise authorized proceedings. If this were Congress' intent, it would parallel the pattern arguably followed in other statutes enacted during the same era. See Richard A. Merrill, *FDA and the Effects of Substantive Rules*, 35 Food Drug Cosm.L.J. 270 (1980).

In an important article, Professor Thomas Merrill and Kathryn Tongue Watts challenge the courts' recent approach to the question whether Congress has given an agency authority to adopt substantive rules, the approach epitomized by the *Petroleum Refiners,* a case that Merrill and Watts criticize.

> Throughout the Progressive and New Deal eras, Congress followed a drafting convention that signaled to agencies whether particular rulemaking grants conferred authority on them to make rules with the force of law as opposed to mere housekeeping rules. That convention was simple and easy to apply in most cases: if Congress specified in the statute that a violation of agency rules would subject the offending party to the imposition of some sanction—meaning civil or criminal penalty, loss of permit, license, or benefits, or other adverse legal consequence—then the grant was understood to confer power to make rules with the force of law. Conversely, if Congress made no provision for sanctions for rule violations, it was understood that the grant authorized only procedural or interpretative rules. This convention was followed from the second decade of the twentieth century through the enactment of the APA, and can be discerned in statutes enacted as recently as 1967.
>
> The most remarkable thing about this drafting convention is that modern administrative lawyers are not aware of its existence. How could a convention consistently followed by Congress during the formative years of the administrative state simply disappear from legal consciousness? The explanation, we suggest, lies in the fact that during the time the convention was developed and followed by Congress, no prominent appellate decision was rendered in which the court found it necessary to determine whether Congress had conferred authority on an agency to make rules with the force of law. * * *
>
> The collective amnesia about the drafting convention was eventually to have important consequences. In the 1960s, courts and commentators began to urge expanded use of rulemaking by agencies reduced emphasis on adjudication. Eventually, two influential federal appellate judges who strongly favored greater use of rulemaking—Judges J. Skelly Wright of the D.C. Circuit and Henry Friendly of the Second Circuit—took advan-

tage of the absence of any authoritative statement endorsing the convention to author important opinions construing facially ambiguous rulemakings grants to the Federal Trade Commission (FTC) and the Food and Drug Administration (FDA) as authorizing legislative rulemaking. These holdings were inconsistent with what Congress had intended, as measured by the convention. Although some commentators expressed unease over the decisions authorizing legislative rulemaking by the FTC and the FDA, no effort was made in Congress or the Supreme Court to reverse them.

Soon, the assumption took hold that facially ambiguous rulemaking grants always include the authority to adopt rules having the force of law. In 1991, for example, the Supreme Court upheld a legislative rule promulgated by the National Labor Relations Board (NLRB) pursuant to its general rulemaking grant under the National Labor Relations Act [*American Hosp. Ass'n v. NLRB*, 499 U.S. 606, discussed *infra*, p. 487]. Although the case involved the first broad-scale exercise of legislative rulemaking by the NLRB since its creation in 1935, no Justice questioned whether the NLRB had the authority to promulgate such a rule. * * *

Thomas W. Merrill and Kathryn Tongue Watts, *Agency Rules with the Force of Law: The Original Convention*, 116 Harv. L. Rev. 467 (2002).

3. *The Subsequent History of FTC Rulemaking*. Soon after the decision in *Petroleum Refiners*, Congress amended the FTC Act to confirm, but at the same time constrain, the Commission's rulemaking authority. The Magnuson–Moss Warranty–Federal Trade Commission Improvement Act, 88 Stat. 2183, Pub.L.No. 93–637 (1975):

a. Confirmed the agency's authority to adopt legislative rules implementing section 5's broad prohibition of unfair or deceptive acts or practices, and permitted it to sue to recover civil penalties for violations of such rules.

b. Subjected FTC rulemaking to procedural requirements that include some trial-type features. The agency was required, for example, to permit oral submissions, receive rebuttal testimony, and allow cross-examination on "disputed material facts" when "necessary for fair determination * * * of the rulemaking proceeding."

c. Accorded FTC orders in adjudicatory proceedings enforcing section 5 a status akin to that of legislative rules, at least for some purposes. Amended section 5(m)(B) permits the FTC to enforce a final cease and desist order determining that a practice is unfair or deceptive against persons not parties to the original proceeding who thereafter engage in the practice "with actual knowledge that [it] * * * is unfair or deceptive and is unlawful. * * *"

It was 1977 before the Commission sought to use its congressionally confirmed authority to adopt trade regulation rules defining and proscribing unfair practices. By 1980 the agency had begun more than two dozen rulemaking proceedings addressed to practices in a wide range of industries, including vocational schools, funeral services, used car sales, and the merchandising of prescription drugs, hearing aids, and home insulation. However, only three of these proceedings had then been completed—one by the agency's withdrawal of its proposed rule. See Barry Boyer, *Report On The*

Trade Regulation Rulemaking Procedures Of The FTC (Executive Summary) (1979), in U.S. Administrative Conference: Recommendations and Reports 41 (1980). Professor Boyer's report documents many of the problems that the Commission encountered in attempting to use this "new" authority, including lack of technical personnel, lack of experience, and lack of information. A major impediment to completion of the rulemaking proceedings that the agency began was the statutory requirement for trial-type hearings on critical factual issues, a topic to which we shall return.

The Commission also encountered difficulties in the courts and, ultimately, in Congress. Its first trade regulation rule to be reviewed was set aside in *Katharine Gibbs School v. FTC*, 612 F.2d 658 (2d Cir.1979), which held that the agency had failed to document that each of the practices its rule proscribed was "unfair" or "deceptive." The Commission's next encounter with judicial review was also a disappointment. See *American Optometric Association v. Federal Trade Commission*, 626 F.2d 896 (D.C.Cir. 1980). Nearly three decades after the enactment of the 1975 Magnuson–Moss amendments to the 1914 FTC Act, only two court of appeals decisions—both from the mid–80s—have upheld trade regulation rules issued pursuant to those amendments. *Consumers Union of U.S. v. FTC*, 801 F.2d 417 (D.C.Cir.1986) (upholding rule on used cars); *American Financial Services Ass'n v. FTC*, 767 F.2d 957 (D.C.Cir.1985) (upholding rule on credit practices).

In the meantime, Congress amended the Act to limit the impact of the FTC's quasi-legislative powers, and it almost enacted others that would have excluded entire areas of business activity from the Commission's jurisdiction. The Federal Trade Commission Improvements Act of 1980, Pub.L.No. 96–252, was the product of congressional exasperation with the agency's attempts to regulate business practices in several sensitive areas—used car sales, funeral services, and sales of hearing aids, among others. In addition to curtailing the FTC's appropriations, limiting its reauthorization to two years, and demanding that it demonstrate that any trade practice to be proscribed by rule be "prevalent" within the industry, the 1980 Amendments' major change was to subject Commission rules to a one-house Congressional veto. This provision was invalidated after *Chadha* in *Consumers Union of U.S., Inc. v. Federal Trade Commission*, 691 F.2d 575 (D.C.Cir. 1982), *aff'd*, 463 U.S. 1216 (1983).

A 1989 report by a Special Committee of the ABA Section on Antitrust Law to Study the Role of the Federal Trade Commission offered the following assessment of the Commission's use of its authority to promulgate trade regulation rules:

> Magnuson–Moss rulemaking is a costly and uncertain tool. The ponderous nature of the process has been the subject of much comment and criticism. * * * Nothing galvanizes an industry to defend itself like an industry-wide assault such as broad rulemaking. Congress is never more sympathetic than when it is hearing from constituents across the country, as may result from rulemaking. Congress is rarely less deferential than when an agency is engaging in a broad rulemaking process that, unlike law enforcement, resembles activity that is the traditional province of Congress.

Given this, good candidates for broad new rulemaking will be scarce. Rulemaking is not a sensible response to an unfocused belief that the market is working imperfectly. Rather, the FTC should embark on rulemaking only when it is contemplating a particular solution to a wide-spread problem and where it has a legal theory that supports its proposed rule. Restraint is required in selecting rulemaking targets and in defining a rulemaking's scope. The Commission frequently will find that a mix of guides, policy statements, and administrative proceedings will be superior to Magnuson–Moss rulemaking.

4. *Rulemaking by the NLRB*. In *American Hospital Ass'n v. NLRB*, 499 U.S. 606 (1991), the Supreme Court confronted another challenge to an agency's reliance on an administrative regulation to resolve an issue that would otherwise have required—and under the agency's past-practice had been subject to—a full-blown adjudicatory hearing. Section 9(b) of the National Labor Relations Act empowers the NLRB to determine the employee units within an employer's workforce that are entitled to separate representation and collective bargaining rights. For years the Board had made such determinations for hospital employees on a case-by-case basis. But its frequent failure to persuade the courts in individual representation cases that it had fixed the appropriate number of units finally led the Board to adopt a rule specifying that, with few exceptions, eight—and only eight—employee units (e.g., nurses, orderlies) should be recognized in any acute-care hospital.

AHA challenged the Board's rule claiming, among other things, that it violated the agency's statutory obligation to determine the appropriate number of employee bargaining units "in each case." The Supreme Court declined to construe this language as precluding the Board's generic resolution. It pointed to section 6 of the NLRA, which grants the Board "authority from time to time to make * * * such rules and regulations as may be necessary to carry out the provisions" of the Act, and found that the "in each case" language did not modify this general grant of rulemaking power:

> We simply cannot find in the three words "in each case" any basis for the fine distinction that petitioner would have us draw. Contrary to petitioner's contention, the Board's rule is not an irrebuttable presumption; instead, it contains an exception for "extraordinary circumstances." Even if the rule did establish an irrebuttable presumption, it would not differ significantly from the prior rules adopted by the Board. * * * [T]he Board must still apply the rule "in each case." For example, the Board must decide, in each case, among a host of other issues, whether a given facility is properly classified as an acute care hospital and whether particular employees are properly placed in particular units.

For a thoughtful discussion of this, the Labor Board's maiden, venture into rulemaking, see Mark H. Grunewald, *The NLRB's First Rulemaking: An Exercise in Pragmatism*, 41 Duke L.J. 274 (1991).

B. RULEMAKING PROCEDURE

Much of the law of administrative rulemaking is judge-made, although the courts generally have claimed to be interpreting statutory requirements. The concerns reflected in both the judicial decisions that we consider and in Congress' specific directives parallel those set forth at the outset of this chapter: assurance of administrative fidelity to politically sanctioned choices and provision of opportunities to know about, and participate in the formulation of, agency policies.

What are the sources of procedures for agencies to follow in rulemaking? One possible answer is the Constitution, but case law suggests that this rich source of procedural safeguards in administrative adjudication speaks only softly, if at all, in the rulemaking context. Some cases imply that when an agency is engaged in formulating prospective rules of general applicability—regardless of their potential impact—the Constitution imposes no procedural requirements whatever. E.g., *Curlott v. Campbell*, 598 F.2d 1175 (9th Cir.1979); *Love v. United States Department of HUD*, 704 F.2d 100 (3d Cir.1983). The Supreme Court's holdings in *Londoner* and *Bi–Metallic Investment Co.*, *supra* p. 314, are consistent with this conclusion. Although a few cases have held that due process sometimes demands at least notice of and an opportunity to comment on agency rules, e.g., *Burr v. New Rochelle Municipal Housing Authority*, 479 F.2d 1165 (2d Cir.1973); *Williams v. Barry*, 708 F.2d 789 (D.C.Cir. 1983), the conventional view is that the procedural requirements prescribed by the APA or by an agency's program statute satisfy whatever minimum standards the Constitution imposes. See *Vermont Yankee Nuclear Power Corp. v. Natural Resources Defense Council, Inc.*, 435 U.S. 519 (1978), *infra* p. 550; *Air Line Pilots Ass'n v. Quesada*, 276 F.2d 892 (2d Cir.1960), *supra* p. 460. See also Evelyn R. Sinaiko, *Due Process Rights of Participation in Administrative Rulemaking*, 63 Calif.L.Rev. 886 (1975).

The APA recognizes two basic and ostensibly quite different procedural models for making rules. For many years most judicial opinions and commentators assumed that federal agency rulemaking fell under the heading of "informal rulemaking," governed solely by section 553 of the APA, or under the heading of "formal rulemaking," governed also by sections 556 and 557 of the APA or by the analogous requirements of certain program statutes.

1. THE DEMISE OF FORMAL RULEMAKING

As visualized by sections 556 and 557 of the APA, formal rulemaking embodies many features of the judicial trial. In its most elaborate expression, exemplified by Section 701(c) of the Federal Food Drug, and Cosmetic Act, 26 U.S.C. § 371(e), the process includes what is essentially a pleading stage, in which the agency publishes a proposed rule and entertains written responses from parties interested in communicating their views; a trial stage, in which the agency seeks to assemble, through testimony and documentary evidence, subject to cross-examination and rebuttal by all other participants, facts sufficient to justify its rule; and a decision stage, in which the agency head(s) reviews the evidence and formulates a final rule, all elements of which must be supported by evidence in the hearing record. With some differences, this is the same process that the APA prescribes, where it applies, for the adjudication of individual disputes.

This process can be contrasted with so-called "informal rulemaking," pursuant to section 553 of the APA, which is by far the dominant federal model. Section 553 specifies just four steps for the adoption of legislative rules:

> (1) A "general notice of proposed rule making"—setting forth the "time, place, and nature of public proceedings," the "legal authority under which the rule is proposed," and "either the terms or substance of the proposed rule or a description of the subjects and issues involved"—shall be published in the Federal Register;
>
> (2) The agency then "shall give interested persons an opportunity to participate in the rule making through submission of written data, views, or arguments with or without opportunity for oral presentation";
>
> (3) The agency shall, after "consider[ing] the relevant matter presented incorporate in the rules adopted a concise general statement of their basis and purpose."
>
> (4) The agency shall publish the text of the rule.

What is notable about this summary is the steps that are not required: There need be no opportunity for any "hearing" in the sense of oral presentation or live testimony; material need not be submitted in testimonial form or under oath; and no opportunity for cross-examination or rebuttal is mandated.

Requirements for formal rulemaking can be found in only a handful of statutes, most enacted prior to the passage of the APA in 1946. Before the APA there was no "default" rulemaking procedure to which legislative drafters could refer. Moreover, the novelty of grants of administrative authority to prescribe substantive rules and a strong (if not expansive) tradition of regulation through adjudication made it logical for the authors of New Deal laws conferring such power to prescribe trial-type procedures for the adoption of rules. Businesses facing regulation also were insistent that their procedural rights be protected in any new grants of power to administrators. See, e.g., Charles Jackson, Food and Drug Legislation in the New Deal (Princeton, 1970).

As a consequence, formal rulemaking requirements appear in several pre-APA statutes, including (at several places) the Federal Food, Drug, and Cosmetic Act, the Walsh–Healy Act (under which wage rates are set for firms doing business with the government), and a number of laws administered by the U.S. Department of Agriculture.

A handful of post–APA laws, such as the Fair Packaging and Labeling Act, Pub.L.No. 89–755 (now codified at 15 U.S.C. § 2451 *et seq.*), which incorporates the procedures of FD & C Act § 701(e), and the Coal Mine Health and Safety Act of 1969, Pub.L.No. 91–173 (codified at 30 U.S.C. § 801 *et seq.*), require trial-type procedures for the adoption of rules. In the larger context of modern statutes conferring rulemaking power on administrators, however, these are quite clearly exceptions. The great majority of federal statutes authorizing rulemaking do not, expressly or by reference to the APA, trigger procedural requirements of the sort embodied in sections 556 and 557. See *United States v. Florida East Coast Railway, supra* p. 387.

Agencies whose statutes mandated trial-type procedures for the adoption of rules have found these requirements frustrating, so frustrating that some agencies have essentially abandoned the programs to which such requirements apply. In *Wirtz v. Baldor Electric Co*., 337 F.2d 518 (1963), the D.C. Circuit struck down a wage-rate determination by the Secretary of Labor under the Walsh–Healy Act because the Secretary had not provided the parties opposing his determination the opportunity to examine the individual responses of employers to a survey that the department had assured them would be confidential. This, the court held, violated the petitioners rights to see and be able to contest all of the evidence on which the Secretary relied.

FDA, whose statute originally mandated formal rulemaking for several categories of rules—including rules establishing food standards of identity, labeling requirements for dietary supplements, and regulating the accuracy and balance of prescription drug advertising—has experienced similar frustration and responded in similar fashion. By the mid–1970s, FDA had largely abandoned its program for prescribing and updating food standards, and found alternative ways of protecting consumers against the marketing of diluted or debased foods. See, e.g., Richard A. Merrill and Earl M. Collier, "*Like Mother Used to Make:" An Analysis of FDA Food Standards of Identity*, 74 Colum. L. Rev. 561 (1974). Responding to complaints, many from food producers, that the agency had ceased adopting standards for new foods or amending existing standards to provide for nutritional improvement of foods already covered by identity standards, Congress in 1990 amended the FD & C Act to partially exempt this activity from formal rulemaking requirements. Nutritional Labeling and Education Act of 1990, 104 Stat. 2353, Pub. L. No. 101–535. This relaxation of procedures, however, specifically did not apply to dairy products (whose manufacturers opposed any changes in the existing identity standards) or to maple syrup! For a host of reasons, this change has not re-energized FDA's' food standards program.

Critics of formal rulemaking have repeatedly cited FDA's experience to support their claim that trial-type hearings are poorly suited to the formulation of general agency policy. President Jimmy Carter once commented: "It should not have taken 12 years and a hearing record of over 100,000 pages for the FDA to decide what percentage of peanuts there ought to be in peanut butter." 15 Weekly Comp. of Pres.Doc. 482 (March 15, 1979). Another less notorious but even more daunting example is the proceeding that the FDA undertook to prescribe labeling and compositional requirements for nutritional supplements and fortified foods, a proceeding governed by section 701(e) of the FD & C Act. The proceeding began in 1962 with the publication of a proposal. Four years elapsed before the agency published a "final order" subject to objections and requests for a hearing. After a legal skirmish over differences between the proposal and final order, see *Pharmaceutical Manufacturers Association v. Gardner*, 381 F.2d 271 (D.C.Cir.1967), the hearing commenced in 1968; it involved over 100 parties and lasted nearly two years. A court challenge to the first installment of final regulations issued by the agency was successful, *National Nutritional Foods Association v. FDA*, 504 F.2d 761 (2d Cir.1974), partly on the ground that the agency's hearing officer had denied the request of some parties to cross-examine a key witness. By the time the hearing was reopened on remand, that witness had long since departed his position as chair of the NAS–NRC committee (whose recommendations the FDA was seeking to implement), so a substitute had to be found. In the meantime, Congress intervened to amend provisions of the agency's statute which authorized certain of the proposed regulations. The FDA's attempt to reissue revised regulations, based on the amended hearing record but without inviting additional comment on the impact of Congress' action, was set aside in part, *National Nutritional Foods Association v. Kennedy*, 572 F.2d 377 (2d Cir.1978).

The procedural burdens, and resulting delays, that prompted Congress to exempt FDA's food standards from formal rulemaking probably were not unforeseen by the authors of the original FD & C Act (or of other statutes imposing similar requirements). Moreover, such impacts have not always been unintended. Formal rulemaking was mandated to set wage rates under the Fair Labor Standards Act as the result of an amendment sponsored by Senator William Fulbright of Arkansas, which then boasted the second-lowest wage scale in the nation. It cannot have been a disappointment to the Senator's supporters that these procedures made the Labor Department's task difficult to perform. See Jerry L. Mashaw, *Reinventing Government and Regulatory Reform: Studies in the Neglect and Abuse of Administrative Law*, 57 U.Pitt.L.Rev. 405, 416 (1996).

Formal rulemaking has, nevertheless, had its defenders. Trial-type hearings are said to facilitate the full development of information necessary to the formulation of reasonable regulatory policies. They produce a closed evidentiary record that permits meaningful judicial review of an agency's factual premises as well as its policy judgments. Moreover, it is argued, only a trial-type hearing affords affected persons a genuine opportunity to question the agency's factual premises. "[H]e who regulates ought to appear publicly if there is a challenge, and put on the table, subject to cross-examination, the facts on which he grounds his proposal." H. Thomas Austern, *Food Standards: The Balance Between Certainty and Innovation*, 24 Food Drug Cosm.L.J. 440, 451 (1969).

Professor Glen Robinson once defended the use of formal procedures for developing agency policy in an analysis that attacks the very utility of the adjudication/legislation distinction:

> Challenges to the suitability of adjudicative methods (particularly the reliance on testimonial evidence and cross-examination) where the issues involve policy planning, appear to rest in large part on the notion that "policy" * * * is something pure, uncontaminated by particular data and questions, assumptions, opinions and biases which have been regarded as properly the subject of such methods in other contexts. * * *
>
> First, it is doubtful that predictive judgment is radically different from determinations of historical fact. In both cases the determination must almost invariably rest on general conclusions that are inferred from particular factual data and an evaluation of probabilities that may be as appropriate for testimonial proof and cross-examination in one case as in the other.
>
> Second, in some cases testimonial proof and cross-examination can serve a more valuable function in testing forecasts and generalized conclusions underlying future policy planning than in making findings concerning specific past events. * * * Even if there is no dispute about specific identifiable "facts," * * * and even if the [agency's] judgment cannot be proved or disproved * * * it may still be desirable to force [it] through cross-examination of its experts, to disclose the particular premises, including facts, opinions, and reasoning, which underlie its "policy" conclusions. * * * At the very least it puts some burden on the agency to explain and articulate the assumptions and the foundations on which its policy rests. * * *
>
> * * * While delay is unquestionably present in administrative regulation, the problem tends to be exaggerated by reference to extraordinary cases which are not fairly representative of the process as a whole. Even accepting the time honored view that delay is a major problem, it is still questionable how much of it is attributable to reliance on formal procedures. * * *

Glen O. Robinson, *The Making of Administrative Policy: Another Look at Rulemaking and Adjudication and Administrative Procedure Reform*, 118 U.Pa.L.Rev. 485, 521–24 (1970). See Richard J. Pierce, *The Choice Between Adjudicating and Rulemaking for Formulating and Implementing Energy Policy*, 31 Hastings L.J. 1 (1979).

Critics of formal rulemaking have, however, been unconvinced. In a study for the U.S. Administrative Conference, Professor Robert W. Hamilton found that requiring rulemaking to be conducted on the record imposes substantial disadvantages in terms of cost, delay, and agency effectiveness. *Procedures for the Adoption of Rules of General Applicabil-*

ity: The Need for Procedural Innovation in Administrative Rulemaking, 60 Calif.L.Rev. 1276, 1312–13 (1972):

> At worst, these procedures have warped regulatory programs or resulted in virtual abandonment of them. It is surprising to discover that most agencies required to conduct formal hearings in connection with rulemaking in fact did not do so during the previous five years. * * * Thus, the primary impact of these procedural requirements is often not as one might otherwise have expected, the testing of agency assumptions by cross-examination or the testing of agency conclusions by courts on the basis of substantial evidence of record. Rather these procedures either cause the abandonment of the program * * *, the development of techniques to reach the same regulatory goal but without a hearing * * *, or the promulgation of noncontroversial regulations by a process of negotiation and compromise. * * *[172]

It is fair to say that the critics of formal rulemaking have carried the day. The authors are not aware of any modern regulatory statute that prescribes formal rulemaking for the adoption of legislative rules, though several add some bells and whistles to the brief requirements of section 553 of the APA. Yet, as the FTC's experience demonstrates, even these accessories may contribute to obstructing an agency's rulemaking efforts. Many of the statutes that once mandated trial-type procedures have been amended to simplify or expedite the rulemaking process. The few programs subject to such requirements remain dormant.

The debate about rulemaking process, however, has not subsided. If anything, it has become more intense, in large part as a result of procedural requirements and analytical responsibilities that courts have extracted from the language—or assumed purpose—of section 553, a subject to which we turn in Section 3 of this part. But first we examine the role that courts have come to play in reviewing the administrative rulemaking product.

2. SUBSTANTIVE REVIEW AND THE RULEMAKING PROCESS

a. Substantive Review Outside the APA Framework

PACIFIC STATES BOX & BASKET CO. v. WHITE

Supreme Court of the United States, 1935.
296 U.S. 176, 56 S.Ct. 159, 80 L.Ed. 138.

JUSTICE BRANDEIS delivered the opinion of the Court.

[The plaintiff, a California manufacturer of fruit and vegetable containers, challenged an order of the Chief of the Oregon Division of

172. It probably does not need pointing out that valid and non-arbitrary regulations may be controversial. Rulemaking on a record is favored by industry attorneys, I suspect, precisely because it may help to impede or prevent the adoption of quite valid and reasonable regulations which are objectionable to their clients.

Plant Industry prescribing the type, size, and shape of containers for the sale of strawberries and raspberries. The defendant had acted, after investigation, notice, and a public hearing, pursuant to an Oregon statute empowering him to promulgate "official standards for containers of horticultural products * * * in order to promote, protect, further and develop the horticultural interests" of the state. The box company claimed that the new standard had the effect of preventing use of its containers by growers in Oregon. It charged, *inter alia*, that the standard thus violated its rights under the Due Process Clause of the Fourteenth Amendment because it "is arbitrary, capricious, and not reasonably necessary for the accomplishment of any legitimate purpose of the police power." The district court dismissed the company's complaint on the ground that it did not allege facts that would entitle it to relief.]

Plaintiff does not question the reasonableness of the standard so far as it prescribes the capacity of the box or basket. Its challenge is directed solely to the fixing of the dimensions and the form of the container. But to fix both the dimensions and the form may be deemed necessary in order to assure observance of the prescribed capacity and to effect other purposes of the regulation. It may be that in Oregon, where hallocks* have long been in general use, buyers at retail are less likely to be deceived by dealers as to the condition and quantity of these berries if they are sold in containers of the prescribed form and dimensions. It is said that there are 34 other styles or shapes of berry basket in use somewhere in the United States. Obviously, a multitude of shapes and sizes of packages tends to confuse the buyer. Furthermore, the character of the container may be an important factor in preserving the condition of raspberries and strawberries, which are not only perishable but tender. * * *

Different types of commodities require different types of containers; and as to each commodity there may be reasonable difference of opinion as to the type best adapted to the protection of the public. Whether it was necessary in Oregon to provide a standard container for raspberries and strawberries; and, if so, whether that adopted should have been made mandatory, involve questions of fact and of policy, the determination of which rests in the legislative branch of the state government. The determination may be made, if the constitution of the State permits, by a subordinate administrative body. With the wisdom of such a regulation we have, of course, no concern. We may enquire only whether it is arbitrary or capricious. That the requirement is not arbitrary or capricious seems clear. That the type of container prescribed by Oregon is an appropriate means for attaining permissible ends cannot be doubted.

* * *

* * * Plaintiff contends that since the case was heard on motion to dismiss the bill, all allegations therein made must be accepted as true;

* [A hallock is described by the Court as "a type of rectangular till box with perpendicular sides and a raised bottom." The plaintiff manufactured a cup-shaped container known as a "tin-top" or "metal rim."]

and, among others, the charge that "there is no necessity for the particular orders relating to strawberries or raspberries" "based on considerations of public health, or to prevent fraud or deception, or any other legitimate use of the police power, and the particular container described * * * does not of necessity promote, protect, further or develop the horticultural interests of the State"; and that its necessary effect is "to grant a monopoly to manufacturers of the so-called hallocks." The order here in question deals with a subject clearly within the scope of the police power. When such legislative action "is called in question, if any state of facts reasonably can be conceived that would sustain it, there is a presumption of the existence of that state of facts, and one who assails the classification must carry the burden of showing by a resort to common knowledge or other matters which may be judicially noticed, or to other legitimate proof, that the action is arbitrary." * * *

* * * It is urged that this rebuttable presumption of the existence of a state of facts sufficient to justify the exertion of the police power attaches only to acts of legislature; and that where the regulation is the act of an administrative body, no such presumption exists, so that the burden of proving the justifying facts is upon him who seeks to sustain the validity of the regulation. The contention is without support in authority or reason, and rests upon misconception. Every exertion of the police power, either by the legislature or by an administrative body, is an exercise of delegated power. Where it is by a statute, the legislature has acted under power delegated to it through the Constitution. Where the regulation is by an order of an administrative body, that body acts under a delegation from the legislature. The question of law may, of course, always be raised whether the legislature had power to delegate the authority exercised. But where the regulation is within the scope of authority legally delegated, the presumption of the existence of facts justifying its specific exercise attaches alike to statutes, to municipal ordinances, and to orders of administrative bodies. Here there is added reason for applying the presumption of validity; for the regulation now challenged was adopted after notice and public hearing as the statute required. It is contended that the order is void because the administrative body made no special findings of fact. But the statute did not require special findings; doubtless because the regulation authorized was general legislation, not an administrative order in the nature of a judgment directed against an individual concern. * * *

Notes

1. *Substantive Constitutional Review*. The box company's challenge to the Oregon container rule relied centrally on the Due Process Clause of the Fourteenth Amendment. Students will recall the history of the Supreme Court's treatment of similar challenges to state statutes during the first half of this century. After initially embracing the notion that "due process" imposes substantive limits on state (and federal) legislation in the economic arena, see *Lochner v. New York*, 198 U.S. 45 (1905), the Court during the

New Deal quickly retreated to a posture of substantial indifference to legislative motives or reasoning. Compare Justice Douglas' statements in *Williamson v. Lee Optical*, 348 U.S. 483 (1955): "The day is gone when this Court uses the Due Process Clause of the Fourteenth Amendment to strike down state laws, regulatory of business and industrial conditions, because they may be unwise, improvident, or out of harmony with a particular school of thought." On an initial reading, therefore, Justice Brandeis' deference to Oregon's rule seems unsurprising.

As most readers will appreciate, the Supreme Court has not in all instances been indifferent to the substantive content of state laws challenged as unconstitutional. Challenges invoking guarantees of the Bill of Rights have continued to elicit more searching review of legislative judgments, as have claims based on the Equal Protection Clause of the Fourteenth Amendment. The Court has also developed special requirements for congressional forays into enforcement of the Civil War Amendments' non-discrimination requirements. (See discussion in Chapter 9, *infra* at 1230.) Predictably, the Court's willingness to scrutinize the substance of statutes that are perceived to affect important personal rights has extended to administrative rules as well. See, e.g., *Bob Jones University v. United States*, 461 U.S. 574 (1983) (reviewing IRS regulations for conformity with the first amendment's guarantee of freedom of religion); *Red Lion Broadcasting Co. v. FCC*, 395 U.S. 367 (1969) (reviewing FCC rules for conformity with the first amendment's guarantee of free speech). But the Supreme Court has never disavowed or, indeed, obviously departed from its posture in *Pacific States Box* on the intensity of constitutional review of administrative rules dealing with traditional subjects of governmental regulation.

2. *Relevance of Agency Procedure*. Justice Brandeis concludes his opinion by noting that "[h]ere there is added reason for applying the presumption of validity; for the regulation now challenged was adopted after notice and public hearing as the statute required." Why should the procedures followed by an administrative rulemaker make a difference? Did the hearing conducted by Oregon officials afford sufficient protection for this out-of-state box company? Does Justice Brandeis supply any evidence that the box company knew about, much less participated in, the hearing? Does he (or did the Oregon agency) attempt to relate what the agency did to what it heard from the hearing participants? Indeed, assuming that procedures allowing the introduction of outside views are meant to inform agency decision making, does Brandeis require that the Oregon agency point to any facts or reasons that would justify its rule?

b. *Substantive Review Under the APA*

By its terms, section 553 makes the opportunity for an oral hearing optional. It says nothing about the form or time for the submission of "data, views, or argument," nor does it mention the materials the agency is likely to have consulted in developing its proposal. It is not obvious that the agency must make those materials public, confine its decision to any identifiable "record," or refrain from consultation with any individual, group, or other governmental body. Judging from the bare language of section 553, an agency apparently need only announce its intention to adopt a rule dealing with a specified topic, allow some reasonable (but unspecified) period for the submission of written comments, and then promulgate a final regulation accompanied by only a "concise" and "general" statement of reasons.

The APA's brief requirements for rulemaking were almost irrelevant in the regulatory environment of 1946. In that era major prosecutorial agencies, such as the FTC and NLRB, did not engage in rulemaking. Licensing agencies like the FCC and the FPC rarely did so and did not have their authority to adopt legislative rules confirmed until the *Storer* and *Texaco* decisions. Other major agencies, such as the ICC and the SEC, did issue regulations, but these generally enunciated broad principles (e.g., that proxy solicitations should not contain "misleading" information) that would be applied and developed in adjudicatory proceedings, or set forth "safe harbor" rules that assured affected parties that conforming conduct would not be considered to violate some broad prohibition of their governing statutes. Outside IRS rulemaking, "bright line" rules were to be found mostly in contract, grant or benefit programs that were exempt from § 553 by its own terms.

By the 1960s, the regulatory environment was changing rapidly. The FTC (and other agencies), long criticized for inertia and ineffectiveness, had begun to flex newly discovered rulemaking muscles. Congressional reinforcement and expansion of regulatory mandates forced agencies like the FDA to attempt to regulate by general rule in order to fulfill their new responsibilities. More importantly, Congress was about to create a host of new health and safety agencies—the National Highway Traffic Safety Administration, the Occupational Safety and Health Administration, the Consumer Product Safety Commission, and (following the initiative of President Nixon) the Environmental Protection Agency—whose statutory mandates were defined largely by directives to make rules. The laws supposedly "regulating" automobile safety, occupational safety and health, consumer product safety, and human health and the environment were largely non-self-executing. They imposed few statutory rules of conduct; rather, they left the setting of standards to the discretion of these newly created regulators.

Congress was not wholly inattentive to this reorientation of agency activity. But initially it did little to enlarge the procedural protections for those whose interests would be affected by the new social regulatory agencies beyond inserting provisions in their organic statutes permitting immediate judicial review of the rules that they adopted. Sometimes it added that such rules had to be supported by "substantial evidence." These invitations to pre-enforcement judicial review meant that many (and for some agencies most) rules would potentially be subject to immediate judicial scrutiny. Instructions to demand "substantial evidence," coupled with a radical shift in the subject matter and scope of federal regulation, virtually assured that the courts called on to review these rules would be impelled to elaborate, and perhaps rethink, administrative law's prior understanding of the APA's basic requirements for rulemaking.

Legal attacks on the work product of federal agencies (new and old) featured a novel blend of substantive and procedural arguments. This is hardly surprising. As we noted in Chapter 4, *supra* at 343, claims that an agency's procedures were inadequate and that its evidence was insubstantial reveal the ease with which substance and procedure can be made interchangeable, or reinforcing. Moreover, Congress' inclusion of the "substantial evidence" standard in several statutes suggested an assumption about the creation of a "record" for both agency decision and judicial review that again linked substance and procedure. Finally, insistent demands to bring these new forms of regulation into alignment with historic notions of administrative power and the rule of law presented courts with a unique challenge to their own legitimacy. If the "hands off" posture of *Pacific States Box* was foreclosed by the APA itself and by modern statutes providing for pre-enforcement review, how were courts to avoid the Lochnerian excesses that provided the constitutional backdrop for Justice Brandeis' restraint in that case? In THE STRUGGLE FOR AUTO SAFETY (1990), Professor Jerry L. Mashaw and David L. Harfst framed the dilemma this way:

> The twin shoals of judicial policymaking on the one hand and unconstrained administrative discretion on the other are hardly novel landmarks when steering for the safe harbor of judicial legitimacy. They are traversed routinely by judicial navigators. But in the context of judging the abstract legality of rules under vague statutory criteria, the task of maintaining the confidence of passengers and crew is made more difficult by the absence of some important aids to navigation. The conventional lawyerly moves for separating law and policy or for camouflaging their inseparability when reviewing agency adjudications are largely unavailable. When reviewing the abstract legality of rules it is simply preposterous to claim (1) that the court is addressing not these broad issues of policy but only the agency's application of law to fact in the adjudication of narrowly focused claims of right, or (2) that these interpretive issues are routinely decided in agency enforcement proceedings and, therefore, have long legal histories that constrain both the agency's and the judiciary's roles. To take the latter claim first, not only are the questions novel, but the norms put at issue are designed precisely to confer policy discretion on the administrator. In virtually all cases, the claim that the court is just interpreting the law, not setting (or "rubber stamping") agency policy, will convince no one.
>
> The facts of rulemaking review proceedings similarly belie the claim that the courts are here merely engaged in reviewing run-of-the-mill administrative dispute settlements. The parties look more like legislative claimants than ordinary litigants. They often are tangentially affected business interests, such as the insurance industry, or ideological champions of the Left or Right, such as the Center for Auto Safety or the Pacific Legal Foundation. Even the directly

affected manufacturers may be litigating for strategic competitive advantage * * * rather than to protect any conventional form of property interest. And no matter who is litigating, the judgment usually will bind everyone. The question is the validity of the rule, not the propriety of its application. The litigant's "rights" and the "rights" of the public are indistinguishable.

The line between law and policy can also disappear in judicial review of agency adjudication. The pre-enforcement review of rules facilitated by the Motor Vehicle Safety Act is but a recognition of the changing structure of federal administrative regulation. Yet no amount of scholarly celebration of this so-called public law litigation is likely to eliminate judicial anxiety in the face of a task that calls for repeated, transparent, and general policy choices. The task must be redefined to integrate it with a more conventional conception of judicial competence. For it is on that convention that the judiciary's political legitimacy depends.

The cases that follow provide one, albeit prominent, example of this process of redefinition, and its implications. At base, it is a process of transforming rationality review into a search for an adequate reasoning process while simultaneously harnessing procedural protection to the information demands of complex technical decision making. The result is a proceduralized substantive review that seeks to move agency decision making processes toward the pursuit of substantive rationality. But, as in most legal transformations, the new wine is served from old bottles—here the spare requirements of section 553 of the APA.

Our first principal case, *Automotive Parts & Accessories Association v. Boyd*, involves what can now be recognized as a typical challenge to agency rules promulgated under a modern regulatory statute. At the time, however, the case, though not entirely without precedent, raised novel questions about agency process and, more significantly for our purposes, the responsibility of agencies to explain and document the bases for their rules. The D.C. Circuit's opinion, which has become a staple of U.S. administrative law, set the tone for much that was to follow in the developing common law of judicial review of administrative rulemaking. The petitioners in *Auto Parts* contended that the respondent, the Secretary of Transportation, failed to follow mandated procedures for the adoption of regulations and, in addition, failed to justify the regulations' substantive requirements. Our immediate concern is with the latter claim—and the court's response to it—but the reader should recall the conjunction of these claims and be attentive, as Judge McGowan surely was, to the interplay between the procedures an agency may follow in adopting rules and the character of the evidence and reasons that will suffice to sustain their content.

AUTOMOTIVE PARTS & ACCESSORIES ASSOCIATION v. BOYD

United States Court of Appeals, District of Columbia Circuit, 1968.
407 F.2d 330.

McGowan, Circuit Judge.

These consolidated review proceedings are among the first to be initiated under the National Traffic and Motor Vehicle Safety Act of 1966 (Safety Act), 15 U.S.C. §§ 1381–1409. The object of this challenge is Motor Vehicle Safety Standard No. 202, which requires that, effective January 1, 1969, all new passenger cars manufactured for sale in this country must be factory-equipped with front seat head restraints which meet specific federal standards. Petitioners are not motor car manufacturers but, rather, a manufacturer of auto accessories including head restraints (Sterling Products Co., Inc.), and two trade associations representing persons engaged in the auto accessory business (Automotive Parts & Accessories Association, Inc. (APAA), and Automotive Service Industry Association (ASIA)). Their common grievance appears to flow not from the recognition and establishment of the head restraint as an essential safety device but from the adverse impact upon their business inherent in a vehicle standard which necessarily requires that the head restraints be factory installed.[1] * * *

It was on November 30, 1966, that the respondent Boyd first issued a notice of proposed rule making under the Act. That notice related to twenty-three suggested safety standards, only one of which involved head restraints. Written comments were invited to be submitted by January 3, 1967. On the following January 31, respondent Bridwell issued rules as to twenty of the proposed subjects; he did not act with respect to head restraints because he thought it desirable to seek further information. Accordingly, on the same day, he issued a new notice of proposed rule making with respect to head restraints, and he invited written comments to be submitted by the following May. As a part of the consideration process, a meeting was held by respondents on November 14, 1967, with both car and accessory manufacturers, and other interested persons. On December 22, 1967, a notice was issued embodying the proposed Standard, and written comments about it were invited by January 26, 1968. The Standard was promulgated on February 12 thereafter.

The Standard as issued reflected certain alterations responsive to comments received, but the announcement accompanying it noted that the changes proposed by those interested in accessory equipment had been rejected for the reasons indicated. Various participants in the

1. The Safety Act provides that the Secretary of Transportation can issue (1) safety standards *for motor vehicles* which require that no automobile can be manufactured for sale without meeting the standard (vehicle standard), or (2) safety standards for motor vehicle *equipment* (equipment standard) which require that all such equipment manufactured for sale must meet that standard.

proceedings, including petitioners, filed petitions for reconsideration. On May 20, 1968, petitioners were sent a letter by respondents denying their request for the reasons stated therein.

Petitioners' central claim is that the Standard is invalid because this manner of proceeding was unauthorized from the beginning since it did not comport with the [trial-type hearing] requirements of Sections [556] and [557] of the APA. This is not a complaint which petitioners appear to have directed to respondents during the course of the proceeding itself, nor in their request for reconsideration. There is, thus, a serious question as to whether they should now be permitted to press the matter for the first time here. Respondents have, however, chosen to deal with it on the merits, and the public interest in the effective administration of the new Safety Act argues for our doing the same.

The question, as we have said, turns upon whether Congress, under the Safety Act, required the rule "to be made on the record after opportunity for agency hearing."* The Safety Act contents itself with what is, in this context, the somewhat Delphic pronouncement that "[t]he Administrative Procedure Act shall apply to all orders establishing, amending, or revoking a Federal motor vehicle safety standard under this subchapter." Since the APA contains both Section [553], on the one hand, and Sections [556] and [557], on the other, this treatment falls somewhat short of the apogee of the legislative draftsman's art. In any event, the classic conditions are present for recourse to legislative history for illumination of the Congressional purposes vis-a-vis formal and informal rule making.

What emerges from this quest is reasonably explicit, and it points away from where petitioners would have us go. The Senate version of the Safety Act expressly stated that rules would be prescribed in accordance with Sections 3, 4, and 5 of the APA, and that "[n]othing in this title or in the Administrative Procedure Act shall be construed to make Sections 7 and 8 [556 and 557 of the codified APA] * * * applicable." The House bill, on the other hand, simply stated that the APA would apply, without discriminating among its parts. In explaining this provision, however, the accompanying committee report stated that "The Secretary may utilize either the informal rule making procedure of section 4 [553] of the APA or the more formal and extensive procedures of the act * * *." In conference the language of the House version was adopted. In explaining the Conference Bill on the floor of the Senate, Senator Magnuson, the sponsor of the Act and a conferee, pointed out that the change in no way threatened the legitimacy of informal rule making procedures, but instead was only to allow the Secretary to adopt formal procedures should he wish to do so in a particular instance:

* [Judge McGowan's reference here is to the final sentence of section 553(c) of the APA which reads: "When rules are required by statute to be made on the record after opportunity for an agency hearing, sections 556 and 557 of this title apply instead of this subsection."]

> With respect to sections [556] and [557] of the Administrative Procedure Act, which apply to formal hearings, the Senate bill had expressly provided that these sections would not apply to standard-setting procedures under the act. *It was the clear understanding of the conferees, however, that under the language of the House bill, the Secretary will utilize the informal rulemaking procedures of section [553] of the Administrative Procedure Act; and that he need hold a formal hearing under sections [556] and [557] only if he determines that such hearing is desirable.* (Emphasis added).

Quite apart from this concrete evidence of Congressional intent, an examination of other provisions of the Act, as well as the particular function which the Secretary is to perform, serves to reinforce the view that informal rule making was appropriate. First, the Act provides for the Secretary to consult informally with the National Motor Vehicle Safety Advisory Council, as well as various state, interstate and legislative committees. Also, the Act contemplates that, within the Department, experimentation and research will be used to generate data useful in formulating safety standards. Both of these approaches are far more consistent with informal than with formal rule making. More importantly, they only further emphasize the inherently legislative nature of the task which the Act delegates to the Secretary and his subordinates. In this context, where the Department is concerned with the issuance of rules requiring basic policy determinations rather than the resolution of particular factual controversies, the informal procedures provided by Section [553] of the APA are appropriate.

In the face of this formidable threat to their position from both the legislative history and the general structure of the Act itself, petitioners refer to the judicial review provisions of the Safety Act, and argue that they make manifest a Congressional intent that the "rules are required by statute to be made on the record after opportunity for an agency hearing," and therefore are to be the product of formal rule making. This is said to be implicit in (1) the requirement that, where review is sought of an order establishing a standard, there shall be filed in court "the record of the proceedings on which the Secretary based his order," (2) the jurisdiction given the court to review safety standards "in accordance with" Section [706] of the APA, and (3) the provision made for a remand by the court, at the request of a petitioner for the taking of additional evidence. Petitioners argue that all these aspects of the judicial review contemplated and authorized by the Safety Act are instinct with the idea of a record compiled in formal evidentiary hearings, from which record the agency makes findings and conclusions required to be supported, in the familiar adjudicatory sense, by substantial evidence in the record. Otherwise, so it is said, the judicial review provisions would be meaningless.

We are not persuaded that this is so, at least when the matter is weighed against the backdrop of legislative history set forth above. As to petitioners' first contention, there *is* a record compiled in a Section [553] proceeding, and available for filing in court. It consists of the submissions made in response to the invitations issued for written comments. And, as to the third, a court *could*, at the instance of a petitioner dissatisfied with the state of such a record, remand it to the agency for the receipt of further expressions of views and related information. * * *

Petitioners press closely upon us the reference in the judicial review provisions of the Safety Act[9] to Section 10 of the Administrative Procedure Act. They point to paragraph (e) of Section 10 [§ 706] which, as its title indicates, is generally concerned with the scope of the review by a court of agency action, and, in particular, to subparagraph (B)(5) which directs that the court shall set aside agency action "unsupported by substantial evidence in a case subject to [Sections 7 and 8] or otherwise reviewed on the record of an agency hearing provided by statute." We think that this language of Section 10, although not free from ambiguity, suggests that this "substantial evidence" standard for judicial review is addressed to the review of formal hearings, either under Sections 7 and 8 or other special statutory provision. Since we have found that a formal hearing is not required by the Safety Act, Subsection (B)(5) by its own terms appears to have no application to this case. This is not to say, however, that Congress has given no guidance as to the proper standards for judicial review of informal proceedings. Section 10(e) [§ 706(e)] is, as noted above, addressed in the large to scope of review, and subsection (B)(5) is only one of its components. The other standards set out in that section, all of which would apply to informal rule making, allow an appellate court to apply 10(e) quite apart from subsection (B)(5).

In any event, although the judicial review provisions of the Safety Act and the APA contain some terms which are normally associated with formal evidentiary hearings, we refuse to infer that Congress, in this unnecessarily oblique way, intended to require the procedures of formal rule making for the issuance of safety standards. To do so would be to negate the specific legislative history and general Congressional purpose which in our view clearly demonstrate that issuance of standards by informal rule making was to be permissible.

* * * Section 4(b) of the APA [§ 533(c)] says in terms that the agency, after considering the relevant matter received by it in response to its invitation of comments, "shall incorporate in the rules adopted a concise general statement of their basis and purpose."

We think * * * that the statement in the text of the promulgation of the Standard, when considered in the light of the reasons stated by the Administrator's denial of rehearing, is "a concise general statement" which passes muster under Section 4 of the APA.[12] However, on the

9. 15 U.S.C. § 1394(a)(3) provides:

> Upon the filing of the petition referred to in paragraph (1) of this subsection, the court shall have jurisdiction to review the order in accordance with [APA § 10], and to grant appropriate relief as provided in such section.

12. The statement in the text of the standard simply stated:

> This standard specifies requirements for head restraints to reduce the frequency and severity of neck injury in rear-end and other collisions.

33 Fed.Reg. 2916 (1968). The reasoning of the Administrator's denial of rehearing is

occasion of this first challenge to the implementation of the new statute it is appropriate for us to remind the Administrator of the ever present possibility of judicial review, and to caution against an overly literal reading of the statutory terms "concise" and "general." These adjectives must be accommodated to the realities of judicial scrutiny, which do not contemplate that the court itself will, by a laborious examination of the record, formulate in the first instance the significant issues faced by the agency and articulate the rationale of their resolution. We do not expect the agency to discuss every item of fact or opinion included in the submissions made to it in informal rule making. We do expect that, if the judicial review which Congress has thought it important to provide is to be meaningful, the "concise general statement of * * * basis and purpose" mandated by Section 4 will enable us to see what major issues of policy were ventilated by the informal proceedings and why the agency reacted to them as it did.

Because the "concise general statement" envisaged by Congress is something different from the detailed "findings and conclusions" on all "material issues of fact, law, or discretion" referred to in Section 8, there will inevitably be differences of emphasis and approach in the application of the judicial review standards prescribed in APA § 10. An adversary lawsuit, which most closely resembles the formal hearing of Sections 7 and 8, throws up issues of law and fact in a form quite unlike those which take shape in informal rule making, which has many analogies to a legislative committee hearing. When the issue on appeal is whether a rule made in informal proceedings meets the criteria of Section 10, the court must necessarily go about the application of that standard in a manner unlike its review of findings of fact and conclusions of law compiled in a formal proceeding.

This exercise need be no less searching and strict in its weighing of whether the agency has performed in accordance with the Congressional purposes, but, because it is addressed to different materials, it inevitably varies from the adjudicatory model. The paramount objective is to see whether the agency, given an essentially legislative task to perform, has carried it out in a manner calculated to negate the dangers of arbitrariness and irrationality in the formulation of rules for general application in the future. With this concept of the scope of review enjoined upon us by the interaction of the Safety Act and Section 10 of the APA, we turn to petitioners' attack upon the merits of the Standard.

Petitioner APAA, by letters dated November 20, 1967 and January 22, 1968, responded to the invitation to comment extended in the notices of proposed rule making. It also, jointly with petitioner Sterling, filed a petition for reconsideration after the Standard had been promulgated. * * * In all three documents, objection was made to any standard which

discussed at length in the second part of this opinion. That a court may consider the statement of an agency in denying a request for rehearing in deciding whether the requirements of APA § 4(b) have been met is shown by *Logansport Broadcasting Corp. v. United States*, 210 F.2d 24, 27–28 (1954).

would require factory implemented head restraints because, quite apart from depriving petitioners of sales, it would result, so it was said, in:

a. higher costs for the consumer;

b. an aggravation of monopolistic conditions in the auto industry;

c. longer delays and lead times in implementing the original standard, as well as subsequent improvements;

d. encouragement of minimum standards; and

e. deprivation of consumers' choice.

It was further argued that, if the standard were to apply to the equipment and not to the vehicles themselves (in other words, if all head restraints had to meet the Federal standards but there was no requirement that they be in place as the cars leave the factory), there would be:

a. continual improvement and innovation through competition;

b. consumer choice (allowing each consumer to buy a head restraint which was best for a person of his size); and

c. faster implementation of the standard.

It was also urged that there were no technical reasons why head restraints had to be factory installed, that the independent manufacturers had already produced millions of head restraints, and that installation was simple and inexpensive; and that "any possible ease in enforcement * * * cannot and should not be the sole criteria" for preferring factory implementation.

The alternative suggested by petitioners to factory implementation was to permit consumers to select the particular head restraint which best suited their needs from among competing brands certified to be in compliance with Federal standards. In short, consumers would choose head restraints as they might choose the color of their car. And, if it were felt that head restraints should be mandatory, then the regulation should simply require installation before delivery.

In the order promulgating Standard No. 202, the Administrator responded to several comments received from different parties. The following was directed toward petitioner's submissions:

> A comment from an equipment manufacturer and an equipment manufacturer's association asserted that the Standard should not require that motor vehicle manufacturers provide head restraints at the time of vehicle manufacture, but that each customer should be free to equip his vehicle with head restraints of his own choice, maintaining that the installation of head restraints is a relatively simple matter and that there appears to be virtually no technological advantage in requiring factory installation. The Administration has determined that safety dictates that head restraints be provided on all passenger cars manufactured on or after January 1, 1969, and that a head restraint standard that merely specified performance requirements for head restraint equipment would not insure that all

passenger cars would be so equipped, and would not, therefore, meet the need for safety. Furthermore, the Administration has determined that the performance of a head restraint is dependent upon the strength of the structure of the seat to which it is attached, as well as the compatibility of the head restraint with its anchorage to the seat structure.

In response to the petitioners' petition for reconsideration, the Administrator further elaborated his reasons for rejection in a three page letter, dated May 20, 1968. The Administrator first noted that "Your submissions concede, and indeed strongly champion the safety protection and benefit to the public provided by head restraint devices in vehicles. * * * [but] you would have us make the matter of affording this kind of protection optional with the purchaser of the vehicle in order to preserve a part of your business." The Administrator stated that he did not have the authority under the Act to require purchasers of vehicles to install equipment, and said that petitioners misconstrued the law if they thought the Act allows the Administrator to establish equipment standards applicable to equipment rather than to vehicles and then "to require purchasers of vehicles to install such equipment."

* * *

After noting that most of the arguments in the petition for reconsideration had been made earlier, the Administrator stated that:

> Among the reasons for not adopting the recommendations made in the comments and denying the Petition for Reconsideration are:
>
> (1) a head restraint standard promulgated as an equipment standard would not result in all passenger cars being equipped with head restraints on or after the effective date of the standard, but instead would make available head restraints that meet a standard which could be installed in vehicles if vehicle owners, at their option, so desired. This would therefore not meet the need for safety.
>
> (2) The performance of a head restraint system is dependent upon the interrelation between the head restraint, the structure of the seat and the seat anchorage.
>
> (3) An equipment standard in lieu of a vehicle performance standard would result in a restriction of design that would dictate that head restraints be add-on equipment without allowing other design options such as making the head restraint an integral part of the seat.
>
> In addition it is determined that an earlier effective date of Standard No. 202 would not be reasonable or practicable for Standard No. 202 in its present form; and that revision of Standard 202 to make such an effective date possible, such as your request that head restraints be optional add-on equipment, would result in a substantial reduction in the protection afforded the public.

And, in a paragraph which perhaps best summarizes the Administrator's reasons for rejecting petitioners' position, he wrote:

> In weighing petitioners' contentions with regard to Standard No. 202 the public interest was clearly on the side of a vehicle performance requirement which would require the vehicle manufacturer to install the device using any design he might choose to provide a requisite level of protection against whiplash injuries. In issuing the standard this consideration far outweighed the possible economic disadvantage that such a decision might impose on the petitioners and best accomplished the stated purpose and policy of the National Traffic and Highway Safety Act of 1966 "To reduce traffic accidents and deaths and injuries to persons resulting from traffic accidents. (15 U.S.C. 1381.)"

The question before us is whether these responses to the objections raised by petitioners adequately reflect, in the language of Section 4, a rational "consideration of the relevant matter presented" as embodied in "a concise general statement of [the] basis and purpose" of the Standard under view. We think they do, and that the picture they present is one of conscientious attention to the objections raised to the proposed rule, and their reasoned disposition on the basis of technical information and other relevant considerations which we have no basis for rejecting. The principal elements in the decision to require factory installation appear to have been (1) greater ease of enforcement and consequent assurance of the extension of protection to consumers and (2) the enhancement of protection due to the relationship between the head restraint and the structure of which it is a part. The one seems evident to us as a matter of common experience, while the other is amply supported by expert opinion in the record. The record also supports the reasonableness of the effective date of January 1, 1969, as against petitioners' insistence upon greater haste.

For the first time in this court, petitioners change gears and question the contributions of head restraints to the cause of safety. They assert in their brief that:

> "A considerable amount of evidence and material was submitted in the course of the Administrative proceedings suggesting that a head restraint standard was not needed to protect the public against 'unreasonable risk' of injury, that head restraints could increase safety hazards for individual drivers and passengers, that any standard with regard to head restraints should continue to make their use optional, and that there was a lack of reliable information with regard to the entire subject matter."

This "evidence and material" was not, of course, forthcoming from petitioners, since at that time they were busily applauding the Administrator's apparent purpose to impose the blessings of head restraints upon the motoring public, albeit chiding him at the same time for being so slow about it. The sources of this "evidence and material" were, of course, mainly the motor car manufacturers who tended to greet the proposed rule with controlled rapture and who generally argued that the restraints should be optional and not mandatory.

Petitioners now tell us that the Administrator did not, by appropriate findings, deal adequately with these objections, and that, although those who propounded them are not here attacking the Standard, the Standard should be set aside for this reason. This is, to say the least, a soaringly expansive concept of the scope to be afforded on judicial review to a participant in a rule making proceeding. Having urged upon the Administrator the adoption of a mandatory requirement of head restraints because of their contribution to safety, petitioners now tell us to set the order aside because it did not answer the arguments of those who said that the safety aspects were so dubious as to justify, at most, an optional system. We find it hard to take petitioners seriously on this score, despite their effort to analogize themselves to private attorneys general with an unlimited right to expose all dangers to the public interest.

In any event, we find substantial support in the record for a conclusion that the contribution of head restraints to consumer safety is such as to warrant their inclusion in all newly-manufactured motor cars. There can be no question but that the Administrator, on the basis of the submission made to him, could reasonably determine that the benefits from mandatory head restraints far outweighed any disadvantages from such restraints due to decreased visibility, or other possible adverse effects upon safety. On the one hand, the benefits from the reduction of neck injuries in rear-end crashes were clearly identifiable from information and specific data contained in submissions from such independent sources as the Office of Biomechanics Research Center of Wayne State University, and the American Association for Automotive Medicine, as well as a substantial statistical compilation within the Department. The evidence that head restraints might lead to significant safety disadvantages, on the other hand, seems rather speculative. The Administrator must of necessity consider many variables, and make "trade-offs" between various desiderata in deciding upon a particular standard for auto safety. On the record before us, we think it clear that Standard No. 202 meets the substantive requirements of the Safety Act.[18]

18. Section 103 of the Vehicle Safety Act provides:

> (a) * * * Each such Federal motor vehicle safety standard shall be practicable, shall meet the need for motor vehicle safety, and shall be stated in objective terms.
>
> * * *
>
> (f) In prescribing standards under this section, the Secretary shall
>
> (1) consider relevant available motor vehicle safety data, including the results of research, development, testing and evaluation activities conducted pursuant to this chapter;
>
> (2) consult with the Vehicle Equipment Safety Commission, and such other state or interstate agencies (including legislative committees) as he deems appropriate;
>
> (3) consider whether any such proposed standard is reasonable, practicable and appropriate for the particular type of motor vehicle or item of motor vehicle equipment for which it is prescribed; and
>
> (4) consider the extent to which such standards will contribute to carrying out the purposes of this chapter.

Thus, having appraised all of petitioners' claims against the Standard, we find no occasion to interfere with its operation. Rule makers, as the delegatees of legislative power, are no more likely than their delegators to make everybody happy with a particular exercise of that power. Our function is to see only that the result is reasonable and within the range of authority conveyed, that it has been formulated in the manner prescribed, and that the disappointed have had the opportunity provided by Congress to try to make their views prevail. On all these counts we are satisfied by the record before us. The petitions for review are

Denied.

Notes

1. *Arbitrariness Under the APA.* Judge McGowan focuses on the requirement in section 553(c) of the APA that an agency "shall incorporate in the rules adopted a concise general statement of their basis and purpose." Since the court purports to be reviewing only for arbitrariness, conventional doctrine would suggest that any colorable explanation could sustain the agency's rule. And the court's apparent acceptance of the Secretary's obvious and very brief statement—that the "standard specifies requirements for head restraints to reduce the frequency and severity of head injury in rear-end and other collisions"—might suggest this is all that was required. Yet Judge McGowan's scrutiny of the Secretary's justification for the head restraint rule is far more searching than would be the case if "arbitrary or capricious" were taken in its constitutional sense. He quotes liberally from portions of the Federal Register publication in which the Secretary explains his choices and also cites passages from the Secretary's denial of reconsideration. These sources together provide an explanation for the head restraint rule that, while by no means prolix, is more detailed than the APA language (or the court's footnote 12) might suggest. In surveying these materials, Judge McGowan seems to demand, first, that the agency provide reasons for its choices—not merely summarize the purpose of its rule. Further, he implies that the reasons offered must be inherently plausible—the enhanced enforceability of requiring manufacturer-installed headrests—or supported by data in the rulemaking record—the strength advantages of manufacturer-installation.

Although a statement of basis and purpose is required to be "incorporated" in the rule, this command has not been enforced literally. Rarely has an agency rule been overturned because the required explanation failed to appear in the Federal Register text. Reviewing courts have discerned an agency's rationale in other documents prepared contemporaneously by agency decision makers and sometimes inferred it from the content of the rule itself. See, e.g., *Alabama Association of Insurance Agents v. Board of Governors*, 533 F.2d 224 (5th Cir.1976), *cert. denied*, 435 U.S. 904 (1978) (employing amicus briefs and the records of adjudicatory hearings applying the rule to discern the agency's "basis and purpose"). Yet the jurisprudence is hardly uniform. Many cases reject the use of any agency-generated explanations or data put forward in support of a rule, but subsequent to its issuance, as "post hoc rationalizations," see *Tabor v. Joint Board for Enrollment of*

Actuaries, 566 F.2d 705 (D.C.Cir.1977); *Rodway v. United States Department of Agriculture*, 514 F.2d 809 (D.C.Cir.1975), and refuse to parse the record for supporting data not relied upon in the agency's contemporaneous rationale. E.g., *Kennecott Copper Corp. v. EPA*, 462 F.2d 846 (D.C.Cir.1972). The concerns reflected in such rulings seem to include (1) a desire to provide information to potential litigants who, if well-informed, might pursue further administrative procedures (such as a request for rehearing) rather than judicial review; (2) a desire to force agencies to be more explicitly rational in justifying their choices, thereby (presumably) guarding against unknown influences that might have corrupted the administrative process; and (3) a desire to force reconsideration of superficially implausible decisions.

Even these requirements might be thought demanding in light of early, authoritative interpretations of the APA. The APA legislative history contains the following explanation of section 553(c)'s "concise general statement" requirement: "The agency must analyze and consider all relevant matter presented. The required statement * * * should not only relate to the data so presented but with reasonable fullness explain the actual basis and objectives of the rule." S. Doc. No. 248, 79th Cong., 2d Sess. 201, 259 (1946). The Attorney General's Manual on the Administrative Procedure Act (1947) expressed the opinion that where such statements would be important as an aid to interpretation, "findings of fact and conclusions of law are not necessary. Nor is there required an elaborate analysis of the rules or of the considerations upon which the rules were issued. Rather, the statement is intended *to advise the public* of the general basis and purpose of the rules." *Id.* at 32 (emphasis supplied).

2. *The Evolution of Informal Rulemaking*. For many years the procedural requirements and judicial review standards of the APA were viewed as symmetrical: When a statute required an agency's action to be based "on the record after opportunity for an agency hearing," the substantial evidence standard applied; when an agency could proceed informally—in making rules or reaching other decisions—its actions were reviewable under the "arbitrary and capricious" standard. But the nexus between agency procedure and the scope of substantive review went beyond the explicit linkages of the APA. If, as Judge McGowan acknowledges, the Secretary had been required to follow sections 556 and 557, he would necessarily have generated an extensive formal record—including direct testimony or written statements of witnesses, cross-examination, exhibits, findings of fact, and conclusions of law—resembling the record in a civil trial. The "record" yielded by the typical informal rulemaking during the late 1960's looked very different. Indeed, few observers saw the process as producing a recognizable "record"—either for internal decision or court review. And without such a record agencies could not be expected to provide "findings of fact and conclusions of law," as the Attorney General's manual recognized.

To be sure, informal rulemaking always generated a good deal of paper. Even in 1967, a conscientious agency might have assembled voluminous analyses, data, and reports in developing a proposed rule. But these sources might not all be public, and they probably would not have been assembled into an organized record even when presented to agency decision makers. The agency's notice of proposed rulemaking probably set forth the text of its contemplated rule, usually accompanied by a few paragraphs describing what the rule was supposed to accomplish. Rarely, however, did a proposal summarize or analyze the data on which the agency relied or explain its tentative choices among competing approaches.

A proposed rule might elicit numerous written comments, which would be collected as they were submitted, usually at the end of the comment period. Comments followed (and still follow) no standard form; they ranged from brief expostulatory letters to lengthy briefs of law and fact. Comments have never been required to address issues in a particular order, so agency analysts had to array submissions around some predetermined matrix of issues. If comments were later arranged in other than chronological sequence, this would have been done to meet the needs of the agency—not to satisfy any requirement of the APA. Sometimes comments remained unassembled, unindexed, and possibly even unread long after a rulemaking concluded.

An agency's final regulation would be published in the Federal Register, accompanied by general assurances that the comments had been considered. Changes in the rule's text might reveal such consideration, and specific references to comments that had prompted changes were common. But few agencies made a serious effort to canvass all of the issues raised or to explain how they had resolved them. (In this respect, the Secretary of Transportation may have been unusually conscientious.) An agency's Federal Register publication typically consisted of the final text of the rule and a brief explanation of its rationale, a so-called "preamble." The NHTSA's head restraint rule took up slightly more than one three-column page in the Federal Register, of which roughly half was introductory discussion or "preamble"; the balance was the text of the rule itself. As we shall discover, however, agency practice in informal rulemaking has changed dramatically since the late 1960s, in part in response to judicial review. For discussions of this evolution, see James V. DeLong, *Informal Rulemaking and the Integration of Law and Policy*, 65 Va.L.Rev. 257 (1979); Colin S. Diver, *Policymaking Paradigms in Administrative Law*, 95 Harv.L.Rev. 393 (1981); William F. Pedersen, *Formal Records and Informal Rulemaking*, 85 Yale L.J. 38 (1975).

A dramatic, if extreme, example of this transformation is the rulemaking that FDA initiated in August 1995 to establish rules governing the manufacture, design, production, and marketing of cigarettes and smokeless tobacco products. FDA had never before asserted jurisdiction over conventional tobacco products, and it realized that it would confront claims that it lacked jurisdiction to regulate at all. Its central rationale for regulating—that tobacco products contain a drug, nicotine, which has been shown to be addictive—depended upon a mountain of complex scientific evidence. And the requirements that it proposed had to be justified in terms of a very complicated statute. FDA's notice of proposed rulemaking—which referred to but did not reproduce or incorporate the volumes of evidence that it claimed supported its case—ran over 450 pages in the Federal Register. 60 Fed.Reg. 41313 (August 11, 1995).

This proposal brought forth a veritable avalanche of comments, from both proponents of the agency's initiative (many national health organizations added data, and interpretations of the agency's data, to the record) and opponents (including advertising agencies, sponsors of advertised events, such as the Winston Cup racing series, and tobacco manufacturers). According to the *Washington Post*, FDA received over 700,000 separate communications. Because many of these comments turned out to be duplicates, the agency was able to whittle the pile that required close attention to a "mere" 93,000! The agency contracted with Oracle Corporation to adapt its computer system to organize the comments. Accounts differ on how many FDA employees were assigned to read, digest, and draft responses. Estimates range from 25 to over 100, most of whom apparently devoted their full time to the task, beginning around Christmas when the comment period closed, until late July, when the agency was prepared to issue—and attempt to document and explain—its final regulations. See John Schwartz, *Comments Couldn't Kill Tobacco Rule Process*, Wash. Post, Feb. 19, 1997, at A19. The preamble to FDA's final regulations, omitting its responses to the major legal objections which were dealt with elsewhere, ran 217 pages of Federal Register text. 61 Fed.Reg. 44395 (Aug. 28, 1996). Then, in a separate volume of the August 28 issue, FDA took more than 650 additional pages to address the legal challenges to its jurisdiction and to its conduct of the rulemaking. 61 Fed.Reg. 44619 (Aug. 28, 1996).

Why FDA felt it necessary to make this heroic investment in a single rulemaking has many explanations. Without doubt, the momentous nature of the agency's initiative, coupled with the assurance that it would be challenged in court, caused the agency to take special pains. But the cases that follow leave no doubt that agencies may not assume automatic deference to their factual premises or their practical reasoning. The steps that FDA attempted to take to protect its tobacco regulations from judicial reversal surely reflected special caution but their motivation was not exceptional.

NATIONAL TIRE DEALERS & RETREADERS ASSOCIATION, INC. v. BRINEGAR

United States Court of Appeals, District of Columbia Circuit, 1974.
491 F.2d 31.

WILKEY, CIRCUIT JUDGE.

Petitioner National Tire Dealers and Retreaders Association, Inc. (NTDRA) seeks review of Federal Motor Vehicle Safety Standard No. 117. * * *

Petitioner focuses its challenge on paragraph S6.3.2 of Standard No. 117, which requires that all pneumatic passenger tires retreaded on or after 1 February 1974 have the following information *permanently* molded into or on one sidewall of the tire: size, maximum inflation pressure and load; actual number of plies or ply rating; the words "tubeless" or "tube-type," as applicable; and the words "bias/belted" or "radial," as applicable.[3] The administrative record does not adequately

3. 49 C.F.R. § 571.117a (1972) reads in pertinent part:

S6.3.2 Each retreaded pneumatic tire produced on or after [February 1, 1974] shall be permanently labeled in at least one

demonstrate that these requirements are practicable, nor does it establish any more than a remote relation between the requirements and motor vehicle safety. The Act mandates that motor vehicle safety standards promulgated thereunder be "practicable" and "meet the need for motor vehicle safety." Therefore, we vacate that portion of the Order establishing Motor Vehicle Safety Standard No. 117 which relates to permanent labeling of tire size, maximum inflation pressure, ply rating, tubeless or tube-type, and bias/belted or radial construction. However, since section 201 of the Act commands that the Secretary promulgate permanent labeling standards with respect to actual number of plies and maximum permissible load,[5] the portion of Standard No. 117 relating to those characteristics must remain in effect.[6]

* * *

The stated purpose of the National Traffic and Motor Vehicle Safety Act of 1966 is "to reduce traffic accidents and deaths and injuries to persons resulting from traffic accidents." Thus, "each * * * Federal motor vehicle safety standard * * * shall meet the need for motor vehicle safety." The Act defines "motor vehicle safety" as "the performance of motor vehicles or motor vehicle equipment in such a manner that the public is protected against *unreasonable risk* of accidents

location on the completed retreaded tire, in letters and numerals not less than three thirty-seconds of an inch that are molded into or onto the tire sidewall, with the following information:

(a) The tire's size designation;

(b) The tire's maximum permissible inflation pressure, either as it appears on the casing or as set forth in Table I;

(c) The tire's maximum load, either as it appears on the casing or as set forth in Table I;

(d) The actual number of plies, ply rating, or both;

(e) The word "tubeless" if the tire is a tubeless tire, or the words "tube-type" if the tire is a tube-type tire;

(f) The word "bias/belted" if the tire is of bias-belted construction;

(g) The word "radial" if the tire is of radial construction.

5. 15 U.S.C. § 1421 (1970):

In all standards for pneumatic tires established under subchapter I of this chapter, the Secretary shall require that tires subject thereto be permanently and conspicuously labeled with such safety information as he determines to be necessary to carry out the purposes of this chapter. Such labeling shall include—* * *

(3) the actual number of plies in the tire.

(4) the maximum permissible load for the tire. * * *

The Secretary may require that additional safety related information be disclosed to the purchaser of a tire at the time of sale of the tire.

6. We would note further that section 201 mandates permanent labeling of retreaded tires with information about "the composition of the material used in the ply of the tire." 15 U.S.C. § 1421(2) (1970). Standard No. 117, however, contains no requirement relating to ply composition. The reason for this omission is set forth in the preamble to Standard No. 117:

The proposed requirement that the tire be labeled with the generic name of its cord material is not retained. The comments have argued, and NHTSA agrees, that in the case of retreaded tires this information is not substantially related to safety. This, combined with the fact that it appears only on certain casings, where it must if it is to be relabeled, has convinced the NHTSA that at present the requirement should not be included in the standard.

37 Fed.Reg. 5952 (1972). Since Congress apparently concluded that permanent labeling of ply material is safety-related, the Secretary was powerless to conclude otherwise and thus erred in omitting a ply material requirement from Standard No. 117.

occurring as a result of the design, construction or performance of motor vehicles and is also protected against *unreasonable risk* of death or injury to persons in the event accidents do occur. * * * "

The general requirement that retreaded tires be labeled with the items of information specified in paragraph S6.3.2 of Standard No. 117 clearly bears a substantial relation to the Act's purpose of achieving motor vehicle safety. * * *

* * *

But the issue here is what relation *permanent* labeling has to avoidance of those hazards. Petitioner recognizes the importance of labeling retreaded tires with the information required by Standard No. 117, and states:

> The retreading industry can and will record such information as is available on a label affixed to the retreaded tire so that the information will be known to the consumer at the time of purchase.

However, petitioner asserts that *the Secretary "has not found* that the information required by S6.3.2 can meet the need for motor vehicle safety *only if it is permanently labeled into the retreaded tire*."

A permanent labeling requirement is clearly unnecessary to protect original purchasers of retreaded tires. A non-permanent, affixed label can supply such purchasers with all the information specified in Standard No. 117 and thus permit them to select tires of proper size and construction. Therefore, lack of permanent labeling could become a factor affecting safety only in the event that a retreaded tire is resold or put to some different use after the affixed label has worn off. The Secretary raised this possibility in the preamble to Standard No. 117:

> Tires * * * may be subject to many applications during their useful life. They are transferred from wheel to wheel and from vehicle to vehicle, and each time this takes place the information on the tire sidewall becomes important. Permanent labeling is therefore required if the information is to perform its function, as it can be readily assumed that affixed labels will last little longer than the first time the tire is mounted.

The Secretary has supplied no illustrations or references to the record to amplify these observations. We can hypothesize two situations in which lack of permanent labeling could conceivably affect safety:

1. An original purchaser of retreaded tires wishes to replace one or more of those tires, and he needs to match up his new tire or tires with the remaining retreads.

2. Someone wishes to purchase retreaded tires from the original purchaser or from some other second-hand source.

There is no suggestion in the record or briefs of how frequently these hypothetical situations arise. They might occur so rarely that a costly and burdensome permanent labeling requirement geared to ensure safety in such situations is unreasonable. Furthermore, it is not clear that a second-hand purchaser of retreads or an original owner who seeks replacements is dependent on the tires' labeling for information necessary to proper match-ups, inflation, and loading. The Secretary's brief observes that an expert can determine many of the critical characteristics of a tire by mere inspection. Therefore, even in the hypothetical situations posed above, a permanent labeling requirement may not make a significant contribution to the Act's goal of enhancing the safety of motor vehicles. If there is a significant nexus between the permanent labeling requirement of Standard No. 117 and the goal of safety, it does not appear in the briefs or in the record of the rule-making proceedings.

As noted above, however, section 201 of the Act mandates that new and retreaded pneumatic tires be "permanently and conspicuously labeled" with safety information which the Secretary "determines to be necessary to carry out the purposes" of the Act. The section further provides, "Such labeling shall include * * * (3) the actual number of plies in the tire. (4) the maximum permissible load for the tire. * * * " Thus, Congress has determined that permanent labeling of ply and load information on retreaded tires bears a significant relation to safety. Although our discussion of the relation of Standard No. 117 to safety applies with equal logic to permanent labeling of ply and load information, we must faithfully carry out the express mandate of Congress. No administrative procedure test applies to an act of Congress. Consequently, that portion of Standard No. 117 relating to permanent labeling of ply and load information must stand.

The apparently remote relationship between the permanent labeling requirements of Standard No. 117 and the goal of motor vehicle safety might be tolerable if those standards imposed no significant burden on the tire retreading industry. However, there are numerous indications in the record that permanent labeling of retreaded tires with the information required by Standard No. 117 would be economically unfeasible. In the face of these indications, the Secretary offers mere assertions, unsupported by any citations to the record, that the requirements are practicable. Therefore, the Secretary's Order establishing the permanent labeling requirements of Standard No. 117 is an "arbitrary" agency action that must be set aside under section 10(e) of the APA.

Section 103(a) of the Act provides that each "Federal motor vehicle safety standard shall be practicable. * * * " Section 103(f) further provides, "In prescribing standards under this section, the Secretary shall * * * (3) consider whether any such proposed standard is reasonable, practicable and appropriate for the particular type of motor vehicle or item of motor vehicle equipment for which it is prescribed." * * *

The record in the case at bar contains considerable comment to the effect that the permanent labeling required by Standard No. 117 would be unreasonably costly and economically unfeasible. The basic problem is that most tire casings received by retreaders either do not bear permanent labeling or the information required by Standard No. 117 or are labeled in a location where the markings are subject to obliteration during the retreading process. While permanent labeling of new tires has been required for several years by Motor Vehicle Safety Standard No. 109, the *location* of the labeling was not specified until the Department of Transportation promulgated an amendment, effective 1 July 1973, which requires that one sidewall bear the requisite information between the "maximum section width and bead." This belated recognition of the practicalities of the retreading process will ensure that the markings are not buffed off during retreading so that, eventually, as the Department explained, "retreaders need not relabel tires in meeting the requirements of Standard No. 117."

The amended requirements for new tire labeling have little impact on the current inventories of new tire casings maintained by the retreading industry. It has been estimated that only about one third of the casings presently in supply bear the requisite labeling in a location where it is not subject to buffing off during the retreading process. Therefore, Standard No. 117 would force the retreading industry to choose between two equally undesirable alternatives. First, retreaders might use only those new tire casings that bear the requisite information in a permanent location. This course of action would necessarily result in a two-thirds reduction in the volume of retreaded tire production and inevitably cause severe economic dislocation in the industry. Second, retreaders could mold the required information into the tire sidewalls during the retreading process. However, the comments of retreaders in the administrative record indicate that this, too, is far from an economically feasible alternative.

Apparently the retreading process cannot be economically adapted to labeling each tire permanently with the seven items of information required by Standard No. 117. * * * In order to label tires permanently with the requisite information during this process "it would be necessary for an employee to work with handtools on a mold that would have a temperature somewhere between 250 and 300 degrees F., exposing him to the danger of burns in an effort to change the varied plates with this information on it as each tire is changed in the mold." Altering the mold plates in this fashion would be necessary for almost every tire run through the production lines, since the size, number of plies, construction, maximum pressure, and other characteristics vary from tire to tire. * * *

One retreader has summarized the economic unfeasibility of the permanent labeling requirements specified in Standard No. 117:

> As an experiment, we ran a series of casings that had labeling in the shoulder area that would be removed in the retreading process. Our experience has indicated that the best we can do with a relabeling program is to be 80% effective, and our additional cost is more than $2.50 per retread. This is an increase of 30%.

Of course, the court need not accept at face value the self-serving comments of interested members of the retreading industry. However, such comments raise serious doubts about the practicability of Standard

No. 117. In the face of these doubts, the Secretary offers only unsupported and unconvincing assertions that the permanent labeling requirements are practicable and economically feasible, and, in so doing, attempts to equate the data required for safety with that already required for recordkeeping.[40] However, the information required by the Identification and Record Keeping Regulations is significantly different. It consists of such items as the name of the manufacturer and week in which the tire was retreaded. With the exception of the latter, these items do not vary from tire to tire as do the items specified in Standard No. 117; the week of retreading can easily be changed at the start of each week while the retreading molds are cool. The Administration's further suggestion that casings could be sorted into uniform groups before retreading to minimize the frequency of alterations in the retreading mold appears reasonable, but there is nothing in the record to indicate whether such a sorting process would be practicable and not unreasonably costly.

Ultimately the Secretary's position rests on the following statement that appears in the Administration's Denial of Petitions for Reconsideration:

> Many of the petitions request the NHTSA to furnish data supporting specific decisions and determinations reflected in the standard. The decisions and determinations embodied in this standard are based on all the information at the agency's disposal, together with the informed judgment and expertise of agency personnel. Documentary materials relating to NHTSA decisions regarding the standard are part of the public docket. The agency is not obliged by law, nor does it consider it appropriate, to categorize or interpret those records as supporting particular statements or decisions made on rule-making issuances.

While it is true that an agency may act after informal rule-making procedures "upon the basis of information available in its own files, and upon the knowledge and expertise of the agency," in the case at bar the Secretary's allusions to information and knowledge outside the record are unpersuasive in light of the powerful doubts raised by the on-the-record comments of petitioner and others about the practicability of the permanent labeling requirements. The Secretary's statement of the reasons for his conclusion that the requirements are practicable is not so inherently plausible that the court can accept it on the agency's mere *ipse dixit*. We are compelled to conclude that the Secretary's practicabili-

40. In the preamble to Standard No. 117, the National Highway Traffic Safety Administration stated:

> The NHTSA disagrees with industry claims that permanent labeling presents unreasonable technical problems. *Methods for permanent labeling developed for compliance with the Tire Identification and Recordkeeping Regulations (49 CFR Part 574) can be readily adapted to meet these requirements.* In fact, of all the information required in today's amendment, only the "size" and "maximum load rating" will vary to a significant amount from casing to casing. Each of the other items of required information can be applied uniformly to large groups of casings and need not be changed from tire to tire if proper sorting is done before retreading occurs.

37 Fed.Reg. 5952 (1972) (emphasis supplied.) * * *

ty determination was arbitrary and thus requires us to set aside Standard No. 117 under section 10(e) of the APA.[45]

* * *

Notes

1. *Substance? Procedure? Or, Both?* The *Brinegar* decision might be explained in either substantive or procedural terms. Either the Secretary failed to marshal evidence that permanent labeling of retreaded tires would be "practicable" (substantive failure), or he failed to respond (procedural failure) to the retreaders' claims that permanent labeling would not be "Practicable." But perhaps this is backwards. Failure to marshal sufficient evidence could be characterized as a procedural lapse, while declaring labeling to be practicable in the teeth of uncontradicted evidence of impracticability, might be thought to be substantively irrational. In other words, substance and procedure tend to merge in rationality review of rules.

Does this matter? As was suggested earlier, the proceduralization of rationality review may preserve judicial capital. It may also preserve agency policy discretion. The conclusion of invalidity in *Brinegar* leads only to a remand for reconsideration. With additional support and explanation the agency is free to issue the rule without substantive change.

2. *What Distinguishes* Brinegar *From* Auto Parts? The Secretary of Transportation followed similar procedures in the two cases and, according to Judge Wilkey, the court applied the same standard of review. Judge Robinson was the only member of the court of appeals who participated in both cases; and in a separate opinion he explained his concurrence in *Brinegar* as follows (491 F.2d at 41–43):

> The problem * * * is that the Secretary's standard calls for permanent labeling on each retreaded tire of six individual characteristics of that tire. The methodology of permanent labeling on which the industry settled is insertion into the retread matrix of a slug that accomplishes the labeling. The number of combinations of characteristics is vast; a change of slugs becomes necessary each time a change of a single characteristic occurs, and the standard would currently intercept an estimated 20 million of the tires now retreaded annually. The administrative record echoes the many complaints that operational and economic havoc in the retreading industry will be the inevitable result.
>
> In this milieu, I agree that the Secretary was summoned to focus on these realities. The Act directs the Secretary to consider, among other things, whether standards he proposes are "practicable," and as the

45. It must be noted that by enacting section 201 of the Motor Vehicle Safety Act, * * * Congress apparently concluded that permanent labeling of retreads with the actual number of plies and maximum permissible load would be practicable. Therefore, we are powerless to overturn the corresponding portions of Safety Standard No. 117 on the ground of impracticability. Consequently, retreaders will be compelled permanently to label their tires with the actual number of plies, maximum permissible load and, pursuant to section 201(2) of the Act, "the composition of the material used in the ply of the tire." While permanent labeling of these three items will likely be difficult and costly for retreaders, it should not be as burdensome as the labeling of all seven items specified in Standard No. 117 would be.

legislative history denotes, it does not suffice to view merely the "technological ability to achieve the goal of a particular standard." "[E]conomic factors" as well must be scrutinized, and these include "reasonableness of cost" and "feasibility." * * *

* * * One may search the record before us for acceptable support for the Secretary's conclusion that the test of practicality was met, but the search will be in vain. That, in my view, is the fatal flaw in the Secretary's case.

3. *Judicial Scrutiny of Congressional Judgments.* The inference is strong that the retreaders' primary objections were to the size and maximum load requirements which, as the Secretary acknowledged, may preclude presorting of casings into large groups. But these parts of the rule are upheld. What accounts for the court's contrasting treatment of these requirements? Did Congress make a more convincing factual case for its maximum load requirement than the Secretary made for permanent size labeling?

4. *Arbitrary or Capricious v. Substantial Evidence Review.* The *Brinegar* case was only one of many decisions that appeared to challenge the conventional assumption that review for arbitrariness was less demanding than review for substantial evidence. See, e.g., *Bunny Bear, Inc. v. Peterson,* 473 F.2d 1002 (1st Cir.1973). This assumption has been characterized as mistaken:

> The essential constraint of the "substantial evidence" test is not that it requires a higher degree of support for an agency determination (the arbitrary and capricious standard itself would probably be violated by a determination made on the basis of insubstantial evidence) but rather, that it requires this support to be contained within the confines of the public record made pursuant to the provisions of sections 556 and 557 of the Administrative Procedure Act.

Antonin Scalia & Frank Goodman, *Procedural Aspects of the Consumer Product Safety Act,* 20 U.C.L.A.L.Rev. 899, 934 (1973).

Several statutes passed by Congress during the 1970s displaced the APA's apparent symmetry between the procedures required for rulemaking and the applicable standard for review. But far from accepting the proposition that the "arbitrary or capricious" standard can be as demanding as the "substantial evidence" test, Congress has generally assumed that the latter *is* more rigorous—and with that objective in mind specifically incorporated it in several statutes that authorize rules to be made through informal rulemaking. One example is the Consumer Product Safety Act, 15 U.S.C. § 2051 *et seq.*, which empowers the Consumer Product Safety Commission to adopt product safety rules through notice and comment procedures, with the added requirement that interested parties be allowed to make oral representations, but specifies that such rules must be "supported by substantial evidence on the record as a whole." The Occupational Safety and Health Act, 29 U.S.C. § 651 *et seq.*, similarly authorizes essentially informal rulemaking while prescribing substantial evidence review. This hybrid was the product of a compromise between those members of Congress who wanted informal rulemaking with review under the arbitrary or capricious standard and those, including many who opposed the basic legislation, who held out for formal procedures with substantial evidence review. See *Industrial Union*

Department, AFL–CIO v. Hodgson, 499 F.2d 467, 469 (D.C.Cir.1974), where Judge McGowan lamented that "the federal courts * * * surely have some claim to be spared additional burdens deriving from the illogic of legislative compromise."

MOTOR VEHICLE MANUFACTURERS ASSOCIATION OF U.S., INC. v. STATE FARM MUTUAL AUTOMOBILE INSURANCE CO.

Supreme Court of the United States, 1983.
463 U.S. 29, 103 S.Ct. 2856, 77 L.Ed.2d 443.

JUSTICE WHITE delivered the opinion of the Court.

* * * While a consensus exists that the current loss of life on our highways is unacceptably high, improving safety does not admit to easy solution. * * * Before changes in automobile design could be mandated, the effectiveness of these changes had to be studied, their costs examined, and public acceptance considered. This task called for considerable expertise and Congress responded by enacting the National Traffic and Motor Vehicle Safety Act of 1966, (Act), 15 U.S.C. §§ 1381 *et seq.* The Act * * * directs the Secretary of Transportation or his delegate to issue motor vehicle safety standards that "shall be practicable, shall meet the need for motor vehicle safety, and shall be stated in objective terms." * * *

The Act also authorizes judicial review under the provisions of the Administrative Procedure Act (APA) of all "orders establishing, amending, or revoking a Federal motor vehicle safety standard." Under this authority, we review today whether NHTSA acted arbitrarily and capriciously in revoking the requirement in Motor Vehicle Safety Standard 208 that new motor vehicles produced after September 1982 be equipped with passive restraints to protect the safety of the occupants of the vehicle in the event of a collision. Briefly summarized, we hold that the agency failed to present an adequate basis and explanation for rescinding the passive restraint requirement * * *.

As originally issued by the Department of Transportation in 1967, Standard 208 simply required the installation of seatbelts in all automobiles. It soon became apparent that the level of seatbelt use was too low to reduce traffic injuries to an acceptable level. The Department therefore began consideration of "passive occupant restraint systems"—devices that do not depend for their effectiveness upon any action taken by the occupant except that necessary to operate the vehicle. Two types of automatic crash protection emerged: automatic seatbelts and airbags. * * * The life-saving potential of these devices was immediately recognized, and in 1977, after substantial on-the-road experience with both devices, it was estimated by NHTSA that passive restraints could prevent approximately 12,000 deaths and over 100,000 serious injuries annually.

In 1969, the Department formally proposed a standard requiring the installation of passive restraints, thereby commencing a lengthy series of proceedings. In 1970, the agency revised Standard 208 to include passive protection requirements, and in 1972, the agency amended the standard to require full passive protection for all front seat occupants of vehicles manufactured after August 15, 1975. In the interim, vehicles built between August 1973 and August 1975 were to carry either passive restraints or lap and shoulder belts coupled with an "ignition interlock" that would prevent starting the vehicle if the belts were not connected. On review, the agency's decision to require passive restraints was found to be supported by "substantial evidence" and upheld. *Chrysler Corp. v. Dep't of Transportation*, 472 F.2d 659 (C.A.6 1972).

In preparing for the upcoming model year, most car makers chose the "ignition interlock" option, a decision which was highly unpopular, and led Congress to amend the Act to prohibit a motor vehicle safety standard from requiring or permitting compliance by means of an ignition interlock or a continuous buzzer designed to indicate that safety belts were not in use. The 1974 Amendments also provided that any safety standard that could be satisfied by a system other than seatbelts would have to be submitted to Congress where it could be vetoed by concurrent resolution of both houses. 15 U.S.C. § 1410b(b)(2).[6]

The effective date for mandatory passive restraint systems was extended for a year until August 31, 1976. But in June 1976, Secretary of Transportation William Coleman initiated a new rulemaking on the issue. After hearing testimony and reviewing written comments, Coleman extended the optional alternatives indefinitely and suspended the passive restraint requirement. Although he found passive restraints technologically and economically feasible, the Secretary based his decision on the expectation that there would be widespread public resistance to the new systems. He instead proposed a demonstration project involving up to 500,000 cars installed with passive restraints, in order to smooth the way for public acceptance of mandatory passive restraints at a later date.

Coleman's successor as Secretary of Transportation disagreed. Within months of assuming office, Secretary Brock Adams decided that the demonstration project was unnecessary. He issued a new mandatory passive restraint regulation, known as Modified Standard 208. The Modified Standard mandated the phasing in of passive restraints beginning with large cars in model year 1982 and extending to all cars by model year 1984. The two principal systems that would satisfy the Standard were airbags and passive belts; the choice of which system to install was left to the manufacturers. In *Pacific Legal Foundation v. Dep't of Transportation*, 593 F.2d 1338 (C.A.D.C.), *cert. denied*, 444 U.S. 830 (1979), the Court of Appeals upheld Modified Standard 208 as a rational, nonarbitrary regulation consistent with the agency's mandate

6. * * * [T]he issue was not submitted to Congress until a passive restraint requirement was reimposed by Secretary Adams in 1977. To comply with the Amendments, NHTSA proposed new warning systems to replace the prohibited continuous buzzers. More significantly, NHTSA was forced to rethink an earlier decision which contemplated use of the interlocks in tandem with detachable belts.

under the Act. The standard also survived scrutiny by Congress, which did not exercise its authority under the legislative veto provision of the 1974 Amendments.

Over the next several years, the automobile industry geared up to comply with Modified Standard 208. * * * In February 1981, however, Secretary of Transportation Andrew Lewis reopened the rulemaking due to changed economic circumstances and, in particular, the difficulties of the automobile industry. Two months later, the agency ordered a one-year delay in the application of the standard to large cars, extending the deadline to September 1982, and at the same time, proposed the possible rescission of the entire standard. After receiving written comments and holding public hearings, NHTSA issued a final rule that rescinded the passive restraint requirement contained in Modified Standard 208.

In a statement explaining the rescission, NHTSA maintained that it was no longer able to find, as it had in 1977, that the automatic restraint requirement would produce significant safety benefits. This judgment reflected not a change of opinion on the effectiveness of the technology, but a change in plans by the automobile industry. In 1977, the agency had assumed that airbags would be installed in 60% of all new cars and automatic seatbelts in 40%. By 1981 it became apparent that automobile manufacturers planned to install the automatic seatbelts in approximately 99% of the new cars. For this reason, the life-saving potential of airbags would not be realized. Moreover, it now appeared that the overwhelming majority of passive belts planned to be installed by manufacturers could be detached easily and left that way permanently. Passive belts, once detached, then required "the same type of affirmative action that is the stumbling block to obtaining high usage levels of manual belts." For this reason, the agency concluded that there was no longer a basis for reliably predicting that the standard would lead to any significant increased usage of restraints at all.

In view of the possibly minimal safety benefits, the automatic restraint requirement no longer was reasonable or practicable in the agency's view. The requirement would require approximately $1 billion to implement and the agency did not believe it would be reasonable to impose such substantial costs on manufacturers and consumers without more adequate assurance that sufficient safety benefits would accrue. In addition, NHTSA concluded that automatic restraints might have an adverse effect on the public's attitude toward safety. Given the high expense and limited benefits of detachable belts, NHTSA feared that many consumers would regard the standard as an instance of ineffective regulation, adversely affecting the public's view of safety regulation and, in particular, "poisoning popular sentiment toward efforts to improve occupant restraint systems in the future."

State Farm Mutual Automobile Insurance Co. and the National Association of Independent Insurers filed petitions for review of NHTSA's rescission of the passive restraint standard. The United States Court of Appeals for the District of Columbia Circuit held that the agency's rescission of the passive restraint requirement was arbitrary and capricious. 680 F.2d 206 (1982). * * *

* * *

* * * Both the Motor Vehicle Safety Act and the 1974 Amendments concerning occupant crash protection standards indicate that motor vehicle safety standards are to be promulgated under the informal rulemaking procedures of § 553 of the Administrative Procedure Act. The agency's action in promulgating such standards therefore may be set aside if found to be "arbitrary, capricious, an abuse of discretion, or otherwise not in accordance with law." We believe that the rescission or modification of an occupant protection standard is subject to the same test. * * *

Petitioner Motor Vehicle Manufacturers Association (MVMA) disagrees, contending that the rescission of an agency rule should be judged by the same standard a court would use to judge an agency's refusal to promulgate a rule in the first place—a standard Petitioner believes considerably narrower than the traditional arbitrary and capricious test and "close to the borderline of nonreviewability." We reject this view. The Motor Vehicle Safety Act expressly equates orders "revoking" and "establishing" safety standards; neither that Act nor the APA suggests that revocations are to be treated as refusals to promulgate standards. Petitioner's view would render meaningless Congress' authorization for judicial review of orders revoking safety rules. Moreover, the revocation of an extant regulation is substantially different than a failure to act. Revocation constitutes a reversal of the agency's former views as to the proper course. A "settled course of behavior embodies the agency's informed judgment that, by pursuing that course, it will carry out the policies committed to it by Congress. There is, then, at least a presumption that those policies will be carried out best if the settled rule is adhered to." Accordingly, an agency changing its course by rescinding a rule is obligated to supply a reasoned analysis for the change beyond that which may be required when an agency does not act in the first instance.

In so holding, we fully recognize that "regulatory agencies do not establish rules of conduct to last forever," and that an agency must be given ample latitude to "adapt their rules and policies to the demands of changing circumstances." But the forces of change do not always or necessarily point in the direction of deregulation. In the abstract, there is no more reason to presume that changing circumstances require the rescission of prior action, instead of a revision in or even the extension of current regulation. If Congress established a presumption from which judicial review should start, that presumption—contrary to petitioners' views—is not *against* safety regulation, but *against* changes in current policy that are not justified by the rulemaking record. While the removal of a regulation may not entail the monetary expenditures and other costs of enacting a new standard, and accordingly, it may be easier for an agency to justify a deregulatory action, the direction in which an agency chooses to move does not alter the standard of judicial review established by law.

The Department of Transportation accepts the applicability of the "arbitrary and capricious" standard. It argues that under this standard, a reviewing court may not set aside an agency rule that is rational, based on consideration of the relevant factors and within the scope of the authority delegated to the agency by the statute. We do not disagree with this formulation.[9] * * *

* * *

The ultimate question before us is whether NHTSA's rescission of the passive restraint requirement of Standard 208 was arbitrary and capricious. We conclude, as did the Court of Appeals, that it was. We also conclude, but for somewhat different reasons, that further consideration of the issue by the agency is therefore required. * * *

The first and most obvious reason for finding the rescission arbitrary and capricious is that NHTSA apparently gave no consideration whatever to modifying the Standard to require that airbag technology be utilized. Standard 208 sought to achieve automatic crash protection by requiring automobile manufacturers to install either of two passive restraint devices: airbags or automatic seatbelts. There was no suggestion in the long rulemaking process that led to Standard 208 that if only one of these options were feasible, no passive restraint standard should be promulgated. Indeed, the agency's original proposed standard contemplated the installation of inflatable restraints in all cars. Automatic belts were added as a means of complying with the standard because they were believed to be as effective as airbags in achieving the goal of occupant crash protection. At that time, the passive belt approved by the agency could not be detached. Only later, at a manufacturer's behest, did the agency approve of the detachability feature—and only after assurances that the feature would not compromise the safety benefits of the restraint. Although it was then foreseen that 60% of the new cars would contain airbags and 40% would have automatic seatbelts, the ratio between the two was not significant as long as the passive belt would also assure greater passenger safety.

The agency has now determined that the detachable automatic belts will not attain anticipated safety benefits because so many individuals will detach the mechanism. Even if this conclusion were acceptable in its entirety, standing alone it would not justify any more than an amendment of Standard 208 to disallow compliance by means of the one technology which will not provide effective passenger protection. It does not cast doubt on the need for a passive restraint standard or upon the efficacy of airbag technology. * * * Given the effectiveness ascribed to

9. The Department of Transportation suggests that the arbitrary and capricious standard requires no more than the minimum rationality a statute must bear in order to withstand analysis under the Due Process Clause. We do not view as equivalent the presumption of constitutionality afforded legislation drafted by Congress and the presumption of regularity afforded an agency in fulfilling its statutory mandate.

airbag technology by the agency, the mandate of the Safety Act to achieve traffic safety would suggest that the logical response to the faults of detachable seatbelts would be to require the installation of airbags. At the very least this alternative way of achieving the objectives of the Act should have been addressed and adequate reasons given for its abandonment. But the agency not only did not require compliance through airbags, it did not even consider the possibility in its 1981 rulemaking. Not one sentence of its rulemaking statement discusses the airbags-only option. * * *

The automobile industry has opted for the passive belt over the airbag, but surely it is not enough that the regulated industry has eschewed a given safety device. * * *

Although the agency did not address the mandatory airbags option the Court of Appeals noted that "airbags seem to have none of the problems that NHTSA identified in passive seatbelts," petitioners recite a number of difficulties that they believe would be posed by a mandatory airbag standard. * * * But these are not the agency's reasons for rejecting a mandatory airbag standard. Not having discussed the possibility, the agency submitted no reasons at all. The short—and sufficient—answer to petitioners' submission is that the courts may not accept appellate counsel's *post hoc* rationalizations for agency action. * * *

* * * It is true that a rulemaking "cannot be found wanting simply because the agency failed to include every alternative device and thought conceivable by the mind of man * * * regardless of how uncommon or unknown that alternative may have been. * * *" But the airbag is more than a policy alternative to the passive restraint standard; it is a technological alternative within the ambit of the existing standard. We hold only that given the judgment made in 1977 that airbags are an effective and cost-beneficial life-saving technology, the mandatory passive-restraint rule may not be abandoned without any consideration whatsoever of an airbags-only requirement.

Although the issue is closer, we also find that the agency was too quick to dismiss the safety benefits of automatic seatbelts. NHTSA's critical finding was that, in light of the industry's plans to install readily detachable passive belts, it could not reliably predict "even a 5 percentage point increase as the minimum level of expected usage increase." * * *

* * * We agree with petitioners that just as an agency reasonably may decline to issue a safety standard if it is uncertain about its efficacy, an agency may also revoke a standard on the basis of serious uncertainties if supported by the record and reasonably explained. Rescission of the passive restraint requirement would not be arbitrary and capricious simply because there was no evidence in direct support of the agency's conclusion. It is not infrequent that the available data does not settle a regulatory issue and the agency must then exercise its judgment in moving from the facts and probabilities on the record to a policy

conclusion. Recognizing that policymaking in a complex society must account for uncertainty, however, does not imply that it is sufficient for an agency to merely recite the terms "substantial uncertainty" as a justification for its actions. The agency must explain the evidence which is available, and must offer a "rational connection between the facts found and the choice made." * * *

In this case, the agency's explanation for rescission of the passive restraint requirement is *not* sufficient to enable us to conclude that the rescission was the product of reasoned decisionmaking. To reach this conclusion, we do not upset the agency's view of the facts, but we do appreciate the limitations of this record in supporting the agency's decision. We start with the accepted ground that if used, seatbelts unquestionably would save many thousands of lives and would prevent tens of thousands of crippling injuries. * * * [T]he safety benefits of wearing seatbelts are not in doubt and it is not challenged that were those benefits to accrue, the monetary costs of implementing the standard would be easily justified. We move next to the fact that there is no direct evidence in support of the agency's finding that detachable automatic belts cannot be predicted to yield a substantial increase in usage. The empirical evidence on the record, consisting of surveys of drivers of automobiles equipped with passive belts, reveals more than a doubling of the usage rate experienced with manual belts. Much of the agency's rulemaking statement—and much of the controversy in this case—centers on the conclusions that should be drawn from these studies. The agency maintained that the doubling of seatbelt usage in these studies could not be extrapolated to an across-the-board mandatory standard because the passive seatbelts were guarded by ignition interlocks and purchasers of the tested cars are somewhat atypical. Respondents insist these studies demonstrate that Modified Standard 208 will substantially increase seatbelt usage. We believe that it is within the agency's discretion to pass upon the generalizability of these field studies. This is precisely the type of issue which rests within the expertise of NHTSA, and upon which a reviewing court must be most hesitant to intrude.

But accepting the agency's view of the field tests on passive restraints indicates only that there is no reliable real-world experience that usage rates will substantially increase. * * * [S]tatements that passive belts will not yield substantial increases in seatbelt usage apparently take no account of the critical difference between detachable automatic belts and current manual belts. A detached passive belt does require an affirmative act to reconnect it, but—unlike a manual seat belt—the passive belt, once reattached, will continue to function automatically unless again disconnected. Thus, inertia—a factor which the agency's own studies have found significant in explaining the current low usage rates for seatbelts—works in *favor* of, not *against*, use of the protective device. Since 20 to 50% of motorists currently wear seatbelts on some occasions, there would seen to be grounds to believe that seatbelt use by occasional users will be substantially increased by the detachable passive belts. Whether this is in fact the case is a matter for the agency to decide, but it must bring its expertise to bear on the question.

The agency is correct to look at the costs as well as the benefits of Standard 208. * * * When the agency reexamines its findings as to the likely increase in seatbelt usage, it must also reconsider its judgment of the reasonableness of the monetary and other costs associated with the Standard. In reaching its judgment, NHTSA should bear in mind that Congress intended safety to be the preeminent factor under the Motor Vehicle Safety Act. * * *

The agency also failed to articulate a basis for not requiring nondetachable belts under Standard 208. It is argued that the concern of the agency with the easy detachability of the currently favored design would be readily solved by a continuous passive belt, which allows the occupant to "spool out" the belt and create the necessary slack for easy extrication from the vehicle. * * *

By failing to analyze the continuous seatbelts in its own right, the agency has failed to offer the rational connection between facts and judgment required to pass muster under the arbitrary and capricious standard. We agree with the Court of Appeals that NHTSA did not suggest that the emergency release mechanisms used in nondetachable belts are any less effective for emergency egress than the buckle release system used in detachable belts. In 1978, when General Motors obtained the agency's approval to install a continuous passive belt, it assured the agency that nondetachable belts with spool releases were as safe as detachable belts with buckle releases. NHTSA was satisfied that this belt design assured easy extricability: "the agency does not believe that the use of [such] release mechanisms will cause serious occupant egress problems * * *." While the agency is entitled to change its view on the acceptability of continuous passive belts, it is obligated to explain its reasons for doing so.

The agency also failed to offer any explanation why a continuous passive belt would engender the same adverse public reaction as the ignition interlock, and, as the Court of Appeals concluded, "every indication in the record points the other way." We see no basis for equating the two devices: the continuous belt, unlike the ignition interlock, does not interfere with the operation of the vehicle. More importantly, it is the agency's responsibility, not this Court's, to explain its decision.

"An agency's view of what is in the public interest may change, either with or without a change in circumstances. But an agency changing its course must supply a reasoned analysis. * * * " We do not accept all of the reasoning of the Court of Appeals but we do conclude that the agency has failed to supply the requisite "reasoned analysis" in this case. Accordingly, we vacate the judgment of the Court of Appeals and remand the case to that court with directions to remand the matter to the NHTSA for further consideration consistent with this opinion.

So ordered.

JUSTICE REHNQUIST, with whom THE CHIEF JUSTICE, JUSTICE POWELL, and JUSTICE O'CONNOR join, concurring in part and dissenting in part.

* * * I agree that, since the airbag and continuous spool automatic seatbelt were explicitly approved in the standard the agency was rescinding, the agency should explain why it declined to leave those requirements intact. In this case, the agency gave no explanation at all. Of course, if the agency can provide a rational explanation, it may adhere to its decision to rescind the entire standard.

I do not believe, however, that NHTSA's view of detachable automatic seatbelts was arbitrary and capricious. * * *

* * * It seems to me that the agency's explanation, while by no means a model, is adequate. The agency acknowledged that there would probably be some increase in belt usage, but concluded that the increase would be small and not worth the cost of mandatory detachable automatic belts. The agency's obligation is to articulate a "rational connection between the facts found and the choice made." I believe it has met this standard. * * *

The agency's changed view of the standard seems to be related to the election of a new President of a different political party. It is readily apparent that the responsible members of one administration may consider public resistance and uncertainties to be more important than do their counterparts in a previous administration. A change in administration brought about by the people casting their votes is a perfectly reasonable basis for an executive agency's reappraisal of the costs and benefits of its programs and regulations. As long as the agency remains within the bounds established by Congress,* it is entitled to assess administrative records and evaluate priorities in light of the philosophy of the administration.

Notes

1. *Legitimacy of Political Justifications*. As Justice Rehnquist's opinion intimates, rescission of the passive restraint standard was proposed by the Reagan Administration as part of a larger package of "regulatory relief" for the automobile industry. See GEORGE C. EADS & MICHAEL FIX, RELIEF OR REFORM?: REAGAN'S REGULATORY DILEMMA 125–33 (1984). This reason for the action was only hinted at in NHTSA's statement of basis and purpose accompanying rescission of the passive restraints rule. Apparently, the Administrator did not believe that he could simply say: "There has been an election since this rule was promulgated. The Carter administration thought passive restraints were a good idea; we do not. This disagreement reflects a fundamental difference in ideology. When in doubt the Carter administration chose to pursue protection of the public safety, notwithstanding the substantial economic costs and the intrusions on individual choice that such a posture

* Of course, a new administration may not choose not to enforce laws of which it does not approve, or to ignore statutory standards in carrying out its regulatory functions. But in this case, as the Court correctly concludes, Congress has not required the agency to require passive restraints.

entailed. Faced with these competing considerations, we make the contrary choice." Why should such an explanation not suffice to justify an essentially legislative decision?

2. *Scope of Secretary's Discretion Under the Safety Act.* In his 1976 notice of proposed rulemaking (NPRM), Secretary Coleman listed several "issues to be addressed" in the passive restraint proceedings. He described one issue in the following terms:

> The goal of motor vehicle safety expressed in the statute is clear and unequivocal. The question arises, however, as to the precise nature of the government's duty in this area and how to achieve the important end of motor vehicle safety while preserving, to the extent possible, both individual freedom of choice and the role of the marketplace in making economic decisions. In the democratic society in which we live, I believe it is my responsibility as a Federal official to consider these important concerns when prescribing safety standards.
>
> Under the terms of the Safety Act, the Federal government's duty in prescribing safety standards is to protect the public "against unreasonable risk of death or injury to persons in the event accidents do occur." I believe that what constitutes an "unreasonable" risk of death or injury is a difficult but critical issue. * * *
>
> In considering a mandate of any particular crash protection system, such as passive restraints, we are talking about government regulations which restrict individuals' freedom to choose the degree of safety protection they want and how much they are willing to pay for it. Individuals should be able to exercise some freedom of choice about how much they are willing to pay for safety protection in private transportation systems. Those who put a premium on freedom of choice contend that is not the role of the Federal government to protect citizens absolutely from deaths and injuries in automotive accidents. Rather, government should only ensure that adequate protection is provided which individuals can avail themselves of if they so choose. On the other hand, the stated purpose of the Safety Act is unequivocally "to reduce deaths and injuries to persons resulting from traffic accidents." While safety standards must be "reasonable," according to the statute, individual freedom of choice is not one of the statutorily explicit prescribed considerations and, arguably, should not be allowed to interfere arbitrarily with the basic purposes of the Act.
>
> Mandating passive restraints in motor vehicles might create, additionally, a problem of equity. The issuance of a passive restraint standard will result in the manufacture of vehicles equipped with air bags or passive belts rather than lap and shoulder seat belts. These passive restraint-equipped vehicles will cost more, but, in tests to date, have been found to provide no materially greater protection to those individuals who already use lap and shoulder seat belts. Nevertheless, these individuals will have to pay more for their automobiles, without any measurable benefit, to help provide passive restraints to those who choose not to wear seat belts. Thus, those who currently wear seat belts would be forced to subsidize those who do not. How public policy should

> deal with such a subsidy is an issue upon which I would welcome comment.
>
> Government regulation in the safety area, as elsewhere, tends to limit the role of the marketplace in making economic decisions, and thereby also to inhibit innovation. Certainly, mandating passive restraints does not comport with the ideal of a free enterprise economy. On the other hand, there are limitations to the benefits that the free market can provide. Some people supported the original passage of the Safety Act because they concluded that the traditional marketplace mechanism was not effective in satisfying our society's need for automotive safety. It is difficult to believe, for instance, that there would be seat belts in every car today if their installation had had to rely on the demands of the marketplace. The extent to which Federal regulations governing occupant crash protection should strive to preserve the role of the marketplace is an issue upon which I invite discussion.

41 Fed.Reg. 24,071 (June 14, 1976).

Suppose NHTSA Administrator Peck had wanted to rely on lack of "unreasonable risk," "individual freedom of choice," "equity" or the encouragement of "innovation" as bases for rescinding Standard 208. Could he have written a reversal-proof statement of basis and purpose? What "facts" would be relevant to a decision premised on any of these grounds?

3. *Proceedings on Remand.* Pursuant to the Supreme Court's remand in *State Farm,* DOT reopened the Standard 208 proceedings and issued a final rule on July 17, 1984. That rule required the achievement of full passive protection in all automobiles marketed after the 1989 model year. Manufacturers were allowed to choose among passive technologies including airbags, enhanced padding of the automobile interior, and either detachable or nondetachable automatic belts. In addition, the rule provided that should states containing two-thirds of the U.S. population adopt qualifying mandatory seatbelt usage laws (MULs) prior to April 1, 1989, the passive restraints requirement of new Standard 208 would be rescinded.

This so-called "trap door" provision in the July 1984 version of Standard 208 brought State Farm and other parties back to court. The petitioners all, in various ways, claimed that the automatic rescission feature of the new rule was "arbitrary and capricious." But the court of appeals in *State Farm Mutual Automobile Insurance Co. v. Dole,* 802 F.2d 474 (D.C.Cir.1986), failed to reach most of these claims because in its opinion they were not yet ripe for review. Looking at the existing stock of mandatory use laws, it appeared to the court highly unlikely that between 1986 and 1989 sufficient states would pass MULs that complied with the features outlined in the Secretary's regulation. Indeed, the clear trend among the states seemed to be to pass mandatory use laws which self-consciously failed to satisfy the Secretary's conditions in order that these laws not be counted against the two-thirds criterion. The "trap door" provision of DOT's 1984 passive restraint rule was never triggered. See Ellen L. Theroff, *Preemption of Airbag Litigation: Just a Lot of Hot Air?,* 76 Va.L.Rev. 577, 584–85 n. 37 (1990).

Only New York asserted claims going beyond the "trap door" provision. The State argued that it was arbitrary and capricious for the department (1) to permit the option of meeting the passive restraint requirement with detachable automatic belts; (2) to fail to require airbags in all cars; and (3) to fail altogether to consider the option of requiring both airbags and non-detachable belts. The court of appeals' analysis of these issues is revealing:

> The Secretary fully considered the suggestion that, as among automatic belts, only non-detachable rather than detachable belts be deemed to meet the federal standard. Her refusal to embrace the idea was based primarily upon two factors. First, since a non-detachable belt is, according to the Secretary, "the most coercive type of automatic restraint," imposing that particular requirement would create a "serious adverse public reaction." New York contends that this conclusion "is admitted to be pure speculation and belied by surveys of consumer attitudes in the record." New York fails, however, to support this contention with any citations to the record or to otherwise buttress its position. The Secretary, by contrast, cites surveys finding that 10 to 20 percent of the public would be likely to cut non-detachable belts, thereby defeating the system. This sort of consideration is entirely appropriate to weigh in the balance * * *.
>
> New York next attacks the Secretary's failure to mandate airbags in all cars.
>
> Her ultimate decision not to require airbags, but to provide incentives for their employment, was based on two factors. First, despite their admitted safety benefits, airbags are costly: According to Department estimates, they would cost $320 more per car than manual belts; in addition, their replacement cost is an estimated $800, making it likely that many airbags would not be replaced once used. In light of these cost estimates, the Secretary concluded that the safety benefits of airbags would not be worth their high cost.
>
> New York vehemently challenges the agency's cost-benefit analysis in this arena of human safety. Specifically, New York complains that the standard takes into account neither the factor of pain and suffering nor the value of human life itself. Not so. The Final Rule devoted several pages to a discussion of the relative effectiveness of airbags, seat belts, and passive restraints in reducing fatalities and serious injuries.
>
> In a related vein, New York takes the Secretary to task for relying upon the Department's own cost estimates rather than lower estimates found in the record. Again, we cannot say that the Secretary's cost estimates are arbitrary, particularly in light of other cost estimates submitted by the automobile manufacturers that run much higher than the Secretary's. In our view, such details of cost-benefit analysis are "most appropriately entrusted to the expertise of an agency," especially where, as here, the evidence runs in contrary directions.
>
> The second basis for the Secretary's decision was public acceptability. As a threshold matter, the Secretary recognized that public acceptability would depend to a great extent on the cost of airbags to consumers, concluding that "only a small percentage appears willing to pay more than $400" for the devices. She also took cognizance of public fears about chemicals used to deploy airbags, the possibility of inadver-

tent deployment of the devices, and the sense of insecurity harbored by some people at not having a belt wrapped around them. The Secretary reasoned that even though these fears are largely unfounded they must nonetheless be taken seriously. She opined that "[i]t may be easier to overcome these concerns if airbags are not the only way of complying with an automatic occupant protection requirement." New York's only response to this point is a single survey indicating that airbags enjoy a higher level of public acceptability than either automatic or manual belts. Particularly in light of a contrary public opinion survey and numerous public comments going in a contrary direction, we cannot say that the Secretary's refusal to give determinative weight to the survey championed by New York descended to the depths of arbitrary and capricious action.

New York's final attack on the Final Rule is that the Secretary failed to consider the alternative of requiring *both* airbags and non-detachable automatic belts. The Government contends, however, that the Secretary did in fact consider this alternative and advanced adequate reasons for rejecting it.

As to the substance of the decision not to require both devices, we cannot discern any significant defects in the Secretary's reasoning. Having concluded that non-detachable automatic belts posed public-acceptability concerns sufficient to preclude requiring manufacturers to install them (rather than detachable belts), the Secretary could reasonably decide not to require that non-detachable belts be used in tandem with airbags. While not articulated with crystalline clarity, the Secretary's discussion of this issue passes muster under the "arbitrary and capricious" standard.

4. *Proceduralized Substantive Review and "Technology Forcing" Regulation*. In *Regulation and Legal Culture: The Case of Motor Vehicle Safety*, 4 Yale J. on Reg. 257 (1987), Jerry L. Mashaw and David L. Harfst consider the effects of judicial review on NHTSA's regulatory behavior:

> * * * Established as a rulemaking agency to force the technology of automobile safety design, NHTSA indeed functioned in a rulemaking mode from roughly its inception in 1966 until about 1974. NHTSA's promulgated rules, however, have had extremely modest technology-forcing effects. The rules that have become operational have required off-the-shelf technologies, many of which were already in widespread, if not universal, use at the time of the standards' promulgation. Since the mid–1970s, NHTSA has instead concentrated on its alternative statutory power to force the recall of motor vehicles that contain "defects" related to safety performance. It has thus retreated to a traditional form of case-by-case adjudication which requires little, if any, technological sophistication and which has no known effects on vehicle safety.

In the authors' view, this result was promoted by a "proceduralized" substantive judicial review that helped NHTSA's regulatory opponents to delay and ultimately to derail the agency's rulemaking efforts. Judicial demands that the agency explain its technical judgments and document the factual predicate for its actions simply played into the automobile manufacturers' hands.

> From the manufacturers' standpoint, finding a gap, or many gaps, in any regulation would be child's play. Moreover, automakers need only point out these technological inadequacies and give them some credibility to force the Agency to document the technical merits of any detail in its standards.

Meanwhile, influenced in part by parallel developments in products liability law, the courts relaxed the evidentiary requirement for the issuance of a recall order.

Although Mashaw and Harfst are careful neither to ascribe NHTSA's flight to recalls (informal adjudications) wholly (or even predominately) to "proceduralized" judicial review of rules, nor to condemn the doctrinal approach that reviewing courts have developed, they clearly believe that the match between agency mission and judicial review creates serious, perhaps insurmountable problems:

> The Agency has been allowed to pursue neither safety nor regulatory relief without thoroughly justifying its actions in terms of a reliable factual predicate and its statutory mandate. The Agency may operate in a domain beset by factual uncertainty, but it cannot offer uncertainty as a predicate for its acts.
>
> These apparently reasonable judicial requirements may nevertheless be uniquely disabling to an agency having NHTSA's standard-setting mandate. The National Traffic and Motor Vehicle Safety Act presumes that at least some standards will be "technology-forcing." NHTSA is supposed to improve the state of the art in automobile safety design. Yet, it is to do this by setting performance standards, not design standards. The statute presumes that the automobile industry will engage in the innovative engineering necessary to make the automobile operate in accordance with these performance requirements.
>
> This division of function between the agency and the industry is eminently sensible. Both engineering know-how and the incentives to reduce compliance costs lie with the industry. Yet the division of responsibility produces something of a paradox when the agency seeks to justify its requirements. If the agency adopts standards requiring only the use of well-known and widely-tested safety devices, thus merely writing into performance criteria language the characteristics of existing designs, it will carry out only a limited portion of its technology-forcing mandate—a demand that manufacturers incorporate known and proven safety advances into their products. But to the extent that NHTSA does more to force technology, it will be attempting to speed up a process of experiential and incremental engineering advance. The ultimate success of that endeavor could not possibly be demonstrable at the time the technology-forcing regulatory power is exercised.
>
> * * * The unhappy position of technology-forcing in the context of rationality review is but one difficulty with the judicial posture that has developed in the course of reviewing NHTSA's rules. The "decision

process" rather than "decision product" cast of judicial review for reasonableness, while it seems restrained and appropriate for "generalist judges" reviewing an "expert agency," has even more general, unfortunate consequences.

First, it invites courts to invalidate reasonable judgments that are badly explained or perhaps inexplicable in straightforward logical fashion. The search for a "rational process" tends to collapse incremental learning in real time—a process that may entail tentative commitments, revised technical and interpretive perspectives, false starts, lucky guesses, new information, or an evolving technological, economic and political environment—into an analytical exercise of the "If A, then B" sort. This approach is both pernicious and self-defeating.

It is pernicious because it gives enormous leverage to the status quo, whether the status quo is no rule * * * or the continuance of a rule. * * * The fits, starts, and reversals of real decisionmaking look, from a rational-analytic perspective, like the fumblings of an incompetent or misguided administrator. It is self-defeating because this approach to review instructs administrators to write a rational-analytic account of their decisions in order to withstand judicial review. If the courts really are interested in the decision process, they are unlikely to learn much about it. The current approach to judicial review virtually assures that no administrator will find it prudent to reveal the agency's real process of decision.

Second, the process approach leads courts to imagine that remands for further consideration or explanation have a modest effect on an agency's regulatory policy choice. Courts, after all, are not judging the reasonableness of the agency's policy; that is for the agency to decide. Judges see themselves as merely shaping up the process of rational bureaucratic decisionmaking. But this view enormously underestimates the potential impact of a judicial remand, particularly one premised, as most are, on the incompleteness of the agency's decision process.

Any remand occurs long after the rulemaking docket has been closed and the staff has been reassigned. Often the remand finds the agency with a new administrator and a new agenda. The idea that an agency can or will quickly turn to remedying the factual or analytic defects in its remanded rule is surely naive, however minor those problems might appear in the abstract. Delay will be measured in years * * * not months. And, of course, delay means that rulemaking will go forward in a new political, economic, and technological context that will radically alter the perceived rationality of the rule. Rather than the rule shaping reality, reality will reshape the rule.

We shall return later to a further discussion of various "impediments" to agency legislative rulemaking, their purported effects on regulatory outputs, and the means by which agencies seek to avoid rulemaking while still formulating and implementing general policies.

3. THE PROCEDURAL REQUIREMENTS OF APA SECTION 553

a. Notice and Opportunity for Comment

UNITED STATES v. NOVA SCOTIA FOOD PRODUCTS CORP.

United States Court of Appeals, Second Circuit, 1977.
568 F.2d 240.

GURFEIN, CIRCUIT JUDGE.

This appeal involving a regulation of the Food and Drug Administration is not here upon a direct review of agency action. It is an appeal from a judgment of the District Court * * * enjoining the appellants, after a hearing, from processing hot smoked whitefish except in accordance with time-temperature-salinity (T–T–S) regulations contained in 21 C.F.R. Part 122 (1977). * * *

* * *

The regulations cited above require that hot-process smoked fish be heated by a controlled heat process that provides a monitoring system positioned in as many strategic locations in the oven as necessary to assure a continuous temperature through each fish of not less than 180° F. for a minimum of 30 minutes for fish which have been brined to contain 3.5% water phase salt or at 150° F. for a minimum of 30 minutes if the salinity was at 5% water phase. * * *

Government inspection of appellants' plant established without question that the minimum T–T–S requirements were not being met. There is no substantial claim that the plant was processing whitefish under "insanitary conditions" in any other material respect. Appellants, on their part, do not defend on the ground that they were in compliance, but rather that the requirements could not be met if a marketable whitefish was to be produced. They defend upon the grounds that the regulation is invalid (1) because it is beyond the authority delegated by the statute; (2) because the FDA improperly relied upon undisclosed evidence in promulgating the regulation and because it is not supported by the administrative record; and (3) because there was no adequate statement setting forth the basis of the regulation. We reject the contention that the regulation is beyond the authority delegated by the statute, but we find serious inadequacies in the procedure followed in the promulgation of the regulation and hold it to be invalid as applied to the appellants herein.

The hazard which the FDA sought to minimize was the outgrowth and toxin formation of Clostridium botulinum Type E spores of the bacteria which sometimes inhabit fish. There had been an occurrence of several cases of botulism traced to consumption of fish from inland waters in 1960 and 1963 which stimulated considerable bacteriological research. These bacteria can be present in the soil and water of various regions. They can invade fish in their natural habitat and can be further disseminated in the course of evisceration and preparation of the fish for cooking. A failure to destroy such spores through an adequate brining, thermal, and refrigeration process was found to be dangerous to public health.

The Commissioner of Food and Drugs ("Commissioner"), employing informal "notice-and-comment" procedures under 21 U.S.C. § 371(a), issued a proposal for the control of C. botulinum bacteria Type E in fish. * * *

* * * Responding to the Commissioner's invitation in the notice of proposed rulemaking, members of the industry, including appellants and the intervenor-appellant, submitted comments on the proposed regulation.

The Commissioner thereafter issued the final regulations in which he adopted certain suggestions made in the comments, including a suggestion by the National Fisheries Institute, Inc. ("the Institute"), the intervenor herein. The original proposal provided that the fish would have to be cooked to a temperature of 180° F. for at least 30 minutes, if the fish have been brined to contain 3.5% water phase salt, with no alternative. In the final regulation, an alternative suggested by the intervenor "that the parameter of 150°F. for 30 minutes and 5% salt in the water phase be established as an alternate procedure to that stated in the proposed regulation for an interim period until specific parameters can be established" was accepted, but as a permanent part of the regulation rather than for an interim period.

The intervenor suggested that "specific parameters" be established. This referred to particular processing parameters for different species of fish on a "species by species" basis. Such "species by species" determination was proposed not only be the intervenor but also by the Bureau of Commercial Fisheries of the Department of the Interior. That Bureau objected to the general application of the T–T–S requirement proposed by the FDA on the ground that application of the regulation to all species of fish being smoked was not commercially feasible, and that the regulation should therefore specify time-temperature-salinity requirements, as developed by research and study, on a species-by-species basis. The Bureau suggested that "wholesomeness considerations could be more practically and adequately realized by reducing processing temperature and using suitable concentrations of nitrite and salt." The commissioner took cognizance of the suggestion, but decided, nevertheless, to impose the T–T–S requirement on *all* species of fish (except chub * * *).

He did acknowledge, however, in his "basis and purpose" statement * * * that "adequate times, temperatures and salt concentrations have not been demonstrated for each individual species of fish presently smoked." The Commissioner concluded, nevertheless, that "the processing requirements of the proposed regulations are the safest now known to prevent the outgrowth and toxin formation of *C. botulinum* Type E."

He determined that "the conditions of current good manufacturing practice for this industry should be established without further delay."

The Commissioner did not answer the suggestion by the Bureau of Fisheries that nitrite and salt as additives could safely lower the high temperature otherwise required, a solution which the FDA had accepted in the case of chub. Nor did the Commissioner respond to the claim of Nova Scotia through its trade association the Association of Smoked Fish Processors, Inc., Technical Center that "[t]he proposed process requirements suggested by the FDA for hot processed smoked fish are neither commercially feasible nor based on sound scientific evidence obtained with the variety of smoked fish products to be included under this regulation."

Nova Scotia, in its own comment, wrote to the Commissioner that "the heating of certain types of fish to high temperatures will completely destroy the product." * * * We have noted above that the response given by the Commissioner was in general terms. He did not specifically aver that the T–T–S requirements as applied to whitefish were, in fact, commercially feasible. * * *

Appellants contend that there is an inadequate administrative record upon which to predicate judicial review, and that the failure to disclose to interested persons the factual material upon which the agency was relying vitiates the element of fairness which is essential to any kind of administrative action. Moreover, they argue that the "concise general statement of * * * basis and purpose" by the Commissioner was inadequate.

The question of what is an adequate "record" in informal rulemaking has engaged the attention of commentators for several years. The extent of the administrative record required for judicial review of informal rulemaking is largely a function of the scope of judicial review. Even when the standard of review is whether the promulgation of the rule was "arbitrary, capricious, an abuse of discretion, or otherwise not in accordance with law," as specified in 5 U.S.C. § 706(2)(A), judicial review must, nevertheless, be based on the "whole record" (*id.*). Adequate review of a determination requires an adequate record, if the review is to be meaningful. What will constitute an adequate record for meaningful review may vary with the nature of the administrative action to be reviewed. Review must be based on the whole record even when the judgment is one of policy, except that findings of fact such as would be required in an adjudicatory proceeding or in a formal "on the record" hearing for rulemaking need not be made. Though the action was informal, without an evidentiary record, the review must be "thorough, probing, [and] in depth." * * *

With respect to the content of the administrative "record," the Supreme Court has told us that in informal rulemaking, "the focal point for judicial review should be the administrative record already in existence, not some new record made initially in the reviewing court." See *Camp v. Pitts*, 411 U.S. 138 (1973).

No contemporaneous record was made or certified.[13] When, during the enforcement action, the basis for the regulation was sought through pretrial discovery, the record was created by searching the files of the FDA and the memories of those who participated in the process of rulemaking. This resulted in what became Exhibit D at the trial of the injunction action. Exhibit D consists of (1) Tab A containing the comments received from outside parties during the administrative "notice-and-comment" proceeding and (2) Tabs B through L consisting of scientific data and the like upon which the Commissioner now says he relied but which was not made known to the interested parties.

Appellants object to the exclusion of evidence in the District Court "aimed directly at showing that the scientific evidence relied upon by the FDA was inaccurate and not based upon a realistic appraisal of the true facts. Appellants attempted to introduce scientific evidence to demonstrate that in fixing the processing parameters FDA relied upon tests in which ground fish were injected with many millions of botulism [sic] spores and then tested for outgrowth at various processing levels whereas the spore levels in nature are far less and outgrowth would have been prevented by far less stringent processing parameters." The District Court properly excluded the evidence.

In an enforcement action, we must rely exclusively on the record made before the agency to determine the validity of the regulation. The exception to the exclusivity of that record is that "there may be independent judicial fact-finding when issues that were not before the agency are raised in a proceeding to *enforce* non-adjudicatory agency action." *Overton Park*, 401 U.S. at 415 (1971). (Emphasis added.)

Though this is an enforcement proceeding and the question is close, we think that the "issues" *were* fairly before the agency and hence that *de novo* evidence was properly excluded by Judge Dooling. Our concern is, rather, with the manner in which the agency treated the issues tendered.

The key issues were (1) whether, in the light of the rather scant history of botulism in whitefish, that species should have been considered separately rather than included in a general regulation which failed to distinguish species from species; (2) whether the application of the proposed T–T–S requirements to smoked whitefish made the whitefish commercially unsaleable; and (3) whether the agency recognized that prospect, but nevertheless decided that the public health needs should prevail even if that meant commercial death for the whitefish industry. The procedural issues were whether, in the light of these key questions, the agency procedure was inadequate because (i) it failed to disclose to interested parties the scientific data and the methodology upon which it

13. A practice developed in the early years of the APA of not making a formal contemporaneous record, but rather, when challenged, to put together a historical record of what had been available for agency consideration at the time the regulation was promulgated.

relied; and (ii) because it failed utterly to address itself to the pertinent question of commercial feasibility.

The history of botulism occurrence in whitefish, as established in the trial record, which we must assume was available to the FDA in 1970, is as follows. Between 1899 and 1964 there were only eight cases of botulism reported as attributable to hot-smoked whitefish. In all eight instances, vacuum-packed whitefish was involved. All of the eight cases occurred in 1960 and 1963. The industry has abandoned vacuum-packing, and there has not been a single case of botulism associated with commercially prepared whitefish since 1963, though 2,750,000 pounds of whitefish are processed annually. Thus, in the seven-year period from 1964 through 1970, 17.25 million pounds of whitefish have been commercially processed in the United States without a single reported case of botulism. The evidence also disclosed that defendant Nova Scotia has been in business some 56 years, and that there has never been a case of botulism illness from the whitefish processed by it.

Interested parties were not informed of the scientific data, or at least of a selection of such data deemed important by the agency, so that comments could be addressed to the data. Appellants argue that unless the scientific data relied upon by the agency are spread upon the public records, criticism of the methodology used or the meaning to be inferred from the data is rendered impossible.

We agree with appellants in this case, for although we recognize that an agency may resort to its own expertise outside the record in an informal rulemaking procedure, we do not believe that when the pertinent research material is readily available and the agency has no special expertise on the precise parameters involved, there is any reason to conceal the scientific data relied upon from the interested parties. * * * This is not a case where the agency methodology was based on material supplied by the interested parties themselves. Here all the scientific research was collected by the agency, and none of it was disclosed to interested parties as the material upon which the proposed rule would be fashioned.[15] Nor was an articulate effort made to connect the scientific requirements to available technology that would make commercial survival possible, though the burden of proof was on the agency. This required it to "bear a burden of adducing a reasoned presentation supporting the reliability of its methodology."

Though a reviewing court will not match submission against counter-submission to decide whether the agency was correct in its conclusion on scientific matters (unless that conclusion is arbitrary), it will consider whether the agency has taken account of all "relevant factors and whether there has been a clear error of judgment." * * *

15. We recognize the problem posed by Judge Leventhal in *International Harvester*, 478 F.2d 615 (D.C.Cir.1973), that a proceeding might never end if such submission required a reply *ad infinitum*. Here the exposure of the scientific research relied on simply would have required a single round of comment addressed thereto.

If the failure to notify interested persons of the scientific research upon which the agency was relying actually prevented the presentation of relevant comment, the agency may be held not to have considered all "the relevant factors." We can think of no sound reasons for secrecy or reluctance to expose to public view (with an exception for trade secrets or national security) the ingredients of the deliberative process. Indeed, the FDA's own regulations now specifically require that every notice of proposed rulemaking contain "references to all data and information on which the Commissioner relies for the proposal (copies or a full list of which shall be a part of the administrative file on the matter * * *)." 21 C.F.R. § 10.40(b)(1) (1977). And this is, undoubtedly, the trend.

We think that the scientific data should have been disclosed to focus on the proper interpretation of "insanitary conditions." When the basis for a proposed rule is a scientific decision, the scientific material which is believed to support the rule should be exposed to the view of interested parties for their comment. One cannot ask for comment on a scientific paper without allowing the participants to read the paper. Scientific research is sometimes rejected for diverse inadequacies of methodology; and statistical results are sometimes rebutted because of a lack of adequate gathering technique or of supportable extrapolation. Such is the stuff of scientific debate. To suppress meaningful comment by failure to disclose the basic data relied upon is akin to rejecting comment altogether. For unless there is common ground, the comments are unlikely to be of a quality that might impress a careful agency. The inadequacy of comment in turn leads in the direction of arbitrary decision-making. We do not speak of findings of fact, for such are not technically required in the informal rulemaking procedures. We speak rather of what the agency should make known so as to elicit comments that probe the fundamentals. Informal rulemaking does not lend itself to a rigid pattern. Especially, in the circumstance of our broad reading of statutory authority in support of the agency, we conclude that the failure to disclose to interested persons the scientific data upon which the FDA relied was procedurally erroneous. Moreover the burden was upon the agency to articulate rationally why the rule should apply to a large and diverse class, with the same T–T–S parameters made applicable to all species.

Appellants additionally attack the "concise general statement" required by APA, 5 U.S.C. § 553, as inadequate. We think that, in the circumstances, it was less than adequate. It is not in keeping with the rational process to leave vital questions, raised by comments which are of cogent materiality, completely unanswered. The agencies certainly have a good deal of discretion in expressing the basis of a rule, but the agencies do not have quite the prerogative of obscurantism reserved to legislatures.

* * *

The Secretary was squarely faced with the question whether it was necessary to formulate a rule with specific parameters that applied to all species of fish, and particularly whether lower temperatures with the addition of nitrite and salt would not be sufficient. Though this alternative was suggested by an agency of the federal government, its suggestion, though acknowledged, was never answered.

Moreover, the comment that to apply the proposed T–T–S requirements to whitefish would destroy the commercial product was neither discussed nor answered. We think that to sanction silence in the face of such vital questions would be to make the statutory requirement of a "concise general statement" less than an adequate safeguard against arbitrary decision-making.

* * *

One may recognize that even commercial infeasibility cannot stand in the way of an overwhelming public interest. Yet the administrative process should disclose, at least, whether the proposed regulation is considered to be commercially feasible, or whether other considerations prevail even if commercial infeasibility is acknowledged. This kind of forthright disclosure and basic statement was lacking in the formulation of the T–T–S standard made applicable to whitefish. It is easy enough for an administrator to ban everything. In the regulation of food processing, the worldwide need for food also must be taken into account in formulating measures taken for the protection of health. In the light of the history of smoked whitefish to which we have referred, we find no articulate balancing here sufficient to make the procedure followed less than arbitrary.

* * *

We cannot, on this appeal, remand to the agency to allow further comments by interested parties, addressed to the scientific data now disclosed at the trial below. We hold in this enforcement proceeding, therefore, that the regulation, as it affects non-vacuum-packed not-smoked whitefish, was promulgated in an arbitrary manner and is invalid.

Notes

1. *Proceduralized Substantive Review.* Judge Gurfein's opinion provides yet another illustration of the close linkage between review of agency rulemaking procedures and review of the substance of the rules agencies adopt. His criticisms of the FDA's failure to respond to the suggestion that nitrite be permitted as an alternative preservative and its silence on the matter of commercial infeasibility are redolent of judicial treatment of the tire retread rule in *Brinegar* and of the withdrawal of the passive restraints rule in *State Farm.* In addition, however, Judge Gurfein addresses other defects in FDA's conduct of the smoked fish rulemaking.

2. *The Right to Comment in Informal Rulemaking.* Because FDA was operating under section 553 of the APA, Judge Gurfein's criticisms of the procedures it followed have been accepted as having general import. He

chastises the FDA for failing—at the time it proposed the regulations—to disclose scientific studies concerning the risk of botulism and methods of preventing it in fish. He observes that the agency's practice by the time the case was decided was to do so and notes that "this is undoubtedly the trend," among federal agencies generally. One can perhaps understand how the FDA in 1969 neglected to mention these studies—all of them, incidentally, available in the published literature—when one learns that the agency was not then maintaining a contemporaneous record in rulemakings. The studies surfaced as part of the "record" for review that FDA lawyers compiled by scouring the agency's files and collecting all of the materials they thought agency officials *might have* consulted when the regulations were adopted. It is thus hardly surprising that the reconstructed record contained materials the defendants may not have seen, and certainly had not had their attention drawn to, when the regulations were proposed.

The court's reaction to this omission reflects two concerns. Judge Gurfein comments on the special importance of the need for adversarial review of scientific evidence—"the stuff of scientific debate." But his objection goes further: the FDA's failure to invite comment on the data was "akin to rejecting comment altogether." The suggestion is that even in informal rulemaking there must be opportunity for critique and rebuttal of the facts that the agency accepts as justifying its rules. But would not an even more effective way of meeting an adversary's case involve cross-examination and submission of rebuttal evidence once the effects of that examination are revealed, i.e., trial-type procedures? Could the court mandate such procedures under section 553?

3. *Review Based on the "Administrative Record."* Judge Gurfein's second concern relates to the exclusiveness of the rulemaking record. His ruling effectively forced agencies generally to adopt what by 1977 had become standard FDA practice, i.e., disclosing the sources on which it relied when publishing a proposed rule and collecting them, with all of the comments, in a package that could be characterized as the "record" for possible judicial review. (The reader will recall that in *Auto Parts* Judge McGowan similarly suggested that such materials could constitute the "record" of informal rulemaking.) Judge Gurfein then accepts the FDA's claim that review of any challenges to its regulations should be confined to this "administrative record," a ruling supported by Supreme Court precedent. But is the agency itself likewise limited to the "record" it assembles during the rulemaking? Presumably it cannot present new evidence in court, but may it consider any materials that came to it after the time for public comment?

In an influential article written before Judge Gurfein's decision, *Formal Records and Informal Rulemaking*, 85 Yale L.J. 38, 61 (1975), William L. Pedersen argued:

> The central loss in discarding the adjudicatory model in favor of notice and comment rulemaking was * * * the focused and defined record which all the procedures used in adjudication were intended to produce. This record served as the basis for decision both at the agency level and on review. There is at present in informal rulemaking no

parallel requirement that the record certified to the court be the fruit of special procedures designed to produce it.

Could the Gurfein/McGowan characterization of the "record" in informal rulemaking be considered an adequate response to this criticism?

There is little doubt that Pedersen's critique influenced judicial interpretation of the procedural requirements of section 553 of the APA. In *Solite Corp. v. U.S. Environmental Protection Agency*, 952 F.2d 473, 484 (D.C.Cir. 1991), a challenge to EPA hazardous waste regulations, the court declared:

> The APA requires that a notice of proposed rulemaking include "either the terms or substance of the proposed rule or a description of the subjects and issues involved," and that the agency "give interested persons an opportunity to participate in the rulemaking through submission of written data, views, or arguments." Integral to the notice requirement is the agency's duty "to identify and make available technical studies and data that it has employed in reaching its conclusions."

Judge Gurfein's insistence that an agency engaged in rulemaking make sure that the critical studies and other material that it relies upon be made public in time for affected persons to digest and respond to the agency's "evidence" has implications for its handling of comments that include supporting or rebuttal information. If such information is genuinely new and not simply cumulative, the agency may be obligated to publish a notice of its submission and allow additional time for the filing of responsive comments. Compare *Air Transport Ass'n v. FAA*, 169 F.3d 1 (D.C.Cir.1999) (failure to allow comments on critical new information denied petitioners fair notice), with *Building Industry Ass'n of Superior California v. Norton*, 247 F.3d 1241 (D.C.Cir.2001) (study received after comment period need not be closed if it merely addressed issues that were fully ventilated during the comment period).

4. *Notice of Issues and Alternatives*. Unlike formal rulemaking or civil court proceedings, the procedures outlined in section 553 do not provide obvious opportunities for identifying contested issues of fact or policy that an agency must resolve in framing final regulations. Notices of proposed rulemaking (NPRMs) now typically describe the problem proposed rules are intended to address, set forth a contemplated regulatory text, and often specify issues on which comment is particularly invited. Even so, NPRMs may treat the agency's premises only briefly and may fail to discuss alternative approaches. Later reflection may surface new issues within the agency, or thoughtful comments may uncover chinks in its analysis or advance new solutions. When the agency is persuaded to depart from its proposed solution, it may confront claims that its original notice did not adequately describe the options it was considering.

In *Wagner Electric Corp. v. Volpe*, 466 F.2d 1013 (3d Cir.1972), one of the first such challenges, the court set aside changes in the Department of Transportation's safety standard for automobile turn signals on the ground that the Secretary's proposal had not afforded interested persons adequate notice of the criteria he ultimately adopted. The proposal had recited that the Secretary was considering the elimination of sampling and permissible failure rates for turn signals, thereby requiring all signals produced to meet existing performance criteria. A number of manufacturers objected to the proposed change unless the performance criteria were relaxed, but none submitted data directed to specific modifications in those criteria. Without inviting additional comments, the Secretary adopted a final rule that eliminated the sampling and failure rate specifications *and* relaxed performance criteria. The Third Circuit concluded that the Secretary's procedure had deprived manufacturers, state agencies, and consumer groups of an effective opportunity to submit their views on what, if any, changes should be made in the performance criteria for turn signals.

Contrast *South Terminal Corp. v. EPA*, 504 F.2d 646, 658–59 (1st Cir.1974), in which the petitioners challenged EPA's plan to reduce automobile pollution around Boston. EPA had proposed an on-street parking ban during certain hours, a $5 surcharge for off-street parking, and a one-day-a-week ban on automobile travel on Boston's circumferential highway which relied on a windshield sticker system. The final plan deleted the sticker system and the parking surcharge, which had been heavily criticized, and substituted reductions in parking spaces, preferential treatment for car pools, special review of new parking facilities, and semi-annual for annual inspection of automobiles. The petitioners contended that the final regulations departed so "radically" from the proposal as to have denied them an effective opportunity for comment. Judge Campbell rejected this claim:

> Although the changes were substantial, they were in character with the original scheme and were additionally foreshadowed in proposals and comments advanced during the rulemaking. Parties had been warned that strategies might be modified in light of their suggestions. * * *
>
> A hearing is intended to educate an agency to approaches different from its own; in shaping the final rule it may and should draw on the comments tendered. The plan seems a logical outgrowth of the hearing and related procedures. * * * As the Court of Appeals for the District of Columbia Circuit recently said:
>
>> The requirement of submission of a proposed rule for comment does not automatically generate a new opportunity for comment merely because the rule promulgated by the agency differs from the rule it proposed, partly at least in response to submissions.[51] *International Harvester Co. v. Ruckelshaus*, 478 F.2d 615, 632 (D.C.Cir.1973).
>
> Cases cited by petitioners in which there was no notice or opportunity to comment or submit evidence are not in point, nor is their reliance on *Wagner Electric Corp. v. Volpe*. A circumscribed announcement, as in the latter case, that standards for testing an automotive product would be revised, is not to be compared to EPA's comprehensive notice. The instant notice left no doubt that EPA would consider all reasonable alternatives for cutting down vehicle use.

5. *Information and Analysis in Rulemaking*. To a large degree the making of rules is an exercise in empiricism—learning about a problem and formulating a response on the basis of evidence and analysis. Agencies have

51. "A contrary rule would lead to the absurdity that in rule-making under the APA the agency can learn from the comments on its proposals only at the peril of starting a new procedural round of commentary."

many ways of gathering information to support regulations. Some make it a practice of holding public meetings when a problem emerges in order to elicit ideas about how it should respond. This is one means of avoiding the dilemma posed by the *Wagner Electric* case on the one hand and claims of unresponsiveness on the other. Another option, sometimes mandated by statute, is to discuss contemplated rules with an advisory committee which includes experts in the field or, representatives of affected interests. The agency may then develop a formal proposal for submission to the usual notice-and-comment procedure of the APA. See Federal Insecticide, Fungicide, and Rodenticide Act, 7 U.S.C. § 136w(d); Occupational Safety and Health Act, 29 U.S.C. § 656.

Advisory committees perform a variety of functions in the regulatory process, including the review or development of proposed regulations. In highly technical areas they provide a means of enlisting expertise that the government probably could not attract from full-time employees. Congress has sometimes mandated consultation with an advisory committee as a prelude to rulemaking. See, e.g., the Toxic Substances Control Act, 15 U.S.C. §§ 2601, 2629, and the Medical Device Amendments to the Food, Drug, and Cosmetic Act, 21 U.S.C. §§ 351–360. Amendments in 1981 to the Consumer Product Safety Act obligate the CPSC to establish a panel of outside scientists to review its staff's findings whenever the agency contemplates regulation of a product believed to pose a risk of cancer, mutagenic damage, or birth defects. See Richard A. Merrill, *CPSC Regulation of Cancer Risks in Consumer Products: 1972–1981*, 67 Va.L.Rev. 1261 (1981).

Another approach favored by some agencies is to publish an advance notice of proposed rulemaking (ANPRM) which describes the problem and outlines alternative solutions and invites comments from the public before a proposed rule is advanced. This device may help to meet objections that agency decision makers made up their minds about the desired outcome before they published a proposed rule. An ANPRM, can provide a genuine opportunity for the public to influence the content of agency policy. It can also permit the agency to identify pockets of resistance to, or arguments against, new policies before committing its full energies and prestige to an unpopular initiative. Amendments to the Consumer Product Safety Act in 1981 obligate the CPSC to proceed in this fashion when it contemplates setting a standard for, or banning, a consumer product. Consumer Product Safety Amendments of 1981, Pub.L.No. 97–35, § 1206, amending 15 U.S.C. § 2077.

Agencies are often criticized for relying on information supplied by the potential targets—or beneficiaries—of regulation. But in many circumstances, persons outside an agency may be in a better position to supply the information on which rules should be based and perhaps in some cases even better equipped to make judgments about what rules should contain. It is arguable, for example, that the tire retreaders in *Brinegar* were better able than the Secretary of Transportation to assess the technological feasibility of permanent imprinting of various types of information. However, an agency's need to tap private information or expertise creates the risk that it will hear only one side of an issue. This risk is particularly worrisome when an agency's rules have immediate impact on groups whose interests sharply diverge. During the 1970s, several agencies experimented with providing financial support for organizations or individuals whose viewpoints might not otherwise be expressed on the public record. The Magnuson–Moss Amendments to the FTC Act specifically authorized the Federal Trade Commission to provide support for "public participation" in trade regulation rule proceedings. Other agencies asserted authority to fund "public interest" participants based on their organic laws or inherent authority. The FDA's five-year effort to implement such a program, however, was nullified in *Pacific Legal Foundation v. Goyan*, 664 F.2d 1221 (4th Cir.1981), which contains language that casts doubt on the authority of other agencies, save for those, like the FTC, that have been expressly empowered to fund public participation. See Barry Boyer, *Funding Public Participation in Agency Proceedings: The Federal Trade Commission Experience*, 70 Geo.L.J. 51 (1981); Carl W. Tobias, *Of Public Funds and Public Participation: Resolving the Issue of Agency Authority to Reimburse Public Participations in Administrative Proceedings*, 82 Colum.L.Rev. 906 (1982).

Several agencies, including OSHA and EPA, rely on contract services for many of the studies and investigations needed for regulatory decision making. Occasionally, however, this practice has led to court challenges to the agency's underlying rule. An example is *United Steelworkers of America v. Marshall*, 647 F.2d 1189 (D.C.Cir.1980), *cert. denied*, 453 U.S. 913 (1981), a challenge to OSHA's lead standard.

> The record shows that OSHA did make rather broad requests for help from the consultants. * * * OSHA relied heavily on David Burton Associates (DBA) and Nicholas Ashford and his Center for Policy Alternatives (CPA) in examining the data on feasibility and developing a "technology-forcing" rationale for the standard. The agency hired a number of other expert consultants, giving them fairly broad mandates to summarize and evaluate data in the record, prepare record data for computer processing, and help draft portions of the Preamble and the final standard. LIA [Lead Industry Association] argues that such reliance on outsiders invites abuse, even if one assumes the honesty of the ones in this case, since hired hands have a financial incentive to tell the agency what it wants to hear, and have no civil service protection against retaliation for telling uncomfortable truths.
>
> LIA asserts that no case has considered and upheld the legality of such reliance. But neither can LIA locate a case or statute forbidding such a practice * * *. If anything, the law generally bearing on the issue supports OSHA here. The OSH Act empowers the agency to employ expert consultants, and OSHA might have possessed that power even without express statutory authority. * * *
>
> LIA's position thus comes down to the challenge that OSHA has violated the principle of *Morgan v. United States*, 298 U.S. 468, 480–81 (1936) (*Morgan I*): "The one who decides must hear," and an agency denies the parties a true hearing if the official who acts for the agency has not personally confronted the evidence and the arguments. * * * [A]pplying the general principle of *Morgan I*, we see that LIA cannot buttress its general allegation of excessive reliance with any specific proof that the Assistant Secretary failed to confront personally the essential evidence and arguments in setting the final standard. * * *

> [W]e note that in the lengthy Preamble and Attachments to the final standard the decisionmaker reviewed the evidence and explained the evidentiary bases for each part of the standard. Moreover, the Assistant Secretary demonstrated her independence from the consultants by strongly criticizing some of their conclusions on the key issue of feasibility.
>
> * * *
>
> LIA's second attack goes to *specific* uses of consultants, and alleges damage to the state of the rulemaking record, rather than to the Assistant Secretary's fulfillment of her personal responsibility. After closing the record, OSHA sought help from outside consultants in reviewing the record and preparing the Preamble. Two consultants were primary. The agency asked David Burton and DBA to help review the record to determine the feasibility of a permissible air-lead standard of 50 μg/m3, as opposed to the 100 μg/m3 standard the agency had proposed in the original notice of rulemaking, and on which most of the public commentary had focused. And OSHA asked Nicholas Ashford and CPA to analyze, in light of the record, the possibility of making a correlation between air-lead levels and blood-lead levels. Both these consultants had previously aided OSHA by supplying on-the-record reports and testifying as expert witnesses at the public hearings. Both fulfilled the new requests by submitting written reports, of 117 and 192 pages respectively, neither of which the agency has released or placed in the rulemaking record. LIA contends that the reports are illegal *ex parte* communications which * * * constitute "secret briefs" and off-the-record evidence which LIA was deprived of a chance to rebut and the court a chance to review.
>
> * * * [T]he documents show that the communications between the agency and the consultants were simply part of the deliberative process of drawing conclusions from the public record. The consultants acted after the record was closed as the functional equivalent of agency staff. * * *
>
> When performed by agency *staff*, this sort of sophisticated review of evidence has always been recognized as legitimate participation in the deliberative process. * * *

Another avenue for information-based challenges to agency rulemaking may exist under the so-called Data Quality Act, contained in Sec. 515 of the Treasury and General Government Appropriations Act for Fiscal Year 2001, Pub. L. No. 106–554. That DQA directed OMB to issue, by September 30, 2001, "policy and procedural guidance" to those federal agencies subject to the Paperwork Reduction Act that would require such agencies (1) to issue data quality guidelines "ensuring and maximizing the quality, objectivity, utility, and integrity of information (including statistical information) disseminated" by the agency "in fulfillment of the purposes and provisions" of that act and (2) to establish "administrative mechanisms allowing affected persons to seek and obtain correction of information maintained and disseminated by the agency that does not comply with the guidelines."

The DQA's implications for rulemaking are unclear. OMB has interpreted the new law as applying to rulemaking, although wording of the DQA is not wonderfully clear on this point. The "good news" for agencies, under the OMB interpretation, is that OMB has concluded that no special administrative mechanisms need be created to deal with data quality challenges during rulemaking. In a September 5, 2002 memorandum to the President's Management Council, OIRA Director John Graham indicated that separate data quality assessments would be unnecessary and duplicative when rulemaking, adjudications, and other administrative procedures already allow for comments and complaints. OMB has defined the "quality, objectivity, utility, and integrity of information" stringently. Guidelines for Ensuring and Maximizing the Quality, Objectivity, Utility, and Integrity of Information Disseminated by Federal Agencies, 67 Fed. Reg. 8452 (Feb. 22, 2002). These definitions may give OIRA additional grounds to second-guess agency rulemaking processes during regulatory review and could conceivably provide additional grounds for judicial review, a point not addressed by the DQA.

b. Hearings in Informal Rulemaking

Section 553(c) on its face does not *require* an agency to provide any opportunity for oral communications, and the typical informal rulemaking proceeding does not include a hearing of any recognizable kind. The lack of opportunity for oral exchange generally, and specifically the effective foreclosure of cross-examination, have been criticized by some scholars, see Robinson, p. 492 *supra*; but see William F. Dixon, *Rulemaking and the Myth of Cross-Examination*, 34 Admin.L.Rev. 389 (1982). And in several statutes enacted in the 1970s, Congress, while consciously avoiding requiring full-blown formal rulemaking, directed the agency to provide *some* opportunity for oral presentation, and in some instances cross-examination. See, e.g., Occupational Safety and Health Act, 84 Stat. 1590 (1972), codified at 29 U.S.C. §§ 651, 655; Magnuson–Moss Warranty–Federal Trade Commission Improvements Act, 88 Stat. 2183 (1975), codified at 15 U.S.C. § 57a(c)(2); Clean Air Act Amendments of 1977, 91 Stat. 776–7, codified at 42 U.S.C. § 7607(d).

In the early 1970s a series of judicial rulings endorsed a similar approach without explicit legislative sanction. The D.C. Circuit and the Fourth Circuit purported to require agencies making rules based on the resolution of complex technical issues to provide participants at least limited trial-type procedures. E.g., *International Harvester Co. v. Ruckelshaus*, 478 F.2d 615 (D.C.Cir.1973); *Appalachian Power Co. v. EPA*, 477 F.2d 495 (4th Cir.1973); *Walter Holm & Co. v. Hardin*, 449 F.2d 1009 (D.C.Cir.1971).

The most notable of these cases was *Mobil Oil Corp. v. Federal Power Commission*, 483 F.2d 1238 (D.C.Cir.1973), a suit to review an order setting minimum rates charged by natural gas pipelines for transporting liquid hydrocarbons. The petitioners raised a host of objections to the Commission's order, among them the claim that the agency had improperly denied them the opportunity to cross-examine the evidence on which it relied on allocating pipeline costs between gaseous and liquid products. Though the Natural Gas Act specified that it could act only "after a hearing," the Commission contended that, under *Florida East Coast*, it need only comply with section 553.

Judge Wilkey's opinion agreed that the FPC was not statutorily required to engage in formal rulemaking, but held the agency was still obligated to accord the petitioners a broader opportunity to contest its factual premises than traditional informal procedures could assure:

> Flexibility in fitting administrative procedures to particular functions is critically important in evaluating the APA and has been a dominant theme in a number of opinions by this court. No court, to our knowledge, has ever treated the explicit language of section 553 on the one hand and sections 556 and 557 on the other as expressing every type of procedure that might be called for in a particular situation. * * *
>
> The Natural Gas Act explicitly states that factual determinations must be supported by "substantial evidence." Unlike many other forms of rulemaking, rate-making necessarily rests upon findings of facts.
>
> * * * Clearly some evidence supporting the FPC's finding must be in the record. *More importantly for our purposes, the rule that the "whole record" be considered—both evidence for and against—means that the procedures must provide some mechanism for interested parties to introduce adverse evidence and criticize evidence introduced by others.* This process of introduction and criticism helps assure that the factual basis of the FPC rates will be accurate and provides the reviewing court with a record from which it can determine if the agency has properly exercised its discretion. * * *
>
> Informal comments simply cannot create a record that satisfies the substantial evidence test. Even if controverting *information* is submitted in the form of comments by adverse parties, the procedure employed cannot be relied upon as adequate. A "whole record," as that phrase is used in this context, does not consist merely of the raw data introduced by the parties. It includes the process of testing and illumination ordinarily associated with adversary, adjudicative procedures. Without this critical element, informal comments, even by adverse parties, are two halves that do not make a whole. Thus, it is adversary procedural devices which permit testing and elucidation that raise information from the level of mere inconsistent data to evidence "substantial" enough to support rates. * * *

These rulings had little practical impact. Only the Department of Agriculture, following *Walter Holm & Co. v. Hardin*, 449 F.2d 1009 (D.C.Cir.1971), ever held an evidentiary hearing with opportunity for cross-examination. In each of the other cases the agency was able, usually with the agreement of the parties involved, to resolve the disputed issues without resorting to formal proceedings. Stephen F. Williams, *"Hybrid Rulemaking" Under the Administrative Procedure Act: A Legal and Empirical Analysis*, 42 U.Chi.L.Rev. 401, 434 (1975);

see also Richard B. Stewart, *The Development of Administrative and Quasi–Constitutional Law in Judicial Review of Environmental Decisionmaking: Lessons from the Clean Air Act*, 62 Iowa L.Rev. 713 (1977). The courts of appeals' creativity, however, eventually provoked the following response from the Supreme Court.

VERMONT YANKEE NUCLEAR POWER CORP. v. NATURAL RESOURCES DEFENSE COUNCIL, INC.

Supreme Court of the United States, 1978.
435 U.S. 519, 98 S.Ct. 1197, 55 L.Ed.2d 460.

JUSTICE REHNQUIST delivered the opinion of the Court.

* * * [I]n *United States v. Allegheny–Ludlum Steel Corp.*, 406 U.S. 742 (1972), and *United States v. Florida East Coast R. Co.*, we held that generally speaking * * * section [553] of the [Administrative Procedure] Act established the maximum procedural requirements which Congress was willing to have the courts impose upon agencies in conducting rulemaking procedures.[1] * * * This is not to say necessarily that there are no circumstances which would ever justify a court in overturning agency action because of a failure to employ procedures beyond those required by the statute. But such circumstances, if they exist, are extremely rare.

Even apart from the Administrative Procedure Act this Court has for more than four decades emphasized that the formulation of procedures was basically to be left within the discretion of the agencies to which Congress had confided the responsibility for substantive judgments. * * *

* * * [T]he Court of Appeals for the District of Columbia Circuit * * * seriously misread or misapplied this statutory and decisional law. * * *

Under the Atomic Energy Act of 1954, 42 U.S.C. § 2011 *et seq.*, the [Nuclear Regulatory] Commission was given broad regulatory authority over the development of nuclear energy. Under the terms of the Act, a utility seeking to construct and operate a nuclear power plant must obtain a separate permit or license at both the construction and the operation stage of the project. In order to obtain the construction permit, the utility must file a preliminary safety analysis report, an environmental report, and certain information regarding the antitrust implications of the proposed project. This application then undergoes exhaustive review by the Commission's staff and by the Advisory Committee on Reactor Safeguards (ACRS), a group of distinguished experts in the field

1. While there was division in this Court in *United States v. Florida East Coast R. Co.*, with respect to the constitutionality of such an interpretation in a case involving ratemaking, which JUSTICE DOUGLAS and JUSTICE STEWART felt was "adjudicatory" within the terms of the Act, the cases in the Court of Appeals for the District of Columbia Circuit which we review here involve rulemaking procedures in their most pristine sense.

appeared the agency employed all the procedures required by § 553 and more, the court determined the proceedings to be inadequate and overturned the rule. Accordingly, the Commission's determination with respect to Vermont Yankee's license was also remanded for further proceedings.

* * *

* * * The court conceded that absent extraordinary circumstances it is improper for a reviewing court to prescribe the procedural format an agency must follow, but it likewise clearly thought it entirely appropriate to "scrutinize the record as a whole to insure that genuine opportunities to participate in a meaningful way were provided. * * *" The court also refrained from actually ordering the agency to follow any specific procedures, but there is little doubt in our minds that the ineluctable mandate of the court's decision is that the procedures afforded during the hearings were inadequate. * * *

In prior opinions [e.g., *Londoner v. Denver*, 210 U.S. 373 (1908)] we have intimated that even in a rulemaking proceeding when an agency is making a " 'quasi-judicial' " determination by which a very small number of persons are " 'exceptionally affected, in each case upon individual grounds,' " in some circumstances additional procedures may be required in order to afford the aggrieved individuals due process.[16] It might also be true, although we do not think the issue is presented in this case and accordingly do not decide it, that a totally unjustified departure from well-settled agency procedures of long standing might require judicial correction.

But this much is absolutely clear. Absent constitutional constraints or extremely compelling circumstances the "administrative agencies 'should be free to fashion their own rules of procedure and to pursue methods of inquiry capable of permitting them to discharge their multitudinous duties.' " * * *

* * *

Respondent NRDC argues that § 553 of the Administrative Procedure Act merely establishes lower procedural bounds and that a court may routinely require more than the minimum when an agency's proposed rule addresses complex or technical factual issues or "Issues of Great Public Import." We have, however, previously shown that our decisions reject this view. We also think the legislative history, even the part which it cites, does not bear out its contention. * * *

There are compelling reasons for construing [§ 553] in this manner. In the first place, if courts continually review agency proceedings to determine whether the agency employed procedures which were, in the court's opinion, perfectly tailored to reach what the court perceives to be the "best" or "correct" result, judicial review would be totally unpredict-

16. Respondent NRDC does not now argue that additional procedural devices were required under the Constitution. Since this was clearly a rulemaking proceeding in its purest form, we see nothing to support such a view.

able. And the agencies, operating under this vague injunction to employ the "best" procedures and facing the threat of reversal if they did not, would undoubtedly adopt full adjudicatory procedures in every instance. Not only would this totally disrupt the statutory scheme, through which Congress enacted "a formula upon which opposing social and political forces have come to rest," but all the inherent advantages of informal rulemaking would be totally lost.

Secondly, it is obvious that the court in these cases reviewed the agency's choice of procedures on the basis of the record actually produced at the hearing, and not on the basis of the information available to the agency when it made the decision to structure the proceedings in a certain way. This sort of Monday morning quarterbacking not only encourages but almost compels the agency to conduct all rulemaking proceedings with the full panoply of procedural devices normally associated only with adjudicatory hearings.

Finally, and perhaps most importantly, this sort of review fundamentally misconceives the nature of the standard for judicial review of an agency rule. The court below uncritically assumed that additional procedures will automatically result in a more adequate record because it will give interested parties more of an opportunity to participate in and contribute to the proceedings. But informal rulemaking need not be based solely on the transcript of a hearing held before an agency. Indeed, the agency need not even hold a formal hearing. Thus, the adequacy of the "record" in this type of proceeding is not correlated directly to the type of procedural devices employed, but rather turns on whether the agency has followed the statutory mandate of the Administrative Procedure Act or other relevant statutes. If the agency is compelled to support the rule which it ultimately adopts with the type of record produced only after a full adjudicatory hearing, it simply will have no choice but to conduct a full adjudicatory hearing prior to promulgating every rule. In sum, this sort of unwarranted judicial examination of perceived procedural short-comings of a rulemaking proceeding can do nothing but seriously interfere with that process prescribed by Congress.

* * *

There remains, of course, the question of whether the challenged rule finds sufficient justification in the administrative proceedings that it should be upheld by the reviewing court. Judge Tamm, concurring in the result reached by the majority of the Court of Appeals, thought that it did not. There are also intimations in the majority opinion which suggest that the judges who joined it likewise may have thought the administrative proceedings an insufficient basis upon which to predicate the rule in question. We accordingly remand so that the Court of Appeals may review the rule as the Administrative Procedure Act provides. * * *

Notes

1. *Substance v. Procedure.* Again, what difference is there between a remand to an agency premised on the inadequacy of the agency's procedure for testing evidence in informal rulemaking and a remand premised on the inadequacy of the factual support for a rule because the record fails to illuminate adequately issues that some participants considered critical to the agency's decision and on which they are prepared to offer rebuttal evidence?

2. *Proceedings on Remand.* Justice Rehnquist's invitation to the court of appeals to focus on the factual bases for the NRC's conclusion did not end the *Vermont Yankee* litigation. Even before the Supreme Court's decision, the NRC had begun proceedings to reformulate its "generic rule" assessing the environmental effects of the nuclear fuel cycle. Its final rule, promulgated before the case was reheard in the D.C. Circuit, forecast that long-term isolation of waste fuel would have no adverse environmental effects, that permanent waste storage facilities could be developed, and that these facilities would perform as expected. The rule was accompanied by a table of numerical values that purported to quantify the environmental effects of nuclear power generation, which were to be drawn on in evaluating any nuclear power facility. The NRC declined to factor acknowledged uncertainties into the tabular values, and went on to state that "no further discussion of such environmental effects [in individual licensing proceedings] shall be required." In *NRDC v. U.S. NRC*, 685 F.2d 459 (D.C.Cir.1982), Judge Bazelon once more set aside the NRC's action, this time on substantive grounds. Noting that the APA required the court to set aside agency action that is "arbitrary and capricious" or "not in accordance with law," Bazelon pointed out that section 102(2)(C) of NEPA demands that federal agencies fully consider and disclose the environmental impact of their actions.

Judge Bazelon's chief concern was that the NRC had excluded a critical issue at the heart of the debate over nuclear power—the problem of permanent disposal of spent fuel—from consideration by those who have the authority to issue or deny licenses. Analyzed either as a factual finding or as a decision making device by which the Commission retained exclusive responsibility for considering the uncertainties concerning long-term waste disposal, the rule was invalid: "NEPA requires an agency to consider the environmental risks of a proposed action in a manner that allows the existence of such risks to influence the agency's decision to take the action." The court also found that the original and interim rules which accompanied Table S–3 violated NEPA because they could be interpreted as cutting off any inquiry by the licensing board into the health, socioeconomic, and cumulative environmental impacts of waste disposal.

Judge Bazelon was not content to rest his decision solely on the special requirements of NEPA (and the APA's command to set aside action "not in accordance with law"):

> * * * [T]he same result can be reached under the arbitrary and capricious standard. Under that standard, as stated above, our inquiry focuses upon whether the zero-release assumption is based on "consideration of the relevant factors." Under NEPA, significant uncertainty

surrounding the environmental effect of a proposed action is relevant to an agency's decision to rule generically that the effect will not occur. For an agency to go forward in the face of significant uncertainty and issue such a rule indicates either a failure to consider a relevant factor or a clear error in judgment. Because that is precisely what the Commission did in promulgating the Table S–3 Rule, we could also conclude that its action was arbitrary and capricious.

Predictably, the case returned to the Supreme Court, which again reversed the D.C. Circuit. *Baltimore Gas & Electric Co. v. NRDC*, 462 U.S. 87 (1983). Writing for a unanimous court, Justice O'Connor held that the court of appeals exceeded its proper role in reviewing the NRC's informed resolution of difficult and controversial issues, and discouraged the courts from becoming embroiled in the debate over the wisdom of nuclear energy. "Resolution of these fundamental policy questions lies * * * with Congress and the agencies to which Congress has delegated authority, as well as with state legislatures and, ultimately, the populace as a whole." Justice O'Connor found that the NRC's extensive hearings on the uncertainties of waste disposal were sufficient to satisfy NEPA's requirements. Her opinion went on to rule that the NRC's use of a zero value to represent the environmental impact of long term storage of nuclear waste was not arbitrary because it was but one figure in a larger table of reasonably conservative values. Moreover, she recognized the NRC was making predictions "at the frontiers of science," not findings of fact, and stressed that in such situations "* * * a reviewing court must generally be at its most deferential."

3. *Commentary on* Vermont Yankee. The Court's *Vermont Yankee* decision provoked a large secondary literature. Among the most provocative analyses is Nathaniel L. Nathanson, *The* Vermont Yankee Nuclear Power *Opinion: A Masterpiece of Statutory Misinterpretation*, 16 San Diego L.Rev. 183 (1979), whose title makes clear the author's viewpoint. Professor Nathanson argued persuasively that the Court misinterpreted the governing statutes in *Vermont Yankee*—the Hobbs Act and the Atomic Energy Act—which together with their legislative history reveal that Congress expected that NRC regulations would be adopted in on-the-record proceedings meeting the requirements of sections 556 and 557 of the APA. He went on to suggest that the agency's procedures in fact probably met those requirements. Nathanson also challenged Justice Rehnquist's earlier holding in *Florida East Coast Railway* that formal rulemaking is required only when an agency's governing statute specifies that rules are "to be made on the record after opportunity for an agency hearing." Nathanson contended that the framers of the APA expected that rules destined for review on the record in the courts of appeals would be the product of formal proceedings. By contrast, rules adopted pursuant to the procedures of section 553 were to be evaluated on the basis of the factual record compiled in enforcement suits in district courts. Professor Nathanson's analysis thus casts doubt on the many decisions, like *Nova Scotia Food Products Corp.*, that assume judicial review of rules promulgated in section 553 rulemaking will be based on, and confined to, an administrative record.

Professor, now Justice, Antonin Scalia assessed *Vermont Yankee* more sympathetically but offered a historical explanation for the judicial propensity to demand that agencies provide procedural safeguards beyond the bare essentials historically associated with section 553:

> Consider two categories of massive post-APA change in the particular area of informal rulemaking:
>
> 1. Not until 1956 [*Storer Broadcasting*] was it established that an agency charged with issuing and denying licenses in adjudicatory hearings could establish generic disqualifying factors in informal rulemaking, thereby avoiding adversarial procedures on those issues. Not until 1968 was it established that a major rate-making agency (the FPC) had implicit authority to fix rates on an areawide basis rather than company by company, enabling the avoidance of constitutional and statutory requirements for an adjudicatory hearing. And not until 1973 [*Petroleum Refiners*] was it judicially determined that the FTC, one of the oldest of the regulatory agencies, had authority to prohibit unfair trade practices by rule, as opposed to operating exclusively through individual "cease-and-desist" proceedings.
>
> Decisions such as these have facilitated what is perhaps the most notable development in federal government administration during the past two decades: "The contrivance of more expeditious administrative methods"—that is, the constant and accelerating flight away from individualized, adjudicatory proceedings to generalized disposition through rulemaking. * * *
>
> 2. Another post-APA development of monumental importance was the establishment in 1967 [*Abbott Laboratories*, in Chapter 7, *infra*] of the principle that rules could be challenged in court directly rather than merely in the context of an adjudicatory enforcement proceeding against a particular individual, combined with the doctrine (clearly enunciated in 1973) that "the focal point for judicial review should be the administrative record already in existence, not some new record made initially in the reviewing court." * * *
>
> The cumulative effect of these developments was that by the mid-1970s vast numbers of issues of the sort which in 1946 would have been resolved in a formal adjudicatory context before the agency, or even in an adjudicatory judicial proceeding, were being resolved in informal rulemaking and informal adjudication; that the courts were expected to provide, in the words of one of the Supreme Court's more expansive descriptions (which it probably now regrets), "a thorough, probing, in-depth review" of that agency action, but taking the agency record as it was and without conducting any additional evidentiary proceedings. * * *

Antonin Scalia, Vermont Yankee: *The APA, The D.C. Circuit, and the Supreme Court*, 1978 Sup.Ct.Rev. 345 (1979). See also Stephen Breyer, Vermont Yankee *and the Courts' Role in the Nuclear Energy Controversy*, 91 Harv.L.Rev. 1833 (1978); Clark Byse, Vermont Yankee *and the Evolution of Administrative Procedure: A Somewhat Different View*, 91 Harv.L.Rev. 1823 (1978); Richard B. Stewart, Vermont Yankee *and the Evolution of Administrative Procedure*, 91 Harv.L.Rev. 1805 (1978).

c. *Ex Parte Contacts in Rulemaking*

By 1977, both agencies and courts understood that rules were to be based (and reviewed) on a "record," even when the agency's proceeding was subject only to the requirements of section 553. General acceptance of this proposition blurred the historical distinction between formal procedures in which decisions were based *exclusively* on the evidentiary record and informal processes in which the "record" consisted of whatever information the agency drew upon in reaching a decision, regardless of how it gained access to the information. That agencies should not rely on any material not placed in the record as possible support for their decisions seems a logical corollary of *Nova Scotia*'s requirement that parties have an opportunity to comment on the crucial factual and theoretical bases for agency rules.

But the concept of an exclusive record for decision might mean more, as a panel of the D.C. Circuit demonstrated in *Home Box Office, Inc. v. FCC*, 567 F.2d 9 (1977), *cert. denied*, 434 U.S. 829 (1977). The case involved regulations that restricted the program fare cablecasters and subscription broadcast television stations could offer. The court's opinion focused on the FCC's conduct during the informal rulemaking proceedings:

> It is apparently uncontested that a number of participants before the Commission sought out individual commissioners or Commission employees for the purpose of discussing ex parte and in confidence the merits of the rules under review here. * * *
>
> Although it is impossible to draw any firm conclusions about the effect of ex parte presentations upon the ultimate shape of the pay cable rules, the evidence is certainly consistent with often-voiced claims of undue industry influence over Commission proceedings, and we are particularly concerned that the final shaping of the rules we are reviewing here may have been by compromise among the contending industry forces, rather than by exercise of the independent discretion in the public interest the Communications Act vests in individual commissioners. * * *
>
> Even the possibility that there is here one administrative record for the public and this court and another for the Commission and those "in the know" is intolerable. * * * [I]t is the obligation of this court to test the actions of the Commission for arbitrariness or inconsistency with delegated authority. Yet here agency secrecy stands between us and fulfillment of our obligation. Moreover, where, as here, an agency justifies its actions by reference only to information in the public file while failing to disclose the substance of other relevant information that has been represented to it, a reviewing court cannot presume that the agency has acted properly, but must treat the agency's justifications as a fictional account of the actual decisionmaking process and must perforce find its actions arbitrary.

> * * * Even if the Commission had disclosed to this court the substance of what was said to it ex parte, it would still be difficult to judge the truth of what the Commission asserted it knew about the television industry because we would not have the benefit of an adversarial discussion among the parties.
>
> Equally important is the inconsistency of secrecy with fundamental notions of fairness implicit in due process and with the ideal of reasoned decisionmaking on the merits which undergirds all of our administrative law. * * *

The court went on to prescribe guidelines for future agency rulemaking:

> [I]t should be clear that information gathered ex parte from the public which becomes relevant to a rulemaking will have to be disclosed at some time. On the other hand, we recognize that informal contacts between agencies and the public are the "bread and butter" of the process of administration and are completely appropriate so long as they do not frustrate judicial review or raise serious questions of fairness. Reconciliation of these considerations in a manner which will reduce procedural uncertainty leads us to conclude that communications which are received prior to issuance of a formal notice of rulemaking do not, in general, have to be put in a public file. Of course, if the information contained in such a communication forms the basis for agency action, then, under well established principles, that information must be disclosed to the public in some form. Once a notice of proposed rulemaking has been issued, however, any agency official or employee who is or may reasonably be expected to be involved in the decisional process of the rulemaking proceeding, should "refus[e] to discuss matters relating to the disposition of a [rulemaking proceeding] with any interested private party, or an attorney or agent for any such party, prior to the [agency's] decision * * *," * * *. If ex parte contacts nonetheless occur, we think that any written document or a summary of any oral communication must be placed in the public file established for each rulemaking docket immediately after the communication is received so that interested parties may comment thereon.

Within a few months another panel of the D.C. Circuit, which included Judge MacKinnon who had dissented in *Home Box Office*, limited that ruling. *Action for Children's Television v. FCC*, 564 F.2d 458 (D.C.Cir.1977), involved a challenge to the FCC's failure to adopt proposed regulations for improving children's programming. The primary reason the Commission offered for its decision to terminate the rulemaking was its belief that proposals developed by the broadcast industry for self-regulation could adequately serve the objectives of the proposed rules. The industry proposals had been discussed by broadcaster representatives with members of the Commission in meetings that were not announced or open to the public, and the agency afforded no opportunity for public comment on the proposals before it terminated its proceeding. The petitioners challenged the Commission's decision not to regulate based in part on its undeniable "violation" of *Home Box Office*. However, the *Action for Children's Television* panel first refused to apply the earlier ruling retroactively and then proceeded to narrow its prospective application:

> If we go as far as *Home Box Office* does in its ex parte ruling in ensuring a "whole record" for our review, why not go further to require the decisionmaker to summarize and make available for public comment every status inquiry from a Congressman or any germane material—say a newspaper editorial—that he or she reads or their evening-hour ruminations? In the end, why not administer a lie-detector test to ascertain whether the required summary is an accurate and complete one? The problem is obviously a matter of degree, and the appropriate line must be drawn somewhere. In light of what must be presumed to be Congress' intent not to prohibit or require disclosure of all ex parte contacts during or after the public comment stage, we would draw that line at the point where the rulemaking proceedings involve "competing claims to a valuable privilege." It is at that point where the potential for unfair advantage outweighs the practical burdens, which we imagine would not be insubstantial, that such a judicially conceived rule would place upon administrators. * * *
>
> * * * Private groups were not competing for a specific valuable privilege. Furthermore, this case does not raise serious questions of fairness. Chairman Wiley met with representatives of NAB, as Chairman Burch had met with representatives of ACT, and there is no indication that he "gave to any interested party advantages not shared by all." * * *

The D.C. Circuit's decision in *Action for Children's Television* thus limited the constraints on ex parte communications first recognized in *Sangamon Valley Television Corp. v. United States*, 269 F.2d 221 (D.C.Cir.1959), to rulemaking undertaken to resolve "competing claims to a valuable privilege." (*Sangamon Valley* involved an FCC proceeding to determine which of two communities would be assigned a television station; under Commission rules, only one of the communities could be awarded the station, and each had a single prospective licensee.)

Other courts of appeals appeared less concerned about ex parte contacts in rulemaking. Compare the Second Circuit's curt dismissal of a complaint about ex parte communications in rulemaking between members of the Federal Trade Commission "and an allegedly biased staff" as "more properly addressed to Congress." *Katharine Gibbs School, Inc. v. FTC*, 612 F.2d 658 (2d Cir.1979). See Ernest Gellhorn and Glen O. Robinson, *Rulemaking "Due Process": An Inconclusive Dialogue*, 48 U.Chi.L.Rev. 201 (1981).

Glen Robinson, himself a former member of the FCC, sees a conflict between quasi-judicial procedural requirements designed to protect the integrity of administrative decision making and the practical necessities of information gathering in a quasi-political environment. In *The Federal*

Communications Commission: An Essay on Regulatory Watchdogs, 64 Va.L.Rev. 169, 228–30 (1978), Professor Robinson wrote:

> Militating against a ban on ex parte communications is the loss of flexibility, speed, and efficiency (in the narrow sense of minimized procedural costs) that would arise if all contacts with agency decisionmakers were restricted to on-the-record communications. Indeed, such a ban would cause more than a loss of efficiency, because the additional procedural burdens almost certainly would reduce the amount of available information. * * * In many cases, informal outside consultation is a useful means to cut through a mass of formal documentary material buried in elephantine dockets and to cull out the essential information.
>
> Ex parte contacts also are an important check on the reliability of staff information. Students of bureaucracy have noted that large organizations rarely exhibit a free flow of information from lower to higher echelons due to obstacles such as conflicting self-interests among members of the different echelons. Because staff information and interpretation is not always reliable, ex parte contacts outside the agency are an important means of avoiding "staff capture." * * *
>
> In support of some restraint on ex parte communications, it must be acknowledged that a totally laissez-faire rulemaking process provides a fertile bed for arbitrary administrative action. For example, when interested persons—without providing notice to others—are able to present their facts and arguments to individual agency members and staff, the rulemaking process imposes no check on the reliability of information presented to the decisionmakers. * * * Allowing unfettered ex parte communications also undermines the incentive for interested persons to submit carefully prepared studies and briefs because their work is lost so easily in the shuffle of off-the-record encounters.
>
> The arguments for and against ex parte communications are balanced sufficiently to commend a solution somewhere between the extremes of laissez-faire and flat prohibition. I believe that most of the desired goals of a ban could be achieved by a system requiring all decisionmakers to record both the fact and the essential content of all communications with interested persons regarding any substantive issue within the Commission's concern. Such a record would be available to the public—including, of course, all persons interested in particular proceedings, to which such discussions pertain. * * *

The position advocated by Professor Robinson is essentially that first adopted by the FDA in its regulations governing agency rulemaking, see 42 Fed.Reg. 4680 (1977), and later accepted by other agencies.

The problem of ex parte communications during rulemaking assumes greater complexity in a world where it is not just regulated firms or private policy advocates who wish to influence the making of regulatory policy. As described in Chapter 3, *supra*, beginning in the 1970s, presidents and their immediate staffs have exhibited increasing interest in the decisions and actions of heads of agencies and other appointed officials. President Reagan established a formal framework for White House oversight of agency rulemaking, a framework whose essential dimensions have been embraced by the first President Bush, President Clinton, and President George W. Bush.

The erection of this managerial edifice not only brought new voices into what had been a highly decentralized process of policy formation; it created an additional forum, ostensibly a higher forum, to which arguments, objections, and information about proposed regulations could be, and very soon were, addressed. These developments immediately raised novel issues of administrative procedure and institutional authority. Indeed, some of these issues surfaced even before President Reagan's issuance of E.O. 12291, during a Carter Administration that sought to exert increased centralized control over policy but through less formal means.

Communications between agency decision makers and OMB or White House staff on proposed regulations inevitably involve meetings and telephone calls as well as the exchange of written memos. Accusations that such intra-executive consultations might be improper, brought the matter to the Department of Justice in 1978. The specific context was Secretary of the Interior's consideration of proposed regulations under the Surface Mining Control and Reclamation Act of 1977, 30 U.S.C. § 1201 *et seq.* The Justice Department offered the following advice on the procedures the Secretary should follow in discussing the proposed regulations with representatives of the Council of Economic Advisers (CEA):

> * * * [I]t is our conclusion that there is no prohibition against communications within the Executive Branch after the close of the comment period on these proposed rules. Nothing in the relevant statutes or in the decisions of the D.C. Circuit suggest the existence of a bar against full and detailed consultations between those charged with promulgating the rules and the President's advisers. The rulings of the D.C. Circuit, however, do suggest that it might be inappropriate for interested persons outside the Executive Branch to have so-called ex parte communications with you and your staff. If that is so, we think it logical to conclude that the D.C. Circuit would disapprove of CEA or other advisers to the President serving as a conduit for those same ex parte communications.

The Justice Department letter went on to describe the procedure that it recommended and that the Secretary had followed:

> (1) The CEA staff compiled a record of all of the oral and written communications they may have had with private persons interested in the proposed regulations. This catalog sets forth the content of all of these communications as accurately and fully as is

possible. For the sake of completeness, it also includes recollections of CEA conversations with other Executive Branch offices.

(2) Following receipt and review of this material, OSM [Office of Surface Mining] made it available to the public in the document room at the Department of Interior. At the same time OSM published in the *Federal Register* for Thursday, January 4, 1979, a statement acknowledging, and explaining the reason for, this addition to the administrative record. The statement also announced the reopening of the record to allow comments on factual material contained in the submission. * * *

(3) Once the compilation was made publicly available and the notice was transmitted to the *Federal Register* for publication, the Chairman [of the CEA] and/or his staff conferred with OSM on particular portions of the proposed rules. * * *

(4) Although we have been advised that no changes were made in the proposed rules as a result of these consultations, we did counsel that if any communications made during this consultation process did become in part the basis for the Secretary's final decision concerning the rulemaking, their relationship to that decision would be fully spelled out with the promulgation of the final rule. There would, however, be no need to reopen the record again prior to the final decision unless you propose to rely on other information that was not included in the record at some stage and subjected to reasonable public comment in advance of your final decision.

(5) During the period of consultation, the participants were instructed to refrain from having any communications with other persons interested in the rulemaking, including other Executive branch officials, if those officials have either directly or indirectly had contacts with non-Government persons having an interest in this rulemaking.

The executive branch is not the only political institution active in an agency's rulemaking environment. Senators and Representatives can hold hearings, write letters, make telephone calls and demand meetings with agency personnel. In hotly contested rulemaking proceedings agencies are awash in a sea of politically inspired comments, meetings and pressures. In what circumstances should ex parte political activity undermine the legal validity of an agency rule?

SIERRA CLUB v. COSTLE

United States Court of Appeals, District of Columbia Circuit, 1981.
657 F.2d 298.

WALD, CIRCUIT JUDGE.

This case concerns the extent to which new coal-fired steam generators that produce electricity must control their emissions of sulfur dioxide and particulate matter into the air. In June of 1979 EPA revised the regulations called "new source performance standards" ("NSPS" or "standards") governing emission control by coal burning power plants. On this appeal we consider challenges to the revised NSPS brought by environmental groups which contend that the standards are too lax and by electric utilities which contend that the standards are too rigorous. * * *

* * *

* * * The new standards increase pollution controls for new coal-fired electric power plants by tightening restrictions on emissions of sulfur dioxide and particulate matter. Sulfur dioxide emissions are limited to a maximum of 1.2 lbs./MBtu [pounds per million British thermal units] (or 520 ng/j) [nanograms per joule] and a 90 percent reduction of potential uncontrolled sulfur dioxide emissions is required except when emissions to the atmosphere are less than 0.60 lbs./MBtu (or 260 ng/j). When sulfur dioxide emissions are less than 0.60 lbs./MBtu potential emissions must be reduced by no less than 70 percent. In addition, emissions of particulate matter are limited to 0.03 lbs./MBtu (or 13 ng/j).

Petitioners in this case are Sierra Club and the State of California Air Resources Board ("CARB"), which oppose the variable 70 to 90 percent reduction requirement of the NSPS; Appalachian Power Co. ("APCO"), *et al.*, a group comprised of APCO, the Edison Electric Institute, the National Rural Electric Cooperative Association, and 86 individual utilities ("Electric Utilities"), which challenge both the maximum 90 percent reduction requirement and the 0.03 lbs./MBtu limit on emissions of particulate matter; and the Environmental Defense Fund ("EDF"), which challenges the 1.2 lbs./MBtu ceiling imposed by the NSPS.

* * *

Coal is the dominant fuel used for generating electricity in the United States. When coal is burned, it releases sulfur dioxide and particulate matter into the atmosphere. At the very least these pollutants are known to cause or contribute to respiratory illnesses. * * * In 1976 power plant emissions accounted for 64 percent of the total estimated sulfur dioxide emissions and 24 percent of the total estimated particulate matter emissions in the entire country.

EPA's revised NSPS are designed to curtail these emissions. EPA predicts that the new standards would reduce national sulfur dioxide emissions from new plants by 50 percent and national particulate matter emissions by 70 percent by 1995. The cost of the new controls, however, is substantial. EPA estimates that utilities will have to spend tens of billions of dollars by 1995 on pollution control under the new NSPS. * * * Not surprisingly, coal burning power plants' already preeminent share of electric power produced in the United States will grow over the remainder of this century.

* * *

V. THE 1.2 LBS./MBTU EMISSION CEILING

EPA proposed and ultimately adopted a 1.2 lbs./MBtu ceiling for total sulfur dioxide emissions which is applicable regardless of the percentage of sulfur dioxide reduction attained. The 1.2 lbs./MBtu standard is identical to the emission ceiling required by the former standard. The achievability of the standard is undisputed.

EDF challenges this part of the final NSPS on procedural grounds, contending that although there may be evidence supporting the 1.2 lbs./MBtu standard, EPA should have and would have adopted a stricter standard if it had not engaged in post-comment period irregularities and succumbed to political pressures. * * *

A. *EPA's Rationale for the Emission Ceiling*

EPA explained in the preamble to the proposed rule that two primary factors were considered in selecting the 1.2 lbs./MBtu ceiling: FGD [flue gas wet scrubbing] performance, and the impact of the ceiling on high sulfur coal reserves. * * *

Following the September 1978 proposal the joint interagency working group investigated options lower than the 1.2 lbs./MBtu ceiling, according to EPA, in order "to take full advantage of the cost effectiveness benefits of a joint coal washing/scrubbing strategy on high-sulfur coal." The joint working group reasoned that since coal washing is relatively inexpensive, an emission ceiling which would require 90 percent scrubbing in addition to coal washing "could substantially reduce emissions in the East and Midwest at a relatively low cost." Since coal washing is a widespread practice, it was thought that the 1.2 lbs./MBtu proposal would not have a seriously detrimental impact upon Eastern coal production. During phase two EPA analyzed 10 different full control and partial control options with its econometric model. These various options included emission ceilings at the 1.2 lbs./MBtu, 0.80 lbs./MBtu and the 0.55 lbs./MBtu levels. The modeling results, published before the close of the public comment period in December 1978, confirmed the joint working group's conclusion that the 1.2 lbs./MBtu standard should be lowered. The results of the phase two modeling exercise were cited by internal EPA memoranda in January and March 1979 as a basis for lowering the 1.2 lbs./MBtu standard. After the phase two modeling, however, EPA undertook "a more detailed analysis of regional coal producing impacts," using BOM [Bureau of Mines] seam by seam data on the sulfur content of the reserves and the coal washing potential for those reserves. This analysis identified the amount of reserves that would require more than 90 percent scrubbing of *washed* coal to meet alternative ceilings.

As a result of concerns expressed on the record by NCA and others about the impacts of more rigorous emission ceilings, EPA called a meeting of principal participants in the rulemaking for April 15, 1979. At the meeting EPA presented its new analysis which showed that a 0.55 lbs./MBtu limit would require more than 90 percent scrubbing on 5 to 10 percent of Northern Appalachian reserves and 12 to 25 percent of Eastern Midwest reserves. A 0.80 ceiling would require more than 90 percent scrubbing on less than 5 percent of the reserves in each of these regions. * * *

* * * The agency's analysis, according to EPA, showed that up to 22 percent of high sulfur coal reserves in the Eastern Midwest and parts of the Northern Appalachian coal regions would require more than 90 percent reduction if emissions were held to a 1.0 lbs./MBtu standard. Thus, although acknowledging that stricter controls were technically feasible, EPA chose to retain the 1.2 lbs./MBtu standard because "conservatism in utility perceptions of scrubber performance could create a significant disincentive against the use of these coals and disrupt the coal markets in these regions." EPA concluded that "[a] more stringent emission limit would be counter to one of the basic purposes of the 1977 Amendments, that is, encouraging the use of higher sulfur coals."

B. EDF's Procedural Attack

EDF alleges that as a result of an "ex parte blitz" by coal industry advocates conducted after the close of the comment period, EPA backed away from adopting the .55 lbs./MBtu limit, and instead adopted the higher 1.2 lbs./MBtu restriction. EDF asserts that even before the comment period had ended EPA had already narrowed its focus to include only options which provided for the .55 lbs./MBtu ceiling. EDF also claims that as of March 9, 1979, the three proposals which EPA had under active consideration all included the more stringent .55 lbs./MBtu ceiling, and the earlier 1.2 lbs./MBtu ceiling had been discarded. Whether or not EDF's scenario is credible, it is true that EPA did circulate a draft NSPS with an emissions ceiling below the 1.2 lbs./MBtu level for interagency comment during February, 1978. Following a "leak" of this proposal, EDF says, the so-called "ex parte blitz" began. "Scores" of pro-industry "ex parte" comments were received by EPA in the post-comment period, states EDF, and various meetings with coal industry advocates—including Senator Robert Byrd of West Virginia—took place during that period. These communications, EDF asserts, were unlawful and prejudicial to its position.

* * *

The comment period for the NSPS began on September 19, 1978, and closed on January 15, 1979. After January 15, EPA received almost 300 written submissions on the proposed rule from a broad range of interests. EPA accepted these comments and entered them all on its administrative docket. EPA did not, however, officially reopen the comment period, nor did it notify the public through the Federal Register or by other means that it had received and was entering the "late" comments. According to EDF, most of the approximately 300 late comments were received after the "leak" of the new .55 lbs./MBtu proposal.

EDF claims that of the 138 late comments from non-government sources, at least 30 were from "representatives of the coal or utility industries," and of the 53 comments from members of Congress, 22 were either forwarded by the Congressmen from industry interests, or else were prepared and submitted by Congressmen as advocates of those interests.

EDF objects to nine different meetings. A chronological list and synopsis of the challenged meetings follows:

1. *March 14, 1979*—This was a one and a half hour briefing at the White House for high-level officials from the Department of Energy (DOE), the Council of Economic Advisors (CEA), the White House staff, the Department of Interior, the Council on Environmental Quality (CEQ), the Office of Management and Budget (OMB), and the National Park Service. The meeting was reported in a May 9, 1979 memorandum from EPA to Senator Muskie's staff, responding to the Senator's request for a monthly report of contacts between EPA staff and other federal officials concerning the NSPS. A summary of the meeting and the materials distributed were docketed on May 30, 1979.

2. *April 5, 1979*—This * * * meeting was attended by representatives of EPA, DOE, NCA, EDF, Congressman Paul Simon's office, ICF, Inc. (who performed the microanalysis), and Hunton & Williams (who represented the Electric Utilities). The participants were notified in advance of the agenda for the meeting. Materials relating to EPA's and NCA's presentations during the meeting were distributed and copies were later put into the docket along with detailed minutes of the meeting. Follow up calls and letters between NCA and EPA came on April 20, 23, and 29, commenting or elaborating upon the April 5 data. All of these follow up contacts were recorded in the docket.

3. *April 23, 1979*—This was a 30–45 minute meeting held at then Senate Majority Leader Robert Byrd's request, in his office, attended by EPA Administrator Douglas Costle, Chief Presidential Assistant Stuart Eizenstat, and NCA officials. A summary of this meeting was put in the docket on May 1, 1979, and copies of the summary were sent to EDF and to other parties. In its denial of the petition for reconsideration, EPA was adamant that no new information was transmitted to EPA at this meeting.

4. *April 27, 1979*—This was a briefing on dry scrubbing technology conducted by EPA for representatives of the Office of Science and Technology Policy, the Council on Wage and Price Stability, DOE, the President's domestic policy staff, OMB, and various offices within EPA. A description of this briefing and copies of the material distributed were docketed on May 1, 1979.

5. *April 30, 1979*—At 10:00 a.m., a one hour White House briefing was held for the President, the White House staff, and high ranking members of the Executive Branch "concerning the issues and options presented by the rulemaking." This meeting was noted on an EPA official's personal calendar which EDF obtained after promulgation in

response to its FOIA request, but was never noted in the rulemaking docket.

6. *April 30, 1979*—At 2:30 p.m., a technical briefing on dry scrubbing technology at the White House was conducted by EPA for the White House staff. A short memorandum describing this briefing was docketed on May 30, 1979.

7. *May 1, 1979*—Another White House briefing was held on the subject of FGD technology. A description of the meeting and materials distributed were docketed on May 30, 1979.

8. *May 1, 1979*—EPA conducted a one hour briefing of staff members of the Senate Committee on Environmental and Public Works concerning EPA's analysis of the effect of alternative emission ceilings on coal reserves. The briefing was "substantially the same as the briefing given to Senator Byrd on May 2, 1980." No persons other than Committee staff members and EPA officials attended the briefing. This meeting, like the one at 10:00 a.m. on April 30, was never entered on the rulemaking docket but was listed on an EPA official's calendar obtained by EDF in response to its FOIA request. * * *

9. *May 2, 1979*—This was a brief meeting between Senator Byrd, EPA, DOE and NCA officials held ostensibly for Senator Byrd to hear EPA's comments on the NCA data. A 49 word, not very informative, memorandum describing the meeting was entered on the docket on June 1, 1979. * * *

C. *Standard for Judicial Review of EPA Procedures*

This court's scope of review is delimited by the special procedural provisions of the Clean Air Act, which declare that we may reverse the Administrator's decision for procedural error only if (i) his failure to observe procedural requirements was arbitrary and capricious, (ii) an objection was raised during the comment period, or the grounds for such objection arose only after the comment period and the objection is "of central relevance to the outcome of the rule," and (iii) "the errors were so serious and related to matters of such central relevance to the rule that there is a substantial likelihood that the rule would have been significantly changed if such errors had not been made." The essential message of so rigorous a standard is that Congress was concerned that EPA's rulemaking not be casually overturned for procedural reasons, and we of course must respect that judgment.

Our authority to reverse informal administrative rulemaking for procedural reasons is also informed by *Vermont Yankee Nuclear Power Corp. v. Natural Resources Defense Council, Inc.* * * *

D. *Statutory Provisions Concerning Procedure*

The procedural provisions of the Clean Air Act specifying the creation and content of the administrative rulemaking record are contained in section 307. * * *

* * * [T]he 1977 Amendments required the agency to establish a "rulemaking docket" for each proposed rule which would form the basis of the record for judicial review. The docket must contain, *inter alia* (1) "notice of the proposed rulemaking * * * accompanied by a statement of its basis and purpose," and a specification of the public comment period; (2) "all written comments and documentary information on the proposed rule received from any person * * * during the comment period[;] [t]he transcript of public hearings, if any[;] and [a]ll documents * * * which become available after the proposed rule has been published and which the Administrator determines are of central relevance to the rulemaking. * * *"; (3) drafts of proposed rules submitted for interagency review, and all documents accompanying them and responding to them; and (4) the promulgated rule and the various accompanying agency documents which explain and justify it.

In contrast to other recent statutes,* there is no mention of any restrictions upon "ex parte" contacts. However, the statute apparently did envision that participants would normally submit comments, documentary material, and oral presentations during a prescribed comment period. Only two provisions in the statute touch upon the post-comment period, one of which, as noted immediately *supra*, states that "[a]ll documents which become available after the proposed rule has been published and which the Administrator determines are of central relevance to the rulemaking shall be placed in the docket as soon as possible after their availability." But since all the post-comment period written submissions which EDF complains of were in fact entered upon the docket, EDF cannot complain that this provision has been violated.

* * *

E. Validity of EPA's Procedures During The Post–Comment Period

The post-comment period communications about which EDF complains vary widely in their content and mode; some are written documents or letters, others are oral conversations and briefings, while still others are meetings where alleged political arm-twisting took place. For analytical purposes we have grouped the communications into categories and shall discuss each of them separately. * * *

Although no express authority to admit post-comment documents exist, the statute does provide that:

> All documents which become available after the proposed rule has been published and which the Administrator determines are of central relevance to the rulemaking shall be placed in the docket as soon as possible after their availability.

* [The only statute Judge Wald cites is the Federal Trade Commission Act, as amended in 1980, 94 Stat. at 379–80. Congress does not generally appear inclined to restrict ex parte communications with agencies engaged in rulemaking, perhaps because such restrictions might be thought to impede the ability of individual members to convey their views on important pending rulemakings.]

This provision, in contrast to others in the same subparagraph, is not limited to the comment period. Apparently it allows EPA not only to put documents into the record after the comment period is over, but also to define which documents are of "central relevance" so as to require that they be placed in the docket. The principal purpose of the drafters was to define in advance, for the benefit of reviewing courts, the record upon which EPA would rely in defending the rule it finally adopted; it was not their purpose to guarantee that every piece of paper or phone call related to the rule which was received by EPA during the post-comment period be included in the docket. EPA thus has authority to place post-comment documents into the docket, but it need not do so in all instances.

Such a reading of the statute accords well with the realities of Washington administrative policymaking, where rumors, leaks, and overreactions by concerned groups abound, particularly as the time for promulgation draws near. In a proceeding such as this, one of vital concern to so many interests—industry, environmental groups, as well as Congress and the Administration—it would be unrealistic to think there would not naturally be attempts on all sides to stay in contact with EPA right up to the moment the final rule is promulgated. The drafters of the 1977 Amendments were practical people, well versed in such activity, and we decline now to infer from their silence that they intended to prohibit the lodging of documents with the agency at any time prior to promulgation. Common sense, after all, must play a part in our interpretation of these statutory procedures.

EPA of course could have extended, or reopened, the comment period after January 15 in order formally to accommodate the flood of new documents; it has done so in other cases. But under the circumstances of this case, we do not find that it was necessary for EPA to reopen the formal comment period. In the first place, the comment period lasted over four months, and although the length of the comment period was not specified in the 1977 Amendments, the statute did put a premium on speedy decisionmaking by setting a one year deadline from the Amendments' enactment to the rules' promulgation. EPA failed to meet that deadline, and subsequently entered into a consent decree where it promised to adopt the final rules by March 19, 1979, over seven months late. EPA also failed to meet that deadline, and it was once more extended until June 1, 1979 upon agreement of the parties pursuant to court order. Reopening the formal comment period in the late spring of 1979 would have confronted the agency with a possible violation of the court order, and would further have frustrated the Congressional intent that these rules be promulgated expeditiously.

If, however, documents of central importance upon which EPA intended to rely had been entered on the docket too late for any meaningful public comment prior to promulgation, then both the structure and spirit of section 307 would have been violated. * * *

The case before us, however, does not present an instance where documents vital to EPA's support for its rule were submitted so late as to preclude any effective public comment. The vast majority of the written comments referred to earlier * * * were submitted in ample time to afford an opportunity for response. Regarding those documents submitted closer to the promulgation date, our review does not reveal that they played any significant role in the agency's support for the rule. The decisive point, however, is that EDF itself has failed to show us any particular document or documents to which it lacked an opportunity to respond, and which also were vital to EPA's support for the rule.

* * *

The statute does not explicitly treat the issue of post-comment period meetings with individuals outside EPA. Oral face-to-face discussions are not prohibited anywhere, anytime, in the Act. The absence of such prohibition may have arisen from the nature of the informal rulemaking procedures Congress had in mind. Where agency action resembles judicial action, where it involves formal rulemaking, adjudication, or quasi-adjudication among "conflicting private claims to a valuable privilege," the insulation of the decisionmaker from ex parte contacts is justified by basic notions of due process to the parties involved. But where agency action involves informal rulemaking of a policymaking sort, the concept of ex parte contacts is of more questionable utility.

Under our system of government, the very legitimacy of general policymaking performed by unelected administrators depends in no small part upon the openness, accessibility, and amenability of these officials to the needs and ideas of the public from whom their ultimate authority derives, and upon whom their commands must fall. As judges we are insulated from these pressures because of the nature of the judicial process in which we participate; but we must refrain from the easy temptation to look askance at all face-to-face lobbying efforts, regardless of the forum in which they occur, merely because we see them as inappropriate in the judicial context.[503] Furthermore, the importance to effective regulation of continuing contact with a regulated industry, other affected groups, and the public cannot be underestimated. Informal contacts may enable the agency to win needed support for its program, reduce future enforcement requirements by helping those regulated to anticipate and shape their plans for the future, and spur the provision of information which the agency needs. The possibility of course exists that in permitting ex parte communications with rulemakers we create the danger of "one administrative record for the public and

503. *See* remarks of Carl McGowan (Chief Judge, U.S. Court of Appeals, D.C. Circuit), Ass'n of Amer. Law Schools, Section on Admin. Law (San Antonio, Texas, Jan. 4, 1981):

> I think it likely that ambivalence will continue to pervade the ex parte contact problem until we face up to the question of whether legislation by informal rulemaking under delegated authority is, in terms of process, to be assimilated to lawmaking by the Congress itself, or to the adversary trial carried on in the sanitized and insulated atmosphere of the courthouse. Anyone with experience of both knows that a courtroom differs markedly in style and tone from a legislative chamber. The customs, the traditions, the mores, if you please, of the processes of persuasion, are emphatically not the same. What is acceptable in the one is alien to the other.

this court and another for the Commission." Under the Clean Air Act procedures, however, "[t]he promulgated rule may not be based (in part or whole) on any information or data which has not been placed in the docket. * * *" Thus EPA must justify its rulemaking solely on the basis of the record it compiles and makes public. * * *

Lacking a statutory basis for its position, EDF would have us extend our decision in *Home Box Office, Inc. v. FCC* to cover all meetings with individuals outside EPA during the post-comment period. Later decisions of this court, however, have declined to apply *Home Box Office* to informal rulemaking of the general policymaking sort involved here, and there is no precedent for applying it to the procedures found in the Clean Air Act Amendments of 1977.

It still can be argued, however, that if oral communications are to be freely permitted after the close of the comment period, then at least some adequate summary of them must be made in order to preserve the integrity of the rulemaking docket, which under the statute must be the sole repository of material upon which EPA intends to rely. The statute does not require the docketing of all post-comment period conversations and meetings, but we believe that a fair inference can be drawn that in some instances such docketing may be needed in order to give practical effect to section 307(d)(4)(B)(i), which provides that all *documents* "of central relevance to the rulemaking" shall be placed in the docket as soon as possible after their availability. This is so because unless oral communications of central relevance to the rulemaking are also docketed in some fashion or other, information central to the justification of the rule could be obtained without ever appearing on the docket, simply by communicating it by voice rather than by pen, thereby frustrating the command of section 307 that the final rule not be "based (in part or whole) on any information or data which has not been placed in the docket." * * *[513]

Turning to the particular oral communications in this case, we find that only two of the nine contested meetings were undocketed by EPA. The agency has maintained that, as to the May 1 meeting where Senate staff people were briefed on EPA's analysis concerning the impact of alternative emissions ceilings upon coal reserves, its failure to place a summary of the briefing in the docket was an oversight. We find no evidence that this oversight was anything but an honest inadvertence;

513. EPA's own internal procedures are consistent with this interpretation of the statute. EPA allows meetings with "interested persons" in the period between proposal and promulgation but "[i]n all cases, however, a written summary of the significant points made at the meetings must be placed in the comment file." Memorandum from the Administrator, Ex Parte Contacts in EPA Rulemaking, App. of Lodged Documents, Schedule C–1 (Aug. 4, 1977). This requirement applies "to every form of discussion with outside interested persons," in meetings or over the telephone, "as long as the discussion is significant." "All new data or significant arguments presented at the meeting should be reflected in the memorandum."

Many commentators agree that ex parte comments during informal rulemaking should not be restricted; but there is also agreement that at least those communications which produce *significant new information* should be noted on a public record.

furthermore, a briefing of this sort by EPA which simply provides background information about an upcoming rule is not the type of oral communication which would require a docket entry under the statute.

The other undocketed meeting occurred at the White House and involved the President and his White House staff. * * *

We note initially that section 307 makes specific provision for including in the rulemaking docket the "written comments" of other executive agencies along with accompanying documents on any proposed draft rules circulated in advance of the rulemaking proceeding. Drafts of the final rule submitted to an executive review process prior to promulgation, as well as all "written comments," "documents," and "written responses" resulting from such interagency review process, are also to be put in the docket prior to promulgation. This specific requirement does not mention informal meetings or conversations concerning the rule which are not part of the initial or final review processes, nor does it refer to oral comments of any sort. Yet it is hard to believe Congress was unaware that intra-executive meetings and oral comments would occur throughout the rulemaking process. We assume, therefore, that unless expressly forbidden by Congress, such intra-executive contacts[520] may take place, both during and after the public comment period; the only real issue is whether they must be noted and summarized in the docket.

The court recognizes the basic need of the President and his White House staff to monitor the consistency of executive agency regulations with Administration policy. He and his White House advisors surely must be briefed fully and frequently about rules in the making, and their contributions to policymaking considered. The executive power under our Constitution, after all, is not shared—it rests exclusively with the President. The idea of a "plural executive," or a President with a council of state, was considered and rejected by the Constitutional Convention. Instead the Founders chose to risk the potential for tyranny inherent in placing power in one person, in order to gain the advantages of accountability fixed on a single source. To ensure the President's control and supervision over the Executive Branch, the Constitution—and its judicial gloss—vests him with the powers of appointment and removal, the power to demand written opinions from executive officers, and the right to invoke executive privilege to protect consultative privacy. In the particular case of EPA, Presidential authority is clear since it has never

520. In this case we need not decide the effect upon rulemaking proceedings of a failure to disclose so-called "conduit" communications, in which administration or inter-agency contacts serve as mere conduits for private parties in order to get the latter's off-the-record views into the proceeding. EDF alleges that many of the executive comments here fell into that category. We note that the Department of Justice Office of Legal Counsel has taken the position that it may be improper for White House advisers to act as conduits for outsiders. It has therefore recommended that Council of Economic Advisers officials summarize and place in rulemaking records a compilation of all written or oral comments they receive relevant to particular proceedings. * * * EDF has given us no reason to believe that a policy similar to this was not followed here, or that unrecorded conduit communications exist in this case; we therefore decline to authorize further discovery simply on the unsubstantiated hypothesis that some such communications may be unearthed thereby.

been considered an "independent agency," but always part of the Executive Branch.

The authority of the President to control and supervise executive policymaking is derived from the Constitution; the desirability of such control is demonstrable from the practical realities of administrative rulemaking. Regulations such as those involved here demand a careful weighing of cost, environmental, and energy considerations. They also have broad implications for national economic policy. Our form of government simply could not function effectively or rationally if key executive policymakers were isolated from each other and from the Chief Executive. Single mission agencies do not always have the answers to complex regulatory problems. An overworked administrator exposed on a 24–hour basis to a dedicated but zealous staff needs to know the arguments and ideas of policymakers in other agencies as well as in the White House.

We recognize, however, that there may be instances where the docketing of conversations between the President or his staff and other Executive Branch officers or rulemakers may be necessary to ensure due process. This may be true, for example, where such conversations directly concern the outcome of adjudications or quasi-adjudicatory proceedings; there is no inherent executive power to control the rights of individuals in such settings. Docketing may also be necessary in some circumstances where a statute like this one *specifically requires* that essential "information or data" upon which a rule is based be docketed. But in the absence of any further Congressional requirements, we hold that it was not unlawful in this case for EPA not to docket a face-to-face policy session involving the President and EPA officials during the post-comment period, since EPA makes no effort to base the rule on any "information or data" arising from that meeting. Where the President himself is directly involved in oral communications with Executive Branch officials, Article II considerations—combined with the strictures of *Vermont Yankee*—require that courts tread with extraordinary caution in mandating disclosure beyond that already required by statute.

The purposes of full-record review which underlie the need for disclosing ex parte conversations in some settings do not require that courts know the details of every White House contact, including a Presidential one, in this informal rulemaking setting. After all, any rule issued here with or without White House assistance must have the requisite factual support in the rulemaking record, and under this particular statute the Administrator may not base the rule in whole or in part on any "*information or data*" which is not in the record, no matter what the source. The courts will monitor all this, but they need not be omniscient to perform their role effectively. Of course, it is always possible that undisclosed Presidential prodding may direct an outcome that is factually based on the record, but different from the outcome that would have obtained in the absence of Presidential involvement. In such a case, it would be true that the political process did affect the outcome in a way the courts could not police. But we do not believe that Congress intended that the courts convert informal rulemaking into a rarified technocratic process, unaffected by political considerations or the presence of Presidential power. In sum, we find that the existence of intra-Executive Branch meetings during the post-comment period, and the failure to docket one such meeting involving the President, violated neither the procedures mandated by the Clean Air Act nor due process.

Finally, EDF challenges the rulemaking on the basis of alleged Congressional pressure, citing principally two meetings with Senator Byrd. EDF asserts that under the controlling case law the political interference demonstrated in this case represents a separate and independent ground for invalidating this rulemaking. But among the cases EDF cites in support of its position, only *D.C. Federation of Civic Associations v. Volpe* [459 F.2d 1231 (D.C.Cir.1971), *cert. denied*, 405 U.S. 1030 (1972)] seems relevant to the facts here.

* * *

D.C. Federation * * * requires that two conditions be met before an administrative rulemaking may be overturned simply on the grounds of Congressional pressure. First, the content of the pressure upon the Secretary is designed to force him to decide upon factors not made relevant by Congress in the applicable statute. Representative Natcher's threats were of precisely that character, since deciding to approve the bridge in order to free the "hostage" mass transit appropriation was not among the decisionmaking factors Congress had in mind when it enacted the highway approval provisions of Title 23 of the United States Code. Second, the Secretary's determination must be affected by those extraneous considerations.

In the case before us, there is no persuasive evidence that either criterion is satisfied. Senator Byrd requested a meeting in order to express "strongly" his already well-known views that the SO_2 standards' impact on coal reserves was a matter of concern to him. EPA initiated a second responsive meeting to report its reaction to the reserve data submitted by the NCA. In neither meeting is there any allegation that EPA made any commitments to Senator Byrd. The meetings did underscore Senator Byrd's deep concerns for EPA, but there is no evidence he attempted actively to use "extraneous" pressures to further his position. Americans rightly expect their elected representatives to voice their grievances and preferences concerning the administration of our laws. We believe it entirely proper for Congressional representatives vigorously to represent the interests of their constituents before administrative agencies engaged in informal, general policy rulemaking, so long as individual Congressmen do not frustrate the intent of Congress as a whole as expressed in statute, nor undermine applicable rules of procedure. Where Congressmen keep their comments focused on the substance of the proposed rule—and we have no substantial evidence to cause us to believe Senator Byrd did not do so here—administrative agencies are expected to balance Congressional pressure with the pressures emanating from all other sources. To hold otherwise would deprive the agencies of legitimate sources of information and call into question the validity of nearly every controversial rulemaking. * * *

Note

Ex Parte Contacts and OMB Regulatory Review. During the Reagan and first Bush Administrations, a persistent point of controversy surrounding OMB oversight of rulemaking was the secrecy of the dialogue between agency officials and OMB reviewers. The early reluctance of OMB to document these exchanges fueled accusations that reviewers had effectively displaced agency heads as final decision makers, and imported into the deliberations arguments and perhaps even factual information that never appeared in the public record, yet formed the basis for the final rules. See Alan B. Morrison, *OMB Interference with Agency Rulemaking: The Wrong Way to Write a Regulation*, 99 Harv.L.Rev. 1059 (1986); Note, *OMB Intervention in Agency Rulemaking: The Case for Broadened Record Review*, 95 Yale L.J. 1789 (1986). The Clinton version of OMB's regulatory oversight process sought to defuse such anxieties by substantially increasing public access to information about the OMB-agency dialogue. See Chapter 3, *supra* at p. 287. President George W. Bush has left the Clinton requirements in place and actually expanded public access to the materials exchanged between OMB and agency heads. It is possible to track OMB deliberations and rulemaking-related meetings and communications through the web site: http://www.whitehouse.gov/omb/oira.

d. Bias and Prejudgment in Rulemaking

In judicial proceedings it is well established that the trier of fact should have no prior knowledge of the facts at issue and no personal connection with any of the parties that could conceivably affect his or her judgment. In the context of formal administrative adjudication, the judicial standard of ignorance of the facts is compromised. Cases may be initiated by agency heads who are ultimately responsible for deciding, on the record, whether the facts alleged have been proved. Even so, proof that an adjudicating official had made up his or her mind about the facts before hearing the parties' evidence would clearly be disqualifying. See, e.g., *Withrow v. Larkin*, 421 U.S. 35 (1975); *Goldberg v. Kelly*, in Chapter 4, *supra*. Bias resulting from personal relationships or financial self-interest likewise disqualifies an adjudicator. E.g., *Gibson v. Berryhill*, 411 U.S. 564 (1973).

The distinction between potentially disqualifying financial interests or personal relationships, on the one hand, and familiarity with the facts or policies to be determined, on the other, has particular importance in the context of administrative rulemaking. The problem of financial interests is addressed, at the federal level, by detailed conflict of interest laws. An official whose position would allow influence over rules that could affect his or her financial interests must either dispose of those interests or at the very least refrain from any participation in related agency decisions. See the discussion of the Ethics in Government Act, *supra* p. 169. The potential influence of nonfinancial personal relationships is more difficult to police, but perhaps also less likely to undermine the integrity of agency rulemaking.

Thus, the more important question is what, if any, evidence of prejudgment ought to disqualify agency officials who have authority to make rules. Because rulemaking under section 553 has, *Vermont Yankee* notwithstanding, become more formal, arguments for adopting, or at least adapting, the prohibitions applicable in formal adjudication have often been advanced. "Prejudgment," however, is a broad indictment that could embrace prior familiarity with specific facts in dispute, well-publicized views about appropriate regulatory policy, or some earlier interpretation of relevant statutory language—in short, a variety of circumstances that might suggest the lack of a perfectly "open mind." Which, if any, of these should provide a basis for challenging agency rules? See Peter L. Strauss, *Disqualification of Decisional Officials in Rulemaking*, 80 Colum.L.Rev. 990 (1980).

ASSOCIATION OF NATIONAL ADVERTISERS, INC. v. FTC

United States Court of Appeals, District of Columbia Circuit, 1979.
627 F.2d 1151, *cert. denied*, 447 U.S. 921, 100 S.Ct. 3011, 65 L.Ed.2d 1113 (1980).

TAMM, CIRCUIT JUDGE.

Plaintiffs, appellees here, brought an action in the United States District Court for the District of Columbia to prohibit Michael Pertschuk, Chairman of the Federal Trade Commission (Commission), from participating in a pending rulemaking proceeding concerning children's advertising. The district court, citing this court's decision in *Cinderella Career & Finishing Schools, Inc. v. FTC*, 425 F.2d 583 (D.C.Cir.1970), found that Chairman Pertschuk had prejudged issues involved in the rulemaking and ordered him disqualified. * * *

On April 27, 1978, the Commission issued a Notice of Proposed Rulemaking that suggested restrictions regarding television advertising directed toward children. * * * The Commission explained that it had decided to propose a rule limiting children's advertising after consideration of a staff report that discussed

> facts which suggest that the televised advertising of any product directed to young children who are too young to understand the selling purpose of, or otherwise comprehend or evaluate, commercials may be unfair and deceptive within the meaning of Section 5 of the Federal Trade Commission Act, requiring appropriate remedy. The Report also discloses facts which suggest that the current televised advertising of sugared products directed to older children may be unfair and deceptive, again requiring appropriate remedy.

The Commission invited interested persons to comment upon any issue raised by the staff proposal.

On May 8, 1978, the Association of National Advertisers, Inc. (ANA), the American Association of Advertising Agencies (AAAA), the American

Advertising Federation (AAF), and the Toy Manufacturers of America, Inc. (TMA) petitioned Chairman Pertschuk to recuse himself from participation in the children's advertising inquiry. The petition charged that Pertschuk had made public statements concerning regulation of children's advertising that demonstrated prejudgment of specific factual issues sufficient to preclude his ability to serve as an impartial arbiter. The charges were based on a speech Pertschuk delivered to the Action for Children's Television (ACT) Research Conference in November 1977, on several newspaper and magazine articles quoting Chairman Pertschuk's views on children's television, on the transcript of a televised interview, and on a press release issued by the Commission during the summer of 1977.

On July 13, 1978, Chairman Pertschuk declined to recuse himself from the proceeding. * * * Five days later, the Commission, without Pertschuk participating, also determined that Pertschuk need not be disqualified.

In August 1978, ANA, AAAA, AAF, and TMA petitioned the district court to declare that Chairman Pertschuk should be disqualified from participating in the children's television proceeding. * * * The plaintiffs introduced copies of three letters, sent by Chairman Pertschuk on the day after he delivered the ACT speech, as additional evidence of his alleged prejudgment. * * *

On November 3, 1978, the district court ruled on cross-motions for summary judgment. The court, relying on *Cinderella*, found that Chairman Pertschuk "has prejudged and has given the appearance of having prejudged issues of fact involved in a fair determination of the Children's Advertising rulemaking proceeding." Accordingly, the court granted the plaintiffs' motion for summary judgment and ordered Pertschuk enjoined from further participation. This appeal followed.

* * *

Evidentiary hearings, although not necessary to determine legislative facts, nevertheless may be helpful in certain circumstances. For example, Congress, when it enacted the Magnuson–Moss Act, recognized that special circumstances might warrant the use of evidentiary proceedings in determining legislative facts. Under section 18(c)(1)(B) and section 18(c)(2)(B), the Commission must conduct a hearing, with a limited right of cross-examination, when it resolves disputed issues of material fact. The legislative history of the Magnuson–Moss Act states that "[t]he only disputed issues of material fact to be determined for resolution by the Commission are those issues characterized as issues of specific fact in contrast to legislative fact."

Although neither the Conference Report nor subsequent congressional debate amplify the term "specific fact," its genesis can be traced to a recommendation of the Administrative Conference of the United States (ACUS). Prior to congressional action on the Magnuson–Moss Act, ACUS promulgated Recommendation No. 72–5, which suggested that

Congress should not require trial-type procedures "for making rules of general applicability, except that it may sometimes appropriately require such procedures for resolving issues of specific fact." 1 C.F.R. § 305.72–5. In a letter dated July 27, 1973, then-ACUS Chairman Antonin Scalia answered Congressman Moss's request for a definition of the term "specific fact:"

> Conference Recommendation 72–5 is addressed exclusively to agency rulemaking of *general* applicability. In such a proceeding, almost by definition, adjudicative facts are not at issue, and the agency should ordinarily be free to, and ordinarily would, proceed by the route of written comments, supplemented, perhaps, by a legislative-type hearing. Yet there may arise occasionally in such rulemaking proceedings factual issues which, though not adjudicative, nevertheless justify exploration in a trial-type format—because they are sufficiently narrow in focus and sufficiently material to the outcome of the proceeding to make it reasonable and useful for the agency to resort to trial-type procedure to resolve them. These are what the Recommendation refers to as issues of specific fact.

A review of this and subsequent ACUS correspondence demonstrates that the term "specific fact" refers to a category of legislative fact, the resolution of which may be aided by the type of adversarial procedures inherent in an evidentiary proceeding with limited cross-examination. Nothing in the legislative history or background of section 18 suggests, however, that Congress believed that the use of evidentiary hearings transformed the nature of the proceedings from rulemaking to adjudication or altered the factual predicate of rulemaking from legislative to adjudicative fact. Accordingly, the appellees' contention that the *Cinderella* standard must be applied to section 18 rulemaking because it invokes the same type of factual judgments as Commission adjudication is simply incorrect. * * *

Had Congress amended section 5 of the FTC Act to declare certain types of children's advertising unfair or deceptive, we would barely pause to consider a due process challenge. No court to our knowledge has imposed procedural requirements upon a legislature before it may act. Indeed, any suggestion that congressmen may not prejudge factual and policy issues is fanciful. A legislature must have the ability to exchange views with constituents and to suggest public policy that is dependent upon factual assumptions. Individual interests impinged upon by the legislative process are protected, as Justice Holmes wrote, "in the only way that they can be in a complex society, by [the individual's] power, immediate or remote, over those who make the rule." *Bi–Metallic Investment Co. v. State Board of Equalization*, 239 U.S. 441, 445 (1915).

Congress chose, however, to delegate its power to proscribe unfair or deceptive acts or practices to the Commission because "there were too many unfair practices for it to define." In determining the due process standards applicable in a section 18 proceeding, we are guided by its nature as rulemaking. When a proceeding is classified as rulemaking, due process ordinarily does not demand procedures more rigorous than those provided by Congress. *See Vermont Yankee Nuclear Power Corp. v. NRDC*, 435 U.S. 519. Accordingly, we must apply a disqualification standard that is consistent with the structure and purposes of section 18.

* * *

The legitimate functions of a policymaker, unlike an adjudicator, demand interchange and discussion about important issues. We must not impose judicial roles upon administrators when they perform functions very different from those of judges. * * *

* * *

* * * [A] Commissioner should be disqualified only when there has been a clear and convincing showing that the agency member has an unalterably closed mind on matters critical to the disposition of the proceeding. The "clear and convincing" test is necessary to rebut the presumption of administrative regularity. The "unalterably closed mind" test is necessary to permit rulemakers to carry out their proper policy-based functions while disqualifying those unable to consider meaningfully a section 18 hearing.

We view the statements offered as grounds for disqualification as a whole to discern whether they evidence a clear and convincing showing that Chairman Pertschuk has an unalterably closed mind on matters critical to the children's television proceeding. * * *

Chairman Pertschuk's remarks, considered as a whole, represent discussion, and perhaps advocacy, of the legal theory that might support exercise of the Commission's jurisdiction over children's advertising. The mere discussion of policy or advocacy on a legal question, however, is not sufficient to disqualify an administrator. To present legal and policy arguments, Pertschuk not unnaturally employed the factual assumptions that underlie the rationale for Commission action. The simple fact that the Chairman explored issues based on legal and factual assumptions, however, did not necessarily bind him to them forever. Rather, he remained free, both in theory and in reality, to change his mind upon consideration of the presentations made by those who would be affected. * * *

The appellees have a right to a fair and open proceeding; that right includes access to an impartial decisionmaker. Impartial, however, does not mean uninformed, unthinking, or inarticulate. The requirements of due process clearly recognize the necessity for rulemakers to formulate policy in a manner similar to legislative action. The standard enunciated today will protect the purposes of a section 18 proceeding, and, in so doing, will guarantee the appellees a fair hearing.

We would eviscerate the proper evolution of policymaking were we to disqualify every administrator who has opinions on the correct course of his agency's future action. Administrators, and even judges, may hold policy views on questions of law prior to participating in a proceeding.

The factual basis for a rulemaking is so closely intertwined with policy judgments that we would obliterate rulemaking were we to equate a statement on an issue of legislative fact with unconstitutional prejudgment. The importance and legitimacy of rulemaking procedures are too well established to deny administrators such a fundamental tool.

Finally, we eschew formulation of a disqualification standard that impinges upon the political process. An administrator's presence within an agency reflects the political judgment of the President and Senate. As Judge Prettyman of this court aptly noted, a "Commission's view of what is best in the public interest may change from time to time. Commissions themselves change, underlying philosophies differ, and experience often dictates changes." *Pinellas Broadcasting Co. v. FCC*, 230 F.2d 204, 206 (D.C.Cir.1956), *cert. denied*, 350 U.S. 1007 (1956). We are concerned that implementation of the *Cinderella* standard in the rulemaking context would plunge courts into the midst of political battles concerning the proper formulation of administrative policy. We serve as guarantors of statutory and constitutional rights, but not as arbiters of the political process. Accordingly, we will not order the disqualification of a rulemaker absent the most compelling proof that he is unable to carry out his duties in a constitutionally permissible manner.

Reversed.

LEVENTHAL, CIRCUIT JUDGE, concurring.

The application of [the court's] test to agencies must take into account important differences in function and functioning between the agencies and court systems. In fulfilling the functions of applying or considering the validity of a statute, or a government program, the judge endeavors to put aside personal views as to the desirability of the law or program, and he is not disqualified because he personally deems the program laudable or objectionable. In the case of agency rulemaking, however, the decisionmaking officials are appointed precisely to implement statutory programs, and with the expectation that they have a personal disposition to enforce them vigilantly and effectively. They work with a combination rather than a separation of functions, in legislative modes, and take action on the basis of information coming from many sources, even though that provides a mindset before a proceeding is begun, subject to reconsideration in the light of the proceeding.

MACKINNON, CIRCUIT JUDGE (dissenting in part and concurring in part).

* * *

The majority opinion holds, and I agree with such holding, that "The appellees have a right to a fair and open proceeding; that right includes access to an *impartial decisionmaker*." However, the majority considers that one qualifies as an "impartial decisionmaker" unless he is shown by clear and convincing evidence to have an *unalterably closed mind* on matters critical to the children's television proceeding. This rule would establish a legal principle that evidence of bias and prejudice would not be disqualifying unless it could surmount a fence that is horse high, pig tight and bull strong. In my view that is too much protection for a biased decisionmaker. In a great many instances it would deprive the public of decisionmakers that are actually "impartial."

The current case * * * illustrates how strong evidence of prejudgment can be played down to almost sanitize the attitudes expressed. * * *

* * * On TV's Today Show on October 31, 1977 [Chairman Pertschuk] admitted that "the implicit indication of [his] personal opinions in these replies are [sic] self-evident." By this statement he recognized that it is the *implicit indications* of his personal opinions that should be evaluated. He next stated: "I have some serious doubt as to whether any television advertising should be directed at a 3 or 4 or 5 year old, a preschooler * * * we have never treated children as commercial objects in our society." This expresses a very firm opinion that, by its advertising, television *was* treating such children as "commercial objects"—presumably trigger words in his vocabulary.

Next, in response to the question whether he would like to see the Federal Trade Commission ban children's advertising *altogether* he replied "not necessarily. But we've not excluded the possibility of bans on certain advertising of certain products to children." In the next paragraph, in an apparent attempt to save the Commission from the taint of any bias that his personal statements indicate, he attempts to spread the responsibility by stating that there are 4 other Commissioners and consequently his views do not bind the others. However, a Commission is prohibited from acting with even *one* biased Commissioner. Then the Chairman stated that the Commission has "not as a body yet approached the question of a remedy for the *evils we see* in children's advertising." So the Commission (we) had already determined that the advertising was "evil." Apparently, the only issue was what remedy to apply.

Next, in his speech to the Action for Children's Television Research Conference at Boston on November 8, 1977, he referred to the "*moral myopia* of children's television advertising." (Emphasis added.) He also stated that "advertisers *seize* on the child's trust and *exploit* it as a weakness for their gain." (Emphasis added.) These remarks evidence definite conclusions, definite opinions and a biased slant. Later he stated: "using sophisticated techniques like fantasy and animation, they [TV advertisers] *manipulate* children's attitudes." (Emphasis added.) This also indicates a prejudgment of the purpose and intent of TV advertisers.

He then argued:

> Why isn't [the] * * * principle [that those responsible for children's well being are entitled to the support of laws designed to aid discharge of that responsibility] applicable to television advertising directed at young children? Why shouldn't established legal prece-

> dents embodying this public policy be applied to protect children from this *form of exploitation*? In short, why isn't such advertising unfair within the meaning of the Federal Trade Commission Act and, hence, unlawful? (Emphasis added.)

Can any reasonable person contend that such remarks do not indicate that he has prejudged TV advertising and decided that it *exploits* children? * * *

Finally, we come to several letters written by the Chairman. * * *

November 9, 1977

MEMORANDUM

TO: Coleman McCarthy

FROM: Mike Pertschuk

Coleman, I know you share my concern in raising public consciousness to the part we play as a society for permitting children to be made commercial objects. I thought you'd want to see this statement in which I've tried to establish underpinnings for a *fundamental assault* on television advertising directed toward young children.

(Emphasis added.)

* * *

November 17, 1977

Honorable Donald Kennedy
Food and Drug Administration
Parklawn Building
5600 Fishers Lane
Rockville, Maryland 20852

Dear Don:

Setting legal theory aside, the truth is that we've been drawn into this issue because of the *conviction*, which I know you share, that one of the *evils* flowing from the *unfairness* of children's advertising is the resulting distortion of children's perceptions of nutritional values. I see, at this point, our logical process as follows: children's advertising is inherently unfair. As a policy planning agency we have to make judgments as to our priorities. The first area in which we choose to act is an area in which a substantial controversy exists as to the health consequences of encouraging consumption of sugared products (not just cereals). With this formulation we do not have to prove the health consequences of sugared cereals. What we do have to prove is that there is a substantial health controversy regarding the health consequences of sugar—a much lower burden of proof.

I'm convinced that the convergence of public policies regarding the commercial exploitation of children with the health controversy over sugared products give us a stronger base and frankly deal directly with the underlying concerns which prompt our action.

Sincerely yours,

Michael Pertschuk

(Emphasis added.)

* * *

Thus, if the Notice of Rulemaking were truthful, so far as Chairman Pertschuk's views were concerned, it would have stated in substance:

> The Commission has decided to make a fundamental assault upon Children's Advertising on TV because we are convinced that it is *evil*, unfair and allowed solely because of the moral myopia of the public and the industry. We solicit comments as to whether it should be prohibited entirely or to some lesser degree.

* * *

It is true that legislators are not required to make findings of fact to support their legislation and that they cannot be disqualified by any court for bias, but there are other safeguards in the legislative process that compensate for the absence of such safeguards as are expressly imposed or implicit in the administrative process. First of all, legislators are *elected* by the voters of their district, and those in the House are elected for a relatively short term—only two years. They can be turned out very quickly if any bias they disclose offends their constituents. Secondly, there is a protection in the sheer size of Congress—535 members of the House and Senate—that implicitly diffuses bias and guarantees that impermissible bias of individual members will not control. There is safety in numbers and a biased Congressman soon loses influence among the other members, if he ever acquired any. Also, the two house system and the Presidential veto are tremendous guarantees that legislation will not be the result of individual bias or even the impermissible bias of one house. * * *

Notes

Open–Minded Rule Makers. So far as the authors have been able to discover, no rule adopted by a federal agency has been set aside on the ground that the agency officials responsible for its adoption had made up their minds before formal public proceedings commenced.

e. *Exemptions From Section 553's Requirements*

The Basic Structure. Section 553 of the APA contains three kinds of exemptions from all or some of its requirements:

Subsection 553(a) categorically exempts rules relating to military or foreign affairs functions, agency management and personnel, and "public property, loans, grants, benefits, or contracts." At face value, these exemptions exclude a very large slice of the contemporary activities of the federal government.

Subsection 553(b) contains two other types of exemptions from the obligation to provide notice and permit comment on proposed rules. The first of these—for "interpretative rules, general statements of policy, or rules of agency organization, procedure, or practice"—focuses chiefly on the legal status of the agency pronouncement rather than its subject matter. The second exemption ostensibly is available for any rule otherwise subject to section 553 when circumstances lead the agency "for good cause" to find, and document, "that notice and public procedure thereon are impracticable, unnecessary, or contrary to the public interest."

The definitive treatment of the exemption for rules relating to public property, loans, grants, benefits, or contracts is still Arthur Earl Bonfield, *Public Participation in Federal Rulemaking Relating to Public Property, Loans, Grants, Benefits, or Contracts*, 118 U.Pa.L.Rev. 540 (1970). As Professor Bonfield points out, the exclusion of these fields may reflect congressional, and perhaps judicial, attitudes toward claims to do business with or obtain financial support from the government, attitudes reflected in the since discredited distinction between "rights" and "privileges." Congress clearly believed that the government should be able to transact its own business without unnecessary procedural impediments, perhaps underestimating the extent to which that "business" affects members of the public.

Unhappiness with section 553 (a)'s broad exemptions led the Administrative Conference of the United States to recommend that, notwithstanding the APA, agencies responsible for government grants, benefits, and contracts should, whenever feasible, follow the rulemaking requirements of section 533. Recommendation No. 16, U.S. Administrative Conference, Recommendations and Reports 29–30 (1970). Some agencies did precisely this, in effect committing themselves to provide notice of and permit comment on proposed rules to which the exclusion might otherwise apply. See, e.g., 36 Fed.Reg. 2532 (1971); 47 Fed.Reg. 26,860 (1982).

There remain important areas of government activity, such as the contracts and procurement area, where statutory rulemaking requirements do not apply. Voluntary compliance with section 553 coupled with grudging judicial interpretation of the exclusions, however, have narrowed their impact. See, e.g., *Vigil v. Andrus*, 667 F.2d 931 (10th Cir.1982).

Subsection (b)'s exemption for "rules of agency * * * procedure" has provoked somewhat more litigation. Reviewing courts have often been skeptical of efforts to invoke this exception when agencies make important changes in even concededly procedural rules. For example, the FDA was unsuccessful when it attempted to defend its failure to provide opportunity for comment on voluminous new procedures for rulemaking, adjudication, and informal agency proceedings. Unquestionably the regulations were in form "rules of agency * * * procedure," but they were unprecedented in their ambition and scope. The district court simply refused to accept that regulations occupying more than 150 pages in the Federal Register could legitimately be exempt from the rulemaking requirements of section 553. *American College of Neuropsychopharmacology v. Weinberger*, 1975 Developments, Food, Drug, Cosm.L.Rep. (CCH) ¶ 38,025 (D.D.C. July 31, 1975). See also *Air Transport Association of America v. Department of Transportation*, 900 F.2d 369 (D.C.Cir. 1990), *remanded for possible mootness*, 498 U.S. 1077 (1991), *vacated*, 933 F.2d 1043 (D.C.Cir.1991) (would have required notice and comment for FAA regulations governing notice, settlement procedures, discovery, hearing and appeal rights, and penalties in formal adjudications).

Compare *James V. Hurson Associates, Inc. v. Glickman*, 229 F.3d 277 (D.C.Cir.2000). The plaintiffs, described by the court as a "courier/expediting firm," created a successful business by processing requests for USDA label approval for meat and poultry processing firms. For decades USDA had accepted mail applications for label approval or disposed of applications in face-to-face meetings with the processing firms or their representatives. The latter mode elicited much quicker action by the agency, which explains the popularity of the plaintiffs' enterprise. In 1998, USDA Secretary Glickman, without providing any opportunity for public comment, revised the departmental regulations to eliminate face-to-face processing of label approval requests, effectively putting the plaintiffs out of business. Glickman defended his action against their claim that he had violated section 553 on the ground that the regulations were rules of agency procedure. The court of appeals agreed.

> But even if the USDA's elimination of face-to-face *did* impose a substantial burden on food processors, that burden would not convert the rule into a substantive one that triggers the APA's notice-and-comment requirement. Appellant has cited no case in which this Court has required notice-and-comment rulemaking for an especially burdensome procedural rule. Nor could it, for we recognize that "the impact of a rule has no bearing on whether it is legislative or interpretative. * * * " *American Postal Workers Union v. United States Postal Serv.*, 707 F.2d 548, 560 (D.C.Cir.1983); *accord Cabais v. Egger*, 690 F.2d 234, 237 (D.C.Cir.1982). * * * The same is true of procedural rules. We conclude, therefore, that an otherwise-procedural rule does not become a substantive one, for notice-and-comment purposes, simply because it imposes a burden on regulated parties.

Compare *Chamber of Commerce of the United States v. U.S. Department of Labor*, 174 F.3d 206 (D.C.Cir.1999) (rejecting claim that a DOL rule providing for inspection of employers that failed to adopt a comprehensive safety and health program was procedural under section 553 of the APA),

The exemptions that have occasioned the greatest controversy and invited the greatest judicial probing into the relations between the promulgating agency and persons affected by its actions are those for "interpretative" rules and "general statements of policy," about which Professor Michael Asimow, *Nonlegislative Rulemaking and Regulatory Reform*, 1985 Duke L.J. 381, has provided this analysis:

> The theoretical difference between legislative and nonlegislative rules is clear. A legislative rule is essentially an administrative statute—an exercise of previously delegated power, new law that completes an incomplete legislative design. Legislative rules frequently prescribe, modify, or abolish duties, rights, or exemptions. In contrast, nonlegislative rules do not exercise delegated lawmaking power and thus are not administrative statutes. Instead, they provide guidance to the public and to agency staff and decisionmakers. They are not legally binding on members of the public.
>
> Interpretive rules and policy statements serve distinct functions. An interpretive rule clarifies or explains the meaning of words used in a statute, a previous agency rule, or a judicial or agency adjudicative decision. A policy statement, on the other hand, indicates how an agency hopes or intends to exercise discretionary power in the course of performing some other administrative function. For example, a policy statement might indicate what factors will be considered and what goals will be pursued when an agency conducts investigation, prosecution, legislative rulemaking, or formal or informal adjudication.

AMERICAN MINING CONGRESS v. MINE SAFETY & HEALTH ADMINISTRATION

United States Court of Appeals, District of Columbia Circuit, 1993.
995 F.2d 1106.

WILLIAMS, Circuit Judge:

This case presents a single issue: whether Program Policy Letters of the Mine Safety and Health Administration, stating the agency's position that certain x-ray readings qualify as "diagnoses" of lung disease within the meaning of agency reporting regulations, are interpretive rules under the Administrative Procedure Act. We hold that they are.

* * *

The Federal Mine Safety and Health Act, 30 U.S.C. § 801 *et seq.*, extensively regulates health and safety conditions in the nation's mines and empowers the Secretary of Labor to enforce the statute and relevant regulations. In addition, the Act requires "every operator of a * * * mine * * * [to] establish and maintain such records, make such reports, and provide such information, as the Secretary * * * may reasonably require from time to time to enable him to perform his functions." The Act makes a general grant of authority to the Secretary to issue "such regulations as * * * [he] deems appropriate to carry out'' any of its provisions.

Pursuant to its statutory authority, the Mine Safety and Health Administration (acting on behalf of the Secretary of Labor) maintains regulations known as ''Part 50'' regulations, which cover the ''Notification, Investigation, Reports and Records of Accidents, Injuries, Illnesses, Employment, and Coal Production in Mines.'' These were adopted via notice-and-comment rulemaking. Subpart C deals with the ''Reporting of Accidents, Injuries, and Illnesses'' and requires mine operators to report to the MSHA within ten days ''each accident, occupational injury, or occupational illness'' that occurs at a mine. See 30 C.F.R. § 50.20(a). Of central importance here, the regulation also says that whenever any of certain occupational illnesses are ''diagnosed,'' the operator must similarly report the diagnosis within ten days. *Id.* (emphasis added). Among the occupational illnesses covered are ''silicosis, asbestosis, coal worker's pneumoconiosis, and other pneumoconioses.'' An operator's failure to report may lead to citation and penalty.

As the statute and formal regulations contain ambiguities, the MSHA from time to time issues Program Policy Letters (''PPLs'') intended to coordinate and convey agency policies, guidelines, and interpretations to agency employees and interested members of the public. See MSHA Administrative Policy and Procedures Manual, Volume II, ¶ 112 (July 17, 1990); MSHA Program Information Bulletin No. 88–03 (August 19, 1988). One subject on which it has done so—apparently in response to inquiries from mine operators about whether certain x-ray results needed to be reported as ''diagnoses''—has been the meaning of the term diagnosis for purposes of Part 50.

The first of the PPLs at issue here, PPL No. 91–III–2 (effective September 6, 1991), stated that any chest x-ray of a miner who had a history of exposure to pneumonoconiosis-causing dust that rated 1/0 or higher on the International Labor Office (ILO) classification system would be considered a ''diagnosis that the x-rayed miner has silicosis or one of the other pneumonoconioses'' for the purposes of the Part 50 reporting requirements. (The ILO classification system uses a 12–step scale to measure the concentration of opacities (i.e., areas of darkness or shading) on chest x-rays. A 1/0 rating is the fourth most severe of the ratings). The 1991 PPL also set up a procedure whereby, if a mine operator had a chest x-ray initially evaluated by a relatively unskilled reader, the operator could seek a reading by a more skilled one; if the latter rated the x-ray below 1/0, the MSHA would delete the ''diagnosis'' from its files. * * *

The second letter, PPL No. P92–III–2 (effective May 6, 1992), superseded the 1991 PPL but largely repeated its view about a Part 50 diagnosis. In addition, the May 1992 PPL stated the MHSA's position that mere diagnosis of an occupational disease or illness within the meaning of Part 50 did not automatically entitle a miner to benefits for disability or impairment under a workers' compensation scheme. The

PPL also said that the MSHA did not intend for an operator's mandatory reporting of an x-ray reading to be equated with an admission of liability for the reported disease.

The final PPL under dispute, PPL No. P92–III–2 (effective August 1, 1992), replaced the May 1992 PPL and again restated the MSHA's basic view that a chest x-ray rating above 1/0 on the ILO scale constituted a "diagnosis" of silicosis or some other pneumoconiosis. The August 1992 PPL also modified the MSHA's position on additional readings. Specifically, when the first reader is not a "B" reader (i.e., one certified by the National Institute of Occupational Safety and Health to perform ILO ratings), and the operator seeks a reading from a "B" reader, the MSHA will stay enforcement for failure to report the first reading. If the "B" reader concurs with the initial determination that the x-ray should be scored a 1/0 or higher, the mine operator must report the "diagnosis." If the "B" reader scores the x-ray below 1/0, the MSHA will continue to stay enforcement if the operator gets a third reading, again from a "B" reader; the MSHA then will accept the majority opinion of the three readers.

The MSHA did not follow the notice and comment requirements of 5 U.S.C. § 553 in issuing any of the three PPLs. In defending its omission of notice and comment, the agency relies solely on the interpretive rule exemption of § 553(b)(3)(A).

* * *

The distinction between those agency pronouncements subject to APA notice-and-comment requirements and those that are exempt has been aptly described as "enshrouded in considerable smog," *General Motors Corporation v. Ruckelshaus*, 742 F.2d 1561, 1565 (D.C.Cir.1984) (en banc); *see also American Hospital Association v. Bowen*, 834 F.2d 1037, 1046 (D.C.Cir.1987) (calling the line between interpretive and legislative rules "fuzzy"); *Community Nutrition Institute v. Young*, 818 F.2d 943, 946 (D.C.Cir.1987) (quoting authorities describing the present distinction between legislative rules and policy statements as "tenuous," "blurred" and "baffling").

Given the confusion, it makes some sense to go back to the origins of the distinction in the legislative history of the Administrative Procedure Act. Here the key document is the Attorney General's Manual on the Administrative Procedure Act (1947), which offers "the following working definitions:"

> Substantive rules—rules, other than organizational or procedural under section 3(a)(1) and (2), issued by an agency pursuant to statutory authority and which implement the statute, as, for example, the proxy rules issued by the Securities and Exchange Commission pursuant to section 14 of the Securities Exchange Act of 1934 (15 U.S.C. 78n). Such rules have the force and effect of law.

> Interpretative rules—rules or statements issued by an agency to advise the public of the agency's construction of the statutes and rules which it administers. * * *
>
> General statements of policy—statements issued by an agency to advise the public prospectively of the manner in which the agency proposes to exercise a discretionary power.

Our own decisions have often used similar language, inquiring whether the disputed rule has "the force of law." We have said that a rule has such force only if Congress has delegated legislative power to the agency and if the agency intended to exercise that power in promulgating the rule.

On its face, the "intent to exercise" language may seem to lead only to more smog, but in fact there are a substantial number of instances where such "intent" can be found with some confidence. The first and clearest case is where, in the absence of a legislative rule by the agency, the legislative basis for agency enforcement would be inadequate. The example used by the Attorney General's Manual fits exactly—the SEC's proxy authority under § 14 of the Securities Exchange Act of 1934, 15 U.S.C. § 78n. Section 14(b), for example, forbids certain persons, "to give, or to refrain from giving a proxy" "in contravention of such rules and regulations as the Commission may prescribe." The statute itself forbids nothing except acts or omissions to be spelled out by the Commission in "rules or regulations." The present case is similar, as to Part 50 itself, in that § 813(h) merely requires an operator to maintain "such records * * * as the Secretary * * * may reasonably require from time to time." Although the Secretary might conceivably create some "requirements" ad hoc, clearly some agency creation of a duty is a necessary predicate to any enforcement against an operator for failure to keep records. Analogous cases may exist in which an agency may offer a government benefit only after it formalizes the prerequisites.

Second, an agency presumably intends a rule to be legislative if it has the rule published in the Code of Federal Regulations; 44 U.S.C. § 1510 limits publication in that code to rules "having general applicability and legal effect."

Third, " 'if a second rule repudiates or is irreconcilable with [a prior legislative rule], the second rule must be an amendment of the first; and, of course, an amendment to a legislative rule must itself be legislative.' " *National Family Planning & Reproductive Health Ass'n v. Sullivan*, 979 F.2d 227, 235 (D.C.Cir.1992).

* * *

In an occasional case we have appeared to stress whether the disputed rule is one with "binding effect"—"binding" in the sense that the rule does not " 'genuinely leave[ ] the agency * * * free to exercise discretion.' " *State of Alaska v. DOT*, 868 F.2d at 445 (quoting *Community Nutrition Institute v. Young*, 818 F.2d 943, 945–46 (D.C.Cir.1987)).

That inquiry arose in a quite different context, that of distinguishing policy statements, rather than interpretive rules, from legislative norms.

* * *

But while a good rule of thumb is that a norm is less likely to be a general policy statement when it purports (or, even better, has proven) to restrict agency discretion, restricting discretion tells one little about whether a rule is interpretive. Nor is there much explanatory power in any distinction that looks to the use of mandatory as opposed to permissive language. While an agency's decision to use "will" instead of "may" may be of use when drawing a line between policy statements and legislative rules, the endeavor miscarries in the interpretive/legislative rule context. Interpretation is a chameleon that takes its color from its context; therefore, an interpretation will use imperative language—or at least have imperative meaning—if the interpreted term is part of a command; it will use permissive language—or at least have a permissive meaning—if the interpreted term is in a permissive provision.

A non-legislative rule's capacity to have a binding effect is limited in practice by the fact that agency personnel at every level act under the shadow of judicial review. If they believe that courts may fault them for brushing aside the arguments of persons who contest the rule or statement, they are obviously far more likely to entertain those arguments. And, as failure to provide notice-and-comment rulemaking will usually mean that affected parties have had no prior formal opportunity to present their contentions, judicial review for want of reasoned decision-making is likely, in effect, to take place in review of specific agency actions implementing the rule. * * * Because the threat of judicial review provides a spur to the agency to pay attention to facts and arguments submitted in derogation of any rule not supported by notice and comment, even as late as the enforcement stage, any agency statement not subjected to notice-and-comment rulemaking will be more vulnerable to attack not only in court but also within the agency itself.

Not only does an agency have an incentive to entertain objections to an interpretive rule, but the ability to promulgate such rules, without notice and comment, does not appear more hazardous to affected parties than the likely alternative. Where a statute or legislative rule has created a legal basis for enforcement, an agency can simply let its interpretation evolve ad hoc in the process of enforcement or other applications (e.g., grants). The protection that Congress sought to secure by requiring notice and comment for legislative rules is not advanced by reading the exemption for "interpretive rule" so narrowly as to drive agencies into pure ad hocery—an ad hocery, moreover, that affords less notice, or less convenient notice, to affected parties.

Accordingly, insofar as our cases can be reconciled at all, we think it almost exclusively on the basis of whether the purported interpretive rule has "legal effect," which in turn is best ascertained by asking (1) whether in the absence of the rule there would not be an adequate legislative basis for enforcement action or other agency action to confer benefits or ensure the performance of duties, (2) whether the agency has published the rule in the Code of Federal Regulations, (3) whether the agency has explicitly invoked its general legislative authority, or (4) whether the rule effectively amends a prior legislative rule. If the answer to any of these questions is affirmative, we have a legislative, not an interpretive rule.

Here we conclude that the August 1992 PPL is an interpretive rule. The Part 50 regulations themselves require the reporting of diagnoses of the specified diseases, so there is no legislative gap that required the PPL as a predicate to enforcement action. Nor did the agency purport to act legislatively, either by including the letter in the Code of Federal Regulations, or by invoking its general legislative authority under 30 U.S.C. § 811(a). The remaining possibility therefore is that the August 1992 PPL is a de facto amendment of prior legislative rules, namely the Part 50 regulations.

A rule does not, in this inquiry, become an amendment merely because it supplies crisper and more detailed lines than the authority being interpreted. If that were so, no rule could pass as an interpretation of a legislative rule unless it were confined to parroting the rule or replacing the original vagueness with another.

Although petitioners cite some definitions of "diagnosis" suggesting that with pneumoconiosis and silicosis, a diagnosis requires more than a chest x-ray—specifically, additional diagnostic tools as tissue examination or at least an occupational history,—MSHA points to some administrative rules that make x-rays at the level specified here the basis for a finding of pneumoconiosis. A finding of a disease is surely equivalent, in normal terminology, to a diagnosis, and thus the PPLs certainly offer no interpretation that repudiates or is irreconcilable with an existing legislative rule.

We stress that deciding whether an interpretation is an amendment of a legislative rule is different from deciding the substantive validity of that interpretation. An interpretive rule may be sufficiently within the language of a legislative rule to be a genuine interpretation and not an amendment, while at the same time being an incorrect interpretation of the agency's statutory authority. Here, petitioners have made no attack on the PPLs' substantive validity. Nothing that we say upholding the agency's decision to act without notice and comment bars any such substantive claims.

Notes

1. *Intent to Bind or Constrain*. In *Community Nutrition Institute v. Young*, 818 F.2d 943 (D.C.Cir.1987), the plaintiff challenged FDA's failure to comply with the APA rulemaking requirements in adopting so-called "action levels" for food contaminants. The Federal Food, Drug, and Cosmetic Act prohibits the marketing of any food containing "any [added] poisonous or deleterious substance that may render it injurious to health." 21 U.S.C.

§ 342(a)(1). For years FDA has adopted confidential "action levels" for ubiquitous contaminants, such as lead and mercury, to guide its field inspectors in their assessments of whether specific foods should be seized and destroyed. In the 1970s, the agency began to make these action levels public, and it briefly contemplated, but then decided against, a practice of proposing new action levels for public comment before making them official.

CNI's basic objection was to FDA's failure to set lower limits on aflatoxin, a potent but naturally occurring carcinogenic contaminant of grains and nuts. However, its formal legal argument was that FDA's action levels served as legislative rules and they had not been adopted in compliance with the APA. FDA responded that its action levels "represent nothing more than nonbinding statements of agency enforcement policy." The court of appeals disagreed. The majority acknowledged, as FDA itself conceded, that in any enforcement proceeding the agency would have to prove a violation of the Act itself and not merely non-compliance with an action level. While action levels were thus not binding on food producers, the court was convinced that "FDA has bound itself" by announcing enforcement guidelines from which *it* did not deviate. Then–Circuit Judge Kenneth Starr dissented, emphasizing that "the action level does not have the force of law in the subsequent [enforcement] proceeding. Indeed, it has no force at all."

CNI v. Young has been criticized for imposing procedural obligations that will discourage agencies from publicizing its enforcement criteria, and thereby providing notice to affected parties of what actions they might take to avoid legal challenge. See Peter Strauss, *The Rulemaking Continuum*, 41 Duke L.J. 1463, 1483–84 (1992). FDA responded to the decision in a notice stating that it would not treat its action levels as binding on producers or as limiting its own discretion to initiate enforcement against products that met their specifications. See 53 Fed.Reg. 5043 (1988); 54 Fed.Reg. 16128 (1989); 55 Fed.Reg. 20782 (1990).

2. *What Does it Mean to "Interpret?" Hoctor v. United States Dep't of Agriculture*, 82 F.3d 165 (7th Cir.1996), grew out of USDA efforts to force Hoctor, a dealer in exotic animals (lions, tigers, and ligers), to erect an eight–foot high fence around the perimeter of his establishment. Hoctor's failure to provide such fencing, USDA claimed, violated a regulation, entitled "structural strength," which in its critical words provided that "the facility must be constructed of such material and of such strength as appropriate for the animals involved. The * * * facilities shall be structurally sound and shall be maintained in good repair to protect the animals from injury and to contain the animals." 9 C.F.R. § 3.125(a). The regulation had been adopted in accordance with the requirements of the APA, but the agency policy requiring fencing 8–feet high had not.

Judge Posner mused about the agency's authority, under the Animal Welfare Act, a statute passed for the protection of animals, to impose a restriction to protect humans:

> [W]e may also assume that the containment of dangerous animals is a proper concern of the Department * * * even though the purpose of the Act is to protect animals from people rather than people from animals. Even Big Cats are not safe outside their compounds, and with a lawyer's ingenuity the Department's able counsel reminded us at argument that

if one of those Cats mauled or threatened a human being, the Cat might get into serious trouble and thus it is necessary to protect human beings from Big Cats in order to protect the Cats from human beings, which is the important thing under the Act. * * * The [agency's] internal memorandum also justifies the eight-foot requirement as a means of protecting the animals from animal predators, though one might have supposed the Big Cats able to protect themselves against the native Indiana fauna.

Having thus satisfied himself regarding the agency's substantive authority, Judge Posner turned to the Government's attempt to justify as "interpretive" the USDA's memorandum prescribing an eight-foot high fence:

* * * The only ground on which the Department defends sanctioning Hoctor for not having a high enough fence is that requiring an eight-foot-high perimeter fence for dangerous animals is an interpretation of the Department's own structural-strength regulation. * * * The Department's counsel made the wonderful lawyer's argument that the eight-foot rule is consistent with the regulation because a fence lower than eight feet has zero structural strength between its height (here six feet) and the eight-foot required minimum. The two feet by which Hoctor's fence fell short could not have contained a groundhog, let alone a liger, since it was empty space.

* * * [I]f the eight-foot rule were deemed one of those minimum standards that the Department is required by statute to create, it could not possibly be thought an interpretive rule. For what would it be interpreting? When Congress authorizes an agency to create standards, it is delegating legislative authority, rather than itself setting forth a standard which the agency might then particularize through interpretation. Put differently, when a statute does not impose a duty on the persons subject to it but instead authorizes (or requires—it makes no difference) an agency to impose a duty, the formulation of that duty becomes a legislative task entrusted to the agency.

The common sense of requiring notice and comment rulemaking for legislative rules is well illustrated by the facts of this case. There is no process of cloistered, appellate-court type reasoning by which the Department of Agriculture could have excogitated the eight-foot rule from the structural-strength regulation. The rule is arbitrary in the sense that it could well be different without significant impairment of any regulatory purpose. But this does not make the rule a matter of indifference to the people subject to it. There are thousands of animals dealers, and some unknown fraction of these face the prospect of having to tear down their existing fences and build new, higher ones at great cost. The concerns of these dealers are legitimate and since, as we are stressing, the rule could well be otherwise, the agency was obliged to listen to them before setting on a final rule and to provide some justification for that rule. * * * Notice and comment is the procedure by which persons affected by legislative rules are enabled to communicate their concerns in a comprehensive and systematic fashion to the legislating agency. The Department's lawyer speculated that if the notice and comment route had been followed in this case the Department would have received thousands of comments. The greater the public interest in a rule, the greater reason to allow the public to participate in its formation.

3. *The Permissible Scope of Agency "Interpretation."* In *Shalala v. Guernsey Memorial Hospital*, 514 U.S. 87 (1995), the hospital challenged a decision of the Secretary of Health and Human Services requiring it to amortize—rather than charge to a single year—an accounting loss resulting from the refinancing of its bonds. The Secretary based her decision on a guideline published in the Medicare Provider Reimbursement Manual but never promulgated, after public comment, in accordance with the APA. The guideline purported to interpret a regulation promulgated pursuant to the APA, 42 C.F.R. § 413.20(a), which specified in part that:

> Standardized definitions, accounting, statistics, and reporting practices that are widely accepted in the hospital and related fields, are followed [in determining provider payments under the Medicare statute]. Changes in these practices and systems will not be required in order to determine costs payable under the principles of reimbursement. Essentially the methods of determining costs payable under Medicare involve making use of data available from the institution's basis accounts, as usually maintained, to arrive at equitable and proper payment for services to beneficiaries.

The hospital contended that this regulation committed HHS to follow "generally accepted accounting principles," which, it maintained, dictated that accounting losses of the sort it incurred should be booked in the year of refinancing. The Secretary contended that the regulation did not oblige her to reimburse according to GAAP and that her guideline was a reasonable, and thus valid, interpretation. A majority of the Court, in an opinion by Justice Kennedy, agreed:

> The Secretary's reading of her regulations is consistent with the Medicare statute. Rather than requiring adherence to GAAP, the statute merely instructs the Secretary * * * to "consider, among other things, the principles generally applied by national organizations or established prepayment organizations which have developed such principle in computing the amount of payment * * * to providers of services." 42 U.S.C. § 1395x(v)(1)(A).
>
> Nor is there any basis for suggesting that the Secretary has a statutory duty to promulgate regulations that, either by default rule or by specification, address every conceivable question in the process of determining equitable reimbursement. * * * The APA does not require that all the specific applications of a rule evolve by further, more precise rules rather than by adjudication. See *NLRB v. Bell Aerospace Co.*, 416 U.S. 267 (1974); *SEC v. Chenery Corp.*, 332 U.S. 194 (1947).

Four Justices dissented in an opinion by Justice O'Connor. It was her view that HHS was obligated to promulgate regulations determining the methods by which reasonable Medicare costs are to be calculated. Only if the Secretary's regulation were read as mandating GAAP could she be understood to have fulfilled this duty. Because, Justice O'Connor argued, GAAP dictated that defeasance losses should be booked in the year incurred, and not amortized, the Secretary's guideline was in substance an amendment of the regulation—and invalid because it had not been promulgated in compliance with APA rulemaking requirements.

The issue addressed in *Hoctor* and *Guernsey Memorial Hospital*—the permissible scope of agency interpretations of their own regulations—has been the focus of several recent cases. The problem is to some degree inescapable. Almost any general set of words will allow some uncertainty—some room for debate—about their meaning in specific contexts. Consider, as an example, the USDA's directive that "the facility must be constructed of such material and of such strength as to be appropriate for the animals involved." Translating such language into concrete instructions for different types of facilities—or animals—is an expected and, the courts have recognized, authorized agency responsibility. But in the process of interpretation and application cases often arise that invite claims of surprise or accusations of inconsistency in, or even reversal of, agency policy. In responding to such claims courts must strike a balance between the need for administrative flexibility and the desire of private parties to know about, and have an opportunity to question, agency demands before they are imposed.

Paralyzed Veterans of America v. D.C. Arena L.P., 117 F.3d 579 (D.C.Cir. 1997), and *Caruso v. Blockbuster–Sony Music Entertainment Centre at the Waterfront*, 174 F.3d 166 (3d Cir.1999), grappled with essentially the same competing arguments over the validity of a Department of Justice interpretation of a DOJ regulation implementing the Americans with Disabilities Act. The regulation in question, styled a "standard," addressed the obligations of sports and entertainment arenas to provide accommodation for customers who use wheelchairs. Specifically, it required that such individuals be provided sitting areas that afforded "lines of sight comparable to those for members of the public."

The issue, in each case, was whether DOJ was justified in interpreting this language to require that most wheelchair areas afford clear lines of sight over standing spectators. And the arguments of the arena owners in each case were similar: DOJ's standard on its face did not provide notice of its ultimate interpretation, which, each claimed, departed from its original albeit informal statements. The D.C. Circuit acknowledged:

> It is certainly not open to an agency to promulgate mush and then give it concrete form only through subsequent less formal "interpretations." That technique would circumvent section 553, the notice and comment procedures of the APA.

But the court found that "the Department never authoritatively adopted a position contrary to its manual interpretation, and as such it is a permissible construction of the [standard]." Turning then to the appellants' claim that the interpretation itself was a legislative rule that had not been adopted in compliance with section 553 of the APA, it offered this analysis:

> The distinction between an interpretative and substantive rule * * * turns on how tightly the agency's interpretation is drawn linguistically from the actual language of the statute or rule. If the statute or rule to be interpreted is itself very general, using terms like "equitable" or "fair," and the "interpretation" really provides all the guidance, then the latter will more likely be a substantive regulation. Here, however, the government's position is driven by the actual meaning it ascribes to

the phrase "lines of sight comparable"—the "legal base upon which the rule rests." In this cases, even "in the absence of the [interpretation] there would [] be an adequately [regulatory] basis for enforcement action to * * * ensure the performance of duties." *American Mining Congress*, 995 F.2d at 1112. In other words, the government arguably could have relied on the regulation itself, even without the manual interpretation, to seek lines of sight over standing spectators.

The Third Circuit in *Caruso, supra*, squarely disagreed with the D.C. Circuit's conclusion, largely because it believed that in promulgating its standard DOJ had announced that it was not then ruling on the question whether "comparable lines of sight" required vision over standing spectators. Hence, its manual interpretation represented a new rule—or the amendment of an existing rule—which had not been adopted in compliance with the APA.

For additional support for the proposition that an agency's novel interpretation of an existing substantive regulation requires compliance with section 553, see *Shell Offshore Inc. v. Babbitt*, 238 F.3d 622 (5th Cir.2001); *Alaska Professional Hunters Ass'n v. FAA*, 177 F.3d 1030 (D.C.Cir.1999). See also *Utility Solid Waste Activities Group v. EPA*, 236 F.3d 749 (D.C.Cir.2001) (holding that agency may not correct an admitted error in a promulgated regulation without complying with the notice and comment requirements of the APA).

A court confronted with a claim that an agency's interpretation of a regulation amounts to an amendment of the regulation, i.e., the adoption of a new rule, may be faced with a choice between upholding the agency's logical response to an unanticipated problem and vindicating the claimant's right to fair notice of the law's requirements. On at least two occasions the D.C. Circuit has settled on a compromise solution, upholding the agency's interpretation as reasonable under *Chevron, U.S.A. v. Natural Resources Defense Council*, 467 U.S. 837 (1984), discussed at length in Chapter 7, *infra*, but denying enforcement against a party who, from the regulation's language, could not have anticipated the agency's position. *General Electric Co. v. U.S. EPA*, 53 F.3d 1324 (D.C.Cir.1995); *Trinity Broadcasting of Florida, Inc. v. FCC*, 211 F.3d 618 (D.C.Cir.2000).

4. *Other Exemptions*. In addition to its categorical exemptions, subsection 553(b) contemplates that circumstances surrounding promulgation of a concededly legislative rule may sometimes justify omission of notice and opportunity for comment. Courts have, however, insisted that the agency invoke the "good cause" exception at the time its rule is issued, rather than when it is challenged, and they have closely scrutinized the reasons offered to support the claim that public rulemaking is "impractical, unnecessary, or contrary to the public interest." For a thorough discussion of the issues raised by this third exception to section 553, see Ellen R. Jordan, *The Administrative Procedure Act's "Good Cause" Exemption*, 36 Admin.L.Rev. 113 (1984).

C. IMPLEMENTING ADMINISTRATIVE POLICY WITHOUT LEGISLATIVE RULES

1. INSTITUTIONAL IMPEDIMENTS TO RULEMAKING

Rulemaking is not simply, or even primarily, a matter of complying with certain procedural forms for announcing agency policy; it is an exercise in policy formation, which takes place within a specialized and hierarchical organization of the kind described in Chapter 1. To appreciate the potential complexity of this process, consider the steps that would be required if the Justice Department's Civil Division, an important component of its litigation staff, contemplated the adoption of a new rule governing contacts by division employees with members of the press concerning ongoing litigation. This would not be a complicated rule. It would ostensibly apply to only one agency and affect only indirectly persons outside the government. Because it concerns a matter of internal agency management, no statute, including the APA, would require the Civil Division to follow any public process in formulating its rule. See APA § 553(b). Furthermore, the rule would not depend on technical data or rely on specialized expertise. In short, this is an atypical rule, not because imaginary, but because the subject is not complex and because the Justice Department is subject to more effective central control than many other parts of the federal government. Even in this environment, however, developing such a rule would not be easy.

The notion that there should be a rule governing Civil Division contacts would never get beyond that unit until staff attorneys prepared a proposal, accompanied by a supporting memorandum, that met the approval of the Assistant Attorney General in charge. Once that step was completed, the proposal would likely be forwarded to the Associate or Deputy Attorney General, who, in turn, would circulate the proposal among all other interested units of the Department for their comment. Given the rule's subject matter, other "interested" units would include the entire remainder of the Department, including, for example, the FBI.

There then would ensue a more or less free-form negotiation among the Civil Division and the other divisions, offices, and bureaus within the Department of Justice that sought to influence (or stifle) the proposed policy. The ultimate goal of the proposal's authors would be a draft regulation that reflected sufficient departmental consensus to warrant presentation to the Attorney General for final "sign off." It would be surprising if the circulation and review of multiple drafts, and responsive comments, on a topic so sensitive, even though not highly technical, took less than six months.

Now consider an agency process to formulate a rule with greater public impact or raising more technical issues. A good, if perhaps extreme example, is the National Highway Traffic Safety Agency's passive restraint rule, which in one version was the subject of the

Supreme Court's *State Farm* decision, *supra* p. 520. Producing a rule setting requirements for protecting automobile occupants in the event of a crash, whatever decision the agency might ultimately make, would present a much more formidable bureaucratic challenge. The agency would (as it did) quickly recognize that it would need information in the possession of outsiders, chiefly but not exclusively automobile manufacturers. In addition to soliciting ideas and data from its own staff units, of which two or more might be concerned, NHTSA would want to find ways of obtaining the manufacturers' own research results as well as tapping their views about alternatives. As work progressed internally, agency analysts would very likely discover data gaps that no existing sources could fill, and then explore ways of filling them—perhaps by contracting to have research done. The agency would almost certainly wish to consult with other private groups, perhaps conduct workshops or symposia, and possibly schedule advisory committee meetings. To secure higher level approval for any proposal, the members of the agency staff directly responsible for the work would periodically have to organize and refine their presentation of available data and analyses so that their superiors could meaningfully review available options without retracing every step of the policy formation process undertaken at lower levels.

Even after completing their internal assessment and arriving at a tentative policy, agency managers might conclude that it was sufficiently controversial to warrant publication of a so-called "advance notice of proposed rulemaking" As mentioned earlier, an ANPRM is a notice, published in the daily Federal Register, in which an agency announces that it is considering proposing the adoption or amendment of a rule. Before publication of an ANPRM, agency staff would have to prepare a draft proposal with supporting documents for approval by the agency head (or heads), which of course would require the sort of extended internal consultation described above.

This process could be repeated several times before agency managers decided that they had a draft rule ready to be proposed. (Between 1967 and 1986 NHTSA published 67 different documents in the Federal Register—ranging from notices of meetings and requests for information to NPRMs and final regulations—relating to its passive restraints rule.) In most cases, as we have already learned, the APA requires the agency then to publish in the Federal Register a notice of proposed rulemaking (NPRM), inviting comments from the public. The comments it receives, of course, may dictate additional rounds of internal consultation and perhaps even additional fact-gathering. Analyzing and preparing responses to the salient comments on a controversial or complex proposed rule, a process perhaps made more rigorous by decisions such as *Brinegar* and *Nova Scotia*, is itself a considerable task, requiring the work of many disciplines. Given the demands of this decision making process, promulgating a major rule on an important subject inside a full calendar year would represent a significant, indeed often a heroic, achievement.

Professor Peter L. Strauss, who once undertook a study of policy formation in the Department of the Interior, offered these comments on the internal obstacles to formulating rules at that agency:

> The failure to use rulemaking is far less a product of conscious departmental choice than a result of impediments to the making of rules created by the Department's internal procedures. The channels which lead to rulemaking, and to a lesser extent other forms of legislative policy statement * * * are so clogged with obstacles, and the flow through them so sluggish, that staff members hesitate to use them. * * * And like an adult game of "Telephone," Department personnel complain, what is suggested at the outset for possible rulemaking is often unrecognizable when and if a formal proposal ultimately emerges. Absent commitment at the highest levels, the process is one that is easily blocked at almost any stage by determined opposition. As a result, rulemaking may be consciously avoided by an individual with an idea for policy change when other means for achieving the same policy ends appear to be available.

Rules, Adjudications, and Other Sources of Law in an Executive Department: Reflections on the Interior Department's Administration of the Mining Law, 74 Colum.L.Rev. 1231, 1245–46 (1974).

Furthermore, most agencies are subject, as described in Chapters 2 and 3, to additional review requirements imposed by one or more of the Regulatory Flexibility Act, the Unfunded Mandates Act, the National Environmental Policy Act, or the Paperwork Reduction Act, not to mention those imposed by Presidential orders mandating consultation with OMB. For a thorough (and depressing) summary of the multiple steps an agency must follow to develop and promulgate a legislative rule, see Mark Seidenfeld, *A Table of Requirements for Federal Administrative Rulemaking*, 27 Fla. St. L. Rev. 533 (2000).

For contrasting views on the likelihood that the OMB review process would, for that reason alone, cause agencies to abandon rulemaking in favor of other regulatory techniques, compare Antonin Scalia, *Back to Basics: Making Law Without Making Rules*, Regulation, July/August 1981, at 25, with Richard K. Berg, *Re-Examining Policy Procedures: The Choice Between Rulemaking and Adjudication*, 38 Admin.L.Rev. 149 (1986). Although Berg predicted that an administration determined to *deregulate* would find it useful, indeed essential, to facilitate rulemaking by agencies, the number of new and revised rules (which would include rules repealing existing regulations) dropped significantly during President Reagan's first term. The trend toward fewer rules reversed under President George H.W. Bush, however, partly because Congress enacted several laws, including the 1990 Clean Air Act Amendments, that mandated issuance of a huge number of new regulations. See Jonathan Rauch, *The Regulatory President*, Nat'l J., Nov. 30, 1991 at 2902. Indeed, the pace of regulatory activity so increased in 1991 that President Bush, following a recommendation by his Competitiveness Council, announced in January, 1992, a 90–day moratorium on new federal rules, supposedly as an aid to economic recovery. He apparently thought the moratorium a sufficient success to order, on April 29, 1992, a further 120–day extension. Most of the regulations delayed involved health, safety, and the environment.

The external impediments embodied in requirements for regulatory analysis are replicated within agencies' internal structures in order to protect against delay or embarrassment in the course of the external review process, including court review. The staffs dedicated to creating "bullet-proof" environmental impact statements, regulatory flexibility, cost-benefit, or paperwork reduction analyses, and to protecting the agency from judicial reversal, can transform the process of rule development into a set of internal barricades that require enormous resources—and uncommon persistence—to overwhelm. For a history of this process within NHTSA, see Jerry L. Mashaw and David L. Harfst, *Inside the National Highway Traffic Safety Administration: Legal Determinants of Bureaucratic Organization and Performance*, 57 U.Chi.L.Rev. 443 (1990).

Finally, rules, once promulgated, must be maintained. They become the focus of outside petitions for enforcement, waiver, repeal, or amendment—the latter two initiatives, if pursued, demanding the same process that generated the rule in the first place. Mashaw and Harfst report, for example, that NHTSA's Standard 108 (on automobile lighting) was amended 37 times and was the subject of 122 notices in the Federal Register between 1967 and 1980. Three staff members were assigned full time to the standard's maintenance, and the agency received (and probably still receives) a petition to amend the rule, on average, once a month. With a sufficient inventory of rules, an agency might be able to do nothing other than attend to their updating. It is hardly surprising, therefore, that agencies sometimes seek to avoid the procedural requirements for rulemaking, either by exploiting the exceptions to section 553, or by utilizing other regulatory techniques.

2. DISCRETION TO ADJUDICATE

For some agencies, rulemaking might hold little appeal—even if modern legislative and White House requirements did not make rulemaking difficult. For decades the FTC found it possible to combat "unfair" or "deceptive" trade practice without once drawing on its dormant rulemaking authority, as did the NLRB in implementing the National Labor Relations Act prohibitions against "unfair" labor practices. The adoption of rules defining and elaborating statutory requirements may not be necessary if the statute also contains—as do both the FTC Act and the NLRA—language prohibiting, in general terms, the conduct Congress meant to proscribe.

There are, of course, many statutes—and especially many modern environmental statutes—that, to be operational, require the adoption of rules. A very early example, rare when it was enacted in 1890, is Section 361(a) of the Public Health Service Act, 42 U.S.C. § 264, which in part provides:

> The Surgeon General [now FDA], with the approval of the Secretary is authorized to make and enforce such regulations as in his judgment are necessary to prevent the introduction transmission, or spread of communicable diseases from foreign countries into the States or possessions, or form one State or possession into any other State or possession. * * * [T]he Surgeon General may provide for such inspection, fumigation, disinfection, sanitation, pest extermination, destruction of animals or articles found to be so infected or contaminated as to be sources of dangerous infection to human beings, and other measures, as in his judgment may be necessary.

This grant of authority is remarkably open-ended, but, notably, it does not contain any restriction or prohibition that may be directly enforced. Unless and until the Surgeon General, or the FDA to which the Surgeon General's authority has been delegated, adopts regulations, the statute provides no basis for enforcement.

The FTC Act, however, is different. As interpreted in *Petroleum Refiners*, and later confirmed by the Magnuson–Moss Amendments, the Act empowers the Commission to formulate regulatory policy either through rulemaking or in the course of disposing of individual proceedings to enforce the broad language of section 5.

Petroleum Refiners suggests that rulemaking offers an agency strategic advantages in developing and implementing policy, including avoidance of formal hearings or court suits, immediate general application, and clarity and prospectivity that invite widespread compliance. Judge Wright's opinion also argued that rulemaking held advantages for persons potentially subject to the FTC's octane posting policy—notably, advance notice of legal requirements and an opportunity to participate in their formulation. Our immediate concern here is whether the latter interests should constrain an agency's choice between rulemaking and adjudication.

SECURITIES & EXCHANGE COMMISSION v. CHENERY CORP.

Supreme Court of the United States, 1947.
332 U.S. 194, 67 S.Ct. 1575, 91 L.Ed. 1995.

JUSTICE MURPHY delivered the opinion of the Court.

This case is here for the second time. In *S.E.C. v. Chenery Corp.*, 318 U.S. 80, we held that an order of the Securities and Exchange Commission could not be sustained on the grounds upon which that agency acted. We therefore directed that the case be remanded to the Commission for such further proceedings as might be appropriate. On remand, the Commission reexamined the problem, recast its rationale and reached the same result. The issue now is whether the Commission's action is proper in light of the principles established in our prior decision.

When the case was first here, we emphasized a simple but fundamental rule of administrative law. That rule is to the effect that a reviewing court, in dealing with a determination or judgment which an administrative agency alone is authorized to make, must judge the propriety of such action solely by the grounds invoked by the agency. If those grounds are inadequate or improper, the court is powerless to affirm the administrative action by substituting what it considers to be a more adequate or proper basis. To do so would propel the court into the domain which Congress has set aside exclusively for the administrative agency.

We also emphasized in our prior decision an important corollary of the foregoing rule. If the administrative action is to be tested by the basis upon which it purports to rest, that basis must be set forth with such clarity as to be understandable.

Applying this rule and its corollary, the Court was unable to sustain the Commission's original action. The Commission had been dealing with the reorganization of the Federal Water Service Corporation (Federal), a holding company registered under the Public Utility Holding Company Act of 1935. During the period when successive reorganization plans proposed by the management were before the Commission, the officers, directors and controlling stockholders of Federal purchased a substantial amount of Federal's preferred stock on the over-the-counter market. Under the fourth reorganization plan, this preferred stock was to be converted into common stock of a new corporation; on the basis of the purchases of preferred stock, the management would have received more than 10% of this new common stock. It was frankly admitted that the management's purpose in buying the preferred stock was to protect its interest in the new company. It was also plain that there was no fraud or lack of disclosure in making these purchases.

But the Commission would not approve the fourth plan so long as the preferred stock purchased by the management was to be treated on a parity with the other preferred stock. It felt that the officers and directors of a holding company in process of reorganization under the Act were fiduciaries and were under a duty not to trade in the securities of that company during the reorganization period. And so the plan was amended to provide that the preferred stock acquired by the management, unlike that held by others, was not to be converted into the new common stock; instead, it was to be surrendered at cost plus dividends accumulated since the purchase dates. As amended, the plan was approved by the Commission over the management's objections.

* * * The Commission appeared to have treated the preferred stock acquired by the management in accordance with what it thought were standards theretofore recognized by courts. If it intended to create new standards growing out of its experience in effectuating the legislative policy, it failed to express itself with sufficient clarity and precision to be so understood. Hence the order was judged by the only standards clearly invoked by the Commission. On that basis, the order could not stand * * *. The opinion further noted that neither Congress nor the Commis-

sion had promulgated any general rule proscribing such action as the purchase of preferred stock by Federal's management. * * *

After the case was remanded to the Commission, Federal Water and Gas Corp. (Federal Water), the surviving corporation under the reorganization plan, made an application for approval of an amendment to the plan to provide for the issuance of new common stock of the reorganized company. This stock was to be distributed to the members of Federal's management on the basis of the shares of the old preferred stock which they had acquired during the period of reorganization, thereby placing them in the same position as the public holders of the old preferred stock. The intervening members of Federal's management joined in this request. The Commission denied the application in an order issued on February 8, 1945. That order was reversed by the Court of Appeals, which felt that our prior decision precluded such action by the Commission.

The latest order of the Commission definitely avoids the fatal error of relying on judicial precedents which do not sustain it. This time, after a thorough reexamination of the problem in light of the purposes and standards of the Holding Company Act, the Commission has concluded that the proposed transaction is inconsistent with the standards of §§ 7 and 11 of the Act. It has drawn heavily upon its accumulated experience in dealing with utility reorganizations. And it has expressed its reasons with a clarity and thoroughness that admit of no doubt as to the underlying basis of its order.

The argument is pressed upon us, however, that the Commission was foreclosed from taking such a step following our prior decision. It is said that, in the absence of findings of conscious wrongdoing on the part of Federal's management, the Commission could not determine by an order in this particular case that it was inconsistent with the statutory standards to permit Federal's management to realize a profit through the reorganization purchases. All that it could do was to enter an order allowing an amendment to the plan so that the proposed transaction could be consummated. Under this view, the Commission would be free only to promulgate a general rule outlawing such profits in future utility reorganizations; but such a rule would have to be prospective in nature and have no retroactive effect upon the instant situation.

We reject this contention, for it grows out of a misapprehension of our prior decision and of the Commission's statutory duties. We held no more and no less than that the Commission's first order was unsupportable for the reasons supplied by that agency. But when the case left this Court, the problem whether Federal's management should be treated equally with other preferred stockholders still lacked a final and complete answer. Still unsettled * * * was the answer the Commission might give were it to bring to bear on the facts the proper administrative and statutory considerations, a function which belongs exclusively to the Commission in the first instance. * * * The administrative process had taken an erroneous rather than a final turn.

The absence of a general rule or regulation governing management trading during reorganization did not affect the Commission's duties in relation to the particular proposal before it. The Commission was asked to grant or deny effectiveness to a proposed amendment to Federal's reorganization plan whereby the management would be accorded parity treatment on its holdings. It could do that only in the form of an order, entered after a due consideration of the particular facts in light of the relevant and proper standards. That was true regardless of whether those standards previously had been spelled out in a general rule or regulation.

It is true that our prior decision explicitly recognized the possibility that the Commission might have promulgated a general rule dealing with this problem under its statutory rule-making powers, in which case the issue for our consideration would have been entirely different from that which did confront us. But we did not mean to imply thereby that the failure of the Commission to anticipate this problem and to promulgate a general rule withdrew all power from that agency to perform its statutory duty in this case. To hold that the Commission had no alternative in this proceeding but to approve the proposed transaction, while formulating any general rules it might desire for use in future cases of this nature, would be to stultify the administrative process. That we refuse to do.

Since the Commission, unlike a court, does have the ability to make new law prospectively through the exercise of its rule-making powers, it has less reason to rely upon ad hoc adjudication to formulate new standards of conduct within the framework of the Holding Company Act. The function of filling in the interstices of the Act should be performed, as much as possible, through this quasi-legislative promulgation of rules to be applied in the future. But any rigid requirement to that effect would make the administrative process inflexible and incapable of dealing with many of the specialized problems which arise. Not every principle essential to the effective administration of a statute can or should be cast immediately into the mold of a general rule.

* * * [P]roblems may arise in a case which the administrative agency could not reasonably foresee, problems which must be solved despite the absence of a relevant general rule. Or the agency may not have had sufficient experience with a particular problem to warrant rigidifying its tentative judgment into a hard and fast rule. Or the problem may be so specialized and varying in nature as to be impossible of capture within the boundaries of a general rule. In those situations, the agency must retain power to deal with the problems on a case-to-case basis if the administrative process is to be effective. There is thus a very definite place for the case-by-case evolution of statutory standards. And the choice made between proceeding by general rule or by individual, ad hoc litigation is one that lies primarily in the informed discretion of the administrative agency.

Hence we refuse to say that the Commission, which had not previously been confronted with the problem of management trading during reorganization, was forbidden from utilizing this particular proceeding for announcing and applying a new standard of conduct. That such action might have a retroactive effect was not necessarily fatal to its validity. Every case of first impression has a retroactive effect, whether the new principle is announced by a court or by an administrative agency. But such retroactivity must be balanced against the mischief of producing a result which is contrary to a statutory design or to legal and equitable principles. If that mischief is greater than the ill effect of the retroactive application of a new standard, it is not the type of retroactivity which is condemned by law.

[After reviewing the SEC's regulatory rationale and the record before it, the Court concluded that the order was "based upon substantial evidence and * * * consistent with the authority granted (to the SEC) by Congress."]

The "fair and equitable" rule of § 11(e) and the standard of what is "detrimental to the public interest or the interest of investors or consumers" under § 7(d)(6) and § 7(e) were inserted by the framers of the Act in order that the Commission might have broad powers to protect the various interests at stake. The application of those criteria, whether in the form of a particular order or a general regulation, necessarily requires the use of informed discretion by the Commission. The very breadth of the statutory language precludes a reversal of the Commission's judgment save where it has plainly abused its discretion in these matters. Such an abuse is not present in this case. * * *

Reversed.

JUSTICE BURTON concurs in the result.

* * *

JUSTICE JACKSON, dissenting.

* * * The reversal of the position of this Court is due to a fundamental change in prevailing philosophy. The basic assumption of the earlier opinion as therein stated was, "But before transactions otherwise legal can be outlawed or denied their usual business consequences, they must fall under the ban of some standards of conduct prescribed by an agency of government authorized to prescribe such standards * * *." *S.E.C. v. Chenery Corp.*, 318 U.S. 80, 92–93. The basic assumption of the present opinion is stated thus: "The absence of a general rule or regulation governing management trading during reorganization did not affect the Commission's duties in relation to the particular proposal before it." This puts in juxtaposition the two conflicting philosophies which produce opposite results in the same case and on the same facts. The difference between the first and the latest decision of the Court is thus simply the difference between holding that administrative orders must have a basis in law and a holding that absence of a legal basis is no ground on which courts may annul them.

As there admittedly is no law or regulation to support this order, we peruse the Court's opinion diligently to find on what grounds it is now held that the Court of Appeals, on pain of being reversed for error, was required to stamp this order with its approval. We find but one. That is the principle of judicial deference to administrative experience * * *. The Court's reasoning adds up to this: The Commission must be sustained because of its accumulated experience in solving a problem with which it had never before been confronted!

Of course, thus to uphold the Commission by professing to find that it has enunciated a "new standard of conduct" brings the Court squarely against the invalidity of retroactive law-making. But the Court does not falter. "That such action might have a retroactive effect was not necessarily fatal to its validity." "But such retroactivity must be balanced against the mischief of producing a result which is contrary to a statutory design or to legal and equitable principles." Of course, if what these parties did really was condemned by "statutory design" or "legal and equitable principles," it could be stopped without resort to a new rule and there would be no retroactivity to condone. * * * Now I realize fully what Mark Twain meant when he said, "The more you explain it, the more I don't understand it."

* * * This administrative authoritarianism, this power to decide without law, is what the Court seems to approve in so many words: "The absence of a general rule or regulation governing management trading during reorganization did not affect the Commission's duties * * *." This seems to me to undervalue and to belittle the place of law, even in the system of administrative justice. * * *

Notes

1. *The Durability of* Chenery. In *Chenery II*, the Supreme Court ruled that an agency has broad discretion to choose between rulemaking and adjudication. In *National Labor Relations Board v. Wyman–Gordon Co.*, 394 U.S. 759 (1969), a majority of the Supreme Court, in two opinions that disagreed over the disposition of that case, briefly fueled speculation that this discretion might be subject to some limitations. The NLRB had brought suit to force Wyman–Gordon to comply with an order entered in a union representation proceeding directing the company to supply the union organizers with a roster of its employees. The Board's order, issued without a hearing, recited for its authority an earlier decision in another representation case involving the Excelsior Underwear Company. In the *Excelsior* proceeding, ostensibly involving just the one company and its employees, the Board had invited briefs from several employer and union organizations on the general question whether it should for the first time construe the National Labor Relations Act as imposing on employers the obligation to share the names of the potential electorate. After considering the briefs, the Board concluded that the Act should be so construed—but it decided that, as a matter of fairness to Excelsior, its ruling should be made prospective only.

When Wyman–Gordon was summarily directed to supply the list *Excelsior* had held was obligatory under the NLRA, it claimed that the Board was invoking a "rule" that had not been adopted through rulemaking. The Board, citing *Chenery*, responded by arguing that it was entitled to implement its policy either through rulemaking or, as in this instance, through adjudication.

Writing for a plurality of four, Justice Fortas criticized the Board for purporting to announce a general rule without engaging in rulemaking but then agreed to uphold its order in this case:

> The "rule" created in *Excelsior* was not published in the Federal Register, which is the statutory and accepted means of giving notice of a rule as adopted; only selected organizations were given notice of the "hearing," whereas notice in the Federal Register would have been general in character; under the Administrative Procedure Act, the terms or substance of the rule would have to be stated in the notice of hearing, and all interested parties would have an opportunity to participate in the rule making.
>
> The Solicitor General does not deny that the Board ignored the rule-making provisions of the Administrative Procedure Act. But he appears to argue that *Excelsior's* command is a valid substantive regulation, binding upon this respondent as such, because the Board promulgated it in the *Excelsior* proceeding, in which the requirements for valid adjudication had been met. This argument misses the point. There is no question that, in an adjudicatory hearing, the Board could validly decide the issue whether the employer must furnish a list of employees to the union. But that is not what the Board did in *Excelsior*. The Board did not even apply the rule it made to the parties in the adjudicatory proceeding, the only entities that could properly be subject to the order in that case. Instead, the Board purported to make a rule: i.e., to exercise its quasi-legislative power.
>
> Adjudicated cases may and do, of course, serve as vehicles for the formulation of agency policies, which are applied and announced therein. They generally provide a guide to action that the agency may be expected to take in future cases. Subject to the qualified role of *stare decisis* in the administrative process, they may serve as precedents. But this is far from saying, as the Solicitor General suggests, that commands, decisions, or policies announced in adjudication are "rules" in the sense that they must, without more, be obeyed by the affected public.
>
> In the present case, however, the respondent itself was specifically directed by the Board to submit a list of the names and addresses of its employees for use by the unions in connection with the election. This direction, which was part of the order directing that an election be held, is unquestionably valid.
>
> Because the Board in an adjudicatory proceeding directed the respondent itself to furnish the list, the decision of the Court of Appeals for the First Circuit must be reversed.

Justice Black, joined by Justices Brennan and Marshall, concurred in the result but repudiated the plurality's criticism of the Board's procedure:

I cannot subscribe to the criticism * * * of the procedure followed by the Board. * * * Nor can I accept the novel theory by which the opinion manages to uphold enforcement of the *Excelsior* practice in spite of what it considers to be statutory violations present in the procedure by which the requirement was adopted.

Most administrative agencies, like the Labor Board here, are granted two functions by the legislation creating them: (1) the power under certain conditions to make rules having the effect of laws, that is, generally speaking, quasi-legislative power; and (2) the power to hear and adjudicate particular controversies, that is quasi-judicial power. Congress gave the Labor Board both of these separate but almost inseparable related powers. No language in the National Labor Relations Act requires that the grant or the exercise of one power was intended to exclude the Board's use of the other.

Nor does any language in the Administrative Procedure Act require such a conclusion. * * * [S]o long as the matter involved can be dealt with in a way satisfying the definition of either "rule making" or "adjudication" under the Administrative Procedure Act, that Act, along with the Labor Relations Act, should be read as conferring upon the Board the authority to decide, within its informed discretion, whether to proceed by rule making or adjudication. * * *

In the present case there is no dispute that all the procedural safeguards required for "adjudication" were fully satisfied in connection with the Board's *Excelsior* decision, and it seems plain to me that that decision did constitute "adjudication" within the meaning of the Administrative Procedure Act, even though the requirement was to be prospectively applied. The Board did not abstractly decide out of the blue to announce a brand new rule of law to govern labor activities in the future, but rather established the procedure as a direct consequence of the proper exercise of its adjudicatory powers. * * *

Apart from the fact that the decisions whether to accept a "new" requirement urged by one party and, if so, whether to apply it retroactively to the other party are inherent parts of the adjudicatory process, I think the opposing theory accepted by the Court of Appeals and by the prevailing opinion today is a highly impractical one. In effect, it would require an agency like the Labor Board to proceed by adjudication only when it could decide, *prior* to adjudicating a particular case, that any new practice to be adopted would be applied retroactively. Obviously, this decision cannot properly be made until all the issues relevant to adoption of the practice are fully considered in connection with the final decision of that case. If the Board were to decide, after careful evaluation of all the arguments presented to it in the adjudicatory proceeding, that it might be fairer to apply the practice only prospectively, it would be faced with the unpleasant choice of either starting all over again to evaluate the merits of the question, this time in a "rule-making" proceeding, or overriding the considerations of fairness and applying its order retroactively anyway, in order to preserve the validity of the new practice and avoid duplication of effort. I see no good reason to impose any such inflexible requirement on the administrative agencies.

Only Justices Douglas and Harlan dissented from the result, essentially on the ground that the NLRB had twice violated the APA, first by promulgating a rule without complying with the procedures of section 553 and then by summarily applying the *Excelsior* "rule" to Wyman–Gordon. Justice Douglas wrote:

> I am willing to assume that, if the Board decided to treat each case on its special facts and perform its adjudicatory function in the conventional way, we should have no difficulty in affirming its action. The difficulty is that it chose a different course in the *Excelsior* case and, having done so, it should be bound to follow the procedures prescribed in the [Administrative Procedure] Act as my Brother Harlan has outlined them.
>
> * * *
>
> * * * [I]t is no answer to say that the order under review was "adjudicatory." * * * [A]n agency is not adjudicating when it is making a rule to fit future cases. A rule like the one in *Excelsior* is designed to fit all cases at all times. It is not particularized to special facts. It is a statement of far-reaching policy covering all future representation elections.

2. *Bell Aerospace*. The Labor Board's power, through adjudication, to announce new principles of law was challenged again in *NLRB v. Bell Aerospace Co.*, 416 U.S. 267 (1974). In that case the Board had appeared to depart from prior law by holding that certain buyers for the company, though recognized as "managerial employees"—a class long considered outside the protection of the Labor Act—had the right to organize and bargain because their unionization would not create a conflict of interest on labor-management relations questions—the agency's new touchstone of statutory coverage. The Second Circuit, in an opinion by Judge Friendly, invalidated the change in policy on the ground, among others, that the Board's failure to use rulemaking was contrary to the considered dictum of six Justices in *Wyman–Gordon*.

The Supreme Court reversed. Justice Powell began his opinion for the court by rejecting the Board's reinterpretation of the Labor Act, holding that Congress had indeed intended that all "managerial employees" were to be excluded from its protections. But Powell went on to hold that the agency could, in adjudicatory proceedings on remand, find that Bell's buyers were not truly "managerial employees." His opinion contained the following reaffirmation of *Chenery*:

> The views expressed in *Chenery II* and *Wyman–Gordon* make plain that the Board is not precluded from announcing new principles in an adjudicative proceeding and that the choice between rulemaking and adjudication lies in the first instance within the Board's discretion. Although there may be situations where the Board's reliance on adjudication would amount to an abuse of discretion or a violation of the Act, nothing in the present case would justify such a conclusion. Indeed, there is ample indication that adjudication is especially appropriate in the instant context. As the Court of Appeals noted, "[t]here must be tens of thousands of manufacturing, wholesale and retail units which

employ buyers, and hundreds of thousands of the latter." Moreover, duties of buyers vary widely depending on the company or industry. It is doubtful whether any generalized standard could be framed which would have more than marginal utility. The Board thus has reason to proceed with caution, developing its standards in a case-by-case manner with attention to the specific character of the buyers' authority and duties in each company. The Board's judgment that adjudication best serves this purpose is entitled to great weight.

The possible reliance of industry on the Board's past decisions with respect to buyers does not require a different result. It has not been shown that the adverse consequences ensuing from such reliance are so substantial that the Board should be precluded from reconsidering the issue in an adjudicative proceeding. Furthermore, this is not a case in which some new liability is sought to be imposed on individuals for past actions which were taken in good-faith reliance on Board pronouncements. Nor are fines or damages involved here. In any event, concern about such consequences is largely speculative, for the Board has not yet finally determined whether these buyers are "managerial."

3. *Consequences of NLRB's Failure to Make Rules*. Several "fairness" values seem to be at stake in the choice between formulating general policy by rule and making policy in the course of adjudication. One is the availability of prior warning about the consequences of primary conduct. Another is the availability of an opportunity for affected parties to participate in developing policy. A third is agency adherence to consistent policies, that is, assurance that like cases are resolved under the same standards or criteria. However, more than fairness is at stake in the debate over the Labor Board's preference for adjudication. There is also the question of whether an agency that concentrates largely on deciding cases is in a position to develop sound policy. In its brief in *Wyman–Gordon*, the Board observed:

> Unlike some other administrative agencies, the Board itself cannot initiate its own processes. * * * Lacking independent authority to investigate or oversee the industrial scene generally, the Board frequently becomes aware of a problem * * * only when it is raised in the context of a particular case. Thus, the bulk of the Board's experience has been accumulated through the adjudication of issues brought to it by outside parties.

Using this statement as a point of departure, Merton C. Bernstein, in *The NLRB's Adjudication–Rule Making Dilemma under the Administrative Procedure Act*, 79 Yale L.J. 571, 577–92 (1970), offered this critique:

> * * * Litigation occurs where labor-management relations have been disrupted, if they ever existed. Seeing only diseased conditions * * * is a dubious way of becoming acquainted with healthy labor relationships. Nor do Board members experience extensive exposure to industrial relations outside of litigation. * * *
>
> I suggest that an enormous number of Board doctrines are based upon untested suppositions. For example, we have had more than twenty-five years of litigation about organizing activities on and off company property but little data on how employees actually react to various organizing devices. We simply do not know what makes an

employee feel fear in election situations. We do not even know whether substantial groups of employees regard Board elections as truly secret. If many do not, the whole Board election process is askew.

What the Board needs is a body of information it has not been getting. Whenever the Board is able to obtain such information, however, the data and conclusions should be subject to critical commentary by the affected public and interested critics *before* the Board acts upon it. For that task, formal rule making on notice seems indispensable. * * *

For a corroborating assessment of the Board's development of policy governing representation elections, see JULIAS G. GETMAN, STEPHEN B. GOLDBERG & JEANNE B. HERMAN, UNION REPRESENTATION ELECTIONS: LAW & REALITY (1976).

The Labor Board departed from the pattern criticized by these accounts when it adopted a rule fixing the number of bargaining units in health care facilities, see *American Hospital Ass'n v. NLRB*, 499 U.S. 606 (1991), *supra*, p. 487.

3. REQUIRED RULEMAKING

MORTON v. RUIZ

Supreme Court of the United States, 1974.
415 U.S. 199, 94 S.Ct. 1055, 39 L.Ed.2d 270.

JUSTICE BLACKMUN delivered the opinion of the Court.

This case presents a narrow but important issue in the administration of the federal general assistance program for needy Indians:

> Are general assistance benefits available only to those Indians living *on* reservations in the United States (or in areas regulated by the Bureau of Indian Affairs in Alaska and Oklahoma), and are they thus unavailable to Indians (outside Alaska and Oklahoma) living *off*, although near, a reservation?

* * *

* * * The respondents, Ramon Ruiz and wife, Anita, are Papago Indians and United States citizens. In 1940 they left the Papago Reservation in Arizona to seek employment 15 miles away at the Phelps–Dodge copper mines at Ajo. Mr. Ruiz found work there, and they settled in a community at Ajo called the "Indian Village" and populated almost entirely by Papagos. Practically all the land and most of the homes in the Village are owned or rented by Phelps–Dodge. The Ruizes have lived in Ajo continuously since 1940 and have been in their present residence since 1947. A minor daughter lives with them. They speak and understand the Papago language but only limited English. Apart from Mr. Ruiz' employment with Phelps–Dodge, they have not been assimilated into the dominant culture, and they appear to have maintained a close tie with the nearby reservation.

In July 1967, 27 years after the Ruizes moved to Ajo, the mine where he worked was shut down by a strike. It remained closed until the following March. * * *

On December 11, 1967, Mr. Ruiz applied for general assistance benefits from the Bureau of Indian Affairs (BIA). He was immediately notified by letter that he was ineligible for general assistance because of the provision (in effect since 1952) in 66 Indian Affairs Manual 3.1.4 (1965) that eligibility is limited to Indians living "on reservations" and in jurisdictions under the BIA in Alaska and Oklahoma. An appeal to the Superintendent of the Papago Indian Agency was unsuccessful. A further appeal to the Phoenix Area Director of the BIA led to a hearing, but this, too, proved unsuccessful. The sole ground for the denial of general assistance benefits was that the Ruizes resided outside the boundaries of the Papago Reservation.

* * *

[After lengthy discussion of BIA practice and congressional understanding, as ventilated in numerous appropriations hearings, the Court concluded that Congress had not consciously restricted relief funds to Indians who resided on reservations. The legislation authorizing the payment of benefits to needy Indians did not contain any express residential criteria of eligibility.]

Having found that the congressional appropriation was intended to cover welfare services at least to those Indians residing "on or near" the reservation, it does not necessarily follow that the Secretary is without power to create reasonable classifications and eligibility requirements in order to allocate the limited funds available to him for this purpose. * * * But in such a case the agency must, at a minimum, let the standard be generally known so as to assure that it is being applied consistently and so as to avoid both the reality and the appearance of arbitrary denial of benefits to potential beneficiaries.

Assuming, *arguendo*, that the Secretary rationally could limit the "on or near" appropriation to include only the smaller class of Indians who lived directly "on" the reservation plus those in Alaska and Oklahoma, the question that remains is whether this has been validly accomplished. The power of an administrative agency to administer a congressionally created and funded program necessarily requires the formulation of policy and the making of rules to fill any gap left, implicitly or explicitly, by Congress. In the area of Indian affairs, the Executive has long been empowered to promulgate rules and policies, and the power has been given explicitly to the secretary and his delegates at the BIA. This agency power to make rules that affect substantial individual rights and obligations carries with it the responsibility not only to remain consistent with the governing legislation, but also to employ procedures that conform to the law. No matter how rational or consistent with congressional intent a particular decision might be, the determination of eligibility cannot be made on an *ad hoc* basis by the dispenser of the funds.

The Administrative Procedure Act was adopted to provide, *inter alia*, that administrative policies affecting individual rights and obligations be promulgated pursuant to certain stated procedures so as to avoid the inherently arbitrary nature of unpublished *ad hoc* determinations. * * *

* * *

* * * [T]he BIA has chosen not to publish its eligibility requirements for general assistance in the Federal Register or in the CFR. This continues to the present time. The only official manifestation of this alleged policy of restricting general assistance to those directly on the reservations is the material in the Manual which is, by BIA's own admission, solely an internal-operations brochure intended to cover policies that "do not relate to the public." Indeed, at oral argument the Government conceded that for this to be a "real legislative rule," itself endowed with the force of law, it should be published in the Federal Register.

Where the rights of individuals are affected, it is incumbent upon agencies to follow their own procedures. This is so even where the internal procedures are possibly more rigorous than otherwise would be required. The BIA, by its Manual, has declared that all directives that "inform the public of privileges and benefits available" and of "eligibility requirements" are among those to be published. The requirement that, in order to receive general assistance, an Indian must reside directly "on" a reservation is clearly an important substantive policy that fits within this class of directives. Before the BIA may extinguish the entitlement of these otherwise eligible beneficiaries, it must comply, at a minimum, with its own internal procedures.

The Secretary has presented no reason why the requirements of the Administrative Procedure Act could not or should not have been met. The BIA itself has not attempted to defend its rule as a valid exercise of its "legislative power," but rather depends on the argument that Congress itself has not appropriated funds for Indians not directly on the reservations. The conscious choice of the Secretary not to treat this extremely significant eligibility requirement, affecting rights of needy Indians, as a legislative-type rule, renders it ineffective so far as extinguishing rights of those otherwise within the class of beneficiaries contemplated by Congress is concerned.

The overriding duty of our Federal Government to deal fairly with Indians wherever located has been recognized by this Court on many occasions. Particularly here, where the BIA has continually represented to Congress, when seeking funds, that Indians living near reservations are within the service area, it is essential that the legitimate expectation of these needy Indians not be extinguished by what amounts to an unpublished *ad hoc* determination of the agency that was not promulgated in accordance with its own procedures, to say nothing of those of the Administrative Procedure Act. The denial of benefits to these respondents under such circumstances is inconsistent with "the distinctive obligation of trust incumbent upon the Government in its dealings with these dependent and sometimes exploited people." * * *

Even assuming the lack of binding effect of the BIA policy, the Secretary argues that the residential restriction in the Manual is a longstanding interpretation of the Snyder Act by the agency best suited to do this, and that deference is due its interpretation. * * *

* * * In order for an agency interpretation to be granted deference, it must be consistent with the congressional purpose. It is evident to us that Congress did not itself intend to limit its authorization to only those Indians directly on, in contrast to those "near," the reservation, and that, therefore, the BIA's interpretation must fail. * * *

The judgment of the Court of Appeals is affirmed and the case is remanded for further proceedings consistent with this opinion.

Notes

1. *The Puzzles of* Morton v. Ruiz. The Court's opinion in *Morton v. Ruiz* raises a host of questions. The many pages we have omitted were devoted to demonstrating that the BIA never informed Congress that it was limiting benefits to on-reservation Indians and that members of Congress would have been disapproving had they known. The Court then obliquely acknowledges what the agency long realized: It did have funds sufficient to support both on-and nearby Indians. And thus it suggests that the BIA could have implemented the policy it adopted if it had proceeded in accordance with the APA. But near the end of the opinion Justice Blackmun comes close to saying that the BIA policy violated the United States' trust obligation to Indians and that was inconsistent with congressional intent.

The puzzles deepen when one asks: Was Mr. Ruiz singled out? Is there any evidence that the BIA granted benefits to some Indians living off reservations but not to others? Why was its policy set forth in a manual distributed to all BIA offices—and available to any member of the public—if not to assure that all offices consistently adhered to the policy? And why did the government concede that the BIA policy was not binding if, as seems likely, the agency could have relied on Section 553's exception for rules implementing grants and benefits programs?

2. *A Retreat from* Chenery? Professor Ralph F. Fuchs, *Development and Diversification in Administrative Rule Making*, 72 Nw.U.L.Rev. 83, 102 (1977), did not think so:

> The Court's exclusion of case-by-case development of eligibility standards, without advance notice of the standards, arose at least in part because they affected "substantial individual rights and obligations. * * *" It would be a mistake to conclude on the basis of the *Ruiz* holding that the use of agency adjudication to develop policy generally is newly restricted by the decision. The Court's reaffirmation in *NLRB v. Bell Aerospace Co.*, decided two months later, of the Board's authority to develop new policies by adjudication, emphasizes the point. In *Bell Aerospace*, the *Ruiz* decision was neither cited nor distinguished and seemingly was not regarded as relevant to the regulation of collective labor relations.

3. *Non-Delegation Redux?* The opinion in *Sun Ray Drive-In Dairy, Inc. v. Oregon Liquor Control Com'n*, 16 Or.App. 63, 517 P.2d 289 (1973), *supra* p. 78, remains probably the most notable state court ruling directing an agency to adopt rules setting forth its policies for disposing of individual cases or claims. However, the fundamental issue in *Sun Ray* was not whether the liquor control agency had properly chosen another process for making policy, but whether it had any discernible policy at all. The applicant's claim was that it was entitled to a hearing on its application, but could not obtain a fair one when it was impossible to know what the issues were and, therefore, what facts might be relevant.

While the result in *Sun Ray* has been influential in the development of state administrative law, see Arthur Earl Bonfield, *State Law in the Teaching of Administrative Law: A Critical Analysis of the Status Quo,* 61 Tex. L. Rev. 95 (1982), the case has had only a few federal parallels. Compare, e.g., *Holmes v. New York City Housing Auth.*, 398 F.2d 262 (2d Cir.1968); *Hornsby v. Allen*, 326 F.2d 605 (5th Cir.1964). In *Hornsby*, the district court was instructed to enjoin the denial of liquor licenses by the City of Atlanta unless and until "ascertainable standards" of such denials had been established by the Board of Aldermen. The *Holmes* court held that a complaint alleging that the Housing Authority had established no standards governing the selection of nonpreference applicants for public housing in New York City stated a cause of action under the Due Process Clause.

Note that in *Sun–Ray, Holmes,* and *Hornsby,* a claim that might have been viewed as a complaint about the absence of statutory standards was put forward in the context of a claim of denial to a fair hearing. As we saw in *American Trucking, supra,* Chapter 2, the Supreme Court is decidedly unsympathetic to the argument—arguably accepted by the *Sun–Ray Drive–In* court—that an improper delegation of authority should be, or could be, cured by requiring an agency to adopt rules.

4. *Abuse of Discretion.* In *Ford Motor v. FTC*, 673 F.2d 1008 (9th Cir.1981), *cert. denied*, 459 U.S. 999 (1982), the Ninth Circuit vacated an order of the Federal Trade Commission addressed to the respondent's practice in giving credit to purchasers of cars that it later repossessed. Francis Ford's practice conformed to that of a car dealers nationwide and the Commission brought parallel section 5 proceedings against Ford Motor Company, Chrysler, and General Motors, their finance companies, and one other dealer. All of the respondents eventually consented to decrees against their practice, except for Francis Ford, which unsuccessfully resisted the charge in formal hearings before the agency. On appeal, Francis Ford contended that the Commission should have proceeded by rulemaking. Citing the dictum in *Bell Aerospace* that "there may be situations where the [agency's] reliance on adjudication would amount to an abuse of discretion," the court of appeals agreed.

> Ultimately * * * we are persuaded to set aside this order because the rule of the case made below will have general application. It will not apply just to Francis Ford. Credit practices similar to those of Francis Ford are widespread in the car dealership industry; and the U.C.C. section the F.T.C. wishes us to interpret exists in 49 states. The F.T.C. is aware of this. It has already appended a "Synopsis of Determination"

to the order, apparently for the purpose of advising other automobile dealerships of the results of this adjudication. To allow the order to stand as presently written would do far more than remedy a discrete violation of a singular Oregon law as the F.T.C. contends; it would create a national interpretation of U.C.C. § 9–504 and in effect enact the precise rule the F.T.C. has proposed, but not yet promulgated.

In 1978 Congress amended the Consolidated Farm and Rural Development Act, 7 U.S.C. § 1981a, to authorize the Secretary of Agriculture to defer payment of principal and interest on federally-funded or insured mortgages held by farmers faced with severe economic hardship. Apparently the Secretary of Agriculture concluded that this authority should rarely if ever be exercised. The Farmers Home Administration took no steps to notify individual debtors about the availability of deferral relief and routinely turned down the requests it received. In *Allison v. Block*, 723 F.2d 631 (8th Cir.1983), the court of appeals held that the Secretary's failure to adopt any standards for the mortgage relief program was unlawful:

> In our view, section 1981a creates a right to have certain uniform procedures established and requires the Secretary to develop substantive standards applicable to deferral applications.
>
> We do not decide in what manner the Secretary must develop the substantive standards applicable to section 1981a deferral requests. * * * Although we believe that formal rulemaking would better insure a uniform set of substantive standards to govern section 1981a requests, we recognize that the Secretary may decide to develop the criteria through adjudicative processes which give some precedential effect to prior FmHA loan deferral decisions. * * *

The Eighth Circuit's willingness to defer to the Secretary's choice of methods for developing standards proved to be a minority view. In *Matzke v. Block*, 732 F.2d 799 (10th Cir.1984), the Tenth Circuit, citing *Wyman–Gordon* and quoting *Morton v. Ruiz*, declared that:

> The statute contains the admonition that the authority of the Secretary is "in addition" to what he now has. The newness would indicate a need for rulemaking. The Act mentioned "request" and a "showing." This contemplates an application and some procedure or hearing for the "showing." Congress felt there was an urgent need for relief and it seems a bit late to begin the accumulation of decisional guides. * * *

In *Curry v. Block*, 738 F.2d 1556 (11th Cir.1984), Judge Clark acknowledged the split of authority but embraced the view of the Tenth Circuit:

> Although *Morton v. Ruiz* may overstate an administrative agency's obligation to exercise its rulemaking authority, we find that under the circumstances of this case, in which many farmers across the nation are in dire need of the relief Congress intended to be made available to them, the Secretary's implementation of this program through adjudication would be an abuse of discretion. In any event, even if neither *Morton v. Ruiz* nor the exigencies of this case required rulemaking, this court has previously held that the Secretary is bound by his July 24, 1971 pronouncement making the procedural requirements of Section 4 of the Administrative Procedure Act, 5 U.S.C. § 553, applicable to

matters relating to "loans," and, therefore, the Secretary is so bound in the instant case.

See also *First Bancorporation v. Board of Governors of the Federal Reserve System*, 728 F.2d 434 (10th Cir.1984) (Board's attempt "to propose legislative policy by an adjudicative order" was abuse of discretion).

5. *Values at Stake.* The cases on agency discretion to choose between rulemaking and adjudication, together with those on agency use of rulemaking to avoid adjudication, raise issues that are analogues of the vagueness versus rigidity problems encountered by legislative drafters, which we considered in Chapter 2. In either context, the specificity of legal rules substantially determines the ratio between discretion exercised at the stage of rule enunciation and that exercised at the stage of rule application. And the Supreme Court has come to essentially the same practical conclusion concerning the role of judicial review in both contexts—the agency's choice will be respected save in exceptional circumstances.

Yet the concerns in the two contexts are hardly identical. Separation of powers generally is not an issue in the case of administrative choice of legal form. The allocation of discretion implicated by the choice will be confined to different stages of the agency's own processes. And while vague legislative delegations are sometimes thought to have serious implications for judicial review, a hard look at an agency's choice of substantive policy seems equally feasible when reviewing adjudicatory decisions (e.g., *Bell Aerospace*) and when reviewing rules (e.g., *State Farm*). Moreover, statutory rigidity is particularly difficult to soften at the stage of application without implying an administrative discretion similar to prosecutorial discretion that entirely escapes judicial review.

While these distinctions might suggest the appropriateness of greater judicial vigilance when reviewing legislative choices concerning the specificity of legal rules than when reviewing similar choices by administrators, there are countervailing considerations. Legislators lack the procedural options, contextual flexibility, and unified leadership of administrative agencies. Judicial second-guessing of legislative judgments concerning the tradeoffs between overgeneralization and underspecification would therefore be particularly disruptive. Intensive review would be more likely to disable than to improve legislative policy choice. Moreover, by long constitutional tradition judicial reexamination itself raises graver separation of powers problems when legislative action is at issue.

Judicial consideration of "appropriate specificity" issues has made little doctrinal headway in either context. The "nondelegation" and "irrebuttable presumption" doctrines are, respectively, ineffectual and dislocating restraints on legislative choice. "Arbitrariness" perhaps captures, but hardly explains, the basis for invalidation of analogous administrative decisions. In a heroic attempt to give some structure to the multiple concerns that inhabit this policy space, Professor Colin S. Diver concludes:

> * * * [C]ourts are repeatedly drawn into controversies about the appropriate precision of administrative rules as they review the legality of actions predicated upon them. When is a rule so opaque that its application denies a person "due process of law?" When is it an "abuse of discretion" to ground actions on an accretion of ad hoc rationales

rather than on a more comprehensive directive? When does the application of a rule become so mechanistic that it denies an individualized hearing guaranteed by statute? At what point does its application to borderline cases become arbitrary and capricious or deny equal protection of the law?

To a large degree, answers to these questions depend on the peculiar statutory or doctrinal context in which they arise. Regulatory incongruities that impair speech or disadvantage suspect minorities will receive far less tolerance, for instance, than those that burden economic interests. Some statutory schemes will display greater legislative concern for individualized treatment or clarity of regulatory exposition than others.

But even after allowing for such doctrinal or statutory peculiarities, there still remains an irreducible core of legal controversy about rule precision that yields only to an indwelling jurisprudential principle of fairness or propriety.

The difficulty of the task counsels broad deference to administrators' choice of rule formulations. Not only are administrators better equipped for "social-cost accounting," but * * * the political "marketplace" can often be relied upon to restrain administrative excesses. Courts, however, cannot wholly escape their editorial responsibility, precisely because the formal dimensions of a rule are so intertwined with its substantive and procedural legality. * * * Courts should, first of all, reserve their closest scrutiny for rules least likely to be subject to effective political discipline. [C]ourts should be most sensitive to the plaint of the unorganized beneficiary of regulatory protection and the adversarially disadvantaged public assistance recipient.

When courts are drawn into disputes about regulatory precision, they should be sensitive to the inevitable tradeoffs among transparency, accessibility, and congruence. They should look for evidence of the factors that drive rules toward one extreme or the other—for example, the high social costs of misspecification error associated with rules of reason, the large rule application costs and quality control problems associated with per se rules. Prohibitory rules should presumptively be more transparent than licensure rules, liability rules more transparent than remedial rules, external rules more transparent than internal rules. In many ways, of course, homilies like this misrepresent the complexity of the subject. But they serve to remind us that "social-cost accounting," for all its intimidating connotations, is really the sophisticated and sensitive application of common sense. * * *

Colin S. Diver, *The Optimal Precision of Administrative Rules*, 93 Yale L.J. 65, 106–09 (1983).

Rules Must Be Followed Until Changed by Rules

Many cases hold that an agency must follow its own rules until it changes them, even though it might not have been obligated to adopt those rules in the first instance. *Morton v. Ruiz* may have turned in part on the BIA's failure to comply with its own manual's mandate that it publish all of its eligibility criteria. Justice Blackmun stressed that, "where the rights of individuals are affected, it is incumbent upon agencies to follow their own procedures."

The long line of authority supporting the proposition that an agency must comply with its own rules stems from three cases decided during the 1950s. The petitioner in the first of these cases, *United States ex rel. Accardi v. Shaughnessy*, 347 U.S. 260 (1954), sought habeas corpus after denial of his application for suspension of deportation. He alleged that the decision of the Board of Immigration Appeals, which had affirmed a finding of deportability, was not the product of deliberations on the merits but a response to the Attorney General's public announcement that he planned to deport certain "unsavory characters" and his subsequent circulation throughout the INS of a confidential list that included Accardi's name. The Court found that the Attorney General's actions, if proved, deprived the petitioner of the Board's independent consideration contemplated by Justice Department regulations. While it conceded that the Board was appointed by the Attorney General and served at his pleasure, the Court held that, having accorded the Board "discretionary authority as broad as the statute confers," the Attorney General could not thereafter dictate its decision.

Service v. Dulles, 354 U.S. 363 (1957), was a challenge to the Secretary of State's termination of a Foreign Service Officer whose loyalty had been reviewed through departmental procedures. The Secretary purported to rely solely on the Loyalty Review Board's finding that there was reasonable doubt as to Service's loyalty; he expressly disclaimed having read any of the briefs in the case or having undertaken an independent review of the evidence. This omission, according to the Supreme Court, violated the State Department regulations governing removal of Foreign Service Officers, which prescribed that "the decision shall be reached after consideration of the complete file, arguments, briefs, and testimony presented." "While it is of course true that under the [statute] the Secretary was not obligated to impose upon himself these more rigorous substantive and procedural standards," the court wrote, "having done so he could not, so long as the Regulations remained unchanged, proceed without regard to them." The Court read *Accardi* as announcing the principle "that regulations validly prescribed by a government administrator are binding upon him as well as the citizen * * * even when the administrative action is discretionary in nature."

Vitarelli v. Seaton, 359 U.S. 535 (1959), also involved the dismissal of a federal employee on loyalty grounds. Vitarelli was removed from the Department of the Interior following a hearing at which the Department adduced no evidence and presented no witnesses; the hearing board relied exclusively on reported prior activities and friendships, whose significance Vitarelli sought vigorously to contest. When Vitarelli sued, the Department expunged his record, eliminated all reference to doubts about his loyalty, and relied simply on the ground that, as a Schedule A employee, he could be dismissed at any time for any reason. It conceded that in this instance it had not followed the procedural safeguards prescribed by its own regulations for such cases: (1) it failed to afford Vitarelli specific notice of the charges against him; (2) it failed to limit questioning of witnesses to the relevant issues; and (3) it failed to afford him an opportunity to confront and cross-examine witnesses whose confidentiality was not protected. "Having chosen to proceed against petitioner on security grounds, the Secretary here, as in *Service*, was bound by the regulations which he himself had promulgated for dealing with such cases, even though without such regulations he could have discharged petitioner summarily."

It is hard to doubt that the charged political context of these cases influenced their outcome. In an era when the "right-privilege" dichotomy still claimed support, the Court's insistence on "scrupulous observance" of self-imposed procedural safeguards provided a useful middle ground between outright rejection of the accompanying constitutional claims and judicial restructuring of agency procedures. It should also be observed that the Court's rulings in *Accardi, Service*, and *Vitarelli* did not prevent the agencies from resuming their proceedings—in compliance with applicable regulations—to pursue the results they had originally sought. Compare *Nader v. Bork*, 366 F.Supp. 104 (D.D.C.1973) (holding that the Acting Attorney General had violated Department of Justice regulations in firing Watergate Special Prosecutor Archibald Cox).

Accardi, Service, and *Vitarelli* do not purport to be grounded in the Due Process Clause. What, then, is the legal basis for the Court's insistence that agencies follow their own regulations? One possibility, of course, is that the Due Process Clause *is* applicable, and obligates an agency to follow whatever procedures it prescribes for itself. See, e.g., *Courts v. Economic Opportunity Authority*, 451 F.Supp. 587 (S.D.Ga. 1978). Such an interpretation could also be thought to promote the equality of treatment of like-situated individuals (and, presumably, firms) that is a recognized counterpart of the equal protection clause of the Fourteenth Amendment. See, e.g., *Bolling v. Sharpe*, 347 U.S. 497 (1954). See also Note, *Violations by Agencies of Their Own Regulations*, 87 Harv.L.Rev. 629 (1974). However, there is hardly a hint of such reasoning in any of these holdings. And in *Board of Curators of the University of Missouri v. Horowitz*, 435 U.S. 78 (1978), the Court, in a footnote, dismissed the proposition that the *Accardi–Service–Vitarelli* doctrine is grounded in the Constitution, claiming instead that the decisions "enunciate principles of federal administrative law rather than of constitutional law binding on the states."

Another possible source of the doctrine is APA § 706 which directs a reviewing court to set aside "arbitrary" or "capricious" agency action. It would not be far-fetched to argue that an agency's unexplained failure to comply with its own regulations amounts to "arbitrary" action. But the APA was relied on by petitioners in only two of the three cases and is not mentioned in any of the opinions.

The Supreme Court has not been unwaivering in insisting that agencies comply with their own regulations. In *American Farm Lines v. Black Ball Freight Service*, 397 U.S. 532 (1970), the Court sustained the ICC award of temporary operating authority to American Farm Lines (AFL). Pursuant to statute, AFL had sought such authority in order to serve the Department of Defense. AFL's application included a statement from the DOD outlining the need for the service, but it failed to describe efforts to obtain it from other carriers—as ICC regulations appeared to require. Writing for the Court, Justice Douglas found that the Commission was nonetheless entitled to treat the application as adequate, explaining:

> The failure of the Caputo statement to provide these particular specifics did not prejudice the carriers in making precise and informed objections to AFL's application. The briefest perusal of the objecting carriers' replies, which cover some 156 pages in the printed record of these appeals, belies any such contention. Neither was the statement so devoid of information that it, along with the replies of the protesting carriers, could not support a finding that AFL's service was required to meet DOD's immediate and urgent transportation needs.
>
> We agree with the Commission that the rules were promulgated for the purpose of providing the "necessary information" for the Commission "to reach an informed and equitable decision" on temporary authority applications. * * * The rules were not intended primarily to confer important procedural benefits upon individuals in the face of otherwise unfettered discretion as in *Vitarelli v. Seaton*, 359 U.S. 535; nor is this a case in which an agency required by rule to exercise independent discretion has failed to do so. *Accardi v. Shaughnessy*, 347 U.S. 260; *Yellin v. United States*, 374 U.S. 109. Thus there is no reason to exempt this case from the general principle that "[i]t is always within the discretion of a court or an administrative agency to relax or modify its procedural rules adopted for the orderly transaction of business before it when in a given case the ends of justice require it. The action of either in such a case is not reviewable except upon a showing of substantial prejudice to the complaining party."

In *United States v. Caceres*, 440 U.S. 741 (1979), the Court refused to overturn the conviction for attempted bribery of an IRS agent by a taxpayer against whom evidence was obtained through electronic surveillance carried out without the Department of Justice approval required by IRS regulations. Writing for the majority, Justice Stevens observed:

> Our decisions * * * demonstrate that the IRS was not required by the Constitution to adopt these regulations. It is equally clear that the violations of agency regulations disclosed by this record do not raise any constitutional questions.

> * * * No claim is, or reasonably could be, made that if the IRS had more promptly addressed this request to the Department of Justice, it would have been denied. * * *
>
> Nor is this a case in which the Due Process Clause is implicated because an individual has reasonably relied on agency regulations promulgated for his guidance or benefit and has suffered substantially because of their violation by the agency. * * *
>
> Finally, the Administrative Procedure Act provides no grounds for judicial enforcement of the regulation violated in this case. * * * Agency violations of their own regulations, whether or not also in violation of the Constitution, may well be inconsistent with the standards of agency action which the APA directs the courts to enforce. * * *
>
> But this is not an APA case, and the remedy sought is not invalidation of the agency actions.

The decision triggered a dissent by Justices Marshall and Brennan, who viewed the *Accardi–Service–Vitarelli* line of cases as "resting on due process foundations." In their view, therefore, the courts were obligated to exclude evidence obtained in violation of agency regulations.

4. NON–ADJUDICATION ALTERNATIVES TO MAKING RULES

While the adoption (and enforcement) of legislative rules has been one of the most important, and most visible, functions performed by federal administrators, most agencies have other means at their disposal for making and implementing regulatory policy. In many situations an agency can elicit the same degree of compliance by announcing what conduct is desired, e.g., by issuing a statement of policy or interpretative rule. As we have seen, this does not require compliance with section 553 of the APA, unless, of course, a reviewing court believes that the agency is actually treating its policy as a legislative rule. According to Professor Michael Asimow, such announcements often have the same practical effect as a legislative rule:

> Most members of the public assume that all agency rules are valid, correct and unalterable. Consequently, most people attempt to conform to them rather than to mount costly, time-consuming, and usually futile challenges. Although legislative and nonlegislative rules are conceptually distinct and although their legal effect is profoundly different, the real-world consequences are usually identical.

Nonlegislative Rulemaking and Regulatory Reform, 1985 Duke L.J. 381, 384.

Anyone familiar with the activities of federal regulators knows that virtually every agency is the source of dozens, indeed hundreds, of communications each year that never appear in the Federal Register and yet are designed to influence the conduct either of private parties, agency employees, or both. Personnel manuals, guides for the processing of applications, press releases, speeches, forms and instructions for filling them out—these are just some of the diverse instruments available to, and utilized by, federal administrators to affect private behavior, i.e., to govern. For a comprehensive examination of these and other mechanisms, accompanied by the claim that many more should be subject to the APA's rulemaking requirements, see ROBERT ANTHONY, INTERPRETIVE RULES, POLICY STATEMENTS, GUIDANCES, MANUALS AND THE LIKE—SHOULD FEDERAL AGENCIES USE THEM TO BIND THE PUBLIC?, Report to the U.S. Administrative Conference (1991).

Of course, there can be limits to the effectiveness of such informal tools. A lack of resources to monitor compliance is often the most important. But there are institutional limits as well. An agency's ability to formulate the policy it wants carried out is often a function of its organizational coherence. Agencies with a stable workforce, well-established functions, and broadly-accepted responsibilities are likely to be more successful in achieving internal agreement on, and adherence to, their policies than agencies whose pathways are less well worn.

An agency's success in implementing its policies, once agreed upon, is subject to other variables. In programs that function by issuing approvals or dispensing largesse, administrators are likely to exercise greater leverage over affected private parties than administrators who must take the initiative if they desire to influence private conduct. Thus one is not surprised to discover that the FDA's standards for testing food additives and drugs—very few of which have ever been promulgated as regulations—are generally complied with by producers who realize that they require the agency's eventual approval before a new product can be marketed. Administrators of public benefit programs at almost any level possess comparable leverage over beneficiaries.

An agency's reputation as expert and its ability to turn the public spotlight on recalcitrant private parties can be important assets as well. For example, the FDA is responsible for regulating the safety of all food products, most of which do not require premarket approval. Its authority over food sanitation, for example, must be exercised in the same fashion that the police officer "regulates" traffic offenders, i.e., by observation and prosecution. When it seizes a food as "adulterated," the FDA theoretically appears in court in the same posture as a public prosecutor, whose views about the defendant's guilt are not officially entitled to any deference. The FDA's judgment that the bacteria level in food renders it "unfit," however, commands deference from courts precisely because the agency is considered expert on the subject. Food distributors understand this and rarely resist the FDA's efforts to enforce its policies. The agency's expected success in court is translated into considerable extra-statutory influence during the investigation process, where an FDA's inspector's statement that a food *appears* adulterated may be sufficient to precipitate its withdrawal from commerce.

The field inspection context illustrates another agency power to elicit compliance with policies that are nowhere embodied in rules but that possess many rule-like characteristics, e.g., they are prescriptive, general, and prospective. But it is also a setting that permits the exercise of unguided and sometimes arbitrary authority. The threat implicit in an OSHA inspector's report of deficiencies may be enough to elicit compliance with *ad hoc* demands that may not enjoy the endorsement of agency management. Professor Kenneth Culp Davis repeatedly emphasized the importance of rulemaking as a device for controlling such decentralized enforcement discretion. See, e.g., KENNETH CULP DAVIS, DISCRETIONARY JUSTICE (1969).

Agencies like the EPA and the FDA that have previously generated a large body of regulations, often in order to get a regulatory program up and running, face a major task in explaining to regulated parties what those regulations require. Like many statutes, many regulations are couched in general terms—e.g., subjects of clinical trials of drugs must have given their "informed consent" to participate—that often require elaboration or explication to make their application in specific cases clear. With the passage of time, the gap between general language and concrete application may widen, yet the impediments to amending regulations to bring them up to date can be more formidable than those that faced the regulations' original authors who may have done their work before passage of such laws as the Regulatory Flexibility Act and the invigoration of OMB review. In addition, agencies continually discover issues they wished that their regulations resolved but on which they may be silent.

One increasingly prominent response to such realities at the EPA and the FDA, and doubtless other agencies, has been the issuance of what both of those agencies call "guidance" or "guidance documents." These are formal statements, addressed to regulated entities or sometimes partners in regulation, such as state environmental agencies, that explain what the agency understands its formal regulations to require. Or they may describe a "safe harbor," a course of conduct that may not represent the only way to satisfy legally binding general language but that the agency promises will be viewed as compliance.

So prominent and wide-ranging has the issuance of "guidance" become that some agencies, notably the FDA, have adopted what could be viewed as regulations describing its use and prescribing procedures for its issuance. See The Food and Drug Administration's Development, Issuance, and Use of Guidance Documents, 62 Fed. Reg. 8961 (1997). (The agency was careful, however, not to label the contents "regulations" and took pains to be sure they appeared in the Notices—and not the Proposed Rules or Final Rules section of the Federal Register.)

FDA's description of its guidance practices began with a definition of the term "guidance document":

> The purpose of guidance documents are to: (1) Provide assistance to the regulated industry by clarifying requirements that have been imposed by Congress or issued in regulations by FDA and by explaining how industry may comply with those statutory and

> regulatory requirements and (2) provide specific review and enforcement approaches to help ensure that FDA's employees implement the agency's mandate in an effective, fair, and consistent manner. Certain guidance documents provide information about what the agencies considers to be the important characteristics of preclinical and clinical test procedures, manufacturing practices, and scientific protocols. Others explain FDA's views on how one may comply with the relevant statutes and regulations and how one may avoid enforcement actions.
>
> The term "guidance documents" includes documents prepared for FDA staff, applicants/sponsors, and the public that: (1) Relate to the processing, content, and evaluation/approval of submissions; (2) relate to the design, production, manufacturing, and testing of regulated products; (3) describe the agency's policy and regulatory approach to an issue; or (4) establish inspection and enforcement policies and procedures. "Guidance documents" do not include documents relating to internal FDA procedures, agency reports, general information documents provided to consumers, speeches, journal articles and editorials, media interviews, press materials, warning letters, or other communications directed to individual persons or firms.

The FDA then addressed, no doubt with an eye on the case law surrounding the APA exception for interpretative rules, the legal status of documents that fit the foregoing definition:

> Guidance documents do not themselves establish legally enforceable rights ore responsibilities and are not legally binding on the public or the agency. Rather, they explain how the agency believes the statutes and regulations apply to certain regulated activities. However, because a guidance document represents the agency's current thinking on the subject addressed in the document, FDA's decisionmakers will take steps to ensure that their staff do not deviate from the guidance document without appropriate justification and appropriate supervisory concurrence.

The FDA description of what it called its "good guidance practices" then proceeded to address the processes the agency would follow in developing "guidance documents." With respect to so-called Level 1 guidance—directed primarily to "regulated industry" and setting forth first interpretations of statutory or regulatory requirements, or major changes in existing interpretations, the agency promised to "solicit public input prior to implementation." This would ordinarily be accomplished by publishing a notice in the Federal Register announcing the availability of a draft and posting of the draft on the FDA home page. For less significant Level 2 guidance, FDA said it would invite public comment upon issuance of a document, i.e., after its adoption. In a pungent analysis of the FDA's "good guidance practice" notice, Professor Lars Noah criticized the agency for its apparent attempt to back away from any promise to treat any of its guidance documents as self-binding and, thus, as affording assured safe harbors. *The FDA's New Policy on Guidelines: Having Your Cake and Eating it Too*, 47 Cath. U. L.Rev. 113 (1997).

The FDA's unusual, indeed remarkable, effort to systematize its processes for advice- and instruction-giving elicited general support from most sectors of the industries that the agency regulates and many representatives of consumer organizations and other beneficiary groups. And it provoked a surprising response from Congress in the Food and Drug Administration Modernization Act of 1997 (FDMA). Broadly speaking, section 405 of FDMA, codified as section 701(h) of the FDCA, 21 U.S.C. 371(h), embodied in FDA's governing statute the basic requirements of advance notice, opportunity for comment, and monitoring of personnel to assure consistent application that the agency had voluntary embraced. FDA was instructed to adopt regulations—in accordance with the rulemaking requirements of the APA—to convert its "good guidance practices" into binding regulations. Pursuant to this directive, the FDA proposed implementing regulations on February 14, 2000, 65 Fed. Reg. 7322, and completed this rulemaking on September 19, 2000. 65 Fed. Reg. 56468.

The FDA's "good guidance" project is a dramatic illustration of the volume and scope of messages sent by that agency—and many other agencies—to individuals and firms that they regulate and to citizens who monitor their performance. One issue that pervades this flow of information and advice is which of these directives are binding in practice because agency officials treat them as binding. A subsidiary issue is whether such directives can be traced to statutes or regulations that were properly adopted. In a recent case involving complex "guidance" that the EPA issued to explain to cooperating state agencies the meaning of its Clean Air Act regulations for state implementation plans. Judge Randolph of the D.C. Circuit offered this jaundiced view:

> The phenomenon we see in this case is familiar. Congress passes a broadly worded statute. The agency follows with regulations containing broad language, open-ended phrases, ambiguous standards, and the like. Then as years pass, the agency issues circulars or guidance or memoranda, explaining, interpreting, defining and often expanding the commands in the regulations. One guidance may yield another and then another and so on. Several words in a regulation may spawn hundreds of pages of text as the agency offers more and more detail regarding what its regulations demand of regulated entities. Law is made, without notice and comment, without public participation, and without publication in the Federal Register or the Code of Federal Regulations. With the advent of the Internet, the agency does not need these official publications to ensure widespread circulation; it can inform those affected publications to ensure widespread circulation; it can inform those affected simply by posting its new guidance or memoranda or policy statement on its web site. An agency operating this way gains a large advantage. "It can issue or amend its real rules, i.e., its interpreta-

> tive rules and policy statements, quickly and inexpensively without following any statutorily prescribed procedures." Richard J. Pierce, Jr., *Seven Ways to Deossify Agency Rulemaking*, 47 Admin. L. Rev. 59, 85 (1995). The agency may also think there is another advantage—immunizing its lawmaking from judicial review.

Appalachian Power Co. v. EPA, 208 F.3d 1015 (D.C.Cir.2000). If the EPA hoped its latest interpretation of its Clean Air Act regulations would escape judicial review, it was disappointed. The court of appeals first held that its guidance amounted to a final rule, subject to immediate review, and then that its interpretation went so far beyond the underlying regulations that it amounted to an amendment—which had not been adopted in accordance with the APA.

Agency reliance on "guidance" may be increasing, not simply as adjunct to rulemaking but as an alternative. Professor Todd D. Rakoff has observed:

> If an agency, without promulgating a nominally—legally—binding regulation, generates a set of detailed guidelines for its inspectors to enforce, it in effect still establishes the law for all those unwilling to pay the expense, or suffer the ill-will of challenging the agency in court. * * *
>
> While it is difficult to document statistically, agencies seem to be resorting increasingly to this mechanism for accomplishing their tasks without paying the procedural price of rulemaking or adjudication. Certainly, the number of lawsuits objecting to the practice, in one guise or another, has greatly increased in the last decade-and-a-half.

The Choice Between Formal and Informal Modes of Administrative Regulation, 52 Admin. L. Rev. 159, 167 (2000).

D. REFORM OF FEDERAL AGENCY RULEMAKING PROCEDURES

Is Rulemaking "Ossification" Stifling Law Making?

In 1990, the then-General Counsel of EPA, E. Donald Elliott, lamented what he termed the "ossification" of informal rulemaking. Remarks at a Symposium on "Assessing the Environmental Protection Agency After Twenty Years: Law, Politics, and Economics," at Duke University School of Law (Nov. 15, 1990). Elliott described a slow-down in the number of new regulations issued by EPA, a rise in the time and resources required to develop new rules, and the mounting frustration of agency policymakers. Soon afterwards Professor Thomas McGarity made Elliott's phrase the basis for a detailed analysis of the legal and bureaucratic environment in which agencies must now make rules. *Some Thoughts on 'Deossifying' the Rulemaking Process*, 41 Duke L.J. 1385 (1992).

In documenting Elliott's complaint, McGarity studied the experiences of OSHA, NHTSA, the FTC, and the CPSC, as well as EPA, and offered these conclusions:

> [I]t is much harder for an agency to promulgate a rule now than it was twenty years ago. Agency explanations for rules are far more lengthy and intricate than they were in the 1960s and early 1970s. * * *
>
> The agencies also take much longer to write the lengthy preambles and technical support documents and to address public comments on proposed rules * * *
>
> Important rulemaking initiatives grind along at such a deliberate pace that they are often consigned to regulatory purgatory, never to be resurrected again * * *
>
> Once an agency has endured the considerable expense and turmoil of writing a rule, it has every incentive to leave well enough alone. Even when forced by statute to revisit existing rules, an agency is very reluctant to change them.

McGarity saw more than administrative inefficiency and frustration. In his view, the mounting impediments to the promulgation of regulations undermined the very purpose of congressional enactments:

> Since most regulatory statutes were enacted to accomplish progressive public policy goals, the ossification of the informal rulemaking process hinders or defeats the agency's pursuit of those goals. To some extent, the fact that the air and waters of the United States are still polluted, workplaces still dangerous, motor vehicles still unsafe, and consumers still being deceived is attributable to the expense and burdensomeness of the informal rulemaking process.

Id. at 1390.

Though Professor McGarity looked at the whole legal environment, he laid much of the blame for ossification on "highly skeptical" judicial review, a view that received support from many regulators and other scholars. See, e.g., CARNEGIE COMMISSION, RISK AND THE ENVIRONMENT: IMPROVING REGULATORY DECISIONMAKING (1993); Richard J. Pierce, *Rulemaking and the Administrative Procedure Act*, 32 Tulsa L.J. 185 (1996); Peter Strauss, *The Rulemaking Continuum*, 41 Duke L.J. 1463 (1992).

A number of cases have been cited as illustrative. One is *Gulf South Insulation v. U.S. Consumer Product Safety Commission*, 701 F.2d 1137 (5th Cir.1983), which struck down a CPSC ban on urea-formaldehyde foam insulation that had been based on the finding that inhaled formaldehyde posed an unreasonable risk of cancer. The agency's finding that formaldehyde is a carcinogen, which had been endorsed by a government-wide group of scientists assembled to review the data, rested on a state-of-the-art study in rodents. The Fifth Circuit found fault with several parts of the agency's risk assessment, including its sampling of escaping formaldehyde in insulated homes and its reliance on an invalidated extrapolation model. But what drew particular attention was the court's dismissal of the animal study as reliable evidence. See, e.g., Richard A. Merrill, *The Legal System's Response to Scientific Uncertainty: The Role of Judicial Review*, 4 Fundamental & Applied Toxicology S418 (1984); Howard Latin, *Good Science, Bad Regulation, and Toxic Risk Assessment*, 5 Yale J. on Reg. 89 (1988).

A second example is *Corrosion Proof Fittings v. EPA*, 947 F.2d 1201 (5th Cir.1991), which struck down EPA's first comprehensive use of its authority to restrict or ban a dangerous substance under section 6(a) of the Toxic Substances Control Act. EPA had spent nearly a decade developing a rule restricting the production and use of asbestos and, in the process, addressed the many different settings in which workers and consumers were exposed to this material. The final regulations imposed a series of limits on production and application of asbestos, including ultimate bans on most uses. The court faulted EPA for failing to weigh the costs and benefits of all plausible options, short of banning, for each of the several categories of uses to which its rule applied. Professor McGarity offered this assessment of the ruling's impact:

> Faced with the daunting prospect of meeting the [Fifth Circuit's] information-gathering and analytical requirements, EPA may be forgiven if it elects to channel its limited resources in other directions. Unless the statute is amended to send a clear message to the reviewing courts that something less than a thoroughgoing analysis of every listed option will do, EPA's first section 6(a) rulemaking will undoubtedly be its last.

41 Duke L.J. at 1423.

Not all students of regulation agree with the charge that "hard look" judicial review is *a*, much less *the*, major cause of rulemaking "ossification." In *Thirty Years of Administrative Law in the D.C. Circuit*, 11 Pike & Fischer's AdLaw Bulletin, No. 13, 1, 4–5 (1997), Circuit (and formerly Chief) Judge Patricia Wald had this to say:

> Personally, I've never been entirely convinced there was a strong empirical as opposed to anecdotal basis for the "ossification" critique, but it did gain momentum, and perhaps put some courts a bit on the defensive. Over the years the D.C. Circuit has shown a fairly steady rate of reversal or remand of agency decisions—around 22%. And my own research shows that most of our reversals are due to failure of the agency to give an adequate explanation for its decision, not for lack of substantial evidence to undergird its findings. Nonetheless every few years or so, some massive—five years in the making—agency rulemaking is overturned by the courts, and the "ossification" criticism flares up anew.
>
> Those cases are not typical, however. My minisurvey of one year's rulemaking in our circuit showed that of 36 major agency rules that came up for review, the agency's judgment was affirmed wholly in 19 cases, and in the bulk of the other 17, most of the rule was upheld. In four cases, the notice and comment requirement had not been followed; in six cases the agency's explanation for its

> choices was not deemed adequate; in seven cases the court said it read the statute wrong. A second D.C. Circuit survey of 135 agency cases of all kinds showed substantial evidence challenges were made in only 13%.
>
> In my view, the major obstacle for agencies on review is convincing a court that they have made rational choices and considered all the arguments and evidence. I've said elsewhere—and I repeat it here—a lot of the misfires came down to matters of miscommunication; agencies often simply fail to address an important objection or give no coherent reason at all for a policy determination. Forty-six percent of challenges on appeal are to the arbitrary and capricious nature of the decision; and twice as many remands are for this reason as for any other.* * * In the end, it is amassing the evidence and organizing it around key principles which will convince a court the agency has made a reasoned decision. * * *

See also Patricia Wald, *Judicial Review in Midpassage: The Uneasy Partnership Between Courts and Agencies Plays On*, 32 Tulsa L.J. 221 (1996).

Several authors have proposed solutions to the problem of "ossification." Acknowledging that by no means all agency rules have been stifled by the procedural requirements of the APA or close review by the courts, Professor Peter Strauss has argued that procedural diversity should replace the APA's unitary model. "[S]imple notice and comment rulemaking is not adequate for rules * * * that require the private sector to expend many millions of dollars to avoid exposing workers or the public to relatively slight concentrations of particular chemicals thought to cause cancer over longer periods of exposure. Given both the uncertainties and the stakes, exposure of the agency's data and reasoning to public view and response, alongside the simple fact of its proposal, seems essential." Strauss would, however, demand much less in the way of procedural formality and rigorous analysis for simple rules. See Peter L. Strauss, *From Expertise to Politics: The Transformation of American Rulemaking*, 31 Wake Forest L.Rev. 745 (1996). Professor Ronald Levin has put this suggestion in concrete form. In *Direct Final Rulemaking*, 64 G.Wash.L.Rev. 1 (1995), Levin advocates the following procedure:

> [A]n agency publishes a rule in the Federal Register with a statement that the rule will become effective unless the agency receives an adverse comment or a written notice that someone intends to submit an adverse comment. * * * If even one person files an adverse comment or notice, the agency must withdraw the rule. Typically it will then immediately republish the substance of the direct rule as a proposed rule, thus initiating the ordinary notice-and-comment process.

Levin's proposal for unclogging the rulemaking pipeline would not remove any of the obstructions to the adoption of controversial regulations. And its implicit invitation to dispense with public comment could exacerbate a quite different, though possibly related, problem identified by Professor Robert Anthony—the propensity of agencies to treat statements of policy and informal "guidance" documents as though they had the force of binding regulations. In a series of articles, Professor Anthony has argued that more, rather than fewer, agency pronouncements should be subject to the discipline of the APA rulemaking process. See, e.g., *Interpretive Rules, Policy Statements, Guidances, Manuals, and the Like—Should Federal Agencies Use Them to Bind the Public?*, 41 Duke L.J. 1311 (1992); Robert A. Anthony & David A. Codvilla, *Pro–Ossification: A Harder Look at Agency Policy Statement*, 31 Wake Forest L.Rev. 667 (1996).

Professor McGarity examined several measures that might be taken by agencies or by Congress to facilitate the rulemaking process. Uncontroversially, he endorsed efforts to streamline internal agency procedures. He saw value in exploring negotiated rulemaking for some regulations. He urged OMB's OIRA to relax its fact-gathering and analytical demands on agencies. And he also suggested that agencies consider adopting what he termed "lite" regulations—regulations that imposed restrictions less rigorous than the statute might allow—on the theory that they would be easier to support and less likely to provoke judicial review and yet could achieve most of the benefits of more costly, and inevitably contested, regulations. See McGarity, 41 Duke L.J. at 1436–62.

However, most scholars, including Professor McGarity himself, have seen such measures as mere palliatives. Their main target has continued to be relentlessly skeptical "hard look" judicial review. McGarity has argued that Congress should amend 706 of the APA—and presumably the counterpart provisions of program statutes—to substitute for the arbitrary or capricious test a new more lenient standard—a "new metaphor." Courts should be instructed to accord agency decision makers wider latitude for judgment and even error. See McGarity, 41 Duke L.J. at 1452; Thomas O. McGarity, *The Courts and the Ossification of Rulemaking: A Response to Professor Seidenfeld*, 75 Tex. L.Rev. 525 (1997). There is, however, no evidence that members of Congress have been persuaded. Nor has there been any more support for Professor Mashaw's suggestion that judicial review of rules should not be routinely available until the agency seeks to enforce them. See Jerry L. Mashaw, *Improving the Environment of Agency Rulemaking: An Essay on Management, Games, and Accountability*, 57 Law & Contemp. Probs. 185 (1994). According to Mashaw, with this shift in timing, judicial review would cease to be an attractive means for simply delaying implementation of agency policy, and courts would confront challenges to the agency's factual premises and policy judgments in the more revealing context of concrete application.

Professor Pierce has been equally critical of what he considers dysfunctionally intrusive judicial review of agency regulations. See, e.g., Richard J. Pierce, 32 Tulsa L.Rev. at 191–97. Surprisingly, however, he sees closer oversight by Congress as the answer. Applauding the enactment of the Congressional Review Act, discussed at p. 110 *supra*, Pierce pronounced the legal framework for agency rulemaking nearly complete:

> [W]e now have in place two-thirds of a new legal environment that would combine our social values in a new way so as to maximize our ability to further those values simultaneously. We have had systematic Presidential review of major rules for over a dozen years. * * * [A]n agency can [now] issue a rule only if it survives review by both of the politically accountable branches of government. * * *
>
> At the same time, the new rulemaking process will further the social goals of enhancing efficiency and fairness in government operations. It will have this effect by creating an environment in which agencies can maximize their reliance on rules and rulemakings: the primary sources of efficiency and fairness in implementing benefit programs and regulatory programs. * * *
>
> With the addition of the congressional review chapter to the APA, then, we need to make only one further change in law to deossify rulemaking. Courts should be limited to two narrow, but important roles, in the rulemaking process. They should retain the power to hold a rule unconstitutional, and they should retain the power to hold a rule invalid because it is inconsistent with a statute.

So far, there is little evidence that Congress is interested in lowering the barriers to agency rulemaking. The enactment of the Congressional Review Act appears to reflect a belief that even after surviving the OIRA review process and meeting statutorily mandated analytical requirements, some rules will still be unacceptable to sitting legislators. As Professor Mashaw has highlighted in *Reinventing Government and Regulatory Reform: Studies in the Neglect and Abuse of Administrative Law*, 57 U.Pitt.L.Rev. 405 (1996), excerpted in Chapter 1, in recent years Congress has enacted a series of laws whose requirements further encumber agency rulemaking. These include the Unfunded Mandates Reform Act of 1995, 2 U.S.C. 1531 (1995), *supra* p. 166, which "codifies many of the analytical requirements * * * contained in presidential executive orders" [and] "makes a number of these requirements more burdensome":

> In particular, it requires coordination and consultation with state, local, and tribal governments which might be affected by regulation and the inclusion of a summary of their comments in the rationale for any proposed rule. In addition, the agency must identify regulatory alternatives and "select the least costly, most cost-effective or least burdensome alternative."

Compliance with these analytical requirements is also made judicially reviewable.

That same year, Congress amended the Paperwork Reduction Act, Pub.L.No. 104–13, *supra* p. 164, overturning a Supreme Court ruling that the Act did not apply to rules requiring private parties to provide information to third parties, in the form of product labels or other mandated disclosures. The amended law enables OMB "to second guess any agency's decision to use information as a regulatory technique." A year later, Congress adopted major amendments to the Regulatory Flexibility Act, Pub.L.No. 104–121, § 241, requiring—again subject to judicial review—that agencies undertake "special analyses to identify and avoid any disproportionate impact [of their rules] on small business." See Strauss, 31 Wake Forest L.Rev. at 768. Surveying these developments, Professor Strauss concludes that American law has so far failed to develop "means of encouraging attention and responsibility without imposing debilitating costs. * * * Current procedural requirements produce a procedural matrix so clogged and expensive that agencies are driven to evade, to seek out alternatives. * * * Congress's recent actions and some of the current proposals threaten to complicate this picture further."

Professor Mashaw's assessment of the incentive effects of the combination of skeptical judicial review and escalating analytical demands by Congress is even more pessimistic:

> [T]his use of law to defeat law-making may ultimately undermine administrative law itself. * * * If the programs crippled by these "reforms"—importantly the health and safety programs that must regulate by rules—retain substantial public support, then legal technicality will eventually come to be seen as the enemy of effective governance. * * *
>
> Alternatively, the new hyperlegalism may remain, but be honored mostly in the breach. Many agencies can avoid using the regulatory techniques that are to be "reformed." Agencies such as the Food and Drug Administration, the Federal Communications Commission, or the Federal Energy Regulatory Commission, with broad licensing, certification, or rule-making authority can control whole industries without ever issuing a single regulation. The Securities and Exchange Commission and the banking regulatory agencies can probably be equally effective through threats of prosecution, even raised eyebrows. The losses then will be in the form of openness, consistency, and, perhaps, rationality * * * Discretion will be exercised, but it will be informal and hidden because the processes of formal action have become too legalistic to be utilized.

Is There a Third Way?

Professor Mashaw's gloomy pronouncements suggest that American administrative regulation is trapped between demands for effective regulation and demands for rationality and legal and political accountability that stifle regulatory effectiveness. He predicts that the result will be evasion of legal requirements, illustrated perhaps by the FDA's guidelines documents, or the abandonment of regulatory requirements, illustrated perhaps by his previously cited study (with David Harfst) of the collapse of rulemaking at the National Highway Traffic Safety Administration. Others see possibilities for the reconciliation of society's conflicting demands in new approaches to regulatory strategy.

In a much cited book, RESPONSIVE REGULATIONS: TRANSCENDING THE DEREGULATION DEBATE (1992), Ian Ayres and John Braithwaite urge that governments seek to accommodate regulated parties when developing and implementing regulatory policies, reserving "rulish" requirements for those situations in which cooperation cannot be garnered. Ayres and Braithwaite are not blind to the difficulties of "responsive" or cooperative regulation. They suggest a staged approach in which the first option is always "self-regulation". When that fails the government should try what they term "enforced self regulation", a process in which companies write the rules tailored to their unique circumstances, but under a government mandate to do so. Enforcement would then be auditing to see that firms live up to their commitments. If these flexible and cooperative strategies failed, the government might then turn to traditional regulation, often through rulemaking. Others have sounded similar themes.

These suggestions raise at least two questions: First, are they new? Second, would these *reforms* be *improvements*? The answers to both seem to be "yes" and "no." The government has always relied extensively on persuasion, negotiation and self-regulation, including mandated self-regulation. And it often borrows rules from private associations. But there are new developments as well, indeed constant experimentation with ways of breaking regulatory logjams and inducing cooperative behavior. Whether these reforms work better than "classical" regulation remains hotly contested.

Reliance on Private Parties. Privately-created rules of conduct have long been influential in governmental regulatory programs. A study for the U.S. Administrative Conference by Professor Robert W. Hamilton, *The Role of Nongovernmental Standards in the Development of Mandatory Federal Standards Affecting Safety or Health*, 56 Tex.L.Rev. 1329 (1978), documents the pervasiveness of private standard-setting. It ranges from the familiar testing of electrical equipment by Underwriters Laboratory—whose certification has been made a legal requirement by most local building codes—to the work of non-profit organizations, such as the American Society for Testing and Materials, the National Fire Protection Association, and the American National Standards Institute (ANSI), the latter an association of standard-setting organizations.

Official reliance on private voluntary standards can be grouped under three headings. The existence of a generally observed private standard for a product or process may cause an agency to turn its attention to other problems; private standards may thus obviate government regulation.

A second approach relies on private standards as the starting point for the development of mandatory government requirements. The so-called "offeror" provisions of the original Consumer Product Safety Act, 15 U.S.C. § 2058, and the 1976 Medical Device Amendments to the Food, Drug, and Cosmetic Act, 21 U.S.C. § 360d, represent variants of this approach. In both laws Congress sought to encourage private sector groups to submit proposals for mandatory standards, including specifically proposals based on existing voluntary standards. In neither instance, however, have Congress' expectations been realized. Theresa M. Schwartz, *The Consumer Product Safety Commission: A Flawed Product of the Consumer Decade*, 51 Geo.Wash.L.Rev. 32 (1982); Robert B. Leflar, *Public Accountability and Medical Device Regulation*, 2 Harv.J.L. & Tech. 1 (1989).

At the extreme, an agency may simply adopt private standards as its own. Incorporation of U.L. certification to determine eligibility for government procurement or compliance with local building codes is an illustration of this approach. A more dramatic example is the Occupational Safety and Health Act, which authorized OSHA, within two years of passage, to adopt—and without public rulemaking—existing "national consensus standards" for workplace hazards. 29 U.S.C. § 655(a). Pursuant to this authority, OSHA adopted wholesale several thousand published standards addressed to worker safety. OSHA's lack of discrimination, according to some observers, was a major cause of its subsequent unpopularity within the business community. Many of these borrowed standards were obsolete, their coverage was incomplete, and their focus, e.g., the color of ladders or the height of toilets, often invited ridicule. Steven Kelman, *Occupational Safety and Health Administration*, in JAMES Q. WILSON, ED., THE POLITICS OF REGULATION 236 (1980); Albert L. Nichols and Richard J. Zeckhauser, *Government Comes to the Workplace: An Assessment of OSHA*, Pub.Int.No. 49, p. 39 (1977).

Professor Robert Hamilton began his study of private standard-setting believing that the agreed-upon practices of industry groups would hardly fulfill the needs and objectives of regulatory programs. He emerged with a revised view:

> [My starting] assumptions for the most part were oversimplified, at least with regard to the standards developed by the best procedures followed by the private sector. Such procedures develop standards that deserve serious consideration for regulatory use and certainly much greater respect than they have been accorded in the past.

Prospects for the Nongovernmental Development of Regulatory Standards, 32 Am.U.L.Rev. 455, 459 (1983). Professor Hamilton nonetheless identified several features of private standard-setting that ought to engender caution before the results are incorporated into governmental mandate. First, private standards may undesirably constrain innovation and competition. Second, private procedures for standards development rarely afford affected interests equivalent opportunities for participation. Hamilton further points out that the criteria embodied in private standards may often subordinate values that the agency or Congress wants given prominence.

Negotiated Rulemaking. Another, much-publicized reform accepts the premise that federal rulemaking is in substantial part a political exercise. The founding father and leading proponent of "negotiated rulemaking," Philip J. Harter, in *Negotiating Regulations: A Cure for Malaise*, 71 Geo.L.J. 1, 7, 18–21 (1982), offered this critique of the conventional rulemaking:

> [It] has become a surrogate for direct participation in the political decision because parties have no means of direct participation in the policy choice. Parties can limit the agency's range of choices only by influencing the record. As a result, the process of developing the record has become bitterly adversarial.
>
> * * * Because the parties advocate the extreme, they may be reluctant to provide data to the agency and to each other because they fear the data may be misused or reveal weaknesses in the extreme position. * * *
>
> * * * Moreover, the adversarial process tends to warp the quality of the scientific and technical information submitted. Because the parties must develop the best arguments for the positions they advocate, qualifications, limitations, and expressions of doubt are lost. * * *

Harter advocated a different approach to the formulation of agency rules:

> * * * Negotiations among directly affected groups conducted within both the existing policies of the statute authorizing the regulation and the existing policies of the agency, would enable the parties to participate directly in the establishment of the rule. The significant concerns of each could be considered frontally. Direct participation in rulemaking through negotiations is preferable to entrusting the decision to the wisdom and judgment of the agency, which is essential under the basic provisions of the APA, or to relying on the more formal, structured method of hybrid rulemaking in which it is difficult for anyone to make the careful trade offs necessary for an enlightened regulation. A regulation that is developed by and has the support of the respective interests would have a political legitimacy that regulations developed under any other process arguably lack. * * *

The process that Harter and others envisioned, e.g., Note, *Rethinking Regulation: Negotiation as an Alternative to Traditional Rulemaking*, 94 Harv.L.Rev. 1871 (1981), was designed to produce agreement among the principal interested parties on a text that served as the responsible agency's notice of proposed rulemaking. Harter visualized a series of carefully structured meetings among principals to identify points of dispute, areas of agreement, and avenues of accommodation—all off the record and outside the glare of public attention that assertedly generates overstatement and rigidity.

Several agencies have experimented with negotiated rulemaking. Their experience has been analyzed by Professor Henry H. Perritt, e.g., *Negotiated Rulemaking Before Federal Agencies: Evaluation of Recommendations by the Administrative Conference of the United States*, 74

Geo.L.J. 1625 (1986); *Administrative Alternative Dispute Resolution: The Development of Negotiated Rulemaking and Other Processes*, 14 Pepperdine L.Rev. 863 (1987). Professor Perritt points out that in three of four early cases in which the process was employed, the authorizing agency produced final regulations that were not challenged in court. He stresses the importance of agency involvement in the negotiation process itself. In the one instance where agency personnel avoided an active role—the attempt to negotiate a revised OSHA standard for benzene following the Supreme Court's rejection of OSHA's initial effort, *infra* p. 846—the private negotiators were unable to reach agreement.

By no means all observers support negotiated rulemaking, however. In *When Smoke Gets in Your Eyes: Regulatory Negotiation and the Public Interest—EPA's Woodstove Standards*, 18 Environ.L. 55 (1987), Professor William Funk recounts the successful effort, sponsored by EPA, to negotiate a proposed performance standard for woodstoves under section 111 of the Clean Air Act. Funk concludes that the resulting proposed rule—to which all of the participants assented—"is not authorized by the Clean Air Act, and that the process of developing the rule by regulatory negotiation directly contributed to this unlawful proposal." He describes a process in which achieving consensus becomes so important that the parties neglect, or even ignore, the constraints imposed by the agency's statute.

> [I]t is my thesis that the theory and principles of regulatory negotiation are at war with the theory and principles of American administrative law applicable to rulemaking. * * * [T]he parties to the rule are happy with it; therefore, it matters not whether the rule is rational or lawful. Discretion delegated to the agency by Congress is effectively exercised by the group of interested parties, constrained only by the need to obtain consensus. The law no longer directs or even necessarily constrains the outcome but has become merely a factor in the give-and-take necessary to achieve consensus.

A less certain skeptic, Judge Patricia M. Wald of the D.C. Circuit, pointed out the challenges courts might face in reviewing negotiated rules. *Negotiation of Environmental Disputes: A New Rule for the Courts?*, 10 Colum.J.Envtl.L. 1 (1985). She noted that courts are accustomed to treating agency explanations as true accounts of their reasoning, and examining rulemaking records to determine whether they contain adequate support. Furthermore, the courts operate at the conclusion of a process structured to allow participation by any interested person and to curb preferential access by any private party. Judge Wald's speculations prompted Philip J. Harter to respond. In *The Role of Courts in Regulatory Negotiation—A Response to Judge Wald*, 11 Colum.J.Envtl.L. 51 (1986), he argued that a court reviewing a rule produced through negotiation must first be satisfied that the rule is within the agency's statutory authority to adopt. Harter acknowledged that a process that relies less on documentation and that may fail to reveal all of the agency's reasoning could present a problem for courts responsible for assuring that rules are not "arbitrary or capricious." He suggested that judges should focus instead on the negotiation process—demanding representation of the full range of affected interests and exploration of all reasonable alternatives.

Based on Harter's 1982 study, the U.S. Administrative Conference twice recommended that Congress authorize negotiated rulemaking as an alternative to section 553 procedures. After eight years, Congress enacted the Negotiated Rulemaking Act of 1990, Pub.L.No. 101–648, 104 Stat. 4949, which generally tracks Harter's original proposal.

In one of the few opinions interpreting the Negotiated Rulemaking Act, *USA Group Loan Services Inc. v. Riley*, 82 F.3d 708 (7th Cir.1996), the Seventh Circuit was asked to overturn Department of Education regulations defining the obligations and liabilities of processors of student loans. Among the petitioners' challenges was the claim that DOE had failed to live up to a Department official's promise to base its proposal on whatever consensus resulted from a negotiation hosted by the agency. Circuit Judge Posner gave this argument, and the Negotiated Rulemaking Act, rather short shrift:

> We have doubts about the propriety of the official's promise to abide by a consensus of the regulated industry, but we have no doubt that the Negotiated Rulemaking Act did not make the promise enforceable. The practical effect of enforcing it would be to the make the Act extinguish notice and comment rulemaking in all cases in which it was preceded by negotiated rulemaking; the comments would be irrelevant if the agency were already bound by promises that it had made to the industry. There is no textual or other clue that the Act meant to do this. Unlike collective bargaining negotiations * * * the Act does not envisage that the negotiations will end in a binding contract. The Act simply creates a consultation process in advance of the more formal arms' length procedure of notice and comment rulemaking.
>
> The complaint about the Secretary's refusal to adhere to the proposal to cap the services' liability misconceives the nature of negotiation. The Secretary proposed the cap in an effort to be accommodating and deflect the industry's wrath. The industry, in retrospect improvidently, rejected the proposal, holding out for no liability. So, naturally, the Secretary withdrew the proposal. A rule that places a ceiling on the offeror's demands would destroy negotiation. * * * By the same token, the negotiating position of the parties in negotiated rulemaking ought not be admissible in a challenge to the rule eventually promulgated when the negotiation failed.

Professor Harter sharply criticized this opinion: "While the court reaches what is probably the right conclusion, it displays a remarkable ignorance of the process and provides only a superficial analysis." *First Judicial Review of Reg–Neg a Disappointment*, Admin. & Regulatory L. News, Fall, 1996.

More recent assessments of negotiated rulemaking confirm its relatively limited popularity and question its legitimacy or practical utility.

In *Bargaining Toward the New Millennium: Regulatory Negotiation and the Subversion of the Public Interest*, 46 Duke L.J. 1351 (1997), Professor William Funk expands upon his original charge that the process undermines accountability for regulatory choices. And in *Assessing Consensus: The Promise and Performance of Negotiated Rulemaking*, 46 Duke L.J. 1255 (1997), Professor Cary Coglianese delivers the following devastating assessment: "Negotiated rulemaking saves no appreciable amount of time nor reduces the rate of litigation."

If U.S. agencies were to move in the direction of negotiating important rules, their practice would more closely resemble European norms for the formulation of general administrative policy. In Britain, for example, both formal and informal consultation of private groups, sometimes designated by statute, is common. See PAUL P. CRAIG, ADMINISTRATIVE LAW (1999). See also WILLIAM SAFRAN, THE FRENCH POLITY (6th ed. 2002). For a comparative assessment of administrative procedures for establishing health standards, see RONALD BRICKMAN, ET AL., CONTROLLING CHEMICALS: THE POLITICS OF REGULATION IN EUROPE AND THE UNITED STATES (1985).

Collaborative Regulation. The Environmental Protection Agency has one of the widest jurisdictions and most onerous regulatory tasks of all federal regulatory agencies. Its regulatory processes are also notoriously adversarial and sclerotic. During the 1990s the EPA, therefore, experimented with several programs that attempt to promote voluntary regulation. One, its Project XL (for eXcellence and Leadership) allows regulated entities to develop their own proposals for controlling pollution. If those proposals provide "superior" environmental results, the EPA will waive various regulatory requirements that would otherwise foreclose the implementation of the proposed pollution control plan. Proponents of alternative strategies for pollution control must seek stakeholder approval for their projects, that is, state and local government agencies, public interest organizations and members of local communities must have an opportunity to participate in the proposal's development. For details, see Regulatory Reinvention (XL) Pilot Project, 60 Fed. Reg. 27,282, 27,287 (1995) and Notice of Modifications to Project XL, 62 Fed. Reg. 19,872, 19,873 (1997).

The EPA has also attempted to rely on positive publicity to reduce emissions from toxic chemicals, to encourage the installation of energy-efficient lighting and to spur the development of energy saving computers. See Pollution Prevention Strategy, 56 Fed. Reg. 7849 (1991); and Eric W. Orts, *Reflexive Environmental Law*, 89 N.W. U. L. Rev. 1227 (1995). Cooperation with the EPA gains firms favorable publicity. By contrast, publication by the EPA of its Toxic Release Inventory (TRI), under the Emergency Planning and Community Right to Know Act, 42 U.S.C. §§ 11001–11050 (1986), employs negative publicity to encourage reductions in the release of toxics.

Commentators differ on whether the Environmental Protection Agency's attempts to be "responsive," "reflexive," or "collaborative" produce superior results, or are simply further evidence that the agency is incapable of carrying out its formal regulatory tasks and has retreated to "softer" techniques that are unlikely to produce results. Eric Orts, in the article cited above, thinks EPA's efforts have been, on the whole, more beneficial than not. And much higher marks are given the TRI by its former general counsel, E. Donald Elliott, *Environmental TQM: Anatomy of a Pollution Control Program That Works!*, 92 Mich. L. Rev. 1840 (1994). Others are much less sanguine. Sidney A. Shapiro and Randy Rabinowitz in a pair of articles, *Punishment v. Cooperation in Regulatory Enforcement: A Case Study of OSHA*, 49 Admin. L. Rev. 713 (1997), and *Voluntary Regulatory Compliance in Theory and in Practice: The Case of OSHA*, 52 Admin. L. Rev. 97 (2000) agree that some mixture of cooperation and punishment should be included in an optimal enforcement policy. The problem is that the literature and agency experience provide no clear guidance on what mix is the optimal one. Shapiro and Rabinowitz believe that voluntary compliance programs have the potential to provide superior regulatory performance but only in "narrowly circumscribed circumstances." They also conclude that "even when voluntary compliance is effected, it is likely that it provides less protection than does regulation." For a broad review of regulatory reform (meaning usually "rulemaking reform") efforts from the 1970s to the beginning of the 21st century, see Sidney A. Shapiro, *Administrative Law After the Counter–Reformation: Restoring Faith in Pragmatic Government*, 48 Kan. L. Rev. 689 (2000).

Chapter 6

GOVERNMENT INFORMATION ACQUISITION AND DISCLOSURE

The federal government acquires and stores more information than any other institution in American society. Some of this information is obtained specifically for the purposes of law enforcement, including the development and enforcement of regulatory policy. Much is compiled in implementing public benefits programs, and a good deal is the byproduct of the government's activities as purchaser—of weapons systems, space shuttles, and office supplies—and owner/manager of buildings and real estate. Indeed, one can hardly conceive of a governmental function for which administrators do not require, or unavoidably receive, information from private parties. Government recourse to that information poses familiar but significant issues of privacy and individual liberty.

By the same token, government is the repository of vast stores of information of enormous importance to the public. Besides the near-endless data that would be of use to entrepreneurs, planners, and researchers of all sorts, government agencies hold information critical to the assessment of their performance by Congress, the press, and the public generally. The responsible management and distribution of this information is itself a costly enterprise, and a recurring theme throughout this chapter is the inevitable tradeoff between facilitating public access to government information and preserving government's resources for serving the public in other ways.

In this chapter we explore, first, the principles applicable to the government's authority to demand that private parties produce information or allow access to their premises and, second, the competing obligations imposed on federal administrators to afford access to government records and to protect confidential and sensitive information in government files.

A. INVESTIGATION AND DISCOVERY

Sound decision making obviously requires good information. Federal administrative agencies accordingly devote substantial effort to data collection and analysis. Indeed, a primary activity of some bodies, like the Department of Commerce, consists of acquiring and disseminating information to assist either other governmental activities or private firms and individuals. In some cases an agency may be its own best source of needed information. The Social Security Administration's own personnel are probably in a better position than anyone outside the government to supply data about its caseload of disability claims, about the costs of processing these claims, and perhaps even about the aggregate effects of government disability benefits on the economy and/or the health and well-being of claimants. Often, however, beneficiaries or subjects of regulation are closer to the facts than any government official. The retreaders of tires whom we encountered in *Brinegar*, for example, in Chapter 5, seemed better equipped to supply information about prevailing industry practices and available technology than employees of the National Highway Traffic Safety Administration.

Agencies obtain needed information from private parties in a variety of ways. Most of it is provided voluntarily, or at least without formal objection. Individuals or businesses often desire to supply information to administrators in order to obtain some benefit—such as welfare assistance, a government loan, a license to market a product, a larger allocation of publicly controlled resources, or protective regulation. While in such cases the submission of information may be initiated by the party seeking governmental favor, the responsible agency usually has made known in a general way the type of information it requires in order to act favorably. Frequently, the agency's needs are made known more specifically, as when the FDA prescribes the contents of applications for approval to market new drugs.

However, some information that government officials require to develop policy, adjudicate cases, or initiate enforcement action is not willingly disclosed. The difficult questions, and most of the law in this area, relate to the power of governmental bodies to compel the production of information. Our attention will focus on three techniques for compelling access to information: (1) the power to subpoena or otherwise order testimony or the production of documents; (2) the power to require the maintenance of records and the submission of reports; and (3) the power physically to enter and explore private premises to obtain information. This preoccupation with the compulsory production of information is justified not only by the difficulty and interest of the questions presented, but by the fact that the extent of voluntary disclosure of information is likely to depend significantly on the scope of official power to demand production.

Several issues recur in our examination of government power to compel disclosure. One is the existence of statutory or inherent authority to order disclosure in a particular context. A second is the scope of legally recognized "privileges" to withhold information, or at least to insist upon its confidential treatment, even in the face of a lawful demand for production. Central to this latter inquiry are the constitutional limits on forced production of information, grounded in the Fourth Amendment's guarantee of security for homes and personal effects and in the Fifth Amendment's protection against forced self-incrimination.

1. AUTHORITY TO SUBPOENA WITNESSES AND DOCUMENTS

While the courts have liberally interpreted express statutory grants of information-gathering authority to administrators, Congress must have conferred such power; no administrator possesses inherent authority to conduct inspections, require reports, or issue subpoenas. The original provisions of the Federal Trade Commission Act are typical. Section 6(a) of the Act expansively empowered the FTC "[t]o gather and compile information concerning, and to investigate from time to time the organization, business, conduct, practices and management of any corporation engaged in commerce * * * and its relation to other corporations and to individuals, associations, and partnerships." 15 U.S.C. § 46(a) (1970). Section 9, 15 U.S.C. § 49, authorized the use of compulsory process in support of the Commission's investigatory and enforcement activities:

> For the purposes of sections [1–6] * * * the Commission, or its duly authorized agent or agents, shall at all reasonable times have access to, for the purpose of examination, and the right to copy any documentary evidence of any corporation being investigated or proceeded against; and the Commission shall have power to require by subpoena the attendance and testimony of witnesses and the production of all such documentary evidence relating to any matter under investigation. * * *
>
> * * * And in case of disobedience to a subpoena the Commission may invoke the aid of any court of the United States in requiring the attendance and testimony of witnesses and the production of documentary evidence.
>
> Any of the district courts of the United States within the jurisdiction of which such inquiry is carried on may, in case of contumacy or refusal to obey a subpoena issued to any corporation or other person, issue an order requiring such corporation or other person to appear before the Commission, or to produce documentary evidence if so ordered, or to give evidence touching the matter in question; and any failure to obey such order of the court may be punished by such court as a contempt thereof.*

* The 1975 Magnuson–Moss Warranty–Federal Trade Commission Improvement Act, 88 Stat. 2183, Pub.L.No. 93–637, broadened the FTC's investigatory jurisdiction to include individuals and partnerships, as well as corporations. That an investigation is directed at an entity other than a corporation is probably not significant under modern decisions concerning the permissible reach of agency subpoena power, save in circumstances that implicate the Fifth Amendment.

Despite this broad language, judicial reaction to the FTC's initial attempts to compel the production of evidence was hostile. In 1923, spurred by a Senate resolution, the Commission undertook an investigation of charges that two tobacco manufacturers, American and P. Lorillard, had unlawfully controlled the prices at which jobbers resold their products. Before issuing a formal complaint the agency ordered each company to produce "all letters and telegrams received by the Company from, or sent by it to all of its jobber customers, between January 1, 1921, to December 31, 1921, inclusive." The companies resisted this demand, essentially on constitutional grounds, and were upheld by the district court in which the Commission sought enforcement of its order. In *FTC v. American Tobacco Co.*, 264 U.S. 298, 305–07 (1924), the Supreme Court, through Justice Holmes, affirmed:

> [T]he Commission claims an unlimited right of access to the respondents' papers with reference to the possible existence of practices in violation of § 5.
>
> The mere facts of carrying on a commerce not confined within state lines and of being organized as a corporation do not make men's affairs public, as those of a railroad company now may be. Anyone who respects the spirit as well as the letter of the Fourth Amendment would be loath to believe that Congress intended to authorize one of its subordinate agencies to sweep all our traditions into the fire and to direct fishing expeditions into private papers on the possibility that they may disclose evidence of crime. We do not discuss the question whether it could do so if it tried, as nothing short of the most explicit language would induce us to attribute to Congress that intent. * * * It is contrary to the first principles of justice to allow a search through all the respondents' records, relevant or irrelevant, in the hope that something will turn up. * * *
>
> The right of access given by the statute is to documentary evidence—not to all documents, but to such documents as are evidence. The analogies of the law do not allow the party wanting evidence to call for all documents in order to see if they do not contain it. Some ground must be shown for supposing that the documents called for do contain it. Formerly in equity the ground must be found in admissions in the answer. We assume that the rule to be applied here is more liberal, but still a ground must be laid and the ground and the demand must be reasonable. A general subpoena in the form of these petitions would be bad. Some evidence of the materiality of the papers demanded must be produced. * * *
>
> We have considered this case on the general claim of authority put forward by the Commission. The argument for the Government attaches some force to the investigations and proceedings upon which the Commission had entered. The investigations and complaints seem to have been only on hearsay or suspicion—but, even if they were induced by substantial evidence under oath, the rudimen-

tary principles of justice that we have laid down would apply. We cannot attribute to Congress an intent to defy the Fourth Amendment or even to come so near to doing so as to raise a serious question of constitutional law.

Holmes' opinion assumed, almost without discussion, that the Fourth Amendment guarantee against "unreasonable searches and seizures" imposes limits on the government's power to obtain evidence through administrative subpoenas. His reading seriously threatened the FTC's authority to investigate activities prior to issuing a complaint charging actual violations of the Act. For the agency might often have no secure basis for determining whether violations had been committed before it had an opportunity to examine the very information Holmes seemed to put out of reach.

Holmes' ruling inhibited administrative investigations for almost two decades, but by World War II the Court was displaying greater sympathy toward agency demands for information. In *Endicott Johnson Corp. v. Perkins*, 317 U.S. 501, 508–10 (1943), the Secretary of Labor sought enforcement of a subpoena issued in connection with an investigation of compliance with the Walsh–Healey Act. The subpoena sought information concerning the contractors' payrolls at plants that arguably were not covered by the Act. The district court held that it first had to determine whether the Act applied to the plants and contracts about which the Secretary sought information, asserting that if it did not, the subpoena was not in aid of an authorized function. This time, the Supreme Court reversed, marking the beginnings of a retreat from *American Tobacco*:

> The matter which the Secretary was investigating and was authorized to investigate was an alleged violation of this Act and these contracts. Her scope would include determining what employees these contracts and the Act covered. It would also include whether the payments to them were lower than the scale fixed pursuant to the Act. She could not perform her full statutory duty until she examined underpayments wherever the coverage extended. * * *
>
> Nor was the District Court authorized to decide the question of coverage itself. The evidence sought by the subpoena was not plainly incompetent or irrelevant to any lawful purpose of the Secretary in the discharge of her duties under the Act, and it was the duty of the District Court to order its production for the Secretary's consideration. * * * The consequence of the action of the District Court was to disable the Secretary from rendering a complete decision on the alleged violation as Congress had directed her to do, and that decision was stated by the Act to be conclusive as to matters of fact for purposes of the award of government contracts. * * *
>
> The subpoena power delegated by the statute as here exercised is so clearly within the limits of Congressional authority that it is

not necessary to discuss the constitutional questions urged by the petitioner. * * *

Oklahoma Press Publishing Co. v. Walling, 327 U.S. 186, 201–14 (1946), marked a decisive step in the evolution of modern doctrine governing the exercise of administrative subpoena powers. There the Department of Labor, in an investigation to determine compliance with the Fair Labor Standards Act, subpoenaed extensive records of the respondent newspaper company before charging any violation. The Court rejected the newspaper's arguments that such extensive inquiry, prior to any formal complaint, was not authorized by the FLSA (which expressly incorporated the investigatory provisions of the FTC Act) or, if authorized, was barred by the Fourth Amendment.

> [T]his case presents an instance of "the most explicit language" which leaves no room for questioning Congress' intent. The very purpose of the subpoena and of the order, as of the authorized investigation, is to discover and procure evidence, not to prove a pending charge or complaint, but upon which to make one if, in the Administrator's judgment, the facts thus discovered should justify doing so.
>
> Accordingly, if §§ 9 and 11(a) are not to be construed as authorizing enforcement of the orders, it must be, as petitioners say, because this construction would make them so dubious constitutionally as to compel resort to an interpretation which saves rather than to one which destroys or is likely to do so. * * * The Court has adopted this course at least once in this type of case [citing *American Tobacco*].
>
> The primary source of misconception concerning the Fourth Amendment's function lies perhaps in the identification of cases involving so-called "figurative" or "constructive" search with cases of actual search and seizure. Only in this analogical sense can any question related to search and seizure be thought to arise in situations which, like the present ones, involve only the validity of authorized judicial orders. * * *
>
> The confusion obscuring the basic distinction between actual and so-called "constructive" search has been accentuated where the records and papers sought are of corporate character, as in these cases. Historically private corporations have been subject to broad visitorial power, both in England and in this country. And it long has been established that Congress may exercise wide investigative power over them, analogous to the visitorial power of the incorporating state, when their activities take place within or affect interstate commerce. Correspondingly it has been settled that corporations are not entitled to all of the constitutional protections which private individuals have in these and related matters. * * *
>
> Without attempt to summarize or accurately distinguish all of the cases, the fair distillation, in so far as they apply merely to the production of corporate records and papers in response to a subpoe-

na or order authorized by law and safeguarded by judicial sanction, seems to be that the Fifth Amendment affords no protection by virtue of the self-incrimination provision, whether for the corporation or for its officers; and the Fourth, if applicable, at the most guards against abuse only by way of too much indefiniteness or breadth in the things required to be "particularly described," if also the inquiry is one the demanding agency is authorized by law to make and the materials specified are relevant. The gist of the protection is in the requirement, expressed in terms, that the disclosure sought shall not be unreasonable.

* * * It is not necessary, as in the case of a warrant, that a specific charge or complaint of violation of law be pending or that the order be made pursuant to one. It is enough that the investigation be for a lawfully authorized purpose, within the power of Congress to command. This has been ruled most often perhaps in relation to grand jury investigations, but also frequently in respect to general or statistical investigations authorized by Congress. The requirement of "probable cause, supported by oath or affirmation," literally applicable in the case of a warrant, is satisfied in that of an order for production by the court's determination that the investigation is authorized by Congress, is for a purpose Congress can order, and the documents sought are relevant to the inquiry. Beyond this the requirement of reasonableness, including particularity in "describing the place to be searched, and the persons or things to be seized," also literally applicable to warrants, comes down to specification of the documents to be produced adequate, but not excessive, for the purposes of the relevant inquiry. Necessarily, as has been said, this cannot be reduced to formula; for relevancy and adequacy or excess in the breadth of the subpoena are matters variable in relation to the nature, purposes and scope of the inquiry.

When these principles are applied to the facts of the present cases, it is impossible to conceive how a violation of petitioners' rights could have been involved. Both were corporations. The only records or documents sought were corporate ones. No possible element of self-incrimination was therefore presented or in fact claimed. All the records sought were relevant to the authorized inquiry,[46] the purpose of which was to determine two issues, whether petitioners were subject to the Act and, if so, whether they were violating it. These were subjects of investigation authorized by

46. The subpoena in No. 61 called for production of:

> "All of your books, papers, and documents showing the hours worked by and wages paid to each of your employees between October 28, 1938, and the date hereof, including all payroll ledgers, time sheets, time cards and time clock records, and all your books, papers and documents showing the distribution of papers outside the State of Oklahoma, the dissemination of news outside the State of Oklahoma, the source and receipt of news from outside the State of Oklahoma, and the source and receipt of advertisements of nationally advertised goods."

The specification in No. 63 was substantially identical except for the period of time covered by the demand.

§ 11(a), the latter expressly, the former by necessary implication. It is not to be doubted that Congress could authorize investigation of these matters. In all these respects,[48] the specifications more than meet the requirements long established by many precedents. * * *

We think * * * that the courts of appeals were correct in the view that Congress has authorized the Administrator, rather than the district courts in the first instance, to determine the question of coverage in the preliminary investigation of possibly existing violations; in doing so to exercise his subpoena power for securing evidence upon that question, by seeking the production of petitioners' relevant books, records, and papers; and, in case of refusal to obey his subpoena, issued according to the statute's authorization, to have the aid of the district court in enforcing it. No constitutional provision forbids Congress to do this. * * *

In *Oklahoma Press*, as in *Endicott Johnson*, the Court held that the issue of the agency's jurisdiction—at least where resolution depends on a factual determination such as whether employees are engaged in the production of goods for the government—is for the agency to decide in the first instance. The Court's vindication of agency power to compel disclosure thus closely parallels contemporaneous judicial affirmations of an agency's authority to conduct enforcement proceedings without judicial interruption to resolve challenges to its jurisdiction prior to completion of the administrative process. See *Myers v. Bethlehem Shipbuilding Corp.*, 303 U.S. 41 (1938); *cf. Federal Trade Commission v. Standard Oil Co.*, 449 U.S. 232 (1980), discussed in Chapter 7 *infra*.

Oklahoma Press was reaffirmed in *Donovan v. Lone Steer, Inc.*, 464 U.S. 408 (1984), a case arising out of investigations of compliance with the Fair Labor Standards Act. The respondents refused to comply with the Secretary of Labor's subpoena duces tecum, claiming that the Act violated the Fourth Amendment insofar as it authorized issuance of a subpoena without a prior judicial warrant. The district court agreed, concluding that this result was demanded by *Marshall v. Barlow's, Inc.*, 436 U.S. 307 (1978), *infra* p. 687. The Court dismissed the suggestion that the Secretary's entry into a public motel and restaurant lobby to serve the subpoena was a "search" covered by the Fourth Amendment, and ruled that judicial supervision of enforcement of the subpoena under *Oklahoma Press* fully protected the respondent's rights.

The Judicial Role in Enforcement of Agency Subpoenas

Endicott Johnson and *Oklahoma Press* appear to recognize only three basic limitations on agency subpoena powers: (1) any demand for

48. The description was made with all of the particularity the nature of the inquiry and the Administrator's situation would permit. See note 46. The specifications more than meet the requirements long established by many precedents. * * * The subpoenas were limited to the books, papers and documents of the respective corporations, to which alone they were addressed. They required production at specified times and places in the cities of publication and stated the purpose of the investigation to be one affecting the respondent, pursuant to the provisions of §§ 9 and 11(c), "regarding complaints of violations by said company of Sections 6, 7, 11(c), 15(a)(1), 15(a)(2) and 15(a)(5) of the Act."

information must fall within the authority conferred on an agency by statute; (2) any information demanded must be relevant to a proper subject of agency inquiry; and (3) a demand for information must not be unreasonable. A recipient of a subpoena who wishes to contest the agency's demand on any of these grounds may either seek a judicial order to quash or simply fail to comply. In the latter case the agency must obtain a judicial order directing compliance, disobedience of which may entail punishment for contempt. This two-step procedure thus affords an opportunity for judicial scrutiny of an agency's authority to compel the production of information and of the propriety of its exercise in the particular case before there can be any penalty for non-compliance. It should also be noted that an order enforcing an agency's subpoena ordinarily does not preclude later objection to the admissibility of evidence produced in formal agency proceedings.

Within Statutory Authorization. An agency generally must find authority to issue subpoenas (or other formal demands for information) in its governing statute. Thus, for example, *Serr v. Sullivan*, 390 F.2d 619 (3d Cir.1968), upheld a refusal to respond to a demand for information issued to permit holders by the Treasury Department's Alcohol and Tobacco Tax Division. Although the ATTD had been given broad authority to grant and withhold permits, its statute did not expressly authorize the agency to issue subpoenas or to conduct special investigations of permittees. This general principle is reiterated in APA § 555(c): "Process, requirement of a report, inspection, or other investigative act or demand may not be issued, made, or enforced except as authorized by law."

Compare *United States v. Exxon Corp.*, 628 F.2d 70 (D.C.Cir.1980), *cert. denied*, 446 U.S. 964 (1980), in which the Secretary of Energy's authority to subpoena information for use in studies under the Petroleum Marketing Practices Act (PMPA) was challenged. The court of appeals held that the subpoena power conferred by the Department of Energy Organization Act, the department's chartering statute, could support the Secretary's demand despite the absence of subpoena power in the PMPA. The court reasoned that the latter act merely confirmed the department's authority to conduct a study that it could have undertaken under its organic law. Circuit Judge Wilkey dissented, pointing out that neither the PMPA nor its legislative history contained a single word about use of subpoenas to obtain information for authorized studies. See Comment, *Department of Energy Needs No Express Grant of Subpoena Power to Study Oil Company Fuel Sales Subsidization*, 56 Notre Dame Law. 515 (1981).

While an agency's demand for information must relate to a subject within its investigatory authority, the party upon whom demand is made need not be within the agency's regulatory jurisdiction. Thus, *Freeman v. Brown Brothers Harriman & Co.*, 357 F.2d 741 (2d Cir.1966), *cert. denied*, 384 U.S. 933 (1966), sustained the Secretary of Agriculture's attempt to compel a bank to disclose information about the account of a depositor over whom the Secretary lacked jurisdiction. The information was relevant to determining whether another company concededly subject to regulation had paid illegal rebates to the bank's customer—a permissible subject of inquiry.

United States v. Minker, 350 U.S. 179 (1956), represents a departure from the general judicial willingness to construe grants of subpoena authority generously. In a denaturalization proceeding the INS sought to compel the appearance and testimony of Minker, the person whose citizenship was threatened, pursuant to a statute authorizing the issuance of subpoenas for "witnesses." Weighing the serious consequences of denaturalization and impressed by arguments that drew analogies to the Fifth Amendment's protection against self-incrimination, a majority of the Supreme Court concluded that the statutory term "witness" should not be read to include the persons under investigation.

Statutes sometimes specify the purposes for which the power to issue subpoenas is conferred. This may give rise to claims that the "real" objective of an agency in demanding documents or testimony is inconsistent with the limited purposes for which the power was given. See *United States v. O'Connor*, 118 F.Supp. 248 (D.Mass.1953), refusing to enforce a facially legitimate subpoena demanding information from a taxpayer when the issuing IRS official admitted he had sometimes used his subpoena power to aid Justice Department prosecution of criminal tax fraud cases. But the Supreme Court has made clear that the burden in such circumstances rests on the taxpayer (or, presumably, any other recipient of a subpoena) to show that the agency's demand represents an abuse of its power. *United States v. Powell*, 379 U.S. 48 (1964). See also *United States v. Litton Industries, Inc.*, 462 F.2d 14 (9th Cir.1972) (court will not assume FTC might misuse information otherwise properly demanded from subject of merger investigation). Some recipients of subpoenas have met this burden. In *Shasta Minerals & Chemical Co. v. SEC*, 328 F.2d 285 (10th Cir.1964), the Commission, having subpoenaed the company's list of shareholders, failed to respond to affidavits alleging systematic persecution and harassment of the company and its president. The court of appeals ruled that the district judge, before ordering enforcement, should have explored the accuracy of the corporation's allegations which presented material questions of "whether or not the Commission acted arbitrarily or outside of its statutory authority." See also *SEC v. Wheeling–Pittsburgh Steel Corp.*, 648 F.2d 118 (3d Cir.1981); Comment, *Bad Faith and the Abuse-of-Process Defense to Administrative Subpoenas*, 82 Colum.L.Rev. 811 (1982).

In *United States v. LaSalle National Bank*, 437 U.S. 298 (1978), the Supreme Court explored the scope of the "bad faith" defense to enforcement of an IRS administrative summons. The Court there overturned the Seventh Circuit's refusal to enforce a summons issued under 26 U.S.C. § 7602 to a bank that had custody of the taxpayer's records. The district court had found as a fact that the investigating agent sought the records "solely" for purposes of obtaining evidence of criminal conduct by the taxpayer—an objective the appellate court believed beyond the authority conferred by section 7602. In reversing, the Court observed that *Donaldson v. United States*, 400 U.S. 517 (1971), had sustained the IRS' use of the summons where criminal prosecution was a potential outcome of its investigation, and it confirmed that section 7602 authorizes use of a summons "in aid of a tax investigation that could have both civil and criminal consequences" until the Service formally recommends prosecution to the Department of Justice—so long as it acts in "good faith." The Court then quoted its summary of the components of good faith from *United States v. Powell, supra:*

> [The Service] must show that the investigation will be conducted pursuant to a legitimate purpose, that the inquiry may be relevant to the purpose, that the information sought is not already within the Commissioner's possession, and that the administrative steps required by the Code have been followed. * * * [A] court may not permit its process to be abused. Such an abuse would take place if the summons had been issued for an improper purpose, such as to harass the taxpayer or to put pressure on him to settle a collateral dispute, or for any other purpose reflecting on the good faith of the particular investigation.

The Court proceeded to hold that the summons should have been enforced in this case. Conceding that the investigating agent's purpose may have been to develop evidence for prosecution, it stressed that the Service as a whole retained responsibility to "calculate and to collect civil fraud penalties and fraudulently reported or unreported taxes." The institutional channels for review of the agent's findings, moreover, assured that the Service retained ability to explore these options as well. To show that a summons was issued in "bad faith," the opponent of enforcement had the heavy burden of disproving "the actual existence of a valid civil tax determination or collection purpose *by the Service.* * * * "

In an opinion joined by three other members of the Court, Justice Stewart would have reversed on a more objective ground: He believed that a section 7602 summons was lawful even when the Service's sole interest was in criminal prosecution, so long as it had not yet referred the case to the Department of Justice.

Germane to a Lawful Subject of Inquiry. Courts may insist that information whose production is demanded be potentially relevant to a proper subject of investigation. This requirement has occasionally led to refusal to enforce demands for information that failed adequately to disclose the purpose for which it was sought. As Circuit Judge Bazelon wrote in *Montship Lines Ltd. v. Federal Maritime Board*, 295 F.2d 147, 154–55 (D.C.Cir.1961), "[w]hat is 'reasonably relevant' depends on the purpose and nature of the investigation undertaken by the agency." There, the Board's failure to state its purpose "precluded a determination of relevancy." See *Hellenic Lines Ltd. v. Federal Maritime Board*, 295 F.2d 138, 140 (D.C.Cir.1961) (recitation that Board was acting " * * * pursuant to the responsibilities vested * * * by the interest of the Board's regulatory duties under that Act" held inadequate). The courts will not demand the specificity of code pleading, however, particularly when the precise direction of investigation has yet to be determined. In *Pacific Westbound Conference v. United States*, 332 F.2d 49, 52–53 (9th Cir.1964), the court sustained a Federal Maritime Commission demand for information that was challenged on the authority of *Montship* and *Hellenic Lines*:

> The statement of purpose set forth in the order here under review * * * is far more comprehensive than that which was found inadequate in Hellenic Lines, Ltd. That statement of purpose appears to us to be about as complete and specific as it could possibly be, considering the fact that, as the Commission had a right to do, it had not yet determined that any agreements, rates or fares were unlawful but was seeking information to ascertain the measure of compliance with the named regulatory statutes and the need of future Commission action in fulfillment of its statutory duties.

When an agency's investigation has acquired a focus that focus must be disclosed and the requirement that relevance be shown may become more demanding. Thus, in *United States v. Associated Merchandising Corp.*, 261 F.Supp. 553 (S.D.N.Y.1966), the FTC, in connection with a proceeding charging violations of the Robinson–Patman Act, demanded the disclosure of documents by respondents that embraced some two million invoices and went well beyond any transactions charged in its complaint. Relying in part on a Commission rule requiring a showing of "good cause" for the production of documents, the court refused enforcement as to several items it concluded were not germane to the agency's specific charges.

The cases make clear that an agency need not conclusively demonstrate the legal relevance of information in advance of obtaining it. The test appears to be one of "possible relevance" to matters properly subject to investigation. And, according to the D.C. Circuit, *FTC v. Texaco, Inc.*, 555 F.2d 862 (D.C.Cir.), *cert. denied*, 431 U.S. 974 (1977), the courts have only a limited role in assuring adherence to this standard. For a suggestion that courts should demand more, see Note, *Reasonable Relation Reassessed: The Examination of Private Documents by Federal Regulatory Agencies*, 56 N.Y.U.L.Rev. 742 (1981).

Specific and Not Unreasonably Burdensome. Closely related to the requirement that an agency explain the purpose of its demand for information in sufficient detail to demonstrate relevance is the requirement that the material sought be identified with reasonable precision. A subpoena may be so general in describing the information sought as to defy assessment of compliance. For example, a demand for "all documents bearing upon * * *" specific events or activities may not afford guidance as to whether particular papers must be produced. Yet it is rarely possible for an agency to identify with specificity everything it desires when it has never had an opportunity to examine the documents it is demanding. In such situations, the agency will usually attempt to identify the types of documents that might be useful and, often, specify the period of time in which it is interested. The resulting demand for, e.g., "all bank statements and cancelled checks for 1961 and 1962" cannot really be faulted for imprecision—the recipient knows what is demanded—but it may be overbroad or burdensome.

In *Kerr Steamship Co. v. United States*, 284 F.2d 61 (2d Cir.1960), *appeal dismissed as moot*, 369 U.S. 422 (1962), the court sustained a demand that carriers produce "a list identifying every contract * * * involving the water-borne commerce of the United States" made between it and any other carrier or "any freight forwarder, terminal operator, stevedore, or ship's agent" pertaining to seven specified types of activities. The court concluded that this demand was as definite as the subject-matter under investigation permitted. It promised that no carrier that attempted to comply in good faith would risk imposition of any penalties for non-compliance. Contrast *United States v. Theodore*, 479 F.2d 749 (4th Cir.1973), which held too "vague" and "burdensome" an IRS demand on a preparer of tax returns to produce all returns prepared and all work records compiled for all of its clients between 1969 and 1971. The objection to generality, in addition to reflecting a concern for relevance, also often reflects a suspicion that an agency has demanded more information than it needs, given the burden on the respondent of assembling it or functioning without it.

The federal courts generally take seriously their responsibility to restrain indiscriminate demands for disclosure. In *CAB v. Hermann*, 353 U.S. 322 (1957), the Supreme Court upheld a district court order enforcing a subpoena for records whose production would require examination of more than a million documents, but it also sustained that part of the court's order that staggered compliance with the Board's demand so that the respondent would not be deprived of all of its records at once. According to *FTC v. Texaco, Inc.*, 555 F.2d 862 (D.C.Cir.), *cert. denied*, 431 U.S. 974 (1977), the primary responsibility for assuring that an agency's demand is not unreasonably burdensome lies with the district courts, whose determinations should be reversed only for abuse of discretion.

Issued by Proper Authority. Occasionally, an agency's demand for information will be resisted on the ground that it has not been issued by the proper official. The FTC Act, for example, authorizes only the Commission members to issue subpoenas. Obviously, it would be tremendously burdensome if a Commissioner personally had to evaluate and authorize each of the many thousand demands for information the FTC issues each year. Thus, it is common in the FTC, the NLRB, and other agencies operating under similar statutory grants of power for members to sign subpoenas in blank, leaving to subordinates the job of filling in the details when a specific demand for information is issued. The courts have approved this practice. *NLRB v. Lewis*, 249 F.2d 832 (9th Cir.1957), *affirmed*, 357 U.S. 10 (1958). Similarly, the courts will sustain a formal subdelegation of authority to sign and issue subpoenas, unless that statutory language or history clearly precludes such a result. In *Fleming v. Mohawk Wrecking & Lumber Co.*, 331 U.S. 111 (1947), the Supreme

Court upheld such a subdelegation by the OPA administrator, based on a general grant of authority to delegate his powers to subordinates and his general rulemaking powers. Compare *Cudahy Packing Co. v. Holland*, 315 U.S. 357 (1942). In *Fleming*, as in so many other contexts, the Court's willingness to accord flexibility at the administrative level seems tied to its awareness that a recipient of a subpoena could obtain a judicial hearing before facing the risk of contempt.

Notice of Investigation

The custodians of subpoenaed material may not always have an interest in assuring that investigative demands comply with the foregoing limitations if they are not themselves the focus of the investigation. In *SEC v. Jerry T. O'Brien, Inc.*, 467 U.S. 735 (1984), the Supreme Court overturned a Ninth Circuit ruling that the SEC was obligated to notify the "target" of its investigation when it demanded records from third parties. The Court found no support for such an obligation in the due process clause of the Fifth Amendment or in the statutes administered by the Commission. It then proceeded to consider—and to dismiss—the argument that such notice was essential to protect the "right" of a target to have any investigation of its affairs carried out in compliance with the authority, relevance, propriety, and reasonableness standards set forth in *United States v. Powell*, 379 U.S. 48 (1964), *supra*:

> Two considerations underlie our decision on this issue. First, administration of the notice requirement advocated by respondents would be highly burdensome for both the Commission and the courts. The most obvious difficulty would involve identification of the persons and organizations that should be considered "targets" of investigation. The SEC often undertakes investigations into suspicious securities transactions without any knowledge of which of the parties involved may have violated the law. * * * Even in cases in which the Commission could identify with reasonable ease the principal targets of its inquiry, another problem would arise. In such circumstances, a person not considered a target by the Commission could contend that he deserved that status and therefore should be given notice of subpoenas issued to others. To assess a claim of this sort, a district court would be obliged to conduct some kind of hearing to determine the scope and thrust of the ongoing investigation. Implementation of this new remedy would drain the resources of the judiciary as well as the Commission.
>
> Second, the imposition of a notice requirement on the SEC would substantially increase the ability of persons who have something to hide to impede legitimate investigations by the Commission. A target given notice of every subpoena issued to third parties would be able to discourage the recipients from complying, and then further delay disclosure of damaging information by seeking intervention in all enforcement actions brought by the Commission. More seriously, the understanding of the progress of an SEC inquiry that would flow from knowledge of which persons had received subpoe-

nas would enable an unscrupulous target to destroy or alter documents, intimidate witnesses, or transfer securities or funds so that they could not be reached by the Government. Especially in the context of securities regulation, where speed in locating and halting violations of the law is so important, we would be loathe to place such potent weapons in the hands of persons with a desire to keep the Commission at bay. * * *

Recognition of Constitutional and Other Privileges

American courts recognize numerous "privileges" to withhold information or testimony otherwise properly demanded in judicial proceedings. The most notable of these, of course, is the privilege guaranteed by the Fifth Amendment (and, as against the states, by the fourteenth) to refuse to provide self-incriminating evidence. It is well accepted that this privilege attaches in administrative proceedings. Because efforts to compel testimony in administrative proceedings are uncommon, the privilege here focuses principally on the right to withhold documentary materials.

The privilege against self-incrimination is subject to several important limitations. First, it justifies the withholding only of information that may expose one to criminal prosecution; other damaging consequences of disclosure, ranging from embarrassment to loss of employment to potential civil liability, may not be the basis for resisting an agency's demand. The distinction between potential criminal liability and other legal consequences can pose difficulties when the recipient of a subpoena simultaneously is exposed to criminal and civil investigations, as happens with some frequency. In such circumstances, a court may defer the civil proceedings (and any accompanying demand for information) until the criminal proceedings have concluded, but it is not obligated to do so. For discussion of the circumstances that are to be considered in making this judgment, see *SEC v. Dresser Industries, Inc.*, 628 F.2d 1368 (D.C.Cir.) (en banc), *cert. denied*, 449 U.S. 993 (1980).

Second, and more important in the administrative context, the privilege is not available to corporations, or other non-natural persons, such as associations, nor may the custodians of a corporation's records refuse to produce those records because they contain matter that may incriminate them. They may claim the privilege only for evidence that belongs to them. See generally Note, *The Constitutional Rights of Associations to Assert the Privilege Against Self-Incrimination*, 112 U.Pa.L.Rev. 394 (1964).

Third, one who is custodian for another individual's records may not refuse to produce them, for the privilege is personal. In *Fisher v. United States*, 425 U.S. 391 (1976), the Court sustained enforcement of an IRS summons seeking documents that the taxpayers had retrieved from their accountants and delivered to attorneys who were representing them in the investigation. The attorneys could claim no Fifth Amendment privilege in the documents, which belonged either to the taxpayers or their accountants. Nor did forced production of documents in the attorneys' hands violate the taxpayers' Fifth Amendment rights even though they might contain incriminating material; "the privilege protects a person only against being incriminated by his own compelled testimonial communications," 425 U.S. at 409, and the summons imposed no compulsion on them. See also *United States v. Rylander*, 460 U.S. 752 (1983), where the Court upheld the petitioner's conviction for civil contempt of an order enforcing an IRS summons. The petitioner had, by affidavit, denied that he still possessed the demanded documents but refused to testify at the contempt hearing on the ground that he might incriminate himself. The Court concluded that he had thus failed to sustain his burden of showing that the documents were not in his possession.

Statutory grants of immunity from prosecution constitute another important limitation on the Fifth Amendment privilege. In *Ullmann v. United States*, 350 U.S. 422 (1956), the Supreme Court upheld the Federal Immunity Act, which accorded witnesses immunity from prosecution under federal or state law for any activities revealed during compelled testimony. In *Kastigar v. United States*, 406 U.S. 441 (1972), and *Zicarelli v. New Jersey State Commission of Investigation*, 406 U.S. 472 (1972), the Court reaffirmed *Ullmann* and held, moreover, that statutory immunity need only protect the compelled witness against the *use* of his or her testimony in a subsequent prosecution; the unwilling witness may still be prosecuted if the authorities can demonstrate that the evidence they intend to use was "derived from a legitimate source wholly independent of the compelled testimony." Thus, the Court sanctioned statutes according only "use," as contrasted with "transactional," immunity, such as the law invoked in *Ullman*.

The extent to which other testimonial privileges limit agency demands for information is a matter of uncertainty. Statutes conferring power on agencies to obtain information habitually ignore the issue, so guidance must be found exclusively in judicial decisions. In *McMann v. SEC*, 87 F.2d 377, 378 (2d Cir.1937), *cert. denied*, 301 U.S. 684 (1937), Judge Learned Hand rejected a claim of customer-broker privilege but at the same time observed: "[W]e assume * * * that the conduct of investigations under these statutes is subject to the same testimonial privileges as judicial proceedings. * * * " No later case has embraced so broad a formulation, although several have considered the availability of specific privileges to withhold information. The attorney-client privilege has received a sympathetic hearing, as in *CAB v. Air Transport Association*, 201 F.Supp. 318 (D.D.C.1961), where the court observed: "The attorney-client privilege is deeply imbedded and is part of the warp and woof of the common law." The leading case on this point is now *Upjohn Co. v. United States*, 449 U.S. 383 (1981), which held that the attorney-client privilege extended to communications from the company's employees to its general counsel. The Court also held that an IRS summons may not demand production of attorneys' "work product," even in the face of claims of necessity or inability to obtain the information in other ways.

Courts have also sometimes recognized the privilege of patients to prevent disclosure of information in the possession of their physicians and the like privilege of one spouse to prevent the compelled testimony of the other, but they have consistently rejected claims based on the relation between client and accountant. The Supreme Court has held that federal law recognizes a privilege protecting confidential communications between psychotherapists and patients, a privilege that extends also to patients and licensed social workers engaged in psychotherapy. *Jaffee v. Redmond*, 518 U.S. 1 (1996). For a general discussion of the area, see Note, *Privileged Communications Before Federal Administrative Agencies: The Law Applied in the District Courts*, 31 U.Chi.L.Rev. 395 (1964).

UNIVERSITY OF PENNSYLVANIA v. EQUAL EMPLOYMENT OPPORTUNITY COMMISSION

Supreme Court of the United States, 1990.
493 U.S. 182, 110 S.Ct. 577, 107 L.Ed.2d 571.

JUSTICE BLACKMUN delivered the opinion of the Court.

I

The University of Pennsylvania, petitioner here, is a private institution. It currently operates 12 schools, including the Wharton School of Business, which collectively enroll approximately 18,000 full-time students.

In 1985, the University denied tenure to Rosalie Tung, an associate professor on the Wharton faculty. Tung then filed a sworn charge of discrimination with respondent Equal Employment Opportunity Commission (EEOC or Commission). As subsequently amended, the charge alleged that Tung was the victim of discrimination on the basis of race, sex, and national origin, in violation of § 703(a) of Title VII of the Civil Rights Act of 1964, 42 U.S.C. § 2000e–2(a), as amended, which makes it unlawful "to discriminate against any individual with respect to his compensation, terms, conditions, or privileges of employment, because of such individual's race, color, religion, sex, or national origin."

In her charge, Tung stated that the Department Chairman had sexually harassed her and that, in her belief, after she insisted that their relationship remain professional, he had submitted a negative letter to the University's Personnel Committee which possessed ultimate responsibility for tenure decisions. She also alleged that her qualifications were "equal to or better than" those of five named male faculty members who had received more favorable treatment. Tung noted that the majority of the members of her Department had recommended her for tenure, and stated that she had been given no reason for the decision against her, but had discovered of her own efforts that the Personnel Committee had attempted to justify its decision "on the ground that the Wharton School is not interested in China-related research." This explanation, Tung's charge alleged, was a pretext for discrimination: "simply their way of saying they do not want a Chinese–American, Oriental, woman in their school."

The Commission undertook an investigation into Tung's charge, and requested a variety of relevant information from petitioner. When the University refused to provide certain of that information, the Commission's Acting District Director issued a subpoena seeking, among other things, Tung's tenure-review file and the tenure files of the five male faculty members identified in the charge. Petitioner refused to produce a number of the tenure-file documents. It applied to the Commission for modification of the subpoena to exclude what it termed "confidential peer review information," specifically, (1) confidential letters written by Tung's evaluators; (2) the Department Chairman's letter of evaluation; (3) documents reflecting the internal deliberations of faculty committees considering applications for tenure, including the Department Evaluation Report summarizing the deliberations relating to Tung's application for tenure; and (4) comparable portions of the tenure-review files of the five males. The University urged the Commission to "adopt a balancing approach reflecting the constitutional and societal interest inherent in the peer review process" and to resort to "all feasible methods to minimize the intrusive effects of its investigations."

The Commission denied the University's application. It concluded that the withheld documents were needed in order to determine the merit of Tung's charges. The Commission found: "There has not been enough data supplied in order for the Commission to determine whether there is reasonable cause to believe that the allegations of sex, race and national origin discrimination are true." The Commission rejected petitioner's contention that a letter, which set forth the Personnel Committee's reasons for denying Tung tenure, was sufficient for disposition of the charge.

The University continued to withhold the tenure-review materials. The Commission then applied to the United States District Court for the Eastern District of Pennsylvania for enforcement of its subpoena. The court entered a brief enforcement order.

The Court of Appeals for the Third Circuit affirmed the enforcement decision. 850 F.2d 969 (1988). * * *

II

As it had done before the Commission, the District Court, and the Court of Appeals, the University raises here essentially two claims. First, it urges us to recognize a qualified common-law privilege against disclosure of confidential peer review materials. Second, it asserts a First Amendment right of "academic freedom" against wholesale disclosure of the contested documents. With respect to each of the two claims, the remedy petitioner seeks is the same: a requirement of a judicial finding of particularized necessity of access, beyond a showing of mere relevance, before peer review materials are disclosed to the Commission.

A

Petitioner's common-law privilege claim is grounded in Federal Rule of Evidence 501. This provides in relevant part:

> "Except as otherwise required by the Constitution * * * or provided by Act of Congress or in rules prescribed by the Supreme Court * * *, the privilege of a witness * * * shall be governed by the principles of the common law as they may be interpreted by the courts of the United States in light of reason and experience."

The University asks us to invoke this provision to fashion a new privilege that it claims is necessary to protect the integrity of the peer review process, which in turn is central to the proper functioning of many colleges and universities. These institutions are special, observes petitioner, because they function as "centers of learning, innovation and discovery."

We do not create and apply an evidentiary privilege unless it "promotes sufficiently important interests to outweigh the need for probative evidence * * *." *Trammel v. United States*, 445 U.S. 40, 51 (1980).

Moreover, although Rule 501 manifests a congressional desire "not to freeze the law of privilege" but rather to provide the courts with flexibility to develop rules of privilege on a case-by-case basis, we are disinclined to exercise this authority expansively. We are especially reluctant to recognize a privilege in an area where it appears that Congress has considered the relevant competing concerns but has not provided the privilege itself. The balancing of conflicting interests of this type is particularly a legislative function. * * *

When Title VII was enacted originally in 1964, it exempted an "educational institution with respect to the employment of individuals to perform work connected with the educational activities of such institution." § 702, 78 Stat. 255. Eight years later, Congress eliminated that specific exemption by enacting § 3 of the Equal Employment Opportunity Act of 1972, 86 Stat. 103. This extension of Title VII was Congress' considered response to the widespread and compelling problem of invidious discrimination in educational institutions. The House Report focused specifically on discrimination in higher education, including the lack of access for women and minorities to higher ranking (i.e., tenured) academic positions. See H.R.Rep.No. 92–238, pp. 19–20 (1971). Significantly, opponents of the extension claimed that enforcement of Title VII would weaken institutions of higher education by interfering with decisions to hire and promote faculty members. Petitioner therefore cannot seriously contend that Congress was oblivious to concerns of academic autonomy when it abandoned the exemption for educational institutions.

The effect of the elimination of this exemption was to expose tenure determinations to the same enforcement procedures applicable to other employment decisions. The Commission's enforcement responsibilities are triggered by the filing of a specific sworn charge of discrimination.

The Act obligates the Commission to investigate a charge of discrimination to determine whether there is "reasonable cause to believe that the charge is true." § 2000e–5(b). If it finds no such reasonable cause, the Commission is directed to dismiss the charge. If it does find reasonable cause, the Commission shall "endeavor to eliminate [the] alleged unlawful employment practice by informal methods of conference, conciliation, and persuasion." *Ibid.* If attempts at voluntary resolution fail, the Commission may bring an action against the employer. § 2000e–5(f)(1).

To enable the Commission to make informed decisions at each stage of the enforcement process, § 2000e–8(a) confers a broad right of access to relevant evidence:

> "[T]he Commission or its designated representative shall at all reasonable times have access to, for the purposes of examination, and the right to copy any evidence of any person being investigated * * * that relates to unlawful employment practices covered by [the Act] and is relevant to the charge under investigation."

If an employer refuses to provide this information voluntarily, the Act authorizes the Commission to issue a subpoena and to seek an order enforcing it. § 2000–9 (incorporating 29 U.S.C. § 161).

On their face, § 2000e–8(a) and § 2000e–9 do not carve out any special privilege relating to peer review materials, despite the fact that Congress undoubtedly was aware, when it extended Title VII's coverage, of the potential burden that access to such material might create. Moreover, we have noted previously that when a court is asked to enforce a Commission subpoena, its responsibility is to "satisfy itself that the charge is valid and that the material requested is 'relevant' to the charge * * * and more generally to assess any contentions by the employer that the demand for information is too indefinite or has been made for an illegitimate purpose." It is not then to determine "whether the charge of discrimination is 'well founded' or 'verifiable.' " *EEOC v. Shell Oil Co.*, 466 U.S., at 72, n. 26.

The University concedes that the information sought by the Commission in this case passes the relevance test set forth in Shell Oil. Petitioner argues, nevertheless, that Title VII affirmatively grants courts the discretion to require more than relevance in order to protect tenure-review documents. Although petitioner recognizes that Title VII gives the Commission broad "power to seek access to all evidence that may be 'relevant to the charge under investigation,' " it contends that Title VII's subpoena enforcement provisions do not give the Commission an unqualified right to acquire such evidence. This interpretation simply cannot be reconciled with the plain language of the text of § 2000e–8(a), which states that the Commission "shall * * * have access" to "relevant" evidence (emphasis added). The provision can be read only as giving the Commission a right to obtain that evidence, not a mere license to seek it.

Although the text of the access provisions thus provides no privilege, Congress did address situations in which an employer may have an interest in the confidentiality of its records. The same § 2000e–8 which gives the Commission access to any evidence relevant to its investigation also makes it "unlawful for any officer or employee of the Commission to make public in any manner whatever any information obtained by the Commission pursuant to its authority under this section prior to the institution of any proceeding" under the Act. A violation of this provision subjects the employee to criminal penalties. To be sure, the protection of confidentiality that § 2000–8(e) provides is less than complete.[5] But this, if anything, weakens petitioner's argument. Congress apparently considered the issue of confidentiality, and it provided a modicum of protection. * * *

We readily agree with petitioner that universities and colleges play significant roles in American society. Nor need we question, at this point, petitioner's assertion that confidentiality is important to the proper functioning of the peer review process under which many academic institutions operate. The costs that ensue from disclosure, however, constitute only one side of the balance. As Congress has recognized, the costs associated with racial and sexual discrimination in institutions of higher learning are very substantial. Few would deny that ferreting out this kind of invidious discrimination is a great if not compelling governmental interest. Often, as even petitioner seems to admit, disclosure of peer review materials will be necessary in order for the Commission to determine whether illegal discrimination has taken place. Indeed, if there is a "smoking gun" to be found that demonstrates discrimination in tenure decisions, it is likely to be tucked away in peer review files. * * *

Moreover, we agree with the EEOC that the adoption of a requirement that the Commission demonstrate a "specific reason for disclosure," beyond a showing of relevance, would place a substantial litigation-producing obstacle in the way of the Commission's efforts to investigate and remedy alleged discrimination. A university faced with a disclosure request might well utilize the privilege in a way that frustrates the EEOC's mission.

Acceptance of petitioner's claim would also lead to a wave of similar privilege claims by other employers who play significant roles in furthering speech and learning in society. What of writers, publishers, musicians, lawyers? It surely is not unreasonable to believe, for example, that confidential peer reviews play an important part in partnership determinations at some law firms. We perceive no limiting principle in petitioner's argument. Accordingly, we stand behind the breakwater Congress has established: unless specifically provided otherwise in the statute, the EEOC may obtain "relevant" evidence. Congress has made the choice. If it dislikes the result, it of course may revise the statute.

B

As noted above, petitioner characterizes its First Amendment claim as one of "academic freedom." * * * Petitioner places special reliance on

5. The prohibition on Commission disclosure does not apply, for example, to the charging party. See *EEOC v. Associated Dry Goods Corp.*, 449 U.S. 590, 598–604 (1981).

Justice Frankfurter's opinion, concurring in the result, in *Sweezy v. New Hampshire*, 354 U.S. 234, 263 (1957), where the Justice recognized that one of "four essential freedoms" that a university possesses under the First Amendment is the right to "determine for itself on academic grounds *who may teach*" (emphasis added).

Petitioner contends that it exercises this right of determining "on academic grounds who may teach" through the process of awarding tenure. A tenure system, asserts petitioner, determines what the university will look like over time. "In making tenure decision, therefore, a university is doing nothing less than shaping its own identity."

Petitioner next maintains that the peer review process is the most important element in the effective operation of a tenure system. A properly functioning tenure system requires the faculty to obtain candid and detailed written evaluations of the candidate's scholarship, both from the candidate's peers at the university and from scholars at other institutions. These evaluations, says petitioner, traditionally have been provided with express or implied assurances of confidentiality. It is confidentiality that ensures candor and enables an institution to make its tenure decisions on the basis of valid academic criteria.

Building from these premises, petitioner claims that requiring the disclosure of peer review evaluations on a finding of mere relevance will undermine the existing process of awarding tenure, and therefore will result in a significant infringement of petitioner's First Amendment right of academic freedom. As more and more peer evaluations are disclosed to the EEOC and become public, a "chilling effect" on candid evaluations and discussions of candidates will result. And as the quality of peer review evaluations declines, tenure committees will no longer be able to rely on them. "This will work to the detriment of universities, as less qualified persons achieve tenure causing the quality of instruction and scholarship to decline." Compelling disclosure of materials "also will result in divisiveness and tension, placing strain on faculty relations and impairing the free interchange of ideas that is a hallmark of academic freedom." The prospect of these deleterious effects on American colleges and universities, concludes petitioner, compels recognition of a First Amendment privilege.

In our view, petitioner's reliance on the so-called academic freedom cases is somewhat misplaced. In those cases government was attempting to control or direct the content of the speech engaged in by the university or those affiliated with it. * * *

Fortunately, we need not define today the precise contours of any academic-freedom right against governmental attempts to influence the content of academic speech through the selection of faculty or by other means, because petitioner does not allege that the Commission's subpoenas are intended to or will in fact direct the content of university discourse toward or away from particular subjects or points of view. Instead, as noted above, petitioner claims that the "quality of instruction and scholarship [will] decline" as a result of the burden EEOC subpoenas place on the peer review process.

Also, the cases upon which petitioner places emphasis involved direct infringements on the asserted right to "determine for itself on academic grounds who may teach." * * * In contrast, the EEOC subpoena at issue here effects no such usurpation. The Commission is not providing criteria that petitioner must use in selecting teachers. Nor is it preventing the University from using any criteria it may wish to use, except those—including race, sex, and national origin—that are proscribed under Title VII. * * *

That the burden of which the University complains is neither content-based nor direct does not necessarily mean that petitioner has no valid First Amendment claim. Rather, it means only that petitioner's claim does not fit neatly within any right of academic freedom that could be derived from the cases on which petitioner relies. In essence, petitioner asks us to recognize an expanded right of academic freedom to protect confidential peer review materials from disclosure. * * * [W]e think the First Amendment cannot be extended to embrace petitioner's claim.

First, by comparison with the cases in which we have found a cognizable First Amendment claim, the infringement the University complains of is extremely attenuated. * * *

In effect, petitioner says no more than that disclosure of peer review materials makes it more difficult to acquire information regarding the "academic grounds" on which petitioner wishes to base its tenure decisions. But many laws make the exercise of First Amendment rights more difficult. For example, a university cannot claim a First Amendment violation simply because it may be subject to taxation or other government regulation, even though such regulation might deprive the university of revenue it needs to bid for professors who are contemplating working for other academic institutions or in industry.

In addition to being remote and attenuated, the injury to academic freedom claimed by petitioner is also speculative. As the EEOC points out, confidentiality is not the norm in all peer review systems. Moreover, some disclosure of peer evaluations would take place even if petitioner's "special necessity" test were adopted. Thus, the "chilling effect" petitioner fears is at most only incrementally worsened by the absence of a privilege. Finally, we are not so ready as petitioner seems to be to assume the worst about those in the academic community. Although it is possible that some evaluators may become less candid as the possibility of disclosure increases, others may simply ground their evaluations in specific examples and illustrations in order to deflect potential claims of bias or unfairness. Not all academics will hesitate to stand up and be counted when they evaluate their peers. * * *

Because we conclude that the EEOC subpoena process does not infringe any First Amendment right enjoyed by petitioner, the EEOC need not demonstrate any special justification to sustain the constitutionality of Title VII as applied to tenure peer review materials in general or to the subpoena involved in this case.[9] * * *

The judgment of the Court of Appeals is affirmed. It is so ordered.

Note

Confidentiality and Peer Review. There is persistent controversy in higher education whether peer review materials that are part of tenure and promotion processes should be made available to faculty candidates. Many institutions, like the University of Pennsylvania, prefer confidentiality on the ground that disclosure of peer review materials would chill candid appraisals and compromise professional relationships. Other institutions believe that anonymity invites abuse, deem an "open file" system to be fairer to faculty candidates, and regard the availability of review materials to the candidate to be an important check on their quality. Imagine yourself counsel to a university with a confidential review system. Would you regard the *University of Pennsylvania* case as raising a substantial argument for change—namely, that, without an open file system, your university might be inviting antidiscrimination litigation as the only available lever to force disclosure of a disappointed candidate's files? Or would you regard the arguments favoring confidentiality as sufficiently persuasive to justify leaving the system in place, acknowledging that occasional litigation may result in a breach of the system?

Responsibility for Enforcement

A practical problem that confronts federal agencies when the recipient of a subpoena resists compliance is the need to persuade the Department of Justice to seek enforcement. In addition to rendering the process more cumbersome, the need to apply to the Justice Department to initiate enforcement may inhibit an agency's investigations to the extent that it must anticipate the Department's attitudes when deciding to issue or seek enforcement of subpoenas. This does not mean that the Department of Justice is uncooperative or that its views are antithetical to agency policies, but its enthusiasm for their programs is rarely likely to match their own. Moreover, the Department of Justice may be inclined to weigh administrative, law enforcement, or budgetary considerations in responding to agency requests that would never occur to most agencies. The result of this external scrutiny of agency investigative activities ordinarily may be benign, but the possibilities for conflict and misunderstanding are obvious. See generally *S & E Contractors, Inc. v. United States*, 406 U.S. 1 (1972).

2. REPORTING AND RECORD KEEPING REQUIREMENTS

From the agency perspective, an efficient method of obtaining information for policy formulation, license approval, or enforcement action is

9. We * * * do not consider the question, not passed upon by the Court of Appeals, whether the District Court's enforcement of the Commission's subpoena will allow petitioner to redact information from the contested materials before disclosing them.

to require persons subject to regulation to compile it. This device shifts the burden and cost of acquiring information to private parties, recognizing that they are often in a better position to obtain the facts. It makes good sense, for example, to require that an applicant for approval to market a new drug supply information about its composition, method and place of manufacture, and proposed labeling, rather than force the FDA to discover these facts for itself. It is also common practice to require applicants to provide the results of tests to determine a product's compliance with legal standards, e.g., a drug's safety and effectiveness.

Requirements to collect, maintain, and report information pervade both federal and state licensing programs. Similarly, income tax laws rely primarily on taxpayers to supply needed information about their liability for tax. Even in areas where administrative responsibilities are primarily of a policing type—aimed at preventing or punishing prohibited conduct—record-keeping and reporting requirements are common.

Basic Doctrine

An agency's demand for the production of or access to required records may raise many legal questions similar to those that surround the exercise of agency subpoena power. A principal difference is that here the agency has ordered the assembly and retention of information, as well as its production for regulatory use. The Supreme Court has generally endorsed such demands when authorized by Congress, subject to conditions of relevance and reasonableness that pertain to subpoenas as well.

The mainspring case is *United States v. Morton Salt Co.*, 338 U.S. 632 (1950). The FTC had previously found several salt producers and their trade association guilty of violating section 5 of the FTC Act. The Seventh Circuit affirmed, with modifications, a cease and desist order which directed the respondents to file reports of compliance within 90 days and reserved jurisdiction to enter further orders to enforce compliance. Later, under section 6 of the Act, the Commission ordered Morton and others to file additional special reports demonstrating compliance with the original decree. The court of appeals affirmed a lower court refusal to enforce this order, on the grounds, *inter alia*, that the Commission lacked authority to require such additional reports and that its order violated the fourth and Fifth Amendments.

The Supreme Court reversed. Justice Jackson's opinion began by recognizing differences between the Commission's role and that of a court following the conclusion of litigation:

> The court in this case advisedly left it to the Commission to receive the report of compliance and to institute any contempt proceedings. This was in harmony with our system. When the process of adjudication is complete, all judgments are handed over to the litigant or executive officers, such as the sheriff or marshal, to execute. Steps which the litigant or executive department lawfully

> takes for their enforcement are a vindication rather than a usurpation of the court's power. * * *
>
> This case illustrates the difference between the judicial function and the function the Commission is attempting to perform. The respondents argue that since the Commission made no charge of violation either of the decree or the statute, it is engaged in a mere "fishing expedition" to see if it can turn up evidence of guilt. We will assume for the argument that this is so. * * *
>
> We must not disguise the fact that sometimes, especially early in the history of the federal administrative tribunal, the courts were persuaded to engraft judicial limitations upon the administrative process. The courts could not go fishing, and so it followed neither could anyone else. * * * More recent views have been more tolerant of it than those which underlay many older decisions.
>
> The only power that is involved here is the power to get information from those who best can give it and who are most interested in not doing so. Because judicial power is reluctant if not unable to summon evidence until it is shown to be relevant to issues in litigation, it does not follow that an administrative agency charged with seeing that the laws are enforced may not have and exercise powers of original inquiry. * * * When investigative and accusatory duties are delegated by statute to an administrative body, it, too, may take steps to inform itself as to whether there is probable violation of the law.

Jackson concluded that the FTC's order infringed neither the court of appeals' jurisdiction nor sections 552 and 555 of the APA, and that it was within the agency's statutory authority. He then proceeded to consider the company's constitutional claims:

> While they may and should have protection from unlawful demands made in the name of public investigation, corporations can claim no equality with individuals in the enjoyment of a right to privacy. They are endowed with public attributes. They have a collective impact upon society, from which they derive the privilege of acting as artificial entities. The Federal Government allows them the privilege of engaging in interstate commerce. Favors from government often carry with them an enhanced measure of regulation. Even if one were to regard the request for information in this case as caused by nothing more than official curiosity, nevertheless law-enforcing agencies have a legitimate right to satisfy themselves that corporate behavior is consistent with the law and the public interest.
>
> Of course a governmental investigation into corporate matters may be of such a sweeping nature and so unrelated to the matter properly under inquiry as to exceed the investigatory power. But it is sufficient if the inquiry is within the authority of the agency, the demand is not too indefinite and the information sought is reasonably relevant. "The gist of the protection is in the requirement, expressed in terms, that the disclosure sought shall not be unreason-

able." Nothing on the face of the Commission's order transgressed these bounds.

* * * Before the courts will hold an order seeking information reports to be arbitrarily excessive, they may expect the supplicant to have made reasonable efforts before the Commission itself to obtain reasonable conditions. Neither respondent raised objection to the order's sweep, nor asked any modification, clarification or interpretation of it. Both challenged, instead, power to issue it. * * *

If respondents had objected to the terms of the order, they would have presented or at least offered to present evidence concerning any records required and the cost of their books, matters which now rest on mere assertions in their briefs. The Commission would have had opportunity to disclaim any inadvertent excesses or to justify their demands in the record. We think these respondents could have obtained any reasonable modifications necessary, but, if not, at least could have made a record that would convince us of the measure of their grievance rather than ask us to assume it.

An agency's demand that records be kept or reports submitted, of course, must be authorized by statute and properly adopted. A general rule requiring periodic reports from persons within its regulatory jurisdiction, for example, can be successfully resisted if the agency failed to observe proper rulemaking procedures. The procedures required, however, may vary with context. For example, in *Morton Salt*, the FTC's order did not purport to apply generally, and rulemaking procedures would thus not have been appropriate, but the agency must have afforded Morton the opportunities for objection and argument that any respondent would have in any cease-and-desist proceeding.

While *Morton Salt* appears to confirm the FTC's authority to adopt general reporting requirements, as well as to require reports of particular respondents by order, these powers are distinct and each arguably must be supported by law. However, an agency that possesses clear authority to enjoin individual violations may have some inherent power to demand compliance information from a respondent, even though Congress has accorded it no general authority to require records and reports. E.g., *In re FTC Line of Business Report Litigation*, 595 F.2d 685 (D.C.Cir.1978).

Fifth Amendment Limits

The issue that has most often arisen in disputes over an individual's failure to produce required information is whether the agency's demand violates the Fifth Amendment privilege against self-incrimination.

In *Shapiro v. United States*, 335 U.S. 1 (1948), the petitioner was convicted of violating regulations issued under the Emergency Price Control Act, a wartime economic measure. Evidence supporting the conviction was obtained from records that OPA rules required but that were of the sort that persons in the same business (selling fruits and vegetables) would maintain in the ordinary course. The petitioner, after first resisting production of the records in response to a subpoena, yielded them; but he claimed that he was entitled to immunity from prosecution under section 202(g) of the Act, which incorporated the Compulsory Testimony Act of 1893, a law according transactional immunity to persons required to testify or produce evidence before the ICC. The court of appeals held that, because they were required to be kept by valid regulations, the records "thereby became public documents, as to which no constitutional privilege against self-incrimination attaches" and to which "accordingly the [statutory] immunity did not extend."

Writing for the Court, Chief Justice Vinson agreed that Congress had not intended to extend immunity so far "as to confer a bonus for the production of information otherwise obtainable." He proceeded to consider whether this construction of the statute raised constitutional doubts:

> It may be assumed at the outset that there are limits which the Government cannot constitutionally exceed in requiring the keeping of records which may be inspected by an administrative agency and may be used in prosecuting statutory violations committed by the record-keeper himself. But no serious misgiving that those bounds have been overstepped would appear to be evoked when there is a sufficient relation between the activity sought to be regulated and the public concern so that the Government can constitutionally regulate or forbid the basic activity concerned, and can constitutionally require the keeping of particular records, subject to inspection by the Administrator. It is not questioned here that Congress has constitutional authority to prescribe commodity prices as a war emergency measure, and that the licensing and recordkeeping requirements of the Price Control Act represent a legitimate exercise of that power. Accordingly, the principle enunciated in the *Wilson* case [*Wilson v. United States*, 221 U.S. 361 (1911)] is clearly applicable here: namely, that the privilege which exists as to private papers cannot be maintained in relation to "records required by law to be kept in order that there may be suitable information of transactions which are the appropriate subjects of governmental regulation and the enforcement of restrictions validly established." [*Davis v. United States*, 328 U.S. 582 (1946).]
>
> * * * In the case at bar, it cannot be doubted that the sales record which petitioner was required to keep as a licensee under the Price Control Act has "public aspects." Nor can there be any doubt that when it was obtained by the Administrator through the use of a subpoena, as authorized specifically by § 202(b) of the statute, it was "legally obtained" and hence "available as evidence." The record involved in the case at bar was a sales record required to be maintained under an appropriate regulation, its relevance to the lawful purpose of the Administrator is unquestioned, and the transaction which it recorded was one in which the petitioner could lawfully engage solely by virtue of the license granted to him under the statute.

This discussion provoked the following dissenting comments from Justice Frankfurter:

> If records merely because required to be kept by law *ipso facto* became public records, we are indeed living in glass houses. Virtually every major public law enactment—to say nothing of State and local legislation—has record-keeping provisions. In addition to record-keeping requirements, is the network of provisions for filing reports. * * *
>
> * * * [T]he authorities give no support to the broad proposition that because records are required to be kept by law they are public records and, hence, non-privileged. Private records do not thus become "public" in any critical or legally significant sense; they are merely the records of an industry or business regulated by law. Nor does the fact that the Government either may make, or has made, a license a prerequisite for the doing of business make them public in any ordinary use of the term. While Congress may in time of war, or perhaps in circumstances of economic crisis, provide for the licensing of every individual business, surely such licensing requirements do not remove the records of a man's private business from the protection afforded by the Fifth Amendment. Just as the licensing of private motor vehicles does not make them public carriers, the licensing of a man's private business, for tax or other purposes, does not under our system, at least so I had supposed, make him a public officer.
>
> Different considerations control where the business of an enterprise is, as it were, the public's. Clearly the records of a business licensed to sell state-owned property are public records. And the records of a public utility, apart from the considerations relevant to corporate enterprise, may similarly be treated as public records. This has been extended to the records of "occupations which are *malum in se*, or so closely allied thereto, as to endanger the public health, morals or safety."
>
> Here the subject matter of petitioner's business was not such as to render it public. Surely, there is nothing inherently dangerous, immoral, or unhealthy about the sale of fruits and vegetables. Nor was there anything in his possession or control of the records to cast a cloud on his title to them. They were the records that he customarily kept. I find nothing in the Act, or in the Court's construction of the Act, that made him a public officer. He was being administered, not administering. Nor was he in any legitimate sense of the word a "custodian" of the records. * * *
>
> The phrase "required to be kept by law," then, is not a magic phrase by which the legislature opens the door to inroads upon the Fifth Amendment. Statutory provisions * * *, requiring the keeping of records and making them available for official inspection, are constitutional means for effective administration and enforcement. It follows that those charged with the responsibility for such admin-

istration and enforcement may compel the disclosure of such records in conformity with the Fourth Amendment. But it does not follow that such disclosures are beyond the scope of the protection afforded by the Fifth Amendment. For the compulsory disclosure of a man's "private books and papers, to convict him of crime or to forfeit his property, is contrary to the principles of a free government. It is abhorrent to the instincts of an Englishman; it is abhorrent to the instincts of an American. It may suit the purposes of despotic power; but it cannot abide the pure atmosphere of political liberty and personal freedom."

Notes

1. *The Fifth Amendment and Required Record Keeping.* The decision in *Shapiro* left unanswered many questions concerning the limits on administrative record keeping and reporting requirements. For example, does anything in the Court's opinion indicate that Congress could not constitutionally require records to be kept by participants in any activity it had prohibited? See Bernard D. Meltzer, *Required Records, the McCarran Act, and the Privilege Against Self-Incrimination*, 18 U.Chi.L.Rev. 687 (1951).

Should it make a difference that the records the government requires are records an individual would ordinarily maintain anyway? See *California Bankers Association v. Shultz*, 416 U.S. 21 (1974), discussed *infra* at p. 675.

2. *Registration of Potentially Subversive Activity.* In *Albertson v. Subversive Activities Control Board*, 382 U.S. 70, 79 (1965), the Court overturned, on Fifth Amendment grounds, SACB orders instructing named individuals to register with the Attorney General as members of the Communist Party. Those named in the orders faced substantial penalties in the form of fines or imprisonment for failure to register, while proof of their party membership would support conviction under both the Smith Act and the Subversive Activities Control Act. Writing for a unanimous Court, Justice Brennan declared:

> Petitioners' claims are not asserted in an essentially noncriminal and regulatory area of inquiry, but against an inquiry in an area permeated with criminal statutes, where response to any of the [registration] form's questions in context might involve the petitioners in the admission of a crucial element of a crime.

His opinion made no reference to *Shapiro*, perhaps because the case involved a requirement to report, and not the maintenance of required records.

Albertson grew out of a protracted controversy between federal security officials and the American Communist party. In *Communist Party of the United States v. Subversive Activities Control Board*, 367 U.S. 1 (1961), the Supreme Court avoided the Fifth Amendment issue presented by the Subversive Activities Control Act's registration requirements by ruling that, since individual members might invoke the Fifth Amendment when ordered to register and since, in any case, the Attorney General might accept their claims, their attack was premature. But as *Albertson* indicates, this subterfuge was short-lived. Following the ruling on the merits, the D.C. Circuit struck down the whole registration procedure as "hopelessly at odds with the protections afforded by the Fifth Amendment." *Communist Party of the United States v. United States*, 384 F.2d 957 (D.C.Cir.1967).

Required Records of Unlawful Activity

In 1968 the Supreme Court again addressed the Fifth Amendment's limitations on compulsory record-keeping and reporting. The petitioner in *Marchetti v. United States*, 390 U.S. 39 (1968), a professional gambler, was convicted for wilfully failing to register with the IRS and to pay an occupation tax for engaging in the business of accepting wagers, as required by 26 U.S.C. §§ 4411 and 4412, and for conspiring to evade payment of the occupational tax. Following the verdict, Marchetti moved unsuccessfully to arrest judgment, claiming that the statutory obligations to register and to pay the occupational tax violated his constitutional privilege against self-incrimination. The Second Circuit affirmed his convictions.

Justice Harlan, who wrote for the Court, began by observing that "every aspect of petitioner's wagering activities thus subjected him to possible state or federal prosecution." He went on to describe the consequences of compliance with the Code's licensing and reporting requirements:

> Information obtained as a consequence of the federal wagering tax laws is readily available to assist the efforts of state and federal authorities to enforce these penalties. Section 6107 of Title 26 requires the principal internal revenue offices to provide to prosecuting officers a listing of those who have paid the occupational tax. Section 6806(c) obliges taxpayers either to post the revenue stamp "conspicuously" in their principal places of business, or to keep it on their persons, and to produce it on the demand of Treasury officers. Evidence of the possession of a federal wagering tax stamp, or of payment of the wagering taxes, has often been admitted at trial in state and federal prosecutions for gambling offenses; such evidence has doubtless proved useful even more frequently to lead prosecuting authorities to other evidence upon which convictions have subsequently been obtained. * * *
>
> In these circumstances, it can scarcely be denied that the obligations to register and to pay the occupational tax created for petitioner "real and appreciable," and not merely "imaginary and unsubstantial," hazards of self-incrimination. Petitioner was confronted by a comprehensive system of federal and state prohibitions against wagering activities; he was required, on pain of criminal prosecution, to provide information which he might reasonably suppose would be available to prosecuting authorities, and which would surely prove a significant "link in a chain" of evidence tending to establish his guilt. * * * It would appear to follow that petitioner's assertion of the privilege as a defense to this prosecution was entirely proper, and accordingly should have sufficed to prevent his conviction.

> Nonetheless, this Court has twice concluded that the privilege against self-incrimination may not appropriately be asserted by those in petitioner's circumstances. * * *

The Court then proceeded to overrule two of its prior decisions, *United States v. Kahriger*, 345 U.S. 22 (1953), and *Lewis v. United States*, 348 U.S. 419 (1955), both of which had held that registration and occupational tax requirements did not infringe the Fifth Amendment privilege against self-incrimination. The Court rejected the basic premises of those decisions, viz., that a person who engaged in activities subject to registration and taxation voluntarily "waived" the privilege, and that the privilege did not protect against disclosure of future activities. It then turned to *Shapiro*:

> We think that neither *Shapiro* nor the cases upon which it relied are applicable here.[14] * * *
>
> * * * First, petitioner Marchetti was not, by the provisions now at issue, obliged to keep and preserve records "of the same kind as he has customarily kept"; he was required simply to provide information, unrelated to any records which he may have maintained, about his wagering activities. * * * Second, whatever "public aspects" there were to the records at issue in *Shapiro*, there are none to the information demanded from Marchetti. The Government's anxiety to obtain information known to a private individual does not without more render that information public; if it did, no room would remain for the application of the constitutional privilege. Nor does it stamp information with a public character that the Government has formalized its demands in the attire of a statute; if this alone were sufficient, the constitutional privilege could be entirely abrogated by any Act of Congress. Third, the requirements at issue in *Shapiro* were imposed in "an essentially noncriminal and regulatory area of inquiry" while those here are directed at a "selective group inherently suspect of criminal activities." Cf. *Albertson v. SACB*. The United States' principal interest is evidently the collection of revenue, and not the punishment of gamblers, but the characteristics of the activities about which information is sought, and the composition of the groups to which inquiries are made, readily distinguish this situation from that in *Shapiro*. * * *
>
> * * * We emphasize that we do not hold that these wagering tax provisions are as such constitutionally impermissible; we hold only that those who properly assert the constitutional privilege as to

14. The United States has urged that this case is not reached by *Shapiro* simply because petitioner was required to submit reports, and not to maintain records. Insofar as this is intended to suggest that the crucial issue respecting the applicability of *Shapiro* is the method by which information reaches the Government, we are unable to accept the distinction. We perceive no meaningful difference between an obligation to maintain records for inspection, and such an obligation supplemented by a requirement that those records be filed periodically with officers of the United States. * * *

these provisions may not be criminally punished for failure to comply with the requirements. * * *

Notes

1. *Post*–Marchetti *Developments*. In two companion cases, the Court invalidated other federal revenue and registration requirements. *Grosso v. United States*, 390 U.S. 62 (1968), involved a conviction for willful failure to pay the federal excise tax on wagers. Again writing for the majority, Justice Harlan distinguished *Shapiro* on the grounds that the excise tax provisions were not primarily "regulatory" in purpose, that the information required to be disclosed by the taxpayer had not acquired any "public records" character, and that it was by no means clear that the information was of a kind persons engaged in wagering could customarily keep. In *Haynes v. United States*, 390 U.S. 85 (1968), the same majority overturned a conviction for knowing possession of a sawed-off shotgun which the petitioner had not registered with the Secretary of the Treasury as required by 26 U.S.C. § 5841. See also *Leary v. United States*, 395 U.S. 6 (1969), where the Court struck down, as violative of the Fifth Amendment, a provision of the Internal Revenue Code requiring persons dealing in marijuana to register and file tax returns covering all transfers of marijuana. *Mackey v. United States*, 401 U.S. 667 (1971), held that *Marchetti* did not apply retroactively to invalidate a prior conviction for income tax evasion based on wagering tax returns. But cf. *United States v. United States Coin and Currency*, 401 U.S. 715 (1971). See *United States v. Freed*, 401 U.S. 601 (1971) (upholding amended record-keeping requirements of National Firearms Act).

2. *False Responses to Invalid Information Demands*. *Marchetti* does not prevent prosecution of one who responds falsely to an invalid reporting requirement. In *United States v. Knox*, 396 U.S. 77 (1969), the Court reversed the dismissal of an indictment charging the defendants with furnishing false information on wagering tax forms. Justice Harlan's majority opinion held that *Marchetti* would have protected the defendants if they had filed no forms at all, but did not apply where they had "voluntarily" supplied false information.

3. *Distinguishing Regulatory from Penal Requirements*. Several lower courts have attempted to discern the line between reporting and record keeping requirements whose purpose is "regulatory" and those whose purpose is penal. In *Application of Nadelson*, 353 F.Supp. 971 (S.D.N.Y.1973), the court ordered production of records by a process server under grand jury investigation for engaging in "sewer service." The records were required to be kept by a regulation of the New York City Department of Consumer Affairs. The district judge distinguished *Marchetti*, et al., emphasizing that here the activity for which records were required was not one that the government had sought to prohibit altogether. Instead, required record keeping was simply one feature of a general regulatory program designed to protect the public interest. The fact that the applicant's records might disclose evidence of crime did not, without more, bring them within the protection of the Fifth Amendment. Similarly, in *United States v. Warren*, 453 F.2d 738 (2d Cir.), *cert. denied*, 406 U.S. 944 (1972), records required to be maintained by persons engaged in dispensing controlled drugs were held

to fall within the *Shapiro* rationale as "part of a regulatory scheme with public purposes." See also *United States v. Reiff*, 435 F.2d 257 (7th Cir. 1970), *cert. denied*, 401 U.S. 938 (1971); *United States v. Silverman*, 449 F.2d 1341 (2d Cir.1971), *cert. denied*, 405 U.S. 918 (1972) (affirming attorney's conviction for income tax evasion based in part on reports of contingent fees required by state law to be filed in court).

4. *Relationship Between Fourth and Fifth Amendment Protections.* May records lawfully required under *Shapiro* be examined by agency officials on the maker's premises without a warrant? The issue has arisen infrequently in litigation. In *United States ex rel. Terraciano v. Montanye*, 493 F.2d 682 (2d Cir.), *cert. denied*, 419 U.S. 875 (1974), the court of appeals upheld the warrantless examination of the required records of a pharmacist, but implied that if a statutorily authorized warrantless search were not sufficiently limited in the nature of the material sought and the manner of access, the Fourth Amendment might require an intruding official to obtain a warrant.

Other cases that have grappled with the elusive relationship between the fourth and Fifth Amendments in the context of required records have achieved no consensus. In a curious opinion a three-judge court in *Stark v. Connally*, 347 F.Supp. 1242 (N.D.Cal.1972), *modified sub nom. California Bankers Association v. Shultz*, 416 U.S. 21 (1974), struck down certain reporting provisions of the Bank Secrecy Act and implementing Treasury Department regulations on the ground that they authorized unreasonable searches and seizures within the meaning of the Fourth Amendment. The provisions required banks automatically to report the details of virtually all domestic transactions in order to facilitate discovery of wrongdoing by bank customers. In reversing this portion of the lower court's decision, Justice Rehnquist's plurality opinion discerned a rational relationship between the record keeping and reporting requirements and the congressional objective of scrutinizing the business operations of organized crime. Rehnquist interpreted the legislative history and implementing regulations as indicating that access to records of domestic transactions could be obtained only by proper legal process, e.g., by subpoena. Despite estimates that the Act would require banks each year to photocopy between 20 and 30 billion checks, weighing some 166 million pounds, the plurality opinion suggested that banks may have been keeping similar records for their own purposes in the past. Although the opinion characterized the bank petitioners as parties to the financial transactions of their customers, it can be read as sustaining record keeping requirements imposed on third parties having information about activities or persons who are the targets of regulation.

5. *Possession of Records and the Fifth Amendment.* Another line of cases holds that if the demanded records are not in the respondent's possession, the privilege is lost. See, e.g., *Andresen v. Maryland*, 427 U.S. 463 (1976); *Couch v. United States*, 409 U.S. 322 (1973); *cf. United States v. LaSalle National Bank*, 437 U.S. 298 (1978). See generally Note, *Formalism, Legal Realism, and Constitutionally Protected Privacy Under the Fourth and Fifth Amendments*, 90 Harv.L.Rev. 945 (1977).

Costs of Government–Mandated Records and Reports

Record keeping and reporting requirements can impose substantial burdens on those subject to them. For example, a requirement that every industrial enterprise continuously monitor the contents of its liquid waste or smoke emissions could necessitate the employment of additional personnel, the maintenance of testing and sample storage facilities, and enormous amounts of paper work. It has been estimated that the premarket notification requirement for new chemicals, prescribed by the 1976 Toxic Substances Control Act, imposes on average a cost of between $9,000 and $41,000 for each compound introduced—a cost that exceeds the expected return on most new chemicals, though it is dwarfed by the yield of the relatively few significant innovations. According to the same estimate, this "reporting charge" has diminished the rate of introduction of new chemicals in this country by 250 to 700 a year. Such costs may be easily absorbed by large businesses, but not all drug or chemical manufacturers are large, and many dischargers of industrial waste are small enterprises. Moreover, it is to be expected that so far as possible the expense of record keeping and reporting will be passed on to customers, as a cost of doing business. See generally EPA, Impact of TSCA Premanufacturing Notification Requirements (December 1978).

Although judicial tolerance of administrative reporting requirements obviously permits agencies wide latitude in demanding information, other supervising institutions may exercise stricter oversight. Until 1980, all new information requirements had to be approved for most executive agencies by OMB, while independent regulatory commissions had to submit their proposals to the Government Accounting Office, an agency of Congress. 44 U.S.C. §§ 3501–512. Congress established this division of authority between OMB and the GAO in 1973, *inter alia*, to protect the "independence" of regulatory commissions. In 1980, at the urging of the Carter Administration, Congress substantially overhauled the regime for administrative oversight of agency reporting and recordkeeping requirements by enacting the Paperwork Reduction Act, Pub. L.No. 96–511, now codified at 44 U.S.C. §§ 3501 et seq. While the new law made modest changes in the criteria for review and approval of proposed agency requirements, its major changes were the restoration and invigoration of OMB's oversight role for all agencies, both executive and independent, and the elimination of most categorical and agency-specific exemptions to centralized review. The Act reflected broad concerns about the impact of federal regulation generally on the nation's economic vitality. See OMB, Paperwork and Red Tape (September 1979). Authorization for the Act lapsed during the Bush-41 Administration because of a controversy over Congress' access to information concerning OMB's regulatory oversight activities, as discussed in Chapter 3, *supra*. Settlement of the interbranch access issues led to enactment of the Paperwork Reduction Act Amendments of 1995, Pub.L.No. 104–12, 109 Stat. 163 (1995), which reauthorized the Act and made few substantive changes.

The Paperwork Act is nominally administered by the Director of OMB, but contemplates that the Director's duties will be performed by the Administrator of an Office of Information and Regulatory Affairs (OIRA), created for this purpose. The Act amends the Federal Reports

Act of 1942, which had been construed as inapplicable to three-quarters of all federal information demands on the private sector. See S.Rep.No. 96–930, 96th Cong., 2d Sess. 75 (1980). In addition to creating a central office in OMB to formulate government information management policies and to oversee agency demands, the Act requires that each agency head designate a senior official to oversee the agency's compliance with the Act and, with OMB's concurrence, exercise that body's final approval authority. In the Information Technology Management Reform Act of 1996, P.L. 104–106, this official was redesignated as the agency Chief Information Officer, or CIO.

Before imposing a new demand for information on the private sector, an agency must first persuade OIRA that the new requirement meets ten statutory criteria, including that it "is necessary for the proper performance of the functions of the agency, * * * and will have practical utility." 44 U.S.C. § 3506(c)(3). OIRA's refusal to approve a request is final, unless the request comes from an independent agency and a majority of its members vote to override the "veto." OIRA may not veto a proposal to obtain information that is demanded by an agency's organic legislation, but the Act requires that it have an opportunity to review such proposals.

The Paperwork Reduction Act also directs OMB to establish general policies and procedures for controlling the government's collection of information. The Act enunciated an original goal of reducing the burden of federally-mandated paperwork by 25 percent by the end of Fiscal Year 1983; the 1995 Amendments contemplate 10 percent reductions during both fiscal year 1996 and fiscal year 1997, followed by 5 per cent reductions in each of the following four fiscal years. OMB is to provide Congress an annual report estimating the hours required to comply with each agency's reporting obligations.

Examples of the paperwork burdens imposed by federal agencies and of efforts to reduce those burdens appear annually in a report to Congress concerning the federal Information Collection Budget. A 1997 report to Congress indicates what continue to be the major sources of reporting requirements:

> [T]he Department of the Treasury, including the IRS, continues to account for the great majority—80%—of the Federal information collection burden in FY 1996* * *. The Department of Labor is the second largest agency in terms of information collection burden, accounting for 18% of the non-Treasury burden. The Defense Department is third, accounting for more than 11% of the burden excluding Treasury. The Federal Trade Commission and the Securities and Exchange Commission are fourth and fifth, respectively. The rest of the top ten are the Department of Health and Human Services, the Department of Agriculture, the Environmental Protection Agency, the Department of Transportation, and the Department of Education* * *.

OMB, Reports to Congress under the Paperwork Reduction Act of 1995 (1997), available at http://www.whitehouse.gov/omb/inforeg/prar-eprt.html. A few of the claimed 1996–97 claimed "burden reduction accomplishments" are illustrative:

- The Food and Consumer Service [of USDA] published a final rule that established a new system to help schools use nutrient-based menu planning for meals in the National School Lunch and School Breakfast Programs. The rule eliminated regulatory requirements for edit checks and the maintenance of records to prove the nonprofit status of schools. As a result, paperwork burden was reduced by almost 16 million hours.
- Defense. DoD has significantly reduced the data delivery burdens imposed on its contractors. As part of contract performance, contractors are required to supply large amounts of information, including drawings, maintenance manuals, test reports, parts lists, software documentation, and cost and scheduling data. DoD has reduced the number of these data item descriptions in its master catalog by 400 (of 1300), reducing the burden on contractors by over 30 million hours.
- The Office of Water efforts to reduce reporting focused on the National Pollutant Discharge Elimination System (NPDES) Monitoring Report. Guidance was developed to reduce existing monitoring and reporting requirements for facilities that consistently comply with their permit limits, consistently discharge higher quality water than required by their permits, or implement strong facility management plans. The burden associated with the NPDES Monitoring Report will be reduced by about 4.7 million hours once the program is fully implemented.

Notwithstanding such "victories," presidential claims of significant annual reductions in the paperwork burden deserve careful scrutiny. The very title of a 1989 assessment by the General Accounting Office implied a skeptical view: General Accounting Office, Paperwork Reduction: Little Real Burden Change in Recent Years (1989). A candid report transmitting to Congress the Information Collection Budget for FY 2002 offered a sobering estimate of the likelihood of meeting Congress' paperwork reduction targets, and a revealing appraisal of the institutional context that makes such goals elusive.

OMB OFFICE OF INFORMATION AND REGULATORY AFFAIRS, MANAGING INFORMATION COLLECTION AND DISSEMINATION FISCAL YEAR 2002

21–22 (April 10, 2002).

In reviewing the Federal Government's experience implementing the 1995 PRA, OMB has learned a number of lessons. * * *

The Government's Need for Information Continues to Grow. * * * [T]he Federal Government provides the American people with a wide array of protections and services. * * * To carry out all of these responsibilities carefully and effectively, the Federal Government collects information. * * * [N]ew legislative initiatives and amendments to existing laws typically require more—not less—data collection by affected agencies. In addition, even in the absence of legislative changes, agency statutory and program responsibilities can expand over time due to a number of factors beyond the agency's direct control, such as economic growth and the number of people to be served. Since the PRA was first enacted in 1980, the size of the U.S. population has increased by over a quarter and U.S. gross domestic product has more than tripled.

The 1995 PRA, in its core paperwork review provisions, recognizes that for a burden reduction target to be "practicable," the target must be consistent with the ability of agencies to carry out their statutory and program responsibilities. While an underlying goal of the 1995 PRA is to minimize Federal paperwork burden on the public, it also affirms the importance of information to the successful completion of agency missions. Furthermore, the PRA charges OMB with the responsibility of weighing the burdens of information collection on the public against the practical utility the information will have for the agency. Specifically, the 1995 PRA provides that "[b]efore approving a proposed collection of information, the [OMB] Director shall determine whether the collection of information by the agency is necessary for the proper performance of the functions of the agency, including whether the information shall have practical utility." Under this authority, if an agency information collection request meets the practical utility, burden, and other PRA criteria for approval, OMB will approve it in accordance with the PRA, notwithstanding the effect of this approval on burden reduction targets. The 1995 Act does not grant OMB the authority to disapprove a collection of information simply because an approval would cause the agency to exceed the agency's paperwork burden reduction goal stated in the ICB.

Burden Reduction Goals Continue to be Difficult to Achieve. To encourage agencies to achieve the fundamental purposes of the PRA, the 1995 Act reinstituted a requirement that OMB, in consultation with the agencies, establish "annual agency goals" to reduce paperwork burden on the public to the "maximum practicable" extent "in each agency." These goals called for government-wide reductions of paperwork burdens of 10 percent for FY 1996 and FY 1997, and 5 percent for each of the four following years, FY 1998–2001. The goals served to stimulate agency efforts to reduce paperwork burdens and were implemented through the annual process by which OMB and the agencies developed the Information Collection Budget.

Due to a variety of factors, * * * agencies did not achieve the 1995 PRA's government-wide burden reduction goals. Although this record may be disappointing, it is important to consider the nature and purpose of these goals. The decision to set targets at 5 and 10 percent was not based on an analysis of the amount of burden reduction that agencies could and should achieve. Rather, Congress set goals that agencies should aspire to meet while also performing their missions. Under the PRA, burden reduction can be achieved only to the extent that it does not interfere with agencies' ability to meet their programmatic responsibilities. This constraint has affected the Government's historical performance on burden reduction. Since the initial passage of the Paperwork Reduction Act in 1980, the aggregate of the agencies' annual paperwork burden reduction goals has met the statutorily set government-wide goal in only one year–1982.

CIOs Face Challenges in Meeting Their PRA Responsibilities. In making CIOs accountable for evaluating agencies' need for information, estimating reporting burdens, and generally overseeing agency plans for the management and use of information, Congress ensures that senior agency management is focused on PRA compliance. Since the passage of the 1995 PRA, however, CIO responsibilities have expanded, largely as a result of increased E–Gov activities. The attention CIOs pay to information technology, in turn, has made it more difficult for CIOs to focus on their PRA responsibilities. While the objectives of agency IT initiatives overlap considerably with those of the PRA–for example, reducing reporting burdens and disseminating information more efficiently—CIO resources are spread over more areas than was the case when the 1995 PRA was enacted.

Moreover, OMB's process for reviewing agency information collection requests has proven to be labor-intensive for CIOs and their staffs. The PRA clearance process, for example, includes a public notice of a 60–day public comment period and a second notice of a 30–day OMB review. This workload has been exacerbated by the three-year OMB approval cycle. Currently, OIRA reviews roughly 3,000 PRA clearance packages a year, only a quarter of which are first-time requests to collect information. If the current limit on OMB approval time was extended, agencies would process fewer information collections annually. For example, a four-year OMB approval period would reduce the number of annual OMB clearances by about 19 percent.

FY 2001 Information Collection Totals
(millions of hours)

	FY 2000 Total Hours Needed	FY 2001 Program Changes		FY 2001 Changes Due to New Statute or Agency Action		FY 2001 Adjustments		FY2001 Total Hours Needed
Government Total	7,361.72	158.70	2.2%			104.85	1.4%	7,651.42
Agency								
Agriculture	75.19	5.77	7.7%	2.08	2.8%	5.86	7.8%	86.72
Commerce*	38.57	-28.60	-74.1%	-28.59	-74.1%	0.45	1.2%	10.29
Defense	93.62	-0.68	-0.7%	-0.65	-0.7%	-0.19	-0.2%	92.05
Education	41.98	-1.45	-3.4%	-1.57	-3.7%	-0.01	0.0%	40.49
Energy	2.92	0.97	33.1%	-0.02	-0.7%	-0.04	-1.4%	3.85
Health and Human Services	173.71	2.19	1.3%	1.57	0.9%	10.93	6.3%	186.61
Housing and Urban Development	12.46	-0.45	-3.6%	-0.48	-3.9%	0.04	0.3%	12.05
Interior	5.64	1.87	33.2%	-0.02	-0.4%	-0.17	-3.0%	7.56
Justice	36.82	0.25	0.7%	3.07	8.3%	3.45	9.4%	40.53
Labor	181.59	-0.04	0.0%	-2.41	-1.3%	4.71	2.6%	186.11
State	29.19	-0.08	-0.3%	-0.11	-0.4%	-13.84	-47.4%	16.56
Transportation**	117.65	-42.39	-36.0%	1.07	0.9%	5.11	4.3%	80.34
Treasury	6,156.80	214.17	3.5%	214.46	3.5%	44.79	0.7%	6,415.85
Veterans Affairs	5.98	-0.01	-0.2%	-0.05	-0.8%	-0.72	-12.0%	5.31
Environmental Protection Agency	128.75	0.94	0.7%	0.72	0.6%	1.18	0.9%	130.77

*Note that a large portion of Commerce's decrease in burden is attributed to the periodic nature of Census collections.

** Due to a PRA violation, the program change total for FY 2001 includes a reduction of 42,464,327 hours. DOT inadvertently allowed OMB's approval of a Federal Motor Carrier Safety Administration collection, Driver's Record of Duty Status, to expire on September 30, 2001. DOT continued to use this collection in violation of the PRA until it obtained a reinstatement of OMB's approval on March 4, 2002.

Source: OFFICE OF MANAGEMENT AND BUDGET OFFICE OF INFORMATION AND REGULATORY AFFAIRS, MANAGING INFORMATION COLLECTION AND DISSEMINATION FISCAL YEAR 2002, at 65 (Apr. 10, 2002).

3. PHYSICAL INSPECTIONS

Many statutes authorize administrative inspections as a means of policing compliance with regulatory requirements. Such provisions are common in laws whose focus is the protection of the public health or the collection of revenue. Probably the most pervasive government inspection program exists in the meat and poultry industries, where resident federal inspectors supervise slaughtering and packing operations from beginning to end, throughout the work day. On-site inspection or visitation also has obvious utility in the enforcement of pollution controls, housing ordinances, and health and fire regulations. But government intrusions into private premises, however benign their purpose or peaceful their execution, raise constitutional issues. Indeed, the clash between the requirements of efficient enforcement and the values protected by the Fourth Amendment is more obvious here than in the subpoena context, for agency subpoenas customarily threaten no violation of the physical integrity of a citizen's home or business. While our attention will be focused on the constitutional issues, this focus should not obscure other issues that may be raised by an agency's attempt to conduct physical inspections. For example, here too clear statutory authority is surely a prerequisite to the conduct of any administrative search or inspection.

Basic Premises

Notwithstanding the prevalence of state and federal laws authorizing physical inspections, it was not until 1959 that the Supreme Court squarely faced the question whether administrative searches are subject to the same constitutional restrictions as those conducted by police officers engaged in enforcing the criminal law. Repeated visits to this question since *Frank v. Maryland*, 359 U.S. 360 (1959), however, have yet to produce a coherent set of governing principles. In *Frank* the Court upheld, by a five-to-four vote, a state conviction of a homeowner who refused to permit a municipal health inspector to enter his premises without a search warrant—in substance recognizing warrantless administrative inspections as "reasonable" under the Fourth Amendment. Within eight years, however, the Court had revised its view of the Fourth Amendment's applicability in this context.

Camara v. Municipal Court, 387 U.S. 523 (1967), and *See v. Seattle*, 387 U.S. 541 (1967), mark the beginnings of contemporary doctrine. The Court overturned convictions for refusing legislatively authorized peaceful inspections of an apartment and a warehouse, upholding each defendant's claim that he was entitled to insist on a search warrant. Writing for the majority in both cases, Justice White rejected attempts to distinguish these contexts from customary police searches for evidence of crime and from one another:

> It is surely anomalous to say that the individual and his private property are fully protected by the Fourth Amendment only when the individual is suspected of criminal behavior. For instance, even the most law-abiding citizen has a very tangible interest in limiting the circumstances under which the sanctity of his home may be broken by official authority, for the possibility of criminal entry under the guise of official sanction is a serious threat to personal and family security. * * * Like most regulatory laws, fire, health, and housing codes are enforced by criminal processes. In some cities, discovery of a violation by the inspector leads to a criminal complaint. Even in cities where discovery of a violation produces only an administrative compliance order, refusal to comply is a criminal offense, and the fact of compliance is verified by a second inspection, again without a warrant. Finally, as this case demonstrates, refusal to permit an inspection is itself a crime, punishable by fine or even by jail sentence.
>
> The *Frank* majority suggested, and appellee reasserts, two other justifications for permitting administrative health and safety inspections without a warrant. First, it is argued that these inspections are "designed to make the least possible demand on the individual occupant." The ordinances authorizing inspections are hedged with

safeguards, and at any rate the inspector's particular decision to enter must comply with the constitutional standard of reasonableness even if he may enter without a warrant. In addition, the argument proceeds, the warrant process could not function effectively in this field. The decision to inspect an entire municipal area is based upon legislative or administrative assessment of broad factors such as the area's age and condition. Unless the magistrate is to review such policy matters, he must issue a "rubber stamp" warrant which provides no protection at all to the property owner.

In our opinion, these arguments unduly discount the purposes behind the warrant machinery contemplated by the Fourth Amendment. Under the present system, when the inspector demands entry, the occupant has no way of knowing whether enforcement of the municipal code involved requires inspection of his premises, no way of knowing the lawful limits of the inspector's power to search, and no way of knowing whether the inspector himself is acting under proper authorization. These are questions which may be reviewed by a neutral magistrate without any reassessment of the basic agency decision to canvass an area. Yet, only by refusing entry and risking a criminal conviction can the occupant at present challenge the inspector's decision to search. And even if the occupant possesses sufficient fortitude to take this risk, as appellant did here, he may never learn any more about the reason for the inspection than that the law generally allows housing inspectors to gain entry. The practical effect of this system is to leave the occupant subject to the discretion of the official in the field. This is precisely the discretion to invade private property which we have consistently circumscribed by a requirement that a disinterested party warrant the need to search. We simply cannot say that the protections provided by the warrant procedure are not needed in this context; broad statutory safeguards are no substitute for individualized review, particularly when those safeguards may only be invoked at the risk of a criminal penalty.

The final justification for warrantless administrative searches is that the public interest demands such a rule: it is vigorously argued that the health and safety of entire urban populations is dependent upon enforcement of minimum fire, housing, and sanitation standards, and that the only effective means of enforcing such codes is by routine systematized inspection of all physical structures. * * * [W]e think this argument misses the mark. The question is not, at this stage at least, whether these inspections may be made, but whether they may be made without a warrant. * * * It has nowhere been urged that fire, health, and housing code inspection programs could not achieve their goals within their confines of a reasonable search warrant requirement. * * *

In *See*, Justice White asserted: "The businessman, like the occupant of a residence, has a constitutional right to go about his business free from unreasonable official entries upon his private commercial property."

Accordingly, "the basic component of a reasonable search under the Fourth Amendment—that it not be enforced without a suitable warrant procedure—is applicable in this context, as in others, to business premises as well as to residential premises."

Having concluded that the occupant of private residential or business premises is entitled to demand a warrant to inspect, Justice White considered the kind of showing an inspector must make to obtain a magistrate's approval for a nonconsensual inspection:

> * * * "[P]robable cause" is the standard by which a particular decision to search is tested against the constitutional mandate of reasonableness. To apply this standard, it is obviously necessary first to focus upon the governmental interest which allegedly justifies official intrusion upon the constitutionally protected interests of the private citizen. * * *
>
> There is unanimous agreement among those most familiar with this field that the only effective way to seek universal compliance with the minimum standards required by municipal codes is through routine periodic inspections of all structures. It is here that the probable cause debate is focused, for the agency's decision to conduct an area inspection is unavoidably based on its appraisal of conditions in the area as a whole, not on its knowledge of conditions in each particular building. * * *
>
> * * * [T]here can be no ready test for determining reasonableness other than by balancing the need to search against the invasion which the search entails. But we think that a number of persuasive factors combine to support the reasonableness of area code-enforcement inspections. First, such programs have a long history of judicial and public acceptance. Second, the public interest demands that all dangerous conditions be prevented or abated, yet it is doubtful that any other canvassing technique would achieve acceptable results. Many such conditions—faulty wiring is an obvious example—are not observable from outside the building and indeed may not be apparent to the inexpert occupant * * *. Finally, because the inspections are neither personal in nature nor aimed at the discovery of evidence of crime, they involve a relatively limited invasion of the urban citizen's privacy. * * *
>
> Having concluded that the area inspection is a "reasonable" search of private property within the meaning of the Fourth Amendment, it is obvious that "probable cause" to issue a warrant to inspect must exist if reasonable legislative or administrative standards for conducting an area inspection are satisfied with respect to a particular dwelling. Such standards, which will vary with the municipal program being enforced, may be based upon the passage of time, the nature of the building (e.g., a multi-family apartment house), or the condition of the entire area, but they will not necessarily depend upon specific knowledge of the condition of the particular dwelling. It has been suggested that so to vary the

probable cause test from the standard applied in criminal cases would be to authorize a "synthetic search warrant" and thereby to lessen the overall protections of the Fourth Amendment. But we do not agree. The warrant procedure is designed to guarantee that a decision to search private property is justified by a reasonable governmental interest. But reasonableness is still the ultimate standard. * * *

Since our holding emphasizes the controlling standard of reasonableness, nothing we say today is intended to foreclose prompt inspections, even without a warrant, that the law has traditionally upheld in emergency situations. On the other hand, in the case of most routine area inspections, there is no compelling urgency to inspect at a particular time or on a particular day. Moreover, most citizens allow inspections of their property without a warrant. Thus, as a practical matter and in light of the Fourth Amendment's requirement that a warrant specify the property to be searched, it seems likely that warrants should normally be sought only after entry is refused unless there has been a citizen complaint or there is other satisfactory reason for securing immediate entry. * * *

A familiarity with the procedure for the issuance of search warrants is helpful in understanding the debate in *Camara* and *See* and later cases. The principal safeguard afforded by a warrant requirement is that it forces law enforcement officers to establish a factual basis for the search of private premises before any entry is made, and thus forestalls *post hoc* attempts to justify conduct that could not have been justified at the time. Typically, an officer seeking a warrant must appear before a magistrate—a judge or other judicial officer—and persuade the magistrate that "probable cause" exists to support two conclusions: (1) that the items the officer hopes to find in the search are in some way connected with unlawful, usually criminal, activity; and (2) that the items are likely to be found on the premises to be searched. Most often, the officer presents supporting information in the form of a sworn affidavit. Very occasionally this will be supplemented by affidavits of other witnesses. Frequently, but by no means always, the officer seeking the warrant will testify before the magistrate. No one is present to represent the person whose premises are to be searched.

Theoretically, the requirement of "probable cause" demands information that, if true, would make it more probable than not that the items sought are indeed connected with unlawful activity and will be found on the premises. But it is clear that magistrate decisions can follow no mathematical formula. Decisions often must be made hastily and, in situations where warrant applications tend to be duplicative, are probably made casually. Moreover, the information offered to establish "probable cause" need not be admissible in a criminal trial or administrative proceeding likely to grow out of the search.

Exceptions and Elaborations

The Supreme Court continued to wrestle after *Camara* and *See* with the Fourth Amendment's applicability to administrative searches and inspections and with the adequacy of procedures for the issuance of warrants. Three years later, the Court recognized an exception to the warrant requirement for businesses with a history of regulation—embracing a distinction that Justice Brennan had suggested in his concurring opinion in the latter case.

In *Colonnade Catering Corp. v. United States*, 397 U.S. 72 (1970), a licensed liquor dealer challenged the legality of a forced and warrantless entry of a locked storeroom which led to his conviction for violating an Internal Revenue Code prohibition against refilling bottles used for the sale of alcoholic beverages. The Court overturned the conviction on the ground that the statutory authorization to inspect licensees could not be read as affording IRS agents the option to break in if access were denied. But in dictum the majority validated the statutory penalty for refusal to permit inspection without a warrant, on the ground that alcoholic beverage licensees had historically been subject to broader administrative scrutiny and control.

In *United States v. Biswell*, 406 U.S. 311 (1972), this "exception" to *Camara* and *See* appeared to expand. The 1968 Federal Gun Control Act, 18 U.S.C. § 923(g), authorizes the premises of registered gun dealers to be entered and inspected by Treasury Department agents during business hours. When agents arrived to inspect Biswell's pawn shop they acknowledged they did not have a warrant, but he acquiesced in their search of his premises after being shown a copy of the statutory provision authorizing entry. Convicted of unauthorized dealing in firearms based on evidence found during the inspection, Biswell claimed that the agents' conduct was unlawful under *See* and that he could not be understood as having waived his constitutional right to demand a warrant. A majority of the Court upheld his conviction:

> Here, the search was not accompanied by any unauthorized force, and if the target of the inspection had been a federally licensed liquor dealer, it is clear under *Colonnade* that the Fourth Amendment would not bar a seizure of illicit liquor. * * *
>
> * * * Federal regulation of the interstate traffic in firearms is not as deeply rooted in history as is governmental control of the liquor industry, but close scrutiny of this traffic is undeniably of central importance to federal efforts to prevent violent crime and to assist the States in regulating the firearms traffic within their borders. Large interests are at stake, and inspection is a crucial part of the regulatory scheme, since it assures that weapons are distributed through regular channels and in a traceable manner and makes possible the prevention of sales to undesirable customers and the detection of the origin of particular firearms.
>
> It is also apparent that if the law is to be properly enforced and inspection made effective, inspections without warrant must be deemed reasonable official conduct under the Fourth Amendment. In *See v. City of Seattle* the mission of the inspection system was to discover and correct violations of the building code, conditions that

were relatively difficult to conceal or to correct in a short time. Periodic inspection sufficed, and inspection warrants could be required and privacy given a measure of protection with little if any threat to the effectiveness of the inspection system there at issue. * * * Here, if inspection is to be effective and serve as a credible deterrent, unannounced, even frequent, inspections are essential. In this context, the prerequisite of a warrant could easily frustrate inspection; and if the necessary flexibility as to time, scope, and frequency is to be preserved, the protections afforded by a warrant would be negligible.

It is also plain that inspections for compliance with the Gun Control Act pose only limited threats to the dealer's justifiable expectations of privacy. When a dealer chooses to engage in this pervasively regulated business and to accept a federal license, he does so with the knowledge that his business records, firearms and ammunition will be subject to effective inspection. Each licensee is annually furnished with a revised compilation of ordinances that describe his obligations and define the inspector's authority. * * *

We have little difficulty in concluding that where, as here, regulatory inspections further urgent federal interests, and the possibilities of abuse and the threat to privacy are not of impressive dimensions, the inspection may proceed without a warrant where specifically authorized by statute.

MARSHALL v. BARLOW'S, INC.

Supreme Court of the United States, 1978.
436 U.S. 307, 98 S.Ct. 1816, 56 L.Ed.2d 305.

JUSTICE WHITE delivered the opinion of the Court.

Section 8(a) of the Occupational Safety and Health Act of 1970 (OSHA or Act)[1] empowers agents of the Secretary of Labor (Secretary) to search the work area of any employment facility within the Act's jurisdiction. The purpose of the search is to inspect for safety hazards and violations of OSHA regulations. No search warrant or other process is expressly required under the Act.

On the morning of September 11, 1975, an OSHA inspector entered the customer service area of Barlow's, Inc., an electrical and plumbing installation business located in Pocatello, Idaho. The president and

1. "In order to carry out the purposes of this chapter, the Secretary, upon presenting appropriate credentials to the owner, operator, or agent in charge, is authorized—

"(1) to enter without delay and at reasonable times any factory, plant, establishment, construction site, or other area, workplace or environment where work is performed by an employee of an employer; and

"(2) to inspect and investigate during regular working hours and at other reasonable times, and within reasonable limits and in a reasonable manner, any such place of employment and all pertinent conditions, structures, machines, apparatus, devices, equipment, and materials therein, and to question privately any such employer, owner, operator, agent, or employee." 29 U.S.C. § 657(a).

general manager, Ferrol G. "Bill" Barlow, was on hand; and the OSHA inspector, after showing his credentials, informed Mr. Barlow that he wished to conduct a search of the working areas of the business. Mr. Barlow inquired whether any complaint had been received about his company. The inspector answered no, but that Barlow's, Inc., had simply turned up in the agency's selection process. The inspector again asked to enter the nonpublic area of the business; Mr. Barlow's response was to inquire whether the inspector had a search warrant. The inspector had none. Thereupon, Mr. Barlow refused the inspector admission to the employee area of his business. He said he was relying on his rights as guaranteed by the Fourth Amendment of the United States Constitution.

Three months later, the Secretary petitioned the United States District Court for the District of Idaho to issue an order compelling Mr. Barlow to admit the inspector.[3] The requested order was issued on December 30, 1975, and was presented to Mr. Barlow on January 5, 1976. Mr. Barlow again refused admission, and he sought his own injunctive relief against the warrantless searches assertedly permitted by OSHA. * * *

This court has already held that warrantless searches are generally unreasonable, and that this rule applies to commercial premises as well as homes. * * *

These same cases [*Camara* and *See*] also held that the Fourth Amendment prohibition against unreasonable searches protects against warrantless intrusions during civil as well as criminal investigations. * * * It therefore appears that unless some recognized exception to the warrant requirement applies, *See v. Seattle* would require a warrant to conduct the inspection sought in this case.

The Secretary urges that an exception from the search warrant requirement has been recognized for "pervasively regulated business[es]," *United States v. Biswell*, and for "closely regulated" industries "long subject to close supervision and inspection." *Colonnade Catering Corp. v. United States*. These cases are indeed exceptions, but they represent responses to relatively unique circumstances. Certain industries have such a history of government oversight that no reasonable expectation of privacy could exist for a proprietor over the stock of such an enterprise. Liquor (*Colonnade*) and firearms (*Biswell*) are industries of this type; when an entrepreneur embarks upon such a business, he has voluntarily chosen to subject himself to a full arsenal of governmental regulation. * * *

The clear import of our cases is that the closely regulated industry of the type involved in *Colonnade* and *Biswell* is the exception. The Secretary would make it the rule. Invoking the Walsh–Healey Act of 1936, the Secretary attempts to support a conclusion that all businesses involved in interstate commerce have long been subjected to close supervision of employee safety and health conditions. But the degree of

3. A regulation of the Secretary, 29 CFR § 1903.4 (1977), requires an inspector to seek compulsory process if an employer refuses a requested search.

federal involvement in employee working circumstances has never been of the order of specificity and pervasiveness that OSHA mandates. It is quite unconvincing to argue that the imposition of minimum wages and maximum hours on employers who contracted with the Government under the Walsh–Healey Act prepared the entirety of American interstate commerce for regulation of working conditions to the minutest detail. Nor can any but the most fictional sense of voluntary consent to later searches be found in the single fact that one conducts a business affecting interstate commerce; under current practice and law, few businesses can be conducted without having some effect on interstate commerce.

* * *

The Secretary nevertheless stoutly argues that the enforcement scheme of the Act requires warrantless searches, and that the restrictions on search discretion contained in the Act and its regulations already protect as much privacy as a warrant would. The Secretary thereby asserts the actual reasonableness of OSHA searches, whatever the general rule against warrantless searches might be. * * *

The Secretary submits that warrantless inspections are essential to the proper enforcement of OSHA because they afford the opportunity to inspect without prior notice and hence to preserve the advantages of surprise. While the dangerous conditions outlawed by the Act include structural defects that cannot be quickly hidden or remedied, the Act also regulates a myriad of safety details that may be amenable to speedy alteration or disguise. The risk is that during the interval between an inspector's initial request to search a plant and his procuring a warrant following the owner's refusal of permission, violations of this latter type could be corrected and thus escape the inspector's notice. To the suggestion that warrants may be issued *ex parte* and executed without delay and without prior notice, thereby preserving the element of surprise, the Secretary expresses concern for the administrative strain that would be experienced by the inspection system, and by the courts, should *ex parte* warrants issued in advance become standard practice.

We are unconvinced, however, that requiring warrants to inspect will impose serious burdens on the inspection system or the courts, will prevent inspections necessary to enforce the statute, or will make them less effective. In the first place, the great majority of businessmen can be expected in normal course to consent to inspection without warrant; the Secretary has not brought to this Court's attention any widespread pattern of refusal.[11] In those cases where an owner does insist on a warrant, the Secretary argues that inspection efficiency will be impeded by the advance notice and delay. The Act's penalty provisions for giving advance notice of a search and the Secretary's own regulations indicate

11. We recognize that today's holding itself might have an impact on whether owners choose to resist requested searches; we can only await the development of evidence not present on this record to determine how serious an impediment to effective enforcement this might be.

that surprise searches are indeed contemplated. However, the Secretary has also promulgated a regulation providing that upon refusal to permit an inspector to enter the property or to complete his inspection, the inspector shall attempt to ascertain the reasons for the refusal and report to his superior, who shall "promptly take appropriate action, including compulsory process, if necessary." 29 CFR § 1903.4 (1977). The regulation represents a choice to proceed by process where entry is refused; and on the basis of evidence available from present practice, the Act's effectiveness has not been crippled by providing those owners who wish to refuse an initial requested entry with a time lapse while the inspector obtains the necessary process. Indeed, the kind of process sought in this case and apparently anticipated by the regulation provides notice to the business operator. If this safeguard endangers the efficient administration of OSHA, the Secretary should never have adopted it, particularly when the Act does not require it. Nor is it immediately apparent why the advantages of surprise would be lost if, after being refused entry, procedures were available for the Secretary to seek an *ex parte* warrant and to reappear at the premises without further notice to the establishment being inspected.[15]

Whether the Secretary proceeds to secure a warrant or other process, with or without prior notice, his entitlement to inspect will not depend on his demonstrating probable cause to believe that conditions in violation of OSHA exist on the premises. Probable cause in the criminal law sense is not required. For purposes of an administrative search such as this, probable cause justifying the issuance of a warrant may be based not only on specific evidence of an existing violation but also on a showing that "reasonable legislative or administrative standards for conducting an * * * inspection are satisfied with respect to a particular [establishment]." *Camara v. Municipal Court.* A warrant showing that a specific business has been chosen for an OSHA search on the basis of a general administrative plan for the enforcement of the Act derived from neutral sources such as, for example, dispersion of employees in various types of industries across a given area, and the desired frequency of searches in any of the lesser divisions of the area, would protect an employer's Fourth Amendment rights. We doubt that the consumption of enforcement energies in the obtaining of such warrants will exceed manageable proportions.

Finally, the Secretary urges that requiring a warrant for OSHA inspectors will mean that, as a practical matter, warrantless-search provisions in other regulatory statutes are also constitutionally infirm. The reasonableness of a warrantless search, however, will depend upon the specific enforcement needs and privacy guarantees of each statute. Some of the statutes cited apply only to a single industry, where regulations might already be so pervasive that a *Colonnade–Biswell*

15. Insofar as the Secretary's statutory authority is concerned, a regulation expressly providing that the Secretary could proceed *ex parte* to seek a warrant or its equivalent would appear to be as much within the Secretary's power as the regulation currently in force and calling for "compulsory process."

exception to the warrant requirement could apply. Some statutes already envision resort to federal-court enforcement when entry is refused, employing specific language in some cases and general language in others. In short, we base today's opinion on the facts and law concerned with OSHA and do not retreat from a holding appropriate to that statute because of its real or imagined effect on other, different administrative schemes.

Nor do we agree that the incremental protections afforded the employer's privacy by a warrant are so marginal that they fail to justify the administrative burdens that may be entailed. The authority to make warrantless searches devolves almost unbridled discretion upon executive and administrative officers, particularly those in the field, as to when to search and whom to search. A warrant, by contrast, would provide assurances from a neutral officer that the inspection is reasonable under the Constitution, is authorized by statute, and is pursuant to an administrative plan containing specific neutral criteria.[20] Also, a warrant would then and there advise the owner of the scope and objects of the search, beyond which limits the inspector is not expected to proceed. These are important functions for a warrant to perform, functions which underlie the Court's prior decisions that the Warrant Clause applies to inspections for compliance with regulatory statutes. We conclude that the concerns expressed by the Secretary do not suffice to justify warrantless inspections under OSHA or vitiate the general constitutional requirement that for a search to be reasonable a warrant must be obtained. * * *

JUSTICE STEVENS, with whom JUSTICE BLACKMUN and JUSTICE REHNQUIST join, dissenting.

The Fourth Amendment contains two separate Clauses, each flatly prohibiting a category of governmental conduct. The first Clause states that the right to be free from unreasonable searches "shall not be violated"; the second unequivocally prohibits the issuance of warrants except "upon probable cause." In this case the ultimate question is whether the category of warrantless searches authorized by the statute is "unreasonable" within the meaning of the first Clause.

* * *

The warrant requirement is linked "textually * * * to the probable-cause concept" in the Warrant Clause. The routine OSHA inspections are, by definition, not based on cause to believe there is a violation on the premises to be inspected. Hence, if the inspections were measured

20. The application for the inspection order filed by the Secretary in this case represented that "the desired inspection and investigation are contemplated as a part of an inspection program designed to assure compliance with the Act and are authorized by Section 8(a) of the Act." The program was not described, however, or any facts presented that would indicate why an inspection of Barlow's establishment was within the program. The order that issued concluded generally that the inspection authorized was "part of an inspection program designed to assure compliance with the Act."

against the requirements of the Warrant Clause, they would be automatically and unequivocally unreasonable.

Because of the acknowledged importance and reasonableness of routine inspections in the enforcement of federal regulatory statutes such as OSHA, the Court recognizes that requiring full compliance with the Warrant Clause would invalidate all such inspection programs. Yet, rather than simply analyzing such programs under the "Reasonableness" Clause of the Fourth Amendment, the Court holds the OSHA program invalid under the Warrant Clause and then avoids a blanket prohibition on all routine, regulatory inspections by relying on the notion that the "probable cause" requirement in the Warrant Clause may be relaxed whenever the Court believes that the governmental need to conduct a category of "searches" outweighs the intrusion on interests protected by the Fourth Amendment.

The Court's approach disregards the plain language of the Warrant Clause and is unfaithful to the balance struck by the Framers of the Fourth Amendment—"the one procedural safeguard in the Constitution that grew directly out of the events which immediately preceded the revolutionary struggle with England." * * *

Since the general warrant, not the warrantless search, was the immediate evil at which the Fourth Amendment was directed, it is not surprising that the Framers placed precise limits on its issuance. The requirement that a warrant only issue on a showing of particularized probable cause was the means adopted to circumscribe the warrant power. While the subsequent course of Fourth Amendment jurisprudence in this Court emphasizes the dangers posed by warrantless searches conducted without probable cause, it is the general reasonableness standard in the first Clause, not the Warrant Clause, that the Framers adopted to limit this category of searches. It is, of course, true that the existence of a valid warrant normally satisfies the reasonableness requirement under the Fourth Amendment. But we should not dilute the requirements of the Warrant Clause in an effort to force every kind of governmental intrusion which satisfies the Fourth Amendment definition of a "search" into a judicially developed, warrant-preference scheme.

Fidelity to the original understanding of the Fourth Amendment, therefore, leads to the conclusion that the Warrant Clause has no application to routine, regulatory inspections of commercial premises. If such inspections are valid, it is because they comport with the ultimate reasonableness standard of the Fourth Amendment. * * *

Congress has determined that regulation and supervision of safety in the workplace furthers an important public interest and that the power to conduct warrantless searches is necessary to accomplish the safety goals of the legislation. In assessing the public interest side of the Fourth Amendment balance, however, the Court today substitutes its judgment for that of Congress on the question of what inspection authority is needed to effectuate the purposes of the Act. * * *

The Court's analysis does not persuade me that Congress' determination that the warrantless-inspection power as a necessary adjunct of the exercise of the regulatory power is unreasonable. It was surely not unreasonable to conclude that the rate at which employers deny entry to inspectors would increase if covered businesses, which may have safety violations on their premises, have a right to deny warrantless entry to a compliance inspector. The Court is correct that this problem could be avoided by requiring inspectors to obtain a warrant prior to every inspection visit. But the adoption of such a practice undercuts the Court's explanation of why a warrant requirement would not create undue enforcement problems. For, even if it were true that many employers would not exercise their right to demand a warrant, it would provide little solace to those charged with administration of OSHA; faced with an increase in the rate of refusals and the added costs generated by futile trips to inspection sites where entry is denied, officials may be compelled to adopt a general practice of obtaining warrants in advance. While the Court's prediction of the effect a warrant requirement would have on the behavior of covered employers may turn out to be accurate, its judgment is essentially empirical. On such an issue, I would defer to Congress' judgment regarding the importance of a warrantless-search power to the OSHA enforcement scheme.

* * *

The Court * * * concludes that the deference accorded Congress in *Biswell* and *Colonnade* should be limited to situations where the evils addressed by the regulatory statute are peculiar to a specific industry and that industry is one which has long been subject to Government regulation. The Court reasons that only in those situations can it be said that a person who engages in business will be aware of and consent to routine, regulatory inspections. I cannot agree that the respect due the congressional judgment should be so narrowly confined.

In the first place, the longevity of a regulatory program does not, in my judgment, have any bearing on the reasonableness of routine inspections necessary to achieve adequate enforcement of that program. Congress' conception of what constitute urgent federal interests need not remain static. The recent vintage of public and congressional awareness of the dangers posed by health and safety hazards in the workplace is not a basis for according less respect to the considered judgment of Congress. Indeed, in *Biswell*, the Court upheld an inspection program authorized by a regulatory statute enacted in 1968. The Court there noted that "[f]ederal regulation of the interstate traffic in firearms is not as deeply rooted in history as is governmental control of the liquor industry, but close scrutiny of this traffic is undeniably" an urgent federal interest. Thus, the critical fact is the congressional determination that federal regulation would further significant public interests, not the date that determination was made.

In the second place, I see no basis for the Court's conclusion that a congressional determination that a category of regulatory inspections is reasonable need only be respected when Congress is legislating on an industry-by-industry basis. The pertinent inquiry is not whether the inspection program is authorized by a regulatory statute directed at a single industry, but whether Congress has limited the exercise of the inspection power to those commercial premises where the evils at which the statute is directed are to be found. * * *

Finally, the Court would distinguish the respect accorded Congress' judgment in *Colonnade* and *Biswell* on the ground that businesses engaged in the liquor and firearms industry " 'accept the burdens as well as the benefits of their trade. * * *.' " In the Court's view, such businesses consent to the restrictions placed upon them, while it would be fiction to conclude that a businessman subject to OSHA consented to routine safety inspections. In fact, however, consent is fictional in both contexts. Here, as well as in *Biswell*, businesses are required to be aware of and comply with regulations governing their business activities. In both situations, the validity of the regulations depends not upon the consent of those regulated, but on the existence of a federal statute embodying a congressional determination that the public interest in the health of the Nation's work force or the limitation of illegal firearms traffic outweighs the businessman's interest in preventing a Government inspector from viewing those areas of his premises which relate to the subject matter of the regulation. * * *[11]

I respectfully dissent.

Notes

1. *Impact on OSHA.* Justice White speculates that the obligation to obtain a warrant when inspection is refused will not prove a serious burden for OSHA because most employers will in fact consent. And one commentator later observed: "Although a final judgment cannot be made at this time, it appears that the Court's decision will *not* have a significant adverse impact on OSHA enforcement." Mark A. Rothstein, *OSHA Inspections After Marshall v. Barlow's, Inc.*, 1979 Duke L.J. 63, 84. Rothstein pointed out that in the three to four months immediately after the ruling, "approximately 11,000 inspections were attempted by OSHA, and employers demanded warrants in fewer than 500 cases." However, it is unclear whether the passage of time will make employers more familiar with, and thus more inclined to insist upon, the agency's warrant obligation, or diminish resistance as the decision fades from memory. There appear to be no studies of the systemic effects of the Court's ruling, which in any case would be difficult to conduct because of shifts in the agency's enforcement emphasis prompted by independent concerns.

11. The decision today renders presumptively invalid numerous inspection provisions in federal regulatory statutes. E.g., 30 U.S.C. § 813 (Federal Coal Mine Health and Safety Act of 1969); 30 U.S.C. §§ 723, 724 (Federal Metal and Nonmetallic Mine Safety Act); 21 U.S.C. § 603 (inspection of meat and food products). That some of these provisions apply only to a single industry, as noted above, does not alter this fact. And the fact that some "envision resort to federal-court enforcement when entry is refused" is also irrelevant since the OSHA inspection program invalidated here requires compulsory process when a compliance inspector has been denied entry.

2. *Showing Necessary to Obtain a Warrant.* The first part of *Barlow's* two-part standard—"specific evidence of an existing violation," is usually satisfied by evidence of employee complaints. Note, *FDA, EPA, and OSHA Inspections—Practical Considerations in Light of Marshall v. Barlow's, Inc.*, 39 Md.L.Rev. 715, 732 (1980). In *In re Establishment Inspection of Gilbert & Bennett Manufacturing Co.*, 589 F.2d 1335, 1339 (7th Cir.), *cert. denied, Chromalloy American Corp. v. Marshall*, 444 U.S. 884 (1979), the court of appeals held that an OSHA warrant application did not have to identify the employee mailing the complaint nor establish the complainant's credibility; however, it must do more than recite that a complaint has been received. Some information concerning the nature of the alleged violation must be provided to establish the presence of probable cause. See also *Martin v. International Matex Tank Terminals—Bayonne*, 928 F.2d 614 (3d Cir.1991) (allegations of political motive underlying employee complaints not relevant to determination whether complaints provide probable cause for search).

Barlow's also allows issuance of a warrant based on "a general administrative plan derived from neutral sources." Thus the Court contemplated that OSHA could obtain warrants on the basis of some showing that the generic characteristics of the employer's establishment made it a logical target for inspection. The agency may not, however, conflate the two parts of the probable cause standard. In *In re Establishment Inspection of Northwest Airlines, Inc.*, 587 F.2d 12 (7th Cir.1978), the court separated OSHA's claim of a reasonable investigation program from the claim involving an employee complaint, and held that the agency had not provided sufficient information about its inspection program to justify a warrant. *In re Establishment Inspection of Urick Property*, 472 F.Supp. 1193 (W.D.Pa.1979), denied OSHA's warrant application on grounds that it had not described or demonstrated the neutrality of its inspection plan. See also *Marshall v. Weyerhaeuser Co.*, 456 F.Supp. 474 (D.N.J.1978). Verified allegations that an employer operates in an industry with a high risk of accident, that the establishment fits criteria for selection within the industry (e.g., size, time since last inspection, accident record), and that these criteria are regularly followed will usually suffice. See *In the Matter of the Establishment Inspection of Trinity Industries, Inc.*, 898 F.2d 1049 (5th Cir.1990) (permissible to target factory for search based on high rate of work days lost on account of injuries). See generally Robert E. Rader, *OSHA Warrants and Administrative Probable Cause*, 33 Baylor L.Rev. 97, 101 (1981).

3. *Scope of Authorized Inspection.* The courts will generally allow broader scope for routine inspections than inspections based on employee complaints. See, e.g., *In re Establishment Inspection of Gilbert & Bennett Manufacturing Co.*, 589 F.2d 1335, 1343 (7th Cir.1979), *cert. denied, Chromalloy American Corp. v. Marshall*, 444 U.S. 884 (1979). ("The scope of an OSHA inspection warrant must be as broad as the subject matter regulated by the statute and restricted only by the limitations imposed by Congress and the reasonableness requirement of the Fourth Amendment.") The courts have divided over the propriety of so-called "wall-to-wall" warrants often sought by OSHA inspectors, with most inclined to confine inspections to the area cited in the complaint that initially supplies the justification for the warrant. For an argument that both these polar approaches are wrong, see Note, *Permissible Scope of OSHA Inspection Warrants*, 66 Corn.L.Rev.

1254 (1981). See also *Martin v. International Matex Tank Terminals—Bayonne*, *supra* (upholding wall-to-wall inspection warrant based on specific allegations that violations permeated facility).

In *Marshall v. Pool Offshore Co.*, 467 F.Supp. 978 (W.D.La.1979), the court held that the OSHA warrants were too broad since they permitted the agency to inspect all records pursuant to an investigation of employee accidents caused by offshore drilling rigs. Under this reasoning, a warrant that fails to specify which records may be inspected may be overly broad. The court in *Pool Offshore* also held that the warrants were invalid because they gave OSHA inspectors the power to question *any* employee found on the rigs. In *Marshall v. Wollaston Alloys, Inc.*, 479 F.Supp. 1102 (D.Mass.1979), the court found that general language in a warrant could not be used to permit private employee interviews. Thus courts generally seem "unwilling to accept '*boilerplate*' recitations of statutory authority when the agency is capable of specifying the extent of its search." Note, *FDA, EPA and OSHA Inspections—Practical Considerations in Light of* Marshall v. Barlow's, Inc., 39 Md.L.Rev. 715, 740 (1980).

Consent to Search

Acquiescence in an officer's request for entry may under some circumstances obviate the need for a warrant. The traditional rubric is that, to be valid, any waiver of constitutional safeguards must be knowing and voluntary. In the regulatory context, however, the standard appears to be less strict. For example, in *United States v. Thriftimart, Inc.*, 429 F.2d 1006 (9th Cir.), *cert. denied*, 400 U.S. 926 (1970), the court upheld the convictions of a corporation and responsible officers for violating federal food sanitation requirements. Evidence of the offenses was obtained during a plant inspection by FDA agents, who obtained entry without a warrant. The inspectors had presented a formal notice of inspection and request for permission to enter the defendants' premises, reciting their general inspection authority under the Federal Food, Drug and Cosmetic Act. The inspectors did not advise the defendants that they were entitled to insist that a warrant be obtained. The Ninth Circuit found the inspection valid and sustained the convictions. The court noted that in *Camara* and *See* the Supreme Court had acknowledged that it was not necessary for inspectors to seek a warrant before being denied permission to inspect, and suggested that a different measure of "consent" should apply to administrative inspections. Emphasizing that the record was barren of evidence that the defendants were uninformed of their rights, surprised by the inspectors' visit, or coerced into admitting them, the court found it entirely plausible that a business owner might consciously adopt a policy of full cooperation with regulatory officials. See also *United States v. J.B. Kramer Grocery Co.*, 418 F.2d 987 (8th Cir.1969) (voluntary consent to inspection obviates need for warrant, but whether consent was given is issue for trier of fact); *Stephenson Enterprises, Inc. v. Marshall*, 578 F.2d 1021 (5th Cir.1978). In *Weyerhaeuser Co. v. Marshall*, 592 F.2d 373 (7th Cir.1979), the court of appeals held that an employer who had consented "under protest" to an

OSHA inspection conducted pursuant to a warrant had preserved his right later to challenge the warrant's validity.

In *Wyman v. James*, 400 U.S. 309 (1971), the notion of "consent" to inspections that are an integral part of a governmental regulatory scheme took root in a different context. Mrs. James, who received welfare payments on behalf of her son under the Aid to Families with Dependent Children program, was stricken from New York's list of eligible recipients after she declined to allow her caseworker to conduct a home visit without a warrant. In a curious opinion by Justice Blackmun, the Court paid homage to *Camara*'s interpretation of the Fourth Amendment but found its teachings inapplicable to this case:

> This natural and quite proper protective attitude, however, is not a factor in this case, for the seemingly obvious and simple reason that we are not concerned here with any search by the New York social service agency in the Fourth Amendment meaning of that term. It is true that the governing statute and regulations appear to make mandatory the initial home visit and the subsequent periodic "contacts" (which may include home visits) for the inception and continuance of aid. It is also true that the caseworker's posture in the home visit is perhaps, in a sense, both rehabilitative and investigative. But this latter aspect, we think is given too broad a character and far more emphasis than it deserves if it is equated with a search in the traditional criminal law context. We note, too, that the visitation in itself is not forced or compelled, and that the beneficiary's denial of permission is not a criminal act. If consent to the visitation is withheld, no visitation takes place. The aid then never begins or merely ceases, as the case may be. There is no entry of the home and there is no search.

Assuming, *arguendo*, that the home visit, "despite its interview nature, does possess some of the characteristics of a search," Justice Blackmun held that it "does not descend to the level of unreasonableness." Its objective was to protect the interests of the child and assure proper expenditure of aid provided by the state which, as a donor of charity, was entitled to a "gentle means, of limited extent and of practical and considerate application, of achieving that assurance." Furthermore, Mrs. James had advance notice of the visit, could adjust its timing, and offered "no specific complaint of any unreasonable intrusion of her home. * * *."

Justice Douglas, dissenting, viewed the case as one in which the state had attempted to "buy up" the constitutional rights of persons dependent on public largesse. While the home visit had benevolent as well as investigatory objectives, it clearly represented governmental invasion of the "sanctity of the sanctuary of the *home*" and should not escape the requirements of the Fourth Amendment.

Professor Burt was not persuaded by the Court's reasons for refusing to require a warrant for welfare home visitations:

> The beneficent purposes of this compulsory visit—either on behalf of the resisting parent or her child—do not necessarily establish the inapplicability of the Fourth Amendment search warrant requirement. * * * As Justice Marshall stated in his *Wyman* dissent, the housing code program in *Camara* was potentially beneficial for the inspected homeowner as well as for his neighbors, who were necessarily affected by the condition of his house. *Camara* cannot be distinguished on this ground from the welfare home visit. Nor can *Camara* be convincingly distinguished from *Wyman* on the ground that the sanction available for refusal to permit housing inspector access, though formally labeled a "criminal" penalty, was more onerous than the total loss of support threatened in *Wyman*. * * *

Robert A. Burt, *Forcing Protection on Children and Their Parents: The Impact of* Wyman v. James, 69 Mich.L.Rev. 1259, 1302 (1971).

Are the premises that underlie an administrative system of warrant-based searches less compatible with programs of public assistance than with the activities of building or fire or health inspectors? If the Court had insisted in *Wyman v. James* that warrants were required for visitations, the welfare agency would have been required to meet some standard of "probable cause." If the primary purpose of its visits was to assure the proper use of public funds, then arguably it would be reasonable to issue a warrant simply on a showing that the target household is receiving such funds. If the primary purpose of its visits was to protect children against abuse and deprivation, then it might be difficult to defend any probable cause standard that would give the agency greater access to the homes of welfare recipients than the government generally has to the homes of families not receiving public assistance.

It would be exceedingly difficult in a public assistance context to assess the consensual nature of warrantless visits. Dependency on public assistance may engender an effective compulsion always to cooperate fully with welfare officials. Applying the standard of "knowing and voluntary waiver" in such a setting is problematic. See generally Joel F. Handler, *Controlling Official Behavior in Welfare Administration*, 54 Calif.L.Rev. 479 (1966).

On the general subject of "unconstitutional conditions" and the doctrine's utility (or lack of it) for assessing such issues as the fairness of conditioning public assistance on warrantless access to the home, see Kathleen Sullivan, *Unconstitutional Conditions*, 102 Harv.L.Rev. 1413 (1989); Richard A. Epstein, *Foreward: Unconstitutional Conditions, State Power and the Limits of Consent*, 102 Harv.L.Rev. 4 (1988); Cass Sunstein, *Why the Unconstitutional Conditions Doctrine is an Anachronism (With Particular Reference to Religion, Speech, and Abortion)*, 70 B.U.L.Rev. 593 (1990).

"Pervasively Regulated" Businesses After *Barlow's*

Just three years after *Barlow's*, *Donovan v. Dewey*, 452 U.S. 594 (1981), confronted the Court with the challenge to section 103(a) of the Federal Mine Safety and Health Act, the inspection provision that the dissenters in *Barlow's* had forecast the majority's approach would jeopardize. But *Dewey* confounded their prediction. Section 103(a) resembles the provision of the OSH Act struck down in *Barlow's*, expressly authorizing unannounced, warrantless inspections of "any coal or other mine" and permitting imposition of civil penalties for denial or entry. Douglas Dewey had refused entry to a federal mine inspector who sought to inspect his stone quarry without a search warrant. The Secretary of Labor proposed a civil penalty of $1000, upheld by an administrative law judge, and brought suit to enjoin Dewey from refusing to permit warrantless inspections of the quarry. The district court granted summary judgment against the government, holding that section 103(a) violated the Fourth Amendment.

Writing for the Court, Justice Marshall read *Barlow's* narrowly and found that the Mine Safety Act's authorization of warrantless inspections fell within the *Biswell–Colonnade* line of authority (452 U.S. at 602–06):

> * * * As an initial matter, it is undisputed that there is a substantial federal interest in improving the health and safety conditions in the Nation's underground and surface mines. In enacting the statute, Congress was plainly aware that the mining industry is among the most hazardous in the country and that the poor health and safety record of this industry has significant deleterious effects on interstate commerce. Nor is it seriously contested that Congress in this case could reasonably determine, as it did with respect to the Gun Control Act in *Biswell*, that a system of warrantless inspections was necessary "if the law is to be properly enforced and inspection made effective." In designing an inspection program, Congress expressly recognized that a warrant requirement could significantly frustrate effective enforcement of the Act. * * * We see no reason not to defer to this legislative determination. * * *
>
> Because a warrant requirement clearly might impede the "specific enforcement needs" of the Act, the only real issue before us is whether the statute's inspection program, in terms of the certainty and regularity of its application, provides a constitutionally adequate substitute for a warrant. We believe that it does. Unlike the statute at issue in *Barlow's*, the Mine Safety and Health Act applies to industrial activity with a notorious history of serious accidents and unhealthful working conditions. The Act is specifically tailored to address those concerns, and the regulation of mines it imposes is sufficiently pervasive and defined that the owner of such a facility cannot help but be aware that he "will be subject to effective inspection." First, the Act requires inspection of *all* mines and specifically defines the frequency of inspection. * * * Second, the

standards with which a mine operator is required to comply are all specifically set forth in the Act or in Title 30 of the Code of Federal Regulations. * * * Thus, rather than leaving the frequency and purpose of inspections to the unchecked discretion of Government officers, the Act establishes a predictable and guided federal regulatory presence. * * *

Finally, the Act provides a specific mechanism for accommodating any special privacy concerns that a specific mine operator might have. The Act prohibits forcible entries, and instead requires the Secretary, when refused entry into a mining facility, to file a civil action in federal court to obtain an injunction against future refusals. This proceeding provides an adequate forum for the mine owner to show that a specific search is outside the federal regulatory authority, or to seek from the district court an order accommodating any unusual privacy interests that the mine owner might have. * * *

* * * [I]t is the pervasiveness and regularity of the federal regulation that ultimately determines whether a warrant is necessary to render an inspection program reasonable under the Fourth Amendment. * * * Of course, the duration of a particular regulatory scheme will often be an important factor in determining whether it is sufficiently pervasive to make the imposition of a warrant requirement unnecessary. But if the length of regulation were the only criterion, absurd results would occur. Under appellees' view, new or emerging industries, including ones such as the nuclear power industry that pose enormous potential safety and health problems, could never be subject to warrantless searches even under the most carefully structured inspection program simply because of the recent vintage of regulation.

The Fourth Amendment's central concept of reasonableness will not tolerate such arbitrary results, and we therefore conclude that warrantless inspection of stone quarries, like similar inspections of other mines covered by the Act, are constitutionally permissible. * * *

A bemused Justice Stevens agreed with the majority that the present case was distinguishable from *Barlow's* and thus found it unnecessary to "confront the more difficult question whether *Camara* represented such a fundamental misreading of the Fourth Amendment that it should be overruled." Justice Stewart, a member of the majority in *Frank* and of the minority in *Camara*, felt compelled to dissent:

> I must * * * accept the law as it is, and the law is now established that administrative inspections are searches within the meaning of the Fourth Amendment. As such, warrantless administrative inspections of private property without consent, are, like other searches, constitutionally invalid except in a few precisely defined circumstances. * * *

> * * * [A]s explained in *Barlow's*, the *Colonnade–Biswell* exception is a single and narrow one: the exception applies to businesses that are both pervasively regulated *and* have a long history of regulation. Today the Court conveniently discards the latter portion of the exception. Yet the very rationale for the exception—that the "businessman * * * in effect consents to the restrictions placed upon him"—disappears without it. It can hardly be said that a businessman consents to restrictions on his business when those restrictions are not imposed until *after* he has entered the business. * * *
>
> As I read today's opinion, Congress is left free to avoid the Fourth Amendment industry by industry even though the Court held in *Barlow's* that Congress could not avoid that Amendment all at once. Congress after today can define any industry as dangerous, regulate it substantially, and provide for warrantless inspections of its members. * * *

The Supreme Court's erratic treatment of warrantless administrative searches was continued in *New York v. Burger*, 482 U.S. 691 (1987), which involved New York's statute regulating automobile junkyards. A 1979 amendment specifically authorized warrantless inspections to determine compliance with the law's requirements. In the course of such an inspection, to which Burger did not at the time object, New York police officers discovered stolen vehicles and parts. Burger was subsequently prosecuted for possession of stolen property and unregistered operation as a vehicle dismantler.

Writing for the majority, Justice Blackmun held that the New York regulatory and inspection scheme fell within the exception to the warrant requirement the Court had recognized in *Biswell* and *Donovan v. Dewey*. Though recent in origin—because automobile usage and dismantling are relatively recent activities—New York's statute, like others elsewhere, established that the operation of a junkyard devoted to automobile dismantling has become a "closely regulated business." The rise in motor vehicle theft and its association with the dismantling business provided New York ample justification to regulate dismantlers' activities. Further, the state's statute put operators on notice that inspections would be made, described their scope, and specified who could conduct them. The statute reflected reasonable regulatory goals of ensuring that vehicle dismantlers are legitimate business operators and that stolen vehicles or parts that pass through junkyards can be identified.

Justice Brennan, in an opinion joined by Justice Marshall and, in part, by Justice O'Connor, objected to the majority's facile extension of *Biswell* and *Donovan*. He thought it preposterous to characterize vehicle dismantling as a "closely regulated business:"

> The provisions governing vehicle dismantling in New York simply are not extensive. A vehicle dismantler must register and pay a fee, display the registration in various circumstances, maintain a

> police book, and allow inspections. Of course, the inspections themselves cannot be cited as proof of pervasive regulation justifying elimination of the warrant requirement; that would be obvious bootstrapping. * * * New York City, like many States and municipalities, imposes similar, and often more stringent licensing, recordkeeping, and other regulatory requirements on a myriad of trades and businesses. Few substantive qualifications are required of an aspiring vehicle dismantler; no regulation governs the condition of the premises, the method of operation, the hours of operation, the equipment utilized, etc. This scheme stands in marked contrast to, e.g., the mine safety regulations relevant in *Dewey*.
>
> In sum, if New York City's administrative scheme renders the vehicle-dismantling business closely regulated, few businesses will escape such a finding.

And Brennan found in New York's statute virtually no restrictions on how or when warrantless inspections could be conducted. Justice Marshall alone joined in his conclusion that the "fundamental defect" of the New York scheme was that "it authorizes searches intended solely to uncover evidence of criminal acts."

> [O]n the Court's reasoning, administrative inspections would evade the requirements of the Fourth Amendment so long as they served an abstract administrative goal, such as the prevention of automobile theft. A legislature cannot abrogate constitutional protections simply by saying that the purpose of an administrative search scheme is to prevent a certain type of crime. If the Fourth Amendment is to retain meaning in the commercial context, it must be applied to searches for evidence of criminal acts even if those searches would also serve an administrative purpose, unless that administrative purpose takes the concrete form of seeking an administrative violation.

Notes

1. *Warrantless Searches—Generally*. The varied contexts of administrative searches and inspections may make development of a coherent jurisprudence impossible—or at least unlikely. In contexts other than those we have already encountered, the Court has followed a wavering line between demands for warrant protection and claims of administrative necessity.

Another "exception" was recognized only eight days after the decision in *Barlow's*. In *Michigan v. Tyler*, 436 U.S. 499 (1978), the Court sustained the right of fire fighters engaged in combatting a fire to conduct contemporaneous searches of the smoldering premises to determine the cause of the blaze. Except in such "emergencies," however, a warrant would be required for either routine inspections to monitor fire hazards or after-the-event investigations into the causes of fires already extinguished.

Several cases have upheld the validity of warrantless searches of airplane passengers and visitors to federal office buildings. See, e.g., *United*

States v. Davis, 482 F.2d 893, 908 (9th Cir.1973): "The essence of these decisions [of the Supreme Court] is that searches conducted as part of a general regulatory scheme in furtherance of an administrative purpose, rather than as part of a criminal investigation to secure evidence of crime, may be permissible under the Fourth Amendment though not supported by a showing of probable cause directed to a particular place or person to be searched." See also *Barrett v. Kunzig*, 331 F.Supp. 266 (M.D.Tenn.1971), *cert. denied*, 409 U.S. 914 (1972).

By contrast, in *Almeida–Sanchez v. United States*, 413 U.S. 266 (1973), the Supreme Court invalidated a warrantless Border Patrol search conducted under the authority of a federal statute and regulations permitting warrantless automobile stops and searches within 100 air miles of the border. But three years later, in *United States v. Martinez–Fuerte*, 428 U.S. 543 (1976), the Court upheld the INS practice of routinely stopping vehicles at fixed checkpoints in California and Texas near the Mexican border. The Court stressed the limited discretion accorded to the inspecting officers, which justified confidence in the control exercised by INS headquarters officials as a safeguard against abuse.

2. *Warrantless Searches—Open Spaces*. There is a reasonably well-established exception to the warrant requirement for observations that are made without intrusion onto private property or into work or business areas that have some plausible claim to privacy. In *Air Pollution Variance Board v. Western Alfalfa Corp.*, 416 U.S. 861, 864–65 (1974), the Court sustained the warrantless visual inspection of the smoke being emitted from the respondent's chimneys. To take a visual reading of the respondent's emissions a Colorado health inspector came onto the respondent's property without its knowledge or consent. His findings later supported the board's conclusion that the respondent was violating applicable air quality standards. Justice Douglas' opinion held that *Camara* and *See* were not applicable:

> The field inspector did not enter the plant or offices. He was not inspecting stakes, boilers, scrubbers, flues, grates, or furnaces; nor was his inspection related to respondent's files or papers. He had sighted what anyone in the city who was near the plant could see in the sky—plumes of smoke. * * * The field inspector was on respondent's property but we are not advised that he was on premises from which the public was excluded. * * * The invasion of privacy * * *, if it can be said to exist, is abstract and theoretical.

See also *Stephenson Enterprises, Inc. v. Marshall*, 578 F.2d 1021, 1024 n. 2 (5th Cir.1978).

Dow Chemical Co. v. United States, 476 U.S. 227 (1986), presented a high-tech variant of the facts in *Western Alfalfa*. After Dow officials had declined EPA's request to inspect its 2000–acre Midland production facility, the agency, instead of seeking a warrant, employed a commercial aerial photographer to fly over the area and take photographs. The photographer used a conventional aerial mapping camera, capable of recording features that the naked human eye could not detect. When Dow became aware of EPA's surveillance it brought suit for an injunction, claiming that it was both unauthorized and violative of the Fourth Amendment.

A bare majority of the Supreme Court upheld the EPA's observations, concluding that they did not amount to a search. The majority recognized that the case fell somewhere between the facts of *Oliver v. United States*, 466 U.S. 170 (1984), which held that an individual could not claim any expectation of privacy in "open fields," and precedents protecting the privacy of the curtilage of a dwelling. It concluded, however, that Dow's "industrial complex is more comparable to an open field and as such it is open to the view and observation of persons in aircraft lawfully in the public airspace immediately above or sufficiently near the area for the reach of cameras." The majority stressed that the photographer had used only standard aerial mapping equipment, rather than some highly advanced technology. "It may well be * * * that surveillance of private property by using highly sophisticated surveillance equipment not generally available to the public, such as satellite technology, might be constitutionally proscribed absent a warrant. But the photographs here are not so revealing of intimate details as to raise constitutional concerns."

Three Justices joined in a dissenting opinion by Justice Powell, who rejected the majority's suggestion that the Court's precedents established that occupants of commercial property have less expectation of privacy than householders.

> Rather, the exception [allowing Congress to prescribe warrantless inspections of regulated business establishments] is based on a determination that the reasonable expectation of privacy that the owner of a business does enjoy may be adequately protected by the regulatory scheme itself. * * * [A]bsent a sufficiently defined and regular program of warrantless inspections, the Fourth Amendment's warrant requirement is fully applicable in the commercial complex.

3. *Warrantless Searches and High Technology.* In his *Dow Chemical* dissent, Justice Powell not only stressed Dow's efforts to protect its commercial privacy, but went out of his way to describe the sophistication and acuity of the photographic methods used here. "For nearly twenty years, this Court has adhered to a standard that ensured that Fourth Amendment rights would retain their vitality as technology expanded the Government's capacity to commit unsuspected intrusions into private areas and activities." The majority's ruling, Powell predicted, "will not protect Fourth Amendment rights, but rather will permit their gradual decay as technology advances." If Justice Powell were correct, then the Court would, in essence, be turning its back on *Katz v. United States*, 389 U.S. 347 (1967), the seminal decision in which the Court held that the use of electronic wiretapping amounted to a search under circumstances where the target of the search had, in the circumstances presented, "an expectation of privacy that society is prepared to recognize as reasonable."

So far, however, the Court has not abandoned *Katz*. In *Kyllo v. United States*, 533 U.S. 27 (2001), the defendant in a prosecution for manufacturing marijuana was initially unsuccessful in challenging the warrantless use of thermal imaging equipment to find probable cause for a subsequent physically intrusive search of his home. Kyllo argued to the district court that the thermal imaging was itself a search that required such cause. In this case, Department of the Interior agents, who suspected he was growing marijuana in his home, knew that "[i]ndoor marijuana growth typically requires high-intensity lamps." They used a thermal imager, which detects infrared radiation, to scan Kyllo's apartment complex from the street. The scan showed two areas of the house substantially warmer than the rest of his house, as well as his neighbor's homes. A federal magistrate issued a search warrant of the interior of the house based on tips from informants, Kyllo's utility bills, and the thermal imaging. The Supreme Court reversed:

> While it may be difficult to refine *Katz* when the search of areas such as telephone booths, automobiles, or even the curtilage and uncovered portions of residences is at issue, in the case of the search of the interior of homes—the prototypical and hence most commonly litigated area of protected privacy—there is a ready criterion, with roots deep in the common law, of the minimal expectation of privacy that *exists*, and that is acknowledged to be reasonable. To withdraw protection of this minimum expectation would be to permit police technology to erode the privacy guaranteed by the Fourth Amendment. We think that obtaining by sense-enhancing technology any information regarding the interior of the home that could not otherwise have been obtained without physical "intrusion into a constitutionally protected area," constitutes a search—at least where (as here) the technology in question is not in general public use.

4. *Warrantless Searches—Public Schools*. Public education has provided another important context for the development of law concerning warrantless administrative searches. In *New Jersey v. T.L.O.*, 469 U.S. 325 (1985), the Court reviewed a challenge by a student whose principal (with the Dickensian name of Mr. Choplick) had discovered marijuana in her purse. The principal searched the purse for cigarettes after a teacher reported personally observing the student smoking in violation of school rules. Upon opening the purse, the principal saw rolling papers in plain view, which triggered a more thorough inspection of the purse, which, in turn, produced the marijuana and drug paraphernalia.

The Supreme Court held that school children have sufficient legitimate expectations of privacy, notwithstanding the peculiar custodial nature of the school environment, to render the Fourth Amendment applicable to public schools. Nonetheless, because of school authorities' special interest in maintaining a swift and informal disciplinary process, the Court held the warrant clause inapplicable to student searches conducted without police involvement. Furthermore, the Court said, school officials needed only a "reasonable suspicion," not probable cause to justify a search. Student searches must be reasonable at their inception, that is, based on reasonable grounds to believe that the search will uncover evidence of a school rule violation, and must be reasonable in scope and method, that is, "reasonably related to the objectives of the search and not excessively intrusive in light of the age and sex of the student and the nature of the infraction."

Justice Brennan dissented from the majority's lowering of the probable cause standard on the ground that its incremental burden on school authorities had not been shown to justify the relaxation of constitutional protections. Justice Stevens regarded the particular search in *T.L.O.* as unreasonable because the purse search was based only on a hunch, the infraction was not serious, the possession of cigarettes would not have proven illicit smoking, and the privacy invasion was significant.

Many earlier cases had anticipated *T.L.O.'s* reasonableness standard, and the case law regarding the reasonableness of targeting particular students for search is fairly extensive. See, e.g., *Cason v. Cook*, 810 F.2d 188 (8th Cir.1987); *Cales v. Howell Public Schools*, 635 F.Supp. 454 (E.D.Mich. 1985); *Bilbrey by Bilbrey v. Brown*, 738 F.2d 1462 (9th Cir.1984). Lower courts, however, had split prior to *T.L.O.* on the applicability of the Fourth Amendment to student locker searches. *State v. Engerud*, 94 N.J. 331, 463 A.2d 934 (1983), held the Fourth Amendment applicable to a locker search because a student's locker is his or her "home away from home," and the existence of a master key no more vitiates a student's expectation of privacy in a locker than such a key eliminates a guest's privacy expectation in a hotel room. The Supreme Court's similar reasoning in a subsequent case involving the search of a public employee's office, desk, and filing cabinets supports the result in *Engerud*. *O'Connor v. Ortega*, 480 U.S. 709 (1987). But see *Zamora v. Pomeroy*, 639 F.2d 662 (10th Cir.1981).

In *Vernonia School District 47J v. Acton*, 515 U.S. 646 (1995), the Court extended *T.L.O.* to uphold a public school district's random urinalysis requirement for participation in interscholastic athletics. The Court relied on the following theory of consent in concluding that student-athletes have a reduced expectation of privacy: "By choosing to 'go out for the team,' they voluntarily subject themselves to a degree of regulation even higher than that imposed on students generally." 515 U.S. at 657. In the jurisprudence of warrantless searches, context, indeed, is everything because the Supreme Court did not regard the reduced expectation of privacy held by political candidates for high office to be sufficient justification for subjecting them to drug testing. *Chandler v. Miller*, 520 U.S. 305 (1997). The Court deemed the prospect of drug users holding high state office not to present a sufficiently "concrete danger demanding departure from the Fourth Amendment's main rule." 520 U.S. at 319. Compare *National Treasury Employees Union v. Von Raab*, 489 U.S. 656 (1989) (upholding a Customs Service drug-testing program for employees who apply for promotion to positions involving the interdiction of illegal drugs or requiring them to carry firearms or handle classified materials).

5. *Multiple–Use Searches.* The permissible seepage into criminal law enforcement of evidence obtained pursuant to civil investigative standards—an issue addressed by the Supreme Court with regard to subpoenas in *United States v. LaSalle National Bank*, discussed *supra*, at p. 651—has taken on special significance with regard to physical searches in light of intensified government efforts to obtain so-called "foreign intelligence information." "Foreign intelligence information," with regard to American citizens, is defined by statute as information that is "necessary to the ability of the United States to protect against" attacks, grave hostile acts, sabotage, international terrorism, or clandestine intelligence activities by "a foreign power or by an agent of a foreign power." 50 U.S.C. § 403–5d(2). When Congress first enacted a statutory procedure for securing warrants to support foreign intelligence searches, it was concerned entirely with electronic surveillance—not usually a tool of civil law enforcement. Foreign Intelligence Surveillance Act of 1978 (FISA), Pub.L. 95–511, 92 Stat. 1783. Nonetheless,

consistent with the evolving doctrine on administrative warrants, Congress adopted a standard for FISA searches more expansive than the probable cause requirement applicable to criminal searches, requiring only that a proposed search be targeted at foreign intelligence information. 18 U.S.C. § 1804. Also, and yet more creatively, it chartered a unique and largely secret judicial tribunal, the Foreign Intelligence Surveillance Court, to adjudicate FISA warrant applications. Congress extended the jurisdiction of that court to the authorization of physical searches in 1994. See 50 U.S.C. § 1822. In 2001, Congress created authority to seek subpoenas targeting "books, records, papers, documents, and other items" related to a United States person if necessary "to protect against international terrorism or clandestine intelligence activities." 50 U.S.C. § 1861.

Although FISA does not address the matter, the Foreign Intelligence Surveillance Court—presumably recognizing its extraordinary procedural character—sought for over twenty years to prevent the Justice Department from using its FISA search authority to expand its conduct of criminal investigations. In 2002, however, following the enactment of the Uniting and Strengthening America by Providing Appropriate Tools Required to Intercept and Obstruct Terrorism (USA PATRIOT) Act, Pub. L. 107–56, 115 Stat. 272 (2001), Attorney General John Ashcroft issued regulations permitting the Department's Criminal Division to direct intelligence cases and to seek authority pursuant to FISA to conduct intelligence searches that might also be useful for criminal prosecution. Although the Foreign Intelligence Surveillance Court initially rejected the regulations as impermissibly blending intelligence and criminal investigatory purposes, the Foreign Intelligence Surveillance Court of Review—in a rare opinion (and, uniquely, a public opinion overturning the lower court)—upheld the regulations and rebuked the FISA court generally for questioning the permissibility of using intelligence searches for criminal law enforcement purposes. *In re Sealed Case*, 310 F.3d 717 (Foreign Int.Surv.Ct.Rev.2002).

B. ACCESS TO INFORMATION HELD BY THE FEDERAL GOVERNMENT

Its broad demands on private individuals and organizations to keep records and submit reports has made the federal government a vast depository of information that is potentially of interest to third parties. Furthermore, the government itself creates information—through its own numerous investigatory activities and by manipulating data obtained from private parties—that also excites curiosity. Perhaps of greatest general interest is information about the activities and plans of government administrators themselves: What issues are before them? What arguments are they hearing and from whom? What staff advice are they receiving? What small part of the files assembled by subordinates are they exposed to? When are they planning to act? Access to information about the deliberations of government officials has value for individuals and businesses whose affairs will be affected by the decisions to be made. For organs of the press, it is key to their functioning, both in the competitive world of the commercial media and in the world of politics, where their performance is believed important to our system of self-government.

But public access to information in government hands, even, perhaps especially, information about what officials are planning, may not always be desirable. We all would probably acknowledge that there is a core of facts about the operations of the military that should be secret, though we might differ about its dimensions. Most would concede that law enforcement authorities should be entitled, at least for a time, to conduct investigations in confidence. And recalling that much—indeed perhaps the majority—of the information in government hands comes from private individuals and organizations, we would stipulate that some of it ought not be routinely available to third parties, either at all or at least without notice to the provider. The protections accorded by the Fourth and Fifth Amendments for interests in privacy and autonomy suggest that government should not become the automatic transfer agent for all information that it obtains from private sources.

In this section, we shall explore the legal doctrines governing private access to information that the government obtains or creates, including the limitations on such access that are intended to protect interests in commercial secrecy and personal privacy.

1. CLAIMS TO ACCESS TO GOVERNMENT INFORMATION

The circumstances under which, and purposes for which, a person may wish to obtain information in the possession of the government are virtually limitless. Nevertheless, it is instructive to categorize the circumstances and purposes which have predominated in claims of right to government information. First are claims asserted for the purpose of preparing for or engaging in contested legal proceedings. A second category consists of attempts to gain access to the deliberations of public agencies and officials for the purpose of overseeing public decision making. A final, residual group of claims to access might be characterized as "proprietary"—claims inspired by the desire to obtain for commercial, academic, or other purposes generally useful information in the government's possession. While not prominent in litigation, this final group of claims makes up the bulk of the requests to agencies for information. A particular demand for information may, and often does, fit into more than one category, but the legal principles traditionally applicable to each category are quite distinct.

Claims of access for purposes of contested legal proceedings have traditionally been governed by the procedural rules regulating discovery and by limitations on the government's ability to enforce regulatory requirements without adequate disclosure of their factual and judgmental bases. Thus, the ability of a litigant to obtain official material, whether for purposes of litigation with the government, e.g., *United States v. Reynolds*, 345 U.S. 1 (1953), or with a third party, e.g., *Carl Zeiss Stiftung v. V. E. B. Carl Zeiss, Jena*, 40 F.R.D. 318 (D.D.C.1966), *affirmed per curiam*, 384 F.2d 979 (D.C.Cir.1967), *cert. denied*, 389 U.S.

952 (1967), has depended upon general federal rules governing discovery in civil or criminal litigation. These rules customarily require the courts to balance the claimant's need for the information against the consequences of disclosure for the government and are enforced through the traditional modes of subpoenas and interlocutory orders. Similarly, discovery in administrative adjudication has been governed by agency rules of procedure. See generally Edward A. Tomlinson, *Discovery in Agency Adjudication*, 1971 Duke L.J. 89. Although under common discovery practices not all potentially relevant factual material need be made available at trial, when it is a party to formal proceedings the government will be required to choose between exposing its evidence to rebuttal and cross-examination and risking a failure to prove its case. *Wirtz v. Baldor Electric Co.*, 337 F.2d 518 (D.C.Cir.1963). Moreover, the government may not enforce or rely upon secret law—regulatory requirements that are not published or filed as required by law.

Claims for access to government information for purposes of contested legal proceedings thus have two dominant characteristics: (1) a relatively limited set of circumstances gives rise to requests for disclosure, and (2) reasonably well-developed procedural rules govern the degree to which disclosure may be required and determine the legal consequences of non-disclosure.

The second category of claims embraces a somewhat less cohesive set of what we term "oversight" demands and is subject to an evolving set of legal principles. In terms of applicable legal doctrine, a major subset of these claims involves requirements for disclosure of the factual basis and rationale for official decisions in order to facilitate judicial review. These claims invoke the familiar "findings" requirement applicable to formal administrative proceedings or the requirement that the complete administrative record be disclosed to a court called upon to determine whether there is adequate support for an administrative determination. Such claims are, of course, subject to limitations on court review, such as the judicial reluctance to inquire into the internal decision processes of an agency or official.

Another type of oversight claim is represented by legislative demands for information from executive officers relating to the latter's areas of administrative responsibility. Here the applicable legal principles include only the negligible limitations on the legislative power of investigation, see, e.g., Ernest J. Eberling, Congressional Investigations: A Study of the Origin and Development of the Power of Congress to Investigate and Punish for Contempt (1928, reprinted 1973); John C. Grabow, Congressional Investigations: Law and Practice (1988), and the amorphous doctrine of "executive privilege"—that is, the asserted right of the executive branch to treat as confidential information relating to state secrets, disclosures of informers, and internal processes of policy formation. See discussion *infra* pp. 736–739.

Finally, there are claims by private persons for access either to the decision process itself or to the documents that support and explain formulated policy. To the extent that such claims do not relate to contested proceedings and are not asserted in aid of judicial review, they are premised on statutes requiring that certain decision processes be carried on in "public," see Government in the Sunshine Act, 5 U.S.C. § 552b; Note, *Open Meeting Statutes: The Press Fights For The "Right to Know,"* 75 Harv.L.Rev. 1199 (1962), or that agency records be available to persons requesting access to them.

The unifying feature of oversight claims is that they relate to fundamental aspects of the American constitutional system—judicial review of administrative action, separation of powers, mutual checks and balances in the constitutional order—and to the democratic ideal of an informed and vigilant electorate.

"Proprietary claims," our catch-all third category, have no strong foundation in prior law. Prior to the Freedom of Information Act, the individual citizen had no distinct property interest in government information, nor do First Amendment freedoms to disseminate or to receive information voluntarily transmitted imply a right to obtain information from the government over its protest. See generally Lillian R. BeVier, *An Informed Public, an Informing Press: The Search for a Constitutional Principle*, 68 Calif.L.Rev. 482 (1980); Note, *The Rights of the Public and the Press to Gather Information*, 87 Harv.L.Rev. 1505 (1974). That information in the government's possession might be useful to private parties for myriad social, economic, and intellectual purposes is no doubt true, but we would not ordinarily expect the mere desire to obtain information in another's possession to be translated into a legal right of access without some firm policy basis for honoring the claim. Nevertheless, the Freedom of Information Act (hereafter sometimes "FOIA"), 5 U.S.C. § 552, by eliminating any requirement that a person requesting government information show why it should be made available, seems to place proprietary claims on the same footing as claims growing out of formal legal proceedings and claims relating to oversight activities. For a forceful demonstration of this point, see *U.S. Department of Justice v. Tax Analysts*, 492 U.S. 136 (1989), requiring the Justice Department to make available to the publisher of a weekly tax service copies of all district court tax decisions that the Department receives. The Department argued unsuccessfully that it was not required to bear the burden of making available already public documents Tax Analysts could—and had previously—sought from the district courts themselves. The Court was unwilling to infer an exemption for agency information already available from other sources, because of both the FOIA's specific wording and the volume of litigation the Court thought such an exemption would invite.

The apparent anomaly of the FOIA's treatment of strong and weak claims as legal equivalents is readily explicable: It is often difficult to determine the true or primary purpose of requests for government information. Moreover, Congress was convinced that the existing disclosure provisions of the APA were used by bureaucrats to shield most of their activities from effective citizen oversight. To avoid abusive nondisclosure, therefore, Congress provided a means of access to government information which cut across analytically distinct categories of requests and which, by its very breadth, has become the standard against which any claim for information (with the possible exception of requests from Congress, see 5 U.S.C. § 552(c)) may ultimately be judged.

2. THE FEDERAL FREEDOM OF INFORMATION ACT

The FOIA, 5 U.S.C. § 552, deals both with "secret law" and with the much larger universe of government documents or records that lack legal force. Section 552(a) restates the Federal Register Act's requirements for agency publication of organization, procedures, and general rules or policies, and it further requires that decisions, statements of policy and interpretation, and staff manuals containing instructions affecting the public shall be indexed and made available for public inspection and copying. Failure to comply with these subsections precludes agency reliance on the unpublished or unavailable materials save with respect to a person who otherwise has actual and timely notice of them. Subsection (3) then provides that agencies shall, on request by any person in accordance with agency rules governing such requests, make available all other "identifiable records." This obligation is enforceable by expedited suit in a federal district court, in which the recalcitrant agency has the burden of justifying its refusal. Paragraph (b) of section 552 exempts nine categories of records from the reach of paragraph (a), and paragraph (c) limits agency authority to withhold information to those exemptions "specifically stated."

Passage of the FOIA gave rise to two contrasting fears. Critics argued that the elimination of any necessity for showing "good cause" or even a "lawful purpose" for a request, combined with an exhaustive listing of exemptions, would prevent courts and agencies from making sound equitable judgments in particular cases concerning the balance of benefits over costs of disclosure. They predicted that the FOIA would result in burdensome fishing expeditions that would fail to promote—and perhaps hinder—sensible public policy objectives. The contrasting fear was that the potential breadth of some of the exemptions, the grant of agency power to prescribe the form of requests and to set fees for disclosure, and the necessity of bringing suit to force disclosure would make the Act a paper tiger. For a relatively early assessment of these competing forecasts, see generally Note, *The Freedom of Information Act: A Seven–Year Assessment*, 74 Colum.L.Rev. 895 (1974).

In amendments to the Act in 1974 Congress displayed a preoccupation with strengthening the requirements for disclosure. For example, the amended Act (1) stipulates that a request need only "reasonably describe" desired documents, thus eliminating the requirement that a request be for "identifiable documents," (2) directs that agencies, except in "unusual circumstances," respond to requests for documents within ten days by stating whether they intend to comply with the request, (3) authorizes the award of attorneys' fees to successful private litigants, and (4) requires a disciplinary investigation of any employee found by a court to have acted arbitrarily and capriciously in withholding information. See Pub.L.No. 93–502, 88 Stat. 1561 (1974).

Attempts to quantify the cost and utility of an enterprise as vast as federal information management—or even the role in that process of the FOIA—are bound to be controversial. The House Report on the 1974 amendments to the FOIA predicted that the additional government-wide costs of program administration entailed by the amendments were likely to be $50,000 in fiscal 1974 and $100,000 for each of the following five years. In fact, the annual cost of FOIA administration, apart from litigation costs, rose to roughly $50 million by the 1980s. This sum might be assessed either as a truly significant commitment or as a small fraction of the over $1 billion that the government spends annually to publish informational and promotional material for public consumption. See PETER HERNON & CHARLES R. MCCLURE, FEDERAL INFORMATION POLICIES IN THE 1980S: CONFLICTS AND ISSUES (1987).

In 1976, Congress amended one FOIA exemption to make it more difficult for another statute to be used as a basis for withholding information. Prior to 1976, 5 U.S.C. § 552(b)(3) exempted from mandatory disclosure any record "specifically exempted from disclosure by statute." As amended, the (b)(3) exemption is available only if the relevant statute mandates nondisclosure or "establishes particular criteria for withholding or refers to particular types of matters to be withheld."

The FOIA was amended yet again by the Freedom of Information Reform Act, a portion of the Anti–Drug Abuse Act of 1986, Pub.L.No. 99–570. The 1986 amendments changed the FOIA in two chief areas. Section 552(a)(4)(A), the provision regulating the fees agencies may charge requesters of records, now empowers the Office of Management and Budget to establish fee guidelines in accordance with stated criteria, and to prescribe a uniform fee schedule for all agencies. In addition, the amended act, for the first time, allows agencies to distinguish between requests for records for commercial use and other requests, and to charge commercial requesters fees for document search and review, as well as for duplication. A second cluster of amendments appears in section 552(b)(7), the so-called "law enforcement exemption," and in new section 552(c). These amendments were intended to make it easier for law enforcement agencies to deny requests for records whose disclosure could prejudice ongoing investigations or damage law enforcement activities generally. The 1986 amendments to the FOIA and their legislative history are analyzed in Note, *Developments under the Freedom of Information Act—1986*, 1987 Duke L.J. 521.

In 1996, Congress enacted the Electronic Freedom of Information Act Amendments of 1996, Pub.L.No. 104–231, 110 Stat. 3048, which, as the title suggests, dealt in part with the proliferation of electronic records since the original enactment of FOIA. The 1996 Amendments make clear that records covered by the Act include agency information maintained in an electronic format, and require that a request for information in a particular "form or format" (electronic or paper, for example) shall be honored if the record is "readily reproducible" in that "form or format." 5 U.S.C. § 552(a)(3)(B). Additionally, agencies are required to make available through computer telecommunications, wherever possible, any records they are required to make available for public inspection or copying.

The 1996 Amendments also sought to tackle the problem of agency delays in responding to FOIA requests. To help the agencies, Congress extended the originally prescribed 10–day response time to 20 days and authorized the promulgation of rules to establish "multitrack processing" for different types of requests. On the other hand, agencies are required to adopt regulations providing for the "expedited processing" of requests based on "compelling need" and "in other cases determined by the agency." Under 5 U.S.C. § 552(a)(5)(E)(v), "compelling need" exists when delay "could reasonably be expected to pose an imminent threat to the life or physical safety of an individual" or when the request is made by "a person primary engaged in disseminating information" and there is "urgency to inform the public" about some government activity. As amended, FOIA also limits the situations in which agencies may assert the existence of "unusual circumstances" justifying delayed responses to requests.

Perhaps unsurprisingly, in the wake of September 11, 2001, Congress reconsidered the general trend towards open access to government records. In enacting the Homeland Security Act of 2002, Congress provided that information voluntarily provided by non-federal parties to the newly created Department of Homeland Security would not be subject to public disclosure under the Freedom of Information Act if such information related to infrastructure vulnerabilities or other vulnerabilities to terrorism. Pub.L. 107–296, Title II, § 214, 116 Stat. 2152, codified at 6 U.S.C. § 133.

In the following excerpt, prepared for an international audience, Professor Glen Robinson provides what is still a cogent introduction to the structure of the FOIA:

G. ROBINSON, ACCESS TO GOVERNMENT INFORMATION: THE AMERICAN EXPERIENCE

14 Federal L.Rev. 35 (1983).

Section 3 [of the original APA] mandated publication of a variety of information about agency decision-making, except in a situation "requiring secrecy in the public interest." This provision for "secrecy in the public interest" permitted agency evasion of publication requirements. Secondly, s[ection] 3(b) required agencies to make available "all final opinions or orders in the adjudication of cases." But this requirement did not extend to opinions or orders "required for good cause to be held confidential." The vagueness with which this exception was phrased made it susceptible to inappropriate application. This same "good cause" language was repeated in s[ection] 3(c), which provided access to public records generally. These records were to be available to "persons properly and directly concerned except information held confidential for good cause found." In addition to the invitation to evasion presented by a "good cause" exception, this sub-section also provided another route to nondisclosure by allowing agencies to determine the standing of persons wishing access to information. A fourth weakness of s[ection] 3 was that it supplied no remedy to a citizen wrongfully denied access to information. The lack of any remedy made possible a too heavy reliance on the vague language of the section to withhold government records. * * *

* * * Eventually the Freedom of Information Bill passed through Congress virtually unopposed despite universal departmental hostility to its broad disclosure principles and its new remedy for requesters of information. Two groups allied to support passage of this law allowing public access to government information. Bar groups and other administrative reformers pressed for the Bill in order to secure publication of agency rules and opinions. These groups were joined by the press which pushed even harder for the FOI Act to gain access to more newsworthy documents disclosing agency activities. * * *

The new Act was revolutionary in its basic approach to the question of government disclosure and public access. The FOI Act established a broad norm of disclosure and access with relatively narrow exceptions. It removed all restrictions on who was entitled to information or the purpose for which it may be obtained. * * *

The coverage of the FOI Act is co-extensive with the Administrative Procedure Act itself and extends to virtually every executive department, bureau, agency or official, the Office of the President being a notable exception.[22] Congress and the courts are not agencies within the meaning of the APA and hence are not within the Act.

In general terms the Act imposes three distinct obligations with respect to disclosure of, or access to, agency records and information:

The first is to publish in the Federal Register descriptions of its organization; methods of operation; general substantive rules and policies; and rules of procedure.

The second is to make available for public inspection and copying, agency opinions and orders, statements of general policy and interpretation not published in the Federal Register, administrative staff manuals and staff instructions that affect a member of the public.

The third is to disclose agency records to any person who requests and reasonably describes such records. Agencies may charge reasonable fees for document search and duplication but are admonished to waive or

22. In *Kissinger v. Reporters Committee for Freedom of the Press*, 445 U.S. 136 (1980), the Court distinguished between the "Executive Office of the President" and the "Office of the President," the latter being limited to the President, his immediate personal staff and other executive office staff whose *sole* function is to advise the President. * * *

reduce fees where disclosure benefits the general public. * * * Judicial enforcement of the disclosure requirement is provided in the form of immediate *de novo* review of agency denials of disclosure requests; including *in camera* review of the documents requested where the court deems it necessary to determine their exempt status. * * *

Most of the attention and most of the controversy over the FOI Act has centered on the disclosure of agency records. Interpretive problems can be conveniently aggregated into two general categories: those specifically concerned with the scope of the nine exemptions, and those involving general issues of definition, implementation and enforcement. * * *

Exemption one embraces what is sometimes called "state secrets," in its narrowest sense: information required to be kept secret in the interest of national defense or foreign policy. As amended in 1974 the exemption is limited to information that is *properly* classified pursuant to Executive Order, which has been interpreted to permit judicial review of the substantive reasonableness as well as the procedural regularity of individual classifications.[39] For this purpose *in camera* examination of specific documents is authorised, but discretionary in the district court. Given the indefinite constitutional dimensions of executive privilege it remains uncertain how far courts may go in ordering disclosure of classified information. A similar ambiguity arises in connection with exemptions five (inter/intra agency memoranda) and seven (investigatory files) which also involve aspects of the executive privilege. * * *

Exemption three, covering all information which Congress in other statutes has required or permitted to be held confidential, also requires little attention. As amended in 1976 the exemption embraces only those statutes that are directed at the particular type of information in question or that specify particular criteria by which confidentiality shall be determined.[46] * * *

Exemption four, covering trade secrets and confidential commercial or financial information, has been among the most controversial of the nine exemptions. Unlike exemption three the number and variety of cases calling for interpretation is essentially open-ended. * * *

39. * * * As originally drafted, exemption one of the U.S. FOI Act was interpreted to preclude judicial review of the reasonableness of the classification. See *Environmental Protection Agency v. Mink*, 410 U.S. 73 (1973). The 1974 amendments overruled *Mink* and provided for *de novo* review of classifications and *in camera* scrutiny of documents themselves where necessary to determine the reasonableness of the classifications. See Attorney General's Memorandum on the 1974 Amendments to The Freedom of Information Act (1975) 1–4 ("Attorney General's Memorandum"). However, legislative history indicates that "*de novo* review" in this context requires courts to give "substantial weight" to an agency's affidavit concerning the details of the classified status of the disputed record.

46. The 1976 amendment, enacted as a rider to the Sunshine Act * * * was intended to overrule *Federal Aviation Administration v. Robertson*, 422 U.S. 255 (1975), where the Supreme Court construed the exemption to cover statutes that gave broad discretion to agencies to withhold documents. * * *

Exemption five, covering intra-agency and inter-agency memoranda and letters, was intended to incorporate the broad common law executive privilege for confidential internal communications. Unfortunately, the contours of that privilege have never been well defined, presenting substantial interpretive problems as to the scope of the exemption. * * *

Exemption six, protecting personnel and medical files whose disclosure would cause unwarranted invasion of personal privacy, is similar to exemption four in several respects. As with exemption four, the *primary* thrust of the exemption is to protect the interests of persons outside the agency about whom the information is pertinent (though in both cases the agency may have an interest in maintaining confidentiality as a means of protecting its ability to obtain information) and the exemption is essentially open-ended in requiring evaluation of the harm of disclosure to the individual in each case. Exemption six has been interpreted to require an explicit balancing of the interest in privacy against the interest in disclosure. Thus, predictability is sacrificed for greater refinement in measuring the competing interests. * * *

Exemption seven protects investigatory records compiled for law enforcement purposes where disclosure would harm any of several specified interests: enforcement proceedings generally, impartial adjudication, personal privacy, confidentiality of investigative sources, or techniques and safety of enforcement personnel. * * * Responding to what it perceived as an overly expansive judicial interpretation of the scope of the exemption Congress narrowed its scope in 1974 by specifying particular interests to be protected. * * * The greater specificity added in 1974 did not, needless to say, resolve all interpretive problems. * * *

As might be expected, substantive issues concerning the scope of disclosure (or, equivalently, the scope of the exemptions) have been the paramount concern over the years. * * * [This has tended] to obscure procedural problems of implementation and enforcement, problems that are in a sense more fundamental to the actual working of the disclosure system.

* * * [P]rovision for direct and immediate judicial enforcement was among the most important, if not the most important, reforms wrought by the 1966 Act. Faithful to the active role of the judiciary throughout American public law, the courts have been more than mere enforcement agents of Congress assuring compliance with statutory directives, they have been "creative" interpreters of public policy—indeed virtual lawmakers in their own right. * * *

As Professor Robinson notes, judicial decisions under the FOIA have also emphasized the dominant goal of disclosure of covered records. But in mediating the conflicting claims of litigants, the courts have had to deal more particularly than has Congress with the interplay of dominant and subsidiary legislative purposes in the Act and with its integration into the preexisting structure of common law, statutory, and constitutional principles. We cannot here pursue the judicial approaches to enforcement of the Act down the many byways that crisscross the jurisprudential terrain. Instead, we focus on two recurrent issues: (1) the extent to which the investigatory and decision making processes of government agencies should be exposed to public examination, and on what conditions; and (2) the accommodation of competing claims of access to information in the government's possession, on the one hand, and protection of the interests of businesses and individuals who provided that information, on the other. At the conclusion of this section we briefly examine the debate over the systemic effects of the FOIA.

3. THE GOVERNMENT'S INTERESTS IN CONFIDENTIAL ADVICE AND DISCUSSION

NLRB v. SEARS, ROEBUCK & CO.

Supreme Court of the United States, 1975.
421 U.S. 132, 95 S.Ct. 1504, 44 L.Ed.2d 29.

JUSTICE WHITE delivered the opinion of the Court.

The National Labor Relations Board (the Board) and its General Counsel seek to set aside an order of the United States District Court directing disclosure to respondent, Sears, Roebuck & Co. (Sears), pursuant to the Freedom of Information Act, of certain memoranda, known as "Advice Memoranda" and "Appeals Memoranda," and related documents generated by the Office of the General Counsel in the course of deciding whether or not to permit the filing with the Board of unfair labor practice complaints.

* * *

Sears claims, and the courts below ruled, that the memoranda sought are expressions of legal and policy decisions already adopted by the agency and constitute "final opinions" and "instructions to staff that affect a member of the public," both categories being expressly disclosable under § 552(a)(2) of the Act, pursuant to its purposes to prevent the creation of "secret law." In any event, Sears claims, the memoranda are nonexempt "identifiable records" which must be disclosed under § 552(a)(3). The General Counsel, on the other hand, claims that the memoranda sought here are not final opinions under § 552(a)(2) and that even if they are "identifiable records" otherwise disclosable under § 552(a)(3), they are exempt under § 552(b), principally as "intra-agency" communications under § 552(b)(b)(5) (Exemption 5), made in the course of formulating agency decisions on legal and policy matters.

I

Crucial to the decision of this case is an understanding of the function of the documents in issue in the context of the administrative process which generated them. We deal with this matter first. Under § 1 et seq. of the National Labor Relations Act, the process of adjudicating unfair labor practice cases begins with the filing by a private party of a "charge." Although Congress has designated the Board as the principal body which adjudicates the unfair labor practice case based on such charge, the Board may adjudicate only upon the filing of a "complaint"; and Congress has delegated to the Office of General Counsel "on behalf of the Board" the unreviewable authority to determine whether a complaint shall be filed. In those cases in which he decides that a complaint shall issue, the General Counsel becomes an advocate before the Board in support of the complaint. In those cases in which he decides not to issue a complaint, no proceeding before the Board occurs at all. The practical effect of this administrative scheme is that a party believing himself the victim of an unfair labor practice can obtain neither adjudication nor remedy under the labor statute without first persuading the Office of General Counsel that his claim is sufficiently meritorious to warrant Board consideration.

In order to structure the considerable power which the administrative scheme gives him, the General Counsel has adopted certain procedures for processing unfair labor practice charges. Charges are filed in the first instance with one of the Board's 31 Regional Directors, to whom the General Counsel has delegated the initial power to decide whether or not to issue a complaint. A member of the staff of the Regional Office then conducts an investigation of the charge, which may include interviewing witnesses and reviewing documents. If, on the basis of the investigation, the Regional Director believes the charge has merit, a settlement will be attempted, or a complaint issued. If the charge has no merit in the Regional Director's judgment, the charging party will be so informed by letter with a brief explanation of the reasons. In such a case, the charging party will also be informed of his right to appeal within 10 days to the Office of the General Counsel in Washington, D.C.

If the charging party exercises this right, the entire file in the possession of the Regional Director will be sent to the Office of Appeals in the General Counsel's Office in Washington, D.C. * * * The charging party may make a written presentation of his case as of right and an oral presentation in the discretion of the General Counsel. If an oral presentation is allowed, the subject of the unfair labor practice charge is notified and allowed a similar but separate opportunity to make an oral presentation. In any event, a decision is reached by the Appeals Committee; and the decision and the reasons for it are set forth in a memorandum called the "General Counsel's Minute" or the "Appeals Memorandum." This document is then cleared through the General Counsel himself. If the case is unusually complex or important, the General Counsel will have been brought into the process at an earlier stage and will have had a hand in the decision and the expression of its basis in the Appeals Memorandum. In either event, the Appeals Memorandum is then sent to the Regional Director who follows its instructions. If the appeal is rejected and the Regional Director's decision not to issue a complaint is sustained, a separate document is prepared and sent by the

General Counsel in letter form to the charging party, more briefly setting forth the reasons for the denial of his appeal.[6] The Appeals Memoranda, whether sustaining or overruling the Regional Directors, constitute one class of documents at issue in this case.

The appeals process affords the General Counsel's Office in Washington some opportunity to formulate a coherent policy, and to achieve some measure of uniformity, in enforcing the labor laws. The appeals process alone, however, is not wholly adequate for this purpose: when the Regional Director initially decides to file a complaint, no appeal is available and when the Regional Director decides not to file a complaint, the charging party may neglect to appeal. Accordingly * * * the General Counsel requires the Regional Directors, before reaching an initial decision in connection with charges raising certain issues specified by the General Counsel, to submit the matter to the General Counsel's "Advice Branch," also located in Washington, D.C. In yet other kinds of cases, the Regional Directors are permitted to seek the counsel of the Advice Branch.

When a Regional Director seeks "advice" from the Advice Branch, he does so through a memorandum which sets forth the facts of the case, a statement of the issues on which advice is sought, and a recommendation. * * * The General Counsel will decide the issue submitted, and his "final determination" will be communicated to the Regional Director by way of an Advice Memorandum. The memorandum will briefly summarize the facts, against the background of which the legal or policy issue is to be decided, set forth the General Counsel's answer to the legal or policy issue submitted together with a "detailed legal rationale," and contain "instructions for the final processing of the case." Depending upon the conclusion reached in the memorandum, the Regional Director will either file a complaint or send a letter to the complaining party advising him of the Regional Director's decision not to proceed and informing him of his right to appeal. It is these Advice Memoranda which constitute the other class of documents of which Sears seeks disclosure in this case.

II

This case arose in the following context. By letter dated July 14, 1971, Sears requested that the General Counsel disclose to it pursuant to the Act all Advice and Appeals Memoranda issued within the previous five years on the subjects of "the propriety of withdrawals by employers or unions from multi-employer bargaining, disputes as to commencement date of negotiations, or conflicting interpretations in any other context of the Board's *Retail Associates* (120 NLRB 388) rule." The letter also sought the subject-matter index or digest of Advice and Appeals Memo-

6. In April 1971, the General Counsel ceased preparing a separate Appeals Memorandum in every case, and ceased preparing one in any case in which the Regional Director's decision not to issue a complaint was sustained. In this latter class of cases, the General Counsel adopted the policy of expanding the letter sent to the charging party and sending the Regional Director a copy of the letter.

randa.[10] The letter urged disclosure on the theory that the Advice and Appeals Memoranda are the only source of agency "law" on some issues. By letter dated July 23, 1971, the General Counsel declined Sears' disclosure request in full. The letter stated that Advice Memoranda are simply "guides for a Regional Director" and are not final; that they are exempt from disclosure under 5 U.S.C. § 552(b)(5) as "intra-agency memoranda" which reflect the thought processes of the General Counsel's staff; and that they are exempt pursuant to 5 U.S.C. § 552(b)(7) as part of the "investigative process." The letter said that Appeals Memoranda were not indexed by subject matter and, therefore, the General Counsel was "unable" to comply with Sears' request. In further explanation of his decision, with respect to Appeals Memoranda, the General Counsel wrote to Sears on August 4, 1971, and stated that Appeals Memoranda which ordered the filing of a complaint were not "final opinions." The letter further stated that those Appeals Memoranda which *were* "final opinions, i.e., those in which an appeal was denied" and which directed that no complaint be filed, numbered several thousand, and that in the General Counsel's view they had no precedential significance. Accordingly, if disclosable at all, they were disclosable under 5 U.S.C. § 552(a)(3) relating to "identifiable records." The General Counsel then said that Sears had failed adequately to identify the material sought and that he could not justify the expenditure of time necessary for the agency to identify them.

On August 4, 1971, Sears filed a complaint pursuant to the Act seeking a declaration that the General Counsel's refusal to disclose the Advice and Appeals Memoranda and indices thereof requested by Sears violated the Act, and an injunction enjoining continued violations of the Act. * * * The answer denied that the Act required disclosure of any of the documents sought but referred to a letter of the same date in which the General Counsel informed Sears that he would make available the index to Advice Memoranda and also all Advice and Appeals Memoranda in cases which had been closed—either because litigation before the Board had been completed or because a decision not to file a complaint had become final. He stated, however, that he would not disclose the memoranda in open cases; that he would, in any event, delete names of witnesses and "security sensitive" matter from the memoranda he did disclose; and that he did not consider the General Counsel's Office bound to pursue this new policy "in all instances" in the future.

Not wholly satisfied with the voluntary disclosures offered and made by the General Counsel, Sears moved for summary judgment and the

10. Sears was then in the process of preparing an appeal to the General Counsel in Washington from a refusal by the Regional Director to file a complaint with the Board in response to an unfair labor practice charge earlier filed by Sears with the Regional Director in Seattle, Wash. * * *

Sears' right under the Act are neither increased nor decreased by reason of the fact that it claims an interest in the Advice and Appeals Memoranda greater than that shared by the average member of the public. The Act is fundamentally designed to inform the public about agency action and not to benefit private litigants. Accordingly, we will not refer again to Sears' underlying unfair labor practice charge.

General Counsel did likewise. Sears thus continued to seek memoranda in open cases. Moreover, Sears objected to the deletions in the memoranda in closed cases and asserted that many Appeals Memoranda were unintelligible because they incorporated by reference documents which were not themselves disclosed and also referred to "the 'circumstances of the case' " which were not set out and about which Sears was ignorant. * * *

III

It is clear, and the General Counsel concedes, that Appeals and Advice Memoranda are at the least "identifiable records" which must be disclosed on demand, unless they fall within one of the Act's exempt categories. It is also clear that, if the memoranda do fall within one of the Act's exempt categories, our inquiry is at an end, for the Act "does not apply" to such documents. Thus our inquiry, strictly speaking, must be into the scope of the exemptions which the General Counsel claims to be applicable—principally Exemption 5 relating to "intra-agency memorandums." * * * The General Counsel argues * * * that no Advice or Appeals Memorandum is a final opinion made in the adjudication of a case and that all are "intra-agency" memoranda within the coverage of Exemption 5. He bases this argument in large measure on what he claims to be his lack of adjudicative authority. It is true that the General Counsel lacks any authority finally to adjudicate an unfair labor practice claim in favor of the claimant; but he does possess the authority to adjudicate such a claim against the claimant through his power to decline to file a complaint with the Board. We hold for reasons more fully set forth below that those Advice and Appeals Memoranda which explain decisions by the General Counsel not to file a complaint are "final opinions" made in the adjudication of a case and fall outside the scope of Exemption 5; but that those Advice and Appeals Memoranda which explain decisions by the General Counsel to file a complaint and commence litigation before the Board are not "final opinions" made in the adjudication of a case and do fall within the scope of Exemption 5.

The parties are in apparent agreement that Exemption 5 withholds from a member of the public documents which a private party could not discover in litigation with the agency. Since virtually any document not privileged may be discovered by the appropriate litigant, if it is relevant to his litigation, and since the Act clearly intended to give any member of the public as much right to disclosure as one with a special interest therein, it is reasonable to construe Exemption 5 to exempt those documents, and only those documents, normally privileged in the civil discovery context. The privileges claimed by petitioners to be relevant to his case are (i) the "generally * * * recognized" privilege for "confidential intra-agency advisory opinions * * *," disclosure of which "would be 'injurious to the consultative functions of government * * *' " (sometimes referred to as "executive privilege"), and (ii) the attorney-client and attorney work-product privileges generally available to all litigants.

That Congress had the Government's executive privilege specifically in mind in adopting Exemption 5 is clear. The precise contours of the privilege in the context of this case are less clear, but may be gleaned from expressions of legislative purpose and the prior case law. The cases uniformly rest the privilege on the policy of protecting the "decision making processes of government agencies"; and focus on documents "reflecting advisory opinions, recommendations and deliberations comprising part of a process by which governmental decisions and policies are formulated." The point, plainly made in the Senate Report, is that the "frank discussion of legal or policy matters" in writing might be inhibited if the discussion were made public; and that the "decisions" and "policies formulated" would be the poorer as a result. * * * [A]s we have said in an analogous context, "[h]uman experience teaches that those who expect public dissemination of their remarks may well temper candor with a concern for appearances * * * to the *detriment of the decision-making process*." *United States v. Nixon*, 418 U.S. 683, 705 (1974) (emphasis added).[17]

Manifestly, the ultimate purpose of this long-recognized privilege is to prevent injury to the quality of agency decisions. The quality of a particular agency decision will clearly be affected by the communications received by the decisionmaker on the subject of the decision prior to the time the decision is made. However, it is difficult to see how the quality of a decision will be affected by communications with respect to the decision occurring after the decision is finally reached; and therefore equally difficult to see how the quality of the decision will be affected by forced disclosure of such communications, as long as prior communications and the ingredients of the decisionmaking process are not disclosed. Accordingly, the lower courts have uniformly drawn a distinction between predecisional communications, which are privileged,[18] and communications made after the decision and designed to explain it, which are not.[19] This distinction is supported not only by the lesser injury to

17. Our remarks in *United States v. Nixon* were made in the context of a claim of "executive privilege" resting solely on the Constitution of the United States. No such claim is made here and we do not mean to intimate that any documents involved here are protected by whatever constitutional content the doctrine of executive privilege might have.

18. Our emphasis on the need to protect pre-*decisional* documents does not mean that the existence of the privilege turns on the ability of an agency to identify a specific decision in connection with which a memorandum is prepared. Agencies are, and properly should be, engaged in a continuing process of examining their policies; this process will generate memoranda containing recommendations which do not ripen into agency decisions; and the lower courts should be wary of interfering with this process.

19. We are aware that the line between predecisional documents and postdecisional documents may not always be a bright one. Indeed, even the prototype of the postdecisional document—the "final opinion"—serves the dual function of explaining the decision just made and providing guides for decisions of similar or analogous cases arising in the future. In its latter function, the opinion is predecisional; and the manner in which it is written may, therefore, affect decisions in later cases. For present purposes it is sufficient to note that final opinions are *primarily* postdecisional—looking back on and explaining, as they do, a decision already reached or a policy already adopted—and that their disclosure poses a negligible risk of denying to agency decisionmakers the uninhibited advice which is so important to agency decisions.

the decisionmaking process flowing from disclosure of postdecisional communications, but also, in the case of those communications which explain the decision, by the increased public interest in knowing the basis for agency policy already adopted. The public is only marginally concerned with reasons supporting a policy which an agency has rejected, or with reasons which might have supplied, but did not supply, the basis for a policy which was actually adopted on a different ground. In contrast, the public is vitally concerned with the reasons which did supply the basis for an agency policy actually adopted. These reasons, if expressed within the agency, constitute the "working law" of the agency and have been held by the lower courts to be outside the protection of Exemption 5. Exemption 5, properly construed, calls for "disclosure of all 'opinions and interpretations' which embody the agency's effective law and policy, and the withholding of all papers which reflect the agency's group thinking in the process of working out its policy and determining what its law shall be."

This conclusion is powerfully supported by the other provisions of the Act. The affirmative portion of the Act, expressly requiring indexing of "final opinions," "statements of policy and interpretations which have been adopted by the agency," and "instructions to staff that affect a member of the public," represents a strong congressional aversion to "secret [agency] law," and represents an affirmative congressional purpose to require disclosure of documents which have "the force and effect of law." We should be reluctant, therefore, to construe Exemption 5 to apply to the documents described in 5 U.S.C. § 552(a)(2); and with respect at least to "final opinions," which not only invariably explain agency action already taken or an agency decision already made, but also constitute "final dispositions" of matters by an agency, we hold that Exemption 5 can never apply.

It is equally clear that Congress had the attorney's work-product privilege specifically in mind when it adopted Exemption 5 and that such a privilege had been recognized in the civil discovery context by the prior case law. The Senate Report states that Exemption 5 "would include the working papers of the agency attorney and documents which would come within the attorney-client privilege if applied to private parties," and the case law clearly makes the attorney's work-product rule of *Hickman v. Taylor*, 329 U.S. 495 (1947), applicable to Government attorneys in litigation. Whatever the outer boundaries of the attorney's work-product rule are, the rule clearly applies to memoranda prepared by an attorney in contemplation of litigation which set forth the attorney's theory of the case and his litigation strategy.

Applying these principles to the memoranda sought by Sears, it becomes clear that Exemption 5 does not apply to those Appeals and Advice Memoranda which conclude that no complaint should be filed and which have the effect of finally denying relief to the charging party; but that Exemption 5 does protect from disclosure those Appeals and Advice Memoranda which direct the filing of a complaint and the commencement of litigation before the Board.

Under the procedures employed by the General Counsel, Advice and Appeals Memoranda are communicated to the Regional Director *after* the General Counsel, through his Advice and Appeals Branches, has decided whether or not to issue a complaint; and represent an explanation to the Regional Director of a legal or policy decision already adopted by the General Counsel. In the case of decisions *not* to file a complaint, the memoranda effect as "final" a "disposition" as an administrative decision can—representing, as it does, an unreviewable rejection of the charge filed by the private party. Disclosure of these memoranda would not intrude on predecisional processes, and protecting them would not improve the quality of agency decisions, since when the memoranda are communicated to the Regional Director, the General Counsel has already reached his decision and the Regional Director who receives them has no decision to make—he is bound to dismiss the charge. Moreover, the General Counsel's decisions not to file complaints together with the Advice and Appeals Memoranda explaining them, are precisely the kind of agency law in which the public is so vitally interested and which Congress sought to prevent the agency from keeping secret.[22] * * *

The General Counsel contends, however, that the Appeals Memoranda represent only the first step in litigation and are not final; and that Advice Memoranda are advisory only and not binding on the Regional Director, who has the discretion to file or not to file a complaint. The contentions are without merit. Plainly, an Appeals Memorandum is the first step in litigation only when the appeal is sustained and it directs the filing of a complaint;[23] and the General Counsel's current characterization of an Advice Memorandum is at odds with his own description of the function of an Advice Memorandum in his statement to the House Committee. That statement says that the Advice Branch establishes "*uniform* policies" in those legal areas with respect to which Regional Directors are "required" to seek advice until a "definitive" policy is arrived at. This is so because if Regional Directors were "free" to interpret legal issues "the *law* could, as a practical matter and before Board decision of the issue, be one thing in one Region and conflicting in others." Therefore, the Advice Memorandum is created after consider-

22. The General Counsel argues that he makes no law, analogizing his authority to decide whether or not to file a complaint to a public prosecutor's authority to decide whether a criminal case should be brought, and claims that he does not adjudicate anything resembling a civil dispute. Without deciding whether a public prosecutor makes "law" when he decides not to prosecute or whether memoranda explaining such decisions are "final opinions," it is sufficient to note that the General Counsel's analogy is far from perfect. The General Counsel, unlike most prosecutors, may authorize the filing of a complaint with the Board only if a private citizen files a "charge." Unlike the victim of a crime, the charging party will, if a complaint is filed by the General Counsel, become a party to the unfair labor practice proceeding before the Board. And, if an unfair labor practice is found to exist, the ensuing cease-and-desist order will, unlike the punishment of the defendant in a criminal case, coerce conduct by the wrongdoer flowing particularly to the benefit of the charging party. For these reasons, we have declined to characterize the enforcement of the laws against unfair labor practices either as a wholly public or wholly private matter.

23. The General Counsel himself in his letter to Sears of August 4, 1971, referred to the Appeals Memoranda "in which an appeal was denied" as "final opinions."

ation of "prior advice determinations in similar or related cases" and contains "instructions for the final processing of the case." In light of this description, we cannot fault the District Court for concluding that the Advice Memorandum achieves a *pro tanto* withdrawal from the Regional Director of his discretion to file or not to file a complaint. Nor can we avoid the conclusion that Advice Memoranda directing dismissal of a charge represent the "law" of the agency. Accordingly, Advice and Appeals Memoranda directing that a charge be dismissed fall outside of Exemption 5 and must be disclosed.

For essentially the same reasons, these memoranda are "final opinions" made in the "adjudication of cases" which must be indexed pursuant to 5 U.S.C. § 552(a)(2)(A). * * *

Advice and Appeals Memoranda which direct the filing of a complaint, on the other hand, fall within the coverage of Exemption 5. The filing of a complaint does not finally dispose even of the General Counsel's responsibility with respect to the case. The case will be litigated before and decided by the Board; and the General Counsel will have the responsibility of advocating the position of the charging party before the Board. The Memoranda will inexorably contain the General Counsel's theory of the case and may communicate to the Regional Director some litigation strategy or settlement advice. Since the Memoranda will also have been prepared in contemplation of the upcoming litigation, they fall squarely within Exemption 5's protection of an attorney's work product. At the same time, the public's interest in disclosure is substantially reduced by the fact * * * that the basis for the General Counsel's legal decision will come out in the course of litigation before the Board; and that the "law" with respect to these cases will ultimately be made not by the General Counsel but by the Board or the courts.

We recognize that an Advice or Appeals Memorandum directing the filing of a complaint—although representing only a decision that a legal issue is sufficiently in doubt to warrant determination by another body—has many of the characteristics of the documents described in 5 U.S.C. § 552(a)(2). Although not a "final opinion" in the "adjudication" of a "case" because it does not effect a "final disposition," the memorandum does explain a decision already reached by the General Counsel which has real operative effect—it permits litigation before the Board; and we have indicated a reluctance to construe Exemption 5 to protect such documents. We do so in this case only because the decisionmaker—the General Counsel—must become a litigating party to the case with respect to which he has made his decision. The attorney's work-product policies which Congress clearly incorporated into Exemption 5 thus come into play and lead us to hold that the Advice and Appeals Memoranda directing the filing of a complaint are exempt whether or not they are, as the District Court held, "instructions to staff that affect a member of the public."

Petitioners assert that the District Court erred in holding that documents incorporated by reference in nonexempt Advice and Appeals Memoranda lose any exemption they might previously have held as "intra-agency" memoranda.[27] We disagree.

The probability that an agency employee will be inhibited from freely advising a decisionmaker for fear that his advice, *if adopted*, will become public is slight. First, when adopted, the reasoning becomes that of the agency and becomes *its* responsibility to defend. Second, agency employees will generally be encouraged rather than discouraged by public knowledge that their policy suggestions have been adopted by the agency. Moreover, the public interest in knowing the reasons for a policy actually adopted by an agency supports the District Court's decision below. Thus, we hold that, if an agency chooses *expressly* to adopt or incorporate by reference an intra-agency memorandum previously covered by Exemption 5 in what would otherwise be a final opinion, that memorandum may be withheld only on the ground that it falls within the coverage of some exemption other than Exemption 5.

Petitioners also assert that the District Court's order erroneously requires it to produce or create explanatory material in those instances in which an Appeals Memorandum refers to the "circumstances of the case." We agree. The Act does not compel agencies to write opinions in cases in which they would not otherwise be required to do so. It only requires disclosure of certain documents which the law requires the agency to prepare or which the agency has decided for its own reasons to create. * * *

IV

Finally, petitioners argue that the Advice and Appeals Memoranda are exempt, pursuant to 5 U.S.C. §§ 552(b)(2) and (7) (Exemptions 2 and 7), and that the documents incorporated therein are protected by Exemption 7. With respect to the Advice and Appeals Memoranda, we decline to reach a decision on these claims for the reasons set forth below, and with respect to the documents incorporated therein, we remand for further proceedings.

Exemption 7 provided, at the time of Sears' request for documents and at the time of the decisions of the courts below, that the Act does not apply to "investigatory files compiled for law enforcement purposes except to the extent available by law to a party other than an agency." Noting support in the legislative history for the proposition that this exemption applies to the civil "enforcement" of the labor laws, the General Counsel asserts that the "documentation underlying advice and appeals memoranda are 'investigatory files' " and that he "believes" the memoranda are themselves similarly exempt in light of the "purposes" of Exemption 7. * * *

27. It should be noted that the documents incorporated by reference are in the main factual documents which are probably not entitled to Exemption 5 treatment in the first place.

* * * Congress has amended Exemption 7 since petitioners filed their brief in this case. * * * The legislative history clearly indicates that Congress disapproves of those cases, relied on by the General Counsel, which relieve the Government of the obligation to show that disclosure of a particular investigatory file would contravene the purposes of Exemption 7. The language of the amended Exemption 7 and the legislative history underlying it clearly reveal a congressional intent to limit application of Exemption 7 to agency records so that it would apply only to the extent that "the production of such records would interfere with enforcement proceedings, deprive a person of a right to a fair trial or an impartial adjudication, constitute [an] * * * unwarranted invasion of personal privacy, disclose the identity of an informer, or disclose investigative techniques and procedures."

Any decision of the Exemption 7 issue in this case would have to be under the Act, as amended, and, apart from the General Counsel's failure to raise the issue, the lower courts have had no opportunity to pass on the applicability of the Act, as amended, to Advice and Appeals Memoranda, since the amendment occurred after the decision by the Court of Appeals.

The General Counsel's claim that Advice and Appeals Memoranda are documents "related solely to the internal personnel rules and practices of an agency" and therefore protected by Exemption 2 was raised neither in the District Court nor in the Court of Appeals and we decline to reach it for the reasons set forth above.

* * *

THE CHIEF JUSTICE concurs in the judgment.

MR. JUSTICE POWELL took no part in the consideration or decision of this case.

Notes

1. *Exemption 5 and Its Limits.* Of the nine exemptions contained in the FOIA, exemption 5 is potentially the most far-reaching. Although this exemption might arguably include almost any agency-authored document, its application has been restricted in two ways, as the *Sears* opinion suggests.

a. It is accepted that exemption 5 does not protect factual material. This limitation is supported both by the legislative history of the FOIA and by the underlying policy of the exemption—protection of the free flow of ideas and opinions in agency policy making. Because the disclosure of factual information presumably does not hinder that flow, factual material is treated as outside the exemption. See *Soucie v. David*, 448 F.2d 1067 (D.C.Cir.1971); *Environmental Protection Agency v. Mink*, 410 U.S. 73 (1973).

Montrose Chemical Corp. v. Train, 491 F.2d 63 (D.C.Cir.1974), refined the factual-deliberative distinction by refusing to order disclosure of factual summaries of public administrative hearings prepared by agency attorneys to aid the EPA Administrator in making a decision concerning the cancellation of registrations for DDT. The court reasoned that such summaries, although largely factual, were prepared as part of the deliberative process which the exemption was designed to protect. Access to the basic facts, as distinguished from the summaries, was available to the plaintiff in a 9200-page public hearing record.

b. A second limitation on exemption 5, confirmed in *Sears*, is that documents containing statements of agency policy or interpretations of law and documents forming the basis for completed decisions must be disclosed even though they contain recommendatory and judgmental materials. In *American Mail Line, Limited v. Gulick*, 411 F.2d 696 (D.C.Cir.1969), the plaintiffs sued to enjoin the withholding of an advisory memorandum which the agency had quoted in part in its cryptic final decision and had referred to as supplying the justification for its order. The memorandum was found not to be within the intra-agency exemption because its incorporation in the agency's decision made it disclosable as part of a "final decision" under section 552(a)(2)(A). See also *General Services Administration v. Benson*, 415 F.2d 878 (9th Cir.1969), where the court allowed the party demanding disclosure to prove by extrinsic means that memoranda contained "statements of policy and interpretations * * * adopted by the agency."

2. *Distinguishing "Decisions" from "Deliberations" Under Exemption 5.* Effecting the disclosure of secret law while also protecting the free flow of ideas during the process of policy formation may require the drawing of fine lines. *Sterling Drug, Inc. v. FTC*, 450 F.2d 698 (D.C.Cir.1971), is exemplary. The appellant, a diversified drug and cosmetic company, was charged with violating Clayton Act § 7 by acquiring Lehn & Fink Products Corp., producers of "Lysol" brand disinfectants and deodorizers. Prior to any formal proceedings on the complaint, Sterling requested documents concerning the Commission's earlier approval of Miles Laboratories' acquisition of the S.O.S. Company from the General Foods Corporation. The FTC had ordered General Foods to divest itself of S.O.S. and, as a part of that divestiture proceeding, had approved Miles as the purchaser. In approving the General Foods plan the agency had stated that it had "entirely relied upon the information submitted by General Foods and its approval [was] conditioned upon this information being accurate and complete."

Sterling hoped to show that its acquisition of Lehn & Fink was so similar to the approved Miles–S.O.S. acquisition that the FTC could not consistently charge Sterling with violating section 7. It unsuccessfully requested disclosure of three groups of informal Commission memoranda relating to that earlier case. The court concluded that the documents were clearly of the type protected by exemption 5, but recognized that this determination did not necessarily dispose of the case. Sterling had argued that under *Gulick* the documents were required to be disclosed "in order to provide access to the basis for the agency decision [approving the Miles–S.O.S. acquisition] and its rationale." The court responded:

> * * * [W]e feel it is necessary to divide the Commission memoranda into three categories—those prepared by the Commission staff, those prepared by individual members of the Commission, and those prepared, or at least issued, by the Commission itself. With regard to the first category, we do not believe *Gulick* supports appellant's position. Here

the Commission has not indicated publicly that staff memoranda contained the rationale for this decision, and we do not agree with Sterling's assertion that this must of necessity be the case. To begin with, most of these memoranda were written after the Commission's decision in Miles–S.O.S. and were directed toward the litigation in the Sterling–Lehn & Fink case. * * *

The staff memoranda submitted to the Commission prior to the Miles–S.O.S. decision undoubtedly contain ideas which affected that decision to some extent. However, our experience with the decision-making process leads us to believe that the material in these memoranda was probably filtered and refined by the Commission, with the result that its ultimate decision was something more than, or at least different from, the sum of its "parts." * * *

* * * Sterling contends * * * that disclosure is only warranted in this case because the Commission did not issue an opinion giving the reason for its *Miles–S.O.S.* decision and that requiring disclosure in this case and others like it will have the salutary effect of requiring agencies to issue an opinion with every order. Although persuasive in the abstract, this reasoning is unrealistic when applied to the everyday world of overburdened administrative agencies. Agencies are required to issue opinions with many of their orders, but it is completely unreasonable to suppose that every agency order can be accompanied by an opinion. The probable effect of a decision requiring disclosure of the staff memoranda would thus be to inhibit "a full and frank exchange of opinions" at least in that class of cases where opinions are not, and as practical matter cannot be, issued. We decline to make such a decision. * * *

We also feel that *Gulick* does not compel disclosure of the two memoranda written by individual Commissioners. Although the Commissioners were obviously parties to the *Miles–S.O.S.* decision and probably discussed the grounds for that decision to some extent in their memoranda, these memoranda do not necessarily contain a full and accurate account of the grounds for the decision. * * *

* * * [But we] are primarily motivated by our belief that there is a great need to preserve the free flow of ideas between Commissioners. * * * In our opinion any attempt to separate a Commissioner's statements as to the basis for a past decision from his views regarding the disposition of a current case and to disclose the former might well infringe upon these essential communications. * * *

With regard to the memoranda issued by the Commission, however, we think the philosophy underlying *Gulick* requires a different result. These memoranda were prepared by the individuals directly responsible for the *Miles–S.O.S.* decision and, as documents emanating from the Commission as a whole, they are presumably neither argumentative in nature nor slanted to reflect a particular Commissioner's view. Hence, the danger that any explanation they may give of Miles–S.O.S. is not the correct one is greatly reduced. We also feel the policy of promoting the free flow of ideas within the agency does not apply here, for private transmittals of binding agency opinions and interpretations should not be encouraged. These are not the ideas and theories which go into the making of the law, they are the law itself, and as such should be made available to the public.

3. *Who May Invoke Exemption 5?* Closely related to the problem of distinguishing "decisions" from "deliberations" is the problem of determining what bodies are "agencies" under the APA—whose decisions must be indexed and disclosed. In *Renegotiation Board v. Grumman Aircraft Engineering Corp.*, 421 U.S. 168 (1975), *reversing*, 482 F.2d 710 (D.C.Cir.1973), Grumman sought disclosure of the reports of Regional Boards in certain classes of disputes involving competitors and contractors as well as the reports of divisions of the Board itself. Disclosure was resisted under exemption 5 on the ground that the Regional Boards' reports were merely advisory and that the division reports were not final decisions because they required the concurrence of the entire Board.

The Supreme Court agreed that both types of reports fell within exemption 5. Its opinion describes the roles played by the two entities in the elaborate system for recovering excess profits earned by government contractors:

> It is undisputed that the Regional Boards had no legal authority to decide whether a contractor had received "excessive profits" in Class A cases. In such cases, the Regional Boards could investigate and recommend, but only the Board could decide. The reports were prepared long before the Board reached its decision. The Board used the Regional Board Report as a basis for discussion and, even when it agreed with the Regional Board's conclusion, it often did so as a result of an analysis of the flexible statutory factors completely different from that contained in the Regional Board Report. * * *
>
> The Court of Appeals' attempt to impute decisional authority to Regional Boards by analogizing their final recommendations to the final decisions of United States district courts must fail. The decision of a United States district court, like the decision of the General Counsel of the NLRB discussed in *NLRB v. Sears, Roebuck & Co.* has real operative effect independent of "review" by a court of appeals: absent appeal by one of the parties, the decision has the force of law; and, even if an appeal is filed, the court of appeals will be bound, within limits, by certain of the district court's conclusions. The recommendation of a Regional Board, by contrast, has no operative effect independent of the review: consideration of the case by the Board is not dependent on the decision by a party to "appeal"—such consideration is an inevitable event without which there is no agency decision; and the recommendation of the Regional Board carries no *legal* weight whatever before the Board—review by the latter is, as the Court of Appeals conceded, *de novo*. * * *
>
> It is equally clear that a division of the Board has no legal authority to decide. Once again, it may analyze and recommend, but the power to decide remains with the full Board. The evidence is uncontradicted that the Division Reports were prepared before the Board reached its decision, were used by the full Board as a basis for discussion, and, as the Chairman testified, were "prepared for and designed to assist the

members of the Board in their deliberations"; nor is the discussion limited to the material and analysis contained in the Division Report. Following the discussion, *any* Board member may disagree with the report's conclusion or agree with it for reasons other than those contained in the report. * * *

4. *Exemption 5 as a Temporary Exemption.* In *Federal Open Market Committee v. Merrill,* 443 U.S. 340 (1979), the Court recognized a different facet of the government's interest in avoiding disclosure of documents articulating administrative policy. Merrill was a Georgetown University law student who sought immediate disclosure of monthly documents, called Domestic Policy Directives, issued by the FOMC, a body composed of the Governors of the Federal Reserve System and representatives of system banks. Each month's Domestic Policy Directive set forth goals to guide the Federal Reserve System's agent in the sale of government securities during the coming month. At the end of each month, the expiring directive was routinely made public as part of the FOMC's approved minutes.

The committee denied Merrill's request on the practical grounds that "immediate release" of the Domestic Policy Directive and tolerance ranges for growth in the money supply and the interest rate on federal securities "would make it difficult to implement limited or gradual changes in monetary policy" and "would permit large institutional investors * * * to obtain an unfair advantage over small investors." The committee advanced a battery of legal arguments to legitimize these pragmatic objections to disclosure, but ultimately relied exclusively on exemption 5. In a tortuous opinion, the Supreme Court sustained this claim.

Justice Blackmun agreed that the Domestic Policy Directives were "inter-agency or intra-agency memorandums or letters," but noted that they were also clearly definitive statements of FOMC policy during the months they were effective. And the Committee could hardly claim an absolute exemption from disclosure in the face of its own practice of publicizing the directives as soon as they expired. For Blackmun, the central question under the language of exemption 5 was whether a civil court would be entitled to recognize a privilege to delay discovery of the directives. In concluding that it would, he had the following comments on the exemption's scope:

> Preliminarily, we note that it is not clear that Exemption 5 was intended to incorporate every privilege known to civil discovery. There are, to be sure, statements in our cases construing Exemption 5 that imply as much. * * * Heretofore, however, this Court has recognized only two privileges in Exemption 5, and, as *NLRB v. Sears, Roebuck & Co.*, emphasized, both these privileges are expressly mentioned in the legislative history of that Exemption. Moreover, material that may be subject to some other discovery privilege may also be exempt from disclosure under one of the other eight exemptions of FOIA, particularly Exemptions 1, 4, 6, and 7. * * *
>
> The most plausible of the three privileges asserted by the FOMC[17] is based on Fed.Rule Civ.Proc. 26(c)(7), which provides that a district

17. The two other privileges advanced by the FOMC are a privilege for "official government information" whose disclosure would be harmful to the public interest, and court, "for good cause shown," may order "that a trade secret or other confidential research, development, or commercial information not be disclosed or be disclosed only in a designated way." The Committee argues that the Domestic Policy Directives constitute "confidential * * * commercial information," at least during the month in which they provide guidance to the Account Manager, and that they therefore would be privileged from civil discovery during this period. * * *

The Court found support in the FOIA's legislative history for recognizing the government's interest in temporarily withholding documents prepared in the course of awarding procurement contracts, whose premature release could prejudice negotiations. It distinguished this interest from the other, ostensibly central, objective of exemption 5:

> * * * The purpose of the privilege for predecisional deliberations is to insure that a decisionmaker will receive the unimpeded advice of his associates. The theory is that if advice is revealed, associates may be reluctant to be candid and frank. It follows that documents shielded by executive privilege remain privileged even after the decision to which they pertain may have been effected, since disclosure at any time could inhibit the free flow of advice, including analysis, reports, and expression of opinion within the agency. The theory behind a privilege for confidential commercial information generated in the process of awarding a contract, however, is not that the flow of advice may be hampered, but that the Government will be placed at a competitive disadvantage or that the consummation of the contract may be endangered. Consequently, the rationale for protecting such information expires as soon as the contract is awarded or the offer withdrawn. * * *
>
> * * * We are mindful that "the discovery rules can only be applied under Exemption 5 by way of rough analogies," and, in particular, that the individual FOIA applicant's need for information is not to be taken into account in determining whether materials are exempt under Exemption 5. Nevertheless, the sensitivity of the commercial secrets involved, and the harm that would be inflicted upon the Government by premature disclosure, should continue to serve as relevant criteria in determining the applicability of this Exemption 5 privilege. Accordingly, we think that if the Domestic Policy Directives contain sensitive information not otherwise available, and if immediate release of these Directives would significantly harm the Government's monetary functions or commercial interests, then a slight delay in the publication of the Directives, such as that authorized by 12 CFR § 271.5, would be permitted under Exemption 5. * * *

Because the district court had made no findings respecting the FOMC's claims of adverse impact, the Court declined to "consider whether, or to what extent, the * * * Directives would in fact be afforded protection in civil discovery." It accordingly remanded the case for further proceedings.

Justice Stevens dissented, in an opinion joined by Justice Stewart:

a privilege based on Fed.Rule Civ.Proc. 26(c)(2), which permits a court to order that discovery "may be had only on specified terms and conditions, including a designation of the time or place." In light of our disposition of this case, we do not consider whether either asserted privilege is incorporated in Exemption 5.

* * * [The] Court's temporary exemption is inconsistent with the structure of the Act. Under FOIA, all information must be released, in the specified manner—i.e., in this case, "currently"—unless it fits into one of nine categories. As to material in those categories, the Act simply "*does not apply*." Between "current" release and total exemption, therefore, the statute establishes no middle ground. Accordingly, I cannot agree with the Court's recognition of a third alternative for "exempt" material to which the Act nonetheless applies—albeit on a delayed basis. If there is to be a new category subject to full disclosure but only after a "slight delay," I believe it should be created by Congress rather than the Court. * * *

5. *Exemption 5 and Civil Discovery Privileges. United States v. Weber Aircraft Corp.*, 465 U.S. 792 (1984), upheld nondisclosure of witness statements assembled by the Air Force in investigating the causes of major crashes of military aircraft. Under Air Force regulations, the "sole purpose" of such investigations is to take action to prevent future accidents. Witnesses are not sworn and are assured their statements will not be used or released for any other purpose, though the Air Force Judge Advocate General may release "factual material" and "nonpersonal evidence" from the investigators' report when required by law or court order.

When his F–106B failed in flight, Captain Richard Hoover ejected from the aircraft, sustaining serious injuries. Hoover sued several companies responsible for the design and manufacture of the ejection equipment. In response to the defendants' motion to discover "all Air Force investigative reports pertaining to the accident," the Air Force refused to release the statements given by Captain Hoover and the airman who had rigged and maintained his parachute equipment. Weber sought disclosure under the FOIA, and sued when it was refused. Justice Stevens upheld the Air Force's refusal in an opinion that explored the relation between exemption 5 and privileges from civil discovery:

> The plain language of the statute itself, as construed by our prior decisions, is sufficient to resolve the question presented. The statements of the two witnesses are unquestionably "intra-agency memorandums or letters" and, since the *Machin* privilege normally protects them from discovery in civil litigation, they "would not be available by law to a party other than [the Air Force] in litigation with [the Air Force]." * * *
>
> Respondents read [*Federal Open Market Committee v.*] *Merrill* as limiting the scope of Exemption 5 to privileges explicitly identified by Congress in the legislative history of the FOIA. But in *Merrill* we were confronted with a claimed exemption that was not clearly covered by a recognized pretrial discovery privilege. We held that Exemption 5 protected the Federal Open Market Committee's Domestic Policy Directives although it was not entirely clear that they fell within any recognized civil discovery privilege because statements in the legislative history supported an inference that Congress intended to recognize such a privilege. Thus, the *holding* of *Merrill* was that a privilege that was mentioned in the legislative history of Exemption 5 is incorporated by

the Exemption—not that all privileges not mentioned are excluded. * * *

Moreover, respondents' contention that they can obtain through the FOIA material that is normally privileged would create an anomaly in that the FOIA could be used to supplement civil discovery. We have consistently rejected such a construction of the FOIA. We do not think that Congress would have intended that the weighty policies underlying discovery privileges could be so easily circumvented.

The recognition of civil discovery privileges under exemption 5 creates an exception to the usual rule that all requesters stand on an equal footing in seeking FOIA access to records. For example, in *U.S. Department of Justice v. Julian*, 486 U.S. 1 (1988), the Court held that federal inmates could use the FOIA to obtain actual copies of all those portions of their presentence investigations that they were permitted to read under the Parole Commission and Reorganization Act of 1976 and the Federal Rules of Criminal Procedure. The Court recognized that such reports would ordinarily not be available to third parties in litigation, but held that the privilege was irrelevant to document requests from the inmates themselves.

6. *The Government in the Sunshine Act and Deliberative Meetings.* A companion statute to the FOIA in terms of opening government to popular scrutiny is the federal open meetings law, called the "Government in the Sunshine Act," 5 U.S.C. § 552b. The basic structure of the two statutes is the same. Each enacts a presumption of public access to certain categories of material. Covered agencies are granted discretion to withhold access if the information or meeting to be "accessed" falls within one of a series of prescribed exceptions. Judicial review is made available if access is denied. Under each statute, the burden is on the agency to sustain the validity of any refusal to provide access.

The statutes, however, do differ in two major ways. First, unlike the FOIA, the Sunshine Act covers only agencies that are headed by collegial bodies, such as the Federal Trade Commission or the Securities and Exchange Commission, and not single-headed agencies, such as the EPA or OMB. Second, the Sunshine Act omits any protection for intra-agency policy discussions. Indeed, the Act clearly contemplates public access to some such discussions within multi-headed agencies.

The differences between the Sunshine Act and the FOIA are vividly demonstrated in *Common Cause v. Nuclear Regulatory Commission*, 674 F.2d 921 (D.C.Cir.1982). The plaintiffs there challenged the NRC's decision to exclude the public from a series of meetings at which members would review the agency's budget requests to be forwarded to OMB for fiscal year 1982. The NRC formally asserted its authority to close the meetings on the grounds they would disclose (a) information relating to internal NRC personnel rules and practices, § 552b(c)(2), (b) information of a personal nature constituting an unwarranted invasion of privacy, § 552b(c)(6), and (c) information the disclosure of which would frustrate the proposed implementation of agency action, § 552b(c)(9)(B). A fair statement is that the real impetus for the NRC's position was its concern that open budget meetings would weaken its position in negotiations with OMB because publicity would alert OMB to the NRC's "item-shifting, exaggeration, and fallback positions."

The court rejected each of the NRC's technical arguments. The court held that exemptions (2) and (6) were not intended to shield deliberations on the managerial performance of agency executives, the only personnel matters likely to arise at the closed meetings. The court held further that exemption (9)(B), concerning the frustration of agency action, was aimed to forestall any unwanted effect that premature disclosure of government policy deliberations might have on private decision making, not on decision making by other agencies within the federal government. The NRC failed to show that disclosure of its budget deliberations would impede the agency's regulatory role, while the Act's goals of enhancing public confidence, encouraging higher quality work, and stimulating well-informed public debate were all consistent with open meetings.

Note, however, that, if the deliberations opened to scrutiny in *Common Cause v. NRC* had been embodied in written form, they would have been protected from disclosure under the FOIA. Under the FOIA, such deliberations could have been confined to predecisional documents exempt from mandatory disclosure under exemption 5. Is it inconsistent that pre-decisional, deliberative memos are not mandatorily accessible, but such meetings are? Should Congress have included a blanket exemption for meetings that are "deliberative" or "predecisional?"

Of course, any broad exemption for deliberative meetings would have rendered the Sunshine Act and its mission virtually meaningless. Under such a statute, only votes and the most general information about agency meetings would have to have been disclosed. The superficial anomaly in the two acts is best understood as reflecting Congress's suppositions that agencies need some outlet for tentative, frank discussion, especially among staff, that written documents are more central to the daily operation of the agencies than are the occasional plenary meetings, and that deliberating in public is part of the job description for the members of multi-member agencies.

A regime of protecting documents, but opening meetings is surely more sensible than the converse because the Sunshine Act exposes the deliberative activities only of those agency officials most accustomed to the limelight and thus least likely to be chilled in their behavior. It is probably easier, as a matter of statutory implementation, to distinguish predecisional documents from final decisions than predecisional from decisional meetings, and, of course, there are far fewer agency meetings than there are written records.

The 1995 Amendments to the Act, Pub.L. 104–66, 109 Stat. 734, somewhat expand the range of information that agencies are required to report annually to Congress concerning their activities covered by the Act, 5 U.S.C. § 552b(j), but do not alter the agencies' legal obligations with respect to open meetings themselves.

7. *Is Deliberative Confidentiality Necessary*? The justification offered to sustain some immunity from public disclosure for policy discussion within the executive branch is that some such "deliberative privilege" is necessary to protect the quality of decision making. A forceful challenge to this supposition appears in Gerald Wetlaufer, *Justifying Secrecy: An Objection to the General Deliberative Privilege*, 65 Ind.L.J. 845 (1990). The "chilling effect" of potential publicity is often explained in terms of bureaucrats' fears

of embarrassment should their politically unpopular or less-than-fully-considered views be aired generally. Even if prospective publicity had no such effect—that is, even if publicity did not chill candor per se—is it plausible that possible disclosure would discourage full written communications anyway? Might administrators be fearful that the need to explain to Congress or to the press every aspect of their developing views would itself be an unacceptable burden on their scarcest resource, time?

Executive Privilege

Exemption 5 is sometimes described as codifying—or at least incorporating—the executive's "privilege" to limit congressional or judicial (and thus presumably public) inquiry into its deliberative processes—whether by review of internal documents or examination of participants. But the elusive doctrine of executive privilege implies more than confidentiality of papers and discussions, for it is sometimes asserted as providing the President immunity from supervision by either the Congress or the courts. Thus the doctrine, whatever its scope, seems potentially farther reaching than the protection afforded by exemption 5. Yet the language of exemption 5 surely bears on the scope of any immunity the President's advisors may assert against mandatory disclosure of executive documents.

An ambitious presidential view of the reach of "executive privilege" was set forth in a 1958 memorandum by Attorney General William Rogers, which identified five categories of information privileged from disclosure:

1. military and diplomatic secrets and foreign affairs;
2. information made confidential by statute;
3. investigations relating to pending litigation, and investigative files and reports;
4. information relating to internal governmental affairs privileged from disclosure in the public interest; and
5. records incidental to the making of policy including inter-departmental memoranda, advisory opinions, recommendations of subordinates and informal working papers.

Within the boundaries of these five categories, Presidents have occasionally claimed that executive privilege to withhold documents in the public interest is "absolute," that is, not subject to review by the courts or Congress. This absolute view of the privilege has been urged by the executive branch on various occasions throughout American history, and the debate over executive privilege has focused as much on the issue of whether the President has the unreviewable discretionary authority under the Constitution to withhold some kinds of information from the Congress or the courts as it has on the scope of the privilege. See generally RAOUL BERGER, EXECUTIVE PRIVILEGE: A CONSTITUTIONAL MYTH (1974).

Three principal arguments have been advanced to support the claim of absolute presidential privilege. Proponents maintain that the privilege is inherent in the office of the President as chief of state and the embodiment of executive authority. Second, they cite the need for confidentiality between Presidents and their advisors in order to generate candor. Finally, it is argued that an absolute view of the privilege is necessitated by the constitutional separation of powers—the branches of government are equals and an absolute executive privilege is required to maintain that equality. Although the issue of executive privilege was raised as early as Washington's administration, the historical record is inconclusive concerning the intentions of the founding generation and the views of early Presidents regarding the proper exercise of the privilege. (That this record is subject to quite different interpretations may be seen in the majority and dissenting opinions in *Nixon v. Sirica*, 487 F.2d 700, 709, 775–81 (D.C.Cir.1973).)

For many years, the leading judicial treatment of executive privilege was *United States v. Reynolds*, 345 U.S. 1, 11 (1953). There, the widow of a civilian killed in the crash of an Air Force plane sought copies of the Air Force investigative reports, which the Secretary of the Air Force claimed were privileged documents. In a confusing opinion, the Supreme Court upheld the government's claim of privilege, yet granted the judiciary the power to determine whether the privilege was applicable, while failing to clarify the scope of judicial review of the executive's claim. As a guideline for review, the Court adopted a necessity formula:

> In each case, the showing of necessity [for disclosure] which is made will determine how far the court should probe in satisfying itself that the occasion for invoking the privilege is appropriate. Where there is a strong showing of necessity, the claim of privilege should not be lightly accepted, but even the most compelling necessity cannot overcome the claim of privilege if the court is ultimately satisfied that military secrets are at stake.

Nothing approaching a definitive statement of the constitutional basis for executive privilege and the role of judicial review was forthcoming until the Watergate tapes case, *United States v. Nixon*, 418 U.S. 683 (1974). There the Court considered both whether the "presidential privacy" branch of the privilege was absolute and whether a specific exercise of the privilege was justified. Although the Court recognized a constitutional basis for the privilege—its relation to the effective discharge of presidential powers—it specifically rejected the dual notions that the privacy privilege was absolute and that its exercise in particular cases was immune from judicial scrutiny. Rather, the legitimate needs of the judicial process (and presumably the legislative process also) may outweigh presidential privilege. More specifically, the Court held that although presidential communications are presumptively privileged, a generalized assertion of privilege based solely on concerns for presidential privacy must yield to a demonstrated specific need of constitutional dimensions, in this case the need (supported by the Sixth Amendment) for evidence in a pending criminal trial. See generally *Symposium: United States v. Nixon*, 22 U.C.L.A.L.Rev. 1 (1974).*

The relationship between the doctrine of executive privilege and the FOIA remains poorly defined. Certain of the Act's exemptions codify various facets of the common law privilege: exemption 1 embodies at least part of the "state secrets" privilege; exemption 5 covers much, if not all, of the "official information" privilege; and exemption 9 deals with the informant's privilege, albeit obliquely. However, information relating to internal governmental affairs that should remain confidential "in the public interest"—the most open-ended of Attorney General Rogers' claimed categories of privilege—is not mentioned (save as it may be covered by one or another of the remaining exemptions in particular instances).

Moreover, under § 552(c), the FOIA may not be invoked to withhold records from Congress. Thus, the exemptions are of only indirect relevance to the often contentious interbranch disputes concerning the availability of executive privilege claims against Congress. For detailed

* In *In re Sealed Case*, 116 F.3d 550 (D.C.Cir.1997), arising from the independent counsel investigation of former USDA Secretary Mike Espy, the court held that communications made by presidential advisers in the course of preparing advice for the President also come under the presidential communications privilege even when the communications were not made directly to the President. As explained by Judge Wald:

> Presidential advisers do not explore alternatives only in conversations with the President or pull their final advice to him out of thin air—if they do, their advice is not likely to be worth much. Rather, the most valuable advisers will investigate the factual context of a problem in detail, obtain input from all others with significant expertise in the area, and perform detailed analyses of several different policy options before coming to closure on a recommendation for the Chief Executive. The President himself must make decisions relying substantially, if not entirely, on the information and analysis supplied by advisers. "Even the most sensitive issues of national security must be brought to the point of presidential decision by staff, who assemble data and views, and then winnow and shape them for the President." Peter L. Strauss, *The Place of Agencies in Government: Separation of Powers and the Fourth Branch*, 84 Colum.L.Rev. 573, 661 (1984). In the vast majority of cases, few if any of the documents advisers generate in the course of their own preparation for rendering advice to the President, other than documents embodying their final recommendations, will ever enter the Oval Office. Yet these pre-decisional documents are usually highly revealing as to the evolution of advisers' positions and as to the different policy options considered along the way. If these materials are not protected by the presidential privilege, the President's access to candid and informed advice could well be significantly circumscribed.

116 F.3d at 570–71. The court nonetheless noted important limits to this privilege:

> [T]he privilege should apply only to communications authored or solicited and received by those members of an immediate White House adviser's staff who have broad and significant responsibility for investigating and formulating the advice to be given the President on the particular matter to which the communications relate* * *. [T]he privilege only applies to communications that these advisers and their staff author or solicit and receive in the course of performing their function of advising the President on official government matters.

Id. at 573. To overcome this privilege in court, Judge Wald determined, a litigant must meet the following standard of need: "A party seeking to overcome a claim of presidential privilege must demonstrate: first, that each discrete group of the subpoenaed materials likely contains important evidence; and second, that this evidence is not available with due diligence elsewhere." *Id.* at 575.

discussions of such disputes, see Peter M. Shane, *Legal Disagreement and Negotiation in a Government of Laws: The Case of Executive Privilege Claims Against Congress*, 71 Minn.L.Rev. 461–542 (1987); Peter M. Shane, *Negotiating for Knowledge: Administrative Responses to Congressional Demands for Information*, 44 Admin.L.Rev. 197 (1992).

Presumably, if executive privilege is constitutionally based and if the FOIA's stated exemptions do not exhaust the scope of the privilege, the declaration that its exemptions are exhaustive would have to give way. The constitutional basis of the privilege might also be thought to render inappropriate the FOIA's allocation of the burden of proof in all cases to the executive department claiming exemption. The *Reynolds* necessity doctrine suggests that the party requesting disclosure bears at least an initial burden of justification, and *Nixon v. Sirica* is not necessarily to the contrary. But the latter case did not arise in an FOIA context, nor did it involve a specific claim of privilege.

In *Environmental Protection Agency v. Mink*, 410 U.S. 73 (1973), the court skirted an opportunity to address the possible collision between statutory directives to release information, such as the FOIA, and the constitutional dimensions of executive privilege. In holding that the courts could not review the reasonableness of executive classification of documents under exemption 1, the Court relied expressly on its understanding of the original FOIA. It acknowledged that Congress could overturn that interpretation (as it soon did), while noting that Congress' power was inhibited by an undefined, yet constitutionally-based, executive privilege.

In *Wolfe v. Department of Health and Human Services*, 839 F.2d 768 (D.C.Cir.1988) (*en banc*), the court overturned a lower court ruling that the plaintiffs were entitled to disclosure, under the FOIA, of departmental records documenting the receipt and transmittal to OMB of proposed and final regulations recommended by the FDA, a component of HHS. Speaking for six other colleagues, Judge Bork held that the records were protected by the "deliberative process" privilege embodied in exemption 5. The executive branch had consistently maintained that any legislatively or judicially compelled disclosure of documents relevant to OMB's regulatory review function would implicate serious questions of executive privilege. In 1993, however, President Clinton—through Executive Order 12,866, discussed in Chapter 3, *supra*—directed OMB henceforth to make public not only the information sought in *Wolfe*, but, following the publication of a regulatory action, "all documents exchanged between OIRA and the agency during the review by OIRA." President George W. Bush not only kept this provision of the Clinton Order in place, but it is possible now to check the status of regulations under review, as well as records of meetings and outside consultations with regard to rules under review, over the OMB web site! These developments will presumably complicate any efforts by future Presidents to reassert the privileged status of such information.

Judicial Techniques for Monitoring Agency Compliance With the FOIA

Environmental Protection Agency v. Mink upheld, and Congress latter confirmed, the courts' general authority to satisfy themselves personally that all non-exempt records are released. In that case the late Congresswoman Patsy Mink and 32 other members of the House sued to obtain the report and recommendations of a high-level interdepartmental committee concerning a planned underground nuclear test at Amchitka Island, Alaska. EPA, which had possession of the documents, resisted disclosure on the grounds that some were classified "in the interest of the national defense or foreign policy," and the remainder were covered by exemption 5. The Court held that the propriety of executive classification of documents was not subject to judicial review and, further, that the district court was not entitled to conduct an in camera inspection of classified documents to segregate their possible "nonsecret components." With respect to documents withheld under exemption 5, however, the Court made clear that segregable factual portions were subject to mandatory disclosure and that it would be appropriate for the district court to inspect them *in camera*, notwithstanding their top-level origin, if it was not satisfied that the government had justified withholding.

In one respect the debate over *in camera* inspection can be viewed as the procedural counterpart of the dispute over absolute executive privilege. The argument against *in camera* inspection roughly parallels the argument for denying judicial review in toto: The executive branch has a much surer feel for the types of disclosures that might injure the national interest than have district judges who confront these questions only occasionally and who cannot be fully aware of the implications of apparently innocuous data for other sensitive areas of executive branch operations. In *Mink* the Court came very close to accepting this argument for exemption 1 materials. The Congress, however, disagreed. The 1974 Freedom of Information Act Amendments expressly authorized *in camera* inspections with respect to "any" claimed exemption and also modified exemption 1 to make it clear that the exemption applies only to those documents that "are in fact properly classified pursuant to such Executive Order." President Ford vetoed the amendments on the ground that they unconstitutionally infringed the necessary discretion of the Executive to maintain secrecy in the national interest, but the Congress overrode his veto.

Beyond the constitutional issues, questions of judicial efficiency and workload are also at stake in a court's decision whether to engage in *in camera* inspection of withheld documents. In *Vaughn v. Rosen*, 484 F.2d 820 (D.C.Cir.1973), *cert. denied*, 415 U.S. 977 (1974), for example, a law professor sought all Civil Service Commission documents evaluating government personnel management programs. The CSC denied the request and justified its posture in an affidavit merely asserting that all the documents were protected by at least one of several exemptions. Faced with the prospect of reviewing voluminous documents to determine the validity of this claim, the district court accepted the agency's affidavit as sufficient proof of exemption, but the court of appeals reversed. In its view the district court should have required the agency to submit a particularized analysis (known now as a "*Vaughn* index") that correlated the claimed exemptions with the documents or portions of documents purportedly exempted from disclosure. Otherwise broad agency claims of exemption covering voluminous documents would destroy the capacity of the district courts to engage in a serious *de novo* review of claimed exemptions. Should inspection be necessary after receipt of the agency's detailed justification for its refusal to disclose, the district court was advised that it might appoint a special master to assist.

See also *Ash Grove Cement Co. v. FTC*, 511 F.2d 815 (D.C.Cir.1975), where the district court, after initially refusing to examine the demanded materials until the FTC described with particularity each document for which it claimed an exemption, accepted the agency's affidavit as sufficient to render *in camera* inspection unnecessary. The court of appeals reversed, requiring the district court to inspect *in camera* at least a sample of the requested documents and indicating the need for more detailed summaries to fulfill the demands of *Vaughn*.

Resistance to *in camera* inspections need not be predicated wholly on separation of powers or judicial efficiency grounds. Such inspections are necessarily ex parte and, therefore, may provide less opportunity for a requesting party to know and meet the agency's claims than would a particularized affidavit. Together these considerations suggest that there is much more to the *in camera* inspections issue than simply the need of the judiciary for "the facts" upon which it may base a de novo finding. For a useful discussion, see Comment, *In Camera Inspections Under the Freedom of Information Act*, 41 U.Chi.L.Rev. 557 (1974).

Residual Judicial Discretion to Refuse to Order Mandatory Disclosures

Cases under the FOIA sometimes present a court with disputes in which the adverse consequences of disclosure seem to dwarf the importance of the requester's interest in the records at issue. In such cases, a court may be tempted to search for a rationale to justify the agency's decision to withhold. The case law, however, generally supports the proposition that such rationales must be found within the Act's nine exemptions; courts apparently retain no discretion to refuse to order disclosure of non-exempt records. In the words of Judge Butzner in *Wellford v. Hardin*, 444 F.2d 21, 25 (4th Cir.1971): "It is not the province of the courts to restrict that legislative judgment under the guise of judicially balancing the same interests that Congress has considered." But see *Federal Open Market Committee v. Merrill*, *supra* p. 731.

The court's refusal to balance "the same interests Congress has considered" may be viewed as a renunciation of the traditional discretion of a court of equity to determine whether an available remedy should, under all the circumstances, be granted. This narrow view of the judicial function under the FOIA is supported by the language of section 552(c), but subsection (a)(3) states merely that the district courts have "jurisdiction to enjoin" the withholding of records, not that the courts "shall" enjoin such withholding in every case. Nor does the legislative history speak unmistakably on this issue. The Senate Report accompanying the original Act, for example, states generally that "[i]t is essential that agency personnel, *and the courts as well*, be given definitive guidelines in setting information policies." S.Rep.No. 813, 89th Cong., 1st Sess. 3 (1965) (emphasis added). By contrast, the House Report states: "The Court will have authority *whenever it considers such action equitable and appropriate* to enjoin the agency from withholding its records." H.R.Rep. No. 1497, 89th Cong., 2d Sess. 9 (1966) (emphasis added).

In *Soucie v. David*, 448 F.2d 1067, 1077 (D.C.Cir.1971), the court opined that "Congress did not intend to confer on district courts a general power to deny relief on equitable grounds apart from the exemptions in the Act itself," language repeated in *Getman v. NLRB*, 450 F.2d 670, 678 (D.C.Cir.1971), and echoed in *Wellford*. However, in *Consumers Union v. Veterans Administration*, 301 F.Supp. 796, 808 (S.D.N.Y.1969), the court refused to require release of a VA scoring system and quality index for hearing aids because in the court's view "the danger of the public being misled * * * and the disruption of the VA programs that [disclosure] * * * would cause outweighs any benefits." See also *General Services Administration v. Benson*, 415 F.2d 878, 880 (9th Cir.1969).

In *Renegotiation Board v. Bannercraft Clothing Co.*, 415 U.S. 1 (1974), three contractors involved in separate renegotiation proceedings obtained a district court injunction barring further proceedings until the Board complied with their FOIA requests for disclosure of pertinent records. Although it acknowledged that the district court had power under the FOIA to issue such an injunction, the Supreme Court, divided five to four, held that the contractors were required to exhaust their administrative remedies (i.e., to complete the renegotiation proceedings) before invoking the equity power of the district court. The FOIA, according to the majority, was not intended "to change the Renegotiation Act's purposeful design of negotiation without interruption for judicial review." 415 U.S. at 22.

The relationship between ongoing agency proceedings and contemporaneous demands for records claimed to be germane to their outcome was also at issue in *Forsham v. Harris*, 445 U.S. 169 (1980). The narrow question was whether data recorded by private clinicians engaged in a federally-funded study of drugs for diabetes constituted "agency records" subject to mandatory disclosure under the FOIA. Investigators from both the sponsoring institute and the FDA were legally entitled to have access to the data to verify the study findings, and the FDA had proposed major changes in the labeling of the drugs based on those findings as reported. The plaintiffs were several prominent diabetologists who sought access to the actual patient records because of suggestions that the reported findings, indicating that the drugs might *increase* patients' risk of heart attack, were erroneous and possibly even fraudulent. The Court held, that notwithstanding the agencies' financial support of the study and their right to obtain access to the data, the records could not be considered "agency records" subject to FOIA because they belonged to and remained in the custody of the investigators and study coordinator. But it did not disagree with the court of appeals' statement that the FDA would have to make public the key portions of the study records if it ultimately decided to issue a rule based on the reported study results. See *Forsham v. Califano*, 587 F.2d 1128 (D.C.Cir.1978); *cf. United States v. Nova Scotia Food Products*, *supra* p. 535. See also *Kissinger v. Reporters Committee for Freedom of the Press*, 445 U.S. 136 (1980) (holding that materials delivered to the Library of Congress were no longer "agency records").

NLRB v. ROBBINS TIRE & RUBBER CO.

Supreme Court of the United States, 1978.
437 U.S. 214, 98 S.Ct. 2311, 57 L.Ed.2d 159.

JUSTICE MARSHALL delivered the opinion of the Court.

The question presented is whether the Freedom of Information Act (FOIA) requires the National Labor Relations Board to disclose, prior to its hearing on an unfair labor practice complaint, statements of witnesses whom the Board intends to call at the hearing. Resolution of this question depends on whether production of the material prior to the hearing would "interfere with enforcement proceedings" within the meaning of Exemption 7(A) of FOIA.

I

Following a contested representation election in a unit of respondent's employees, the Acting Regional Director of the NLRB issued an unfair labor practice complaint charging respondent with having committed numerous violations of § 8(a)(1) of the National Labor Relations Act (NLRA), during the pre-election period. A hearing on the complaint was scheduled for April 27, 1976. On March 31, 1976, respondent wrote to the Acting Regional Director and requested, pursuant to FOIA, that he make available for inspection and copying, at least seven days prior to the hearing, copies of all potential witnesses' statements collected during the Board's investigation. The Acting Regional Director denied this request on April 2, on the ground that this material was exempt from the disclosure requirements of FOIA. * * * He placed particular reliance on Exemption 7(A), which provides that disclosure is not required of "matters that are * * * investigatory records compiled for law enforcement purposes, but only to the extent that the production of such records would * * * interfere with enforcement proceedings."

Respondent appealed to the Board's General Counsel. Before expiration of the 20–day period within which FOIA requires such appeals to be decided, respondent filed this action in the United States District Court for the Northern District of Alabama, pursuant to 5 U.S.C. § 552(a)(4)(B). The complaint sought not only disclosure of the statements, but also a preliminary injunction against proceeding with the unfair labor practice hearing pending final adjudication of the FOIA claim and a permanent injunction against holding the hearing until the documents had been disclosed. * * * The District Court held that, since the Board did not claim that release of the documents at issue would pose any unique or unusual danger of interference with this particular enforcement proceeding, Exemption 7(A) did not apply. It therefore directed the Board to provide the statements for copying on or before April 22, 1976, or at least five days before any hearing where the person making the statement would be called as a witness.

On the Board's appeal, the United States Court of Appeals for the Fifth Circuit commenced its discussion by observing that while "[t]his is a [FOIA] case, * * * it takes on the troubling coloration of a dispute about the discovery rights * * * in [NLRB] proceedings." It concluded * * * that the legislative history of certain amendments to FOIA in 1974 demonstrated that Exemption 7(A) was to be available only where there was a specific evidentiary showing of the possibility of actual interference in an individual case.

* * *

II

* * *

Exemption 7 as originally enacted permitted nondisclosure of "investigatory files compiled for law enforcement purposes except to the extent available by law to a private party." In 1974, this exemption was rewritten to permit the nondisclosure of "investigatory records compiled for law enforcement purposes," but only to the extent that producing such records would involve one of six specified dangers. The first of these, with which we are here concerned, is that production of the records would "interfere with enforcement proceedings."

* * *

The starting point of our analysis is with the language and structure of the statute. We can find little support in the language of the statute itself for respondent's view that determinations of "interference" under Exemption 7(A) can be made only on a case-by-case basis. Indeed, the literal language of Exemption 7 as a whole tends to suggest that the contrary is true. The Exemption applies to:

> "investigatory records compiled for law enforcement purposes, but only to the extent that the production of such records would (A) interfere with enforcement proceedings, (B) deprive a person of a right to a fair trial or an impartial adjudication, (C) constitute an unwarranted invasion of personal privacy, (D) disclose the identity of a confidential source and, in the case of a record compiled by a criminal law enforcement authority in the course of a criminal investigation, or by an agency conducting a lawful national security

intelligence investigation, confidential information furnished only by the confidential source, (E) disclose investigative techniques and procedures, or (F) endanger the life or physical safety of law enforcement personnel."

There is a readily apparent difference between subdivision (A) and subdivisions (B), (C), and (D). The latter subdivisions refer to particular cases—"a person," "an unwarranted invasion," "a confidential source"—and thus seem to require a showing that the factors made relevant by the statute are present in each distinct situation. By contrast, since subdivision (A) speaks in the plural voice about "enforcement proceedings," it appears to contemplate that certain generic determinations might be made.

Respondent points to other provisions of FOIA in support of its interpretation. It suggests that, because FOIA expressly provides for disclosure of segregable portions of records and for *in camera* review of documents, and because the statute places the burden of justifying nondisclosure on the Government, the Act necessarily contemplates that the Board must specifically demonstrate in each case that disclosure of the particular witness' statement would interfere with a pending enforcement proceeding. We cannot agree. The *in camera* review provision is discretionary by its terms, and is designed to be invoked when the issue before the District Court could not be otherwise resolved; it thus does not mandate that the documents be individually examined in every case. Similarly, although the segregability provision requires that nonexempt portions of documents be released, it does not speak to the prior question of what material is exempt. Finally, the mere fact that the burden is on the Government to justify nondisclosure does not, in our view, aid the inquiry as to what kind of burden the Government bears.

* * *

In originally enacting Exemption 7, Congress recognized that law enforcement agencies had legitimate needs to keep certain records confidential, lest the agencies be hindered in their investigations or placed at a disadvantage when it came time to present their cases. Foremost among the purposes of this Exemption was to prevent "harm [to] the Government's case in court," S.Rep.No. 813, 89th Cong., 1st Sess. (1965), by not allowing litigants "earlier or greater access" to agency investigatory files than they would otherwise have. Indeed, in an unusual, post-passage reconsideration vote, the Senate modified the language of this Exemption specifically to meet Senator Humphrey's concern that it might be construed to require disclosure of "statements of agency witnesses" prior to the time they were called on to testify in agency proceedings.

Senator Humphrey was particularly concerned that the initial version of the Exemption passed by the Senate might be "susceptible to the interpretation that once a complaint of unfair labor practice is filed by the General Counsel of the NLRB, access could be had to the statements of all witnesses, whether or not these statements are relied upon to support the complaint." * * *

In light of this history, the Board is clearly correct that the 1966 Act was expressly intended to protect against the mandatory disclosure through FOIA of witnesses' statements prior to an unfair labor practice proceeding. * * *

In 1974 Congress acted to amend FOIA in several respects. The move to amend was prompted largely by congressional disapproval of our decision in *EPA v. Mink*, 410 U.S. 73 (1973), regarding the availability of *in camera* review of classified documents. Congress was also concerned that administrative agencies were being dilatory in complying with the spirit of the Act and with court decisions interpreting FOIA to mandate disclosure of information to the public. As the amending legislation was reported out of the respective Committees, no change in Exemption 7 was recommended. The 1974 amendment of Exemption 7 resulted instead from a proposal on the floor by Senator [Philip] Hart during Senate debate.

* * *

* * * [T]he thrust of congressional concern in its amendment of Exemption 7 was to make clear that the Exemption did not endlessly protect material simply because it was in an investigatory file. * * *

In the face of this history, respondent relies on Senator Hart's floor statement that "it is only relevant" to determine whether an interference would result "in the context of the particular enforcement proceeding." Respondent argues that this statement means that in each case the court must determine whether the material of which disclosure is sought would actually reveal the Government's case prematurely, result in witness intimidation, or otherwise create a demonstrable interference with the particular case.

We believe that respondent's reliance on this statement is misplaced. Although Congress could easily have required in so many words that the Government in each case show a particularized risk to its individual "enforcement proceedin[g]," it did not do so; the statute, if anything, seems to draw a distinction in this respect between subdivision (A) and subdivisions (B), (C), and (D). Senator Hart's words are ambiguous, moreover, and must be read in light of his primary concern: that by extending blanket protection to anything labeled an investigatory file, the D.C. Circuit had ignored Congress' original intent. His remarks plainly do not preclude a court from considering whether "particular" *types* of enforcement proceedings, such as NLRB unfair labor practice proceedings, will be interfered with by particular types of disclosure.

* * *

What Congress clearly did have in mind was that Exemption 7 permit nondisclosure only where the Government "specif[ies]" that one of the six enumerated harms is present, and the court, reviewing the question *de novo*, agrees that one of those six "reasons" for nondisclosure applies. Thus, where an agency fails to "demonstrat[e] that the * * * documents [sought] relate to any ongoing investigation or * * * would jeopardize any future law enforcement proceedings," Exemption 7(A) would not provide protection to the agency's decision. While the Court of Appeals was correct that the amendment of Exemption 7 was designed to eliminate "blanket exemptions" for Government records simply because they were found in investigatory files compiled for law enforcement purposes, we think it erred in concluding that no generic determinations of likely interference can ever be made. We conclude that Congress did not intend to prevent the federal courts from determining that, with respect to particular kinds of enforcement proceedings, disclosure of particular kinds of investigatory records while a case is pending would generally "interfere with enforcement proceedings."

III

The remaining question is whether the Board has met its burden of demonstrating that disclosure of the potential witnesses' statements at this time "would interfere with enforcement proceedings." A proper resolution of this question requires us to weigh the strong presumption in favor of disclosure under FOIA against the likelihood that disclosure at this time would disturb the existing balance of relations in unfair labor practice proceedings, a delicate balance that Congress has deliberately sought to preserve and that the Board maintains is essential to the effective enforcement of the NLRA. Although reasonable arguments can be made on both sides of this issue, for the reasons that follow we conclude that witness statements in pending unfair labor practice proceedings are exempt from FOIA disclosure at least until completion of the Board's hearing.

Historically, the NLRB has provided little prehearing discovery in unfair labor practice proceedings and has relied principally on statements such as those sought here to prove its case. While the NLRB's discovery policy has been criticized, the Board's position that § 6 of the NLRA, 29 U.S.C. § 156, commits the formulation of discovery practice to its discretion has generally been sustained by the lower courts. A profound alteration in the Board's trial strategy in unfair labor practice cases would thus be effectuated if the Board were required, in every case in which witnesses' statements were sought under FOIA prior to an unfair labor practice proceeding, to make a particularized showing that release of these statements would interfere with the proceeding.[17]

Not only would this change the substantive discovery rules, but it would do so through mechanisms likely to cause substantial delays in the adjudication of unfair labor practice charges. In addition to having a duty under FOIA to provide public access to its processes, the NLRB is charged with the duty of effectively investigating and prosecuting viola-

17. If the Court of Appeals' ruling below were not reversed, the Board anticipated that prehearing requests for witnesses' statements under FOIA would be made by employer-respondents in virtually all unfair labor practice proceedings.

tions of the labor laws. To meet its latter duty, the Board can be expected to continue to claim exemptions with regard to prehearing FOIA discovery requests, and numerous court contests will thereby ensue. Unlike ordinary discovery contests, where rulings are generally not appealable until the conclusion of the proceedings, an agency's denial of an FOIA request is immediately reviewable in the district court, and the district court's decision can then be reviewed in the court of appeals. The potential for delay and for restructuring of the NLRB's routine adjudications of unfair labor practice charges from requests like respondent's is thus not insubstantial.

* * *

The most obvious risk of "interference" with enforcement proceedings in this context is that employers or, in some cases, unions will coerce or intimidate employees and others who have given statements, in an effort to make them change their testimony or not testify at all. This special danger flowing from prehearing discovery in NLRB proceedings has been recognized by the courts for many years, and formed the basis for Senator Humphrey's particular concern. Indeed, Congress recognized this danger in the NLRA itself, and provided in § 8(a)(4) that it is an unfair labor practice for an employer "to discharge or otherwise discriminate against an employee because he has filed charges or given testimony under this subchapter." Respondent's argument that employers will be deterred from improper intimidation of employees who provide statements to the NLRB by the possibility of a § 8(a)(4) charge misses the point of Exemption 7(A); the possibility of deterrence arising from *post hoc* disciplinary action is no substitute for a prophylactic rule that prevents the harm to a pending enforcement proceeding which flows from a witness' having been intimidated.

The danger of witness intimidation is particularly acute with respect to current employees—whether rank and file, supervisory, or managerial—over whom the employer, by virtue of the employment relationship, may exercise intense leverage. Not only can the employer fire the employee, but job assignments can be switched, hours can be adjusted, wage and salary increases held up, and other more subtle forms of influence exerted. A union can often exercise similar authority over its members and officers. * * * While the risk of intimidation (at least from employers) may be somewhat diminished with regard to statements that are favorable to the employer, those known to have already given favorable statements are then subject to pressure to give even more favorable testimony.

Furthermore, both employees and nonemployees may be reluctant to give statements to NLRB investigators at all, absent assurances that unless called to testify in a hearing, their statements will be exempt from disclosure until the unfair labor practice charge has been adjudicated. Such reluctance may flow less from a witness' desire to maintain complete confidentiality—the concern of Exemption 7(D)—than from an all too familiar unwillingness to "get too involved" unless absolutely necessary. Since the vast majority of the Board's unfair labor practice proceedings are resolved short of hearing, without any need to disclose witness statements, those currently giving statements to Board investigators can have some assurance that in most instances their statements will not be made public (at least until after the investigation and any adjudication is complete).[20] The possibility that an FOIA-induced change in the Board's prehearing discovery rules will have a chilling effect on the Board's sources cannot be ignored.[21]

In short, prehearing disclosure of witnesses' statements would involve the kind of harm that Congress believed would constitute an "interference" with NLRB enforcement proceedings: that of giving a party litigant earlier and greater access to the Board's case than he would otherwise have. * * * While those drafting discovery rules for the Board might determine that this "interference" is one that should be tolerated in order to promote a fairer decisionmaking process, that is not our task in construing FOIA.

The basic purpose of FOIA is to ensure an informed citizenry, vital to the functioning of a democratic society, needed to check against corruption and to hold the governors accountable to the governed. Respondent concedes that it seeks those statements solely for litigation discovery purposes, and that FOIA was *not* intended to function as a private discovery tool. Most, if not all, persons who have sought prehearing disclosure of Board witnesses' statements have been in precisely this posture—parties respondent in Board proceedings.[23] Since we are dealing here with the narrow question whether witnesses' statements must be released five days prior to an unfair labor practice hearing, we cannot see how FOIA's purposes would be defeated by deferring disclosure until after the Government has "presented its case in court." * * *

The judgment of the Court of Appeals is, accordingly,

Reversed.

[The concurring opinion of JUSTICE STEVENS, joined by the CHIEF JUSTICE and JUSTICE REHNQUIST, is omitted.]

JUSTICE POWELL, with whom JUSTICE BRENNAN joins, concurring in part and dissenting in part.

20. According to the Board, 94% of all unfair labor practice charges filed are resolved short of hearing; in the remaining 6% that go to hearing, many potential witnesses are not actually called to testify, since their testimony is cumulative.

21. Respondent argues that the Court of Appeals was correct in concluding that this danger is nonexistent with respect to a witness scheduled to testify, since the Board under its own discovery rules will turn over those statements once the witness has actually testified. This argument falters, first, on the fact that only those portions of the witness' statements relating to his direct examination or the issues raised in the pleadings are disclosed under the Board's discovery rules. In addition, to uphold respondent's FOIA request would doubtless require the Board in many cases to turn over statements of persons whom it did not actually call at the adjudicatory hearings.

23. This is not to suggest that respondent's rights are in any way diminished by its being a private litigant, but neither are they enhanced by respondent's particular, litigation-generated need for these materials.

* * *

* * * Exemption 7(A) requires that the Board demonstrate a reasonable possibility that disclosure would "interfere with enforcement proceedings * * *." In my view, absent a particularized showing of likely interference, statements of all witnesses—other than current employees in proceedings against employers (or union members in proceedings against unions)—are subject to the statutory presumption in favor of disclosure. In contrast to the situation of current employees or union members, there simply is no basis for presuming a particular likelihood of employer interference with union representatives or others not employed by the charged party, or, in a proceeding against a union, of union interference with employer representatives and other nonmembers of the union or the bargaining unit. Similarly, I am unwilling to presume interference with respect to disclosure of favorable statements by current employees, and would require the Board to show a reasonable possibility of employer reprisal. * * *

There may be exceptional cases that would permit the Board to withhold all witness statements for the duration of an unfair labor practice proceeding. Such a situation could arise where prehearing revelation would divulge incompletely developed information which, if prematurely disclosed, may interfere with the proceedings before the Board, or where the facts of a case suggest a strong likelihood that the charged party will attempt to interfere with any and all of the Board's witnesses. The Act requires, however, that the Board convince a federal court that there is a reasonable possibility of this kind of interference. * * *

Notes

1. *Judicial Balancing and Exemption 7.* Although most of the FOIA exemptions are couched in categorical rather than contextual terms—embodying legislative judgments about the appropriate balance between access and confidentiality—a few, like exemption 6 and exemptions 7(A) and (D), appear to require some balancing to determine whether or not records are disclosable. The FOIA's directives that courts shall review agency denials *de novo* and that agencies bear the burden of justifying withholding would seem to accord agencies little, if any, room to strike this balance themselves. But is this not precisely what the NLRB has accomplished through its discovery rules, which the Court upholds in *Robbins Tire*?

Judicial willingness to recognize any "generic" exclusions under an exemption that appears to call for balancing appears destined to accord some deference to the agency's initial striking of the balance. Is it not inevitable that an agency will have a comparative advantage in assessing the likely consequences of disclosure of documents of a particular kind?

On the other hand, the interpretation of exemption 7(A) urged by the respondent—requiring the NLRB to demonstrate that disclosure of specific documents would interfere with a specific pending proceeding—would have significant implications for the courts as well as the Board. Unless the Board were to revise its judgment that disclosure of witness statements would often interfere with its enforcement efforts, it would routinely decline FOIA requests. Many of those denials would be litigated, requiring in each instance a district judge to determine after a hearing whether disclosure of the demanded materials would interfere with a pending unfair labor practice proceeding.

The Court reaffirmed the technique of categorical judicial balancing in a later case involving exemption 7(C), which pertains to law enforcement records whose production would "constitute an unwarranted invasion of personal privacy." In *U.S. Department of Justice v. Reporters Committee For Freedom of the Press*, 489 U.S. 749 (1989), the Court upheld the FBI's refusal to disclose to reporters its "rap sheets" or compiled criminal records on certain named individuals. Although each of the facts recounted in the records was likely already to have been made public, the Court determined that the compilation of such data in a centralized database nonetheless implicated serious privacy concerns. Moreover, the Court agreed that the invasion of privacy would be "unwarranted," because disclosure of the records would reveal nothing about the quality of the government's performance of its duties, and would thus not advance what the Court deemed to be the central purpose of the FOIA.

The Court rejected a generic approach to Exemption 7(D), however, in *Department of Justice v. Landano*, 508 U.S. 165 (1993). In response to a habeas petitioner's FOIA request for FBI files concerning his case, the Government argued "that a presumption of confidentiality arises whenever any individual or institutional source supplies information to the Bureau during a criminal investigation." The Court unanimously rejected so broad a presumption as unreasonable, while hinting that more narrowly asserted categorical claims might be upheld: "[I]t is reasonable to infer that paid informants normally expect their cooperation with the FBI to be kept confidential* * *. [T]he character of the crime at issue may be relevant to determining whether a source cooperated with the FBI with an implied assurance of confidentiality. So too may the source's relation to the crime* * *. We think this more particularized approach is consistent with Congress' intent to provide 'workable rules' of FOIA disclosure." 508 U.S. at 178–180.

2. *When Are Records "Compiled" Under Exemption 7?* A recurring difficulty in interpreting section 552(b)(7) involves records that were not originally compiled for law enforcement purposes, but that later took on law enforcement significance. In *John Doe Agency v. John Doe Corp.*, 493 U.S. 146 (1989), the Court held, over a strenuous dissent by Justices Scalia and Marshall, that such records could be exempted from mandatory disclosure under section 552(b)(7) if they were "recompiled" for law enforcement purposes at a later date. The case before the Court involved 1978 correspondence between a corporation and the Defense Contract Auditing Agency (DCAA) concerning the proper accounting treatment of certain costs charged to particular contracts. In 1985, a U.S. Attorney instituted investigative proceedings concerning possible fraud by the corporation. The corporation lodged an FOIA request with the DCAA, seeking all documents relating to its 1978 correspondence. On the U.S. Attorney's advice, the DCAA withheld the documents, which were transferred two days later to the FBI. Six

members of the Court voted to remand the case to determine whether, notwithstanding the late timing of the transfer of records, the targeted documents had, in fact, been compiled for law enforcement purposes after the onset of the grand jury investigation. Justice Stevens, agreeing with the majority that "recompilation" was possible under exemption 7, dissented on the ground that the FOIA required the government to shoulder the burden of proving the fact of compilation, which it clearly had not done. The majority did not say whether a "compilation for law enforcement purposes" sufficient to invoke exemption 7 could occur after an FOIA request had been filed.

3. *Agency Incentives to Invoke FOIA Exemptions. Robbins Tire* illustrates a context of government information gathering in which the agency has a strong incentive not only to claim exemption from the FOIA, but a strong incentive to assert that claim in all cases where it has plausibility. In many circumstances, however, an agency may have little at stake in disclosure—save as its inability to safeguard providers' interests in confidentiality may undermine their continuing willingness to provide information voluntarily. See *National Parks and Conservation Association v. Morton*, 498 F.2d 765 (D.C.Cir.1974).

In 1977, the Carter Administration took steps to encourage agencies with little at stake in disclosure *not* to invoke section 552(b) exemptions. Attorney General Bell issued a memorandum to federal agencies that limited the defenses the Justice Department would be willing to invoke in defending agency decisions to withhold particular records. In particular, his memo said that the Justice Department, in deciding whether to defend a decision to withhold, would consider:

1. Whether the denial had a substantial legal basis;
2. Whether litigation would bear an acceptable risk of adverse impact on other agencies if it were lost;
3. Whether there would be a "sufficient prospect of actual harm to legitimate public or private interests," if disclosed, to justify defense; and
4. Whether the DOJ knew enough about the case to support a judgment that the agency denial satisfied the above three criteria.

1 James T. O'Reilly, Federal Information Disclosure 3–16 (2d ed. 1990).

This memorandum was reinforced by a set of "Procedures and Standards on Refusals to Defend FOIA Suits," which further limited the defenses agencies could invoke to sustain the withholding of documents. The Reagan Justice Department withdrew those standards and announced its willingness to defer more generally to agency decisions to invoke any exemptions technically available to resist mandatory disclosure. *Id.* Both Presidents Bush followed the policy of the Reagan Justice Department in this respect, while, under President Clinton, the Justice Department reverted to a litigating position akin to that of the Carter Administration. Which allocation of decision making authority within the executive makes more sense?

4. PROTECTING PRIVATE INTERESTS IN INFORMATION IN THE GOVERNMENT'S POSSESSION

The FOIA represents an emphatic statement in favor of general public access to information in the government's possession. But it is not surprising to find that persons who relinquish information to the government, whether voluntarily or under compulsion, are often reluctant to have it seen by anyone else. The kinds of information sought to be protected range from personal records about private individuals to the practices of businesses to scientific studies of new products and technologies. The motives of providers to prevent public access even as they yield information to the government are obvious and, in some instances, compelling.

Exemptions 4 and 6 of the FOIA evidence Congress' recognition that other interests sometimes override the public interest in knowledge of government plans and actions. And numerous federal statutes prescribe confidential treatment for categories of information in government hands. Notable examples are the Privacy Act of 1974 and 18 U.S.C. § 1905, which makes it a criminal offense for government officials, without legal authorization, to disclose trade secret information acquired in performing their duties. But the FOIA exemptions merely relieve an agency of the obligation to disclose in response to a request; they do not demand that an agency keep exempt material secret. Moreover, the effectiveness of prohibitions against disclosure found in section 1905 and other statutes depends, in the first instance, on the willingness of other government officials—in the Department of Justice—to enforce them against violators. In these circumstances, it is not surprising that providers of information to the government have sought more effective measures to protect their interests in confidentiality.

CHRYSLER CORP. v. BROWN

Supreme Court of the United States, 1979.
441 U.S. 281, 99 S.Ct. 1705, 60 L.Ed.2d 208.

JUSTICE REHNQUIST delivered the opinion of the Court.

* * *

This case belongs to a class that has been popularly denominated "reverse-FOIA" suits. The Chrysler Corp. (hereinafter Chrysler) seeks to enjoin agency disclosure on the grounds that it is inconsistent with the FOIA and 18 U.S.C. § 1905, a criminal statute with origins in the 19th century that proscribes disclosure of certain classes of business and personal information. We agree with the Court of Appeals for the Third Circuit that the FOIA is purely a disclosure statute and affords Chrysler no private right of action to enjoin agency disclosure. But we cannot agree with that court's conclusion that this disclosure is "authorized by law" within the meaning of § 1905. Therefore, we vacate the Court of Appeals' judgment and remand so that it can consider whether the documents at issue in this case fall within the terms of § 1905.

As a party to numerous Government contracts, Chrysler is required to comply with Executive Orders 11246 and 11375, which charge the Secretary of Labor with ensuring that corporations that benefit from Government contracts provide equal employment opportunity regardless of race or sex. The U.S. Department of Labor's Office of Federal Contract Compliance Programs (OFCCP) has promulgated regulations which require Government contractors to furnish reports and other information about their affirmative-action programs and the general composition of their work forces.

The Defense Logistics Agency (DLA) * * * of the Department of Defense is the designated compliance agency responsible for monitoring Chrysler's employment practices. OFCCP regulations require that Chrysler make available to this agency written affirmative action programs (APP's) and annually submit Employer Information Reports, known as EEO–1 Reports. * * *

Regulations promulgated by the Secretary of Labor provide for public disclosure of information from records of the OFCCP and its compliance agencies. Those regulations state that notwithstanding exemption from mandatory disclosure under the FOIA, 5 U.S.C. § 552,

> "records obtained or generated pursuant to Executive Order 11246 (as amended) * * * shall be made available for inspection and copying * * * if it is determined that the requested inspection or copying furthers the public interest and does not impede any of the functions of the OFCC[P] or the Compliance Agencies except in the case of records disclosure of which is prohibited by law."

It is the voluntary disclosure contemplated by this regulation, over and above that by the FOIA, which is the gravamen of Chrysler's complaint in this case.

This controversy began on May 14, 1975, when the DLA informed Chrysler that third parties had made an FOIA request for disclosure of the 1974 AAP for Chrysler's Newark, Del., assembly plant and an October 1974 CIR [Complaint Investigation Report] for the same facility. Nine days later Chrysler objected to release of the requested information, relying on OFCCP's disclosure regulations and on exemptions to the FOIA. Chrysler also requested a copy of the CIR, since it had never seen it. DLA responded the following week that it had determined that the requested material was subject to disclosure under the FOIA and the OFCCP disclosure rules, and that both documents would be released five days later.

On the day the documents were to be released Chrysler filed a complaint in the United States District Court for Delaware seeking to enjoin release of the Newark documents. * * *

Chrysler made three arguments in support of its prayer for an injunction: that disclosure was barred by the FOIA; that it was inconsistent with 18 U.S.C. § 1905, 42 U.S.C. § 2000e–8(e), and 44 U.S.C. § 3508, which for ease of reference will be referred to as the "confidentiality statutes"; and finally that disclosure was an abuse of agency discretion insofar as it conflicted with OFCCP rules. * * *

* * *

In contending that the FOIA bars disclosure of the requested equal employment opportunity information, Chrysler relies on the Act's nine exemptions and argues that they require an agency to withhold exempted material. In this case it relies specifically on Exemption 4:

"(b) [FOIA] does not apply to matters that are—

* * *

"(4) trade secrets and commercial or financial information obtained from a person and privileged or confidential * * *."

Chrysler contends that the nine exemptions in general, and Exemption 4 in particular, reflect a sensitivity to the privacy interests of private individuals and nongovernmental entities. That contention may be conceded without inexorably requiring the conclusion that the exemptions impose affirmative duties on an agency to withhold information sought. In fact, that conclusion is not supported by the language, logic, or history of the Act.

The organization of the Act is straightforward. Subsection (a), 5 U.S.C. § 552(a), places a general obligation on the agency to make information available to the public and sets out specific modes of disclosure for certain classes of information. Subsection (b), 5 U.S.C. § 552(b), which lists the exemptions, simply states that the specified material is not subject to the disclosure obligations set out in subsection (a). By its terms, subsection (b) demarcates the agency's obligation to disclose; it does not foreclose disclosure.

That the FOIA is exclusively a disclosure statute is, perhaps, demonstrated most convincingly by examining its provision for judicial relief. Subsection (a)(4)(B) gives federal district courts "jurisdiction to enjoin the agency from withholding agency records and to order the production of any agency records improperly withheld from the complainant." 5 U.S.C. § 552(a)(4)(B). That provision does not give the authority to bar disclosure * * *. Congress appreciated that, with the expanding sphere of governmental regulation and enterprise, much of the information within Government files has been submitted by private entities seeking Government contracts or responding to unconditional reporting obligations imposed by law. There was sentiment that Government agencies should have the latitude, in certain circumstances, to afford the confidentiality desired by these submitters. But the Congressional concern was the *agency's* need or preference for confidentiality; the FOIA by itself protects the submitters' interest in confidentiality only to the extent that this interest is endorsed by the agency collecting the information.

* * *

This conclusion is further supported by the legislative history. * * *

We therefore conclude that Congress did not limit an agency's discretion to disclose information when it enacted the FOIA. It necessarily follows that the Act does not afford Chrysler any right to enjoin agency disclosure.

Chrysler contends, however, that even if its suit for injunctive relief cannot be based on the FOIA, such an action can be premised on the Trade Secrets Act, 18 U.S.C. § 1905. The act provides:

> "Whoever, being an officer or employee of the United States or of any department or agency thereof, publishes, divulges, discloses, or makes known in any manner or to any extent not authorized by law any information coming to him in the course of his employment or official duties or by reason of any examination or investigation made by, or return, report or record made to or filed with, such department or agency or officer or employee thereof, which information concerns or relates to the trade secrets, processes, operations, style of work, or apparatus, or to the identity, confidential statistical data, amount or source of any income, profits, losses, or expenditures of any person, firm, partnership, corporation, or association; or permits any income return or copy thereof or any book containing any abstract or particulars thereof to be seen or examined by any person except as provided by law; shall be fined not more than $1,000, or imprisoned not more than one year, or both; and shall be removed from office or employment."

There are necessarily two parts to Chrysler's argument: that § 1905 is applicable to the type of disclosure threatened in this case, and that it affords Chrysler a private right of action to obtain injunctive relief.

The Court of Appeals held that § 1905 was not applicable to the agency disclosure at issue here because such disclosure was "authorized by law" within the meaning of the Act. The court found the source of that authorization to be the OFCCP regulations that DLA relied on in deciding to disclose information on the Hamtramck and Newark plants. Chrysler contends here that these agency regulations are not "law" within the meaning of § 1905.

* * *

The regulations relied on by the respondents in this case as providing "authoriz[ation] by law" within the meaning of § 1905 certainly affect individual rights and obligations; they govern the public's right to information in records obtained under Executive Order 11246 and the confidentiality rights of those who submit information to OFCCP and its compliance agencies. It is a much closer question, however, whether they are the product of a congressional grant of legislative authority.

* * * Since materials that are exempt from disclosure under the FOIA are * * * outside the ambit of that Act, the Government cannot

rely on the FOIA as congressional authorization for disclosure regulations that permit the release of information within the Act's nine exemptions.

* * *

The relationship between any grant of legislative authority and the disclosure regulations becomes more remote when one examines § 201 of the Executive Order. It speaks in terms of rules and regulations "necessary and appropriate" to achieve the purposes of the Executive Order. Those purposes are an end to discrimination in employment by the Federal Government and those who deal with the Federal Government. One cannot readily pull from the logic and purposes of the Executive Order any concern with the public's access to information in Government files or the importance of protecting trade secrets or confidential business statistics.

* * *

The respondents argue, however, that even if these regulations do not have the force of law by virtue of Executive Order 11246, an explicit grant of legislative authority for such regulations can be found in 5 U.S.C. § 301, commonly referred to as the "housekeeping statute." It provides:

> "The head of an Executive department or military department may prescribe regulations for the government of his department, the conduct of its employees, the distribution and performance of its business, and the custody, use, and preservation of its records, papers, and property. This section does not authorize withholding information from the public or limiting the availability of records to the public."

The antecedents of § 301 go back to the beginning of the Republic, when statutes were enacted to give heads of early Government departments authority to govern internal departmental affairs. * * *

* * * [T]here is nothing in the legislative history of § 301 to indicate it is a substantive grant of legislative power to promulgate rules authorizing the *release* of trade secrets or confidential business information. It is indeed a "housekeeping statute," authorizing what the APA terms "rules of agency organization, procedure or practice" as opposed to "substantive rules."

This would suggest that regulations pursuant to § 301 could not provide the "authoriz[ation] by law" required by § 1905. * * *

* * *

We reject [as well] Chrysler's contention that the Trade Secrets Act affords a private right of action to enjoin disclosure in violation of the statute. In *Cort v. Ash*, 422 U.S. 66 (1975) [*infra* Chapter 9], we noted that this Court has rarely implied a private right of action under a criminal statute, and where it has done so "there was at least a statutory basis for inferring that a civil cause of action of some sort lay in favor of someone." Nothing in § 1905 prompts such an inference. Nor are other pertinent circumstances outlined in *Cort* present here. As our review of the legislative history of § 1905—or lack of same—might suggest, there is no indication of legislative intent to create a private right of action. Most importantly, a private right of action under § 1905 is not "necessary to make effective the congressional purpose," for we find that review of DLA's decision to disclose Chrysler's employment data is available under the APA.

While Chrysler may not avail itself of any violations of the provisions of § 1905 in a separate cause of action, any such violations may have a dispositive effect on the outcome of judicial review of agency action pursuant to § 10 of the APA. Section 10(a) of the APA provides that "[a] person suffering legal wrong because of agency action, or adversely affected or aggrieved by agency action * * * is entitled to judicial review thereof." * * *

Both Chrysler and the respondents agree that there is APA review of DLA's decision. They disagree on the proper scope of review. Chrysler argues that there should be *de novo* review, while the respondents contend that such review is only available in extraordinary cases and this is not such a case.

* * * For the reasons previously stated, we believe any disclosure that * * * violates § 1905 is "not in accordance with law" within the meaning of 5 U.S.C. § 706(2)(A). *De novo* review by the District Court is ordinarily not necessary to decide whether a contemplated disclosure runs afoul of § 1905. The District Court in this case concluded that disclosure of some of Chrysler's documents was barred by § 1905, but the Court of Appeals did not reach the issue. We shall therefore vacate the Court of Appeals' judgment and remand for further proceedings consistent with this opinion in order that the Court of Appeals may consider whether the contemplated disclosures would violate the prohibition of § 1905.[49] Since the decision regarding this substantive issue—the scope of § 1905—will necessarily have some effect on the proper form of judicial review pursuant to § 706(2), we think it unnecessary, and therefore unwise, at the present stage of this case for us to express any additional views on that issue.

Vacated and remanded.

[The concurring opinion of JUSTICE MARSHALL is omitted.]

49. Since the Court of Appeals assumed for purposes of argument that the material in question was within an exemption to the FOIA, that court found it unnecessary expressly to decide that issue and it is open on remand. We, of course, do not here attempt to determine the relative ambits of Exemption 4 and § 1905, or to determine whether § 1905 is an exempting statute within the terms of the amended Exemption 3, 5 U.S.C. § 552(b)(3). Although there is a theoretical possibility that material might be outside Exemption 4 yet within the substantive provisions of § 1905, and that therefore the FOIA might provide the necessary "authoriz[ation] by law" for purposes of § 1905, that possibility is at most of limited practical significance in view of the similarity of language between Exemption 4 and the substantive provisions of § 1905.

* * *

Notes

1. *Scope of Section 1905.* The Supreme Court's *Chrysler* decision had been awaited as the definitive ruling on issues raised by the growing stream of "reverse FOIA" suits by suppliers of information to the government. The Court's opinion provides relatively clear guidance on the elements of such suits, with the notable exception of the persistent issue of the scope of § 1905. On that issue, the Court has never spoken decisively, and the legislative history of the provision is no more helpful. Because providers of information to the government frequently are as concerned about the timing as about the occurrence of disclosure, e.g., if the information relates to decisions not yet implemented, many "reverse FOIA" suits are brought to delay release and may never yield rulings on the underlying issues of confidentiality.

2. *Notice to Suppliers of Information.* As the *Chrysler* opinion describes, it has been the practice of the Department of Defense, as well as many other agencies, to give notice to suppliers of information before releasing it, thus affording an opportunity for them to protect their "property" by administrative appeal or judicial challenge. But no court has held that such notice is legally required, and one early opinion that discussed the issue at length held that it is not. See *Pharmaceutical Manufacturers Association v. Weinberger*, 401 F.Supp. 444 (D.D.C.1975), 411 F.Supp. 576 (D.D.C.1976).

Business interests have long complained about the failure of some agencies to notify them about the impending release of sensitive materials they have submitted to the government, and have pointed to instances in which concededly confidential information has been released by mistake. Efforts have been made to include a mandatory notification provision in amendments to the FOIA itself, but none has succeeded. In part in response to these complaints, President Reagan in 1987 issued Executive Order No. 12,600, "Predisclosure Notification Procedures for Confidential Commercial Information," 52 Fed.Reg. 23,781. Sections of the order require each agency subject to the FOIA "to the extent permitted by law" to "establish procedures to notify submitters of records containing confidential commercial information * * * when those records are requested. * * * " if the agency "determines that it may be required to disclose the records." Section 2 of the order defines "confidential commercial information" as records "that *arguably contain material exempt from release*" (emphasis supplied) under exemption 4 of the FOIA "because disclosure could reasonably be expected to cause substantial competitive harm." Section 4 obligates agencies to provide notified submitters an opportunity to "object to the disclosure * * * and to state all grounds upon which disclosure is opposed." In turn, section 5 requires agencies to provide a written explanation when such objections are not sustained.

Section 3 of Executive Order No. 12,600 distinguishes between records submitted prior to January 1, 1988, and all others. In regard to the former category of records, agencies are required to provide predisclosure notice if the records have within ten years been designated by the submitter as confidential or if the agency "has reason to believe" that disclosure "could reasonably be expected to cause substantial competitive harm." Submitters of records after January 1, 1988, are to be given an opportunity to designate portions whose disclosure they claim could result in competitive harm.

Section 8 outlines the circumstances in which these mandated procedures need not be followed:

Sec. 8. The notice requirements of this Order need not be followed if:

(a) The agency determines that the information should not be disclosed;

(b) The information has been published or has been officially made available to the public;

(c) Disclosure of the information is required by law (other than 5 U.S.C. 552);

(d) The disclosure is required by an agency rule that (1) was adopted pursuant to notice and public comment, (2) specifies narrow classes of records submitted to the agency that are to be released under the Freedom of Information Act, and (3) provides in exceptional circumstances for notice when the submitter provides written justification, at the time the information is submitted or a reasonable time thereafter, that disclosure of the information could reasonably be expected to cause substantial competitive harm.

(e) The information requested is not designated by the submitter as exempt from disclosure in accordance with agency regulations promulgated pursuant to section 7, when the submitter had an opportunity to do so at the time of submission of the information or a reasonable time thereafter, unless the agency has substantial reason to believe that disclosure of the information would result in competitive harm; or

(f) The designation made by the submitter in accordance with agency regulations promulgated pursuant to section 7 appears obviously frivolous; except that, in such case, the agency must provide the submitter with written notice of any final administrative disclosure determination within a reasonable number of days prior to the specified disclosure date.

3. *Further Reading*. Still useful pre-*Chrysler* secondary literature on "reverse FOIA" litigation includes Daniel Gorham Clement, *The Rights of Submitters to Prevent Agency Disclosure of Confidential Business Information: The Reverse Freedom of Information Act Lawsuit*, 55 Tex.L.Rev. 587 (1977); Comment, *Reverse–Freedom of Information Act Suits: Confidential Information in Search of Protection*, 70 Nw.U.L.Rev. 995 (1976); Note, *Protection from Government Disclosure—The Reverse–FOIA Suit*, 1976 Duke L.J. 330 (1976). For more recent developments, see James T. O'Reilly, Federal Information Disclosure Ch. 10 (2d ed. 1990); Comment, *De Novo Review in Reverse Freedom of Information Act Suits*, 50 Ohio St.L.J. 1307 (1989); and Note, *Protecting Confidential Business Information from Federal Agency Disclosure After* Chrysler Corp. v. Brown, 80 Colum.L.Rev. 109 (1980).

Exemption of Proprietary Information

Exemption 4 has been one of the most frequently invoked, and its coverage and implementation have increasingly generated concern within the business community as the FOIA has become a mechanism for industrial "espionage." A common objective of businesses is to find out what competitors are doing; if one's competitors must share that information with the government, what better way of finding out than an FOIA request?

The most frequently cited statement of the scope of exemption 4, *National Parks and Conservation Association v. Morton*, 498 F.2d 765 (D.C.Cir.1974), grew out of a request to the National Park Service for financial records submitted by park concessionaires. The Service claimed that the materials were exempt from disclosure as "commercial or financial information obtained from a person and privileged or confidential." Because the parties agreed that the information sought was not privileged, the court focused on its confidentiality.

Judge Tamm identified two justifications for the FOIA's exemption of commercial records: "(1) encouraging cooperation by those who are not obliged to provide information to the government and (2) protecting the rights of those who must." He went on to conclude that information should be considered "confidential" for purposes of exemption 4 if its disclosure would either impair the government's ability to obtain such information in the future, or "cause substantial harm to the competitive position of the person from whom the information was obtained." The finding that a provider of information would not ordinarily have made it public, by itself, would not justify withholding. Because the Park Service was authorized to require the submission of the records in question, disclosure could not imperil its ability to obtain information in the future. But the court could not, on the record before it, determine whether disclosure would harm the concessionaires' competitive position; though in one sense monopolists, the concessionaires could face competition from other applicants for their exclusive franchise to do business in the parks.

The "trade secret" language of exemption 4 has generated fewer disputes than the "confidential commercial information" language at issue in *Morton*, *supra*, but it is hardly self-defining. Several agencies and many courts have embraced the broad definition of "trade secret" in the Restatement of Torts § 757, comment b (1939). The D.C. Circuit, in *Public Citizen Health Research Group v. FDA*, 704 F.2d 1280 (D.C.Cir. 1983), however, adopted a restrictive interpretation of this term, limiting protection to information about the "productive process" as distinct from more general matters of commercial confidentiality. Accord *Anderson v. Department of Health and Human Services*, 907 F.2d 936 (10th Cir.1990).

Protection of Personal Privacy

Exemption 6 excludes from the FOIA's coverage "personnel and medical files and similar files the disclosure of which would constitute a clearly unwarranted invasion of personal privacy." In 1974 Congress amended exemption 7 to permit withholding of information in investigatory files where disclosure would result in an "unwarranted" invasion of personal privacy.

The language and legislative history of exemption 6 confirm that it alone of the nine original exemptions contemplates case-by-case balancing. The question is what factors are to be balanced in determining whether disclosure is "clearly unwarranted?"

The plaintiffs in *Department of the Air Force v. Rose*, 425 U.S. 352 (1976), were student editors of a law review who requested access to case summaries, with names and identifying information deleted, of honor and ethics hearings at the Air Force Academy. The Air Force denied their request even though such summaries were routinely posted on bulletin boards at the Academy. The Court rejected the contention that the summaries were covered by exemptions 2 and 6 and affirmed a ruling ordering the Air Force to submit the summaries to the district court for an in camera inspection and to cooperate in redacting the records to delete all names and identifying information. Noting that "the general thrust of the exemption [2] is simply to relieve agencies of the burden of assembling and maintaining for public inspection matter in which the public could not reasonably be expected to have an interest," the majority found it inapplicable to the case summaries because they were not routine matters of internal significance, but rather were matters of significant public interest. The majority held that the phrase in exemption 6 "the disclosure of which would constitute a clearly unwarranted invasion of personal privacy" modified "personnel and medical files" as well as "similar files." Thus limited to "clearly unwarranted" invasions of privacy, the exemption required balancing "the individual's right of privacy against the preservation of the basic purpose of the * * * Act 'to open agency action to the light of public scrutiny.'" This balance would be achieved by the district court's in camera inspection and expurgation of the case summaries.

The plaintiffs in *United States Department of State v. Ray*, 502 U.S. 164 (1991), were a Florida lawyer who represented undocumented Haitian nationals seeking political asylum in the United States and three of his clients. They sought to prove in immigration proceedings that Haitians who had immigrated illegally to the United States would face a well-founded fear of persecution if returned to their homeland and were therefore refugees entitled to asylum. In order to test the Government's assertion that undocumented Haitian nationals had not been persecuted upon their return to Haiti, the plaintiffs made a series of FOIA requests to three Government agencies for reports of interviews by State Department personnel with persons who had been involuntarily returned to Haiti. The Department of State produced 25 documents containing information about involuntary Haitian returnees, but deleted the names of the Haitian nationals from 17 of the documents that reported on the actual individual interviews, claiming authority under exemption 6 to withhold their identities.

The Supreme Court unanimously upheld the State Department's position. The Court concluded that disclosure of the names would significantly impinge on the interviewees' privacy because (1) the redacted summaries contained significant personal information about the interviewees; (2) disclosure would embarrass and perhaps endanger persons who had cooperated with a State Department investigation; and (3) the interviewees had disclosed private information under assurances of confidentiality. Invasion of these privacy interests was "clearly unwarranted" because unredacted portions of the released documents provided full information about the State Department's performance of its duty to monitor Haitian compliance with that government's promise not to persecute returnees. Moreover, the Court discerned no weighty public interest in the possibility that a release of the interviewees' names might lead the plaintiffs to additional information outside government files because nothing in the record suggested either that the reports were inaccurate or that further questioning of those already interviewed would produce any relevant information not already released.

The Court has made clear that, where the potential for invasion of privacy has been shown, the importance of the information sought in light of the needs of the individual requester is *not* to be considered in deciding whether the invasion of privacy is "clearly unwarranted:"

> "[T]he only relevant public interest in the FOIA balancing analysis" is "the extent to which disclosure of the information sought would 'she[d] light on an agency's performance of its statutory duties' or otherwise let citizens know 'what their government is up to.' " " '[T]he purposes for which the request for information is made,' " * * * have no bearing on whether information must be disclosed under FOIA.

Bibles v. Oregon Natural Desert Association, 519 U.S. 355, 355–56 (1997) (citations omitted).

FOIA's Relationship to the Privacy Act and Other Statutes

Exemptions 6 and 7 are not the Act's only safeguards of personal privacy interests. Exemption 3's reference to material "specifically exempted from disclosure by statute" reaches scores, if not hundreds (see H.R.Rep.No. 1497, 89th Cong., 2d Sess. 10 (1966)), of existing statutory prohibitions against disclosure of information held by the government, many of which are designed to protect individual privacy.

In the Privacy Act of 1974, Pub.L.No. 93–579, 5 U.S.C. § 552a, Congress enlarged the legal protections for individual privacy. The basic objectives of that law are to restrict dissemination of information about individuals both within and outside the government, to assure that such information usually is not released to third parties without the knowledge and consent of the individuals, and to afford individuals a procedure for challenging the accuracy of information about them in government files.

The Act is not comprehensive, however, in protecting information regarding individuals because it applies only to records within a "system of records," that is, a group of agency records "from which information is retrieved by the name of the individual or by some identifying number, symbol, or other identifying particular assigned to the individual." 5 U.S.C. § 552a(a)(5). The Act creates two presumptive rules, each subject to numerous exceptions: first, a presumption against disclosing covered records to third-parties; second, presumptive access to covered records for the subjects of those records.

For a decade after its enactment, the relationship of the Privacy Act to the FOIA was unclear. Although issues concerning the interplay between the statutes may arise in a number of contexts, the two issues of persistent concern were these: (1) If a record need not be disclosed to its subject under the Privacy Act, does it become exempt from disclosure under exemption 3 of the FOIA? (2) If a record is protected from disclosure under the Privacy Act and exempt from mandatory disclosure under the FOIA, may an agency nonetheless disclose that record pursuant to an FOIA request?

Prior to 1984, there was a split in the circuits concerning whether the Privacy Act qualified as a statute "specifically exempting" material from disclosure under exemption 3 of the FOIA. The D.C. and the Third Circuits held that it did not, see, e.g., *Greentree v. United States Customs Service*, 674 F.2d 74 (D.C.Cir.1982); *Porter v. United States Department of Justice*, 717 F.2d 787 (3d Cir.1983), while the Seventh and Fifth Circuits held that it did. See *Shapiro v. Drug Enforcement Administration*, 721 F.2d 215 (7th Cir.1983); *Painter v. FBI*, 615 F.2d 689 (5th Cir.1980). Congress eliminated the ambiguity in 1984, by enacting 5 U.S.C. § 552a(q)(2), which expressly prohibits relying on Privacy Act exemptions to withhold records from individuals that would otherwise be accessible to them under the FOIA. It is likewise the case that an agency may not rely on FOIA exemptions to withhold from an individual a record to which that person is entitled under the Privacy Act. 5 U.S.C. § 552a(q)(1).

The answer to the second question is likewise negative. The Privacy Act exempts from its general prohibition against third-party disclosure those records concerning individuals that are "required" to be disclosed under the FOIA. 5 U.S.C. § 552a(b)(2). If an agency could rely on a FOIA exemption to protect a record from mandatory disclosure, it would seem to follow that FOIA disclosure is not "required," and, therefore, for Privacy Act purposes, not permitted. *Brown v. FBI*, 658 F.2d 71 (2d Cir.1981); *Bartel v. FAA*, 725 F.2d 1403 (D.C.Cir.1984). This interpretation, however, when implemented in light of the limited balancing sanctioned by decisions such as *Bibles v. Oregon Natural Desert Association, supra*, can produce significant policy tensions, as illustrated in the following case:

DEPARTMENT OF DEFENSE v. FEDERAL LABOR RELATIONS AUTHORITY

Supreme Court of the United States, 1994.
510 U.S. 487, 114 S.Ct. 1006, 127 L.Ed.2d 325.

JUSTICE THOMAS delivered the opinion of the Court.

This case requires us to consider whether disclosure of the home addresses of federal civil service employees by their employing agency pursuant to a request made by the employees' collective-bargaining representative under the Federal Service Labor–Management Relations Statute, 5 U.S.C. §§ 7101–7135 (1988 ed. and Supp. IV), would constitute a "clearly unwarranted invasion" of the employees' personal privacy within the meaning of the Freedom of Information Act, 5 U.S.C. § 552. Concluding that it would, we reverse the judgment of the Court of Appeals.

I

The controversy underlying this case arose when two local unions[1] requested the petitioner federal agencies[2] to provide them with the names and home addresses of the agency employees in the bargaining units represented by the unions. The agencies supplied the unions with the employees' names and work stations, but refused to release home addresses.

In response, the unions filed unfair labor practice charges with respondent Federal Labor Relations Authority (Authority), in which they contended that the Federal Service Labor–Management Relations Statute (Labor Statute), 5 U.S.C. §§ 7101–7135 (1988 ed. and Supp. IV), required the agencies to divulge the addresses. The Labor Statute generally provides that agencies must, "to the extent not prohibited by law," furnish unions with data that is necessary for collective-bargaining purposes. § 7114(b)(4). The agencies argued that disclosure of the home addresses was prohibited by the Privacy Act of 1974 (Privacy Act), 5 U.S.C. § 552a (1988 ed. and Supp. IV)* * *. [T]he Authority rejected that argument and ordered the agencies to divulge the addresses.

A divided panel of the United States Court of Appeals for the Fifth Circuit granted enforcement of the Authority's orders. The panel majority agreed with the Authority that the unions' requests for home addresses fell within a statutory exception to the Privacy Act. That Act does not bar disclosure of personal information if disclosure would be "required

1. Local 1657 of the United Food and Commercial Workers Union represents a bargaining unit composed of employees of the Navy CBC Exchange in Gulfport, Mississippi. Local 1345 of respondent American Federation of Government Employees, AFL–CIO, represents a worldwide bargaining unit composed of employees of the Army and Air Force Exchange, which is headquartered in Dallas, Texas.

2. Petitioners are the U.S. Department of Defense, U.S. Department of the Navy, Navy CBC Exchange, Construction Battalion Center, Gulfport, Mississippi, and the U.S. Department of Defense, Army and Air Force Exchange, Dallas, Texas.

under section 552 of this title [the Freedom of Information Act (FOIA)]." 5 U.S.C. § 552a(b)(2). The court below observed that FOIA, with certain enumerated exceptions, generally mandates full disclosure of information held by agencies. In the view of the Court of Appeals, only one of the enumerated exceptions—the provision exempting from FOIA's coverage personnel files "the disclosure of which would constitute a clearly unwarranted invasion of personal privacy," 5 U.S.C. § 552(b)(6) (Exemption 6)—potentially applied to this case.

In determining whether Exemption 6 applied, the Fifth Circuit balanced the public interest in effective collective bargaining embodied in the Labor Statute against the interest of employees in keeping their home addresses private. The court recognized that, in light of our decision in *Department of Justice v. Reporters Committee for Freedom of Press*, 489 U.S. 749 (1989), other Courts of Appeals had concluded that the only public interest to be weighed in the Exemption 6 balancing analysis is the extent to which FOIA's central purpose of opening agency action to public scrutiny would be served by disclosure. Rejecting that view, however, the panel majority reasoned that Reporters Committee "has absolutely nothing to say about * * * the situation that arises when disclosure is initially required by some statute other than the FOIA, and the FOIA is employed only secondarily." In such cases, the court ruled that "it is proper for the federal court to consider the public interests embodied in the statute which generates the disclosure request."

Applying this approach, the court concluded that, because the weighty interest in public sector collective bargaining identified by Congress in the Labor Statute would be advanced by the release of the home addresses, disclosure "would not constitute a clearly unwarranted invasion of privacy." In the panel majority's view, because Exemption 6 would not apply, FOIA would require disclosure of the addresses; in turn, therefore, the Privacy Act did not forbid the agencies from divulging the addresses, and the Authority's orders were binding. The dissenting judge argued that Reporters Committee controlled the case and barred the agencies from disclosing their employees' addresses to the unions* * *.

II

Like the Court of Appeals, we begin our analysis with the terms of the Labor Statute, which governs labor-management relations in the federal civil service. Consistent with the congressional finding that "labor organizations and collective bargaining in the civil service are in the public interest," 5 U.S.C. § 7101(a), the Labor Statute requires an agency to accord exclusive recognition to a labor union that is elected by employees to serve as the representative of a bargaining unit. § 7111(a). An exclusive representative must represent fairly all employees in the unit, regardless of whether they choose to become union members. § 7114(a)(1). The Labor Statute also imposes a duty on the agency and the exclusive representative to negotiate in good faith for the purpose of arriving at a collective-bargaining agreement. § 7114(a)(4).

To fulfill its good-faith bargaining obligation, an agency must, inter alia, "furnish to the exclusive representative involved, or its authorized representative, upon request and, to the extent not prohibited by law, data * * * (B) which is reasonably available and necessary for full and proper discussion, understanding, and negotiation of subjects within the scope of collective bargaining." § 7114(b)(4)(B) (emphasis added). The Authority has determined that the home addresses of bargaining unit employees constitute information that is "necessary" to the collective-bargaining process because through them, unions may communicate with employees more effectively than would otherwise be possible* * *. This determination, which has been upheld by several Courts of Appeals, is not before us. Nor is there any dispute that the addresses are "reasonably available." Therefore, unless disclosure is "prohibited by law," agencies such as petitioners must release home addresses to exclusive representatives upon request.

Petitioners contend that the Privacy Act prohibits disclosure. This statute provides in part:

"No agency shall disclose any record which is contained in a system of records by any means of communication to any person, or to another agency, except pursuant to a written request by, or with the prior written consent of, the individual to whom the record pertains, unless disclosure of the record would be * * * (2) required under section 552 of this title [FOIA]." 5 U.S.C. § 552a(b)(2) (1988 ed. and Supp. IV).

The employee addresses sought by the unions are "records" covered by the broad terms of the Privacy Act. Therefore, unless FOIA would require release of the addresses, their disclosure is "prohibited by law," and the agencies may not reveal them to the unions.[4]

We turn, then, to FOIA* * *. [A]lthough this case requires us to follow a somewhat convoluted path of statutory cross-references, its proper resolution depends upon a discrete inquiry: whether disclosure of the home addresses "would constitute a clearly unwarranted invasion of [the] personal privacy" of bargaining unit employees within the meaning of FOIA. For guidance in answering this question, we need look no further than to our decision in *Department of Justice v. Reporters Committee for Freedom of Press*, 489 U.S. 749 (1989).

4. The written-consent provision of the Privacy Act is not implicated in this case. The unions already have access to the addresses of their members and to those of nonmembers who have divulged this information to them. It is not disputed that the unions are able to contact bargaining unit employees at work and ask them for their home addresses. In practical effect, the unions seek only those addresses that they do not currently possess: the addresses of non-union employees who have not revealed this information to their exclusive representative. We also note that we are not asked in this case to consider the potential applicability of any other Privacy Act exceptions, such as the "routine use" exception. See 5 U.S.C. § 552a(b)(3). Respondents rely solely on the argument that the unions' requests for home addresses fall within the Privacy Act's FOIA exception.

Reporters Committee involved FOIA requests addressed to the Federal Bureau of Investigation that sought the "rap sheets" of several individuals. In the process of deciding that the FBI was prohibited from disclosing the contents of the rap sheets, we reaffirmed several basic principles that have informed our interpretation of FOIA. First, in evaluating whether a request for information lies within the scope of a FOIA exemption, such as Exemption 6, that bars disclosure when it would amount to an invasion of privacy that is to some degree "unwarranted," "a court must balance the public interest in disclosure against the interest Congress intended the [e]xemption to protect."

Second, the only relevant "public interest in disclosure" to be weighed in this balance is the extent to which disclosure would serve the "core purpose of the FOIA," which is "contribut[ing] significantly to public understanding of the operations or activities of the government."

Third, "whether an invasion of privacy is warranted cannot turn on the purposes for which the request for information is made." Because "Congress 'clearly intended' the FOIA 'to give any member of the public as much right to disclosure as one with a special interest [in a particular document],' " except in certain cases involving claims of privilege, "the identity of the requesting party has no bearing on the merits of his or her FOIA request."

III

The principles that we followed in *Reporters Committee* can be applied easily to this case. We must weigh the privacy interest of bargaining unit employees in nondisclosure of their addresses against the only relevant public interest in the FOIA balancing analysis—the extent to which disclosure of the information sought would "she[d] light on an agency's performance of its statutory duties" or otherwise let citizens know "what their government is up to."

The relevant public interest supporting disclosure in this case is negligible, at best. Disclosure of the addresses might allow the unions to communicate more effectively with employees, but it would not appreciably further "the citizens' right to be informed about what their government is up to." 489 U.S., at 773 (internal quotation marks omitted). Indeed, such disclosure would reveal little or nothing about the employing agencies or their activities* * *.

Apparently realizing that this conclusion follows ineluctably from an application of the FOIA tenets we embraced in *Reporters Committee*, respondents argue that *Reporters Committee* is largely inapposite here because it dealt with an information request made directly under FOIA, whereas the unions' requests for home addresses initially were made under the Labor Statute, and implicated FOIA only incidentally through a chain of statutory cross-references. In such a circumstance, contend respondents, to give full effect to the three statutes involved and to allow unions to perform their statutory representational duties, we should import the policy considerations that are made explicit in the Labor

Statute into the FOIA Exemption 6 balancing analysis. If we were to do so, respondents are confident we would conclude that the Labor Statute's policy favoring collective bargaining easily outweighs any privacy interest that employees might have in nondisclosure.

We decline to accept respondents' ambitious invitation to rewrite the statutes before us and to disregard the FOIA principles reaffirmed in *Reporters Committee*. The Labor Statute does not, as the Fifth Circuit suggested, merely "borro[w] the FOIA's disclosure calculus for another purpose." Rather, it allows the disclosure of information necessary for effective collective bargaining only "to the extent not prohibited by law." 5 U.S.C. § 7114(b)(4). Disclosure of the home addresses is prohibited by the Privacy Act unless an exception to that Act applies. The terms of the Labor Statute in no way suggest that the Privacy Act should be read in light of the purposes of the Labor Statute. If there is an exception, therefore, it must be found within the Privacy Act itself. Congress could have enacted an exception to the Privacy Act's coverage for information "necessary" for collective-bargaining purposes, but it did not do so. In the absence of such a provision, respondents rely on the exception for information the disclosure of which would be "required under [FOIA]." § 552a(b)(2). Nowhere, however, does the Labor Statute amend FOIA's disclosure requirements or grant information requestors under the Labor Statute special status under FOIA.[5] Therefore, because all FOIA requestors have an equal, and equally qualified, right to information, the fact that respondents are seeking to vindicate the policies behind the Labor Statute is irrelevant to the FOIA analysis* * *.

Against the virtually nonexistent FOIA-related public interest in disclosure, we weigh the interest of bargaining unit employees in nondisclosure of their home addresses. Because a very slight privacy interest would suffice to outweigh the relevant public interest, we need not be exact in our quantification of the privacy interest. It is enough for present purposes to observe that the employees' interest in nondisclosure is not insubstantial* * *.

Because the privacy interest of bargaining unit employees in nondisclosure of their home addresses substantially outweighs the negligible FOIA-related public interest in disclosure, we conclude that disclosure would constitute a "clearly unwarranted invasion of personal privacy." 5 U.S.C. § 552(b)(6). FOIA, thus, does not require the agencies to divulge the addresses, and the Privacy Act, therefore, prohibits their release to the unions.

5. In this regard, see Department of Veterans Affairs, 958 F.2d, at 512 ("Nowhere in the [Labor Statute] does its language indicate that the disclosure calculus required by FOIA should be modified. Nowhere do we find a qualification that the policies of collective bargaining should be integrated into FOIA"); Department of Treasury, 884 F.2d, at 1453 ("Privacy Act exception b(2) speaks only of FOIA. We do not believe we are entitled to engage in the sort of imaginative reconstruction that would be necessary to introduce collective bargaining values into the [FOIA] balancing process").

IV

Respondents argue that our decision will have a number of untoward effects. First, they contend that without access to home addresses, public sector unions will be unable to communicate with and represent effectively all bargaining unit employees. Such a result, they believe, thwarts the collective-bargaining policies explicitly embodied in the Labor Statute. According to respondents, it is illogical to believe that Congress intended the Privacy Act and FOIA to be interpreted in a manner that hinders the effectuation of the purposes motivating the Labor Statute.

Respondents, however, place undue emphasis on what they perceive to be the impulses of the Congress that enacted the Labor Statute, and neglect to consider the language in that statute that calls into play the limitations of the Privacy Act. Speculation about the ultimate goals of the Labor Statute is inappropriate here; the statute plainly states that an agency need furnish an exclusive representative with information that is necessary for collective-bargaining purposes only "to the extent not prohibited by law." 5 U.S.C. § 7114(b)(4). Disclosure of the addresses in this case is prohibited "by law," the Privacy Act. By disallowing disclosure, we do no more than give effect to the clear words of the provisions we construe, including the Labor Statute* * *.

Second, respondents fear that our ruling will allow agencies, acting pursuant to the Privacy Act, to refuse to provide unions with other employee records, such as disciplinary reports and performance appraisals, that the unions need in order to perform their duties as exclusive bargaining representatives. This concern is not presented in this case, however, and we do not address it.

Finally, respondents contend that our decision creates an unnecessary and unintended disparity between public and private sector unions. While private sector unions assertedly are entitled to receive employee home address lists from employers under the National Labor Relations Act, as interpreted by the National Labor Relations Board, respondents claim that federal sector unions now will be needlessly barred from obtaining this information, despite the lack of any indication that Congress intended such a result. See *Department of Treasury*, 884 F.2d, at 1457–1461 (R. Ginsburg, J., concurring). We do not question that, as a general matter, private sector labor law may provide guidance in parallel public sector matters. This fact has little relevance here, however, for unlike private sector employees, federal employees enjoy the protection of the Privacy Act, and that statute prohibits the disclosure of the address lists sought in this case. To the extent that this prohibition leaves public sector unions in a position different from that of their private sector counterparts, Congress may correct the disparity* * *.

[The concurring opinions of Justices SOUTER and GINSBURG are omitted.]

Note

General commentaries on the Privacy Act include Hanus and Relyea, *A Policy Assessment of the Privacy Act of 1974*, 25 Am.U.L.Rev. 555 (1976), and Report of the Privacy Protection Study Commission, Personal Privacy in an Information Society (1977).

5. IMPACT AND REFORM OF THE FOIA

For legislation that is ostensibly ancillary to the central functions of government agencies, the FOIA has stimulated not only an extraordinary volume of litigation but also continuous, often strident debate over its effects, its costs, and its value. During the latter years of the Carter Administration and throughout President Reagan's first term, some congressional critics of the Act, encouraged by the Department of Justice, pressed for further amendments designed mainly to reduce the cost of administering the law and broaden certain of the exemptions. But other informed observers, including spokespersons for public interest organizations, claimed that the agencies responsible for compliance with FOIA have been persistently recalcitrant in fulfilling their obligations.

In an acerbic commentary, *The Freedom of Information Act Has No Clothes*, Regulation, March/April 1982, at 15, Professor (now Justice) Scalia dramatized two of the most often cited defects of the FOIA: its expense and its indiscriminate exposure of information about the internal workings, not of government, but of private organizations who must provide it information:

> The Freedom of Information Act (FOIA) is part of the basic weaponry of modern regulatory war, deployable against regulators and regulated alike. It differs, however, from other weaponry in the conflict, in that it is largely immune from arms limitation debate. * * * It is the Taj Mahal of the Doctrine of Unanticipated Consequences, the Sistine Chapel of Cost–Benefit Analysis Ignored. * * *
>
> * * * [T]he 1974 amendments were estimated by Congress to cost $100,000 a year. They have in fact cost many millions of dollars—no one knows precisely how much. The main reason is that the amendments forbid the government from charging the requester for the so-called processing costs. Responding to a request generally requires three steps: (1) searching for the requested documents; (2) reviewing or "processing" them to determine whether any of the material they contain is exempt from disclosure, to decide whether the exemption should be asserted, and, if so, to make the line-by-line deletions; and (3) duplicating them. Before 1974, the cost for all of this work was chargeable to the requester; since 1974, step two has been at the government's expense. In many cases, it is the most costly part of the process, often requiring the personal attention of high-level personnel for long periods of time. If, for example, material in an investigative file is requested, someone familiar with the investigation must go through the material line by line to delete

those portions, and only those portions, that would disclose a confidential source or come within one of the other specific exceptions to the requirement of disclosure. Moreover, even steps one and three are at the government's expense "where the agency determines that waiver or reduction of the fee is in the public interest because furnishing the information can be considered as primarily benefiting the general public." Even where the agency parsimoniously refuses to grant this waiver, the more generous judiciary sometimes mandates it—which happened for example, in the case of the FOIA request by the Rosenberg children. * * *

Other features of the amendments reflect the same unthinking extravagance and disregard of competing priorities. Although federal agencies carry out a great many important activities, rarely does the law impose a specific deadline for agency action. Yet the FOIA requester is entitled by law to get an answer to his request within ten working days—and, if it is denied, to get a ruling on his appeal within another twenty. * * * So the investigative agent who is needed to review a file must lay aside his other work and undertake that task as his top priority. * * *

In the courts, the statute provides that FOIA appeals shall take precedence on the docket over all cases and shall be assigned for hearing and trial or for argument at the earliest practicable date and expedited in every way. * * *

But the most ironic absolute defect of the '74 amendments was perhaps unintended at the time and seems to have gone virtually unnoticed since. The amendments have significantly reduced the privacy, and hence the autonomy, of all our nongovernmental institutions—corporations, labor unions, universities, churches, political and social clubs—all those private associations that form, as Tocqueville observed, diverse centers of power apart from what would otherwise be the all-powerful democratic state. * * * [V]irtually all activities of private institutions may be subjected to *governmental investigation*—and increasingly are, to ensure compliance with the innumerable requirements of federal laws and regulations. * * *

* * * The way things now work, the government may obtain almost anything in the course of an investigation; and once the investigation is completed the public (or, more specifically, the opponents or competitors of the investigated institution) may obtain all that the investigative file contains, unless one of a few narrow exemptions applies. There is an exemption (though the agency has discretion not to invoke it) for confidential commercial information. But there is none that protects an institution's consultative and deliberative processes—the minutes of a university's faculty meetings, for example. It is noteworthy that internal consultation and advice within the government itself is exempted from disclosure since, as the 1966 House Committee Report explained, "a full and frank exchange of opinions would be impossible if all internal

communications were made public." But no such exemption exists for the internal communications of private organizations that come into the government's hands. * * *

The defects of the Freedom of Information Act cannot be cured as long as we are dominated by the obsession that gave them birth—that the first line of defense against an arbitrary executive is do-it-yourself oversight by the public and its surrogate, the press. On that assumption, the FOIA's excesses are not defects at all, but merely the necessary price for our freedoms. It is a romantic notion, but the facts simply do not bear it out. The major exposes of recent times, from CIA mail openings to Watergate to the FBI COINTELPRO operations, owe virtually nothing to the FOIA but are primarily the product of the institutionalized checks and balances within our system of representative democracy. This is not to say that public access to government information has no useful role—only that it is not the ultimate guarantee of responsible government, justifying the sweeping aside of all other public and private interests at the mere invocation of the magical words "freedom of information." * * *

A contrasting viewpoint, though equally critical of experience under the FOIA, is provided by Professor Robert A. Vaughn, an occasional patron of the Act, see *Vaughn v. Rosen*, 484 F.2d 820 (D.C.Cir.1973), *cert. denied*, 415 U.S. 977 (1974). In *Our Government Stymies Open Government*, Washington Post, July 1, 1984 at C1, Vaughn inveighed against the propensity of government agencies to impede its operation:

The Founding Fathers would be proud of the act—unless they could see how the peoples' government often frustrates its purpose. * * *

* * * [D]ozens of [judicial opinions] issued since 1979 * * * indict the federal government for subverting the spirit and intent of the Freedom of Information Act by delay, intransigence, evasion and even open hostility toward those attempting to avail themselves of their legal rights.

So costly and difficult has the government made it for the public to gain speedy access to information that the Freedom of Information Act may become useless for all but the most-patient and the best-financed citizens. * * *

No doubt some of the problems, including the huge backlog of cases, often result from circumstances beyond the control of agencies, such as the heavy volume of requests and inadequate resources to cope with it. But * * * delays are sometimes motivated by hostility and are used by the government to its own tactical advantage. * * *

The act's current deadlines for response to requests have limited practical significance. The volume of requests and inadequate resources devoted to processing them guarantee large backlogs.

Courts have recognized the practical problems faced by the government by deferring judicial review if an agency is processing its backlog in good faith. The backlog itself has become an issue for the courts. * * *

The courts understandably prefer that cases be resolved without judicial intervention, given that the process of judicial review can be as lengthy as the delay at the agency level. (The administrative office of the United States Courts found that the median time between the filing of an FOIA suit and its disposition in district courts was eight months for the year ending June 30, 1981. And 10 percent of the cases took more than 23 months.)

As things now stand, courts have limited ability to evaluate the reasons for a backlog—and little power to modify the practices of government agencies. One federal court expressed the limitations of judicial enforcement this way: "To be sure, the court deplores the 10–month delay between plaintiffs' request and the agency's action on their appeal, but the staggering practicalities of the 'FOIA explosion' render [other judicial action] both unrealistic and probably unenforceable."

Confronted with delays by government departments, the costs of seeking judicial review and the courts' inability to deal with delay, requesters are left to bargain with the same bureaucracy from which they are seeking information. This procedure discourages individuals and journalists, in particular, from using the act and undoubtedly helps explain why the main users are large organizations, corporations and well-funded interest groups.

One modification made by Congress in 1974 was the establishment of a complicated procedure under which a federal court could initiate an investigation by the executive branch leading to possible disciplining of federal officials who arbitrarily or capriciously withhold information. * * *

But in the 10 years since that provision was passed, the courts have referred only a handful of cases to the agency authorized to investigate: the Office of Special Counsel in the Merit Systems Protection Board, and no federal official has *ever* been disciplined under the provision.

G. ROBINSON, ACCESS TO GOVERNMENT INFORMATION: THE AMERICAN EXPERIENCE

14 Federal L.Rev. 35 (1983).

The real issues of enforcement * * * relate to such matters as administrative costs of disclosure, and benefits of confidentiality of private and governmental information versus the benefits of openness—these are the important elements to be weighed. * * *

The concern over administrative costs is not new; the agencies have for some time complained of the burdens imposed by the heavy volume of requests generated by the liberal disclosure policies and the strict compliance requirements imposed by Congress and the courts. * * *

* * * [T]he common complaint that the fiscal burden is unacceptably high seems to me somewhat overdrawn. We do not have sufficiently detailed cost accounts for FOI Act related activity, but a recent estimate puts the aggregate annual administrative costs at more than $50 million. It is not clear what functions the estimate covers, but it is probably an underestimate; for example, the above estimate does not include judicial enforcement *or* other "indirect" costs. Suppose to allow for all unaccounted costs we estimate the costs at $100 million. To those who balance their cheque books each month, this will seem a royal sum, but in the mega-dimensional budgetary world in which the United States Government operates, $100 million is a trifle. It is indeed far less than the United States Government spends annually in support of programmes to disseminate information abroad. If one supposes that the information needs of United States citizens are entitled to the same respect as those of foreigners, one would have to imagine a large adjustment to the present estimate before costs would warrant serious concern in terms of budgetary impact.

Moreover, one would still not be in a position to declare the budgetary burden to be an important problem without some attention to the benefits of public access to information. To date no one has devised any method for measuring these intangible benefits in quantitative terms. * * *

The real case for increasing the fee level—or for other cost-related administrative reforms—is not a macroeconomic budgetary argument. * * * The real case for cost recovery is more in the nature of a microeconomic rationale of forcing a cost discipline on particular kinds of requests. In this context, the proposal to recoup some of the profits earned by the sale of commercially valuable information by FOI Act requesters is especially noteworthy.

Part of the FOI Act-spawned cottage industry * * * is the thriving business in merchandising FOI Act services or information obtained through the FOI Act, particularly trade secrets or other confidential business information about competitors.[85] While commercialisation is in the best tradition of Yankee entrepreneurship, it is also a minor embar-

85. See *Government, Business and the People's Right to Know* (1978) 3 Media Law Reporter 20–21 (discussing FOI Act service bureaus). See also Montgomery, Peters & Weinburg, *The Freedom of Information Act: Strategic Opportunities and Threats* (1978) Sloan Management Review 1–2 (use of FOI Act to obtain trade secrets and other information about competitors).

The merchandising of FOI Act services and information is not, of course, confined to obtaining business secrets. One enterprising company promotes its "Freedom of Information Kit" with an advertisement that promises: "Here's How to Find Out Which 'Enemies List' You're On—Within 10 Working Days." Weinstein, *"Open Season on 'Open Government'"* (19 June 1979) New York Times Magazine, 32, 85–86. * * *

rassment to the public interest objectives that supposedly guided Congress. * * *

The real point is that whatever Congress contemplated about the public or private uses to which information would be put, it surely did not intend, through the FOI Act, to put its processes of information gathering at the *free* disposal of private interests except where the information had public benefits over and above those reflected in commercial information markets. * * * I do not suggest that disclosure requirements themselves be redefined in terms of public versus private purpose—that disclosure be restricted to those who seek to use it "in the public interest." In the abstract such a distinction would be hard to observe if not wholly meaningless. There is no necessary *conflict* between public and private welfare. The conflict arises when, in the name of public welfare, one group is able to secure *special, distinctive* private benefits at the public expense.

The existence of a private market for commercially valuable information obtained from the government highlights a more basic complaint about the FOI Act than the *free* access to commercially valuable information. The more basic complaint is that the FOI Act has been used to obtain confidential commercial information the disclosure of which is harmful to legitimate business interests. * * *

Exemption four has not, however, * * * prevented some "leakage" of legitimately privileged business information. We do not have reliable evidence as to the magnitude of the problem. The very existence of an apparently successful business devoted to selling commercially valuable information is some evidence that the problem is not imaginary, but as with other claims of FOI Act abuse, the evidence of serious injury from disclosure of confidential commercial information is a bit thin—certainly it is less robust than the expressions of concern by businessmen.

Some of the "leakage" of legitimately confidential information is unintended—the product of careless treatment by agency personnel. But the more significant problem appears to be deliberate disclosure by agencies. * * * The larger problem here is defining the scope of agency discretion. Agency discretion in "reverse FOI Act" cases is subject to judicial review, but the review standards are not as demanding as for judicial determination of the scope of the exemption itself. The asymmetry between judicial review of agency action in FOI Act and reverse-FOI Act cases thus favours disclosure. * * *

* * * At least in terms of a simple increase in the *quantitative* flow of information from government agency files to the public I do not think there can be much question about the effectiveness of the FOI Act.

As to whether the public has significantly benefitted from that information, this is more problematical. * * *

Absent a calculus for quantitative measurement we must resort to general "principles"—faith informed by intuition. It has always been a professed article of faith that an informed public is vital to democratic society. * * * [G]iven our social, political commitment to open, even relatively indiscriminate dissemination of information generally, it is hard to make government disclosure of information dependent on some *specified* positive benefit to the individual or to the society. We simply take that as an axiom of our political and social system that information is good and more information is better.

To be sure, in neither the private nor the public sector are we so committed to the free flow of information as to be indifferent to the costs of unrestrained dissemination. In the private sector we have a complex set of laws designed to limit various kinds of information in order to protect a variety of interests from being injured (suffering costs). Protection of trademarks and copyrights, business "secrets," personal privacy; protection against various forms of misleading or otherwise injurious information (defamation) are illustrative of efforts to prevent certain costs caused by free flow of information. To the extent that these restrictions on information are recognized in the private sector they are properly protected in the public sector. The government should not allow itself to be the vehicle for undermining protected interests in the name of promoting "open government."

This much seems plain. Less plain is the recognition to be given to secrets about the government processes themselves. To what extent should democratic government be forced to operate in a fishbowl? * * *

* * * [G]overnment politicians and bureaucrats are close kin to ordinary people; their personal preferences are very similar to those of people outside government, as are the motives that drive their behaviour. In particular, they probably have about the same mixture of self-interest and "public interest" motivation as others. Of course, politicians and bureaucrats operate in a different environment, with different kinds of freedoms and constraints than those that others confront. Bureaucrats in particular are not subject directly or indirectly to market discipline. Their behaviour is subject to the control of official superiors, or public constituents, but performance standards lack objective measures.

In any environment individuals have a natural self-interest incentive to control information about themselves in order favourably to influence other persons' perceptions of them and of their behaviour. If there is anything distinctive about the public sector environment in this respect, it is the degree to which bureaucrats or politicians are able to control information about their activities and the extent to which evaluations of them and their performance depends on information within their control.

In the private sector, consumer evaluation of the firm's product does not typically depend on public perusal of intracorporate records. Direct experience of the product, measured against competitive substitutes, is normally considered a better measure of the firm's "output." Evaluation of the "output" of the "public firm" of bureaucrats and politicians is not so easily measured by external criteria. Indeed, we need some internal information from the "public firm" even to determine what the relevant output is. It follows that a degree of access to government information, concerning its activities in particular, is essential in order to make the political "marketplace" work.

The above argument merely restates in the somewhat stilted style of academic theory the homely common sense of elementary civics: there are no better guarantees that entrusted power will be well used than an *informed* and critical public *attitude.* The FOI Act makes a positive, if modest, contribution to that guarantee.

See also Hon. Patricia Wald, *The Freedom of Information Act: A Short Case Study in the Perils and Paybacks of Legislating Democratic Values*, 33 Emory L.J. 649 (1984).

Chapter 7

SUITS TO REVIEW ADMINISTRATIVE ACTION

A. INTRODUCTION

1. THE PUBLIC LAW REMEDIAL SYSTEM

Our discussion of agency process in previous chapters has proceeded on the general assumption that judicial remedies were available to protect private rights by testing the legality of administrative action. Our discussion repeatedly raised questions, however, concerning the limits of this "judicial review" function—often drawing attention to the tension between judicial oversight and control and administrative efficacy. Yet, these remedial concerns have been secondary to our interests in exploring the relationships of agencies to the President and Congress, or in observing the means through which agencies accomplish their public purposes within whatever procedural or substantive constraints are enforced through judicial review.

In the three chapters that follow we focus explicitly on the structure of the public law remedial system. Here our interests will be in the public law analogues of familiar private law remedial issues: questions of judicial jurisdiction; of the necessary elements of a "claim" or "cause of action"; of the types of relief available; and of the scope of peremptory defenses that preclude judicial decision on the merits of claims. While legal doctrine abounds, clearly discernible beneath the surface of the technical legal rules are broader concerns about the appropriate legal structure of the administrative state.

Remedial issues in the public law system can be conceptualized in several ways. Our chapter divisions reflect our choice to address them as emerging from three broad and interrelated categories of claims. The first type of remedial claim, considered in Chapter 7, we call "Suits to Review Administrative Action." Here we deal with the most conventional remedies in federal public law—injunctions either prohibitory or mandatory in form, often accompanied by a formal declaration of legal rights and obligations. It is here that the public law system of remedies differs most sharply from the private law system because, in federal public law, the injunction is the most common and least problematic remedy a claimant can pursue.

Often judicial review in this injunctive mode is expressly authorized by a statutory provision that establishes judicial jurisdiction, specifies the form and timing of review proceedings, indicates who can seek review, and empowers the reviewing court to affirm, reverse, or remand particular agency decisions. In other cases, plaintiffs proceed under more general grants of federal jurisdiction, e.g., 21 U.S.C. § 1331, and the questions of *who* may seek review, *when*, and *how* review is to occur are matters of administrative common law—or its close analogue, interpretation of the Constitution or the judicial review provisions of the APA. Whatever the form of proceeding and the specific doctrinal issues raised, such review actions are recognized as oriented broadly to public law concerns. The social function of "judicial review" as we conceptualize it here is the maintenance of the rule of law, given the constraints on judicial authority inherent in a system committed also to a separation of governmental powers.

In Chapter 8 we consider a category of claims that we denominate claims for "Relief from Officially Inflicted Injuries." As in the more common form of review proceedings examined in Chapter 7, plaintiffs who seek damages or specific performance from the government, or from government officials, also invariably question the legality of administrative conduct. To that degree, suits against the government and its officials sounding essentially in tort, contract, or property also invite judicial review of administrative action. Yet, both the doctrinal categories relevant to these suits and their broader orientation differ from the so-called review proceedings. Whereas review proceedings raise threshold issues of "standing," "ripeness," "exhaustion of administrative remedies," and "reviewability," the linguistic conventions of our second category of remedies emphasize doctrinal questions of "sovereign" and "official" immunity. This shift in the language of judicial discourse is not merely cosmetic. Suits for "relief" rather than "review" tend to emphasize concerns that are more like those encountered in the private law context—questions such as the appropriateness of spreading risks of loss, or the potential for damage actions to provide incentives for the regulation of primary conduct. More than "maintaining the rule of law," courts operating in this remedial mode seem to be concerned with "corrective justice," on the one hand, and balancing incentives for government officials, on the other.

A final category of claims, explored in Chapter 9, we term suits for "Beneficiary Enforcement." Here, rather than suing federal officials, either to review their decisions or to remedy the effects of their behavior, plaintiffs seek to enforce duties owed to them under federal statutes or constitutional provisions by private persons or by federal, state, and local officials. In this mode the remedial system directly implements federal public law. Or, perhaps we should say, federal public law raises questions of whether it *should* be directly implemented by private lawsuits. Here the characteristic doctrinal concerns have to do with the existence or nonexistence of "implied rights of action" and with the potentially "primary jurisdiction" of federal administrators to enforce public law.

This third category has a decidedly hybrid character. Beneficiary suits invoke statutes or the Constitution in a fashion reminiscent of a petition for review. Yet the claims also have a flavor of actions in tort or contract: the plaintiff often seeks damages or an injunctive order that looks rather like specific performance of a duty to a third-party beneficiary. Moreover, the policy questions that surround these actions implicate both the essentially public law concerns of separation of powers and the more characteristically private law concerns of spreading risks and influencing primary conduct.

The following table attempts to fix these ideas somewhat more concretely by noting the divergent characteristics of the three types of claims we shall be discussing.

FIGURE 1

Claim Type	**Social Function**	**Broad Issue Orientation**	**Forms of Action**	**Doctrinal Categories**
Review of Legality of Official Action	Maintain Rule of Law	Public law concerns, particularly separation of powers	General or specific statutory proceeding	Standing, Ripeness, Exhaustion of Administrative Remedies, Reviewability
Relief from Officially Inflicted Injuries	Corrective Justice	Private Law Concerns —Risk Spreading —Incentives	Tort or contract action (damages or specific performance)	Sovereign and Official Immunity
Beneficiary Enforcement of Public Law	Implementation	Hybrid	Suit on a statute or contract (including 42 U.S.C. § 1983)	Implied rights of action, Primary jurisdiction

But we should note immediately that this categorization of remedial prototypes masks many similarities and cross-cutting doctrinal concerns. Each category of claims raises issues that may be framed in terms of the existence of federal court jurisdiction. Questions of the effect on administrative power or discretion of recognizing a particular judicial remedy—broadly speaking, separation of powers questions—are likewise pervasive. And, obviously, the existence or nonexistence of a particular type of judicial remedy in part defines what it means to be a citizen or "rights holder" in our liberal democratic, but ubiquitously administrative, state.

Indeed, given the numerous overlaps among the categories, our treatment of rights of action under 42 U.S.C. § 1983 as suits for beneficiary enforcement may be viewed by some as arbitrary if not capricious. This categorization reflects our belief that the remedial conceptualization of § 1983 actions should mirror the implementation concerns that attend the allocation to non-federal officials of the power to effectuate federal policies. Hence, we see private suits against state officials under § 1983 as attempts to implement federal rights where "cooperative federalism" has left or placed the concrete realization of those rights in local hands.

One can obviously view § 1983 actions differently. They can be seen as "review proceedings" that subject state and local implementors of federal norms to the same sort of judicial supervision available against federal implementors. In this guise, for example, § 1983 becomes the means by which a Medicaid beneficiary obtains review opportunities similar to those available to a person insured under Medicare. (The former program is state administered and partially state funded, subject to federal conditions for the receipt of federal grant dollars; the latter is wholly funded and administered by the federal government.) And, in yet another incarnation, § 1983 actions raise critical issues of public tort law. Indeed, such suits have generated much of the modern law of official immunity.

The conceptualization that we offer in these chapters is, therefore, but one of many possible visions. Yet, together these three categories of claims canvass the principal remedial interests of most citizens of the American administrative state. To take a concrete (if hypothetical) example, shrimpers whom the FDA prevents from marketing their allegedly contaminated catch will want to know the possibilities for "review" vis-a-vis the FDA. They may have a similar, perhaps even livelier, interest in the prospects for recovering damages from either the U.S. Government or from an errant FDA official, should the agency's allegations prove incorrect. And these same shrimpers also may want to consider suit against the upstream chemical company whose violation of the Federal Water Pollution Control Act produced the contamination that affected their livelihoods and/or against the state officials responsible for administering that statute. These three interrelated sets of remedial possibilities—claims for "review," for "relief," and for "enforcement"—are the subjects of the chapters that follow.

2. THE MULTIPLE CONUNDRA OF JUDICIAL REVIEW

Judicial review exposes the tensions between two insistent demands: that the government respect the law and that courts not run the government. Balancing these demands lies at the base of a series of questions that are raised by almost every instance of judicial review of administrative action.

How intensely should courts scrutinize administrative decisionmaking? Although only a small share of the decisions of federal administrators are actually tested in court, the ever-present possibility of judicial challenge, plus government lawyers' routine attention to judicial precedent, give federal courts substantial power to influence the path of public administration. That the courts' role is critical, however, does not render that role self-defining. If courts were to police agencies by assessing every administrative decision from scratch (de novo), any efficiency or other gains that Congress seeks by vesting authority in administrators would be nullified. Moreover, such a role would threaten to usurp policy authority from both Congress and the executive. On the other hand, a *Pacific States Box* treatment of administrative decisions, see Chapter 5, could render the courts' role superfluous. Thus, determining the appropriate intensity of judicial oversight—conventionally termed "scope of review"—is of paramount importance in adjusting the courts' relationship to the other institutions of government.

Who should be able to demand judicial review? In private law, to say that one party owes a legal duty to another is tantamount to declaring that the party owed that duty has a judicially enforceable right to relief if that duty is breached. Government officers also have duties, but they derive from legislative prescriptions of official functions and, in form at least, are owed to the public at large. The role of the government officer, i.e., of one charged with public functions and ultimately, if remotely, responsible politically to the general citizenry, raises difficult questions concerning how official compliance with statutory directives should be policed and who should do the policing.

For example, should any citizen's general interest in the proper administration of law confer "standing" to seek a remedy against an officer who performs some function improperly? Or should a citizen be required to show that the official has invaded some personal interest or "right" belonging to the citizen? If the former premise is accepted, the federal courts may exceed their historic function of deciding concrete controversies and, simultaneously, their Article III jurisdiction. If they adopt the latter posture, however, legal control of the conduct of government officials might be confined to the boundaries of legal redress for private wrongs. Yet, in a liberal democratic state the merger of private and public law remedies is not obviously appropriate. A basic presupposition of such a polity is that private conduct should be restricted only by specific legal proscription and by the duty to avoid unnecessary injury to one's neighbors. Limitations on judicial remedies in private law and criminal law thus embody a general policy of non-interference with private autonomy. Actions by government officials, on the other hand, are presumptively lawful only if within the boundaries of some empowering statute. Recognition of broad judicial jurisdiction to confine officials within statutory limits would therefore support both individual autonomy and democratic control. Yet, the very notion of representative democracy suggests that every disagreement about policy should not be resolved or resolvable by lawsuit. Where is the balance to be struck?

How can the "legal" be distinguished from the "political?" Similar problems are encountered on the duty side of the equation. The breadth of the officer's duty—to the citizenry as a whole—may imply the exercise of political judgment not subject to the rational elaboration of coherent principles associated with court enforcement of legal rights. Does the political nature of administration thus defy judicial scrutiny? And, if not generally, in what contexts? What if the official appeals to administrative necessity rather than political discretion? To what extent should the potential for interference with efficient execution of public business be considered in defining remedies against public officers? Should such considerations influence the existence as well as the extent of such remedies? Their timing?

Such basic questions—who can obtain review, what official actions are subject to review, to what extent, and when—are recurrent themes in the jurisprudence of judicial review of administrative action. Instead of the "right-duty-remedy" language encountered in the discussion of private law remedies, however, these issues are generally discussed in terms of such conceptual headings as "standing," "reviewability," "ripeness," and, as we have seen in prior chapters, "scope of judicial review."

B. SCOPE OF REVIEW

The Supreme Court's decisions on the appropriate intensity of judicial review of administrative action do not fit any neat categorization that reveals a single explanatory variable. Scope of review cases have been categorized variously by (a) the nature of the agency determination being challenged (law/fact/mixed), (b) the nature of the process that produced the challenged decision (formal/informal, adjudication/rulemaking), (c) the intensity of review characteristic of the historical period or particular court whose cases are being featured ("soft glance"/"hard look"); (d) the substantive arena or "technicality" of the decisions reviewed (communications regulation/social security benefits; regulation of carcinogens/certification of bargaining units); or (e) some combination of the above. We have opted for (e). Our objective is only to help organize reflection on the issues raised, not to stress the one or two variables that we believe "explain" the cases.

1. PRESUMPTIVE BUT LIMITED REVIEW: THE *OVERTON PARK* ICON

CITIZENS TO PRESERVE OVERTON PARK, INC. v. VOLPE

Supreme Court of the United States, 1971.
401 U.S. 402, 91 S.Ct. 814, 28 L.Ed.2d 136.

Opinion of the Court by JUSTICE MARSHALL, announced by JUSTICE STEWART.

* * * We are concerned in this case with § 4(f) of the Department of Transportation Act of 1966, as amended, and § 18(a) of the Federal–Aid Highway Act of 1968, 23 U.S.C. § 138.[3] These statutes prohibit the

3. "It is hereby declared to be the national policy that special effort should be made to preserve the natural beauty of the countryside and public park and recreation lands, wildlife and waterfowl refuges, and historic sites. * * * After the effective date of the Federal–Aid Highway Act of 1968, the Secretary shall not approve any program or project which requires the use of any publicly owned land from a public park,

Secretary of Transportation from authorizing the use of federal funds to finance the construction of highways through public parks if a "feasible and prudent" alternative route exists. If no such route is available, the statutes allow him to approve construction through parks only if there has been "all possible planning to minimize harm" to the park.

Petitioners, private citizens as well as local and national conservation organizations, contend that the Secretary has violated these statutes by authorizing the expenditure of federal funds for the construction of a six-lane interstate highway through a public park in Memphis, Tennessee. * * *

* * *

Petitioners contend that the Secretary's action is invalid without * * * formal findings and that the Secretary did not make an independent determination but merely relied on the judgment of the Memphis City Council. They also contend that it would be "feasible and prudent" to route I–40 around Overton Park either to the north or to the south. And they argue that if these alternative routes are not "feasible and prudent," the present plan does not include "all possible" methods for reducing harm to the park. * * *

Respondents argue that it was unnecessary for the Secretary to make formal findings, and that he did, in fact, exercise his own independent judgment which was supported by the facts. In the District Court, respondents introduced affidavits, prepared specifically for this litigation, which indicated that the Secretary had made the decision and that the decision was supportable. These affidavits were contradicted by affidavits introduced by petitioners, who also sought to take the deposition of a former Federal Highway Administrator who had participated in the decision to route I–40 through Overton Park.

The District Court and the Court of Appeals found that formal findings by the Secretary were not necessary and refused to order the deposition of the former Federal Highway Administrator because those courts believed that probing of the mental processes of an administrative decisionmaker was prohibited. And, believing that the Secretary's authority was wide and reviewing courts' authority narrow in the approval of highway routes, the lower courts held that the affidavits contained no basis for a determination that the Secretary had exceeded his authority.

We agree that formal findings were not required. But we do not believe that in this case judicial review based solely on litigation affidavits was adequate.

recreation area, or wildlife and waterfowl refuge of national, State, or local significance as determined by the Federal, State, or local officials having jurisdiction thereof, or any land from an historic site of national, State, or local significance as so determined by such officials unless (1) there is no feasible and prudent alternative to the use of such land, and (2) such program includes all possible planning to minimize harm to such park, recreational area, wildlife and waterfowl refuge, or historic site resulting from such use." 23 U.S.C.A. § 138 (1964 ed., Supp. V).

[The language of section 4(f) of the Transportation Act is virtually identical.]

A threshold question—whether petitioners are entitled to any judicial review—is easily answered. Section 701 of the Administrative Procedure Act provides that the action of "each authority of the Government of the United States," which includes the Department of Transportation, is subject to judicial review except where there is a statutory prohibition on review or where "agency action is committed to agency discretion by law." In this case, there is no indication that Congress sought to prohibit judicial review and there is most certainly no "showing of 'clear and convincing evidence' of a * * * legislative intent" to restrict access to judicial review. *Abbott Laboratories v. Gardner*, [*infra*, p. 961].

Similarly, the Secretary's decision here does not fall within the exception for action "committed to agency discretion." This is a very narrow exception. The legislative history of the Administrative Procedure Act indicates that it is applicable in those rare instances where "statutes are drawn in such broad terms that in a given case there is no law to apply."

* * *

Despite the clarity of the statutory language, respondents argue that the Secretary has wide discretion. They recognize that the requirement that there be no "feasible" alternative route admits of little administrative discretion. For this exemption to apply the Secretary must find that as a matter of sound engineering it would not be feasible to build the highway along any other route. Respondents argue, however, that the requirement that there be no other "prudent" route requires the Secretary to engage in a wide-ranging balancing of competing interests. They contend that the Secretary should weigh the detriment resulting from the destruction of parkland against the cost of other routes, safety considerations, and other factors, and determine on the basis of the importance that he attaches to these other factors whether, on balance, alternative feasible routes would be "prudent."

But no such wide-ranging endeavor was intended. It is obvious that in most cases considerations of cost, directness of route, and community disruption will indicate that parkland should be used for highway construction whenever possible. Although it may be necessary to transfer funds from one jurisdiction to another, there will always be a smaller outlay required from the public purse when parkland is used since the public already owns the land and there will be no need to pay for right-of-way. And since people do not live or work in parks, if a highway is built on parkland no one will have to leave his home or give up his business. Such factors are common to substantially all highway construction. Thus, if Congress intended these factors to be on an equal footing with preservation of parkland there would have been no need for the statutes.

Congress clearly did not intend that cost and disruption of the community were to be ignored by the Secretary. But the very existence of the statutes indicates that protection of parkland was to be given paramount importance. * * * If the statutes are to have any meaning, the Secretary cannot approve the destruction of parkland unless he finds that alternative routes present unique problems.

Plainly, there is "law to apply" and thus the exemption for action "committed to agency discretion" is inapplicable. But the existence of judicial review is only the start: the standard for review must also be determined. For that we must look to § 706 of the Administrative Procedure Act, which provides that a "reviewing court shall * * * hold unlawful and set aside agency action, findings, and conclusions found" not to meet six separate standards. In all cases agency action must be set aside if the action was "arbitrary, capricious, an abuse of discretion, or otherwise not in accordance with law" or if the action failed to meet statutory, procedural, or constitutional requirements. In certain narrow, specifically limited situations, the agency action is to be set aside if the action was not supported by "substantial evidence." And in other equally narrow circumstances the reviewing court is to engage in a *de novo* review of the action and set it aside if it was "unwarranted by the facts."

Petitioners * * * contend that the "substantial evidence" standard of § 706(2)(E) must be applied. In the alternative, they claim that § 706(2)(F) applies and that there must be a *de novo* review to determine if the Secretary's action was "unwarranted by the facts." Neither of these standards is, however, applicable.

Review under the substantial-evidence test is authorized only when the agency action is taken pursuant to a rulemaking provision of the Administrative Procedure Act itself, or when the agency action is based on a public adjudicatory hearing. The Secretary's decision to allow the expenditure of federal funds to build I–40 through Overton Park was plainly not an exercise of a rulemaking function. And the only hearing that is required by either the Administrative Procedure Act or the statutes regulating the distribution of federal funds for highway construction is a public hearing conducted by local officials for the purpose of informing the community about the proposed project and eliciting community views on the design and route. 23 U.S.C. § 128 (1964 ed., Supp. V). The hearing is nonadjudicatory, quasi-legislative in nature. It is not designed to produce a record that is to be the basis of agency action—the basic requirement for substantial-evidence review.

Petitioners' alternative argument also fails. *De novo* review of whether the Secretary's decision was "unwarranted by the facts" is authorized by § 706(2)(F) in only two circumstances. First, such *de novo* review is authorized when the action is adjudicatory in nature and the agency factfinding procedures are inadequate. And, there may be independent judicial factfinding when issues that were not before the agency are raised in a proceeding to enforce nonadjudicatory agency action. Neither situation exists here.

Even though there is no *de novo* review in this case and the Secretary's approval of the route of I–40 does not have ultimately to meet the substantial-evidence test, the generally applicable standards of

§ 706 require the reviewing court to engage in a substantial inquiry. Certainly, the Secretary's decision is entitled to a presumption of regularity. But that presumption is not to shield his action from a thorough, probing, in-depth review.

The court is first required to decide whether the Secretary acted within the scope of his authority. This determination naturally begins with a delineation of the scope of the Secretary's authority and discretion. * * * Also involved in this initial inquiry is a determination of whether on the facts the Secretary's decision can reasonably be said to be within that range. * * *

Scrutiny of the facts does not end, however, with the determination that the Secretary has acted within the scope of his statutory authority. Section 706(2)(A) requires a finding that the actual choice made was not "arbitrary, capricious, an abuse of discretion, or otherwise not in accordance with law." To make this finding the court must consider whether the decision was based on a consideration of the relevant factors and whether there has been a clear error of judgment. Although this inquiry into the facts is to be searching and careful, the ultimate standard of review is a narrow one. The court is not empowered to substitute its judgment for that of the agency.

The final inquiry is whether the Secretary's action followed the necessary procedural requirements. Here the only procedural error alleged is the failure of the Secretary to make formal findings and state his reason for allowing the highway to be built through the park.

Undoubtedly, review of the Secretary's action is hampered by his failure to make such findings, but the absence of formal findings does not necessarily require that the case be remanded to the Secretary. Neither the Department of Transportation Act nor the Federal–Aid Highway Act requires such formal findings. * * *

* * * The lower courts based their review on the litigation affidavits that were presented. These affidavits were merely "post hoc" rationalizations which have traditionally been found to be an inadequate basis for review. And they clearly do not constitute the "whole record" compiled by the agency: the basis for review required by § 706 of the Administrative Procedure Act.

Thus it is necessary to remand this case to the District Court for plenary review of the Secretary's decision. That review is to be based on the full administrative record that was before the Secretary at the time he made his decision. But since the bare record may not disclose the factors that were considered or the Secretary's construction of the evidence it may be necessary for the District Court to require some explanation in order to determine if the Secretary acted within the scope of his authority and if the Secretary's action was justifiable under the applicable standard.

The court may require the administrative officials who participated in the decision to give testimony explaining their action. Of course, such inquiry into the mental processes of administrative decisionmakers is usually to be avoided. *United States v. Morgan*, 313 U.S. 409, 422 (1941). And where there are administrative findings that were made at the same time as the decision, as was the case in *Morgan*, there must be a strong showing of bad faith or improper behavior before such inquiry may be made. But here there are no such formal findings and it may be that the only way there can be effective judicial review is by examining the decisionmakers themselves.

The District Court is not, however, required to make such an inquiry. It may be that the Secretary can prepare formal findings * * * that will provide an adequate explanation for his action. Such an explanation will, to some extent, be a "post hoc rationalization" and thus must be viewed critically. If the District Court decides that additional explanation is necessary, that court should consider which method will prove the most expeditious so that full review may be had as soon as possible.

Reversed and remanded.

[The separate opinion of Justice Black is omitted.]

Notes

1. *Presumption of Reviewability and the Distinctiveness of Public Law.* Justice Marshall cites *Abbott Laboratories v. Gardner*, 387 U.S. 136 (1967), *infra* p. 961, for the proposition that actions of administrators are presumed to be judicially reviewable. And surely *Overton Park* is resounding support for this proposition. The Court entertains a challenge by a group of citizens, who as individuals apparently have slight stake in the routing of the highway, to an administrative determination for which Congress has prescribed no procedures and which, as a matter of custom, results in no formal documentation or written explanation. Nor has Congress anywhere specifically authorized judicial review of such decisions. This is not to say that the circumstances surrounding the Secretary of Transportation's decision cannot be fitted into the shape of a lawsuit; it is to suggest that the prevailing judicial willingness to engage in review of administrative actions, of which *Overton Park* is exemplary, extends well beyond those situations in which clashes between private and official interests appear close analogues of disputes in the private law system.

2. *Requiring an Informal Record.* The federal aid highway program involved in *Overton Park* is a quintessential example of the progressive legal formalization of federal developmental and managerial functions that have substantial social, economic, and political impacts. One of the principal techniques for managing the "externalities" of public as well as private activities is to subject those activities to consideration of a broader range of values. Statutory requirements for broadened consideration of federal activities inhabit both the framework statutes discussed in Chapter 2 and many amendments to the basic laws that authorize these so-called "proprietary" programs. As *Overton Park* demonstrates, these criteria provide a "law to

apply" that is sufficient to allow judicial review of the Transportation Secretary's decision.

The conclusion that judicial review is appropriate has its own progressive logic. A court cannot review the activities of highway officials stretching over many years except on the basis of some sort of "record." If the Federal Highway Administration were simply to dump on the District Court all of the paperwork relating to the planning, design, approval, and construction of I–40 through Memphis, the judge would be buried and soon lost. Hence, the Supreme Court requires an explanation with some "findings" by the Secretary in order to structure judicial evaluation of the underlying record. The Secretary's decision and its "rationale" will then be tested against the material in the record.

3. *The Bureaucratization of Politics*. The implications for the administrative process of such "record" review are predictable. Any official who knows that his or her action will be tested by reference to a record must somehow build one that will support the decision that is made. This requires the development of administrative routines which can be followed by subordinates—in this case the federal district engineers and the Federal Highway Administration—to assure that appropriate information is assembled on the crucial questions of feasibility and prudence. The prospect of judicial review thus reinforces the inexorable bureaucratization of those agency functions that it touches.

That such a bureaucratic process did not exist at the time of *Overton Park* is evident from the subsequent history of the case. Given the Supreme Court's remarkably narrow conception of "prudent" and its broad conception of "all possible planning," Secretary Volpe was certainly unlikely to have developed (or had developed for him) a record that would justify the decision to use parkland. And, after numerous days of trial on remand, it became clear that neither the contemporaneous record nor the recollections of the various persons involved in the project would provide a sufficient record upon which to uphold the Secretary's decision. The district court therefore remanded the matter to the Secretary. In the face of the Supreme Court's interpretation of 23 U.S.C. § 138, Secretary Volpe declined to approve the parkland route. But this decision, too, was overturned. *Citizens to Preserve Overton Park, Inc. v. Volpe*, 357 F.Supp. 846 (W.D.Tenn.1973). The second reversal came in a suit by the State of Tennessee, which objected to the Secretary's refusal to approve the Overton Park route on the ground that he had specified no other route that would be either feasible or prudent. The state's argument, with which the district court agreed, was that without such a finding the Secretary, in rejecting the park route, had not complied with the findings requirement of the Supreme Court's *Overton Park* opinion.

This turn of events should not be surprising. The Secretary had before him a record on the basis of which both the Tennessee Highway Department, in consultation with the Memphis City Council, and the Federal Highway Administrator had concluded that there was no feasible or prudent alternative to the Overton Park route. It seems unlikely that the same record would support a finding that a particular alternative route was both feasible and prudent. In the end, however, the Secretary's decision on remand was upheld. The Sixth Circuit held that the district court was wrong to interpret section 4(f) as demanding the specification of an alternative route as a necessary element in justifying a refusal to find that there was "no feasible or prudent alternative." *Citizens to Preserve Overton Park v. Brinegar*, 494 F.2d 1212 (6th Cir.1974), *cert. denied*, 421 U.S. 991 (1975).

More important, perhaps, than the law it made, the *Overton Park* litigation illustrates the difficulty of inserting a rationalistic model of decision making—records, formal findings, and judicial review—into the highly flexible, dynamic, and inherently political process of highway construction. But to understand this point, some history is necessary. Until the Federal Aid Road Act of 1916, roads were normally built and maintained by localities and turnpike companies. See generally Ross D. Netherton, *Intergovernmental Relations Under the Federal Aid Highway Program*, 1 Urb.L.Ann. 15, 16–17 (1968). The federal government's participation in road building was premised on the notion that there was a national interest in providing a linked system of toll free roads for the movement of persons and goods in interstate commerce. Thus, in providing aid, the federal government required that monies be spent pursuant to an overall design or long-range plan for the development of highway networks. This system's conception entailed some coordination of local activity if not outright displacement of local authority. The federal legislation therefore required that states have highway departments with sufficient authority and responsibility to approve all projects and to certify their compliance with any requirements of federal law.

The interests of localities were, however, not forgotten in the federal highway program. Congress over the years strengthened the role of local governing bodies by requirements for local public hearings; for state certification that projects were consistent with the goals and objectives of local urban planning; for cooperative planning between localities and state highway departments; and for consideration of the views of local governing bodies on highway projects within standard metropolitan statistical areas.

At the time of the Supreme Court's *Overton Park* decision the involvement of localities in highway planning was reinforced by the Intergovernmental Cooperation Act (ICA) of 1968, 42 U.S.C. §§ 4201–4244. As implemented by circulars and directives from the Office of Management and Budget, compliance with the ICA was integrated with other federal policies as well. Thus, for example, section 102(2)(C) of the NEPA, 42 U.S.C. § 4332(2)(C), was synthesized with the ICA by the requirement that localities make, or be given the opportunity to make, comments on environmental quality questions arising in the planning and construction of highways. See DOT Order 5610.1A (Oct. 4, 1971). Section 128 of Title 23 also required that state highway departments certify that their projects were consistent with area planning objectives, and section 134(a) required that all projects be based on "a continuing comprehensive transportation planning process carried on cooperatively by States and local communities. * * * " 23 U.S.C. § 134(a).

In short, the Federal Aid Highways Act, combined with other structural requirements of federal legislation, created a complex web of intergovernmental relationships. And, as in all such relationships there were cross currents, conflicts, and constituent pressures that required continuous negotiation and accommodation among the three levels of actors in the process.

See generally MARTHA DERTHICK, THE INFLUENCE OF FEDERAL GRANTS: PUBLIC ASSISTANCE IN MASSACHUSETTS (1970). Indeed, the DOT decision reviewed in *Overton Park* was but the culminating event in a process that comprised extensive, even redundant local meetings, disputes, demonstrations, elections and other indicia of wide-spread public political participation. Peter L. Strauss, *Revisiting* Overton Park: *Political and Judicial Controls Over Administrative Actions Affecting the Community*, 39 U.C.L.A.L.Rev. 1251 (1992).

This is not to say that all was "blooming, buzzing confusion" in the administration of the Federal Aid Highways program. As in all bureaucracies, the administration of the program was, and is, surrounded and in part structured by highly detailed statements of the various standards that must be satisfied, as well as the procedural steps through which satisfaction is to be demonstrated. See generally FEDERAL HIGHWAY ADMINISTRATION, REVIEW OF FEDERAL-AID HIGHWAY PROGRAMS (1970). But this was not a grant process that functioned like the applications process for graduate fellowships or research grants. State highway departments did not engage separately in something called "highway planning" and then apply for federal aid which was approved on the basis of a review of documentary evidence demonstrating compliance with federal standards. Instead, the FHWA delegated virtually all of its grant approval authority to its division engineer in each state. That engineer worked constantly with the state highway department to improve the state's planning and engineering capabilities in connection with ongoing projects. The objective of federal officials was not to "build a record" that demonstrated compliance with all federal standards, but to get the best possible job out of quite diverse state highway departments in relation to those standards. Moreover, the federal engineer had to remember at all times that the state agency was embedded in state politics and was therefore also required to negotiate with, and take account of, local interests and local officials.

In this connection, one should note that 23 U.S.C. § 138's protection for parklands at issue in *Overton Park* demanded that the Secretary make certain findings only to the extent that the project involved a park having local significance as determined by elected local representatives. And while there was no claim in the *Overton Park* case that the Memphis City Council had determined Overton Park to be insignificant, it is equally clear that the Tennessee State Department of Highways, in consultation with those same elected officials, had determined and certified that the planned route through Overton Park was consistent with the Memphis transportation planning process. In short, the Secretary's initial determination that there was no feasible or prudent alternative had been made within the context of an ongoing process of intergovernmental consultation.

From this perspective one might question the Supreme Court's approach to the interpretation of the Federal Aid Highways Act. For that interpretation suggests that Congress intended that a Washington-based administrative official should determine, on the basis of narrow federal criteria, the appropriate utilization of local public property. Moreover, that decision was to be made in a "rational" fashion, presumably giving little weight to the political accommodations and trade-offs built into the general structure, or to the dynamics of the intergovernmental system from which the decision emerged.

Judicial review thus tends to push administrative action into a conceptual mold that employs clear divisions of function, sharp criteria for judgment, and detailed explanation for decisions. Questions of administrative discretion or judgment are sharply formulated by the well-drawn complaints of anti-highway plaintiffs. Or, as the second district court remand in *Overton Park* suggests, by pro-highway plaintiffs as well. The influences of history, intergovernmental politics, and of the nonscientific or nonrational side of planning, tend to be ignored.

At the very least, the influence of these factors on decision making is difficult to reproduce in a "record" that is accessible for judicial review. Such factors appear, therefore, in the mouths of administrative defendants to be lame explanations for apparent incompetence or for the evasion of legislative mandates. The Administrator, thus, seems trapped between a Congress, which found comprehensive rationalization of his or her program impossible, and a reviewing court, which insisted that all exercises of judgment be explicable in terms of some cogently articulated policy. For a more extended discussion of the Federal Aid Highways Program, see Jerry L. Mashaw, *The Legal Structure of Frustration: Alternative Strategies for Public Choice Concerning Federally Aided Highway Construction*, 122 U.Pa.L.Rev. 1 (1973).

4. *Requiring a Contemporaneous Rationale*. The Supreme Court in *Overton Park* says that the reasons offered in court by the Secretary for his decision cannot provide a basis for determining its legality because those reasons appear in affidavits prepared for litigation. They are, in the Court's terms, "post hoc rationalizations." The Court then remands to the district court, anticipating that it will, in turn, have to remand the case to the Secretary for a new "explanation" which, as the Court recognizes, will itself be "to some extent, * * * a post hoc rationalization." In countless cases after *Overton Park*, courts have rejected explanations offered for agency decisions on the ground that they were post hoc rationalizations. Yet it is not obvious why post hoc rationalizations should be objectionable—at least in the case of informal actions that are not required by the APA, or by an agency's organic statute, to be accompanied by contemporaneous reasons.

Why are after-the-fact rationalizations any more suspect than contemporaneous reason giving? To be sure, the ordinary meaning of *rationalize* is "to provide plausible but untrue reasons or motives for a course of conduct." Webster's Third New International Dictionary (Unabridged) 1885 (1971). Presumably this is to be distinguished from *explain*, which is "to make manifest: present in detail * * * to make plain or understandable * * * to give the meaning or significance of." Are reasons given after a decision has been made more likely to be disingenuous than reasons provided contemporaneously? Are the latter more likely to be genuine?

Indeed, is it not always the case that reason giving follows decision making? "Post hoc-ness" seems to be merely a matter of degree. Few psychologists or psychoanalysts since JAMES HARVEY ROBINSON, THE MIND IN THE MAKING (1921), have believed that articulated reasons capture much of the truth about human motivation. Although he disagreed strongly with the baleful line of reading, thinking, and teaching about judicial opinions that Robinson's position supported, Karl Llewellyn nevertheless said:

> I do not think that, save on occasions normally impossible to spot, an opinion reflects with any accuracy a third of the variegated great and petty motivating stimuli that have somehow combined to produce the particular decision, or that it shows the weight of such factors as it may happen to mention expressly, nor yet the manner of their interaction.

KARL N. LLEWELLYN, THE COMMON LAW TRADITION: DECIDING APPEALS 131 (1960). If this is true, the Supreme Court would have been equally justified in suggesting to the district court in *Overton Park* that it view *all* reasons given by administrators skeptically.

There may, though, be grounds for rejecting the sort of post hoc rationalization that confronted the Court in the *Overton Park* case. Statements made in litigation affidavits may not reflect the thinking of administrators, but rather of their lawyers. Again, however, this is hardly a decisive objection. As we noted in Chapter 4, the Court has accepted "collegial" or "organizational" decisions as a fact of life in bureaucracy. And presumably an administrator has access to the agency's legal staff in informal proceedings as in other settings. Moreover, having once been reversed in court, it seems highly unlikely that any prudent administrator would formulate a new rationale for decision without relying heavily on legal counsel.

This observation prompts one to wonder what might be going on in a case like *Local 814, International Brotherhood of Teamsters v. NLRB*, 546 F.2d 989 (D.C.Cir.1976), *cert. denied*, 434 U.S. 818 (1977). There the court had remanded to the Board a decision that was apparently inconsistent with another NLRB case that had been decided almost simultaneously. In upholding the Board's re-rationalization following remand, the court suggested that the *Overton Park* proscription against post hoc rationalization did not preclude the Board from rendering a valid decision based on an "amplified articulation." This, the court reasoned, was not a "post hoc rationalization," because it did not violate the purpose of the Supreme Court's prohibition in *Overton Park*, to wit, upholding "agency action on the basis of rationales offered by anyone other than the proper decisionmakers." Apparently the court convinced itself that the agency officials who draft "amplified articulations" are different from those who prepare litigation affidavits.

Other cases suggest different theories for the prohibition against post hoc rationalizations. They include the difficulty reviewing courts face in parsing the agency record without the assistance of a contemporaneous rationale and the similar difficulty for petitioners who wish to seek reconsideration within the agency. However, since briefs can focus a court on the relevant portions of the record, it is hard to see why judges cannot accept the same advice from agency post hoc rationalizations, however provided. And any litigant who may petition for reconsideration can also request clarification of the agency's rationale.

A more plausible explanation for the Supreme Court's reaction in *Overton Park* is that it was searching for some device to force administrators to reason *within* applicable statutory criteria *at the time* they are making decisions. For surely it is only through such a reasoning process that statutory criteria take on life and force. That the prohibition against post hoc rationalizations is likely to have only modest impact is perhaps not a decisive argument against it, given the Court's limited arsenal of weapons to induce administrative fidelity to statutory commands. Moreover, in *Overton Park* it was clear that, under the Court's interpretation of the statute, the Secretary had misconstrued his authority. On the other hand, where an agency is acting within its authority and offers, post hoc, a rationale that, if contemporaneously made, would have justified its action, a remand for a rearticulation of reasons in a "decisional context" may be pointless.

2. INTERPRETATIONS OF LAW: THE *CHEVRON* DOCTRINE

CHEVRON, U.S.A., INC. v. NATURAL RESOURCES DEFENSE COUNCIL, INC.

Supreme Court of the United States, 1984.
467 U.S. 837, 104 S.Ct. 2778, 81 L.Ed.2d 694.

JUSTICE STEVENS delivered the opinion of the Court.

In the Clean Air Act Amendments of 1977, Congress enacted certain requirements applicable to States that had not achieved the national air quality standards established by the Environmental Protection Agency (EPA) pursuant to earlier legislation. The amended Clean Air Act required these "nonattainment" States to establish a permit program regulating "new or modified major stationary sources" of air pollution. Generally, a permit may not be issued for a new or modified major stationary source unless several stringent conditions are met. The EPA regulation promulgated to implement this permit requirement allows a State to adopt a plantwide definition of the term "stationary course."[2] Under this definition, an existing plant that contains several pollution-emitting devices may install or modify one piece of equipment without meeting the permit conditions if the alteration will not increase the total emissions from the plant. The question presented by these cases is whether EPA's decision to allow States to treat all of the pollution-emitting devices within the same industrial grouping as though they were encased within a single "bubble" is based on a reasonable construction of the statutory term "stationary source."

I

The EPA regulations containing the plantwide definition of the term stationary source were promulgated on October 14, 1981. * * * The Court of Appeals set aside the regulations. *Natural Resources Defense Council, Inc. v. Gorsuch*, 685 F.2d 718 (1982).

2. "(i) 'Stationary source' means any building, structure, facility, or installation which emits or may emit any air pollutant subject to regulation under the Act.

"(ii) 'Building, structure, facility, or installation' means all of the pollutant-emitting activities which belong to the same industrial grouping, are located on one or more contiguous or adjacent properties, and are under the control of the same person (or persons under common control) except the activities of any vessel." 40 CFR §§ 51.18(j)(1)(i) and (ii) (1983).

The court observed that the relevant part of the amended Clean Air Act "does not explicitly define what Congress envisioned as a 'stationary source,' to which the permit program * * * should apply," and further stated that the precise issue was not "squarely addressed in the legislative history." In light of its conclusion that the legislative history bearing on the question was "at best contradictory," it reasoned that "the purposes of the nonattainment program should guide our decision here." Based on two of its precedents concerning the applicability of the bubble concept to certain Clean Air Act programs, the court stated that the bubble concept was "mandatory" in programs designed merely to maintain existing air quality, but held that it was "inappropriate" in programs enacted to improve air quality. Since the purpose of the permit program—its "raison d'etre," in the court's view—was to improve air quality, the court held that the bubble concept was inapplicable in these cases under its prior precedents. It therefore set aside the regulations embodying the bubble concept as contrary to law. * * *

The basic legal error of the Court of Appeals was to adopt a static judicial definition of the term "stationary source" when it had decided that Congress itself had not commanded that definition.

II

When a court reviews an agency's construction of the statute which it administers, it is confronted with two questions. First, always, is the question whether Congress has directly spoken to the precise question at issue. If the intent of Congress is clear, that is the end of the matter; for the court as well as the agency, must give effect to the unambiguously expressed intent of Congress.[9] If, however, the court determines Congress has not directly addressed the precise question at issue, the court does not simply impose its own construction on the statute, as would be necessary in the absence of an administrative interpretation. Rather, if the statute is silent or ambiguous with respect to the specific issue, the question for the court is whether the agency's answer is based on a permissible construction of the statute.[11]

"The power of an administrative agency to administer a congressionally created * * * program necessarily requires the formulation of policy and the making of rules to fill any gap left, implicitly or explicitly, by Congress." *Morton v. Ruiz*, 415 U.S. 199, 231 (1974). If Congress has explicitly left a gap for the agency to fill, there is an express delegation of authority to the agency to elucidate a specific provision of the statute by regulation. Such legislative regulations are given controlling weight unless they are arbitrary, capricious, or manifestly contrary to the statute. Sometimes the legislative delegation to an agency on a particular

9. The judiciary is the final authority on issues of statutory construction and must reject administrative constructions which are contrary to clear congressional intent.

11. The court need not conclude that the agency construction was the only one it permissibly could have adopted to uphold the construction, or even the reading the court would have reached if the question initially had arisen in a judicial proceeding.

question is implicit rather than explicit. In such a case, a court may not substitute its own construction of a statutory provision for a reasonable interpretation made by the administrator of an agency.

We have long recognized that considerable weight should be accorded to an executive department's construction of a statutory scheme it is entrusted to administer, and the principle of deference to administrative interpretations

> "has been consistently followed by this Court whenever decision as to the meaning or reach of a statute has involved reconciling conflicting policies, and a full understanding of the force of the statutory policy in the given situation has depended upon more than ordinary knowledge respecting the matters subjected to agency regulations.
>
> "* * * If this choice represents a reasonable accommodation of conflicting policies that were committed to the agency's care by the statute, we should not disturb it unless it appears from the statute or its legislative history that the accommodation is not one that Congress would have sanctioned." *United States v. Shimer*, 367 U.S. 374, 382, 383 (1961).

In light of these well-settled principles it is clear that the Court of Appeals misconceived the nature of its role in reviewing the regulations at issue. Once it determined, after its own examination of the legislation, that Congress did not actually have an intent regarding the applicability of the bubble concept to the permit program, the question before it was not whether in its view the concept is "inappropriate" in the general context of a program designed to improve air quality, but whether the Administrator's view that it is appropriate in the context of this particular program is a reasonable one. Based on the examination of the legislation and its history which follows, we agree with the Court of Appeals that Congress did not have a specific intention on the applicability of the bubble concept in these cases, and conclude that the EPA's use of that concept here is a reasonable policy choice for the agency to make. * * *

[In the omitted portions of its opinion the Court reviews the statutory and regulatory history of the definition of a "stationary source" under the 1970 Clean Air Act and of a "major stationary source" in section 172(b)(6) of the Clean Air Amendments of 1977. Based on this review the Court was persuaded that, at least prior to 1980, neither Congress, nor for that matter EPA, had embraced any stable policy concerning when a "source" might be considered to be a whole plant ("the bubble concept") rather than its components.]

VI

* * * In August 1980, however, the EPA adopted a regulation that, in essence, applied the basic reasoning of the Court of Appeals in these cases. The EPA took particular note of the two then-recent Court of Appeals decisions, which had created the bright-line rule that the "bub-

ble concept" should be employed in a program designed to maintain air quality but not in one designed to enhance air quality. Relying heavily on those cases, EPA adopted a dual definition of "source" for nonattainment areas that required a permit whenever a change in either the entire plant, or one of its components, would result in a significant increase in emissions even if the increase was completely offset by reductions elsewhere in the plant. The EPA expressed the opinion that this interpretation was "more consistent with congressional intent" than the plantwide definition because it "would bring in more sources or modifications for review," but its primary legal analysis was predicated on the two Court of Appeals decisions.

In 1981 a new administration took office and initiated a "Government-wide reexamination of regulatory burdens and complexities." In the context of that review, the EPA reevaluated the various arguments that had been advanced in connection with the proper definition of the term "source" and concluded that the term should be given the same definition in both nonattainment areas and PSD areas.

In explaining its conclusion, the EPA first noted that the definitional issue was not squarely addressed in either the statute or its legislative history and therefore that the issue involved an agency "judgment as how to best carry out the Act." It then set forth several reasons for concluding that the plantwide definition was more appropriate. It pointed out that the dual definition "can act as a disincentive to new investment and modernization by discouraging modifications to existing facilities" and "can actually retard progress in air pollution control by discouraging replacement of older, dirtier processes or pieces of equipment with new, cleaner ones." Moreover, the new definition "would simplify EPA's rules by using the same definition of 'source' for PSD [Prevention of Serious Deterioration], nonattainment new source review and the construction moratorium. This reduces confusion and inconsistency." Finally, the agency explained that additional requirements that remained in place would accomplish the fundamental purposes of achieving attainment with NAAQS's [National Ambient Air Quality Standards] as expeditiously as possible. These conclusions were expressed in a proposed rulemaking in August 1981 that was formally promulgated in October.

VII

In this Court respondents expressly reject the basic rationale of the Court of Appeals' decision. * * * They contend that the text of the Act requires the EPA to use a dual definition—if either a component of a plant, or the plant as a whole, emits over 100 tons of pollutant, it is a major stationary source. They thus contend that the EPA rules adopted in 1980, insofar as they apply to the maintenance of the quality of clean air, as well as the 1982 rules which apply to nonattainment areas, violate the statute.

Our review of the EPA's varying interpretations of the word "source"—both before and after the 1977 Amendments—convinces us that the agency primarily responsible for administering this important legislation has consistently interpreted it flexibly—not in a sterile textual vacuum, but in the context of implementing policy decisions in a technical and complex arena. The fact that the agency has from time to time changed its interpretation of the term "source" does not, as respondents argue, lead us to conclude that no deference should be accorded the agency's interpretation of the statute. An initial agency interpretation is not instantly carved in stone. On the contrary, the agency, to engage in informed rulemaking, must consider varying interpretations and the wisdom of its policy on a continuing basis. Moreover, the fact that the agency has adopted different definitions in different contexts adds force to the argument that the definition itself is flexible, particularly since Congress has never indicated any disapproval of a flexible reading of the statute.

The arguments over policy that are advanced in the parties' briefs create the impression that respondents are now waging in a judicial forum a specific policy battle which they ultimately lost in the agency and in the 32 jurisdictions opting for the "bubble concept," but one which was never waged in the Congress. Such policy arguments are more properly addressed to legislators or administrators, not to judges. In these cases, the Administrator's interpretation represents a reasonable accommodation of manifestly competing interests and is entitled to deference: the regulatory scheme is technical and complex, the agency considered the matter in a detailed and reasoned fashion, and the decision involves reconciling conflicting policies. Congress intended to accommodate both interests, but did not do so itself on the level of specificity presented by these cases. Perhaps that body consciously desired the Administrator to strike the balance at this level, thinking that those with great expertise and charged with responsibility for administering the provision would be in a better position to do so; perhaps it simply did not consider the question at this level; and perhaps Congress was unable to forge a coalition on either side of the question, and those on each side decided to take their chances with the scheme devised by the agency. For judicial purposes, it matters not which of these things occurred.

Judges are not experts in the field, and are not part of either political branch of the Government. Courts must, in some cases, reconcile competing political interests, but not on the basis of the judges' personal policy preferences. In contrast, an agency to which Congress has delegated policymaking responsibilities may, within the limits of that delegation, properly rely upon the incumbent administration's views of wise policy to inform its judgments. While agencies are not directly accountable to the people, the Chief Executive is, and it is entirely appropriate for this political branch of the Government to make such policy choices—resolving the competing interests which Congress itself either inadvertently did not resolve, or intentionally left to be resolved by the agency charged with the administration of the statute in light of everyday realities.

When a challenge to an agency construction of a statutory provision, fairly conceptualized, really centers on the wisdom of the agency's policy, rather than whether it is a reasonable choice within a gap left open by Congress, the challenge must fail. In such a case, federal judges—who have no constituency—have a duty to respect legitimate policy choices made by those who do. The responsibilities for assessing the wisdom of such policy choices and resolving the struggle between competing views of the public interest are not judicial ones. * * *

Note

Is Chevron an Innovation? Judging by the frequency with which lower courts—not to mention government briefs—cite *Chevron* and by the continuing avalanche of law review commentary, *Chevron* is widely regarded as a major change in the direction of the Court's thinking on deference to agency statutory interpretation. But is the Court's approach in *Chevron* truly novel?

Consider the agency decision under review. The Clean Air Act Amendments of 1977 imposed certain requirements on areas whose air had not yet met established national air quality standards. Each state containing such a "nonattainment area" was required to submit an implementation plan for achieving the standards. That plan had to require a permit for any modification or construction of a major "stationary source" in a nonattainment area if the facility's emissions would include a pollutant for which the area was out of compliance. Permits could be issued only if the permit applicant demonstrated, among other things, that:

1. Total emissions from the proposed source together with all other emissions from the area would represent reasonable further progress towards attainment, that is, total emissions would be lower than before construction; and

2. It would install equipment capable of achieving the "lowest achievable emissions rate," the most stringent level of control imposed by the Act.

The EPA, however, wanted to allow states to forego treating as a modified source any modification of an existing plant if the modified technology together with remaining old plant would not produce greater total emissions than the original plant. In substance, a proprietor would be entitled to treat all pollution-emitting devices within an industrial grouping as though they were inside a single "bubble." This approach would permit plant owners to trade old equipment for more efficient new equipment, even if the new equipment was not capable of achieving the lowest achievable emissions rate. The EPA saw the alternative as continued operation of old polluting equipment, which would be wasteful. The legal question facing EPA was whether it could legitimately exclude such upgraded plants from the category of "modified major stationary sources" for which the Clean Air Act explicitly requires permits.

One might expect the Court in reviewing the EPA's answer to ask two questions. First, was its interpretation of its authority either dictated or proscribed by the Act? If the Act defined "modified major stationary source" to exclude changes that would improve a plant's overall emission levels, EPA would have been obligated to adopt the bubble strategy. On the other hand, if the statute prohibited a bubble approach, or prohibited EPA from basing its decision on criteria that rendered the bubble strategy attractive, EPA's interpretation would have been barred. The Court would have to decide for itself whether the statute dictated such results. Presumably, this is what Justice Stevens means by saying, "If the intent of Congress is clear, that is the end of the matter."

If EPA's interpretation were neither dictated nor proscribed by statute, the remaining inquiry would be whether its reading was permissible. That is, would a definition of "modified major stationary source" that permitted "bubbling" be a sufficiently appropriate means of accomplishing Congress' purposes as to be implicitly authorized? At this stage, matters of legal interpretation and policy choice converge. That is, the arguments EPA would make for the permissibility of its statutory "interpretation" would be all but identical to the arguments it would advance to support the rationality of its rule. Judicial deference at *Chevron*'s "Step Two" appears to be deference to the same sorts of expert determinations and policy inferences to which courts are expected to defer under the "arbitrary or capricious" standard of 5 U.S.C. § 706. In *Overton Park* terms, EPA would argue that its decision "was based on a consideration of the relevant factors" and was rational. *Overton Park* indicates that the scope of review on this issue is narrow. Again, on this view, *Chevron* seems conventional in its approach.

This perhaps explains Justice Stevens' statement that courts should defer to reasonable agency interpretations at "Step Two" whether the absence of a clear statutory answer is the product of a deliberate congressional choice to delegate interpretive authority, a policy impasse, or mere oversight. Because EPA's defense of its "interpretation" is essentially the defense of an implementation strategy, for which *Overton Park* prescribes deferential review, it would seem odd to forego such deference because the agency's policy reasoning is de facto its legal interpretation as well. Justice Stevens' conclusion that "a court may not substitute its own construction of a statutory provision for a reasonable interpretation made by the administrator of the agency," might have been put more clearly as: "When an agency has articulated a rational approach for implementing a statute, a court should not invent a statutory requirement that the agency adopt some different approach that the court would have preferred."

What may have been novel in *Chevron* was Justice Stevens' description of the circumstances in which a court should move from de novo examination of statutory language to a deferential search for agency reasonableness. He writes that a court should determine for itself if "Congress has directly spoken to the precise question at issue." A court, however, should defer to a reasonable agency interpretation "if the statute is silent or ambiguous." Reading this language for all it's worth—a reading that *would* cast doubt on *Overton Park*—there are few statutory phrases in which an agency could not find sufficient ambiguity to allow substitution of its own interpretation.

The starkness of Justice Stevens' formulation may reflect a tacit goal often ascribed to Supreme Court opinion writing, namely, to send a generalized direction to lower courts about how to approach their task, not a technical message about legal doctrine. In *Chevron*, the behavioral signal might be: "Lighten up." Because Justice Stevens puts the Court's direction so strongly, however, "*Chevron*" has become a central feature of contemporary administrative law argumentation.

UNITED STATES v. MEAD CORP.

Supreme Court of the United States, 2001.
533 U.S. 218, 121 S.Ct. 2164, L.Ed.2d 292.

JUSTICE SOUTER delivered the opinion of the Court.

The question is whether a tariff classification ruling by the United States Customs Service deserves judicial deference. The Federal Circuit rejected Customs's invocation of *Chevron U.S.A. Inc. v. Natural Resources Defense Council, Inc.,* in support of such a ruling, to which it gave no deference. We agree that a tariff classification has no claim to judicial deference under *Chevron,* there being no indication that Congress intended such a ruling to carry the force of law, but we hold that under *Skidmore v. Swift Co.*, 323 U.S. 134 (1944), the ruling is eligible to claim respect according to its persuasiveness.

I

A

Imports are taxed under the Harmonized Tariff Schedule of the United States (HTSUS), 19 U.S.C. § 1202. Title 19 U.S.C. § 1500(b) provides that Customs "shall, under rules and regulations prescribed by the Secretary [of the Treasury] * * * fix the final classification and rate of duty applicable to * * * merchandise" under the HTSUS. Section 1502(a) provides that

> "[t]he Secretary of the Treasury shall establish and promulgate such rules and regulations not inconsistent with the law (including regulations establishing procedures for the issuance of binding rulings prior to the entry of the merchandise concerned), and may disseminate such information as may be necessary to secure a just, impartial, and uniform appraisement of imported merchandise and the classification and assessment of duties thereon at the various ports of entry."[1]

The Secretary provides for tariff rulings before the entry of goods by regulations authorizing "ruling letters" setting tariff classifications for particular imports. 19 CFR § 177.8 (2000). A ruling letter

> "represents the official position of the Customs Service with respect to the particular transaction or issue described therein and is

1. The statutory term "ruling" is defined by regulation as "a written statement * * * that interprets and applies the provisions of the Customs and related laws to a specific set of facts." 19 CFR § 177.1(d)(1) (2000).

binding on all Customs Service personnel in accordance with the provisions of this section until modified or revoked. In the absence of a change of practice or other modification or revocation which affects the principle of the ruling set forth in the ruling letter, that principle may be cited as authority in the disposition of transactions involving the same circumstances." § 177.9(a).

After the transaction that gives it birth, a ruling letter is to "be applied only with respect to transactions involving articles identical to the sample submitted with the ruling request or to articles whose description is identical to the description set forth in the ruling letter." § 177.9(b)(2). As a general matter, such a letter is "subject to modification or revocation without notice to any person, except the person to whom the letter was addressed," § 177.9(c), and the regulations consequently provide that "no other person should rely on the ruling letter or assume that the principles of that ruling will be applied in connection with any transaction other than the one described in the letter." Since ruling letters respond to transactions of the moment, they are not subject to notice and comment before being issued, may be published but need only be made "available for public inspection," 19 U.S.C. § 1625(a), and, at the time this action arose, could be modified without notice and comment under most circumstances, 19 CFR § 177.10(c) (2000). A broader notice-and-comment requirement for modification of prior rulings was added by statute in 1993, and took effect after this case arose.[3]

Any of the 46 port-of-entry Customs offices may issue ruling letters, and so may the Customs Headquarters Office, in providing "[a]dvice or guidance as to the interpretation or proper application of the Customs and related laws with respect to a specific Customs transaction [which] may be requested by Customs Service field offices * * * at any time, whether the transaction is prospective, current, or completed," 19 CFR § 177.11(a) (2000). Most ruling letters contain little or no reasoning, but simply describe goods and state the appropriate category and tariff. A few letters, like the Headquarters ruling at issue here, set out a rationale in some detail.

B

Respondent, the Mead Corporation, imports "day planners," three-ring binders with pages having room for notes of daily schedules and phone numbers and addresses, together with a calendar and suchlike.

3. As amended by legislation effective after Customs modified its classification ruling in this case, 19 U.S.C. § 1625(c) provides that a ruling or decision that would "modify * * * or revoke a prior interpretive ruling or decision which has been in effect for at least 60 days" or would "have the effect of modifying the treatment previously accorded by the Customs Service to substantially identical transactions" shall be "published in the Customs Bulletin. The Secretary shall give interested parties an opportunity to submit, during not less than the 30-day period after the date of such publication, comments on the correctness of the proposed ruling or decision. After consideration of any comments received, the Secretary shall publish a final ruling or decision in the Customs Bulletin within 30 days after the closing of the comment period. The final ruling or decision shall become effective 60 days after the date of its publication."

The tariff schedule on point falls under the HTSUS heading for "[r]egisters, account books, notebooks, order books, receipt books, letter pads, memorandum pads, diaries and similar articles," HTSUS subheading 4820.10, which comprises two subcategories. Items in the first, "[d]iaries, notebooks and address books, bound; memorandum pads, letter pads and similar articles," were subject to a tariff of 4.0 per cent at the time in controversy. Objects in the second, covering "[o]ther" items, were free of duty.

Between 1989 and 1993, Customs repeatedly treated day planners under the "other" HTSUS subheading. In January 1993, however, Customs changed its position, and issued a Headquarters ruling letter classifying Mead's day planners as "Diaries * * *, bound" subject to tariff under subheading 4820.10.20. That letter was short on explanation, but after Mead's protest, Customs Headquarters issued a new letter, carefully reasoned but never published, reaching the same conclusion. This letter considered two definitions of "diary" from the Oxford English Dictionary, the first covering a daily journal of the past day's events, the second a book including " 'printed dates for daily memoranda and jottings; also * * * calendars. * * * ' " Customs concluded that "diary" was not confined to the first, in part because the broader definition reflects commercial usage and hence the "commercial identity of these items in the marketplace." As for the definition of "bound," Customs concluded that HTSUS was not referring to "bookbinding," but to a less exact sort of fastening described in the Harmonized Commodity Description and Coding System Explanatory Notes to Heading 4820, which spoke of binding by " 'reinforcements or fittings of metal, plastics, etc.' "

* * * Mead then went to the United States Court of Appeals for the Federal Circuit. While the case was pending there this Court decided *United States v. Haggar Apparel Co.*, 526 U.S. 380 (1999), holding that Customs regulations receive the deference described in *Chevron U.S.A. Inc. v. Natural Resources Defense Council, Inc.* The appeals court requested briefing on the impact of *Haggar*, and the Government argued that classification rulings, like Customs regulations, deserve *Chevron* deference.

The Federal Circuit, however, * * * held that Customs classification rulings should not get *Chevron* deference, owing to differences from the regulations at issue in *Haggar*. Rulings are not preceded by notice and comment as under the Administrative Procedure Act (APA), 5 U.S.C. § 553, they "do not carry the force of law and are not, like regulations, intended to clarify the rights and obligations of importers beyond the specific case under review." The appeals court thought classification rulings had a weaker *Chevron* claim even than Internal Revenue Service interpretive rulings, to which that court gives no deference; unlike rulings by the IRS, Customs rulings issue from many locations and need not be published.

The Court of Appeals accordingly gave no deference at all to the ruling classifying the Mead day planners and rejected the agency's reasoning as to both "diary" and "bound." It thought that planners were not diaries because they had no space for "relatively extensive notations about events, observations, feelings, or thoughts" in the past. And it concluded that diaries "bound" in subheading 4810.10.20 presupposed "unbound" diaries, such that treating ring-fastened diaries as "bound" would leave the "unbound diary" an empty category.

We granted certiorari, in order to consider the limits of *Chevron* deference owed to administrative practice in applying a statute. We hold that administrative implementation of a particular statutory provision qualifies for *Chevron* deference when it appears that Congress delegated authority to the agency generally to make rules carrying the force of law, and that the agency interpretation claiming deference was promulgated in the exercise of that authority. Delegation of such authority may be shown in a variety of ways, as by an agency's power to engage in adjudication or notice-and-comment rulemaking, or by some other indication of a comparable congressional intent. The Customs ruling at issue here fails to qualify, although the possibility that it deserves some deference under *Skidmore* leads us to vacate and remand.

II

A

When Congress has "explicitly left a gap for an agency to fill, there is an express delegation of authority to the agency to elucidate a specific provision of the statute by regulation," and any ensuing regulation is binding in the courts unless procedurally defective, arbitrary or capricious in substance, or manifestly contrary to the statute. But whether or not they enjoy any express delegation of authority on a particular question, agencies charged with applying a statute necessarily make all sorts of interpretive choices, and while not all of those choices bind judges to follow them, they certainly may influence courts facing questions the agencies have already answered. * * * The fair measure of deference to an agency administering its own statute has been understood to vary with circumstances, and courts have looked to the degree of the agency's care, its consistency, formality, and relative expertness, and to the persuasiveness of the agency's position. * * * Justice Jackson summed things up in *Skidmore* v. *Swift & Co.*:

> "The weight [accorded to an administrative] judgment in a particular case will depend upon the thoroughness evident in its consideration, the validity of its reasoning, its consistency with earlier and later pronouncements, and all those factors which give it power to persuade, if lacking power to control."

Since 1984, we have identified a category of interpretive choices distinguished by an additional reason for judicial deference. This Court in *Chevron* recognized that Congress not only engages in express delegation of specific interpretive authority, but that "[s]ometimes the legislative delegation to an agency on a particular question is implicit." Congress, that is, may not have expressly delegated authority or responsibility to implement a particular provision or fill a particular gap. Yet it can still be apparent from the agency's generally conferred authority and other statutory circumstances that Congress would expect the agency to be able to speak with the force of law when it addresses ambiguity in the statute or fills a space in the enacted law, even one about which "Congress did not actually have an intent" as to a particular result. When circumstances implying such an expectation exist, a reviewing court has no business rejecting an agency's exercise of its generally conferred authority to resolve a particular statutory ambiguity simply because the agency's chosen resolution seems unwise, but is obliged to accept the agency's position if Congress has not previously spoken to the point at issue and the agency's interpretation is reasonable.

We have recognized a very good indicator of delegation meriting *Chevron* treatment in express congressional authorizations to engage in the process of rulemaking or adjudication that produces regulations or rulings for which deference is claimed. It is fair to assume generally that Congress contemplates administrative action with the effect of law when it provides for a relatively formal administrative procedure tending to foster the fairness and deliberation that should underlie a pronouncement of such force. Thus, the overwhelming number of our cases applying *Chevron* deference have reviewed the fruits of notice-and-comment rulemaking or formal adjudication. That said, and as significant as notice-and-comment is in pointing to *Chevron* authority, the want of that procedure here does not decide the case, for we have sometimes found reasons for *Chevron* deference even when no such administrative formality was required and none was afforded. The fact that the tariff classification here was not a product of such formal process does not alone, therefore, bar the application of *Chevron*.

There are, nonetheless, ample reasons to deny *Chevron* deference here. * * *

B

No matter which angle we choose for viewing the Customs ruling letter in this case, it fails to qualify under *Chevron*. On the face of the statute, to begin with, the terms of the congressional delegation give no indication that Congress meant to delegate authority to Customs to issue classification rulings with the force of law. We are not, of course, here making any global statement about Customs's authority, for it is true that the general rulemaking power conferred on Customs, see 19 U.S.C. § 1624, authorizes some regulation with the force of law, or "legal norms," as we put it in *Haggar*. It is true as well that Congress had classification rulings in mind when it explicitly authorized, in a parenthetical, the issuance of "regulations establishing procedures for the issuance of binding rulings prior to the entry of the merchandise concerned," 19 U.S.C. § 1502(a). The reference to binding classifications does not, however, bespeak the legislative type of activity that would naturally bind more than the parties to the ruling, once the goods classified are admitted into this country. And though the statute's direction to disseminate "information" necessary to "secure" uniformity, seems to assume that a ruling may be precedent in later transactions, precedential value alone does not add up to *Chevron* entitlement; interpretive rules may sometimes function as precedents, and they enjoy no *Chevron* status as a class. In any event, any precedential claim of a classification ruling is counterbalanced by the provision for independent review of Customs classifications by the [Court of International Trade]; the scheme for CIT review includes a provision that treats classification rulings on par with the Secretary's rulings on "valuation, rate of duty, marking, restricted merchandise, entry requirements, drawbacks, vessel repairs, or similar matters," § 1581(h); see § 2639(b). It is hard to imagine a congressional understanding more at odds with the *Chevron* regime.

It is difficult, in fact, to see in the agency practice itself any indication that Customs ever set out with a lawmaking pretense in mind when it undertook to make classifications like these. Customs does not generally engage in notice-and-comment practice when issuing them, and their treatment by the agency makes it clear that a letter's binding character as a ruling stops short of third parties; Customs has regarded a classification as conclusive only as between itself and the importer to whom it was issued, and even then only until Customs has given advance notice of intended change. Other importers are in fact warned against assuming any right of detrimental reliance.

Indeed, to claim that classifications have legal force is to ignore the reality that 46 different Customs offices issue 10,000 to 15,000 of them each year. Any suggestion that rulings intended to have the force of law are being churned out at a rate of 10,000 a year at an agency's 46 scattered offices is simply self-refuting. Although the circumstances are less startling here, with a Headquarters letter in issue, none of the relevant statutes recognizes this category of rulings as separate or different from others; there is thus no indication that a more potent delegation might have been understood as going to Headquarters even when Headquarters provides developed reasoning, as it did in this instance.

Nor do the amendments to the statute made effective after this case arose disturb our conclusion. The new law requires Customs to provide notice-and-comment procedures only when modifying or revoking a prior classification ruling or modifying the treatment accorded to substantially identical transactions; and under its regulations, Customs sees itself obliged to provide notice-and-comment procedures only when "changing a practice" so as to produce a tariff increase, or in the imposition of a restriction or prohibition, or when Customs Headquarters determines that "the matter is of sufficient importance to involve the interests of domestic industry." * * *

In sum, classification rulings are best treated like "interpretations contained in policy statements, agency manuals, and enforcement guidelines." *Christensen v. Harris County*, 529 U.S., at 587. They are beyond the *Chevron* pale.

C

To agree with the Court of Appeals that Customs ruling letters do not fall within *Chevron* is not, however, to place them outside the pale of any deference whatever. *Chevron* did nothing to eliminate *Skidmore*'s holding that an agency's interpretation may merit some deference whatever its form, given the "specialized experience and broader investigations and information" available to the agency, and given the value of uniformity in its administrative and judicial understandings of what a national law requires. There is room at least to raise a *Skidmore* claim here, where the regulatory scheme is highly detailed, and Customs can bring the benefit of specialized experience to bear on the subtle questions in this case. * * * A classification ruling in this situation may therefore at least seek a respect proportional to its "power to persuade," *Skidmore, supra.* Such a ruling may surely claim the merit of its writer's thoroughness, logic and expertness, its fit with prior interpretations, and any other sources of weight.

D

Underlying the position we take here, like the position expressed by Justice Scalia in dissent, is a choice about the best way to deal with an inescapable feature of the body of congressional legislation authorizing administrative action. That feature is the great variety of ways in which the laws invest the Government's administrative arms with discretion, and with procedures for exercising it, in giving meaning to Acts of Congress. * * *

Although we all accept the position that the Judiciary should defer to at least some of this multifarious administrative action, we have to decide how to take account of the great range of its variety. If the primary objective is to simplify the judicial process of giving or withholding deference, then the diversity of statutes authorizing discretionary administrative action must be declared irrelevant or minimized. If, on the other hand, it is simply implausible that Congress intended such a broad range of statutory authority to produce only two varieties of administrative action, demanding either *Chevron* deference or none at all, then the breadth of the spectrum of possible agency action must be taken into account. Justice Scalia's first priority over the years has been to limit and simplify. The Court's choice has been to tailor deference to variety. This acceptance of the range of statutory variation has led the Court to recognize more than one variety of judicial deference, just as the Court has recognized a variety of indicators that Congress would expect *Chevron* deference. * * *

The Court * * * said nothing in *Chevron* to eliminate *Skidmore*'s recognition of various justifications for deference depending on statutory circumstances and agency action; *Chevron* was simply a case recognizing that even without express authority to fill a specific statutory gap, circumstances pointing to implicit congressional delegation present a particularly insistent call for deference. * * *

We think, in sum, that Justice Scalia's efforts to simplify ultimately run afoul of Congress's indications that different statutes present different reasons for considering respect for the exercise of administrative authority or deference to it. Without being at odds with congressional intent much of the time, we believe that judicial responses to administrative action must continue to differentiate between *Chevron* and *Skidmore,* and that continued recognition of *Skidmore* is necessary for just the reasons Justice Jackson gave when that case was decided.

* * *

JUSTICE SCALIA, dissenting.

Today's opinion makes an avulsive change in judicial review of federal administrative action. Whereas previously a reasonable agency application of an ambiguous statutory provision had to be sustained so long as it represented the agency's authoritative interpretation, henceforth such an application can be set aside unless "it appears that Congress delegated authority to the agency generally to make rules carrying the force of law," as by giving an agency "power to engage in adjudication or notice-and-comment rulemaking, or * * * some other [procedure] indicating comparable congressional intent," and "the agency interpretation claiming deference was promulgated in the exercise of that authority." What was previously a general presumption of authority in agencies to resolve ambiguity in the statutes they have been authorized to enforce has been changed to a presumption of no such authority, which must be overcome by affirmative legislative intent to the contrary. And whereas previously, when agency authority to resolve ambiguity did not exist the court was free to give the statute what it considered the best interpretation, henceforth the court must supposedly give the agency view some indeterminate amount of so-called *Skidmore* deference. We will be sorting out the consequences of the *Mead* doctrine, which has today replaced the *Chevron* doctrine, for years to come. * * *

I

* * *

The Court's new doctrine is neither sound in principle nor sustainable in practice.

As to principle: The doctrine of *Chevron*—that all *authoritative* agency interpretations of statutes they are charged with administering deserve deference—was rooted in a legal presumption of congressional intent, important to the division of powers between the Second and Third Branches. When, *Chevron* said, Congress leaves an ambiguity in a statute that is to be administered by an executive agency, it is presumed that Congress meant to give the agency discretion, within the limits of reasonable interpretation, as to how the ambiguity is to be resolved. By committing enforcement of the statute to an agency rather than the courts, Congress committed its initial and primary interpretation to that branch as well.

There is some question whether *Chevron* was faithful to the text of the Administrative Procedure Act (APA), which it did not even bother to cite.[2] But it was in accord with the origins of federal-court judicial review. Judicial control of federal executive officers was principally exercised through the prerogative writ of mandamus. That writ generally would not issue unless the executive officer was acting plainly beyond the scope of his authority. * * *

The basis in principle for today's new doctrine can be described as follows: The background rule is that ambiguity in legislative instructions to agencies is to be resolved not by the agencies but by the judges. Specific congressional intent to depart from this rule must be found—and while there is no single touchstone for such intent it can generally be found when Congress has authorized the agency to act through (what the Court says is) relatively formal procedures such as informal rulemaking and formal (and informal?) adjudication, and when the agency in fact employs such procedures. The Court's background rule is contradicted by the origins of judicial review of administrative action. But in addition, the Court's principal criterion of congressional intent to supplant its background rule seems to me quite implausible. There is no necessary connection between the formality of procedure and the power of the entity administering the procedure to resolve authoritatively questions of law. The most formal of the procedures the Court refers to—formal adjudication—is modeled after the process used in trial courts, which of course are not generally accorded deference on questions of law. The purpose of such a procedure is to produce a closed record for determination and review of the facts—which implies nothing about the power of the agency subjected to the procedure to resolve authoritatively questions of law.

As for informal rulemaking: While formal adjudication procedures are *prescribed* (either by statute or by the Constitution), informal rulemaking is more typically *authorized* but not required. Agencies with such authority are free to give guidance through rulemaking, but they may proceed to administer their statute case-by-case, "making law" as they implement their program (not necessarily through formal adjudication).

2. Title 5 U.S.C. § 706 provides that, in reviewing agency action, the court shall "decide all relevant questions of law"—which would seem to mean that all statutory ambiguities are to be resolved judicially. It could be argued, however, that the legal presumption identified by *Chevron* left as the only "questio[n] of law" whether the agency's interpretation had gone beyond the scope of discretion that the statutory ambiguity conferred. Today's opinion, of course, is no more observant of the APA's text than *Chevron* was—and indeed is even more difficult to reconcile with it. Since the opinion relies upon actual congressional intent to suspend § 706, rather than upon a legal presumption against which § 706 was presumably enacted, it runs head-on into the provision of the APA which specifies that the Act's requirements (including the requirement that judges shall "decide all relevant questions of law") cannot be amended except expressly.

See *NLRB v. Bell Aerospace Co.*, 416 U.S. 267 (1974); *SEC v. Chenery Corp.*, 332 U.S. 194 (1947). Is it likely—or indeed even plausible—that Congress meant, when such an agency chooses rulemaking, to accord the administrators of that agency, *and their successors*, the flexibility of interpreting the ambiguous statute now one way, and later another; but, when such an agency chooses case-by-case administration, to eliminate all future agency discretion by having that same ambiguity resolved authoritatively (and forever) by the courts? Surely that makes no sense. It is also the case that certain significant categories of rules—those involving grant and benefit programs, for example, are exempt from the requirements of informal rulemaking. Under the Court's novel theory, when an agency takes advantage of that exemption its rules will be deprived of *Chevron* deference, *i.e.*, authoritative effect. Was this either the plausible intent of the APA rulemaking exemption, or the plausible intent of the Congress that established the grant or benefit program?

Some decisions that are neither informal rulemaking nor formal adjudication are required to be made personally by a Cabinet Secretary, without any prescribed procedures. Is it conceivable that decisions specifically committed to these high-level officers are meant to be accorded no deference, while decisions by an administrative law judge left in place without further discretionary agency review, are authoritative? This seems to me quite absurd, and not at all in accord with any plausible actual intent of Congress.

As for the practical effects of the new rule:

The principal effect will be protracted confusion. As noted above, the one test for *Chevron* deference that the Court enunciates is wonderfully imprecise: whether "Congress delegated authority to the agency generally to make rules carrying the force of law, * * * as by * * * adjudication[,] notice-and-comment rulemaking, or * * * some other [procedure] indicating comparable congressional intent." But even this description does not do justice to the utter flabbiness of the Court's criterion, since, in order to maintain the fiction that the new test is really just the old one, applied consistently throughout our case law, the Court must make a virtually open-ended exception to its already imprecise guidance: In the present case, it tells us, the absence of notice-and-comment rulemaking (and "[who knows?] [of] some other [procedure] indicating comparable congressional intent") is not enough to decide the question of *Chevron* deference, "for we have sometimes found reasons for *Chevron* deference even when no such administrative formality was required and none was afforded." The opinion then goes on to consider a grab bag of other factors—including the factor that used to be the sole criterion for *Chevron* deference: whether the interpretation represented the *authoritative* position of the agency. It is hard to know what the lower courts are to make of today's guidance.

Another practical effect of today's opinion will be an artificially induced increase in informal rulemaking. Buy stock in the GPO. Since informal rulemaking and formal adjudication are the only more-or-less safe harbors from the storm that the Court has unleashed; and since formal adjudication is not an option but must be mandated by statute or constitutional command; informal rulemaking—which the Court was once careful to make voluntary unless required by statute, will now become a virtual necessity. * * * Agencies will now have high incentive to rush out barebones, ambiguous rules construing statutory ambiguities, which they can then in turn further clarify through informal rulings entitled to judicial respect.

Worst of all, the majority's approach will lead to the ossification of large portions of our statutory law. Where *Chevron* applies, statutory ambiguities remain ambiguities subject to the agency's ongoing clarification. * * * For the indeterminately large number of statutes taken out of *Chevron* by today's decision, however, ambiguity (and hence flexibility) will cease with the first judicial resolution. *Skidmore* deference gives the agency's current position some vague and uncertain amount of respect, but it does not, like *Chevron*, *leave* the matter within the control of the Executive Branch for the future. Once the court has spoken, it becomes *unlawful* for the agency to take a contradictory position; the statute now *says* what the court has prescribed. * * *

* * *

And finally, the majority's approach compounds the confusion it creates by breathing new life into the anachronism of *Skidmore*, which sets forth a sliding scale of deference owed an agency's interpretation of a statute that is dependent "upon the thoroughness evident in [the agency's] consideration, the validity of its reasoning, its consistency with earlier and later pronouncements, and all those factors which give it power to persuade, if lacking power to control"; in this way, the appropriate measure of deference will be accorded the "body of experience and informed judgment" that such interpretations often embody. Justice Jackson's eloquence notwithstanding, the rule of *Skidmore* deference is an empty truism and a trifling statement of the obvious: A judge should take into account the well-considered views of expert observers.

It was possible to live with the indeterminacy of *Skidmore* deference in earlier times. But in an era when federal statutory law administered by federal agencies is pervasive, and when the ambiguities (intended or unintended) that those statutes contain are innumerable, totality-of-the-circumstances *Skidmore* deference is a recipe for uncertainty, unpredictability, and endless litigation. To condemn a vast body of agency action to that regime (all except rulemaking, formal (and informal?) adjudication, and whatever else might now and then be included within today's intentionally vague formulation of affirmative congressional intent to "delegate") is irresponsible. * * *

III

To decide the present case, I would adhere to the original formulation of *Chevron*. * * *

* * *

There is no doubt that the Customs Service's interpretation represents the authoritative view of the agency. Although the actual ruling letter was signed by only the Director of the Commercial Rulings Branch of Customs Headquarters' Office of Regulations and Rulings, the Solicitor General of the United States has filed a brief, cosigned by the General Counsel of the Department of the Treasury, that represents the position set forth in the ruling letter to be the official position of the Customs Service. No one contends that it is merely a "post hoc rationalizatio[n]" or an "agency litigating positio[n] wholly unsupported by regulations, rulings, or administrative practice."

There is also no doubt that the Customs Service's interpretation is a reasonable one, whether or not judges would consider it the best. I will not belabor this point, since the Court evidently agrees: An interpretation that was unreasonable would not merit the remand that the Court decrees for consideration of *Skidmore* deference.

Notes

1. *The Relevance of Agency Process.* Although Justice Souter seems to treat the procedure an agency follows to arrive at a legal ruling as merely evidence of Congress's intent to confer law-making authority, there were suggestions prior to *Mead* that an agency's process had independent, possibly decisive, significance. *Christensen v. Harris County*, 529 U.S. 576 (2000), to which Justice Souter refers, involved a provision of the Fair Labor Standards Act that permits local governments, instead of paying over-time, to grant their employees "compensatory time" for work in excess of 40 hours. Harris County asked the Assistant Administrator of the Labor Department's Wage and Hours Division whether the county could require its employees to use their accrued "comp hours" rather than be compensated for them. The Assistant Administrator responded in an "Opinion Letter," interpreting the statute to permit such a directive only if permitted by a previously negotiated agreement between the county and the employees.

In an opinion by Justice Thomas, the Court held that the agency's interpretation of FLSA was not entitled to *Chevron* deference.

> Here * * * we confront an interpretation contained in an opinion letter, not one arrived at after, for example, a formal adjudication or notice-and-comment rulemaking. Interpretations such as those in opinion letters—like interpretations contained in policy statements, agency manuals, and enforcement guidelines, all of which lack the force of law—do not warrant *Chevron*-style deference.

Justice Thomas then went on to declare that interpretations in such non-binding formats are "entitled to respect" under *Skidmore*. Justice Scalia concurred separately, previewing his *Mead* objection to the Court's references to *Skidmore*. Following his preferred approach, Justice Scalia acknowledged that the interpretation contained in the agency's letter represented its authoritative position, but he found that interpretation not "reasonable."

In the term following *Mead*, the Court again addressed the importance of agency process—or, in Justice Thomas's words, "format"—in determining whether an agency's statutory interpretation merits *Chevron* deference or merely some lesser degree of respect. The issue in *Barnhart v. Walton*, 535 U.S. 212 (2002), was whether the Commissioner of Social Security's interpretation of the statutory term "disability" was entitled to *Chevron* deference. The SSA had for many years taken the positions that, to be classified as disabled, a claimant had to suffer from an inability to engage in substantial gainful activity that would have lasted, or would have been expected to last, for at least 12 months and, further, that a claimant's earlier return to work precluded a finding of disability. These positions, however, had only recently been set forth in regulations adopted in accordance with the APA's requirements, and Walton argued that the agency's interpretation therefore should not be given deference.

Writing for eight Justices, Justice Breyer concluded that the statute did not either mandate or preclude the SSA interpretation and found the agency's interpretation reasonable under Step 2 of *Chevron*. Addressing Walton's contention that *Chevron* deference should not be accorded because the interpretation was not the genuine product of public rulemaking, Justice Breyer responded:

> We have previously rejected similar arguments. *Smiley v. Citibank (South Dakota), N.A.*, 517 U.S. 735 (1996); *United States v. Morton*, 467 U.S. 822 (1984). Regardless, the [SSA's] interpretation is one of long standing. And the fact that the Agency previously reached its interpretation through means less formal than "notice and comment" rulemaking does not automatically deprive that interpretation of the judicial deference otherwise its due. * * * *Mead* pointed to instances in which the Court has applied *Chevron* deference to agency interpretations that did not emerge out of notice-and-comment rulemaking. It indicated that whether a court should give such deference depends in significant part upon the interpretive method used and the nature of the question at issue. * * *
>
> In this case, the interstitial nature of the legal question, the related expertise of the Agency, the importance of the question to administration of the statute, the complexity of that administration, and the careful consideration the Agency has given the question over a long period of time all indicate that *Chevron* provides the appropriate legal lens through which to view the legality of the Agency interpretation here at issue.

Once again Justice Scalia, though he agreed with the majority's result, concurred separately:

> I do not believe * * * that "particular deference" is owed "to an agency interpretation of 'longstanding' duration." That notion is an anachronism—a relic of the pre-*Chevron* days, when there was thought to be only one "correct" interpretation of a statutory text. * * * But once it is accepted, as it was in *Chevron*, that there is a range of permissible interpretations, and that the agency is free to move from one to another, so long as the most recent interpretation is reasonable its antiquity should make no difference.

A vocal defender of the Court's opinion in *Mead*, Professor Robert A. Anthony objected to what he saw as signs of back-sliding in *Barnhart*. Focusing on the passages in Justice Breyer's opinion quoted above, Professor Anthony feared they "could sow the seeds of grievous confusion in the law of *Chevron* deference." He favored a reading of the cases that presumptively limited such deference to interpretations that are the product of rulemaking or formal adjudication. *Keeping* Chevron *Pure*, 5 The Green Bag 371 (2002).

2. *In What Language Must Congress Clearly Speak?* According to Justice Steven's *Chevron* majority opinion, a reviewing court should, first, determine whether Congress has spoken directly to the "precise issue" purportedly resolved by the agency's interpretation. If it has done so, then the courts, as well as the agency, are bound. An important question, then, is what sources may a court consult in deciding whether Congress has spoken directly. The words of the statute itself would seem an obvious starting (and, for some Justices, stopping) place, but some decisions demonstrate that "directly" does not necessary mean "explicitly."

In *Immigration and Naturalization Service v. Cardoza–Fonseca*, 480 U.S. 421 (1987), the Court was faced with the question whether the INS had legitimately concluded that the legal standards for suspension of deportation and for the discretionary grant of asylum were functionally the same. To be entitled to suspension of deportation an alien must establish that "it is more likely than not that" he "would be subject to persecution" in the country to which he would be returned. To be eligible for asylum, an alien must show "a well-founded fear of persecution" if returned to his home country. By regulation, the INS had interpreted these statutory standards to require the same showing. That is, an alien seeking asylum would also have show that he or she would *probably*—"more likely than not"—be persecuted if returned.

While Justice Stevens, writing for the majority, conceded that the meaning of each statutory phrase might be a matter of debate—and thus, under Step 2, the appropriate focus of an inquiry into the reasonableness of the agency's interpretation—he concluded that Congress had indeed spoken directly to the precise issue before the Court (and the INS), namely, whether the two standards were congruent. By its use of different language, Stevens argued, Congress had made clear that the two standards were not the same. A fear could be "well-founded" without having a more than 50 per cent probability of being an accurate prediction. On this point Justice Scalia, who wrote separately, concurred.

Another notable example of the Court's willingness to find clarity at Step 1 is *FDA v. Brown & Williamson Tobacco Corp.*, 529 U.S. 120 (2000). From the FDA's perspective, the issue in that case was whether cigarettes fell within the broad definitions of "drug" and "device" in the Federal Food, Drug, and Cosmetic Act, and thus within the agency's regulatory jurisdiction. The two definitions are in material respects identical; a product satisfies either if it is "intended to affect the structure or function of the body of man." FDA contended that the nicotine in cigarettes has pharmacological effects, that smokers desire and seek those effects, and that the makers of cigarettes market them with the intention of satisfying smoker desires. The Court, five-four, in an opinion by Justice O'Connor, did not dispute that this language was capacious enough to encompass cigarettes, but it nonetheless rejected FDA's argument, finding, at Step 1, that Congress had spoken directly to the question whether the FD & C Act should apply to cigarettes—and ruled out the possibility.

The evidence for Congress's rejection, according to Justice O'Connor, was apparent in two places. First, it was evident in the requirements that the FD & C Act prescribes for therapeutic drugs and medical devices, which must be found both safe and effective in order to be marketed. Since on the FDA's own reasoning cigarettes were not and could not be found "safe," it seemed inevitable that the agency would have to ban them entirely. And this outcome could not be squared with the second source of evidence of Congress's intent, specifically, a series of statutes that imposed distinctive labeling and advertising restrictions on cigarettes by name but that, at the same time, revealed that Congress intended to permit their continued marketing.

3. *Statutory Ambiguity and the Battle of the Dictionaries.* Justice Scalia, perhaps more than any other Justice, searches for the meaning—and thus the clarity or ambiguity—of statutory language in dictionaries. His opinion for the Court in *MCI v. AT & T*, 512 U.S. 218 (1994), is illustrative. Section 203 of the Federal Communications Act requires common carriers to file tariffs with the FCC, but authorizes the FCC to "modify any requirement made by or under * * * this section." The FCC decided to make tariff filing optional for all nondominant long distance carriers, and MCI proceeded to bill on the basis of tariffs that it had not filed. Justice Scalia agreed with AT & T that the FCC had exceeded its authority to "modify" the requirements of Section 203. Exempting nondominant carriers from tariff filing was too fundamental a change to be authorized by the word, "modify."

> The word "modify"—like a number of other English words employing the root "mod-" (deriving from the Latin word for "measure"), such as "moderate," "modulate," "modest," and "modicum,"—has a connotation of increment or limitation. Virtually every dictionary we are aware of says that "to modify" means to change moderately or in minor fashion. *See, e.g.*, Random House Dictionary of the English Language 1236 (2d ed. 1987) ("to change somewhat the form or qualities of; alter partially; amend"); Webster's Third New International Dictionary 1452 (1976) ("to make minor changes in the form or structure of: alter without transforming"); 9 Oxford English Dictionary 952 (2d ed. 1989) ("[t]o make partial changes in; to change (an object) in respect of some of its qualities; to alter or vary without radical transformation"); Black's Law Dictionary 1004 (6th ed. 1990) ("[t]o alter; to change in incidental or subordinate features; enlarge; extend; amend; limit; reduce").
>
> In support of their position, petitioners cite dictionary definitions contained in or derived from a single source, Webster's Third New International Dictionary 1452 (1976) ("Webster's Third"), which includes among the meanings of "modify," "to make a basic or important change in."[2] Petitioners contend that this establishes sufficient ambigui-

2. Petitioners also cite Webster's Ninth New Collegiate Dictionary 763 (1991), which includes among its definitions of "modify," "to make basic or fundamental changes in often to give a new orientation to or to serve a new end." They might also

ty to entitle the Commission to deference in its acceptance of the broader meaning, which in turn requires approval of its permissive detariffing policy. * * *

Most cases of verbal ambiguity in statutes involve * * * a selection between accepted alternative meanings shown as such by many dictionaries. One can envision (though a court case does not immediately come to mind) having to choose between accepted alternative meanings, one of which is so newly accepted that it has only been recorded by a single lexicographer. * * * But what petitioners demand that we accept as creating an ambiguity here is a rarity even rarer than that: a meaning set forth in a single dictionary (and, as we say, its progeny) which not only supplements the meaning contained in all other dictionaries, but contradicts one of the meanings contained in virtually all other dictionaries. Indeed, contradicts one of the alternative meanings contained in the out-of-step dictionary itself—for as we have observed, Webster's Third itself defines "modify" to connote both (specifically) major change and (specifically) minor change. It is hard to see how that can be. When the word "modify" has come to mean both "to change in some respects" and "to change fundamentally" it will in fact mean neither of those things. It will simply mean "to change," and some adverb will have to be called into service to indicate the great or small degree of the change.

If that is what the peculiar Webster's Third definition means to suggest has happened—and what petitioners suggest by appealing to Webster's Third—we simply disagree. "Modify," in our view, connotes moderate change. * * * It is perhaps [sic] gilding the lily to add this: In 1934, when the Communications Act became law—the most relevant time for determining a statutory term's meaning Webster's Third was not yet even contemplated. To our knowledge all English dictionaries provided the narrow definition of "modify," including those published by G. & C. Merriam Company. See Webster's New International Dictionary 1577 (2d ed.1934); Webster's Collegiate Dictionary 628 (4th ed.1934). We have not the slightest doubt that is the meaning the statute intended.

Putting aside the merits of the FCC decision, does the central notion of institutional comity that prompted the *Chevron* opinion, and that permeates Justice Scalia's *Mead* dissent, seem in danger here of receding altogether into a mist of dictionary fetishism?

4. *Agency Interpretations of Their Jurisdiction.* The Court has not yet squarely addressed whether *Chevron* deference is owed to agency interpretations of statutory provisions that describe and define the boundaries of

have cited Webster's Eighth New Collegiate Dictionary 739 (1973), which contains that same definition; and Webster's Seventh New Collegiate Dictionary 544 (1963), which contains the same definition as Webster's Third New International Dictionary quoted in text. The Webster's New Collegiate Dictionaries, published by G. & C. Merriam Company of Springfield, Massachusetts, are essentially abridgments of that company's Webster's New International Dictionaries, and recite that they are based upon those lengthier works. The last New Collegiate to be based upon Webster's Second New International, rather than Webster's Third, does not include "basic or fundamental change" among the accepted meanings of "modify." See Webster's New Collegiate Dictionary 541 (6th ed. 1949).

agency authority. In *Law and Administration After* Chevron, 90 Colum. L. Rev. 2071 (1990), Professor Cass R. Sunstein concluded that *Chevron* deference should not be given:

> Because congressional instructions are crucial here, courts should probably refuse to defer to agency decisions with respect to issues of jurisdiction—again, if we assume that the distinction between jurisdictional and non-jurisdictional questions is easily administrable. The principal reason is that Congress would be unlikely to want agencies to have the authority to decide on the extent of their own powers. To accord such power to agencies would be to allow them to be judges in their own cause, in which they are of course susceptible to bias.

In *Mississippi Power & Light Co. v. Mississippi ex rel. Moore*, 487 U.S. 354 (1988), which found that FERC's regulatory authority preempted state authority to review certain utility management decisions, Justice Scalia said in concurrence: "[T]he rule of deference applies even to an agency's interpretation of its own statutory jurisdiction." But Justice Brennan countered: "Our agency deference cases have always been limited to statutes the agency was entrusted to administer."

As Professor Sunstein implicitly acknowledges, it may be difficult to distinguish issues of jurisdiction from other issues of agency authority. Any claim that a statute *permits* the adoption of a rule that it neither mandates nor proscribes is *pro tanto* an "interpretation" of the scope of the agency's authority. Yet there are cases in which the Court's failure to defer seems to reflect judicial anxiety about agency overreaching. In *Dole v. United Steelworkers*, 494 U.S. 26 (1990), the Court held that OMB lacked authority under the Paperwork Reduction Act (PRA), 44 U.S.C. § 3501 *et seq.*, to review rules requiring an agency's regulated entities to disclose information directly to employees, consumers, or others. The Department of Labor had promulgated a standard requiring employers to label containers of hazardous substances to inform their employees of the potential hazards posed by such substances at their workplace. OMB disapproved the regulation pursuant to its authority under the PRA to approve "information collection requests" by executive agencies. The Act then defined "information collection requests" as "a written report form, application form, schedule, questionnaire, reporting or recordkeeping requirement, collection of information requirement, or other similar method calling for the collection of information." 44 U.S.C. § 3502(11). "Collection of information," in turn, was defined as:

> the obtaining or soliciting of facts or opinions by an agency through the use of written report forms, application forms, schedules, questionnaires, reporting or recordkeeping requirements, or other similar methods calling for either—
>
> > (A) answers to identical questions posed to, or identical reporting or recordkeeping requirements imposed on, ten or more persons, other than agencies, instrumentalities, or employees of the United States; or
> >
> > (B) answers to questions posed to agencies, instrumentalities, or employees of the United States which are to be used for general statistical purposes.

44 U.S.C. § 3502(4).

The Court held that this language obviously did not apply to requirements for the collection and disclosure of information to parties other than the government, and, accordingly, no *Chevron* deference was due. The majority stated: "The common-sense view of 'obtaining or soliciting facts by an agency' is that the phrase refers to an agency's efforts to gather facts for its own use * * *." The point hardly seemed free from ambiguity, however, because the majority resorted to "a consideration of the object and structure of the Act as a whole," to buttress its assertion of plain meaning. Justice White, joined by Chief Justice Rehnquist, disputed the majority's divination of clarity, finding the Act "not clear and unambiguous" and OMB's reading "permissible" under *Chevron*.

The D.C. Circuit, at least, believes that the Supreme Court accords *Chevron* deference to explicit agency interpretations of their statutory jurisdiction. In *Oklahoma Natural Gas Co. v. F.E.R.C.*, 28 F.3d 1281 (D.C.Cir. 1994), the court observed:

> Although not directly ruling on the matter of deference on such issues, the Supreme Court has in practice deferred even on jurisdictional issues. See *Reiter v. Cooper*, 507 U.S. 258 (1993) (applying *Chevron* to ICC's determination that statute did not grant it "initial jurisdiction * * * with respect to the award of reparations"); *Commodity Futures Trading Comm'n v. Schor*, 478 U.S. 833 (1986) (applying *Chevron* to scope of Commission's jurisdiction over counterclaims); *NLRB v. City Disposal Systems, Inc.*, 465 U.S. 822 (1984) (pre-*Chevron* decision expressly rejecting proposition that a different level of deference guides review of "a jurisdictional or legal question concerning the coverage of" the National Labor Relations Act). So have we.

See Patricia M. Wald, *Judicial Review in Midpassage: The Uneasy Partnership Between Courts and Agencies Plays On*, 32 Tulsa L.J. 221, 243 (1996). See generally Comment, Chevron *Deference to Agency Interpretations that Delimit the Scope of the Agency's Jurisdiction*, 62 U.Chi.L.Rev. 957 (1994).

The cigarette manufacturers in *FDA v. Brown & Williamson Tobacco Corp.*, *supra*, argued that no deference should be accorded the FDA's interpretation of the FD & C Act definitions that define the agency's jurisdiction, but the majority found it unnecessary to reach this issue since it was convinced that Congress had clearly placed cigarettes beyond the agency's reach, and thus the issue of reasonableness under step 2 did not arise. See also *Federal Election Commission v. NRA Political Victory Fund*, 513 U.S. 88 (1994), where the Court, without mentioning *Chevron*, expressly declined to defer to the FEC's interpretation of provisions of the Federal Election Campaign Act as authorizing the agency to conduct certain litigation independently of the Attorney General.

5. *The Relevance of Legislative History*. The post-*Chevron* jurisprudence reveals a continuing debate within the Supreme Court over interpretive method. In *Cardoza–Fonseca, supra*, Justice Scalia, who agreed with the majority's result and much of its reasoning, devoted his separate concurrence to attacking the portion of Justice Steven's opinion in which Stevens sought to show that the legislative history of the separate provisions of the Immigration and National Act confirmed the conclusion drawn from the text

alone—that Congress did not consider the two standards to be congruent. Justice Scalia took sharp exception to this methodology:

> The Court first implies that courts may substitute their interpretation of a statute for that of an agency whenever, "[e]mploying traditional tools of statutory construction," they are able to reach a conclusion as to the proper interpretation of the statute. But this approach would make deference a doctrine of desperation, authorizing courts to defer only if they would otherwise be unable to construe the enactment at issue. This is not an interpretation but an evisceration of *Chevron*.

Justice Scalia's arguments have drawn congressional attention in negotiating the language of statutes. Joan Biskupic, *Congress Keeps Eye on Justices as Court Watches Hill's Words*, 49 Cong.Q.Weekly Rept. 2863 (1991). Scalia's approach, if embraced by the full Court, would be of great importance to agencies, which historically have relied on their influence in the legislative process to assure the inclusion in committee reports and floor debates of material that could later be cited to support their views on statutory meaning. The commentary on textualism in statutory interpretation includes many useful sources, including William N. Eskridge, Jr., *The New Textualism*, 37 U.C.L.A.L.Rev. 621 (1990); Jerry L. Mashaw, *Textualism, Constitutionalism, and the Interpretation of Federal Statutes*, 32 Wm. & Mary L.Rev. 827 (1991); Patricia M. Wald, *supra*, 32 Tulsa L.J. 221, 241–43; Note, *Justice Scalia's Use of Sources in Statutory and Constitutional Interpretation: How Congress Always Loses*, 1990 Duke L.J. 160; and *Conference on Statutory Interpretation: The Role of Legislative History in Judicial Interpretation—A Discussion Between Judge Kenneth W. Starr and Judge Abner J. Mikva*, 1987 Duke L.J. 361.

6. Chevron's *Influence in the Lower Federal Courts*. Courts of appeals and many scholars have read *Chevron* as representing a genuinely significant departure. Professors Peter Schuck and Donald Elliott found that, during the six months following *Chevron*, courts of appeals upheld agency decisions 10 per cent more often than in the previous six months. Further, the grounds for remands to agencies shifted markedly from objections to the agency's interpretation of the substantive law to (a) failures to follow prescribed procedures, (b) failure to sustain fact-finding, and (c) failure to state an adequate rationale. Furthermore, court of appeals citations to *Chevron* have, in recent years, far outpaced citations to *Overton Park*. PETER SCHUCK & E. DONALD ELLIOTT, TO THE CHEVRON STATION: AN EMPIRICAL STUDY OF FEDERAL ADMINISTRATIVE LAW, Report to the U.S. Administrative Conference (1989).

Judge Patricia M. Wald, formerly Chief Judge of the D.C. Circuit, provided the following assessment of *Chevron*'s influence on how lower courts—and the lawyers who appear before them—approach issues of statutory interpretation.

> *Chevron*, in my view, is as much of a landmark decision as exists in administrative law. Until 1984, * * * the prevailing wisdom was that a court could decide what a statute meant, giving whatever deference it considered "due" to agency expertise in interpreting it. Since 1984 most courts faced with a challenge to the agency's interpretation or its statutory authority invoke the *Chevron* two-step litany verbatim. * * *

Recently, much attention has focused on the effect that the rise of textualism, particularly on the Supreme Court, has had on the application of *Chevron*. * * * Implicit in textualism is the belief that the plain meaning of statutory provisions can usually be discerned. This belief makes textualism's advocates more inclined to find under the *Chevron* step one inquiry that Congress has spoken with precision as to the meaning of a statutory provision, thereby obviating the need to defer, under *Chevron* step two, to any reasonable interpretation offered by the agency. * * *

Textualism has not taken as big a hold on the D.C. Circuit as on the Supreme Court. * * * Even in *Chevron* step one we usually supplant [sic] our textual reading with references to legislative history. And unlike the Supreme Court, we continue to use the *Chevron* formula consistently as the governing standard for deciding any challenge to any agency interpretation. * * *

* * * [W]e often disagree about whether a case should be decided under *Chevron* step one or *Chevron* step two, that is, whether Congress has made its intent crystal clear or whether there is an ambiguity for the agency to resolve. This may come down to how judges identify the precise question at issue, since at one level of generality the statute may answer it under *Chevron* step one, but at a more refined level there may be an ambiguity. * * * I sense another unarticulated factor at play as well in our *Chevron* one or two disagreements, which is simply that if the agency's position is to be upheld, many judges. * * * would prefer to do so under *Chevron* step two than *Chevron* step one. Proceeding to *Chevron* step two allows the court in close cases to acknowledge linguistic and structural ambiguities identified by the petitioners, yet conclude that the agency's interpretation is still reasonable, given the broad deference to which the agency is entitled. It also allows the agencies some elbow room to change * * * practices in the future if events and experience dictate.

Chevron was a preemptive strike to force the courts out of the business of telling the agencies what they could do, or could not do, when the law itself was not clear. The Supreme Court said, in effect we will find a general congressional intent to leave it to the agency where there is any doubt about what the law means. * * * But the ongoing debates suggest that *Chevron* is still a work in progress. It clearly has critics who would like to return to an era of greater judicial freedom to construe statutes as judges see fit. I believe these critics are unlikely to prevail, but it is indisputably true that not even *Chevron*'s one-two exercise can cabin judicial discretion entirely. * * * With the power to decide such matters as what the precise issue is, whether Congress has spoken clearly to it, and if not, whether the agency has come up with a reasonable construction, all things considered, judges retain significant control over the interpretation of agency-administered statutes.

Patricia M. Wald, *Judicial Review in Midpassage*, 32 Tulsa L.J. 221, 241–44, 247 (1996).

7. *Dueling Canons*. *Chevron's* teaching may conflict with other familiar canons of statutory construction. For example, in *EEOC v. Aramco*, 499 U.S.

244 (1991), where the Court held the EEOC lacked jurisdiction to enforce Title VII of the Civil Rights Act outside the U.S., Justice Scalia concurred separately to state that *Chevron* was applicable to the EEOC's claim of jurisdiction. He would ordinarily have accorded the agency deference, but the presumption against extraterritoriality made it unreasonable to "give effect to mere implications from the statutory language as the EEOC has done."

Compare *Rust v. Sullivan*, 500 U.S. 173 (1991), in which a five-to-four majority upheld HHS regulations barring government-funded family planning services from providing "counseling concerning the use of abortion as a method of family planning or provid[ing] referral for abortion as a method of family planning." The regulations were issued pursuant to a statute that authorized funding for "voluntary family planning projects which shall offer a broad range of acceptable and effective family planning methods and services," but with respect to abortion, provided: "None of the funds appropriated under this subchapter shall be used in programs where abortion is a method of family planning."

Only Justice Stevens regarded the statute as clear in limiting the Secretary to preventing the use of government funds to *conduct* abortions; all the other Justices thought the statute ambiguous. However, Justices Blackmun, O'Connor, and Marshall thought *Chevron* was trumped by the canon that favors construing statutes to avoid serious constitutional difficulties. Concluding that the statute would be constitutional as construed by HHS, the majority refused to apply that canon and instead invoked *Chevron*. In a succinct dissent, Justice O'Connor argued that the preference for constitutionally unproblematic statutory interpretation should be followed whenever a contrary interpretation would raise a serious constitutional issue, and not only when a majority would actually find the agency's interpretation unconstitutional on the merits.

8. *Interpreting Regulations—To Whom Is Deference Owed?* Long before *Chevron* it was routine for courts to accord "substantial deference" to agency interpretations of their own regulations. See *Lyng v. Payne*, 476 U.S. 926, 939 (1986). Courts are supposed to defer to any reasonable agency interpretation not obviously belied by the regulatory language. See also *Thomas Jefferson University v. Shalala*, 512 U.S. 504 (1994) (giving controlling weight to HHS Secretary's interpretation of Medicare regulation governing reimbursement of hospitals for cost of educational activities); cf. *Stinson v. United States*, 508 U.S. 36 (1993) (according "controlling weight" to a U.S. Sentencing Commission Manual commenting on the Commission's Guidelines, on the ground that the commentary is functionally analogous to an agency's interpretation of its own regulations).

Martin v. OSHRC, 499 U.S. 144 (1991), however, posed the unusual question: to which agency does a court owe deference when two that share administrative responsibility offer "reasonable but conflicting interpretations" of an ambiguous regulation? The Occupational Safety and Health Act authorizes the Secretary of Labor, acting through the Occupational Safety and Health Administration (OSHA), to set and enforce workplace health and safety standards. It also creates a three-member independent board within the Labor Department—the Occupational Safety and Health Review Commission (OSHRC)—to adjudicate enforcement actions that the Department brings pursuant to the Secretary's standards. The *Martin* case involved allegations that an employer equipped certain of its employees with ill-fitting respirators that failed to protect wearers against carcinogenic emissions. The Secretary urged that the responsibility to provide tight-fitting respirators was imposed by a regulation requiring an employer to "institute a respiratory protection program." OSHRC concluded, however, that the cited regulation required no more than training in the proper use of respirators. A standard for fit, it argued, was established by a different regulation, which was not urged by the Secretary as a basis for liability in this case.

The Court resolved this dispute in favor of the body to which Congress had given primary responsibility for statutory enforcement. It found that the Secretary had "sole responsibility" for enforcement, and that the structure and history of the Act implied that the Secretary's responsibilities included the power to render authoritative interpretations of implementing regulations. In so interpreting the Act, however, the Court did not cite deference to the Secretary's *statutory* interpretation as a basis for its conclusion. See also *Pauley v. BethEnergy Mines, Inc.*, 501 U.S. 680 (1991) (allocating deference in the administration of a statute first implemented by one agency, then another). See generally Daniel Lovejoy, *The Ambiguous Basis for Chevron Deference: Multiple–Agency Statutes*, 88 Va. L. Rev. 879 (2002).

9. *A Source of Sources.* In addition to the sources already cited, other helpful articles exploring these issues, but displaying widely varying degrees of enthusiasm for the Court's opinion in *Chevron* include Steven G. Breyer, *Judicial Review of Questions of Law and Policy*, 38 Admin.L.Rev. 363 (1986); Clark Byse, *Judicial Review of Administrative Interpretation of Statutes: An Analysis of* Chevron*'s Step Two*, 2 Admin.L.J. 255 (1988); Cynthia R. Farina, *Statutory Interpretation and the Balance of Power in the Administrative State*, 89 Colum.L.Rev. 452 (1989); Thomas W. Merrill and Kristin E. Hickman, Chevron*'s Domain*, 89 Geo.L.J. 833 (2001); Antonin Scalia, *Judicial Deference to Administrative Interpretations of Law*, 1989 Duke L.J. 511; and Kenneth W. Starr, *Judicial Review in the Post-*Chevron *Era*, 3 Yale J. on Reg. 283 (1986).

3. FINDINGS OF FACT AND THE "SUBSTANTIAL EVIDENCE" TEST

Virtually all statutes that prescribe formal adjudicatory process for administrative decision making also provide for judicial review of the resulting decisions. Review is usually placed in the courts of appeals and confined to the record of the administrative hearing. Challengers to such decisions may raise issues of procedural regularity, jurisdiction, statutory interpretation and—typically—the question whether the record contains "substantial evidence" to support the agency decision.

There are many variations on this basic scheme. For example, the thousands of appeals from SSA disability hearings are lodged, for obvious practical reasons, in the federal district courts. Statutory review provisions also use different language to describe the degree of evidentiary support necessary to support an agency's finding. Nevertheless, the dominant approach is that articulated by APA § 706: "substantial evidence review" is available for federal agency decisions—meaning, almost always, agency adjudications—that are the product of formal evidentiary proceedings.

The image of judges searching administrative records for "substantial evidence," does not begin to capture the essence of judicial review of agency adjudication. Indeed, no generalization can do so. As the preceding materials attest, agencies make law and policy in the course of adjudication, as well as determine facts. Issues of law, policy, and fact shade together at the margins. Their resolution in any particular adjudication is related to the whole course of an agency's adjudicatory and regulatory activity in complex and subtle ways—perceptible perhaps only to those immersed in the administrative routine. And yet protection from the skewed perceptions and bureaucratic imperatives produced by total immersion in program tasks is one basic justification for judicial review by generalist judges. Deciding what evidence amounts to "substantial evidence"—or, more broadly, how a court's appropriate "scope of review" is to be defined—is not a matter of finding the right verbal formula, but rather of striking the right balance between generalized legal ideals and the particularized objectives of administration.

To put the question in this way is to suggest that many considerations are likely to be relevant to the scope of review actually exercised by a reviewing court—the type of issue presented (constitutional, statutory, evidentiary), the impact of a decision either way on the agency's effectiveness, the social importance of the agency's function, the political history of the agency and its governing statutes, the consistency of the judgment under review with past actions, general public and judicial confidence in the agency's competence and integrity, the "equities" of the particular case, and a host of other factors. Not surprisingly, this contextual approach to defining the scope of review to be exercised in a specific case—including, in thousands of cases, the meaning of "substantial evidence"—constantly fuels litigation and provides multitudinous occasions for judicial eloquence as well as despair. Perhaps no one has done better than the late Judge Harold Leventhal in *Greater Boston Television Corp. v. FCC*, 444 F.2d 841, 851–52 (D.C.Cir.1970), *cert. denied*, 403 U.S. 923 (1971), when he described the court as looking for some "combination of danger signals" that warrant close scrutiny and perhaps justify a reversal or remand. Judge Leventhal further suggested that the relationship between court and agency has a dynamic, almost an organic character. In his view, the review function:

> combines judicial supervision with a salutary principle of judicial restraint, an awareness that agencies and courts together constitute a 'partnership' in the furtherance of the public interest and are 'collaborative instrumentalities of justice.' The court is in a real sense part of the total administrative process, and not a hostile stranger to the office of first instance.

Judge Leventhal was hardly writing on a clean slate. Thirty years earlier the Attorney General's Committee had observed:

> Judicial review of administrative action has developed even as the common law itself, gradually, from case to case, in response to the pressures of particular situations, the teachings of experience, the guidance of ideal and general principle, and the influence of legislation—with the courts playing a chief role in the development. As an incident of the administrative process, it shares many features of that process. * * * Like the agencies, judicial review is a complex of old and new, of historical survivals and purposive innovations.

Attorney General's Committee On Administrative Procedure, Administrative Procedure In Government Agencies, S.Doc.No. 8, 77th Cong., 1st Sess. 75–76 (1941).

A feel for this evolving common law can be gained only by exposure to hundreds of cases, not a handful. Every case in this book contributes to the process of acculturation. In this section, where we focus explicitly on the issue of scope of review, we can provide only a snapshot of the interactions among analytic distinctions, history, functional concerns, and equity that determine the relationship between adjudicatory agencies and reviewing courts. We have chosen to feature cases involving the National Labor Relations Board, an agency whose decisions have elicited some of the most often cited judicial pronouncements on the scope of judicial review of agency adjudication.

NLRB v. HEARST PUBLICATIONS

Supreme Court of the United States, 1944.
322 U.S. 111, 64 S.Ct. 851, 88 L.Ed. 1170.

JUSTICE RUTLEDGE delivered the opinion of the Court.

These cases arise from the refusal of respondents, publishers of four Los Angeles daily newspapers, to bargain collectively with a union representing newsboys who distribute their papers on the streets of that city. Respondents' contention that they were not required to bargain because the newsboys are not their "employees" within the meaning of that term in the National Labor Relations Act, 49 Stat. 450, 29 U.S.C. § 152,[1] presents the important question which we granted certiorari to resolve.

The proceedings before the National Labor Relations Board were begun with the filing of four petitions for investigation and certification by Los Angeles Newsboys Local Industrial Union No. 75. Hearings were held in a consolidated proceeding after which the Board made findings of fact and concluded that the regular full-time newsboys selling each paper

1. Section 2(3) of the Act provides that "The term 'employee' shall include any employee, and shall not be limited to the employees of a particular employer, unless the Act explicitly states otherwise, and shall include any individual whose work has ceased as a consequence of, or in connection with, any current labor dispute or because of any unfair labor practice, and who has not obtained any other regular and substantially equivalent employment, but shall not include any individual employed as an agricultural laborer, or in the domestic service of any family or person at his home, or any individual employed by his parent or spouse."

were employees within the Act and that questions affecting commerce concerning the representation of employees had arisen. It designated appropriate units and ordered elections. At these the union was selected as their representative by majorities of the eligible newsboys. After the union was appropriately certified, the respondents refused to bargain with it. Thereupon proceedings under § 10 were instituted, a hearing was held and respondents were found to have violated §§ 8(1) and 8(5) of the Act. They were ordered to cease and desist from such violations and to bargain collectively with the union upon request.

Upon respondents' petitions for review and the Board's petitions for enforcement, the Circuit Court of Appeals, one judge dissenting, set aside the Board's orders. Rejecting the Board's analysis, the Court independently examined the question whether the newsboys are employees within the Act, decided that the statute imports common-law standards to determine that question, and held the newsboys are not employees. * * *

The papers are distributed to the ultimate consumer through a variety of channels, including independent dealers and newsstands often attached to drug, grocery or confectionery stores, carriers who make home deliveries, and newsboys who sell on the streets of the city and its suburbs. Only the last of these are involved in this case.

The newsboys work under varying terms and conditions. They may be "bootjackers," selling to the general public at places other than established corners, or they may sell at fixed "spots." They may sell only casually or part-time, or full-time; and they may be employed regularly and continuously or only temporarily. The units which the Board determined to be appropriate are composed of those who sell full-time at established spots. Those vendors, misnamed boys, are generally mature men, dependent upon the proceeds of their sales for their sustenance, and frequently supporters of families. Working thus as news vendors on a regular basis, often for a number of years, they form a stable group with relatively little turnover, in contrast to schoolboys and others who sell as bootjackers, temporary and casual distributors.

* * *

The newsboys' compensation consists in the difference between the prices at which they sell the papers and the prices they pay for them. The former are fixed by the publishers and the latter are fixed either by the publishers or, in the case of the News, by the district manager. In practice the newsboys receive their papers on credit. They pay for those sold either sometime during or after the close of their selling day, returning for credit all unsold papers. Lost or otherwise unreturned papers, however, must be paid for as though sold. Not only is the "profit" per paper thus effectively fixed by the publisher, but substantial control of the newsboys' total "take home" can be effected through the ability to designate their sales areas and the power to determine the number of papers allocated to each. While as a practical matter this power is not exercised fully, the newsboys' "right" to decide how many papers they will take is also not absolute. In practice, the Board found, they cannot determine the size of their established order without the cooperation of the district manager. And often the number of papers they must take is determined unilaterally by the district managers.

In addition to effectively fixing the compensation, respondents in a variety of ways prescribe, if not the minutiae of daily activities, at least the broad terms and conditions of work. This is accomplished largely through the supervisory efforts of the district managers, who serve as the nexus between the publishers and the newsboys. The district managers assign "spots" or corners to which the newsboys are expected to confine their selling activities. Transfers from one "spot" to another may be ordered by the district manager for reasons of discipline or efficiency or other cause. Transportation to the spots from the newspaper building is offered by each of respondents. Hours of work on the spots are determined not simply by the impersonal pressures of the market, but to a real extent by explicit instructions from the district managers. Adherence to the prescribed hours is observed closely by the district managers or other supervisory agents of the publishers. Sanctions, varying in severity from reprimand to dismissal, are visited on the tardy and the delinquent. By similar supervisory controls minimum standards of diligence and good conduct while at work are sought to be enforced. However wide may be the latitude for individual initiative beyond those standards, district managers' instructions in what the publishers apparently regard as helpful sales techniques are expected to be followed. Such varied items as the manner of displaying the paper, of emphasizing current features and headlines, and of placing advertising placards, or the advantages of soliciting customers at specific stores or in the traffic lanes are among the subjects of this instruction. Moreover, newsboys are furnished with sales equipment, such as racks, boxes and change aprons, and advertising placards by the publishers. In this pattern of employment the Board found that the newsboys are an integral part of the publishers' distribution system and circulation organization. * * *

[After concluding that "employee" in the NLRA was not intended to vary with state common law, the Court addressed the more concrete issue of statutory interpretation.]

The mischief at which the Act is aimed and the remedies it offers are not confined exclusively to "employees" within the traditional legal distinctions separating them from "independent contractors." Myriad forms of service relationship, with infinite and subtle variations in the terms of employment, blanket the nation's economy. Some are within this Act, others beyond its coverage. Large numbers will fall clearly on one side or on the other, by whatever test may be applied. But intermediate there will be many, the incidents of whose employment partake in part of the one group, in part of the other, in varying proportions of weight. And consequently the legal pendulum, for purposes of applying the statute, may swing one way or the other, depending upon the weight of this balance and its relation to the special purpose at hand.

* * *

Interruption of commerce through strikes and unrest may stem as well from labor disputes between some who, for other purposes, are technically "independent contractors" and their employers as from disputes between persons who, for those purposes, are "employees" and their employers. Inequality of bargaining power in controversies over wages, hours and working conditions may as well characterize the status of the one group as of the other. The former, when acting alone, may be as "helpless in dealing with an employer," as "dependent * * * on his daily wage" and as "unable to leave the employ and to resist arbitrary and unfair treatment" as the latter. For each, "union * * * [may be] essential to give * * * opportunity to deal on equality with their employer." And for each, collective bargaining may be appropriate and effective for the "friendly adjustment of industrial disputes arising out of differences as to wages, hours, or other working conditions." In short, when the particular situation of employment combines these characteristics, so that the economic facts of the relation make it more nearly one of employment than of independent business enterprise with respect to the ends sought to be accomplished by the legislation, those characteristics may outweigh technical legal classification for purposes unrelated to the statute's objectives and bring the relation within its protections.

* * *

It is not necessary in this case to make a completely definitive limitation around the term "employee." That task has been assigned primarily to the agency created by Congress to administer the Act. Determination of "where all the conditions of the relation require protection" involves inquiries for the Board charged with this duty. Everyday experience in the administration of the statute gives it familiarity with the circumstances and backgrounds of employment relationships in various industries, with the abilities and needs of the workers for self-organization and collective action, and with the adaptability of collective bargaining for the peaceful settlement of their disputes with their employers. The experience thus acquired must be brought frequently to bear on the question who is an employee under the Act. Resolving that question, like determining whether unfair labor practices have been committed, "belongs to the usual administrative routine" of the Board.

In making that body's determinations as to the facts in these matters conclusive, if supported by evidence, Congress entrusted to it primarily the decision whether the evidence establishes the material facts. Hence in reviewing the Board's ultimate conclusions, it is not the court's function to substitute its own inferences of fact for the Board's, when the latter have support in the record. Undoubtedly questions of statutory interpretation, especially when arising in the first instance in judicial proceedings, are for the courts to resolve, giving appropriate weight to the judgment of those whose special duty is to administer the questioned statute. *Norwegian Nitrogen Products Co. v. United States*,

288 U.S. 294; *United States v. American Trucking Associations*, 310 U.S. 534. But where the question is one of specific application of a broad statutory term in a proceeding in which the agency administering the statute must determine it initially, the reviewing court's function is limited. Like the commissioner's determination under the Longshoremen's & Harbor Workers' Act, that a man is not a "member of a crew" (*South Chicago Coal & Dock Co. v. Bassett*, 309 U.S. 251) or that he was injured "in the course of employment" (*Parker v. Motor Boat Sales, Inc.*, 314 U.S. 244) and the Federal Communications Commission's determination that one company is under the "control" of another (*Rochester Telephone Corp. v. United States*, 307 U.S. 125), the Board's determination that specified persons are "employees" under this Act is to be accepted if it has "warrant in the record" and a reasonable basis in law.

In this case the Board found that the designated newsboys work continuously and regularly, rely upon their earnings for the support of themselves and their families, and have their total wages influenced in large measure by the publishers, who dictate their buying and selling prices, fix their markets and control their supply of papers. Their hours of work and their efforts on the job are supervised and to some extent prescribed by the publishers or their agents. Much of their sales equipment and advertising materials is furnished by the publishers with the intention that it be used for the publisher's benefit. Stating that "the primary consideration in the determination of the applicability of the statutory definition is whether effectuation of the declared policy and purposes of the Act comprehend securing to the individual the rights guaranteed and protection afforded by the Act," the Board concluded that the newsboys are employees. The record sustains the Board's findings and there is ample basis in the law for its conclusion.

* * *

JUSTICE ROBERTS.

* * *

I think it plain that newsboys are not "employees" of the respondents within the meaning and intent of the National Labor Relations Act. When Congress, in § 2(3), said "The term 'employee' shall include any employee, * * * " it stated as clearly as language could do it that the provisions of the Act were to extend to those who, as a result of decades of tradition which had become part of the common understanding of our people, bear the named relationship. Clearly also Congress did not delegate to the National Labor Relations Board the function of defining the relationship of employment so as to promote what the Board understood to be the underlying purpose of the statute. The question who is an employee, so as to make the statute applicable to him, is a question of the meaning of the Act and, therefore, is a judicial and not an administrative question. * * *

Judicial Review of the NLRB and the Substantial Evidence Test

The "warrant in the record and a reasonable basis in law" formulation in *Hearst* signals a judicial deference that was replicated in many other early Labor Board cases. Although the Wagner Act, which established the NLRB, provided that "the findings of the Board as to facts, if supported by evidence, shall be conclusive," the Supreme Court read the Act to require Board determinations to be supported by "substantial evidence." *Washington, Virginia & Maryland Coach Co. v. NLRB*, 301 U.S. 142, 147 (1937). However, this requirement imposed only modest demands on agency fact-finding. "Substantial evidence" was defined to mean something "more than a mere scintilla * * * or such relevant evidence as a reasonable mind might accept as adequate to support a conclusion." *Consolidated Edison Co. v. NLRB*, 305 U.S. 197, 229 (1938). The Board's findings of fact would not be disturbed unless the record was "wholly barren of evidence." Id. See also *NLRB v. Columbian Enameling and Stamping Co.*, 306 U.S. 292 (1939). These judicial glosses on the text of the Wagner Act were translated into reflexive deference in practice. Board determinations were approved whenever the Court could find record evidence that, when viewed in isolation, substantiated its findings. Indeed, congressional critics charged that the Court made a practice of sustaining Board decisions based on little more than "hearsay, opinion, and emotional speculation in place of factual evidence." Intermediate Report of the House Special Committee to Investigate the National Labor Relations Board, 76th Cong., 3rd Sess. 76 (1940).

Influential members of the judiciary also found the Supreme Court's performance unsatisfactory. In *NLRB v. Standard Oil Co.*, 138 F.2d 885, 887 (2d Cir.1943), Judge Learned Hand characterized the Supreme Court's interpretation of the "substantial evidence" test as "momentous" judicial "abdication." Other judges begrudgingly accepted the Supreme Court's definition of the scope of review, but with undeferential cynicism:

> We have recognized (or tried to) that findings must be sustained, even when they are contrary to the great weight of the evidence, and we have ignored, or at least endeavored to ignore, the shocking injustices which such findings, opposed to the overwhelming weight of the evidence, produce. We must confess that at times we have apparently failed to recognize that evidence which would not appeal to any rational appraiser of the truth, may yet fall within the field of "some evidence." On the assumption that such evidence would not be sufficient to sustain a finding in an ordinary civil suit, we have rejected it. We have at times set aside the findings of the Board, but only * * * when the findings were so overwhelmingly opposed by the evidence as to require it. Our conclusions have not met with the approval of the Supreme Court to whose superior judgment we bow.

Wilson & Co. v. NLRB, 126 F.2d 114, 117 (7th Cir.1942).

Congress reacted, first, with oversight hearings and, ultimately, legislation. In condemnatory tones, House Resolution 258 created a Special Committee of the House of Representatives to investigate the NLRB. The Senate Judiciary Committee held similar hearings. Appearing before the Senate committee, Dean Blythe Stason echoed the prevailing dissatisfaction with the Supreme Court's interpretation of the substantial evidence test in reviewing Labor Board decisions:

> Construed grammatically, the term "substantial evidence" might conceivably—although not reasonably—mean little more than a sort of modified "scintilla" rule—the rule formerly regarded as sufficient to block a motion for directed verdict in jury cases. So defined, the requirement simply calls for a searching of the record to find some relevant testimony which can be regarded as substantial to support the order, ignoring all countervailing testimony introduced by the opposing party. There are decisions apparently adopting this modified scintilla method of applying the substantial evidence rule. In fact, in two recent Supreme Court decisions in Labor Board cases, the *NLRB v. Waterman Steamship Corporation*, 309 U.S. 206 (1940), and *NLRB v. Bradford Dyeing Association*, 310 U.S. 318 (1940), this scintilla technique seems to have been followed, at least so far as the method is revealed by the written opinion of the Court. * * *

Hearings on S.674 Before a Subcomm. of the Senate Judiciary Committee, Part 3, 77th Cong., 1st Sess. 1355–56 (1941).

Earlier testimony in this spirit added to the pressure for legislative action, and in 1940, both Houses of Congress passed the so-called Walter–Logan bill, providing generally for stricter review of agency determinations of fact. H.R. 6324, S. 915, 76th Cong., 1st Sess. The legislation was vetoed by President Roosevelt, who believed that it imposed other unduly rigid limitations on the administrative process, and threatened to preempt the separate investigation of administrative agencies then being conducted by the Attorney General's Committee.

The Final Report of the Attorney General's Committee, released in January, 1941, noted the widespread dissatisfaction with the prevailing scope of review of agency adjudications. The committee majority concluded, however, that Congress should not attempt to correct the problem by legislation. Changing the prevailing statutory standard, the majority thought, would not eliminate the discretionary aspect of judicial review and might encourage involvement by the federal courts in inefficient reconsideration of evidentiary questions. Attorney General's Committee on Administrative Procedure in Government Agencies, S.Doc.No. 8, 77th Cong., 1st Sess. 75–76 (1941).

The dissenting members of the Attorney General's Committee favored a general reform of the scope of review standard and in particular criticized the Supreme Court's treatment of NLRB findings of fact as "unsatisfactory" and "unfair." Under the prevailing interpretation of the scope of review, they argued, "if what is called 'substantial evidence' is found anywhere in the record to support conclusions of fact, the courts are said to be obliged to sustain the decision without reference to how heavily the countervailing evidence may preponderate. * * * Under this interpretation, the courts need to read only one side of the case and, if they find any evidence there, the administrative action is to be sustained and the record to the contrary is to be ignored." They recommended that the courts be allowed to "set aside decisions *clearly* contrary to the *manifest* weight of the evidence." *Id.* at 211 (emphasis in original). This led them to advocate a formula for judicial review that would extend to "findings of fact, including inferences and conclusions of fact," "unsupported, upon the *whole* record, by substantial evidence." *Id.*

The substance of the minority position found its way into the statute books, both as section 10(e) (now section 706) of the APA and as part of the 1947 amendments to the National Labor Relations Act. The stage was thus set for *Universal Camera Corp. v. NLRB*, 340 U.S. 474 (1951), which involved the effect of a hearing examiner's initial decision on the substantiality of the record evidence supporting a contrary Board decision.

In brief, Universal Camera was charged with unfairly dismissing one of its supervisory employees, who had testified at an NLRB hearing concerning representation for the company's maintenance employees. According to the employer, the supervisor had been fired for refusing to discipline a worker. The supervisor countered that his discharge suspiciously took place nearly a month after his alleged insubordination and that the person who ordered his discharge had earlier accused him of perjury before the NLRB, expressing then his obvious hostility towards the supervisor's continuing employment. The hearing examiner believed the employer's account, but the NLRB reversed. Narrowly construed, the question before the Court was whether the examiner's decision, reflecting his personal exposure to the witnesses' testimony, was a part of the whole record on which the NLRB's decision had to be judged, and if so, what weight it should have. But the Court recognized that broader questions were involved. After recounting the movement to enlarge judicial review of NLRB decisions, the Court concluded that the addition of the requirement that its findings of fact be supported "by substantial evidence on the record considered as a whole," 29 U.S.C. § 141(e), legislated a much more demanding standard of review, and "expressed a mood" of dissatisfaction with the excessive deference previously afforded Board decisions:

> From the legislative story we have summarized, two concrete conclusions do emerge. One is the identity of aim of the Administrative Procedure Act and the Taft–Hartley Act regarding the proof with which the Labor Board must support a decision. The other is that now Congress has left no room for doubt as to the kind of scrutiny which a Court of Appeals must give the record before the Board to satisfy itself that the Board's order rests on adequate proof. * * *

Whether or not it was ever permissible for courts to determine the substantiality of evidence supporting a Labor Board decision merely on the basis of evidence which in and of itself justified it, without taking into account contradictory evidence or evidence from which conflicting inferences could be drawn, the new legislation definitively precludes such a theory of review and bars its practice. The substantiality of evidence must take into account whatever in the record fairly detracts from its weight. This is clearly the significance of the requirement in both statutes that courts consider the whole record. Committee reports and the adoption in the Administrative Procedure Act of the minority views of the Attorney General's Committee demonstrate that to enjoin such a duty on the reviewing court was one of the important purposes of the movement which eventuated in that enactment.

To be sure, the requirement for canvassing "the whole record" in order to ascertain substantiality does not furnish a calculus of value by which a reviewing court can assess the evidence. Nor was it intended to negative the function of the Labor Board as one of those agencies presumably equipped or informed by experience to deal with a specialized field of knowledge, whose findings within that field carry the authority of an expertness which courts do not possess and therefore must respect. Nor does it mean that even as to matters not requiring expertise a court may displace the Board's choice between two fairly conflicting views, even though the court would justifiably have made a different choice had the matter been before it *de novo*. Congress has merely made it clear that a reviewing court is not barred from setting aside a Board decision when it cannot conscientiously find that the evidence supporting that decision is substantial, when viewed in the light that the record in its entirety furnishes, including the body of evidence opposed to the Board's view.

There remains, then, the question whether enactment of these two statutes has altered the scope of review other than to require that substantiality be determined in the light of all that the record relevantly presents.

* * * We should fail in our duty to effectuate the will of Congress if we denied recognition to expressed Congressional disapproval of the finality accorded to Labor Board findings by some decisions of this and lower courts, or even of the atmosphere which may have favored those decisions.

We conclude, therefore, that the Administrative Procedure Act and the Taft–Hartley Act direct that courts must now assume more responsibility for the reasonableness and fairness of Labor Board decisions than some courts have in the past. Reviewing courts must be influenced by a feeling that they are not to abdicate the conventional judicial function. Congress has imposed on them responsibility for assuring that the Board keeps within reasonable bounds. * * *

> The Board's findings are entitled to respect; but they must nonetheless be set aside when the record before a Court of Appeals clearly precludes the Board's decision from being justified by a fair estimate of the worth of the testimony of witnesses or its informed judgment on matters within its special competence or both. * * * Whether on the record as a whole there is substantial evidence to support agency findings is a question which Congress has placed in the keeping of the Courts of Appeals.

Whether the "new mood" ushered in by the APA, the Wagner Act, and *Universal Camera* has persisted is difficult to determine. In one of the few general studies of the subject, *Judicial Review of Agency Decisions: The Labor Board and the Court*, 1968 Sup.Ct.Rev. 53, 71–73, 74–75, Professor (now Judge) Ralph Winter suggested that the dual aspects of the judicial stance enunciated in *Universal Camera* may produce a peculiar dynamic—a retreat by the Board into the facts of cases in ways that both elude serious judicial review and avoid the agency's responsibilities to develop reasoned and politically responsive labor relations policy:

> The Supreme Court is of course responsible for establishing the proper doctrine and attitudes concerning the scope of review of Labor Board decisions involving questions of law or mixed fact and law. The opinions of the Court, however, do not establish a coherent view of the scope of that review. In some cases they seem to show great deference to Board discretion and experience both in establishing doctrine and in changing it. In others, deference is expressed but not in fact shown. In yet others, the Court talks and acts as though it is merely reviewing the decisions of another court.
>
> If the verbiage of the Court has not articulated a meaningful role for judicial review, however, there is a clear trend apparent. The Supreme Court has in fact shown little deference to Board discretion in exercising the power delegated to it and has demonstrated little interest in the Board's views of its experience or in seeing that the Board acts as a specialized agency. And more frequently than not, the Court has employed a broad scope of review that has permitted it to substitute its own judgment. * * *
>
> Nor is it only in reversing the Board that the Court impinges on the functions of the agency. If the Board is affirmed by an opinion that approves the decision below as being the only one possible, rather than as a correct one within the realm of agency discretion, a future Board will be precluded from changing the rule because the doctrine of *stare decisis* will lead to judicial reversal of its decision. Thus, the rigid distinction between mandatory and nonmandatory subjects of bargaining has become embedded in the law as the result of a Supreme Court decision and no longer seems subject to Board reversal. The Board's ability to experiment and to be politically responsive has thus been unduly narrowed.

> The Court in short has failed to permit the Board sufficient discretion in statutory interpretation and in doctrinal change over time. It has behaved as though the Board's only function is to "flesh out" the statute and has focused almost entirely on the coherence of the body of law developed through judicial review. Over time the Court has permitted less and less discretion to the Board and has adopted the policy-making functions for itself.

So much for the portion of *Universal Camera* that holds Congress intended the courts to "assume more responsibility for the reasonableness and fairness of Labor Board decisions." But Professor Winter went on to question *Universal Camera's* approach to findings of fact in a fashion that very nearly turns the conventional wisdom about scope of review on its head:

> The discussion to this point has focused almost entirely on the scope of judicial review of Board decisions on matters of law or mixed fact and law and has not encompassed Board findings of adjudicative facts. The present test, based on the Administrative Procedure and Taft–Hartley Acts, requires courts merely to determine whether such findings are supported by substantial evidence viewing the record as a whole. And, as elaborated by Justice Frankfurter in the *Universal Camera* decision, the report of a trial examiner is entitled only to "such probative force as it intrinsically commands." The Board, therefore, has greater power to reverse a trial examiner on issues of adjudicative fact than a court has to reverse the Board.
>
> I have doubts regarding the propriety of this scope of review of Board findings. The conduct of the Board, because it is a politically responsive agency, must be carefully scrutinized to insure that this responsiveness affects only principles of general application and that the Board otherwise behaves in an even-handed fashion. In the absence of such controls, the agency might decide cases on an ad hoc basis. There is, however, an evident danger in entrusting the Board with substantial control of findings of adjudicative fact because whatever controls are exercised through judicial review of questions of law can easily be circumvented by carefully contrived findings of fact. And whatever expertness the Board may bring to questions of fact seems to me outweighed by the dangers created by its political responsiveness. I would, therefore, tentatively suggest a statutory amendment limiting the substantial evidence test to cases in which the Board affirms the factual findings of trial examiners—assuming they can be made truly independent—and compelling the Board to apply the same test to those findings when it reviews them initially. Or, if the trial examiners are thought in some way to be infected by the agency, the courts might be permitted to apply a "weighing the evidence" test that would increase the scope of their review of Board decisions and not vary the Board's control of the examiners.

To be sure, these are only partially formulated proposals, and then only tentatively suggested. But it seems to me that the reasons for permitting the Board greater leeway in establishing legal principles imply a need for greater restrictions on its power to find facts. And, paradoxically, therefore, the scope of judicial review of matters of law ought to be narrower than that of matters of fact.

Thirty years later, a divided Supreme Court provided an illustration of what the implementation of Judge Winter's approach might look like. In *Allentown Mack Sales and Service, Inc. v. NLRB*, 522 U.S. 359, (1998), the new owners of a car dealership refused to recognize the bargaining status of the union it "inherited," claiming a good-faith reasonable doubt as to the employees' continuing support of the union. Based on its doubt, the employer arranged an independent poll of the employees, who voted 19 to 13 against the union. In a subsequent unfair labor practice proceeding, an ALJ concluded that the employer lacked the "objective reasonable doubt" about the union's majority status that, under the Board's interpretation of the NLRA, would have permitted the employer to conduct a poll and to refuse to bargain on the poll's outcome. The Board agreed and ordered the employer to recognize and bargain with the union; the D.C. Circuit upheld the order.

On review, the Supreme Court first upheld the Board's "reasonable doubt" standard for the permissible use of independent employer polls, even though the Board had adopted the very same standard for a unilateral withdrawal of recognition and for employer initiation of a Board-supervised election—both of which would represent far more drastic confrontations with an existing union and which thus might be thought to require a more demanding preliminary justification on the employer's part. The employer had argued that the Board's policy in this respect "irrationally permits employers to poll only when it would be unnecessary and legally pointless to do so." The Court conceded that the Board's standard "is in some respects a puzzling policy," but did "not find it so irrational as to be 'arbitrary [or] capricious' within the meaning of the Administrative Procedure Act."

The Court disagreed, however, as to whether substantial evidence existed to support the NLRB's conclusion that the employer "ha[d] not demonstrated that it held a reasonable doubt, based on objective considerations, that the Union continued to enjoy the support of a majority of the bargaining unit employees." The Board had adopted the ALJ's finding that six of Allentown's 32 employees had made "statements which could be used as objective considerations supporting a good-faith reasonable doubt as to continued majority status by the Union." Moreover, according to the Court:

> [T]he most significant evidence excluded from consideration by the Board consisted of statements of two employees regarding not merely their own support of the union, but support among the work force in general. Kermit Bloch, who worked on the night shift, told an Allentown manager "the entire night shift did not want the Union."

The ALJ refused to credit this, because "Bloch did not testify and thus could not explain how he formed his opinion about the views of his fellow employees." Unsubstantiated assertions that other employees do not support the union certainly do not establish *the fact of that disfavor* with the degree of reliability ordinarily demanded in legal proceedings. But under the Board's enunciated test for polling, it is not the fact of disfavor that is at issue (the poll itself is meant to establish that), but rather the existence of a reasonable uncertainty on the part of the employer regarding that fact. On that issue, absent some reason for the employer to know that Bloch had no basis for his information, or that Bloch was lying, reason demands that the statement be given considerable weight.

Another employee who gave information concerning overall support for the union was Ron Mohr, who told Allentown managers that "if a vote was taken, the Union would lose" and that "it was his feeling that the employees did not want a union." The ALJ again objected irrelevantly that "there is no evidence with respect to how he gained this knowledge." In addition, the Board held that Allentown "could not legitimately rely on [the statement] as a basis for doubting the Union's majority status," because Mohr was "referring to Mack's existing employee complement, not to the individuals who were later hired by [Allentown]." This basis for disregarding Mohr's statements is wholly irrational. Local 724 had never won on election, or even an informal poll, within the actual unit of 32 Allentown employees. Its claim to represent them rested entirely on the Board's presumption that the work force of a successor company has the same disposition regarding the union as did the work force of the predecessor company, if the majority of the new work force came from the old one. The Board cannot rationally adopt that presumption for purposes of imposing the duty to bargain, and adopt precisely the opposite presumption (*i.e,* contend that there is no relationship between the sentiments of the two work forces) for purposes of determining what evidence tends to establish a reasonable doubt regarding union support.

In light of this evidence, the Court found that the NLRB lacked a sufficient basis to deny the existence of reasonable doubt on the part of the employer as to the union's continued majority status. (It availed the Board nothing to argue that it had found an absence of reasonable doubt in other cases in which employers could have argued doubt as forcefully as did Allentown Mack. According to the majority, so long as "reasonable doubt" was the NLRB's articulated standard, it could not justify departing from that standard in one case by an arguably arbitrary departure from that standard in a precedent case).

Chief Justice Rehnquist, along with Justices O'Connor, Kennedy, and Thomas, concurred in the judgment and in the majority's holding with regard to substantial evidence review, but dissented from upholding the "reasonable doubt" standard in the first place. Justice Breyer, Stevens, Souter, and Ginsburg concurred in upholding the Board's standard, but would also have upheld the Board's fact-finding. They thought the Board's finding reasonable, based on the totality of evidence before the ALJ and the Board's consistent approach in weighing various categories of such evidence as presented in polling disputes. For example: "The Board, drawing upon both reason and experience, has said it will 'view with suspicion and caution' one employee's statements 'purporting to represent the views of other employees.' "

Note

Does the Choice of Standard Make a Difference? As we noted in Chapter 5, Congress seems to presume that "substantial evidence" review is meant to be more searching than review under the "arbitrary and opinion" standard. Yet, it is hard to imagine the *Allentown Mack* majority upholding the Labor Board whether the standard was "substantial evidence," "arbitrary and capricious," or "clearly erroneous"—the standard normally applied by appellate courts to lower court findings. Indeed, the practical effects of employing one standard rather than another are difficult to detect, and courts rarely have to address the question of which standard applies—much less whether it makes any difference.

Dickinson v. Zurko, 527 U.S. 150 (1999), is an exception. There the Supreme Court had occasion to address the difference between appellate court review of lower court fact findings and judicial review of agency factual determinations. The issue was whether the Federal Circuit had correctly applied the judicial "clearly erroneous" standard in reviewing the determination of the Patent and Trademark Office's Board of Patent Appeals and Interferences or should it, instead, have applied the substantial evidence standard of section 706 of the APA? The Federal Circuit justified its use of the former, ostensibly less deferential standard, on the ground that "clearly erroneous" had been its test long before the APA was passed and called attention to 5 U.S.C. § 559, which specifies that the APA "does not limit or repeal additional requirements * * * recognized by law." Writing for the Court majority, Justice Breyer was not persuaded. He found the pre-APA practice far less clear than the Federal Circuit claimed and the evidence that Congress meant in the APA to establish a uniform standard for court review of agency adjudications convincing.

That done, Justice Breyer struggled to describe the difference between the two standards of review:

> This Court has described the APA court/agency "substantial evidence" standard as requiring a court to ask whether a "reasonable mind might accept" a particular evidentiary record as "adequate to support a conclusion." *Consolidated Edison v. NLRB*, 305 U.S. 197 at 229 (1938). It has described the court/court "clearly erroneous" standard in terms of whether a reviewing judge has a "definite and firm conviction" that an error has been committed. *United States v. United States Gypsum Co.*, 333 U.S. 364, 395 (1948). And it has suggested that the former is somewhat less strict than the latter. *Universal Camera*, 340 U.S., at 477, 488. * * *

The upshot in terms of judicial review is some practical difference in outcome depending on which standard is used. The court/agency standard * * * is somewhat less strict than the court/court standard. But the difference is a subtle one—so fine that (apart from the present case) we have failed to uncover a single instance in which a reviewing court conceded that use of one standard rather than the other would in fact have produced a different outcome.

The difficulty of finding such a case may in part reflect the basic similarity of the reviewing task, which requires judges to apply logic and experience to an evidentiary record, whether that record was made in a court or by an agency. It may in part reflect the difficulty of attempting to capture in a form of words intangible factors such as judicial confidence in the fairness of the factfinding process. It may in part reflect the comparatively greater importance of case-specific factors, such as a finding's dependence upon agency expertise or the presence of internal agency review, which factors will often prove more influential in respect to outcome than will the applicable standard of review.

No other member of the Court disputed Justice Breyer's description but three Justices—Chief Justice Rehnquist, Justice Kennedy, and Justice Ginsburg—found the evidence for a pre-APA adherence to the "clearly erroneous" standard convincing and interpreted section 559 as recognizing this exception from the APA's presumptively uniform rule.

In *Association of Data Processing Service Organizations, Inc. v. Board of Governors of the Federal Reserve System*, 745 F.2d 677 (D.C.Cir.1984), Justice (then-Judge) Scalia argued that "substantial evidence" and "arbitrary or capricious" review imposed essentially identical substantive demands:

> When the arbitrary or capricious standard is performing [the] function of assuring factual support, there is no substantive difference between what it requires and what would be required by the substantial evidence test, since it is impossible to conceive of a "nonarbitrary" factual judgment supported only by evidence that is not substantial in the APA sense—i.e., not " 'enough to justify, if the trial were to a jury, a refusal to direct a verdict when the conclusion sought to be drawn * * * is one of fact for the jury.' " * * *
>
> [T]his does not consign paragraph (E) of the APA's judicial review section [requiring review of fact finding for "substantial evidence" in on-the-record proceedings] to pointlessness. The distinctive function of paragraph (E)—what it achieves that paragraph (A) does not—is to require substantial evidence to be found within the record of closed-record proceedings to which it exclusively applies. The importance of that requirement should not be underestimated. It is true that, as the Supreme Court said in *Camp v. Pitts*, 411 U.S. 138, 142 (1973), even informal agency action (not governed by paragraph (E)) must be reviewed only on the basis of "the administrative record already in existence." But that is quite a different and less onerous requirement, meaning only that whether the administrator was arbitrary must be determined on the basis of what he had before him when he acted, and not on the basis of "some new record made initially in the reviewing

> court." That "administrative record" might well include crucial material that was neither shown to nor known by the private parties in the proceeding * * *. It is true that, in informal rulemaking, at least the most critical factual material that is used to support the agency's position on review must have been made public in the proceeding and exposed to refutation. That requirement, however, does not extend to all data, and it only applies in rulemaking and not in other informal agency action, since it derives not from the arbitrary or capricious test but from the command of 5 U.S.C. § 533(c) that "the agency * * * give interested persons an opportunity to participate in the rule making."

Justice Scalia's account notwithstanding, the impression that the substantial evidence standard is more demanding persists among many lawyers, judges, scholars, and members of Congress. Note, in particular, the statement in Justice Marshall's dissenting opinion in *Industrial Union Dept. v. American Petroleum Inst.*, 448 U.S. 607, 705 (1980): "This [the substantial evidence] standard represents a legislative judgment that regulatory action should be subject to review more stringent than the traditional 'arbitrary and capricious' standard for informal rulemaking."

The Impact of Judicial Oversight on Agency Adjudication

Federal administrative agencies conduct hundreds of thousands of formal adjudications every year, each theoretically subject to judicial review. The Social Security Administration, the Labor Department, the Treasury Department, and the Immigration and Naturalization Service are the source of the vast majority of these decisions, but regulatory agencies, like the NLRB, the SEC, the FTC, and the FCC also decide hundreds of contested cases annually. By one now-dated count, SAMUEL KRISLOV & LLOYD D. MUSOLF, EDS., THE POLITICS OF REGULATION 2 (1964), 120 different federal agencies were engaged in formal adjudication of rights and duties under various federal statutory regimes in the early 1960s. The number now is surely larger. Of this vast caseload only a small percentage are ever pressed to judicial review. While the thousands of SSA disability cases filed in the federal district courts are a source of continuing judicial displeasure, these appeals routinely represent less than 5 per cent of ALJ decisions following hearings and fewer than 1 per cent of initial disability decisions.

That courts are exposed to considerably less than the tip of the iceberg of agency adjudications, and to a far-from-representative sample, raises two fundamental questions: (1) What effect can intermittent judicial scrutiny have on the general course of administrative adjudication? (2) Are the perceptible effects of judicial review, on the whole, beneficial? While both questions are complex and the evidence available to answer them incomplete, the materials that we have already explored are suggestive. The impact of court review will obviously depend to some degree on the basis for the judicial judgment and on the capacity of the agency to respond to judicial direction. A decision such as *Goldberg v. Kelly*, *supra* p. 322, which holds certain routine procedures unconstitutional and prescribes minimums for the future, should have a much greater impact than a remand for lack of substantial evidence in a specific case, even if that remand is by the Supreme Court. But, as the administrative response to *Goldberg* also demonstrates, the uneven capacity of agencies to implement judicial direction may make the ultimate effects of judicial review quite unpredictable. Moreover, the very uncertainty of consequences raises substantial questions about the desirability of "effective" judicial intervention. See also JERRY L. MASHAW, BUREAUCRATIC JUSTICE 187–88 (1983) (describing similar dynamic problems in response to the hearing delay cases cited in *Heckler v. Campbell*).

Agency recalcitrance can also affect the efficacy of judicial review, for whatever impact the Court might anticipate when it interprets an agency's statutory authority could be undermined by findings of fact in particular adjudications. Notice that following the remand in *Bell Aerospace*, discussed in Chapter 5, the NLRB retained the power to find as a "fact" that the company's buyers were not managerial employees. The Board's previous noncompliance with court opinions suggests a strong predisposition to do so.

Agency resistance to court decisions with which they disagree need not necessarily entail the subterfuge of masking policy judgments in factual findings. Federal administrative agencies generally exercise national jurisdiction; the territorial powers of reviewing courts end at the district or circuit boundary. Opinions in one district or circuit need not be followed elsewhere—indeed, where circuit rulings conflict, could not be. Moreover, having lost one case, the agency may not acquiesce even in that local jurisdiction.

Nonetheless, agency "nonacquiescence" in the decisions of lower federal courts remains a highly controversial practice that has stirred indignation in both Congress and the judiciary, as well as substantial law review commentary. See, e.g., Don T. Coenen, *The Constitutional Case Against Intracircuit Nonacquiescence*, 75 Minn.L.Rev. 1339 (1991), Samuel Estreicher and Richard L. Revesz, *The Uneasy Case Against Intracircuit Nonacquiescence*, 99 Yale L.J. 831 (1990); Mathew Diller and Nancy Morawetz, *Intracircuit Nonacquiesnce and the Breakdown of the Rule of Law: A Response to Estreicher and Revesz*, 99 Yale L.J. 801 (1990); Samuel L. Estreicher and Richard Revesz, *Nonacquiescence by Federal Administrative Agencies*, 98 Yale L.J. 679 (1989).

Agencies may not display substantially greater fidelity to the dictates of Supreme Court decisions. In THE SUPREME COURT AND ADMINISTRATIVE AGENCIES (1968), Professor Martin Shapiro made a careful study of the U.S. Patent Office. Although the Patent Office rules on patentability and issues patents, the ultimate authority to determine patentability presumably lies with the federal courts in cases challenging a patent or involving claims of infringement. Beginning in the 1930s, a sharp divergence emerged between the Patent Office's and the Supreme Court's conceptions of patentability. In the base period 1920–29, the Court invalidated about 50 per cent of the patents challenged before it. The percentage invalidated increased dramatically thereafter; between 1934 and 1966 the Court sustained only two patents on the merits.

One should not conclude from two or three examples that judicial review of agency adjudication is generally ineffectual because agencies are recalcitrant. Others have suggested that the more common judicial/agency interaction is accommodation, not conflict, *e.g.*, Joseph V. Fiorino, *Judicial–Administrative Interaction in Regulatory Policy Making: The Case of the Federal Power Commission*, 28 Ad.L.Rev. 41 (1976). Yet these examples, combined with the tiny percentage of agency decisions that reach the courts for review, do make one wonder about the systemic utility of judicial review of administrative adjudication.

The central value of judicial review may lie in its residual guarantee of justice in individual cases. From this perspective judicial review protects the citizen from the extremes of bureaucratic tunnel vision or incompetence—extremes revealed, one hopes, by the lack of substantial evidence in the record or by some other "danger signal" that can be converted into a legal claim. Somewhat more broadly, judicial review is a protection against official illegality. Agencies zealously pursuing particular programs on the basis of specialized knowledge should not be expected simultaneously to maintain a detached perspective about the impact of their actions on tangential statutory, constitutional, or common law rights—or to display modesty in interpreting the extent of their own jurisdiction. Judicial review thus polices the boundaries of agency power and sustains general substantive and procedural norms where the latter compete with the implementation of particular programs.

That judicial review should help assure justice and protect the rule of law is as conventional as it is plausible. Indeed, it is its commonsensical character that gives judicial review the power to legitimate administrative action. The assurance that the courts remain open to check administrative lawlessness is surely one of the major means by which the administrative apparatus of the modern welfare state has been accommodated to an historically liberal-individualist political ideology. See, *e.g.*, *Amalgamated Meat Cutters v. Connally*, 337 F.Supp. 737 (D.D.C. 1971), excerpted in Chapter 2, *supra*.

More recently, it has become common to think of judicial review as more than a mere check at the boundaries of agency power or a case-by-case oversight for inequity. Whether or not one is attracted by Judge Harold Leventhal's description of court-agency "partnership," it is difficult not to imagine that reviewing courts are in some sense co-inhabitants of a legislatively-created arena for the formulation and implementation of policy. To believe otherwise is to believe in sharper boundaries among fact, law, and policy than most contemporary lawyers can discern. Moreover, because the judicial process of review is now accessible to many individuals and groups affected by agency action, judicial review may play a democratizing role. See, e.g., Richard B. Stewart, *The Reformation of American Administrative Law*, 88 Harv.L.Rev. 1667 (1975). This is true partly because parties who can invoke judicial review, by virtue of that power alone, necessarily gain some leverage in negotiations with the agency over protection of their interests. In this way political pluralism, as Professor Lowi has lamented, *supra* p. 88, can be maintained all the way to the stage of concrete implementation. Moreover, a judiciary constantly compelled to resolve disputes concerning administrative action cannot be expected continuously to maintain a neat division between agency and judicial discretion. Judicial conceptions of appropriate policy are insinuated into the administrative process even as the judiciary struggles to understand and maintain a proper respect for agency action. In the view of some commentators, the judiciary has a special claim to represent social or public values in our particular brand of constitutional democracy. See, e.g., Philip Bobbitt, Constitutional Fate (1982); Owen M. Fiss, *Forward: The Forms of Justice*, 93 Harv.L.Rev. 1 (1979); Harry H. Wellington, *The Nature of Judicial Review*, 91 Yale L.J. 486 (1982).

That these functional hypotheses concerning the role of judicial review—ensuring individualized justice, maintaining the rule of law, legitimating the administrative state, and democratizing bureaucratic choices among competing values—may be plausible, however, does not make them true. And, if true, their pursuit within the current structure of judicial review of agency adjudication may nevertheless be sub-optimal or even deleterious. Such a conclusion might be applicable generally or, as Judge Winter's critique suggests, one reached about particular agencies or functions.

Nor is Winter alone in his criticism. In their study of the SSA disability program, Social Security Hearings and Appeals 125–150 (1978), Jerry L. Mashaw and his colleagues found little evidence that judicial review either produced justice in individual cases or maintained the appropriate norms of the program. They concluded that judicial review should be retained on the sole ground that to remove it might impair the perceived legitimacy of SSA administration. But surely that conclusion, too, is suspect. Others have concluded that judicial oversight has pressed SSA toward defensive administrative actions that are widely considered dysfunctional. See Symposium, *Judicial Review of Social Security Disability Decisions: A Proposal for Change*, 11 Tex.Tech L.Rev. 215 (1980). Does the possible legitimation value of review outweigh the potential costs of dysfunctional administrative adaptation? And if legitimacy flows from functional assumptions about justice and the rule of law that are either demonstrably false or problematic, how much weight should the former have? Is judicial review merely a prop supporting what Murray Edelman has termed the "expressive function" of administrative agencies: "to create and sustain an impression that ensures acquiescence in the public in the face of private tactics that might otherwise be expected to produce resentment, protest and resistance." MURRAY J. EDELMAN, THE SYMBOLIC USES OF POLITICS 56 (1964). See also THURMAN WESLEY ARNOLD, THE SYMBOLS OF GOVERNMENT 34 (1935).

Students of other programs question the capacity of reviewing courts to understand the subtle interconnections of the discrete decisions they are called upon to review with the broader programs and policies that those decisions seek to implement. These misunderstandings produce "a multitude of unintended and undesirable consequences." R. SHEP MELNICK, REGULATION AND THE COURTS 351–52 (1983).

One of Melnick's case studies is instructive. The 1970 Clean Air Act gave the EPA responsibility, in effect, to authorize local enforcement of federal air quality standards by approving state implementation plans (SIPs). Because of federal statutory deadlines the original SIP approval process was hurried. Many states had very meager information about prevailing air quality. They therefore adopted draconian control requirements with escape clauses in the form of "variance" provisions that could be used to tailor enforcement to the facts as they become known. EPA approved these SIPs, recognizing the critical role that variances would play in both the state and the federal enforcement efforts.

This enforcement calculus was upset by judicial intervention. In 1973, the Natural Resources Defense Council (NRDC) filed suit in six federal courts of appeals to force the EPA to disapprove the variance provisions in most state plans. The ensuing interaction between the federal courts and the federal and state pollution control agencies over the variance issue is summarized by Melnick:

> Fearing that administrative leniency would undermine the Clean Air Act's rigid deadlines, several circuit courts prohibited the EPA from allowing states to grant polluters variances after 1975. The EPA first ignored these decisions and then announced ambiguous guidelines designed to appease the courts. These guidelines angered state enforcement officials, many of whom either cut back on their activities or stopped talking with the federal agency. The EPA responded by issuing new guidelines that reassured the states but flew in the face of the court orders. While the Supreme Court eventually reversed the decisions that had caused the EPA so much trouble, it could not repair the damage already done. * * *

Why was judicial review of EPA's actions under the state implementation plans so misinformed? Why was it that no court—not even the Supreme Court, which sided with the EPA—recognized that variances formed the linchpin of state and federal enforcement efforts? The reasons Melnick offers rehearse some of the institutional explanations advanced by others:

> The adjudicatory process failed to probe the inadequacies of the original SIPs, the weakness of state and federal enforcement programs, or the different ways in which the EPA and the states used variances. The original cases were argued and decided well before the EPA had had any experience enforcing the act. Neither the EPA's lawyers nor the NRDC anticipated what was to come. More disturbing still was the failure of the government's attorneys to explain the problem candidly to the Supreme Court in 1975. The EPA's Office of General Counsel and the Department of Justice, themselves far removed from the centers of enforcement, insisted upon arguing "the law" and declined to complicate their argument with a discussion of the fact of widespread noncompliance. Public

> admission that SIPs were vague, confused, and unreasonable or that the EPA lacked credible enforcement sanctions might further weaken enforcement. Neither the NRDC nor the business groups that intervened in the case saw any advantage in explaining these bleak facts to the Court.

See also BRUCE A. ACKERMAN & WILLIAM T. HASSLER, CLEAN COAL/DIRTY AIR 25 (1981). Melnick also comments on the democratizing effects of the SIP episode:

> Once again court decisions gave environmental groups greater access to EPA decisionmaking. The EPA's 1974 variance guidelines were the direct result of negotiations with the NRDC. But in the long run these guidelines served only to diminish the influence of environmentalists. Rather than granting fewer concessions to polluters, state officials merely made their concessions in a less formal manner. Consequently, their actions were less subject to scrutiny by environmentalists—and by the EPA. It is interesting to note that the NRDC at first approved of the EPA's rules on variances and only later chose to bring suit. They chose wrong.

At a broader level, Melnick questions whether the contribution of the courts to the development of policy reveals a "partnership" in good working order:

> Taken as a whole, the consequences of court action under the Clean Air Act are neither random nor beneficial. * * * Court action has encouraged legislators and administrators to establish goals without considering how they can be achieved, exacerbating the tendency of these institutions to promise far more than they can deliver. The policymaking system of which the federal courts are now an integral part has produced serious inefficiency and inequities, has made rational debate and conscious political choice difficult, and has added to frustration and cynicism among participants of all stripes.

Here, Melnick is speaking not just of judicial review of adjudication, but of judicial review of all forms of agency action under the Clean Air Act.

4. REVIEW OF SCIENCE-BASED DECISIONS: THE INTERPLAY OF FACT, POLICY, AND INTERPRETATION

In Chapter 5, we examined judicial review of informal agency rulemaking, focusing on the courts' merger of rationality review with demands for procedural formality. We now revisit the subject to pose a more conventional issue: With what intensity should courts scrutinize agency decisions, especially legislative rules, based on technical evidence and policy judgment at what Judge Carl McGowan once termed the "frontiers of science?"

INDUSTRIAL UNION DEPARTMENT v. AMERICAN PETROLEUM INSTITUTE

Supreme Court of the United States, 1980.
448 U.S. 607, 100 S.Ct. 2844, 65 L.Ed.2d 1010.

JUSTICE STEVENS announced the judgment of the Court and delivered an opinion, in which THE CHIEF JUSTICE and JUSTICE STEWART joined and in Parts I, II, III–A–C and E of which JUSTICE POWELL joined.

The Occupational Safety and Health Act of 1970, 29 U.S.C. § 651 *et seq.* (the Act), was enacted for the purpose of ensuring safe and healthful working conditions for every working man and woman in the Nation. This litigation concerns a standard promulgated by the Secretary of Labor to regulate occupational exposure to benzene, a substance which has been shown to cause cancer at high exposure levels. The principal question is whether such a showing is a sufficient basis for a standard that places the most stringent limitation on exposure to benzene that is technologically and economically possible.

* * * The basic definition of an "occupational safety and health standard" is found in § 3(8), which provides:

> "The term 'occupational safety and health standard' means a standard which requires conditions, or the adoption or use of one or more practices, means, methods, operations, or processes, reasonably necessary or appropriate to provide safe or healthful employment and places of employment."

Where toxic materials or harmful physical agents are concerned, a standard must also comply with § 6(b)(5), which provides:

> "The secretary, in promulgating standards dealing with toxic materials or harmful physical agents under this subsection, shall set the standard which most adequately assures, to the extent feasible, on the basis of the best available evidence, that no employee will suffer material impairment of health or functional capacity even if such employee has regular exposure to the hazard dealt with by such standard for the period of his working life. Development of standards under this subsection shall be based upon research, demonstrations, experiments, and such other information as may be appropriate. In addition to the attainment of the highest degree of health and safety protection for the employee, other considerations shall be the latest available scientific data in the field, the feasibility of the standards, and experience gained under this and other health and safety laws."

Wherever the toxic material to be regulated is a carcinogen, the Secretary has taken the position that no safe exposure level can be determined and that § 6(b)(5) requires him to set an exposure limit at the lowest technologically feasible level that will not impair the viability of the industries regulated. * * *

On pre-enforcement review * * * the United States Court of Appeals for the Fifth Circuit held the regulation invalid. 581 F.2d 493 (1978). The court concluded that OSHA had exceeded its standard-setting authority because it had not shown that the new benzene exposure limit was "reasonably necessary or appropriate to provide safe or healthful employment" as required by § 3(8), and because § 6(b)(5) does "not give OSHA the unbridled discretion to adopt standards designed to create absolutely risk-free workplaces regardless of costs." Reading the two provisions together, the Fifth Circuit held that the Secretary was under a duty to determine whether the benefits expected from the new standard bore a reasonable relationship to the costs that it imposed. The court noted that OSHA had made an estimate of the costs of compliance, but that the record lacked substantial evidence of any discernible benefits.

We agree with the Fifth Circuit's holding that § 3(8) requires the Secretary to find, as a threshold matter, that the toxic substance in question poses a significant health risk in the workplace and that a new, lower standard is therefore "reasonably necessary or appropriate to provide safe or healthful employment and places of employment." Unless and until such a finding is made, it is not necessary to address the further question whether the Court of Appeals correctly held that there must be a reasonable correlation between costs and benefits, or whether, as the federal parties argue, the Secretary is then required by § 6(b)(5) to promulgate a standard that goes as far as technologically and economically possible to eliminate the risk. * * *

I.

Benzene is a familiar and important commodity. It is a colorless, aromatic liquid that evaporates rapidly under ordinary atmospheric conditions. Approximately 11 billion pounds of benzene were produced in the United States in 1976. Ninety-four per cent of that total was produced by the petroleum and petrochemical industries, with the remainder produced by the steel industry as a byproduct of coking operations. Benzene is used in manufacturing a variety of products including motor fuels (which may contain as much as 2 per cent benzene), solvents, detergents, pesticides, and other organic chemicals.

* * *

Industrial health experts have long been aware that exposure to benzene may lead to various types of nonmalignant diseases. * * * In 1969 the American National Standards Institute (ANSI) adopted a national consensus standard of 10 ppm averaged over an 8–hour period with a ceiling concentration of 25 ppm for 10–minute periods or a maximum peak concentration of 50 ppm. In 1971, after the Occupational Safety and Health Act was passed, the Secretary adopted this consensus standard as the federal standard, pursuant to 29 U.S.C. § 655(a).

* * * In the late 1960s and early 1970s a number of epidemiological studies were published indicating that workers exposed to high concen-

trations of benzene were subject to a significantly increased risk of leukemia. * * *

Between 1974 and 1976 additional studies were published which tended to confirm the view that benzene can cause leukemia, at least when exposure levels are high. * * * NIOSH stated that these studies provided "conclusive" proof of a causal connection between benzene and leukemia. Although it acknowledged that none of the intervening studies had provided the dose-response data it had found lacking two years earlier, NIOSH nevertheless recommended that the exposure limit be set as low as possible. * * *

* * *

In the spring of 1976, NIOSH had selected two Pliofilm plants in St. Mary's and Akron, Ohio, for an epidemiological study of the link between leukemia and benzene exposure. In April 1977, NIOSH forwarded an interim report to OSHA indicating at least a five-fold increase in the expected incidence of leukemia for workers who had been exposed to benzene at the two plants from 1940 to 1949. The report submitted to OSHA erroneously suggested that exposures in the two plants had generally been between zero and 15 ppm during the period in question.[16] * * *

In its published statement giving notice of the proposed permanent standard, OSHA did not ask for comments as to whether or not benzene presented a significant health risk at exposures of 10 ppm or less. Rather, it asked for comments as to whether 1 ppm was the minimum feasible exposure limit. * * * [T]his formulation of the issue to be considered by the Agency was consistent with OSHA's general policy with respect to carcinogens. Whenever a carcinogen is involved, OSHA will presume that no safe level of exposure exists in the absence of clear proof establishing such a level and will accordingly set the exposure limit at the lowest level feasible. * * * The fact that OSHA did not ask for comments on whether there was a safe level of exposure for benzene was indicative of its further view that a demonstration of such absolute safety simply could not be made.

* * *

As presently formulated, the benzene standard is an expensive way of providing some additional protection for a relatively small number of employees. According to OSHA's figures, the standard will require capital investments in engineering controls of approximately $266 million, first-year operating costs (for monitoring, medical testing, employee

16. * * * Industry representatives argued at the [rulemaking] hearing that this evidence indicated that the exposure levels had been very high, as they had been in the other epidemiological studies conducted in the past. NIOSH witnesses, however, simply stated that actual exposure levels for the years in question could not be determined; they did agree, however, that their study should *not* be taken as proof of a five-fold increase in leukemia risk at 10–15 ppm. In its explanation of the permanent standard, OSHA agreed with the NIOSH witnesses that no dose-response relationship could be inferred from the study. * * *

training, and respirators) of $187 million to $205 million and recurring annual costs of approximately $34 million. The figures outlined in OSHA's explanation of the costs of compliance to various industries indicate that only 35,000 employees would gain any benefit from the regulation in terms of a reduction in their exposure to benzene. Over two-thirds of these workers (24,450) are employed in the rubber-manufacturing industry. Compliance costs in that industry are estimated to be rather low with no capital costs and initial operating expenses estimated at only $34 million ($1,390 per employee); recurring annual costs would also be rather low, totaling less than $1 million. By contrast, the segment of the petroleum refining industry that produces benzene would be required to incur $24 million in capital costs and $600,000 in first-year operating expenses to provide additional protection for 300 workers ($82,000 per employee), while the petrochemical industry would be required to incur $20.9 million in capital costs and $1 million in initial operating expenses for the benefit of 552 employees ($39,675 per employee).[29]

Although OSHA did not quantify the benefits to each category of worker in terms of decreased exposure to benzene, it appears from the economic impact study done at OSHA's direction that those benefits may be relatively small. Thus, although the current exposure limit is 10 ppm, the actual exposures outlined in that study are often considerably lower. For example, for the period 1970–1975 the petrochemical industry reported that, out of a total of 496 employees exposed to benzene, only 53 were exposed to levels between 1 and 5 ppm and only 7 (all at the same plant) were exposed to between 5 and 10 ppm.

II.

* * * Any discussion of the 1 ppm exposure limit must, of course, begin with the agency's rationale for imposing that limit. The written explanation of the standard fills 184 pages of the printed appendix. Much of it is devoted to a discussion of the voluminous evidence of the adverse effects of exposure to benzene at levels of concentration well above 10 ppm. This discussion demonstrates that there is ample justification for regulating occupational exposure to benzene and that the prior limit of 10 ppm, with a ceiling of 25 ppm (or a peak of 50 ppm), was reasonable. It does not, however, provide direct support for the Agency's conclusion that the limit should be reduced from 10 ppm to 1 ppm.

The evidence in the administrative record of adverse effects of benzene exposure at 10 ppm is sketchy at best. OSHA noted that there was "no dispute" that certain nonmalignant blood disorders, evidenced by a reduction in the level of red or white cells or platelets in the blood,

29. The high cost per employee in the latter two industries is attributable to OSHA's policy of requiring engineering controls rather than allowing respirators to be used to reduce exposures to the permissible limit. The relatively low estimated cost per employee in the rubber industry is based on OSHA's assumption that other solvents and adhesives can be substituted for those that contain benzene and that capital costs will therefore not be required.

could result from exposures of 25–40 ppm. It then stated that several studies had indicated that relatively slight changes in normal blood values could result from exposures below 25 ppm and perhaps below 10 ppm. OSHA did not attempt to make any estimate based on these studies of how significant the risk of nonmalignant disease would be at exposures of 10 ppm or less. Rather, it stated that because of the lack of data concerning the linkage between low-level exposures and blood abnormalities, it was impossible to construct a dose-response curve at this time.[33] OSHA did conclude, however, that the studies demonstrated that the current 10 ppm exposure limit was inadequate to ensure that no single worker would suffer a nonmalignant blood disorder as a result of benzene exposure. * * * OSHA did not state, however, that the nonmalignant effects of benzene exposure justified a reduction in the permissible exposure limit to 1 ppm. * * *

With respect to leukemia, evidence of an increased risk (i.e., a risk greater than that borne by the general population) due to benzene exposures at or below 10 ppm was even sketchier. Once OSHA acknowledged that the NIOSH study it had relied upon in promulgating the emergency standard did not support its earlier view that benzene had been shown to cause leukemia at concentrations below 25 ppm, there was only one study that provided any evidence of such an increased risk. That study, conducted by the Dow Chemical Co., uncovered three leukemia deaths, versus 0.2 expected deaths, out of a population of 594 workers; it appeared that the three workers had never been exposed to more than 2 to 9 ppm of benzene. The authors of the study, however, concluded that it could not be viewed as proof of a relationship between low-level benzene exposure and leukemia because all three workers had probably been occupationally exposed to a number of other potentially carcinogenic chemicals at other points in their careers and because no leukemia deaths had been uncovered among workers who had been exposed to much higher levels of benzene. In its explanation of the permanent standard, OSHA stated that the possibility that these three leukemias had been caused by benzene exposure could not be ruled out and that the study, although not evidence of an increased risk of leukemia at 10 ppm, was therefore "consistent with the findings of many studies that there is an excess leukemia risk among benzene exposed employees." The Agency made no finding that the Dow study, any other empirical evidence, or any opinion testimony demonstrated that exposure to benzene at or below the 10 ppm level had ever in fact caused leukemia. * * *

In the end OSHA's rationale for lowering the permissible exposure limit to 1 ppm was based, not on any finding that leukemia has ever been caused by exposure to 10 ppm of benzene and that it will *not* be

33. OSHA's comments with respect to the insufficiency of the data were addressed primarily to the lack of data at low exposure levels. OSHA did not discuss whether it was possible to make a rough estimate, based on the more complete epidemiological and animal studies done at higher exposure levels, of the significance of the risks attributable to those levels, nor did it discuss whether it was possible to extrapolate from such estimates to derive a risk estimate for low-level exposures.

caused by exposure to 1 ppm, but rather on a series of assumptions indicating that some leukemias might result from exposure to 10 ppm and that the number of cases might be reduced by reducing the exposure level to 1 ppm. In reaching that result, the Agency first unequivocally concluded that benzene is a human carcinogen. Second, it concluded that industry had failed to prove that there is a safe threshold level of exposure to benzene below which no excess leukemia cases would occur. In reaching this conclusion OSHA rejected industry contentions that certain epidemiological studies indicating no excess risk of leukemia among workers exposed to levels below 10 ppm were sufficient to establish that the threshold level of safe exposure was at or above 10 ppm. It also rejected an industry witness' testimony that a dose-response curve could be constructed on the basis of the reported epidemiological studies and that this curve indicated that reducing the permissible exposure limit from 10 to 1 ppm would prevent at most one leukemia and one other cancer death every six years.[38]

Third, the Agency applied its standard policy with respect to carcinogens, concluding that, in the absence of definitive proof of a safe level, it must be assumed that *any* level above zero presents *some* increased risk of cancer. As the federal parties point out in their brief, there are a number of scientists and public health specialists who subscribe to this view, theorizing that a susceptible person may contract cancer from the absorption of even one molecule of a carcinogen like benzene.

Fourth, the Agency reiterated its view of the Act, stating that it was required by § 6(b)(5) to set the standard either at the level that has been demonstrated to be safe or at the lowest level feasible, whichever is higher. If no safe level is established, as in this case, the Secretary's interpretation of the statute automatically leads to the selection of an exposure limit that is the lowest feasible. Because of benzene's importance to the economy, no one has ever suggested that it would be feasible to eliminate its use entirely, or to try to limit exposures to the small amounts that are omnipresent. Rather, the Agency selected 1 ppm as a workable exposure level and then determined that compliance with that level was technologically feasible and that "the economic impact of * * * [compliance] will not be such as to threaten the financial welfare of the affected firms or the general economy." * * *

III.

Our resolution of the issues in these cases turns, to a large extent, on the meaning of and the relationship between § 3(8), which defines a health and safety standard as a standard that is "reasonably necessary and appropriate to provide safe or healthful employment," and § 6(b)(5), which directs the Secretary in promulgating a health and safety standard

38. OSHA rejected this testimony in part because it believed the exposure data in the epidemiological studies to be inadequate to formulate a dose-response curve. It also indicated that even if the testimony was accepted—indeed as long as there was any increase in the risk of cancer—the Agency was under an obligation to "select the level of exposure which is most protective of exposed employees."

for toxic materials to "set the standard which most adequately assures, to the extent feasible, on the basis of the best available evidence, that no employee will suffer material impairment of health or functional capacity * * *."

In the Government's view, § 3(8)'s definition of the term "standard" has no legal significance or at best merely requires that a standard not be totally irrational. It takes the position that § 6(b)(5) is controlling and that it requires OSHA to promulgate a standard that either gives an absolute assurance of safety for each and every worker or reduces exposures to the lowest level feasible. The Government interprets "feasible" as meaning technologically achievable at a cost that would not impair the viability of the industries subject to the regulation. The respondent industry representatives, on the other hand, argue that the Court of Appeals was correct in holding that the "reasonably necessary and appropriate" language of § 3(8), along with the feasibility requirement of § 6(b)(5), requires the Agency to quantify both the costs and the benefits of a proposed rule and to conclude that they are roughly commensurate.

In our view, it is not necessary to decide whether either the Government or industry is entirely correct. For we think it is clear that § 3(8) does apply to all permanent standards promulgated under the Act and that it requires the Secretary, before issuing any standard, to determine that it is reasonably necessary and appropriate to remedy a significant risk of material health impairment. * * *

* * *

By empowering the Secretary to promulgate standards that are "reasonably necessary or appropriate to provide safe or healthful employment and places of employment," the Act implies that, before promulgating any standard, the Secretary must make a finding that the workplaces in question are not safe. But "safe" is not the equivalent of "risk-free." There are many activities that we engage in every day—such as driving a car or even breathing city air—that entail some risk of accident or material health impairment; nevertheless, few people would consider these activities "unsafe." Similarly, a workplace can hardly be considered "unsafe" unless it threatens the workers with a significant risk of harm.

Therefore, before he can promulgate *any* permanent health or safety standard, the Secretary is required to make a threshold finding that a place of employment is unsafe—in the sense that significant risks are present and can be eliminated or lessened by a change in practices. This requirement applies to permanent standards promulgated pursuant to § 6(b)(5), as well as to other types of permanent standards. * * *

* * *

In the absence of a clear mandate in the Act, it is unreasonable to assume that Congress intended to give the Secretary the unprecedented power over American industry that would result from the Government's view of §§ 3(8) and 6(b)(5), coupled with OSHA's cancer policy. Expert testimony that a substance is probably a human carcinogen—either because it has caused cancer in animals or because individuals have contracted cancer following extremely high exposures—would justify the conclusion that the substance poses some risk of serious harm no matter how minute the exposure and no matter how many experts testified that they regarded the risk as insignificant. That conclusion would in turn justify pervasive regulation limited only by the constraint of feasibility. In light of the fact that there are literally thousands of substances used in the workplace that have been identified as carcinogens or suspect carcinogens, the Government's theory would give OSHA power to impose enormous costs that might produce little, if any, discernible benefit.

If the Government were correct in arguing that neither § 3(8) nor § 6(b)(5) requires that the risk from a toxic substance be quantified sufficiently to enable the Secretary to characterize it as significant in an understandable way, the statute would make such a "sweeping delegation of legislative power" that it might be unconstitutional under the Court's reasoning in *A.L.A. Schechter Poultry Corp. v. United States* and *Panama Refining Co. v. Ryan*. A construction of the statute that avoids this kind of open-ended grant should certainly be favored.

* * *

As we read the statute, the burden was on the Agency to show, on the basis of substantial evidence, that it is at least more likely than not that long-term exposure to 10 ppm of benzene presents a significant risk of material health impairment. * * *

In this case OSHA did not even attempt to carry its burden of proof. The closest it came to making a finding that benzene presented a significant risk of harm in the workplace was its statement that the benefits to be derived from lowering the permissible exposure level from 10 to 1 ppm were "likely" to be "appreciable." The Court of Appeals held that this finding was not supported by substantial evidence. Of greater importance, even if it were supported by substantial evidence, such a finding would not be sufficient to satisfy the Agency's obligations under the act.

* * *

Contrary to the Government's contentions, imposing a burden on the Agency of demonstrating a significant risk of harm will not strip it of its ability to regulate carcinogens, nor will it require the Agency to wait for deaths to occur before taking any action. First, the requirement that a "significant" risk be identified is not a mathematical straitjacket. It is the Agency's responsibility to determine, in the first instance, what it considers to be a "significant" risk. Some risks are plainly acceptable and others are plainly unacceptable. If, for example, the odds are one in a billion that a person will die from cancer by taking a drink of chlorinated water, the risk clearly could not be considered significant. On the other hand, if the odds are one in a thousand that regular inhalation of gasoline vapors that are 2 per cent benzene will be fatal, a reasonable person might well consider the risk significant and take appropriate steps to decrease or eliminate it. Although the Agency has no duty to calculate the exact probability of harm, it does have an obligation to find that a significant risk is present before it can characterize a place of employment as "unsafe."

Second, OSHA is not required to support its finding that a significant risk exists with anything approaching scientific certainty. Although the Agency's findings must be supported by substantial evidence, § 6(b)(5) specifically allows the Secretary to regulate on the basis of the "best available evidence." * * * Thus, so long as they are supported by a body of reputable scientific thought, the Agency is free to use conservative assumptions in interpreting the data with respect to carcinogens, risking error on the side of overprotection rather than underprotection.

Finally, the record in this case and OSHA's own rulings on other carcinogens indicate that there are a number of ways in which the Agency can make a rational judgment about the relative significance of the risks associated with exposure to a particular carcinogen.[64]

* * *

Because our review of these cases has involved a more detailed examination of the record than is customary, it must be emphasized that we have neither made any factual determinations of our own, nor have we rejected any factual findings made by the Secretary. We express no opinion on what factual findings this record might support, either on the basis of empirical evidence or on the basis of expert testimony; nor do we express any opinion on the more difficult question of what factual determinations would warrant a conclusion that significant risks are

64. For example, in the coke-oven emissions standard, OSHA had calculated that 21,000 exposed coke-oven workers had an annual excess mortality of over 200 and that the proposed standard might well eliminate the risk entirely. 41 Fed.Reg. 46742, 46750 (1976), upheld in *American Iron & Steel Inst. v. OSHA*, 577 F.2d 825 (C.A.3 1978), *cert. granted* [448 U.S. at 909]. In hearings on the coke-oven emissions standard, the Council on Wage and Price Stability estimated that 8 to 35 lives would be saved each year, out of an estimated population of 14,000 workers, as a result of the proposed standard. Although noting that the range of benefits would vary depending on the assumptions used, OSHA did not make a finding as to whether its own staff estimate or CWPS's was correct, on the ground that it was not required to quantify the expected benefits of the standard or to weigh those benefits against the projected costs.

In other proceedings, the Agency has had a good deal of data from animal experiments on which it could base a conclusion on the significance of the risk. For example, the record on the vinyl chloride standard indicated that a significant number of animals had developed tumors of the liver, lung, and skin when they were exposed to 50 ppm of vinyl chloride over a period of 11 months. One hundred out of 200 animals died during that period. * * *

In this case the Agency did not have the benefit of the animal studies, because scientists have been unable as yet to induce leukemia in experimental animals as a result of benzene exposure. It did, however, have a fair amount of epidemiological evidence, including both positive and negative studies. Although the Agency stated that this evidence was insufficient to construct a precise correlation between exposure levels and cancer risks, it would at least be helpful in determining whether it is more likely than not that there is a significant risk at 10 ppm.

present which make promulgation of a new standard reasonably necessary or appropriate. The standard must, of course, be supported by the findings actually made by the Secretary, not merely by findings that we believe he might have made.

In this case the record makes it perfectly clear that the Secretary relied squarely on a special policy for carcinogens that imposed the burden on industry of proving the existence of a safe level of exposure, thereby avoiding the Secretary's threshold responsibility of establishing the need for more stringent standards. In so interpreting his statutory authority, the Secretary exceeded his power.

* * *

[CHIEF JUSTICE BURGER'S concurring opinion is omitted.]

JUSTICE POWELL, concurring in part and concurring in the judgment.

* * * I agree that §§ 6(b)(5) and 3(8) of the Occupational Safety and Health Act of 1970 must be read together. * * * When OSHA acts to reduce existing national consensus standards, therefore, it must find that (i) currently permissible exposure levels create a significant risk of material health impairment; and (ii) a reduction of those levels would significantly reduce the hazard.

* * *

Although I regard the question as close, I do not disagree with the plurality's view that OSHA has failed, on this record, to carry its burden of proof on the threshold issues summarized above. But even if one assumes that OSHA properly met this burden, I conclude that the statute also requires the agency to determine that the economic effects of its standard bear a reasonable relationship to the expected benefits. An occupational health standard is neither "reasonably necessary" nor "feasible," as required by statute, if it calls for expenditures wholly disproportionate to the expected health and safety benefits.

* * * OSHA's interpretation of § 6(b)(5) would force it to regulate in a manner inconsistent with the important health and safety purposes of the legislation we construe today. Thousands of toxic substances present risks that fairly could be characterized as "significant." Even if OSHA succeeded in selecting the gravest risks for earlier regulation, a standard-setting process that ignored economic considerations would result in a serious misallocation of resources and a lower effective level of safety than could be achieved under standards set with reference to the comparative benefits available at a lower cost. I would not attribute such an irrational intention to Congress. * * *

JUSTICE REHNQUIST, concurring in the judgment.

* * * According to the Secretary * * * § 6(b)(5) imposes upon him an absolute duty, in regulating harmful substances like benzene for which no safe level is known, to set the standard for permissible exposure at the lowest level that "can be achieved at bearable cost with available technology." * * *

* * * According to respondents, § 6(b)(5), as tempered by § 3(8), requires the Secretary to demonstrate that any particular health standard is justifiable on the basis of a rough balancing of costs and benefits.

In considering these alternative interpretations, my colleagues manifest a good deal of uncertainty, and ultimately divide over whether the Secretary produced sufficient evidence that the proposed standard for benzene will result in any appreciable benefits at all. This uncertainty, I would suggest, is eminently justified, since I believe that this litigation presents the Court with what has to be one of the most difficult issues that could confront a decisionmaker: whether the statistical possibility of future deaths should ever be disregarded in light of the economic costs of preventing those deaths. I would also suggest that the widely varying positions advanced in the briefs of the parties and in the opinions of Justice Stevens, The Chief Justice, Justice Powell, and Justice Marshall demonstrate, perhaps better than any other fact, that Congress, the governmental body best suited and most obligated to make the choice confronting us in this litigation, has improperly delegated that choice to the Secretary of Labor and, derivatively, to this Court.

* * *

* * * Especially in light of the importance of the interests at stake, I have no doubt that the provision at issue, standing alone, would violate the doctrine against uncanalized delegations of legislative power. For me the remaining question, then, is whether additional standards are ascertainable from the legislative history of statutory context of § 6(b)(5) or, if not, whether such a standardless delegation was justifiable in light of the "inherent necessities" of the situation. * * *

The legislative history contains nothing to indicate that the language "to the extent feasible" does anything other than render what had been a clear, if somewhat unrealistic, standard largely, if not entirely, precatory. There is certainly nothing to indicate that these words, as used in § 6(b)(5), are limited to technological and economic feasibility. * * *

* * *

* * * [I]n some cases this Court has abided by a rule of necessity, upholding broad delegations of authority where it would be "unreasonable and impracticable to compel Congress to prescribe detailed rules" regarding a particular policy or situation. But no need for such an evasive standard as "feasibility" is apparent in the present cases. In drafting § 6(b)(5), Congress was faced with a clear, if difficult, choice between balancing statistical lives and industrial resources or authorizing the Secretary to elevate human life above all concerns save massive dislocation in an affected industry. * * * That Congress chose, intentionally or unintentionally, to pass this difficult choice on to the Secretary is evident from the spectral quality of the standard it selected. * * *

As formulated and enforced by this Court, the nondelegation doctrine serves three important functions. First, and most abstractly, it ensures to the extent consistent with orderly governmental administration that important choices of social policy are made by Congress, the branch of our Government most responsive to the popular will. * * * Second, the doctrine guarantees that, to the extent Congress finds it necessary to delegate authority, it provides the recipient of that authority with an "intelligible principle" to guide the exercise of the delegated discretion. * * * Third, and derivative of the second, the doctrine ensures that courts charged with reviewing the exercise of delegated legislative discretion will be able to test that exercise against ascertainable standards. * * *

I believe the legislation at issue here fails on all three counts. The decision whether the law of diminishing returns should have any place in the regulation of toxic substances is quintessentially one of legislative policy. For Congress to pass that decision on to the Secretary in the manner it did violates, in my mind, John Locke's caveat * * * that legislatures are to make laws, not legislators. Nor, as I think the prior discussion amply demonstrates, do the provisions at issue or their legislative history provide the Secretary with any guidance that might lead him to his somewhat tentative conclusion that he must eliminate exposure to benzene as far as technologically and economically possible. Finally, I would suggest that the standard of "feasibility" renders meaningful judicial review impossible.

* * *

I would invalidate the first sentence of § 6(b)(5) of the Occupational Safety and Health Act of 1970 as it applies to any toxic substance or harmful physical agent for which a safe level, that is, a level at which "no employee will suffer material impairment of health or functional capacity even if such employee has regular exposure to [that hazard] for the period of his working life," is, according to the Secretary, unknown or otherwise "infeasible." Absent further congressional action, the Secretary would then have to choose, when acting pursuant to § 6(b)(5), between setting a safe standard or setting no standard at all. * * *

JUSTICE MARSHALL, with whom JUSTICE BRENNAN, JUSTICE WHITE, and JUSTICE BLACKMUN join, dissenting.

In cases of statutory construction, this Court's authority is limited. If the statutory language and legislative intent are plain, the judicial inquiry is at an end. Under our jurisprudence, it is presumed that ill-considered or unwise legislation will be corrected through the democratic process; a court is not permitted to distort a statute's meaning in order to make it conform with the Justices' own views of sound social policy.

Today's decision flagrantly disregards these restrictions on judicial authority. The plurality ignores the plain meaning of the Occupational Safety and Health Act of 1970 in order to bring the authority of the Secretary of Labor in line with the plurality's own views of proper regulatory policy. * * *

The plurality's discussion of the record in this case is both extraordinarily arrogant and extraordinarily unfair. It is arrogant because the plurality presumes to make its own factual findings with respect to a variety of disputed issues relating to carcinogen regulation. * * * And the plurality's discussion is unfair because its characterization of the Secretary's report bears practically no resemblance to what the Secretary actually did in this case. Contrary to the plurality's suggestion, the Secretary did not rely blindly on some Draconian carcinogen "policy." If he had, it would have been sufficient for him to have observed that benzene is a carcinogen, a proposition that respondents do not dispute. Instead, the Secretary gathered over 50 volumes of exhibits and testimony and offered a detailed and evenhanded discussion of the relationship between exposure to benzene at all recorded exposure levels and chromosomal damage, aplastic anemia, and leukemia. In that discussion he evaluated, and took seriously, respondents' evidence of a safe exposure level.

The hearings on the proposed standard were extensive, encompassing 17 days from July 19 through August 10, 1977. The 95 witnesses included epidemiologists, toxicologists, physicians, political economists, industry representatives, and members of the affected work force. Witnesses were subjected to exhaustive questioning by representatives from a variety of interested groups and organizations.

* * *

* * * [T]he Secretary's determinations must be upheld if supported by "substantial evidence in the record considered as a whole." 29 U.S.C. § 655(f). This standard represents a legislative judgment that regulatory action should be subject to review more stringent than the traditional "arbitrary and capricious" standard for informal rulemaking. * * * As we have emphasized, however, judicial review under the substantial evidence test is ultimately deferential. The agency's decision is entitled to the traditional presumption of validity, and the court is not authorized to substitute its judgment for that of the Secretary. If the Secretary has considered the decisional factors and acted in conformance with the statute, his ultimate decision must be given a large measure of respect.

The plurality is insensitive to three factors which, in my view, make judicial review of occupational safety and health standards under the substantial evidence test particularly difficult. First, the issues often reach a high level of technical complexity. In such circumstances the courts are required to immerse themselves in matters to which they are unaccustomed by training or experience. Second, the factual issues with which the Secretary must deal are frequently not subject to any definitive resolution. * * * Causal connections and theoretical extrapolations may be uncertain. Third, when the question involves determination of the acceptable level of risk, the ultimate decision must necessarily be based on considerations of policy as well as empirically verifiable facts. Factual determinations can at most define the risk in some statistical way; the judgment whether that risk is tolerable cannot be based solely on a resolution of the facts.

* * *

* * * On this record, the Secretary could conclude that regular exposure above the 1 ppm level would pose a definite risk resulting in material impairment to some indeterminate but possibly substantial number of employees. * * * Nothing in the Act purports to prevent the Secretary from acting when definitive information as to the quantity of a standard's benefits is unavailable. Where, as here, the deficiency in knowledge relates to the extent of the benefits rather than their existence, I see no reason to hold that the Secretary has exceeded his statutory authority.

The plurality avoids this conclusion through reasoning that may charitably be described as obscure. * * *

At the outset, it is important to observe that "reasonably necessary or appropriate" clauses are routinely inserted in regulatory legislation, and in the past such clauses have uniformly been interpreted as general provisos that regulatory actions must bear a reasonable relation to those statutory purposes set forth in the statute's substantive provisions. * * *

The plurality suggests that under the "reasonably necessary" clause, a workplace is not "unsafe" unless the Secretary is able to convince a reviewing court that a "significant" risk is at issue. That approach is particularly embarrassing in this case, for it is contradicted by the plain language of the Act. The plurality's interpretation renders utterly superfluous the first sentence of § 655(b)(5) * * *. By so doing, the plurality makes the test for standards regulating toxic substances and harmful physical agents substantially identical to the test for standards generally—plainly the opposite of what Congress intended. * * *

The plurality is obviously more interested in the consequences of its decision than in discerning the intention of Congress. But since the language and legislative history of the Act are plain, there is no need for conjecture about the effects of today's decision. * * * I do not pretend to know whether the test the plurality erects today is, as a matter of policy, preferable to that created by Congress and its delegates: the area is too fraught with scientific uncertainty, and too dependent on considerations of policy, for a court to be able to determine whether it is desirable to require identification of a "significant" risk before allowing an administrative agency to take regulatory action. But in light of the tenor of the plurality opinion, it is necessary to point out that the question is not one-sided, and that Congress' decision to authorize the Secretary to promulgate the regulation at issue here was a reasonable one.

* * *

* * * If the plurality means to require the Secretary realistically to "quantify" the risk in order to satisfy a court that it is "significant," the

record shows that the plurality means to require him to do the impossible. But regulatory inaction has very significant costs of its own. The adoption of such a test would subject American workers to a continuing risk of cancer and other serious diseases; it would disable the Secretary from regulating a wide variety of carcinogens for which quantification simply cannot be undertaken at the present time.

There are encouraging signs that today's decision does not extend that far. My Brother Powell concludes that the Secretary is not prevented from taking regulatory action "when reasonable quantification cannot be accomplished by any known methods." The plurality also indicates that it would not prohibit the Secretary from promulgating safety standards when quantification of the benefits is impossible. The Court might thus allow the Secretary to attempt to make a very rough quantification of the risk imposed by a carcinogenic substance, and give considerable deference to his finding that the risk was significant. If so, the Court would permit the Secretary to promulgate precisely the same regulation involved in these cases if he had not relied on a carcinogen "policy," but undertaken a review of the evidence and the expert testimony and concluded, on the basis of conservative assumptions, that the risk addressed is a significant one. Any other interpretation of the plurality's approach would allow a court to displace the agency's judgment with its own subjective conception of "significance," a duty to be performed without statutory guidance.

Notes

1. *What Was Wrong with the Benzene Rule?* According to Justice Stevens, the 1 ppm standard was invalid because OSHA failed to find that exposure to benzene at 10 ppm (the current standard) or below posed a "significant" risk to worker health. This conclusion—that OSHA failed to find a necessary "fact"—can also be understood as a holding that the agency misinterpreted Congress's instructions when it concluded that section 6(b)(5) obliged it to set the lowest feasible standard so long as benzene posed any risk whatever to exposed workers. Indeed, given OSHA's 184–page explanation of its reasoning, based on 50 volumes of testimony and exhibits, it might have been difficult for the Court to overturn the agency's conclusions while accepting its interpretation of the statute. But this account of the Court's opinion makes it difficult to reconcile with *Chevron*—also authored by Justice Stevens four years later—and adds substance to Justice Marshall's charge that the plurality was determined to "write" the statute it believed Congress should have passed. In portions of his dissent that are omitted Marshall argued that the plurality's construction of the statute was contrived and unpersuasive. Assuming that the OSH Act is not so clear that Justice Stevens was entitled to interpret its provisions de novo, his more traditional approach in the benzene case arguably confirms that *Chevron* did indeed represent a shift in judicial deference to agency statutory interpretations.

Although Justice Stevens' opinion strongly suggests that the plurality was influenced by its belief that the benzene rule imposed high costs with limited benefits, a year later the Court held explicitly that OSHA standards regulating toxic chemicals and other "harmful physical agents" under section 6(b)(5)—once the risk is found to be significant—need not show a positive cost-benefit ratio. They need only be shown to be technologically achievable and affordable. *American Textile Manufacturers Inst. v. Donovan*, 452 U.S. 490 (1981) (upholding OSHA's cotton dust standard). But see *International Union, United Automobile, Aerospace & Agricultural Implement Workers of America, UAW v. Occupational Safety and Health Administration*, 938 F.2d 1310 (D.C.Cir.1991) (rejecting OSHA's similar significant risk/feasibility analysis in setting safety standards as an unreasonable interpretation of its authority under another statutory provision).

2. *Benzene Redux*. OSHA reopened the benzene rule in 1983 in light of new epidemiological studies and a completed animal experiment showing carcinogenicity. Following a lengthy attempt at a mediated standard and litigation over delay in issuing a rule, OSHA in 1985 reproposed the same 1 ppm standard that the Supreme Court had earlier rejected, plus a short-term (that is, 15–minute) exposure standard of 5 ppm. Following extensive public comment, informal hearings, and further litigation, OSHA published the 1 ppm standard as a final rule in 1987. After initially filing petitions for judicial review, however, both industry and union challengers withdrew their suits.

In repromulgating its 1 ppm standard for benzene, OSHA asserted and presumably believed that its augmented record would show that worker exposure at levels at and below 10 ppm did pose a significant risk. And the industry challengers presumably concluded that this finding was not likely to be overturned (or possibly they discovered that compliance would cost much less than they had previously claimed). In subsequent post-benzene proceedings to set standards under section 6(b)(5), OSHA has generally accepted the burden of showing that the risk posed by current exposure levels is significant. In one notable instance this proved a difficult challenge. Criticized for its slow pace in regulating worker exposure to toxic chemicals, OSHA in 1988 commenced what it styled a "generic rulemaking" to establish new "permissible exposure limits" or PEL's for over 400 chemicals already subject to regulation. In analyzing the risks posed by current levels of exposure, the agency grouped the chemicals into eight categories defined by the adverse health effects they could cause and then offered categorical conclusions about their risks.

This effort did not satisfy the Eleventh Circuit, which in *AFL–CIO v. OSHA*, 965 F.2d 962 (11th Cir.1992), set aside OSHA's new PEL's because OSHA had not attempted to estimate the magnitude of the risk posed by *each* chemical. The court professed to be willing to accord OSHA a good deal of freedom to interpret meager data and apply conservative assumptions in assessing the risk of individual chemicals, but it insisted that the statute, as interpreted by the Supreme Court in the Benzene case required OSHA to find that current exposure levels of any chemical it proposed to regulate in fact pose a significant risk to worker health. The Department of Justice, reflecting the deregulatory policies of the Bush Administration, declined to permit the filing of a petition for certiorari and the incoming Clinton Administration decided not to pursue the matter. See Daniel A. Graff, *Safe*

Workplaces? Judicial Review of OSHA's Updated Air Contaminant Standards in AFL–CIO v. OSHA, 11 Lab.Law. 151 (1995).

3. *Quantitative Risk Assessment.* The benzene case was the Supreme Court's first encounter with a discipline that now informs much regulatory decision making. "Risk assessment" has not only become an influential analytical tool but has inspired a mushrooming literature, the formation of a national professional society (The Society for Risk Analysis), the establishment of university-based centers and degree programs, as well as congressional proposals for reform of agency rulemaking. The subject is too complex to describe comprehensively here, but a brief introduction to the methodology OSHA initially rejected—and has since embraced—may assist understanding of the case.

In deciding whether to reduce worker exposure to benzene, OSHA was confronted with a paradigmatic dilemma. Scientists had convincing evidence from epidemiological studies—observational studies of exposed populations—that benzene at high levels increased the "natural" or "background" incidence of leukemia. It is important to understand that some workers in almost any work environment would "naturally" experience leukemia even if they were not exposed to benzene. But, as is often the case, the exposures demonstrated to cause leukemia in a few workers were considerably higher than those currently being experienced. It would take a long time to find out, from observing workers currently exposed, whether the levels allowed by the 10 ppm standard would cause any additional cases of leukemia, much less how many.

If OSHA had possessed good information about the levels of exposure that had been shown to cause cancer, it might have been able to construct what is called "dose-response curve" from which it could project the possible increased incidence of cancer at lower levels, levels that had never been tested. But this information was missing, as it often is. A generation ago few companies kept good records of what chemicals their workers were exposed to, much less how much, and the workers themselves had no way of knowing. This problem, too, recurs in the regulation of air and water pollutants, pesticides, and even pharmaceuticals, about whose use and human exposure levels we may think we know more.

Yet OSHA would not accept the industry argument that, because no workers exposed to 10 ppm had been shown to have leukemia, exposures below that level should be assumed safe. This was because, as Justice Stevens pointed out, the agency had concluded—in common with FDA, EPA, and probably even today most scientists—that, for any compound shown capable of causing cancer, no finite safe, or "threshold" dose could be presumed.

In another context, OSHA might have done what EPA and FDA for years have routinely done: They rely on the results of animal experiments (where exposures are carefully controlled and recorded) to supply a numerical basis for extrapolation of those results to humans (while making appropriate adjustments for differences in size). Indeed, in many programs, regulators necessarily rely exclusively on animal experiments to estimate human risk. This is inevitable where Congress has called for regulation before any human exposure to a chemical or product is permitted, as in the case of pesticides and food additives such as saccharin. (Only for humans drugs, which require premarket approval, do we allow testing on humans. In this single instance, we rely on the theory that the patients on whom the drugs are tested have possible therapeutic benefits to gain.) But OSHA did not have the option of relying on experimental results in animals because the few experiments on benzene had not shown it to be carcinogenic at any level.

By 1980, when the benzene case was decided, it had become accepted practice among other federal agencies to attempt quantitative estimates of the risk posed by carcinogenic chemicals at lower levels of exposure than those administered in animal studies or observed in retrospective studies of humans. This was (and is) done using one of a variety of mathematical models that project, from the increased incidence observed at high doses, the risk that might be expected at lower exposure levels—levels in what is termed the "unobserved region" of the dose-response curve. As performed by FDA and EPA, this exercise did not (and does not) ignore the "no threshold" assumption, which is incorporated into all of the models used.

Thus described, quantitative risk assessment for carcinogens may appear to be a straightforward exercise, capable of yielding precise and reliable estimates of the risk posed by chemicals such as benzene. This is quite misleading. The methodology inevitably incorporates a host of assumptions that cannot be proved and relies on data that are almost always incomplete. We do not know, for example, that the "no threshold" assumption holds for many, indeed most, chemicals. It holds for radiation apparently, but few chemicals have been tested sufficiently to confirm its wider application. We do not know that laboratory animals are always good surrogates for humans, or, if two species have been tested, which species should be assumed to be the closer match. We do not know that the dose-response relationship is the same for animals and humans, or the same for humans throughout the range of possible exposures. And we often lack good information about how much of a chemical humans are actually exposed to, so that any estimate of the risk they face is in a real sense speculative. Uncertainty is thus a pervasive characteristic of regulatory risk assessments. But the technique continues to be used because there are no better alternatives.

It seems likely that the Justices were aware of the theoretical possibility of performing a risk assessment for benzene—extrapolating from the high doses shown to cause leukemia to the much lower exposures currently faced by workers. Moreover, as Justice Stevens points out in a footnote, OSHA itself was familiar with the methodology. EPA and FDA declined to support OSHA's refusal to attempt a risk assessment for benzene, believing that, both as a scientific and a political matter, regulators could not simply invoke the "no threshold" assumption to justify reducing exposure to any carcinogen to zero or as close to it as possible. OSHA's reluctance to join them in this view was partly a product of the meager exposure data for benzene (and the lack of good dose-response data from animal studies). But it also reflected an unwillingness to acknowledge publicly that, in deciding how to protect workers from dangerous chemicals, some protective measures might simply be considered too expensive.

From the broader perspective of federal regulation, the Supreme Court's decision was a watershed. Justice Stevens' sage, if indirect, opinion not only confirmed the legitimacy of quantitative risk assessment; it effectively made reliance on the methodology obligatory. In most subsequent disputes over regulatory decisions to protect human health, the question has not been whether a risk assessment was required but whether the assessment offered by the agency was plausible. In this respect, Judge McGowan's opinion in the *Tyson* case, *infra*, and the Fifth Circuit's highly skeptical opinion in *Gulf South Insulation*, *infra*, are illustrative of this focus of judicial review.

The risk assessment literature is voluminous and even a selective listing of references would inevitably be distorted and incomplete. For a lucid and still influential account of quantitative risk assessment for chemical carcinogens, and a penetrating discussion of its numerous uncertainties, see NATIONAL RESEARCH COUNCIL RISK ASSESSMENT IN THE FEDERAL GOVERNMENT: MANAGING THE PROCESS (1983).

Review of Regulatory Decisions Made in the Face of Uncertainty

The benzene case illustrates the challenges of judicial review of agency decisions that rest on a resolution of complex issues, where the limitations of current knowledge leave substantial uncertainties. Judge Carl McGowan recognized this problem in *Industrial Union Department, AFL–CIO v. Hodgson*, 499 F.2d 467, 473–76 (D.C.Cir.1974), an unsuccessful challenge to OSHA's first health standard, for asbestos:

> One question generated by [the statute's provision for substantial evidence review] * * * is whether the determinations in question here are of the kind to which substantial evidence review can appropriately be applied.
>
> From extensive and often conflicting evidence, the Secretary in this case made numerous factual determinations. With respect to some of those questions, the evidence was such that the task consisted primarily of evaluating the data and drawing conclusions from it. The court can review that data in the record and determine whether it reflects substantial support for the Secretary's findings. But some of the questions involved in the promulgation of these standards are on the frontiers of scientific knowledge, and consequently as to them insufficient data is presently available to make a fully informed factual determination. Decision making must in that circumstance depend to a greater extent upon policy judgments and less upon purely factual analysis. * * *
>
> * * *
>
> Regardless of the manner in which the task of judicial review is articulated, policy choices of this sort are not susceptible to the same type of verification or refutation by reference to the record as are some factual questions. Consequently, the court's approach must necessarily be different no matter how the standards of review are labeled. * * *

* * *

> What we are entitled to at all events is a careful identification by the Secretary, when his proposed standards are challenged, of the reasons why he chooses to follow one course rather than another. Where that choice purports to be based on the existence of certain determinable facts, the Secretary must, in form as well as substance, find those facts from evidence in the record. By the same token, when the Secretary is obliged to make policy judgments where no factual certainties exist or where facts alone do not provide the answer, he should so state and go on to identify the considerations he found persuasive.

Judge McGowan's opinion was just one early chapter in a continuing dialogue among the judges on the D.C. Circuit about the appropriate intensity and focus of judicial review of decisions that rested heavily on scientific evidence and judgment.

Ethyl Corp. v. EPA, 541 F.2d 1 (D.C.Cir.), *cert. denied*, 426 U.S. 941 (1976), involved a challenge to EPA regulations requiring a step-wise reduction in the lead content of gasoline. The Clean Air Act authorized the EPA Administrator to promulgate regulations controlling or prohibiting the manufacture, distribution, or sale of "any fuel or fuel additive for use in a * * * motor vehicle engine * * * if any emission products of such fuel or fuel additive will endanger the public health or welfare." 42 U.S.C. § 1857f–6c(c)(1)(A), now incorporated and revised in 42 U.S.C. § 7545(c). In interpreting the statutory phrase "will endanger," Judge Wright endorsed and elaborated Judge McGowan's *Hodgson* analysis of the requisite factual support for an agency's disposition of unresolvable scientific questions:

> Where a statute is precautionary in nature, the evidence difficult to come by, uncertain, or conflicting because it is on the frontiers of scientific knowledge, the regulations designed to protect the public health, and the decision that of an expert administrator, we will not demand rigorous step-by-step proof of cause and effect. Such proof may be impossible to obtain if the precautionary purpose of the statute is to be served. Of course, we are not suggesting that the Administrator has the power to act on hunches or wild guesses. * * * He must take account of available facts, of course, but his inquiry does not end there. The Administrator may apply his expertise to draw conclusions from suspected, but not completely substantiated, relationships between facts, from trends among facts, from theoretical projections from imperfect data, from probative preliminary data not yet certifiable as "fact," and the like. * * *

Judge Wright's majority opinion in *Ethyl*, however, goes one step beyond *Hodgson* by explicitly freeing the agency, in areas on the frontiers of scientific knowledge, from "the procedural [as well as] the substantive rigor proper for questions of fact." At the same time Judge Wright emphasized that his approach still contemplated a substantial role for reviewing courts. His majority opinion and Judge Wilkey's dissent filled more than thirty-eight pages of the Federal Reporter with conflicting analyses of the scientific evidence bearing on the health hazards of lead additives to gasoline. "The more technical the case," Judge Wright observed, "the more intensive must be the court's effort to understand the evidence, for without an appropriate understanding of the case before it the court cannot properly perform its appellate function."

In a concurring opinion Chief Judge Bazelon took issue with the latter suggestion. He offered an alternative approach:

> I agree with the court's construction of the statute that the Administrator is called upon to make "essentially legislative policy judgments" in assessing risks to public health. But I cannot agree that this automatically relieves the Administrator's decision from the "procedural * * * rigor proper for questions of fact." Quite the contrary, this case strengthens my view that
>
> > * * * in cases of great technological complexity, the best way for courts to guard against unreasonable or erroneous administrative decisions is not for the judges themselves to scrutinize the technical merits of each decision. Rather, it is to establish a decision-making process that assures a reasoned decision that can be held up to the scrutiny of the scientific community and the public.
>
> This record provides vivid demonstration of the dangers implicit in the contrary view * * * which would have judges "steeping" themselves "in technical matters to determine whether the agency 'has exercised a reasoned discretion.'" It is one thing for judges to scrutinize FCC judgments concerning diversification of media ownership to determine if they are rational. But I doubt judges contribute much to improving the quality of the difficult decisions which must be made in highly technical areas when they take it upon themselves to decide, as did the panel in this case, that "in assessing the scientific and medical data the Administrator made clear errors of judgment." The process of making a de novo evaluation of the scientific evidence inevitably invites judges of opposing views to make plausible-sounding, but simplistic, judgments of the relative weight to be afforded various pieces of technical data. * * *
>
> Because substantive review of mathematical and scientific evidence by technically illiterate judges is dangerously unreliable, I continue to believe we will do more to improve administrative decision-making by concentrating our efforts on strengthening administrative procedures. * * *

In a separate statement, Judge Harold Leventhal responded:

> * * * Congress has been willing to delegate its legislative powers broadly—and courts have upheld such delegation—because there is court review to assure that the agency exercises the delegated power within statutory limits, and that it fleshes out objectives

within those limits by an administration that is not irrational or discriminatory. * * *

Our present system of review assumes judges will acquire whatever technical knowledge is necessary as background for decision of the legal questions. It may be that some judges are not initially equipped for this role, just as they may not be technically equipped initially to decide issues of obviousness and infringement in patent cases. If technical difficulties loom large, Congress may push to establish specialized courts. Thus far, it has proceeded on the assumption that we can both have the important values secured by generalist judges and rely on them to acquire whatever technical background is necessary. * * *

* * * Once the presumption of regularity in agency action is challenged with a factual submission, and even to determine whether such a challenge has been made, the agency's record and reasoning has to be looked at. If there is some factual support for the challenge, there must either be evidence or judicial notice available explicating the agency's result, or a remand to supply the gap.

While Judge Leventhal may be correct in suggesting that judicial abdication of substantive review cannot be reconciled with the APA, one may still question whether federal judges are equipped to reexamine an agency's resolution of complex scientific questions. The difficulty of combining the deference and skepticism that seems called for is captured in *American Petroleum Institute v. EPA*, 661 F.2d 340, 349 (5th Cir. 1981):

In summary, we must accord the agency considerable, but not too much deference; it is entitled to exercise its discretion, but only so far and no further; and its decision need not be ideal or even, perhaps, correct so long as not "arbitrary" or "capricious" and so long as the agency gave at least minimal consideration to the relevant facts as contained in the record.

The Supreme Court's decision in *Vermont Yankee*, excerpted in Chapter 5, *supra*, discouraged, and apparently was intended to discourage, Judge Bazelon's desire to concentrate judicial efforts "on strengthening administrative procedures." It is more difficult to assess whether reviewing courts have, as a group, seized Judge Leventhal's challenge to become intimately familiar with the substance underlying agency decisions. Advocates for either view can find examples to support their account. Judge McGowan had occasion to revisit OSHA's discharge of its responsibilities in *Public Citizen Health Research Group v. Tyson*, 796 F.2d 1479 (D.C.Cir.1986), which upheld OSHA's standard for long-term worker exposure to ethylene oxide. In an opinion that closely tracked the agency's reasoning, McGowan upheld the standard against attacks on virtually every intermediate conclusion reflected in the agency's risk assessment:

AEOU attacks each piece of evidence, suggesting that no individual piece proves a relationship between EtO exposure and various adverse health effects. This approach disregards the marginal contribution that each piece of evidence makes to the total picture. While some of OSHA's evidence suffers from shortcomings, such incomplete proof is inevitable when the Agency regulates on the frontiers of scientific knowledge.

* * * OSHA need not "prove" its assertions in the manner AEOU demands. * * * Rather, OSHA need only gather evidence from which it can reasonably draw the conclusion it has reached. We in no way denigrate the "searching and careful" nature of our inquiry. Our function, however, is only to search for substantial evidence, not proof positive. * * *

* * * When the evidence can be reasonably interpreted as supporting the need for regulation, we must affirm the agency's conclusion, despite the fact that the same evidence is susceptible of another interpretation.

Gulf South Insulation v. U.S. Consumer Product Safety Commission, 701 F.2d 1137 (5th Cir.1983), provides an extreme contrasting example, and arguably illustrates the potential pitfalls of Judge Leventhal's approach in less adept hands. There the court struck down for, among other reasons, lack of factual foundation a CPSC ban on urea formaldehyde foam insulation. The Commission had based its decision on the results of a state-of-the-art animal experiment conducted at the Chemical Industry Institute of Toxicology (CIIT), which found that formaldehyde fumes caused nasal cancer in mice. The agency, with the endorsement of an inter-agency group of scientists, extrapolated this result to humans housed in UF foam-insulated homes and concluded that the risk they faced was unreasonable. The Fifth Circuit had this to say about the agency's reliance on the animal test data:

While the Commission correctly notes that the epidemiologic evidence is not conclusive, its exclusive reliance on the Chemical Institute study in its Global 79 [the extrapolation model used] risk assessment is equally unsupportable. * * * [I]n a study as small as this one [240 rats exposed for 24 months] the margin of error is inherently large. For example, had 20 fewer rats, or 20 more, developed carcinomas, the risk predicted by Global 79 would be altered drastically.

* * * The Federal Panel's findings that the Chemical Institute study was valid and that formaldehyde should be presumed to pose a cancer risk to man do not authenticate the use of the study's results, and only those results, to predict exactly the cancer risk UFFI poses to man. As Dr. Higginson aptly stated, it is not good science to rely on a single experiment, particularly one involving only 240 subjects, to make precise estimates of cancer risk.

And in a footnote, the court offered these additional comments on the CPSC risk assessment:

> At least two of the assumptions are of questionable validity. The Commission assumed that at identical exposure levels the effective dose for rats is the same as that for humans. The industry points out that the effective dose for mice is much less than that for rats and argues that it is far more sensible to assume that rats equal mice than that rats equal humans.
>
> Probably the most controversial assumption incorporated into Global 79 is that the risk of cancer from formaldehyde is linear at low dose—in other words that there is no threshold below which formaldehyde poses no risk of cancer. As the Commission acknowledges, this assumption leads inescapably to the conclusion that ambient air is carcinogenic, albeit to a lesser extent than UFFI.

Debate over the courts' handling of scientific evidence, in civil litigation as well as in the context of reviewing agency fact-finding, has if anything intensified since the Supreme Court's famous "benzene" decision. A cascade of civil suits seeking damages for disease assertedly caused by consumer products, chemicals, and industrial wastes has confronted the courts with disputes over the kind of evidence necessary to prove both that a substance can cause disease and probably did cause the plaintiff's disease. This issue reached the Supreme Court in a case in which the parents of a deformed child sued the maker of a drug, Bendectin, that the mother had taken during pregnancy. Accepting arguments advanced by the National Academy of Sciences and the American Association for the Advancement of Science, among others, the Court in *Daubert v. Merrell Dow Pharmaceuticals*, 509 U.S. 579 (1993), ruled that, to be admissible in federal court, an expert's testimony had to meet the standards for acceptance within the scientific community. And, to implement this limitation, the Court instructed federal trial judges to undertake a careful screening of proffered evidence before allowing its introduction and evaluation by a jury.

The Supreme Court reaffirmed this ruling in *General Electric Co. v. Joiner,* 522 U.S. 136 (1997), and later extended it to expert engineering testimony in *Kumho Tire Co. v. Carmichael*, 526 U.S. 137 (1999). The Court's so-called *Daubert* trilogy has significantly affected the conduct of toxic tort suits in the federal courts and in the many states that have accepted its teachings, directly or by adopting the Federal Rules of Evidence. See Margaret A. Berger, *Upsetting the Balance Between Adverse Interests: The Impact of the Supreme Court's Trilogy on Expert Testimony in Toxic Tort Litigation,* 64 Law & Contemp. Probs. 289 (2001); Michael D. Green, *The Road Less Well–Traveled (and Seen): Contemporary Lawmaking in Products Liability,* 49 DePaul L. Rev. 377 (1999). Trial courts clearly are devoting more attention to screening scientific evidence. Some observers contend that the *Daubert* trilogy has tilted the playing field in tort cases in favor of defendants. See Lucinda M. Finley, *Guarding the Gate to the Courthouse: How Trial Judges Are Using Their Evidentiary Screening Role to Remake Tort Causation Rules,* 49 DePaul L. Rev. 335 (1999); Michael H. Graham, *Gatekeeping*

Test of Daubert, Kumho, *and Proposed Amended Rule 702 of the Federal Rules of Evidence,* 54 Miami L. Rev. 317 (2000).

The controversies kindled by *Daubert* have unquestionably dominated scholarly criticism of the legal system's handling of scientific evidence, but debate about the capacity of regulatory agencies to process such evidence expertly and objectively has not abated. The pages devoted to this subject in the past generation would fill a large library. See STEPHEN BREYER, BREAKING THE VICIOUS CIRCLE: TOWARD EFFECTIVE RISK REGULATION (1993); Lester B. Lave, *Does the Surgeon General Need a Statistics Advisor?* in CHANCE: NEW DIRECTIONS FOR STATISTICS AND COMPUTING 33 (1990); W. KIP VISCUSI, FATAL TRADEOFFS: PUBLIC AND PRIVATE RESPONSIBILITIES FOR RISK 263–65 (1992); Sam Kazman, *Death by Regulation,* 14(4) Regulation 18 (1991); Janet L. McQuaid, Note, *Risk Assessment of Hazardous Air Pollutants Under the EPA's Final Benzene Rules and the Clean Air Act Amendments of 1990,* 70 Tex. L. Rev. 427 (1991); Leslie Roberts, *Counting on Science at EPA*, 249 Science 616 (1990). Within this literature several themes recur. One relates to the professional qualifications of agency personnel, and expresses itself in recommendations for increased staffing and the rewarding of scientific talent, as well as strong support for the role of advisory committees composed of experts drawn from outside the government. See the discussion of the Federal Advisory Committee Act, Chapter 2 *supra.* See also STEPHEN BREYER, BREAKING THE VICIOUS CIRCLE: TOWARD EFFECTIVE RISK REGULATION 59–68 (1993); SHELIA JASANOFF, THE FIFTH BRANCH: SCIENCE ADVISORS AS POLICYMAKERS 4–9, 39–57 (1990); NATIONAL RESEARCH COUNCIL, RISK ASSESSMENT IN THE FEDERAL GOVERNMENT: MANAGING THE PROCESS 151–175 (National Academy Press 1983); Sheila Jasanoff, *Procedural Choices in Regulatory Science,* 4 Risk: Issues in Health & Safety 143 (1993), available at http://www.fplc.edu/risk/vol4/spring/jasanoff.htm.

A second theme is exemplified by two recent pieces of legislation, each buried in appropriations bills enacted in the waning hours of a Congress. The so-called Shelby Amendment, Omnibus Consolidated and Emergency Supplemental Appropriations Act, 1999, Pub. L. No. 105–277, 112 Stat. 2681–495 (1998), and the Data Quality Act, Treasury and General Government Appropriations Act for Fiscal Year 2001, § 515, Pub. L. No. 106–554, 114 Stat. 2763 (2000), are designed to enable critics of information—including, prominently, scientific information relied on or disseminated by government—to probe its origins and accuracy and, if appropriate, demand its retraction or correction. The Shelby Amendment, which bears the name of the Alabama Senator who sponsored its enactment, obligates government agencies to disclose, under the Freedom of Information Act, the raw data generated by researchers funded by federal dollars whose published results become a basis for regulatory action—not necessarily, or indeed ordinarily, action by the agency that funded the research. This "mandatory discovery" statute was a response to EPA's reliance on a famous study of the health effects of air pollution, which had been conducted (using federal funds) at the Harvard School of Public Health. Opponents of a proposed EPA rule demanded access to the researchers' supporting data, collected over several years under a promise of confidentiality. The opponents hoped to expose the researchers' biases and mistakes. EPA declined to provide the data, which it did not possess, and the researchers, too, refused access, citing their pledge of confidentiality.

Proponents of the Shelby Amendment sought to fill this "gap" in administrative procedural law. On its face the amendment would appear to allow any person to demand access to the data generated or collected as part of any federally funded research project, whether or not the reported results were relied on in regulatory decision making. The alarm voiced by spokespersons for university-based research led OMB to publish a narrowed interpretation which effectively limits "Shelby access" to research relied on to support regulatory action. Guidelines for Ensuring and Maximizing the Quality, Objectivity, Utility, and Integrity of Information Disseminated by Federal Agencies; Republication, 67 Fed. Reg. 8452 (Feb. 22, 2002). Thus far, the amendment has been invoked infrequently.

The Data Quality Act has a much broader reach than Shelby. It applies to all executive branch agencies and it covers all information that they "disseminate," for any purpose. Furthermore, its obligations attach regardless of whether or not any agency seeks or intends to make use of the information to support regulation. The Act's key requirements are two: An agency must establish and follow internal procedures to assure the reliability, objectivity, and quality of any information it disseminates. And it must afford an opportunity for any private party who disputes the accuracy, objectivity, or quality of disseminated information to seek its correction or withdrawal. Some believe that the Data Quality Act was authored by the same former OMB official who claims to have inspired Shelby and was likewise aimed at EPA, specifically that agency's implementation of the Superfund provision that obligates the agency to publish an annual account of pollutants released into the environment by industrial sources. See Frederick R. Anderson, *Data Quality Act,* Nat'l L. J., Oct. 14, 2002, at 1; *New Data Quality Law Could Challenge Agency Assessments,* Risk Pol'y Rep., Mar. 19, 2001, at 4; *Agencies 'Adapt' Data Quality Act Guidelines, available at http://www.ombwatch.org/article/articleprint/740/-1/39.*

One other proposal for "reforming" agency analyses of scientific evidence has gathered endorsements recently, though it has not yet attracted judicial acceptance or legislative codification. Drawing on *Daubert's* apparent demand for "good science" in civil litigation, Alan Raul and others have argued that the principle should be extended to the administrative arena. Their proposal is not addressed to formal agency adjudication, the administrative process most analogous to a civil trial, but to the courts before which agency decisions (rules as well as orders) are challenged. Raul wants reviewing courts to apply the same rigorous standards to agency factual determinations as *Daubert* directs trial judges to apply in screening proffered expert testimony. See Alan Charles Raul & Julie M. Zampa, *Deeper Judicial Scrutiny Needed for*

Agencies' Use of Science, 24 No. 7 Andrews Asbestos Litig. Rep. 9 (Feb. 28, 2002); Nancy S. Bryson & Richard J. Mannix, *Good Science, Junk Science, and Regulatory Science: Is There a Role for the* Daubert *Guidelines in Administrative Rulemaking?*, 8 Envtl. Qual. Mgmt. 89 (1998); Charles D. Weller & David B. Graham, *New Approaches to Environmental Law and Agency Regulation: The* Daubert *Litigation Approach,* 30 Envtl. L. Rep. 10557, 10568 (July 2000).

The Supreme Court's benzene decision spawned a vast body of commentary, much of it focused on the historical accuracy of the majority's interpretation of the OSH Act. Like Colin S. Diver, in *Policymaking Paradigms in Administrative Law*, 95 Harv.L.Rev. 393 (1981), however, William H. Rodgers, Jr., saw in the case broader lessons about the relationship between courts and agencies.

WILLIAM H. RODGERS, JR., JUDICIAL REVIEW OF RISK ASSESSMENTS: THE ROLE OF DECISION THEORY IN UNSCRAMBLING THE BENZENE DECISION

11 Envtl. L. 301 (1981).

There are three prominent contenders for the most suitable descriptive theory of contemporary administrative decisionmaking. * * * The first is what may be called the classical theory, which views the administrator as a surrogate for the legislative policymaker. Rulemaking, under this view, is a free-wheeling and many-splendored process in which the administrator reaches out for information from any source—hearings, libraries, whispers in the hall. Decisionmaking is perceived to be intuitive, involving as it does horsetrading among the interests and the deft balancing of value choices. * * *

A second model, in many ways the converse of the first, could be called the rational or formal model of administrative decisionmaking. * * * These [various] decision methods to a large degree depend upon the identification of alternatives, the projection of consequences, and the conscious selection of a "best" decision. * * *

* * * A decision is not a negotiated bill of accord, with a little bit here and there for the prominent interests and bearing the stamp of consensus; it is perceived as correct and definitive, carefully developed and imposed. * * *

A third, and now eminently popular, theory of administrative decisionmaking is the theory of successive limited comparisons, known less elegantly as the science of muddling through. This is my own nominee, in essential particulars, for the theory best capturing the realities of how agencies decide. * * * Like the classicists, the muddlers reach out to the interest groups and engage them in negotiation and searches for common criteria, or at least agreed-upon processes. They are similarly familiar, however, with the techniques and methods of formal decisionmaking, although the data which is received is altered and shaped to take into account financial, informational, administrative, and political limits. * * *

The choice of administrative decisionmaking models and their legislative counterparts strongly influences one's normative perceptions of appropriate judicial review. Acceptance of the classical free-wheeling agency model begets a mild regime of review. Administrative knowhow, and ergo judicial deference, extends even to the reading of the legislative charter and the interpretation to be accorded legal terms. * * *

By contrast, the assumption that agency decisionmakers are supposed to be rational in the strictest sense of the term encourages a regime of close judicial scrutiny. If the goal is an ideal "best" decision, departures from standards of perfection are viewed with intolerance. Interpretation of the legislative charter should be closely supervised as this charter sets the ultimate bounds of the formal inquiry undertaken. * * * There is little judicial tolerance for political balancing or policy guesswork from the agencies, for the results are supposed to be scientifically derived, and whatever the meaning of the scientific method, it is thought to yield results supportable by evidence and to differ sharply from political tradeoff.

* * * Procedural oversight and interest representation are also important because of the strong process orientation of strategic decisionmaking. Explanations of what was done and why must be demanded by the courts to protect against the dangers of subjectivity associated with incremental decisions under uncertain criteria. The essence of the contemporary hard look doctrine of judicial review is to compel explanations of methodology and identification of the criteria for judgment. * * *

* * * Justice Stevens' plurality opinion [in the benzene case] comes close to adopting the rational decisionmaking model, and demonstrates the vulnerability of that model to judicial nitpicking over evidentiary gaps in the record supporting the supposedly ideal decision. * * * Justice Powell comes down somewhere between the muddling and the rational decisionmaking model, honoring the agency's ability to make predictive judgments but finding insubstantial evidence to support the conclusion that the risk perceived was a significant one. The dissenters are probably believers in muddling, and the analysis adopted is consistent with that theory. Justice Marshall's opinion, however, together with the Stevens and Powell opinions, makes clear that the choice of theory does not automatically dictate results. Courts overseeing administrative muddlers must distinguish between explanations, which are sharply scrutinized, and predictive judgments to which deference is owed. * * *

C. THE AVAILABILITY OF JUDICIAL REVIEW

1. INTRODUCTION

Statutory and Nonstatutory Review. Overton Park confirms that judicial review of administrative action is presumptively available, but the presumption is rebuttable. Indeed, the structure and operational premises of our judicial system pose recurring issues of when, where, and by whom judicial review may be secured. In part, the issues are rooted in the Constitution. Article III sets the outer limits of federal judicial authority, and the Court has derived from its restrictions certain principles of standing that limit the parties who may invoke the federal courts' power. Moreover, the "sovereign immunity" of the United States against being sued without its consent is long established. *Cohens v. Commonwealth of Virginia,* 19 U.S. (6 Wheat.) 264 (1821). But the issues are also statutory. The lower federal courts are courts of limited jurisdiction and entirely of Congress' creation. Any litigant who desires to challenge the action of a federal agency or official in federal court must thus be able to demonstrate that some statute authorizes the court to hear the case. Statutes likewise establish the terms on which Congress agrees to waive the government's sovereign immunity from suit.

In many cases, these threshold issues provoke little controversy. For example, if a party is challenging the legality of federal action by way of defense in an enforcement proceeding, the government's initiation of suit has usually (but not always) answered the questions whether the parties have sufficiently adverse interests to create a "case" under Article III, and whether now is an appropriate time to challenge the legality of the agency's action. Likewise, if a litigant is a named party to an agency proceeding that has resulted in adverse agency action against that litigant, whether that litigant is an appropriate challenger to the agency's order is not likely to be questioned.

Beyond such cases, the degree of difficulty posed by threshold issues of judicial power and the way they are analyzed will vary according to the statutory framework within which a judicial challenge is brought. For example, many regulatory statutes purport explicitly to provide particular parties a right to challenge the legality of agency action taken pursuant to that statute. In these cases of so-called "specific statutory review," an agency may, of course, question whether *this* litigant is within the class of parties Congress has authorized to sue or whether the litigant has complied with statutory limits on the venue or timing of suit. Those questions will be answered based on judicial interpretation of the intent underlying the explicit grant of a right of review. The specific statutory review provision, however, will generally be regarded as conferring jurisdiction and waiving sovereign immunity for any suit within its purview.

With respect to certain agency functions, however, an agency's organic act or program statute may say nothing about judicial review. Courts may still have authority to review actions under those statutes, because the APA provides, with certain exceptions: "A person suffering legal wrong because of agency action, or adversely affected or aggrieved by agency action, is entitled to judicial review thereof," 5 U.S.C. § 702, and, "final agency action for which there is no other adequate remedy in a court [is] subject to judicial review," 5 U.S.C. § 704. Review pursuant to these provisions—sometimes inaptly termed "nonstatutory review"—

does require threshold determinations whether the suit is one over which the litigant's chosen court has jurisdiction, whether sovereign immunity bars suit, whether the action is appropriately timed, and whether the litigant has standing to sue. What makes the phrase "nonstatutory review" inapt, of course, is that each of these questions requires recourse to *some* statute for its answer, usually at least the APA plus the provisions of the U.S. Code establishing the relevant category of federal court jurisdiction. Yet the doctrine courts have constructed in interpreting these statutes has a strong common law flavor.

Jurisdiction. In the federal system, suits for injunctive relief or declaratory judgment conventionally serve as the primary vehicles for relief against unlawful agency action. Such suits typically begin in U.S. district court under 28 U.S.C. § 1331, which confers original jurisdiction over claims "arising under federal law." Because that statute no longer demands that at least $10,000 be in controversy, it is not generally necessary to invoke other statutes that also confer jurisdiction without regard to amount in controversy, e.g., over claims involving acts of Congress regulating commerce, 28 U.S.C. § 1337, or for the protection of civil rights, 28 U.S.C. § 1343(4). This is not to deny, however, that the interpretation of the "arising under" language of § 1331 has triggered extensive litigation. For a comprehensive review, see PETER W. LOW & JOHN C. JEFFRIES, FEDERAL COURTS AND THE LAW OF FEDERAL-STATE RELATIONS 450–76 (4th ed. 1998).

Readers should not make the still-common mistake of assuming that the broad language of the APA itself establishes federal court jurisdiction. The Supreme Court has had occasion, as recently as 1999, to reiterate its long-standing position that the APA is not a grant of subject-matter jurisdiction. See *Your Home Visiting Nurse Services, Inc. v. Shalala*, 525 U.S. 449, 457–58 (1999); *Califano v. Sanders*, 430 U.S. 99 (1977).

There is a further possibility that once a litigant presents a colorable claim over which jurisdiction clearly exists, the court will treat other claims, not independently within its jurisdiction, as "pendent." See, *e.g.*, *Hagans v. Lavine*, 415 U.S. 528 (1974). But, note that an action for declaratory relief cannot be used as an independent basis for "appending" other claims because the Declaratory Judgments Act authorizes that form of relief only where the claim is otherwise within the court's jurisdiction. 28 U.S.C. § 2201.

While the jurisprudence elaborating the exceptions to "presumptive" review can be complex and confusing, a great advantage of the current statutory structure is that it spares litigants the arcane difficulties of the writ system. Although the "great writ," habeas corpus, has a venerable role in the federal courts, other prerogative writs have had inauspicious histories. One explanation is the generally flexible use of injunctions by federal courts, coupled with the generous authorization of specific statutory review. In addition, writs commonly pursued in the state courts, certiorari and mandamus, have been narrowly confined by the federal courts. See *Degge v. Hitchcock*, 229 U.S. 162 (1913); *United States ex rel. McLennan v. Wilbur*, 283 U.S. 414, 420 (1931). Moreover, before 1962, federal courts outside of the District of Columbia lacked jurisdiction to issue either writ. See generally Clark Byse and Joseph V. Fiocca, *Section 1361 of the Mandamus and Venue Act of 1962 and "Nonstatutory" Judicial Review of Federal Administrative Action*, 81 Harv.L.Rev. 308 (1967).

Sovereign Immunity. Stated in formal terms, sovereign immunity means simply that the sovereign (read "the government") may not be sued without its consent. But as a doctrine, its history is cloudy and its rationale obscure. In *United States v. Lee*, 106 U.S. 196, 207 (1882), Justice Miller observed that "the principle has never been discussed or the reasons for it given, but it has always been treated as an established doctrine." Moreover, despite the vitriolic criticism of sovereign immunity by academics and others, the Supreme Court has never been willing to "disestablish" the doctrine. See *Larson v. Domestic and Foreign Commerce Corp.*, 337 U.S. 682, 704 (1949), holding that the government should not be "stopped in its tracks by any plaintiff who presents a disputed question." At that level of generality, the *Larson* case almost suggests a general presumption against judicial review.

But this was not the reality of judicial review, even when *Larson* was decided in 1949. As Kenneth Culp Davis later noted:

> The plain, clear, visible reality is, as no one knows better than the Supreme Court Justices, that courts including the Supreme Court are constantly interfering with the public administration and constantly stopping the government in its tracks. Many of the great constitutional decisions throughout our history have stopped the government in its tracks and have interfered in public administration.

Kenneth Culp Davis, Administrative Law Treatise, § 27.00–7 at 915 (1970 Supp.). That "reality" was made possible by the legal fiction that a suit against the *official* was not a suit against the *government* barred by sovereign immunity. Yet, as the *Larson* case itself noted, the fiction could be exposed. Suit could be entertained only to the extent that it was not "really against the government" or where the challenged action could be described as either "unconstitutional" or completely outside the official's authority or jurisdiction (*ultra vires*).

The effort to determine whether suits were "really against the government" and the interpretive conundra that resulted from attempts to distinguish between *ultra vires* and merely illegal action produced a chaotic jurisprudence. See Roger O. Cramton, *Nonstatutory Review of Federal Administrative Action: The Need for Statutory Reform of Sovereign Immunity, Subject Matter Jurisdiction, and Parties Defendant*, 68 Mich.L.Rev. 387, 392 (1970). Congress came to the rescue in 1976, Pub.L.No. 94–574, 90 Stat. 2721, by amending APA § 702 to include the following language:

> An action in a court of the United States seeking relief other than money damages and stating a claim that an agency or an officer or employee thereof acted or failed to act in an official capacity or under color of legal authority shall not be dismissed nor relief therein be denied on the ground that it is against the United States or that the United States is an indispensable party. The United States may be named as a defendant in any such action, and a judgment or decree may be entered against the United States.

This clear waiver for claims, other than those for "money damages," now ordinarily eliminates the barrier of sovereign immunity where a plaintiff seeks the standard public law remedies of injunction or declaratory judgment.

Accordingly, in the modern legal environment, it can be presumed that most final decisions of federal administrators are subject to judicial review in some court, at some time. The ubiquitously-cited *Overton Park* decision and *Abbott Laboratories*, *infra* p. 961, are the cornerstones of the prevailing judicial posture. Litigants may proceed under specific statutory review provisions, through "nonstatutory" review suits, and by way of defense in enforcement actions, without confronting initial and theoretically absolute barriers to review. The remaining barriers are largely those functional and prudential limits thought (by courts) necessary to maintain appropriate separation of powers, to promote administrative efficiency, and to prevent a multiplicity of judicial proceedings. Yet, even in a contemporary jurisprudence whose intellectual style is purposive and policy-oriented, we shall encounter limitations on or barriers to judicial review that are reminiscent of the jurisprudence of sovereign immunity and limited federal question jurisdiction.

2. REVIEWABILITY

a. Statutory Preclusion

Section 701(a) of the APA declares that the Act's judicial review provisions apply "except to the extent that—(1) statutes preclude judicial review; or (2) agency action is committed to agency discretion by law." The APA thus recognizes that Congress, or perhaps a court, may appropriately decide that *some* agency actions should not be subject to judicial reexamination.

Language in federal statutes purporting to *bar* judicial review of final administrative decisions is uncommon. Indeed, the prevalent pattern in modern federal regulatory and social legislation is to describe the availability and terms of judicial review in copious detail. However, congressional efforts to *limit* or *channel* review are not unusual, and every statute that provides for review also raises issues of exclusivity, i.e., of implied "preclusion" of review by other routes.

Congressional channelling of challenges to administrative action or limits on judicial oversight of what might be considered internal decision making requirements do not weaken the general edifice of presumptive review. Occasionally, however, Congress has attempted to bar judicial review of specific types of decisions altogether. For their part courts have generally resisted these efforts, as a series of decisions under the laws providing benefits to military veterans illustrates.

In *Tracy v. Gleason*, 379 F.2d 469 (D.C.Cir.1967), the estate of a deceased veteran sought review of a Veterans Administration determination that the decedent was not entitled to disability benefits for the years 1949–1960. The VA had paid Tracy benefits through 1949 before terminating them because of his failure to file an income form. The VA's notice of termination had been sent to St. Elizabeth's Hospital where, as its records showed, Tracy had been confined since 1936 suffering from severe mental illness. No member of Tracy's family knew about his eligibility for benefits until 1960. When the VA refused payment for the intervening eleven years, Tracy's family brought suit. The district court granted the VA's motion to dismiss for lack of jurisdiction, relying on 38 U.S.C. § 211(a), which then provided:

> [T]he decision of the Administrator on any question of law or fact concerning a claim for benefits * * * shall be final and conclusive and no other official or any court of the United States shall have power or jurisdiction to review any such decision.

The court of appeals avoided this statutory bar to review. It reasoned that the dispute did not grow out of a disposition of a "claim" but rather was the result of an action by the VA Administrator to terminate benefits previously conferred: "[A]fter the claim has been allowed and benefits have been awarded, there is, strictly speaking, no longer a mere claim which the Administrator may unreviewably reject if he chooses. The veteran is then * * * a *beneficiary*, and the Administrator's subsequent termination of his benefits should not be immune from judicial scrutiny * * *. [C]ertainly, [Congress] did not so provide in § 211(a)."

Three years later, in response to *Tracy*, Congress amended 38 U.S.C. § 211(a) to read:

> On and after October 17, 1940 * * * the decisions of the Administrator [of Veterans' Affairs] on any question of law or fact under any law administered by the Veterans' Administration providing benefits for veterans and their dependents or survivors shall be final and conclusive and no other official or any court of the United States shall have power or jurisdiction to review any such decision by an action in the nature of mandamus or otherwise.

JOHNSON v. ROBISON

Supreme Court of the United States, 1974.
415 U.S. 361, 94 S.Ct. 1160, 39 L.Ed.2d 389.

JUSTICE BRENNAN delivered the opinion of the Court.

A draftee accorded Class I–O conscientious objector status and completing performance of required alternative civilian service does not qualify under 38 U.S.C. * * * 1652(a)(1) as a "veteran who * * * served on active duty" * * *, and is therefore not an "eligible veteran" entitled under 38 U.S.C. § 1661(a) to veterans' educational benefits provided by the Veterans' Readjustments Benefits Act of 1966. Appellants, the Administration and the Administrator of Veterans' Affairs, for that reason, denied the application for educational assistance of appellee Robison, a conscientious objector who filed his application after he satisfactorily completed two years of alternative civilian service at the Peter Bent Brigham Hospital, Boston. Robison thereafter commenced this class action * * * seeking a declaratory judgment that 38 U.S.C. §§ 101(21), 1652(a)(1), and 1661(a), read together, violated the First Amendment's guarantee of religious freedom and the Fifth Amendment's guarantee of equal protection of the laws. * * *

We consider first appellants' contention that § 211(a) bars federal courts from deciding the constitutionality of veterans' benefits legislation. Such a construction would, of course, raise serious questions concerning the constitutionality of § 211(a),[8] and in such case "it is a cardinal principle that this Court will first ascertain whether a construction of the statute is fairly possible by which the [constitutional] question[s] may be avoided."

Plainly, no explicit provision of § 211(a) bars judicial consideration of appellee's constitutional claims. * * * The prohibitions would appear to be aimed at review only of those decisions of law or fact that arise in the *administration* by the Veterans' Administration of a *statute* providing benefits for veterans. A decision of law or fact "under" a statute is made by the Administrator in the interpretation or application of a particular provision of the statute to a particular set of facts. Appellee's constitutional challenge is not to any such decision of the *Administrator*, but rather to a decision of *Congress* to create a statutory class entitled to benefits that does not include I–O conscientious objectors who performed alternative civilian service. * * *

* * * No-review clauses similar to § 211(a) have been a part of veterans' benefits legislation since 1933. While the legislative history accompanying these precursor no-review clauses is almost nonexistent, the Administrator, in a letter written in 1952 in connection with a revision of the clause under consideration by the Subcommittee of the House Committee on Veterans' Affairs, comprehensively explained the policies necessitating the no-review clause and identified two primary purposes: (1) to insure that veterans' benefits claims will not burden the courts and the Veterans' Administration with expensive and time-consuming litigation, and (2) to insure that the technical and complex determinations and applications of Veterans' Administration policy connected with veterans' benefits decisions will be adequately and uniformly made.

8. Compare *Ex parte McCardle*, 7 Wall. 506 (1869); *Sheldon v. Sill*, 8 How. 441 (1850), with *Martin v. Hunter's Lessee*, 1 Wheat. 304 (1816); *St. Joseph Stock Yards Co. v. United States*, 298 U.S. 38, 84 (1936) (Brandeis, J., concurring). See Hart, *The Power of Congress to Limit the Jurisdiction of Federal Courts: An Exercise in Dialectic*, 66 Harv.L.Rev. 1362 (1953).

* * *

Congress perceived * * * [*Tracy v. Gleason*] as a threat to the dual purposes of the no-review clause. First, the interpretation would lead to an inevitable increase in litigation with consequent burdens upon the courts and the Veterans' Administration. * * *

Second, Congress was concerned that the judicial interpretation of § 211(a) would involve the courts in day-to-day determination and interpretation of Veterans' Administration policy. * * *

* * * Nothing whatever in the legislative history of the 1970 amendment, or predecessor no-review clauses, suggests any congressional intent to preclude judicial cognizance of constitutional challenges to veterans' benefits legislation. Such challenges obviously do not contravene the purposes of the no-review clause, for they cannot be expected to burden the courts by their volume, nor do they involve technical considerations of Veterans' Administration policy. We therefore conclude, in agreement with the District Court, that a construction of § 211(a) that does not extend the prohibitions of that section to actions challenging the constitutionality of laws providing benefits for veterans is not only "fairly possible" but is the most reasonable construction, for neither the text nor the scant legislative history of § 211(a) provides the "clear and convincing" evidence of congressional intent required by this Court before a statute will be construed to restrict access to judicial review. See *Abbott Laboratories v. Gardner*, 387 U.S. 136, 141 (1967).

Notes

1. *Cutting § 211(a)'s Preclusion Language Down to Size*. In *Traynor v. Turnage*, 485 U.S. 535 (1988), the Court once again grappled with 38 U.S.C. § 211(a). Petitioners were honorably discharged veterans who sought VA approval to receive educational benefits beyond the ordinary 10–year period from discharge, claiming that they had been disabled by alcoholism much of the time. The VA denied their request, relying on an agency regulation characterizing primary alcoholism as "willful misconduct" that made extension of benefits unjustified. The petitioners sought review, claiming that the Administrator's refusal to extend the benefit period violated due process and equal protection, and that the VA's regulation conflicted with § 504 of the Rehabilitation Act. The D.C. Circuit held that their suit was not barred by § 211(a) but upheld the VA regulation (and its denial of benefits) on the merits.

The Supreme Court affirmed both rulings. Responding to the government's argument that review was precluded, Justice White commented:

> Section 211(a) insulates from review decisions * * * made in interpreting or applying a particular provision * * * to a particular set of facts. But the cases now before us involve the issue whether the law sought to be administered is valid in light of a subsequent statute whose enforcement is not the exclusive domain of the Veterans' Administration. There is no claim that the regulation at issue is inconsistent with the statute under which it was issued; and there is no challenge to the Veterans'

Administration's construction of any statute dealing with veterans' benefits. * * * Permitting these cases to go forward will not undermine the purposes of § 211(a) any more than did the result in *Johnson*.

On the merits, Justice White found that the VA regulation confining primary alcoholics to the 10–year period for servicemen's education benefits comported with Congress' judgment that benefits should not be extended for veterans whose failure to exhaust them within the period was attributable to "willful misconduct." He found nothing in the text or history of the Rehabilitation Act that revealed an intention to displace the VA's "irrebuttable presumption."

Justices Blackmun, Brennan, and Marshall dissented from the Court's judgment on the merits.

Pub.L.No. 100–687, Nov. 18, 1988, which converted the VA into the Cabinet-level Department of Veterans Affairs, also created an "Article I" court, the United States Court of Veterans' Appeals, to review veterans' cases. Although most VA regulations and adjudications are made subject to review by the new court, no action establishing a schedule of disability ratings is subject to review in any court. The scope of review provision applicable to veterans' claims also departs nominally from the APA model by substituting the "clearly erroneous" for the "substantial evidence" rule. (This feature may not, as intended, shrink but rather expand the authority of judges to second-guess administrative findings. See *Dickinson v. Zurko*, 527 U.S. 150 (1999), discussed at p. 838 *supra*.) Review of Court of Veterans' Appeals decisions is available in the Federal Circuit, limited to the facial validity of a "statute or regulation or any interpretation thereof."

2. *Judicial Construction of Express Preclusion Provisions*. To characterize the judicial attitude toward statutes that preclude review as "uncharitable" may be an overgeneralization. The Supreme Court has routinely acquiesced in statutory language making agency decisions on property claims "final and conclusive." See, e.g., *Schilling v. Rogers*, 363 U.S. 666 (1960); *Work v. United States ex rel. Rives*, 267 U.S. 175 (1925). In cases involving personal liberty, however, the Court has construed preclusion clauses very narrowly. For example, in *Shaughnessy v. Pedreiro*, 349 U.S. 48 (1955), it ruled that a clause making deportation orders of the Immigration and Naturalization Service "final" referred to "administrative finality" and was not meant to limit judicial review. And in a long series of Selective Service cases during the 1960s, the Court steadily pushed back the borders of nonreviewability. See generally Note, *Judicial Review of Selective Service Classifications*, 56 Va.L.Rev. 1288 (1970), and the one major case decided after 1970, *Fein v. Selective Service System Local Board No. 7*, 405 U.S. 365 (1972).

The Court's latter predisposition was evident in *Reno v. Catholic Social Services (CSS)*, 509 U.S. 43 (1993). The Court there disposed of two suits that attacked different INS regulations promulgated in connection with the alien legalization program created by the Immigration Reform and Control Act of 1986. The Act required aliens applying for legalization to demonstrate their "continuous physical presence" in the United States since November 6, 1986, which could be broken only by "brief, casual and innocent absences." The INS, however, purported to consider an absence after May 1, 1987, "brief, casual and innocent" only if the alien had obtained INS permission to leave the United States prior to his or her departure. Similarly, the Act required an alien applying for legalization to show "continuous unlawful residence" in the United States. Under INS's regulations, however, an alien who had gone abroad and secured reentry into the United States by presenting facially valid documentation to immigration authorities would fail this requirement.

The Court held that district courts could entertain otherwise procedurally proper suits challenging the legality of INS regulations if the suits did not refer to or rely on the denial of any individual application. The 1986 Act made no provision whatever for such suits, but it did specify that a denial of an alien's application for adjustment of status could be reviewed only in the Court of Appeals and "only in the judicial review of an order of deportation." The provision went on to say: "There shall be no administrative or judicial review of a determination respecting an application for adjustment of status under this section except in accordance with this subsection." The Court held that this jurisdictional limitation was simply inapplicable to suits that did not involve individual applications for status adjustment. As for the statute's failure expressly to authorize review, the Court relied on the APA's presumption of reviewability.

Immigration and Naturalization Service v. St. Cyr, 533 U.S. 289 (2001), is in the same spirit. There a deportable alien sought habeas corpus to challenge an INS determination barring him for consideration for discretionary waiver of deportation. St. Cyr, a citizen of Haiti, was admitted to the United States as a lawful permanent resident in 1986. In 1996, he pled guilty to a state charge of selling a controlled substance. That conviction made him deportable, but at the time the federal immigration statutes permitted an alien so situated to seek discretionary relief from the Attorney General. Later that year Congress passed the Illegal Immigration Reform and Immigration Responsibility Act (IIRIRA), 110 Stat. 3009–546, and the Antiterrorism and Effective Death Penalty Act, 110 Stat. 1214, each of which, in the Attorney General's view, made aliens who had been convicted of a crime such as St. Cyr's ineligible for discretionary administrative relief. The new laws also contained language designed to channel and limit judicial review of a variety of INS decisions reached in applying and enforcing the immigration laws. One of these provisions, section 1252(a)(2)(C) of IIRIRA, provides in relevant part:

> Notwithstanding any other provision of law, no court shall have jurisdiction to review any final order of removal against an alien who is removable by reason of having committed [one or more enumerated] criminal offense[s] [including drug-trafficking offenses of the sort of which St. Cyr had been convicted]. * * *

St. Cyr challenged not the denial of a waiver of deportation but the INS's determination that the statutes restricting the Attorney General's discretion applied retroactively—to an alien whose conviction occurred prior to the statutes' passage. He contended that this was not Congress's intent and that retroactive application would violate due process. Writing for five members of the Court Justice Stevens held that Congress, in the IIRIRA, had failed to make clear that it intended to foreclose relief via habeas corpus, and observed:

> A construction of the amendments at issue that would entirely preclude review of a pure question of law [the question of retroactivity] by any court would give rise to substantial constitutional questions.

The central constitutional question, which would have to be confronted if section 1252(a)(2)(C) were interpreted as the government contended, was whether such an interpretation could be reconciled with Article I, § 9, cl. 2, of the Constitution, which narrowly limits the circumstances in which the "privilege of the writ of habeas corpus" may be suspended. The majority avoided this question by invoking the "plain statement rule," thus allowing review of the INS ruling via habeas corpus. On the merits, the Court majority ruled that the limits on the Attorney General's authority to waive deportation should not apply to aliens whose convictions pre-dated their enactment.

Justice Stevens' opinion provoked a blunt rejoinder from Justice Scalia, writing for the Chief Justice and Justices O'Connor and Thomas. He read the IIRIRA as "categorically and unequivocally" precluding judicial review of deportation orders in cases like the present one. "Unquestionably, unambiguously, and unmistakably, IIRIRA expressly supersedes § 2241's general provision for habeas corpus."

At the conclusion of his dissenting opinion, Justice Scalia turned briefly to what he termed the "insubstantial" claims of the majority that to read the new laws as precluding review by habeas corpus might violate due process or the federal courts' authority under Article III:

> The Due Process Clause does not "[r]equir[e] [j]udicial [d]etermination [o]f" respondent's claim. Respondent has no legal entitlement to suspension of deportation, no matter how appealing his case. [T]he Attorney General's suspension of deportation [is] "an act of grace" which is accorded pursuant to her 'unfettered discretion,' and [can be likened as Judge Learned Hand observed,] to "a judge's power to suspend the execution of a sentence, or the President's to pardon a convict." * * *
>
> Article III, § 1's investment of the "judicial Power of the United States" in the federal courts does not prevent Congress from committing the adjudication of respondent's legal claim wholly to "non-Article III federal adjudicative bodies." The notion that Article III requires every Executive determination, on a question of law or of fact, to be subject to judicial review has no support in our jurisprudence. Were it correct, the doctrine of sovereign immunity would not exist, and the APA's general permission of suits challenging administrative action would have been superfluous. Of its own force, Article III does no more than commit to the courts matters that are the stuff of the traditional actions at common law tried by the courts at Westminister in 1789.

Ultimately, the numerous "preclusion" cases may be reconcilable only on the most fundamental level—an evaluation of the degree to which the foreclosure of judicial review in a particular case is thought to undermine the sense of the rule of law that obtains only because the courthouse door is open. Judge John Minor Wisdom's dissenting statement in *Caulfield v. United States Department of Agriculture*, 293 F.2d 217, 228 (5th Cir.1961), *petition for cert. dismissed*, 369 U.S. 858 (1962), remains one of the most cogent analyses of the issue:

> The only common denominator of the decided cases I am able to discern is the broad principle, loosely applied, that finality language will be whittled down to size—to fit the Court's sense of fundamental fairness, whenever that sense is offended by denial of judicial review. I do not say that the courts decide reviewability cases guided only by their own notions of abstract justice. If courts rationalize fair play in terms of "jurisdiction," "statutory construction," "due process," or some other legal concept it is always, I hope, in proper context, considering the circumstances of the case and the interplay of policy, statute, and regulation; reducing the subjective element by weighing the presence or absence of constitutional safeguards, the reasonableness of the regulatory scheme, the effectiveness of administrative relief, the adequacy of administrative check on initial action, the comparative qualifications of courts on the one hand or administrative tribunals on the other hand to decide the particular question at issue, the nature of the judicial review prayed for, the nature of the administrative action, and many other factors, some at cross-purposes.

3. *Partial Preclusion*. As Judge Wisdom's statement suggests, courts are likely to be less reluctant to enforce preclusion language—even to abort constitutional challenges—where the statutory provision merely channels litigation into a particular form or forum. For example, *Johnson v. Robison* was distinguished in *Weinberger v. Salfi*, 422 U.S. 749 (1975), where the plaintiffs challenged the constitutionality of "duration-of-relationship" eligibility requirements for surviving wives and stepchildren under the Social Security Act. Although that act provides for review in a federal district court on appeal from a formal administrative adjudication, plaintiffs premised jurisdiction on 28 U.S.C. § 1331 in the face of language in section 405(h) of the Act, which provides:

> No action against the United States, the Secretary, or any officer or employee thereof shall be brought under [any provision of] Title 28 to recover on any claim arising under [Title II of the Social Security Act].

The district court, interpreting this language as merely codifying a requirement to exhaust administrative remedies, concluded that it made no sense to insist that the plaintiffs first pursue an administrative claim for benefits when the Secretary lacked authority, under the very requirements they challenged, to grant it.

The Supreme Court, per Justice Rehnquist, disagreed with the district court's interpretation of section 405(h), holding that it flatly precluded any suit seeking Title II benefits, even one challenging the constitutionality of statutory eligibility provisions prior to their implementation. Rehnquist contrasted section 405(h)'s language with the provision that the Court had eluded in *Johnson v. Robison*:

> Its reach is not limited to decisions of the Secretary on issues of law or fact. Rather, it extends to any "action" seeking "to recover on any [Social Security] claim"—irrespective of whether resort to judicial pro-

cesses is necessitated by discretionary decisions of the Secretary or by his non-discretionary applications of allegedly unconstitutional statutory restrictions.

> There is another reason why *Johnson v. Robison* is inapposite. It was expressly based, at least in part, on the fact that if § 211(a) reached constitutional challenges to statutory limitations, then absolutely no judicial consideration of the issue would be available. * * * In the present case * * * [§ 405(g) of] the Social Security Act itself provides jurisdiction for constitutional challenges to its provisions.

Justice Rehnquist then examined the requirements of section 405(g), which prescribes a final decision by the Secretary "after a hearing," commencement of suit within 60 days of that decision, and filing in the district where the plaintiff resides or transacts business. He read the latter two of these requirements as waivable by the parties, but the first he considered "central to the requisite grant of subject-matter jurisdiction." At this juncture, he confronted a difficulty, for section 405(g) seems to make a Secretarial decision after an evidentiary hearing a prerequisite to suit—and it was clear that the Secretary would not grant a hearing, much less benefits, to a claimant whose application revealed failure to comply with the challenged duration-of-relationship requirements. Judge Rehnquist escaped this conundrum by holding that jurisdiction under section 405(g) could be sustained if a plaintiff had pursued a claim for benefits far enough to permit the Secretary to conclude that only the allegedly unconstitutional eligibility criteria precluded an award:

> Plainly these purposes [of the statutory limitation] have been served once the Secretary has satisfied himself that the only issue is the constitutionality of a statutory requirement, a matter which is beyond his jurisdiction to determine, and that the claim is neither otherwise invalid nor cognizable under a different section of the Act.

Salfi was followed and reaffirmed in *Heckler v. Ringer*, 466 U.S. 602 (1984).

The potential reach of the "channeling" language of section 405(g) of the Social Security Act, relied on in *Salfi*, has been the focus of several subsequent decisions by the Supreme Court. Readers may recall that in *Mathews v. Eldridge*, p. 337 *supra*, the plaintiff, Eldridge, challenged the Social Security Administration's failure to provide a hearing before suspending his disability benefits without waiting for the available post-termination hearing referred to by the statute. The Court was unconvinced by the government's argument that his suit was premature, even though, unlike *Salfi*, the Secretary had not waived exhaustion in Eldridge's case. Where a plaintiff had satisfied the non-waivable jurisdictional requirement of presenting and receiving an administrative ruling on his claim, the Court was unwilling to demand exhaustion of procedures that were being challenged as inadequate to provide adequate relief. But this exception to the Social Security Act's requirements was carefully circumscribed:

> * * * Salfi suggested that under § 405(g) the power to determine when finality has occurred ordinarily rests with the Secretary since ultimate responsibility for the integrity of the administrative program is his. But cases may arise where a claimant's interest in having a

particular issue resolved promptly is so great that deference to the agency's judgment is inappropriate. This is such a case.

Eldridge's constitutional challenge is entirely collateral to his substantive claim of entitlement. Moreover, there is a crucial distinction between the nature of the constitutional claim asserted here and that raised in Salfi. A claim to a predeprivation hearing as a matter of constitutional right rests on the proposition that full relief cannot be obtained at a postdeprivation hearing. In light of the Court's prior decision, Eldridge has raised at least a colorable claim that because of his physical condition and dependency upon the disability benefits, an erroneous termination would damage him in a way not recompensable through retroactive payments. Thus, unlike the situation in Salfi, denying Eldridge's substantive claim "for other reasons" would not answer his constitutional challenge.

Bowen v. Michigan Academy of Family Physicians, 476 U.S. 667 (1986), however, seemed to recognize potentially broad exception to *Salfi's* holding that judicial review of SSA determinations could only be obtained by following the elaborate administrative review provisions set forth in the Act and HHS regulations. *Michigan Academy* was a suit brought under 28 U.SC. § 1331 challenging the lawfulness of HHS regulations that governed procedures for calculating benefits under Medicare Part B. In holding the suit proper, the Court distinguished challenges to general SSA standards or procedures from suits challenging the agency's determination of the amount of benefits to which a provider or beneficiary was entitled. The latter were governed by *Salfi*, but the former apparently could be based on the district court's federal question jurisdiction.

But *Shalala v. Illinois Council on Long Term Care, Inc.*, 529 U.S. 1 (2000), substantially narrowed, if it did not nullify, the route to court around *Salfi* that the Court had opened in *Michigan Academy*. An association of nursing homes sued the HHS Secretary, relying on 28 U.S.C. § 1331, claiming that certain Medicare regulations violated the Medicare Act and the U.S. Constitution. The government contested jurisdiction, relying on *Salfi*, and the Court majority, in an opinion by Justice Breyer, agreed. He read *Michigan Academy* narrowly, as applying only where application of section 405(h) would preclude judicial review altogether, a possibility that he rejected in the case at hand.

Justice Scalia filed a short dissent, in which he declared: "In my view, preenforcement review is better described as the background rule, which can be displaced by any reasonable implication from the statute." Justice Thomas, writing for Justice Stevens, Kennedy, and (in part) Scalia, authored a lengthy dissent in which he first sought to show that 405(h) was not intended to bar a suit like that of the nursing homes and then invoked the "longstanding canon that 'judicial review of executive action "will not be cut off unless there is persuasive reason to believe that such was the purpose of Congress." '* * * Contrary to the Secretary's representation, the presumption favors not merely judicial review 'at some point,' but *preenforcement* judicial review." See also *Board of Governors of the Federal Reserve System v. MCorp Financial Inc.*, 502 U.S. 32 (1991) rebuffing an attempt to create a general exception to statutory nonreviewability in cases of *ultra vires* action and see also the series of cases, summarized in *Broward Gardens Tenants Ass'n v. U.S. Environmental Protection Agency*, 311 F.3d 1066 (11th Cir. 2002) (construing section 113(h) of the Comprehensive Environmental Response, Compensation, and Liability Act (also known as Superfund), 42 U.S.C. § 9601 "to bar jurisdiction over constitutional, as well as statutory claims challenging the adequacy of a remedial plan.")

4. *Implied Statutory Preclusion*. Like the explicit preclusion cases, implied preclusion almost always involves actions that are reviewable in some form at some time. But, given judicial skepticism of preclusion in any form, implicit preclusion is a limited category reserved for rather special, verging on unique, circumstances. *Morris v. Gressette*, 432 U.S. 491 (1977), is an illustration. Under section 5 of the 1965 Voting Rights Act, no covered state may implement changes in "any voting qualification, or prerequisite to voting, or standard, practice, or procedure with respect to voting" without first pursuing one of two routes of approval. 42 U.S.C. § 1973c (1982). A state may initiate a declaratory judgment action in the District Court of the District of Columbia to obtain a determination that the proposed change "does not have the purpose and will not have the effect of denying or abridging the right to vote on account of race or color"—an action in which it bears the burden of proof. Alternatively, the state may submit the change to the Attorney General, who has 60 days in which to object. If no objection is forthcoming in that period, the change may be implemented.

The facts of *Morris v. Gressette* are complicated. The State of South Carolina submitted a revised reapportionment plan to the Attorney General while litigation challenging an earlier version was still pending in a South Carolina district court. Before the Attorney General took any action, the district court held the new plan constitutional. Soon afterwards the Attorney General announced that he would not interpose any objection because he felt constrained to defer to the court's ruling. Civil rights groups promptly filed suit in the District of Columbia, seeking review of the Attorney General's failure to exercise his authority to object to the plan; the district court there ordered him to make "a reasoned decision in accordance with his statutory responsibility," and the D.C. Circuit affirmed. Two of the plaintiffs then filed suit in South Carolina to enjoin implementation of the reapportionment plan, only to be met by a ruling that the Attorney General's determination under section 5—in this case to defer to the South Carolina district court's determination of constitutionality—was not subject to judicial review under either the Voting Rights Act or the APA.

The Supreme Court agreed. While it conceded that no statutory language barred review of the Attorney General's exercise of his authority under section 5, it found that the legislative history of the Voting Rights Act evidenced a congressional intent to preclude such challenges. The alternative route of approval for state election laws was intended to be expeditious. The Court stressed that this result—according unreviewable discretion to the Attorney General—did not bar direct judicial challenges to such laws once adopted, though it conceded that the plaintiffs in such a case, and not the state, would bear the burden of proof on the issue of constitutionality.

The Court likewise found review implicitly precluded in *Block v. Community Nutrition Institute*, 467 U.S. 340 (1984). The issue was whether ultimate consumers of dairy products could obtain judicial review of milk market orders issued by the Secretary of Agriculture under the authority of the Agricultural Marketing Agreement Act of 1937, 7 U.S.C. § 601 *et seq.* The Court had already construed the Act as implicitly authorizing judicial review at the behest of dairy producers, *Stark v. Wickard*, 321 U.S. 288 (1944), and the Act expressly provides a mechanism by which handlers of dairy products may obtain review of the Secretary's market orders, 7 U.S.C. § 608c(15), requiring that they first exhaust the administrative remedies made available by the Secretary. According to Justice O'Connor:

> [T]he statutory scheme * * * makes * * * clear Congress' intention to limit the classes entitled to participate in the development of market orders. The Act contemplates a cooperative venture among the Secretary, handlers, and producers the principal purposes of which are to raise the price of agricultural products and to establish an orderly system for marketing them. Handlers and producers—but not consumers—are entitled to participate in the adoption and retention of market orders. 7 U.S.C. §§ 608c(8), (9), (16)(B). The Act provides for agreements among the Secretary, producers, and handlers, 7 U.S.C. § 608(2), for hearings among them, §§ 608(5), 608c(3), and for votes by producers and handlers, §§ 608c(8)(A), (9)(B), (12), 608c(19). Nowhere in the Act, however, is there an express provision for participation by consumers in any proceeding. In a complex scheme of this type, the omission of such a provision is sufficient reason to believe that Congress intended to foreclose consumer participation in the regulatory process.

The Court further determined that "[a]llowing consumers to sue the Secretary would severely disrupt this complex and delicate administrative scheme." At the very least, it would be strange to permit consumers to obtain a form of review unavailable to those whose activities are regulated.

Block v. CNI is nonetheless a peculiar "preclusion" case. The challenged actions are fully reviewable, just not at the behest of these plaintiffs. Hence, it might be more appropriate to view *Block v. CNI* as involving one of those rare instances in which Congress has denied standing to a particular category of persons who may be adversely affected by official action.

5. *NLRB Certification of Bargaining Units.* NLRB decisions defining the bargaining status of labor organizations may be the only category of agency decisions that have frequently been held unreviewable because implicitly barred by statute. The classic case is *Switchmen's Union v. National Mediation Board*, 320 U.S. 297 (1943), where Justice Douglas held unreviewable the Board's decision to include yardmen in a unit with all other operating railroad employees rather than to permit them to vote for separate representation. Although the Railway Labor Act neither explicitly authorized nor precluded review of such decisions, the Court concluded that Congress intended its certification decisions to be final. In *Brotherhood of Railway and Steamship Clerks v. Association for Benefit of Non–Contract Employees*, 380 U.S. 650 (1965), the Court again held that the Board's determination of the proper election unit, following an investigation that was procedurally proper, was beyond review. The holding of nonreviewability in these cases recognizes the necessities of the collective bargaining context. If employers or competing unions could get review of every certification of a bargaining unit prior

to contract negotiations, labor-management relations would produce much litigation and little bargaining. Judicial acknowledgment of nonreviewability here reflects a fear that attempts to assure "legality" through judicial review will effectively frustrate congressional policy. These sorts of functional concerns make "implied preclusion" cases almost indistinguishable from the analysis of the category of claims that we take up next—decisions committed to agency discretion by law."

Implied preclusion may thus be more susceptible to functional considerations that limit its scope. For example, in *Leedom v. Kyne*, 358 U.S. 184 (1958), the Court entertained review of an NLRB certification decision that included both professional and nonprofessional employees in a bargaining unit. The NLRA expressly prohibits such a certification, unless approved by a majority of the professional employees involved. The NLRB conceded no vote had been taken, but insisted its certification decisions could be challenged only when the employer or the union later sought review or enforcement of an unfair labor practice order. The Court described the professionals' suit as "not one to 'review,' in the sense of that term as used in the Act, a decision of the Board made within its jurisdiction. Rather, it is one to strike down an order of the Board made in excess of its delegated powers and contrary to a specific prohibition in the Act. * * * "

Limiting Review at the Enforcement Stage

Although bald preclusions of review are rare, Congress sometimes seeks to forestall challenges to agency regulations in the context of enforcement proceedings by providing an immediate, time-limited, and possibly exclusive mode of review elsewhere. These provisions are almost mirror images of the Social Security Act provisions at issue in *Salfi* and *Eldridge*, which tend to delay review until enforcement or implementation. *Yakus v. United States*, 321 U.S. 414 (1944), which upheld review of the government's wartime price control orders limited to pre-enforcement review, affirmed the general proposition that Congress may do so. Yet, Congress' specification in an agency's statute of a time and place for judicial review may pose two puzzles. First, if the statute specifies that its route of review is exclusive, are there circumstances in which the provision may be avoided on grounds of unfairness? Second, should the route of review delineated in a specific statutory review provision be presumed exclusive whenever no alternative is mentioned? The APA's statement that review may be had in enforcement proceedings "except to the extent that prior, adequate and exclusive opportunity" for review has been afforded recognizes, but does little more than restate, these questions.

Adamo Wrecking Co. v. United States, 434 U.S. 275 (1978), illustrates the first problem. The petitioner was prosecuted for violating the EPA's "National Emission Standard for Asbestos" while demolishing a building. The EPA's "standard" prescribed demolition procedures designed to limit the dispersal of asbestos fibers in old insulation, but it did not, for quite practical reasons, purport to set a ceiling on fibers discharged by pollution sources (as conventional emissions standards do). Adamo persuaded the district court to dismiss the charge on the ground that EPA's so-called "standard" was not of the kind authorized by the Clean Air Act of 1970. On appeal, the court of appeals held that section 307(b) of the Act, 42 U.S.C. § 1857h–5(b), precluded consideration of Adamo's claim. That provision stated:

> (1) A petition for review of action of the Administrator in promulgating * * * any emission standard under section 112 * * * may be filed only in the United States Court of Appeals for the District of Columbia. * * * Any such petition shall be filed within 30 days from the date of such promulgation or approval, or after such date if such petition is based solely on grounds arising after such 30th day.
>
> (2) Action of the Administrator with respect to which review could have been obtained under paragraph (1) shall not be subject to judicial review in civil or criminal proceedings for enforcement.

No challenge had been made under this provision to the building demolition rule when it was promulgated.

The Supreme Court reversed the lower court, saying, in part:

> We conclude * * * that a federal court in which a criminal prosecution under § 113(c)(1)(C) of the Clean Air Act is brought may determine whether or not the regulation which the defendant is alleged to have violated is an "emission standard" within the meaning of the Act. We are aware of the possible dangers that flow from this interpretation; district courts will be importuned, under the guise of making a determination as to whether a regulation is an "emission standard," to engage in judicial review in a manner that is precluded by § 307(b)(2) of the Act. This they may not do. The narrow inquiry to be addressed by the court in a criminal prosecution is not whether the Administrator has complied with appropriate procedures in promulgating the regulation in question, or whether the particular regulation is arbitrary, capricious, or supported by the administrative record. Nor is the court to pursue any of the other familiar inquiries which arise in the course of an administrative review proceeding. The question is only whether the regulation which the defendant is alleged to have violated is on its face an "emission standard" within the broad limits of the congressional meaning of that term.

In a concurring opinion, Justice Powell went further to raise doubts about the constitutionality of the limited opportunity for review afforded by the Clean Air Act to persons facing criminal prosecution:

> If the constitutional validity of § 307(b) of the Clean Air Act had been raised by petitioner, I think it would have merited serious consideration. * * *
>
> Although I express no considered judgment, I think *Yakus* is at least arguably distinguishable. The statute there came before the Court during World War II, and it can be viewed as a valid exercise

> of the war powers of Congress under Art. I, § 8, of the Constitution.
> * * *
>
> The 30–day limitation on judicial review imposed by the Clean Air Act would afford precariously little time for many affected persons even if some adequate method of notice were afforded. It also is totally unrealistic to assume that more than a fraction of the persons and entities affected by a regulation—especially small contractors scattered across the country—would have knowledge of its promulgation or familiarity with or access to the Federal Register. Indeed, following *Yakus*, and apparently concerned by * * * Justice Rutledge's eloquent dissent, Congress amended the most onerous features of the Emergency Price Control Act.
>
> I join the Court's opinion with the understanding that it implies no view as to the constitutional validity of the preclusion provisions of § 307(b) in the context of a criminal prosecution.

A majority echoed Justice Powell's concerns in *United States v. Mendoza–Lopez*, 481 U.S. 828 (1987), which considered whether a deported alien prosecuted for unlawful reentry may challenge the validity of the underlying deportation order. Mendoza claimed, and the district court (after listening to a tape recording of the proceeding) agreed, that his deportation hearing had been fundamentally flawed. The immigration judge failed to explain Mendoza's rights to appeal or to seek suspension of deportation and thus Mendoza's waiver of those rights could not be considered knowing or intelligent. The district court accordingly dismissed the indictments. The government sought review, claiming that the deportation order, although once directly reviewable, was not subject to collateral attack as a defense to prosecution.

The Supreme Court rejected the government's claim, even though it conceded that section 1326 of the Immigration and Nationality Act did not purport to allow for such challenges. Justice Marshall observed that a reading of the statute to allow criminal prosecution "for reentry after *any* deportation, regardless of how violative of the rights of the alien the deportation proceeding may have been," would violate due process:

> Our cases establish that where a determination made in an administrative proceeding is to play a critical role in the subsequent imposition of a criminal sanction, there must be *some* meaningful review of the administrative proceeding. This principle means at the very least that where the defects in an administrative proceeding foreclose judicial review of that proceeding, an alternative means of obtaining judicial review must be made available before the administrative order may be used to establish conclusively an element of a criminal offense.

Justice Marshall argued that *Yakus*, "motivated by the exigencies of wartime, dealt with the propriety of regulations rather than the legitimacy of adjudicatory procedure, and, most significantly, turned on the fact that adequate judicial review of the validity of the regulation was available in another forum."

Chief Justice Rehnquist, dissenting with Justices White and O'Connor, thought that the respondent had not demonstrated those "exceptional circumstances" that would make denial of collateral review a violation of due process. Justice Scalia, also dissenting, perceived no constitutional impediment to Congress' "mak[ing] it a felony for deportees—irrespective of the legality of their deportations—to reenter the United States illegally."

Concern about potential unfairness of foreclosing review in subsequent enforcement proceedings may induce a narrow construction of preenforcement review provisions, where a provision authorizing preenforcement review limits that review to a particular court. *Chrysler Corp. v. EPA*, 600 F.2d 904 (D.C.Cir.1979), for example, involved review under a provision authorizing exclusive court of appeals review of EPA "action * * * promulgating any standard or regulation under section 6, 17, or 18 of this Act." Noise Control Act of 1972, 42 U.S.C. § 4901 *et seq.* The court held that it lacked jurisdiction under the section to review regulations describing the procedures EPA would use in enforcing noise requirements for trucks, including record keeping, inspection, and recall requirements. The EPA and all but one of the petitioners had urged the court to accept jurisdiction in order to avoid bifurcation of suits challenging both substantive standards and enforcement procedures. The court, however, adopted a reading of the statute that allowed subsequent challenge to the enforcement procedures because "of possible unfairness, particularly to small manufacturers who may lack resources to monitor the Administrator's actions to assure protection of the opportunity to contest regulations affecting their interests." See generally Thomas O. McGarity, *Multi–Party Forum Shopping for Appellate Review of Administrative Action*, 129 U.Pa.L.Rev. 302 (1980); Paul R. Verkuil, *Congressional Limitations on Judicial Review of Rules*, 57 Tul.L.Rev. 733 (1983).

Litigants should not assume that courts will be lenient in implementing statutory provisions that restrict the timing or venue of challenges to agency action. In enforcing a 90–day time limit on review of regulations that the petitioner mistakenly concluded were not ripe for review, the D.C. Circuit said:

> We have entertained untimely claims only in a limited number of exceptional circumstances where the petitioner lacked a meaningful opportunity to challenge the agency action during the review period due to, for example, inadequate notice that the petitioner would be affected by the action, confusion in the law as to the proper forum for review, and lack of ripeness during the review period.

Eagle–Picher Industries, Inc. v. United States Environmental Protection Agency, 759 F.2d 905 (D.C.Cir.1985). That court likewise held, in *Telecommunications Research and Action Center (TRAC) v. FCC*, 750 F.2d 70 (D.C.Cir.1984), that suits challenging an agency's delay in acting must be brought exclusively in the courts of appeals that would have jurisdiction to review its ultimate action unless Congress specifically directs otherwise.

Later cases have limited this ruling. It does not apply to an attack on the constitutionality of an agency's enabling act if it does not arise in the context of a challenge to some final agency action. See *Time Warner Entertainment Co.,L.P. v. FCC,* 810 F.Supp. 1302 (D.D.C.1992), *affirmed* 93 F.3d 957, 965 (D.C.Cir.1996). And *TRAC* may not dictate filing in the court of appeals when a suit challenges different agency actions, one under a provision making court of appeals jurisdiction exclusive while the others fall within the original jurisdiction of the district courts. See *City of Kansas City, Mo. v. U.S. Dept. of Housing and Urban Development*, 669 F.Supp. 525 (D.D.C.1987), *affirmed* 861 F.2d 739 (D.C.Cir. 1988).

Constitutional Restraints on Statutory Preclusion of Review

The *Robison* Court suggests that an interpretation of 38 U.S.C. § 211(a) that would preclude judicial review of constitutional claims would itself raise a serious constitutional question. In the view of most scholars and probably a majority of the current Justices, the question goes to the essence of separation of powers, for in general terms the issue is the extent to which the Congress may render the federal courts impotent by controlling their jurisdiction. Yet, the latest case the *Robison* Court cites as bearing on the matter was decided in 1936—a testament perhaps both to congressional restraint in exercising its authority to regulate the courts' jurisdiction and to the Supreme Court's facility at avoiding the issue. See generally WilliamVan Alstyne, *A Critical Guide to Ex Parte McCardle*, 15 Ariz.L.Rev. 229 (1973).

Professor Henry Hart, in the article cited at footnote 8 of the *Robison* opinion, took the position (which is supported by the broad language of the three cases also cited) that the jurisdiction of the federal courts, save the original jurisdiction of the Supreme Court conferred by the Constitution itself, is under Article III subject to the control of the Congress. Hart argued that the vindication of federal rights, including federal constitutional rights, could constitutionally be left to the state courts operating under the supremacy clause. (Under what conditions these courts are required to host such cases remains uncertain. See *Alden v. Maine*, 527 U.S. 706 (1999).) He acknowledged that Congress could not, by restricting court jurisdiction, accomplish what it cannot do by direct substantive prescription. It could not, for example, take property without due process by forbidding any court to hear a claim for compensation. But this caveat would not necessarily constrain Congress' power to remove jurisdiction from the federal courts to hear appeals from administrative bodies, for the Court has never held that there is a due process right to judicial review. See *Ortwein v. Schwab*, 410 U.S. 656 (1973).

The only judicial authority potentially adverse to Professor Hart's view is a series of cases (one of which, *St. Joseph Stock Yards*, is cited in *Robison*) which apparently held that a court cannot be statutorily barred from investigating *de novo* certain "jurisdictional" or "constitutional" facts that determine the agency's power to act. In this respect *St. Joseph Stock Yards* confirmed the prior holding of *Ohio Valley Water Co. v. Ben Avon Borough*, 253 U.S. 287 (1920), that, when a regulatory commission's rate order was challenged as "confiscatory," the utility must have the opportunity for judicial review of the agency's underlying factual determinations. Failing to afford review of these "constitutional" facts, the Supreme Court held, would violate due process.

A parallel doctrine emerged in *Ng Fung Ho. v. White*, 259 U.S. 276 (1922). The petitioner challenged a deportation order of the Secretary of Labor on the ground that he was a citizen and not deportable. The Court held that the petitioner was entitled to a *de novo* judicial determination on the question of citizenship because his allegations went to the Secretary's "jurisdiction" to act. The Court reiterated this "jurisdictional fact" doctrine ten years later in *Crowell v. Benson*, 285 U.S. 22 (1932), holding that employers were entitled to *de novo* judicial review of "fundamental" or "jurisdictional" facts, e.g., the existence of a master-servant relationship and the occurrence of the injury on navigable waters, underlying an award pursuant to the Longshoremen's and Harbor Workers' Compensation Act.

These cases called forth an avalanche of critical commentary, which stressed the possibilities they created for transferring much of administrative fact-finding to the judicial arena. The doctrines they enunciated are now generally considered moribund, although never explicitly rejected by the Supreme Court. See PETER L. STRAUSS, TODD RAKOFF, & CYNTHIA R. FARINA, GELLHORN & BYSE'S ADMINISTRATIVE LAW 973–78 (10th ed. 2003). Professor Louis Jaffe, however, argued that these cases establish at least the limited proposition that a judicial test of the propriety of an administrative order is constitutionally necessary where enforcement ultimately involves execution against person or property through judicial process. LOUIS L. JAFFE, JUDICIAL CONTROL OF ADMINISTRATIVE ACTION 381–89 (1965). Professor Henry Hart agreed with this analysis because he believed that Congress may not, having provided judicial jurisdiction, instruct the courts to ignore relevant issues of law. 66 Harv.L.Rev. at 1373–74. But he did not think that this negated the power of Congress to remove federal judicial jurisdiction entirely. The Hart approach thus implies that Congress may grant or withhold, but not redefine, the "judicial power" under Article III; or at least may redefine it only within limits that continue to permit review of constitutional issues, though not necessarily issues of "constitutional fact."

Professor Hart's theory of plenary congressional power to define and control the federal courts' jurisdiction is so riddled with exceptions that the exceptions swallow most of the rule. Once it is admitted that judicial enforcement of administrative orders constitutionally implies judicial review to determine that property and personal liberty are not taken without due process of law, virtually all regulatory administrative action becomes reviewable—to some indeterminate degree—as a matter of constitutional necessity. Moreover, Hart's fundamental thesis is questionable. For it may be argued that without a federal judicial power sufficient to resolve basic constitutional conflicts, the Constitution's separation and limitation of governmental powers are empty promises. We should surely be cautious in concluding that the framers granted Congress an authority over judicial jurisdiction that could warp the constitutional system. See, e.g., Theodore Eisenberg, *Congressional Authority to Restrict Lower Federal Court Jurisdiction*, 83 Yale L.J. 498 (1974); Martin H. Redish and Curtis E. Woods, *Congressional Power to Control the Jurisdiction of Lower Federal Courts: A Critical Review and a New Synthesis*, 124 U.Pa.L.Rev. 45 (1975); Akhil Reed Amar, *A Neo–Federalist View of Article III: Separating the Two Tiers of Federal Jurisdiction*, 65 B.U.L.Rev. 205 (1985), and *The Two–Tiered Structure of the Judiciary Act of 1789*, 138 U.Pa.L.Rev. 1499 (1990); Martin H. Redish, *Text, Structure and Common Sense in the Interpretation of Article III*, 138 U.Pa.L.Rev. 1633 (1990).

b. Decisions "Committed to Agency Discretion" By Law

WEBSTER v. DOE

Supreme Court of the United States, 1988.
486 U.S. 592, 108 S.Ct. 2047, 100 L.Ed.2d 632.

CHIEF JUSTICE REHNQUIST delivered the opinion of the Court.

Section 102(c) of the National Security Act of 1947, provides that:

> "[T]he Director of Central Intelligence may, in his discretion, terminate the employment of any officer or employee of the Agency whenever he shall deem such termination necessary or advisable in the interests of the United States * * *."

50 U.S.C. § 403(c). In this case we decide whether, and to what extent, the termination decisions of the Director under § 102(c) are judicially reviewable.

I

Respondent John Doe was first employed by the Central Intelligence Agency (CIA or Agency) in 1973 as a clerk-typist. He received periodic fitness reports that consistently rated him as an excellent or outstanding employee. By 1977, respondent had been promoted to a position as a covert electronics technician.

In January 1982, respondent voluntarily informed a CIA security officer that he was a homosexual. Almost immediately, the Agency placed respondent on paid administrative leave pending an investigation of his sexual orientation and conduct. On February 12 and again on February 17, respondent was extensively questioned by a polygraph officer concerning his homosexuality and possible security violations. Respondent denied having sexual relations with any foreign nationals and maintained that he had not disclosed classified information to any of his sexual partners. After these interviews, the officer told respondent that the polygraph tests indicated that he had truthfully answered all questions. The polygraph officer then prepared a five-page summary of his interviews with respondent, to which respondent was allowed to attach a two-page addendum.

On April 14, 1982, a CIA security agent informed respondent that the Agency's Office of Security had determined that respondent's homosexuality posed a threat to security, but declined to explain the nature of the danger. Respondent was then asked to resign. When he refused to do so, the Office of Security recommended to the CIA Director (petitioner's predecessor) that respondent be dismissed. After reviewing respondent's records and the evaluations of his subordinates, the Director "deemed it necessary and advisable in the interests of the United States to terminate [respondent's] employment with this Agency pursuant to section 102(c) of the National Security Act * * *." Respondent was also advised that, while the CIA would give him a positive recommendation in any future job search, if he applied for a job requiring a security clearance the Agency would inform the prospective employer that it had concluded that respondent's homosexuality presented a security threat.

Respondent then filed an action against petitioner in United States District Court for the District of Columbia. Respondent's amended complaint asserted a variety of statutory and constitutional claims against the Director. Respondent alleged that petitioner's decision to terminate his employment violated § 706 of the Administrative Procedure Act (APA), because it was arbitrary and capricious, represented an abuse of discretion, and was reached without observing the procedures required by law and CIA regulations. He also complained that the Director's termination of his employment deprived him of constitutionally protected rights to property, liberty, and privacy in violation of the First, Fourth, Fifth, and Ninth Amendments. Finally, he asserted that his dismissal transgressed the procedural due process and equal protection of the laws guaranteed by the Fifth Amendment. * * *

Petitioner moved to dismiss respondent's amended complaint on the ground that § 102(c) of the National Security Act (NSA) precludes judicial review of the Director's termination decisions under §§ 701, 702, and 706 of the APA. * * *

The District Court denied petitioner's motion to dismiss, and granted respondent's motion for partial summary judgment. The court determined that the APA provided judicial review of petitioner's termination decisions made under § 102(c) of the NSA, and found that respondent had been unlawfully discharged because the CIA had not followed the procedures described in its own regulations. The District Court declined, however, to address respondent's constitutional claims. Respondent was ordered reinstated to administrative leave status, and the Agency was instructed to reconsider his case using procedures that would supply him with the reasons supporting any termination decision and provide him with an opportunity to respond.

A divided panel of the Court of Appeals for the District of Columbia Circuit vacated the District Court's judgment and remanded the case for further proceedings. The Court of Appeals first decided that judicial review under the APA of the Agency's decision to terminate respondent was not precluded by §§ 701(a)(1) or (a)(2). Turning to the merits, the Court of Appeals found that, while an agency must normally follow its own regulations, the CIA regulations cited by respondent do not limit the Director's discretion in making termination decisions. Moreover, the regulations themselves state that, with respect to terminations pursuant to § 102(c), the Director need not follow standard discharge procedures, but may direct that an employee "be separated immediately and without regard to any suggested procedural steps." The majority thus concluded that the CIA regulations provide no independent source of procedural or substantive protection.

The Court of Appeals went on to hold that respondent must demonstrate that the Director's action was an arbitrary and capricious exercise of his power to discharge employees under § 102(c). Because the record below was unclear on certain points critical to respondent's claim for relief, the Court of Appeals remanded the case to District Court for a determination of the reason for the Director's termination of respondent. * * *

II

* * * Section 701(a) * * * limits application of the entire APA to situations in which judicial review is not precluded by statute, see § 701(a)(1), and the agency action is not committed to agency discretion by law, see § 701(a)(2).

In *Citizens to Preserve Overton Park v. Volpe*, 401 U.S. 402 (1971), this Court explained the distinction between §§ 701(a)(1) and (a)(2). Subsection (a)(1) is concerned with whether Congress expressed an intent to prohibit judicial review; subsection (a)(2) applies "in those rare instances where 'statutes are drawn in such broad terms that in a given case there is no law to apply.' "

We further explained what it means for an action to be "committed to agency discretion by law" in *Heckler v. Chaney*, 470 U.S. 821 (1985). Heckler required the Court to determine whether the Food and Drug Administration's decision not to undertake an enforcement proceeding against the use of certain drugs in administering the death penalty was subject to judicial review. We noted that, under § 701(a)(2), even when Congress has not affirmatively precluded judicial oversight, "review is not to be had if the statute is drawn so that a court would have no meaningful standard against which to judge the agency's exercise of discretion." * * *

Both *Overton Park* and *Heckler* emphasized that § 701(a)(2) requires careful examination of the statute on which the claim of agency illegality is based (the Federal–Aid Highway Act of 1968 in *Overton Park* and the Federal Food, Drug, and Cosmetic Act in *Heckler*). In the present case, respondent's claims against the CIA arise from the Director's asserted violation of § 102(c) of the National Security Act. As an initial matter, it should be noted that § 102(c) allows termination of an Agency employee whenever the Director "shall *deem* such termination necessary or advisable in the interests of the United States" (emphasis added), not simply when the dismissal is necessary or advisable to those interests. This standard fairly exudes deference to the Director, and appears to us to foreclose the application of any meaningful judicial standard of review. Short of permitting cross-examination of the Director concerning his views of the Nation's security and whether the discharged employee was inimical to those interests, we see no basis on which a reviewing court could properly assess an Agency termination decision. The language of § 102(c) thus strongly suggests that its implementation was "committed to agency discretion by law."

So too does the overall structure of the National Security Act. Passed shortly after the close of the Second World War, the NSA created the CIA and gave its Director the responsibility "for protecting intelligence sources and methods from unauthorized disclosure." Section 102(c) is an integral part of that statute, because the Agency's efficacy, and the Nation's security, depend in large measure on the reliability and trustworthiness of the Agency's employees. As we recognized in *Snepp v. United States*, 444 U.S. 507, 510 (1980), employment with the CIA entails a high degree of trust that is perhaps unmatched in government service.

This overriding need for ensuring integrity in the Agency led us to uphold the Director's use of § 102(d)(3) of the NSA to withhold the identities of protected intelligence sources in *CIA v. Sims*, 471 U.S. 159 (1985). In denying respondent's Freedom of Information Act requests in Sims to produce certain CIA records, we stated that "[t]he plain meaning of the statutory language, as well as the legislative history of the National Security Act, * * *, indicates that Congress vested in the Director of Central Intelligence very broad authority to protect all sources of intelligence information from disclosure." Section 102(c), that portion of the NSA under consideration in the present case, is part and parcel of the entire Act, and likewise exhibits the Act's extraordinary deference to the Director in his decision to terminate individual employees.

We thus find that the language and structure of § 102(c) indicate that Congress meant to commit individual employee discharges to the Director's discretion, and that § 701(a)(2) accordingly precludes judicial review of these decisions under the APA. We reverse the Court of Appeals to the extent that it found such terminations reviewable by the courts.

III

In addition to his claim that the Director failed to abide by the statutory dictates of § 102(c), respondent also alleged a number of constitutional violations in his amended complaint. Respondent charged that petitioner's termination of his employment deprived him of property and liberty interests under the Due Process Clause, denied him equal protection of the laws, and unjustifiably burdened his right to privacy. Respondent asserts that he is entitled, under the APA, to judicial consideration of these claimed violations.[7] * * *

Petitioner maintains that, no matter what the nature of respondent's constitutional claim, judicial review is precluded by the language and intent of § 102(c). In petitioner's view, all Agency employment termination decisions, even those based on policies normally repugnant to the Constitution, are given over to the absolute discretion of the Director, and are hence unreviewable under the APA. We do not think § 102(c) may be read to exclude review of constitutional claims. We emphasized in *Johnson v. Robison* that where Congress intends to preclude judicial review of constitutional claims its intent to do so must be clear. In *Weinberger v. Salfi*, 422 U.S. 749 (1975), we reaffirmed that view. We require this heightened showing in part to avoid the "serious constitutional question" that would arise if a federal statute were construed to deny any judicial forum for a colorable constitutional claim.

Our review of § 102(c) convinces us that it cannot bear the preclusive weight petitioner would have it support. As detailed above, the section does commit employment termination decisions to the Director's discretion, and precludes challenges to these decisions based upon the statutory language of § 102(c). A discharged employee thus cannot complain that his termination was not "necessary or advisable in the interests of the United States," since that assessment is the Director's alone. Subsections (a)(1) and (a)(2) of § 701, however, remove from judicial review only those determinations specifically identified by Congress or "committed to agency discretion by law." Nothing in § 102(c) persuades us that Congress meant to preclude consideration of colorable constitutional claims arising out of the actions of the Director pursuant to that section; we believe that a constitutional claim based on an individual discharge may be reviewed by the District Court. We agree with the Court of Appeals that there must be further proceedings in the District Court on this issue.

Petitioner complains that judicial review even of constitutional claims will entail extensive "rummaging around" in the Agency's affairs to the detriment of national security. But petitioner acknowledges that Title VII claims attacking the hiring and promotion policies of the Agency are routinely entertained in federal court, and the inquiry and discovery associated with those proceedings would seem to involve some

7. We understand that petitioner concedes that the Agency's failure to follow its own regulations can be challenged under the APA as a violation of § 102(c). The Court of Appeals, however found that the CIA's own regulations plainly protect the discretion granted the Director by § 102(c), and that the regulations "provide[ ] no independent source of procedural or substantive protections." Thus, since petitioner prevailed on this ground below and does not seek further review of the question here, we do not reach that issue.

of the same sort of rummaging. Furthermore, the District Court has the latitude to control any discovery process which may be instituted so as to balance respondent's need for access to proof which would support a colorable constitutional claim against the extraordinary needs of the CIA for confidentiality and the protection of its methods, sources, and mission.

Petitioner also contends that even if respondent has raised a colorable constitutional claim arising out of his discharge, Congress in the interest of national security may deny the courts the authority to decide the claim and to order respondent's reinstatement if the claim is upheld. For the reasons previously stated, we do not think Congress meant to impose such restrictions when it enacted § 102(c) of the NSA. Even without such prohibitory legislation from Congress, of course, traditional equitable principles requiring the balancing of public and private interests control the grant of declaratory or injunctive relief in the federal courts. On remand, the District Court should thus address respondent's constitutional claims and the propriety of the equitable remedies sought. * * *

JUSTICE KENNEDY took no part in the consideration or decision of this case.

JUSTICE O'CONNOR, concurring in part and dissenting in part.

I agree that the Administrative Procedure Act (APA) does not authorize judicial review of the employment decisions referred to in § 102(c) of the National Security Act. Because § 102(c) does not provide a meaningful standard for judicial review, such decisions are clearly "committed to agency discretion by law" within the meaning of § 701(a)(2) of the APA. I do not understand the Court to say that the exception in § 701(a)(2) is necessarily or fully defined by reference to statutes "drawn in such broad terms that in a given case there is no law to apply." * * *

I disagree, however, with the Court's conclusion that a constitutional claim challenging the validity of an employment decision covered by § 102(c) may nonetheless be brought in a Federal District Court. Whatever may be the exact scope of Congress' power to close the lower federal courts to constitutional claims in other contexts, I have no doubt about its authority to do so here. The functions performed by the Central Intelligence Agency and the Director of Central Intelligence lie at the core of "the very delicate, plenary and exclusive power of the President as the sole organ of the federal government in the field of international relations." The authority of the Director of Central Intelligence to control access to sensitive national security information by discharging employees deemed to be untrustworthy flows primarily from this constitutional power the President, and Congress may surely provide that the inferior federal courts are not used to infringe on the President's constitutional authority. Section § 102(c) plainly indicates that Congress has done exactly that, and the Court points to nothing in the structure, purpose, or legislative history of the National Security Act that would suggest a different conclusion. * * *

JUSTICE SCALIA, dissenting.

I agree with the Court's apparent holding in Part II of its opinion, * * * [b]ut because I do not see how a decision can, either practically or legally, be both unreviewable and yet reviewable for constitutional defect, I regard Part III of the opinion as essentially undoing Part II. I therefore respectfully dissent from the judgment of the Court.

I

Before proceeding to address Part III of the Court's opinion, which I think to be in error, I must discuss one significant element of the analysis in Part II. * * * Our precedents amply show that "commit[ment] to agency discretion by law" includes, but is not limited to, situations in which there is "no law to apply." * * *

The "no law to apply" test can account for the nonreviewability of certain issues, but falls far short of explaining the full scope of the areas from which the courts are excluded. For the fact is that there is no governmental decision that is not subject to a fair number of legal constraints precise enough to be susceptible of judicial application—beginning with the fundamental constraint that the decision must be taken in order to further a public purpose rather than a purely private interest; yet there are many governmental decisions that are not at all subject to judicial review. A United States Attorney's decision to prosecute, for example, will not be reviewed on the claim that it is prompted by personal animosity. Thus, "no law to apply" provides much less than the full answer to whether § 701(a)(2) applies.

The key to understanding the "committed to agency discretion by law" provision of § 701(a)(2) lies in contrasting it with the "statutes preclude judicial review" provision of § 701(a)(1). Why "statutes" for preclusion, but the much more general term "law" for commission to agency discretion? The answer is * * * that the latter was intended to refer to "the 'common law' of judicial review of agency action,"—a body of jurisprudence that had marked out, with more or less precision, certain issues and certain areas that were beyond the range of judicial review. That jurisprudence included principles ranging from the "political question" doctrine, to sovereign immunity (including doctrines determining when a suit against an officer would be deemed to be a suit against the sovereign), to official immunity, to prudential limitations upon the courts' equitable powers, to what can be described no more precisely than a traditional respect for the functions of the other branches reflected in the statement in *Marbury v. Madison*, that "[w]here the head of a department acts in a case, in which executive discretion is to be exercised; in which he is the mere organ of executive will; it is again repeated, that any application to a court to control, in any respect, his conduct, would be rejected without hesitation." Only if all that "common law" were embraced within § 701(a)(2) could it have been true that, as was generally understood, "[t]he intended result of [§ 701(a)] is to restate the existing law as to the area of reviewable agency action." Attorney General's Manual on the Administrative Procedure Act 94 (1947). Because that is the meaning of the provision, we have continued to take into account for purposes of determining reviewability, post-APA as before, not only the text and structure of the statute under which the agency acts, but such factors as whether the decision involves "a sensitive and inherently discretionary judgment call," whether it is the sort of decision that has traditionally been nonreviewable, and whether review would have "disruptive practical consequences." * * *

All this law, shaped over the course of centuries and still developing in its application to new contexts, cannot possibly be contained within the phrase "no law to apply." It is not surprising, then, that although the Court recites the test it does not really apply it. Like other opinions relying upon it, this one essentially announces the test, declares victory and moves on. It is not really true " 'that a court would have no meaningful standard against which to judge the agency's exercise of discretion.' " The standard set forth in § 102(c) of the National Security Act of 1947, 50 U.S.C. § 403(c), "necessary or advisable in the interests of the United States," at least excludes dismissal out of personal vindictiveness, or because the Director wants to give the job to his cousin. * * *

If and when this Court does come to consider the reviewability of a dismissal such as the present one on the ground that it violated the agency's regulations—a question the Court avoids today, the difference between the "no law to apply" test and what I consider the correct test will be crucial. * * *

II

* * * I turn, then, to the substance of the Court's warning that judicial review of all "colorable constitutional claims" arising out of the respondent's dismissal may well be constitutionally required. What could possibly be the basis for this fear? Surely not some general principle that all constitutional violations must be remediable in the courts. The very text of the Constitution refutes that principle, since it provides that "[e]ach House shall be the Judge of the Elections, Returns and Qualifications of its own Members," Art. I, § 5, and that "for any Speech or Debate in either House, [the Senators and Representatives] shall not be questioned in any other Place," Art. I, § 6. Claims concerning constitutional violations committed in these contexts—for example, the rather grave constitutional claim that an election has been stolen—cannot be addressed to the courts. Even apart from the strict text of the Constitution, we have found some constitutional claims to be beyond judicial review because they involve "political questions." * * *

Perhaps, then, the Court means to appeal to a more limited principle, that although there may be areas where judicial review of a constitutional claim will be denied, the scope of those areas is fixed by the

Constitution and judicial tradition, and cannot be affected by Congress, through the enactment of a statute such as § 102(c). That would be a rather counter-intuitive principle, especially since Congress has in reality been the principal determiner of the scope of review, for constitutional claims as well as all other claims, through its waiver of the pre-existing doctrine of sovereign immunity. On the merits of the point, however: It seems to me clear that courts would not entertain, for example, an action for backpay by a dismissed Secretary of State claiming that the reason he lost his Government job was that the President did not like his religious views—surely a colorable violation of the First Amendment. I am confident we would hold that the President's choice of his Secretary of State is a "political question." But what about a similar suit by the Deputy Secretary of State? Or one of the Under Secretaries? Or an Assistant Secretary? Or the head of the European Desk? Is there really a constitutional line that falls at some immutable point between one and another of these offices at which the principle of unreviewability cuts in, and which cannot be altered by congressional prescription? I think not. I think Congress can prescribe, at least within broad limits, that for certain jobs the dismissal decision will be unreviewable—that is, will be "committed to agency discretion by law."

Once it is acknowledged, as I think it must be, (1) that not all constitutional claims require a judicial remedy, and (2) that the identification of those that do not can, even if only within narrow limits, be determined by Congress, then it is clear that the "serious constitutional question" feared by the Court is an illusion. Indeed, it seems to me that if one is in a mood to worry about serious constitutional questions the one to worry about is not whether Congress can, by enacting § 102(c), give the President, through his Director of Central Intelligence, unreviewable discretion in firing the agents that he employs to gather military and foreign affairs intelligence, but rather whether Congress could constitutionally permit the courts to review all such decisions if it wanted to. * * *

I think it entirely beyond doubt that if Congress intended, by § 701(a)(2) of the APA, to exclude judicial review of the President's decision (through the Director of Central Intelligence) to dismiss an officer of the Central Intelligence Agency, that disposition would be constitutionally permissible.

III

I turn, then, to whether that executive action is, within the meaning of § 701(a)(2), "committed to agency discretion by law." My discussion of this point can be brief, because the answer is compellingly obvious. Section 102(c) of the National Security Act of 1947, 61 Stat. 498, states:

> Notwithstanding * * * the provisions of any other law, the Director of Central Intelligence, may, in his discretion, terminate the employment of any officer or employee of the Agency whenever he shall

> deem such termination necessary or advisable in the interests of the United States * * *.

50 U.S.C. § 403(c). Further, as the Court declares, § 102(c) is an "integral part" of the National Security Act, which throughout exhibits "extraordinary deference to the Director." Given this statutory text, and given (as discussed above) that the area to which the text pertains is one of predominant executive authority and of traditional judicial abstention, it is difficult to conceive of a statutory scheme that more clearly reflects that "commit[ment] to agency discretion by law" to which § 701(a)(2) refers. * * *

Even if we were to assume, * * *, contrary to all reason, that every constitutional claim is ipso facto more worthy, and every statutory claim less worthy, of judicial review, there would be no basis for writing that preference into a statute that makes no distinction between the two. * * * There is no more textual basis for reading this statute as barring only nonconstitutional claims than there is to read it as barring only claims with a monetary worth of less than $1 million. * * *

The Court seeks to downplay the harm produced by today's decision by observing that "petitioner acknowledges that Title VII claims attacking the hiring and promotion policies of the Agency are routinely entertained in federal court." Assuming that those suits are statutorily authorized, I am willing to accept the Director's assertion that, while suits regarding hiring or promotion are tolerable, a suit regarding dismissal is not. Like the Court, I have no basis of knowledge on which I could deny that—especially since it is obvious that if the Director thinks that a particular hiring or promotion suit is genuinely contrary to the interests of the United States he can simply make the hiring or grant the promotion, and then dismiss the prospective litigant under § 102(c). The harm done by today's decision is that, contrary to what Congress knows is preferable, it brings a significant decision-making process of our intelligence services into a forum where it does not belong. Neither the Constitution, nor our laws, nor common sense gives an individual a right to come into court to litigate the reasons for his dismissal as an intelligence agent.

Today's result, however, will have ramifications far beyond creation of the world's only secret intelligence agency that must litigate the dismissal of its agents. If constitutional claims can be raised in this highly sensitive context, it is hard to imagine where they cannot. The assumption that there are any executive decisions that cannot be hauled into the courts may no longer be valid. Also obsolete may be the assumption that we are capable of preserving a sensible common law of judicial review. I respectfully dissent.

Notes

1. Webster *on Remand.* On remand, the district court concluded that CIA regulations gave Doe a post-probation property interest in his clerk-

typist position, and that his discharge without a statement of reasons why his homosexuality posed a security threat and without an opportunity to respond to those reasons violated due process. *Doe v. Webster*, 769 F.Supp. 1 (D.D.C.1991). Reliance on CIA regulations served to distinguish the case from *Doe v. Cheney*, 885 F.2d 898 (D.C.Cir.1989), in which the court found that the plaintiff, an employee of the National Security Agency, lacked any liberty or property interest in his security clearance on which to base a due process claim against its revocation based on allegations that he engaged in homosexual conduct with foreign nationals.

2. *The Importance of Constitutional Claims*. The majority's insistence in *Webster* that a legislative attempt to preclude review of constitutional claims would be troubling sends a strong message. This is, after all, a case involving (a) a congressional determination to make the Director's statutory discretion unreviewable, (b) a decision involving national security decision making, as to which federal courts are usually highly deferential, and (c) a constitutional context in which the Court has not always been hospitable to substantive due process claims. Compare *Bowers v. Hardwick*, 478 U.S. 186 (1986). Yet, Justice Scalia argues, as he has in other cases, e.g., *INS v. St.Cyr, supra* p. 882, that the preclusion of constitutional claims is no more or less troubling than a preclusion of statutory claims.

Justice Scalia identifies a number of specific respects in which the Constitution seems to imply an absence of judicial review of claims of constitutional right. He infers from these specific examples a general interpretive premise that such preclusions are not constitutionally exceptional. Recall, however, that, in his *Morrison v. Olson* dissent, Justice Scalia implicitly refused to find as a general principle that branches of the federal government may exhibit shared or overlapping powers despite specific ways in which the Constitution expressly contemplates the sharing of powers. Is there a principled way of determining when constitutional "specifics" illustrate a general principle to be construed broadly (à la the *Webster* dissent) and when they are merely exceptions to another principle, and should themselves be construed narrowly (à la the *Morrison* dissent)?

3. *Distinguishing Section 701(a)'s Grounds for Nonreviewability*. It should be obvious that the line between the two exceptions to reviewability in 5 U.S.C. § 701 is not sharp. The same statute may in one case be described as "precluding review" and in another as "committing decisions to agency discretion." This is especially likely if claims of nonreviewability under both headings involve identical functional assessments of the impact of judicial review on a particular statutory program. Recall, from the notes following *Johnson v. Robison*, that the Court has found implicit statutory preclusion based on its functional interpretation of how particular programs were intended to operate. *Morris v. Gressette, supra*; *Block v. Community Nutrition Institute, Inc., supra*. The D.C. Circuit has likewise expressed its view that "pragmatic considerations" underlie an inference of commitment to discretion: "Among the important considerations are 'the need for judicial supervision to safeguard the interests of the plaintiffs[,] the impact of review on the effectiveness of the agency in carrying out its congressionally assigned role[,] and the appropriateness of the issues raised for judicial review.'" *Investment Co. Institute v. FDIC*, 728 F.2d 518, 526–27 (D.C.Cir.1984). This formula—the best known of the judicial balancing tests of reviewability in

use prior to *Heckler v. Chaney*, *infra* p. 922—originated in *Hahn v. Gottlieb*, 430 F.2d 1243 (1st Cir.1970).

Indeed, the potential interchangeability of § 701(a)'s twin exceptions to review is nicely illustrated by two cases, one of them *Hahn v. Gottlieb*, in which tenants residing in federally subsidized housing unsuccessfully sought review of the FHA's approval of rent increases proposed by their landlords. In *Hahn v. Gottlieb*, Judge Coffin determined that the FHA's decision whether to approve rent increases was committed to the agency's discretion by law. He regarded the FHA's "economic and managerial" decisions as ill-suited for judicial assessment, and concluded that costly and time-consuming judicial review of such decisions could both (1) undermine plaintiffs' interests by prompting yet higher rents or a lower rate of investor participation in FHA housing programs and (2) undermine FHA performance by unduly formalizing its decision making. Addressing the same issue in *Langevin v. Chenango Court, Inc.*, 447 F.2d 296 (2d Cir.1971), Judge Friendly disagreed with Judge Coffin's assertion that courts were ill-equipped to assess the reasonableness of rent increase approvals. He inferred, however, that the Federal Housing Act precluded judicial review because Congress would not likely intend that courts review an agency's discretionary administration of a contract Congress authorized it to make. The managerial nature of FHA's responsibilities and the potential impact on the FHA of a high volume of judicial appeals of its decisions were also factors substantiating the inference that Congress intended to preclude review of rent increase approvals.

The significance of the difference in approach between the First and Second Circuits is a matter of debate. One might assume that a decision couched in terms of legislative preclusion affords the courts less room for maneuver in the future—requiring either a confession of error or new legislation to allow review. But since paragraph (2) of section 701(a) appears to include categories of cases in which *Congress* has decided that review should not be available, this intuition may be wrong. Yet the sources consulted in determining the applicability of 701(a)(2) often seem so malleable that one has the impression that judicial self-restraint is at work when review is withheld.

Hahn and *Langevin* are relatively unusual in withholding substantive review of the FHA's approval of rent increases—though both acknowledge that the issue might have looked different if the tenants had alleged an outright violation of the Housing Act or of the Constitution. As one might expect, however, decisions finding particular actions committed to agency discretion often arise in areas traditionally viewed as imbued with official discretion. These include matters of agency management not involving the discharge of personnel, *e.g.*, *Kletschka v. Driver*, 411 F.2d 436 (2d Cir.1969) (VA decisions to withdraw physician's research grant and transfer him to less desirable location nonreviewable); disposing of public lands, *e.g.*, *Ferry v. Udall*, 336 F.2d 706 (9th Cir.1964), *cert. denied*, 381 U.S. 904 (1965); *United States v. Walker*, 409 F.2d 477 (9th Cir.1969); and defense and foreign affairs, *Curran v. Laird*, 420 F.2d 122 (D.C.Cir.1969) (en banc). Even in these areas, statutory nonreviewability is the exception, however, not the rule.

4. *Nonreviewability of Agency Budget Reallocations.* The congressional appropriations process is one of the most important mechanisms for the legislative control of agency behavior. As consensus-building between the branches has become more difficult, Congress has turned increasingly to so-called appropriations "riders" as a means of giving specific directions to agencies. Thus, for example, Congress, if dissatisfied with a particular agency rulemaking, may enact an appropriations measure for the agency that includes language like: "No funds herein appropriated may be expended for the purpose of implementing" the rule Congress does not like. Such a restriction constrains the agency only for the duration of the annual act, but is more likely to be veto-proof than a bill amending the agency's substantive authorities.

Generally, however, Congress appropriates funds for agencies in "lump sums" that the agency may deploy in its discretion for a variety of specific purposes, so long as each of the initiatives relates to the general purpose of the lump sum. Congress is rarely surprised by the actual use of funds because the lump sum totals reflect projections for the use of funds that the agency submits as part of its appropriations testimony and in informal negotiations with Congress.

Clearly an agency redeployment of lump-sum appropriations from one initiative to another is a "final agency action" that can have significant programmatic impacts. In *Lincoln v. Vigil*, 508 U.S. 182 (1993), disabled Indian children challenged a decision by the Indian Health Service to close a program providing direct services to Indian children in the Southwest with "emotional, educational, physical, or mental handicaps," and to shift such funds to the support of a national mental health treatment program. The Service thought the reallocation would advance "our goal of increased mental health services for all Indian [c]hildren." The children who had been receiving targeted services contended that the decision violated the Service's legal obligations to them. The Supreme Court, however, held the agency decision unreviewable, observing:

> The allocation of funds from a lump-sum appropriation is [an] administrative decision traditionally regarded as committed to agency discretion. After all, the very point of a lump-sum appropriation is to give an agency the capacity to adapt to changing circumstances and meet its statutory responsibilities in what it sees as the most effective or desirable way.

In the Court's view, subjecting reallocation decisions to judicial review would undermine Congress's intention to allow flexibility in administration, and interfere with the "complicated balancing of a number of factors which are peculiarly within [an agency's] expertise."

5. *Constitutional Commitment to Discretion.* Justice Scalia must surely be right that the "law" that may commit decisions "to agency discretion" is not limited to statutes. When a dispute involves the exercise of power constitutionally vested in the President, however, the question of review is usually analyzed in "political question" terms. And when an agency operates in a domain charged with executive prerogative, the "political" nature of the activity will influence judicial assessment of whether the statutory function has been committed to agency discretion. For example, in *Curran v. Laird*,

420 F.2d 122 (D.C.Cir.1969) (en banc), the National Maritime Union sought to enforce the requirement of 10 U.S.C. § 2631 that supplies for the military forces be shipped *only* in United States vessels. The government admitted using foreign vessels, but only when U.S. ships were not available. The union conceded that unavailability might justify failure to follow the letter of the statute, but contended that U.S. ships were "unavailable" only because the Secretary had failed to activate portions of the reserve fleet. Judge Leventhal balked at reviewing in any fashion the Secretary's decision:

> The range of executive judgments involved are likely to involve estimates as to when, where, and how much cargo will have to be moved in the future—not only military but also foreign aid cargoes. The decisions also require a judgment of the feasibility of providing sustained employment for a reactivated vessel.
>
> This court cannot sit in judgment to review a determination which involves appraisals like those outlined. The manifest difficulties cannot be obviated by construing the statute as requiring only that the authorities "consider" the feasibility of employing the reserve fleet ships for transporting military cargoes. There is no satisfactory exit once the judiciary crosses the threshold and enters the domain of these matters. * * *
>
> Even restricted review requires probing the surface and going beyond mere conclusory affidavits setting forth the department's reasons. Any other approach belies the notion that these matters before us are not in fact necessarily committed to agency discretion. Settled doctrine does not permit us to accept at face value administrative determinations without at least surveying a record.
>
> We do not deal with officials who are operating under discernible statutory standards, or a mandate to develop standards to assure even-handed justice. They are rather likely to be called on to make and revise judgments freely, perhaps to draw heavily on information from sources abroad or in the domain of the military in making global guesstimates. Not all operations of government are subject to judicial review, even though they may have a profound effect on our lives.

Judges Wright, Bazelon, and Robinson would have reviewed to determine whether the Secretary had at least considered activating the reserve fleet and had "reason for passing over it."

Where decision making authority has been assigned by Congress (or the Constitution?) to the executive without instructions or any apparent limits on its exercise, it is nonetheless possible that the delegate may, for its own purposes, establish criteria and procedures for decision that can provide the basis for at least limited judicial oversight. *Miami Nation of Indians of Indiana v. U.S. Department of the Interior*, 255 F.3d 342 (7th Cir.2001), sought judicial review of the Interior Secretary's refusal to recognize the Nation as an Indian tribe entitled to the status and benefits Congress has by statute provided. The court of appeals, in an opinion by Chief Judge Posner, held that the Secretary's decision was reviewable:

> Article I of the Constitution authorizes Congress to regulate commerce with Indians. As an original matter, the power to recognize an

> Indian tribe might be thought quintessentially and exclusively Presidential, like the power to recognize (or not recognize) a foreign nation. * * * [T]he analogy to recognition of foreign governments has prevailed to the extent that Congress has delegated to the executive branch the power of recognition of Indian tribes without setting forth any criteria to guide the exercise of that power. * * *
>
> * * *
>
> * * * It comes as no surprise, therefore, that "the action of the federal government in recognizing or failing to recognize a tribe has traditionally been held to be a political one not subject to judicial review."
>
> But this conclusion assumes that the executive branch has not sought to canalize the discretion of its subordinate officials by means of regulations that require them to base recognition of Indian tribes on the kinds of determination, legal or factual, that courts routinely make. By promulgating such regulations [as Interior had done in 1978] the executive brings the tribal recognition process within the scope of the Administrative Procedure Act. And the Act has been interpreted (1) to require agencies, on pain of being found to have acted arbitrarily and capriciously, to comply with their own regulations * * * and (2) to make compliance with the regulations judicially reviewable, provided there is law to apply to determine compliance. * * *

In addressing this last qualification Judge Posner went on to observe:

> [A]s the "law to apply" provision of the APA makes clear, the fact that a regulation has been promulgated doesn't automatically make compliance with the regulation a justiciable issue. It depends on what the regulation says; it may not set forth sufficiently law-like criteria to provide guideposts for a reasoned judicial decision.

Judge Posner then turned to the text of the Interior regulations, which set forth seven criteria that a tribe must satisfy to be eligible for recognition, including historical continuity, occupancy of a specific area, maintenance of tribal authority over community members, adherence to a written governing document, and documentation of tribal membership. Judge Posner found that these criteria posed factual and legal questions of "the sort * * * that courts are equipped to answer." He then proceeded to evaluate the Interior Department's explanation for its refusal to recognize the tribe and, save for an error he found harmless, concluded that its decision should be upheld.

c. *Review of Agency Inaction*

The traditional law of judicial review of administrative action is largely the product of a concern to protect private interests from unlawful *assertions* of governmental authority. In recent years, however, much attention has been given to the failure of administrative agencies to enforce existing standards or to develop standards adequate to protect the public interest. Judicial review is frequently sought not to restrain, but to stimulate, administrative action. See, e.g., *Allen v. Wright*, *infra* p. 1054. See generally Note, *Judicial Review of Administrative Inaction*, 83

Colum.L.Rev. 627 (1983); Merrick B. Garland, *Deregulation and Judicial Review*, 98 Harv.L.Rev. 505 (1985); Cass R. Sunstein, *Deregulation and the Hard–Look Doctrine*, 1983 Sup.Ct.L.Rev. 177.

That such suits should confront objections of nonreviewability is not surprising. Statutes often provide for review of agency action but seldom address the question of inaction. Moreover, an agency's decision to initiate enforcement proceedings is closely analogous to the decision to prosecute criminal offenders, and such prosecutorial judgments have traditionally been considered beyond review. *E.g., Smith v. United States*, 411 U.S. 908 (1973). And one searches in vain for enforceable restraints on congressional decisions to delay, defer, or wholly ignore demands for the enactment of new legislation. This analogy to administrative selection of subjects for rulemaking suggests the difficulty of framing a legal challenge to an agency's failure to adopt new rules. The questions raised by the materials in this section thus implicate two central issues: First, should agency enforcement choices be insulated from judicial review to the same extent as the judgments of criminal prosecutors? Second, should the federal courts have a role in overseeing agency priorities for rulemaking?

(1) Review of Enforcement Discretion

An inevitable part of agenda setting in any agency with prosecutorial powers is deciding what cases *not* to bring. Consider, as an example, the NLRB, whose General Counsel has "final authority, in respect of the investigation of charges and issuance of [unfair labor practice] complaints * * *, and in respect of the prosecution of such complaints before the Board, * * *." 29 U.S.C. § 153. The General Counsel has delegated the authority to issue complaints to NLRB Regional Directors, whose decisions *not* to file complaints may be appealed to the General Counsel.

Private parties disappointed by NLRB decisions not to prosecute have often sought to challenge the exercise of enforcement discretion by the General Counsel and Regional Directors. A leading illustration is *Dunn v. Retail Clerks Int'l Ass'n*, 307 F.2d 285 (6th Cir.1962), which involved a hotly contested union election in which the employer had hired a photographer to take pictures of union representatives aggressively electioneering among employees during the period of the vote. Union members allegedly "swarmed" onto the floors of the plaintiff's stores, campaigned among employees in a way that interfered with their work, and mingled with the employees in line to vote. When the union lost, it alleged unfair voter intimidation through the use of the employer's photographer, and the NLRB Regional Director set the election aside based on the employer's practices. He refused, however, to issue a complaint against the union for unfair electioneering. The court held that it lacked authority to enjoin the General Counsel or Regional Director to pursue the employer's complaint, even though the situation alleged was, if accurately depicted, "a pretty horrible situation."

The federal courts have consistently followed the *Dunn* approach to NLRA enforcement, although disappointed complainants have continued to pursue judicial review of decisions not to initiate unfair labor practice proceedings. The single inroad on the NLRB General Counsel's discretion to prosecute unfair labor practices involved allegations that a nonprosecution decision was based purely on a misinterpretation of law. In *Southern California District Council v. Ordman*, 318 F.Supp. 633 (C.D.Cal.1970), the General Counsel had refused to consider a complaint on the ground that it had been filed more than six months after the alleged unfair labor practice; 29 U.S.C. § 160(b) requires that the complaints be filed within six months. The court held that his refusal to consider the complaint on this ground was reviewable to determine whether he had misconstrued the statute. The court found that the General Counsel had indeed mistaken the time at which the alleged unfair labor practice should be held to have occurred and ordered him to consider the complaint as timely filed.

In making known his reasons for dismissing the complaint in *Southern California District* the NLRB General Counsel acted in accordance with the Board's Rules, Regulations and Statement of Procedures, which in 1968 provided:

> *Sec. 102.19 Appeal to the general counsel from refusal to issue or reissue.*
>
> (a) If, after the charge has been filed, the regional director declines to issue a complaint, or having withdrawn a complaint pursuant to § 102.18, refuses to reissue it, he shall so advise the parties in writing, accompanied by a simple statement of the procedural or other grounds for his action. The person making the charge may obtain a review of such action by filing an appeal with the general counsel in Washington, D.C., and filing a copy of the appeal with the regional director, within 10 days from the service of the notice of such refusal to issue or reissue by the regional director * * *. Consideration of an appeal untimely filed is within the discretion of the general counsel upon good cause shown. * * *
>
> (c) The general counsel may sustain the regional director's refusal to issue or reissue a complaint, stating the grounds of his affirmance, or may direct the regional director to take further action; the general counsel's decision shall be served on all the parties. * * *

Although *Dunn* may seem very hard law, the exception to review recognized in *Southern California District Council* is not obviously a move in the right direction. There is no requirement that the Board maintain the system of appeals and written reasons prescribed in its regulations. If the courts are willing to review only when reasons are given and if internal review of decisions not to initiate enforcement is burdensome (which it certainly might be for an agency like the NRLB which rejects thousands of petitions each year), the course the Board should follow seems clear.

In a pair of cases the D.C. Circuit seemed to send the same message to the Securities and Exchange Commission concerning its "no-action" letters (letters which indicate to a complaining party that the Commission will take no enforcement action on the complaint). Compare *Medical Committee for Human Rights v. SEC*, 432 F.2d 659 (D.C.Cir.1970), *cert. granted*, 401 U.S. 973 (1971), *vacated as moot*, 404 U.S. 403 (1972), with *Kixmiller v. SEC*, 492 F.2d 641 (D.C.Cir.1974). In the latter opinion the court explained the distinction between the two cases:

> * * * [In] *Medical Committee*, * * * after the staff announced that it would not recommend action respecting a company's omission of a stockholder's proposal from its proxy materials, the Commission examined the staff's no-action determination and accepted it. As our opinion in *Medical Committee* recounted, the Commission, "after reviewing the petitioner's proxy claim," "exercised its discretion to review [the] controversy," and "approved the recommendation of the [staff] that no objection be raised." * * * In sum, *Medical Committee* involved a no-action ruling by the staff which was sanctioned by the Commission, and that, we held, constituted administrative action subject to judicial review.
>
> In sharp contrast to that decision is the Commission's refusal here to in any way probe or pass on the staff's no-action position. The distinction is between the Commission's reexamination and affirmance of the staff's conclusion on the one hand, and the Commission's declension of any review or adjudication on the other. We recognized the vitality of that distinction when in *Medical Committee* we admonished that the availability of judicial review of a staff no-action decision respecting proxy proposals "depends upon the Commission's initial determination to review the staff decision." That precondition is not met here.

The court then went on to hold that the full Commission's refusal to review the staff determination in *Kixmiller* was unreviewable:

> The Securities Exchange Act of 1934 provides that "the Commission may, in its discretion, make such investigations as it deems necessary," and that "it may in its discretion bring an action" in court. An agency's decision to refrain from an investigation or an enforcement action is generally unreviewable and, as to the agency before us, the specifications of the Act leave no doubt on that score.

An agency's failure to act on complaints about activities that appear to violate its law is likely to be the product of a complex set of reasons, usually innocent if not always convincing. These often include conscious allocation of resources to other problems that the agency considers (or has been directed by the President or urged by Congress to consider) more serious. No agency has resources adequate to enforce its relevant statutes completely or comprehensively, nor would we wish it to do so. The Internal Revenue Service, for example, cannot conceivably audit all income tax returns and, predictably, it has adopted criteria for selecting the relatively few returns that will be carefully reviewed, *e.g.*, those revealing substantial charitable deductions or investments in tax shelters.

Such choices do not always reflect simply a desire to maximize the "impact" of limited enforcement resources. Or perhaps it is more accurate to say that administrative agencies often employ quite catholic measures of "impact." An illustration is the FDA, whose managers self-consciously reevaluate the agency's priorities on a regular basis. The objective is to allocate total agency resources, measured both in human energy (*e.g.*, inspector time, laboratory analyst time) and dollars among a huge array of activities that range across several different product lines. The main criterion used is cost-effective health promotion but the managers also consider what has been termed "public interest," which can be a proxy for "potential public embarrassment." If health protection were the sole criterion, the FDA would allocate its resources differently. Prevention of food-borne disease through regular inspection of production and storage establishments, in its view, contributes significantly to prolonging life and preventing morbidity. Review of food additives, by contrast, has been considered less important as a public health safeguard. But the FDA has always devoted substantial resources to the latter activity, partly because it believes that consumers are anxious about food additive safety and their advocates have significant influence with Congress and the press. For one account of the FDA's priority-setting process, see DISCUSSION OF FDA PRIORITIES: FISCAL YEAR 1986 PLANNING PROCESS (March 1984).

The FDA's experience in regulating food sanitation provides another illustration of resource constraints on agency enforcement activities. In the early 1970s, as again a generation later, considerable attention was being given in Congress to the adequacy of the FDA's oversight of food production and distribution practices. At Hearings before the Subcommittee on Public Health and Environment of the House Committee on Interstate and Foreign Commerce, 92d Cong., 1st Sess. (1971), the following colloquy occurred:

> [FDA Commissioner Dr. Charles] EDWARDS. * * * Every time an emergency situation or a natural disaster occurs, it is necessary for us to suspend food inspections, suspend planned food analyses and our normal program operations. * * *
>
> CONGRESSMAN ROY. How many food plants are presently subject to your inspection?
>
> DR. EDWARDS. We figure there are approximately 60,000 food establishments which come under our jurisdiction. * * *
>
> MR. ROY. And you presently have 250 inspectors in the field. * * *
>
> CONGRESSMAN ROGERS. Doctor, what is your need for manpower to do an effective job in inspecting the 60,000 food plants coming within your jurisdiction: 1,500 inspectors, is that a sufficient figure?
>
> DR. EDWARDS. I think in that order of magnitude; yes. * * *

MR. ROGERS. That would amount to how much money?

DR. EDWARDS. $75 to $85 million.

MR. ROGERS. About the amount of your total budget now?

DR. EDWARDS. It is getting fairly close; yes. * * *

The realization that an agency cannot and will not proceed against all claimed violations obviously invites demands to know what criteria it uses in selecting those it will pursue. Our concern here is not with the content of such criteria, which differ widely from agency to agency, but with public access to such information. Agencies have had varying success in resisting disclosure of their internal enforcement criteria under the FOIA. A desire to retain the *in terrorem* effects of the written law helps explain the unwillingness of many law enforcement officers to reveal their working guides for prosecution. But every agency has such guides, and some agencies may find it useful to make them known.

Once more, the FDA serves as an example. For decades it maintained so-called "action levels" for contaminants of food—levels that, if detected, will lead to seizure. In 1972, in response to food distributors, who claimed the knowledge would contribute to voluntary compliance, as well as to demands for open government, the FDA formally announced that all of its action levels would be disclosed upon request. 37 Fed.Reg. 6497 (Mar. 30, 1972). The reaction was disconcerting. Citizens wrote the agency and their congressmen, expressing dismay that foods such as bay leaves could have up to "5 per cent insect infested pieces" or up to "1 milligram rodent excreta per pound" and still be sold! An FDA official's defensive retort that if food were required to be pure, "there would be no food sold in the United States" was hardly reassuring. See The Washington Post, March 29, 1972, § B, at 2.

DUNLOP v. BACHOWSKI

Supreme Court of the United States, 1975.
421 U.S. 560, 95 S.Ct. 1851, 44 L.Ed.2d 377.

JUSTICE BRENNAN delivered the opinion of the Court.

On February 13, 1973, the United Steelworkers of America (USWA) held district officer elections in its several districts. Respondent Bachowski (hereinafter respondent) was defeated by the incumbent in the election for that office in District 20. After exhausting his remedies within USWA, respondent filed a timely complaint with petitioner, the Secretary of Labor, alleging violations of § 401 of the Labor–Management Reporting and Disclosure Act of 1959 (LMRDA), 29 U.S.C. § 481, thus invoking 29 U.S.C. §§ 482(a), (b) which require that the Secretary investigate the complaint and decide whether to bring a civil action to set aside the election.[2] * * * After completing his investigations, the

2. * * * "(b) Investigation of complaint; commencement of civil action by Secretary; jurisdiction; preservation of assets.

"The Secretary shall investigate [a union member's] complaint and, if he finds probable cause to believe that a violation

Secretary * * * advised respondent by letter dated November 7, 1973, that "[b]ased on the investigative findings, it has been determined * * * that civil action to set aside the challenged election is not warranted."

On November 7, 1973, respondent filed this action against the Secretary and USWA in the District Court for the Western District of Pennsylvania. * * * [That court] concluded that [it] lacked "authority" to find that the action was capricious and to order him to file suit. * * *

The Court of Appeals held, *first*, that the District Court had jurisdiction of respondent's suit under 28 U.S.C. § 1337 as a case arising under an Act of Congress regulating commerce, the LMRDA; *second*, that the Administrative Procedure Act, 5 U.S.C. §§ 702 and 704, subjected the Secretary's decision to judicial review as "final agency action for which there is no other adequate remedy in a court," and that his decision was not, as the Secretary maintained, agency action pursuant to "(1) statutes [that] preclude judicial review; or (2) agency action [that] is committed to agency discretion by law," excepted by § 701(a) from judicial review; and, *third*, that the scope of judicial review—governed by § 706(2)(A), "to ensure that the Secretary's actions are not arbitrary, capricious, or an abuse of discretion."—entitled respondent, who sought "to challenge the factual basis for [the Secretary's] conclusion either that no violations occurred or that they did not affect the outcome of the election," "to a sufficiently specific statement of the factors upon which the Secretary relied in reaching his decision * * * so that [respondent] may have information concerning the allegations contained in his complaint." * * *

We agree that 28 U.S.C. § 1337 confers jurisdiction upon the District Court to entertain respondent's suit, and that the Secretary's decision not to sue is not excepted from judicial review by 5 U.S.C. § 701(a); rather, §§ 702 and 704 subject the Secretary's decision to judicial review under the standard specified in § 706(2)(A). We hold, however, that the Court of Appeals erred insofar as its opinion construes § 706(2)(A) to authorize a trial-type inquiry into the factual bases of the Secretary's conclusion that no violations occurred affecting the outcome of the election. We accordingly reverse the judgment of the Court of Appeals insofar as it directs further proceedings on remand consistent with the opinion of that court * * *.

In the absence of an express prohibition in the LMRDA, the Secretary * * * bears the heavy burden of overcoming the strong presumption that Congress did not mean to prohibit all judicial review of his decision. * * * *Abbott Laboratories v. Gardner*, 387 U.S. 136 (1967); *Citizens to Preserve Overton Park v. Volpe*, 401 U.S. 402 (1971).

of this subchapter has occurred and has not been remedied, he shall, within sixty days after the filing of such complaint, bring a civil action against the labor organization as an entity in the district court of the United States in which such labor organization maintains its principal office to set aside the invalid election, if any, and to direct the conduct of an election or hearing and vote upon the removal of officers under the supervision of the Secretary * * *."

The Secretary urges that the structure of the statutory scheme, its objectives, its legislative history, the nature of the administrative action involved, and the conditions spelled out with respect thereto, combine to evince a congressional meaning to prohibit judicial review of his decision. We have examined the materials the Secretary relies upon. They do not reveal to us any congressional purpose to prohibit judicial review. Indeed, there is not even the slightest intimation that Congress gave thought to the matter of the preclusion of judicial review. * * *

* * * Our examination of the relevant materials persuades us, however, that although no purpose to prohibit all judicial review is shown, a congressional purpose narrowly to limit the scope of judicial review of the Secretary's decision can, and should, be inferred in order to carry out congressional objectives in enacting the LMRDA.

Two conclusions follow from [a] * * * survey of our decisions: (1) since the statute relies upon the special knowledge and discretion of the Secretary for the determination of both the probable violation and the probable effect, clearly the reviewing court is not authorized to substitute its judgment for the decision of the Secretary not to bring suit; (2) therefore, to enable the reviewing court intelligently to review the Secretary's determination, the Secretary must provide the court and the complaining witness with copies of a statement of reasons supporting his determination. * * *

Moreover, a statement of reasons serves purposes other than judicial review. Since the Secretary's role as lawyer for the complaining union member does not include the duty to indulge a client's usual prerogative to direct his lawyer to file suit, we may reasonably infer that Congress intended that the Secretary supply the member with a reasoned statement why he determined not to proceed. * * * Finally, a "reasons" requirement promotes thought by the Secretary and compels him to cover the relevant points and eschew irrelevancies, and as noted by the Court of Appeals in this case, the need to assure careful administrative consideration "would be relevant even if the Secretary's decision were unreviewable."

The necessity that the reviewing court refrain from substitution of its judgment for that of the Secretary thus helps define the permissible scope of review. Except in what must be the rare case, the court's review should be confined to examination of the "reasons" statement, and the determination whether the statement, without more, evinces that the Secretary's decision is so irrational as to constitute the decision arbitrary and capricious. Thus, review may not extend to cognizance or trial of a complaining member's challenges to the factual bases for the Secretary's conclusion either that no violations occurred or that they did not affect the outcome of the election. * * * If * * * the Court concludes * * * there is a rational and defensible basis [stated in the reasons statement] for [the Secretary's] determination, then that should be an end of this matter, for it is not the function of the Court to determine whether or not the case should be brought or what its outcome would be. * * *

The District Court, pursuant to the Court of Appeals' order of remand, ordered the Secretary to furnish a statement of reasons. The petitioner did not cross-petition from the order, and petitioner and USWA conceded that the order was proper in this case. The Secretary furnished the statement and it is attached as an Appendix to this opinion. Its adequacy to support a conclusion whether the Secretary's decision was rationally based or was arbitrary and capricious, is a matter of initial determination by the District Court. * * *[12]

CHIEF JUSTICE BURGER, concurring.

I join in the opinion of the Court with the understanding that the Court has fashioned an exceedingly narrow scope of review of the Secretary's determination not to bring an action on behalf of a complainant to set aside an election. The language and purposes of § 401 of the Labor–Management Reporting and Disclosure Act of 1959 have required the Court to define a scope of review much narrower than applies under 5 U.S.C. § 706(a)(A) in most other administrative areas. The Court's holding must be read as providing that the determination of the Secretary not to challenge a union election may be held arbitrary and capricious only where the Secretary's investigation, as evidenced by his statement of reasons, shows election irregularities that affected its outcome as to the complainant, and that notwithstanding the illegal conduct so found the Secretary nevertheless refuses to bring an action and advances no rational reason for his decision.

JUSTICE REHNQUIST, concurring in the result in part and dissenting in part.

The parties to this case will have to be excused if they react with surprise to the opinion of the Court. Instead of deciding the issue presented in the Secretary of Labor's petition for certiorari, the Court decides an issue about which the parties no longer disagree; to compound the confusion, the reasoning adopted by the Court to resolve the issue it does decide is quite unusual unless it is intended to foreshadow disposition of the issue upon which the Court purports to reserve judgment. * * *

* * * The single question presented by the Secretary's petition for certiorari is:

> "Whether a disappointed union office seeker may invoke the judicial process to compel the Secretary of Labor to bring an action under Title IV of the Labor–Management Reporting and Disclosure Act of 1959 to set aside a union election."

12. USWA argues that Arts. II and III of the Constitution "do not countenance a court order requiring the executive branch, against its wishes, to institute a lawsuit in federal court." "[A] judicial direction that such an action be brought would violate the separation of powers * * * [and] because the Secretary agrees with the union that Title IV does not require a new election, the lawsuit would be one lacking the requisite adversity of interests to constitute a 'case' or 'controversy' as required by Article III." Since we do not consider at this time the question of the court's power to order the Secretary to file suit, we need not address those contentions.

* * * It seems to me that prior decisions of this Court establish that the Secretary's decision to file or not to file a complaint under § 482 is precisely the kind of "agency action * * * committed to agency discretion by law" exempted from the judicial-review provisions of the APA. * * *

The Court recognizes the power of these arguments, if only by understatement, when it acknowledges that any argument for judicial review of the Secretary's determination "obviously presents some difficulty in light of the strong evidence that Congress deliberately gave exclusive enforcement authority to the Secretary." In my view the parties to this litigation are entitled to adjudication of the issue upon which this Court granted certiorari. I would accordingly reverse the judgment of the Court of Appeals insofar as it held that the Secretary's refusal to institute an action under 29 U.S.C. § 482 is judicially reviewable under the provisions of the APA, 5 U.S.C. §§ 701–706.

Notes

1. *The Textual Basis for* Bachowski. Without elaboration, the Supreme Court agreed in a footnote with the Third Circuit's reasons, 502 F.2d 79 (3d Cir.1974), for finding the Secretary's decision not to file suit under the L–MRDA reviewable. 421 U.S. at 568 n. 7. In brief, the circuit court rejected the Secretary's claim as invoking a principle of "absolute prosecutorial discretion," which "should be limited to those civil cases which, like criminal prosecutions, involve the vindication of societal or governmental interests, rather than the protection of individual rights." The court regarded the L–MRDA, as intended, instead, to vindicate the rights of "individual unions members" who, without secretarial intervention, "are left without a remedy."

The circuit court also thought section 482(b), *supra* p. 914 n.2, provided law to apply to the review of the Secretary's enforcement discretion. The court read that section as *mandating* prosecution if an investigation yielded probable cause to believe that a violation had occurred affecting the outcome of an election, and no settlement remedying the violation could be reached. Is 482(b) readily distinguishable from the relevant language of the National Labor Relations Act, which provides: "Whenever it is charged that any person has engaged in or is engaging in any * * * unfair labor practice, the Board * * * shall have power to issue * * * a complaint," 29 U.S.C. § 160(b)?

Is *Bachowski* distinguishable from *Dunn* on the ground that review in *Bachowski* would interfere less with the Secretary's allocation of enforcement resources? On the ground that the employer in *Dunn* had a weaker interest in protection from unfair labor practices than a candidate for union office has in protection from rigged elections?

2. *Requiring Reasons for Nonenforcement.* Does *Bachowski* solve the problem of discouraging reasoned public explanation posed by the *Dunn–Southern California District Council* and the *Medical Committee–Kixmiller* cases? From what source can the court derive a requirement of reasoned decision making that is not itself based upon a prior determination that

judicial review is available or that an on-the-record hearing is required? Does APA § 555(e) support such a requirement?

3. *Nonenforcement and Public Interests.* The Eighth Circuit reached a result similar to *Bachowski* in a case construing the duty of the NLRB to seek an injunction against secondary boycotts. *Terminal Freight Handling Co. v. Solien*, 444 F.2d 699, 708–09 (8th Cir.1971), *cert. denied*, 405 U.S. 996 (1972). The statutory language defining the Regional Director's duty in *Solien*, 29 U.S.C. § 160(1) (1970), was virtually identical to the language of the L–MRDA involved in *Bachowski*. However, the court's ruling in *Solien*, that the Director's failure to bring suit was reviewable, was based on the potentially grave and immediate damage to the *public* from secondary boycotts. The court then went on to describe the standard of review that should apply:

> We * * * conclude the "and that a complaint should issue" phrase reflects Congress' intention that the regional director retain limited prosecutorial discretion once he has made a reasonable cause determination. We think it is clearly within his discretion to make an initial demand upon the union to cease its unlawful activity. However, if he is unable to secure cessation upon such summary demand and negotiation, he must then petition for temporary injunctive relief and issue a complaint (or vice-versa) * * *.
>
> The Director of course may still negotiate settlements in lieu of injunctive relief in cases in which he has petitioned for injunctive relief such as was done here, and undoubtedly such settlements will be approved by the district court in most instances. If a settlement in lieu of injunctive relief negotiated by the regional director fails to adequately protect the public interest, the district court can override the settlement and grant injunctive relief.

4. *Settlement Discretion.* This "negotiated settlement" exception to required prosecution outlined in *Solien* may undercut the ruling's value for litigants who doubt an agency's enforcement zeal. Moreover, an attempt to intervene in negotiations prior to the initiation of enforcement proceedings in order to shape the direction of the informal agency process may well be rebuffed. In *Action on Safety and Health v. FTC*, 498 F.2d 757 (D.C.Cir. 1974), the plaintiffs had been denied participation in "pre-complaint" negotiations between the FTC and Volvo concerning the latter's advertising—negotiations which ultimately resulted in a consent decree. In declining to review the Commission's refusal to allow intervention, the court first described the Commission's consent order procedure:

> Under these rules the Commission may notify a "proposed respondent" of its intention to institute a formal proceeding against him. Such notification contains a form of the proposed complaint which the Commission will issue, as well as the proposed order which the Commission will seek. If the proposed respondent elects, within 10 days, to attempt a settlement, negotiations begin between the Commission's staff and the proposed respondent. If the parties are unable to agree, the Commission may commence formal adjudicative procedure. If, however, an agreement is reached and accepted by the Commission, the provisionally accepted consent order is placed on the public record for a period of 30

days, during which time any interested party may file comments or views with the Commission. After reviewing any such public comments, the Commission may withdraw its acceptance of the consent order either as originally proposed or as modified in light of comments received.

The court then had this to say concerning the possibility of judicial review:

> * * * Congress granted great discretion to the Commission to determine whether a potential respondent has violated the Act and whether a proceeding by the Commission against the violator would be in the public interest. Neither the Federal Trade Commission Act nor the Commission's Rules of Procedure grant appellants any right to intervene in consent negotiations. Rather, the power to prescribe consent negotiation procedure is part of the general enforcement power of the Commission, and such enforcement decisions are generally not subject to judicial review. In this area, concerned as it is with questions of administrative policy and allocation of scarce Commission resources, "the Commission alone is empowered to develop that enforcement policy best calculated to achieve the ends contemplated by Congress and to allocate its available funds and personnel in such a way as to execute its policy efficiently and economically." *Moog Industries, Inc. v. FTC*, 355 U.S. 411, 412 (1958).
>
> Whether or not the denial of appellants' motion to intervene in the negotiations is agency action committed entirely to agency discretion is a question which must be answered by viewing the *source* of the Commission's power to act. We believe that the whole consent negotiation procedure was promulgated by the Commission pursuant to its broad enforcement discretion. As such, we hold that the decision to grant or deny intervention is an agency action committed to agency discretion and therefore is specifically exempt from judicial review under § 701(a)(2) of the APA.

By contrast, *Local 1219, American Federation of Government Employees v. Donovan*, 683 F.2d 511 (D.C.Cir.1982), extended judicial review to the Secretary of Labor's enforcement of the provisions of the 1978 Civil Service Reform Act, 5 U.S.C. § 7101 et seq., which govern federal employee elections. In that case, the Secretary had reached a settlement with the union on charges of unfair election procedures, one that did not set aside any past election but called for Department supervision of the 1982 election of national union officers. Four union locals and 86 individual members challenged the settlement as inconsistent with 5 U.S.C. § 7120, which authorizes settlement agreement "providing for appropriate remedial action" but directs that failing agreement, enforcement proceedings "shall" be instituted. Writing for the court, Judge Wald rejected the government's claim that the Secretary's decision to settle was not subject to review but then upheld the settlement based on the adequacy of the agency's statement of reasons in support of its agreement.

5. *A Balancing Approach to Nonreviewability Claims. Investment Co. Institute v. FDIC*, 728 F.2d 518 (D.C.Cir.1984), is a reminder that regulatory context will significantly affect a court's willingness to entertain such challenges. In that case a majority, over the dissent of Chief Judge Wright, set aside a district court order to the Federal Deposit Insurance Corporation

to "take up and decide the merits of [ICI's] petition seeking a declaration that" a plan by Boston Five Cents Savings Bank to sell mutual fund shares through subsidiaries violated the federal banking laws and "meanwhile to order the [bank] to halt its allegedly unlawful conduct." The court held, first, that the district court lacked jurisdiction to issue its order under 12 U.S.C. § 1818.* It then addressed more broadly the FDIC's enforcement rule and concluded that the agency's decision whether to consider the merits of ICI's petition was "committed to agency discretion by law:"

> Whether a particular agency decision is committed to agency discretion depends, broadly speaking, on whether there is law to apply in making and reviewing the decision, which in turn depends, we have said, on "pragmatic considerations as to whether an agency determination is the proper subject of judicial review." *Natural Resources Defense Council, Inc. v. SEC*, 606 F.2d 1031, 1043 (D.C.Cir.1979). Among the important considerations are "the need for judicial supervision to safeguard the interests of the plaintiffs[,] the impact of review on the effectiveness of the agency in carrying out its congressionally assigned role[,] and the appropriateness of the issues raised for judicial review." Each consideration points to nonreviewability of the FDIC's refusal to take up ICI's petition.
>
> In this case, there is no significant need for judicial supervision to safeguard ICI's rights. In *New York Stock Exchange v. Bloom*, 562 F.2d 736 (D.C.Cir.1977), *cert. denied*, 435 U.S. 942 (1978), this court held that judicial review was not needed to protect the rights of ICI, whose position in that case was virtually identical to its position here. The court gave two reasons for this conclusion. First, since there was no agency decision applicable to ICI, ICI was not exposed to any burden of compliance or risk of penalty for noncompliance. Second, nothing was shown to cast doubt on the ability of ICI to bring an action directly against the bank whose conduct it thought unlawful, an action that, though possibly inconvenient, was an alternative form of relief. Both these reasons apply with full force in this case, and we therefore

* In relevant part, that section confers authority on the FDIC as follows:

> If, in the opinion of the appropriate Federal banking agency, any insured depository institution, depository institution which has insured deposits, or any institution-affiliated party is * * * violating or has violated, or the agency has reasonable cause to believe that the depository institution or any institution-affiliated party is about to violate, a law, rule, or regulation, * * * the agency may issue and serve upon the depository institution or such party a notice of charges in respect thereof. The notice shall contain a statement of the facts constituting the alleged violation or violations or the unsafe or unsound practice or practices, and shall fix a time and place at which a hearing will be held to determine whether an order to cease and desist therefrom should issue against the depository institution or the institution-affiliated party. * * * [I]f upon the record made at any such hearing, the agency shall find that any violation or unsafe or unsound practice specified in the notice of charges has been established, the agency may issue and serve upon the depository institution or the institution-affiliated party an order to cease and desist from any such violation or practice. Such order may, by provisions which may be mandatory or otherwise, require the depository institution or its institution-affiliated parties to cease and desist from the same, and, further, to take affirmative action to correct the conditions resulting from any such violation or practice.

12 U.S.C. § 1818(B)(1).

conclude, as we did in the earlier case, that the hardship to ICI is not substantial enough to justify judicial review.

Regarding the second consideration—whether review would hamper agency effectiveness—we have a less than fully satisfactory basis for making an independent judgment. The FDIC informs us that it supervises some nine thousand state-chartered banks and conducts some twenty thousand bank examinations each year. It informs us, too, that several hundred banks are in danger of failure and therefore require especially close monitoring. It tells us the exercise of its heavy and profound regulatory responsibilities would be severely disrupted if every person seeking FDIC action on a petition seeking enforcement action could invoke judicial review of a simple FDIC refusal to consider the merits of the petition. ICI makes no response to these representations, and we find them quite plausible. * * *

* * * [A]gency action is not the exclusive form of relief for ICI's complaint, as it was for the complaint at issue in *Dunlop v. Bachowski*, 421 U.S. 560 (1975), there being no reason to believe that ICI could not bring an action directly against the bank whose conduct it thinks unlawful. Nor has the FDIC initiated an action that it subsequently decided to terminate. * * * Nor is there the slightest evidence of a consistent policy of abdicating a statutory duty. * * * The FDIC decision here was a simple exercise of "prosecutorial" discretion not to invoke a non-exclusive remedy for allegedly unlawful conduct. That discretion about how to exercise a "general enforcement power" is inappropriate for review where there are no standards to govern the agency exercise of discretion, the statutory language is wholly permissive, the statute itself severely limits the scope of judicial review, and the agency decision involves budgetary constraints and enforcement priorities that we are ill-equipped to evaluate.

Thus, there is "no law to apply" in reviewing a simple refusal to take enforcement action. There might, of course, be some law to apply in deciding whether the practice challenged by ICI is unlawful; it is even imaginable that there might be law to apply in deciding whether the practice is unsafe or unsound. But the FDIC has made no such determination. It has merely decided not to exercise its power under section 1818, and the statute lays down no standards to guide the FDIC in deciding whether to make a finding on the issues of unlawfulness, unsoundness, or unsafeness, let alone in deciding whether to take enforcement action once it has made such a finding. There is, in short, no basis in the statute for a court to use in reviewing the FDIC decision at issue in this case.

HECKLER v. CHANEY

Supreme Court of the United States, 1985.
470 U.S. 821, 105 S.Ct. 1649, 84 L.Ed.2d 714.

Justice Rehnquist delivered the opinion of the Court.

* * *

Respondents are several prison inmates convicted of capital offenses and sentenced to death by lethal injection of drugs. They petitioned the

Food and Drug Administration (FDA), alleging that under the circumstances the use of these drugs for capital punishment violated the Federal Food, Drug, and Cosmetic Act, 52 Stat. 1040, as amended, 21 U.S.C. § 301 et seq. (FDCA), and requesting that the FDA take various enforcement actions to prevent these violations. The FDA refused their request. We review here a decision of the Court of Appeals for the District of Columbia Circuit, which held the FDA's refusal to take enforcement actions both reviewable and an abuse of discretion, and remanded the case with directions that the agency be required "to fulfill its statutory function."

I

Respondents have been sentenced to death by lethal injection of drugs under the laws of the States of Oklahoma and Texas. Those States, and several others, have recently adopted this method for carrying out the capital sentence. Respondents first petitioned the FDA, claiming that the drugs used by the States for this purpose, although approved by the FDA for the medical purposes stated on their labels, were not approved for use in human executions. They alleged that the drugs had not been tested for the purpose for which they were to be used, and that, given that the drugs would likely be administered by untrained personnel, it was also likely that the drugs would not induce the quick and painless death intended. They urged that use of these drugs for human execution was the "unapproved use of an approved drug" and constituted a violation of the Act's prohibitions against "misbranding."[1] They also suggested * * * that the FDA was required to approve the drugs as "safe and effective" for human execution before they could be distributed in interstate commerce. See 21 U.S.C. § 355. They therefore requested the FDA to take various investigatory and enforcement actions to prevent these perceived violations; they requested the FDA to affix warnings to the labels of all the drugs stating that they were unapproved and unsafe for human execution, to send statements to the drug manufacturers and prison administrators stating that the drugs should not be so used, and to adopt procedures for seizing the drugs from state prisons and to recommend the prosecution of all those in the chain of distribution who knowingly distribute or purchase the drugs with intent to use them for human execution.

The FDA Commissioner responded, refusing to take the requested actions. The Commissioner first detailed his disagreement with respondents' understanding of the scope of FDA jurisdiction over the unapproved use of approved drugs for human execution, concluding that FDA jurisdiction in the area was generally unclear but in any event should not be exercised to interfere with this particular aspect of state criminal justice systems. He went on to state:

1. See 21 U.S.C. § 352(f): "A drug or device shall be deemed to be misbranded * * * [u]nless its labeling bears (1) adequate directions for use * * *."

"Were FDA clearly to have jurisdiction in the area, moreover, we believe we would be authorized to decline to exercise it under our inherent discretion to decline to pursue certain enforcement matters. The unapproved use of approved drugs is an area in which the case law is far from uniform. Generally, enforcement proceedings in this area are initiated only when there is a serious danger to the public health or a blatant scheme to defraud. We cannot conclude that those dangers are present under State lethal injection laws, which are duly authorized statutory enactments in furtherance of proper State functions * * *."

* * * The District Court granted summary judgment for petitioner. * * *

A divided panel of the Court of Appeals for the District of Columbia Circuit reversed. * * *

The court found "law to apply" in the form of a FDA policy statement which indicated that the agency was "obligated" to investigate the unapproved use of an approved drug when such use became "widespread" or "endanger[ed] the public health." 718 F.2d, at 1186 (citing 37 Fed.Reg. 16504 (1972)). The court held that this policy statement constituted a "rule" and was considered binding by the FDA. * * *

The Court of Appeals' decision addressed three questions: (1) whether the FDA had jurisdiction to undertake the enforcement actions requested, (2) whether if it did have jurisdiction its refusal to take those actions was subject to judicial review, and (3) whether if reviewable its refusal was arbitrary, capricious, or an abuse of discretion. In reaching our conclusion that the Court of Appeals was wrong, however, we need not and do not address the thorny question of the FDA's jurisdiction. For us, this case turns on the important question of the extent to which determinations by the FDA *not to exercise* its enforcement authority over the use of drugs in interstate commerce may be judicially reviewed. That decision in turn involves the construction of two separate but necessarily interrelated statutes, the APA and the FDCA. * * *

This Court has not had occasion to interpret [the] second exception in § 701(a) in any great detail. On its face, the section does not obviously lend itself to any particular construction; indeed, one might wonder what difference exists between § (a)(1) and § (a)(2). The former section seems easy in application; it requires construction of the substantive statute involved to determine whether Congress intended to preclude judicial review of certain decisions. That is the approach taken with respect to § (a)(1) in cases such as *Dunlop v. Bachowski*. But one could read the language "committed to agency discretion *by law*" in § (a)(2) to require a similar inquiry. In addition, commentators have pointed out that construction of § (a)(2) is further complicated by the tension between a literal reading of § (a)(2), which exempts from judicial review those decisions committed to agency "discretion," and the primary scope of review prescribed by § 706(2)(A)—whether the agency's action was "arbitrary, capricious, or an *abuse of discretion.*" How is it, they ask, that an action committed to agency discretion can be unreviewable and yet courts still can review agency actions for abuse of that discretion? See 5 K. Davis, Administrative Law § 28:6 (1984) (hereafter Davis); Berger, *Administrative Arbitrariness and Judicial Review*, 65 Colum.L.Rev. 55, 58 (1965). The APA's legislative history provides little help on this score. Mindful, however, of the common-sense principle of statutory construction that sections of a statute generally should be read "to give effect, if possible, to every clause * * *," we think there is a proper construction of § (a)(2) which satisfies each of these concerns.

This Court first discussed § (a)(2) in *Citizens to Preserve Overton Park v. Volpe* * * * [where it] addressed the "threshold question" of whether the agency's action was at all reviewable. After setting out the language of § 701(a), the Court stated:

> In this case, there is no indication that Congress sought to prohibit judicial review and there is most certainly no "showing of 'clear and convincing evidence' of a * * * legislative intent" to restrict access to judicial review. * * * Similarly, the Secretary's decision here does not fall within the exception for action "committed to agency discretion." This is a very narrow exception * * *. The legislative history of the Administrative Procedure Act indicates that it is applicable in those rare instances where "statutes are drawn in such broad terms that in a given case there is no law to apply."

The above quote answers several of the questions raised by the language of § 701(a), although it raises others. First, it clearly separates the exception provided by § (a)(1) from the § (a)(2) exception. The former applies when Congress has expressed an intent to preclude judicial review. The latter applies in different circumstances; even where Congress has not affirmatively precluded review, review is not to be had if the statute is drawn so that a court would have no meaningful standard against which to judge the agency's exercise of discretion. In such a case, the statute ("law") can be taken to have "committed" the decisionmaking to the agency's judgment absolutely. This construction avoids conflict with the "abuse of discretion" standard of review in § 706—if no judicially manageable standards are available for judging how and when an agency should exercise its discretion, then it is impossible to evaluate agency action for "abuse of discretion." In addition, this construction satisfies the principle of statutory construction mentioned earlier, by identifying a separate class of cases to which § 701(a)(2) applies.

To this point our analysis does not differ significantly from that of the Court of Appeals. That court purported to apply the "no law to apply" standard of *Overton Park*. We disagree, however, with that court's insistence that the "narrow construction" of § (a)(2) required application of a presumption of reviewability even to an agency's decision not to undertake certain enforcement actions. Here we think the Court of Appeals broke with tradition, case law, and sound reasoning.

Overton Park did not involve an agency's refusal to take requested enforcement action. It involved an affirmative act of approval under a statute that set clear guidelines for determining when such approval should be given. Refusals to take enforcement steps generally involve precisely the opposite situation, and in that situation we think the presumption is that judicial review is not available. This Court has recognized on several occasions over many years that an agency's decision not to prosecute or enforce, whether through civil or criminal process, is a decision generally committed to an agency's absolute discretion. See *United States v. Batchelder*, 442 U.S. 114, 123–124 (1979); *United States v. Nixon*, 418 U.S. 683, 693 (1974); *Vaca v. Sipes*, 386 U.S. 171, 182 (1967); *Confiscation Cases*, 7 Wall. 454 (1869). This recognition of the existence of discretion is attributable in no small part to the general unsuitability for judicial review of agency decisions to refuse enforcement.

The reasons for this general unsuitability are many. First, an agency decision not to enforce often involves a complicated balancing of a number of factors which are peculiarly within its expertise. Thus, the agency must not only assess whether a violation has occurred, but whether agency resources are best spent on this violation or another, whether the agency is likely to succeed if it acts, whether the particular enforcement action requested best fits the agency's overall policies, and indeed, whether the agency has enough resources to undertake the action at all. An agency generally cannot act against each technical violation of the statute it is charged with enforcing. The agency is far better equipped than the courts to deal with the many variables involved in the proper ordering of its priorities. * * *

In addition to these administrative concerns, we note that when an agency refuses to act it generally does not exercise its *coercive* power over an individual's liberty or property rights, and thus does not infringe upon areas that courts often are called upon to protect. Similarly, when an agency does act to enforce, that action itself provides a focus for judicial review, inasmuch as the agency must have exercised its power in some manner. The action at least can be reviewed to determine whether the agency exceeded its statutory powers. Finally, we recognize that an agency's refusal to institute proceedings shares to some extent the characteristics of the decision of a prosecutor in the Executive Branch not to indict—a decision which has long been regarded as the special province of the Executive Branch, inasmuch as it is the executive who is charged by the Constitution to "take care that the Laws be faithfully executed."

We of course only list the above concerns to facilitate understanding of our conclusion that an agency's decision not to take enforcement action should be presumed immune from judicial review under § 701(a)(2). For good reasons, such a decision has traditionally been "committed to agency discretion," and we believe that the Congress enacting the APA did not intend to alter that tradition. * * * In so stating, we emphasize that the decision is only presumptively unreviewable; the presumption may be rebutted where the substantive statute has provided guidelines for the agency to follow in exercising its enforcement powers. * * *

Dunlop [*v. Bachowski*] is * * * thus consistent with a general presumption of unreviewability of decisions not to enforce. The statute being administered quite clearly withdrew discretion from the agency and provided guidelines for exercise of its enforcement power. Our decision that review was available was not based on "pragmatic considerations" * * * that amount to an assessment of whether the interests at stake are important enough to justify intervention in the agencies' decisionmaking. The danger that agencies may not carry out their delegated powers with sufficient vigor does not necessarily lead to the conclusion that courts are the most appropriate body to police this aspect of their performance. That decision is in the first instance for Congress, and we therefore turn to the FDCA to determine whether in this case Congress has provided us with "law to apply." * * *

[Justice Rehnquist parsed the language of the FDCA and found no relevant language resembling the articulated criteria for action or the mandatory tone of the statute at issue in *Dunlop v. Bachowski*. Describing the FDA's "policy statement" as "singularly unhelpful," the Court found it both vague and contradicted by a general FDA regulation characterizing its enforcement discretion as unreviewable.]

We therefore conclude that the presumption that agency decisions not to institute proceedings are unreviewable under § 701(a)(2) of the APA is not overcome by the enforcement provisions of the FDCA. The FDA's decision not to take the enforcement actions requested by respondents is therefore not subject to judicial review under the APA. The general exception to reviewability provided by § 701(a)(2) for action "committed to agency discretion" remains a narrow one, but within that exception are included agency refusals to institute investigative or enforcement proceedings, unless Congress has indicated otherwise. In so holding, we essentially leave to Congress, and not to the courts, the decision as to whether an agency's refusal to institute proceedings should be judicially reviewable. No colorable claim is made in this case that the agency's refusal to institute proceedings violated any constitutional rights of respondents, and we do not address the issue that would be raised in such a case. *Cf. Johnson v. Robison*, 415 U.S. 361 (1974); *Yick Wo v. Hopkins*, 118 U.S. 356 (1886). The fact that the drugs involved in this case are ultimately to be used in imposing the death penalty must not lead this Court or other courts to import profound differences of opinion over the meaning of the Eighth Amendment to the United States Constitution into the domain of administrative law.

The judgment of the Court of Appeals is Reversed.

[The concurring opinion of Justice Brennan is omitted.]

Justice Marshall, concurring in the judgment.

* * * In my view, the "presumption of unreviewability" announced today is a product of that lack of discipline that easy cases make all too easy. * * * Because this "presumption of unreviewability" is fundamentally at odds with rule-of-law principles firmly embedded in our jurisprudence, because it seeks to truncate an emerging line of judicial authority subjecting enforcement discretion to rational and principled constraint, and because, in the end, the presumption may well be indecipherable, one can only hope that it will come to be understood as a relic of a particular factual setting in which the full implications of such a presumption were neither confronted nor understood.

I write separately to argue for a different basis of decision: that refusals to enforce, like other agency actions, are reviewable in the absence of a "clear and convincing" congressional intent to the contrary, but that such refusals warrant deference when, as in this case, there is nothing to suggest that an agency with enforcement discretion has abused that discretion.

In response to respondents' petition, the FDA Commissioner stated that it would not pursue the complaint

> "under our inherent discretion to decline to pursue certain enforcement matters. The unapproved use of approved drugs is an area in which the case law is far from uniform. Generally, enforcement proceedings in this area are initiated only when there is a serious danger to the public health or a blatant scheme to defraud. We cannot conclude that those dangers are present under State lethal injection laws. * * * [We] decline, as a matter of enforcement discretion, to pursue supplies of drugs under State control that will be used for execution by lethal injection."

The FDA may well have been legally required to provide this statement of basis and purpose for its decision not to take the action requested. Under the Administrative Procedure Act, such a statement is required when an agency denies a "written application, petition, or other request of an interested person made in connection with any agency proceedings." 5 U.S.C. § 555(e). Whether this written explanation was legally required or not, however, it does provide a sufficient basis for holding, on the merits, that the FDA's refusal to grant the relief requested was within its discretion.

First, respondents on summary judgment neither offered nor attempted to offer any evidence that the reasons given for the FDA's refusal to act were other than the reasons stated by the agency. Second * * * the FDCA is not a mandatory statute that requires the FDA to prosecute all violations of the Act. Thus, the FDA clearly has significant discretion to choose which alleged violations of the Act to prosecute. Third, the basis on which the agency chose to exercise this discretion—that other problems were viewed as more pressing—generally will be enough to pass muster. Certainly it is enough to do so here, where the number of people currently affected by the alleged misbranding is around 200, and where the drugs are integral elements in a regulatory scheme over which the States exercise pervasive and direct control. * * *

The Court, however, * * * transforms the arguments for deferential review on the merits into the wholly different notion that "enforcement" decisions are presumptively unreviewable altogether. * * *

* * * [T]o support its newfound "presumption of unreviewability," the Court resorts to completely undefined and unsubstantiated references to "tradition," and to citation of four cases.

Yet these cases hardly support such a broad presumption with respect to agency refusal to take enforcement action. The only one of these cases to involve administrative action, *Vaca v. Sipes*, suggests, in dictum, that the General Counsel of the National Labor Relations Board has unreviewable discretion to refuse to initiate an unfair labor practice complaint. To the extent this dictum is sound, later cases indicate that unreviewability results from the particular structure of the National Labor Relations Act and the explicit statutory intent to withdraw review found in 29 U.S.C. § 153(d), rather than from some general "presumption of unreviewability" of enforcement decisions. *See NLRB v. Sears, Roebuck & Co.*, 421 U.S. 132, 138 (1975). Neither *Vaca* nor *Sears, Roebuck* discuss the APA. The half-sentence cited from *Nixon*, which states that the Executive has "absolute discretion to decide whether to prosecute a case," is the only apparent support the Court actually offers for even the limited notion that prosecutorial discretion in the criminal area is unreviewable. But that half-sentence is of course misleading, for *Nixon* held it an abuse of that discretion to attempt to exercise it contrary to validly promulgated regulations. Thus, *Nixon* actually stands for a very different proposition than the one for which the Court cites it: faced with a specific claim of abuse of prosecutorial discretion, *Nixon* makes clear that courts are not powerless to intervene. * * *

* * * [A]rguments about prosecutorial discretion do not necessarily translate into the context of agency refusals to act. * * * Criminal prosecutorial decisions vindicate only intangible interests, common to society as a whole, in the enforcement of the criminal law. The conduct at issue has already occurred; all that remains is society's general interest in assuring that the guilty are punished. See *Linda R.S. v. Richard D.* In contrast, requests for administrative enforcement typically seek to prevent concrete and future injuries that Congress has made cognizable—injuries that result, for example, from misbranded drugs, such as alleged in this case, or unsafe nuclear power plants, to obtain palpable benefits that Congress has intended to bestow—such as labor union elections free of corruption, see *Dunlop v. Bachowski*. Entitlements to receive these benefits or to be free of these injuries often run to specific classes of individuals whom Congress has singled out as statutory beneficiaries. The interests at stake in review of administrative enforcement decisions are thus more focused and in many circumstances more pressing than those at stake in criminal prosecutorial decisions. * * *

Perhaps more important, the *sine qua non* of the APA was to alter inherited judicial reluctance to constrain the exercise of discretionary administrative power—to rationalize and make fairer the exercise of such discretion. Since passage of the APA, the sustained effort of administrative law has been to "continuously narro[w] the category of actions considered to be so discretionary as to be exempted from review." Shapiro, *Administrative Discretion: The Next Stage*, 92 Yale L.J. 1487, 1489, n. 11 (1983). * * *

The "tradition" of unreviewability upon which the majority relies is refuted most powerfully by a firmly entrenched body of lower court case law that holds reviewable various agency refusals to act. * * * The lower courts, facing the problem of agency inaction and its concrete effects more regularly than do we, have responded with a variety of solutions to assure administrative fidelity to congressional objectives: a demand that an agency explain its refusal to act, a demand that explanations given be further elaborated, and injunctions that action "unlawfully withheld or unreasonably delayed" be taken. Whatever the merits of any particular solution, one would have hoped the Court would have acted with greater respect for these efforts by responding with a scalpel rather than a blunderbuss.

To be sure, the Court no doubt takes solace in the view that it has created only a "presumption" of unreviewability, and that "this presumption may be rebutted where the substantive statute has provided guidelines for the agency to follow in exercising its enforcement powers." But this statement implies far too narrow a reliance on positive law, either statutory or constitutional, as the sole source of limitations on agency discretion not to enforce. In my view, enforcement discretion is also channelled by traditional background understandings against which the APA was enacted and which Congress hardly could be thought to have intended to displace in the APA. For example, a refusal to enforce that stems from a conflict of interest, that is the result of a bribe, vindictiveness or retaliation, or that traces to personal or other corrupt motives ought to be judicially remediable. Even in the absence of statutory "guidelines" precluding such factors as bases of decision, Congress should not be presumed to have departed from principles of rationality and fair process in enacting the APA. Moreover, the agency may well narrow its own enforcement discretion through historical practice, from which it should arguably not depart in the absence of explanation, or through regulations and informal action. Traditional principles of rationality and fair process do offer "meaningful standards" and "law to apply" to an agency's decision not to act, and no presumption of unreviewability should be allowed to trump these principles. * * *

Notes

1. *Categorical Refusal to Enforce?* Justice Rehnquist suggests that an agency's categorical failure to enforce a statutory prohibition might be

subject to judicial review. But could it not be argued that this was precisely what the plaintiffs in *Chaney* alleged? They did not challenge the FDA's failure to interfere with the execution of a specific capital defendant, but rather its refusal to challenge the practice, in several states, of using FDA-approved medicines for a purpose for which they were not approved. Furthermore, engaging in review would not have forced the FDA to focus attention and resources on a matter that it considered unimportant, or to deliberate about issues it would otherwise have ignored. The agency had already considered and responded to the plaintiffs' petition and thereby created a "record" that a court could examine. In light of these circumstances, one could read the Supreme Court's opinion as a very strong statement about the nonreviewability of agency refusals to enforce. On the other hand, the special circumstances of the litigation, representing an attack on the death penalty, caution against overreading. Indeed, Chief Justice Rehnquist appears to go out of his way to emphasize that decisions not to enforce are only "presumptively unreviewable," and then adds two provocative statements, at first in a footnote: "Nor do we have a situation where it could justifiably be found that the agency has 'consciously and expressly adopted a general policy' that is so extreme as to amount to an abdication of its statutory responsibilities." And, just before in the text, Rehnquist cautioned: "[I]n establishing this presumption in the APA, Congress did not set agencies free to disregard legislative direction in the statutory scheme that the agency administers." 470 U.S. at 832, 833. This language has inspired more than a few attempts by private litigants to characterize an agency's failure to enforce as reflecting systematic abdication of its statutory duties—and thus reviewable.

2. *Review of Remedial Discretion*. Although its language has been less categorical than in *Chaney*, the Supreme Court has similarly limited review of the "back end" of enforcement discretion, namely, the agency's choice of remedy once it has charged and proved a violation. In *FTC v. Universal–Rundle Corp.*, 387 U.S. 244 (1967), the Court refused to modify a cease-and-desist order against a party who argued that a prohibition against its continued discriminatory pricing would impose severe financial loss so long as its competitors continued to engage in the prohibited practice. Quoting *Moog Industries, Inc. v. FTC*, 355 U.S. 411 (1958), the Court said:

> The decision as to whether to postpone enforcement of a cease-and-desist order "depends on a variety of factors peculiarly within the expert understanding of the Commission." Thus, "although an allegedly illegal practice may appear to be operative throughout an industry, whether such appearances reflect fact" is a question "that [calls] for discretionary determination by the administrative agency." Because these determinations require the specialized experienced judgment of the Commission, they cannot be overturned by the courts "in the absence of a patent abuse of discretion." Consequently, the reviewing court's inquiry is not whether the evidence adduced in support of a petition for a stay tends to establish certain facts, such as that the industry is engaged in allegedly illegal price discrimination practices; rather, the court's review must be limited to determining whether the Commission's evaluation of the merit of the petition for a stay was patently arbitrary and capricious.
> * * *

> [T]he Federal Trade Commission does not have unbridled power to institute proceedings which will arbitrarily destroy one of many law violators in an industry. This is not such a case. The Commission's refusal to withhold enforcement of the cease-and-desist order against respondent was based upon a reasonable evaluation of the merits of the petition for a stay; thus it was not within the scope of the reviewing authority of the court below to overthrow the Commission's determination * * *.

See also *Butz v. Glover Livestock Commission Co., Inc.*, 411 U.S. 182 (1973) (unsuccessful challenge by stockyard operator to USDA's temporary suspension of its registration as a livestock marketing agency; absent a specific statutory requirement to the contrary, "[t]he employment of a sanction within the authority of an administrative agency is * * * not rendered invalid in a particular case because it is more severe than sanctions imposed in other cases.")

The language of *Universal–Rundle* raises the obvious question how a requirement that an agency's behavior be proved "*patently* arbitrary and capricious" differs from the run-of-the-mill "arbitrary and capricious" standard. Would "patent" arbitrariness, for example, require a showing of more than insufficient explanation, perhaps of bad faith or invidious discrimination?

3. *Lower Court Reactions to* Chaney. While the Supreme Court's decision in *Chaney* provided government attorneys with an additional argument against judicial review of agency decisions not to act, its impact on the outcome of cases is less certain. More than a few post-*Chaney* cases uphold claims of unreviewability, see, e.g., *Clementson v. Brock*, 806 F.2d 1402 (9th Cir.1986); *Dubois v. Thomas*, 820 F.2d 943 (8th Cir.1987), and objections to review of inaction have become common. Within two years of the Supreme Court's ruling the D.C. Circuit alone had confronted *Chaney* claims in more than 30 cases and the number has continued to mount. Because nearly a third of all challenges to federal agency decisions come to this circuit, and because the court had previously displayed a greater propensity to review inaction than the other courts of appeals, the D.C. Circuit's treatment of *Chaney* claims is of particular interest.

The court has declined to review agency refusals to initiate enforcement action on several occasions. See, e.g., *Community Nutrition Institute v. Young*, 818 F.2d 943 (D.C.Cir.1987) (holding unreviewable FDA's failure to initiate seizure actions against assertedly adulterated corn products). The court has also sometimes read *Chaney* to bar review of decisions outside the "classic nonenforcement context." See Hon. Patricia Wald, *The Contribution of the D.C. Circuit to Administrative Law* (speech delivered to the ABA Section on Administrative Law, May 1987) (citing *Schering Corp. v. Heckler*, 779 F.2d 683 (D.C.Cir.1985); *Falkowski v. EEOC*, 783 F.2d 252 (D.C.Cir. 1986)).

But other D.C. Circuit cases have found in an agency's statute or regulations enforceable constraints on decisions whether or not to act. An example is *Center for Auto Safety v. Dole*, 846 F.2d 1532 (D.C.Cir.1988), where a majority held that the decision of the Secretary of Transportation not to reopen an investigation of alleged safety defects in Ford automobiles was reviewable, *Chaney* notwithstanding. Chief Judge Wald pointed out that the Motor Vehicle Safety Act gave citizens the right to petition the Secretary to investigate alleged safety violations and required written reasons for any refusal to investigate. Moreover, she wrote, under its regulations, the agency's decision "involves the evaluation of 'technical' evidence about cars as prescribed by the agency's regulations. This court reviews similar decisions 'thousands of times every year' without an impermissible substitution of judgment."

In *International Union, United Automobile, Aerospace & Agricultural Implement Workers v. Brock*, 783 F.2d 237 (D.C.Cir.1986), by contrast, the union unsuccessfully challenged the Secretary of Labor's decision not to act on its complaint that Kawasaki and its law firm had violated provisions of the LMRDA requiring employers to report activities and expenditures designed to prevent unionization. Ascending departmental levels had offered varied explanations for the failure, after investigation, to take action before the Secretary's own statement made clear that, in addition to reservations about the facts of the case, he was revising his interpretation of what sorts of activities were required to be reported. Chief Judge Wald and Judges Bork and D. Ginsberg joined in holding that the Secretary's decision not to initiate enforcement in this case was beyond review under *Chaney*. "[T]he relevant statutory provision here, as in *Chaney*, does not mandate that the Department take enforcement action against each and every violation." But the court went on to hold that the Secretary's changed statutory interpretation was subject to review. "[C]ourts are emphatically qualified to decide whether an agency has acted outside of the bounds of reason * * * There are real and cognizable practical differences distinguishing an agency's announcement of how it will exercise its discretion, from an agency's announcement of what citizen's duties are under a statute like the LMRDA that depends primarily on self-enforcement. Were we to accept the Department's contention, we would be handing agencies carte blanche to avoid review by announcing new interpretations of statutes only in the context of decisions not to take enforcement action." The Secretary's interpretation of the LMRDA was ultimately upheld. *International Union, United Automobile, Aerospace & Agricultural Implement Workers of America v. Dole*, 869 F.2d 616 (D.C.Cir. 1989).

A "legal issues" exception to the *Chaney* presumption is apparently endorsed by other circuits as well. *Montana Air Chapter No. 29, Ass'n of Civilian Technicians, Inc. v. Federal Labor Relations Authority*, 898 F.2d 753 (9th Cir.1990); *Davis Enterprises v. U.S. EPA*, 877 F.2d 1181 (3d Cir.1989), *cert. denied*, 493 U.S. 1070 (1990); *Woodsmall v. Lyng*, 816 F.2d 1241 (8th Cir.1987); *Dina v. Attorney General of U.S.*, 793 F.2d 473 (2d Cir.1986); *Electricities of N.C., Inc. v. Southeastern Power Administration*, 774 F.2d 1262 (4th Cir.1985).

4. *The Relevance of the Availability of a Private Remedy.* In the concluding paragraph of his majority opinion *in Chaney*, Chief Justice Rehnquist alludes, albeit obliquely, to an alternative open to the plaintiffs in this case. Assuming their fundamental goal was to challenge the practice of lethal injection as a means of accomplishing capital punishment, presumably individual death row inmates could obtain review, by direct appeal, habeas corpus, or perhaps even suit against prison authorities, of a claim based on

the Eighth Amendment. Following this lead in *Investment Co. Institute v. FDIC*, 728 F.2d 518 (D.C.Cir.1984), and *New York Stock Exchange v. Bloom*, 562 F.2d 736 (D.C.Cir.1977), *cert. denied*, 435 U.S. 942 (1978), both discussed at pp. 920–921 *supra*, the D.C. Circuit offered the apparent availability of a private remedy against the alleged violator as one reason for declining to review the agency's failure to enforce. But the argument does not necessarily work in reverse. In *Block v. SEC*, 50 F.3d 1078 (D.C.Cir.1995), the claim that, unless the SEC agreed to begin the administrative process that might lead to enforcement, frustrated mutual fund shareholders could have no remedy whatever—under federal or state law—failed to persuade the court to grant review.

5. *Review, Yes, but Lightly.* While Justice Marshall argues vigorously in *Chaney* that the Court should review FDA's refusal to take any steps to curb the use of agency-approved drugs in capital punishment—a use for which they had concededly never been approved—he makes clear that he would not find the agency's refusal to act arbitrary or capricious. Indeed, his opinion suggests that he found the agency's explanation not merely adequate but convincing. This is a reminder, should any be needed, that a court's willingness to review an agency's decision does not assure that it will find fault with the decision on the merits. Most agencies are generally successful in defending their decisions in court.

6. *Further Reading.* In *Reviewing Agency Inaction After* Heckler v. Chaney, 52 Chi.L.Rev. 653 (1985), Professor Cass R. Sunstein, clearly troubled by Justice Rehnquist's broad language, argues that whenever an agency's decision is claimed to be unreviewable, the central issue is whether Congress has set discernible limits on its discretion. This requires "measuring the plaintiff's allegation against the governing substantive statute." If plaintiffs can point to language that arguably confines an agency's decision making, and allege that it ignored or breached those limits, they should be entitled to review on the merits, whether the decision was to act or not act. For a general treatment of this area, see Ronald M. Levin, *Understanding Unreviewability in Administrative Law*, 74 Minn.L.Rev. 689 (1990). A useful pre-*Chaney* analysis is Harvey Saferstein, *Nonreviewability: A Functional Analysis of "Committed to Agency Discretion,"* 82 Harv.L.Rev. 367 (1968).

(2) Review of Discretion to Regulate

AMERICAN HORSE PROTECTION ASSOCIATION, INC. v. LYNG

United States Court of Appeals, District of Columbia Circuit, 1987.
812 F.2d 1.

WILLIAMS, CIRCUIT JUDGE:

The American Horse Protection Association (the "Association") appeals from a grant of summary judgment to the Secretary of Agriculture in its challenge to regulations under the Horse Protection Act, 15 U.S.C. §§ 1821–1831 (1982) (the "Act"). We find that summary judgment was inappropriate in view of the Secretary's failure to offer a satisfactory explanation of his refusal to institute rule making proceedings.

The regulations at issue concern the practice of deliberately injuring show horses to improve their performance in the ring. This practice, called soring, may involve fastening heavy chains or similar equipment, called action devices, on a horse's front limbs. As a result of wearing action devices, the horse may suffer intense pain as its forefeet touch the ground. This pain causes it to adopt a high-stepping gait that is highly prized in Tennessee walking horses and certain other breeds. * * * In the Horse Protection Act, Congress sought to end this practice by forbidding the showing or selling of sored horses. Exercising broadly phrased rulemaking power under 15 U.S.C. § 1828, the Secretary issued regulations that prohibited soring devices and other soring methods in both general and specific terms. The general prohibition, 9 C.F.R. § 11.2(a) (1986), states

> Notwithstanding the provisions of paragraph (b) of this section [containing specific prohibitions], no chain, boot, roller, collar, action device, nor any other device, method, practice, or substance shall be used with respect to any horse at any horse show, horse exhibition, or horse sale or auction if such use causes or can reasonably be expected to cause such horse to be sore.

The regulations' specific prohibitions include the use of chains weighing more than eight or ten ounces (depending on the age of the horse), rollers weighing more than fourteen ounces, and certain padded shoes on young horses. Lighter chains and rollers are not specifically prohibited.

Use of action devices in violation of either the general or specific prohibitions is unlawful under 15 U.S.C. § 1824(7) and may subject the violator to both criminal and civil penalties under 15 U.S.C. § 1825. Under the general prohibition, however, there is no penalty unless the use of the device is shown to have caused soreness or the device can "reasonably be expected to cause" soreness. Use of pain killers may make detection of actual soring difficult. The regulations give no guidance as to when a device not specifically prohibited may reasonably be expected to cause soreness. There are no such definitional difficulties, of course, when a violation involves a device specifically prohibited.

The Association here contends that developments since these regulations were originally promulgated have demonstrated their inadequacy and that, accordingly, the Secretary should revise them in a new rulemaking. In fact, in its original rulemaking the agency made quite clear its recognition that the premises for not enacting broader specific prohibitions might erode. In its notice of proposed rulemaking, it stated that it relied on evidence from three test clinics which appeared to exonerate action devices weighing less than those that it proposed to forbid. When the final rule was issued, the agency stated that it would consider prohibiting all action devices and padded shoes if the practice of soring continued. At the same time it also mentioned that the agency had recently commissioned "a study of soring methods and techniques at a major university" that might eventually result in further changes in the regulations.

This study was conducted at the Auburn University School of Veterinary Medicine between September 1978 and December 1982. The Auburn study evaluated use of eight-and ten-ounce chains and fourteen-ounce rollers—devices that the agency had declined to prohibit on the grounds that they did not cause soring when properly used under actual training conditions. The study concluded that ten-ounce chains caused lesions, bleeding, edema, and inflammation. It also considered the effects of eight-and ten-ounce chains and fourteen-ounce rollers on scarred horses, and found that these devices caused raw lesions. The effects of these devices thus fell within the statutory definition of sore. * * * The Auburn study also made preliminary findings on the effects of padded shoes, suggesting they caused problems not suspected at the time of the initial rulemaking. The Association relies on these results in challenging the Agriculture Department's regulations.

Even before the Auburn study was completed, however, the agency considered revising its regulations on action devices. In a May 1981 letter to the Administrator of the Animal and Plant Health Inspection Service ("APHIS"), the Agriculture Department's Office of General Counsel recognized that soring had not been eliminated and argued that the gaps in the regulations were "undermining the Department's ability to achieve effective enforcement of the law and * * * preventing the attainment of the goal Congress ha[d] set." The letter cited administrative cases interpreting the regulations to allow soring with "legal" action devices, *i.e.*, those not covered by the specific prohibitions.

Bureaucratic activity surged briefly, then ebbed. The Administrator of APHIS endorsed the letter from the Office of General Counsel, "OGC's comments make sense," and asked his staff for recommendations on possible changes. In early 1982, representatives of the Association met with the Administrator to propose a ban on all action devices and pads. In March, the Administrator informed the group by letter that the agency's Veterinary Services staff had already prepared a justification for such a ban and was currently drafting a proposed rulemaking to implement it. In July, he confirmed that such regulations had been drafted and that the agency had intended to publish the proposals "as soon as possible." But, he reported, these plans were now being held in abeyance in order to observe the "self-regulation efforts of the industry."

In March 1984, agency officials met with representatives of the walking horse industry, the Association, and others to discuss enforcement of the Act. The Association again requested a rulemaking. In a letter to the Association discussing this meeting, the Deputy Administrator of Veterinary Services wrote, "The apparent inconsistency of the current regulations regarding the weight of action devices with the law and research performed at Auburn University has been a matter of concern for Veterinary Services and the Office of the General Counsel for some time." Nevertheless, he reported that the agency would withhold publication of the proposed rule pending further studies by the industry. He also reported the industry representatives' remark "that the allowable weight of action devices could not be lowered and still retain the desired gait." Perhaps supposing that industry approval was required for any change in the regulations, the Deputy Administrator said, "We are * * * disappointed that no consideration has been given to restricting the weight of action devices."

The reviewability of a refusal to institute a rulemaking has been a source of some uncertainty since the Supreme Court held refusals to take ad hoc enforcement steps presumptively unreviewable in *Heckler v. Chaney*. Although the Court expressly noted that *Chaney* did not "involve the question of agency discretion not to invoke rulemaking proceedings," its reasoning applies to some extent to a refusal to institute a rulemaking. Our examination of *Chaney* persuades us, however, that it does not bar review of the agency's decision here.

The *Chaney* Court relied on three features of nonenforcement decisions in arriving at its negative presumption. First, such decisions require a high level of agency expertise and coordination in setting priorities. Second, the agency in such situations will not ordinarily be exercising "its *coercive* power over an individual's liberty or property rights." (emphasis in original). Third, such nonenforcement decisions are akin to prosecutorial decisions not to indict, which traditionally involve executive control and judicial restraint. The first and second of these features are likely to be involved in an agency's refusal to institute a rulemaking, but the third is another matter.

Chaney says little about this third feature. To a degree, of course, it recapitulates and underscores the prior points about resource allocation and non-coercion. The analogy between prosecutorial discretion and agency nonenforcement is strengthened, however, by two other shared characteristics. First, both prosecutors and agencies constantly make decisions not to take enforcement steps; such decisions thus are numerous. Second, both types of nonenforcement are typically based mainly on close consideration of the facts of the case at hand, rather than on legal analysis. Refusals to institute rulemakings, by contrast, are likely to be relatively infrequent and more likely to turn upon issues of law. This analysis of the third *Chaney* feature finds support in the Court's distinguishing of cases where an agency "has 'consciously and expressly adopted a general policy' that is so extreme as to amount to an abdication of its statutory responsibilities." Such abdications are likely both to be infrequent and to turn on matters remote from the specific facts of individual cases.

Furthermore, the Administrative Procedure Act ("APA") serves to distinguish between *Chaney* nonenforcement decisions and refusals to institute rulemakings. The *Chaney* Court noted that "when an agency *does* act to enforce, that action itself provides a focus for judicial review" since a court can "at least * * * determine whether the agency exceeded its statutory powers." APA provisions governing agency refusals to initiate rulemakings give a similar focal point. The APA requires agencies to allow interested persons to "petition for the issuance, amendment, or repeal of a rule," 5 U.S.C. § 553(e) (1982), and, when such petitions are denied, to give "a brief statement of the grounds for denial," *id.* § 555(e). These two provisions suggest that Congress expected that agencies denying rulemaking petitions must explain their actions.

Thus, refusals to institute rulemaking proceedings are distinguishable from other sorts of nonenforcement decisions insofar as they are less frequent, more apt to involve legal as opposed to factual analysis, and subject to special formalities, including a public explanation. *Chaney* therefore does not appear to overrule our prior decisions allowing review of agency refusals to institute rulemakings.

The District Court was thus correct in finding that this case requires a determination of whether the Secretary's failure to act was "arbitrary, capricious, an abuse of discretion, or otherwise not in accordance with law" under 5 U.S.C. § 706(2)(A) (1982). Review under the "arbitrary and capricious" tag line, however, encompasses a range of levels of deference to the agency, *see WWHT, Inc. v. FCC*, 656 F.2d 807, 817 (D.C.Cir.1981), and *Chaney* surely reinforces our frequent statements that an agency's refusal to institute rulemaking proceedings is at the high end of the range. Such a refusal is to be overturned "only in the rarest and most compelling of circumstances," *WWHT*, 656 F.2d at 818, which have primarily involved "plain errors of law, suggesting that the agency has been blind to the source of its delegated power."

In these, as in more typical reviews, however, we must consider whether the agency's decisionmaking was "reasoned." * * *

Finally, a refusal to initiate a rulemaking naturally sets off a special alert when a petition has sought modification of a rule on the basis of a radical change in its factual premises. In *Geller v. FCC*, 610 F.2d 973 (D.C.Cir.1979), the regulations at issue had been adopted expressly to facilitate passage of certain legislation, but even after Congress adopted the legislation the agency refused to reconsider them. *Geller* was later summarized by this court as holding that "an agency may be forced by a reviewing court to institute rulemaking proceedings if a significant factual predicate of a prior decision on the subject (either to promulgate or not to promulgate specific rules) has been removed." *WWHT*, 656 F.2d at 819. The Association argues that this principle applies here.

In considering a refusal to grant a rulemaking petition, the court must examine "the petition for rulemaking, comments pro and con * * * and the agency's explanation of its decision to reject the petition." The record before us contains no formal rulemaking petition, but we have no difficulty in characterizing the Association's requests for action as such. Neither the Agriculture Department's regulations, nor the Administrative Procedure Act, specifies any formalities for a rulemaking petition. * * *

The agency's explanation for its refusal to proceed with the rulemaking is contained in its correspondence with the Association (discussed below) and in the two litigation affidavits of the Deputy Administrator of Veterinary Services of the APHIS. In response to the claim that the Auburn study presented new facts that merited a new rulemaking, the Deputy Administrator's first affidavit stated:

> 6. I have reviewed studies and other materials, relating to action devices, presented by humane groups, Walking Horse industry groups, and independent institutions, including the study referred to in the Complaint.
>
> 7. On the basis of this information, I believe that the most effective method of enforcing the Act is to continue the current regulations.

The second affidavit cites statistics indicating that the agency wrote up a generally diminishing number of alleged violations over the period beginning in 1979 and ending in 1984, although the number of horses exhibited and examined did not generally decline.

On the basis of the litigation affidavits, the District Court found that "the agency has provided a rational basis for its conclusion not to regulate. * * * " We cannot agree. The two conclusory sentences quoted above are insufficient to assure a reviewing court that the agency's refusal to act was the product of reasoned decisionmaking. There is no articulation of "the factual and policy bases for [the] decision." We are abjured to take a critical view of an agency's "post hoc rationalization," but under even the most charitable view the agency's post hoc conclusory statement lacks substance. Nor do the figures on reduced findings of violations suffice. These are apparently intended to suggest that soring is being eliminated by dint of agency efforts. Litigation affidavits of Association members suggest, however, that soring continues to be widespread. Furthermore, the agency's correspondence with the Association (which was not discussed by the District Court) casts doubt on the agency's benign interpretation of this data.

In this correspondence the agency indicated that its concerns about the regulations were great enough in 1982 to cause it to draft new ones. The reason given later in 1982 for not publishing these proposed regulations—to give industry self-regulation a chance to work—was by 1984 too stale to justify continued inaction. Moreover, in 1984 the Deputy Administrator admitted the "apparent inconsistency of the current regulations regarding the weight of action devices with the law and the [Auburn] research." In the face of this "apparent inconsistency," the Deputy Administrator passively noted his disappointment that industry representatives "felt that the allowable weight of action devices could not be lowered and still retain the desired gait."

This statement suggests a belief that the Act was a sort of compromise between industry proponents of soring and persons who regarded the practice as barbarous. * * *

We see nothing ambiguous in the Act's treatment of soring methods. The Act was clearly designed to end soring. It explicitly finds that soring is "cruel and inhumane," flatly prohibits the showing in a horse show of "any horse which is sore," and makes it a criminal offense knowingly to do so. Moreover, Congress amended the Act in 1976 "to stop an inhumane and harmful practice that the Congress thought would end when it enacted [the original Act], but which has not in fact ended." S.Rep. 418, 94th Cong., 1st Sess. 1 (1975).

There is no indication in the Act or the legislative history that Congress was concerned with the ability of horse owners to "retain the desired gait," at least insofar as the desired gait required soring. To be sure, the legislative history shows concern for owners who refused to adopt the practice of soring, but instead used "patient, careful training * * * and natural breeding" to achieve the distinctive walk. S.Rep.No. 609, at 1–2. Soring, which causes horses to perform beyond their natural ability, put these owners at a competitive disadvantage. The Act sought to do away not only with the unnecessary cruelty of soring, but also with this unfair competition. But it shows no solicitude for owners who favor soring. * * *

In sum, we conclude that the Secretary has not presented a reasonable explanation of his failure to grant the rulemaking petition of the Association, particularly in light of the apparent message of the Auburn study. Moreover, what he has said strongly suggests that he has been blind to the nature of his mandate from Congress.

The Association seeks an order directing the Secretary to institute rulemaking proceedings. Our cases make clear, however, that such a remedy is appropriate "only in the rarest and most compelling of circumstances." In arguing that the present circumstances qualify, the Association relies on *Geller v. FCC*, 610 F.2d 973 (D.C.Cir.1979). In fact, however, the court in *Geller* merely remanded to the agency to inquire into whether the changed circumstances called for amendment of the earlier rule, leaving it to the agency to choose the form of the inquiry. This remedy is particularly appropriate when the agency has failed to provide an adequate explanation of its denial.

The findings of the Auburn study may or may not remove a "significant factual predicate" of the original rules' gaps. The issues as to the Auburn study's validity and significance lie within the institutional competence of the Secretary. He therefore must be given a reasonable opportunity to explain his decision or to institute a new rulemaking proceeding on action devices and other soring practices.

We vacate the judgment of the District Court and remand to that Court with instructions to remand the case to the Secretary for further consideration consistent with this opinion.

Notes

1. *Varying the Intensity of Review.* The *AHPA* case largely reiterates the D.C. Circuit's pre-*Chaney* approach to the review of agency decisions not to regulate, an approach that might be thought not to raise the same separation of powers concerns implicated in *Bachowski* and *Chaney*. In adjudicatory cases like *Dunn* or *Bachowski*, judicial review of enforcement

discretion could ultimately require an agency to go to court for relief. Ordering an agency to initiate or continue rulemaking deliberations does not immediately raise the spectre of courts creating their own caseload.

AHPA could be read, however, to go even further than pre-*Chaney* decisions. For example, prior cases suggested a possible significant distinction between judicial review of bare petitions and situations like *AHPA* in which an agency has done much, although no rule has been promulgated. Section 555(e), after all, refers to "the denial * * * of a * * * petition * * * of an interested person made *in connection with any agency proceeding*" (emphasis added). Conceivably, the italicized language should be read as limiting Section 555's requirement for responsive reasons to those petitions that animated some agency response other than a bare letter of rejection.

Such a distinction was implicit in pre-*Chaney* discussions of the appropriate stringency of review of nonregulation. In *NRDC v. SEC*, 606 F.2d 1031 (D.C.Cir.1979), the court held reviewable the SEC's refusal to promulgate rules regarding corporations' disclosure of their environmental and equal employment policies. Although calling for highly deferential review, Judge McGowan's opinion is painstaking in arriving at the conclusion that the SEC's position was not arbitrary. What made such careful judicial consideration possible was the time and energy that the SEC had devoted to the possibility of issuing rules before it ultimately decided not to regulate. As the court observed:

> [I]n the context of an agency's non-adoption of a rule, the record and reasons statement will be of little use to a reviewing court unless they are narrowly focused on the particular rule advocated by plaintiff or petitioner. There are an infinite number of rules that an agency could adopt in its discretion; unless the agency has carefully focused its considerations, judicial review will have an undesirably abstract and hypothetical quality. However, in a context like the present one, in which the agency has in fact held extensive rulemaking proceedings narrowly focused on the particular rules at issue, and has explained in detail its reasons for not adopting those rules, we believe that the questions posed will be amenable to at least a minimal level of judicial scrutiny.

Note the implications of this analysis. Because the agency has considered with great care the proposal to regulate, it has generated a record for judicial review. It has also signaled that judicial insistence to think further about the problem is not forcing on the agency a set of issues it thinks trivial, and, to that extent, may be respectful of the agency's own set of priorities. If all this is plausible, would not agencies now be well advised to respond to any rulemaking petition with no more than the following: "Given our limited budget and our sense that other regulatory needs are more urgent, we are denying your petition. Thank you for writing." Would this lead to a remand under *AHPA?*

The competing impulses to insist on reviewability and then review lightly, depending on the materials available, were evident also in *WWHT, Inc. v. Federal Communications Commission*, 656 F.2d 807 (D.C.Cir.1981). The court was there asked to review the FCC's rejection of a petition for rulemaking from producers of subscription television programs. They asked the FCC to make paid programming subject to the agency's general requirement that cable companies carry the signals generated by all television stations within their designated localities. The petition was filed pursuant to specific FCC rules governing requests for rulemaking, 47 C.F.R. § 1.40(a) (1979), and supporting and opposing comments were filed by several parties. After reviewing the comments the Commission denied the request for rulemaking and also denied an ancillary request for a declaratory ruling on the scope of the existing mandatory cable carriage rules.

Although noting that the case for reviewability of the FCC's denial of rulemaking was "even less compelling" than in *NRDC v. SEC, supra*, the court nevertheless thought that limited review could focus on the petition, the comments filed, and the FCC's letter explaining, pursuant to its regulations, its reasons for denying the petition. And, as in *NRDC*, review produced an affirmance of the Commission's determination. Indeed, the court's scrutiny was so limited that the distinction between reviewability and nonreviewability appears elusive.

> For us to seriously indulge petitioner's claims in this case would be to ignore the institutional disruption that would be visited on the Commission by our second guessing its expert determination not to pursue a particular program or policy at a given time. It would also require us to ignore the plain fact that the policy determinations made by the Commission in this case—as to the relative merits of a mandatory cable carriage of subscription television signals—raise issues that are not well suited for determination by this court. These considerations lead us to conclude that our review of the Commission's actions should be *extremely narrow*, consistent with the views heretofore expressed. The Commission's substantive determinations are essentially legislative in this case and are thus committed to the discretion of the agency.

Compare *Center for Auto Safety v. National Highway Traffic Safety Administration*, 710 F.2d 842 (D.C.Cir.1983) (holding that the withdrawal of ANPRM under the Motor Vehicle Information and Cost Saving Act amounted to an informal determination that manufacturer plans for voluntary fuel economy improvement were sufficient to meet statutory goals, but finding that agency's implicit decision not to regulate was not ripe for review). But cf. *Investment Co. Institute v. FDIC*, 728 F.2d 518, 526 n. 6 (D.C.Cir.1984).

2. *Action–Forcing Deadlines*. It should be apparent that the availability of judicial review of agency inaction may depend on the language that Congress used in conveying and structuring the agency's authority. In the 1970s it became fashionable for regulatory statutes, particularly in health, environmental, and energy fields, not only to direct agencies to develop regulations but to "build in" requirements designed to assure that such congressional directions would be followed. One of the most common devices was to set deadlines for action. In many statutes Congress has specified that the administering agency "shall" promulgate regulations addressed to a specific problem or activity within a prescribed period from the date of enactment. An illustration is the 1976 Medical Device Amendments to the Federal Food, Drug, and Cosmetic Act, Pub.L.No. 94–295, 90 Stat. 539 (1976), which included a requirement that the FDA, within 120 days, promulgate regulations governing the use of experimental devices in clinical

research. 21 U.S.C. § 520(g)(2)(A). The purpose of this deadline was to minimize disruption of clinical investigations in hospitals throughout the country without having to delay implementation of the entire scheme for regulation of medical experimentation. In the same legislation, however, Congress also specified that the FDA must afford at least 60 days for public comment on all proposed regulations—leaving the agency, in this case, a total of 60 calendar (not working) days to draft a proposal, evaluate comments, and prepare final rules. The FDA was three years late completing this assignment. See 45 Fed.Reg. 3732 (Jan. 18, 1980).

The FDA's experience with statutory deadlines for issuance of regulations is not unusual. For a treatment of the FDA experience, see PETER BARTON HUTT & RICHARD A. MERRILL, FOOD AND DRUG LAW 1319–24 (2d ed. 1991). See generally EDWIN TOMLINSON, THE EXPERIENCE OF VARIOUS AGENCIES WITH STATUTORY TIME LIMITS APPLICABLE TO LICENSING OR CLEARANCE FUNCTIONS AND TO RULEMAKING, Report of the U.S. Administrative Conference (1978). Courts have taken statutory deadlines seriously by entertaining suits to enforce them, but they rarely demand more than "good faith" efforts at compliance. E.g., *NRDC v. Train*, 510 F.2d 692 (D.C.Cir.1974).

Forest Guardians v. Babbitt, 174 F.3d 1178 (10th Cir.1999), provides a dramatic illustration of the impact of a statutory deadline on both the availability and intensity of judicial review of an agency's failure to regulate. Under the Endangered Species Act the Secretary of the Interior is empowered to publish rules designating specific species as endangered and designating habitat that is critical to their survival. The statute specifies that critical habitat must be designated within one year of the publication a listing a species as endangered. The Secretary listed the Rio Grande silvery minnow as endangered on March 1, 1993, but had not identified critical habitat by the time the plaintiff sued nearly four years later. At the time the Secretary published the final rule designating the silvery minnow as endangered, he explained that habitat listing would be delayed—for this and the remaining 343 proposed species listings—because of Congress's failure to provide sufficient funding for the program. In response to this legislative effort to curb Interior's efforts to protect endangered and threatened species, the Department had issued guidance setting forth a three-tier schedule for working through the backlog, in which designation of critical habitat ranked lowest. When sued for failure to meet the statutory deadline, the Secretary essentially blamed his inaction on lack of appropriations and fell back on the schedule, whose reasonableness the Tenth Circuit did not question.

Assuming that the Interior Department's failure to regulate was subject to review, the court framed the question as "whether resource limitations can justify the Secretary's failure to comply with mandatory, non-discretionary duties imposed by the ESA. We hold that they cannot. * * * " The question, then, was whether the court had discretion to refrain from issuing an injunction ordering the Secretary to identify critical habitat for the silvery minnow. Judge Ebel interpreted the language of section 706(1) of the APA, which provides that a reviewing court "shall * * * compel agency action unlawfully withheld or unreasonably delayed," as leaving the court no choice. "[W]e believe that once a court deems agency delay unreasonable, it must compel agency action." Accordingly, the court remanded the case and ordered the district court to publish "as soon as possible * * * a final regulation, based on such data as may be available at the time, designating * * * the critical habitat for the Rio Grande silvery minnow, as is required by [the ESA]."

3. *Legislative Defaults.* Congress has experimented with a variety of agency-forcing tools to assure implementation of statutory mandates to make rules. One example is the so-called "hammer" provision of the Nutrition Education and Labeling Act of 1990, § 3(b)(2), Pub.L.No. 101–535, 104 Stat. 2353, 2361–2, which directed the FDA to prescribe revolutionary new rules governing nutrition labeling of conventional foods. A Democratic Congress, skeptical that the first Bush Administration would expeditiously implement this new and potentially costly program, enacted a two-stage schedule for rulemaking. FDA was given one year in which to propose regulations and one additional year to complete what all expected to be a massive rulemaking. (This was, without question, the most ambitious rulemaking proceeding that FDA at the time had ever undertaken. Is proposal ran over 200 pages in the Federal Register and attracted several thousand comments, many of them complex and lengthy.) To encourage the FDA to complete the task on time, the statute provided that, if final regulations had not been promulgated within two years of the laws enactment, the proposed regulations would automatically become final.

To the great surprise of many, and after herculean effort, FDA nearly met the prescribed schedule. However, the agency failed, by a few days, to complete the rulemaking within the year prescribed by Congress. This meant that it had to face the question of how it could, consistently with the APA's rulemaking requirements, substitute its "final"—and by almost universal assent superior—regulations for those that it had proposed and that had become final by operation of law. The prospect of having to propose their repeal, invite new comment, and complete the rulemaking a year or more behind schedule was unacceptable. Ultimately, FDA summarily revoked the "hammered final" regulations and published its thoroughly considered regulations as "final," invoking the APA's good cause exception for failure to go through the process once more. For an account of this episode and an analysis of the impact of various legislative strategies to force timely rulemaking, with and without the assistance of the courts, see M. Elizabeth Magill, *Congressional Control Over Agency Rulemaking: The Nutrition Labeling and Education Act's Hammer Provisions*, 50 Food & Drug L.J. 149 (1995).

4. *The Impact of Judicial Review of Agency Failure to Regulate.* Judicial willingness to review an agency's compliance with Congress's prescription for rulemaking may lead to a long and often frustrating relationship. One example is provided by a series of cases in which representatives of migrant workers pursued their demand that OSHA adopt a so-called "field sanitation standard," i.e., a rule designed to assure that farm workers have access to drinking water, lavatories, and other health-protective facilities. OSHA initiated investigations in 1973, referring the matter to an advisory committee which conducted hearings and prepared recommendations. When after more than a year OSHA had taken no further action, groups representing migrant workers sued to force the agency to complete the rulemaking process in accordance with 29 U.S.C. § 655(b), which sets precise time limits for all steps subsequent to consultation with an advisory committee. *Nation-*

al Congress of Hispanic American Citizens v. Usery, 554 F.2d 1196 (D.C.Cir. 1977). While acknowledging that the Secretary of Labor had discretion to decide which workplace hazards to address, the plaintiffs contended that once he had commenced the rulemaking process, he was obligated to adhere to the statutory schedule. The court of appeals disagreed, but it was also unwilling to remit the plaintiffs to the unguided mercies of the agency, and so its order contemplated a continuing role for the judiciary:

> Upon remand the trial court should require the Secretary to file a report as to the present situation on each of these proposed standards, including the timetables governing each. If the court is not satisfied as to the sincerity of the effort of the Secretary in the processing of such standards, it should take such action as the circumstances require; if it is satisfied as to the same, it should hold the case on the docket for further report from the Secretary on the issuance of the standards.

The dispute was back before the court two years later. *National Congress of Hispanic American Citizens (El Congreso) v. Marshall*, 626 F.2d 882 (D.C.Cir.1979), following a district court order directing the Secretary to "complete development of a field sanitation standard * * * as soon as possible." This order was a response to a series of agency submissions, which made clear that the field sanitation standard ranked low on its priorities and would not receive serious attention within "the agency's 18–month planning horizon because of both generally limited agency resources" and its "relatively low priority." Before challenging the order, the Secretary had proffered a schedule that could have yielded a final standard by the end of 1979, but he reiterated that unanticipated problems could cause yet further delays. Shortly afterwards, the government moved to withdraw the schedule, explaining it did not reflect the priorities of the OSHA Administrator, who had been out of the country when it was prepared, and appealed the district court's order.

Writing for the court, Judge Leventhal reaffirmed OSHA's discretion to allocate its resources in accordance with its own assessment of need, the statutory timetable notwithstanding: "So long as his action is rational in the context of the statute, and is taken in good faith, the Secretary has authority to delay development of a standard at any stage as priorities demand." The court, however, felt obliged to review the agency's choice. In performing this function, Leventhal concluded that the district court had exceeded its role:

> The district court's "own view of appropriate priorities" disregarded, without warrant, material findings made by the agency. For example, the Secretary specifically concluded that rulemaking concerning the field sanitation standard would be quite lengthy, involving the allocation of substantial resources (approximately 3600 man-hours). The Secretary also concluded that the greatest hazards to agricultural employees had already been remedied, and that other industries merited allocation of the available resources (the accident rate in the agricultural industry was fifth among eight major groupings). The district court emphasized almost exclusively the number of employees to be benefited, ignoring numerous other criteria considered by the Secretary such as the nature and the severity of the hazard exposure.

> This court is of the view that greater respect is due the Secretary's judgment that promulgation of a cancer policy, a lead standard, an anhydrous ammonia standard and the like, merited higher priority than a field sanitation standard. With its broader perspective, and access to a broad range of undertakings, and not merely the program before the court, the agency has a better capacity than the court to make the comparative judgments involved in determining priorities and allocating resources. The district court impermissibly substituted its judgment for that of the agency.

Even so, Leventhal was not prepared to leave matters as they stood. He concluded with these instructions to the (by now no doubt exasperated) district court:

> Where the Secretary deems a problem significant enough to warrant initiation of the standard setting process, the Act requires that he have a plan to shepherd through the development of the standard—that he takes pains, regardless of the press of other priorities, to ensure that the standard is not inadvertently lost in the process.
>
> It is not enough for the Secretary merely to state that the standard will not be issued over the next 18 months. If other priorities preclude promulgation of a field sanitation standard within that frame, then the Secretary must provide a timetable—at least for the standard in question—which covers a larger period.
>
> Upon remand to the district court, the Secretary should be granted leeway to reconsider the timetable submitted on January 22, 1979, since it was developed without input from the official charged with responsibility for this area. In constructing the timetable, the Secretary need not be constrained, as he would have been under the district court order, to rearrange priorities that were rationally set. But, the Secretary must give due regard to the principle, presumed in the timetable of 29 U.S.C. § 655(b)(2)–(4) and developed here, that once the process of developing a standard begins, a good faith effort must be made to complete it.

While Labor Secretary Marshall submitted a new schedule for completing the rulemaking, the 1980 election intervened before any final decision—and the Reagan Administration found new priorities for OSHA. In March 1984, Labor Secretary Donovan withdrew the 1976 proposal and replaced it with a new proposed standard, 49 Fed.Reg. 7589, 7592 (1984). The new proposal was confined to farms employing 11 or more field laborers because Congress had enacted a rider to the agency's budget prohibiting the Secretary from using agency funds to regulate farms with 10 or fewer workers. Donovan also raised, for the first time, the possibility that no federal standard was needed "in light of" state adoption of local standards and voluntary provision of drinking water and sanitary facilities by employers. In any event, rulemaking was to be completed by February 1985, in accordance with an agreement settling El Congreso's suit.

In January 1985, OSHA sought judicial approval to prolong the rulemaking proceeding through April. The court of appeals found the Secretary to be acting in good faith but warned that "we will look with extreme displeasure on any variance from the schedule and will not hesitate to set a date certain for completion of the administrative proceeding if they unreasonably delay." On April 16, OSHA issued a final decision declining to promulgate any field sanitation standard. It claimed that such a standard would have low priority for enforcement, and asserted that considerations of federalism justified deference to state efforts to provide protection for field workers.

Eight days later, a new Labor Secretary-designate,William Brock, promised in confirmation hearings to reconsider Donovan's "no standard" decision, and in October, 1985, Brock announced that he was revoking it. But Brock declined to promulgate a standard or to issue a new proposal immediately, instead announcing that he would delay action for two additional years to give state governments an opportunity to implement their own standards. In the course of his decision, Brock acknowledged the "clear evidence * * * of unacceptable risks to the health of farmworkers arising from the currently inadequate provision of sanitary facilities and drinking water," and conceded that "further regulation is required to deal with the farmworkers' health problems." 50 Fed.Reg. 42,600 (1985). He concluded, however, that state regulation would be preferable to a federal standard.

Predictably, this decision was challenged in court, and on February 6, 1987, it was overturned by the D.C. Circuit in *Farmworker Justice Fund, Inc. v. Brock*, 811 F.2d 613 (D.C.Cir.1987). Optimistically describing the case as "culminating" a 14–year old effort, Judge Wald quickly dispensed with the suggestion that judicial review of OSHA's failure to act was barred by *Heckler v. Chaney*. Moving to the merits, she found Brock's deference to state regulation to be inconsistent with the congressional judgment embodied in the 1972 Occupational Safety and Health Act. "[T]he Secretary may not withhold or delay issuance of a standard within his jurisdiction because he holds a different vision of the federal government's role in this field than the role envisioned by Congress and enacted into law. * * * " Judge Wald conceded that the agency could weigh the adequacy of state regulation in assessing the need for federal intervention, but held that in this instance the Secretary's assessment of the likelihood of effective state control was simply unsupported. Accordingly, invoking section 706(1) of the APA, the court ordered the Secretary to issue a federal field sanitation standard for farmworkers within 30 days. Judge Williams dissented on the merits, though he did agree that OSHA's decision not to issue the standard was reviewable, *Chaney* notwithstanding.

On April 28, 1987, OSHA finally promulgated a field sanitation standard closely resembling its 1984 proposal. On petition for rehearing, the panel in *FJF v. Brock* withdrew its opinion as moot. 817 F.2d 890 (D.C.Cir.1987).

3. TIMING

Establishing that a claim is in principle reviewable does not insure that a court will reach the merits. An agency decision may not be challenged prematurely, as gauged under the doctrines of "finality," "ripeness," and "exhaustion." Although the requirement that agency action be "final" is statutory, 5 U.S.C. § 704, while "ripeness" and "exhaustion" are judicially crafted, the three doctrines implement overlapping policies: avoiding judicial interruptions in the administrative process; giving agencies leeway to develop expert judgment and maintain program integrity; and maximizing the likelihood that judicial challenges, once brought, will be sharply focused and based on reviewable records. The overlap of the doctrines is illustrated by *Ticor Title Insurance Co. v. FTC*, 814 F.2d 731 (D.C.Cir.1987), in which a panel unanimously dismissed as premature the petitioner's facial challenge to the constitutionality of FTC enforcement proceedings, but split three ways over whether exhaustion, finality, or ripeness doctrine best explained the result.

a. Requiring Final Agency Action

The requirement that agency action be "final" before it may be reviewed by a court would seem straightforward, and in most cases it is easily (and obviously) satisfied. A litigant who is the subject of enforcement proceedings brought before an agency must ordinarily wait until the administrative process has concluded with an order to change or cease conduct, or pay a penalty, before challenging the agency's accusations, findings, or procedures by petition or suit for judicial review. Until the administrative process has run its course and the litigant confronts such an order, it typically has suffered no legally cognizable injury, and there remains the possibility that the agency itself may change its view of the facts or of the law.

While satisfaction of the principle of finality is easy to discern in most cases, sometimes administrative decisions are the product of a multi-stage process. And many challenges to agency action raise multiple issues, which may be definitively disposed of at different stages of the administrative process. Thus it is frequently necessary to ask, with respect to a particular issue, when the administrative process will have yielded a definitive, and final, decision.

DALTON v. SPECTER

Supreme Court of the United States.

511 U.S. 462, 114 S.Ct. 1719, 128 L.Ed.2d 497 (1994).

CHIEF JUSTICE REHNQUIST delivered the opinion of the Court.

Respondents sought to enjoin the Secretary of Defense (Secretary) from carrying out a decision by the President to close the Philadelphia Naval Shipyard.[1] This decision was made pursuant to the Defense Base Closure and Realignment Act of 1990 (1990 Act). The Court of Appeals held that judicial review of the decision was available to ensure that various participants in the selection process had complied with procedural mandates specified by Congress. We hold that such review is not available.

The decision to close the shipyard was the end result of an elaborate selection process prescribed by the 1990 Act. Designed "to provide a fair

1. Respondents are shipyard employees and their unions; members of Congress from Pennsylvania and New Jersey; the States of Pennsylvania, New Jersey, and Delaware, and officials of those States; and the city of Philadelphia. Petitioners are the Secretary of Defense; the Secretary of the Navy; and the Defense Base Closure and Realignment Commission and its members.

process that will result in the timely closure and realignment of military installations inside the United States," § 2901(b), the Act provides for three successive rounds of base closings—in 1991, 1993, and 1995, respectively. For each round, the Secretary must prepare closure and realignment recommendations, based on selection criteria he establishes after notice and an opportunity for public comment.

The Secretary submits his recommendations to Congress and to the Defense Base Closure and Realignment Commission (Commission), an independent body whose eight members are appointed by the President, with the advice and consent of the Senate. The Commission must then hold public hearings and prepare a report, containing both an assessment of the Secretary's recommendations and the Commission's own recommendations for base closures and realignments. Within roughly three months of receiving the Secretary's recommendations, the Commission has to submit its report to the President.

Within two weeks of receiving the Commission's report, the President must decide whether to approve or disapprove, in their entirety, the Commission's recommendations. If the President disapproves, the Commission has roughly one month to prepare a new report and submit it to the President. If the President again disapproves, no bases may be closed that year under the Act. If the President approves the initial or revised recommendations, the President must submit the recommendations, along with his certification of approval, to Congress. Congress may, within 45 days of receiving the President's certification (or by the date Congress adjourns for the session, whichever is earlier), enact a joint resolution of disapproval. If such a resolution is passed, the Secretary may not carry out any closures pursuant to the Act; if such a resolution is not passed, the Secretary must close all military installations recommended for closure by the Commission.

In April 1991, the Secretary recommended the closure or realignment of a number of military installations, including the Philadelphia Naval Shipyard. * * * The Commission did not concur in all of the Secretary's recommendations, but it agreed that the Philadelphia Naval Shipyard should be closed. In July 1991, President Bush approved the Commission's recommendations, and the House of Representatives rejected a proposed joint resolution of disapproval by a vote of 364 to 60.

Two days before the President submitted his certification of approval to Congress, respondents filed this action under the Administrative Procedure Act (APA), 5 U.S.C. § 701 *et seq.*, and the 1990 Act. Their complaint contained three counts, two of which remain at issue. Count I alleged that the Secretaries of Navy and Defense violated substantive and procedural requirements of the 1990 Act in recommending closure of the Philadelphia Naval Shipyard. Count II made similar allegations regarding the Commission's recommendations to the President, asserting specifically that, *inter alia*, the Commission used improper criteria, failed to place certain information in the record until after the close of public hearings, and held closed meetings with the Navy.

* * * The Court of Appeals first acknowledged that the actions challenged by respondents were not typical of the "agency actions" reviewed under the APA, because the 1990 Act contemplates joint decisionmaking among the Secretary, Commission, President, and Congress. The Court of Appeals then reasoned that because respondents sought to enjoin the implementation of the President's decision, respondents (who had not named the President as a defendant) were asking the Court of Appeals "to review a presidential decision." The Court of Appeals decided that there could be judicial review of the President's decision because the "actions of the President have never been considered immune from judicial review solely because they were taken by the President." It held that certain procedural claims, such as respondents' claim that the Secretary failed to transmit to the Commission all of the information he used in making his recommendations, and their claim that the Commission did not hold public hearings as required by the Act, were thus reviewable. The dissenting judge took the view that the 1990 Act precluded judicial review of all statutory claims, procedural and substantive.

Shortly after the Court of Appeals issued its opinion, we decided *Franklin v. Massachusetts*, 505 U.S. 788 (1992), in which we addressed the existence of "final agency action" in a suit seeking APA review of the decennial reapportionment of the House of Representatives. The Census Act requires the Secretary of Commerce to submit a census report to the President, who then certifies to Congress the number of Representatives to which each State is entitled pursuant to a statutory formula. We concluded both that the Secretary's report was not "final agency action" reviewable under the APA, and that the APA does not apply to the President. After we rendered our decision in *Franklin*, petitioners sought our review in this case. Because of the similarities between *Franklin* and this case, we granted the petition for certiorari, vacated the judgement of the Court of Appeals, and remanded for further consideration in light of *Franklin*.

On remand, the same divided panel of the Court of Appeals adhered to its earlier decision, and held that *Franklin* did not affect the reviewability of respondents' procedural claims. *Specter v. Garrett*, 995 F.2d 404 (1993) (*Specter II*). Although apparently recognizing that APA review was unavailable, the Court of Appeals felt that adjudging the President's actions for compliance with the 1990 Act was a "form of constitutional review," and that *Franklin* sanctioned such review. Petitioners again sought our review, and we granted certiorari. We now reverse.

I

We begin our analysis on common ground with the Court of Appeals. In *Specter II*, that court acknowledged, at least tacitly, that respondents' claims are not reviewable under the APA. A straightforward application of *Franklin* to this case demonstrates why this is so. *Franklin* involved a suit against the President, the Secretary of Commerce, and various public officials, challenging the manner in which seats in the House of

Representatives had been apportioned among the States. The plaintiffs challenged the method used by the Secretary of Commerce in preparing her census report, particularly the manner in which she counted federal employees working overseas. The plaintiffs raised claims under both the APA and the Constitution. In reviewing the former, we first sought to determine whether the Secretary's action, in submitting a census report to the President, was "final" for purposes of APA review. * * * Because the President reviewed (and could revise) the Secretary's report, made the apportionment calculations, and submitted the final apportionment report to Congress, we held that the Secretary's report was "not final and therefore not subject to review."

We next held that the President's actions were not reviewable under the APA, because the President is not an "agency" within the meaning of the APA. * * * We thus concluded that the reapportionment determination was not reviewable under the standards of the APA. In reaching our conclusion, we noted that the "President's actions may still be reviewed for constitutionality."

In this case, respondents brought suit under the APA, alleging that the Secretary and the Commission did not follow the procedural mandates of the 1990 Act. But here, as in *Franklin*, the prerequisite to review under the APA—"final agency action"—is lacking. The reports submitted by the Secretary of Defense and the Commission, like the report of the Secretary of Commerce in *Franklin*, "carr[y] no direct consequences" for base closings. The action that "will directly affect" the military bases is taken by the President, when he submits his certification of approval to Congress. Accordingly, the Secretary's and Commission's reports serve "more like a tentative recommendation than a final and binding determination." The reports are, "like the ruling of a subordinate official, not final and therefore not subject to review." The actions of the President, in turn, are not reviewable under the APA because, as we concluded in *Franklin*, the President is not an "agency."

* * * Respondents appear to argue that the President, under the 1990 Act, has little authority regarding the closure of bases. See Brief for Respondents 29 (pointing out that the 1990 Act does not allow "the President to ignore, revise or amend the Commission's list of closures. He is only permitted to accept or reject the Commission's closure package in its entirety"). Consequently, respondents continue, the Commission's report must be regarded as final. This argument ignores the *ratio decidendi* of *Franklin*.

First, respondents underestimate the President's authority under the Act, and the importance of his role in the base closure process. Without the President's approval, no bases are closed under the Act, the Act, in turn, does not by its terms circumscribe the President's discretion to approve or disapprove the Commission's report. Second, and more fundamentally, respondents' argument ignores "the core question" for determining finality: "whether the agency has completed its decision-making process, and whether the result of that process is one that will directly affect the parties." That the President cannot pick and choose among bases, and must accept or reject the entire package offered by the Commission, is immaterial. What is crucial is the fact that "[t]he President, not the [Commission], takes the final action that affects" the military installations. Accordingly, we hold that the decisions made pursuant to the 1990 Act are not reviewable under the APA.

Although respondents apparently sought review exclusively under the APA, the Court of Appeals nevertheless sought to determine whether non-APA review, based on either common law or constitutional principles, was available. * * *

II

Seizing upon our statement in *Franklin* that presidential decisions are reviewable for constitutionality, the Court of Appeals asserted that "there is a constitutional aspect to the exercise of judicial review in this case—an aspect grounded in the separation of powers doctrine." It reasoned, relying primarily on *Youngstown Sheet & Tube Co. v. Sawyer*, 343 U.S. 579 (1952), that whenever the President acts in excess of his statutory authority, he also violates the constitutional separation of powers doctrine. Thus, judicial review must be available to determine whether the President has statutory authority "for whatever action" he takes. In terms of this case, the Court of Appeals concluded that the President's statutory authority to close and realign bases would be lacking if the Secretary and Commission violated the procedural requirements of the Act in formulating their recommendations.

Accepting for purposes of decision here the propriety of examining the President's actions, we nonetheless believe that the Court of Appeals' analysis is flawed. Our cases do not support the proposition that every action by the President, or by another executive official, in excess of his statutory authority is *ipso facto* in violation of the Constitution. On the contrary, we have often distinguished between claims of constitutional violations and claims that an official has acted in excess of his statutory authority. * * *

In *Larson v. Domestic & Foreign Commerce Corp.*, 337 U.S. 682, 691, n. 11 (1949), for example, we held that sovereign immunity would not shield an executive officer from suit if the officer acted either "unconstitutionally *or* beyond his statutory powers." (Emphasis added). If all executive actions in excess of statutory authority were *ipso facto* unconstitutional, as the Court of Appeals seemed to believe, there would have been little need in *Larson* for our specifying unconstitutional and ultra vires conduct as separate categories.

Our decision in *Youngstown* does not suggest a different conclusion. In *Youngstown*, the Government disclaimed any statutory authority for the President's seizure of steel mills. The only basis of authority asserted was the President's inherent constitutional power as the Executive and the Commander-in-Chief of the Armed Forces. Because no statutory authority was claimed, the case necessarily turned on whether the

Constitution authorized the President's actions. *Youngstown* thus involved the conceded *absence* of *any* statutory authority, not a claim that the President acted in excess of such authority. The case cannot be read for the proposition that an action taken by the President in excess of his statutory authority necessarily violates the Constitution.

The decisions cited above establish that claims simply alleging that the President has exceeded his statutory authority are not "constitutional" claims, subject to judicial review under the exception recognized in *Franklin*. As this case demonstrates, if every claim alleging that the President exceeded his statutory authority were considered a constitutional claim, the exception identified in *Franklin* would be broadened beyond recognition. * * *

So the claim raised here is a statutory one: The President is said to have violated the terms of the 1990 Act by accepting procedurally flawed recommendations. * * * We may assume for the sake of argument that some claims that the President has violated a statutory mandate are judicially reviewable outside the framework of the APA. See *Dames & Moore v. Regan*, 453 U.S. 654 (1981). But longstanding authority holds that such review is not available when the statute in question commits the decision to the discretion of the President.

* * *

In a case analogous to the present one, *Chicago & Southern Air Lines, Inc. v. Waterman S. S. Corp.*, 333 U.S. 103 (1948), an airline denied a certificate from the Civil Aeronautics Board to establish an international air route sought judicial review of the denial. Although the Civil Aeronautics Act, 49 U.S.C. § 646 (1946 ed.), generally allowed for judicial review of the Board's decisions, and did not explicitly exclude judicial review of decisions involving international routes of domestic airlines, we nonetheless held that review was unavailable.

In reasoning pertinent to this case, we first held that the Board's certification was not reviewable because it was not final until approved by the President. * * * We then concluded that the President's decision to approve or disapprove the orders was not reviewable, because "the final orders embody Presidential discretion as to political matters beyond the competence of the courts to adjudicate." We fully recognized that the consequence of our decision was to foreclose judicial review:

> "The dilemma faced by those who demand judicial review of the Board's order is that before Presidential approval it is not a final determination * * * and after Presidential approval the whole order, both in what is approved without change as well as in amendments which he directs, derives its vitality from the exercise of *unreviewable Presidential discretion*."

Although the President's discretion in *Waterman S. S. Corp.* derived from the Constitution, we do not believe the result should be any different when the President's discretion derives from a valid statute.

The 1990 Act does not at all limit the President's discretion in approving or disapproving the Commission's recommendations. The Third Circuit seemed to believe that the President's authority to close bases depended on the Secretary's and Commission's compliance with statutory procedures. This view of the statute, however, incorrectly conflates the duties of the Secretary and Commission with the authority of the President. The President's authority to act is not contingent on the Secretary's and Commission's fulfillment of all the procedural requirements imposed upon them by the 1990 Act. Nothing in § 2903(e) requires the President to determine whether the Secretary or Commission committed any procedural violations in making their recommendations, nor does § 2903(e) prohibit the President from approving recommendations that are procedurally flawed. Indeed, nothing in § 2903(e) prevents the President from approving or disapproving the recommendations for whatever reason he sees fit.

How the President chooses to exercise the discretion Congress has granted him is not a matter for our review. * * *

III

* * *

Respondents tell us that failure to allow judicial review here would virtually repudiate *Marbury v. Madison*, and nearly two centuries of constitutional adjudication. But our conclusion that judicial review is not available for respondents' claim follows from our interpretation of an Act of Congress, by which we and all federal courts are bound. The judicial power of the United States conferred by Article III of the Constitution is upheld just as surely by withholding judicial relief where Congress has permissibly foreclosed it, as it is by granting such relief where authorized by the Constitution or by statute.

The judgment of the Court of Appeals is

Reversed.

[The concurring opinion of Justice Blackmun is omitted.]

JUSTICE SOUTER, with whom JUSTICE BLACKMUN, JUSTICE STEVENS, and JUSTICE GINSBURG join, concurring in part and concurring in the judgment.

I join Part II of the Court's opinion because I think it is clear that the President acted wholly within the discretion afforded him by the Defense Base Closure and Realignment Act of 1990 (Act), and because respondents pleaded no constitutional claim against the President, indeed, no claim against the President at all. As the Court explains, the Act grants the President unfettered discretion to accept the Commission's base-closing report or to reject it, for a good reason, a bad reason, or no reason.

It is not necessary to reach the question the Court answers in Part I, whether the Commission's report is final agency action, because the text, structure, and purpose of the Act compel the conclusion that judicial review of the Commission's or the Secretary's compliance with it is precluded. There is, to be sure, a "strong presumption that Congress did not mean to prohibit all judicial review." But although no one feature of the Act, taken alone, is enough to overcome that strong presumption, I believe that the combination present in this unusual legislative scheme suffices.

* * *

[The concurring Justices were at pains to point out that they viewed this statute as unusual. It contained a set of tight and rigid deadlines for determining which bases should be closed and implementing those decisions, and procedures for putting together "political packages" that could garner an affirmative decision by the President and a majority in Congress. Judicial review that might delay or prevent the closure of one or another base would destroy both the decision schedule and the political viability of the Commission's recommended "package." The whole structure and purpose of the Act argued against allowing plaintiffs, such as the ones here, to undo the political compromises painstakingly worked out in the special Commission process.]

Note

Reviewing Presidential Action. For a discussion of possible ways in which the President might be sued, outside the APA, for failure to comply with limitations on authority vested in him by statute, see Jonathan R. Siegel, *Suing the President: Nonstatutory Review Revisited*, 97 Colum.L.Rev. 1612 (1997).

When Is Agency Inaction "Final?"

A pair of cases decided by the D.C. Circuit in 1970 and 1971 pitted environmental advocates who sought to end the use of the pesticide DDT against both the makers of DDT and the agencies that were successively responsible for administering the federal pesticide law, known as FIFRA (Federal Insecticide, Fungicide and Rodenticide Act). In her famous book, SILENT SPRING (1962), Rachel Carson had dramatized the threat that synthetic organic pesticides—and most notably DDT—posed to human health, wildlife, and the ecosystem. At the time, responsibility for administering FIFRA rested with the U.S. Department of Agriculture, then led by Secretary Earl Butz. In 1970, however, when by executive order President Nixon created the new Environmental Protection Agency, authority to administer the statute was reassigned to EPA. Each agency in turn became the target of the Environmental Defense Fund's efforts to force administrative action to curb or ban DDT and, when these efforts failed, of a suit challenging its failure to act. The resulting pair of decisions illustrate not only the elusive contours of the doctrine of finality but the ingenuity of EDF's attorneys.

In 1969, when EDF first petitioned USDA, FIFRA forbade the marketing of any pesticide until it had been "registered" with the

Department. To obtain registration the sponsor of a pesticide had to show, among other requirements, that it would be "safe" for humans who were exposed. DDT had been registered for several different uses some years earlier; for EDF the goal was to secure the withdrawal—in the statute's words, the "cancellation"—of those registrations. The statute authorized USDA (later EPA) to cancel a pesticide's registration if, after a formal adjudicatory hearing, it was found unsafe. It also permitted the agency to suspend immediately, i.e., without any prior hearing, a pesticide that the Secretary believed posed an "imminent hazard" to health.

The multi-stage litigation began with the filing of EDF's petition with USDA demanding that it both (a) initiate the process to cancel the registrations for DDT on the ground that it was unsafe and (b) issue an order immediately suspending further sales of DDT on the ground that the pesticide presented an imminent hazard. Secretary Butz issued notices of cancellation (proposals to cancel) for four minor uses of DDT, solicited comments on the remaining uses, but did not address at all EDF's request that he suspend the use of DDT pending further agency proceedings. Months of silence passed, and finally EDF, despairing that USDA would act in time to forestall further harm from the uses of DDT, filed a petition to review USDA's failure to act on its suspension request in the U.S. Court of Appeals for the D.C. Circuit.

EDF's choice of court on its face may seem surprising since statutes that provide for appellate court review usually contemplate that review will be based on the record of a formal agency hearing. USDA's failure to make any response to EDF's petition, of course, meant that there had been no hearing or other administrative process of any kind. But EDF's choice proved propitious. At the time, the judicial review provisions of FIFRA provided in part:

> Final orders of the [Secretary, later] Administrator * * * shall be subject to judicial review, in accordance with the provisions of subsection (d) of this section.
>
> In a case of actual controversy as to the validity of any order * * * any person who will be adversely affected by such order may obtain judicial review by filing in the [appropriate] United States court of appeals.* * *

7 U.S.C. § 135b(c) and (d). Paragraph (d) further specified that review should be under the substantial evidence standard.

EDF recognized that, to invoke these provisions, it would have to persuade the court of appeals that USDA's utter failure to respond to its petition was a "final order," but it also perceived significant advantage if it were successful with this argument. Perhaps most important, the court's acknowledgment that USDA's failure to act was a "final order" within the meaning of FIFRA's specific statutory review provision would avoid USDA's near-certain objection that its exercise of its enforcement discretion was unreviewable. Further, the general words, "any person who will be adversely affected" surely allowed review by litigants in addition to pesticide registrants and could solve what might otherwise have been a serious standing problem for these plaintiffs (see Section C–4 *infra*). Finally, if EDF were able to establish jurisdiction in the court of appeals it would not only shorten, by one stage, the process for securing judicial relief (appeal of any district court decision in this case was a foregone conclusion), but also bring its challenge before a liberal court whose members were accustomed to reexamining and often "correcting" the actions of federal administrators.

To no one's surprise, the government's immediate response to EDF's petition for review was to challenge the court of appeals' jurisdiction—on the central premise that there was no order, final or otherwise, for it to review. The court, in an opinion by Chief Judge David Bazelon, rejected the government's argument:

> An order expressly denying the request for suspension or for cancellation would clearly be ripe for review. The doctrines of ripeness and finality are designed to prevent premature judicial intervention in the administrative process, before the administrative action has been fully considered, and before the legal dispute has been brought into focus. No subsequent action can sharpen the controversy arising from a decision by the Secretary that the evidence submitted by petitioners does not compel suspension or cancellation of the registration of DDT. In light of the urgent character of petitioners' claim, and the allegation that delay itself inflicts irreparable injury, the controversy is as ripe for judicial consideration as it can ever be.
>
> * * *
>
> * * * [W]hen administrative inaction has precisely the same impact on the rights of the parties as denial of relief, an agency cannot preclude judicial review by casting its decision in the form of inaction rather than in the form of an order denying relief.
>
> With regard to the request for interim suspension of the registration of DDT, we agree that inaction is tantamount to an order denying suspension. The suspension power is designed to protect the public from an "imminent hazard"; if petitioners are right in their claim that DDT presents a hazard sufficient to warrant suspension, then even a temporary refusal to suspend results in irreparable injury on a massive scale. The controversy over interim relief is ripe for judicial resolution, because the Secretary's inaction results in a final disposition of such rights as the petitioners and the public may have to interim relief.
>
> * * *
>
> With respect to the request for notices of cancellation, we are more reluctant to equate a tentative and equivocal delay with an outright denial of the request. * * * Since the issuance of cancellation notices merely triggers that administrative mechanism, it is questionable whether the Secretary may properly defer the decision

> to issue notices in order to engage in a preliminary inquiry not contemplated by the statute.
>
> At some point administrative delay amounts to a refusal to act, with sufficient finality and ripeness to permit judicial review. The present record does not permit us to determine whether that point has been reached here. On remand, the Secretary should either decide on the record whether to issue the remaining requested cancellation notices, or explain the reasons for deferring the decision still further.

As Judge Bazelon's concluding directive to Secretary Butz implies, the court—having ruled that USDA's failure to respond to EDF's demand that the registrations for DDT be suspended amounted to a final order—faced an immediate problem. The Secretary's silence meant he had offered no explanation for his inaction and thus there was no "record" for the court to review. Judge Bazelon would not be stymied, however, and ordered the matter remanded "either for a fresh determination on the question of suspension, or for a statement of reasons for his silent but effective refusal to suspend the registration of DDT."

Within a year the case was back before the court of appeals, but with a new named respondent: William Ruckelshaus, who as EPA Administrator had been delegated responsibility for FIFRA after the Agriculture Secretary had responded to the court's original remand. The Secretary had formally declined to suspend the registrations for DDT, but declared that the possibility of initiating proceedings to cancel most of the remaining uses of DDT was still under consideration. Again writing for the court, Chief Judge Bazelon reaffirmed the court's earlier ruling that a refusal to suspend was a "final order" subject to immediate review, and, reaching the merits, concluded that the Administrator had misinterpreted the statutory standard for ordering suspension. *Environmental Defense Fund, Inc. v. Ruckelshaus*, 439 F.2d 584 (D.C.Cir.1971).

> The statute provides for suspension in order "to prevent an imminent hazard to the public." Congress clearly intended to protect the public from some risks by summary administrative action pending further proceedings. The administrator's problem is to determine which risks fall in that class. The Secretary has made no attempt to deal with that problem, either by issuing regulations relating to suspension, or by explaining his decision in this case. * * *
>
> Since the Secretary has not yet provided an adequate explanation for his decision to deny interim relief in this case, it will be necessary to remand the case once more, for a fresh determination on that issue.

In the course of his treatment of the finality question, Bazelon went out of his way to opine that, had the Secretary granted EDF's request to suspend, the registrants—the makers of DDT—would have been entitled to seek immediate judicial review of that decision even though the agency would simultaneously have begun the formal hearing process that could lead to cancellation. In so doing, he rejected the contrary reasoning of the Seventh Circuit in *Nor–Am Agricultural Products, Inc. v. Hardin*, 435 F.2d 1151 (7th Cir.1970) (en banc), *cert. dismissed*, 402 U.S. 935 (1971).

> [T]he administrative proceedings that follow suspension are equally available after a refusal to suspend. * * * In either event, there is a prospect of further administrative action, but that prospect does not resolve the question of reviewability. The subsequent proceedings are designed solely to resolve the ultimate question whether cancellation is warranted, and not to shed any further light on the question whether there is a sufficient threat of "Imminent hazard" to warrant suspension in the interim. Once the Secretary has made a decision with respect to suspension, whether he decides to grant or to deny that relief, the "imminence" of the hazard is no longer at issue.

But Judge Bazelon agreed with the Seventh Circuit's analysis of the reviewability of EPA decisions initiating, or refusing to initiate, cancellation proceedings.

> * * * [W]e find substantial merit in the distinction suggested by *Nor–Am*. That is, a decision of the Secretary to issue cancellation notices is not reviewable, because it merely sets in motion the administrative process that terminates in a reviewable final order. An unqualified refusal to issue notices, on the other hand, operates with finality as an administrative rejection of the claim that cancellation is required.

Compare *Dow Chemical Co. v. Ruckelshaus*, 477 F.2d 1317 (8th Cir.1973), and *Pax Co. v. United States*, 454 F.2d 93 (10th Cir.1972), in which producers sought immediate district court review of notices to cancel registrations for certain pesticides. Both courts declined to review on the ground that a cancellation notice only initiated the formal administrative process, and did not interrupt continued marketing or use of the pesticides. If the Administrator ultimately cancelled the registrations after hearing, review could be had in a court of appeals.

2. *Challenging the Initiation of Enforcement Proceedings*. The *Nor–Am* and *Dow* situations should be compared with others in which an initial agency move has concrete adverse effects, but wholly preliminary and reversible legal consequences. *FTC v. Standard Oil Co.*, 449 U.S. 232 (1980), is perhaps the best-known example in a standard enforcement context. Following sharp increases in the price of gasoline because of the first Arab oil embargo, the FTC served complaints on eight major oil companies averring that the agency had "reason to believe" that they had committed unfair methods of competition under section 5(b) of the FTC Act. The allegations suggested that the companies had callously used the embargo as a pretext for driving up prices. With administrative trial of the charges still pending, one targeted company, Standard Oil Company of California (Socal), sought an injunction to terminate the proceeding on the ground that the complaint had issued unlawfully.

Socal charged that the FTC had not performed an investigation sufficient to support any suspicions, much less the merits of its allegations, but had issued a complaint solely in response to political pressure from powerful members of Congress to "do something" about gasoline shortages and skyrocketing prices.

In reviewing Socal's claim, the Ninth Circuit held that the issuance of the complaint represented a final agency determination that the FTC had "reason to believe" that violations had occurred, and that the district court could properly review for the limited purpose of insuring that a determination of "reason to believe" had, in fact, been made. 596 F.2d 1381 (9th Cir.1979). The Supreme Court reversed. The Court held that the issuance of the complaint was not reviewable "final agency action" for any purpose, because the agency position it embodied—a belief that Socal had violated the FTC Act—was preliminary and subject to revision or correction in the adjudicatory process. The Court perceived that the complaint imposed no legal burden on Socal. The practical effects, of course, were possible damage to the company's reputation and the burden of participating in litigation that might be baseless, but nonetheless protracted and expensive. The Court treated these latter effects as no more than "part of the burden of living under government."

The majority of eight Justices acknowledged that Socal had no possibility of persuading the FTC to withdraw its complaint, but refused to concede that delaying review of Socal's immediate claim would render it effectively unreviewable. In a solo concurrence, Justice Stevens agreed with Socal on this point:

> If the Commission ultimately prevails on the merits of its complaint, Socal surely will not be granted immunity because the Commission did not uncover the evidence of illegality until after the complaint was filed. On the other hand, if Socal prevails, there will be no occasion to review the contention it now advances because the only relief it seeks is a dismissal of the Commission's complaint.

Stevens nonetheless joined in the judgment on the ground that the filing of a complaint was not intended to be treated reviewable "agency action" under the APA.

3. *Must "Final" Action Be Coercive?* In what may prove an important precedent, the Fourth Circuit declined to review the release, by the EPA, of a scientific study of the health effects of side-stream tobacco smoke. *Flue–Cured Tobacco Cooperative Stabilization Corp. v. EPA,* 313 F.3d 852 (4th Cir.2002). The report represented the consummation of a lengthy research and analysis effort by the agency; the agency's investigatory effort, specifically authorized by Congress, was at an end. But Congress had also expressly denied EPA authority to take regulatory action on the basis of its findings. Thus the EPA report "creates no 'legal rights or obligations' and has no direct regulatory effect on plaintiffs." The possibility that the report cast a cloud over the plaintiffs' commercial prospects and could lay the basis for regulatory action by

other federal or state regulatory bodies did not make it reviewable. The court interpreted the Supreme Court's rulings in *Dalton v. Specter* and *Franklin v. Massachusetts* as confirming that "[a]gency action which carries no 'direct and appreciable legal consequences' is not reviewable under the APA."

b. Ripeness

ABBOTT LABORATORIES v. GARDNER

Supreme Court of the United States, 1967.
387 U.S. 136, 87 S.Ct. 1507, 18 L.Ed.2d 681.

JUSTICE HARLAN delivered the opinion of the Court.

In 1962 Congress amended the Federal Food, Drug, and Cosmetic Act to require manufacturers of prescription drugs to print the "established name" of the drug "prominently and in type at least half as large as that used thereon for any proprietary name or designation for such drug," on labels and other printed material. The "established name" is one designated by the Secretary of Health, Education, and Welfare pursuant to § 502(e)(2) of the Act, 21 U.S.C. § 352(e)(2); the "proprietary name" is usually a trade name under which a particular drug is marketed. The underlying purpose of the 1962 amendment was to bring to the attention of doctors and patients the fact that many of the drugs sold under familiar trade names are actually identical to drugs sold under their "established" or less familiar trade names at significantly lower prices. The Commissioner of Food and Drugs, exercising authority delegated to him by the Secretary, published proposed regulations designed to implement the statute. After inviting and considering comments submitted by interested parties the Commissioner promulgated the following regulation for the "efficient enforcement" of the Act, § 701(a), 21 U.S.C. § 371(a):

> "If the label or labeling of a prescription drug bears a proprietary name or designation for the drug or any ingredient thereof, the established name, if such there be, corresponding to such proprietary name or designation, shall accompany each appearance of such proprietary name or designation."

A similar rule was made applicable to advertisements for prescription drugs.

The present action was brought by a group of 37 individual drug manufacturers and by the Pharmaceutical Manufacturers Association, of which all the petitioner companies are members, and which includes manufacturers of more than 90 per cent of the Nation's supply of prescription drugs. They challenged the regulations on the ground that the Commissioner exceeded his authority under the statute by promulgating an order requiring labels, advertisements, and other printed matter relating to prescription drugs to designate the established name of the particular drug involved every time its trade name is used anywhere in such material.

The District Court, on cross motions for summary judgment, granted the declaratory and injunctive relief sought, finding that the statute did not sweep so broadly as to permit the Commissioner's "every time" interpretation. The Court of Appeals for the Third Circuit reversed without reaching the merits of the case. 352 F.2d 286. It held first that under the statutory scheme provided by the Federal Food, Drug, and Cosmetic Act pre-enforcement[1] review of these regulations was unauthorized and therefore beyond the jurisdiction of the District Court. Second, the Court of Appeals held that no "actual case or controversy" existed and, for that reason, that no relief under the Administrative Procedure Act, or under the Declaratory Judgment Act, was in any event available. * * *

The first question we consider is whether Congress by the Federal Food, Drug, and Cosmetic Act intended to forbid pre-enforcement review of this sort of regulation promulgated by the Commissioner. The question is phrased in terms of "prohibition" rather than "authorization" because a survey of our cases shows that judicial review of a final agency action by an aggrieved person will not be cut off unless there is persuasive reason to believe that such was the purpose of Congress. Early cases in which this type of judicial review was entertained have been reinforced by the enactment of the Administrative Procedure Act, which embodies the basic presumption of judicial review to one "suffering legal wrong because of agency action, or adversely affected or aggrieved by agency action within the meaning of a relevant statute," 5 U.S.C. § 702, so long as no statute precludes such relief or the action is not one committed by law to agency discretion, 5 U.S.C. § 701(a). The Administrative Procedure Act provides specifically not only for review of "[a]gency action made reviewable by statute" but also for review of "final agency action for which there is no other adequate remedy in a court," 5 U.S.C. § 704. The legislative material elucidating that seminal act manifests a congressional intention that it cover a broad spectrum of administrative actions,[2] and this Court has echoed that theme by noting that the Administrative Procedure Act's "generous review provisions" must be given a "hospitable" interpretation. * * *

Given this standard, we are wholly unpersuaded that the statutory scheme in the food and drug area excludes this type of action. The Government relies on no explicit statutory authority for its argument that pre-enforcement review is unavailable, but insists instead that because the statute includes a specific procedure for such review of certain enumerated kinds of regulations, not encompassing those of the kind involved here, other types were necessarily meant to be excluded from any pre-enforcement review. The issue, however, is not so readily

1. That is, a suit brought by one before any attempted enforcement of the statute or regulation against him.

2. See H.R.Rep.No. 1980, 79th Cong., 2d Sess., 41 (1946): "To preclude judicial review under this bill a statute, if not specific in withholding such review, must upon its face give clear and convincing evidence of an intent to withhold it. The mere failure to provide specially by statute for judicial review is certainly no evidence of intent to withhold review."

resolved; we must go further and inquire whether in the context of the entire legislative scheme the existence of that circumscribed remedy evinces a congressional purpose to bar agency action not within its purview from judicial review. * * *

In this case the Government has not demonstrated such a purpose; indeed, a study of the legislative history shows rather conclusively that the specific review provisions* were designed to give an additional remedy and not to cut down more traditional channels of review. * * *

This conclusion is strongly buttressed by the fact that the Act itself, in § 701(f)(6), states, "The remedies provided for in this subsection shall be in addition to and not in substitution for any other remedies provided by law." This saving clause was passed over by the Court of Appeals without discussion. In our view, however, it bears heavily on the issue, for if taken at face value it would foreclose the Government's main argument in this case. The Government deals with the clause by arguing that it should be read as applying only to review of regulations under the sections specifically enumerated in § 701(e). This is a conceivable reading, but it requires a considerable straining both of language and of common understanding. The saving clause itself contains no limitations, and it requires an artificial statutory construction to read a general grant of a right to judicial review begrudgingly, so as to cut out agency actions that a literal reading would cover. * * *

The only other argument of the Government requiring attention on the preclusive effect of the statute is that *Ewing v. Mytinger & Casselberry, Inc.*, 339 U.S. 594, counsels a restrictive view of judicial review in the food and drug area. In that case the Food and Drug Administrator found that there was probable cause that a drug was "adulterated" because it was misbranded in such a way as to be "fraudulent" or "misleading to the injury or damage of the purchaser or consumer." Multiple seizures were ordered through libel actions. The manufacturer of the drug brought an action to challenge directly the Administrator's finding of probable cause. This Court held that the owner could raise his constitutional, statutory, and factual claims in the libel actions themselves, and that the mere finding of probable cause by the Administrator could not be challenged in a separate action. That decision was quite clearly correct, but nothing in its reasoning or holding has any bearing on this declaratory judgment action challenging a promulgated regulation.

The Court in *Ewing* first noted that the "administrative finding of probable cause required by § 304(a) is merely the statutory prerequisite to the bringing of the lawsuit," at which the issues are aired. Such a situation bears no analogy to the promulgation, after formal procedures, of a rule that must be followed by an entire industry. To equate a finding

* [Section 701(e) of the FD & C Act provides for pre-enforcement court of appeals review of certain types of FDA regulations promulgated following formal rulemaking, but clearly does not provide a basis for review of the regulation challenged in this case.]

of probable cause for proceeding against a particular drug manufacturer with the promulgation of a self-operative industry-wide regulation, such as we have here, would immunize nearly all agency rulemaking activities from the coverage of the Administrative Procedure Act.

Second, the determination of probable cause in *Ewing* has "no effect in and of itself"; only some action consequent upon such a finding could give it legal life. As the Court there noted, like a determination by a grand jury that there is probable cause to proceed against an accused, it is a finding which only has vitality once a proceeding is commenced, at which time appropriate challenges can be made. The Court also noted that the unique type of relief sought by the drug manufacturer was inconsistent with the policy of the Act favoring speedy action against goods in circulation that are believed on probable cause to be adulterated. Also, such relief was not specifically granted by the Act, which did provide another type of relief in the form of a consolidation of multiple libel actions in a convenient venue.

The drug manufacturer in *Ewing* was quite obviously seeking an unheard-of form of relief which, if allowed, would have permitted interference in the early stages of an administrative determination as to specific facts, and would have prevented the regular operation of the seizure procedures established by the Act. That the Court refused to permit such an action is hardly authority for cutting off the well-established jurisdiction of the federal courts to hear, in appropriate cases, suits under the Declaratory Judgment Act and the Administrative Procedure Act challenging final agency action of the kind present here.

We conclude that nothing in the Food, Drug, and Cosmetic Act itself precludes this action.

A further inquiry must, however, be made. The injunctive and declaratory judgment remedies are discretionary, and courts traditionally have been reluctant to apply them to administrative determinations unless these arise in the context of a controversy "ripe" for judicial resolution. Without undertaking to survey the intricacies of the ripeness doctrine it is fair to say that its basic rationale is to prevent the courts, through avoidance of premature adjudication, from entangling themselves in abstract disagreements over administrative policies, and also to protect the agencies from judicial interference until an administrative decision has been formalized and its effects felt in a concrete way by the challenging parties. The problem is best seen in a twofold aspect, requiring us to evaluate both the fitness of the issues for judicial decision and the hardship to the parties of withholding court consideration.

As to the former factor, we believe the issues presented are appropriate for judicial resolution at this time. First, all parties agree that the issue tendered is a purely legal one: whether the statute was properly construed by the Commissioner to require the established name of the drug to be used *every time* the proprietary name is employed.[16] Both sides

16. While the "every time" issue has been framed by the parties in terms of statutory *compulsion*, we think that its essentially legal character would not be differ-

moved for summary judgment in the District Court, and no claim is made here that further administrative proceedings are contemplated. It is suggested that the justification for this rule might vary with different circumstances, and that the expertise of the Commissioner is relevant to passing upon the validity of the regulation. This of course is true, but the suggestion overlooks the fact that both sides have approached this case as one purely of congressional intent, and that the Government made no effort to justify the regulation in factual terms.

Second, the regulations in issue we find to be "final agency action" within the meaning of § 10 of the Administrative Procedure Act, 5 U.S.C. § 704, as construed in judicial decisions. An "agency action" includes any "rule," defined by the Act as "an agency statement of general or particular applicability and future effect designed to implement, interpret, or prescribe law or policy." The cases dealing with judicial review of administrative actions have interpreted the "finality" element in a pragmatic way. Thus in *Columbia Broadcasting System v. United States*, 316 U.S. 407, * * * this Court held reviewable a regulation of the Federal Communications Commission setting forth certain proscribed contractual arrangements between chain broadcasters and local stations. The FCC did not have direct authority to regulate these contracts, and its rule asserted only that it would not license stations which maintained such contracts with the networks. Although no license had in fact been denied or revoked, and the FCC regulation could properly be characterized as a statement only of its intentions, the Court held that "Such regulations have the force of law before their sanctions are invoked as well as after. When, as here, they are promulgated by order of the Commission and the expected conformity to them causes injury cognizable by a court of equity, they are appropriately the subject of attack. * * * "

Two more recent cases have taken a similarly flexible view of finality. In *Frozen Food Express v. United States*, 351 U.S. 40, at issue was an Interstate Commerce Commission order specifying commodities that were deemed to fall within the statutory class of "agricultural commodities." Vehicles carrying such commodities were exempt from ICC supervision. An action was brought by a carrier that claimed to be transporting exempt commodities, but which the ICC order had not included in its terms. Although the dissenting opinion noted that this ICC order had no authority except to give notice of how the Commission interpreted the Act and would have effect only if and when a particular action was brought against a particular carrier, and argued that "judicial intervention [should] be withheld until administrative action has reached its complete development," the Court held the order reviewable.

Again, in *United States v. Storer Broadcasting Co.*, 351 U.S. 192, the Court held to be a final agency action within the meaning of the Administrative Procedure Act an FCC regulation announcing a Commis-

ent had it been framed in terms of statutory *authorization* for the requirement.

sion policy that it would not issue a television license to an applicant already owning five such licenses, even though no specific application was before the Commission. The Court stated: "The process of rulemaking was complete. It was final agency action * * * by which Storer claimed to be 'aggrieved.' "

We find decision in the present case following *a fortiori* from these precedents. The regulation challenged here, promulgated in a formal manner after announcement in the Federal Register and consideration of comments by interested parties is quite clearly definitive. There is no hint that this regulation is informal, see *Helco Products Co. v. McNutt*, 78 U.S.App.D.C. 71, 137 F.2d 681 (1943), or only the ruling of a subordinate official, see *Swift & Co. v. Wickham*, D.C., 230 F.Supp. 398, 409, *aff'd*, 364 F.2d 241 (1966), or tentative. It was made effective upon publication, and the Assistant General Counsel for Food and Drugs stated in the District Court that compliance was expected.

The Government argues, however, that the present case can be distinguished from cases like *Frozen Food Express* on the ground that in those instances the agency involved could implement its policy directly, while here the Attorney General must authorize criminal and seizure actions for violations of the statute. In the context of this case, we do not find this argument persuasive. These regulations are not meant to advise the Attorney General, but purport to be directly authorized by the statute. Thus, if within the Commissioner's authority, they have the status of law and violations of them carry heavy criminal and civil sanctions. Also, there is no representation that the Attorney General and the Commissioner disagree in this area; the Justice Department is defending this very suit. It would be adherence to a mere technicality to give any credence to this contention. Moreover, the agency does have direct authority to enforce this regulation in the context of passing upon applications for clearance of new drugs, § 505, 21 U.S.C. § 355, or certification of certain antibiotics, § 507, 21 U.S.C. § 357.

This is also a case in which the impact of the regulations upon the petitioners is sufficiently direct and immediate as to render the issue appropriate for judicial review at this stage. These regulations purport to give an authoritative interpretation of a statutory provision that has a direct effect on the day-to-day business of all prescription drug companies; its promulgation puts petitioners in a dilemma that it was the very purpose of the Declaratory Judgment Act to ameliorate. As the District Court found on the basis of uncontested allegations, "Either they must comply with the every time requirement and incur the costs of changing over their promotional material and labeling or they must follow their present course and risk prosecution." 228 F.Supp. 855, 861. The regulations are clear-cut, and were made effective immediately upon publication; as noted earlier the agency's counsel represented to the District Court that immediate compliance with their terms was expected. If petitioners wish to comply they must change all their labels, advertisements, and promotional materials; they must destroy stocks of printed matter; and they must invest heavily in new printing type and new supplies. The alternative to compliance—continued use of material which they believe in good faith meets the statutory requirements, but which clearly does not meet the regulation of the Commissioner—may be even more costly. That course would risk serious criminal and civil penalties for the unlawful distribution of "misbranded" drugs.

It is relevant at this juncture to recognize that petitioners deal in a sensitive industry, in which public confidence in their drug products is especially important. To require them to challenge these regulations only as a defense to an action brought by the Government might harm them severely and unnecessarily. Where the legal issue presented is fit for judicial resolution, and where a regulation requires an immediate and significant change in the plaintiffs' conduct of their affairs with serious penalties attached to noncompliance, access to the courts under the Administrative Procedure Act and the Declaratory Judgment Act must be permitted, absent a statutory bar or some other unusual circumstance, neither of which appears here. * * *

The Government further contends that the threat of criminal sanctions for noncompliance with a judicially untested regulation is unrealistic; the Solicitor General has represented that if court enforcement becomes necessary, "the Department of Justice will proceed only civilly for an injunction * * * or by condemnation." We cannot accept this argument as a sufficient answer to petitioners' petition. This action at its inception was properly brought and this subsequent representation of the Department of Justice should not suffice to defeat it.

Finally, the Government urges that to permit resort to the courts in this type of case may delay or impede effective enforcement of the Act. We fully recognize the important public interest served by assuring prompt and unimpeded administration of the Pure Food, Drug, and Cosmetic Act, but we do not find the Government's argument convincing. First, in this particular case, a pre-enforcement challenge by nearly all prescription drug manufacturers is calculated to speed enforcement. If the Government prevails, a large part of the industry is bound by the decree; if the Government loses, it can more quickly revise its regulation.

The Government contends, however, that if the Court allows this consolidated suit, then nothing will prevent a multiplicity of suits in various jurisdictions challenging other regulations. The short answer to this contention is that the courts are well equipped to deal with such eventualities. The venue transfer provision, 28 U.S.C. § 1404(a), may be invoked by the Government to consolidate separate actions. Or, actions in all but one jurisdiction might be stayed pending the conclusion of one proceeding. A court may even in its discretion dismiss a declaratory judgment or injunctive suit if the same issue is pending in litigation elsewhere. * * *

Further, the declaratory judgment and injunctive remedies are equitable in nature, and other equitable defenses may be interposed. If a multiplicity of suits are undertaken in order to harass the Government or to delay enforcement, relief can be denied on this ground alone. * * *

In addition to all these safeguards against what the Government fears, it is important to note that the institution of this type of action does not by itself stay the effectiveness of the challenged regulation. There is nothing in the record to indicate that petitioners have sought to stay enforcement of the "every time" regulation pending judicial review. If the agency believes that a suit of this type will significantly impede enforcement or will harm the public interest, it need not postpone enforcement of the regulation and may oppose any motion for a judicial stay on the part of those challenging the regulation. It is scarcely to be doubted that a court would refuse to postpone the effective date of an agency action if the Government could show, as it made no effort to do here, that delay would be detrimental to the public health or safety. * * *

Lastly, although the Government presses us to reach the merits of the challenge to the regulation in the event we find the District Court properly entertained this action, we believe the better practice is to remand the case to the Court of Appeals for the Third Circuit to review the District Court's decision that the regulation was beyond the power of the Commissioner.

Reversed and remanded.

JUSTICE BRENNAN took no part in the consideration or decision of this case.

TOILET GOODS ASSOCIATION v. GARDNER

Supreme Court of the United States, 1967.
387 U.S. 158, 87 S.Ct. 1520, 18 L.Ed.2d 697.

JUSTICE HARLAN delivered the opinion of the Court.

Petitioners in this case are the Toilet Goods Association, an organization of cosmetics manufacturers accounting for some 90 per cent of annual American sales in this field, and 39 individual cosmetics manufacturers and distributors. They brought this action in the United States District Court for the Southern District of New York seeking declaratory and injunctive relief against the Secretary of Health, Education, and Welfare and the Commissioner of Food and Drugs, on the ground that certain regulations promulgated by the Commissioner exceeded his statutory authority under the Color Additive Amendments to the Federal Food, Drug, and Cosmetic Act. * * *

* * *

* * * The Commissioner of Food and Drugs * * * under statutory authority "to promulgate regulations for the efficient enforcement" of the Act, issued the following regulation after due public notice and consideration of comments submitted by interested parties:

> "(a) When it appears to the Commissioner that a person has:
>
> * * *
>
> "(4) Refused to permit duly authorized employees of the Food and Drug Administration free access to all manufacturing facilities,

processes, and formulae involved in the manufacture of color additives and intermediates from which such color additives are derived;

"he may immediately suspend certification service to such person and may continue such suspension until adequate corrective action has been taken."[1]

The petitioners maintain that this regulation is an impermissible exercise of authority, that the FDA has long sought congressional authorization for free access to facilities, processes, and formulae, but that Congress has always denied the agency this power except for prescription drugs. Framed in this way, we agree with petitioners that a "legal" issue is raised, but nevertheless we are not persuaded that the present suit is properly maintainable.

In determining whether a challenge to an administrative regulation is ripe for review a twofold inquiry must be made: first to determine whether the issues tendered are appropriate for judicial resolution, and second to assess the hardship to the parties if judicial relief is denied at that stage.

As to the first of these factors, we agree with the Court of Appeals that the legal issue as presently framed is not appropriate for judicial resolution. This is not because the regulation is not the agency's considered and formalized determination, for we are in agreement with petitioners that under this Court's decisions in *Frozen Food Express v. United States* and *United States v. Storer Broadcasting Co.*, there can be no question that this regulation—promulgated in a formal manner after notice and evaluation of submitted comments—is a "final agency action." * * * Also, we recognize the force of petitioners' contention that the issue as they have framed it presents a purely legal question: whether the regulation is totally beyond the agency's power under the statute, the type of legal issue that courts have occasionally dealt with without requiring a specific attempt at enforcement. * * *

These points which support the appropriateness of judicial resolution are, however, outweighed by other considerations. The regulation serves notice only that the Commissioner *may* under certain circumstances order inspection of certain facilities and data, and that further certification of additives *may* be refused to those who decline to permit a duly authorized inspection until they have complied in that regard. At this juncture we have no idea whether or when such an inspection will be ordered and what reasons the Commissioner will give to justify his order. The statutory authority asserted for the regulation is the power to promulgate regulations "for the efficient enforcement" of the Act, § 701(a). Whether the regulation is justified thus depends not only, as

1. The Color Additive Amendments provide for listings of color additives by the Secretary "if and to the extent that such additives are suitable and safe. * * * " The Secretary is further authorized to provide "for the certification, with safe diluents or without diluents, of batches of color additives. * * * " A color additive is "deemed unsafe" unless it is either from a certified batch or exempted from the certification requirement. A cosmetic containing such an "unsafe" additive is deemed to be adulterated, and is prohibited from interstate commerce.

petitioners appear to suggest, on whether Congress refused to include a specific section of the Act authorizing such inspections, although this factor is to be sure a highly relevant one, but also on whether the statutory scheme as a whole justified promulgation of the regulation. This will depend not merely on an inquiry into statutory purpose, but concurrently on an understanding of what types of enforcement problems are encountered by the FDA, the need for various sorts of supervision in order to effectuate the goals of the Act, and the safeguards devised to protect legitimate trade secrets. We believe that judicial appraisal of these factors is likely to stand on a much surer footing in the context of a specific application of this regulation than could be the case in the framework of the generalized challenge made here.

We are also led to this result by considerations of the effect on the petitioners of the regulation, for the test of ripeness, as we have noted, depends not only on how adequately a court can deal with the legal issue presented, but also on the degree and nature of the regulation's present effect on those seeking relief. * * *

This is not a situation in which primary conduct is affected—when contracts must be negotiated, ingredients tested or substituted, or special records compiled. This regulation merely states that the Commissioner may authorize inspectors to examine certain processes or formulae; no advance action is required of cosmetics manufacturers, who since the enactment of the 1938 Act have been under a statutory duty to permit reasonable inspection of a "factory, warehouse, establishment, or vehicle and all pertinent equipment, finished and unfinished materials; containers, and labeling therein." Moreover, no irremediable adverse consequences flow from requiring a later challenge to this regulation by a manufacturer who refuses to allow this type of inspection. Unlike the other regulations challenged in this action, in which seizure of goods, heavy fines, adverse publicity for distributing "adulterated" goods, and possible criminal liability might penalize failure to comply, a refusal to admit an inspector here would at most lead only to a suspension of certification services to the particular party, a determination that can then be promptly challenged through an administrative procedure,[2] which in turn is reviewable by a court. Such review will provide an adequate forum for testing the regulation in a concrete situation.

It is true that the administrative hearing will deal with the "factual basis" of the suspension, from which petitioners infer that the Commissioner will not entertain and consider a challenge to his statutory

2. See 21 CFR §§ 8.28(b), 130.14–130.26. We recognize that a denial of certification might under certain circumstances cause inconvenience and possibly hardship, depending upon such factors as how large a supply of certified additives the particular manufacturer may have, how rapidly the administrative hearing and judicial review are conducted, and what temporary remedial or protective provisions, such as compliance with a reservation pending litigation, might be available to a manufacturer testing the regulation. In the context of the present case we need only say that such inconvenience is speculative and we have been provided with no information that would support an assumption that much weight should be attached to this possibility.

authority to promulgate the regulation. Whether or not this assumption is correct, given the fact that only minimal, if any, adverse consequences will face petitioners if they challenge the regulation in this manner, we think it wiser to require them to exhaust this administrative process through which the factual basis of the inspection order will certainly be aired and where more light may be thrown on the Commissioner's statutory and practical justifications for the regulation. Judicial review will then be available, and a court at that juncture will be in a better position to deal with the question of statutory authority.

For these reasons the judgment of the Court of Appeals is

Affirmed.

JUSTICE FORTAS [concurring in the portion of the *Toilet Goods* decision set forth above but dissenting in *Abbott Laboratories*], with whom the CHIEF JUSTICE and JUSTICE CLARK join.

* * *

The issues considered by the Court are not constitutional questions. The Court does not rest upon any asserted right to challenge the regulations at this time because the agency lacks authority to promulgate the regulations as to the subject matters involved, or because its procedures have been arbitrary or unreasonable. Its decision is based solely upon the claim of right to challenge these particular regulations at this time on the ground that they are erroneous exercises of the agency's power. It is solely at this point that the Court * * * authorizes threshold or pre-enforcement challenge by action for injunction and declaratory relief to suspend the operation of the regulations in their entirety and without reference to particular factual situations.

With all respect, I submit that established principles of jurisprudence, solidly rooted in the constitutional structure of our Government, require that the courts should not intervene in the administrative process at this stage, under these facts and in this gross, shotgun fashion. * * *

The Administrative Procedure Act and fundamental principles of our jurisprudence insist that there must be some type of effective judicial review of final, substantive agency action which seriously affects personal or property rights. But, "[a]ll constitutional questions aside, it is for Congress to determine how the rights which it creates shall be enforced. * * * In such a case the specification of one remedy normally excludes another." *Switchmen's Union of North America v. National Mediation Board*, 320 U.S. 297, 301 (1943). Where Congress has provided a method of review, the requisite showing to induce the courts otherwise to bring a governmental program to a halt may not be made by a mere showing of the impact of the regulation and the customary hardships of interim compliance. At least in cases where the claim is of erroneous action rather than the lack of jurisdiction or denial of procedural due process, a suit for injunctive or declaratory relief will not lie absent a clear demonstration that the type of review available under the statute would not be "adequate," that the controversies are otherwise "ripe" for judicial decision, and that no public interest exists which offsets the private values which the litigation seeks to vindicate. As I shall discuss, no such showing is or can be made here. * * *

In evaluating the destructive force and effect of the Court's action in these cases, it is necessary to realize that it is arming each of the federal district judges in this Nation with power to enjoin enforcement of regulations and actions under the federal law designed to protect the people of this Nation against dangerous drugs and cosmetics. Restraining orders and temporary injunctions will suspend application of these public safety laws pending years of litigation—a time schedule which these cases illustrate. They are disruptive enough, regardless of the ultimate outcome. The Court's validation of this shotgun attack upon this vital law and its administration is not confined to these suits, these regulations, or these plaintiffs—or even this statute. It is a general hunting license; and I respectfully submit, a license for mischief because it authorizes aggression which is richly rewarded by delay in the subjection of private interests to programs which Congress believes to be required in the public interest. As I read the Court's opinion, it does not seriously contend that Congress authorized or contemplated this type of relief. It does not rest upon the argument that Congress intended that injunctions or threshold relief should be available. The Court seems to announce a doctrine, which is new and startling in administrative law, that the courts, in determining whether to exercise jurisdiction by injunction, will not look to see whether Congress intended that the parties should resort to another avenue of review, but will be governed by whether Congress has "prohibited" injunctive relief. * * *

The regulation in [*Abbott Laboratories*] relates to a 1962 amendment to the Act requiring manufacturers of prescription drugs to print on the labels or other printed material, the "established name" of the drug "prominently and in type at least half as large as that used thereon for any proprietary name or designation for such drug." Obviously, this requires some elucidation, either case-by-case or by general regulation or pronouncement, because the statute does not say that this must be done "every time," or only once on each label or in each pamphlet, or once per panel, etc., or that it must be done differently on labels than on circulars, or doctors' literature than on directions to the patients, etc. This is exactly the traditional purpose and function of an administrative agency. The Commissioner, acting by delegation from the Secretary, took steps to provide for the specification. He invited and considered comments and then issued a regulation requiring that the "established name" appear every time the proprietary name is used. A manufacturer—or other person who violates this regulation—has mislabeled his product. The product may be seized; or injunction may be sought; or the mislabeler may be criminally prosecuted. In any of these actions he may challenge the regulation and obtain a judicial determination.

* * * The Court says that this confronts the manufacturer with a "real dilemma." But the fact of the matter is that the dilemma is no

more than citizens face in connection with countless statutes and with the rules of the SEC, FTC, FCC, ICC, and other regulatory agencies. This has not heretofore been regarded as a basis for injunctive relief unless Congress has so provided. The overriding fact here is—or should be—that the public interest in avoiding the delay in implementing Congress' program far outweighs the private interest; and that the private interest which has so impressed the Court is no more than that which exists in respect of most regulatory statutes or agency rules. Somehow, the Court has concluded that the damage to petitioners if they have to engage in the required redesign and reprint of their labels and printed materials without threshold review outweighs the damage to the public of deferring during the tedious months and years of litigation a cure for the possible danger and asserted deceit of peddling plain medicine under fancy trademarks and for fancy prices which, rightly or wrongly, impelled the Congress to enact this legislation. I submit that a much stronger showing is necessary than the expense and trouble of compliance and the risk of defiance. Actually, if the Court refused to permit this shotgun assault, experience and reasonably sophisticated common sense show that there would be orderly compliance without the disaster so dramatically predicted by the industry, reasonable adjustments by the agency in real hardship cases, and where extreme intransigence involving substantial violations occurred, enforcement actions in which legality of the regulation would be tested in specific, concrete situations. I respectfully submit that this would be the correct and appropriate result. Our refusal to respond to the vastly overdrawn cries of distress would reflect not only healthy skepticism, but our regard for a proper relationship between the courts on the one hand and Congress and the administrative agencies on the other. It would represent a reasonable solicitude for the purposes and programs of the Congress. And it would reflect appropriate modesty as to the competence of the courts. The courts cannot properly—and should not—attempt to judge in the abstract and generally whether this regulation is within the statutory scheme. Judgment as to the "every time" regulation should be made only in light of specific situations, and it may differ depending upon whether the FDA seeks to enforce it as to doctors' circulars, pamphlets for patients, labels, etc. * * *

Notes

1. *Settling the Litigation.* Following the Supreme Court's decision, the *Abbott* case went back to the Third Circuit for resolution on the merits. (The district court, which had found the regulation ripe for review, had also held it invalid.) A few days before scheduled argument, the FDA and the companies agreed to a settlement, on terms that require a manufacturer to disclose the generic name of a drug at least once per page of labeling and advertising, as well as each time the brand name is "featured."

2. *Scope of the Ruling.* Does *Abbott* establish the propriety of pre-enforcement review whenever a litigant is torn between the costs of compli-

ance and the risks of prosecution? Or does *Abbott* mean only that pre-enforcement review is appropriate to test administrative policies that apply irrespective of a litigant's particular circumstances? The drug companies undoubtedly feared that the FDA would pick out the worst offender among them as a "test case" of the legality of its regulation. The companies were also determinedly opposed to the "every time" requirement because they had been successful in persuading physicians to prescribe drugs by brand, rather than generic name. See generally RICHARD HARRIS, THE REAL VOICE (1964). What harm—apart from the loss of a possible tactical advantage—does the FDA suffer by having its regulation reviewed in advance of enforcement?

The Supreme Court's distinction between the rules challenged in *Abbott* and *Toilet Goods* retains significance.

For example, in *Ohio Forestry Ass'n v. Sierra Club*, 523 U.S. 726 (1998), the Sierra Club brought suit to review the land and forest management plan that the U.S. Forest Service had developed for the Wayne National Forest in southern Ohio, pursuant to the 1976 National Forest Management Act. The plan described the areas and number of acres in which the Service would allow logging in the forest, and imposed a ceiling on the amount of timber that could be cut during the ten-year life of the plan, but it did not itself authorize the cutting of any trees. To allow logging, the Service must (a) propose a specific area in which logging may occur, (b) ensure that logging will be consistent with the plan, (c) provide those affected with notice of the proposal and an opportunity to be heard, (d) conduct an environmental analysis of the project, and (e) issue a final decision to permit logging, which affected persons may challenge through an administrative appeals process.

A unanimous Supreme Court, in an opinion by Justice Breyer, ruled that the Wayne National Forest plan was not ripe for judicial review. Though it acknowledged that the plan's adoption "makes logging more likely," the Court concluded that the *Abbott Labs* factors counseled against immediate judicial review. To withhold court consideration would not inflict significant practical harm on the environmental interests that the Sierra Club advanced nor create legal obstacles to a later challenge to any specific proposal to allow logging. Nor would the plan force the club to alter its behavior to avoid future adverse consequences:

> The Sierra Club does say that it will be easier, and certainly cheaper, to mount one legal challenge against the Plan now, than to pursue many challenges to each site-specific logging decision to which the Plan might eventually lead. It does not explain, however, why one initial site-specific victory (if based on the Plan's unlawfulness) could not, through preclusion principles, effectively carry the day. And, in any event, the Court has not considered this kind of litigation cost saving sufficient by itself to justify review in a case that would otherwise be unripe.

Furthermore, Justice Breyer asserted, "From the courts' perspective, review of the Sierra Club's claims regarding logging and clearcutting now would require time-consuming judicial consideration of the details of an elaborate, technically based plan, which predicts consequences that may affect many different parcels of land in a variety of ways, and which effects themselves may change over time." Finally, Justice Breyer noted, Congress has not provided for pre-implementation review of forest plans: "The Plan is consequently unlike agency rules that Congress has specifically instructed the courts to review 'preenforcement.' "

See also *Sierra Club v. Peterson*, 228 F.3d 559 (5th Cir.2000) (holding that plaintiffs, who challenged Forest Service policies governing logging in Texas National Forests, failed to identify specific and "final" logging approvals).

3. *Ripeness in Anticipating a Denial of Government Benefits*. In *Reno v. Catholic Social Services (CSS)*, 509 U.S. 43 (1993), noted p. 881 *supra*, the INS urged that any challenge by undocumented aliens to regulations governing the government's legalization program would be ripe only following the actual denial of an alien's legalization petition. The Court generally agreed, concluding that, in the ordinary case, regulations limiting access to legalization did not adversely affect any alien until that alien had applied for legalization, and been denied. (This holding created a "Catch–22" with the Court's holding in a prior case that the statutory scheme permitted district court review of suits challenging these INS applications so long as the suits did not refer to the denial of a particular application. In other words, once a litigant's claim was ripe, it was jurisdictionally barred in the district court.) The Court observed, however, that a number of aliens might have ripe claims even if they had not yet formally sought and been denied legalization. The INS had apparently authorized a process called "front-desking," involving an informal review of a petitioner's application before filing. Under this process, a petition would not even be accepted for filing if an INS employee determined, prior to filing, that the alien was statutorily ineligible for legalization. The Court remanded for a determination whether, under this process, any plaintiff class member had been refused permission to apply for legalization. If so, that alien's claim would be ripe because the challenged regulation would have been brought to bear on his or her case in "a particularly concrete matter." He or she would not be subject to provisions limiting the forum for a review of denials of applications because there would not be any formal denial to review. Vigorous separate opinions by Justice O'Connor and by Justice Stevens (writing also for White and Blackmun) challenged this reasoning.

It is not easy to reconcile *Reno* with *Northeastern Florida Chapter of Associated General Contractors of America v. Jacksonville*, 508 U.S. 656 (1993). That case allowed non-minority contractors to challenge a racial set-aside ordinance that allegedly made it more difficult for them to compete for public business, even before any class member could show that it would have received business but for the ordinance. It was enough that the contractors were being denied an opportunity to compete equally for a government benefit. Had not the class members in *Reno v. CSS* similarly alleged the denial of an opportunity to apply for legalization, free of an unlawful regulation? Is it a persuasive distinction that the contractors could show that they had a history of bidding on and performing work of the sort now covered by the challenged ordinance? As we shall see below, these timing questions replicate themselves—with no more determinate answers—as courts search for "concrete" and "individualized" injuries sufficient to satisfy the requirements of standing doctrine.

4. *Exclusive Routes for Review.* In *Abbott Labs* there was no doubt that the drug companies could challenge the FDA's rule in subsequent enforcement proceedings; the issue was whether earlier review could be obtained. The uncertainty in this respect stemmed from Congress's failure to make any provision in the FD & C Act for judicial review of regulations adopted pursuant to section 701(a). See Richard A. Merrill, *FDA and the Effects of Substantive Rules*, 35 Food Drug Cosm.L.J. 270 (1980). In more recent regulatory legislation, such an omission would be unusual. Congress usually specifies a procedure by which judicial review of agency rules can be obtained—typically review prior to enforcement. A frequent question, then, is whether the prescribed route of review is exclusive. In some instances, Congress has addressed this issue as well, as it did in section 307(b) of the Clean Air Act, at issue in *Adamo Wrecking*, *supra* p. 889. But language purporting to preclude collateral review is likewise unusual, so that a court must balance the values of finality against the contesting party's interest in obtaining some judicial confirmation of the legality of the standard it is accused of violating.

The "exclusivity" issue has arisen frequently in the context of enforcement of OSHA workplace safety standards, which takes place in proceedings before an administrative law judge whose decision is reviewable by the Occupational Safety and Health Review Commission, an independent quasi-judicial tribunal located within the Labor Department. Most courts have declined to read the statutory review provision, 29 U.S.C. § 655(f), as exclusive, holding that a respondent in an enforcement proceeding can challenge the underlying OSHA standard(s) on substantive or procedural grounds. E.g., *Marshall v. Union Oil Co.*, 616 F.2d 1113 (9th Cir.1980); *Deering Milliken, Inc. v. OSHRC*, 630 F.2d 1094 (5th Cir.1980). Some courts, however, have limited the grounds for collateral attack. *National Industrial Constructors, Inc. v. OSHRC*, 583 F.2d 1048 (8th Cir.1978), for example, held that a respondent could not object to the procedures OSHA had followed in promulgating a standard. The Fourth Circuit, in *Daniel International Corp. v. OSHRC*, 656 F.2d 925 (4th Cir.1981), declined to go this far, but held that the respondent had not demonstrated that it had been prejudiced by the agency's procedural errors. No case has allowed collateral challenge to an OSHA standard on grounds previously rejected in pre-enforcement review proceedings initiated by other parties.

In *Thunder Basin Coal Company v. Reich*, 510 U.S. 200 (1994), the Court held that the statutory review provisions of the Federal Mine Safety and Health Amendments Act of 1977 precluded a preenforcement challenge to the Labor Secretary's interpretation of that Act. Specifically, the Act requires the Secretary to conduct periodic unannounced mine inspections, and provides that a representative authorized by the mineworkers shall be given an opportunity to accompany the Secretary or the Secretary's representative during the physical inspection of the mine. When the petitioner's employees selected as their representatives two UMW employees who did not work for Thunder Basin, the mine operator complained informally to the Mine Safety and Health Administration, which nonetheless required the operator to post information concerning the chosen representatives, as required by MSHA regulations. Even before receiving the MSHA written directive, Thunder Basin filed suit in U.S. district court to challenge MSHA's regulation. The Supreme Court held, however, that provisions of the Act authorizing judicial review of MSHA enforcement were exclusive. Those provisions required mine operators to challenge any MSHA enforcement citations, first, before the Federal Mine Safety and Health Review Commission, and then, in the appropriate Court of Appeals. Although the Act did not expressly preclude preenforcement suits, the Court found such preclusion reasonably discernible from the statute's purposes. The Court held that enforcement of the Federal Mine Safety and Health Amendments Act of 1977 could be undermined by preenforcement review actions. According to the Court, no such danger existed with regard to the FD & C Act, the statute at issue in *Abbott Labs.*

5. *The Relevance of Alternative Relief. New York Stock Exchange, Inc. v. Bloom*, 562 F.2d 736 (D.C.Cir.1977), *cert. denied*, 435 U.S. 942 (1978), introduced a new dimension into the *Abbott Laboratories* ripeness calculus. In that case, the court declined to entertain a suit to review the expressed opinion of the Comptroller of the Currency that automatic stock-purchasing services proposed by Security Pacific National Bank would not violate the Glass–Steagall Act. The Comptroller's opinion was set forth in two letters, the second of which was issued following a request for reconsideration by investment companies, on which the interested parties had been given opportunity to comment.

new factor added

Despite the appearance of considered judgment, the court concluded that the Comptroller's opinion was not ripe for review. Judge McGowan stressed that the Comptroller had "expressly reserved the possibility that his opinion * * * might change if and when he was presented with concrete evidence that AIS [Security Pacific's proposed service] involves the hazards which the Glass–Steagall Act was intended to prevent." He further concluded that a determination of legality would depend on the precise features and effects of the service actually undertaken by Security Pacific. Moreover, "appellants' conduct [was] not directly regulated by the agency action at issue and consequently they [were] not facing a 'Hobson's choice' between burdensome compliance and risky noncompliance." Finally, Judge McGowan suggested that the plaintiffs had an alternative means to protect their interest in being free from unlawful competition:

> Appellants concede, and the Comptroller agrees, that they could bring a private action for injunctive relief, advancing the same substantive claim they have made here directly against any national bank which offers AIS to its customers. Although we have been unable to find any case law squarely on point, and in any event are without power to make an authoritative ruling on the issue since it is not currently before us, we have no reason to believe that appellant would not have a private right of action for injunctive relief under the Glass–Steagall Act. The express language of the statute neither authorizes nor precludes such an action, but under the standards set forth in recent Supreme Court decisions we would suppose, first, that an implied right of action for injunctive relief would exist for appropriate parties and, second, that appellants would qualify as proper plaintiffs.

The *Bloom* court's refusal to review the Comptroller's "tentative" position should not be understood as suggesting that an agency opinion letter can never be ripe for review. In both *National Automatic Laundry and Cleaning Council v. Shultz*, 443 F.2d 689 (D.C.Cir.1971), and *Continental Air Lines, Inc. v. CAB*, 522 F.2d 107 (D.C.Cir.1974) (en banc), the court reviewed statements of agency position embodied in correspondence with regulated firms. In both cases the recipient of the agency's communication faced the choice of immediate compliance or defense against an enforcement proceeding, and in neither case had the agency qualified its statement of applicable legal requirements by reference to as-yet-undetermined factual circumstances.

6. *Mootness*. Just as ripeness doctrine guards against premature litigation, rules of "mootness" enable federal courts to avoid deciding cases no longer justifying judicial intervention. If, at any stage in a lawsuit, the controversy is no longer "live," the court may dismiss. The Supreme Court, however, has characterized the doctrine as "flexible," and courts need not dismiss a controversy as moot if the issue presented is "capable of repetition, yet evading review." *Weinstein v. Bradford*, 423 U.S. 147, 149 (1975).

An illustration of the difficulty of ascertaining mootness is *Doe v. Sullivan*, 938 F.2d 1370 (D.C.Cir.1991), in which the plaintiffs challenged FDA regulations under the FD & C Act 21 U.S.C. § 301 *et seq.*, that permit the Defense Department, upon appropriate administrative findings, to use nonapproved, investigational drugs on military personnel in certain combat situations, without a service member's informed consent. The plaintiffs, a service member and his wife, specifically challenged the applicability of the regulation to two drugs intended to mitigate the effects of possible chemical or biological attack during the Persian Gulf War. A district court dismissed the complaint on the merits, and, by the time the appeal was heard, the United States and allied forces had already defeated Iraq and ceased hostilities. A majority on the court of appeals regarded the question as "capable of repetition," because of increasing worldwide threats of chemical and biological warfare, but "evading review," so long as military encounters could be of brief duration. It then proceeded to affirm the lower court on the merits.

c. *Exhaustion*

The requirement that agency challengers must "exhaust" their administrative remedies before seeking judicial review is designed to avoid premature claims as well as to permit the agency to address objections to its factual or legal premises. The classic statement of the *prospective* requirement to exhaust appears in the oft-cited decision, *Myers v. Bethlehem Shipbuilding Corp.*, 303 U.S. 41 (1938). The NLRB charged the company with unfair labor practices at its Quincy, Massachusetts plant which, according to the Board's allegations, operated in interstate commerce. Bethlehem sued the Board members in district court to enjoin the administrative proceeding, contending that the National Labor Relations Act did not apply because the company did not operate "in interstate or foreign commerce," and that therefore the agency lacked jurisdiction. Bethlehem further contended that "hearings would, at best, be futile; and that the holding of them would result in irreparable damage to the Corporation" through direct costs, loss of time, and loss of employee good will.

The Supreme Court held that the district court lacked power to enjoin the Board's proceedings. Pointing out that the agency's procedures were not under attack and that, under the NLRA, no agency order could affect Bethlehem before it had an opportunity to secure judicial review, the Court concluded that Congress could lawfully vest exclusive jurisdiction in the Board to adjudicate unfair labor practices, with ultimate review in the courts of appeals. Its opinion explained:

> It is true that the Board has jurisdiction only if the complaint concerns interstate or foreign commerce. Unless the board finds that it does, the complaint must be dismissed. And if it finds that interstate or foreign commerce is involved, but the Circuit Court of Appeals concludes that such finding was without adequate evidence to support it, or otherwise contrary to law, the Board's petition to enforce it will be dismissed, or the employer's petition to have it set aside will be granted. Since the procedure before the Board is appropriate and the judicial review so provided is adequate, Congress had power to vest exclusive jurisdiction in the Board and the Circuit Court of Appeals.
>
> The Corporation contends that, since it denies that interstate or foreign commerce is involved and claims that a hearing would subject it to irreparable damage, rights guaranteed by the Federal Constitution will be denied unless it be held that the District Court has jurisdiction to enjoin the holding of a hearing by the Board. So to hold would, as the Government insists, in effect substitute the District Court for the Board as the tribunal to hear and determine what Congress declared the Board exclusively should hear and determine in the first instance. The contention is at war with the long settled rule of judicial administration that no one is entitled to judicial relief for a supposed or threatened injury until the prescribed administrative remedy has been exhausted. That rule has been repeatedly acted on in cases where, as here, the contention is made that the administrative body lacked power over the subject matter.
>
> Obviously, the rule requiring exhaustion of the administrative remedy cannot be circumvented by asserting that the charge on which the complaint rests is groundless and that the mere holding of the prescribed administrative hearing would result in irreparable damage. Lawsuits also often prove to have been groundless; but no way has been discovered of relieving a defendant from the necessity of a trial to establish the fact.

Myers was in many ways the paradigm case for the prospective application of the exhaustion doctrine. The injury about which the company complained was one normally attached to an obligation to protect one's interests in a formal legal proceeding—an injury that might be lessened, but not avoided by shifting to the judicial forum. The issue involved was one requiring factual proof, and it would necessarily be canvassed in the agency proceeding that the company sought to avoid.

Moreover, the claim of lack of jurisdiction was at least disputable, for if the Bethlehem Shipbuilding Corporation did not operate in "interstate commerce," the Board had indeed been accorded very narrow jurisdiction. One therefore should not be surprised to discover that the courts generally have followed a more flexible functional approach to the exhaustion requirement than the *Myers* opinion suggests on its face.

For example, in *AMP Inc. v. Gardner*, 275 F.Supp. 410 (S.D.N.Y. 1967), *affirmed*, 389 F.2d 825 (2d Cir.), *cert. denied*, 393 U.S. 825 (1968), a manufacturer sued to review the FDA's letter ruling that its instrument for ligating blood vessels during surgery was a "drug," which therefore had to go through the FDA's lengthy premarket approval procedures. AMP succeeded in obtaining an immediate, albeit unfavorable, judicial resolution of this threshold "jurisdictional" issue.

A functional analysis could distinguish *AMP* from *Myers* on several grounds: (1) the burden imposed by the available administrative process; (2) the appropriateness of the agency proceeding for resolving the issue raised; and (3) the dependence of the legal issue on the development of a factual record. If AMP were correct that its instrument was not a "drug" but a "device," it would not have had to pursue the FDA's time-consuming premarket approval process. The process was not one in which it would merely have had to contest the agency's jurisdictional claim but one in which it would be required to amass evidence and carry a preliminary burden of proof before the agency would even address the issue it wished to raise. While the NLRB was accustomed to entertaining evidence on and resolving the jurisdictional ("interstate commerce") issue in administrative hearings, the FDA typically assumed that any product a manufacturer chose to submit for approval was a "drug." Finally, the jurisdictional question in *Myers* turned on specific facts—such as the scope of Bethlehem's operations, its sources of supply, the location of its customers—while the issue in *AMP*—whether the company's product was a "drug" or a "medical device"—turned largely on construction of the statute.

A *retrospective* variation of the exhaustion doctrine may apply when a litigant challenges an agency decision from which he or she might earlier have sought administrative relief, but failed to do so. Recognizing that the exhaustion doctrine exists to protect the integrity of agency decision making, courts have realized that programs can be undermined by post-decisional review that forgives a party for unjustifiably bypassing the agency's own internal appeal processes. Invocation of "retrospective exhaustion" can be draconian. Litigants are barred from judicial remedies because they should have sought agency relief, which is now foreclosed to them. Thus, for example, in *McGee v. United States*, 402 U.S. 479 (1971), the Court refused to permit a draftee convicted for failing to report for induction to raise in defense his asserted entitlement to classification as a conscientious objector. He had not sought timely review of his classification by the Selective Service System. Writing for the Court, Justice Marshall said:

> McGee's claims to exempt status * * * depended on the application of expertise by administrative bodies in revolving underlying questions of fact. * * * [P]etitioner's dual failure to exhaust—his failure either to secure a personal appearance or to take an administrative appeal—implicates decisively the policies served by the exhaustion requirement. * * * When a claim to exemption depends ultimately on the careful gathering and analysis of relevant facts, the interest in full airing of the facts within the administrative system is prominent. * * *

By contrast, in *McKart v. United States*, 395 U.S. 185 (1969), the Court declined to apply the exhaustion doctrine to bar review of a draft registrant's claim that his local board had unlawfully reclassified him from IV–A (sole surviving son) to I–A. McKart had failed to pursue an administrative appeal of his reclassification and did not raise his claim until prosecuted for failure to report for induction. The Government contended that this failure to exhaust administrative remedies precluded consideration of his defense. After discussing the policy justifications for the exhaustion doctrine, Justice Marshall explained why it should not be applied in this case:

> * * * We are not here faced with a premature resort to the courts—all administrative remedies are now closed to petitioner. We are asked instead to hold that petitioner's failure to utilize a particular administrative process—an appeal—bars him from defending a criminal prosecution on grounds which could have been raised on that appeal. We cannot agree that application of the exhaustion doctrine would be proper in the circumstances of the present case.
>
> First of all, it is well to remember that use of the exhaustion doctrine in criminal cases can be exceedingly harsh. The defendant is often stripped of his only defense; he must go to jail without having any judicial review of an assertedly invalid order. This deprivation of judicial review occurs not when the affected person is affirmatively asking for assistance from the courts but when the Government is attempting to impose criminal sanctions on him. * * * We must ask, then, whether there is in this case a governmental interest compelling enough to outweigh the severe burden placed on petitioner. Even if there is no such compelling interest when petitioner's case is viewed in isolation, we must also ask whether allowing all similarly situated registrants to bypass administrative appeal procedures would seriously impair the Selective Service System's ability to perform its functions.
>
> The question of whether petitioner is entitled to exemption as a sole surviving son is, as we have seen, solely one of statutory interpretation. The resolution of that issue does not require any particular expertise on the part of the appeal board; the proper interpretation is certainly not a matter of discretion. * * * Since judicial review would not be significantly aided by an additional

administrative decision of this sort, we cannot see any compelling reason why petitioner's failure to appeal should bar his only defense to a criminal prosecution. * * *

We are thus left with the Government's argument that failure to require exhaustion in the present case will induce registrants to bypass available administrative remedies. * * * This argument is based upon the proposition that the Selective Service System will, through its own processes, correct most errors and thus avoid much litigation. The exhaustion doctrine is assertedly necessary to compel resort to these processes. The Government also speculates that many more registrants will risk criminal prosecution if their claims need not carry into court the stigma of denial not only by their local boards, but also by at least one appeal board.

We do not, however, take such a dire view of the likely consequences to today's decision. At the outset, we doubt whether many registrants will be foolhardy enough to deny the Selective Service System the opportunity to correct its own errors by taking their chances with a criminal prosecution and a possibility of five years in jail. The very presence of the criminal sanction is sufficient to ensure that the great majority of registrants will exhaust all administrative remedies before deciding whether or not to continue the challenge to their classifications. And, today's holding does not apply to every registrant who fails to take advantage of the administrative remedies provided by the Selective Service System. * * * In short, we simply do not think that the exhaustion doctrine contributes significantly to the fairly low number of registrants who decide to subject themselves to criminal prosecution for failure to submit to induction. * * *

Notes

1. *Challenges to Defective Procedures*. Litigants have successfully avoided the exhaustion requirement where they challenged the propriety or adequacy of the very administrative procedures to which the doctrine would remit them, see, e.g., *American Federation of Government Employees v. Acree*, 475 F.2d 1289 (D.C.Cir.1973); *Elmo Division of Drive–X Co. v. Dixon*, 348 F.2d 342 (D.C.Cir.1965), and where the potentially available administrative procedure could not be invoked as a matter of right by one in the complainant's position, *Rosado v. Wyman*, 397 U.S. 397 (1970).

Mathews v. Eldridge, 424 U.S. 319 (1976), excerpted in Chapter 4, *supra*, illustrates the first of these "exceptions" to the exhaustion requirement. Eldridge claimed that the Social Security Administration's failure to accord him an evidentiary hearing before terminating his disability benefits violated due process. He brought suit in district court immediately after learning that his benefits had been cut off, and never pursued the post-termination hearing to which the SSA's regulations entitled him. In holding that the Court would entertain his due process claim, Justice Powell wrote:

> * * * The question is whether the denial of Eldridge's claim to continued benefits was a sufficiently "final" decision with respect to his

> constitutional claim to satisfy the statutory exhaustion requirement. Eldridge concedes that he did not exhaust the full set of internal-review procedures provided by the Secretary. As [*Weinberger v. Salfi*] recognized, the Secretary may waive the exhaustion requirement if he satisfies himself, at any stage of the administrative process, that no further review is warranted either because the internal needs of the agency are fulfilled or because the relief that is sought is beyond his power to confer. * * * [T]he power to determine when finality has occurred ordinarily rests with the Secretary since ultimate responsibility for the integrity of the administrative program is his. But cases may arise where a claimant's interest in having a particular issue resolved promptly is so great that deference to the agency's judgment is inappropriate. This is such a case.
>
> Eldridge's constitutional challenge is entirely collateral to his substantive claim of entitlement. Moreover, there is a crucial distinction between the nature of the constitutional claim asserted here and that raised in *Salfi*. A claim to a predeprivation hearing as a matter of constitutional right rests on the proposition that full relief cannot be obtained at a postdeprivation hearing. * * * Eldridge has raised at least a colorable claim that because of his physical condition and dependency upon the disability benefits an erroneous termination would damage him in a way not recompensable through retroactive payments. Thus * * * denying Eldridge's substantive claim "for other reasons" or upholding it "under other provisions" at the post-termination stage would not answer his constitutional challenge.

As this excerpt suggests, in cases like *Eldridge* a court usually will wish to be assured that administrative remedies have been pursued far enough to allow the agency to decide whether there is a non-constitutional basis for resolving the dispute. In *Eldridge* itself, there was no doubt that the SSA would not provide a pre-termination hearing; its published regulations announced precisely the opposite policy. Yet the SSA was not statutorily required to adopt those procedures and, in theory, could have changed its mind if it was prepared to do so in all cases. (In *Weinberger v. Salfi*, 422 U.S. 749 (1975), the Court had enforced what it characterized as a statutory exhaustion requirement for Social Security claims, but it allowed the plaintiff to challenge the constitutionality of eligibility criteria after pursuing a claim far enough through the administrative apparatus to assure that no alternative ground for disposition existed.)

2. *Constitutional Claims*. Many opinions suggest that administrative agencies lack credentials to rule on constitutional challenges to their substantive criteria or procedures, and some speak in terms of lack of jurisdiction to consider constitutional issues. If true, this would suggest that whenever plaintiffs challenge an agency's action as unconstitutional, they need not exhaust administrative remedies. Judicial practice, however, is much less rigid than this analysis suggests. Surely if the practice challenged as unconstitutional is one that the agency chose to employ, it makes sense for a court to be sure that the agency wishes to defend the practice rather than change it. Even where the plaintiff challenges a criterion or procedure that has been prescribed by Congress—as in *McKart*—the agency proceeding may be a superior, or at least adequate, forum for eliciting pertinent facts.

And when a plaintiff combines constitutional with other claims, there are usually strong reasons to allow the agency to address these claims and conclude its proceedings before allowing review. Finally, as *Crowell v. Benson* and *Myers v. Bethlehem Shipbuilding* reveal, allowing parties to repair to court whenever a dispute involves "constitutional" or "jurisdictional" facts could paralyze administrative decisionmaking.

The applicability of exhaustion principles in constitutional cases may also depend on the remedy sought. In *McCarthy v. Madigan*, 503 U.S. 140 (1992), the Court unanimously held that a prisoner need not exhaust the Federal Bureau of Prisons grievance procedure for federal inmates before filing an Eighth Amendment "constitutional tort" suit based on alleged deliberate indifference to his medical needs. (See Chapter 8 on damage actions against government officials.) Finding that Congress had not mandated any such exhaustion, six Justices concluded that "an evaluation of the individual and institutional interests at stake" counseled against the judicial imposition of such a requirement. Three Justices relied solely on the fact that the grievance procedure did not provide for any award of monetary damages, the prisoner's sole requested relief.

3. *Equitable Tolling of Statutory Periods for Review.* The Supreme Court unanimously rebuffed a notably unappealing government attempt to invoke both exhaustion requirements and time limits for judicial review in *Bowen v. City of New York*, 476 U.S. 467 (1986). Claimants to Social Security benefits based on mental disabilities brought a class action challenging a covert SSA directive. That directive mandated a presumption at all stages of the disability adjudication process that persons with severe mental disabilities that were not per se disabling under HHS regulations were able to do at least unskilled work and, therefore, did not qualify for benefits. A district court found that the evidence of a " 'fixed clandestine policy against those with mental illness' was overwhelming." The class included (a) persons recently denied benefits who could still pursue administrative review of their cases, (b) persons whose claims had been decided more than 60 days prior to suit, and who therefore were outside the 60 day statute of limitations on judicial review of disability denials, and (c) persons whose opportunities for administrative review had lapsed, but who were within the statute of limitations.

To the government's attempt to invoke the statute of limitations for the most "stale" claims, the Court responded:

> Petitioners * * * contend that if the 60–day limit is a statute of limitations, it is a condition on the waiver of sovereign immunity and thus must be strictly construed. We have no difficulty agreeing with that statement. Accepting this proposition, however, does not answer the question whether equitable tolling can be applied to this statute of limitations, for in construing the statute we must be careful not to "assume the authority to narrow the waiver that Congress intended," or construe the waiver "unduly restrictively." * * * Petitioners argue that * * * equitable tolling is permissible only in cases in which the public treasury is not directly affected. We decline to hold that the doctrine of equitable tolling is so limited. When application of the doctrine is consistent with Congress' intent in enacting a particular statutory

scheme, there is no justification for limiting the doctrine to cases that do not involve monetary relief.

* * * The statute of limitations we construe in this case is contained in a statute that Congress designed to be "unusually protective" of claimants. Moreover, Congress has authorized the Secretary to toll the 60–day limit, thus expressing its clear intention to allow tolling in some cases. While in most cases the Secretary will make the determination whether it is proper to extend the period within which review must be sought, cases may arise where the equities in favor of tolling the limitations period are "so great that deference to the agency's judgment is inappropriate." * * * [W]e conclude that application of a "traditional equitable tolling principle" to the 60–day requirement of § 405(g) is fully "consistent with the overall congressional purpose" and is "nowhere eschewed by Congress."

We conclude, moreover, that on these facts the equities in favor of tolling are compelling. As the Court of Appeals explained:

> "All of the class members who permitted their administrative or judicial remedies to expire were entitled to believe that their Government's determination of ineligibility was the considered judgment of an agency faithfully executing the laws of the United States. Though they knew of the denial or loss of benefits, they did not and could not know that those adverse decisions had been made on the basis of a systematic procedural irregularity that rendered them subject to court challenge. Where the Government's secretive conduct prevents plaintiffs from knowing of a violation of rights, statutes of limitations have been tolled until such time as plaintiffs had a reasonable opportunity to learn the facts concerning the cause of action. Since in this case the full extent of the Government's clandestine policy was uncovered only in the course of this litigation, all class members may pursue this action notwithstanding the 60–day requirement."

In addition to serving its customary purpose, the statute of limitations embodied in § 405(g) is a mechanism by which Congress was able to move cases to speedy resolution in a bureaucracy that processes millions of claims annually. Thus, the limitation serves both the interest of the claimant and the interest of the Government. Tolling, in the rare case such as this, does not undermine the purpose of the 60–day limitations period when viewed in connection with the underlying statute. Rather, it serves the purpose of the Act where, as the Court of Appeals stated, "the Government's secretive conduct prevents plaintiffs from knowing of a violation of rights * * *."

For claimants within the statute of limitations, but who had failed to obtain a "final decision" from the Secretary as ordinarily required for judicial review, the Court refused to apply the retroactive exhaustion rule:

> [W]e conclude that exhaustion is excused for the same reasons requiring tolling of the statute of limitations. Since "[m]embers of the class could not attack a policy they could not be aware existed," it would be unfair to penalize these claimants for not exhausting under these circumstances.

As for those claimants who may still have had time to exhaust their administrative remedies, the Court concluded:

> The claims in this lawsuit are collateral to the claims for benefits that class members had presented administratively. The class members neither sought nor were awarded benefits in the District Court, but rather challenged the Secretary's failure to follow the applicable regulations.
>
> Moreover, as in *Eldridge*, the claimants in this case would be irreparably injured were the exhaustion requirement now enforced against them. The District Court found that class members not only were denied the benefits they were seeking, but "[t]he ordeal of having to go through the administrative appeal process may trigger a severe medical setback. Many persons have been hospitalized due to the trauma of having disability benefits cut off. Interim benefits will not adequately protect plaintiffs from this harm. Nor will ultimate success if they manage to pursue their appeals." Petitioners do not challenge this finding here * * *. We should be especially sensitive to this kind of harm where the Government seeks to require claimants to exhaust administrative remedies merely to enable them to receive the procedure they should have been afforded in the first place. * * *
>
> [T]he District Court found a systemwide, unrevealed policy that was inconsistent in critically important ways with established regulations. Nor did this policy depend on the particular facts of the case before it; rather, the policy was illegal precisely because it ignored those facts. The District Court found that the policy was being adhered to by state agencies due to pressure from SSA, and that therefore exhaustion would have been futile. Under these unique circumstances, there was nothing to be gained from permitting the compilation of a detailed factual record, or from agency expertise. *Cf. McKart v. United States.*
>
> We do not suggest that every internal policy that is found to be inconsistent with legal requirements, and arguably touches upon the outcome of a class of cases, will justify tolling the statute of limitations or excusing exhaustion. But, whatever the outer bounds of our holding today, this case falls well within them. While "hard" cases may arise, this is not one of them.

4. *Failure to Raise Claims Before the Agency.* One reason for requiring exhaustion of administrative remedies is to allow the agency to consider and respond to objections to its actions or procedures. Does this mean that a litigant's failure to raise an objection before the agency, when there was an opportunity to do so, should preclude judicial consideration of the objection? In *Sims v. Apfel*, 530 U.S. 103 (2000), Ms. Sims unsuccessfully applied for disability and supplemental security benefits. She sought review of this denial from the Social Security Appeals Council, contending that the state agency and then the ALJ who heard her case had erred in analyzing her evidence of disability. The Appeals Council affirmed and Ms. Sims filed suit, claiming that (1) the ALJ had made selective use of the record, (2) that the ALJ's questions to the vocational expert at the hearing were prejudicial and incomplete, and (3) that, given the medical evidence, the ALJ should have ordered a consultative examination.

The district court rejected all three contentions. The Fifth Circuit affirmed as to the first claim but held that it lacked jurisdiction to entertain Ms. Sims' second and third claims because she had not raised them before the agency. In supporting this ruling government counsel argued that the Court "should require issue exhaustion in addition to exhaustion of remedies." By a 5–4 vote, in an opinion by Justice Thomas, the Court declined to accept this argument. Justice Thomas acknowledged that "administrative issue exhaustion" is the "general rule," by analogy to the principle that appellate courts will not consider arguments not raised before trial courts. But he was not persuaded that the analogy fit the facts:

> [T]he desirability of a court imposing a requirement of issue exhaustion depends on the degree to which the analogy to normal adversarial litigation applies in a particular administrative proceeding. Where the parties are expected to develop the issues in an adversarial administrative proceeding, it seems to us that the rationale for requiring issue exhaustion is at its greatest. Where, by contrast, an administrative proceeding is not adversarial, [as in Social Security disability proceedings] we think the reasons for a court to require issue exhaustion are much weaker. * * *
>
> Thus, the * * * analogy to judicial proceedings is at its weakest in this area. The adversarial development of issues by the parties—the "com[ing] to issue"—on which that analogy depends simply does not exist. The [Appeals] Council, not the claimant, has primary responsibility for identifying and developing the issues. We therefore agree * * * that "the general rule [of issue exhaustion] makes little sense in this particular context." * * *

The Chief Justice, and Justices Scalia, Kennedy, and Breyer, in an opinion by Justice Breyer, found the majority's reasoning unconvincing and would have affirmed the Fifth Circuit's opinion.

5. *Exhaustion and Review of Rules.* Government attempts to invoke exhaustion raise different considerations in the context of suits to review agency rules. It is common for comments on a proposed rule to raise dozens, even hundreds, of factual and legal objections to an agency's plans, but, precisely because such comment may provoke changes, the final rule may raise issues that no participant squarely addressed. It is also not uncommon for someone who did not participate in the rulemaking to seek judicial review, perhaps because he or she only learned later that the rule might apply.

It is generally accepted that a litigant need not have participated personally in an agency's rulemaking in order to obtain judicial review of the final rule. But it is not clear whether a challenger may raise only objections that were conveyed in comments or reflected in the agency's narrative explanation for the rule. *American Forest and Paper Ass'n v. U.S. Environmental Protection Agency*, 137 F.3d 291 (5th Cir.1998), holds that a challenger's failure to participate in the agency proceeding does not waive any right to seek judicial review, but also suggests that a non-participant may raise only objections that were raised before the agency.

DARBY v. CISNEROS

Supreme Court of the United States.
509 U.S. 137, 113 S.Ct. 2539, 125 L.Ed.2d 113 (1993).

JUSTICE BLACKMUN delivered the opinion of the Court.**

This case presents the question whether federal courts have the authority to require that a plaintiff exhaust available administrative remedies before seeking judicial review under the Administrative Procedure Act (APA), 5 U.S.C. § 701 *et seq.*, where neither the statute nor agency rules specifically mandate exhaustion as a prerequisite to judicial review. At issue is the relationship between the judicially created doctrine of exhaustion of administrative remedies and the statutory requirements of § 10(c) of the APA.

I

Petitioner R. Gordon Darby is a self-employed South Carolina real estate developer who specializes in the development and management of multifamily rental projects. In the early 1980s, he began working with Lonnie Garvin, Jr., a mortgage banker, who had developed a plan to enable multifamily developers to obtain single-family mortgage insurance from respondent Department of Housing and Urban Development (HUD). * * *

The principal advantage of Garvin's plan was that it promised to avoid HUD's "Rule of Seven." This rule prevented rental properties from receiving single-family mortgage insurance if the mortgagor already had financial interests in seven or more similar rental properties in the same project or subdivision. See 24 CFR § 203.42(a) (1992). Under Garvin's plan, a person seeking financing would use straw purchasers as mortgage-insurance applicants. Once the loans were closed, the straw purchasers would transfer title back to the development company. Because no single purchaser at the time of purchase would own more than seven rental properties within the same project, the Rule of Seven appeared not to be violated. HUD employees in South Carolina apparently assured Garvin that his plan was lawful and that he thereby would avoid the limitation of the Rule of Seven.

Darby obtained financing for three separate multi-unit projects, and, through Garvin's plan, Darby obtained single-family mortgage insurance from HUD. Although Darby successfully rented the units, a combination of low rents, falling interest rates, and a generally depressed rental market forced him into default in 1988. HUD became responsible for the payment of over $6.6 million in insurance claims.

HUD had become suspicious of Garvin's financing plan as far back as 1983. In 1986, HUD initiated an audit but concluded that neither

** THE CHIEF JUSTICE, JUSTICE SCALIA, and JUSTICE THOMAS join all but Part III of this opinion.

Darby nor Garvin had done anything wrong or misled HUD personnel. Nevertheless, in June 1989, HUD issued a limited denial of participation (LDP) that prohibited petitioners for one year from participating in any program in South Carolina administered by respondent Assistant Secretary of Housing.[5] Two months later, the Assistant Secretary notified petitioners that HUD was also proposing to debar them from further participation in all HUD procurement contracts and in any nonprocurement transaction with any federal agency.

Petitioners' appeals of the LDP and of the proposed debarment were consolidated, and an Administrative Law Judge (ALJ) conducted a hearing on the consolidated appeals in December 1989. The judge issued an "Initial Decision and Order" in April 1990, finding that the financing method used by petitioners was "a sham which improperly circumvented the Rule of Seven." The ALJ concluded, however, that most of the relevant facts had been disclosed to local HUD employees, that petitioners lacked criminal intent, and that Darby himself "genuinely cooperated with HUD to try [to] work out his financial dilemma and avoid foreclosure." In light of these mitigating factors, the ALJ concluded that an indefinite debarment would be punitive and that it would serve no legitimate purpose;[6] good cause existed, however, to debar petitioners for a period of 18 months.

Under HUD regulations,

> [t]he hearing officer's determination shall be final unless, pursuant to 24 CFR part 26, the Secretary or the Secretary's designee, within 30 days of receipt of a request decides as a matter of discretion to review the finding of the hearing officer. The 30 day period for deciding whether to review a determination may be extended upon written notice of such extension by the Secretary or his designee. Any party may request such a review in writing within 15 days of receipt of the hearing officer's determination.

24 CFR § 24.314(c) (1992). Neither petitioners nor respondents sought further administrative review of the ALJ's "Initial Decision and Order."

On May 31, 1990, petitioners filed suit in the United States District Court for the District of South Carolina. They sought an injunction and a declaration that the administrative sanctions were imposed for purposes of punishment, in violation of HUD's own debarment regulations, and therefore were "not in accordance with law" within the meaning of § 10(e)(B)(1) of the APA, 5 U.S.C. § 706(2)(A).

5. An LDP precludes its recipient from participating in any HUD "program," which includes "receipt of any benefit or financial assistance through grants or contractual arrangements; benefits or assistance in the form of loan guarantees or insurance; and awards of procurement contracts, notwithstanding any quid pro quo given and whether [HUD] gives anything in return." 24 CFR § 24.710(a)(2) (1992).

6. According to HUD regulations, "[d]ebarment and suspension are serious actions which shall be used only in the public interest and for the Federal Government's protection and not for purposes of punishment." 24 CFR § 24.115(b) (1992).

Respondents moved to dismiss the complaint on the ground that petitioners, by forgoing the option to seek review by the Secretary, had failed to exhaust administrative remedies. The District Court denied respondents' motion to dismiss, reasoning that the administrative remedy was inadequate and that resort to that remedy would have been futile. * * *

The Court of Appeals for the Fourth Circuit reversed. *Darby v. Kemp*, 957 F.2d 145 (1992). It recognized that neither the National Housing Act nor HUD regulations expressly mandate exhaustion of administrative remedies prior to filing suit. The court concluded, however, that the District Court had erred in denying respondents' motion to dismiss, because there was no evidence to suggest that further review would have been futile or that the Secretary would have abused his discretion by indefinitely extending the time limitations for review.

* * *

II

Section 10(c) of the APA bears the caption "Actions reviewable." It provides in its first two sentences that judicial review is available for "final agency action for which there is no other adequate remedy in a court," and that "preliminary, procedural, or intermediate agency action * * * is subject to review on the review of the final agency action." The last sentence of § 10(c) reads:

> Except as otherwise expressly required by statute, agency action otherwise final is final for the purposes of this section whether or not there has been presented or determined an application for a declaratory order, for any form of reconsideration, or, unless the agency otherwise requires by rule and provides that the action meanwhile is inoperative, for an appeal to superior agency authority.

5 U.S.C. § 704.

Petitioners argue that this provision means that a litigant seeking judicial review of a final agency action under the APA need not exhaust available administrative remedies unless such exhaustion is expressly required by statute or agency rule. According to petitioners, since § 10(c) contains an explicit exhaustion provision, federal courts are not free to require further exhaustion as a matter of judicial discretion.

Respondents contend that § 10(c) is concerned solely with timing, that is, when agency actions become "final," and that Congress had no intention to interfere with the courts' ability to impose conditions on the timing of their exercise of jurisdiction to review final agency actions. Respondents concede that petitioners' claim is "final" under § 10(c), for neither the National Housing Act nor applicable HUD regulations require that a litigant pursue further administrative appeals prior to seeking judicial review. However, even though nothing in § 10(c) precludes judicial review of petitioners' claim, respondents argue that federal courts remain free under the APA to impose appropriate exhaustion requirements.[9]

We have recognized that the judicial doctrine of exhaustion of administrative remedies is conceptually distinct from the doctrine of finality:

> [T]he finality requirement is concerned with whether the initial decisionmaker has arrived at a definitive position on the issue that inflicts an actual, concrete injury; the exhaustion requirement generally refers to administrative and judicial procedures by which an injured party may seek review of an adverse decision and obtain a remedy if the decision is found to be unlawful or otherwise inappropriate.

Williamson County Regional Planning Comm'n v. Hamilton Bank, 473 U.S. 172, 193 (1985). Whether courts are free to impose an exhaustion requirement as a matter of judicial discretion depends, at least in part, on whether Congress has provided otherwise, for "of 'paramount importance' to any exhaustion inquiry is congressional intent." We therefore must consider whether § 10(c), by providing the conditions under which agency action becomes "final for the purposes of" judicial review, limits the authority of courts to impose additional exhaustion requirements as a prerequisite to judicial review. * * *

While some dicta in [prior] cases might be claimed to lend support to petitioners' interpretation of § 10(c), the text of the APA leaves little doubt that petitioners are correct. Under § 10(a) of the APA, "[a] person suffering legal wrong because of agency action, or adversely affected or aggrieved by agency action within the meaning of a relevant statute, is entitled to judicial review thereof." 5 U.S.C. § 702 (emphasis added). Although § 10(a) provides the general right to judicial review of agency actions under the APA, § 10(c) establishes when such review is available. When an aggrieved party has exhausted all administrative remedies expressly prescribed by statute or agency rule, the agency action is "final for the purposes of this section" and therefore "subject to judicial review" under the first sentence. While federal courts may be free to apply, where appropriate, other prudential doctrines of judicial administration to limit the scope and timing of judicial review, § 10(c), by its very terms, has limited the availability of the doctrine of exhaustion of administrative remedies to that which the statute or rule clearly mandates.

The last sentence of § 10(c) refers explicitly to "any form of reconsideration" and "an appeal to superior agency authority." Congress clearly was concerned with making the exhaustion requirement unambiguous so that aggrieved parties would know precisely what administra-

9. Respondents also have argued that under HUD regulations, petitioners' debarment remains "inoperative" pending review by the Secretary. See 48 Fed. Reg. 43304 (1983). But this fact alone is insufficient under § 10(c) to mandate exhaustion prior to judicial review, for the agency also must require such exhaustion by rule. Respondents concede that HUD imposes no such exhaustion requirement.

tive steps were required before judicial review would be available. If courts were able to impose additional exhaustion requirements beyond those provided by Congress or the agency, the last sentence of § 10(c) would make no sense. To adopt respondents' reading would transform § 10(c) from a provision designed to " 'remove obstacles to judicial review of agency action,' " *Bowen v. Massachusetts*, 487 U.S., at 904, *quoting Shaughnessy v. Pedreiro*, 349 U.S. 48, 51 (1955), into a trap for unwary litigants. Section 10(c) explicitly requires exhaustion of all intra-agency appeals mandated either by statute or by agency rule; it would be inconsistent with the plain language of § 10(c) for courts to require litigants to exhaust optional appeals as well.

III

Recourse to the legislative history of § 10(c) is unnecessary in light of the plain meaning of the statutory text. Nevertheless, we consider that history briefly because both sides have spent much of their time arguing about its implications. [The Court concluded that nothing in the legislative history argued for a different reading of § 10(c).]

IV

We noted just last Term in a non-APA case that "appropriate deference to Congress' power to prescribe the basic procedural scheme under which a claim may be heard in a federal court requires fashioning of exhaustion principles in a manner consistent with congressional intent and any applicable statutory scheme." *McCarthy v. Madigan*, 503 U.S. 140, 144 (1992). Appropriate deference in this case requires the recognition that, with respect to actions brought under the APA, Congress effectively codified the doctrine of exhaustion of administrative remedies in § 10(c). Of course, the exhaustion doctrine continues to apply as a matter of judicial discretion in cases not governed by the APA. But where the APA applies, an appeal to "superior agency authority" is a prerequisite to judicial review only when expressly required by statute or when an agency rule requires appeal before review and the administrative action is made inoperative pending that review. Courts are not free to impose an exhaustion requirement as a rule of judicial administration where the agency action has already become "final" under § 10(c).

The judgment of the Court of Appeals is reversed, and the case is remanded for further proceedings consistent with this opinion.

It is so ordered.

Note

A Bifurcated Doctrine? Despite the *Darby* Court's unanimity, it is not clear that, prior to *Darby*, the Court had paid attention to the distinction in exhaustion cases between APA-based and non-APA-based challenges to administrative action. Just a year earlier, the Court had written: "[W]here Congress has not clearly required exhaustion, sound judicial discretion governs." *McCarthy v. Madigan*, 503 U.S. 140 (1992) (holding that a prisoner bringing a *Bivens* action, discussed *infra* in Chapter 8, seeking only money damages for an alleged denial of medical care, was not required to exhaust prison administrative remedies). Apparently, in light of *Darby*, the sentence should have concluded: "Unless the disputed action is being challenged pursuant to the Administrative Procedure Act, in which case sound judicial discretion is barred." What makes the APA/non-APA distinction puzzling, of course, is the obvious relevance in all cases challenging administrative action of the same policy issues regarding the timing of review. As the Court noted in *McCarthy*: "Exhaustion * * * serves the twin purposes of protecting administrative agency authority and promoting judicial efficiency." *Id.* at 145. It is a little odd to think Congress intended the APA to foreclose judicial attention to those values in cases in which Congress did not expressly mandate exhaustion.

The *Darby* result purports to flow from the language of the APA. As the Court notes, however, any apparent inconsistency between judicially crafted exhaustion requirements in APA cases and the literal language of 5 U.S.C. § 704 could be resolved by limiting § 704's reach to the conceptually distinct "finality" requirement.

The overlap between "finality" and "exhaustion" is extensive, but not complete. Failure to exhaust can be raised in an enforcement context, for example, but a claim that review was barred because the agency's position had not become final would be self-contradicting. After *Darby*, exhaustion would apparently still be required under the plain language of § 704 in any case for which agency rules mandated an administrative "appeal" from an ALJ decision "to superior agency authority." Would exhaustion be required under § 704 if the agency purported to require losing parties to petition for a discretionary form of superior agency review? Or does "appeal" embrace only the opportunity for a judgment on the merits as of right? If "appeal" means the latter, then any agency attempt to create an administrative certiorari-type review from ALJ decisions is not going to assure the agency control of its supposedly discretionary docket. It can deny discretionary review to a losing party who seeks it, but losing parties, following *Darby*, would not need to seek the agency's discretionary review in the first place.

4. STANDING

Even assuming timely and reviewable claims, not every person who objects to agency action may obtain judicial review. The standing cases seek to identify those parties entitled to judicial review and to explain why some, but not others, may invoke the courts' powers. As suggested earlier, standing often presents no problem. A person subject to adverse agency adjudication or other individuated agency compulsion (*e.g.*, a subpoena), or deprived of property rights by agency action (*e.g.*, through cancellation of a mineral lease on public lands) will have no difficulty demonstrating standing. Yet, parties adversely, but indirectly or only probabilistically, affected by agency action often present themselves to courts in a guise which raises concerns about the sufficiency of their legal interest to proceed. Numerous verbal formulae have attempted, none wholly successfully, to capture the circumstances that render a claim too "abstract," "diffuse," "political," "speculative," or the like, to pass muster as a basis for standing. Countless essays and judicial opinions attempt to explain the functions of, and the basis for, our evolving standing doctrine. But the concept is slippery. For while focused ostensibly on *who* is bringing suit, "standing" is also a place holder for some very general ideas about what it means to have a "cause of action" and what sorts of claims, given our particular constitutional commitment to the separation of powers, should be justiciable in federal courts—ideas that continue to defy cogent and complete articulation.

As with much legal doctrine, where conceptual analysis fails, history often helps. We need to see the seeds of current doctrine in older concepts, and to appreciate how these ideas have been transformed since 1970 to generate current doctrine.

a. Standing Prior to 1970: "Legal Wrongs" and "Public Rights"

Legal Wrongs. The Supreme Court's standing decisions prior to the enactment of the Administrative Procedure Act—though perhaps not a wholly coherent jurisprudence—followed two main doctrinal axes. The first is illustrated by *Alexander Sprunt & Son, Inc. v. United States*, 281 U.S. 249 (1930), a suit challenging an order of the Interstate Commerce Commission establishing railroad rates for the shipment of cotton. ICC orders were then reviewable in the district courts pursuant to the Urgent Deficiencies Act, which provided:

> Except as otherwise provided by Act of Congress, the district courts shall have jurisdiction of any civil action to enforce, enjoin, set aside, annul or suspend, in whole or in part, any order of the [Interstate Commerce Commission].

At the time in dispute, pursuant to ICC orders, railroads serving the Gulf Coast states transported cotton at two different rates, one for domestic cotton and a higher one for cotton intended for export. Sprunt owned a wharfside warehouse on the Texas coast, which compressed and stored cotton in preparation for shipment to other U.S. ports. Although an exporter, Sprunt—like other warehouse owners on the wharf—did not need any transportation service between its plant and the ships carrying its cotton; the ships' tackle could load the cotton directly. Consequently, the railroads had for several years offered Sprunt the lower domestic rate. Export shipments processed through uptown warehouses had to pay an additional 3.5 cents/100 pounds of cotton, assertedly to reflect the additional costs of getting the cotton shipside.

The apparent inequities of this structure prompted investigation by the ICC, which, after extended hearings, found that the existing rate structure was "unduly preferential." It directed that the rates be equalized in any fashion "which would preserve but not increase the carriers' revenues." When the railroads were unable to agree on new rates, the Commission reopened the proceeding and issued an order prescribing adjustments that eliminated Sprunt's competitive advantage.

Sprunt and other similarly situated shippers, along with the railroads, brought suit challenging the ICC's order under the statutory procedure described above, but the railroads did not pursue their objections beyond the district court. The agency challenged the shippers' standing to sue, and the Supreme Court, in an opinion by Justice Brandeis, agreed:

> *First.* The appellants contend that there is no basis for the Commission's finding of undue prejudice and preference. We are of opinion that appellants have no standing, in their own right, to make this attack. * * *
>
> * * * The appellants' position is legally no different from what it would have been if the carriers had filed the rates freely, pursuant to an informal suggestion of the Commission or one of its members; or if the filing had been made by carriers voluntarily after complaint filed before the Commission, which had never reached a hearing, because the rate structure complained of was thus superseded. * * * Since the appellants' economic advantage as shippers was an incident of the supposed right exercised by the carriers, the appellants cannot complain after the carriers are satisfied or prefer not to press their right, if any. * * *
>
> * * * A judgment in appellants' favor would be futile. It would not restore the appellants to the advantage previously enjoyed. If the Commission's order is set aside, the carriers would still be free to continue to equalize the rates; and for aught that appears would continue to do so.
>
> Second. Appellants complain of the order also on the ground that it authorized an increase in the local or domestic delivery rates without a hearing and findings as to the reasonableness of the level of either the old or the new rates. It is urged that § 15 of the Act does not authorize the Commission to fix the rates necessary to remove undue prejudice without such hearing and findings. But plainly appellants cannot, in their own right, be heard to complain in this suit of this part of the order. * * * In prescribing the rate, the Commission in no way prejudiced any preexisting rights or remedies of the appellants. Any question as to the reasonableness of the level of the rate was expressly left open by the Commission. It did not prescribe any rate as the minimum. If appellants are aggrieved by the level of the new rates, they still have their remedy before the Commission under §§ 13 and 15 of the Act.

Alexander Sprunt is the last of a trilogy of Transportation Act standing cases decided by the Court between 1923 and 1930. The first case, *Edward Hines Yellow Pine Trs. v. United States*, 263 U.S. 143 (1923), involved an ICC order requiring that railroads discontinue charges for storage of lumber left in railroad cars after arrival at their destination. These charges were imposed during the First World War to combat a shortage of rolling stock, and the ICC order was premised on a finding that shortage conditions no longer existed. A shipper who did not use car storage for its products, and was therefore advantaged by charges against competitors who did, sought review of the order. The Court found that the plaintiff had sustained no legal injury under the act because his statutory interest was limited to protection against "unjust discrimination." It therefore refused to rule on the legality of the ICC's order. By contrast, in the *Chicago Junction Case*, 264 U.S. 258 (1924), competitors who opposed the acquisition of terminal railroads by the New York Central were permitted to obtain review of an ICC order that approved the acquisitions. The Court found that the plaintiffs, who had lost business because of the Central's control of terminals, had a protected interest under a 1920 amendment to the Act, which required ICC approval of terminal acquisitions and, specifically, consideration of the interests of other carriers.

Later decisions followed the Transportation Act cases in insisting that a plaintiff seeking review demonstrate a "legal right" or "protected interest." In *Tennessee Elec. Power Co. v. TVA*, 306 U.S. 118 (1939), for example, the Court held that private power companies lacked standing to challenge the constitutionality of the act creating the Tennessee Valley Authority since they had no legal right derived from common law, statute, or franchise to be free from governmentally sponsored competition. But after Congress, actuated by concern for private utility companies, amended the Tennessee Valley Authority Act in 1959 to restrict the TVA's area of operations, the Court entertained suit by an injured competitor challenging the TVA's interpretation of the new area limitations. *Hardin v. Ky. Utils. Co.*, 390 U.S. 1 (1968).

Professor Davis, a fierce critic of the "legal right" test, see generally 3 KENNETH CULP DAVIS, ADMINISTRATIVE LAW TREATISE § 22.04 (1958), offered two sources of authority for rejecting it. One was the APA, which he viewed as granting standing to any party "aggrieved in fact"—a reading of section 702 that is certainly not self-evident and has never been embraced by the Supreme Court. Davis also suggested an analogy to the common law.

> The natural system is that of the common law: If A and B are private parties and A hurts B, B has standing to get a determination of the legality of A's action. Why should not the law be the same, whether A is the government, an agency, an officer, or a private party, and whether the injury is to B's person, his physical property or his intangible interests? Is not the natural system the simple one that injury in fact is enough for standing?

Kenneth Culp Davis, *The Liberalized Law of Standing*, 37 U. Chi. L. Rev. 450, 468 (1970).

Professor Jaffe rejected Davis' analogy: "*[T]hat is not the common law*. Rather, * * * if A alleges that B is violating a statute and the court concludes that the statute was not designed to protect A's interest the court will not determine the validity of A's claim." Louis Jaffe, *Standing Again*, 84 Harv. L. Rev. 633, 636 (1971). On that point, Professor Jaffe was clearly correct.

Another criticism of the "legal right" rule was that courts found it difficult to apply. The search for a "legal right" to determine standing suggested that the court was to resolve that issue as a preliminary matter without reaching the merits. But whether a plaintiff's interest is within statutory, common-law, or constitutional protections is clearly a merits question. *Perkins v. Lukens Steel Co.*, 310 U.S. 113 (1940), illustrates the propensity to confuse standing and the merits of the claim. The steel company sought to review an order of the Secretary of Labor under the Walsh–Healy Act establishing minimum rates of pay in the steel industry. Lukens claimed that the Secretary had, in establishing six different steel production regions in the country, misinterpreted what the Congress meant by "locality." But the Court never reached the question of statutory construction; it ruled that the company had no legally protected interest in the proper construction of the Walsh–Healy Act and dismissed the suit. In the Court's view, the Act merely constituted instructions to the government's purchasing agents, and, as in the case of a private agent, the common law affords no remedy against an agent who misinterprets his principal's instructions.

Had the Court carefully considered the purpose of the Walsh–Healy Act's requirement that the Secretary's wage determinations be made in terms of "localities," it would have recognized that provision was designed specifically to protect employers from general standard setting that did not take into account differences in local economic situations. (*Perkins* was overturned by the Fulbright Amendment, Act of June 30, 1952, Pub. L. No. 429, § 301, 66 Stat. 308 (codified as amended at 41 U.S.C. § 43(a) (2000)). Similarly, one might argue that in *Sprunt*, the Court's focus on the Transportation Act obscured the potentially analogous common law tort of interference with advantageous business relationships which might have supported recognition of a legal wrong to the dockside warehouses.

Perkins and *Sprunt* might be explained on other grounds—the former on the Court's reticence to review nonregulatory functions of the government; the latter on Brandeis's interest in protecting fledgling regulatory agencies from disruptive judicial interference. Nevertheless, they suggest that there is some danger that a search for "legal rights," framed as a question of standing, may confuse analysis of whether plaintiffs are asserting a recognized legal right with analysis of the merits of particular claims.

The "legal right" debate raises a broader question: To what degree should a claim for review of agency action be required to track the general requirements of a private law claim, i.e., that the plaintiff has been damaged by the wrongful action or inaction of the defendant (or more succinctly "act," "cause," "damage," "fault")? Some approximation of these elements seems sensible, but close adherence to the content of these private law concepts in public law contexts might improperly restrict review of administrative action. For example, the wrongfulness of a private defendant's conduct often depends upon owing a duty to the plaintiff that is distinct from any duty owed the public generally.

Vigorously applied, this notion would suggest that private parties claiming to be damaged by unlawful official conduct would generally fail to state a cause of action, for official duties are generally owed to the public at large. Similarly, many types of "damage" caused by public officials, such as the denial of a license or other public benefit, would not constitute an actionable "injury" under private law. Nor is an agency's failure properly to exercise its regulatory responsibilities readily characterized as the "proximate cause" of harm resulting from unregulated conduct. Consider here the Court's treatment of "causation" in *Sprunt.*

Judicial review of official action does not serve the same purposes as a private law suit. Review proceedings have public aspects that have been recognized historically to warrant a different approach to the question of whether a cognizable claim has been stated. See generally JOSEPH VINING, LEGAL IDENTITY: THE COMING OF AGE OF PUBLIC LAW (1978); LOUIS L. JAFFE, JUDICIAL REVIEW OF ADMINISTRATIVE ACTION (1965); Cass R. Sunstein, *What's Standing After* Lujan, *Of Citizens Suits, "Injuries," and Article III*, 91 Mich. L. Rev. 163 (1992); Jerry L. Mashaw, *"Rights" in the Federal Administrative State*, 92 Yale L.J. 1129 (1983); Abraham Chayes, *The Supreme Court, 1981 Term—Foreword: Public Law Litigation and the Burger Court*, 96 Harv. L. Rev. 4 (1982).

Public Rights. The second line of pre–1946 standing cases is epitomized by *FCC v. Sanders Bros.*, 309 U.S. 470 (1940). In that case the holder of a broadcast license in East Dubuque, Illinois, challenged the FCC's award of a license to a new station in Dubuque, Iowa, just across the Mississippi River. The challenger claimed, *inter alia*, that the Commission had improperly failed to take into account that the advertising market that the two stations would share was not adequate to support more than one. The Solicitor General responded that the Communications Act of 1934 did not confer on licensees a legal right to be protected from competition and that, on the authority of *Sprunt* and similar cases, Sanders Bros. lacked standing to challenge the Commission's award of a license to a competitor.

The Supreme Court found the case distinguishable from *Sprunt* in light of section 402(b) of the Federal Communications Act, which explicitly authorized appellate review of FCC orders not only by applicants for construction, broadcast, or transfer authorities, but also by "any other person who is aggrieved or whose interests are adversely affected" by any FCC order "granting or denying such authority." The Court analyzed Sanders Brothers' cause of action as follows:

> * * * [R]espondent appealed to the Court of Appeals for the District of Columbia. That court entertained the appeal and held that one of the issues which the Commission should have tried was that of alleged economic injury to the respondent's station by the establishment of an additional station and that the Commission had erred in failing to make findings on that issue. * * *
>
> The petitioner's contentions are that under the Communications Act economic injury to a competitor is not a ground for

refusing a broadcast license and that since this is so, the respondent was not a person aggrieved or whose interests were adversely affected by the Commission's action, within the meaning of § 402(b) of the Act which authorizes appeals from the Commission's orders. * * *

First. We hold that resulting economic injury to a rival station is not, in and of itself, and apart from considerations of public convenience, interest, or necessity, an element the petitioner must weigh, and as to which it must make findings, in passing on an application for a broadcasting license. * * *

This is not to say that the question of competition between a proposed station and one operating under an existing license is to be entirely disregarded by the Commission, and, indeed, the Commission's practice shows that it does not disregard that question. It may have a vital and important bearing upon the ability of the applicant adequately to serve his public; it may indicate that both stations—the existing and the proposed—will go under, with the result that a portion of the listening public will be left without adequate service; it may indicate that, by a division of the field, both stations will be compelled to render inadequate service. These matters, however, are distinct from the consideration that, if a license be granted, competition between the licensee and any other existing station may cause economic loss to the latter. If such economic loss were a valid reason for refusing a license this would mean that the Commission's function is to grant a monopoly in the field of broadcasting, a result which the Act itself expressly negatives. * * *

Second. It does not follow that, because the licensee of a station cannot resist the grant of a license to another, on the ground that the resulting competition may work economic injury to him, he has no standing to appeal from an order of the Commission granting the application.

Section 402(b) of the Act provides for an appeal to the Court of Appeals of the District of Columbia (1) by an applicant for a license or permit, or (2) "by any other person aggrieved or whose interests are adversely affected by any decision of the Commission granting or refusing any such application."

The petitioner insists that as economic injury to the respondent was not a proper issue before the Commission it is impossible that § 402(b) was intended to give the respondent standing to appeal, since absence of right implies absence of remedy. This view would deprive subsection (2) of any substantial effect.

Congress had some purpose in enacting § 402(b)(2). It may have been of [the] opinion that one likely to be financially injured by the issue of a license would be the only person having a sufficient interest to bring to the attention of the appellate court errors of law in the action of the Commission in granting the license. It is within the power of Congress to confer such standing to prosecute an appeal. * * *

Although the *Sanders Bros.* Court states that "it is within the power of Congress to confer such standing," the constitutional issue raised by section 402(b) of the Communications Act was not frivolous. If "legal right" cases like *Sprunt* rested on the constitutional requirement of a "case" or "controversy" and if section 402(b) authorized review where the plaintiff's interest was not otherwise "legally protected," the Act attempted to confer jurisdiction that was not a part of the judicial power of the federal courts. The Supreme Court offered an explanation of *Sanders Bros.* two years later, in *Scripps–Howard Radio, Inc. v. FCC*, 316 U.S. 4 (1942):

> The Communications Act of 1934 did not create new private rights. The purpose of the Act was to protect the public interest in communications * * *. [Economic competitors] have standing only as representatives of the public interest [citing *Sanders Bros.*]. That a Court is called upon to enforce public rights and not the interest of private property does not diminish its power to protect such rights.

In a famous opinion, *Associated Indus. of N.Y. State, Inc. v. Ickes*, 134 F.2d 694 (2d Cir.), *rev'd per curiam on other grounds*, 320 U.S. 707 (1943), Judge Jerome Frank tried to reconcile this approach to standing with the "cases or controversies" requirement by denominating the "person aggrieved" within the meaning of various federal provisions for specific statutory review a "private attorney general." In Frank's view, Congress had the power to direct the Attorney General to bring suit to protect the public interest in federal agency actions and could therefore alternatively direct that such public interest suits be pursued by "persons aggrieved."

Judge Frank's opinion, while later influential, is little more than a play on words. The "private attorney general" rationale proves too much, for it fails to place any limit on the congressional power to expand judicial jurisdiction. Under Judge Frank's theory Congress might just as easily provide for suit by "all green-eyed persons" or, indeed, "all persons." Yet presumably Congress cannot write the case or controversy requirement out of the Constitution. At the same time Frank's opinion reveals too little about the contours of standing under the "any person aggrieved" language of section 402(b) and other specific review provisions; leaving "legal right" behind, the opinion fails to provide any criteria for identifying those "grievances" that confer standing.

Yet, constitutional considerations aside, it clearly matters to a court that a litigant is seeking to invoke an express statutory review provision rather than one or more general grants of federal court jurisdiction. The reason it should matter is captured in the following observation by Kenneth E. Scott, *Standing in the Supreme Court—A Functional Analysis*, 86 Harv. L. Rev. 645, 656 (1973):

> The difference, and it is a vital one, is that Congress has weighed the need for and value of judicial review of a given category of

administrative decisions, and has decided it is warranted. Congress having explicitly made that decision, the Court has before it only the implementing, secondary decision as to whether there is reason not to allow the particular plaintiff in question to be one of those who may invoke the review—and the standing rules tend to become much more liberal.

b. Standing Post–1970: From "Rights" to "Injuries"

Prior to 1970, most lower courts had held that section 702 of the APA merely codified the pre–1946 law of standing: A party had standing to seek review of agency action only if it could show either that it had suffered a "legal wrong" (the *Sprunt* test) or that it was "aggrieved or adversely affected" within the meaning of an express review provision of the statute the agency was purporting to implement (the *Sanders Brothers* doctrine). See Comment, *Judicial Review of Agency Action: The Unsettled Law of Standing*, 69 Mich. L. Rev. 540, 545–46 (1971). That year, however, the Supreme Court decided the following case:

ASSOCIATION OF DATA PROCESSING SERVICE ORGANIZATIONS, INC. v. CAMP

Supreme Court of the United States, 1970.
397 U.S. 150, 90 S.Ct. 827, 25 L.Ed.2d 184.

JUSTICE DOUGLAS delivered the opinion of the Court.

Petitioners sell data processing services to businesses generally. In this suit they seek to challenge a ruling by respondent Comptroller of the Currency that, as an incident to their banking services, national banks, including respondent American National Bank & Trust Company, may make data processing services available to other banks and to bank customers. The District Court dismissed the complaint for lack of standing of petitioners to bring the suit. * * *

Generalizations about standing to sue are largely worthless as such. One generalization is, however, necessary and that is that the question of standing in the federal courts is to be considered in the framework of Article III which restricts judicial power to "cases" and "controversies." As we recently stated in *Flast v. Cohen*, 392 U.S. 83 (1968), "[I]n terms of Article III limitations on federal court jurisdiction, the question of standing is related only to whether the dispute sought to be adjudicated will be presented in an adversary context and in a form historically viewed as capable of judicial resolution." *Flast* was a *taxpayer's* suit. The present is a *competitor's* suit. And while the two have the same Article III starting point, they do not necessarily track one another.

The first question is whether the plaintiff alleges that the challenged action has caused him injury in fact, economic or otherwise. There can be no doubt but that petitioners have satisfied this test. The petitioners not only allege that competition by national banks in the business of providing data processing services might entail some future loss of profits for the petitioners, they also allege that respondent American

National Bank & Trust Company was performing or preparing to perform such services for two customers on whom petitioner Data Systems, Inc., had previously agreed or negotiated to perform such services. The petitioners' suit was brought not only against the American National Bank & Trust Company, but also against the Comptroller of the Currency. The Comptroller was alleged to have caused petitioners injury in fact by his 1966 ruling which stated:

> "Incidental to its banking services, a national bank may make available its data processing equipment or perform data processing services on such equipment for other banks and bank customers." Comptroller's Manual for National Banks ¶ 3500 (October 15, 1966).

> The Court of Appeals viewed the matter differently, stating:

> "[A] plaintiff may challenge alleged illegal competition when as complainant it pursues (1) a legal interest by reason of public charter or contract, * * * (2) a legal interest by reason of statutory protection, * * * or (3) a 'public interest' in which Congress has recognized the need for review of administrative action and plaintiff is significantly involved to have standing to represent the public. * * * "[10]

The "legal interest" test goes to the merits. The question of standing is different. It concerns, apart from the "case" or "controversy" test, the question whether the interest sought to be protected by the complainant is arguably within the zone of interests to be protected or regulated by the statute or constitutional guarantee in question. Thus the Administrative Procedure Act grants standing to a person "aggrieved by agency action within the meaning of a relevant statute." That interest, at times, may reflect "aesthetic, conservational, and recreational" as well as economic values. A person or a family may have a spiritual stake in First Amendment values sufficient to give standing to raise issues concerning the Establishment Clause and the Free Exercise Clause. We mention these noneconomic values to emphasize that standing may stem from them as well as from the economic injury on which petitioners rely here. Certainly he who is "likely to be financially" injured may be a reliable private attorney general to litigate the issues of the public interest in the present case.

Apart from Article III jurisdictional questions, problems of standing, as resolved by this Court for its own governance, have involved a "rule of self-restraint." Congress can, of course, resolve the question one way or another, save as the requirements of Article III dictate otherwise. *Muskrat v. United States*, 219 U.S. 346.

10. The first two tests applied by the Court of Appeals required a showing of a "legal interest." * * * The third test mentioned by the Court of Appeals, which rests on an explicit provision in a regulatory statute conferring standing and is commonly referred to in terms of allowing suits by "private attorneys general," is inapplicable to the present case. See *FCC v. Sanders Bros. Radio Station*, 309 U.S. 470; *Associated Industries v. Ickes*, 134 F.2d 694, vacated on suggestion of mootness, 320 U.S. 707.

Where statutes are concerned, the trend is toward enlargement of the class of people who may protest administrative action. The whole drive for enlarging the category of aggrieved "persons" is symptomatic of that trend. In a closely analogous case we held that an existing entrepreneur had standing to challenge the legality of the entrance of a newcomer into the business, because the established business was allegedly protected by a valid city ordinance that protected it from unlawful competition. *Chicago v. Atchison, T. & S.F.R. Co.*, 357 U.S. 77. In that tradition was *Hardin v. Kentucky Utilities Co.*, 390 U.S. 1. * * *

It is argued that the *Chicago* case and the *Hardin* case are relevant here because of § 4 of the Bank Service Corporation Act of 1962, which provides:

> "No bank service corporation may engage in any activity other than the performance of bank services for banks."

The Court of Appeals for the First Circuit held in *Arnold Tours, Inc. v. Camp*, 408 F.2d 1147, 1153, that by reason of § 4 a data processing company has standing to contest the legality of a national bank performing data processing services for other banks and bank customers:

> "Section 4 had a broader purpose than regulating only the service corporations. It was also a response to the fears expressed by a few senators, that without such a prohibition, the bill would have enabled 'banks to engage in a nonbanking activity,' S.Rep.No. 2105 [87th Cong., 2d Sess., 7–12] (Supplemental views of Senators Proxmire, Douglas, and Neuberger), and thus constitute 'a serious exception to the accepted public policy which strictly limits banks to banking.' (Supplemental views of Senators Muskie and Clark). We think Congress has provided the sufficient statutory aid to standing even though the competition may not be the precise kind Congress legislated against."

We do not put the issue in those words, for they implicate the merits. We do think, however, that § 4 arguably brings a competitor within the zone of interests protected by it. * * *

* * * Both [the Bank Service Corporation and the National Bank] Acts are clearly "relevant" statutes within the meaning of § 702. The Acts do not in terms protect a specified group. But their general policy is apparent; and those whose interests are directly affected by a broad or narrow interpretation of the Acts are easily identifiable. It is clear that petitioners, as competitors of national banks which are engaging in data processing services, are within the class of "aggrieved" persons who, under § 702, are entitled to judicial review of "agency action."

Note

The Novelty of the "Zone of Interests" Test. The *ADAPSO* opinion purports to interpret the Administrative Procedure Act and to further the "trend" toward a more generous conferral of standing. It arguably does neither. The "zone of interests" requirement is found nowhere in the APA, nor is a requirement for "injury in fact." The latter formulation is treated as a gloss on Article III, but one searches in vain for prior jurisprudence that uses or explains either of Justice Douglas' new tests. As one of us has argued, these tests could have been grounded wholly in the language of the APA, although the *ADAPSO* opinion does not seek to do so. Peter M. Shane, *Returning Separation of Powers Analysis to its Normative Roots: The Constitutionality of Qui Tam Actions and Other Private Suits to Enforce Civil Penalties*, 30 Envtl. L. Rep. 11,081, 11,084–85 (2000). Under APA § 702: "A person suffering legal wrong because of agency action, or adversely affected or aggrieved by agency action within the meaning of a relevant statute, is entitled to judicial review thereof." The first category—persons "suffering legal wrong because of agency action"—is not implicated in *ADAPSO*. Thus, in order to satisfy § 702, the Association of Data Processing Organizations had to show that it was "affected or aggrieved" by the Comptroller of the Currency. "Injury" is a plausible construction of that requirement. Further, the Association had to show that it was affected or aggrieved "within the meaning of a relevant statute." This appears to be the basis for the Court's "zone of interests" test. On this reading of § 702, Article III would have no necessary bearing on the *ADAPSO* formulation of the criteria for standing. Unfortunately, the Court is nowhere as clear as this in *ADAPSO*.

Nor is it obvious that Douglas' criteria expand rather than contract the bases for standing. They could do so in non-statutory review cases, like *ADAPSO*, yet contract standing in specific statutory review cases by importing requirements for beneficiary status or direct injury into cases that had never before required a showing of either.

The question whether *ADAPSO* expands or contracts standing demands a highly speculative response. To answer it we would need to know what the pre-*ADAPSO* jurisprudence actually required and how that jurisprudence would have developed. A confident answer to even the first query requires considerable chutzpah. The answer to the second is unknowable. One thing is clear, however, *ADAPSO* did not cement a trend or, indeed, settle anything. It instead set off a struggle over the shape of standing doctrine that shows no sign of abating.

"Zone of Interest" Analysis

Sanders Bros. acknowledged Congress' authority to confer standing by explicitly licensing suit by "any person aggrieved" by agency action, and *ADAPSO* accepts the propriety of exercising judicial authority to resolve any claim brought by persons "injured in fact," if their interests are arguably protected by a relevant statute (or constitutional provision). In a case decided the same day as *ADAPSO*, the Court made clear that others besides economic competitors could take advantage of the expanded availability of standing. *Barlow v. Collins*, 397 U.S. 159 (1970), involved regulations governing USDA payments to tenant farmers under the "upland cotton program" enacted by the Food and Agriculture Act of 1965. Tenant farmers are statutorily permitted to assign such payments as advance security only to help finance "making a crop." Until 1966, USDA regulations excluded from the expenses of "making a crop" the rent paid for a farm, thus precluding landlords from demanding that their tenants assign their upland cotton payments to them. When USDA eliminated that exclusion in 1965 and construed "making a crop" to include farm rental, it enabled farm owners to insist on such assignments as a condition of a lease. Tenant farmers thus lost the only collateral available to them to secure a pre-harvest loan from anyone but their landlords to finance the purchase of every other farm need, such as tools or groceries. The plaintiffs in *Barlow* argued that the new ruling thus left them at the economic mercy of the landlords.

The Court had little trouble upholding the farmers' standing to challenge the agency's revised definition of "making a crop." The new definition clearly removed a protection that they had once enjoyed against the economic power of landlords, and Congress' manifest purpose in enacting the upland cotton program was to protect tenant farmers. As in *ADAPSO*, the relevant statute contained no provision analogous to section 402 of the Federal Communications Act specifically authorizing review of USDA action by anyone.

It was not clear, however, from *ADAPSO* or *Barlow* if the "zone of interests" test asks whether the statute under which standing is asserted must protect a particular *category of claimant* or rather the *particular interests* of statutory beneficiaries in the proper implementation of that statute:

> According to Professor Davis, the Court meant, or should have meant, to say that not the plaintiffs but the "particular interest" they were asserting was within the zone protected by the statutes. This highlights the convenient vagueness of the concept of "interest." In part it has been used to refer to the injury being inflicted on plaintiff, which causes him to seek relief. The injury may be economic and measurable in terms of loss of property or income, or it may be an impairment of other values which he holds; in either case, he sees government action as affecting him in ways he would pay to avoid. On the other hand, "interest" is also used to refer to the constitutional or statutory limitation which he claims the defendant government official is not observing. The greater the particularity with which plaintiff's interest is defined, the more it involves the precise legal issues which he is raising. A determination of whether plaintiff's interest is protected by the statute then comes to turn on a determination of the merits of his legal argument, and we are back to the problem of circularity. On the other hand, a definition of the plaintiff's interest in the most general terms tends to make the search for a protective legislative intent a fiction.

Scott, *supra*, at 664 n. 88. The Court has never wholly cured the vagueness inherent in its interest-based approach. Indeed, the Court cannot without reformulating its criteria, because "injury in fact" preserves one meaning of interest identified by Professor Scott while "zone of interest" analysis preserves the other.

Clarke v. Securities Indus. Ass'n, 479 U.S. 388 (1987), confirms, and perhaps expands, the liberal approach of *ADAPSO* and *Barlow* to the zone of interests test. The Court there upheld the standing of a trade association representing securities brokers, underwriters, and investment bankers to challenge a ruling of the Comptroller of the Currency that would permit national banks to establish or purchase discount brokerage subsidiaries under the National Bank Act's branching provisions, codified as amended at 12 U.S.C. §§ 36, 81 (2000). The Court explained:

> In cases where the plaintiff is not itself the subject of the contested regulatory action, the [*ADAPSO*] test denies a right of review if the plaintiff's interests are so marginally related to or inconsistent with the purposes implicit in the statute that it cannot reasonably be assumed that that Congress intended to permit the suit. The test is not meant to be especially demanding, in particular, there need be no indication of congressional purpose to benefit the would-be plaintiff.

The Court further indicated that the relatively undemanding test was appropriate because it was "most usefully understood" as a gloss on the APA's presumptive grant of judicial review.

Clarke thus also confirms that the "zone of interests" requirement is a so-called "prudential" construct, that is, it is not a limitation on standing mandated by the "case" or "controversy" limits of Article III. If we understand the zone of interests test as a prudential attempt to insure that judicial review does not undermine Congress' intended design for the workings of an administrative program, then there would seem to be a merger between "zone of interests" as a standing concern and the Court's analysis in *Block v. Community Nutrition Inst.*, noted at p. 887, finding implied preclusion under APA § 701(a)(2). Holding consumer challenges to milk pricing orders judicially nonreviewable because Congress had not made consumers a part of the governance scheme for elaborating or challenging milk market orders can be understood as a special, prudential "zone of interests"-type limit on standing.

Statutory preclusion of participation by a particular set of interests is not the only basis for failing the "zone of interests" test. In *Air Courier Conference of America v. Am. Postal Workers Union*, 498 U.S. 517 (1991), postal workers had sued to overturn a postal service regulation that permitted "international remailing" to evade the postal service's statutory monopoly on all carriage of letters in and from the United States. International remailing involves delivery of letters to a courier service which then deposits those letters with the postal system of a foreign nation. Remailing was allowed under the exception in the Private Express Statutes (PES) for "extremely urgent letters." The Postal Workers Union claimed that a blanket exemption for international remailing misconstrued the PES exception. Standing was premised on the theory that the diversion of mail from the postal service would reduce postal employment.

A majority of the Court agreed that the union (and its members) satisfied the injury in fact requirement, but believed that it failed the "zone of interests" test. Carefully reviewing the legislative history of the Postal Service statutes, and the development of the Postal Service letter monopoly, the Court found no congressional purpose to protect employment. The Court admitted that postal workers' interests were included within the Postal Reorganization Act of 1970 (PRA), but found that the only relationship between the PES, upon which the unions relied for their claim, and the labor-management provisions of the PRA was that the latter was a general codification of many postal statutes, which included the PES. In the Court's view it stretched the zone of interests requirement to the breaking point to view the "relevant statute" as everything codified together in the U.S. Code, whether or not the various provisions had any historical or operational relationship with each other.

The Court distinguished *Clarke*, in which the plaintiff had also relied on two separate statutes. However, the Court asserted the two statutes in *Clarke* were integrally related because the provisions of one were explicitly meant to be exceptions to the provisions of the other.

The special concurrence of Justices Stevens, Marshall and Blackmun in *Air Courier Conference* suggests that the majority was reaching out to instruct the courts of appeals that there was some limit to the generosity of the zone of interests interpretation reflected in *Clarke*. As the concurring Justices pointed out, the postal statutes exempt the postal service from the coverage of the Administrative Procedure Act. Hence, in their view, 5 U.S.C. § 702, under which the zone of interests test was developed, had no application to the case. And, because the APA did not apply, a more restrictive standing analysis applied that in their view clearly would exclude the Union's claims.

Air Courier Conference indicates only that the generous standing requirements of *Clarke* have limits when the question is whether a claimant falls within the zone of interests protected or regulated by the relevant statute. The following decision amply demonstrates, however, the Court's deep ambivalence about the scope of those limits:

NATIONAL CREDIT UNION ADMINISTRATION v. FIRST NATIONAL BANK & TRUST CO.

Supreme Court of the United States, 1998.
522 U.S. 479, 118 S.Ct. 927, 140 L.Ed.2d 1.

JUSTICE THOMAS delivered the opinion of the Court, except as to footnote 6.*

Section 109 of the Federal Credit Union Act (FCUA), 48 Stat. 1219, 12 U.S.C. § 1759, provides that "federal credit union membership shall be limited to groups having a common bond of occupation or association, or to groups within a well-defined neighborhood, community, or rural district." Since 1982, the National Credit Union Administration

* Justice Scalia joins the opinion, except as to footnote 6. [Footnote 6 supported the majority's analysis through recourse to legislative history, a method Justice Scalia disfavors.]

(NCUA), the agency charged with administering the FCUA, has interpreted § 109 to permit federal credit unions to be composed of multiple unrelated employer groups, each having its own common bond of occupation. In this case, respondents, five banks and the American Bankers Association, have challenged this interpretation on the ground that § 109 unambiguously requires that the same common bond of occupation unite every member of an occupationally defined federal credit union. We granted certiorari to answer two questions. First, do respondents have standing under the Administrative Procedure Act to seek federal court review of the NCUA's interpretation? Second, under the analysis set forth in *Chevron U.S.A. Inc. v. Natural Resources Defense Council, Inc.*, 467 U.S. 837 (1984), is the NCUA's interpretation permissible? We answer the first question in the affirmative and the second question in the negative. We therefore affirm.

I

A

In 1934, during the Great Depression, Congress enacted the FCUA, which authorizes the chartering of credit unions at the national level and provides that federal credit unions may, as a general matter, offer banking services only to their members. Section 109 of the FCUA, which has remained virtually unaltered since the FCUA's enactment, expressly restricts membership in federal credit unions. In relevant part, it provides:

> "Federal credit union membership shall consist of the incorporators and such other persons and incorporated and unincorporated organizations, to the extent permitted by rules and regulations prescribed by the Board, as may be elected to membership and as such shall each, subscribe to at least one share of its stock and pay the initial installment thereon and a uniform entrance fee if required by the board of directors; except that Federal credit union membership shall be limited to groups having a common bond of occupation or association, or to groups within a well-defined neighborhood, community, or rural district."

12 U.S.C. § 1759.

Until 1982, the NCUA and its predecessors consistently interpreted § 109 to require that the same common bond of occupation unite every member of an occupationally defined federal credit union. In 1982, however, the NCUA reversed its longstanding policy in order to permit credit unions to be composed of multiple unrelated employer groups. It thus interpreted § 109's common bond requirement to apply only to each employer group in a multiple-group credit union, rather than to every member of that credit union. Under the NCUA's new interpretation, all of the employer groups in a multiple-group credit union had to be located "within a well-defined area," but the NCUA later revised this requirement to provide that each employer group could be located within "an area surrounding the [credit union's] home or a branch office that can be reasonably served by the [credit union] as determined by NCUA." Since 1982, therefore, the NCUA has permitted federal credit unions to be composed of wholly unrelated employer groups, each having its own distinct common bond.

B

After the NCUA revised its interpretation of § 109, petitioner AT & T Family Federal Credit Union (ATTF) expanded its operations considerably by adding unrelated employer groups to its membership. As a result, ATTF now has approximately 110,000 members nationwide, only 35 per cent of whom are employees of AT & T and its affiliates. The remaining members are employees of such diverse companies as the Lee Apparel Company, the Coca–Cola Bottling Company, the Ciba–Geigy Corporation, the Duke Power Company, and the American Tobacco Company.

In 1990, after the NCUA approved a series of amendments to ATTF's charter that added several such unrelated employer groups to ATTF's membership, respondents brought this action. Invoking the judicial review provisions of the Administrative Procedure Act (APA), 5 U.S.C. § 702, respondents claimed that the NCUA's approval of the charter amendments was contrary to law because the members of the new groups did not share a common bond of occupation with ATTF's existing members, as respondents alleged § 109 required. ATTF and petitioner Credit Union National Association were permitted to intervene in the case as defendants.

The District Court dismissed the complaint. It held that respondents lacked prudential standing to challenge the NCUA's chartering decision because their interests were not within the "zone of interests" to be protected by § 109, as required by this Court's cases interpreting the APA. The Court of Appeals for the District of Columbia Circuit reversed. * * * On remand, District Court applied the two-step analysis that we announced in *Chevron* and held that the NCUA had permissibly interpreted § 109. * * * The Court of Appeals again reversed. * * * Because of the importance of the issue presented, we granted certiorari.

II

Respondents claim a right to judicial review of the NCUA's chartering decision under § 10(a) of the APA, which provides:

> "A person suffering legal wrong because of agency action, or adversely affected or aggrieved by agency action within the meaning of a relevant statute, is entitled to judicial review thereof."

5 U.S.C. § 702. We have interpreted § 10(a) of the APA to impose a prudential standing requirement in addition to the requirement, imposed by Article III of the Constitution, that a plaintiff have suffered a sufficient injury-in-fact. See, e.g., *Association of Data Processing Service*

Organizations, Inc. v. Camp, 397 U.S. 150 (1970) (*Data Processing*).[4] For a plaintiff to have prudential standing under the APA, "the interest sought to be protected by the complainant [must be] arguably within the zone of interests to be protected or regulated by the statute * * * in question."

Based on * * * our prior cases finding that competitors of financial institutions have standing to challenge agency action relaxing statutory restrictions on the activities of those institutions, we hold the respondents' interest in limiting the markets that federal credit unions can serve is arguably within the zone of interests to be protected by § 109. * * *

A

Although our prior cases have not stated a clear rule for determining when a plaintiff's interest is "arguably within the zone of interests" to be protected by a statute, they nonetheless establish that we should not inquire whether there has been a congressional intent to benefit the would-be plaintiff. * * *

* * *

The proper inquiry is simply "whether the interest sought to be protected by the complainant is arguably within the zone of interests to be protected * * * by the statute." Hence in applying the "zone of interests" test, we do not ask whether, in enacting the statutory provision at issue, Congress specifically intended to benefit the plaintiff. Instead, we first discern the interests "arguably * * * to be protected" by the statutory provision at issue; we then inquire whether plaintiff's interests affected by the agency action in question are among them.

Section 109 provides that "federal credit union membership shall be limited to groups having a common bond of occupation or association, or to groups within a well-defined neighborhood, community, or rural district." 12 U.S.C. § 1759. By its express terms, § 109 limits membership in every federal credit union to members of definable "groups." Because federal credit unions may, as a general matter, offer banking services only to members, § 109 also restricts the markets that every federal credit union can serve. Although these markets need not be small, they unquestionably are limited. The link between § 109's regulation of federal credit union membership and its limitation on the markets that federal credit union can serve is unmistakable. Thus, even if it cannot be said that Congress had the specific purpose of benefiting commercial banks, one of the interests "arguably * * * to be protected" by § 109 is an interest in limiting the markets that federal credit unions can serve. This interest is precisely the interest of respondents affected by the NCUA's interpretation of § 109. As competitors of Federal credit unions, respondents certainly have an interest in limiting the markets

4. In this case, it not disputed that respondents have suffered an injury-in-fact because the NCUA's interpretation allows persons who might otherwise be their customers to be members, and therefore customers, of ATTF.

that federal credit unions can serve, and the NCUA's interpretation has affected that interest by allowing federal credit unions to increase their customer base.[7] Section 109 cannot be distinguished from the statutory provisions at issue in *Clarke* * * * and *Data Processing.* * * *

C

Petitioners attempt to distinguish this case principally on the ground that there is no evidence that Congress, when it enacted the FCUA, was at all concerned with the competitive interests of commercial banks, or indeed at all concerned with competition. * * * The difficulty with this argument is that similar arguments were made unsuccessfully in * * * *Data Processing* * * * and *Clarke.* * * * In each case, we declined to accept the Comptroller's argument. In *Data Processing*, we considered it irrelevant that the statutes in question "did not in terms protect a specified group," because "their general policy [was] apparent[,] and those whose interests [were] directly affected by a broad or narrow interpretation of [the statutes] [were] easily identifiable." * * * The provisions at issue in each of these cases, moreover, could be said merely to be safety-and-soundness provisions, enacted only to protect national banks and their depositors and without a concern for competitive effects. We nonetheless did not hesitate to find standing.

Petitioners also mistakenly rely on our decision in *Air Courier Conference v. Postal Workers*, 498 U.S. 517 (1991). In *Air Courier*, we held that the interest of Postal Service employees in maximizing employment opportunities was not within the "zone of interests" to be protected by the postal monopoly statutes, and hence those employees did not have standing under the APA to challenge Postal Service Regulation suspending its monopoly over certain international operations. We stated that the purposes of the statute were solely to increase the revenues of the Post Office and to ensure that postal services were provided in a manner consistent with the public interest. Only those interests, therefore, and not the interests of Postal Service employees in their employment, were "arguably within the zone of interests to be protected" by the statute. We further noted that although the statute in question regulated competition, the interests of the plaintiff employees had nothing to do with competition. In this case, not only do respondents have "competitive and direct injury," but, as the foregoing discussion makes clear, they possess an interest that is "arguably * * * to be protected" by § 109. * * *

7. Contrary to the dissent's contentions, our formulation does not "eviscerate" or "abolish[ ]" the zone of interests requirement. Nor can it be read to imply that in order to have standing under the APA, a plaintiff must merely have an interest in enforcing the statute in question. * * * Because of the unmistakable link between § 109's express restriction on credit union membership and the limitation on the markets that federal credit unions can serve, there is objectively "some indication in the statute," that respondents' interest is "arguably within the zone of interests to be protected" by § 109. Hence respondents are more than merely incidental beneficiaries of § 109's effects on competition.

III

[The majority went on to find the NCUA's interpretation of § 109 impermissible, relying on the contrary and "unambiguously expressed intent of Congress."]

Affirmed.

JUSTICE O'CONNOR, with whom JUSTICE STEVENS, JUSTICE SOUTER, and JUSTICE BREYER join, dissenting.

I

* * * The "injury respondents complain of," * * * is a loss of respondents' customer base to a competing entity, or more generally, an injury to respondents' commercial interest as a competitor. The relevant question under the zone-of-interests test, then, is whether injury to respondents' commercial interest as a competitor "falls within the zone of interests sought to be protected by the [common bond] provision." For instance, in *Data Processing*, where the plaintiffs—like respondents here—alleged competitive injury to their commercial interest, we found that the plaintiffs had standing because "their commercial interest was sought to be protected by the * * * provision which they alleged had been violated."

The Court adopts a quite different approach to the zone-of-interests test today, eschewing any assessment of whether the common bond provision was intended to protect respondents' commercial interest. * * *

Under the Court's approach, every litigant who establishes injury in fact under Article III will automatically satisfy the zone-of-interests requirement, rendering the zone-of-interests test ineffectual. * * * That result stems from the Court's articulation of the relevant "interest." In stating that the common bond provision protects an "interest in limiting the markets that federal credit unions can serve," the Court presumably uses the term "markets" in the sense of customer markets, as opposed to, for instance, product markets: The common bond requirement and the provisions prohibiting credit unions from serving nonmembers combine to limit the customers a credit union can serve, not the services a credit union can offer.

With that understanding, the Court's conclusion that respondents "have" an interest in "limiting the [customer] markets that federal credit unions can serve" means little more than that respondents "have" an interest in enforcing the statute. The common bond requirement limits a credit union's membership, and hence its customer base, to certain groups, 12 U.S.C. § 1759, and in the Court's view, it is enough to establish standing that respondents "have" an interest in limiting the customers a credit union can serve. The Court's additional observation that respondents' interest has been "affected" by the NCUA's interpretation adds little to the analysis; agency interpretation of a statutory restriction will of course affect a party who has an interest in the restriction. Indeed, a party presumably will bring suit to vindicate an interest only if the interest has been affected by the challenged action. The crux of the Court's zone-of-interests inquiry, then, is simply that the plaintiff must "have" an interest in enforcing the pertinent statute.

A party, however, will invariably have an interest in enforcing a statute when he can establish injury in fact caused by an alleged violation of that statute. An example we used in [*Lujan v.*] *National Wildlife Federation*, 497 U.S. 871 (1990) illustrates the point. There, we hypothesized a situation involving "the failure of an agency to comply with a statutory provision requiring 'on the record' hearings." That circumstance "would assuredly have an adverse effect upon the company that has the contract to record and transcribe the agency's proceedings," and so the company would establish injury in fact. But the company would not satisfy the zone-of-interests test, because "the provision was obviously enacted to protect the interests of the parties to the proceedings and not those of the reporters." Under the Court's approach today, however, the reporting company would have standing under the zone-of-interests test: Because the company is injured by the failure to comply with the requirement of on-the-record hearings, the company would certainly "have" an interest in enforcing the statute.

Our decision in *Air Courier* likewise cannot be squared with the Court's analysis in this case. * * * We concluded that the postal employees did not have standing under the zone-of-interests test, because "the PES were not designed to protect postal employment or further postal job opportunities." * * * [But] the postal employees would have established standing under the Court's analysis in this case: The employees surely "had" an interest in enforcing the statutory monopoly given that suspension of the monopoly caused injury to their employment opportunities. * * *

II

Contrary to the Court's suggestion, its application of the zone-of-interests test in this case is not in concert with the approach we followed in a series of cases in which the plaintiffs, like respondents here, alleged that agency interpretation of a statute caused competitive injury to their commercial interests. In each of those cases, we focused * * * on whether competitive injury to the plaintiff's commercial interest fell within the zone of interests protected by the relevant statute.

It is true, as the Court emphasizes repeatedly, that we did not require in this line of decisions that the statute at issue was designed to benefit the particular party bringing suit. See *Clarke*, supra. * * * In each of the competitor standing cases, though, we found that Congress had enacted an "anti-competition limitation," or, alternatively, that Congress had "legislated against * * * competition," and accordingly, that the plaintiff-competitor's "commercial interest was sought to be protected by the anti-competition limitation" at issue. We determined, in other words, that "the injury [the plaintiff] complained of * * * [fell] within the zone of interests sought to be protected by the [relevant] statutory provision." The Court fails to undertake that analysis here.

III

Applying the proper zone-of-interests inquiry to this case, I would find that competitive injury to respondents' commercial interests does not arguably fall within the zone of interests sought to be protected by the common bond provision. The terms of the statute do not suggest a concern with protecting the business interests of competitors. The common bond provision limits "federal credit union membership * * * to groups having a common bond of occupation or association, or to groups within a well-defined neighborhood, community, or rural district." 12 U.S.C. § 1759. And the provision is framed as an exception to the preceding clause, which confers membership on "incorporators and such other persons and incorporated and unincorporated organizations * * * as may be elected * * * and as such shall each, subscribe to at least one share of its stock and pay the initial installment thereon and a uniform entrance fee." The language suggests that the common bond requirement is an internal organizational principle concerned primarily with defining membership in a way that secures a financially sound organization. There is no indication in the text of the provision or in the surrounding language that the membership limitation was even arguably designed to protect the commercial interests of competitors. Nor is there any nontextual indication to that effect. * * *

The operation of the common bond provision does not likewise denote a congressional desire to legislate against competition. First, the common bond requirement does not purport to restrict credit unions from becoming large, nationwide organizations, as might be expected if the provision embodied a congressional concern with the competitive consequences of credit union growth. * * * More tellingly, although the common bond provision applies to all credit unions, the restriction operates against credit unions individually: The common bond requirement speaks only to whether a particular credit union's membership can include a given group of customers, not to whether credit unions in general can serve that group. * * * In this sense, the common bond requirement does not limit credit unions collectively from serving any customers, nor does it bar any customers from being served by credit unions. The circumstances surrounding the enactment of the FCUA also indicate that Congress did not intend to legislate against competition through the common bond provision. * * *

The requirement of a common bond was thus meant to ensure that each credit union remains a cooperative institution that is economically stable and responsive to its members' needs. As a principle of internal governance designed to secure the viability of individual credit unions in the interests of the membership, the common bond provision was in no way designed to impose a restriction on all credit unions in the interests of institutions that might one day become competitors. * * * That the common bond requirement would later come to be viewed by competitors as a useful tool for curbing a credit union's membership should not affect the zone-of-interests inquiry. The pertinent question under the zone-of-interests test is whether Congress intended to protect certain interests through a particular provision, not whether, irrespective of congressional intent, a provision may have the effect of protecting those interests. * * *

The other major post-*ADAPSO* battleground has been over whether particular plaintiffs satisfy the injury-in-fact requirement. Indeed, although the decades since *ADAPSO* represent but a small slice of Supreme Court history, in 1992 Professor Sunstein found that 109 of the 117 cases discussing standing as an Article III limitation had been decided after 1965. See Cass R. Sunstein, *What's Standing After* Lujan? *Citizens Suits, "Injuries" and Article III*, 91 Mich. L. Rev. 163, 169 (1992). This remarkable fact not only validates the claim that *ADAPSO* unsettled rather than settled the law of standing; it also makes clear that only a sample of the jurisprudence can be treated here. Moreover, because later cases often reinterpret and recharacterize earlier opinions, our organization of these materials has been forced to compromise between conceptual or issue-oriented categories and sequential or historical presentation. We begin with the following, now-famous, case.

SIERRA CLUB v. MORTON

Supreme Court of the United States, 1972.
405 U.S. 727, 92 S.Ct. 1361, 31 L.Ed.2d 636.

JUSTICE STEWART delivered the opinion of the Court.

The Mineral King Valley is an area of great natural beauty nestled in the Sierra Nevada Mountains in Tulare County, California, adjacent to Sequoia National Park. It has been part of the Sequoia National Forest since 1926, and is designated as a national game refuge by special Act of Congress. * * *

The United States Forest Service, which is entrusted with the maintenance and administration of national forests, began in the late 1940s to give consideration to Mineral King as a potential site for recreational development. Prodded by a rapidly increasing demand for skiing facilities, the Forest Service published a prospectus in 1965, inviting bids from private developers for the construction and operation of a ski resort that would also serve as a summer recreation area. The proposal of Walt Disney Enterprises, Inc., was chosen from those of six bidders. * * *

The final Disney plan, approved by the Forest Service in January 1969, outlines a $35 million complex of motels, restaurants, swimming pools, parking lots, and other structures designed to accommodate 14,000 visitors daily. * * * To provide access to the resort, the State of California proposes to construct a highway 20 miles in length. A section of this road would traverse Sequoia National Park, as would a proposed high-voltage power line needed to provide electricity for the resort. Both the highway and the power line require the approval of the Department of the Interior which is entrusted with the preservation and maintenance of the national parks.

Representatives of the Sierra Club, who favor maintaining Mineral King largely in its present state, followed the progress of recreational planning for the valley with close attention and increasing dismay. In June 1969 the Club filed the present suit in the United States District Court for the Northern District of California, seeking a declaratory judgment that various aspects of the proposed development contravene federal laws and regulations governing the preservation of national parks, forests, and game refuges,[2] and also seeking preliminary and permanent injunctions restraining the federal officials involved from granting their approval or issuing permits in connection with the Mineral King project. The petitioner Sierra Club sued as a membership corporation with "a special interest in the conservation and the sound maintenance of the national parks, game refuges and forests of the country," and invoked the judicial-review provisions of the Administrative Procedure Act.

After two days of hearings, the District Court granted the requested preliminary injunction. * * * The respondents appealed, and the Court of Appeals for the Ninth Circuit reversed. With respect to the petitioner's standing, the court noted that there was "no allegation in the complaint that members of the Sierra Club would be affected by the actions of [the respondents] other than the fact that the actions are personally displeasing or distasteful to them," * * *

* * *

The injury alleged by the Sierra Club will be incurred entirely by reason of the change in the uses to which Mineral King will be put, and the attendant change in the aesthetics and ecology of the area. Thus, in referring to the road to be built through Sequoia National Park, the complaint alleged that the development "would destroy or otherwise adversely affect the scenery, natural and historic objects and wildlife of the park and would impair the enjoyment of the park for future generations." We do not question that this type of harm may amount to

2. As analyzed by the District Court, the complaint alleged violations of law falling into four categories. First, it claimed that the special-use permit for construction of the resort exceeded the maximum-acreage limitation placed upon such permits by 16 U.S.C. § 497, and that issuance of a "revocable" use permit was beyond the authority of the Forest Service. Second, it challenged the proposed permit for the highway through Sequoia National Park on the grounds that the highway would not serve any of the purposes of the park, in alleged violation of 16 U.S.C. § 1, and that it would destroy timber and other natural resources protected by 16 U.S.C. §§ 41 and 43. Third, it claimed that the Forest Service and the Department of the Interior had violated their own regulations by failing to hold adequate public hearings on the proposed project. Finally, the complaint asserted that 16 U.S.C. § 45c required specific congressional authorization of a permit for construction of a power transmission line within the limits of a national park.

an "injury in fact" sufficient to lay the basis for standing under § 10 of the APA. Aesthetic and environmental well-being, like economic well-being, are important ingredients of the quality of life in our society, and the fact that particular environmental interests are shared by the many rather than the few does not make them less deserving of legal protection through the judicial process. But the "injury in fact" test requires more than an injury to a cognizable interest. It requires that the party seeking review be himself among the injured.

The impact of the proposed changes in the environment of Mineral King will not fall indiscriminately upon every citizen. The alleged injury will be felt directly only by those who use Mineral King and Sequoia National Park, and for whom the aesthetic and recreational values of the area will be lessened by the highway and ski resort. The Sierra Club failed to allege that it or its members would be affected in any of their activities or pastimes by the Disney development. Nowhere in the pleadings or affidavits did the Club state that its members use Mineral King for any purpose, much less that they use it in any way that would be significantly affected by the proposed actions of the respondents.[8]

The Club apparently regarded any allegations of individualized injury as superfluous, on the theory that this was a "public" action involving questions as to the use of natural resources, and that the Club's longstanding concern with and expertise in such matters were sufficient to give it standing as a "representative of the public." This theory reflects a misunderstanding of our cases involving so-called "public actions" in the area of administrative law.

* * *

The trend of cases arising under the APA and other statutes authorizing judicial review of federal agency action has been toward recognizing that injuries other than economic harm are sufficient to bring a person within the meaning of the statutory language, and toward discarding the notion that an injury that is widely shared is *ipso facto* not an injury sufficient to provide the basis for judicial review. We noted this development with approval in *Data Processing*, in saying that the interest alleged to have been injured "may reflect 'aesthetic, conservational, and recreational' as well as economic values." But broadening the categories of injury that may be alleged in support of standing is a different matter from abandoning the requirement that the party seeking review must himself have suffered an injury.

8. * * * In an *amici curiae* brief filed in this Court by the Wilderness Society and others, it is asserted that the Sierra Club has conducted regular camping trips into the Mineral King area, and that various members of the Club have used and continue to use the area for recreational purposes. These allegations were not contained in the pleadings, nor were they brought to the attention of the Court of Appeals. Moreover, the Sierra Club in its reply brief specifically declines to rely on its individualized interest, as a basis for standing. Our decision does not, of course, bar the Sierra Club from seeking in the District Court to amend its complaint by a motion under Rule 15, Federal Rules of Civil Procedure.

* * * It is clear that an organization whose members are injured may represent those members in a proceeding for judicial review. But a mere "interest in a problem," no matter how longstanding the interest and no matter how qualified the organization is in evaluating the problem, is not sufficient by itself to render the organization "adversely affected" or "aggrieved" within the meaning of the APA. The Sierra Club is a large and long-established organization, with a historic commitment to the cause of protecting our Nation's natural heritage from man's depradations. But if a "special interest" in this subject were enough to entitle the Sierra Club to commence this litigation, there would appear to be no objective basis upon which to disallow a suit by any other bona fide "special interest" organization, however small or short-lived. And if any group with a bona fide "special interest" could initiate such litigation, it is difficult to perceive why any individual citizen with the same bona fide special interest would not also be entitled to do so.

The requirement that a party seeking review must allege facts showing that he is himself adversely affected does not insulate executive action from judicial review, nor does it prevent any public interests from being protected through the judicial process.[15] It does serve as at least a rough attempt to put the decision as to whether review will be sought in the hands of those who have a direct stake in the outcome. That goal would be undermined were we to construe the APA to authorize judicial review at the behest of organizations or individuals who seek to do no more than vindicate their own value preferences through the judicial process. The principle that the Sierra Club would have us establish in this case would do just that.

* * *

JUSTICE DOUGLAS, dissenting.

The critical question of "standing" would be simplified and also put neatly in focus if we fashioned a federal rule that allowed environmental issues to be litigated before federal agencies or federal courts in the name of the inanimate object about to be despoiled, defaced, or invaded by roads and bulldozers and where injury is the subject of public outrage. Contemporary public concern for protecting nature's ecological equilibrium should lead to the conferral of standing upon environmental objects to sue for their own preservation. See Stone, *Should Trees Have Standing?—Toward Legal Rights for Natural Objects*, 45 S.Cal.L.Rev. 450

15. In its reply brief, after noting the fact that it might have chosen to assert individualized injury to itself or to its members as a basis for standing, the Sierra Club states:

> "The Government seeks to create a 'heads I win, tails you lose' situation in which either the courthouse door is barred for lack of assertion of a private, unique injury or a preliminary injunction is denied on the ground that the litigant has advanced private injury which does not warrant an injunction adverse to a competing public interest. Counsel have shaped their cases to avoid this trap."

The short answer to this contention is that the "trap" does not exist. The test of injury in fact goes only to the question of standing to obtain judicial review. Once this standing is established, the party may assert the interests of the general public in support of his claims for equitable relief.

(1972). This suit would therefore be more properly labeled as *Mineral King. v. Morton.*

* * *

The Solicitor General * * * considers the problem in terms of "government by the Judiciary." With all respect, the problem is to make certain that the inanimate objects, which are the very core of America's beauty, have spokesmen before they are destroyed. It is, of course, true that most of them are under the control of a federal or state agency. * * *

Yet the pressures on agencies for favorable action one way or the other are enormous. The suggestion that Congress can stop action which is undesirable is true in theory; yet Congress is too remote to give meaningful direction and its machinery is too ponderous to use very often. The federal agencies of which I speak are not venal or corrupt. But they are notoriously under the control of powerful interests who manipulate them through advisory committees, or friendly working relations, or who have that natural affinity with the agency which in time develops between the regulator and the regulated. * * *

The voice of the inanimate object, therefore, should not be stilled. That does not mean that the judiciary takes over the managerial functions from the federal agency. It merely means that before these priceless bits of Americana (such as a valley, an alpine meadow, a river, or a lake) are forever lost or are so transformed as to be reduced to the eventual rubble of our urban environment, the voice of the existing beneficiaries of these environmental wonders should be heard.

[The dissenting opinion of Justice Blackmun is omitted.]

Notes

1. *Which Harms Count as "Injuries?"* Despite its emphasis on the importance of pleading, the broader message of *Sierra Club v. Morton* was that adverse effects on many noneconomic interests might satisfy the injury in fact requirements of Article III. The Court has since made clear also that the injury in fact that supports a plaintiff's standing need not be tightly connected to the legal claim that represents the gravamen of the lawsuit. In *Duke Power Co. v. Carolina Envtl. Study Group, Inc.*, 438 U.S. 59 (1978), plaintiffs challenged the NRC's issuance of construction permits for two proposed nuclear power plants. Their central legal claim was that the Price–Anderson Act, a statutory limitation on the plants' liability in the event of a nuclear accident, violated the fifth amendment. In the event of a catastrophic accident, plaintiffs asserted, the damages available would so undercompensate the victims as to result in an impermissible taking of private property. No such incident had, of course, occurred at any U.S. nuclear plant, and the harm that would be visited on these plaintiffs were such an unlikely event to occur sometime in the future was entirely speculative.

Plaintiffs' standing, however, was not based on the anticipated shortfall in recovery should a nuclear accident by these yet-to-be-built plants devastate their homes. Instead, they argued that the statutory limitation on liability was key to the plants' ability to attract financing. Without the financing, the plants would not be built. The injuries that supported standing were the radiation that might result if the plants *were* built, plus anticipated thermal degradation of two lakes that the CESG members used for recreation. See also *Wyoming v. Oklahoma*, 502 U.S. 437, (1992), upholding Wyoming's standing to challenge an Oklahoma requirement that coal-fired electric generating plants producing power for sale in that state burn a mixture of coal containing at least 10 per cent of Oklahoma-mined coal. Although the State of Wyoming did not itself sell coal, it was deemed sufficient for standing that Wyoming claimed a loss in its severance tax revenues because of reduced Wyoming coal mining allegedly resulting from Oklahoma's discriminatory restriction.

2. *"Standing" v. "Cause of Action."* The *Sierra Club* opinion raised a host of issues that would bedevil the subsequent jurisprudence. Because many modern regulatory statutes deal with diffuse risks and widespread harms that may be difficult to trace to the acts of particular individuals, it is predictable that citizens will have interests in pursuing instances of governmental non-feasance and will seek to do so by collective means. *Overton Park* had validated the reviewability of governmental inaction in just such a situation and illustrated that the common form of such litigation would be a suit by a group or association rather than by an individual. In pressing the outer limits of this so-called "associational standing" the Sierra Club was opening up general questions about whether associations had recognizable interests that transcended the interests of individual members for standing purposes, as well as exactly what "interests" an association might represent that belonged to its members individually.

The Sierra Club's claim that it had a general interest in the environment that would justify its standing raised in the associational context a traditional concern that courts be restricted to deciding particular controversies rather than serving as a forum for the airing of "generalized grievances." After all, most governmental action affects some interests of citizens or taxpayers. Can we, putting on our citizen or taxpayer hats, come into court claiming to represent that group? And, if so, under what conditions?

Another way to put this question of generalized versus particular grievances is to ask whether there have been some identifiable (and illegal) acts by a governmental defendant that have caused particularized harm to the plaintiffs. And when put in that way, the injury in fact test begins to look, once again, like a requirement of a cause of action having the standard elements of act, cause, damage, and fault. Without ever quite saying that it is searching for the elements of a cause of action, the post-*Sierra Club* jurisprudence has explored these elements in detail. Indeed, it has added yet another inquiry—whether a decision in favor of the plaintiff would be likely to redress (the redressability criterion) the harm that the plaintiff claims to have suffered. (Query, for example, whether enforcement of any of the provisions described in footnote 2 in *Sierra Club* would have benefitted the plaintiff.)

Particular Injuries v. Generalized Grievances

1. *Citizens and Taxpayers*. The Court's primary articulated reason for demanding a particularized injury to support standing is avoiding lawsuits that amount essentially to political grievances, which could be addressed through political processes. Thus, in *United States v. Richardson*, 418 U.S. 166 (1974), the Court dismissed a taxpayer's suit to challenge the nonpublication of the CIA's budget under the "statement and account" clause of Article I, § 9 of the Constitution for lack of standing. The Court described the taxpayer's alleged injury—disabling him from voting with knowledge of incumbent legislators' decisions about intelligence budgeting—as a mere "generalized grievance" that failed to distinguish him from any citizen who objected to the secrecy of the intelligence budget. The Court dealt similarly that year with a challenge to the reserve officer status of certain members of Congress. The plaintiffs there alleged that holding such commissions contravened the "Incompatibility Clause," U.S. Const., Art. I, § 6, which precludes members of Congress from simultaneously holding any office in the executive branch. *Schlesinger v. Reservists Comm. to Stop the War*, 418 U.S. 208 (1974).

Richardson and *Schlesinger* are purportedly premised on Article III. But the search for their true meaning continues to haunt standing analysis. For many subsequent cases strongly suggest that Congress can transform generalized grievances into particularized injuries by explicit, statutory creation of a cause of action. In *Havens Realty Corp. v. Coleman*, 455 U.S. 363 (1982), a private class action, plaintiffs had accused Havens Realty of racial steering in violation of Fair Housing Act of 1968. Havens Realty had been investigated by HOME, a nonprofit fair housing group, that employed black and white "testers" to ask realtors about the availability of housing, with the objective of discovering if they were providing different answers to clients of different races. The named plaintiffs in the suit included a black would-be renter, a black tester, a white tester, and HOME itself. The would-be renter's right to challenge racial steering was clear, but the Court recognized standing also in testers who had no genuine interest in renting apartments and were thus not obviously injured by being denied accurate information.

The Court determined that Congress had conferred on all persons a statutory right to truthful information about housing availability. Because the black tester was denied truthful information, she suffered sufficient injury to permit standing. Because the white tester had received accurate information about housing availability, he could not establish standing on that basis, but, the Court held, white testers would have standing to redress a denial of opportunity to them to live in an integrated neighborhood, so long as the injury was alleged and proved with specificity. HOME was entitled to organizational standing in its suit for damages because the realtor's alleged violations made it more costly for HOME to refer its clients successfully to genuine housing opportunities.

If Congress may create a statutory right to information from realtors, the denial of which satisfies Article III requirements for standing, should Congress not be able to create a statutory right to information from the CIA, the denial of which would also be a legally cognizable injury? And, if so, why did the constitutional provision invoked in *Richardson* not do so?

An answer, of sorts, may emerge from looking at some earlier cases in which citizens and taxpayers were denied standing when pursuing constitutional claims. *Fairchild v. Hughes*, 258 U.S. 126 (1922), dismissed a suit challenging the propriety of the process by which the Nineteenth Amendment was ratified. Justice Brandeis, writing for the Court, stated: "[This is] not a case within a meaning of * * * Article III. * * * Plaintiff has [asserted] only the right, possessed by every citizen, to require that the government be administered according to law and that the public monies be not wasted." The Court dealt in similar terms with *Massachusetts v. Mellon*, 262 U.S. 447 (1923), a taxpayer's suit challenging the propriety of certain federal expenditures, and with *Ex Parte Levitt*, 302 U.S. 633 (1937), a suit contending that Justice Black's appointment to the Supreme Court violated the Ineligibility Clause, Article I, § 6, Cl. 2, of the Constitution.

The thread that may unify all these cases, including *Richardson* and *Schlesinger*, is the nature of the constitutional provision invoked. In each case the plaintiffs were claiming that a "structural" provision of the Constitution, not one directed at preserving particular individual liberties, prohibited the governmental action in question. Under traditional standards, a law that creates a duty to the general public does not, without more, give rise to privately enforceable rights. Hence, for example, it would be highly unlikely for the Court to find that these structural provisions created a private right of action of the sort recognized pursuant to the Fourth Amendment in *Bivens v. Six Unknown Named Agents*, *infra*, Chapter 9.

To be sure, as we explore in Chapters 8 and 9, the question whether a party has standing to pursue an action for injunction or declaratory judgment may not be the same as the question whether that party has a right of action for damages to vindicate the same interest. And, structural limitations may certainly be invoked by parties who are the particular targets of governmental action, as the *Chadha* case clearly illustrates. But, that may just be the point of requiring a particularized injury. Without such an injury—or a congressional statute providing for citizen or taxpayer enforcement of the constitutional provisions in question—the Court may feel that it lacks warrant to pursue issues that look like general "political controversies" and that may arguably be said to be delegated by the Constitution to the other branches of government.

Many will find the Court's hospitality to statutory claims of the sort presented by *Havens Realty*, combined with its inhospitality to interests such as those at stake in *Schlesinger* and *Richardson*, peculiar, if not anomalous. In all of these cases the injury alleged is arguably of a "psychological" character. And, one might have thought that the stake that a citizen has in the structure of constitutional government might be viewed as at least as worthy of judicial attention as the *Havens Realty* tester's right to truthful information.

Indeed, privileging statutorily-conferred over constitutionally-based interests produces both amusing strategic decisions and a bizarre jurisprudence. In *ACLU v. Rabun County Chamber of Commerce, Inc.*, 678 F.2d 1379 (11th Cir.1982), *modified*, 698 F.2d 1098 (11th Cir.1983), the plaintiffs challenged the private placement of a large illuminated cross in a state park. Apparently believing that Supreme Court doctrine cast doubt upon the plaintiffs' standing as constitutionally protected "separationists," the ACLU transformed itself into an organization for the protection of the environment. According to the complaint, the presence of the cross disrupted the camping pleasures of several members and violated their statutorily protected rights to an uncluttered environment. Standing was granted on the environmental theory, although the court was clearly concerned by the complication introduced by the sectarian character of the unwelcome intruder. It is at least ironic that the placement of a cross in a public park complicates, rather than enhances, a claim that would not be problematic were it directed at the discarding of gumwrappers and beer cans. For an excellent attempt to sort out these and other standing conundra, see Gene R. Nichol, Jr., *Rethinking Standing*, 72 Cal. L. Rev. 68 (1984).

The capacity of statutory claims to withstand motions to dismiss or motions for summary judgment for lack of standing where analogous constitutional claims might not may be explicable in terms of the distinction made at the beginning of this chapter between general and specific statutory review. Specific review provisions often grant standing to any person "aggrieved" or "adversely affected" by a government action. In the face of such a congressional instruction, a reviewing court need not, perhaps should not, concern itself with prudential limitations on standing once it has been satisfied that a plaintiff satisfies the constitutional minima. Hence, for example, an objection to standing based on the fact that the plaintiff's arguments amount to "generalized grievances" pervasively shared by the population at large would have no place in the context of a congressional instruction to review at the behest of "any person aggrieved."

This may be the message of two of the Supreme Court's "vote dilution" cases. In *Department of Commerce v. U.S. House of Representatives*, 525 U.S. 316 (1999), the Court ruled that voters who stood to lose a state representative or experience intrastate redistricting because of a Census Bureau plan to use statistical sampling in the 2000 census possessed standing to challenge the statistical sampling plan. The voters and four counties brought suit under a 1998 statute in which Congress designated the Census Bureau plan final agency action and permitted any person aggrieved by the plan to bring suit before a three-judge district court with direct appeal to the U.S. Supreme Court. The district court sustained the voters' motion for summary judgment, ruling that they satisfied standing requirements and that the Bureau's plan violated the Census Act's prohibition against the use of statistical sampling to apportion representatives. The district court granted the voters a permanent injunction against the use of statistical sampling in the apportionment aspect of the 2000 census. On direct appeal, the voters' suit was consolidated with a challenge brought by the U.S. House of Representatives, also before the Supreme Court.

The Supreme Court ruled that the Congressional grant of a cause of action to "aggrieved" persons eliminated any prudential standing concerns and that "several of the appellants" challenging statistical sampling had met the burden of proof regarding Article III standing requirements:

> In support of their motion for summary judgment, appellees submitted the affidavit of Dr. Ronald F. Weber, a professor of government at the University of Wisconsin, which demonstrates that Indiana resident Gary A. Hofmeister has standing to challenge the proposed census 2000 plan. Utilizing data published by the Bureau, Dr. Weber projected year 2000 populations and net undercount rates for all States under the 1990 method of enumeration and under the Department's proposed plan for the 2000 census. He then determined on the basis of these projections how many Representatives would be apportioned to each State under each method and concluded that "it is a virtual certainty that Indiana will lose a seat * * * under the Department's Plan." * * *
>
> Appellee Hofmeister's expected loss of a Representative to the United States Congress undoubtedly satisfies the injury-in-fact requirement of Article III standing. In the context of apportionment, we have held that voters have standing to challenge an apportionment statute because "[t]hey are asserting 'a plain, direct and adequate interest in maintaining the effectiveness of their votes.'" The same distinct interest is at issue here: With one fewer Representative, Indiana residents' votes will be diluted. Moreover, the threat of vote dilution through the use of sampling is "concrete" and "actual or imminent, not 'conjectural' or 'hypothetical.'"

Compare the Court's analysis here with its subsequent decision in *Sinkfield v. Kelley*, 531 U.S. 28 (2000). In *Sinkfield*, the Court held that white voters residing in majority-white districts created under a state redistricting plan with the express purpose of maximizing the number of majority-minority districts in Alabama did not possess standing to challenge the gerrymandering under the Fourteenth Amendment. The Court reasoned that the white voters did not live in a majority-minority district and "neither alleged nor produced any evidence that any of them was assigned to his or her district as a direct result of having 'personally been subjected to a racial classification.'"

It is far from obvious why a purposive plan to assign voters by race made the *Sinkfield* plaintiffs' likelihood of having been assigned because of race more "hypothetical" or "conjectural" than Mr. Hofmeister's risk of personal injury from Indiana's predicted loss of a representative—except, of course, that Congress had provided for broadened standing to enforce the census statutes but not the Fourteenth Amendment. But should this distinction make a difference? The injury-in-fact requirement is said to be an Article III requirement. And, if so, the Court has not explained why, or to what degree, Congress may alter the Article III analysis of injury-in-fact by creating what we might term "interests-in-law." Following the Supreme Court's lead we will return to this question again, and again.

2. *A Special Taxpayer Injury.* Notwithstanding the Court's professed reluctance to entertain "generalized grievances," establishment clause challenges have evoked different judicial treatment. In *Flast v. Cohen*, 392 U.S. 83 (1968), the Court permitted a taxpayer suit to challenge the support of religious schools under the Elementary and Secondary Education Act of 1965. It would have been difficult, if not impossible, to demonstrate that the statutorily authorized use of public funds to support religious schools had any impact on plaintiff's personal tax bill, especially one that would distinguish him from taxpayers generally. The Court nonetheless upheld the plaintiff's standing because (a) the taxpayer alleged an unconstitutional exercise of Congress's spending and taxing powers, and (b) the challenged government program or policy invaded a "specific" limitation on those powers. Apparently, it counts as a taxpayer injury for government to violate such "specific" limits on its authority.

The seeming artificiality of these formal distinctions lead many constitutional lawyers to assume that *Flast* created a relaxed rule of standing for all establishment clause challenges. That interpretation was rejected, however, in *Valley Forge Christian College v. Americans United for Separation of Church and State, Inc.*, 454 U.S. 464 (1982). In a five-to-four opinion, the Court denied standing in a taxpayer suit challenging the federal government's donation of public property to a sectarian college. The majority declared *Flast* inapposite because the transfer of real property was based on Congress' Article IV powers over government property, not on the taxing and spending powers of Article I. True. But, so what?

FEDERAL ELECTION COMMISSION v. AKINS

Supreme Court of the United States, 1998.
524 U.S. 11, 118 S.Ct. 1777, 141 L.Ed.2d 10.

JUSTICE BREYER delivered the opinion of the Court.

I.

* * * As commonly understood, the Federal Election Campaign Act seeks to remedy any actual or perceived corruption of the political process in several important ways. The Act imposes limits upon the amounts that individuals, corporations, "political committees" (including political action committees), and political parties can contribute to a

candidate for federal political office. The Act also imposes limits on the amount these individuals or entities can spend in coordination with a candidate. * * *

This case concerns requirements in the Act that extend beyond these better-known contribution and expenditure limitations. In particular the Act imposes extensive recordkeeping and disclosure requirements upon groups that fall within the Act's definition of a "political committee." Those groups must register with the FEC, appoint a treasurer, keep names and addresses of contributors, track the amount and purpose of disbursements, and file complex FEC reports that include lists of donors giving in excess of $200 per year (often, these donors may be the group's members), contributions, expenditures, and any other disbursements irrespective of their purposes.

* * * The Act states that a "political committee" includes "*any* committee, club, association or other group of persons which receives" more than $1,000 in "contributions" or "which makes" more than $1,000 in "expenditures" in any given year. § 431(4)(A) (emphasis added). * * *

The Act defines the key terms "contribution" and "expenditure" as covering only those contributions and expenditures that are made "for the purpose of influencing any election for Federal office." * * *

This case arises out of an effort by respondents, a group of voters with views often opposed to those of [the American Israeli Public Affairs Committee, hereafter "AIPAC"] to persuade the FEC to treat AIPAC as a "political committee." Respondents filed a complaint with the FEC, stating that AIPAC had made more than $1,000 in qualifying "expenditures" per year, and thereby became a "political committee." * * *

The FEC * * * held that AIPAC was not subject to the disclosure requirements. * * * In the FEC's view, the Act's definition of "political committee" includes only those organizations that have as a "major purpose" the nomination or election of candidates. AIPAC, it added, was fundamentally an issue-oriented lobbying organization, not a campaign-related organization, and hence AIPAC fell outside the definition of a "political committee". * * * The FEC consequently dismissed respondents' complaint.

Respondents filed a petition in Federal District Court seeking review of the FEC's determination dismissing their complaint. The District Court granted summary judgment for the FEC, and a divided panel of the Court of Appeals affirmed. * * * The en banc Court of Appeals reversed, however, on the ground that the FEC's "major purpose" test improperly interpreted the Act's definition of a "political committee." * * * We granted the Government's petition for certiorari. * * *

II.

The Solicitor General argues that respondents lack standing to challenge the FEC's decision not to proceed against AIPAC. He claims that they have failed to satisfy the "prudential" standing requirements upon which this Court has insisted. He adds that respondents have not shown that they "suffer injury in fact," that their injury is "fairly traceable" to the FEC's decision, or that a judicial decision in their favor would "redress" the injury. In his view, respondents' District Court petition consequently failed to meet Article III's demand for a "case" or "controversy."

We do not agree with the FEC's "prudential standing" claim. Congress has specifically provided in the FECA that "any person who believes a violation of this Act * * * has occurred, may file a complaint with the Commission." § 437g(a)(1). It has added that "any party aggrieved by an order of the Commission dismissing a complaint filed by such party * * * may file a petition" in district court seeking review of that dismissal. § 437g(8)(A). History associates the word "aggrieved" with a congressional intent to cast the standing net broadly—beyond the common-law interests and substantive statutory rights upon which "prudential" standing traditionally rested. * * *

Given the language of the statute and the nature of the injury, we conclude that Congress, intending to protect voters such as respondents from suffering the kind of injury here at issue, intended to authorize this kind of suit. Consequently, respondents satisfy "prudential" standing requirements.

Nor do we agree with the FEC or the dissent that Congress lacks the constitutional power to authorize federal courts to adjudicate this lawsuit. Article III, of course, limits Congress' grant of judicial power to "cases" or "controversies." That limitation means that respondents must show, among other things, an "injury in fact"—a requirement that helps assure that courts will not "pass upon * * * abstract, intellectual problems," but adjudicate "concrete, living contests between adversaries." *Coleman v. Miller*. * * * In our view, respondents here have suffered a genuine "injury in fact."

The "injury in fact" that respondents have suffered consists of their inability to obtain information—lists of AIPAC donors (who are, according to AIPAC, its members), and campaign-related contributions and expenditures—that, on respondents' view of the law, the statute requires that AIPAC make public. There is no reason to doubt their claim that the information would help them (and others to whom they would communicate it) to evaluate candidates for public office, especially candidates who received assistance from AIPAC, and to evaluate the role that AIPAC's financial assistance might play in a specific election. Respondents' injury consequently seems concrete and particular. Indeed, this Court has previously held that a plaintiff suffers an "injury in fact" when the plaintiff fails to obtain information which must be publicly disclosed pursuant to a statute. *Public Citizen v. Department of Justice*, 491 U.S. 440, 449 (1989) (failure to obtain information subject to disclosure under Federal Advisory Committee Act "constitutes a sufficiently distinct injury to provide standing to sue"). *See also Havens Realty Corp. v. Coleman.*

The dissent refers to *United States v. Richardson* * * * [where t]he Court held that the plaintiff lacked standing because there was "no 'logical nexus' between the [plaintiff's] asserted status of taxpayer and the claimed failure of the Congress to require the Executive to supply a more detailed report of the [CIA's] expenditures."

In this case, however, the "logical nexus" inquiry is not relevant. Here, there is no constitutional provision requiring the demonstration of the "nexus" the Court believed must be shown in *Richardson* and *Flast.* Rather, there is a statute which, as we previously pointed out * * * does seek to protect individuals such as respondents from the kind of harm they say they have suffered, *i.e.*, failing to receive particular information about campaign-related activities. * * *

The fact that the Court in *Richardson* focused upon taxpayer standing, * * * not voter standing, places that case at still a greater distance from the case before us. We are not suggesting, as the dissent implies, * * * that *Richardson* would have come out differently if only the plaintiff had asserted his standing to sue as a voter, rather than as a taxpayer. Faced with such an assertion, the *Richardson* court would simply have had to consider whether "the Framers * * * ever imagined that *general directives* [of the Constitution] * * * would be subject to enforcement by an individual citizen." But since that answer (like the answer to whether there was taxpayer standing in *Richardson*) would have rested in significant part upon the Court's view of the Accounts Clause, it still would not control our answer in this case. All this is to say that the legal logic which critically determined *Richardson*'s outcome is beside the point here.

The FEC's strongest argument is its contention that this lawsuit involves only a "generalized grievance." (Indeed, if *Richardson* is relevant at all, it is because of its broad discussion of *this* matter, not its basic rationale.) The Solicitor General points out that respondents' asserted harm (their failure to obtain information) is one which is " 'shared in substantially equal measure by all or a large class of citizens.' " (quoting *Warth v. Seldin.)* This Court, he adds, has often said that "generalized grievances" are not the kinds of harms that confer standing. * * *

The kind of judicial language to which the FEC points, however, invariably appears in cases where the harm at issue is not only widely shared, but is also of an abstract and indefinite nature—for example, harm to the "common concern for obedience to law." *L. Singer & Sons v. Union Pacific R. Co.*, 311 U.S. 295, 303 (1940). * * * The abstract nature of the harm—for example, injury to the interest in seeing that the law is obeyed—deprives the case of the concrete specificity that characterized those controversies which were "the traditional concern of the courts at Westminster," *Coleman*, 307 U.S. at 460 (Frankfurter, J., dissenting); and which today prevents a plaintiff from obtaining what would, in effect, amount to an advisory opinion.

Often the fact that an interest is abstract and the fact that it is widely shared go hand in hand. But their association is not invariable, and where a harm is concrete, though widely shared, the Court has found "injury in fact." *See Public Citizen*, 491 U.S. at 449–450 ("The fact that other citizens or groups of citizens might make the same complaint after unsuccessfully demanding disclosure * * * does not lessen [their] asserted injury"). Thus the fact that a political forum may be more readily available where an injury is widely shared (while counseling against, say, interpreting a statute as conferring standing) does not, by itself, automatically disqualify an interest for Article III purposes. Such an interest, where sufficiently concrete, may count as an "injury in fact." This conclusion seems particularly obvious where (to use a hypothetical example) large numbers of individuals suffer the same common-law injury (say, a widespread mass tort), or where large numbers of voters suffer interference with voting rights conferred by law. *Cf. Lujan, supra*, at 572; *Shaw v. Hunt*, 517 U.S. 899, 905 (1996). We conclude that similarly, the informational injury at issue here, directly related to voting, the most basic of political rights, is sufficiently concrete and specific such that the fact that it is widely shared does not deprive Congress of constitutional power to authorize its vindication in the federal courts.

Respondents have also satisfied the remaining two constitutional standing requirements. The harm asserted is "fairly traceable" to the FEC's decision about which respondents complain. Of course, as the FEC points out, * * * it is possible that even had the FEC agreed with respondents' view of the law, it would still have decided in the exercise of its discretion not to require AIPAC to produce the information, * * * see *Heckler v. Chaney*, 470 U.S. 821 (1985), and "take no further action" on its § 441b allegation against AIPAC. But that fact does not destroy Article III "causation," for we cannot know that the FEC would have exercised its prosecutorial discretion in this way. Agencies often have discretion about whether or not to take a particular action. Yet those adversely affected by a discretionary agency decision generally have standing to complain that the agency based its decision upon an improper legal ground. If a reviewing court agrees that the agency misinterpreted the law, it will set aside the agency's action and remand the case—even though the agency (like a new jury after a mistrial) might later, in the exercise of its lawful discretion, reach the same result for a different reason. Thus respondents' "injury in fact" is "fairly traceable" to the FEC's decision not to issue its complaint, even though the FEC might reach the same result exercising its discretionary powers lawfully. For similar reasons, the courts in this case can "redress" respondents' "injury in fact."

Finally, the FEC argues that we should deny respondents standing because this case involves an agency's decision not to undertake an enforcement action—an area generally not subject to judicial review.

* * * In *Heckler*, this Court noted that agency enforcement decisions "have traditionally been 'committed to agency discretion,' " and concluded that Congress did not intend to alter that tradition in enacting the APA. We deal here with a statute that explicitly indicates the contrary.

JUSTICE SCALIA, dissenting with whom JUSTICE O'CONNOR and JUSTICE THOMAS join, dissenting.

I

It is clear that the Federal Election Campaign Act does not intend that *all* persons filing complaints with the Commission have the right to seek judicial review of the rejection of their complaints. This is evident from the fact that the Act permits a complaint to be filed by "any *person* who believes a violation of this Act * * * has occurred," (emphasis added), but accords a right to judicial relief only to "any *party aggrieved by* an order of the Commission dismissing a complaint filed by such party," (emphasis added). The interpretation that the Court gives the latter provision deprives it of almost all its limiting force. *Any voter* can sue to compel the agency to require registration of an entity as a political committee, even though the "aggrievement" consists of nothing more than the deprivation of access to information whose public availability would have been one of the consequences of registration.

This seems to me too much of a stretch. It should be borne in mind that the agency action complained of here is not the refusal to make available information in its possession that the Act requires to be disclosed. A person demanding provision of information that the law requires the agency to furnish—one demanding compliance with the Freedom of Information Act or the Advisory Committee Act, for example—can reasonably be described as being "aggrieved" by the agency's refusal to provide it. What the respondents complain of in this suit, however, is not the refusal to provide information, but the refusal (for an allegedly improper reason) to commence an agency enforcement action against a third person. That refusal *itself* plainly does not render respondents "aggrieved" within the meaning of the Act, for in that case there would have been no reason for the Act to differentiate between "person" in subsection (a)(1) and "party aggrieved" in subsection (a)(8). Respondents claim that each of them is elevated to the special status of a "party aggrieved" by the fact that the requested enforcement action (if it was successful) would have had the effect, among others, of placing certain information in the agency's possession, where respondents, along with everyone else in the world, would have had access to it. It seems to me most unlikely that the failure to produce that effect—*both* a secondary consequence of what respondents immediately seek, *and* a consequence that affects respondents no more and with no greater particularity than it affects virtually the entire population—would have been meant to set apart each respondent as a "party aggrieved" (as opposed to just a rejected complainant) within the meaning of the statute.

This conclusion is strengthened by the fact that this citizen-suit provision was enacted two years after this Court's decision in *United States v. Richardson*, 418 U.S. 166 (1974), which, as I shall discuss at greater length below, gave Congress every reason to believe that a voter's interest in information helpful to his exercise of the franchise was *constitutionally inadequate* to confer standing. * * *

II.

In *Richardson*, we dismissed for lack of standing a suit whose "aggrievement" was precisely the "aggrievement" respondents assert here: the Government's unlawful refusal to place information within the public domain. The only difference, in fact, is that the aggrievement there was more direct, since the Government already had the information within its possession, whereas here the respondents seek enforcement action that will bring information within the Government's possession and *then* require the information to be made public. * * * It is true enough that the narrow question presented in *Richardson* was "whether a federal taxpayer has standing," but the *Richardson* Court did not hold only, as the Court today suggests, that the plaintiff failed to qualify for the exception to the rule of no taxpayer standing established by the "logical nexus" test of *Flast v. Cohen*. The plaintiff's complaint in *Richardson* had also alleged that he was "a member of the electorate," and he asserted injury in that capacity as well. The *Richardson* opinion treated that as fairly included within the taxpayer-standing question, or at least as plainly indistinguishable from it:

"The respondent's claim is that without detailed information on CIA expenditures—and hence its activities—he cannot intelligently follow the actions of Congress or the Executive, *nor can he properly fulfill his obligations as a member of the electorate in voting for candidates seeking national office*.

"*This is surely the kind of a generalized grievance described in both* *Frothingham* and *Flast* since the impact on him is plainly undifferentiated and common to all members of the public." (citations and internal quotation omitted) (emphasis added).

If *Richardson* left voter-standing unaffected, one must marvel at the unaccustomed ineptitude of the American Civil Liberties Union Foundation, which litigated *Richardson*, in not immediately refiling with an explicit voter-standing allegation. Fairly read, and applying a fair understanding of its important purposes, *Richardson* is indistinguishable from the present case.

The Court's opinion asserts that our language disapproving generalized grievances "invariably appears in cases where the harm at issue is not only widely shared, but is also of an abstract and indefinite nature." "Often," the Court says, "the fact that an interest is abstract and the fact that it is widely shared go hand in hand. But their association is not invariable, and where a harm is concrete, though widely shared, the Court has found 'injury in fact.'" If that is so—if concrete generalized grievances (like concrete particularized grievances) are OK, and abstract generalized grievances (like abstract particularized grievances) are bad—one must wonder why we ever *developed* the superfluous distinction between generalized and particularized grievances at all. But of course the Court is wrong to think that generalized grievances have only concerned us when they are abstract. One need go no further than *Richardson* to prove that—unless the Court believes that deprivation of information is an abstract injury, in which event this case could be disposed of on that much broader ground. * * *

The Constitution's line of demarcation between the Executive power and the judicial power presupposes a common understanding of the type of interest needed to sustain a "case or controversy" against the Executive in the courts. A system in which the citizenry at large could sue to compel Executive compliance with the law would be a system in which the courts, rather than of the President, are given the primary responsibility to "take Care that the Laws be faithfully executed," Art. II, § 3. We do not have such a system because the common understanding of the interest necessary to sustain suit has included the requirement, affirmed in *Richardson*, that the complained-of injury be particularized and differentiated, rather than common to all the electorate* * *. If today's decision is correct, it is within the power of Congress to authorize any interested person to manage (through the courts) the Executive's enforcement of any law that includes a requirement for the filing and public availability of a piece of paper. This is not the system we have had, and is not the system we should desire.

Because this statute should not be interpreted to confer upon the entire electorate the power to invoke judicial direction of prosecutions, and because if it is so interpreted the statute unconstitutionally transfers from the Executive to the courts the responsibility to "take Care that the Laws be faithfully executed," Art. II, § 3, I respectfully dissent.

Notes

1. *May Congress Create the Contours of Article III Standing?* Commenting on *Akins*, Professor Cass Sunstein observed that:

> An especially narrow reading of *Akins* would fasten on the following sentence: "We conclude that similarly, the informational injury at issue here, directly related to voting, the most basic of political rights, is sufficiently concrete and specific such that the fact that it is widely shared does not deprive Congress of constitutional power to authorize its vindication in the federal courts." A future court could possibly read *Akins* as crucially about information directly related to voting. Such a court could plausibly say that the *Akins* Court allowed standing for citizens asserting a generalized grievance only because, and to the extent that, the injury involved "the most basic of political rights." * * *

Sunstein, however, argues for a broader, positivist view of what constitutes an injury:

So long as there is an injury, Congress can grant standing to plaintiffs even if their injuries are very widely shared. Whether there is an injury depends largely on what the law says. * * *

The most interesting questions involve Congress's authority to create novel legal interests and to give people the power to bring suit to protect those interests in court. Congress might, for example, give everyone an interest in information of a certain sort (as it did in both FOIA and FECA, and might do in other contexts as well); *Akins* plainly says that this is constitutional. If Congress can do that, perhaps it also has a great deal of room to create novel interests that do not involve information. Perhaps Congress could give all citizens a property interest in the continued existence of endangered species (making each of us beneficial owners of a particular sort), or in maintaining certain land in a pristine state, or in clean air in certain regions of the country, or in a certain kind of telecommunications market. After *Akins*, why is Congress forbidden from saying that all Americans have a property interest in clear skies above the Grand Canyon, a property interest that exists regardless of whether the citizens in question actually visit the Grand Canyon?

A possible answer—not ruled out by current law—is that such a statute would be unconstitutional because those who do not visit the Grand Canyon lack an "injury in fact." The same might be said about the hypothesized cases involving endangered species, land, and telecommunications. But if Congress says that they have an injury in fact, why should courts disagree? Note that "existence value" is often treated as a kind of property interest for purposes of environmental valuation; it is now conventional in contingent valuation studies to consider the amount that people are willing to pay in order to maintain a certain state of affairs. This very practice treats the continued existence of that state of affairs as a kind of property interest. Why can't Congress do the same thing? In any case, a property interest often is no more, and no less, than a cause of action. If Congress attempts to create a cause of action in a certain state of affairs and grants that cause of action to all Americans, there appears to be no constitutional barrier, especially after the *Akins* Court's unambiguous holding that the obstacle to generalized grievances is merely prudential. * * *

If this is true with information, why is it not true with many other interests? Why, for example, is Congress not permitted to give standing to all drivers to challenge acts that increase the risk of accidents on highways; or to give standing to parents of children in schools undergoing desegregation plans to allow them to challenge the grant of tax deductions to segregated schools; or to give standing to automobile purchasers and environmental organizations to ensure that the EPA enforces statutory requirements for fuel economy standards? The best answer is that Congress is indeed permitted to do these things. To the extent that similar cases have come out unfavorably to plaintiffs, it is because the governing statutes, interpreted in the light of relevant prudential requirements, reflect no effort by Congress to do so. *Akins* would not have had standing if Congress had denied him standing. Because of the prudential barrier to generalized grievances, *Akins* would probably not have had standing if FECA had merely incorporated the APA's standing provision. Denials of standing in cases involving novel interests foreign to the existing legal culture are therefore best understood as interpretations of the underlying statute. Congress's challenge for the future—if it genuinely seeks to grant standing—is to think of imaginative ways to create legal interests in the rights it intends to protect. With this point, we end where we began: an assertion of the primacy, for purposes of Article III, of legislative instructions.

Cass R. Sunstein, *Informational Regulation and Informational Standing:* Akins *and Beyond*, 147 U. Pa. L. Rev. 613, 645, 670–73 (1999).

2. *Legislators as Plaintiffs*. Professor Sunstein's arguments notwithstanding, Congress's instructions concerning who should have standing are not always honored. In *Raines v. Byrd*, 521 U.S. 811 (1997), the congressional plaintiffs sued to overturn the Line Item Veto Act under a provision in that statute that allows "any member of Congress or any individual adversely affected" to bring an action in district court challenging the constitutionality of the Act. The Court thus directly confronted the question whether Congress could, consistent with Article III, confer standing on these particular plaintiffs.

It held that Congress could not. In the majority's view, the injury alleged by individual representatives and senators was an injury that was neither personal to them nor concrete or particularized enough to constitute an injury in fact for purposes of Article III. In essence the Court viewed these Congress members as seeking to vindicate an incidental loss of political power that stemmed from Congress' giving the President the authority to engage in line-item vetoes of certain appropriations bills. In the majority's view all that was alleged was a loss of political power, not the loss of any private right. The majority therefore distinguished *Powell v. McCormack*, 395 U.S. 486 (1969), which held that a member's constitutional challenge to his exclusion from the House, and his consequent loss of position and salary, presented an Article III case or controversy.

The Court recognized that it had not always made a clear distinction between the personal particularized interests of legislators and their interests as members of the representative assembly. In *Coleman v. Miller*, 307 U.S. 433 (1939), the Court had allowed a suit by twenty Kansas state senators seeking to invalidate the "ratification" of the proposed "Child Labor Amendment" by the State of Kansas on the ground that an improper vote by the State's Lieutenant Governor had deprived them of the victory to which their votes entitled them. The majority thought *Coleman* distinguishable, however, because there, if the complaining Senators were correct, their votes to ratify the Amendment had been deprived of all validity. *Coleman* was said, therefore, to stand only for the proposition that legislators whose votes would have been sufficient to (approve) defeat a specific legislative act have standing to sue if that legislative action (does not go) goes into effect.

In the instant case, however, the plaintiffs were simply the losing parties in a vote by which the line-item veto statute was passed. Although the Court recognized that because of the law's passage, these plaintiffs' subsequent votes on appropriations bills would have a somewhat different meaning and effect than they had previously, it refused to accept their argument that the law so undermined the effectiveness of their votes that they obtained a personal interest in a determination of its invalidity. The majority characterized their interest instead as a concern about an "abstract dilution" of institutional legislative power that had some indirect effect on them.

The majority opinion in *Raines* garnered only five votes. Justices Souter and Ginsburg concurred specially on the broad ground that general separation of powers principles cautioned against judicial intrusion into this interbranch controversy. They recognized, indeed welcomed, the fact that a private party affected by the line-item veto of a project that benefitted them directly would almost certainly bring the matter to the Court at a latter date. But they believed that "deciding a suit to vindicate an interest outside the government raises no spectre of judicial readiness to enlist on one side of a political tug of war." They were also influenced by the fact that the presence of a private party in the suit placed the judiciary at some remove from political forces and increased the separation in time between political resolution and judicial review.

The concurring Justices found the distinction between the interests asserted by the plaintiffs here and the interests recognized as conferring standing in prior cases as extremely "nice" ones. The distinctions were entirely too nice for Justices Stevens and Breyer. The former could not conceive of how voters could have standing to pursue the question of the apportionment of their state legislature, as individual voters surely do under *Baker v. Carr*, 369 U.S. 186 (1962), and yet hold that there was no particularized injury to representatives denied the opportunity to vote on the bills that actually went into effect after the President's exercise of his line-item veto. Justice Breyer simply could find no difference between this case and *Coleman v. Miller*. Because he, like the majority, would not overrule *Coleman*, he would have found standing in these plaintiffs.

As we know from Chapter 2, *supra*, the line item veto was ultimately held to be unconstitutional. But, how the case came to satisfy standing requirements is not without interest.

Less than two months after the decision in *Raines v. Byrd*, President Clinton exercised his line item veto power. He struck one provision in the Balanced Budget Act of 1997 which would have clarified that the City of New York did not owe the Department of Health and Human Services as much as $2.6 billion in funds that otherwise would be earmarked to finance medical care for the indigent. Clinton also cancelled a limited tax benefit for owners of certain food refiners and processors that sell their stock to eligible farmers' cooperatives.

Two groups of plaintiffs claimed injury from the changes Clinton wrought with his line item veto power, and challenged the line item veto act was unconstitutional. The Supreme Court in *Clinton v. New York*, 524 U.S. 417 (1998) unanimously found that the first group of plaintiffs, the City of New York, two hospital associations, one hospital and two unions representing health care employees, had standing because New York "now has a multibillion dollar contingent liability that had been eliminated" by the provision struck by Clinton. The Court noted that "[u]nder New York statutes that are already in place, it is clear that both the City of New York and the appellee health care providers will be assessed by the State for substantial portions of any recoupment payments that the State may have to make to the Federal Government."

Seven justices also ruled that a farmers' cooperative and an individual farmer and member of the cooperative suffered sufficient injury in fact. The majority reasoned that the plaintiffs lost a "statutory 'bargaining chip' " in their bid to acquire processing facilities. The Court noted that the cooperative had "concrete plans to utilize" the benefits of the provision Clinton struck, and was engaged in negotiations with the owner of a processing plant interested in structuring a tax deferred sale. Moreover, the cooperative was "actively searching" for other processing facilities for possible future purchase if the President's cancellation were reversed. The Court concluded that the deprivation of a statutory bargaining chip "inflicted a sufficient likelihood of economic injury to establish standing." The dissenters broke with the majority's reasoning on this point, arguing that detriment to a bargaining position is insufficient to qualify as an injury.

3. *What About Article II?* Justice Scalia's *Akins* dissent echoes his oft-stated theory of plenary presidential authority under Article II to execute the laws of the United States—a theory that has never attracted the votes of a majority of the Justices. Justice Scalia's approach to standing is grounded in the notion that Article III limits on judicial power are designed in significant part to keep courts from intruding upon this executive power. The fullest explication of his views on executive authority occurs in his *Morrison v. Olson* dissent, but he has argued its implications for federalism as well, *Printz v. United States*, 521 U.S. 898 (1997) (holding it impermissible to command state law enforcement officers to implement federal law), and for so-called qui tam litigation (see Chapter 9). In *Raines*, the Court did articulate its concern that Congress might be inserting itself into the enforcement of the laws in ways that put the judiciary in the middle of interbranch political disputes. However, the majority declined to address the Article II dimensions of generalized grievances.

On the other hand, a concern about intruding on the executive power to harmonize, or attempt to harmonize, execution of the laws has clearly played a role in some cases. Recall the difficulties of the Social Security Administration, illustrated in Chapter 4, when it sought to control the policy discretion of its adjudicators. Rules were helpful but not determinative. And, attempts to manage adjudicative personnel tended to impair the independence of the adjudicatory function. As *Director, Office of Workers' Compensation Programs, Department of Labor v. Newport News Shipbuilding and Dry Dock Company*, 514 U.S. 122 (1995), illustrates, lawsuits might be an alternative means of controlling the discretion of administrative adjudicators. The case involved a determination by an administrative law judge that a particular claimant was only partially rather than totally disabled within the meaning of the Longshore and Harbor Worker's Compensation Act. When this decision was affirmed by the Labor Department's Benefits Review Board, the Director of Worker's Compensation Programs appealed to the Court of Appeals for the Fourth Circuit. The claimant herself declined to join in the appeal, but the Director claimed to have standing under the "any person adversely affected or aggrieved" language of the LHWCA because the ALJ and Review Board determinations interfered with her ability to assure that claimants received the benefits to which they were entitled.

The Supreme Court could find no authority for the proposition that an agency in its "policymaking capacity," absent some specific authorization to appeal, should be considered a person adversely affected or aggrieved because of a dispute with its own adjudicators. Moreover, the Court believed that "to acknowledge the general adequacy of such an interest would put the federal courts into the regular business of deciding inter-branch and intra-agency policy disputes—a role that would be most inappropriate."

The Court was careful to note that the United States could have a particularized interest sufficient to confer standing where it was suing in a "non-governmental" capacity. The government as a shipper by rail, for example, was entitled like any other shipper to invoke administrative and judicial protections available under the Interstate Commerce Act. See *United States v. ICC*, 337 U.S. 426 (1949). And, it was certainly true that, under certain statutory schemes, the United States has been made a party to administrative adjudicatory proceedings and given rights of appeal. Indeed, the Director of Worker's Compensation Program administrator had precisely that position under the Black Lung Benefits Act. The Director's remedy lay, therefore, with Congress—not necessarily a false hope if, as Justice Ginsburg concurring believed, Congress had made a drafting mistake in its 1972 Amendments to the LHWCA.

Associational Standing

Another way to characterize the difficulty in cases such as *Raines* or *Newport News Shipbuilding* might be that the parties serving as plaintiffs were really attempting to vindicate the rights of others. The Director of Worker's Compensation Programs in *Newport News Shipbuilding* was attempting to stand in the shoes of claimants who were not themselves parties to the litigation. And the legislators in *Raines*, who admittedly had a political, representative capacity, were instead seeking to sue as legal representatives of persons who might be harmed directly when the President wielded his new line item veto authority.

The federal courts have been cautious in allowing parties to litigate the legal rights of others. There is no absolute bar to such *jus tertii* claims, but the Supreme Court has required that certain criteria be met: (a) the plaintiff must be injured by the denial of a third party's rights, (b) there must be some obstacle to the third party's independent assertion of rights, and (c) the plaintiff must be an appropriate representative of the third party's interests. Compare *Singleton v. Wulff*, 428 U.S. 106 (1976) (permitting physicians' challenge to the exclusion of abortion services from a state Medicaid scheme on grounds of unconstitutional interference with patients' rights), with *Diamond v. Charles*, 476 U.S. 54 (1986) (denying pediatrician standing as "a doctor, a father, and a protector of the unborn" to appeal injunction against state enforcement of certain provisions of its abortion control law).

The most common examples of third-party claims in administrative law involve suits by public interest groups or industry or labor associations, and here the requirements of third-party standing are somewhat more relaxed. In *International Union, UAW v. Brock*, 477 U.S. 274 (1986), the Supreme Court had occasion to explicate its jurisprudence on the standing of associations to litigate the interests of their members. At issue was a Department of Labor guideline interpreting provisions of the Trade Act of 1974 which provided a federally funded "readjustment allowance" to workers laid off because of competition from imports. The petitioners' claim was that the Labor Department guideline improperly restricted access to the readjustment benefits. The court of appeals had held that individual union member plaintiffs could not appeal because they had not joined as party-defendants the state agencies that had denied their claims. The union was held to lack standing to bring the action on behalf of its members. The Supreme Court reversed both rulings and provided an extensive analysis of the union's standing to sue:

> It has long been settled that "[e]ven in the absence of injury to itself, an association may have standing solely as the representative of its members. *E.g.*, *National Motor Freight Traffic Assn. v. United States*, 372 U.S. 246 (1963)." *Warth v. Seldin*, 422 U.S. 490, 511 (1975). While the "possibility of such representational standing * * * does not eliminate or attenuate the constitutional requirement of a case or controversy," we have found that, under certain circumstances, injury to an organization's members will satisfy Article III and allow that organization to litigate in federal court on their behalf. In *Warth*, *supra*, we set out the nature of these circumstances:
>
> "The association must allege that its members, or any one of them, are suffering immediate or threatened injury as a result of the challenged action of the sort that would make out a justiciable case had the members themselves brought suit. * * * So long as this can be established, and so long as the nature of the claim and of the relief sought does not make the individual participation of each injured party indispensable to proper resolution of the cause, the association may be an appropriate representative of its members, entitled to invoke the court's jurisdiction."
>
> Subsequently, this doctrine was stated as a three-part test:
>
> > "[A]n association has standing to bring suit on behalf of its members when: (a) its members would otherwise have standing to sue in their own right; (b) the interests it seeks to protect are germane to the organization's purpose; and (c) neither the claim asserted nor the relief requested requires the participation of individual members in the lawsuit." *Hunt v. Washington Apple Advertising Comm'n*, 432 U.S. 333, 343 (1977).
>
> Addressing the first part of the analysis in *Hunt*, the Secretary does not dispute petitioners' claim that a large number of UAW

members were denied TRA benefits by their respective state agencies as a result of his Department's interpretation of § 2291(2) between 1975 and 1981. His argument is not that all members whom the UAW purports to represent have suffered no injury. Rather, he relies on 19 U.S.C. § 2311(d), which makes TRA entitlement determinations by state agencies "subject to review in the same manner and to the same extent as determinations under the applicable state law and only in that manner and to that extent," and maintains that not a single member of the UAW—or any other aggrieved TRA claimant—can challenge the 1975 policy directive without running afoul of settled principles of administrative finality and judicial comity, as well as statutory intent. * * *

The Secretary's arguments simply miss the point of petitioners' claims. The statutory challenges raised here will no doubt affect the outcome of individual entitlement determinations if petitioners are successful on the merits of their suit. However, this action does not directly seek TRA benefits. In accordance with § 2231(d), decisions as to the eligibility of individual claimants for benefits will remain the province of state authorities. The question is thus not whether there are any individual members of the UAW who might have circumvented state administrative and judicial processes in order to bring the claims that the UAW now seeks to litigate. Rather, it is whether there are members of the UAW who have yet to receive either the TRA benefits they believe they are due or a final state judgment that would preclude further consideration of their eligibility claims. Such individuals would have the live interest in challenging the Labor Department guidelines that would support standing in this case. And there is no question here that among the UAW's members are many such individuals. * * *

Having found that at least some members of the UAW would have had standing to bring this suit in their own right, we need pause only briefly to consider whether the second of *Hunt's* preconditions for associational standing has been satisfied here. For there is little question that the interests that the UAW seeks to protect in this suit are "germane to the organization's purpose." The UAW's Constitution announces that one of the union's goals is "to work for legislation on a national scale, having as its object the establishment of real social and unemployment insurance, the expense of which is to be borne by the employer and the government." In pursuit of that goal, the leadership of the UAW, along with other representatives of organized labor, lobbied hard for the establishment of the TRA benefit program. * * *

Relying on our decision in *Warth v. Seldin*, 422 U.S. 490 (1975), the Court of Appeals concluded that the UAW had failed to satisfy the last of the preconditions for associational standing set out in *Hunt*. In *Warth*, we noted that even where the members of an association have suffered the sort of injury that might otherwise support a suit by the association, "whether an association has standing to invoke the court's remedial powers on behalf of its members depends in substantial measure on the nature of the relief sought." An organization of construction firms, we held, could not seek damages for the profits and business lost by its members because "whatever injury might have been suffered is peculiar to the individual member concerned, and both the fact and extent of injury would require individualized proof." Each member therefore had to be a party to the suit, and the association lacked standing to proceed on his behalf. Likening the instant case to *Warth*, the Court of Appeals noted that because those UAW members "who had suffered an alleged injury had done so in varying amounts requiring individualized proof," the relief sought here could not be obtained unless "each individual claimant was a party plaintiff."

Like the Secretary in his arguments before this Court, the Court of Appeals misconstrued the nature of petitioners' claims. Neither these claims nor the relief sought required the District Court to consider the individual circumstances of any aggrieved UAW member. The suit raises a pure question of law: whether the Secretary properly interpreted the Trade Act's TRA eligibility provisions. And the relief requested, and granted by the District Court leaves any questions regarding the eligibility of individual TRA claimants to the state authorities given jurisdiction over such questions by 19 U.S.C. § 2311(d). * * *

The Secretary's presentation * * * fails to recognize the special features, advantageous both to the individuals represented and to the judicial system as a whole, that distinguish suits by associations on behalf of their members from class actions. While a class action creates an *ad hoc* union of injured plaintiffs who may be linked only by their common claims, an association suing to vindicate the interests of its members can draw upon a preexisting reservoir of expertise and capital. * * * These resources can assist both courts and plaintiffs. * * *

In addition, the doctrine of associational standing recognizes that the primary reason people join an organization is often to create an effective vehicle for vindicating interests that they share with others. * * * The very forces that cause individuals to band together in an association will thus provide some guarantee that the association will work to promote their interests.

We are not prepared to dismiss out of hand the Secretary's concern that associations allowed to proceed under *Hunt* will not always be able to represent adequately the interests of all their injured members. Should an association be deficient in this regard, a judgment won against it might not preclude subsequent claims by the association's members without offending due process principles. And were we presented with evidence that such a problem existed either here or in cases of this type, we would have to consider how it might be alleviated. However, the Secretary has given us absolutely no reason to doubt the ability of the UAW to proceed here on behalf of its aggrieved members, and his presentation has fallen far short of meeting the heavy burden of persuading us to abandon settled principles of associational standing. * * *

The Supreme Court's apparent invitation in *UAW v. Brock* to challenge associational standing by demonstrating conflicting interests within the union was seized by the defendant in *National Maritime Union of Am. v. Commander, MSC*, 824 F.2d 1228 (D.C.Cir.1987). Yet, notwithstanding the existence of some clearly contradictory interests among the union plaintiff's members, Judge Bork found that the union had standing to represent them. Indeed, he interpreted the Supreme Court's language in *UAW v. Brock* as suggesting that the problem of contradictory interests within an association should be addressed by some technique other than denying it standing. But the opinion does not rest there:

> Most, perhaps all, associations, even though created to serve the members' common interests, will have internal conflicts about appropriate organizational policies. Such conflicts are typically resolved by the association's internal procedures or political structure. Inevitably, some resolutions will harm some members' interests, but that is usually accepted as part of the cost of obtaining the benefits of association. Courts would ordinarily uphold an association's determinations against internal challenge unless it were shown that the organization's own procedures had been violated. It is not obvious to us that this rationale should not apply to an association's internal resolution of conflicts about litigating positions.
>
> This is not to say that dissenting members, who are bound by the association's decision as to the association's litigating position, are also bound as individuals. Without deciding the point, for no union dissidents are before us, several possibilities come to mind. Members, as individuals or groups, if they had standing, could intervene to advance their interests in the merits against the association's position. It may be that they could challenge the association's standing by showing that the procedures for adopting a position had been ignored. A union might present a special case of this. If a union sought a litigation victory that would harm some workers to benefit others, that might give rise to a claim by employees in the bargaining unit that the union had breached its duty of fair representation. In such a situation, the union's duty of fair representation itself, if clearly implicated by the union's requested relief, could perhaps deprive the union of organizational standing. But that duty derives from and reaches no further than the union's authority as exclusive collective bargaining representative of the employees. In this case, none of the Union's claims is within the ambit of their exclusive bargaining authority and the duty of fair representation is not implicated.

For the reasons given, we think that the mere fact of conflicting interests among members of an association does not of itself defeat the association's standing to urge the interests of some members in litigation, even though success may harm the legal interests of other members.

The associational standing cases have seldom been clear as to whether the three criteria they offer are aspects of the Article III case or controversy requirement or merely prudential factors similar to the zone of interests test. *United Food & Commercial Workers Union Local 751 v. Brown Group, Inc.*, 517 U.S. 544 (1996), faced this issue directly in the context of a union suit to recover damages for members laid off without proper notification under the Worker Adjustment and Retraining Notification Act (WARN). Lower courts had almost uniformly held that associations could not collect damages on behalf of their members because the receipt of individual damages would require the "participation of individual members in the lawsuit" within the meaning of the third prong of the test for associational standing. The WARN Act, however, clearly authorized unions to sue for damages on behalf of their members, thus raising the question whether Congress had constitutional authority to abrogate the third prong of the associational standing test.

Justice Souter, writing for a unanimous Court, held that the Act was indeed constitutional:

> There are two ways in which *Hunt* addresses the Article III requirements of injury in fact, causal connection to the defendant's conduct, and redressability. First and most obviously, it guarantees the satisfaction of these elements by requiring an organization suing as representative to include at least one member with standing to present, in his or her own right, the claim (or the type of claim) pleaded by the association. As *Hunt* is most directly addressed to Article III standing, this first prong can only be seen as itself an Article III necessity for an association's representative suit. *Hunt*'s second prong is, at the least, complementary to the first, for its demand that an association plaintiff be organized for a purpose germane to the subject of its member's claim raises an assurance that the association's litigators will themselves have a stake in the resolution of the dispute, and thus be in a position to serve as the defendant's natural adversary. But once an association has satisfied *Hunt*'s first and second prongs, assuring adversarial vigor in pursuing a claim for which member Article III standing exists, it is difficult to see a constitutional necessity for anything more.

Agency Passivity and the Search for a Harmful Act

The paradigmatic suit for review of administrative decisions seeks to relieve a plaintiff of the effects of some allegedly illegal bureaucratic action. Yet, as *State Farm, Bachowski, AHPA v. Lyng,* and other cases illustrate, administrative inaction also poses problems. Indeed, the combination of divided government, continuous expansion of both substantive and procedural implementation responsibilities, and shrinking administrative resources have made administrative inaction the critical complaint of many who rely on government programs for support or protection. As *Akins* demonstrates, when these beneficiaries seek relief, standing joins with issues of reviewability and ripeness to pose obstacles to the review of allegedly unlawful inaction. These problems are variously characterized: as a problem of "injury-in-fact" as in *Akins*, or as issues of causation or redressability, to which we will soon turn. But there also may be a prior question: whether the plaintiff can identify a particular action or failure to act that gives rise to an alleged injury.

In *Lujan v. National Wildlife Fed'n*, 497 U.S. 871 (1990), the National Wildlife Federation alleged that the Interior Department violated several environmental and land management statutes in the course of administering what the NWF called the "land withdrawal review program" of the Bureau of Lands Management (BLM).

Through various statutes, Congress had authorized U.S. citizens to acquire rights in vast portions of federally owned land, but also for the Executive to remove or "withdraw" public lands from the operation of these statutes. In 1976, Congress enacted the Federal Lands Planning and Management Act (FLPMA), to repeal many of the earlier laws and establish a coherent policy in favor of retaining public lands for multiple use management. It directed the Interior Secretary to "prepare and maintain on a continuing basis an inventory of all public lands and their resource and other values," 43 U.S.C. § 1711(a) (1982), required land use planning for public lands, and established criteria to be used for that purpose, 43 U.S.C. § 1712 (1982). It provided that existing classifications of public lands were subject to review in the land use planning process, and that the Secretary could "modify or terminate any such classification consistent with such land use plans." § 1712(d). It also authorized the Secretary to "make, modify, extend, or revoke" withdrawals. 43 U.S.C. § 1714(a) (1982). Finally it directed the Secretary, within 15 years, to review withdrawals in existence in 1976 in 11 western States, § 1714(*l*)(1), and to "determine whether, and for how long, the continuation of the existing withdrawal of the lands would be, in his judgment, consistent with the statutory objectives of the programs for which the lands were dedicated and of the other relevant programs," § 1714(*l*)(2). It was the BLM activities undertaken to comply with these various provisions that the NWF labeled the "land withdrawal review program."

NWF alleged that the reclassification of withdrawn lands and the return of others to the public domain would open the lands up to mining activities and thereby destroy their natural beauty. NWF argued that the BLM violated the FLPMA by failing to "develop, maintain, and, when appropriate, revise land use plans which provide by tracts or areas for the use of the public lands," 43 U.S.C. § 1712(a); failing to submit recommendations as to withdrawals in the 11 western states to the President, § 1714(*l*)(2); failing to consider multiple uses for the disputed lands, § 1732(a); focusing inordinately on such uses as mineral exploitation and development; and failing to provide public notice of decisions,

43 U.S.C. §§ 1701(a)(5), 1712(c)(9), 1712(f), 1739(e) (1982). It also claimed that the BLM had violated NEPA, which requires federal agencies to "include in every recommendation or report on * * * major Federal actions significantly affecting the quality of the human environment, a detailed statement by the responsible official on * * * the environmental impact of the proposed action." 42 U.S.C. § 4332(2)(C) (1982). Finally, NWF claimed that all of the above actions were "arbitrary, capricious, an abuse of discretion, or otherwise not in accordance with law." Its complaint listed specific land status determinations that the NWF sought to challenge, each of which had been taken since January 1, 1981. NWF further alleged that its members used environmental resources that would be damaged by BLM's actions. Two members filed affidavits claiming the use of land "in the vicinity" of the land covered by two of the specifically challenged land use decisions.

In December 1985, the district court granted NWF's motion for a preliminary injunction prohibiting petitioners from "[m]odifying, terminating or altering any withdrawal, classification, or other designation governing the protection of lands in the public domain that was in effect on January 1, 1981," and from "[t]aking any action inconsistent" with any such withdrawal, classification, or designation. In a subsequent order, the court denied a motion to dismiss the complaint for failure to demonstrate standing. The court of appeals initially affirmed both orders, but, on rehearing, vacated the preliminary injunction and remanded for trial on the suit for a permanent injunction.

Back before the district court, petitioners again claimed that NWF had no standing. NWF filed four additional member affidavits, which the district court rejected as untimely. On BLM's Rule 56 motion for summary judgment, the court dismissed for lack of standing. The court concluded that the two original affidavits could not sustain NWF's attempted APA challenge to "each of the 1250 or so individual classification terminations and withdrawal revocations" effected under the land withdrawal review program. The court of appeals reversed, holding both that those affidavits did confer standing and that the district court abused its discretion in refusing to permit the filing of the additional affidavits.

In a complex opinion, the Supreme Court disagreed. Because neither FLPMA nor NEPA creates a statutory right of action, NWF could achieve review under the APA only by demonstrating that it was challenging some "final agency action," and that its asserted injuries met the "zone of interests" test. The Court agreed that NWF had associational standing to represent its members. The Court also thought that each of the original affidavits could be read to complain of a particular "agency action" as that term is defined in section 551. It acknowledged that the injury established by the affidavits met the "zone of interests" test, taking FLPMA and NEPA as the relevant statutes. The Court concluded, however, that the original affidavits failed to show that the interests there described were affected by the challenged decisions.

The Court quoted with approval the district court's conclusion that one affiant had not alleged that her "recreational use and enjoyment extends to the particular 4500 acres covered by the decision to terminate classification [or] to the remainder of the two million acres affected by the termination. All she claims is that she uses lands 'in the vicinity.' The affidavit on its face contains only a bare allegation of injury, and fails to show specific facts supporting the affiant's allegation." The district court found the other affidavit "similarly flawed." The Court concluded that, at least in cases of nonstatutory review, a motion for summary judgment cannot be successfully opposed "by averments which state only that one of [the plaintiff's] members uses unspecified portions of an immense tract of territory, on some portions of which mining activity has occurred or probably will occur by virtue of the governmental action."

As to the later four affidavits, the Court reached a conclusion of potentially greater import for public interest litigation:

> It is impossible that the affidavits would suffice * * * to challenge the entirety of petitioners' so-called "land withdrawal review program." That is not an "agency action" within the meaning of § 702, much less a "final agency action" within the meaning of § 704. The term "land withdrawal review program" (which as far as we know is not derived from any authoritative text) does not refer to a single BLM order or regulation, or even to a completed universe of particular BLM orders and regulations. It is simply the name by which petitioners have occasionally referred to the continuing (and thus constantly changing) operations of the BLM in reviewing withdrawal revocation applications and the classifications of public lands and developing land use plans as required by the FLPMA. It is no more an identifiable "agency action"—much less a "final agency action"—than a "weapons procurement program" of the Department of Defense or a "drug interdiction program" of the Drug Enforcement Administration. As the district court explained, the "land withdrawal review program" extends to, currently at least, "1250 or so individual classification terminations and withdrawal revocations."
>
> Respondent alleges that violation of the law is rampant within this program—failure to revise land use plans in proper fashion, failure to submit certain recommendations to Congress, failure to consider multiple use, inordinate focus upon mineral exploitation, failure to provide required public notice, failure to provide adequate environmental impact statements. Perhaps so. But respondent cannot seek wholesale improvement of this program by court decree, rather than in the offices of the Department or the halls of Congress, where programmatic improvements are normally made. Under the terms of the APA, respondent must direct its attack against some particular "agency action" that causes it harm. Some statutes permit broad regulations to serve as the "agency action," and thus to be the object of judicial review directly, even before the concrete

effects normally required for APA review are felt. Absent such a provision, however, a regulation is not ordinarily considered the type of agency action "ripe" for judicial review under the APA until the scope of the controversy has been reduced to more manageable proportions, and its factual components fleshed out, by some concrete action applying the regulation to the claimant's situation in a fashion that harms or threatens to harm him. (The major exception, of course, is a substantive rule which as a practical matter requires the plaintiff to adjust his conduct immediately. * * *)

In the present case, the individual actions of the BLM identified in the six affidavits can be regarded as rules of general applicability * * *. It may well be * * * that even those individual actions will not be ripe for challenge until some further agency action or inaction more immediately harming the plaintiff occurs. But it is at least entirely certain that the flaws in the entire "program"—consisting principally of the many individual actions referenced in the complaint, and presumably actions yet to be taken as well—cannot be laid before the courts for wholesale correction under the APA, simply because one of them that is ripe for review adversely affects one of respondent's members.

The Court made clear that it would not reach any different conclusion if the NWF sought standing on its own, pursuant to the *Havens Realty* analysis, because BLM actions were frustrating the purposes for which NWF was organized. Even if it were satisfied that NWF had set forth injuries of this sort sufficiently concrete to be cognizable, it still failed to identify any particular "agency action" that was the source of these injuries:

[T]he "Land Withdrawal Review Program" is not an identifiable action or event. With regard to alleged deficiencies in providing information and permitting public participation, as with regard to the other illegalities alleged in the complaint, respondent cannot demand a general judicial review of the BLM's day-to-day operations.

Justices Blackmun, Brennan, Marshall, and Stevens dissented. In their judgment, the affidavits were precise enough to satisfy the requirements of Rule 56(e) to withstand a motion for summary judgment. The affidavits were at least sufficiently precise to enable BLM officials to identify the particular termination orders to which the affiants referred. The dissenters argued that the majority's characterization of the BLM land management program as " '1250 or so individual classification terminations and withdrawal revocations,' " was conclusory and bore more on the scope of the relief ultimately to be awarded should NWF prevail, rather than on the jurisdiction of the district court to entertain the suit.

It seems obvious that effective government (and our constitutional distribution of powers) can be undermined as effectively through delay and indifference as through affirmative maladministration. Yet, as the above case demonstrates, rules of standing, timing, and reviewability may combine to preclude the use of judicial review as a source of accountability when government refuses to act. Is it appropriate to remit such complaints to the political process for remedy? Could the National Wildlife Federation have sought relief through more particularized administrative and judicial proceedings?

The Court concludes that the BLM's multiple decisions do not amount to a coherent "agency action." If, however, NWF is correct in alleging failures to revise land use plans in proper fashion, failures to submit required recommendations to Congress, failures to consider multiple use as required, failures to provide required public notice, and failures to provide adequate environmental impact statements, is there not a point at which such multiple failures coalesce into a policy susceptible to legal challenge?

The immediate impact of *Lujan* on lower court decision making is exemplified by *Foundation on Economic Trends v. Lyng*, 943 F.2d 79 (D.C.Cir.1991). A nonprofit foundation engaged in disseminating information on environmental dangers challenged USDA's failure to issue an environmental impact statement (EIS) under the National Environmental Policy Act (NEPA) with regard to cutbacks in USDA's "germplasm program." That program involves the collection, storage, and distribution of plants, seeds, and plant parts for purposes of genetic research and enhancing the genetic base of U.S. agricultural crops. Upon receiving the Foundation's petition for an EIS, USDA issued a finding that its program changes had "no significant environmental impact," and that, therefore, no EIS was required. Even though USDA apparently regarded its germplasm program as a coherent program, the court of appeals held that plaintiffs lacked standing under *Lujan*: "The 'germplasm preservation program' is no more an 'identifiable action or event' than the 'Land Withdrawal Review Program.' * * * Plaintiffs fail to target their complaint to a particular proposal for federal action and fail to identify any revisions or changes * * * in the germplasm program that would trigger the obligation to prepare" an EIS.

Judge Buckley dissented on the standing issue. He thought the formal finding of no significant environmental impact was clearly final agency action within the meaning of 5 U.S.C. § 704, and that the majority pursued a "contortion" in arguing that interrelated activities that USDA itself considered a program were insufficiently concerted to be one.

On the issues raised in *Lujan*-type suits, see Henry Paul Monaghan, *Federal Statutory Review Under Section 1983 and the APA*, 91 Colum. L. Rev. 233 (1991); Note, *Preserving Review of Undeclared Programs: A Statutory Redefinition of Final Agency Action*, 101 Yale L.J. 643 (1991) (E. Gates Garrity–Rokous).

Causation and Redressability

In the Supreme Court's current formulation, a plaintiff's constitutional standing depends on two elements in addition to the presence of injury-in-fact. There must be a "causal nexus" between a defendant's alleged conduct and the injury the plaintiff had or would suffer. There must also exist a reasonable degree of assurance that the relief a plaintiff seeks would actually redress the injuries alleged. Logically, considerations of causality and redressability are often linked. A court is quite likely to doubt the efficacy of its remedies precisely in those cases in which it is uncertain that the defendant has been the causal agent of the plaintiff's injury. Yet, the requirements generally have independent significance. Compensation might redress the plaintiff's injury, even if the defendant did not cause the harm. And many harms caused by determinate individuals defy the power of lawsuits to provide redress. When unbundled, however, these two issues may seem to have little to do with standing as conventionally conceived, that is, with the question of the plaintiff's concrete adverseness or appropriateness for the vindication of largely public interests. They seem instead to go to the question whether a plaintiff can "state a claim" or "allege a cause of action," and commentators have argued persuasively that casting analysis in these terms would make better sense. See, e.g., William A. Fletcher, *The Structure of Standing*, 98 Yale L.J. 221 (1988).

The debate over how to characterize a motion to dismiss—as a challenge to "standing", "cause of action," or perhaps "subject-matter jurisdiction"—goes on inside the Court as well as outside. The Supreme Court's opinion in *Steel Co. v. Citizens for a Better Environment*, 523 U.S. 83 (1998), is a good example. The respondents brought suit under the Emergency Planning and Community Right-to-Know Act of 1986 (EPCRA), alleging that the Steel Company had failed to make required reports concerning its use and disposal of hazardous chemicals. EPCRA provides that "any person may commence a civil action on his own behalf against. * * * [a]n owner or operator of a facility for failure. * * * to complete and submit an inventory from [required by] * * * this title. * * * " Like most such citizen suit provisions, EPCRA demands that a plaintiff give notice to the public enforcement agency (here, EPA) and to the defendant sixty days prior to filing suit. Upon receiving notice of the respondent's claim, the Steel Company filed the required reports and the EPA declined to prosecute. Citizen for a Better Environment pursued its claim and was met with a motion to dismiss on the grounds that EPCRA fails to provide for suits for purely historical violations. Hence, according to the Steel Company, the respondent's allegations of untimeliness in filing were not a claim on which relief could be granted.

The District Court held for the petitioner, Steel Company, but the Court of Appeals reversed. In both those courts the legal battle was framed as either the failure of the plaintiffs to state a cause of action or the failure of the federal court to have jurisdiction under § 326(c) of EPCRA. Sections 326(c) states "the district court shall have jurisdiction over actions brought under [§ 326(a)] against an owner or operator of a facility to enforce the requirement concerned and to impose any civil penalty provided for the violation of that requirement." Because § 326(a) is the citizen suit provision, the question of jurisdiction resolved itself into the question whether § 326(a) authorized citizen suits for wholly past violations. If it did, the district court had jurisdiction over those violations; if not, the court lacked jurisdiction.

In its petition for certiorari and its brief in Supreme Court, the Steel Company for the first time argued that the respondents lacked standing to bring the action. The Court was unanimous that the Circuit Court decision should be reversed. Only six Justices agreed, however, that the appropriate analysis of the case should be based on an inquiry into the respondents' standing to sue. (Justices Breyer, Kennedy, O'Connor, Scalia, Thomas, and the Chief Justice). Three of these (Justices Breyer, O'Connor and Kennedy) thought that the majority opinion overstated the degree to which a court was required to decide a difficult standing issue when an alternative merits ground that would favor the same party was available.

Justice Stevens, Souter, and Ginsburg believed that the statute provided no cause of action to citizen groups for past violations and therefore that the district court had not been given jurisdiction to determine the claim. Moreover, they were convinced that the Court should have resolved the case on this available ground of lack of statutory jurisdiction, rather than providing an unnecessary decision on Article III standing.

When the Supreme Court produces five opinions to reach the same result one is tempted to conclude that one is witness to the proverbial "tempest in a teapot." This is especially true where, as here, Justice Scalia's standing analysis concluded that none of the remedies that the respondents sought would redress any of the harms that they had claimed to have suffered from the petitioner's prior actions. The difference between saying that, and saying that the respondents had not been given a cause of action under the statute to remedy past harms, seems vanishingly small. Moreover, both the Justices deciding the case on standing grounds and the Justices deciding the case essentially on the cause of action grounds agreed that the respondents would have encountered no "redressability bar" if they had alleged continuing violations or the imminent threat of such violations.

Nevertheless, the difference between the two positions may have substantial effects. By deciding the case on Article III "redressability" grounds the majority seems to be saying that, not only has the Congress not given citizens a right of action for past harms under the EPCRA citizen suit provision, it could not do so consistent with Article III. It is that implication that agitated those Justices who concurred only in the result. We will return to this issue shortly.

But, whatever its implications for Congress' power to confer standing, *Steel Company's* redressability analysis was conventional in requiring that plaintiffs requesting prospective relief demonstrate the probability of future harm. In *City of Los Angeles v. Lyons*, for example, 461 U.S. 95 (1983), the Court held that a victim of a police chokehold could sue for damages, but not injunctive relief. As the Court understood its standing rules, unless the victim could show a likelihood that he would be a *future* target of such a chokehold, a prospective injunction against future brutality would not remedy any injury he had alleged. Thus, in the Court's vernacular, he lacked standing to seek such relief.

In a case like *Lyons* the Court seems to be seeking to prevent the litigation of abstract policy questions, whatever the plaintiff's bitter past experience, and it seems likely that Lyons would have been unable to justify the necessity for injunction at the remedy stage in any event. But many causation/redressability cases are less easy to explain. Indeed, the Court appears markedly uneven in determining which redressability claims are too speculative to support standing.

In *United States v. Students Challenging Regulatory Agency Procedures (SCRAP)*, 412 U.S. 669 (1973), the plaintiffs, a group of environmentally concerned law students, challenged an ICC ruling permitting an increase in certain freight rates. The students alleged that (1) the ICC ruling would lead to higher rates, which (2) would lead to greater costs for users of recyclable beverage containers, which (3) would lead to more nonrecyclable packaging, which (4) would result in greater litter, which (5) would degrade the recreational areas of Washington, D.C. frequented by the students. This chain of reasoning was deemed *not* too speculative to sustain standing!

In *Japan Whaling Ass'n v. Am. Cetacean Soc'y*, 478 U.S. 221 (1986), the Supreme Court held that environmental groups had standing to challenge the failure of the Secretary of Commerce to certify, under the Pelly and Packwood Amendments, 22 U.S.C. § 1978 (1982 & Supp. III 1985); 16 U.S.C. § 1821(e)(2)(A)(I) (1982 & Supp. III 1985), that Japan's whaling practices "diminish the effectiveness" of the International Convention for the Regulation of Whaling. Plaintiffs alleged that Japan's annual whale harvest exceeds quotas established under the Convention. The Court determined that the groups "undoubtedly * * * alleged a sufficient 'injury in fact' in that the whale watching and studying of their members will be adversely affected by continued whale harvesting, and this type of injury is within the 'zone of interests' protected by the Pelly and Packwood Amendments." Without directly discussing redressability, the Court presumably concluded that the Secretary's action, if directed by a court, would so modify Japan's behavior as to assure that whale watching and study could proceed at the same level of quality. The Court ultimately held for the Secretary on the merits.

The Court has even found standing where judicial judgment could not possibly fully redress the plaintiff's injury. *Utah v. Evans*, 536 U.S. 452 (2002), involved Utah's challenge to the Census Bureau's method for filling gaps in data on households collected for purposes of the 2000 census. Using so-called "hot-deck imputation" the Bureau imputes certain relevant information by assuming that the missing information about a particular address or dwelling unit has the same population characteristics as a nearby sample or "donor" address or dwelling unit. Utah claimed that this method violated the census statute's prohibition against using sampling methods and that it violated the Constitution's requirement that the census be an "actual enumeration" of the population. The Census Bureau's "hot deck" method was destined to allot Utah one less congressional representative than if the Bureau had filled in its information gaps with zeros. North Carolina, which stood to gain a representative under the Census Bureau's method intervened in support of the federal government and urged Utah's lack of standing. North Carolina's argument was that changing the Census Bureau's methodology would not necessarily change the allocation of representatives to the states because the final determination in that matter, although based on the Census Bureau's report, was for the President and the Congress. Those parties were neither before the Court nor subject to suit to control their exercises of discretion.

The Supreme Court rejected North Carolina's argument. In the majority's view, if the Census Bureau substituted a new report for the old one, the subsequent calculations resulting in apportionment of House seats would be purely mechanical. The Court thought it unlikely that the President or other executive branch or congressional officials would not abide by an authoritative statement from the Bureau. Hence, if Utah were successful, the practical consequence of the filing of a new report using a different methodology would be to significantly increase the likelihood that Utah's claimed injury would be redressed.

Justice Scalia dissented, in substantial part because he read the census statutes differently than did the majority. Under Justice Scalia's reading there was no power in the President or anyone else to revise the apportionment specified by the Census Bureau because of technical or mechanical errors. Thus, the only way that Utah could receive one of North Carolina's congressional seats was by a new Census, in 2011, or by special congressional statute. He could not see how the petitioners could be considered likely to have their injury redressed when redress depended upon the "unbridled discretion" of a majority of 435 representatives and 100 senators, or two-thirds of those if the President did not agree.

But in a number of notable cases, the Court has found the likelihood of redress too speculative to permit standing.

In *Linda R.S. v. Richard D.*, 410 U.S. 614 (1973), the Court decided, with four justices dissenting, that an unwed mother lacked standing to challenge the failure of Texas officials to enforce the state's criminal child support statute against the father of her illegitimate children. Writing for the Court, Justice Marshall concluded:

> [W]e hold that, in the unique context of a challenge to a criminal statute, appellant has failed to allege sufficient nexus between her injury and the government action which she attacks to justify judicial intervention. To be sure, appellant no doubt suffered an injury stemming from the failure of her child's father to contribute support payments. But the bare existence of an abstract injury meets only the first half of the standing requirement. * * *

> Here, appellant has made no showing that her failure to secure support payments results from the nonenforcement, as to her child's father, of Art. 602. * * * [T]he statute creates a completed offense with a fixed penalty as soon as a parent fails to support his child. Thus, if appellant were granted the requested relief, it would result only in the jailing of the child's father. The prospect that prosecution will, at least in the future, result in payment of support can, at best, be termed only speculative. Certainly the "direct" relationship between the alleged injury and the claims ought to be adjudicated, which previous decisions of this Court suggest is a prerequisite of standing, is absent in this case.

In *Warth v. Seldin*, 422 U.S. 490 (1975), low-income and minority group plaintiffs sought an injunction against restrictive zoning practices in the town of Penfield, N.Y., alleged to deny them the equal protection of the laws. According to their complaint they all desired and had sought accommodation in Penfield, but could find no housing in a price range that closely approximated their ability to pay. The complaint further alleged that the high price of housing in Penfield resulted from a zoning ordinance and pattern of enforcement that excluded virtually all high density uses. In denying the plaintiff's standing the Court concluded:

> Here, by their own admission, realization of petitioners' desire to live in Penfield always has depended on the efforts and willingness of third parties to build low-and moderate-cost housing. The record specifically refers to only two such efforts: that of Penfield Better Homes Corp., in late 1969, to obtain the rezoning of certain land in Penfield to allow the construction of subsidized cooperative townhouses that could be purchased by persons of moderate income and a similar effort by O'Brien Homes, Inc., in late 1971. But the record is devoid of any indication that these projects, or other like projects, would have satisfied petitioners' needs at prices they could afford, or that, were the court to remove the obstructions attributable to respondents, such relief would benefit petitioners. Indeed, petitioners' descriptions of their individual financial situations and housing needs suggest precisely the contrary—that their inability to reside in Penfield is the consequence of the economics of the area housing market, rather than of respondents' assertedly illegal acts.

The low-income plaintiffs in *Warth* were joined by several groups who supported their position: (1) associations of home builders, some of whose members had been refused variances for high density housing; (2) a non-profit corporation, the purpose of which is "to alert citizens to problems of social concern," representing certain Penfield residents who desired to alleviate the critical shortage of low and moderate income housing; and (3) taxpayers in nearby Rochester who claimed that their tax rates were adversely affected by Penfield's refusal to bear its share of the low and moderate income housing burden. The homebuilders were denied "standing" on the essentially "ripeness" ground that they had no current proposals for projects in Penfield. The socially concerned corporation was found to be asserting no constitutional rights of its own or of its members—in short, it had no standing because it had no cause of action. And the Rochester taxpayers, as might be expected, failed the "causal nexus" test, not to mention the requirement of stating a claim.

Justices Douglas, Brennan, White, and Marshall dissented. In an opinion joined by Justices White and Marshall, Justice Brennan commented on the majority's treatment of the standing requirement:

> [O]ne glaring defect of the Court's opinion is that it views each set of plaintiffs as if it were prosecuting a separate lawsuit, refusing to recognize that the interests are intertwined, and that the standing of any one group must take into account its position vis-a-vis the others. * * *
>
> * * * [T]he portrait which emerges from the allegations and affidavits is one of total, purposeful, intransigent exclusion of certain classes of people from the town, pursuant to a conscious scheme never deviated from. Because of this scheme, those interested in building homes for the excluded groups were faced with insurmountable difficulties, and those of the excluded groups seeking homes in the locality quickly learned that their attempts were futile. Yet, the Court turns the very success of the allegedly unconstitutional scheme into a barrier to a lawsuit seeking its invalidation. In effect, the Court tells the low-income minority and building company plaintiffs they will not be permitted to prove what they have alleged—that they could and would build and live in the town if changes were made in the zoning ordinance and its application—because they have not succeeded in breaching, before the suit was filed, the very barriers which are the subject of the suit.

In *Simon v. E. Ky. Welfare Rights Org.*, 426 U.S. 26 (1976), the Court denied standing to an organization of low-income persons who sought to challenge an IRS change in the tax treatment of hospitals serving the poor. Under the challenged policy, a hospital would no longer need to serve indigent patients "to the extent of [the hospital's] financial ability" in order to retain its charitable exemption. The plaintiffs alleged that the change in tax treatment made it less likely that hospitals would offer such services and more likely that the plaintiffs would be excluded from hospital services. The Court responded:

> The complaint here alleged only that petitioners, by the adoption of Revenue Ruling 69–545, had "encouraged" hospitals to deny services to indigents. The implicit corollary of this allegation is that a grant of the respondents' requested relief, resulting in a requirement that all hospitals serve indigents as a condition to favorable tax treatment, would "discourage" hospitals from denying their services to respondents. But it does not follow from the allegation and its corollary that the denial of access to hospital services in fact results from petitioners' new Ruling, or that a court-ordered return by petitioners to their previous policy would result in these respondents' receiving the hospital services they desire. * * *

It is equally speculative whether the desired exercise of the court's remedial powers in this suit would result in the availability to respondents of such services. So far as the complaint sheds light, it is just as plausible that the hospitals to which respondents may apply for service would elect to forego favorable tax treatment to avoid the undetermined financial drain of an increase in the level of uncompensated services. * * *

The Court took a similar view in *Allen v. Wright*, 468 U.S. 737 (1984). There parents of black public school pupils challenged the failure of the Internal Revenue Service to adopt sufficient standards and procedures to fulfill its obligation to deny tax exempt status to racially discriminatory private schools. Writing for the majority, Justice O'Connor described the plaintiffs' injuries and their connection to IRS policies in the following way:

> Respondents allege two injuries in their complaint to support their standing to bring this lawsuit. First, they say that they are harmed directly by the mere fact of Government financial aid to discriminatory private schools. Second, they say that the federal tax exemptions to racially discriminatory private schools in their communities impair their ability to have their public schools desegregated. * * *
>
> Respondents' first claim of injury can be interpreted in two ways. It might be a claim simply to have the Government avoid the violation of law alleged in respondents' complaint. Alternatively, it might be a claim of stigmatic injury, or denigration, suffered by all members of a racial group when the Government discriminates on the basis of race. Under neither interpretation is the claim of injury judicially cognizable.
>
> This Court has repeatedly held that an asserted right to have the Government act in accordance with law is not sufficient, standing alone, to confer jurisdiction on a federal court. * * * Respondents here have no standing to complain simply that their Government is violating the law.
>
> Neither do they have standing to litigate their claims based on the stigmatizing injury often caused by racial discrimination. There can be no doubt that this sort of noneconomic injury is one of the most serious consequences of discriminatory government action and is sufficient in some circumstances to support standing. Our cases make clear, however, that such injury accords a basis for standing only to "those persons who are personally denied equal treatment" by the challenged discriminatory conduct. * * *
>
> If the abstract stigmatic injury were cognizable, standing would extend nationwide to all members of the particular racial groups against which the Government was alleged to be discriminating by its grant of a tax exemption to a racially discriminatory school, regardless of the location of that school. All such persons could claim the same sort of abstract stigmatic injury respondents assert in their

first claim of injury. A black person in Hawaii could challenge the grant of a tax exemption to a racially discriminatory school in Maine. Recognition of standing in such circumstances would transform the federal courts into "no more than a vehicle for the vindication of the value interests of concerned bystanders." *United States v. SCRAP*, 412 U.S. 669, 687 (1973). Constitutional limits on the role of the federal courts preclude such a transformation.

It is in their complaint's second claim of injury that respondents allege harm to a concrete, personal interest that can support standing in some circumstances. The injury they identify—their children's diminished ability to receive an education in a racially integrated school—is, beyond any doubt, not only judicially cognizable but, as shown by cases from *Brown v. Board of Education* to *Bob Jones University v. United States*, 461 U.S. 574 (1983), one of the most serious injuries recognized in our legal system. Despite the constitutional importance of curing the injury alleged by respondents, however, the federal judiciary may not redress it unless standing requirements are met. In this case, respondents' second claim of injury cannot support standing because the injury alleged is not fairly traceable to the Government conduct respondents challenge as unlawful. * * *

The diminished ability of respondents' children to receive a desegregated education would be fairly traceable to unlawful IRS grants of tax exemptions only if there were enough racially discriminatory private schools receiving tax exemptions in respondents' communities for withdrawal of those exemptions to make an appreciable difference in public school integration. Respondents have made no such allegation. It is, first, uncertain how many racially discriminatory private schools are in fact receiving tax exemptions. Moreover, it is entirely speculative, as respondents themselves conceded in the Court of Appeals, whether withdrawal of a tax exemption from any particular school would lead the school to change its policies. It is just as speculative whether any given parent of a child attending such a private school would decide to transfer the child to public school as a result of any changes in educational or financial policy made by the private school once it was threatened with loss of tax-exempt status. It is also pure speculation whether, in a particular community, a large enough number of the numerous relevant school officials and parents would reach decisions that collectively would have a significant impact on the racial composition of the public schools.

Justices Brennan and Stevens in separate opinions complained that the Court was requiring that the plaintiffs prove their case at the pleading stage. Justice Stevens was particularly puzzled that the Court had cited the *Bob Jones* case (which upheld the constitutionality of denying tax-exempt status to racially discriminatory private schools) while seemingly holding that allegations of injury from the provision of government subsidies to an illegal activity failed to provide an appropriate causal link between the harms suffered by the plaintiffs and the government action challenged. He speculated that the Court was in fact confusing the question whether the plaintiffs had standing with the question whether it would be willing to grant the relief that they were seeking—a nationwide mandatory injunction directing the details of IRS enforcement activity.

The Court correctly identified elements of speculation in assessing the likelihood of redressability in *Linda R.S., Warth, Simon,* and *Allen.* But was relief less likely to prove effective in these cases than in *SCRAP* or *Japan Whaling Association?* Do these holdings mask a tacit receptivity to environmental claims (a doubtful proposition because the plaintiffs lost on the merits) or judicial deference to political decision making in the areas of criminal law enforcement, tax policy, and zoning? Dean Gene Nichol has posed his own speculation starkly:

> It may well be, however, that the Supreme Court has no desire to make sense of the standing doctrine. As the doctrine presently exists, standing can apparently be either rolled out or ignored in order to serve unstated and unexamined values. And what a remarkable set of values the standing doctrine has been forced to serve.
>
> The Burger Court has raised the toughest standing hurdles in cases in which minorities have challenged exclusionary zoning practices, patterns of police brutality, and judicial or administrative bias. Poverty plaintiffs have been barred from challenging the discriminatory enforcement of child support obligations, and the tax-exempt status of hospitals that deny them emergency medical services. Litigants seeking to prevent government from contributing valuable property to a religious organization and to force public disclosure of the CIA budget have similarly fallen before an aggressive standing doctrine.
>
> On the other hand, standing requirements have been eased in cases sustaining the constitutionality of the federal subsidy for the nuclear power plant industry, upholding Secretary Watt's offshore leasing policy, affirming the propriety of tuition tax credits to private schools, and condoning government support for chaplains and Christmas crèches. One could perhaps be forgiven for confusing standing's agenda with that of the New Right.

Gene R. Nichol, Jr., *Abusing Standing: A Comment on* Allen v. Wright, 133 U. Pa. L. Rev. 635, 658–59 (1985). Fourteen years later Professor Richard Pierce undertook an analysis of standing cases at both the Supreme Court and Circuit Court levels between 1991 and 1998. In his view, judges' positions on standing were as easy to predict as the votes of their ideological counterparts in the legislature. According to Professor Pierce, all one needs to know is (1) whether the plaintiff is a beneficiary, like an environmental group, or a regulated party, like a manufacturer, and (2) whether the judge is "liberal" or "conservative.". As a stand-in for the latter two categories, "Democrat" or "Republican" works almost as well. Richard J. Pierce, Jr., *Is Standing Law or Politics?*, 77 N.C. L. Rev. 1741 (1999).

The apparent malleability of causation analysis may reflect in part the conventional legal problem of characterization. Should the Court be looking for the likelihood that the recalcitrant father or die-hard segregation academy will reform as a consequence of government action, or to the question whether government inaction has increased the plaintiff's risks of unfavorable treatment? If the latter were viewed as the appropriate way to frame the question, then the inaction complained of in most of the cases just discussed would have produced immediate injury. There may in these cases be an unexpressed oscillation between viewing the creation of increased risks of harm as harm itself, at least for standing purposes, and trying to measure the expected value of some harm whose risk has been increased, but only marginally. To the extent that the cases involve regulatory programs whose basic purpose is to decrease risk, the Court arguably should be focusing on whether the beneficiaries' risks have in fact been increased by failures of implementation because, again arguably, the statute confers a right to whatever level of risk reduction effective implementation would assure.

The question of possible harm versus certain risk is acute where the legal protections involved are largely procedural, as the next case illustrates.

LUJAN v. DEFENDERS OF WILDLIFE

Supreme Court of the United States, 1992.
504 U.S. 555, 112 S.Ct. 2130, 119 L.Ed.2d 351.

Justice Scalia delivered the opinion of the Court with respect to Parts I, II, III–A, and IV, and an opinion with respect to Part III–B, in which The Chief Justice, Justice White, and Justice Thomas join.

This case involves a challenge to a rule promulgated by the Secretary of the Interior interpreting § 7 of the Endangered Species Act of 1973 (ESA), in such fashion as to render it applicable only to actions within the United States or on the high seas. The preliminary issue, and the only one we reach, is whether respondents here, plaintiffs below, have standing to seek judicial review of the rule.

I

The ESA seeks to protect species of animals against threats to their continuing existence caused by man. The ESA instructs the Secretary of the Interior to promulgate by regulation a list of those species which are either endangered or threatened under enumerated criteria, and to define the critical habitat of these species. [Section 7(a)(2)] of the Act then provides, in pertinent part:

> "Each Federal agency shall, in consultation with and with the assistance of the Secretary [of the Interior], insure that any action authorized, funded, or carried out by such agency * * * is not likely

to jeopardize the continued existence of any endangered species or threatened species or result in the destruction or adverse modification of habitat of such species which is determined by the Secretary, after consultation as appropriate with affected States, to be critical."

In 1978, the Fish and Wildlife Service (FWS) and the National Marine Fisheries Service (NMFS) * * * promulgated a joint regulation stating that the obligations imposed by § 7(a)(2) extend to actions taken in foreign nations. 43 Fed.Reg. 874 (1978). The next year, however, the Interior Department began to reexamine its position. A revised joint regulation, reinterpreting § 7(a)(2) to require consultation only for actions taken in the United States or on the high seas was proposed in 1983.

Shortly thereafter, respondents, organizations dedicated to wildlife conservation and other environmental causes, filed this action against the Secretary of the Interior, seeking a declaratory judgment that the new regulation is in error as to the geographic scope of § 7(a)(2) and an injunction requiring the Secretary to promulgate a new regulation restoring the initial interpretation. The District Court granted the Secretary's motion to dismiss for lack of standing. The Court of Appeals for the Eighth Circuit reversed by a divided vote. * * *

II

While the Constitution of the United States divides all power conferred upon the Federal Government into "legislative Powers," Art. I, § 1, "the executive Power," Art. II, § 1, and "the judicial Power," Art. III, § 1, it does not attempt to define those terms. To be sure, it limits the jurisdiction of federal courts to "Cases" and "Controversies," but an executive inquiry can bear the name "case" (the Hoffa case) and a legislative dispute can bear the name "controversy" (the Smoot–Hawley controversy). Obviously, then, the Constitution's central mechanism of separation of powers depends largely upon common understanding of what activities are appropriate to legislatures, to executives, and to courts. In The Federalist No. 48, Madison expressed the view that "it is not infrequently a question of real nicety in legislative bodies whether the operation of a particular measure will, or will not, extend beyond the legislative sphere," whereas "the executive power [is] restrained within a narrower compass and * * * more simple in its nature," and "the judiciary [is] described by landmarks still less uncertain." One of those landmarks * * * is the doctrine of standing. Though some of its elements express merely prudential considerations that are part of judicial self-government, the core component of standing is an essential and unchanging part of the case-or-controversy requirement of Article III.

Over the years, our cases have established that the irreducible constitutional minimum of standing contains three elements. First, the plaintiff must have suffered an "injury in fact"—an invasion of a legally protected interest which is (a) concrete and particularized, *Sierra Club v. Morton*, (b) "actual or imminent, not 'conjectural' or 'hypothetical,' "

Whitmore v. Arkansas, 495 U.S. 149, 155 (1990) (quoting *Los Angeles v. Lyons*). Second, there must be a causal connection between the injury and the conduct complained of—the injury has to be "fairly * * * trace[able] to the challenged action of the defendant, and not * * * the result [of] the independent action of some third party not before the court." *Simon v. Eastern Ky. Welfare Rights Organization*. Third, it must be "likely," as opposed to merely "speculative," that the injury will be "redressed by a favorable decision."

The party invoking federal jurisdiction bears the burden of establishing these elements. Since they are not mere pleading requirements but rather an indispensable part of the plaintiff's case, each element must be supported in the same way as any other matter on which the plaintiff bears the burden of proof, i.e., with the manner and degree of evidence required at the successive stages of the litigation. At the pleading stage, general factual allegations of injury resulting from the defendant's conduct may suffice. * * * In response to a summary judgment motion, however, the plaintiff can no longer rest on such "mere allegations," but must "set forth" by affidavit or other evidence "specific facts," Fed. Rule Civ.Proc. 56(e), which for purposes of the summary judgment motion will be taken to be true. And at the final stage, those facts (if controverted) must be "supported adequately by the evidence adduced at trial."

When the suit is one challenging the legality of government action or inaction, the nature and extent of facts that must be averred (at the summary judgment stage) or proved (at the trial stage) in order to establish standing depends considerably upon whether the plaintiff is himself an object of the action (or forgone action) at issue. If he is, there is ordinarily little question that the action or inaction has caused him injury, and that a judgment preventing or requiring the action will redress it. When, however, as in this case, a plaintiff's asserted injury arises from the government's allegedly unlawful regulation (or lack of regulation) of someone else, much more is needed. In that circumstance, causation and redressability ordinarily hinge on the response of the regulated (or regulable) third party to the government action or inaction—and perhaps on the response of others as well. The existence of one or more of the essential elements of standing "depends on the unfettered choices made by independent actors not before the courts and whose exercise of broad and legitimate discretion the courts cannot presume either to control or to predict," and it becomes the burden of the plaintiff to adduce facts showing that those choices have been or will be made in such manner as to produce causation and permit redressability of injury. Thus, when the plaintiff is not himself the object of the government action or inaction he challenges, standing is not precluded, but it is ordinarily "substantially more difficult" to establish.

III

We think the Court of Appeals failed to apply the foregoing principles in denying the Secretary's motion for summary judgment. Respondents had not made the requisite demonstration of (at least) injury and redressability.

A

Respondents' claim to injury is that the lack of consultation with respect to certain funded activities abroad "increas[es] the rate of extinction of endangered and threatened species." Of course, the desire to use or observe an animal species, even for purely esthetic purposes, is undeniably a cognizable interest for purpose of standing. *See, e.g., Sierra Club v. Morton*. "But the 'injury in fact' test requires more than an injury to a cognizable interest. It requires that the party seeking review be himself among the injured." To survive the Secretary's summary judgment motion, respondents had to submit affidavits or other evidence showing, through specific facts, not only that listed species were in fact being threatened by funded activities abroad, but also that one or more of respondents' members would thereby be "directly" affected apart from their " 'special interest' in the subject."

With respect to this aspect of the case, the Court of Appeals focused on the affidavits of two Defenders' members—Joyce Kelly and Amy Skilbred. Ms. Kelly stated that she traveled to Egypt in 1986 and "observed the traditional habitat of the endangered Nile crocodile there and intend[s] to do so again, and hope[s] to observe the crocodile directly," and that she "will suffer harm in fact as the result of [the] American * * * role * * * in overseeing the rehabilitation of the Aswan High Dam on the Nile * * * and [in] developing * * * Egypt's * * * Master Water Plan." Ms. Skilbred averred that she traveled to Sri Lanka in 1981 and "observed the habitat" of "endangered species such as the Asian elephant and the leopard" at what is now the site of the Mahaweli project funded by the Agency for International Development (AID), although she "was unable to see any of the endangered species"; "this development project," she continued, "will seriously reduce endangered, threatened, and endemic species habitat including areas that I visited * * * [, which] may severely shorten the future of these species"; that threat, she concluded, harmed her because she "intend[s] to return to Sri Lanka in the future and hope[s] to be more fortunate in spotting at least the endangered elephant and leopard." When Ms. Skilbred was asked at a subsequent deposition if and when she had any plans to return to Sri Lanka, she reiterated that "I intend to go back to Sri Lanka," but confessed that she had no current plans: "I don't know [when]. There is a civil war going on right now. I don't know. Not next year, I will say. In the future."

We shall assume for the sake of argument that these affidavits contain facts showing that certain agency-funded projects threaten listed species—though that is questionable. They plainly contain no facts, however, showing how damage to the species will produce "imminent" injury to Mses. Kelly and Skilbred. That the women "had visited" the areas of the projects before the projects commenced proves nothing. As we have said in a related context, " 'Past exposure to illegal conduct does not in itself show a present case or controversy regarding injunctive relief * * * if unaccompanied by any continuing, present adverse effects.' "

Besides relying upon the Kelly and Skilbred affidavits, respondents propose a series of novel standing theories. The first, inelegantly styled "ecosystem nexus," proposes that any person who uses any part of a "contiguous ecosystem" adversely affected by a funded activity has standing even if the activity is located a great distance away. This approach, as the Court of Appeals correctly observed, is inconsistent with our opinion in National Wildlife Federation, which held that a plaintiff claiming injury from environmental damage must use the area affected by the challenged activity and not an area roughly "in the vicinity" of it. It makes no difference that the general-purpose section of the ESA states that the Act was intended in part "to provide a means whereby the ecosystems upon which endangered species and threatened species depend may be conserved." To say that the Act protects ecosystems is not to say that the Act creates (if it were possible) rights of action in persons who have not been injured in fact, that is, persons who use portions of an ecosystem not perceptibly affected by the unlawful action in question.

Respondents' other theories are called, alas, the "animal nexus" approach, whereby anyone who has an interest in studying or seeing the endangered animals anywhere on the globe has standing; and the "vocational nexus" approach, under which anyone with a professional interest in such animals can sue. Under these theories, anyone who goes to see Asian elephants in the Bronx Zoo, and anyone who is a keeper of Asian elephants in the Bronx Zoo, has standing to sue because the Director of the Agency for International Development (AID) did not consult with the Secretary regarding the AID-funded project in Sri Lanka. This is beyond all reason. Standing is not "an ingenious academic exercise in the conceivable," *United States v. Students Challenging Regulatory Agency Procedures (SCRAP)*, but as we have said requires, at the summary judgment stage, a factual showing of perceptible harm. It is clear that the person who observes or works with a particular animal threatened by a federal decision is facing perceptible harm, since the very subject of his interest will no longer exist. It is even plausible—though it goes to the outermost limit of plausibility—to think that a person who observes or works with animals of a particular species in the very area of the world where that species is threatened by a federal decision is facing such harm, since some animals that might have been the subject of his interest will no longer exist, see *Japan Whaling Assn. v. American Cetacean Society*. It goes beyond the limit, however, and into pure speculation and fantasy, to say that anyone who observes or works with an endangered species, anywhere in the world, is appreciably harmed by a single project affecting some portion of that species with which he has no more specific connection.

Besides failing to show injury, respondents failed to demonstrate redressability. Instead of attacking the separate decisions to fund particular projects allegedly causing them harm, respondents chose to challenge a more generalized level of Government action (rules regarding consultation), the invalidation of which would affect all overseas projects. This programmatic approach has obvious practical advantages, but also obvious difficulties insofar as proof of causation or redressability is concerned.

The most obvious problem in the present case is redressability. Since the agencies funding the projects were not parties to the case, the District Court could accord relief only against the Secretary: He could be ordered to revise his regulation to require consultation for foreign projects. But this would not remedy respondents' alleged injury unless the funding agencies were bound by the Secretary's regulation, which is very much an open question.* * * When the Secretary promulgated the regulation at issue here, he thought it was binding on the agencies, see 51 Fed.Reg. 19928 (1986). The Solicitor General, however, has repudiated that position here, and the agencies themselves apparently deny the Secretary's authority.

* * * Assuming that it is appropriate to resolve an issue of law such as this in connection with a threshold standing inquiry, resolution by the District Court would not have remedied respondents' alleged injury anyway, because it would not have been binding upon the agencies. They were not parties to the suit, and there is no reason they should be obliged to honor an incidental legal determination the suit produced. * * * The short of the matter is that redress of the only injury in fact respondents complain of requires action (termination of funding until consultation) by the individual funding agencies; and any relief the District Court could have provided in this suit against the Secretary was not likely to produce that action.

A further impediment to redressability is the fact that the agencies generally supply only a fraction of the funding for a foreign project. AID, for example, has provided less than 10 per cent of the funding for the Mahaweli project. Respondents have produced nothing to indicate that the projects they have named will either be suspended, or do less harm to listed species, if that fraction is eliminated. As in *Simon*, it is entirely conjectural whether the non-agency activity that affects respondents will be altered or affected by the agency activity they seek to achieve. There is no standing.

IV

The Court of Appeals found that respondents had standing for an additional reason: because they had suffered a "procedural injury." The so-called "citizen-suit" provision of the ESA provides, in pertinent part, that "any person may commence a civil suit on his own behalf (A) to enjoin any person, including the United States and any other governmental instrumentality or agency * * * who is alleged to be in violation of any provision of this chapter." 16 U.S.C. § 1540(g). The court held that, because § 7(a)(2) requires interagency consultation, the citizen-suit provision creates a "procedural right" to consultation in all "persons"—so that anyone can file suit in federal court to challenge the Secretary's (or presumably any other official's) failure to follow the assertedly correct consultative procedure, notwithstanding his or her inability to allege any discrete injury flowing from that failure. To understand the remarkable nature of this holding one must be clear about what it does not rest upon: This is not a case where plaintiffs are seeking to enforce a procedural requirement the disregard of which could impair a separate concrete interest of theirs (*e.g.*, the procedural requirement for a hearing prior to denial of their license application, or the procedural requirement for an environmental impact statement before a federal facility is constructed next door to them).[22]

Nor is it simply a case where concrete injury has been suffered by many persons, as in mass fraud or mass tort situations. Nor, finally, is it the unusual case in which Congress has created a concrete private interest in the outcome of a suit against a private party for the Government's benefit, by providing a cash bounty for the victorious plaintiff. Rather, the court held that the injury-in-fact requirement had been satisfied by congressional conferral upon all persons of an abstract, self-contained, noninstrumental "right" to have the Executive observe the procedures required by law. We reject this view.

We have consistently held that a plaintiff raising only a generally available grievance about government—claiming only harm to his and every citizen's interest in proper application of the Constitution and laws, and seeking relief that no more directly and tangibly benefits him than it does the public at large—does not state an Article III case or controversy. * * * [The Court here discusses its holdings in *Fairchild v. Hughes* (a suit challenging the property of the process by which the Nineteenth Amendment was ratified); *Massachusetts v. Mellon* (a taxpayer suit challenging certain federal expenditures); and *Ex parte Levitt* (a suit contending that Justice Black's appointment to the Court violated the Ineligibility Clause).]

More recent cases are to the same effect. In *United States v. Richardson*, we dismissed for lack of standing a taxpayer suit challenging the Government's failure to disclose the expenditures of the Central Intelligence Agency, in alleged violation of the constitutional requirement, Art. I, § 9, cl. 7, that "a regular Statement and Account of the

22. There is this much truth to the assertion that "procedural rights" are special: The person who has been accorded a procedural right to protect his concrete interests can assert that right without meeting all the normal standards for redressability and immediacy. Thus, under our case law, one living adjacent to the site for proposed construction of a federally licensed dam has standing to challenge the licensing agency's failure to prepare an environmental impact statement, even though he cannot establish with any certainty that the statement will cause the license to be withheld or altered, and even though the dam will not be completed for many years. (That is why we do not rely, in the present case, upon the Government's argument that, even if the other agencies were obliged to consult with the Secretary, they might not have followed his advice.) What respondents' "procedural rights" argument seeks, however, is quite different from this: standing for persons who have no concrete interests affected—persons who live (and propose to live) at the other end of the country from the dam.

Receipts and Expenditures of all public Money shall be published from time to time." We held that such a suit rested upon an impermissible "generalized grievance," and was inconsistent with "the framework of Article III" because "the impact on [plaintiff] is plainly undifferentiated and 'common to all members of the public.' " And in *Schlesinger v. Reservists Comm. to Stop the War*, we dismissed for the same reasons a citizen-taxpayer suit contending that it was a violation of the Incompatibility Clause, Art. I, § 6, cl. 2, for Members of Congress to hold commissions in the military Reserves. We said that the challenged action, "standing alone, would adversely affect only the generalized interest of all citizens in constitutional governance. * * * We reaffirm Levitt in holding that standing to sue may not be predicated upon an interest of th[is] kind. * * * " Since Schlesinger we have on two occasions held that an injury amounting only to the alleged violation of a right to have the Government act in accordance with law was not judicially cognizable because " 'assertion of a right to a particular kind of Government conduct, which the Government has violated by acting differently, cannot alone satisfy the requirements of Art. III without draining those requirements of meaning.' " [Citing *Allen* and *Valley Forge*] And only two Terms ago, we rejected the notion that Article III permits a citizen suit to prevent a condemned criminal's execution on the basis of " 'the public interest protections of the Eighth Amendment' "; once again, "this allegation raised only the 'generalized interest of all citizens in constitutional governance' * * * and [was] an inadequate basis on which to grant * * * standing." *Whitmore*, 495 U.S. at 160.

To be sure, our generalized-grievance cases have typically involved Government violation of procedures assertedly ordained by the Constitution rather than the Congress. But there is absolutely no basis for making the Article III inquiry turn on the source of the asserted right. Whether the courts were to act on their own, or at the invitation of Congress, in ignoring the concrete injury requirement described in our cases, they would be discarding a principle fundamental to the separate and distinct constitutional role of the Third Branch—one of the essential elements that identifies those "Cases" and "Controversies" that are the business of the courts rather than of the political branches. "The province of the court," as Chief Justice Marshall said in *Marbury v. Madison*, "is, solely, to decide on the rights of individuals." Vindicating the public interest (including the public interest in Government observance of the Constitution and laws) is the function of Congress and the Chief Executive. The question presented here is whether the public interest in proper administration of the laws (specifically, in agencies' observance of a particular, statutorily prescribed procedure) can be converted into an individual right by a statute that denominates it as such, and that permits all citizens (or, for that matter, a subclass of citizens who suffer no distinctive concrete harm) to sue. If the concrete injury requirement has the separation-of-powers significance we have always said, the answer must be obvious: To permit Congress to convert the undifferentiated public interest in executive officers' compliance with the law into an "individual right" vindicable in the courts is to permit Congress to transfer from the President to the courts the Chief Executive's most important constitutional duty, to "take Care that the Laws be faithfully executed," Art. II, § 3. It would enable the courts, with the permission of Congress, "to assume a position of authority over the governmental acts of another and co-equal department," *Massachusetts v. Mellon*, and to become " 'virtually continuing monitors of the wisdom and soundness of Executive action.' " *Allen*. We have always rejected that vision of our role:

> "When Congress passes an Act empowering administrative agencies to carry on governmental activities, the power of those agencies is circumscribed by the authority granted. This permits the courts to participate in law enforcement entrusted to administrative bodies only to the extent necessary to protect justiciable individual rights against administrative action fairly beyond the granted powers. * * * This is very far from assuming that the courts are charged more than administrators or legislators with the protection of the rights of the people. Congress and the Executive supervise the acts of administrative agents. * * * But under Article III, Congress established courts to adjudicate cases and controversies as to claims of infringement of individual rights whether by unlawful action of private persons or by the exertion of unauthorized administrative power." *Stark v. Wickard*, 321 U.S. 288, 309–310 (1944) (footnote omitted).

"Individual rights," within the meaning of this passage, do not mean public rights that have been legislatively pronounced to belong to each individual who forms part of the public.

Nothing in this contradicts the principle that "the * * * injury required by Art. III may exist solely by virtue of 'statutes creating legal rights, the invasion of which creates standing.' " Warth (quoting *Linda R. S. v. Richard D*). Both of the cases used by Linda R. S. as an illustration of that principle involved Congress' elevating to the status of legally cognizable injuries concrete, de facto injuries that were previously inadequate in law (namely, injury to an individual's personal interest in living in a racially integrated community, see *Trafficante v. Metropolitan Life Ins. Co.*, 409 U.S. 205, 208–212 (1972), and injury to a company's interest in marketing its product free from competition, see *Hardin v. Kentucky Utilities Co.*, 390 U.S. 1, 6 (1968)). As we said in *Sierra Club*, "[Statutory] broadening [of] the categories of injury that may be alleged in support of standing is a different matter from abandoning the requirement that the party seeking review must himself have suffered an injury." Whether or not the principle set forth in Warth can be extended beyond that distinction, it is clear that in suits against the Government, at least, the concrete injury requirement must remain.

Justice Kennedy, with whom Justice Souter joins, concurring in part and concurring in the judgment.

I agree with the Court's conclusion in Part III–A that, on the record before us, respondents have failed to demonstrate that they themselves are "among the injured." * * * While it may seem trivial to require that Mses. Kelly and Skilbred acquire airline tickets to the project sites or announce a date certain upon which they will return, this is not a case where it is reasonable to assume that the affiants will be using the sites on a regular basis, see *Sierra Club v. Morton*, nor do the affiants claim to have visited the sites since the projects commenced. With respect to the Court's discussion of respondents' "ecosystem nexus," "animal nexus," and "vocational nexus" theories, I agree that on this record respondents' showing is insufficient to establish standing on any of these bases. I am not willing to foreclose the possibility, however, that in different circumstances a nexus theory similar to those proffered here might support a claim to standing.

In light of the conclusion that respondents have not demonstrated a concrete injury here sufficient to support standing under our precedents, I would not reach the issue of redressability that is discussed by the plurality in Part III–B.

I also join Part IV of the Court's opinion with the following observations. As Government programs and policies become more complex and far reaching, we must be sensitive to the articulation of new rights of action that do not have clear analogues in our common-law tradition. Modern litigation has progressed far from the paradigm of Marbury suing Madison to get his commission, or Ogden seeking an injunction to halt Gibbons' steamboat operations. In my view, Congress has the power to define injuries and articulate chains of causation that will give rise to a case or controversy where none existed before, and I do not read the Court's opinion to suggest a contrary view. * * *

[JUSTICE STEVENS concurred only in the judgment, finding that the plaintiffs had standing, but that the ESA was properly interpreted not to apply to activities abroad.]

JUSTICE BLACKMUN, with whom JUSTICE O'CONNOR joins, dissenting.

I part company with the Court in this case in two respects. First, I believe that respondents have raised genuine issues of fact—sufficient to survive summary judgment—both as to injury and as to redressability. Second, I question the Court's breadth of language in rejecting standing for "procedural" injuries. I fear the Court seeks to impose fresh limitations on the constitutional authority of Congress to allow citizen suits in the federal courts for injuries deemed "procedural" in nature.

I

To survive petitioner's motion for summary judgment on standing, respondents need not prove that they are actually or imminently harmed. They need show only a "genuine issue" of material fact as to standing. Fed. Rule Civ.Proc. 56(c). * * *

The Court never mentions the "genuine issue" standard. Rather, the Court refers to the type of evidence it feels respondents failed to produce, namely, "affidavits or other evidence showing, through specific facts" the existence of injury. The Court thereby confuses respondents' evidentiary burden (i.e., affidavits asserting "specific facts") in withstanding a summary judgment motion under Rule 56(e) with the standard of proof (i.e., the existence of a "genuine issue" of "material fact") under Rule 56(c).

Were the Court to apply the proper standard for summary judgment, I believe it would conclude that the sworn affidavits and deposition testimony of Joyce Kelly and Amy Skilbred advance sufficient facts to create a genuine issue for trial concerning whether one or both would be imminently harmed by the Aswan and Mahaweli projects. In the first instance, as the Court itself concedes, the affidavits contained facts making it at least "questionable" (and therefore within the province of the factfinder) that certain agency funded projects threaten listed species. The only remaining issue, then, is whether Kelly and Skilbred have shown that they personally would suffer imminent harm.

* * * The Court dismisses Kelly's and Skilbred's general statements that they intended to revisit the project sites as "simply not enough." But those statements did not stand alone. A reasonable finder of fact could conclude, based not only upon their statements of intent to return, but upon their past visits to the project sites, as well as their professional backgrounds, that it was likely that Kelly and Skilbred would make a return trip to the project areas. * * * [T]he fact of their past visits could demonstrate to a reasonable factfinder that Kelly and Skilbred have the requisite resources and personal interest in the preservation of the species endangered by the Aswan and Mahaweli projects to make good on their intention to return again. [R]equiring a "description of concrete plans" or "specification of when the some day [for a return visit] will be" * * * will do little to weed out those who are genuinely harmed from those who are not. More likely, it will resurrect a code-pleading formalism in federal court summary judgment practice, as federal courts, newly doubting their jurisdiction, will demand more and more particularized showings of future harm. Just to survive summary judgment, for example, a property owner claiming a decline in the value of his property from governmental action might have to specify the exact date he intends to sell his property and show that there is a market for the property, lest it be surmised he might not sell again. A nurse turned down for a job on grounds of her race had better be prepared to show on what date she was prepared to start work, that she had arranged daycare for her child, and that she would not have accepted work at another hospital instead. And a Federal Tort Claims Act plaintiff alleging loss of consortium should make sure to furnish this Court with a "description of concrete plans" for her nightly schedule of attempted activities.

The Court also concludes that injury is lacking because respondents' allegations of "ecosystem nexus" failed to demonstrate sufficient proximity to the site of the environmental harm. To support that conclusion, the Court mischaracterizes our decision in *Lujan v. National Wildlife Federation* as establishing a general rule that "a plaintiff claiming injury from environmental damage must use the area affected by the challenged activity." * * * [T]he Court required specific geographical proximity because of the particular type of harm alleged in that case: harm to the plaintiff's visual enjoyment of nature from mining activities. One cannot suffer from the sight of a ruined landscape without being close enough to see the sites actually being mined. Many environmental injuries, however, cause harm distant from the area immediately affected by the challenged action. * * *

The Court also rejects respondents' claim of vocational or professional injury. * * * I am unable to see how the distant location of the destruction necessarily (for purposes of ruling at summary judgment) mitigates the harm to the elephant keeper. If there is no more access to a future supply of the animal that sustains a keeper's livelihood, surely there is harm. * * *

A plurality of the Court suggests that respondents have not demonstrated redressability: a likelihood that a court ruling in their favor would remedy their injury. * * * Petitioner officially and publicly has taken the position that his regulations regarding consultation under § 7 of the Act are binding on action agencies. And he has previously taken the same position in this very litigation. * * * I cannot agree with the plurality that the Secretary (or the Solicitor General) is now free, for the convenience of this appeal, to disavow his prior public and litigation positions. More generally, I cannot agree that the Government is free to play "Three–Card Monte" with its description of agencies' authority to defeat standing against the agency given the lead in administering a statutory scheme.

Emphasizing that none of the action agencies are parties to this suit (and having rejected the possibility of their being indirectly bound by petitioner's regulation), the plurality concludes that "there is no reason they should be obliged to honor an incidental legal determination the suit produced." * * * I wonder if the plurality has not overlooked the extensive involvement from the inception of this litigation by the Department of State and AID. Under principles of collateral estoppel, these agencies are precluded from subsequently relitigating the issues decided in this suit. * * *

In *Montana v. United States*, 440 U.S. 147 (1979), this Court held that the Government was estopped from relitigating in federal court the constitutionality of Montana's gross receipts tax, because that issue previously had been litigated in state court by an individual contractor whose litigation had been financed and controlled by the Federal Government. "Thus, although not a party, the United States plainly had a sufficient 'laboring oar' in the conduct of the state-court litigation to actuate principles of estoppel." In my view, the action agencies have had sufficient "laboring oars" in this litigation since its inception to be bound from subsequent relitigation of the extraterritorial scope of the § 7 consultation requirement. * * *

The second redressability obstacle relied on by the plurality is that "the [action] agencies generally supply only a fraction of the funding for a foreign project." What this Court might "generally" take to be true does not eliminate the existence of a genuine issue of fact to withstand summary judgment. * * *

The Court concludes that any "procedural injury" suffered by respondents is insufficient to confer standing. It rejects the view that the "injury-in-fact requirement [is] satisfied by congressional conferral upon all persons of an abstract, self-contained, noninstrumental 'right' to have the Executive observe the procedures required by law." Whatever the Court might mean with that very broad language, it cannot be saying that "procedural injuries" as a class are necessarily insufficient for purposes of Article III standing.

The Court expresses concern that allowing judicial enforcement of "agencies' observance of a particular, statutorily prescribed procedure" would "transfer from the President to the courts the Chief Executive's most important constitutional duty, to 'take Care that the Laws be faithfully executed,' Art. II, § 3." In fact, the principal effect of foreclosing judicial enforcement of such procedures is to transfer power into the hands of the Executive at the expense—not of the courts—but of Congress, from which that power originates and emanates.

Under the Court's anachronistically formal view of the separation of powers, Congress legislates pure, substantive mandates and has no business structuring the procedural manner in which the Executive implements these mandates. To be sure, in the ordinary course, Congress does legislate in the black-and-white terms of affirmative commands or negative prohibitions on the conduct of officers of the Executive Branch. In complex regulatory areas, however, Congress often legislates, as it were, in procedural shades of gray. That is, it sets forth substantive policy goals and provides for their attainment by requiring Executive Branch officials to follow certain procedures, for example, in the form of reporting, consultation, and certification requirements.

The Court recently has considered two such procedurally oriented statutes. In *Japan Whaling Assn. v. American Cetacean Society*, the Court examined a statute requiring the Secretary of Commerce to certify to the President that foreign nations were not conducting fishing operations or trading which "diminis[h] the effectiveness" of an international whaling convention. The Court expressly found standing to sue. In *Robertson v. Methow Valley Citizens Council*, 490 U.S. 332, 348 (1989), this Court considered injury from violation of the "action-forcing" procedures of the National Environmental Policy Act (NEPA), in particular the requirements for issuance of environmental impact statements.

The consultation requirement of § 7 of the Endangered Species Act is a similar, action-forcing statute. Consultation is designed as an integral check on federal agency action, ensuring that such action does not go forward without full consideration of its effects on listed species. * * *

Congress legislates in procedural shades of gray not to aggrandize its own power but to allow maximum Executive discretion in the attainment of Congress' legislative goals. Congress could simply impose a substantive prohibition on Executive conduct; it could say that no agency action shall result in the loss of more than 5 per cent of any listed species. Instead, Congress sets forth substantive guidelines and allows the Executive, within certain procedural constraints, to decide how best to effectuate the ultimate goal. The Court never has questioned Congress' authority to impose such procedural constraints on Executive power. Just as Congress does not violate separation of powers by structuring the procedural manner in which the Executive shall carry out the laws, surely the federal courts do not violate separation of powers when, at the very instruction and command of Congress, they enforce these procedures. * * *

Ironically, this Court has previously justified a relaxed review of congressional delegation to the Executive on grounds that Congress, in turn, has subjected the exercise of that power to judicial review. *INS v. Chadha*. The Court's intimation today that procedural injuries are not constitutionally cognizable threatens this understanding upon which Congress has undoubtedly relied. In no sense is the Court's suggestion compelled by our "common understanding of what activities are appropriate to legislatures, to executives, and to courts." In my view, it reflects an unseemly solicitude for an expansion of power of the Executive Branch. * * *

Notes

1. *Benefits, Burdens, and the Law of Standing.* In an article published soon after the Supreme Court's decision in *Lujan v. Defenders of Wildlife*, Professor Sunstein noted the striking similarity between then-judge and ex-professor Scalia's 1983 article, *The Doctrine of Standing As an Essential Element of Standing*, published at 17 Suffolk U. L. Rev. 881 (1983), and the analysis presented by Justice Scalia writing for the *Lujan* majority:

> Only recently named a judge, and having taught administrative and constitutional law for many years, Judge Scalia called for a significant shift in the law of standing.
>
> Judge Scalia's argument hinged on a distinction between two kinds of cases: "[W]hen an individual who is the very object of a law's requirement or prohibition seeks to challenge it, he always has standing." But standing should frequently be unavailable when "the plaintiff is complaining of an agency's unlawful failure to impose a requirement or prohibition upon someone else." In the latter case, Judge Scalia contended that there was a serious interference with executive power. Judge Scalia concluded that in cases of the latter sort, courts should hold that Article III imposes "a limit upon even the power of Congress

to convert generalized benefits into legal rights. * * * " The Court had not addressed this important and long-disputed issue before.

In 1992, Justice Antonin Scalia wrote the dramatic opinion for the Supreme Court in *Lujan v. Defenders of Wildlife*, which significantly shifts the law of standing. The opinion hinges on a distinction between two kinds of cases. "When * * * the plaintiff is himself an object of the action (or forgone action) at issue * * * there is ordinarily little question" that he has standing. "When, however * * * a plaintiff's asserted injury arises from the government's allegedly unlawful regulation (or lack of regulation) of someone else, much more is needed." In the latter case, there is the risk of serious interference with executive power, in the form of a "transfer from the President to the courts" of "the Chief Executive's most important constitutional duty," to "take Care that the Laws be faithfully executed." Through Justice Scalia's opinion, the Court held that Article III required invalidation of an explicit congressional grant of standing to "citizens." The Court had not answered this question before.

Lujan may well be one of the most important standing cases since World War II. Read for all it is worth, the decision invalidates the large number of statutes in which Congress has attempted to use the "citizen-suit" device as a mechanism for controlling unlawfully inadequate enforcement of the law. Indeed, the decision ranks among the most important in history in terms of the sheer number of federal statutes that it apparently has invalidated. The citizen suit has becomes a staple of federal environmental law in particular: nearly every major environmental statute provides for citizen standing. The place of the citizen in environmental and regulatory law has now been drawn into sharp question.

Cass R. Sunstein, *What's Standing After* Lujan? *Of Citizen's Suits "Injuries" and Article III*, 91 Mich. L. Rev. 163, 164–66 (1992).

2. *Why* Lujan *Might Matter*. One of the most influential analytic constructs in modern political science is James Q. Wilson's categorization of statutes according to whether their benefits and burdens are concentrated or diffused. JAMES Q. WILSON, POLITICAL ORGANIZATIONS (1973). In Wilson's typology, statutes are of four types: those offering diffuse benefits and diffuse burdens, such as national defense; those providing both concentrated benefits and concentrated burdens, like labor relations regulation; those featuring concentrated benefits and diffuse burdens, such as local pork barrel projects supported by general taxation; and those providing diffuse benefits but imposing concentrated burdens, such as much consumer protection and health and safety legislation.

In Wilson's analysis, each type of statute creates a distinctive form of politics and allows us to assess the difficulty of enacting and implementing each form. For example, bills providing concentrated benefits with diffuse burdens should be supported intensely by those who will prosper by their passage and meet little opposition; it will not be in the interests of the diffuse constituency of potential taxpayers to organize to defeat the legislation. The same intense interests that promote the passage of such legislation can be expected to take continuous action at the administrative level to ensure that the benefits promised are in fact provided.

By contrast, statutes providing diffuse benefits, but imposing concentrated costs, will be strongly opposed by those who are predictably harmed and only weakly supported by the diffuse set of beneficiaries who stand to realize some small gain from their passage and implementation. To be sure, such statutes may pass as an expression of "entrepreneurial" or "movement" politics. But, at the implementation stage those who must pay the costs will remain vigilant (if not obstructionist) while the beneficiaries may lose energy or interest once the leader of the cause has gone on to other issues and ideological fervor has waned.

From this latter perspective, it may seem especially important that virtually any potential beneficiary, and particularly beneficiary groups organized to carry on the battle for environmental protection or consumer welfare, be empowered to sue administrators whose energy lags as their statutes age and opposition becomes more persistent and sophisticated. Citizen suits may seem essential to assure that broad protective statutes do not become memorials to dashed hopes and disappointed expectations. It was precisely this expectation that caused supporters to lobby for citizen suit provisions in modern environmental statutes and, presumably, it was congressional recognition of this danger that led to their widespread adoption in the 1970s and 1980s.

3. *"Citizen Suits" and the Separation of Powers.* As the next case demonstrates, *Lujan v. Defenders of Wildlife* has not "been read for all it is worth." Its more general language was called sharply into question by Justice Blackmun's dissent and by the many articles (other than Sunstein's) that criticized both *Lujan's* rhetoric and its result. Note, moreover, that Justices Kennedy and Souter concur on narrow grounds that do not endorse the broad language of Parts II and IV of the Scalia opinion—the parts quoted by Sunstein. In short, Justice Scalia's attempt to limit beneficiary enforcement, by using the injury-in-fact criterion created by Justice Douglas in *ADAPSO* for precisely the opposite purpose, remains controversial on the Supreme Court, not just among commentators.

Indeed, the Court upheld standing just five years later in an Endangered Species Act suit that seemed to rest on a remedial theory no less speculative than the one advanced in *Lujan*:

> The plaintiffs in *Bennett v. Spear*[23] were two water districts in Oregon and two ranchers in those districts. The plaintiffs sought to challenge a so-called "Biological Opinion" issued by the Fish and Wildlife Service, which concluded that continued operation of a particular irrigation project by the Bureau of Reclamation would likely jeopardize the continued existence of two endangered species of fish. As required by law, the Opinion also identified "reasonable and prudent alternatives" that would avoid jeopardy to the fish habitat, including the maintenance of minimum water levels on two particular reservoirs. The Bureau indicated its intention to follow such alternatives. The plaintiffs argued that the Opinion was unsubstantiated and that conducting the project

23. 520 U.S. 154 (1997).

under the Opinion would reduce the level of available irrigation water and otherwise harm their use of the reservoirs for "recreational, aesthetic and commercial purposes." The Government responded that the plaintiffs had failed to show injury, causality or redressability. In particular, the plaintiffs had not demonstrated that an aggregate diminution in water levels would result in less water going to the plaintiffs. Moreover, any reduction in water level was the result, the Government said, not of the Biological Opinion of the Fish and Wildlife Service, but, rather, of the Reclamation Bureau's independent determination to follow that opinion, which, technically speaking, was not legally compelled. Finally, even if the Opinion were set aside in Court, the Bureau would retain the legal discretion to retain only minimum water levels in the reservoirs.

Justice Scalia, again writing for a majority, nonetheless found that the plaintiffs had standing. Although plaintiffs had not yet shown specific facts to demonstrate that their own water supply would be reduced by the challenged actions, their standing had been dismissed at the pleading stage, where the only question posed should have been whether the complaint stated facts sufficient to make the claim of injury plausible. Plaintiffs met this test.[24] As for the prospect that the Bureau of Reclamation could or would ignore the challenged Biological Opinion and make its own determination of how to proceed, Justice Scalia found that the FWS Biological Opinion had a sufficient impact in affecting the Bureau's legal options to have the requisite causal nexus to any decision to limit reservoir water levels.[25] Moreover, the Bureau's consistent practice of operating the reservoirs at higher levels before the opinion provided a sufficient guarantee of redressability—namely, that the Bureau would maintain high water levels if the Biological Opinion were invalidated.[26]

Bennett was a striking decision, in part, because the Endangered Species Act provisions at stake were the same as those implicated in *Lujan v. Defenders of Wildlife*.* * * Of course, the overall significance of *Bennett* might be limited by the fact that, unlike *Lujan*, which reviewed plaintiffs' standing at the summary judgment stage, *Bennett* involved dismissal at the complaint stage, when the plaintiffs' burden of going forward is less onerous. But * * * a unanimous decision upholding standing in a case where causality and redressability were non-obvious could not help but suggest some limits to the most draconian reading of *Lujan*.

Peter M. Shane, *Returning Separation of Powers Analysis to Its Normative Roots: The Constitutionality of Qui Tam Actions and Other Private Suits to Enforce Civil Penalties*, 20 Envtl. L. Rep. 11,081, 11,089–90 (2000).

Yet, it would not be difficult to describe the path of the Supreme Court's standing jurisprudence from *ADAPSO* to *Lujan* as validating Justice Scalia's basic premise. Directly regulated parties seldom have a standing problem. Nor, as *Bennett v. Spear* illustrates, do those adversely affected by regulatory action although not its addressees. On the other hand beneficiaries, like the

24. Id. at 168.

25. Id. at 168–70.

26. Id. at 170–71.

Lujan plaintiffs, who seek to make regulatory systems have more bite, have often failed to demonstrate the requisite "injury-in-fact." Whether this state of affairs should, or indeed must, be the case is difficult to discern from the design of the Constitution. Justice Scalia's thrust, that limitations on judicial power are necessary to protect the executive power conferred by Article II, confronts Justice Blackmun's parry that judicial review to insure the legality of executive action is critical to preserving the legislative power conferred by Article I.

Adjudicating between these positions is hardly easy. One might surely wonder whether the chief executive's power to execute the law is meant under our constitutional scheme to be policed only by those who oppose rather than those who support the vigorous implementation of statutes. The Constitution may presume such a scheme, but if so, one is tempted to conclude that the presumption is to be found somewhere other than Article II. After all, the President's obligation to "take care that the laws be faithfully executed" seems to make underenforcement a constitutional problem as troubling as overenforcement. On the other hand, it is hardly an argument for Justice Blackmun's position that turning every citizen loose on the executive by means of citizen suits would help Congress in its continuous policy struggles with the Executive Branch. That this might please the assembly exercising Article I power does not mean that it is a part of the constitutional design. It is tempting, therefore, to suggest that talk of Article I and Article II powers, and of the balance of power between Congress and the Chief Executive, should be put aside in standing analysis. Discovering the limits of the judicial power under Article III is the constitutional business of standing doctrine. But this tidy allocation of separation of powers considerations becomes more tenuous where the "standing" conferred by statute permits not only judicial review of administrative action, but also private enforcement of public law.

However, before leaving the subjects of executive and legislative power, it may be useful to think about the ways in which beneficiary enforcement, or its absence, fit our modern understandings of the workings of legislatures and bureaucracies.

FRIENDS OF THE EARTH, INC. v. LAIDLAW ENVIRONMENTAL SERVICES

Supreme Court of the United States, 2000.
528 U.S. 167, 120 S.Ct. 693, 145 L.Ed.2d 610.

JUSTICE GINSBURG delivered the opinion of the Court.

I

In 1972, Congress enacted the Clean Water Act (Act), also known as the Federal Water Pollution Control Act. Section 402 of the Act provides for the issuance, by the Administrator of the Environmental Protection Agency (EPA) or by authorized States, of National Pollutant Discharge Elimination System (NPDES) permits. NPDES permits impose limitations on the discharge of pollutants, and establish related monitoring and reporting requirements, in order to improve the cleanliness and safety of the Nation's waters. * * *

Under § 505(a) of the Act, a suit to enforce any limitation in an NPDES permit may be brought by any "citizen," defined as "a person or persons having an interest which is or may be adversely affected." Sixty days before initiating a citizen suit, however, the would-be plaintiff must give notice of the alleged violation to the EPA, the State in which the alleged violation occurred, and the alleged violator. * * * The Act also bars a citizen from suing if the EPA or the State has already commenced, and is "diligently prosecuting," an enforcement action.

The Act authorizes district courts in citizen-suit proceedings to enter injunctions and to assess civil penalties, which are payable to the United States Treasury. * * * In addition, the court "may award costs of litigation (including reasonable attorney and expert witness fees) to any prevailing or substantially prevailing party, whenever the court determines such award is appropriate."

In 1986, defendant-respondent Laidlaw Environmental Services (TOC), Inc., bought a hazardous waste incinerator facility in Roebuck, South Carolina, that included a wastewater treatment plant. * * * Shortly after Laidlaw acquired the facility, the South Carolina Department of Health and Environmental Control (DHEC) * * * granted Laidlaw an NPDES permit authorizing the company to discharge treated water into the North Tyger River. The permit, which became effective on January 1, 1987, placed limits on Laidlaw's discharge of several pollutants into the river, including—of particular relevance to this case—mercury, an extremely toxic pollutant. * * * Once it received its permit, Laidlaw began to discharge various pollutants into the waterway; repeatedly, Laidlaw's discharges exceeded the limits set by the permit. * * * The District Court later found that Laidlaw had violated the mercury limits on 489 occasions between 1987 and 1995.

On April 10, 1992, plaintiff-petitioners Friends of the Earth (FOE) and Citizens Local Environmental Action Network, Inc. (CLEAN) (referred to collectively in this opinion, together with later joined plaintiff-petitioner Sierra Club, as "FOE") took the preliminary step necessary to the institution of litigation. They sent a letter to Laidlaw notifying the company of their intention to file a citizen suit against it under § 505(a) of the Act after the expiration of the requisite 60–day notice period, i.e., on or after June 10, 1992. Laidlaw's lawyer then contacted DHEC to ask whether DHEC would consider filing a lawsuit against Laidlaw. The District Court later found that Laidlaw's reason for requesting that DHEC file a lawsuit against it was to bar FOE's proposed citizen suit. * * * DHEC agreed to file a lawsuit against Laidlaw; the company's lawyer then drafted the complaint for DHEC and paid the filing fee. On June 9, 1992, the last day before FOE's 60–day notice period expired, DHEC and Laidlaw reached a settlement requiring Laidlaw to pay $100,000 in civil penalties and to make " 'every effort' " to comply with its permit obligations.

On June 12, 1992, FOE filed this citizen suit against Laidlaw under § 505(a) of the Act, alleging noncompliance with the NPDES permit and seeking declaratory and injunctive relief and an award of civil penalties. Laidlaw moved for summary judgment on the ground that FOE had failed to present evidence demonstrating injury in fact, and therefore lacked Article III standing to bring the lawsuit. In opposition to this motion, FOE submitted affidavits and deposition testimony from members of the plaintiff organizations. The record before the District Court also included affidavits from the organizations' members submitted by FOE in support of an earlier motion for preliminary injunctive relief. After examining this evidence, the District Court denied Laidlaw's summary judgment motion, finding—albeit "by the very slimmest of margins"—that FOE had standing to bring the suit.

Laidlaw also moved to dismiss the action on the ground that the citizen suit was barred by DHEC's prior action against the company. The United States, appearing as amicus curiae, joined FOE in opposing the motion. After an extensive analysis of the Laidlaw–DHEC settlement and the circumstances under which it was reached, the District Court held that DHEC's action against Laidlaw had not been "diligently prosecuted"; consequently, the court allowed FOE's citizen suit to proceed. The record indicates that after FOE initiated the suit, but before the District Court rendered judgment, Laidlaw violated the mercury discharge limitation in its permit 13 times. The District Court also found that Laidlaw had committed 13 monitoring and 10 reporting violations during this period. The last recorded mercury discharge violation occurred in January 1995, long after the complaint was filed but about two years before judgment was rendered.

On January 22, 1997, the District Court issued its judgment. It found that Laidlaw had gained a total economic benefit of $1,092,581 as a result of its extended period of noncompliance with the mercury discharge limit in its permit. The court concluded, however, that a civil penalty of $405,800 was adequate in light of the guiding factors listed in 33 U.S.C. § 1319(d). In particular, the District Court stated that the lesser penalty was appropriate taking into account the judgment's "total deterrent effect." In reaching this determination, the court "considered that Laidlaw will be required to reimburse plaintiffs for a significant amount of legal fees." The court declined to grant FOE's request for injunctive relief, stating that an injunction was inappropriate because "Laidlaw has been in substantial compliance with all parameters in its NPDES permit since at least August 1992."

FOE appealed the District Court's civil penalty judgment, arguing that the penalty was inadequate, but did not appeal the denial of declaratory or injunctive relief. Laidlaw cross-appealed, arguing, among other things, that FOE lacked standing to bring the suit and that DHEC's action qualified as a diligent prosecution precluding FOE's litigation. The United States continued to participate as *amicus curiae* in support of FOE.

On July 16, 1998, the Court of Appeals for the Fourth Circuit * * * assumed without deciding that FOE initially had standing to bring the action, but went on to hold that the case had become moot. The appellate court stated, first, that the elements of Article III standing—injury, causation, and redressability—must persist at every stage of review, or else the action becomes moot. Citing our decision in *Steel Co.*, the Court of Appeals reasoned that the case had become moot because "the only remedy currently available to [FOE]—civil penalties payable to the government—would not redress any injury [FOE has] suffered." The court therefore vacated the District Court's order and remanded with instructions to dismiss the action. In a footnote, the Court of Appeals added that FOE's "failure to obtain relief on the merits of [its] claims precludes any recovery of attorneys' fees or other litigation costs because such an award is available only to a 'prevailing or substantially prevailing party.' "

According to Laidlaw, after the Court of Appeals issued its decision but before this Court granted certiorari, the entire incinerator facility in Roebuck was permanently closed, dismantled, and put up for sale, and all discharges from the facility permanently ceased. * * *

II

The Constitution's case-or-controversy limitation on federal judicial authority, Art. III, § 2, underpins both our standing and our mootness jurisprudence, but the two inquiries differ in respects critical to the proper resolution of this case, so we address them separately. Because the Court of Appeals was persuaded that the case had become moot and so held, it simply assumed without deciding that FOE had initial standing. But because we hold that the Court of Appeals erred in declaring the case moot, we have an obligation to assure ourselves that FOE had Article III standing at the outset of the litigation. * * *

In *Lujan v. Defenders of Wildlife*, we held that, to satisfy Article III's standing requirements, a plaintiff must show (1) it has suffered an "injury in fact" that is (a) concrete and particularized and (b) actual or imminent, not conjectural or hypothetical; (2) the injury is fairly traceable to the challenged action of the defendant; and (3) it is likely, as opposed to merely speculative, that the injury will be redressed by a favorable decision. An association has standing to bring suit on behalf of its members when its members would otherwise have standing to sue in their own right, the interests at stake are germane to the organization's purpose, and neither the claim asserted nor the relief requested requires the participation of individual members in the lawsuit. *Hunt v. Washington State Apple Advertising Comm'n.* * * *

The relevant showing for purposes of Article III standing, however, is not injury to the environment but injury to the plaintiff. To insist upon the former rather than the latter as part of the standing inquiry is to raise the standing hurdle higher than the necessary showing for success on the merits in an action alleging noncompliance with an NPDES permit. Focusing properly on injury to the plaintiff, the District Court found that FOE had demonstrated sufficient injury to establish standing. For example, FOE member Kenneth Lee Curtis averred in affidavits that he lived a half-mile from Laidlaw's facility; that he occasionally drove over the North Tyger River, and that it looked and smelled polluted; and that he would like to fish, camp, swim, and picnic in and near the river between 3 and 15 miles downstream from the facility, as he did when he was a teenager, but would not do so because he was concerned that the water was polluted by Laidlaw's discharges. Curtis reaffirmed these statements in extensive deposition testimony. For example, he testified that he would like to fish in the river at a specific spot he used as a boy, but that he would not do so now because of his concerns about Laidlaw's discharges.

Other members presented evidence to similar effect. * * *

These sworn statements, as the District Court determined, adequately documented injury in fact. We have held that environmental plaintiffs adequately allege injury in fact when they aver that they use the affected area and are persons "for whom the aesthetic and recreational values of the area will be lessened" by the challenged activity. *Sierra Club v. Morton.*

Our decision in *Lujan v. National Wildlife Federation*, 497 U.S. 871 (1990), is not to the contrary. In that case an environmental organization assailed the Bureau of Land Management's "land withdrawal review program," a program covering millions of acres, alleging that the program illegally opened up public lands to mining activities. * * * We held that the plaintiff could not survive the summary judgment motion merely by offering "averments which state only that one of [the organization's] members uses unspecified portions of an immense tract of territory, on some portions of which mining activity has occurred or probably will occur by virtue of the governmental action."

In contrast, the affidavits and testimony presented by FOE in this case assert that Laidlaw's discharges, and the affiant members' reasonable concerns about the effects of those discharges, directly affected those affiants' recreational, aesthetic, and economic interests. * * *

Los Angeles v. Lyons, 461 U.S. 95 (1983), relied on by the dissent, does not weigh against standing in this case. In *Lyons*, we held that a plaintiff lacked standing to seek an injunction against the enforcement of a police chokehold policy because he could not credibly allege that he faced a realistic threat from the policy. In the footnote from *Lyons* cited by the dissent, we noted that "the reasonableness of Lyons' fear is dependent upon the likelihood of a recurrence of the allegedly unlawful conduct," and that his "subjective apprehensions" that such a recurrence would even take place were not enough to support standing. Here, in contrast, it is undisputed that Laidlaw's unlawful conduct—discharging pollutants in excess of permit limits—was occurring at the time the complaint was filed. Under *Lyons*, then, the only "subjective" issue here is "the reasonableness of [the] fear" that led the affiants to respond to that concededly ongoing conduct by refraining from use of the North Tyger River and surrounding areas. Unlike the dissent, we see nothing "improbable" about the proposition that a company's continuous and pervasive illegal discharges of pollutants into a river would cause nearby residents to curtail their recreational use of that waterway and would subject them to other economic and aesthetic harms. The proposition is entirely reasonable, the District Court found it was true in this case, and that is enough for injury in fact.

Laidlaw argues next that even if FOE had standing to seek injunctive relief, it lacked standing to seek civil penalties. Here the asserted defect is not injury but redressability. Civil penalties offer no redress to private plaintiffs, Laidlaw argues, because they are paid to the government, and therefore a citizen plaintiff can never have standing to seek them.

Laidlaw is right to insist that a plaintiff must demonstrate standing separately for each form of relief sought. But it is wrong to maintain that citizen plaintiffs facing ongoing violations never have standing to seek civil penalties.

We have recognized on numerous occasions that "all civil penalties have some deterrent effect." More specifically, Congress has found that civil penalties in Clean Water Act cases do more than promote immediate compliance by limiting the defendant's economic incentive to delay its attainment of permit limits; they also deter future violations. * * *

The dissent argues that it is the availability rather than the imposition of civil penalties that deters any particular polluter from continuing to pollute. This argument misses the mark in two ways. First, it overlooks the interdependence of the availability and the imposition; a threat has no deterrent value unless it is credible that it will be carried out. Second, it is reasonable for Congress to conclude that an actual award of civil penalties does in fact bring with it a significant quantum of deterrence over and above what is achieved by the mere prospect of such penalties. A would-be polluter may or may not be dissuaded by the existence of a remedy on the books, but a defendant once hit in its pocketbook will surely think twice before polluting again.[2]

In this case we need not explore the outer limits of the principle that civil penalties provide sufficient deterrence to support redressability. Here, the civil penalties sought by FOE carried with them a deterrent effect that made it likely, as opposed to merely speculative, that the penalties would redress FOE's injuries by abating current violations and preventing future ones—as the District Court reasonably found when it assessed a penalty of $405,800.

2. The dissent suggests that there was little deterrent work for civil penalties to do in this case because the lawsuit brought against Laidlaw by DHEC had already pushed the level of deterrence to "near the top of the graph." This suggestion ignores the District Court's specific finding that the penalty agreed to by Laidlaw and DHEC was far too low to remove Laidlaw's economic benefit from noncompliance, and thus was inadequate to deter future violations. And it begins to look especially far-fetched when one recalls that Laidlaw itself prompted the DHEC lawsuit, paid the filing fee, and drafted the complaint.

Laidlaw contends that the reasoning of our decision in *Steel Co.* directs the conclusion that citizen plaintiffs have no standing to seek civil penalties under the Act. We disagree. *Steel Co.* established that citizen suitors lack standing to seek civil penalties for violations that have abated by the time of suit. We specifically noted in that case that there was no allegation in the complaint of any continuing or imminent violation, and that no basis for such an allegation appeared to exist. In short, *Steel Co.* held that private plaintiffs, unlike the Federal Government, may not sue to assess penalties for wholly past violations, but our decision in that case did not reach the issue of standing to seek penalties for violations that are ongoing at the time of the complaint and that could continue into the future if undeterred.[4]

Satisfied that FOE has standing under Article III to bring this action, we turn to the question of mootness.

The only conceivable basis for a finding of mootness in this case is Laidlaw's voluntary conduct—either its achievement by August 1992 of substantial compliance with its NPDES permit or its more recent shutdown of the Roebuck facility. It is well settled that "a defendant's voluntary cessation of a challenged practice does not deprive a federal court of its power to determine the legality of the practice." "If it did, the courts would be compelled to leave 'the defendant * * * free to return to his old ways.' " In accordance with this principle, the standard we have announced for determining whether a case has been mooted by the defendant's voluntary conduct is stringent: "A case might become moot if subsequent events made it absolutely clear that the allegedly wrongful behavior could not reasonably be expected to recur." *United States v. Concentrated Phosphate Export Assn, Inc.*, 393 U.S. 199, 203 (1968). The "heavy burden of persuading" the court that the challenged conduct cannot reasonably be expected to start up again lies with the party asserting mootness.

4. In insisting that the redressability requirement is not met, the dissent relies heavily on *Linda R. S. v. Richard D.*, 410 U.S. 614 (1973). That reliance is sorely misplaced. In *Linda R. S.*, the mother of an out-of-wedlock child filed suit to force a district attorney to bring a criminal prosecution against the absentee father for failure to pay child support. In finding that the mother lacked standing to seek this extraordinary remedy, the Court drew attention to "the special status of criminal prosecutions in our system" and carefully limited its holding to the "unique context of a challenge to [the non-enforcement of] a criminal statute." Furthermore, as to redressability, the relief sought in *Linda R. S.*—a prosecution which, if successful, would automatically land the delinquent father in jail for a fixed term with predictably negative effects on his earning power—would scarcely remedy the plaintiff's lack of child support payments. * * *

Putting aside its mistaken reliance on *Linda R. S.*, the dissent's broader charge that citizen suits for civil penalties under the Act carry "grave implications for democratic governance" seems to us overdrawn. Certainly the federal Executive Branch does not share the dissent's view that such suits dissipate its authority to enforce the law. In fact, the Department of Justice has endorsed this citizen suit from the outset, submitting amicus briefs in support of FOE in the District Court, the Court of Appeals, and this Court. As we have already noted, supra, at 3, the Federal Government retains the power to foreclose a citizen suit by undertaking its own action. 33 U.S.C. § 1365(b)(1)(B). And if the Executive Branch opposes a particular citizen suit, the statute allows the Administrator of the EPA to "intervene as a matter of right" and bring the Government's views to the attention of the court.

The Court of Appeals justified its mootness disposition by reference to *Steel Co.*, which held that citizen plaintiffs lack standing to seek civil penalties for wholly past violations. In relying on *Steel Co.*, the Court of Appeals confused mootness with standing. The confusion is understandable, given this Court's repeated statements that the doctrine of mootness can be described as "the doctrine of standing set in a time frame: The requisite personal interest that must exist at the commencement of the litigation (standing) must continue throughout its existence (mootness)."

Careful reflection on the long-recognized exceptions to mootness, however, reveals that the description of mootness as "standing set in a time frame" is not comprehensive. As just noted, a defendant claiming that its voluntary compliance moots a case bears the formidable burden of showing that it is absolutely clear the allegedly wrongful behavior could not reasonably be expected to recur. By contrast, in a lawsuit brought to force compliance, it is the plaintiff's burden to establish standing by demonstrating that, if unchecked by the litigation, the defendant's allegedly wrongful behavior will likely occur or continue, and that the "threatened injury [is] certainly impending." Thus, in *Lyons*, as already noted, we held that a plaintiff lacked initial standing to seek an injunction against the enforcement of a police chokehold policy because he could not credibly allege that he faced a realistic threat arising from the policy. Elsewhere in the opinion, however, we noted that a citywide moratorium on police chokeholds—an action that surely diminished the already slim likelihood that any particular individual would be choked by police—would not have mooted an otherwise valid claim for injunctive relief, because the moratorium by its terms was not permanent. The plain lesson of these cases is that there are circumstances in which the prospect that a defendant will engage in (or resume) harmful conduct may be too speculative to support standing, but not too speculative to overcome mootness.

Furthermore, if mootness were simply "standing set in a time frame," the exception to mootness that arises when the defendant's allegedly unlawful activity is "capable of repetition, yet evading review" could not exist. * * * Standing admits of no similar exception; if a plaintiff lacks standing at the time the action commences, the fact that the dispute is capable of repetition yet evading review will not entitle the complainant to a federal judicial forum. * * *

Laidlaw also asserts, in a supplemental suggestion of mootness, that the closure of its Roebuck facility, which took place after the Court of Appeals issued its decision, mooted the case. The facility closure, like Laidlaw's earlier achievement of substantial compliance with its permit requirements, might moot the case, but—we once more reiterate—only if one or the other of these events made it absolutely clear that Laidlaw's permit violations could not reasonably be expected to recur. *Concentrated Phosphate Export Assn.*, 393 U.S. at 203. The effect of both Laidlaw's compliance and the facility closure on the prospect of future violations is a disputed factual matter. FOE points out, for example—and Laidlaw does not appear to contest—that Laidlaw retains its NPDES permit.

These issues have not been aired in the lower courts; they remain open for consideration on remand.

[The majority opinion refrained from ruling on whether FOE was entitled to attorney's fees because "when the Court of Appeals addressed the availability of counsel fees in this case, no order was before it either denying or awarding fees. It is for the District Court, not this Court, to address in the first instance any request for reimbursement of costs, including fees."]

[The concurring opinions of JUSTICE KENNEDY and JUSTICE STEVENS, joined by JUSTICE KENNEDY are omitted. JUSTICE KENNEDY writes that Article II questions should be reserved for a later case as specific attention was not accorded to the issue by the parties and lower courts. The concurring opinion by JUSTICE STEVENS focuses on mootness].

JUSTICE SCALIA, with whom JUSTICE THOMAS joins, dissenting.

* * *

I

* * *Typically, an environmental plaintiff claiming injury due to discharges in violation of the Clean Water Act argues that the discharges harm the environment, and that the harm to the environment injures him. This route to injury is barred in the present case, however, since the District Court concluded after considering all the evidence that there had been "no demonstrated proof of harm to the environment," that the "permit violations at issue in this citizen suit did not result in any health risk or environmental harm," that "all available data * * * fail to show that Laidlaw's actual discharges have resulted in harm to the North Tyger River," and that "the overall quality of the river exceeds levels necessary to support * * * recreation in and on the water."

The Court finds these conclusions unproblematic for standing, because "the relevant showing for purposes of Article III standing * * * is not injury to the environment but injury to the plaintiff." This statement is correct, as far as it goes. We have certainly held that a demonstration of harm to the environment is not enough to satisfy the injury-in-fact requirement unless the plaintiff can demonstrate how he personally was harmed. In the normal course, however, a lack of demonstrable harm to the environment will translate, as it plainly does here, into a lack of demonstrable harm to citizen plaintiffs. While it is perhaps possible that a plaintiff could be harmed even though the environment was not, such a plaintiff would have the burden of articulating and demonstrating the nature of that injury. Ongoing "concerns" about the environment are not enough, for "it is the reality of the threat of repeated injury that is relevant to the standing inquiry, not the plaintiff's subjective apprehensions," At the very least, in the present case, one would expect to see evidence supporting the affidavits' bald assertions regarding decreasing recreational usage and declining home values, as well as evidence for the improbable proposition that Laidlaw's violations, even though harmless to the environment, are somehow responsible for these effects. Plaintiffs here have made no attempt at such a showing, but rely entirely upon unsupported and unexplained affidavit allegations of "concern." * * *

The Court is correct that the District Court explicitly found standing—albeit "by the very slimmest of margins," and as "an awfully close call." That cautious finding, however, was made in 1993, long before the court's 1997 conclusion that Laidlaw's discharges did not harm the environment. * * * Thus no lower court has reviewed the injury-in-fact issue in light of the extensive studies that led the District Court to conclude that the environment was not harmed by Laidlaw's discharges.

Inexplicably, the Court is untroubled by this, but proceeds to find injury in fact in the most casual fashion, as though it is merely confirming a careful analysis made below. Although we have previously refused to find standing based on the "conclusory allegations of an affidavit," *Lujan v. National Wildlife Federation*, the Court is content to do just that today. By accepting plaintiffs' vague, contradictory, and unsubstantiated allegations of "concern" about the environment as adequate to prove injury in fact, and accepting them even in the face of a finding that the environment was not demonstrably harmed, the Court makes the injury-in-fact requirement a sham. If there are permit violations, and a member of a plaintiff environmental organization lives near the offending plant, it would be difficult not to satisfy today's lenient standard.

II

The Court's treatment of the redressability requirement—which would have been unnecessary if it resolved the injury-in-fact question correctly—is equally cavalier. As discussed above, petitioners allege ongoing injury consisting of diminished enjoyment of the affected waterways and decreased property values * * *. But the remedy petitioners seek is neither recompense for their injuries nor an injunction against future violations. Instead, the remedy is a statutorily specified "penalty" for past violations, payable entirely to the United States Treasury * * *. [The Court thus] holds that a penalty payable to the public "remedies" a threatened private harm, and suffices to sustain a private suit.

That holding has no precedent in our jurisprudence, and takes this Court beyond the "cases and controversies" that Article III of the Constitution has entrusted to its resolution. * * *

* * * Although the Court in *Linda R. S.* recited the "logical nexus" analysis of *Flast v. Cohen*, which has since fallen into desuetude, "it is clear that standing was denied * * * because of the unlikelihood that the relief requested would redress appellant's claimed injury." *Duke Power Co. v. Carolina Environmental Study Group, Inc.* * * * Of course precisely the same situation exists here. The principle that "in American jurisprudence * * * a private citizen lacks a judicially cognizable interest in the prosecution or nonprosecution of another" applies no less to

prosecution for civil penalties payable to the State than to prosecution for criminal penalties owing to the State.

The Court's opinion reads as though the only purpose and effect of the redressability requirement is to assure that the plaintiff receive some of the benefit of the relief that a court orders. That is not so. * * * Just as a "generalized grievance" that affects the entire citizenry cannot satisfy the injury-in-fact requirement even though it aggrieves the plaintiff along with everyone else, so also a generalized remedy that deters all future unlawful activity against all persons cannot satisfy the remediation requirement, even though it deters (among other things) repetition of this particular unlawful activity against these particular plaintiffs.

Thus, relief against prospective harm is traditionally afforded by way of an injunction, the scope of which is limited by the scope of the threatened injury. In seeking to overturn that tradition by giving an individual plaintiff the power to invoke a public remedy, Congress has done precisely what we have said it cannot do: convert an "undifferentiated public interest" into an "individual right" vindicable in the courts. The sort of scattershot redress approved today makes nonsense of our statement in *Schlesinger*, that the requirement of injury in fact "insures the framing of relief no broader than required by the precise facts." A claim of particularized future injury has today been made the vehicle for pursuing generalized penalties for past violations, and a threshold showing of injury in fact has become a lever that will move the world.

* * *

Article II of the Constitution commits it to the President to "take Care that the Laws be faithfully executed," Art. II, § 3, and provides specific methods by which all persons exercising significant executive power are to be appointed, Art. II, § 2. [T]he question of the conformity of this legislation with Article II has not been argued—and I, like the Court, do not address it. But * * * it is worth noting the changes in that structure which today's decision allows.

By permitting citizens to pursue civil penalties payable to the Federal Treasury, the Act does not provide a mechanism for individual relief in any traditional sense, but turns over to private citizens the function of enforcing the law. A Clean Water Act plaintiff pursuing civil penalties acts as a self-appointed mini-EPA. Where, as is often the case, the plaintiff is a national association, it has significant discretion in choosing enforcement targets. Once the association is aware of a reported violation, it need not look long for an injured member, at least under the theory of injury the Court applies today. And once the target is chosen, the suit goes forward without meaningful public control. The availability of civil penalties vastly disproportionate to the individual injury gives citizen plaintiffs massive bargaining power—which is often used to achieve settlements requiring the defendant to support environmental projects of the plaintiffs' choosing. *See* Greve, The *Private Enforcement of Environmental Law*, 65 Tulane L. Rev. 339, 355–359 (1990). Thus is a public fine diverted to a private interest.

To be sure, the EPA may foreclose the citizen suit by itself bringing suit. This allows public authorities to avoid private enforcement only by accepting private direction as to when enforcement should be undertaken—which is no less constitutionally bizarre. Elected officials are entirely deprived of their discretion to decide that a given violation should not be the object of suit at all, or that the enforcement decision should be postponed. * * *

III

* * * I am troubled by the Court's too-hasty retreat from our characterization of mootness as "the doctrine of standing set in a time frame." *Arizonans for Official English v. Arizona*, 520 U.S. 43, 68, n. 22 (1997). We have repeatedly recognized that what is required for litigation to continue is essentially identical to what is required for litigation to begin: There must be a justiciable case or controversy as required by Article III. "Simply stated, a case is moot when the issues presented are no longer 'live' or the parties lack a legally cognizable interest in the outcome." * * *

Part of the confusion in the Court's discussion is engendered by the fact that it compares standing, on the one hand, with mootness based on voluntary cessation, on the other hand. The required showing that it is "absolutely clear" that the conduct "could not reasonably be expected to recur" is not the threshold showing required for mootness, but the heightened showing required in a particular category of cases where we have sensibly concluded that there is reason to be skeptical that cessation of violation means cessation of live controversy. For claims of mootness based on changes in circumstances other than voluntary cessation, the showing we have required is less taxing, and the inquiry is indeed properly characterized as one of "standing set in a time frame."

Notes

1. *The Legal Logic of "Injury-in-Fact"*. In its discussions of Article III's demands, the Supreme Court seems caught between a logical position that reads the "case" and "controversy" references out of the Constitution and an incoherent position that preserves them. The logical position is straightforward: Anyone appearing in court presenting a claim of legal right presents a case or controversy. Legal rights arise from both common law and statute. Congress, by passing a statute can change the common law or add to it through statutory prescription. Hence, anytime anyone alleges either a common law or statutory right they have articulated a claim that presents a case or controversy. On this view, the question whether a case or controversy has been presented simply collapses into the question of whether the plaintiff has stated a cause of action. And, on this perfectly logical approach to the matter, a Congress that says that all citizens have a right to have the Secretary of Interior properly interpret the Endangered Species Act has just created a right enforceable in court. This is not the approach taken by the majority in *Laidlaw*, although the dissenters believe that the Court has come

dangerously close to saying that, where congressionally created standing is at issue, anything Congress says goes.

The alternative approach, invented almost by inadvertence by Justice Douglas in *ADAPSO*, demands that the right alleged to be violated result in "injury-in-fact." But what is that? A plaintiff shows up in court saying that he or she has been injured in some specified way. Moreover, says the plaintiff, I have been given a legal right by the Congress to seek redress for my injury. That is the type of argument put forward by the *Laidlaw* plaintiffs.

It is successful there. But, the Court's response, in *Lujan* and a number of other cases, has been that Congress may have given you a right, but it is a right to redress an injury that does not exist. When the plaintiff replies that the injury does indeed exist, otherwise he or she would not be paying lawyers and going to other trouble and expense to pursue the matter, the Court falls back upon its criteria for determining when there is an "injury in fact." But these, of course, are legal criteria. They determine what sorts of injuries a court will recognize as "injury in fact." In short, the question is whether the plaintiff has an injury "in law." The Court cannot determine that question by staring at the facts of the case. Injury in *fact* is an incoherent legal idea.

At this point the debate about whether the plaintiff should be able to proceed must shift to some justification for the particular rules of recognition for injuries that the Court has created, not only as an aspect of self-regulation, but as a constitutional necessity that limits congressional conferral of enforceable legal rights. The Supreme Court's increasingly technical parsing of prior standing doctrine often seems to ignore, if not obscure, these fundamental issues—issues that Justice's Scalia and Thomas have sought to reintroduce via Article II.

2. ADAPSO's *Dashed Hopes and Broken Dreams*. Many standing cases make the point that standing must be demonstrated in a fashion appropriate to the posture of the case, from pleadings through summary judgment to proof at trial. *Laidlaw* merely adds the implication that at some point standing and mootness will overlap. And, should the issue be characterized as "mootness" rather than "standing," the case may be addressed from the perspective of different criteria and burdens of proof. Of course, if Justice Scalia is correct, how the Court characterizes these questions should also depend on what sort of "mootness" is at issue. But, whatever the proper resolution of that debate, the now settled doctrine that plaintiff's standing remains an issue throughout the litigation, merely changing its evidentiary shape as the case proceeds from the pleadings to the merits, makes a mockery of Justice Douglas' ambition in *ADAPSO*—to formulate principles that would separate standing from the merits and permit expeditious disposition of standing questions at preliminary stages of litigation.

3. *Further reading. Laidlaw* has spawned not just articles, but whole symposia devoted both to that case and to other recent "citizen suit" litigation. See, e.g., Symposium, *Citizen Suits and the Future of Standing in the 21st Century: From* Lujan *to* Laidlaw *and Beyond*, 12 Duke Envtl. L. & Pol'y F. 1 (2001).

Chapter 8

DAMAGE ACTIONS AGAINST THE FEDERAL GOVERNMENT AND ITS OFFICERS

A. DAMAGE ACTIONS AGAINST THE GOVERNMENT

The federal government, through its millions of employees, engages in most of the activities that regularly give rise to lawsuits between private parties. This fact means that the range of potential private claims against the government is at least as broad as the variety of legal disputes between private citizens. Typically, a party who sues the government for damages relies on the same body of legal principles that affords protection against similar invasions by other private citizens. If one's tulips have been damaged by a carelessly driven mail delivery truck, any claim for relief must find support in the statutory and common law that generally determines the liability of owners of negligently operated motor vehicles. Even when the government inflicts injuries that are unique, as, for example, when military operations result in the destruction of private property, the property owner may assert a cause of action that is identical or closely analogous to a private law claim.

Beyond these more prosaic damage actions, it is obvious that governmental agencies have special capacities to harm. For government not only has special constitutional duties to refrain from acting, it also undertakes a vast array of protective activities which, if bungled, can produce serious harms, even disaster. It is primarily these special duties, and the government's special defenses, that will occupy us in this section.

As noted in Chapter 7, damage actions against the federal government are not embraced by the sweeping waiver of immunity now found in the APA, 5 U.S.C. § 706. Claims for damages must therefore proceed pursuant to the more circumscribed provisions of special waiver statutes—chief among them the Tucker Act, Act of 1887, ch. 359, 24 Stat.

505 (codified in scattered sections of 28 U.S.C.), and the Federal Tort Claims Act of 1946, 60 Stat. 843 (codified at 28 U.S.C. §§ 1346(b), 2671 et seq.). Both statutes have a long and tortured statutory history, which is paralleled in their subsequent judicial interpretation.

1. THE TUCKER ACT

In 1832, John Quincy Adams complained that private bills seeking monetary relief consumed half the time of Congress, to the detriment of both that body and the public. *See Hearings on* H.R. 5373 *and* H.R. 6463 *Before the House Comm. on the Judiciary*, 77th Cong. 49 (1942). Yet over fifty additional years of experimentation with various modifications of the private bills practice were required to convince Congress to pass the Tucker Act which gave the Court of Claims jurisdiction to render final judgments against the government. Even then, actions sounding in tort were excluded.

As currently codified, the Court of Claims' Tucker Act jurisdiction includes claims "* * * founded either upon the Constitution, or any Act of Congress, or any regulation of an executive department, upon any express or implied contract with the United States, or for liquidated or unliquidated damages in cases not sounding in tort." 28 U.S.C. § 1491(a)(1). Yet notwithstanding this rather sweeping language, the Tucker Act has been narrowly, even grudgingly, interpreted. A flavor of the jurisprudence can be gleaned from the description of one of the leading contemporary cases, *United States v. Testan*, 424 U.S. 392 (1976), in Gregory K. Orme, *Tucker Act Jurisdiction Over Breach of Trust Claims*, 1979 B.Y.U. L. Rev. 855, 860–62:

> *Testan* involved a claim by two government attorneys that their positions should have been classified as GS–14 rather than GS–13. After exhausting their administrative remedies, the attorneys brought suit in the Court of Claims seeking prospective reclassification and an award of back pay. A divided Court of Claims found the administrative refusal to reclassify plaintiffs arbitrary, but the court concluded that it lacked power to mandate the employees' reclassification. A monetary award was deemed permissible but premature until an entitlement to the governmental position was created by the proper authority. Therefore, the case was ordered remanded to the Civil Service Commission. If on remand the Civil Service Commission should order reclassification, that action "could create a legal right which [could then be enforced] by a money judgment." The Supreme Court disagreed.
>
> Justice Blackmun, in an opinion that drew no dissent, * * * articulated the Court's general approach to the case:
>
>> The Tucker Act, of course, is itself only a jurisdictional statute; it does not create any substantive right enforceable against the United States for money damages. The Court of Claims has recognized that the Act merely confers jurisdiction upon it whenever the substantive right exists. * * * We there-

fore must determine whether the two other federal statutes that are invoked by the respondents confer a substantive right to recover money damages from the United States for the period of their allegedly wrongful civil service classifications.

The Court first rejected what it deemed the "implicit" conclusion of the lower court that the Classification Act "gives rise to a claim for money damages for pay lost by reason of the allegedly wrongful classifications." The Court stated that, as a sovereignty, the United States cannot be sued without its consent, " 'and the terms of its consent to be sued in any court define that court's jurisdiction to entertain the suit.' " Such consent to suit " 'cannot be implied but must be unequivocally expressed.' " "Thus," wrote Justice Blackmun, "except as Congress has consented to a cause of action against the United States, 'there is no jurisdiction in the Court of Claims more than in any other court to entertain suits against the United States.' "

The Court also rejected the contention that the Tucker Act itself waived sovereign immunity with respect to all claims "invoking a constitutional provision or a federal statute or regulation." Justice Blackmun wrote that since the claim in issue was not based on contract and was not one for the return of money paid the government, "[i]t follows that the asserted entitlement to money damages depends upon whether any federal statute 'can fairly be interpreted as mandating compensation by the Federal Government for the damage sustained.' " He and his brethren declined "to tamper with these established principles," and held that the Court of Claims lacked jurisdiction.

The Court subjected the Back Pay Act to similar scrutiny and found that it granted "a monetary cause of action only to those who were subjected to a reduction in their duly appointed emoluments or position," not to those who contended they were entitled to positions other than the ones they held. The claimants' suit was ordered dismissed.

The Court's language in *Testan* was indeed so stringent that it could be read to suggest that the Tucker Act is, while jurisdictional, not a waiver of sovereign immunity. The necessary waiver would have to be provided by some other statute specifically making the government liable in damages.

UNITED STATES v. MITCHELL

Supreme Court of the United States, 1983.
463 U.S. 206, 103 S.Ct. 2961, 77 L.Ed.2d 580.

JUSTICE MARSHALL delivered the opinion of the Court.

The principal question in this case is whether the United States is accountable in money damages for alleged breaches of trust in connection with its management of forest resources on allotted lands of the Quinault Indian Reservation.

In the 1850s, the United States undertook a policy of removing Indian tribes from large areas of the Pacific Northwest in order to facilitate the settlement of non-Indians. Pursuant to this policy, the first Governor and Superintendent of Indian Affairs of the Washington Territory began negotiations in 1855 with various tribes living on the west coast of the Territory. The negotiations culminated in a treaty between the United States and the Quinault and Quileute Tribes (Treaty of Olympia). In the Treaty the Indians ceded to the United States a vast tract of land on the Olympic Peninsula in the State of Washington, and the United States agreed to set aside a reservation for the Indians.

* * *

In 1905 the Federal Government began to allot the Quinault Reservation in trust to individual Indians under the General Allotment Act of 1887.[5] * * * By 1935 the entire Reservation had been divided into 2,340 trust allotments, most of which were 80 acres of heavily timbered land. * * *

The forest resources on the allotted lands have long been managed by the Department of the Interior, which exercises "comprehensive" control over the harvesting of Indian timber. The Secretary of the Interior has broad statutory authority over the sale of timber on reservations. Sales of timber "must be based upon a consideration of the needs and best interests of the Indian owner and his heirs," and the proceeds from such sales are to be used for the benefit of the Indians or transferred to the Indian owner. Congress has directed the Secretary to adhere to principles of sustained-yield forestry on all Indian forest lands under his supervision. Under these statutes, the Secretary has promulgated detailed regulations governing the management of Indian timber. The Secretary is authorized to deduct an administrative fee for his services from the timber revenues paid to Indian allottees.

The respondents are 1,465 individuals owning interests in allotments on the Quinault Reservation, an unincorporated association of Quinault Reservation allottees, and the Quinault Tribe, which now holds some portions of the allotted lands. In 1971 respondents filed four actions that were consolidated in the Court of Claims. * * * Respondents sought to recover damages from the United States based on allegations of pervasive waste and mismanagement of timber lands on the Quinault Reservation. More specifically, respondents claimed that the Government (1) failed to obtain a fair market value for timber sold; (2) failed to manage timber on a sustained-yield basis; (3) failed to obtain any payment at all for some merchantable timber; (4) failed to develop a proper system of roads and easements for timber operations and exacted improper charges from allottees for maintenance of roads; (5) failed to pay any interest on certain funds from timber sales held by the Govern-

5. Section 5 of the Act provided that the United States would hold the allotted land for 25 years "in trust for the sole use and benefit of the Indian to whom such allotment shall have been made." The period during which the United States was to hold the allotted land was extended indefinitely by the Indian Reorganization Act of 1934.

ment and paid insufficient interest on other funds; and (6) exacted excessive administrative fees from allottees. Respondents assert that the alleged misconduct constitutes a breach of the fiduciary duty owed them by the United States as trustee under various statutes.

* * *

In *United States v. Mitchell*, 445 U.S. 535 (1980), this Court [held] * * * that the General Allotment Act "created only a limited trust relationship between the United States and the allottees that does not impose any duty upon the Government to manage timber resources." We concluded that "[a]ny right of the respondents to recover money damages for Government mismanagement of timber resources must be found in some source other than [the General Allotment] Act." Since the Court of Claims had not considered respondents' assertion that other statutes render the United States answerable in money damages for the alleged mismanagement in this case, we remanded the case for consideration of these alternative grounds for liability.

On remand, the Court of Claims once again held the United States subject to suit for money damages on most of respondents' claims. The court ruled that the timber management statutes, various federal statutes governing road building and rights of way, statutes governing Indian funds and government fees, and regulations promulgated under these statutes imposed fiduciary duties upon the United States in its management of forested allotted lands. The court concluded that the statutes and regulations implicitly required compensation for damages sustained as a result of the Government's breach of its duties. Thus, the court held that respondents could proceed on their claims. * * *

* * *

It is axiomatic that the United States may not be sued without its consent and that the existence of consent is a prerequisite for jurisdiction. The terminology employed in some of our prior decisions has unfortunately generated some confusion as to whether the Tucker Act constitutes a waiver of sovereign immunity. The time has come to resolve this confusion. For the reasons set forth below, we conclude that by giving the Court of Claims jurisdiction over specified types of claims against the United States, the Tucker Act constitutes a waiver of sovereign immunity with respect to those claims. * * *

For decades this Court consistently interpreted the Tucker Act as having provided the consent of United States to be sued *eo nomine* for the classes of claims described in the Act. * * * These decisions confirm the unambiguous thrust of the history of the Act.

The existence of a waiver is readily apparent in claims founded upon "any express or implied contract with the United States." * * * The source of consent for such suits unmistakably lies in the Tucker Act. Otherwise, it is doubtful that *any* consent would exist, for no contracting officer or other official is empowered to consent to suit against the United States. The same is true for claims founded upon executive regulations. Indeed, the Act makes absolutely no distinction between claims founded upon contracts and claims founded upon other specified sources of law.

In *United States v. Testan*, 424 U.S. 392 (1976), and in *United States v. Mitchell*, this Court employed language suggesting that the Tucker Act does not effect a waiver of sovereign immunity. Such language was not necessary to the decision in either case. Without in any way questioning the result in either case, we conclude that this isolated language should be disregarded. If a claim falls within the terms of the Tucker Act, the United States has presumptively consented to suit.

It nonetheless remains true that the Tucker Act " 'does not create any substantive right enforceable against the United States for money damages.' " A substantive right must be found in some other source of law, such as "the Constitution, or any Act of Congress, or any regulation of an executive department." * * * [A]nd the claimant must demonstrate that the source of substantive law he relies upon " 'can fairly be interpreted as mandating compensation by the Federal Government for the damages sustained.' " * * *

* * * The question in this case is thus analytically distinct: whether the statutes or regulations at issue can be interpreted as requiring compensation. Because the Tucker Act supplies a waiver of immunity for claims of this nature, the separate statutes and regulations need not provide a second waiver of sovereign immunity, nor need they be construed in the manner appropriate to waivers of sovereign immunity.

* * *

Respondents have based their money claims against the United States on various Acts of Congress and executive department regulations. * * *

* * *

The language of these statutory and regulatory provisions directly supports the existence of a fiduciary relationship. For example, § 8 of the 1910 Act, as amended, expressly mandates that sales of timber from Indian trust lands be based upon the Secretary's consideration of "the needs and best interests of the Indian owner and his heirs" and that proceeds from such sales be paid to owners "or disposed of for their benefit." Similarly, even in its earliest regulations, the Government recognized its duties in "managing the Indian forests so as to obtain the greatest revenue for the Indians consistent with a proper protection and improvement of the forests." Office of Indian Affairs, Regulations and Instructions for Officers in Charge of Forests on Indian Reservations 4 (1911). Thus, the Government has "expressed a firm desire that the Tribe should retain the benefits derived from the harvesting and sale of reservation timber."

Moreover, a fiduciary relationship necessarily arises when the Government assumes such elaborate control over forests and property belonging to Indians. All of the necessary elements of a common-law trust are present: a trustee (the United States), a beneficiary (the Indian allottees), and a trust corpus (Indian timber, lands, and funds). "[W]here the Federal government takes on or has control or supervision over tribal monies or properties, the fiduciary relationship normally exists with respect to such monies or properties (unless Congress has provided otherwise) even though nothing is said expressly in the authorizing or underlying statute (or other fundamental document) about a trust fund, or a trust or fiduciary connection." *Navajo Tribe of Indians v. United States*, 624 F.2d 981, 987 (1980).

Our construction of these statutes and regulations is reinforced by the undisputed existence of a general trust relationship between the United States and the Indian people. This Court has previously emphasized "the distinctive obligation of trust incumbent upon the Government in its dealings with these dependent and sometimes exploited people." * * *

Because the statutes and regulations at issue in this case clearly establish fiduciary obligations of the Government in the management and operation of Indian lands and resources, they can fairly be interpreted as mandating compensation by the Federal Government for damages sustained. Given the existence of a trust relationship, it naturally follows that the Government should be liable in damages for the breach of its fiduciary duties. It is well established that a trustee is accountable in damages for breaches of trust. * * *

The recognition of a damages remedy also furthers the purposes of the statutes and regulations, which clearly require that the Secretary manage Indian resources so as to generate proceeds for the Indians. It would be anomalous to conclude that these enactments create a right to the value of certain resources when the Secretary lives up to his duties, but no right to the value of the resources if the Secretary's duties are not performed. * * *

The Government contends that violations of duties imposed by the various statutes may be cured by actions for declaratory, injunctive or mandamus relief against the Secretary, although it concedes that sovereign immunity might have barred such suits before 1976. In this context, however, prospective equitable remedies are totally inadequate. To begin with, the Indian allottees are in no position to monitor federal management of their lands on a consistent basis. * * *

In addition, by the time government mismanagement becomes apparent, the damage to Indian resources may be so severe that a prospective remedy may be next to worthless. For example, if timber on an allotment has been destroyed through Government mismanagement, it will take many years for nature to restore the timber. * * *

We thus conclude that the statutes and regulations at issue here can fairly be interpreted as mandating compensation by the Federal Government for violations of its fiduciary responsibilities in the management of

Indian property. The Court of Claims therefore has jurisdiction over respondents' claims for alleged breaches of trusts.

* * *

JUSTICE POWELL, with whom JUSTICE REHNQUIST and JUSTICE O'CONNOR join, dissenting.

The controlling law in this case is clear. Speaking for the Court in *United States v. Mitchell (Mitchell I)*, Justice Marshall reaffirmed the general principle that a cause of action for damages against the United States " 'cannot be implied but must be unequivocally expressed.' " Where, as here, a claim for money damages is predicated upon an alleged statutory violation, the rule is that the statute does not create a cause of action for damages unless the statute " 'in itself * * * can fairly be interpreted as mandating compensation by the Federal Government for the damage sustained.' "*United States v. Testan*. * * * In sum, whether the United States has created a cause of action turns upon the intent of Congress, not the inclinations of the courts.

Today, the Court appears disinterested in the intent of Congress. It has effectively reversed the presumption that absent "affirmative statutory authority," the United States has not consented to be sued for damages. * * *

The Court does not—and clearly cannot—contend that any of the statutes standing alone reflects the necessary legislative authorization of a damages remedy. * * * Indeed, nothing in the timber-sales statute,[1] the road and right-of-way statutes, or the interest statute, addresses in any respect the institution of damages actions against the United States. Nor is there any indication in the legislative history of the statutes that Congress intended to consent to damages actions for mismanagement of Indian assets by enacting these provisions. The Court does not suggest otherwise.

* * *

The Court makes little or no pretense that it is following doctrine heretofore established. Without pertinent analysis, it simply concludes: "Because the statutes and regulations at issue in this case clearly establish fiduciary obligations of the Government in the management and operation of Indian lands and resources, they can fairly be interpreted as mandating compensation by the Federal Government for damages sustained." * * *

* * * Some of the statutes involved here, to be sure, create substantive duties that the Secretary must fulfill. But this could equally be said of the Classification Act, considered in *Testan*. It requires that pay

1. The only monetary obligation imposed upon the Secretary by § 406 or § 407 is to pay the actual "proceeds" of timber sales to the owners of the land. Thus, while it may well be that those sections would permit an action to compel the Secretary to pay over unlawfully retained proceeds, no statutory basis exists for extending that remedy to profits that arguably or ideally should have been, but were not, earned by the Secretary. * * *

classification ratings of federal employees be carried out pursuant to "the principle of equal pay for substantially equal work," 5 U.S.C. § 5101(1)(A). Although the federal employee in *Testan* alleged a violation of the Act, the Court concluded that a back-pay remedy was unavailable, rejecting the argument that the substantive right necessarily implies a damages remedy. * * *

It is fair to say that the Court is influenced by its view that an injunctive remedy is inadequate to redress the violations alleged—precisely the inference deemed inadmissible in *Testan*. It is the ordinary result of sovereign immunity that unconsented claims for money damages are barred. The fact that damages cannot be recovered without the sovereign's consent hardly supports the conclusion that consent has been given. Yet this, in substance, is the Court's reasoning. If it is saying that a remedy is necessary to redress every injury sustained, the doctrine of sovereign immunity will have been drained of all meaning. Moreover, "many of the federal statutes * * * that expressly provide money damages as a remedy against the United States in carefully limited circumstances would be rendered superfluous."

The Court has made no effort to demonstrate that Congress intended to render the United States answerable in damages upon claims of the kind presented here. The mere application by a court of the label "trust" cannot properly justify disregard of an immunity from damages the Government has never waived. I would reverse the judgment of the Court of Claims.

Notes

1. Mitchell *and the Demand for Unequivocal Statutory Language.* Notwithstanding *Mitchell*, the availability of monetary relief in the U.S. Claims Court remains problematic where the suit is to enforce a federal statutory duty. Where the statute explicitly grants the claimant a cause of action for monetary relief, that statute might also be construed as waiving the sovereign immunity of the United States. In such a case jurisdiction would be appropriately founded in the Claims Court under the Tucker Act, but the Tucker Act's waiver of sovereign immunity would be quite unnecessary. On the other hand, where a statute imposes a duty but does not provide an explicit remedy, a suit to obtain a money judgment must confront the requirement articulated in both *Testan* and *Mitchell*, that the statute be interpreted "as mandating compensation" by the federal government. Given the Supreme Court's recent restrictive jurisprudence concerning implied private rights of action, *see infra* Chapter 9, this may well be an uphill battle.

In at least one post-*Mitchell* case, *Bowen v. Massachusetts*, 487 U.S. 879 (1988), the majority's dictum casts doubt on Claims Court jurisdiction even under a statute—in *Bowen*, the Medicaid statute—which requires the payment of grant-in-aid funds to states which satisfy its specific conditions. And, if the Claims Court lacks jurisdiction even under such a statute, then, as Justice Scalia points out in his *Bowen* dissent, one would be hard-pressed to find any provision of the U.S. Code sufficiently explicit to create a cause of action and thereby supply Claims Court jurisdiction. In short, the Supreme Court's dictum seems to lead straight back to the position espoused in *Testan*. If the statute explicitly grants a cause of action for monetary relief, then the plaintiff has a cause of action and sovereign immunity is waived without the assistance of the Tucker Act, which becomes purely jurisdictional. If the statute does not expressly grant a cause of action, then it cannot be fairly interpreted as "mandating compensation" and the Tucker Act's waiver of sovereign immunity is insufficient to allow judicial relief.

Justice Scalia in *Bowen* ends his critique of the Court's dictum with the optimistic suggestion that "the Court cannot possibly mean what it says today." 487 U.S. at 928–30. A less well-positioned commentator has described the *Bowen* opinion more soberly as reflecting "a fundamental misunderstanding of the nature of the Tucker Act. * * * The Tucker Act itself provides an *express* private right of action; that is its purpose." Gregory C. Sisk, *Two Proposals to Clarify the Tucker Act Jurisdiction of the Claims Court*, 37 Fed. B. News & J. 47 (1990). But neither Justice Scalia nor Mr. Sisk cites any authority that would support his opinion. Moreover, a cursory survey of Shephard's citator confirms that, outside the jurisprudence related to Indian claims, *Testan* remains the more cited authority, notwithstanding the apparent rejection of its reasoning in *Mitchell*.

The stinginess evident in the Court's reading of the Tucker Act in *Bowen* is replicated in *U.S. Department of Energy v. Ohio*, 503 U.S. 607 (1992). There a "citizen suit" was filed by Ohio claiming violations of the Clean Water Act (CWA), 33 U.S.C. § 1251 et seq., and the Resource Conservation and Recovery Act of 1976 (RCRA), 42 U.S.C. § 6901 et seq., in DOE's operation of an Ohio uranium processing plant. The United States conceded that the statutes unambiguously permit suits against the federal government, and unambiguously permit the issuance of injunctions and the levying of fines designed to foster compliance with those injunctions. The United States nonetheless argued, and the Supreme Court agreed, that the acts are insufficiently clear in waiving sovereign immunity to permit the levying against the federal government of civil fines, which the acts clearly authorize as punishment for past violations by all other polluters. Justice White's dissent accused the majority of "stylistic gymnastics" in discovering sufficient ambiguity in the statute to defeat the claim for this one category of monetary relief. The result is all the more interesting, of course, because the EPA could be expected to face unique difficulties in enforcing these statutes against other federal entities—difficulties that citizen suits might be well designed to overcome.

The Supreme Court returned to the specific context of *Mitchell I & II* in a pair of Indian claims cases decided the same day: *United States v. White Mountain Apache Tribe, 123 S.Ct. 1126 (2003)* and *United States v. Navajo Nation, 123 S.Ct. 1079 (2003)*. Both cases sought damages for breach of fiduciary duty in relation to the management of Indian lands, the former for waste in the management of tribal property, the latter for failure to protect tribal interests when approving a mineral lease on tribal lands. In ruling for the White Mountain Apaches and against the Navajo Nation, the Supreme Court attempted to explain more clearly the distinction between its rulings in *Mitchell I* and *Mitchell II*, and the criteria by which courts should determine whether federal statutes create rights compensable in money damages under the Tucker Act (or, as here, its "Indian" counterpart).

In *White Mountain Apache Tribe*, Justice Souter, writing only for himself and Justices O'Connor and Stevens, found that the statutes in question satisfied *Mitchell II*'s requirement that they could be "fairly interpreted as mandating compensation." Justice Souter took care to explain that this "fair interpretation" is not the sort of grudging or "clear statement" interpretation that would satisfy the Court that Congress intended a waiver of sovereign immunity. The Tucker Act provides that. Moreover, the statute need only create duties the breach of which would normally result in damages relief: here the imposition of a trust, combined with allocation of day-to-day use and management of some of the property to the Secretary of Interior. Where that use and management resulted in damage to the property, the United States should be understood to have the usual common law duties of a trustee in management, that is to return the property in good repair or pay damages for waste.

Justice Thomas, writing for himself, the Chief Justice and Justices Scalia and Kennedy, parted company with the plurality just at this point. For the dissenters, this was not a fair interpretation of the statute, but of the common law of trusts. Citing *Testan*, Justice Thomas insisted that any right of action for damages be granted "with specificity." For him, citing *Mitchell II*, that would require statutory language "*unambiguously* provid[ing] that the United States ha[d] undertaken full fiduciary responsibilities" for management of the land in question. Here the statutes provided in so many words that the land was to be held in trust for the tribe. But, as the dissenters read the statute, the management complained of was undertaken pursuant to a provision permitting use by and for the benefit of the United States, not pursuant to a provision further elaborating the duties of the trustee to the tribe. In their view, this was but the sort of "bare trust" that *Mitchell I* had found an insufficient premise for Tucker Act jurisdiction.

Justice Ginsburg concurred specially for herself and Justice Breyer, in order to clarify her position as author of the companion, *Navajo Nation*, decision. In that case, the tribe complained of interference by the Secretary of Interior in its negotiations for mineral leases on tribal lands—leases that by statute demanded the Secretary's approval. The tribe urged that the Secretary's approval power was meant to be exercised for the protection of its interests, but was instead used to coerce the tribe into an agreement on demonstrably unfavorable terms.

Whatever the truth of those factual claims, the case was decided on motions for summary judgment below. Justice Ginburg's majority opinion found that the limited statutory requirement that the Secretary approve lease agreements imposed no fiduciary or managerial duties on the United States. This was not even the "bare trust" rejected as a basis for Tucker Act jurisdiction in *Mitchell I*, much less the detailed fiduciary obligations to manage Indian lands to promote tribal interests that were the basis for the Court's ruling in *Mitchell II*.

Justices Souter, O'Connor, and Stevens dissented. For them the statutory history of the multiple statutes giving federal officials approval power over Indian tribe's alienation of tribal property, including this one, made clear that those approvals have a protective purpose. They have routinely been interpreted to be for the benefit of the tribes to which they apply, and the Department's regulations pursuant to this statute are to the same effect. That, for the dissenters, was enough to establish the sort of fiduciary responsibilities that will support a Tucker Act suit for damages.

Mitchell I and *Mitchell II* thus remain the touchstones of Tucker Act jurisdiction, at least in suits involving Indian claims. The only problem seems to be that these stones have a different feel in the pockets of different Justices.

2. *Dodging the Implied Contract Dodge.* The fiduciary duty or "trusteeship" theory that prevailed in *Mitchell* suggested that the general tenor of statutes might create broad duties on the part of the federal government that go beyond any express obligation. Another way to characterize such claims might be that the statutes authorizing federal transactions with private parties contain *implied* terms that are the equivalent of an explicit contractual undertaking. Yet the Supreme Court has steadfastly maintained that the Tucker Act's jurisdiction to hear and determine claims against the United States founded upon any "express or implied" contract does not include jurisdiction to determine claims where the contract is "implied in law" rather than "implied in fact."

Hercules, Inc. v. United States, 516 U.S. 417 (1996), is exemplary. The Hercules corporation was one of the producers of "Agent Orange," a defoliant used in the Vietnam War. In the late 1970s, Vietnam veterans and their families filed lawsuits against the manufacturers of Agent Orange, including Hercules, claiming that the veterans' exposure to dioxin, a toxic by-product found in Agent Orange, had caused various health problems. These lawsuits led ultimately to a settlement creating a $180 million dollar fund to be distributed to members of the plaintiff class. Hercules and others then sued the United States to recover their share of the settlement fund and the cost of defending the veterans' lawsuits.

The theory of the suit for reimbursement was that the government had implicitly promised to indemnify the manufacturers for any liability resulting from its production. Although there was no explicit indemnity clause in the contracts, the manufacturers pointed out that they had been forced to produce the defoliant under the authority of the Defense Production Act, including in some cases a threat of civil or criminal fines if they failed to do so. The government had also imposed detailed specifications with respect to the production and labeling of the product and had superior knowledge of its hazards, never disclosed to the manufacturers. Finally, the government had complete control over the utilization of the product and, if Agent Orange were implicated at all in the veterans' health problems, the proximate cause of those difficulties may have been the way in which the product and its containers were stored, used, and discarded.

The Supreme Court recognized that, while these circumstances might add up to a general claim that it was "unfair" or "inequitable" for the government to deny indemnification, such a finding would be an implication of law, not of fact. This sort of claim was barred by the Court's clear understanding of the reach of the Tucker Act, that is, that it permitted lawsuits only where the government had waived its immunity by accepting obligations either in statutory or contractual form. Hence, if the petitioners were to prevail, they would have to demonstrate that the government had in fact tacitly agreed to an indemnification provision.

The Court found that the petitioners could not sustain this burden. While the United States might be liable for breach of contractual warranty to one who had suffered harm by following the government's production specifications, that implied warranty extends only to a guarantee that the contractor will be able to perform the contracts satisfactorily if it follows the specifications. Nor could the Court find that the government had in fact agreed to indemnification. Statutes governing Defense Department contract permit indemnification clauses of certain sorts under certain circumstances, but in no case authorize indemnification of the general sort urged by the petitioners. The Court was loath to find that the government had tacitly agreed to indemnification terms that it had no authority to make.

In dissent, Justices Breyer and O'Connor argued that the Court was much too grudging in its reading both of the petitioners' complaint and of the statutes and regulations surrounding the contracts in question. Because the district and circuit courts decided these cases primarily on another ground—the belief that the immunity granted to the contractors under the Defense Production Act made it impossible for any of the government's actions to be the proximate cause of their settlement and litigation costs—the dissenters argued that the petitioners had never had a fair hearing on all the facts and circumstances surrounding their particular contracts. Justice Breyer concluded: "I fear that the practical effect of disposing of the company's claim at this stage of the proceeding will be to make it more difficult. * * * for courts to interpret government contracts * * * [to achieve] the fair allocation of risks that the parties likely intended."

It is clear from other parts of Justice Breyer's dissent that his view of the parties' "likely intent" is highly influenced by what he believes that a "government dealing in good faith with its contractors" *would* have intended. And on that view contracts "implied in fact" and those "implied in law" are virtually impossible to distinguish. The majority's position seems determined to maintain a bright line separation between these categories. Without that separation, implied contract claims verge imperceptibly into statutory implication claims that the Court's clear statement rules are designed to resolve against a finding of waiver. Commentators continue to doubt whether these bright line rules actually promote congressional intent. See John Copeland Nagle, *Waiving Sovereign Immunity in the Age of Clear Statement Rules*, 1995 Wis. L. Rev. 771, and authorities cited therein.

2. THE FEDERAL TORT CLAIMS ACT

As might be imagined from the language of the Tucker Act, the period from its enactment to the 1946 enactment of the Federal Tort Claims Act was punctuated by considerable dispute over what cases "sounded in tort," and were thus beyond Court of Claims jurisdiction under the former law. That period also saw enactment of numerous statutes waiving governmental tort immunity in special circumstances. These ranged from relatively general statutes, such as the Federal Employee's Compensation Act, to statutes waiving governmental immunity for tort suits by oyster growers. See generally WILLIAM B. WRIGHT, THE FEDERAL TORT CLAIMS ACT, ANALYZED AND ANNOTATED, Ch. 2, ¶¶ 2–18 to 2–50 (1964). Agitation for a general waiver of immunity for torts was also persistent. Finally, Congress acquiesced to these pressures in connection with the massive post-war governmental reorganization of 1946.

The Federal Tort Claims Act is codified in numerous sections of Title 28 U.S.C., and as originally enacted included the following significant provisions:

§ 1346. United States as Defendant

(b) Subject to [§§ 2674–80] of this title, the district courts * * * shall have exclusive jurisdiction of civil actions on claims against the United States, for money damages * * * for injury or loss of property, or personal injury or death caused by the negligent or wrongful act or omission of any employee of the Government while acting within the scope of his office or employment, under circumstances where the United States, if a private person, would be liable to the claimant in accordance with the law of the place where the act or omission occurred.

§ 2674. Liability of United States

The United States shall be liable, respecting the provisions of this title relating to tort claims, in the same manner and to the same extent as a private individual under like circumstances, but shall not be liable for interest prior to judgment or for punitive damages. * * *

The statute excepted from this broad waiver several classes of claims, the most important of which, for our purposes, were:

§ 2680. Exceptions

The provisions of [§§ 2674–79] and section 1346(b) of this title shall not apply to—

(a) Any claim based upon an act or omission of an employee of the Government, exercising due care, in the execution of a statute or regulation, whether or not such statute or regulation be valid, or based upon the exercise or performance or the failure to exercise or perform a discretionary function or duty on the part of a federal agency or an employee of the Government, whether or not the discretion involved be abused.

* * *

(h) Any claim arising out of assault, battery, false imprisonment, false arrest, malicious prosecution, abuse of process, libel, slander, misrepresentation, deceit, or interference with contract rights.

Subsection (h) was amended in 1974 to waive immunity for assault, battery, false imprisonment, false arrest, abuse of process or malicious prosecution with regard to the acts of federal "investigative or law enforcement officers." Pub. L. No. 93–253, § 2, 88 Stat. 50.

The critical interest of the subsection (h) exceptions lies in the pressure that the government's continued immunity has put on litigants and courts to expand the liability of federal officials—a subject to which we shall soon turn. The basic waiver provisions and section 2680(a) shape our current interest.

Section 1346(b) not only makes state law the governing norm for tort actions under the FTCA, it reinforces section 2680(a)'s executive and discretionary functions exceptions to liability by making the government liable only where a "private" party would be. Thus the government may escape liability *either* because its actions as the government have no private counterparts to which liability attaches under state law *or* because the action was "governmental" in the senses specified by section 2680(a).

UNITED STATES v. S.A. EMPRESA DE VIACAO AEREA RIO GRANDENSE (VARIG AIRLINES) ET AL.

Supreme Court of the United States, 1984.
467 U.S. 797, 104 S.Ct. 2755, 81 L.Ed.2d 660.

CHIEF JUSTICE BURGER delivered the opinion of the Court.

We granted certiorari in these two cases to determine whether the United States may be held liable under the Federal Tort Claims Act for the negligence of the Federal Aviation Administration in certificating certain aircraft for use in commercial aviation.

I

A. No. 82–1349

On July 11, 1973, a commercial jet aircraft owned by respondent S.A. Empresa de Viacao Aerea Rio Grandense (Varig Airlines) was flying from Rio de Janeiro to Paris when a fire broke out in one of the aft lavatories. The fire produced a thick black smoke, which quickly filled the cabin and cockpit. Despite the pilots' successful effort to land the plane, 124 of the 135 persons on board died from asphyxiation or the effects of toxic gases produced by the fire. Most of the plane's fuselage was consumed by a post-impact fire.

The aircraft involved in this accident was a Boeing 707, a product of the Boeing Co. In 1958 the Civil Aeronautics Agency, a predecessor of the FAA, had issued a type certificate for the Boeing 707, certifying that its designs, plans, specifications, and performance data had been shown to be in conformity with minimum safety standards. Seaboard Airlines originally purchased this particular plane for domestic use; in 1969 Seaboard sold the plane to respondent Varig Airlines, a Brazilian air carrier, which used the plane commercially from 1969 to 1973.

After the accident respondent Varig Airlines brought an action against the United States under the Federal Tort Claims Act seeking damages for the destroyed aircraft. The families and personal representatives of many of the passengers, also respondents here, brought a separate suit under the Act pressing claims for wrongful death. The two actions were consolidated in the United States District Court for the Central District of California.

Respondents asserted that the fire originated in the towel disposal area located below the sink unit in one of the lavatories and alleged that the towel disposal area was not capable of containing fire. In support of their argument, respondents pointed to an air safety regulation requiring that waste receptacles be made of fire-resistant materials and incorporate covers or other provisions for containing possible fires. 14 CFR § 4b.381(d) (1956). Respondents claimed that the CAA had been negligent when it inspected the Boeing 707 and issued a type certificate to an aircraft that did not comply with CAA fire protection standards. The District Court granted summary judgment for the United States on the ground that California law does not recognize an actionable tort duty for inspection and certification activities. The District Court also found that, even if respondents had stated a cause of action in tort, recovery against the United States was barred by two exceptions to the Act: the discretionary function exception, 28 U.S.C. § 2860(a), and the misrepresentation exception, § 2860(h).

The United States Court of Appeals for the Ninth Circuit reversed. 692 F.2d 1205 (1982). The Court of Appeals reasoned that a private person inspecting and certificating aircraft for airworthiness would be liable for negligent inspection under the California "Good Samaritan" rule, see Restatement (Second) of Torts §§ 323 and 324A (1965), and concluded that the United States should be judged by the same rule. * * * Interpreting respondents' claims as arising from the negligence of the CAA inspection rather than from any implicit misrepresentation in the resultant certificate, the Court of Appeals held that the misrepresentation exception did not apply. Finally, the Court of Appeals * * * viewed the inspection of aircraft for compliance with air safety regulations as a function not entailing the sort of policymaking discretion contemplated by the discretionary function exception.

B. No. 82–1350

On October 8, 1968, a DeHavilland Dove aircraft owned by respondent John Dowdle and used in the operation of an air taxi service caught fire in midair, crashed, and burned near Las Vegas, Nev. The pilot, copilot, and two passengers were killed. The cause of the crash was an in-flight fire in the forward baggage compartment of the aircraft. * * *

In the aftermath of the crash, respondent Dowdle filed this action for property damage against the United States under the Federal Tort Claims Act. * * * The United States District Court for the Southern District of California found that the crash resulted from defects in the installation of the gasoline line leading to the cabin heater. The District Court concluded that the installation did not comply with the applicable FAA regulations and held that the Government was negligent in certifying an installation that did not comply with those safety requirements. Accordingly, the District Court entered judgment for respondents.

On appeal, the United States Court of Appeals for the Ninth Circuit reversed and remanded for the District Court to consider whether the California courts would impose a duty of due care upon the Government by applying the "Good Samaritan" doctrine of §§ 323 and 324A of the Restatement (Second) of Torts. * * * On remand, the District Court again entered judgment for respondents, finding that the California "Good Samaritan" rule would apply in this case and would give rise to liability on these facts.

On the Government's second appeal, the Ninth Circuit affirmed the judgment of the District Court. * * *

II

In the Federal Aviation Act of 1958, 49 U.S.C. § 1421(a)(1), Congress directed the Secretary of Transportation to promote the safety of flight of civil aircraft in air commerce by establishing minimum standards for aircraft design, materials, workmanship, construction, and performance. Congress also granted the Secretary the discretion to prescribe reasonable rules and regulations governing the inspection of aircraft, including the manner in which such inspections should be made. Congress emphasized, however, that air carriers themselves retained certain responsibilities to promote the public interest in air safety: the duty to perform their services with the highest possible degree of safety, the duty to make or cause to be made every inspection required by the Secretary, and the duty to observe and comply with all other administrative requirements established by the Secretary.

Congress also established a multistep certification process to monitor the aviation industry's compliance with the requirements developed by the Secretary. Acting as the Secretary's designee, the FAA has promulgated a comprehensive set of regulations delineating the minimum safety standards with which the designers and manufacturers of aircraft must comply before marketing their products. See 14 CFR pts. 23, 25, 27, 29, 31, 33, and 35 (1983). At each step in the certification process, FAA employees or their representatives evaluate materials submitted by aircraft manufacturers to determine whether the manufacturer has satisfied these regulatory requirements. Upon a showing by the manufacturer that the prescribed safety standards have been met, the FAA issues an appropriate certificate permitting the manufacturer to continue with production and marketing.

The first stage of the FAA compliance review is type certification. A manufacturer wishing to introduce a new type of aircraft must first obtain FAA approval of the plane's basic design in the form of a type certificate. After receiving an application for a type certificate, the

Secretary must "make, or require the applicant to make, such tests during manufacture and upon completion as the Secretary * * * deems reasonably necessary in the interest of safety. * * * "49 U.S.C. § 1423(a)(2). By regulation, the FAA has made the applicant itself responsible for conducting all inspections and tests necessary to determine that the aircraft comports with FAA airworthiness requirements. The applicant submits to the FAA the designs, drawings, test reports, and computations necessary to show that the aircraft sought to be certificated satisfies FAA regulations. In the course of the type certification process, the manufacturer produces a prototype of the new aircraft and conducts both ground and flight tests. FAA employees or their representatives then review the data submitted by the applicant and make such inspections or tests as they deem necessary to ascertain compliance with the regulations. If the FAA finds that the proposed aircraft design comports with minimum safety standards, it signifies its approval by issuing a type certificate.

Production may not begin, however, until a production certificate authorizing the manufacture of duplicates of the prototype is issued. To obtain a production certificate, the manufacturer must prove to the FAA that it has established and can maintain a quality control system to assure that each aircraft will meet the design provisions of the type certificate. When it is satisfied that duplicate aircraft will conform to the approved type design, the FAA issues a production certificate, and the manufacturer may begin mass production of the approved aircraft.

Before any aircraft may be placed into service, however, its owner must obtain from the FAA an airworthiness certificate, which denotes that the particular aircraft in question conforms to the type certificate and is in condition for safe operation. It is unlawful for any person to operate an aircraft in air commerce without a valid airworthiness certificate.

An additional certificate is required when an aircraft is altered by the introduction of a major change in its type design. * * * The methods used by FAA employees or their representatives to determine an applicant's compliance with minimum safety standards are generally the same as those employed for basic type certification.

With fewer than 400 engineers, the FAA obviously cannot complete this elaborate compliance review process alone. Accordingly, 49 U.S.C. § 1355 authorizes the Secretary to delegate certain inspection and certification responsibilities to properly qualified private persons. By regulation, the Secretary has provided for the appointment of private individuals to serve as designated engineering representatives to assist in the FAA certification process. These representatives are typically employees of aircraft manufacturers who possess detailed knowledge of an aircraft's design based upon their day-to-day involvement in its development. * * * FAA employees may briefly review the reports and other data submitted by representatives before certificating a subject aircraft.

III

* * *

* * * The legislative materials of the Seventy-seventh Congress illustrate most clearly Congress' purpose in fashioning the discretionary function exception. A Government spokesman appearing before the House Committee on the Judiciary described the discretionary function exception as a "highly important exception."

> "[It is] designed to preclude application of the act to a claim based upon an alleged abuse of discretionary authority by a regulatory or licensing agency—for example, the Federal Trade Commission, the Securities and Exchange Commission, the Foreign Funds Control Office of the Treasury, or others. It is neither desirable nor intended that the constitutionality of legislation, the legality of regulations, or the propriety of a discretionary administrative act should be tested through the medium of a damage suit for tort. The same holds true of other administrative action not of a regulatory nature, such as the expenditure of Federal funds, the execution of a Federal project, and the like.
>
> "On the other hand, the common law torts of employees of regulatory agencies, as well as of all other Federal agencies, would be included within the scope of the bill." Hearings on H.R. 5373 and H.R. 6463 before the House Committee on the Judiciary, 77th Cong., 2d Sess., 28, 33 (1942) (statement of Assistant Attorney General Francis M. Shea) * * *.

The nature and scope of § 2680(a) were carefully examined in *Dalehite v. United States*, 346 U.S. 15 (1953). *Dalehite* involved vast claims for damages against the United States arising out of a disastrous explosion of ammonium nitrate fertilizer, which had been produced and distributed under the direction of the United States for export to devastated areas occupied by the Allied Armed Forces after World War II. Numerous acts of the Government were charged as negligent: the cabinet-level decision to institute the fertilizer export program, the failure to experiment with the fertilizer to determine the possibility of explosion, the drafting of the basic plan of manufacture, and the failure properly to police the storage and loading of the fertilizer.

The Court concluded that these allegedly negligent acts were governmental duties protected by the discretionary function exception and held the action barred by § 2680(a). Describing the discretion protected by § 2680(a) as "the discretion of the executive or the administrator to act according to one's judgment of the best course," the Court stated:

> "It is unnecessary to define, apart from this case, precisely where discretion ends. It is enough to hold, as we do, that the 'discretionary function or duty' that cannot form a basis for suit under the Tort Claims Act includes more than the initiation of programs and activities. It also includes determinations made by executives or administrators in establishing plans, specifications or

schedules of operations. Where there is room for policy judgment and decision there is discretion. It necessarily follows that acts of subordinates in carrying out the operations of government in accordance with official directions cannot be actionable."

Respondents here insist that the view of § 2680(a) expressed in *Dalehite* has been eroded, if not overruled, by subsequent cases construing the Act, particularly *Indian Towing Co. v. United States*, 350 U.S. 61 (1955), and *Eastern Air Lines, Inc. v. Union Trust Co.*, 221 F.2d 62, *aff'd per curiam sub nom. United States v. Union Trust Co.*, 350 U.S. 907 (1955). While the Court's reading of the Act admittedly has not followed a straight line, we do not accept the supposition that *Dalehite* no longer represents a valid interpretation of the discretionary function exception.

Indian Towing Co. v. United States involved a claim under the Act for damages to cargo aboard a vessel that ran aground, allegedly owing to the failure of the light in a lighthouse operated by the Coast Guard. The plaintiffs contended that the Coast Guard had been negligent in inspecting, maintaining, and repairing the light. Significantly, the Government *conceded* that the discretionary function exception was not implicated in *Indian Towing*, arguing instead that the Act contained an implied exception from liability for "uniquely governmental functions." The Court rejected the Government's assertion, reasoning that it would "push the courts into the 'non-governmental'-'governmental' quagmire that has long plagued the law of municipal corporations."

In *Eastern Air Lines, Inc. v. Union Trust Co.*, two aircraft collided in midair while both were attempting to land at Washington National Airport. The survivors of the crash victims sued the United States under the Act, asserting the negligence of air traffic controllers as the cause of the collision. The United States Court of Appeals for the District of Columbia Circuit permitted the suit against the Government. In its petition for certiorari, the Government urged the adoption of a "governmental function exclusion" from liability under the Act and pointed to § 2680(a) as textual support for such an exclusion. The Government stated further that § 2680(a) was "but one aspect of the broader exclusion from the statute of claims based upon the performance of acts of a uniquely governmental nature." This Court summarily affirmed, citing *Indian Towing Co. v. United States*. Given the thrust of the arguments presented in the petition for certiorari and the pointed citation to *Indian Towing*, the summary disposition in *Union Trust Co.* cannot be taken as a wholesale repudiation of the view of § 2680(a) set forth in *Dalehite*.[10]

10. Respondents' reliance upon *Rayonier, Inc. v. United States*, 352 U.S. 315 (1957), is equally misplaced. In *Rayonier* the Court revisited an issue considered briefly in *Dalehite:* whether the United States may be held liable for the alleged negligence of its employees in fighting a fire. In *Dalehite*, the Court held that alleged negligence in firefighting was not actionable under the Act, basing its decision upon "the normal rule that an alleged failure or carelessness of public firemen does not create private actionable rights." In so holding, the *Dalehite* Court did not discuss or rely upon the discretionary function exception. The *Rayonier* Court rejected the reasoning

As in *Dalehite*, it is unnecessary—and indeed impossible—to define with precision every contour of the discretionary function exception. From the legislative and judicial materials, however, it is possible to isolate several factors useful in determining when the acts of a Government employee are protected from liability by § 2680(a). First, it is the nature of the conduct, rather than the status of the actor, that governs whether the discretionary function exception applies in a given case. As the Court pointed out in *Dalehite*, the exception covers "[n]ot only agencies of government * * * but all employees exercising discretion." Thus, the basic inquiry concerning the application of the discretionary function exception is whether the challenged acts of a Government employee—whatever his or her rank—are of the nature and quality that Congress intended to shield from tort liability.

Second, whatever else the discretionary function exception may include, it plainly was intended to encompass the discretionary acts of the Government acting in its role as a regulator of the conduct of private individuals. Time and again the legislative history refers to the acts of regulatory agencies as examples of those covered by the exception, and it is significant that the early tort claims bills considered by Congress specifically exempted two major regulatory agencies by name. This emphasis upon protection for regulatory activities suggests an underlying basis for the inclusion of an exception for discretionary functions in the Act: Congress wished to prevent judicial "second-guessing" of legislative and administrative decisions grounded in social, economic, and political policy through the medium of an action in tort. By fashioning an exception for discretionary governmental functions, including regulatory activities, Congress took "steps to protect the Government from liability that would seriously handicap efficient government operations."

IV

We now consider whether the discretionary function exception immunizes from tort liability the FAA certification process involved in this case. Respondents in No. 82–1349 argue that the CAA was negligent in issuing a type certificate for the Boeing 707 aircraft in 1958 because the lavatory trash receptacle did not satisfy applicable safety regulations. Similarly, respondents in No. 82–1350 claim negligence in the FAA's issuance of a supplemental type certificate in 1965 for the DeHavilland Dove aircraft: they assert that the installation of the fuel line leading to the cabin heater violated FAA airworthiness standards. From the records in these cases there is no indication that either the Boeing 707 trash receptacle or the DeHavilland Dove cabin heater was actually inspected or reviewed by an FAA inspector or representative. Respondents thus argue in effect that the negligent failure of the FAA to inspect certain

of *Dalehite* on the ground that the liability of the United States under the Act is not restricted to that of a municipal corporation or other public body. While the holding of *Rayonier* obviously overrules one element of the judgment in *Dalehite*, the more fundamental aspects of *Dalehite*, including its construction of § 2680(a), remain undisturbed.

aspects of aircraft type design in the process of certification gives rise to a cause of action against the United States under the Act.

The Government, on the other hand, urges that the basic responsibility for satisfying FAA air safety standards rests with the *manufacturer*, not with the FAA. The role of the FAA, the Government says, is merely to police the conduct of private individuals by monitoring their compliance with FAA regulations. According to the Government, the FAA accomplishes its monitoring function by means of a "spot-check" program designed to encourage manufacturers and operators to comply fully with minimum safety requirements. Such regulatory activity, the Government argues, is the sort of governmental conduct protected by the discretionary function exception to the Act. We agree that the discretionary function exception precludes a tort action based upon the conduct of the FAA in certificating these aircraft for use in commercial aviation.

* * * [T]he Secretary of Transportation has the duty to promote safety in air transportation by promulgating reasonable rules and regulations governing the inspection, servicing, and overhaul of civil aircraft. * * *

In the exercise of this discretion, the FAA, as the Secretary's designee, has devised a system of compliance review that involves certification of aircraft design and manufacture at several stages of production. The FAA certification process is founded upon a relatively simple notion: the duty to ensure that an aircraft conforms to FAA safety regulations lies with the manufacturer and operator, while the FAA retains the responsibility for policing compliance. Thus, the manufacturer is required to develop the plans and specifications and perform the inspections and tests necessary to establish that an aircraft design comports with the applicable regulations; the FAA then reviews the data for conformity purposes by conducting a "spot check" of the manufacturer's work.

Respondents' contention that the FAA was negligent in failing to inspect certain elements of aircraft design before certificating the Boeing 707 and DeHavilland Dove necessarily challenges two aspects of the certification procedure: the FAA's decision to implement the "spot-check" system of compliance review, and the application of that "spot-check" system to the particular aircraft involved in these cases. In our view, both components of respondents' claim are barred by the discretionary function exception to the Act.

The FAA's implementation of a mechanism for compliance review is plainly discretionary activity of the "nature and quality" protected by § 2680(a). When an agency determines the extent to which it will supervise the safety procedures of private individuals, it is exercising discretionary regulatory authority of the most basic kind. Decisions as to the manner of enforcing regulations directly affect the feasibility and practicality of the Government's regulatory program; such decisions require the agency to establish priorities for the accomplishment of its policy objectives by balancing the objectives sought to be obtained against such practical considerations as staffing and funding. Here, the FAA has determined that a program of "spot-checking" manufacturers' compliance with minimum safety standards best accommodates the goal of air transportation safety and the reality of finite agency resources. Judicial intervention in such decisionmaking through private tort suits would require the courts to "second-guess" the political, social, and economic judgments of an agency exercising its regulatory function. It was precisely this sort of judicial intervention in policymaking that the discretionary function exception was designed to prevent.

It follows that the acts of FAA employees in executing the "spot-check" program in accordance with agency directives are protected by the discretionary function exception as well. The FAA employees who conducted compliance reviews of the aircraft involved in this case were specifically empowered to make policy judgments regarding the degree of confidence that might reasonably be placed in a given manufacturer, the need to maximize compliance with FAA regulations, and the efficient allocation of agency resources. In administering the "spot-check" program, these FAA engineers and inspectors necessarily took certain calculated risks, but those risks were encountered for the advancement of a governmental purpose and pursuant to the specific grant of authority in the regulations and operating manuals. Under such circumstances, the FAA's alleged negligence in failing to check certain specific items in the course of certificating a particular aircraft falls squarely within the discretionary function exception of § 2680(a).

V

In rendering the United States amenable to some suits in tort, Congress could not have intended to impose liability for the regulatory enforcement activities of the FAA challenged in this case. The FAA has a statutory duty to *promote* safety in air transportation, not to insure it. We hold that these actions against the FAA for its alleged negligence in certificating aircraft for use in commercial aviation are barred by the discretionary function exception of the Federal Tort Claims Act. Accordingly, the judgments of the United States Court of Appeals for the Ninth Circuit are reversed.

"Discretionary Functions" from *Dalehite* to *Gaubert*

As the *Varig* opinion notes, the *Dalehite* case is the foundational authority on the discretionary function exception. *Dalehite*'s test for discretion seemed to distinguish "planning" from "operational" activities. The former were immune; the latter not. Yet the Court also said that "[w]here there is room for policy judgment and decision there is discretion," a locution that seems capable of capturing most conscious and voluntary human conduct. Moreover, the Court found a large number of actions in *Dalehite* that seemed remote from policy judgment—such as selection of the type of bagging to be used and the bagging temperature of the nitrates—embraced in the general "Plan of Activities" concocted by the U.S. Field Director of Ammunition Plants.

Yet the Court soon afterwards took the "liberal" approach to the construction of the FTCA previously described in *Indian Towing* and *Rayonier*.

In response to this Janus-faced posture many lower court opinions prior to *Varig* found a waiver of immunity even where there clearly was "room for policy judgment and decision." In *Griffin v. United States*, 500 F.2d 1059, 1066–67 (3d Cir.1974), for example, the court allowed recovery against the government for the severe injuries suffered following administration of a dose of Sabin polio vaccine that the Division of Biological Standards had released. The DBS had formally promulgated a regulation establishing specifications that its employees were to apply in determining nonvirulence of batches of the vaccine—specifications that many outside experts had criticized as unnecessarily stringent. The DBS had released the batch of vaccine administered to Mrs. Griffin even though it did not meet these specifications. The court disagreed with the government's contention that the decision whether to release the vaccine was discretionary and that the DBS regulation required a judgmental determination:

> We acknowledge that under DBS's construction of the regulation, the implementation called for a judgmental determination as to the degree to which each of the enumerated criteria indicated neurovirulence. * * * The judgment, however, was that of a professional measuring neurovirulence. It was not that of a policy-maker promulgating regulations by balancing competing policy considerations in determining the public interest. * * * At issue was a scientific, but not policy-making, determination as to whether each of the criteria listed * * * was met and the extent to which each such factor accurately indicated neurovirulence. DBS's responsibility was limited to merely executing the policy judgments of the Surgeon General. * * *
>
> The Government's release of Lot 56 was predicated upon its reliance on a factor called "biological variation." Reliance on this factor, however, was not authorized by the regulations. We therefore conclude * * * that DBS's activity was not immunized from judicial review.

See also *Payton v. United States*, 636 F.2d 132 (5th Cir.1981), *modified en banc*, 679 F.2d 475 (5th Cir.1982) (holding certain aspects of a parole board's functions to be "operational" in suit by survivors of persons killed by a prisoner claimed to have been wrongfully released). But the lower court decisions are hardly uniform or consistently liberal in finding a waiver of immunity. See, e.g., Note, *Federal Tort Claims Act: The Development and Application of the Discretionary Function Exemption*, 13 Cum. L. Rev. 535 (1983).

Varig shifted interpretation in the lower courts toward the very broad reading of the discretionary function exception contained in *Dalehite*. Indeed, a substantial number of the courts of appeals read *Varig* to exempt all federal regulatory activity from the coverage of the Federal

Tort Claims Act. See D. Scott Barash, *The Discretionary Function Exception and Mandatory Regulations*, 54 U. Chi. L. Rev. 1300, 1320–22 (1987). See also *Allen v. United States*, 816 F.2d 1417, 1423 n. 8 (10th Cir.1987) (collecting the post-*Varig* authorities up to that point).

This tilt in the direction of restoring governmental immunity under the discretionary function exception apparently went too far. The Supreme Court reentered the fray in *Berkovitz v. United States*, 486 U.S. 531 (1988). Kevan Berkovitz, like Mrs. Griffin, claimed to have contracted polio from the administration of a dose of polio vaccine (Orimune) that was improperly licensed and released by the Division of Biologic Standards at the National Institutes of Health. A divided panel of the Third Circuit Court of Appeals (822 F.2d 1322 (3d Cir.1987)), analogizing the regulatory scheme to the one found in *Varig*, concluded that licensing vaccines and releasing particular batches for use were wholly discretionary actions that could not form the basis for a suit against the United States. The Supreme Court reversed in an extended opinion that seemed to lay out all the possible ways of analyzing the case as an instructional guide for the circuit courts. Walking carefully through the petitioners' allegations, the Court provided the following analysis:

> Petitioners' first allegation with regard to the licensing of Orimune is that the DBS [Division of Biologic Standards of the NIH, now the FDA Center for Biologics Evaluation and Research] issued a product license without first receiving data that the manufacturer must submit showing how the product, at the various stages of the manufacturing process, matched up against regulatory safety standards. The discretionary function exception does not bar a cause of action based on this allegation. The statute and regulations require, as a precondition to licensing, that the DBS receive certain test data from the manufacturer relating to the product's compliance with regulatory standards. The DBS has no discretion to issue a license without first receiving the required test data; to do so would violate a specific statutory and regulatory directive. Accordingly, to the extent that petitioners' licensing claim is based on a decision of the DBS to issue a license without having received the required test data, the discretionary function exception imposes no bar.
>
> Petitioners' other allegation regarding the licensing of Orimune is difficult to describe with precision. Petitioners contend that the DBS licensed Orimune even though the vaccine did not comply with certain regulatory safety standards.[9] This charge may be understood

9. Petitioners point to two specific regulatory standards that the product allegedly failed to satisfy. First, petitioners claim that an original virus strain from which the vaccine was made did not comply with the requirement that the strain be "free of harmful effect upon administration in the recommended dosage to at least 100,000 people susceptible to poliomyelitis." Second, petitioners assert that the strain, a seed virus, a vaccine monopool, and the ultimate vaccine product failed to comply with the regulatory scheme's neurovirulence requirement. Neurovirulence is the capacity of an infectious agent to produce pathologic effects on the central nervous system. In this context, it refers to the vaccine's ability to cause paralytic poliomyelitis. The neurovirulence of a vaccine product is tested by injecting the product into monkeys. The

in any of three ways. First, petitioners may mean that the DBS licensed Orimune without first making a determination as to whether the vaccine complied with regulatory standards. Second, petitioners may intend to argue that the DBS specifically found that Orimune failed to comply with certain regulatory standards and nonetheless issued a license for the vaccine's manufacture. Third, petitioners may concede that the DBS made a determination of compliance, but alleged that this determination was incorrect. Neither petitioners' complaint nor their briefs and argument before this Court make entirely clear their theory of the case.

If petitioners aver that the DBS licensed Orimune either without determining whether the vaccine complied with regulatory standards or after determining that the vaccine failed to comply, the discretionary function exception does not bar the claim. Under the scheme governing the DBS's regulation of polio vaccines, the DBS may not issue a license except upon an examination of the product and a determination that the product complies with all regulatory standards. The agency has no claim to deviate from this mandated procedure.[10] Petitioners' claim, if interpreted as alleging that the DBS licensed Orimune in the absence of a determination that the vaccine complied with regulatory standards, therefore does not challenge a discretionary function. Rather, the claim charges a failure on the part of the agency to perform its clear duty under federal law. When a suit charges an agency with failing to act in accord with a specific mandatory directive, the discretionary function exception does not apply.

If petitioners' claim is that the DBS made a determination that Orimune complied with regulatory standards, but that the determination was incorrect, the question of the applicability of the discretionary function exception requires a somewhat different analysis. In that event, the question turns on whether the manner and method of determining compliance with the safety standards at issue involves agency judgment of the kind protected by the discretionary function exception.[11] Petitioners contend that the determination involves the application of objective scientific standards, whereas the Government asserts that the determination incorporates considerable "policy judgment." In making these assertions, the parties have

product meets the neurovirulence criterion only if a specified number of the animals survive and a "comparative analysis" demonstrate that the neurovirulence of the vaccine product "does not exceed" the neurovirulence of a reference product previously selected by the agency.

10. Even the Government conceded at oral argument that the DBS has no discretion to issue a product license without an examination of the product and a determination that the product complies with regulatory standards. * * *

11. * * * [T]he regulatory standards that petitioners claim were not satisfied in this case are the neurovirulence criterion and the requirement that virus strains be free from harmful effect. The question presented is thus whether the determination that a vaccine product complies with each of these regulatory standards involves judgment of the kind that the discretionary function exception protects.

framed the issue appropriately; application of the discretionary function exception to the claim that the determination of compliance was incorrect hinges on whether the agency officials making that determination permissibly exercise policy choice. The parties, however, have not addressed this question in detail, and they have given us no indication of the way in which the DBS interprets and applies the regulations setting forth the criteria for compliance. Given that these regulations are particularly abstruse, we hesitate to decide the question on the scanty record before us. We therefore leave it to the District Court to decide, if petitioners choose to press this claim, whether agency officials appropriately exercise policy judgment in determining that a vaccine product complies with the relevant safety standards.

The regulatory scheme governing release of vaccine lots is distinct from that governing the issuance of licenses. The former set of regulations places an obligation on manufacturers to examine all vaccine lots prior to distribution to ensure that they comply with regulatory standards. These regulations, however, do not impose a corresponding duty on the Bureau of Biologics. Although the regulations empower the Bureau to examine any vaccine lot and prevent the distribution of a noncomplying lot, see 21 CFR § 610.2(a) (1978), they do not require the Bureau to take such action in all cases. The regulations generally allow the Bureau to determine the appropriate manner in which to regulate the release of vaccine lots, rather than mandating certain kinds of agency action. The regulatory scheme governing the release of vaccine lots is substantially similar in this respect to the scheme discussed in *United States v. Varig Airlines.*

Given this regulatory context, the discretionary function exception bars any claims that challenge the Bureau's formulation of policy as to the appropriate way in which to regulate the release of vaccine lots * * *. In addition, if the policies and programs formulated by the Bureau allow room for implementing officials to make independent policy judgments, the discretionary function exception protects the acts taken by those officials in the exercise of this discretion. * * * The discretionary function exception, however, does not apply if the acts complained of do not involve the permissible exercise of policy discretion. Thus, if the Bureau's policy leaves no room for an official to exercise policy judgment in performing a given act, or if the act simply does not involve the exercise of such judgment, the discretionary function exception does not bar a claim that the act was negligent or wrongful. * * *

Viewed in light of these principles, petitioners' claim regarding the release of the vaccine lot from which Kevan Berkovitz received his dose survives the Government's motion to dismiss. Petitioners allege that, under the authority granted by the regulations, the Bureau of Biologics has adopted a policy of testing all vaccine lots for compliance with safety standards and preventing the distribution to the public of any lots that fail to comply. Petitioners further allege that notwithstanding this policy, which allegedly leaves no room for implementing officials to exercise independent policy judgment, employees of the Bureau knowingly approved the release of a lot that did not comply with safety standards. Thus, petitioners' complaint is directed at a governmental action that allegedly involved no policy discretion. Petitioners, of course, have not proved their factual allegations, but they are not required to do so on a motion to dismiss. If those allegations are correct—that is, if the Bureau's policy did not allow the official who took the challenged action to release a noncomplying lot on the basis of policy considerations—the discretionary function exception does not bar the claim.

Federal regulators' attempts to deal with the many crises in the savings and loan industry gave the Supreme Court yet another opportunity to instruct the lower courts in *United States v. Gaubert*, 499 U.S. 315 (1991). At the time that the events in *Gaubert* occurred, the Federal Homeowners Loan Act authorized the Federal Home Loan Bank Board (FHLBB) to prescribe rules and regulations "for the organization, incorporation, examination, and regulation" of federal savings and loan associations, and to issue charters, "giving primary consideration to the best practices of thrift institutions in the United States," 12 U.S.C. § 1464(a). Exercising this authority with the respect to the Independent American Savings Association (IASA), the FHLBB and the Federal Home Loan Bank–Dallas (FHLB–D) made a substantial number of "informal" demands of IASA. Gaubert, Chairman of the Board and IASA's largest stockholder, was asked to remove himself from management and to post a $25,000,000 security bond to guarantee his representation that IASA's net worth would exceed regulatory minimums. The regulators ultimately requested the removal of all of IASA's management and the appointment of new management and directors recommended by FHLB–D. FHLB–D then became continuously involved in IASA's business operations—recommending the hiring of consultants, advising the institution concerning the timing of voluntary bankruptcies for its subsidiaries, mediating salary disputes and even reviewing drafts of complaints to be used in litigation. The new directors soon announced that IASA had a substantial negative net worth and the Federal Savings and Loan Insurance Corporation (FHLIC) put the institution into receivership.

Gaubert sued, claiming that the incompetent actions of the regulators had destroyed the value of IASA, thus devaluing his stock holdings by $75,000,000 and requiring the forfeiture of his $25,000,000 bond. The Government moved to dismiss on the ground that all the regulators' actions had been within the discretionary function exception to the Federal Tort Claims Act. The district court granted the Government's motion, but the Fifth Circuit Court of Appeals, relying on *Indian Towing*, reversed. The appeals court found that at least those claims concerning the regulators' activities after they assumed supervisory control of IASA's day-to-day affairs were not "policy decisions," which fall within the exception to the FTCA, but were "operational actions" which do not.

The Supreme Court granted certiorari and reversed. The Court was at pains to point out that neither *Indian Towing* nor *Dalehite* supported a strict dichotomy between "planning level" functions which were within the discretionary function exception and "operational activities" which were not. Writing for a near-unanimous court (only Justice Scalia filed a concurring opinion), Justice White once again attempted to give concrete meaning to the elusive distinction between discretionary and nondiscretionary acts.

> Where Congress has delegated the authority to an independent agency or to the executive branch to implement the general provisions of a regulatory statute and to issue regulations to that end, there is no doubt that planning level decisions establishing programs are protected by the discretionary function exception, as is the promulgation of regulations by which the agencies are to carry out the programs. In addition, the actions of Government agents involving the necessary element of choice and grounded in the social, economic, or political goals of the statute and regulations are protected.
>
> * * * Not all agencies issue comprehensive regulations, however. Some establish policy on a case-by-case basis, whether through adjudicatory proceedings or through administration of agency programs. Others promulgate regulations on some topics, but not on others. In addition, an agency may rely on internal guidelines rather than on published regulations. In any event, it will most often be true that the general aims and policies of the controlling statute will be evident from its text.
>
> When established governmental policy, as expressed or implied by statute, regulation, or agency guidelines, allows a Government agent to exercise discretion, it must be presumed that the agent's acts are grounded in policy when exercising that discretion. For a complaint to survive a motion to dismiss, it must allege facts which would support a finding that the challenged actions are not the kind of conduct that can be said to be grounded in the policy of the regulatory regime. The focus of the inquiry is not on the agent's subjective intent in exercising the discretion conferred by statute or regulation, but on the nature of the actions taken and on whether they are susceptible to policy analysis.[7]
>
> In light of our cases and their interpretation of § 2680(a), it is clear that the Court of Appeals erred in holding that the exception does not reach decisions made at the operational or management

7. There are obviously discretionary acts performed by a Government agent that are within the scope of his employment but not within the discretionary function exception because these acts cannot be said to be based on the purposes that the regulatory regime seeks to accomplish. If one of the officials involved in this case drove an automobile on a mission connected with his official duties and negligently collided with another car, the exception would not apply. Although driving requires the constant exercise of discretion, the official's decisions in exercising that discretion can hardly be said to be grounded in regulatory policy.

level of the bank involved in this case. A discretionary act is one that involves choice or judgment; there is nothing in that description that refers exclusively to policy making or planning functions. Day-to-day management of banking affairs, like the management of other businesses, regularly requires judgment as to which of a range of permissible courses is the wisest. Discretionary conduct is not confined to the policy or planning level. "[I]t is the nature of the conduct, rather than the status of the actor, that governs whether the discretionary function exception applies in a given case." *Varig Airlines, supra.*

The Court's first use of the term "operational" in connection with the discretionary function exception occurred in *Dalehite*, where the Court noted that "[t]he decisions held culpable were all responsibly made at a planning rather than operational level and involved considerations more or less important to the practicality of the Government's fertilizer program." 346 U.S. at 42. Gaubert relies upon this statement as support for his argument that the Court of Appeals applied the appropriate analysis to the allegations of the Amended Complaint, but the distinction in *Dalehite* was merely a description of the level at which the challenged conduct occurred. There was no suggestion that decisions made at an operational level could not also be based on policy.

Neither is the decision below supported by *Indian Towing*. There the Coast Guard had negligently failed to maintain a lighthouse by allowing the light to go out. The United States was held liable, not because the negligence occurred at the operational level but because making sure the light was operational "did not involve any permissible exercise of policy judgment." Indeed, the Government did not even claim the benefit of the exception but unsuccessfully urged that maintaining the light was a governmental function for which it could not be liable. The court of appeals misinterpreted *Berkovitz's* references to *Indian Towing* as perpetuating a nonexistent dichotomy between discretionary functions and operational activities. Consequently, once the court determined that some of the actions challenged by Gaubert occurred at an operational level, it concluded, incorrectly, that those actions must necessarily have been outside the scope of the discretionary function exception.

Turning to the question of whether the particular acts alleged by Gaubert were "discretionary" within the meaning of § 2680(a), Justice White continued:

We first inquire whether the challenged actions were discretionary, or whether they were instead controlled by mandatory statutes or regulations. Although the FHLBB, which oversaw the other agencies at issue, had promulgated extensive regulations which were then in effect, see 12 CFR §§ 500–591 (1986), neither party has identified formal regulations governing the conduct in question. As already noted, 12 U.S.C. § 1464(a) authorizes the FHLBB to examine and regulate FSSLA's, "giving primary consideration to the best practices of thrift institutions in the United States." Both the District Court and the Court of Appeals recognized that the agencies possessed broad statutory authority to supervise financial institutions. The relevant statutory provisions were not mandatory, but left to the judgment of the agency the decision of when to institute proceedings against a financial institution and which mechanism to use. * * *

We are unconvinced by Gaubert's assertion that because the agencies did not institute formal proceedings against IASA, they had no discretion to take informal actions as they did. Although the statutes provided only for formal proceedings, there is nothing in the language or structure of the statutes that prevented the regulators from invoking less formal means of supervision of financial institutions. Not only was there no statutory or regulatory mandate which compelled the regulators to act in a particular way, but there was no prohibition against the use of supervisory mechanisms not specifically set forth in statute or regulation.

* * *

Gaubert also argues that the challenged actions fall outside the discretionary function exception because they involved the mere application of technical skills and business expertise. But this is just another way of saying that the considerations involving the day-to-day management of a business concern such as IASA are so precisely formulated that decisions at the operational level never involve the exercise of discretion within the meaning of § 2680(a), a notion that we have already rejected in disapproving the rationale of the Court of Appeals' decision. It may be that certain decisions resting on mathematical calculations, for example, involve no choice or judgment in carrying out the calculations, but the regulatory acts alleged here are not of that genre. Rather, it is plain to us that each of the challenged actions involved the exercise of choice and judgment.

We are also convinced that each of the regulatory actions in question involved the kind of policy judgment that the discretionary function exception was designed to shield. The FHLBB Resolution quoted above,* coupled with the relevant statutory provisions, established governmental policy which is presumed to have been fur-

* [The Resolution stated in pertinent part:

"In each case, based upon an assessment of management's willingness to take appropriate corrective action and the potential harm to the institution if corrective action is not effected, the staff must weigh the appropriateness of available supervisory actions. If the potential harm is slight and there is a substantial probability that management will correct the situation, informal supervisory guidance and oversight is appropriate. If some potential harm to the institution or its customers is likely, a supervisory agreement should be promptly negotiated and implemented. If substantial financial harm may occur to the institution, its customers, or the FSLIC and there is substantial doubt that corrections will be made promptly, a cease-and-desist order should be sought immediately through the Office of General Counsel." FHLBB Resolution No. 82–381 (May 26, 1982).]

thered when the regulators exercised their discretion to choose from various courses of action in supervising IASA. Although Gaubert contends that day-to-day decisions concerning IASA's affairs did not implicate social, economic, or political policies, even the Court of Appeals recognized that these day-to-day "operational" decisions were undertaken for policy reasons of primary concern to the regulatory agencies:

"[T]he federal regulators here had two discrete purposes in mind as they commenced day-to-day operations at IASA. First, they sought to protect the solvency of the Savings and Loan industry at large, and maintain the public's confidence in that industry. Second, they sought to preserve the assets of IASA for the benefit of depositors and shareholders, of which Gaubert was one."

Consequently, Gaubert's assertion that the day-to-day involvement of the regulators with IASA is actionable because it went beyond "normal regulatory activity" is insupportable.

Justice Scalia concurred specially to make clear that, in his view, while the bureaucratic level of the decision maker was not determinative, the level at which a decision was made was nevertheless relevant to the discretionary function inquiry—and often highly probative:

This test [i.e., the one established in *Dalehite, Varig* and *Berkovitz*], by looking not only to the decision but also the officer who made it, recognizes that there is something to the planning vs. operational dichotomy—though the "something" is not precisely what the Court of Appeals believed. Ordinarily, an employee working at the operational level is not responsible for policy decisions, even though policy considerations may be highly relevant to his actions. The dock foreman's decision to store bags of fertilizer in a highly compact fashion is not protected by this exception because, even if he carefully calculated considerations of cost to the government versus safety, it was not his responsibility to ponder such things; the Secretary of Agriculture's decision to the same effect is protected, because weighing those considerations is his task. In *Indian Towing Co. v. United States*, the United States was held liable for, among other things, the failure of Coast Guard maintenance personnel adequately to inspect electrical equipment in a lighthouse; though there could conceivably be policy reasons for conducting only superficial inspections, the decisions had been made by the maintenance personnel, and it was assuredly not their responsibility to ponder such things. This same factor explains why it is universally acknowledged that the discretionary function exception never protects against liability for the negligence of a vehicle driver. The need for expedition vs. the need for safety may well represent a policy choice, *supra*, but the government does not expect its drivers to make that choice on a case-by-case basis.

Moreover, not only is it necessary for application of the discretionary function exception that the decisionmaker be an official who possesses the relevant policy responsibility, but also the decision-maker's close identification with policymaking can be strong evidence that the other half of the test is met—i.e., that the subject-matter of the decision is one that ought to be informed by policy considerations. I am much more inclined to believe, for example, that the manner of storing fertilizer raises economic policy concerns if the decision on that subject has been reserved to the Secretary of Agriculture himself.

The Supreme Court may have done the best that it could in *Berkovitz* and *Gaubert* to provide guidance to lower courts concerning the application of the discretionary function exception. The circuit courts, however, continue to struggle with its application. *Shansky v. United States*, 164 F.3d 688 (1st Cir.1999), is representative. The plaintiff fell down a flight of steps at the Hubbell Trading Post, a national historic site in Ganado, Arizona. She was seriously injured and urged that the Park Service had been negligent in not installing a handrail or a warning sign near the steps. The National Park Service urged successfully that its decision about whether to install safety devices was a discretionary function within the meaning of the discretionary function exception of the FTCA.

With a tight grip on its instructions from the Supreme Court in *Berkovitz* and *Gaubert*, the First Circuit divided the issue into two questions: "Is the conduct itself discretionary?" "If so, is the discretion susceptible to policy-related judgments?" The court viewed the first question as involving a determination of whether there was some binding policy that would require the installation of handrails or warning signs by the Park Service. It found no such policy either in legislation concerning the management of historic sites, Park Service regulations or guidelines, or Park Service practice amounting to the adoption of a binding policy.

The plaintiff urged, nevertheless, that the Park Service had not in fact exercised policy judgment in this case. She offered to demonstrate that, even though the Park Service *might* have balanced questions of safety and maintenance of historic authenticity when refurbishing the Hubbell Trading Post, it had not in fact done so, but merely neglected to provide standard safety devices.

The court, citing authority in other circuits, held that this offered proof was unavailing. The question was not whether governmental officials actually balanced policy considerations in this case, but whether the choice made was *susceptible* of policy choice.

While this formulation might suggest that application of the *Berkovitz–Gaubert* formula should be relatively easy at the stage of a motion to dismiss, the First Circuit went on to qualify its holding: "Let us be perfectly clear. We do not suggest that any conceivable policy justification will suffice to prime the discretionary function pump. Virtually any government action can be traced back to a policy decision of some kind, but an attenuated tie is not enough to show that conduct is grounded in policy * * *. a case-by-case approach is required."

This language might seem to take back virtually all of the protection against fact-based inquiry that the court's earlier criteria for the discretionary function exception had provided. Indeed, the court's citation of *Cope v. Scott*, 45 F.3d 445 (D.C.Cir.1995), with approval suggests as much. The plaintiff in *Cope* had been allowed to demonstrate that, although the National Park Service might have been balancing aesthetic considerations and safety when providing signs on a Park Service road, it in fact had "chosen to manage the road in a manner more amenable to communing through nature than communing with it." Hence, the Park Service was exercising only a technical, safety-assessment type of discretion when signing the road rather than a discretion that involved the exercise of policy choice. That the distinction here is a fine one hardly needs to be emphasized. As the First Circuit acknowledged in *Shansky*, "[c]ase-by-case development has led to some disarray."

Courts and commentators have continued to complain that the discretionary function exception permits neither consistent application of the law nor reasonable compensation for harms caused by the action or inaction of the federal government. Judge Merritt of the Sixth Circuit complained in a 1997 dissenting opinion, for example, that the discretionary function exception has "swallowed, digested and excreted" the FTCA's waiver of immunity. *Rosebush v. U.S.* 119 F.3d 438, 444. Taken together, the critical literature combines impressively comprehensive scholarship, passionate denunciation of the current system, and a host of plausible reform proposals. But Congress seems unmoved. For a collection of critiques and proposals and an argument for displacing the whole tort approach with a worker's-compensation-inspired, limited-liability statute, see James R. Levin, *The Federal Tort Claims Act: A Proposal for Institutional Reform*, 100 Colum. L. Rev. 1538 (2000).

Other Critical Aspects of the Application of the Federal Tort Claims Act

Analogous Private Liability. The FTCA's reference to state law for its basic notions of "duty owed" can be troublesome. The first Supreme Court case to confront the question, *Feres v. United States*, 340 U.S. 135 (1950), held that the government was not liable to service members for injuries that were incidental to military service, even though such injuries were not within the specific FTCA exception for claims arising out of "combatant activities of the military." The Court reasoned that there simply was no recovery on behalf of military personnel for negligence against the government anywhere in American law.

The government pursued this "uniquely governmental" function notion in both *Indian Towing* and *Rayonier*. Those cases involved claims of negligence, respectively, in the operation of a lighthouse and in fighting a fire. Taking a broader view of the reference to private law than in *Feres*, however, the Court in those cases analogized the liability asserted to "good Samaritan" liability. The Court interpreted the FTCA to require that claims only be like some private claim recognized by state law, not the same as some existing private liability. Such a construction seemed essential to avoid remitting both the "waiver" and the "cause or action" issues to state law. For as the Government surely recognized, a requirement of identity would reintroduce immunity wherever state law provided immunity for "governmental functions." Such a result would be anomalous to say the least.

United States v. Muniz, 374 U.S. 150 (1963), was another step in detaching federal tort liability from state law. There federal prisoners were permitted to maintain a negligence suit against their jailers even though in many states such an action was not recognized. The Court viewed the case as one in which the duty of care was fixed by federal statute (18 U.S.C. § 4042) "independent of an inconsistent state rule." One should not conclude, however, that the details of state law are unimportant. The cases are legion in which the specific contours of state common law or statute control the outcome of FTCA litigation. See, e.g., *Aguilar v. United States*, 920 F.2d 1475 (9th Cir.1990) (holding that the FTCA incorporates state statute limiting amount of damages).

Subsequent litigation concerning the *Feres* doctrine suggests that it is based on policy grounds quite independent of the lack of closely analogous private liability under state law. *United States v. Johnson*, 481 U.S. 681 (1987), is exemplary. Lieutenant Commander Johnson was a helicopter pilot serving in the United States Coast Guard. He was killed during a search and rescue operation while under the radar control of Federal Aviation Administration civilian employees. His estate sued the government for the alleged negligence of its civilian air traffic controllers. The United States argued that under the *Feres* doctrine Johnson could not recover.

The Eleventh Circuit found *Feres* inapplicable. It viewed the "*Feres* factual paradigm" as one in which one member of the armed services sues another and in which an investigation of possible liability would involve civilian courts in judging the appropriateness of the conduct of persons acting in the special context of military services. In the Eleventh Circuit's opinion, although the Supreme Court had articulated numerous rationales for the *Feres* doctrine, its primary justification lay in avoiding the effects of civil litigation on military organization and discipline. Applying that understanding to the facts of *Johnson*, the court found "[a]bsolutely no hint * * * that the conduct of any alleged tortfeasor even remotely connected to the military will be scrutinized if this case proceeds to trial."

The Supreme Court reversed. Reviewing the reasons that it had given for the exclusion of suits by military personnel under the Federal Tort Claims Act, the Court identified three controlling bases for the *Feres* doctrine. First was the consideration that the relationship between the government and members of the armed forces is "distinctively federal" in character. Second was the existence of generous statutory disability and death benefits for military personnel outside of the Federal Tort Claims Act. And third was the consideration that such claims, if generally permitted, would involve the judiciary in sensitive military affairs at the potential expense of military discipline and effectiveness. In the Court's view none of these reasons gave critical significance to the status of the alleged tortfeasor. The majority thus reaffirmed the broad statement in *Feres* that suits were barred for injuries that "arise out of or are in the course of activity incident to service."

Justices Scalia, Brennan, Marshall, and Stevens dissented. In a scathing review of the various rationales offered for the *Feres* doctrine, Justice Scalia found none to have any solid justification. Moreover, because the *Feres* doctrine itself had no basis in the text of the Federal Tort Claims Act, he would happily have overruled that precedent, but for the fact that the respondent had not asked the Court to do so. In any event, the four dissenters believed that there was surely no reason to extend the exception beyond the situation that had been presented in *Feres* itself, that is, lawsuits in which both the victim and tortfeasor were members of the armed services.

Notwithstanding its bare majority support, the *Feres* doctrine maintains its vigor in the courts of appeals, and apparently in the Supreme Court as well. Although well-known for its perceived propensity to bend Supreme Court doctrine in the pursuit of its vision of substantive justice, the Ninth Circuit held in *Costo v. United States*, 248 F.3d 863 (9th Cir.2001), that suits related to recreational activities sponsored by the military should be treated the same as any other military activity under *Feres*. The Supreme Court denied certiorari, 534 U.S. 1078 (2002).

Negligent or Wrongful. Section 1346(b) also limits liability to injuries caused by a "negligent or wrongful act." The government's liability for negligence is essentially congruent with that of private persons, subject to the exceptions in section 2680. An official's actions can be shown to have been "negligent" not only by proving that they were taken without the precautions a reasonable person would have taken under the same circumstances, but also by demonstrating that they deviated from a federal statute or regulation promulgated to assure protection of the plaintiff's interests. See *Griffin v. United States*, 500 F.2d 1059 (3d Cir.1974).

The term "wrongful" has been given a narrow construction and expands the government's liability only to the extent of allowing recovery for some trespasses that might not technically be considered negligent. See *Dalehite v. United States*, 346 U.S. 15, 45 (1953); see also Richard A. Merrill, *Compensation for Prescription Drug Injuries*, 59 Va. L. Rev. 1, 71 (1973). An example is *Hatahley v. United States*, 351 U.S. 173 (1956), where the Supreme Court allowed certain Navajo Indians to recover for the destruction of their horses by federal agents purporting to act under federal public lands legislation and the Utah abandoned horse statute. See also *United States v. Praylou*, 208 F.2d 291 (4th

Cir.1953), *cert. denied*, 347 U.S. 934 (1954) (allowing recovery for property damages caused by the crash of government airplane).

In 1972, the Supreme Court laid to rest speculation that the term "wrongful" might permit recovery on a theory of strict or absolute ability. *Laird v. Nelms*, 406 U.S. 797, 801 (1972), was an action for damages caused by a sonic boom from overflying military aircraft. The plaintiff relied on North Carolina precedents imposing absolute liability for harm caused by an ultrahazardous activity. A majority held that the Act did not embrace such a theory: "Congress intended to permit liability essentially based on the intentionally wrongful or careless conduct of Government employees, for which the Government was to be made liable according to state law under the doctrine of *respondeat superior*, but to exclude liability based solely on the ultrahazardous nature of an activity undertaken by the Government."

The necessity of alleging negligence or some other ground of "wrongfulness" closely analogous to negligence is not always an impediment. As the Supreme Court's opinion in *Sheridan v. United States*, 487 U.S. 392 (1988), demonstrates, recharacterizing a tort as a species of negligence may avoid the FTCA's prohibitions on bringing certain intentional tort actions. In *Sheridan* petitioners had been injured when an off-duty serviceman fired several rifle shots into their automobile. The serviceman worked at Bethesda Naval Hospital where, shortly before firing on the petitioners, he had been observed by naval corpsmen as obviously drunk and brandishing a rifle. The corpsmen fled the scene and made no report or warning concerning the incident either to hospital authorities or local police. The petitioners' claim was that the government (through its agents, the corpsmen) had been negligent in allowing the serviceman to leave the hospital in a drunken condition and with a loaded rifle in his possession.

The court of appeals affirmed a district court order dismissing the action on the ground that the claim was barred by 28 U.S.C. § 2680(h), which excepts from the FTCA's coverage any claim "arising out of" an assault or battery, among other intentional torts. The Supreme Court reversed. Given the petitioners' theory, a majority of the Court believed that the assault or battery exception was inapplicable. If under Maryland law a private hospital could on the facts be held negligent on a "good samaritan" theory, then the petitioner's claim arose out of the acts of the naval corpsmen and liability would attach even had the drunken serviceman been a nongovernmental employee, patient, or visitor at the hospital. Justice O'Connor, joined by the Chief Justice and Justice Scalia, disagreed. The dissenters thought it linguistically implausible to say that the petitioner's claim did not "arise out of" an assault and battery. Since the FTCA excluded all such claims, they viewed the Court's opinion as impermissibly narrowing a clear exception to the government's waiver of immunity.

Misrepresentation. The statutory exception for injuries arising out of misrepresentation has produced several controversial decisions. (One torts scholar, Marshall Shapo, *A Representational Theory of Consumer Protection: Doctrine, Function and Legal Liability for Product Disappointment*, 60 Va. L. Rev. 1109 (1974), has suggested that much, if not the whole, of tort law might be unified around a broadly conceived notion of representational harm.) The troublesome cases under the FTCA have involved negligent or reckless misstatements, rather than deliberate deceptions, which would appear to be covered by "deceit." For example, in *Jones v. United States*, 207 F.2d 563 (2d Cir.1953), *cert. denied*, 347 U.S. 921 (1954), owners of oil production rights in certain government land sued to recover damages they sustained when they sold their interest in reliance on an understatement by the U.S. Geological Survey of the land's productive capacity. The court dismissed their action as sounding in misrepresentation. In a well-known case, *United States v. Neustadt*, 366 U.S. 696 (1961), the Supreme Court held that the government was not liable to the purchaser of a house who had relied on an inspection and appraisal conducted by an FHA inspector. The "misrepresentation" exception has also sheltered the government from liability for injuries resulting from erroneous inspection of food products by FDA officers. *Anglo-American & Overseas Corp. v. United States*, 242 F.2d 236 (2d Cir.1957); *Mizokami v. United States*, 414 F.2d 1375 (Ct.Cl.1969).

Constitutional Torts. The FTCA's incorporation of state tort law limits recovery against the government for tort-like violations of individual constitutional rights to situations in which state law recognizes an analogous negligent or intentional tort. *Birnbaum v. United States*, 436 F.Supp. 967 (E.D.N.Y.1977), *reversed on other grounds*, 588 F.2d 319 (2d Cir.1978), for example, permitted an action under the FTCA when CIA agents opened and copied plaintiff's mail. The claim could not be premised on violation of First or Fourth Amendment rights, however, but only on New York law recognizing the tort of invasion of privacy. And, of course, many official acts may not fit easily or at all, within the contours of common law tort notions. See, e.g., *Brown v. United States*, 653 F.2d 196 (5th Cir.1981), *cert. denied*, 456 U.S. 925 (1982) (finding an allegation of false testimony by U.S. official leading to unconstitutional arrest and conviction not actionable under Texas law). This peculiar state of affairs has led to numerous proposals for reform of the Federal Tort Claims Act. Note, *Rejecting Absolute Immunity for Federal Officials*, 71 Cal. L. Rev. 1707, 1708 n.8 (1983). See generally Peter H. Schuck, Suing Government: Citizen Remedies for Official Wrongs (1983).

Actions against the government that are founded on the Constitution but that seek monetary relief for conduct not recognized as tortious by state law might, of course, be thought to fall within the plain language of the Tucker Act. The generally restrictive approach to Tucker Act claims has, however, prevented relief other than that sought pursuant to the Fifth Amendment's just compensation clause. See Note, *Rethinking Sovereign Immunity after* Bivens, 57 N.Y.U. L. Rev. 597, 642–47 (1982).

Strangely enough, exclusion from the waiver provisions of the Federal Tort Claims Act can sometimes redound to a plaintiff's benefit. In *Federal Deposit Insurance Corporation v. Meyer*, 510 U.S. 471 (1994), respondent Meyer brought suit under the Due Process Clause claiming that his summary removal from his position as a senior official in a savings and loan association by the FDIC deprived him of property without due process of law. Meyer claimed that the FDIC was not immune from suit, not because of the Federal Tort Claims Act or the Tucker Act, but because its original legislation included a so-called "sue and be sued" clause that had been interpreted to constitute a broad waiver of the FDIC's immunity from suit. The government countered by arguing that the Federal Tort Claims Act limited the scope of sue and be sued waivers such as the one contained in the FDIC organic statute.

The specific section of the Federal Tort Claims Act at issue, 28 U.S.C. § 2679(a) reads:

> The authority of any federal agency to sue and be sued in its own name shall not be construed to authorize suits against such federal agency on claims which are cognizable under § 1346(b) of this title, and the remedies provided by this title in such cases shall be exclusive.

Because Meyer's constitutional claim would be excluded from the waiver in the Federal Tort Claims Act as one in which the United States would not be liable to the claimant "as a private person" "in accordance with the law of the place where this act or omission occurred," his action was not "cognizable" under § 1346(b). And, if Meyer could not sue under the Federal Tort Claims Act, that Act could hardly provide an exclusive remedy that limited the sue and be sued waiver in the FDIC statute.

Having avoided the immunity defense, Meyer's suit nevertheless failed on the ground that he had no cause of action against the government or one of its bureaus under the Due Process Clause. The Court thus refused to extend the so-called "*Bivens*" action against federal officials for deprivation of constitutional rights to action against the government itself. We will hold discussion of the rationale for that determination until we take up *Bivens* and its progeny in Chapter 9.

Sovereign Immunity and the Battle Over Interpretive Method

The cramped reading of the Tucker Act waiver combined with the often grudging construction of the Federal Tort Claims Act suggest a consistently "strict constructionist" approach to sovereign immunity doctrine, particularly to statutory waivers of immunity. Yet, the "sue and be sued" clause at issue in *Meyer* is characteristic of clauses contained in other statutes establishing federal corporations serving specialized functions, such as, the Federal Deposit Insurance Corporation, the Domestic and Foreign Commerce Corporation, or the Reconstruction Finance Corporation. The Court has often treated these clauses as creating a general presumption that immunity has been waived, and, where not indulging that presumption, has cautioned against interpreting the waiver as either broader or narrower than the Congress intended. See, e.g., *United States v. Kubrick*, 444 U.S. 111 (1979).

The sue and be sued cases also resonate with Supreme Court doctrine from the 1930s and 1940s, instructing that waivers of sovereign immunity should be "liberally construed," e.g., *United States v. Shaw*, 309 U.S. 495, 501 (1940), and characterizing the doctrine of sovereign immunity as "disfavored." *Brady v. Roosevelt S.S. Co.*, 317 U.S. 575, 580 (1943). Hence, up until the early 1990s, it might be fair to characterize the Supreme Court's approach to the interpretation of statutory waivers of immunity as eclectic. To some degree this eclecticism has represented merely the failure to unify or explain divergent lines of jurisprudence having differing historical antecedents. But, as our discussion of the discretionary function exception under the Federal Torts Claims Act illustrates, ambivalence about the degree to which the government's immunity should be expanded or contracted inhabits single lines of cases as well.

There is some evidence, nevertheless, that "strict construction" is becoming the norm in sovereign immunity jurisprudence. One ground for that belief is the gravitational pull of Eleventh Amendment sovereign immunity doctrine which has created a super-strong presumption against waivers of *state* immunity. We will return to this topic in Chapter 9. Another is the general affection of the contemporary Supreme Court for "clear statement rules." See generally William N. Eskridge, Jr., Dynamic Statutory Interpretation, 323–33 (1994); William N. Eskridge, Jr. and Philip P. Frickey, *Quasi-Constitutional Law: Clear Statement Rules or Constitutional Lawmaking*, 45 Vand. L. Rev. 593, 598–629 (1992). The Court's demands for congressional clear statements have ranged across a host of legal issues, including waivers of the federal government's sovereign immunity. This is at once a powerful and a limiting approach to statutory interpretation. Rather than asking what a statute means, clear statement rules ask "does this statute mean x?" Moreover, because the Court is asking whether the statute "clearly" means x, the Court often fails or, indeed refuses, to consider the purposes of a statutory waiver, the legislative history of that and similar provisions, or even whether a construction favoring waiver is the most plausible construction of the statute. Absent unambiguous waiver language on the face of the statutory text, sovereign immunity is preserved. See, e.g., *Ardestani v. INS*, 502 U.S. 129 (1991) (rejecting an attempt to recover attorney's fees under the Equal Access to Justice Act); *United States v. Nordic Village, Inc.*, 503 U.S. 30 (1992) (barring a trustee in bankruptcy from recovering company funds that were fraudulently used to pay individual tax liability); *United States Department of Energy v. Ohio*, see *supra* Chapter 8, Sec. A (barring recovery of civil penalties from the government where a governmental entity violated the Clean Water Act and the Resource Conservation Recovery Act).

Lane v. Pena, 518 U.S. 187 (1996), may be thought of as a "poster child" for the new clear statement approach to waivers of sovereign immunity. The plaintiff was a cadet at the United States Merchant

Marine Academy who had been expelled after being diagnosed with diabetes. After unsuccessfully challenging his separation administratively, petitioner sued the government under § 504(a) of the Rehabilitation Act which provides:

> "No otherwise qualified individual with a disability * * * shall, solely by reason of his or her disability, be excluded from the participation in; be denied the benefits of, or be subjected to discrimination under any program or activity receiving federal financial assistance, or under any program or activity conducted by any Executive agency or by the United States Postal Service."

The district court ordered that Lane be reinstated and awarded compensatory relief. The government did not challenge the reinstatement remedy, but challenged the compensation award urging that the rehabilitation act contained no "unequivocal expression" of congressional intent to waive the government's immunity to monetary damages. The D.C. Circuit agreed.

In affirming the D.C. Circuit's holding, the Supreme Court reviewed its waiver jurisprudence and enunciated four requirements for finding a waiver: (1) "A waiver of the federal government's sovereign immunity must be unequivocally expressed in the statutory text and will not be implied." (2) "[A] waiver of the government's sovereign immunity will be strictly construed, in terms of its scope, in favor of the sovereign." (3) The court required that any waiver of immunity extend "unambiguously" to monetary claims. And, (4), the Court excluded the use of legislative history in interpreting congressional intent. "[T]he unequivocal expression of elimination of sovereign immunity that we insist upon is an expression in statutory text."

Following these criteria the Court could not find an unequivocal statutory expression of a waiver covering Lane's case. The Rehabilitation Act's waiver of sovereign immunity incorporate the provisions of Title 6 of the Civil Rights of 1964, by providing that all such remedies "should be available to any person aggrieved by any act or failure to act by any recipient of federal assistance or federal provider of such assistance under § 504." Although the Department of Transportation is a provider of assistance subject to § 504 and to § 505's waiver of immunity, the Department when running the Merchant Marine Academy is not acting as a provider, but as an "Executive agency." That makes it subject to § 504's nondiscrimination requirements and to non-damage remedies such as reinstatement, but not to a suit for damages.

Lane's further arguments from the structure and the purpose of the statute were quickly rejected. The petitioner argued that it would be completely illogical for Congress to wish to waive federal government immunity when it acts as a mere provider of funds while not waiving federal executive agency immunity when it itself commits a violation of § 504(a). The Court admitted that as it was interpreting it, the statutory scheme was "somewhat bewildering." But, the Court continued, "The lack of perfect correlation on the various provisions does not indicate

* * * that the reading proposed by the government is entirely irrational." Indeed, the Court noted, other statutes, including the Administrative Procedure Act, provide relief against the United States while excluding claims for money damages.

Nor was the Court impressed by Lane's argument based on legislative history. Congress had enacted § 1003 of the Rehabilitation Act in response to the Supreme Court's decision in *Atascadero State Hospital v. Scanlon*, 473 U.S. 234 (1985), which held that Congress had not originally expressed an unmistakable intention under the Rehabilitation Act to abrogate state Eleventh Amendment immunity. Lane argued that, in making states liable under the Act through the addition of § 1003, Congress showed an implicit intention to treat all Rehabilitation Act defendants equally. Once again, it might be difficult to understand why Congress would subject all private parties, states as governmental entities, and the federal government as provider of funds to money damages under the Rehabilitation Act, while excluding non-provider federal defendants. However, there were "conceivable" interpretations of § 1003 that would exclude executive agencies acting in their executive capacity.

The Supreme Court majority's willingness to accept "not irrational" and merely "conceivable" interpretations as negativing the conclusion that Congress had spoken unequivocally prompted an exasperated dissent from Justices Stevens and Breyer. The dissenters concluded:

> The Court's strict approach to statutory waivers of sovereign immunity leads it to concentrate so carefully on textual details that it has lost sight of the primary purpose of judicial construction of Acts of Congress. We appropriately rely on canons of construction as tie-breakers to help us discern Congress' intent when its message is not entirely clear. The presumption against waivers of sovereign immunity serves that neutral purpose in doubtful cases. A rule that refuses to honor such a waiver because it could have been expressed with even greater clarity, or a rule that refuses to accept guidance from relevant and reliable legislative history, does not facilitate—indeed, actually obstructs—the neutral performance of the Court's task of carrying out the will of Congress.
>
> The prompt congressional reaction to our decision in *Atascadero* illustrates the lack of wisdom of the Court's rigid approach to waivers of sovereign immunity. It was true in that case, as it is in this, that Congress could have drafted a clearer statement of its intent. Our task, however, is not to educate busy legislators in the niceties and details of scholarly draftsmanship, but rather to do our best to determine what message they intended to convey. When judge-made rules require Congress to use its valuable time enacting and reenacting provisions whose original intent was clear to all but the most skeptical and hostile reader, those rules should be discarded.

The Court took a similarly restrictive view of language in the Federal Tort Claims Act in *Smith v. United States*, 507 U.S. 197 (1993).

The FTCA generally waives immunity but does not apply to "any claim arising in a foreign country." The petitioner's husband died in Antarctica. The petitioner alleged negligence on the part of the government under the FTCA and countered the government's "foreign country" defense by pointing out that Antarctica was not a country at all, but a denationalized zone protected by various treaties.

Chief Justice Rehnquist's opinion acknowledged that there were statements in prior cases suggesting that the waiver of sovereign immunity in the FTCA should be construed broadly. Indeed, dicta in *Nordic Village* had recently described the FTCA waiver as "sweeping." The Court, however, reaffirmed the principle first stated in *Kubrick* that the waivers should be read neither too broadly nor too narrowly. True to this more balanced methodological commitment, the Chief Justice identified plausible reasons to believe that the foreign country exception should also be applied to a territory like Antarctica.

Some cases raise questions about the consistency of the Supreme Court's commitment to the *Lane v. Pena* "unequivocal statement" principle in sovereign immunity cases. *Meyer*, as we have seen, maintains the broad view of "sue and be sued" clauses. Moreover, in *United States v. Idaho*, 508 U.S. 1 (1993), the Court ruled for the United States under the McCarran Amendment, governing the participation of federal government in state water law adjudication, but quoted its "balanced" approach from *Kubrick* along with admonitions that waivers must be express, strictly construed, and not enlarged beyond their statutory language. And, Justice Ginsberg expressed what she characterized as the Court's "preference for common sense inquiries over formalism" when finding a waiver of immunity in a tax case brought under the provision of 28 U.S.C. § 1346(a)(1) that creates federal jurisdiction over "any civil action against the United States for the recovery of any Internal Revenue tax alleged to be erroneously or illegally assessed or collected." *United States v. Williams*, 514 U.S. 527, 532 (1995). The IRS pointed to other provisions of the Internal Revenue Code that defined "taxpayer" in a way that arguably excluded the petitioner, who had paid taxes assessed against her former husband, under protest, in order to clear title to property received in a divorce settlement. Even Justice Scalia who repeated the clear statement rule, thought the IRS position "implausible." *Id.* at 1620 (Scalia, J., concurring).

Making sense of the sovereign immunity jurisprudence of the 1990s is no simple matter. One might argue that the Court has now established that a generous waiver approach continues under the sue and be sued statutes, that "balance" is to prevail in the interpretation of the Federal Tort Claims Act, and that everywhere else (or almost everywhere else) any claim of waiver of sovereign immunity requires a "clear statement," meaning an unequivocal waiver on the face of the statute. Moreover, where clear statement rules apply, they tend to be decisive. Apparently, clear statements are not unequivocal if there is any plausible contrary interpretation.

On this view doctrinal eclecticism still reigns but the Court's preference for "clear statements" is likely to color interpretation in many, if not most, cases. The invasion of sovereign immunity analysis by the clear statement rule thus further cements sovereign immunity doctrine and revives the basic question of why that doctrine should persist. Commentators generally view clear statement approaches to statutory interpretation as designed to protect crucial public or constitutional values. Why put sovereign immunity into this category? Indeed, in all of the cases just discussed, (and in a Northwestern Law Review article, *Is Justice Irrelevant*, 87 Nw. U. L. Rev. 1121 (1993)), Justice Stevens has attacked the need for sovereign immunity as well as his colleagues' desire to protect it.

No current Justice has responded on the merits to Justice Stevens' complaints. It is virtually impossible to find any commentator who supports the Court's approach. Enlightenment on these matters from Justice Scalia might be particularly pertinent. He is a staunch defender of the contemporary clear statement jurisprudence, but, while a law professor, he wrote one of the most persuasive articles on the incomprehensibility of the continuance of sovereign immunity in the modern American legal system. Antonin Scalia, *Sovereign Immunity and Nonstatutory Review of Federal Administrative Actions: Some Conclusions From the Public–Lands Cases*, 68 Mich. L. Rev. 867 (1970). For a more comprehensive discussion of the clear statement jurisprudence and sovereign immunity, see John Copeland Nagel, *Waiving Sovereign Immunity in an Age of Clear Statement Rule*, 1995 Wis. L. Rev. 771, and authorities there cited.

B. SUITS AGAINST FEDERAL OFFICERS

When the local representative of the Small Business Administration runs over your pet poodle on your way to the market, we expect the case to be disposed of in accordance with the principles that determine the liability of any person who damages the property of another. Indeed, the foundational understanding that officials have no special legal protections when sued for acts not connected with their offices applies equally to the President and to a General Services Administration carpenter's apprentice. *Clinton v. Jones*, 520 U.S. 681 (1997).

When a government employee acting in an official capacity harms the interests of a private party the legal situation changes. Although "judicial review" is presumptively available, we have already observed that, generally speaking, no suit for damages will lie against the U.S. government unless it has consented to be sued. And the exceptions to FTCA consent insulate a substantial range of official actions from a suit for damages against the government. This obstacle to relief alone would be sufficient to focus the plaintiff's attention on the immediate cause of his or her aggrievement, the official. Moreover, the conduct may have seemed sufficiently independent, or so outrageous, to make the official, rather than the government, the obvious target for suit. Not surprisingly, therefore, suits against government officers are common, and the principles that govern their disposition are important elements of the American public law system.

Such suits may be based on a variety of legal theories. The aggrieved party often can rely on established common law principles governing liability for the infliction of harm to person, property, or reputation. Statutes impose special duties on officials and may provide for specific remedies, including damages. For example, the several civil rights acts passed by Congress following the Civil War authorize private suits against state officers for the violation of any right guaranteed by federal law. (We shall leave consideration of suits against non-federal officials for treatment in the next chapter.) Finally, litigants may rely directly on provisions of the Constitution that prohibit specific conduct or protect particular interests as affording an independent basis for private recovery.

1. COMMON LAW ACTIONS AGAINST GOVERNMENT OFFICERS: OFFICIAL IMMUNITY

It requires little imagination to visualize many of the types of suits the wide range of official activities might provoke. Law enforcement officers routinely restrain the freedom of the citizens that they detain or arrest. Often, they use physical force to effect an arrest or carry out a search. Prosecutors devote long hours to achieving the imprisonment, and sometimes even the execution, of persons charged with crimes. Judges render verdicts and impose sentences that result in deprivation of property and freedom. Agency officers issue public statements describing policies or actions that may seriously damage the reputation of an individual, or business, or product. In short, common law theories would support a wide range of claims for damages for harm sustained by private citizens at the hands of government officers.

In a tort action against a government officer the identity of the defendant should not alter the basic elements of the plaintiff's affirmative case, which will be governed by the common law of the jurisdiction. The defendant's identity may, however, preclude suit altogether. For if the plaintiff's claim grows out of activities related to an official function, the defendant certainly will claim "official immunity" from suit. Typically, official immunity is raised by a motion to dismiss for failure to state a claim; although clearly a defensive doctrine, an assertion of official immunity is the functional equivalent of a demurrer. The official claims not merely a *defense to liability* for money damages, but *immunity from suits* for damages.

Official immunity is of relatively recent origin. According to one source, "[early opinions made no distinction between public officers and the ordinary citizen when considering answerability for tortious conduct." WALTER GELLHORN & CLARK BYSE, ADMINISTRATIVE LAW: CASES AND COMMENTS 335 (6th ed. 1974). Indeed, many early decisions imposed liability for official acts that would not even have been characterized as tortious by private law standards. A well-known example is *Miller v. Horton*, 152 Mass. 540, 26 N.E. 100 (1891). The defendant, a state health officer, had ordered the destruction of the plaintiff's horse pursuant to a Massachusetts statute that directed officers to inspect horses believed to be infected with glanders and summarily to destroy and bury diseased animals. Writing for the court, then-state Justice Holmes ruled that the plaintiff could recover damages from the officer personally if the jury found that the horse had not in fact been infected. The defendant could not escape liability by showing that his action had been undertaken reasonably and in good faith, for he had authority to destroy only diseased horses. Other cases imposed liability for official mistakes based on similarly narrow readings of their authority. See, e.g., *Lowe v. Conroy*, 120 Wis. 151, 97 N.W. 942 (1904); *Pearson v. Zehr*, 138 Ill. 48, 29 N.E. 854 (1891).

Nineteenth century decisions thus afforded public officers little protection against liability, much less against suits, based on actions taken in the performance of their public responsibilities:

> * * * [T]he officer was held personally liable not only for his negligence and omissions and for positive torts which he was not authorized to commit, but even for acts he was authorized-in-fact to do if * * * his authority to do those acts was legally insufficient. Good faith, mistake, obedience to orders, or even the noblest intentions, were no better defenses to a personal action for damages. * * * These standards of personal official liability were repeatedly reaffirmed and applied during the same decades around the turn of the century when the Supreme Court was enlarging the immunity of the state; indeed it was only for this reason that the expanding state immunity was considered to be consistent with the tradition of effective redress for positive governmental wrongs.

David E. Engdahl, *Immunity and Accountability for Positive Governmental Wrongs*, 44 U. Colo. L. Rev. 1, 47 (1972).

The same draconian rules were not applied to judges, however. The Supreme Court early recognized the threat to judicial performance that would be posed by allowing disappointed litigants to sue judges personally who had assertedly exceeded their jurisdiction or authority. In *Bradley v. Fisher*, 80 U.S. (13 Wall.) 335, 351–54 (1871), Justice Field explained why judges should be accorded immunity from such suits:

> * * * Where there is clearly no jurisdiction over the subject-matter any authority exercised is a usurped authority, and for the exercise of such authority, when the want of jurisdiction is known to the judge, no excuse is permissible. But where jurisdiction over the subject-matter is invested by law in the judge * * * the manner and extent in which the jurisdiction shall be exercised are generally as much questions for his determination as any other questions involved in the case. * * * [I]f * * * a judge of a criminal court, invested with general criminal jurisdiction over offenses committed within a certain district, should hold a particular act to be a public

offense, which is not by the law made an offense, and proceed to the arrest and trial of a party charged with such act, or should sentence a party convicted to a greater punishment than that authorized by the law upon its proper construction, no personal liability to civil action for such acts would attach to the judge. * * *

* * * The allegation of malicious or corrupt motives could always be made, and if the motives could be inquired into judges would be subjected to the same vexatious litigation upon such allegations, whether the motives had or had not any real existence. * * * [F]or malice or corruption in their action whilst exercising their judicial functions within the general scope of their jurisdiction, the judges of these courts can only be reached by public prosecution in the form of impeachment, or in such other form as may be specially prescribed.

This reasoning eventually prompted federal courts to extend similar immunity to officers other than judges who acted for the judicial branch or were engaged in "quasi-judicial" functions. See *Kendall v. Stokes*, 44 U.S. (3 How.) 87 (1845) (Postmaster General). Still, by the mid-twentieth century the Supreme Court had not recognized any general immunity for administrative officers below Cabinet rank. Such immunity had, however, been strongly supported by Judge Learned Hand in the following famous case.

GREGOIRE v. BIDDLE

United States Court of Appeals, Second Circuit, 1949.
177 F.2d 579, *cert. denied*, 339 U.S. 949, 70 S.Ct. 803, 94 L.Ed. 1363 (1950).

L. HAND, CHIEF JUDGE.

The plaintiff has appealed from a judgment, which dismissed a complaint in two counts because of its "failure to state a claim upon which relief can be granted." The first count alleged that the five defendants were two successive Attorneys–General of the United States, two successive Directors of the Enemy Alien Control Unit of the Department of Justice, and the District Director of Immigration at Ellis Island; and that they arrested the plaintiff on the pretense that he was a German and therefore an enemy alien. In spite of a ruling of the Enemy Alien Hearing Board after a hearing that he was a Frenchman, they kept him in custody from January 5, 1942, until September 18, 1946, when Judge Knox found that he was a Frenchman and released him by an order, which this court affirmed on November 6, 1947. The count ended by alleging that the arrest and imprisonment was "without any authority of law and without any reasonable or colorable cause," and that the defendants "conspired together and maliciously and wilfully entered into a scheme to deprive the plaintiff * * * of his liberty contrary to law." * * * The judge held that the defendants had an absolute immunity from liability, even though their unlawful acts had been induced only by personal ill-will, and dismissed the complaint for that reason.

We lay aside any extenuating facts * * * not because we should not be free to consider them if need were, but, because we think that the complaint should not stand, even though under Rule 9(b) we read the allegation that the defendants arrested the plaintiff "maliciously and wilfully," as though it had specifically alleged that they had acted altogether from personal spite and had been fully aware that they had no legal warrant for arresting or deporting the plaintiff. True, so stated, that seems at first blush a startling proposition; but we think, not only that it necessarily follows from the decision of the Supreme Court in *Yaselli v. Goff;* but that, as a new question, the result is desirable. * * *

[In *Yaselli v. Goff*, 275 U.S. 503 (1927), the Supreme Court affirmed a lower court's decision extending the absolute immunity previously recognized for judges to a special assistant to the Attorney General sued for malicious prosecution. As Judge Hand noted, in *Yaselli* the Supreme Court relied on *Bradley v. Fisher, supra*; *Alzua v. Johnson*, 231 U.S. 106 (1913) (judicial immunity); and *Spalding v. Vilas*, 161 U.S. 483 (1896) (recognizing immunity of cabinet officers, in that instance the Postmaster General).]

It does indeed go without saying that an official, who is in fact guilty of using his powers to vent his spleen upon others, or for any other personal motive not connected with the public good, should not escape liability for the injuries he may so cause; and, if it were possible in practice to confine such complaints to the guilty, it would be monstrous to deny recovery. The justification for doing so is that it is impossible to know whether the claim is well founded until the case has been tried, and that to submit all officials, the innocent as well as the guilty, to the burden of a trial and to the inevitable danger of its outcome, would dampen the ardor of all but the most resolute, or the most irresponsible, in the unflinching discharge of their duties. Again and again the public interest calls for action which may turn out to be founded on a mistake, in the face of which an official may later find himself hard put to it to satisfy a jury of his good faith. There must indeed be means of punishing public officers who have been truant to their duties; but that is quite another matter from exposing such as have been honestly mistaken to suit by anyone who has suffered from their errors. As is so often the case, the answer must be found in a balance between the evils inevitable in either alternative. In this instance it has been thought in the end better to leave unredressed the wrongs done by dishonest officers than to subject those who try to do their duty to the constant dread of retaliation. Judged as res nova, we should not hesitate to follow the path laid down in the books.

The decisions have, indeed, always imposed as a limitation upon the immunity that the official's act must have been within the scope of his powers; and it can be argued that official powers, since they exist only for the public good, never cover occasions where the public good is not their aim, and hence that to exercise a power dishonestly is necessarily to overstep its bounds. A moment's reflection shows, however, that that cannot be the meaning of the limitation without defeating the whole doctrine. What is meant by saying that the officer must be acting within his power cannot be more than that the occasion must be such as would have justified the act, if he had been using his power for any of the purposes on whose account it was vested in him. For the foregoing reasons it was proper to dismiss the first count. * * *

[The court concluded that the plaintiff's second count—which charged violations of federal civil rights statutes—did not apply to the facts alleged in the complaint.]

Judgment affirmed.

BARR v. MATTEO

Supreme Court of the United States, 1959.
360 U.S. 564, 79 S.Ct. 1335, 3 L.Ed.2d 1434.

JUSTICE HARLAN announced the judgment of the Court, and delivered an opinion, in which JUSTICE FRANKFURTER, JUSTICE CLARK, and JUSTICE WHITTAKER join.

We are called upon in this case to weigh in a particular context two considerations of high importance which now and again come into sharp conflict—on the one hand, the protection of the individual citizen against pecuniary damage caused by oppressive or malicious action on the part of officials of the Federal Government; and on the other, the protection of the public interest by shielding responsible governmental officers against the harassment and inevitable hazards of vindictive or ill-founded damage suits brought on account of action taken in the exercise of their official responsibilities. * * *

[This was a libel action brought by two officials of the Office of Housing Expediter against the Acting Director of the agency. The alleged libelous statements appeared in a press release, issued by the defendant in response to congressional criticism of an agency plan, devised by the plaintiffs, for making terminal-leave payments to certain employees some two years before. The press release announced that Barr was suspending the plaintiffs as his first official act, asserted that Barr had consistently opposed their plan for terminal-leave payments, and stated that he regarded the payments, even if legal, as violative of the "spirit" of governing legislation. The Court of Claims subsequently upheld the legality of the terminal-leave plan.]

Respondents sued, charging that the press release, in itself and as coupled with the contemporaneous news reports of senatorial reaction to the plan, defamed them to their injury, and alleging that its publication and terms had been actuated by malice on the part of petitioner. Petitioner defended, *inter alia*, on the ground that the issuance of the press release was protected by either a qualified or an absolute privilege. * * *

* * * The judgment of the trial court was affirmed by the Court of Appeals, which held that "in explaining his decision [to suspend respondents] to the general public [petitioner] * * * went entirely outside his

line of duty" and that thus the absolute privilege, assumed otherwise to be available, did not attach. We * * * remanded the case "with directions to pass upon petitioner's claim of a qualified privilege." On remand the Court of Appeals held that the press release was protected by a qualified privilege, but that there was evidence from which a jury could reasonably conclude that petitioner had acted maliciously, or had spoken with lack of reasonable grounds for believing that his statement was true, and that either conclusion would defeat the qualified privilege. * * * [P]etitioner again sought, and we again granted certiorari to determine whether in the circumstances of this case petitioner's claim of absolute privilege should have stood as a bar to maintenance of the suit despite the allegations of malice made in the complaint.

The law of privilege as a defense by officers of government to civil damage suits for defamation and kindred torts has in large part been of judicial making, although the Constitution itself gives an absolute privilege to members of both Houses of Congress in respect to any speech, debate, vote, report, or action done in session. This Court early held that judges of courts of superior or general authority are absolutely privileged as respects civil suits to recover for actions taken by them in the exercise of their judicial functions, irrespective of the motives with which those acts are alleged to have been performed, *Bradley v. Fisher*, and that a like immunity extends to other officers of government whose duties are related to the judicial process. *Yaselli v. Goff*, 275 U.S. 503 (1927), involving a Special Assistant to the Attorney General. Nor has the privilege been confined to officers of the legislative and judicial branches of the Government and executive officers of the kind involved in *Yaselli*. In *Spalding v. Vilas*, 161 U.S. 483 (1896), petitioner brought suit against the Postmaster General, alleging that the latter had maliciously circulated widely among postmasters, past and present, information which he knew to be false and which was intended to deceive the postmasters to the detriment of the plaintiff. This Court sustained a plea by the Postmaster General of absolute privilege. * * *[8]

The reasons for the recognition of the privilege have been often stated. It has been thought important that officials of government should be free to exercise their duties unembarrassed by the fear of damage suits in respect of acts done in the course of those duties—suits which would consume time and energies which would otherwise be devoted to governmental service and the threat of which might appreciably inhibit the fearless, vigorous, and effective administration of policies of government. * * * [Justice Harlan here quotes at length from *Gregoire v. Biddle, supra*.]

8. The communication in *Spalding v. Vilas* was not distributed to the general public, but only to a particular segment thereof which had a special interest in the subject matter. Statements issued at the direction of Cabinet officers and disseminated to the press in the form of press releases have also been accorded an absolute privilege, so long as their contents and the occasion for their issuance relate to the duties and functions of the particular department.

We do not think that the principle announced in *Vilas* can properly be restricted to executive officers of cabinet rank, and in fact it never has been so restricted by the lower federal courts. The privilege is not a badge or emolument of exalted office, but an expression of a policy designed to aid in the effective functioning of government. The complexities and magnitude of governmental activity have become so great that there must of necessity be a delegation and redelegation of authority as to many functions, and we cannot say that these functions become less important simply because they are exercised by officers of lower rank in the executive hierarchy.

To be sure, the occasion upon which the acts of the head of an executive department will be protected by the privilege are doubtless far broader than in the case of an officer with less sweeping functions. But that is because the higher the post, the broader the range of responsibilities and duties, and the wider the scope of discretion, it entails. It is not the title of his office but the duties with which the particular officer sought to be made to respond in damages is entrusted—the relation of the act complained of to "matters committed by law to his control or supervision," which must provide the guide in delineating the scope of the rule which clothes the official acts of the executive officer with immunity from civil defamation suits.

Judged by these standards, we hold that petitioner's plea of absolute privilege in defense of the alleged libel published at his direction must be sustained. The question is a close one, but we cannot say that it was not an appropriate exercise of the discretion with which an executive officer of petitioner's rank is necessarily clothed to publish the press release here at issue in the circumstances disclosed by this record. Petitioner was the Acting Director of an important agency of government, and was clothed by redelegation with "all powers, duties, and functions conferred on the President by Title II of the Housing and Rent Act of 1947. * * * "The integrity of the internal operations of the agency which he headed, and thus his own integrity in his public capacity, had been directly and severely challenged in charges made on the floor of the Senate and given wide publicity; and without his knowledge correspondence which could reasonably be read as impliedly defending a position very different from that which he had from the beginning taken in the matter had been sent to a Senator over his signature and incorporated in the Congressional Record. The issuance of press releases was standard agency practice, as it has become with many governmental agencies in these times. We think that under these circumstances a publicly expressed statement of the position of the agency head, announcing personnel action which he planned to take in reference to the charges so widely disseminated to the public, was an appropriate exercise of the discretion which an officer of that rank must possess if the public service is to function effectively. It would be an unduly restrictive view of the scope of the duties of a policy-making executive official to hold that a public statement of agency policy in respect to matters of wide public interest and concern is not action in the line of duty. That petitioner was not *required* by law or by direction of his superiors to speak out cannot be controlling in the case of an official of policy-making rank, for the same considerations which underlie the recognition of the privilege as to acts done in connection with a mandatory duty apply with equal force to discretionary acts at those levels of government where the concept of duty encompasses the sound exercise of discretionary authority.

The fact that the action here taken was within the outer perimeter of petitioner's line of duty is enough to render the privilege applicable, despite the allegations of malice in the complaint. * * *

We are told that we should forbear from sanctioning any such rule of absolute privilege lest it open the door to wholesale oppression and abuses on the part of unscrupulous government officials. It is perhaps enough to say that fears of this sort have not been realized within the wide area of government where a judicially formulated absolute privilege of broad scope has long existed. It seems to us wholly chimerical to suggest that what hangs in the balance here is the maintenance of high standards of conduct among those in the public service. To be sure, as with any rule of law which attempts to reconcile fundamentally antagonistic social policies, there may be occasional instances of actual injustice which will go unredressed, but we think that price a necessary one to pay for the greater good. And there are of course other sanctions than civil tort suits available to deter the executive official who may be prone to exercise his functions in an unworthy and irresponsible manner. We think that we should not be deterred from establishing the rule which we announce today by any such remote forebodings.

Reversed.

JUSTICE BLACK, concurring.

I concur in the reversal of this judgment but briefly summarize my reasons because they are not altogether the same as those stated in the opinion of JUSTICE HARLAN. * * *

Mr. Barr was peculiarly well qualified to inform Congress and the public about the Rent Stabilization Agency. Subjecting him to libel suits for criticizing the way the Agency or its employees perform their duties would certainly act as a restraint upon him. So far as I am concerned, if federal employees are to be subjected to such restraints in reporting their views about how to run the government better, the restraint will have to be imposed expressly by Congress and not by the general libel laws of the States or of the District of Columbia. How far the Congress itself could go in barring federal officials and employees from discussing public matters consistently with the First Amendment is a question we need not reach in this case. It is enough for me here that the press release was neither unauthorized nor plainly beyond the scope of Mr. Barr's official business, but instead related more or less to general matters committed by law to his control and supervision.

CHIEF JUSTICE WARREN, with whom JUSTICE DOUGLAS joins, dissenting. * * *

* * * This is not a case where the only interest is in plaintiff's obtaining redress of a wrong. The public interest in limiting libel suits against officers in order that the public might be adequately informed is paralleled by another interest of equal importance: that of preserving the opportunity to criticize the administration of our Government and the action of its officials without being subjected to unfair—and absolutely privileged—retorts. * * *

It is clear that public discussion of the action of the Government and its officials is accorded no more than qualified privilege. * * * Only in a minority of States is a public critic of Government even qualifiedly privileged where his facts are wrong. Thus, at best, a public critic of the Government has a qualified privilege. Yet here the Court has given some amorphous group of officials—who have the most direct and personal contact with the public—an absolute privilege when their agency or their action is criticized. In this situation, it will take a brave person to criticize government officials knowing that in reply they may libel him with immunity in the name of defending the agency and their own position. This extension of *Spalding v. Vilas* can only have the added effect of deterring the desirable public discussion of all aspects of our Government and the conduct of its officials. It will sanctify the powerful and silence debate. This is a much more serious danger than the possibility that a government official might occasionally be called upon to defend his actions and to respond in damages for a malicious defamation. * * *

JUSTICE BRENNAN, dissenting.

* * * In my view, only a qualified privilege is necessary here, and that is all I would afford the officials. A qualified privilege would be the most the law would allow private citizens under comparable circumstances. It would protect the government officer unless it appeared on trial that his communication was (a) defamatory, (b) untrue, and (c) "malicious."[2] We write on almost a clean slate here, and even if *Spalding v. Vilas* allows a Cabinet officer the defense of an absolute privilege in defamation suits, I see no warrant for extending its doctrine to the extent done—apparently to include every official having some color of discretion to utter communications to Congress or the public. * * * Justice Harlan's approach seems to clothe with immunity the most obscure sub-foreman on an arsenal production line who has been delegated authority to hire and fire and who maliciously defames one he discharges.[4]

* * * The opinion's position is simply that there are certain societal interests in relieving federal officials from judicial inquiry into their motives that outweigh all interest in affording relief. * * * "But it is

2. Actual "malice" is required to vitiate a qualified privilege, not simply the "constructive" malice that is inferred from the publication.

4. The opinion's rationale covers the entire federal bureaucracy, as compared to the numerically much less extensive legislative and judicial privileges. And as to the former, the Constitution speaks, and the resolution of the factors involved in the latter is very obviously within the courts' special competence.

stretching the argument pretty far to say that the *mere inquiry into malice* would have worse consequences than the *possibility of actual malice* (which we would not, for a minute, condone). Since the danger that official power will be abused is greatest where motives are improper, the balance here may well swing the other way." Harper and James, Torts (1956), p. 1645. * * *

There is an even more basic objection to the opinion. It deals with large concepts of public policy and purports to balance the societal interests involved in them. It denies the defamed citizen a recovery by characterizing the policy favoring absolute immunity as "an expression of a policy designed to aid in the effective functioning of government." * * * This, I fear, is a gossamer web self-spun without a scintilla of support to which one can point. To come to this conclusion, and to shift the line from the already extensive protection given the public officer by the qualified privilege doctrine, demands the resolution of large imponderables which one might have thought would be better the business of the Legislative Branch. * * *

[I]f the fears expressed materialized and great inconvenience to the workings of the Government arose out of allowing defamation actions subject to a showing of malice, Congress might well be disposed to intervene. * * * We ought not, as I fear we do today, for all practical purposes foreclose such consideration of the problem by expanding on the comparable common-law privilege and wholly immunizing federal officials from defamation suits whenever they can show that their act was incidental to their jobs.

The Rise and Fall of *Barr*-Style Immunity

Some writers expressed doubt that Justice Harlan's opinion in *Barr v. Matteo*, which commanded the support of only four Justices, would long remain the definitive statement of the immunity enjoyed by high-ranking federal administrators. See, e.g., Joel F. Handler & William A. Klein, *The Defense of Privilege in Defamation Suits Against Government Executive Officials*, 74 Harv. L. Rev. 44 (1960); see also R.J. Gray, *Private Wrongs of Public Servants*, 47 Calif. L. Rev. 303 (1959). Very few would have forecast the expansive reading that the opinion received.

During most of the three decades following *Barr* federal courts accorded immunity to virtually any administrative officer who could show that the conduct that was the basis for a common law tort suit fell generally within the scope of his or her assigned responsibilities. The notion that immunity was premised on and limited by a functional concern to protect the exercise of official discretion is surely instinct in *Barr* itself. Yet, in application, the test for whether an officer's actions demanded the exercise of "judgment" or "discretion" seemed to find discretion ubiquitous.

Meanwhile, the law of official immunity was developing apace with respect to two categories of non-common law damage actions against officials—constitutional torts and actions pursuant to 42 U.S.C. § 1983, see *infra* Chapter 9. To put the matter succinctly, courts in those contexts expressed deep skepticism about the necessity for absolute immunity, even where the official's responsibilities were highly discretionary in nature. And, given the significant overlap between constitutional torts and common-law torts recognized in state law, the absolute immunity of federal officials from suits alleging state law harms meshed uneasily with a jurisprudence that provided at most a qualified immunity to most officials, federal or state, alleged to have committed harms proscribed by the Constitution.

In 1988 the Supreme Court revisited the question of federal official immunity for common law torts. In *Westfall v. Erwin*, 484 U.S. 292 (1988), respondents brought a state law personal injury suit against federal civilian employees for negligence in the storage of toxic soda ash. Relying on *Barr v. Matteo*, the district court held the defendants absolutely immune from suit. The court of appeals reversed, interpreting the Supreme Court's post-*Barr* decisions as according absolute immunity only when the acts complained of were within the scope of the employee's duties and also involved the exercise of discretion.

Reinforcing the functional analysis that had emerged in suits alleging constitutional torts, the Supreme Court affirmed. Justice Marshall reasoned that according absolute immunity for nondiscretionary acts would not further the immunity doctrine's central purpose of promoting effective government by insulating decision makers from harassing litigation.

> In deciding whether particular governmental functions properly fall within the scope of absolute immunity * * * courts should be careful to * * * consider whether the contribution to effective government in particular contexts outweighs the potential harm to individual citizens. * * *. We are also of the view, however, that Congress is in the best position to provide guidance for the complex and often highly empirical inquiry into whether absolute immunity is warranted in a particular context.

Congress promptly seized Justice Marshall's invitation to "legislate[ ] standards governing the immunity of federal employees involved in state law tort actions" by enacting the Federal Employees Liability Reform and Tort Compensation Act of 1988, Pub. L. No. 100–694, 102 Stat. 4563. An explicit response to *Westfall v. Erwin*, the 1988 Act purports to eliminate personal liability for common law torts committed by federal employees—of the judicial and legislative as well as the executive branch—when they act within the scope of their employment. It makes suit under the FTCA the exclusive remedy for such torts, even when the government has a defense that prevents recovery. Federal officials may nevertheless remain attractive targets in tort litigation seeking to exploit the statute's exceptions to absolute official immunity; they may still be sued for "egregious misconduct" or for constitutional torts. Moreover, when sued, an official may compel the substitution of the United States as defendant only if the Attorney General—or upon petition, the trial court—certifies that the defendant employee was acting within the scope of his or her office or employment. Proving once again that no administrative task is non-controversial, this certification function has given rise to its own arcane—and conflicting—jurisprudence. See Robert D. Lee, Jr., *Federal Employers Torts and the Westfall Act of 1988*, 56 Pub. Admin. Rev. 334 (1996).

In *Gutierrez de Martinez v. Lamagno*, 515 U.S. 417 (1995), the Supreme Court resolved the sharp conflict among the circuits in favor of judicial review of the Attorney General's certification of a case as one involving conduct of an official within his or her scope of authority. The *Lamagno* case involved a positive certification by a U.S. Attorney (to whom the Attorney General's authority has been delegated). However, because the certification dismissed the individual officer and substituted the United States in a circumstance in which the Federal Tort Claims Act fails to provide relief (the accident occurred in a foreign country), the U.S. Attorney's action would have deprived the petitioner of all relief. Recognizing that the U.S. Attorney had strong incentives to make a certification that absolved the United States of all responsibility (both direct liability and the responsibility to reimburse an officer for damages for actions arising in the line of duty), the Court simply invoked the general presumption in favor of judicial review of administrative action. It then found no persuasive ground upon which to reject that general presumption.

The sharp divergence in the circuit court jurisprudence made plain, of course, that the Westfall Act's language was far from clear. On one hand, the statute states that "upon certification by the Attorney General * * * any civil action or proceeding * * * shall be deemed an action against the United States * * *, and the United States shall be substituted as the party defendant." Not only is this language imperative, but the Act also specifically provides for court review where the Attorney General (or her delegate) refuses to certify an action at the behest of defending employees.

On the other hand, the self-interested nature of the certification process and the specter of having federal court jurisdiction decided conclusively by the actions of a litigant, a U.S. Attorney, suggested that a construction that made the Attorney General's certification conclusive was problematic. A majority of the Court, therefore, viewed the overall statutory scheme as ambiguous on the question of whether certification should be subject to judicial review. And, in case of doubt, presumptions, such as the presumption of judicial review, decide the case.

2. CONSTITUTIONAL ACTIONS AGAINST FEDERAL OFFICERS

The U.S. Constitution, and more particularly the Bill of Rights, forbids a wide variety of interferences with private rights by agencies or officials of government. A familiar example is the Fourth Amendment's prohibition against unreasonable searches and seizures, which the Fourteenth Amendment makes applicable to the states. No provision of the Constitution itself, however, expressly authorizes any remedy, judicial or administrative, for official conduct that violates constitutional rights. The federal courts, nevertheless, have long been prepared to issue injunctions to protect constitutional rights with no statutory authority for such a remedy beyond the bare grant of jurisdiction, in 28 U.S.C. § 1331, over cases "arising under the Constitution, laws, or treaties of the United States." See generally Alfred Hill, *Constitutional Remedies*, 69 Colum. L. Rev. 1109 (1969). Furthermore, the courts have granted what may be termed "defensive" relief for many constitutional violations by invalidating government action taken without observance, or in defiance, of constitutional safeguards. Thus, for example, the courts have refused to enforce statutes found unconstitutional and have struck down criminal convictions obtained through procedures that violate any of the Bill of Rights.

These several remedies are subject to important limitations. Injunctive relief may be adequate when a constitutional violation is only incipient or is likely to be repeated, but it is not a satisfactory remedy for the one-time abridgement of rights that occurred in the past. Moreover, the assurance that a judge will refuse to enforce an unconstitutional statute or will forbid the use of tainted evidence affords scant comfort to the individual who is afraid to resist compliance or to the victim of police brutality who is never brought to trial. Finally, these essentially defensive remedies may not provide adequate incentives to law enforcement officers to refrain from unconstitutional conduct. Accordingly, it may be a matter of some importance whether affirmative remedies are available to protect rights guaranteed by the Constitution.

In *Bell v. Hood*, 327 U.S. 678 (1946), the plaintiffs sought damages for alleged unconstitutional arrests, searches, and seizures conducted by agents of the Federal Bureau of Investigation. The plaintiffs based their claim to damages on the Constitution, not on state law, and they premised federal jurisdiction on the predecessor of 28 U.S.C. § 1331. The lower courts held that the case was not one "arising under the Constitution or laws of the United States," and that they therefore lacked jurisdiction. The Supreme Court reversed, ruling that whether such a cause of action for damages would lie presented an issue sufficiently substantial to support the district court's jurisdiction to decide the case on the merits. On remand, the district court concluded that an action for damages could not be maintained and distinguished the precedents allowing equitable relief against constitutional violations. The case did not go further. Later, in *Wheeldin v. Wheeler*, 373 U.S. 647 (1963), the Supreme Court in dictum indicated doubt about whether a federal court could award damages for constitutional violations without specific statutory authorization. As late as 1971, therefore, the availability of such a remedy—in the absence of congressional authorization—remained uncertain. See Al Katz, *The Jurisprudence of Remedies: Constitutional Legality and Law of Torts in Bell v. Hood*, 117 U. Pa. L. Rev. 1 (1968).

BIVENS v. SIX UNKNOWN NAMED AGENTS OF THE FEDERAL BUREAU OF NARCOTICS

Supreme Court of the United States, 1971.
403 U.S. 388, 91 S.Ct. 1999, 29 L.Ed.2d 619.

JUSTICE BRENNAN delivered the opinion of the Court.

The Fourth Amendment provides that:

> "The right of the people to be secure in their persons, houses, papers, and effects, against unreasonable searches and seizures, shall not be violated. * * *"

In *Bell v. Hood*, we reserved the question whether violation of that command by a federal agent acting under color of his authority gives rise to a cause of action for damages consequent upon his unconstitutional conduct. Today we hold that it does.

This case has its origin in an arrest and search carried out on the morning of November 26, 1965. Petitioner's complaint alleged that on that day respondents, agents of the Federal Bureau of Narcotics acting under claim of federal authority, entered his apartment and arrested him for alleged narcotics violations. The agents manacled petitioner in front of his wife and children, and threatened to arrest the entire family. They searched the apartment from stem to stern. Thereafter, petitioner was taken to the federal courthouse in Brooklyn, where he was interrogated, booked, and subjected to a visual strip search.

* * * [P]etitioner brought suit in Federal District Court. In addition to the allegations above, his complaint asserted that the arrest and search were effected without a warrant, and that unreasonable force was employed in making the arrest; fairly read, it alleges as well that the arrest was made without probable cause. Petitioner claimed to have suffered great humiliation, embarrassment, and mental suffering as a result of the agents' unlawful conduct, and sought $15,000 damages from each of them. The District Court, on respondents' motion, dismissed the complaint on the ground, *inter alia*, that it failed to state a cause of action. The Court of Appeals, one judge concurring specially, affirmed on that basis. * * *

Respondents do not argue that petitioner should be entirely without remedy for an unconstitutional invasion of his rights by federal agents. In respondents' view, however, the rights that petitioner asserts—primarily rights of privacy—are creations of state and not of federal law. Accordingly, they argue, petitioner may obtain money damages to redress invasion of these rights only by an action in tort, under state law, in the state courts. In this scheme the Fourth Amendment would serve merely to limit the extent to which the agents could defend the state law tort suit by asserting that their actions were a valid exercise of federal power: if the agents were shown to have violated the Fourth Amendment, such a defense would be lost to them and they would stand before the state law merely as private individuals. * * *

* * * Respondents seek to treat the relationship between a citizen and a federal agent unconstitutionally exercising his authority as no different from the relationship between two private citizens. In so doing, they ignore the fact that power, once granted, does not disappear like a magic gift when it is wrongfully used. An agent acting—albeit unconstitutionally—in the name of the United States possesses a far greater capacity for harm than an individual trespasser exercising no authority other than his own. Accordingly, as our cases make clear, the Fourth Amendment operates as a limitation upon the exercise of federal power regardless of whether the State in whose jurisdiction that power is exercised would prohibit or penalize the identical act if engaged in by a private citizen. It guarantees to citizens of the United States the absolute right to be free from unreasonable searches and seizures carried out by virtue of federal authority. And "where federally protected rights have been invaded, it has been the rule from the beginning that courts will be alert to adjust their remedies so as to grant the necessary relief." *Bell v. Hood.*

First. Our cases have long since rejected the notion that the Fourth Amendment proscribes only such conduct as would, if engaged in by private persons, be condemned by state law. * * *

Second. The interests protected by state laws regulating trespass and the invasion of privacy, and those protected by the Fourth Amendment's guarantee against unreasonable searches and seizures, may be inconsistent or even hostile. Thus, we may bar the door against an unwelcome private intruder, or call the police if he persists in seeking entrance. The availability of such alternative means for the protection of privacy may lead the State to restrict imposition of liability for any consequent trespass. A private citizen, asserting no authority other than his own, will not normally be liable in trespass if he demands, and is granted, admission to another's house. * * * Nor is it adequate to answer that state law may take into account the different status of one clothed with the authority of the Federal Government. For just as state law may not authorize federal agents to violate the Fourth Amendment, neither may state law undertake to limit the extent to which federal authority can be exercised. The inevitable consequence of this dual limitation on state power is that the federal question becomes not merely a possible defense to the state law action, but an independent claim both necessary and sufficient to make out the plaintiff's cause of action.

Third. That damages may be obtained for injuries consequent upon a violation of the Fourth Amendment by federal officials should hardly seem a surprising proposition. Historically, damages have been regarded as the ordinary remedy for an invasion of personal interests in liberty. Of course, the Fourth Amendment does not in so many words provide for its enforcement by an award of money damages for the consequences of its violation. But "it is * * * well settled that where legal rights have been invaded, and a federal statute provides for a general right to sue for such invasion, federal courts may use any available remedy to make good the wrong done." The present case involves no special factors counseling hesitation in the absence of affirmative action by Congress. We are not dealing with a question of "federal fiscal policy." * * * Nor are we asked in this case to impose liability upon a congressional employee for actions contrary to no constitutional prohibition, but merely said to be in excess of the authority delegated to him by the Congress. Finally, we cannot accept respondents' formulation of the question as whether the availability of money damages is necessary to enforce the Fourth Amendment. For we have here no explicit congressional declaration that persons injured by a federal officer's violation of the Fourth Amendment may not recover money damages from the agents, but must instead be remitted to another remedy, equally effective in the view of Congress. The question is merely whether petitioner, if he can demonstrate an injury consequent upon the violation by federal agents of his Fourth Amendment rights, is entitled to redress his injury through a particular remedial mechanism normally available in the federal courts. *Cf. J.I. Case Co. v. Borak*, 377 U.S. 426, 433 (1964). * * * Having concluded that petitioner's complaint states a cause of action under the Fourth Amendment, we hold that petitioner is entitled to recover money damages for any injuries he has suffered as a result of the agents' violation of the Amendment. * * *

JUSTICE HARLAN, concurring in the judgment.

My initial view of this case was that the Court of Appeals was correct in dismissing the complaint, but for reasons stated in this opinion I am now persuaded to the contrary. Accordingly, I join in the judgment of reversal. * * *

I turn first to the contention that the constitutional power of federal courts to accord Bivens damages for his claim depends on the passage of a statute creating a "federal cause of action." Although the point is not entirely free of ambiguity, I do not understand either the Government or my dissenting Brothers to maintain that Bivens' contention that he is entitled to be free from the type of official conduct prohibited by the Fourth Amendment depends on a decision by the State in which he resides to accord him a remedy. Such a position would be incompatible with the presumed availability of federal equitable relief, if a proper showing can be made in terms of the ordinary principles governing equitable remedies. However broad a federal court's discretion concerning equitable remedies, it is absolutely clear * * * that in a nondiversity suit a federal court's power to grant even equitable relief depends on the presence of a substantive right derived from federal law.

Thus the interest which Bivens claims—to be free from official conduct in contravention of the Fourth Amendment—is a federally protected interest. Therefore, the question of judicial *power* to grant Bivens damages is not a problem of the "source" of the "right"; instead, the question is whether the power to authorize damages as a judicial remedy for the vindication of a federal constitutional right is placed by the Constitution itself exclusively in Congress' hands.

The contention that the federal courts are powerless to accord a litigant damages for a claimed invasion of his federal constitutional rights until Congress explicitly authorizes the remedy cannot rest on the notion that the decision to grant compensatory relief involves a resolution of policy considerations not susceptible of judicial discernment. Thus, in suits for damages based on violations of federal statutes lacking any express authorization of a damage remedy, this Court has authorized such relief where, in its view, damages are necessary to effectuate the congressional policy underpinning the substantive provisions of the statute. *J.I. Case Co. v. Borak* [*infra* Chapter 9, Sec. B]. *Cf. Wyandotte Transportation Co. v. United States*, 389 U.S. 191 (1967).[4]

If it is not the nature of the remedy which is thought to render a judgment as to the appropriateness of damages inherently "legislative," then it must be the nature of the legal interest offered as an occasion for invoking otherwise appropriate judicial relief. But I do not think that the fact that the interest is protected by the Constitution rather than statute or common law justifies the assertion that federal courts are powerless to grant damages in the absence of explicit congressional action authorizing the remedy. * * * [I]t would be at least anomalous to conclude that the federal judiciary—while competent to choose among the range of traditional judicial remedies to implement statutory and common-law policies, and even to generate substantive rules governing primary behavior in furtherance of broadly formulated policies articulated by statute or Constitution—is powerless to accord a damages remedy to vindicate social policies which, by virtue of their inclusion in the Constitution, are aimed predominantly at restraining the Government as an instrument of the popular will.

More importantly, the presumed availability of federal equitable relief against threatened invasions of constitutional interests appears entirely to negate the contention that the status of an interest as constitutionally protected divests federal courts of the power to grant damages absent express congressional authorization.

If explicit congressional authorization is an absolute prerequisite to the power of a federal court to accord compensatory relief regardless of the necessity or appropriateness of damages as a remedy simply because of the status of a legal interest as constitutionally protected, then it seems to me that explicit congressional authorization is similarly prerequisite to the exercise of equitable remedial discretion in favor of constitutionally protected interests. Conversely, if a general grant of jurisdiction

4. The *Borak* case is an especially clear example of the exercise of federal judicial power to accord damages as an appropriate remedy in the absence of any express statutory authorization of a federal cause of action. There we "implied"—from what can only be characterized as an "exclusively procedural provision" affording access to a federal forum—a private cause of action for damages for violation of § 14(a) of the Securities Exchange Act of 1934. We did so in an area where federal regulation has been singularly comprehensive and elaborate administrative enforcement machinery had been provided. The exercise of judicial power involved in *Borak* simply cannot be justified in terms of statutory construction; nor did the *Borak* Court purport to do so. The notion of "implying" a remedy, therefore, as applied to cases like *Borak*, can only refer to a process whereby the federal judiciary exercises a choice among *traditionally available* judicial remedies according to reasons related to the substantive social policy embodied in an act of positive law.

to the federal courts by Congress is thought adequate to empower a federal court to grant equitable relief for all areas of subject-matter jurisdiction enumerated therein, then it seems to me that the same statute is sufficient to empower a federal court to grant a traditional remedy at law. Of course, the special historical traditions governing the federal equity system might still bear on the comparative appropriateness of granting equitable relief as opposed to money damages. That possibility, however, relates, not to whether the federal courts have the power to afford one type of remedy as opposed to the other, but rather to the criteria which should govern the exercise of our power. * * *

The major thrust of the Government's position is that, where Congress has not expressly authorized a particular remedy, a federal court should exercise its power to accord a traditional form of judicial relief at the behest of a litigant, who claims a constitutionally protected interest has been invaded, only where the remedy is "essential," or "indispensable for vindicating constitutional rights." While this "essentiality" test is most clearly articulated with respect to damages remedies, apparently the Government believes the same test explains the exercise of equitable remedial powers. It is argued that historically the Court has rarely exercised the power to accord such relief in the absence of an express congressional authorization and that "[i]f Congress had thought that federal officers should be subject to a law different than state law, it would have had no difficulty in saying so, as it did with respect to state officers. * * *" See 42 U.S.C. § 1983. Although conceding that the standard of determining whether a damage remedy should be utilized to effectuate statutory policies is one of "necessity" or "appropriateness," the Government contends that questions concerning congressional discretion to modify judicial remedies relating to constitutionally protected interests warrant a more stringent constraint on the exercise of judicial power with respect to this class of legally protected interests.

These arguments for a more stringent test to govern the grant of damages in constitutional cases seem to be adequately answered by the point that the judiciary has a particular responsibility to assure the vindication of constitutional interests such as those embraced by the Fourth Amendment. * * * [T]he Bill of Rights is particularly intended to vindicate the interests of the individual in the face of the popular will as expressed in legislative majorities; at the very least, it strikes me as no more appropriate to await express congressional authorization of traditional judicial relief with regard to these legal interests than with respect to interests protected by federal statutes.

The question then, is, as I see it, whether compensatory relief is "necessary" or "appropriate" to the vindication of the interest asserted. In resolving that question, it seems to me that the range of policy considerations we may take into account is at least as broad as the range of those a legislature would consider with respect to an express statutory authorization of a traditional remedy. In this regard I agree with the Court that the appropriateness of according Bivens compensatory relief does not turn simply on the deterrent effect liability will have on federal official conduct.[8] Damages as a traditional form of compensation for invasion of a legally protected interest may be entirely appropriate even if no substantial deterrent effects on future official lawlessness might be thought to result. Bivens, after all, has invoked judicial processes claiming entitlement to compensation for injuries resulting from allegedly lawless official behavior, if those injuries are properly compensable in money damages. I do not think a court of law—vested with the power to accord a remedy—should deny him his relief simply because he cannot show that future lawless conduct will thereby be deterred.

And I think it is clear that Bivens advances a claim of the sort that, if proved, would be properly compensable in damages. The personal interests protected by the Fourth Amendment are those we attempt to capture by the notion of "privacy"; while the Court today properly points out that the type of harm which officials can inflict when they invade protected zones of an individual's life are different from the types of harm private citizens inflict on one another, the experience of judges in dealing with private trespass and false imprisonment claims supports the conclusion that courts of law are capable of making the types of judgment concerning causation and magnitude of injury necessary to accord meaningful compensation for invasion of Fourth Amendment rights.[9]

On the other hand, the limitations on state remedies for violation of common-law rights by private citizens argue in favor of a federal damages remedy. The injuries inflicted by officials acting under color of law, while no less compensable in damages than those inflicted by private parties, are substantially different in kind, as the Court's opinion today discusses in detail. It seems to me entirely proper that these injuries be compensable according to uniform rules of federal law, especially in light of the very large element of federal law which must in any event control the scope of official defenses to liability. * * *

Putting aside the desirability of leaving the problem of federal official liability to the vagaries of common-law actions, it is apparent that some form of damages is the only possible remedy for someone in Bivens' alleged position. It will be a rare case indeed in which an individual in Bivens' position will be able to obviate the harm by securing injunctive

8. And I think it follows from this point that today's decision has little, if indeed any, bearing on the question whether a federal court may properly devise remedies—other than traditionally available forms of judicial relief—for the purpose of enforcing substantive social policies embodied in constitutional or statutory policies. The Court today simply recognizes what has long been implicit in our decisions concerning equitable relief and remedies implied from statutory schemes; that a court of law vested with jurisdiction over the subject matter of a suit has the power—and therefore the duty—to make principled choices among traditional judicial remedies. Whether social prophylactic measures—which at least arguably the exclusionary rule exemplifies—are supportable on grounds other than a court's competence to select among traditional judicial remedies to make good the wrong done is a separate question.

9. The same, of course, may not be true with respect to other types of constitutionally protected interests, and therefore the appropriateness of money damages may well vary with the nature of the personal interest asserted. See *Monroe v. Pape*, 365 U.S. 167, 196 n. 5 (Harlan, J., concurring).

relief from any court. However desirable a direct remedy against the Government might be as a substitute for individual official liability, the sovereign still remains immune to suit. Finally, assuming Bivens' innocence of the crime charged, the "exclusionary rule" is simply irrelevant. For people in Bivens' shoes, it is damages or nothing.

The only substantial policy consideration advanced against recognition of a federal cause of action for violation of Fourth Amendment rights by federal officials is the incremental expenditure of judicial resources that will be necessitated by this class of litigation. There is, however, something ultimately self-defeating about this argument. For if, as the Government contends, damages will rarely be realized by plaintiffs in these cases because of jury hostility, the limited resources of the official concerned, etc., then I am not ready to assume that there will be a significant increase in the expenditure of judicial resources on these claims. * * * And I simply cannot agree with my Brother BLACK that the possibility of "frivolous" claims—if defined simply as claims with no legal merit—warrants closing the courthouse doors to people in Bivens' situation. There are other ways, short of that, of coping with frivolous lawsuits.

On the other hand, if—as I believe is the case with respect, at least, to the most flagrant abuses of official power—damages to some degree will be available when the option of litigation is chosen, then the question appears to be how Fourth Amendment interests rank on a scale of social values compared with, for example, the interests of stockholders defrauded by misleading proxies. Judicial resources, I am well aware, are increasingly scarce these days. Nonetheless, when we automatically close the courthouse door solely on this basis, we implicitly express a value judgment on the comparative importance of classes of legally protected interests. And current limitations upon the effective functioning of the courts arising from budgetary inadequacies should not be permitted to stand in the way of the recognition of otherwise sound constitutional principles.

Of course, for a variety of reasons, the remedy may not often be sought. And the countervailing interests in efficient law enforcement of course argue for a protective zone with respect to many types of Fourth Amendment violations. But, while I express no view on the immunity defense offered in the instant case, I deem it proper to venture the thought that at the very least such a remedy would be available for the most flagrant and patently unjustified sorts of police conduct. Although litigants may not often choose to seek relief, it is important, in a civilized society, that the judicial branch of the Nation's government stand ready to afford a remedy in these circumstances. * * *

CHIEF JUSTICE BURGER, dissenting.

I dissent from today's holding which judicially creates a damage remedy not provided for by the Constitution and not enacted by Congress. We would more surely preserve the important values of the doctrine of separation of powers—and perhaps get a better result—by recommending a solution to the Congress as the branch of government in which the Constitution has vested the legislative power. Legislation is the business of the Congress, and it has the facilities and competence for that task—as we do not. * * *

The problems of both error and deliberate misconduct by law enforcement officials call for a workable remedy. Private damage actions against individual police officers concededly have not adequately met this requirement, and it would be fallacious to assume today's work of the Court in creating a remedy will really accomplish its stated objective. There is some validity to the claims that juries will not return verdicts against individual officers except in those unusual cases where the violation has been flagrant or where the error has been complete, as in the arrest of the wrong person or the search of the wrong house. * * *

I conclude, therefore, that an entirely different remedy is necessary but it is one that in my view is as much beyond judicial power as the step the Court takes today. Congress should develop an administrative or quasi-judicial remedy against the government itself to afford compensation and restitution for persons whose Fourth Amendment rights have been violated. The venerable doctrine of *respondeat superior* in our tort law provides an entirely appropriate conceptual basis for this remedy. If, for example, a security guard privately employed by a department store commits an assault or other tort on a customer such as an improper search, the victim has a simple and obvious remedy—an action for money damages against the guard's employer, the department store. Such a statutory scheme would have the added advantage of providing some remedy to the completely innocent persons who are sometimes the victims of illegal police conduct—something that the suppression doctrine, of course, can never accomplish.

A simple structure would suffice. For example, Congress could enact a statute along the following lines:

(a) a waiver of sovereign immunity as to the illegal acts of law enforcement officials committed in the performance of assigned duties;

(b) the creation of a cause of action for damages sustained by any person aggrieved by conduct of governmental agents in violation of the Fourth Amendment or statutes regulating official conduct;

(c) the creation of a tribunal, quasi-judicial in nature or perhaps patterned after the United States Court of Claims, to adjudicate all claims under the statute;

(d) a provision that this statutory remedy is in lieu of the exclusion of evidence secured for use in criminal cases in violation of the Fourth Amendment; and

(e) a provision directing that no evidence, otherwise admissible, shall be excluded from any criminal proceeding because of violation of the Fourth Amendment.

* * *

JUSTICE BLACK, dissenting.

In my opinion for the Court in *Bell v. Hood*, we did as the Court states, reserve the question whether an unreasonable search made by a federal officer in violation of the Fourth Amendment gives the subject of the search a federal cause of action for damages against the officers making the search. There can be no doubt that Congress could create a federal cause of action for damages for an unreasonable search in violation of the Fourth Amendment. Although Congress has created such a federal cause of action against *state* officials acting under color of state law, it has never created such a cause of action against federal officials. If it wanted to do so, Congress could, of course, create a remedy against federal officials who violate the Fourth Amendment in the performance of their duties. But the point of this case and the fatal weakness in the Court's judgment is that neither Congress nor the State of New York has enacted legislation creating such a right of action. For us to do so is, in my judgment, an exercise of power that the Constitution does not give us.

Even if we had the legislative power to create a remedy, there are many reasons why we should decline to create a cause of action where none has existed since the formation of our Government. * * *

We sit at the top of a judicial system accused by some of nearing the point of collapse. Many criminal defendants do not receive speedy trials and neither society nor the accused are assured of justice when inordinate delays occur. Citizens must wait years to litigate their private civil suits. Substantial changes in correctional and parole systems demand the attention of the lawmakers and the judiciary. If I were a legislator I might well find these and other needs so pressing as to make me believe that the resources of lawyers and judges should be devoted to them rather than to civil damage actions against officers who generally strive to perform within constitutional bounds. There is also a real danger that such suits might deter officials from the *proper* and honest performance of their duties.

All of these considerations make imperative careful study and weighing of the arguments both for and against the creation of such a remedy under the Fourth Amendment. I would have great difficulty for myself in resolving the competing policies, goals, and priorities in the use of resources, if I thought it were my job to resolve those questions. But that is not my task. The task of evaluating the pros and cons of creating judicial remedies for particular wrongs is a matter for Congress and the legislatures of the States. Congress has not provided that any federal court can entertain a suit against a federal officer for violations of Fourth Amendment rights occurring in the performance of his duties. A strong inference can be drawn from creation of such actions against state officials that Congress does not desire to permit such suits against federal officials. * * * Cases could be cited to support the legal proposition which I assert, but it seems to me to be a matter of common understanding that the business of the judiciary is to interpret the laws and not to make them.

I dissent.

The Scope and Impact of "*Bivens* Actions"

The Supreme Court has recognized damage actions based on both the Eighth, *Carlson v. Green*, 446 U.S. 14 (1980); *Hudson v. McMillian*, 503 U.S. 1 (1992); and Fifth Amendments, *Davis v. Passman*, 442 U.S. 228 (1979). Lower courts have included at least the First, Sixth, and (against state officers) Fourteenth Amendments as well. *See* Note, *Rethinking Sovereign Immunity After* Bivens, 57 N.Y.U. L. Rev. 597, 598 n.7 (1982).

The Due Process Clauses of the Fifth and Fourteenth Amendments are sufficiently expansive both in their wording and their historical interpretation to suggest the possibility of a vast domain of "constitutional torts" that might lie against federal or state officials and federal or state governments. The Court has been alert, however, to restrict *Bivens*-style actions in ways that would avoid wholesale transformation of tort actions against officials into constitutional causes of action.

Collins v. Harker Heights, 503 U.S. 115 (1992), illustrates both the potentially expansive scope and the Court's cautious treatment of due process claims. The petitioner sought damages against a city for the death of her husband, a city employee who was asphyxiated while working to unstop a sewer line. The claim was that the decedent had a right under the due process clause of the Fourteenth Amendment "to be free from unreasonable risks of harm * * * and * * * to be protected from the [city's] custom and policy of deliberate indifference toward [its employees'] safety." The city was claimed to have violated this right by following a custom and policy of not training its employees about the dangers of working in sewers and not providing safety equipment and warnings. The Supreme Court was unanimous in holding that these allegations did not state a constitutional violation. Although the Court reaffirmed that the due process clause has a substantive component and that the Fourteenth Amendment was intended to prevent the government from abusing its power or from employing it as an instrument of oppression, these core concerns seemed remote from the facts petitioner alleged. Petitioner did not claim that the city or any of its employees deliberately harmed her husband. Nor was there any suggestion of conduct on the part of the city that might be considered "shocking to the conscience" of the Court. The city's challenged action (or inaction) was therefore not "arbitrary" in a constitutional sense.

The Court has also made clear that the standard for liability under the Eighth Amendment is one of "deliberate indifference" to the well-being of persons subject to punishment or incarceration under federal criminal law. *Estelle v. Gamble*, 429 U.S. 97 (1976); see also *Farmer v. Brennan*, 511 U.S. 825 (1994) ("deliberate indifference describes a state of mind more blameworthy than negligence"). Indeed, in the three decades following *Bivens* the Court has shown increasing reluctance to extend *Bivens* beyond a very limited reading of its core holding.

In *Correctional Services Corp. v. Malesko*, 534 U.S. 61 (2001), the Court considered a *Bivens*-based claim by an inmate of a privately run halfway house. Respondent had sued the Correctional Services Corporation because one of its employees had forced respondent to climb stairs to his fifth floor room rather than use the elevator. Respondent had a heart condition and had been exempted from the general policy that inmates below the sixth floor must use the stairway rather than the elevator. On the way to his bedroom the respondent had a heart attack and fell, resulting in permanent injury.

The district court dismissed the suit on the authority of *FDIC v. Meyer*, 510 U.S. 471 (1994), where the Court had held that *Bivens* actions could not be maintained against federal agencies but only against federal officers. The Second Circuit reversed and remanded, reasoning that while the logic of *Bivens* did not extend to suits against federal agencies that are covered by other doctrines of both liability and immunity, a suit against a private corporation would accomplish the important *Bivens* goal of providing an effective remedy for constitutional violations. The Supreme Court reversed. In a plurality opinion by the Chief Justice, joined fully only by Justices O'Connor and Kennedy, the Court rehearsed much of its post-*Bivens* jurisprudence.

> Since *Carlson* we have consistently refused to extend *Bivens* liability to any new context or new category of defendants. In *Bush v. Lucas*, 462 U.S. 367 (1983), we declined to create a *Bivens* remedy against individual Government officials for a First Amendment violation arising in the context of federal employment. Although the plaintiff had no opportunity to fully remedy the constitutional violation, we held that administrative review mechanisms crafted by Congress provided meaningful redress and thereby foreclosed the need to fashion a new, judicially crafted cause of action. We further recognized Congress' institutional competence in crafting appropriate relief for aggrieved federal employees as a "special factor counseling hesitation in the creation of a new remedy." * * * We have reached a similar result in the military context, even where the defendants were alleged to have been civilian personnel.
>
> In *Schweiker v. Chilicky*, 487 U.S. 412 (1988), we declined to infer a damages action against individual government employees alleged to have violated due process in their handling of Social Security applications. We observed that our "decisions have responded cautiously to suggestions" that *Bivens* remedies be extended into new contexts. In light of these decisions, we noted that "the absence of statutory relief for a constitutional violation * * * does not by any means necessarily imply that courts should award money damages against the officers responsible for the violation." We therefore rejected the claim that a *Bivens* remedy should be implied

simply from want of any other means for challenging a constitutional deprivation in federal court* * *.

Most recently, in *FDIC v. Meyer*, we unanimously declined an invitation to extend *Bivens* to permit suit against a federal agency even though the agency—because Congress had waived sovereign immunity—was otherwise amenable to suit. Our opinion emphasized that "the purpose of *Bivens* is to deter *the officer*," not the agency. We reasoned that if given the choice, plaintiffs would sue a federal agency instead of an individual who could assert qualified immunity as an affirmative defense. To the extent aggrieved parties had less incentives to bring a damages claim against individuals, "the deterrent effects of the *Bivens* remedy would be lost." * * *

From this discussion, it is clear that the claim urged by respondent is fundamentally different from anything recognized in *Bivens* or subsequent cases. In 30 years of *Bivens* jurisprudence we have extended its holding only twice, to provide an otherwise nonexistent cause of action against *individual officers* alleged to have acted unconstitutionally, or to provide a cause of action for a plaintiff who lacked *any alternative remedy* for harms caused by an individual officer's unconstitutional conduct* * *.

Respondent claims that even under *Meyer's* deterrence rationale, implying a suit against private corporations acting under color of federal law is still necessary to advance the core deterrence purpose of *Bivens*. He argues that because corporations respond to market pressures and make decisions without regard to constitutional obligations, requiring payment for the constitutional harms they commit is the best way to discourage future harms. That may be so, but it has no relevance to *Bivens*, which is concerned solely with deterring the unconstitutional acts of individual officers. If deterring the conduct of the policy-making entity was the purpose of *Bivens*, then *Meyer* would have implied a damages remedy against the Federal Deposit Insurance Corporation; it was after all an agency policy that led to *Meyer's* constitutional deprivation. But *Bivens* from its inception has been based not on that premise, but on the deterrence of individual officers who commit unconstitutional acts.

Nor are we confronted with a situation in which claimants in respondent's shoes lack effective remedies. It was conceded at oral argument that alternative remedies are at least as great, and in many respects greater, than anything that could be had under *Bivens*. For example, federal prisoners in private facilities enjoy a parallel tort remedy that is unavailable to prisoners housed in government facilities. * * *

This also makes respondent's situation altogether different from *Bivens*, in which we found alternative state tort remedies to be "inconsistent or even hostile" to a remedy inferred from the Fourth Amendment* * *.

Justice Scalia, joined by Justice Thomas, concurred in an opinion strongly suggesting that they would limit *Bivens* to its facts plus the facts of *Davis v. Passman* and *Carlson v. Green.*

> I join the opinion of the court because I agree that a narrow interpretation of the rationale of *Bivens* would not logically produce its application to the circumstances of this case. The dissent is doubtless correct that a broad interpretation of its rationale would logically produce such application, but I am not inclined (and the Court has not been inclined) to construe *Bivens* broadly.
>
> In joining the Court's opinion, however, I do not mean to imply that, if the narrowest rationale of *Bivens* did apply to a new context, I *would* extend its holding. I would not. *Bivens* is a relic of the heady days in which this Court assumed common-law powers to create causes of action—decreeing them to be "implied" by the mere existence of a statutory or constitutional prohibition. As the Court points out, we have abandoned that power to invent "implications" in the statutory field. There is even greater reason to abandon it in the constitutional field, since an "implication" imagined in the constitution can presumably not even be repudiated by Congress* * *.

Justice Stevens, joined by Justices Souter, Ginsberg, and Breyer dissented. The dissenters argued that the Court's approach, far from avoiding an extension of *Bivens*, had in fact retrenched on *Bivens'* "core premise." The dissenters read *Meyer* as based entirely on a reluctance to create substantial financial burdens for the federal government by creating a cause of action against a federal agency whose waiver of sovereign immunity would have permitted the very sort of lawsuit that *Bivens* presumed to be impossible. In addition, *Meyer* involved a straightforward procedural due process claim, not the substantive due process, or in this case Eighth Amendment claims, that the dissent viewed as lying "in the heartland of substantive *Bivens* claims."

Because *Meyer* did not dispose of the case, the dissenters returned to *Bivens* and sharply criticized the majority's understanding of what that case was about.

> It is ironic that the Court relies so heavily for its holding on this assumption that alternative effective remedies—primarily negligence actions in state court—are available to respondent. Like Justice Harlan, I think it "entirely proper that these injuries be compensable according to uniform rules of federal law, especially in light of the very large element of federal law which must in any event control the scope of official defenses to liability." And aside from undermining uniformity, the Court's reliance on state tort law will jeopardize the protection of the full scope of federal constitutional rights. State law might have comparable causes of action for tort claims like the Eighth Amendment violation alleged here, but other unconstitutional actions by prison employees, such as violations of the Equal Protection or Due Process Clauses, may find no

parallel causes of action in state tort law. Even though respondent here may have been able to sue for some degree of relief under state law because his Eighth Amendment claim could have been pleaded as negligence, future plaintiffs with constitutional claims less like traditional torts will not necessarily be so situated.

Second, the Court claims that the deterrence goals of *Bivens* would not be served by permitting liability here. It cannot be seriously maintained, however, that tort remedies against corporate employers have less deterrent value than actions against their employees. As the Court has previously noted, the "organizational structure" of private prisons "is one subject to the ordinary competitive pressures that normally help private firms adjust their behavior in response to the incentives that tort suits provide—*pressures not necessarily present in government departments.*" *Richardson v. McKnight*, 521 U.S. 399 (1997). Thus, the private corporate entity at issue here is readily distinguishable from the federal agency in Meyer. Indeed, a tragic consequence of today's decision is the clear incentive it gives to corporate managers of privately operated custodial institutions to adopt cost-saving policies that jeopardize the constitutional rights of the tens of thousands of inmates in their custody.

The Court raises a concern with imposing "asymmetrical liability costs on private prison facilities," and further claims that because federal prisoners in Government-run institutions can only sue officers, it would be unfair to permit federal prisoners in private institutions to sue an "officer's employer." Permitting liability in the present case, however, would *produce* symmetry: both private and public prisoners would be unable to sue the principal (*i.e.*, the Government), but would be able to sue the primary federal agent (*i.e.*, the government official or the corporation). Indeed, it is the *Court's* decision that creates asymmetry—between federal and state prisoners housed in private correctional facilities. Under 42 U.S.C. § 1983 [discussed *infra* Chapter 9], a state prisoner may sue a private prison for deprivation of constitutional rights, yet the Court denies such a remedy to that prisoner's federal counterpart. It is true that we have never expressly held that the contours of *Bivens* and § 1983 are identical. The Court, however, has recognized sound jurisprudential reasons for parallelism, as different standards for claims against state and federal actors "would be incongruous and confusing." *Butz v. Economou*, 438 U.S. 478 (1978) * * *.

It is apparent from the Court's critical discussion of the thoughtful opinions of Justice Harlan and his contemporaries, and from its erroneous statement of the question presented by this case as whether *Bivens* "should be extended" to allow recovery against a private corporation employed as a federal agent, that the driving force behind the Court's decision is a disagreement with the holding in *Bivens* itself * * *.

Commentators have been doubtful both about the good sense of allowing suits for constitutional torts against individual officials and about the evidentiary base for retrenching on *Bivens* actions once established. In SUING GOVERNMENT: CITIZENS' REMEDIES FOR OFFICIAL WRONGS (1983), Peter Schuck finds suits against government officers to be doubly perverse: claimants may be under-compensated because of severe limitations on the causes of action afforded, while risk averse public officials (who, with some justification, view merely being sued as a personal calamity) are given incentives to refrain from vigorous execution of their public duties. However sensible, Professor Schuck's arguments have fallen on deaf congressional and Supreme Court ears. Congress, you will remember, excluded constitutional torts from its immunization of federal officials from suit in the Westfall Act. And, of course, in *Meyer*, the Supreme Court passed up the opportunity to extend *Bivens* actions to include federal agencies.

Meanwhile in a pair of widely-cited articles, Professors Eisenberg and Schwab argue that the Supreme Court's retrenchment on *Bivens* actions may be a reaction more to appearance than to reality. They found little evidence that constitutional tort suits are having a major impact on court dockets or on public budgets. And although there have been numerous reports of officials living in fear of § 1983 and *Bivens*-style suits, they could discover no systematic study of the effects of such litigation on public officials' morale or performance. *See* Theodore Eisenberg & Stewart Schwab, *The Reality of Constitutional Tort Litigation*, 72 Cornell L. Rev. 641 (1987); *Explaining Constitutional Tort Litigation*, 73 Cornell L. Rev. 719 (1988).

BUTZ v. ECONOMOU

Supreme Court of the United States, 1978.
438 U.S. 478, 98 S.Ct. 2894, 57 L.Ed.2d 895.

JUSTICE WHITE delivered the opinion of the Court.

* * *

I

Respondent controls Arthur N. Economou and Co., Inc., which was at one time registered with the Department of Agriculture as a commodity futures commission merchant. * * * On February 19, 1970, following an audit, the Department of Agriculture issued an administrative complaint alleging that respondent, while a registered merchant, had willfully failed to maintain the minimum financial requirements prescribed by the Department. After another audit, an amended complaint was issued on June 22, 1970. A hearing was held before the Chief Hearing Examiner of the Department, who filed a recommendation sustaining the administrative complaint. The Judicial Officer of the Department, to whom the Secretary had delegated his decisional authority in enforcement proceedings, affirmed the Chief Hearing Examiner's decision. On respondent's petition for review, the Court of Appeals for the Second Circuit vacated the order of the Judicial Officer. It reasoned that "the essential finding of willfulness * * * was made in a proceeding instituted without the customary warning letter, which the Judicial Officer conceded might well have resulted in prompt correction of the claimed insufficiencies." 494 F.2d 519 (1974).

While the administrative complaint was pending before the Judicial Officer, respondent filed this lawsuit in Federal District Court. Respondent sought initially to enjoin the progress of the administrative proceeding, but he was unsuccessful in that regard. On March 31, 1975, respondent filed a second amended complaint seeking damages. Named as defendants were the individuals who had served as Secretary and Assistant Secretary of Agriculture during the relevant events; the Judicial Officer and Chief Hearing Examiner; several officials in the Commodity Exchange Authority;[2] the Agriculture Department attorney who had prosecuted the enforcement proceeding; and several of the auditors who had investigated respondent or were witnesses against respondent.

The complaint stated that prior to the issuance of the administrative complaints respondent had been "sharply critical of the staff and operations of Defendants and carried on a vociferous campaign for the reform of Defendant Commodity Exchange Authority to obtain more effective regulation of commodity trading." The complaint also stated that some time prior to the issuance of the February 19 complaint, respondent and his company had ceased to engage in activities regulated by the defendants. The complaint charged that each of the administrative complaints had been issued without the notice or warning required by law; that the defendants had furnished the complaints "to interested persons and others without furnishing respondent's answers as well"; and that following the issuance of the amended complaint, the defendants had issued a "deceptive" press release that "falsely indicated to the public that [respondent's] financial resources had deteriorated, when Defendants knew that their statement was untrue and so acknowledge[d] previously that said assertion was untrue."

The complaint then presented 10 "causes of action," some of which purported to state claims for damages under the United States Constitution. For example, the first "cause of action" alleged that respondent had been denied due process of law because the defendants had instituted unauthorized proceedings against him without proper notice and with the knowledge that respondent was no longer subject to their regulatory jurisdiction. The third "cause of action" stated that by means of such actions "the Defendants discouraged and chilled the campaign of criticism [plaintiff] directed against them, and thereby deprived the [plaintiff] of [his] rights to free expression guaranteed by the First Amendment of the United States Constitution."

2. These individuals included the Administrator of the Commodity Exchange Authority, the Director of its Compliance Division, the Deputy Director of its Registration and Audit Division, and the Regional Administrator for the New York Region.

The defendants moved to dismiss the complaint on the ground that "as to the individual defendants it is barred by the doctrine of official immunity. * * * "The defendants relied on an affidavit submitted earlier in the litigation by the attorney who had prosecuted the original administrative complaint against respondent. He stated that the Secretary of Agriculture had had no involvement with the case and that each of the other named defendants had acted "within the course of his official duties."

The District Court, apparently relying on the plurality opinion in *Barr v. Matteo*, held that the individual defendants would be entitled to immunity if they could show that "their alleged unconstitutional acts were within the outer perimeter of their authority and discretionary." * * *

The Court of Appeals for the Second Circuit reversed the District Court's judgment of dismissal with respect to the individual defendants. 535 F.2d 688 (1976). The Court of Appeals reasoned that *Barr v. Matteo* did not "represen[t] the last word in this evolving area," because principles governing the immunity of officials of the Executive Branch had been elucidated in later decisions dealing with constitutional claims against state officials. E.g., *Pierson v. Ray*, 386 U.S. 547 (1967); *Scheuer v. Rhodes*, 416 U.S. 232 (1974); *Wood v. Strickland*, 420 U.S. 308 (1975). These opinions were understood to establish that officials of the Executive Branch exercising discretionary functions did not need the protection of an absolute immunity from suit, but only a qualified immunity based on good faith and reasonable grounds. The Court of Appeals rejected a proposed distinction between suits against state officials sued pursuant to § 1983 and suits against federal officials under the Constitution * * *. After noting that summary judgment would be available to the defendants if there were no genuine factual issues for trial, the Court of Appeals remanded the case for further proceedings.

II

The single submission by the United States on behalf of petitioners is that all of the federal officials sued in this case are absolutely immune from any liability for damages even if in the course of enforcing the relevant statutes they infringed respondent's constitutional rights and even if the violation was knowing and deliberate. Although the position is earnestly and ably presented by the United States, we are quite sure that it is unsound and consequently reject it.

* * *

Bivens established that compensable injury to a constitutionally protected interest could be vindicated by a suit for damages invoking the general federal-question jurisdiction of the federal courts, but we reserved the question whether the agents involved were "immune from liability by virtue of their official position," and remanded the case for that determination. On remand, the Court of Appeals for the Second Circuit, as has every other Court of Appeals that has faced the question, held that the agents were not absolutely immune and that the public interest would be sufficiently protected by according the agents and their superiors a qualified immunity.

In our view, the Courts of Appeals have reached sound results. We cannot agree with the United States that our prior cases are to the contrary and support the rule it now urges us to embrace. Indeed, as we see it, the Government's submission is contrary to the course of decision in this Court from the very early days of the Republic.

The Government places principal reliance on *Barr v. Matteo.* * * * *Barr* clearly held that a false and damaging publication, the issuance of which was otherwise within the official's authority, was not itself actionable and would not become so by being issued maliciously. The Court did not choose to discuss whether the director's privilege would be defeated by showing that he was without reasonable grounds for believing his release was true or that he knew that it was false, although the issue was in the case as it came from the Court of Appeals.

Barr does not control this case. It did not address the liability of the acting director had his conduct not been within the outer limits of his duties, but from the care with which the Court inquired into the scope of his authority, it may be inferred that had the release been unauthorized, and surely if the issuance of press releases had been expressly forbidden by statute, the claim of absolute immunity would not have been upheld. The inference is supported by the fact that Mr. Justice Stewart, although agreeing with the principles announced by Mr. Justice Harlan, dissented and would have rejected the immunity claim because the press release, in his view, was not action in the line of duty. It is apparent also that a quite different question would have been presented had the officer ignored an express statutory or constitutional limitation on his authority.

Barr did not, therefore, purport to depart from the general rule, which long prevailed, that a federal official may not with impunity ignore the limitations which the controlling law has placed on his powers. The immunity of federal executive officials began as a means of protecting them in the execution of their federal statutory duties from criminal or civil actions based on state law. A federal official who acted outside of his federal statutory authority would be held strictly liable for his trespassory acts. For example, *Little v. Barreme*, 2 Cranch [6 U.S.] 170 (1804), held the commander of an American warship liable in damages for the seizure of a Danish cargo ship on the high seas. Congress had directed the President to intercept any vessels reasonably suspected of being en route *to* a French port, but the President had authorized the seizure of suspected vessels whether going *to* or *from* French ports, and the Danish vessel seized was en route *from* a forbidden destination. * * * [T]he seizure at issue was not among that class of seizures that the Executive had been authorized by statute to effect.

Bates v. Clark, 95 U.S. 204 (1877), was a similar case. The relevant statute directed seizures of alcoholic beverages in Indian country, but the seizure at issue, which was made upon the orders of a superior, was not made in Indian country. The "objection fatal to all this class of defenses is that in that locality [the seizing officers] were utterly without any authority in the premises" and hence were answerable in damages.

As these cases demonstrate, a federal official was protected for action tortious under state law only if his acts were authorized by controlling federal law. "To make out his defence he must show that his authority was sufficient in law to protect him." Since an unconstitutional act, even if authorized by statute, was viewed as not authorized in contemplation of law, there could be no immunity defense.

In both *Barreme* and *Bates*, the officers did not merely mistakenly conclude that the circumstances warranted a particular seizure, but failed to observe the limitations on their authority by making seizures not within the category or type of seizures they were authorized to make. *Kendall v. Stokes*, 3 How. [44 U.S.] 87 (1845), addressed a different situation. The case involved a suit against the Postmaster General for erroneously suspending payments to a creditor of the Post Office. Examining and, if necessary, suspending payments to creditors were among the Postmaster's normal duties, and it appeared that he had simply made a mistake in the exercise of the discretion conferred upon him. He was held not liable in damages since "a public officer, acting to the best of his judgment and from a sense of duty, in a matter of account with an individual [is not] liable in an action for an error of judgment." Having "the right to examine into this account" and the right to suspend it in the proper circumstances, the officer was not liable in damages if he fell into error, provided, however, that he acted "from a sense of public duty and without malice."

In *Spalding v. Vilas*, 161 U.S. 483 (1896), on which the Government relies, the principal issue was whether the malicious motive of an officer would render him liable in damages for injury inflicted by his official act that otherwise was within the scope of his authority. The Postmaster General was sued for circulating among the postmasters a notice that assertedly injured the reputation of the plaintiff and interfered with his contractual relationships. * * * Because the Postmaster General in issuing the circular in question "did not exceed his authority, nor pass the line of his duty," it was irrelevant that he might have acted maliciously.

Spalding made clear that a malicious intent will not subject a public officer to liability for performing his authorized duties as to which he would otherwise not be subject to damages liability. But *Spalding* did not involve conduct manifestly or otherwise beyond the authority of the official, nor did it involve a mistake of either law or fact in construing or applying the statute. It did not purport to immunize officials who ignore limitations on their authority imposed by law. Although the "manifestly or palpably" standard for examining the reach of official power may have been suggested as a gloss on *Barreme, Bates,* [and] *Kendall,* none of those cases was overruled. It is also evident that *Spalding* presented no claim that the officer was liable in damages because he had acted in violation of a limitation placed upon his conduct by the United States Constitution. If any inference is to be drawn from *Spalding* in any of these respects, it is that the official would not be excused from liability if he failed to observe obvious statutory or constitutional limitations on his powers or if his conduct was a manifestly erroneous application of the statute.

Insofar as cases in this Court dealing with the immunity or privilege of federal officers are concerned, this is where the matter stood until *Barr v. Matteo*. * * * [W]e are confident that *Barr* did not purport to protect an official who has not only committed a wrong under local law, but also violated those fundamental principles of fairness embodied in the Constitution.[22] Whatever level of protection from state interference is appropriate for federal officials executing their duties under federal law, it cannot be doubted that these officials, even when acting pursuant to congressional authorization, are subject to the restraints imposed by the Federal Constitution.

Although it is true that the Court has not dealt with this issue with respect to federal officers,[23] we have several times addressed the immunity of state officers when sued under 42 U.S.C. § 1983 for alleged violations of constitutional rights. These decisions are instructive for present purposes.

III

Pierson v. Ray, 386 U.S. 547 (1967), decided that § 1983 was not intended to abrogate the immunity of state judges which existed under the common law and which the Court had held applicable to federal judges in *Bradley v. Fisher*. *Pierson* also presented the issue "whether immunity was available to that segment of the executive branch of a state government that is * * * most frequently exposed to situations which can give rise to claims under § 1983—the local police officer." *Scheuer v. Rhodes*, 416 U.S. 232 (1974). Relying on the common law, we held that police officers were entitled to a defense of "good faith and probable cause," even though an arrest might subsequently be proved to be unconstitutional. We observed, however, that "[t]he common law has never granted police officers an absolute and unqualified immunity, and the officers in this case do not claim that they are entitled to one."

In *Scheuer v. Rhodes*, the issue was whether "higher officers of the executive branch" of state governments were immune from liability

22. We view this case, in its present posture, as concerned only with constitutional issues. The District Court memorandum focused exclusively on respondent's constitutional claims. It appears from the language and reasoning of its opinion that the Court of Appeals was also essentially concerned with respondent's constitutional claims. * * *

23. *Doe v. McMillan*, 412 U.S. 306 (1973), did involve a constitutional claim for invasion of privacy—but in the special context of the Speech or Debate Clause. The Court held that the executive officials would be immune from suit only to the extent that the legislators at whose behest they printed and distributed the documents could claim the protection of the Speech or Debate Clause.

under § 1983 for violations of constitutionally protected rights. There, the Governor of a State, the senior and subordinate officers of the state National Guard, and a state university president had been sued on the allegation that they had suppressed a civil disturbance in an unconstitutional manner. We explained that the doctrine of official immunity from § 1983 liability, although not constitutionally grounded and essentially a matter of statutory construction, was based on two mutually dependent rationales:

> "(1) the injustice, particularly in the absence of bad faith, of subjecting to liability an officer who is required, by the legal obligations of his position, to exercise discretion; (2) the danger that the threat of such liability would deter his willingness to execute his office with the decisiveness and the judgment required by the public good."

The opinion also recognized that executive branch officers must often act swiftly and on the basis of factual information supplied by others, constraints which become even more acute in the "atmosphere of confusion, ambiguity, and swiftly moving events" created by a civil disturbance. Although quoting at length from *Barr v. Matteo*, we did not believe that there was a need for absolute immunity from § 1983 liability for these high-ranking state officials. Rather the considerations discussed above indicated:

> "[I]n varying scope, a qualified immunity is available to officers of the executive branch of government, the variation being dependent upon the scope of discretion and responsibilities of the office and all the circumstances as they reasonably appeared at the time of the action on which liability is sought to be based. It is the existence of reasonable grounds for the belief formed at the time and in light of all the circumstances, coupled with good-faith belief, that affords a basis for qualified immunity of executive officers for acts performed in the course of official conduct."

Subsequent decisions have applied the *Scheuer* standard in other contexts. * * *

None of these decisions with respect to state officials furnishes any support for the submission of the United States that federal officials are absolutely immune from liability for their constitutional transgressions. On the contrary, with impressive unanimity, the Federal Courts of Appeals have concluded that federal officials should receive no greater degree of protection from *constitutional* claims than their counterparts in state government. * * *

We agree with the perception of these courts that, in the absence of congressional direction to the contrary, there is no basis for according to federal officials a higher degree of immunity from liability when sued for a constitutional infringement as authorized by *Bivens* than is accorded state officials when sued for the identical violation under § 1983. The constitutional injuries made actionable by § 1983 are of no greater magnitude than those for which federal officials may be responsible. The pressures and uncertainties facing decisionmakers in state government are little if at all different from those affecting federal officials. * * *

The Government argues that the cases involving state officials are distinguishable because they reflect the need to preserve the effectiveness of the right of action authorized by § 1983. But as we discuss more fully below, the cause of action recognized in *Bivens* would similarly be "drained of meaning" if federal officials were entitled to absolute immunity for their constitutional transgressions.

Moreover, the Government's analysis would place undue emphasis on the congressional origins of the cause of action in determining the level of immunity. It has been observed more than once that the law of privilege as a defense to damage actions against officers of Government has "in large part been of judicial making." *Barr v. Matteo*, 360 U.S., at 569. Section 1 of the Civil Rights Act of 1871—the predecessor of § 1983—said nothing about immunity for state officials. It mandated that any person who under color of state law subjected another to the deprivation of his constitutional rights would be liable to the injured party in an action at law. This Court nevertheless ascertained and announced what it deemed to be the appropriate type of immunity from § 1983 liability in a variety of contexts. *Pierson v. Ray; Imbler v. Pachtman; Scheuer v. Rhodes*. The federal courts are equally competent to determine the appropriate level of immunity where the suit is a direct claim under the Federal Constitution against a federal officer.

The presence or absence of congressional authorization for suits against federal officials is of course, relevant to the question whether to infer a right of action for damages for a particular violation of the Constitution. * * *

But once this analysis is completed, there is no reason to return again to the absence of congressional authorization in resolving the question of immunity. Having determined that the plaintiff is entitled to a remedy in damages for a constitutional violation, the court then must address how best to reconcile the plaintiff's right to compensation with the need to protect the decisionmaking processes of an executive department. * * *

IV

* * *

Our system of jurisprudence rests on the assumption that all individuals, whatever their position in government, are subject to federal law:

> "No man in this country is so high that he is above the law. No officer of the law may set that law at defiance with impunity. All officers of the government, from the highest to the lowest, are creatures of the law, and are bound to obey it."

United States v. Lee, 106 U.S. 196 (1882). In light of this principle, federal officials who seek absolute exemption from personal liability for unconstitutional conduct must bear the burden of showing that public policy requires an exemption of that scope.

This is not to say that considerations of public policy fail to support a limited immunity for federal executive officials. We consider here, as we did in *Scheuer*, the need to protect officials who are required to exercise their discretion and the related public interest in encouraging the vigorous exercise of official authority. Yet *Scheuer* and other cases have recognized that it is not unfair to hold liable the official who knows or should know he is acting outside the law, and that insisting on an awareness of clearly established constitutional limits will not unduly interfere with the exercise of official judgment. We therefore hold that, in a suit for damages arising from unconstitutional action, federal executive officials exercising discretion are entitled only to the qualified immunity specified in *Scheuer*, subject to those exceptional situations where it is demonstrated that absolute immunity is essential for the conduct of the public business.[34] * * *

V

Although a qualified immunity from damages liability should be the general rule for executive officials charged with constitutional violations, our decisions recognize that there are some officials whose special functions require a full exemption from liability. In each case, we have undertaken "a considered inquiry into the immunity historically accorded the relevant official at common law and the interests behind it."

In *Bradley v. Fisher*, the Court analyzed the need for absolute immunity to protect judges from lawsuits claiming that their decisions had been tainted by improper motives. The Court began by noting that the principle of immunity for acts done by judges "in the exercise of their judicial functions" had been "the settled doctrine of the English courts for many centuries, and has never been denied, that we are aware of, in the courts of this country." The Court explained that the value of this rule was proved by experience. Judges were often called to decide "[c]ontroversies involving not merely great pecuniary interests, but the liberty and character of the parties, and consequently exciting the deepest feelings." Such adjudications invariably produced at least one losing party, who would "accep[t] anything but the soundness of the decision in explanation of the action of the judge." "Just in proportion to the strength of his convictions of the correctness of his own view of the case is he apt to complain of the judgment against him, and from complaints of the judgment to pass to the ascription of improper motives

34. The Government argued in *Bivens* that the plaintiff should be relegated to his traditional remedy at state law. "In this scheme the Fourth Amendment would serve merely to limit the extent to which the agents could defend the state law tort suit by asserting that their actions were a valid exercise of federal power: if the agents were shown to have violated the Fourth Amendment, such a defense would be lost to them and they would stand before the state law merely as private individuals." Although, as this passage makes clear, traditional doctrine did not accord immunity to officials who transgressed constitutional limits, we believe that federal officials sued by such traditional means should similarly be entitled to a *Scheuer* immunity.

to the judge." *Ibid.* If a civil action could be maintained against a judge by virtue of an allegation of malice, judges would lose "that independence without which no judiciary can either be respectable or useful." Thus, judges were held to be immune from civil suit "for malice or corruption in their action whilst exercising their judicial functions within the general scope of their jurisdiction."[36]

The principle of *Bradley* was extended to federal prosecutors through the summary affirmance in *Yaselli v. Goff*, 275 U.S. 503 (1927), *aff'g*, 12 F.2d 396 (C.A.2 1926). * * *

We recently reaffirmed the holding of *Yaselli v. Goff* in *Imbler v. Pachtman* [424 U.S. 409 (1976)], a suit against a state prosecutor under § 1983. The Court's examination of the leading precedents led to the conclusion that "[t]he common-law immunity of a prosecutor is based upon the same considerations that underlie the common-law immunities of judges and grand jurors acting within the scope of their duties." * * *

Despite these precedents, the Court of Appeals concluded that all of the defendants in this case—including the Chief Hearing Examiner, Judicial Officer, and prosecuting attorney—were entitled to only a qualified immunity. The Court of Appeals reasoned that officials within the Executive Branch generally have more circumscribed discretion and pointed out that, unlike a judge, officials of the Executive Branch would face no conflict of interest if their legal representation was provided by the Executive Branch. The Court of Appeals recognized that "some of the Agriculture Department officials may be analogized to criminal prosecutors, in that they initiated the proceedings against [respondent], and presented evidence therein," but found that attorneys in administrative proceedings did not face the same "serious constraints of time and even information" which this Court has found to be present frequently in criminal cases.

We think that the Court of Appeals placed undue emphasis on the fact that the officials sued here are—from an administrative perspective—employees of the Executive Branch. Judges have absolute immunity not because of their particular location within the Government, but because of the special nature of their responsibilities. * * *

We think that adjudication within a federal administrative agency shares enough of the characteristics of the judicial process that those who participate in such adjudication should also be immune from suits for damages. The conflicts which federal hearing examiners seek to resolve are every bit as fractious as those which come to court. * * * Moreover, federal administrative law requires that agency adjudication contain many of the same safeguards as are available in the judicial process. * * *

36. In *Pierson v. Ray*, 386 U.S. 547 (1967), we recognized that state judges sued on constitutional claims pursuant to § 1983 could claim a similar absolute immunity. * * *

* * *

In light of these safeguards, we think that the risk of an unconstitutional act by one presiding at an agency hearing is clearly outweighed by the importance of preserving the independent judgment of these men and women. We therefore hold that persons subject to these restraints and performing adjudicatory functions within a federal agency are entitled to absolute immunity from damages liability for their judicial acts. Those who complain of error in such proceedings must seek agency or judicial review.

We also believe that agency officials performing certain functions analogous to those of a prosecutor should be able to claim absolute immunity with respect to such acts. * * *

The discretion which executive officials exercise with respect to the initiation of administrative proceedings might be distorted if their immunity from damages arising from that decision was less than complete. While there is not likely to be anyone willing and legally able to seek damages from the officials if they do *not* authorize the administrative proceedings, there is a serious danger that the decision to authorize proceedings will provoke a retaliatory response. An individual targeted by an administrative proceeding will react angrily and may seek vengeance in the courts. A corporation will muster all of its financial and legal resources in an effort to prevent administrative sanctions. * * *

* * *

We believe that agency officials must make the decision to move forward with an administrative proceeding free from intimidation or harassment. Because the legal remedies already available to the defendant in such a proceeding provide sufficient checks on agency zeal, we hold that those officials who are responsible for the decision to initiate or continue a proceeding subject to agency adjudication are entitled to absolute immunity from damages liability for their parts in that decision.

We turn finally to the role of an agency attorney in conducting a trial and presenting evidence on the record to the trier of fact. We can see no substantial difference between the function of the agency attorney in presenting evidence in an agency hearing and the function of the prosecutor who brings evidence before a court. * * * Administrative agencies can act in the public interest only if they can adjudicate on the basis of a complete record. We therefore hold that an agency attorney who arranges for the presentation of evidence on the record in the course of an adjudication is absolutely immune from suits based on the introduction of such evidence.

VI

There remains the task of applying the foregoing principles to the claims against the particular petitioner-defendants involved in this case. Rather than attempt this here in the first instance, we vacate the judgment of the Court of Appeals and remand the case to that court with instructions to remand the case to the District Court for further proceedings consistent with this opinion.

So ordered.

JUSTICE REHNQUIST, with whom THE CHIEF JUSTICE, JUSTICE STEWART, and JUSTICE STEVENS join, concurring in part and dissenting in part.

I concur in that part of the Court's judgment which affords absolute immunity to those persons performing adjudicatory functions within a federal agency, those who are responsible for the decision to initiate or continue a proceeding subject to agency adjudication, and those agency personnel who present evidence on the record in the course of an adjudication. I cannot agree, however, with the Court's conclusion that in a suit for damages arising from allegedly unconstitutional action federal executive officials, regardless of their rank or the scope of their responsibilities, are entitled to only qualified immunity even when acting within the outer limits of their authority. The Court's protestations to the contrary notwithstanding, this decision seriously misconstrues our prior decisions, finds little support as a matter of logic or precedent, and perhaps most importantly, will, I fear, seriously "dampen the ardor of all but the most resolute, or the most irresponsible, in the unflinching discharge of their duties," *Gregoire v. Biddle*, 177 F.2d 579, 581 (C.A.2 1949) (Learned Hand, J.). * * *†

History will surely not condemn the Court for its effort to achieve a more finely ground product from the judicial mill, a product which would both retain the necessary ability of public officials to govern and yet assure redress to those who are the victims of official wrongs. But if such a system of redress for official wrongs was indeed capable of being achieved in practice, it surely would not have been rejected by this Court speaking through the first Mr. Justice Harlan in 1896, by this Court speaking through the second Mr. Justice Harlan in 1959, and by Judge Learned Hand speaking for the Court of Appeals for the Second Circuit in 1948. These judges were not inexperienced neophytes who lacked the vision or the ability to define immunity doctrine to accomplish that result had they thought it possible. Nor were they obsequious toadies in their attitude toward high-ranking officials of coordinate branches of the Federal Government. But they did see with more prescience than the Court does today, that there are inevitable trade-offs in connection with any doctrine of official liability and immunity. They forthrightly accepted

† The ultimate irony of today's decision is that in the area of common-law official immunity, a body of law fashioned and applied by judges, absolute immunity within the federal system is extended only to judges and prosecutors functioning in the judicial system. * * * If one were to hazard an informed guess as to why such a distinction in treatment between judges and prosecutors, on the one hand, and other public officials on the other, obtains, mine would be that those who decide the common law know through personal experience the sort of pressures that might exist for such decisionmakers in the absence of absolute immunity, but may not know or may have forgotten that similar pressures exist in the case of nonjudicial public officials to whom difficult decisions are committed. But the cynical among us might not unreasonably feel that this is simply another unfortunate example of judges treating those who are not part of the judicial machinery as "lesser breeds without the law."

the possibility that an occasional failure to redress a claim of official wrongdoing would result from the doctrine of absolute immunity which they espoused, viewing it as a lesser evil than the impairment of the ability of responsible public officials to govern.

But while I believe that history will look approvingly on the motives of the Court in reaching the result it does today, I do not believe that history will be charitable in its judgment of the all but inevitable result of the doctrine espoused by the Court in this case. That doctrine seeks to gain and hold a middle ground which, with all deference, I believe the teachings of those who were at least our equals suggest cannot long be held. That part of the Court's present opinion from which I dissent will, I fear, result in one of two evils, either one of which is markedly worse than the effect of according absolute immunity to the Secretary and the Assistant Secretary in this case. The first of these evils would be a significant impairment of the ability of responsible public officials to carry out the duties imposed upon them by law. If that evil is to be avoided after today, it can be avoided only by a necessarily unprincipled and erratic judicial "screening" of claims such as those made in this case, an adherence to the form of the law while departing from its substance. Either one of these evils is far worse than the occasional failure to award damages caused by official wrongdoing, frankly and openly justified by the rule of *Spalding v. Vilas, Barr v. Matteo*, and *Gregoire v. Biddle*.

Notes

1. *Absolute Immunity—For Whom and For What?* Since *Economou*, the Supreme Court has returned often to the question of the immunity of federal officials. In *Nixon v. Fitzgerald*, 457 U.S. 731 (1982), the Court held that the President, because of his unique constitutional position, was entitled to absolute immunity for all acts within the "outer perimeter of his official responsibility"—hardly a surprising result.

Harlow v. Fitzgerald, 457 U.S. 800 (1982), presented a more difficult question. In that case, aides to President Nixon asserted absolute immunity from suit for acts taken pursuant to an alleged conspiracy, of which the President was a part, to deprive respondent of his First Amendment rights. The Court rejected this claim with the following explanation:

> In disputing the controlling authority of *Butz*, petitioners rely on the principles developed in *Gravel v. United States*, 408 U.S. 606 (1972). In *Gravel* we endorsed the view that "it is literally impossible * * * for Members of Congress to perform their legislative tasks without the help of aides and assistants" and that "the day-to-day work of such aides is so critical to the Members' performance that they must be treated as the latter's alter egos. * * * "Having done so, we held the Speech and Debate Clause derivatively applicable to the "legislative acts" of a Senator's aide that would have been privileged if performed by the Senator himself.
>
> Petitioners contend that the rationale of *Gravel* mandates a similar "derivative" immunity for the chief aides of the President of the United

States. Emphasizing that the President must delegate a large measure of authority to execute the duties of his office, they argue that recognition of derivative absolute immunity is made essential by all the considerations that support absolute immunity for the President himself.

Petitioners' argument is not without force. Ultimately, however, it sweeps too far. If the President's aides are derivatively immune because they are essential to the functioning of the Presidency, so should the members of the Cabinet—Presidential subordinates some of whose essential roles are acknowledged by the Constitution itself—be absolutely immune. Yet we implicitly rejected such derivative immunity in *Butz*. Moreover, in general our cases have followed a "functional" approach to immunity law. We have recognized that the judicial, prosecutorial, and legislative functions require absolute immunity. But this protection has extended no further than its justification would warrant. In *Gravel*, for example, we emphasized that Senators and their aides were absolutely immune only when performing "acts legislative in nature," and not when taking other acts even "in their official capacity." Our cases involving judges and prosecutors have followed a similar line. The undifferentiated extension of absolute "derivative" immunity to the President's aides therefore could not be reconciled with the "functional" approach that has characterized the immunity decisions of this Court, indeed including *Gravel* itself.

Petitioners also assert an entitlement to immunity based on the "special functions" of White House aides. This form of argument accords with the analytical approach of our cases. For aides entrusted with discretionary authority in such sensitive areas as national security or foreign policy, absolute immunity might well be justified to protect the unhesitating performance of functions vital to the national interest. But a "special functions" rationale does not warrant a blanket recognition of absolute immunity for all Presidential aides in the performance of all their duties. This conclusion too follows from our decision in *Butz*, which establishes that an executive official's claim to absolute immunity must be justified by reference to the public interest in the special functions of his office, not the mere fact of high station.

* * * In order to establish entitlement to absolute immunity a Presidential aide first must show that the responsibilities of his office embraced a function so sensitive as to require a total shield from liability. He then must demonstrate that he was discharging the protected function when performing the act for which liability is asserted.

Applying these standards to the claims advanced by petitioners Harlow and Butterfield, we cannot conclude on the record before us that either has shown that "public policy requires [for any of the functions of his office] an exemption of [absolute] scope."

In *Forrester v. White*, 484 U.S. 219 (1988), the Supreme Court confronted the mirror image of *Butz v. Economou*. Respondent, an Illinois state judge, had authority under state law to appoint and discharge probation officers. After hiring Forrester as a probation officer and later promoting her, respondent demoted and then discharged her. She sought damages under 42 U.S.C. § 1983, alleging that she was demoted and discharged on account of her gender. Respondent claimed that as a judge he was absolutely immune from a suit for civil damages. The district court granted White's motion for summary judgment and the court of appeals affirmed.

The Supreme Court unanimously reversed. Although the Court recognized that its jurisprudence had declared the absolute immunity of judges in broad terms, it was convinced that the functional approach of *Butz* should control. Just as the executive employees exercising adjudicatory functions in *Butz* were entitled to an absolute immunity, so judges exercising administrative functions, such as the hiring and firing of subordinate officials, should have only the qualified immunity that attaches to executive officials beneath the rank of president.

The Supreme Court has also grappled with the questions of when prosecutors are acting as prosecutors and of which court personnel engage in actions that are comparable to those of a judge. In *Buckley v. Fitzsimmons*, 509 U.S. 259 (1993), the Court held that a prosecutor was not entitled to absolute immunity for actions involved when assisting the police in investigation at a crime scene or when giving briefings to the news media. Neither of these functions was peculiarly prosecutorial and both involved actions for which other personnel, such as the police, would receive only a qualified immunity.

In *Antoine v. Byers & Anderson*, 508 U.S. 429 (1993), the Court also provided only a qualified immunity to a court reporter when sued for damages for failing to produce a transcript of a federal criminal trial. The Court reasoned that the court reporter's tasks were not "discretionary" and were therefore not functionally comparable to that of a judge.

2. *Criteria for Qualified Immunity?* The *Harlow* Court also revisited the question of the nature of the qualified immunity available to federal officials, in the process altering the *Butz* formula:

> Qualified or "good faith" immunity is an affirmative defense that must be pleaded by a defendant official. Decisions of this Court have established that the "good faith" defense has both an "objective" and a "subjective" aspect. The objective element involves a presumptive knowledge of and respect for "basic, unquestioned constitutional rights." The subjective component refers to "permissible intentions." Characteristically the Court has defined these elements by identifying the circumstances in which qualified immunity would *not* be available. Referring both to the objective and subjective elements, we have held that qualified immunity would be defeated if an official "*knew or reasonably should have known* that the action he took within his sphere of official responsibility would violate the constitutional rights of the [plaintiff], *or* if he took the action *with the malicious intention* to cause a deprivation of constitutional rights or other injury. * * * " (emphasis added).
>
> The subjective element of the good-faith defense frequently has proved incompatible with our admonition in *Butz* that insubstantial claims should not proceed to trial. Rule 56 of the Federal Rules of Civil Procedure provides that disputed questions of fact ordinarily may not be decided on motions for summary judgment. And an official's subjective

good faith has been considered to be a question of fact that some courts have regarded as inherently requiring resolution by a jury.

In the context of *Butz*'s attempted balancing of competing values, it now is clear that substantial costs attend the litigation of the subjective good faith of government officials. Not only are there the general costs of subjecting officials to the risks of trial—distraction of officials from their governmental duties, inhibition of discretionary action, and deterrence of able people from public service. There are special costs to "subjective" inquiries of this kind. Immunity generally is available only to officials performing discretionary functions. In contrast with the thought processes accompanying "ministerial" tasks, the judgments surrounding discretionary action almost inevitably are influenced by the decisionmaker's experiences, values, and emotions. These variables explain in part why questions of subjective intent so rarely can be decided by summary judgment. Yet they also frame a background in which there often is no clear end to the relevant evidence. Judicial inquiry into subjective motivation therefore may entail broad-ranging discovery and the deposing of numerous persons, including an official's professional colleagues. Inquiries of this kind can be peculiarly disruptive of effective government.

Consistently with the balance at which we aimed in *Butz*, we conclude today that bare allegations of malice should not suffice to subject government officials either to the costs of trial or to the burdens of broadreaching discovery. We therefore hold that government officials performing discretionary functions generally are shielded from liability for civil damages insofar as their conduct does not violate clearly established statutory or constitutional rights of which a reasonable person would have known.

The Supreme Court has continued to struggle with the extent to which immunity should protect government officials, not only from liability, but also from the obligation to stand trial. In *Mitchell v. Forsyth*, 472 U.S. 511 (1985), the respondent's telephone had been tapped pursuant to an authorization from Attorney General John Mitchell "in the exercise of [the President's] authority relating to national security as set forth in 18 U.S.C. § 2511(3)." In the wake of *United States v. United States District Court*, 407 U.S. 297 (1972) (*Keith*), holding that the Fourth Amendment does not permit the use of warrantless wiretaps in cases involving domestic threats to national security, respondents brought suit against Mitchell, who admittedly had authorized the wiretap only in order to gather intelligence needed for domestic national security purposes. Mitchell claimed absolute immunity under *Imbler v. Pachtman*, as well as a qualified immunity pursuant to the objective standard of *Harlow v. Fitzgerald*. The district court denied both forms of immunity. The court of appeals also rejected Mitchell's argument that the national security functions of the Attorney General entitled him to absolute immunity under *Imbler*. With respect to the denial of qualified immunity, the court of appeals held that the district court order was not appealable under the collateral order doctrine of *Cohen v. Beneficial Industrial Loan Corp.*, 337 U.S. 541 (1949).

On certiorari the Supreme Court agreed with both lower courts that *Imbler* absolute immunity applied only to the Attorney General's prosecutorial functions, which were not at issue in this case. The Court also found no blanket immunity for the performance of national security functions. Finding no analogous historical immunity, and believing that national security functions did not carry anything like the continuous risk of entanglement in vexatious litigation that judicial or prosecutorial actions entail, the Court denied Mitchell's claim of absolute immunity. The Court noted that other officials given absolute immunity were either subject to strong forms of political accountability (legislators and the chief executive) or potentially self-correcting hierarchical control (judges) that did not constrain the Attorney General's activities in the name of national security.

The Court was quick to point out, however, that the denial of absolute immunity neither negated the Attorney General's immunity from liability nor necessitated that he establish that immunity by proof of fact at trial:

> We emphasize that the denial of absolute immunity will not leave the Attorney General at the mercy of litigants with frivolous and vexatious complaints. Under the standard of qualified immunity articulated in *Harlow v. Fitzgerald*, the Attorney General will be entitled to immunity so long as his actions do not violate "clearly established statutory or constitutional rights of which a reasonable person would have known." This standard will not allow the Attorney General to carry out his national security functions wholly free from concern for his personal liability; he may on occasion have to pause to consider whether a proposed course of action can be squared with the Constitution and law of the United States. But this is precisely the point of the *Harlow* standard. * * * We do not believe that the security of the Republic will be threatened if its Attorney General is given incentives to abide by clearly established law.

The Court recognized, however, that if the district court's denial of Mitchell's claim to qualified immunity was not immediately appealable, Mitchell might have to go to trial in order to establish his immunity on appeal. This would be true even when no material issue of fact was in dispute at the time of the district court's ruling on the Attorney General's motion for summary judgment.

> At the heart of the issue before us is the question whether qualified immunity shares this essential attribute of absolute immunity—whether qualified immunity is in fact an entitlement not to stand trial under certain circumstances. The conception animating the qualified immunity doctrine as set forth in *Harlow v. Fitzgerald*, 457 U.S. 800 (1982), is that "where an official's duties legitimately require action in which clearly established rights are not implicated, the public interest may be better served by action taken 'with independence and without fear of consequences.'" * * * [T]he "consequences" with which we were concerned in *Harlow* are not limited to liability for money damages; they also include "the general costs of subjecting officials to the risks of trial—distraction of officials from their governmental duties, inhibition of discretionary action, and deterrence of able people from public service." Indeed, *Harlow* emphasizes that even such pretrial matters as discovery

are to be avoided if possible, as "[i]nquiries of this kind can be peculiarly disruptive of effective government."

With these concerns in mind, the *Harlow* Court refashioned the qualified immunity doctrine in such a way as to "permit the resolution of many insubstantial claims on summary judgment" and to avoid "subject[ing] government officials either to the costs of trial or to the burdens of broad-reaching discovery" in cases where the legal norms the officials are alleged to have violated were not clearly established at the time. Unless the plaintiff's allegations state a claim of violation of clearly established law, a defendant pleading qualified immunity is entitled to dismissal before the commencement of discovery. Even if the plaintiff's complaint adequately alleges the commission of acts that violated clearly established law, the defendant is entitled to summary judgment if discovery fails to uncover evidence sufficient to create a genuine issue as to whether the defendant in fact committed those acts. *Harlow* thus recognized an entitlement not to stand trial or face the other burdens of litigation, conditioned on the resolution of the essentially legal question whether the conduct of which the plaintiff complains violated clearly established law. The entitlement is an *immunity from suit* rather than a mere defense to liability; and like an absolute immunity, it is effectively lost if a case is erroneously permitted to go to trial. Accordingly, the reasoning that underlies the immediate appealability of an order denying absolute immunity indicates that the denial of qualified immunity should be similarly appealable: in each case, the district court's decision is effectively unreviewable on appeal from a final judgment.

Turning to the merits of Mitchell's claim, the Court found that when he authorized the wiretaps in question—well over a year before *Keith* was decided—it was not clearly established law that warrantless wiretaps for purposes of domestic national security were unconstitutional under the Fourth Amendment.

Although *Harlow* may have eliminated subjective intent issues from the affirmative defense of qualified immunity, it did not eliminate those issues when they are a part of the plaintiff's underlying cause of action. *Crawford-El v. Britton*, 523 U.S. 574 (1998), involved a claim that the respondent had misdirected the petitioner's personal belongings in connection with his prison transfer in order to punish him for the exercise of his First Amendment rights. Under applicable law an otherwise lawful lapse becomes a constitutional violation if it was not a mere lapse, but a malicious attempt to undermine the exercise of constitutional freedoms.

Recognizing that in this context it would be difficult to protect federal officers at the pleading stage, as *Harlow* seems to require, the D.C. Circuit required that petitioner provide "clear and convincing" evidence of the malicious intent in order to withstand a motion for summary judgment.

The Supreme Court reversed, in a 5–4 decision authored by Justice Stevens. The majority distinguished between a subjective intent factor attached to the affirmative defense of official immunity and the necessary inclusion of an intent allegation in certain constitutional tort claims. In the majority's view *Harlow* excluded the former but had nothing to say about the latter. Finding no authority in statute or the Federal Rules of Civil Procedure to heighten the pleading or proof requirement for the petitioner's

First Amendment claim, the majority found that the circuit court had no warrant for making wholesale changes in the law. The majority was influenced by congressional action in the form of the Prison Litigation Reform Act of 1996. While that statute clearly sought to discourage prisoners from filing unlikely claims, Congress made no change of the sort adopted by the D.C. Circuit's opinion. The majority presumed that, if district courts were unable to deal with frivolous claims using the ordinary techniques of the Federal Rules of Civil Procedure, Congress would again step in to provide needed reforms.

The dissenting Justices argued that the majority's approach was unworkable if *Harlow's* purpose of protecting officials at the pleading or summary judgment stage was to be realized. They were divided, however, concerning what the test should be. Chief Justice Rehnquist, joined by Justice O'Connor, would have held that a defendant in a motive-based tort suit was entitled to immunity so long as the defendant could offer a legitimate reason for the act and the plaintiff was unable to provide "objective evidence" that the offered reason was actually a pretext.

Justices Scalia and Thomas would have clung even more tightly to *Harlow's* objective standard because it is not obvious how to distinguish objective evidence of subjective intent from subjective evidence of subjective intent. Justices Scalia and Thomas would favor a rule that "once the trial court finds that the alleged grounds for the official action were objectively valid (*e.g.,* the person fired for alleged incompetence was indeed incompetent), it would not admit any proof that something other than these reasonable grounds was the genuine motive (*e.g.*, the incompetent person fired was a Republican)." What the objectively-valid evidence was that Crawford–El might have offered in this case, the dissenters did not elaborate.

Justices Scalia and Thomas recognized that their approach would substantially limit intent-based constitutional torts. But, consistent with their view of *Bivens* actions, Justices Scalia and Thomas also believe that the § 1983 jurisprudence bears "scant resemblance" to what Congress intended when enacting the civil rights statutes of the 1860s. Hence, if their objective standard eliminated large categories of constitutional torts, they would find this result consistent with both the Constitution and congressional intent.

3. *The Search for a Fact–Free Qualified Immunity Defense.* As the path from *Butz* to *Crawford-El*, via *Harlow* and *Mitchell*, reveals, protecting officers who may be innocent of wrongdoing from the necessity of trial or exposure to extensive discovery is difficult, perhaps even more difficult than even these cases acknowledge. For, while the question of whether a constitutional right exists and is clearly established easily may be characterized as a question of law, it is difficult to untangle from the facts of particular cases. Moreover, the question whether an official could reasonably have believed that his or her acts were constitutional necessarily implicates the underlying facts—facts that are often hotly contested.

Anderson v. Creighton, 483 U.S. 635 (1987), is a good illustration. Anderson, an FBI agent, entered the Creighton residence without a warrant in pursuit of the prime suspect in a recent bank robbery. The suspect, a family relation, was thought to be living with the Creightons and the latter's vehicle also matched the description of the "getaway car." Mr. Creighton demanded a warrant at the door, but Anderson told him that he had been watching too many police stories on television and that a warrant was unnecessary in this case. The Creightons claimed that the search was both unreasonable and conducted with excessive force. Anderson asserted his qualified immunity from suit and the trial court granted summary judgment. The court of appeals reversed, concluding that summary judgment was inappropriate because factual disputes concerning the circumstances of the search precluded deciding as a matter of law whether the search was supported by probable cause and exigent circumstances—making it lawful without a warrant.

The Supreme Court, through Justice Scalia, reversed again. A major portion of the opinion is devoted to the question of how to analyze a case in which the central question is whether a law enforcement officer had a reasonable belief that a search (or arrest) was reasonable. Both the trial and circuit courts had seemed to treat the case as one in which there was only one question of reasonableness—the Fourth Amendment question of the reasonableness of the search. In Scalia's view, this was error. Even if it were determined that the search was unreasonable as a matter of law, Anderson was still entitled to a qualified immunity if he could have believed reasonably that his search met the constitutional standard.

But, how is a court to frame either question of reasonableness without implicating the facts? If it addresses the question of whether the right to be free from unreasonable searches is clearly established as a matter of constitutional law, then the answer will always be "yes." At that level of generality the right is clearly established and no officer could reasonably believe otherwise. Qualified immunity disappears. On the other hand, if the right to be free from unreasonable searches is never "clearly" established in situations that differ factually from some prior search that has been the subject of adjudication, then qualified immunity protects officers in virtually every case.

Courts must therefore search for some middle ground which takes the circumstances of past cases and the circumstances of the present case into account both when determining whether the right is clearly established and when assessing whether the officer could at the time have reasonably believed that his search was proper, even though later adjudged to be in violation of a "clearly established" constitutional right. Both inquiries lead directly into the invariably contested facts of the case. Indeed, the Supreme Court's insistence that qualified immunity persists in circumstances where a clearly established right has been violated, but the officer could have made a reasonable mistake, makes the facts more, rather than less, relevant. Attempts by circuit courts to fuse the two inquiries to maintain their capacity to resolve cases on the pleadings or at the summary judgment stage have been resisted. See *Saucier v. Katz*, 533 U.S. 194 (2001) (reversing a Ninth Circuit decision that inquiries concerning qualified immunity are duplicative in an excessive force case). Lower court confusion in the face of Supreme Court clarity may result from the greater ease with which the Supreme Court seems to be able to discern that constitutional rights have not been clearly established. See *id.*; see also *Wilson v. Layne*, 526 U.S. 603 (1999) (holding that law enforcement officials had qualified immunity because the

Fourth Amendment violation had not been clearly established at the time officials enforced arrest warrant in the presence of news media).

These difficulties are not limited to Fourth Amendment cases. For a discussion and collection of lower court authorities struggling with the "clearly established" question, see David Rudovsky, *The Qualified Immunity Doctrine and the Supreme Court: Judicial Activism and the Restriction of Constitutional Rights*, 138 U. Pa. L. Rev. 23, 44–46 (1989). See also Note, *Qualified Immunity and the Allocation of Decisionmaking Functions Between Judge and Jury*, 90 Colum. L. Rev. 1045 (1990). The confusions and distortions involved in applying double balancing tests—both at the immunity and the substantive constitutional right stages of judicial consideration—have persuaded some that a return to "rulishness" in immunity doctrine is in order. See Alan K. Chen, *The Ultimate Standard: Qualified Immunity in the Age of Constitutional Balancing Tests*, 81 Iowa L. Rev. 261 (1995). The four dissenters in *Butz* presumably agree.

Chapter 9

BENEFICIARY ENFORCEMENT OF PUBLIC LAW

A. INTRODUCTION

One widely held view of the growth of American administrative law sees the rise of federal benefits and regulatory programs as a response to deficiencies or gaps in the legal protection provided by a limited federal common law and by state systems of private and criminal law. In supplanting or supplementing these court-centered regimes, the activist state has simultaneously produced a significant growth in public bureaucracies. To be sure, states and localities had and have their own administrative regimes. Justifications for national intervention have, therefore, stressed the substantive content of the pre-existing law, as well as the substitution of centralized, expert, and continuous bureaucratic implementation for the episodic decision making of generalist state and federal judges. Yet, national regulatory requirements and social welfare programs do not have to be enforced or implemented by federal officials. The beneficiaries of federal legislation can be given a direct role in the enforcement of federal standards, as a century of private antitrust enforcement attests. Federal programs can also take the form of framework laws which empower and sometimes fund the developmental, regulatory, or social welfare activities of state or local governments, as federal-aid highways legislation illustrates. Indeed, Congress, in recent decades, has found private enforcement of federal public law and schemes of "cooperative federalism" increasingly attractive.

These hybrid forms of administration, that is, federal public law with privatized enforcement or decentralized implementation, raise important remedial issues: When is private rather than public enforcement good public policy? What legal controls should govern the implementing actions of non-federal officials? From one perspective the first question might be answered "most of the time." Providing liberal opportunities for beneficiary enforcement of federal public law would seem an important support for administrative law's putative general project of maintaining the rule of law. As we saw in Chapter 7, beneficiaries of federal programs have limited capacity to require that federal officers carry out their statutory mandates. Opportunities for direct beneficiary enforcement that augment the capacities of federal agencies might be important safeguards against the neglect of individual or group interests that federal laws are designed to protect.

From this same perspective the second question above might be answered, "The same legal controls that apply to federal implementation." Otherwise, there may be a serious gap in the presumption that public officials may be called to account for the legality of their actions. In federal-state cooperative programs federal criteria or standards are implemented concretely only to the extent they are embodied in the criteria or standards of state public law or in the conduct of state and local officials. Because these officials operate under state law and are not subject to the APA, their actions are not subject to presumptive review in the system characterized by the somewhat aspirational language of *Abbott Laboratories* and *Overton Park*. The actions of state officials are normally "reviewable" only pursuant to state administrative law, which might, or might not, provide parallel remedies. This situation would seem to call for the development of some means by which state officials' fidelity to federal criteria or standards can be tested by the putative beneficiaries of federal programs.

From a different perspective, however, beneficiary enforcement or "review" in these contexts is a problematic enterprise. The nonreviewability of federal agency enforcement discretion is meant to protect values like policy consistency, equal treatment, and expert judgment, any of which might be undermined by allowing affected private parties to pursue enforcement on their own. Similarly, federal-state cooperative programs typically embody a delicate political balance between federal and state interests. States are not the mere implementors of federal programs—they are partners in a cooperative enterprise which often relies primarily on state personnel and substantial state funding. Historically, many such programs existed first at the state level. Attempts to fold these programs into the general system of federal judicial review of administrative action misconceives their complex, hybrid character. And, in either case, the insertion of opportunities for private enforcement or review rekindles the ever-present competition between the perspectives of generalist judges and specialized administrators. Indeed, federal or federal-state schemes of regulation may so comprehensively occupy particular fields that the continued recognition of preexisting common law rights, whether state or federal, could be considered dysfunctional.

In this final chapter on remedies, we explore these tensions. We begin with explicit statutory remedies, a technique of ancient origin and important modern applications, particularly in federal environmental statutes. We then review the tortured history of modern attempts to "imply" rights of action from federal regulatory statutes. We turn next to the contemporary use of a civil rights statute dating from 1866, 42 U.S.C. § 1983, to provide remedies, and/or a system of judicial review, for the beneficiaries of federal-state programs. Finally, we take up questions of the partial or complete supersession of common law rights by public law programs. For, as we shall see, in some instances the activist state's attempt to supplement the pre-existing legal order results ultimately in the complete substitution of public law, bureaucratically administered, for private rights, enforceable in the courts of law.

B. EXPLICIT STATUTORY REMEDIES

During the era in which crown courts replaced feudal justice in England and became the primary arenas for litigation, the jurisdictional theory of most actions brought by private persons in the royal courts was that the plaintiff represented or stood in the place of the king ("*Qui tam pro domino rege quam pro seipso*") and that the latter's interests were served by the suit. See generally Note, *The History and Development of Qui Tam*, 1972 Wash.U.L.Q. 81. This historical and purposeful confusion between suits to protect the public interest and suits to protect private interests persists in theory, though not generally in practice, in England. See generally Richard M. Jackson, The Machinery of Justice in England (7th ed. 1977).

However, neither the English theory nor the practice of private prosecution was transplanted effectively to American soil. From the earliest days of the Republic there seems to have been a presumption that criminal laws, and other laws designed to protect public interests, would be enforced by public officers. *Cf. Young v. United States ex rel. Vuitton et Fils S.A.*, 481 U.S. 787 (1987) (courts may appoint private prosecutors in criminal contempt proceedings only if executive branch declines enforcement). There are historically only three explicit exceptions to the monopoly that American statutes normally give public officers over the enforcement of public law:

(1) A crime victim may be permitted to hire counsel to "assist" the public prosecutor. With the prosecutor's assent, this private collaborator may even handle the case, but the prosecution cannot be initiated without the approval of the public officer. See generally Note, *Private Prosecution: A Remedy for District Attorneys' Unwarranted Inaction*, 65 Yale L.J. 209 (1955).

(2) Many early state statutes provided a special *qui tam* or informers suit. The informer or "relator" was in substance a private prosecutor who was rewarded by collecting a portion, often one half, of any criminal fine assessed at the conclusion of a successful prosecution. Most such actions were abolished as state public enforcement capabilities increased.

Only one important federal statute authorizing *qui tam* suits has persisted to the present day. The Federal Informer's Act was passed in 1863 as an amendment to the False Claims Act to promote the prosecution of military contractors who filed fraudulent claims related to federal procurement activities during the Civil War. The statute fell into disfavor, however, during World War II because of a widespread belief that it was producing windfalls for unscrupulous suitors who appropriated information that the Government had relied on to secure criminal indictments as a basis for bringing their *qui tam* actions. In 1943 Congress amended the Informer's Act to bar *qui tam* suits based on information known to the government at the time suit was filed, even if the information had come from the person proposing to sue and even if the government planned to take no action.

These reforms drastically reduced *qui tam* actions under the False Claims Act over the ensuing four decades. The widespread procurement abuses of the Reagan era defense build-up, however, provoked Congress to enact another round of amendments in 1986. 31 U.S.C. §§ 3729–3733 (1988). These amendments sought to steer a cautious course between promoting *qui tam* actions and regulating their use. But once again, unintended effects quickly emerged. Because the 1986 changes failed to exclude suits by current or former public employees based on information obtained within the scope of their employment, federal employees were given a significant financial incentive to ignore opportunities within normal agency channels to correct abuses, in order to enhance the likelihood of success in pursuing a False Claims Act prosecution privately. See *Congress Gropes With Whistleblower Law*, Nat'l L.J., April 27, 1992, at 7.

Nevertheless, the "whistleblower law" has proved a bonanza for both the federal government and for the private bar that specializes in *qui tam* cases. Hundreds of millions of dollars have flowed into the U.S. Treasury, and the plaintiffs' bar is not doing too badly either. See Richard B. Smith, *Honesty Pays Off: John Phillips Fosters a Growing Industry of Whistleblowing*, Wall St. J., Jan. 11, 1995, A–1. See also Ann M. Lininger, *The False Claims Act and Environmental Enforcement*, 16 Va.Envir.L.J. 577 (1997) (arguing that the FCA has also become an "important tool for environmental law enforcement").

The increasing popularity of the False Claims Act gave rise to questions concerning its constitutionality under both Articles II and III of the Constitution. The circuit courts have rejected the Article II defense, mostly on the authority of *Morrison v. Olson*, and the Justice Department has refused to join with defendants in asserting a claim to executive prosecutorial monopoly, impassioned pleas from commentators notwithstanding. See Note, *Fight for Your Right to Litigate: Qui Tam Article II and the President*, 49 Stan. L. Rev. 853 (1997) (Ara Lovitt). See also Robin J. Craig, *Will Separation of Powers Challenges "Take Care" of Environmental Citizen Suits?, Article II, Injury-in-Fact, "Private Enforcers," and Lessons From Qui Tam Litigation*, 72 U. Colo. L. Rev. 93 (2001).

The Article III question was resolved by the Supreme Court in *Vermont Agency of Natural Resources v. United States ex rel. Stevens*, 529 U.S. 765 (2000). Stevens, the *qui tam* relator, brought an action against his former employer claiming that it had defrauded the Environmental Protection Agency out of millions of dollars under various federal grant programs administered by EPA. The case was ultimately dismissed on the ground that states were not "persons" within the meaning of the False Claims Act, but not before the Supreme Court had resolved the question of relator Stevens' standing to prosecute the claim. Writing for the Court, Justice Scalia first disposed of Stevens' arguments that he had standing because he was acting either as an agent of the United States or in his own right based upon his interest in sharing the recovery with the federal government. The majority thought it clear that the federal False Claims Act gave the private relator more than an agency relationship to the lawsuit. Under that statute the action is said to be brought both for the government and "for the person." Moreover, the relator has a right to continue as a party to the action even when the government assumes responsibility for prosecuting the suit, and the statute entitles the relator to a hearing before either a voluntary dismissal of the suit or a settlement over the relator's objection.

On the other hand, the majority did not believe that Stevens could prosecute the suit merely because the statute gave him an interest in the recovery. That mere interest in the outcome of the suit was, in the majority's opinion, no different from the interest of someone who had placed a wager on the litigation. Standing thus requires not only a "concrete private interest in the outcome of the suit," but also that the parties' concrete interest be related to the "injury-in-fact" that gives rise to the lawsuit itself. The *qui tam* relator, however, has suffered no invasion of his rights. Indeed, in the Court's view, any right that the relator might have does not materialize until the litigation is completed and there is a recovery in which he can share.

Nevertheless, the Court found an adequate basis for the relator's suit on the theory that he was an "assignee" of a portion of the government's claim. Although the majority recognized that it had never expressly addressed the question of "representational standing" on the part of assignees, the Court had routinely entertained such suits in the past. This conclusion was strongly reinforced by the history of *qui tam*. Although *qui tam* suits were not recognized as common law actions in the colonies, and in that mode were dying out in England in the late Eighteenth Century, numerous colonial, state and early federal statutes recognized informer suits. On that basis the Court concluded that these suits must have been recognized as "cases and controversies" of the sort referred to in Article III of the Constitution.

(3) Several early federal statutes provided a private civil action for damages, double damages or, as in the antitrust laws, treble damages for violations. Since private damages were doubled or trebled, obviously Congress must have considered the private action more an enforcement device than a suit to compensate a private party who had been harmed by the violation of the statute. It is then but a short step to imagine, as does much of the recent law and economics literature, that the principal policy focus of damage actions, of whatever type, is the deterrence of socially costly conduct.

The large conceptual and practical overlap between the functions of public and private enforcement has not often convinced Congress or the courts, however, to abandon the conceptually tidy distinction between public law and private right. Explicit authorizations of damage actions in modern federal statutes, such as the securities acts of the 1930s or the civil rights laws of the 1960s, tend to be viewed as providing compensation for the infringement of statutorily based private rights, rather than as encouraging private efforts to vindicate the public interest. The latter function is left securely in the hands of public officials, as some of the materials in Chapter 7 illustrate.

A significant exception to the customary division between public and private enforcement appears in many federal environmental statutes. Beginning with the Clean Air Act of 1970, now codified at 42 U.S.C. §§ 7401, 7604, Congress has attached a "citizen suit" provision to most subsequently enacted environmental laws. Although these provisions vary in detail, the Clean Air Act establishes the basic model. "Any person" may commence an action in federal district court against any other person, including the United States or a state (to the extent permitted by the Eleventh Amendment), to enforce any emission standard or limitation promulgated pursuant to the Act or any order of the EPA or state with respect to such standards or limitations. Remedies include injunctions and civil penalties payable to the government. A person who contemplates suit must notify the EPA, the state, and the alleged violator sixty days prior to commencing suit and is barred from instituting suit if the EPA or state is "diligently prosecuting" a civil action for enforcement. The Act provides for intervention of right by the EPA in any citizen suit.

These citizen suit provisions attempt to guard against official inaction by permitting circumvention of the agency's conventional discretion to deploy its enforcement resources. This incursion into the agency's enforcement domain, however, is accomplished ostensibly without interfering with either the agency's allocation of resources or its power to establish environmental quality standards. The action is one to enforce officially prescribed standards or limitations, and the EPA may intervene or not at its discretion. Congress thus hoped to add private resources to the campaign to protect the environment without fragmenting authority to establish substantive requirements or putting agency resources at the disposal of private litigants.

Although citizen suit provisions do not authorize private damage awards, many do permit the award of attorneys' fees and fees for expert witnesses. Thus these statutory provisions incorporate some private incentives to act in the public interest. Nevertheless, most commentators agree (albeit without systematic empirical inquiry) that suits under these provisions were infrequent until the mid–1980s. See David A. Feller, *Private Enforcement of Federal Anti–Pollution Laws Through Citizen Suits: A Model*, 60 Den.L.J. 553, 564–65 (1983). The decline in government enforcement activity during the 1980s seems to have prompted increased citizen enforcement by public interest groups and others. See, e.g., ENVIRONMENTAL LAW INSTITUTE, CITIZENS SUITS AND ANALYSIS OF CITIZEN ENFORCEMENT ACTIONS UNDER EPA–ADMINISTERED STATUTES (1984) (documenting increased interest in private enforcement of the Clean Water Act). Requirements in EPA water discharge permits that dischargers maintain detailed publicly available records of all of their discharges make proof of violations elementary in theory. The polluter is convicted out of its own mouth.

While it is treacherous to generalize about the use of citizen suit provisions in environmental statutes, Michael S. Greve argues that few cases are brought by "citizens," if by that is meant locally concerned individuals or ad hoc groups. *The Private Enforcement of Environmental Law*, 65 Tul.L.Rev. 339 (1990). Most litigation is by well-established national organizations who pursue objectives that are the joint product of (1) their organizational agendas and (2) the economic incentives provided by the structure of citizen suit provisions, the deep pockets of private firms, and the reporting requirements embedded in environmental regulations. According to Greve, the result has been major private enforcement efforts under the Clean Water Act against a class of polluters, industrial dischargers, that accounts for only a small portion of all surface pollution. Private efforts to combat other forms of pollution have languished largely for the same reasons as public efforts, namely, the difficulties of establishing permit limits and attributing pollution to particular sources.

To the extent that local interests do drive "citizen" enforcement actions they are represented primarily in suits brought by local public authorities (who are "citizens" for purposes of these statutes) to stop polluting activity that they believe is inadequately regulated by state and federal pollution control agencies. These local "public citizens" are apparently prepared to pursue the non-degradation desires of their communities beyond the point at which limited public enforcement resources, or sometimes a different perspective, convince the EPA or state agencies to adopt a more tolerant view of noncompliance.

The enlistment of private citizens, or even local public officials, as enforcers of federal law obviously has drawbacks. Principal among them is the possibility that these parties will zealously pursue matters of great interest to them, but in the process impose burdens on particular defendants much heavier than those that others similarly situated are required to bear. There is even the possibility of harassment by private parties who are pursuing objectives only remotely connected to environmental protection.

Weinberger v. Romero–Barcelo, 456 U.S. 305 (1982), provides an example of local enforcement motivated by, at best, attenuated concerns for environmental protection. The litigation was instituted by the Governor of Puerto Rico against the Defense Department, under the Clean Water Act, to enjoin the Navy from discharging bombs into waters surrounding an island off the coast of Puerto Rico. Because the Navy had obtained no water quality permit to discharge any material of any kind into these waters, it clearly was in violation of the Act and of EPA regulations. The underlying dispute, however, had more to do with Puerto Rico's interest in developing tourism in and around the island (which was inhibited, to say the least, by the Navy's utilization of the vicinity for air to ground weapons training) than it did with any effects of discharged ordinance on water quality. Nevertheless, the lower court believed that it had no choice but to issue an injunction ordering the Navy to cease violating the Federal Water Quality Act. The Supreme Court reversed. The Court reasoned that the authorization for citizen suits was not intended to deny a district court the usual judicial discretion to withhold an injunction based upon the equities of a particular case.

Notwithstanding these concerns about misuse, there is strong evidence that citizen suits under some environmental statutes provide a crucial "safety net" that prevents extremely modest federal and state enforcement efforts from resulting in totally inadequate compliance. The political economy of enforcement at the state and federal levels puts enormous pressure on state and federal officials to limit enforcement activity and to settle cases quickly for moderate penalties or mere promises to comply in the future.

The federal government, through the Environmental Protection Agency, theoretically has power to oversee and control enforcement activity throughout the United States. In fact, it is required by federal law, state-federal political relationships and resource constraints to delegate virtually all of its enforcement power to state agencies. While default by state agencies on their enforcement responsibilities can result in reversion of those powers to the federal level, this rarely invoked remedy merely restores formal authority to an agency that has little capacity to do the job itself.

Meanwhile, there are intense pressures on state legislatures, and—through legislatures and governors' offices—on state administrators, to improve or maintain the state "business climate." "Accommodating" enforcement of environmental regulations is thus a common feature of state compliance activity. States and state agencies react to these pressures in varying ways, but the reality, or the perception, of interstate competition for mobile economic resources clearly limits what states are prepared to do. Remember the facts of the *Laidlaw* case in Chapter 7. There the polluting firm's relationship with the state agency was sufficiently amicable that the agency not only entered the suit at the firm's behest, it even permitted the firm to draft its complaint. In these circumstances it was hardly surprising that the district court found that the state agency was not "vigorously prosecuting" an enforcement action that would preclude a citizen suit by environmental organizations.

Citizen suits to enforce environmental statutes are roughly equal in number and effect to all state and federal judicial enforcement efforts. And, while state and federal public authorities may do a good bit more through administrative enforcement techniques, administrative enforcement is much more "cooperative"—and serves up considerably lower penalties—than judicial enforcement. For a review of these matters under the Clean Water Act, see David R. Hodas, *Enforcement of Environmental Law in a Triangular Federal System: Can Three Not be a Crowd When Enforcement Authority is Shared by the United States, the States and their Citizens?*, 54 Md.L.Rev. 1552 (1995).

C. IMPLIED RIGHTS OF ACTION

In *Bivens v. Six Unknown Named Agents*, *supra* p. 1144, the Supreme Court held that violations of the Fourth Amendment by federal law enforcement officers may give rise to a private action for damages. No provision of the Constitution specifically authorized such a remedy, but the Court was not content to remit the victims of unconstitutional conduct to whatever relief state law might afford. It invoked the traditional remedial authority of the federal judiciary to fashion a remedy. Both the majority opinion in *Bivens* and Justice Harlan's concurring opinion referred explicitly to the Court's earlier decision in the following case.

J.I. CASE CO. v. BORAK

Supreme Court of the United States, 1964.
377 U.S. 426, 84 S.Ct. 1555, 12 L.Ed.2d 423.

JUSTICE CLARK delivered the opinion of the Court.

This is a civil action brought by respondent, a stockholder of petitioner J.I. Case Company, charging deprivation of the preemptive rights of respondent and other shareholders by reason of a merger between Case and the American Tractor Corporation. It is alleged that the merger was effected through the circulation of a false and misleading proxy statement by those proposing the merger. The complaint was in two counts, the first based on diversity and claiming a breach of the directors' fiduciary duty to the stockholders. The second count alleged a violation of § 14(a)[1] of the Securities Exchange Act of 1934 with reference to the proxy solicitation material. The trial court held that as to this count it had no power to redress the alleged violations of the Act but was limited solely to the granting of declaratory relief thereon under § 27 of the Act.[2] The court held Wis.Stat., 1961, § 180.405(4), which

1. Section 14(a) of the Securities Exchange Act of 1934, 15 U.S.C. § 78n(a), provides: "It shall be unlawful for any person, by the use of the mails or by any means or instrumentality of interstate commerce or of any facility of any national securities exchange or otherwise to solicit or to permit the use of his name to solicit any proxy or consent or authorization in respect of any security (other than an exempted security) registered on any national securities exchange in contravention of such rules and regulations as the [Securities and Exchange] Commission may prescribe as necessary or appropriate in the public interest or for the protection of investors."

2. Section 27 of the Act, 15 U.S.C. § 78aa, provides in part: "The district courts of the United States * * * shall have exclusive jurisdiction of violations of this title or the rules and regulations thereunder, and of all suits in equity and actions at law brought to enforce any liability or duty

requires posting security for expenses in [stockholder] derivative actions, applicable to both counts, except that portion of Count 2 requesting declaratory relief. It ordered the respondent to furnish a bond in the amount of $75,000 thereunder and, upon his failure to do so, dismissed the complaint, save that part of Count 2 seeking a declaratory judgment. On interlocutory appeal the Court of Appeals reversed on both counts, holding that the District Court had the power to grant remedial relief and that the Wisconsin statute was not applicable. * * * We consider only the question of whether § 27 of the Act authorizes a federal cause of action for rescission or damages to a corporate stockholder with respect to a consummated merger which was authorized pursuant to the use of a proxy statement alleged to contain false and misleading statements violative of § 14(a) of the Act. * * *

* * * The claims pertinent to the asserted violation of the Securities Exchange Act were predicated on diversity jurisdiction as well as on § 27 of the Act. They alleged: that petitioners, or their predecessors, solicited or permitted their names to be used in the solicitation of proxies of Case stockholders for use at a special stockholders' meeting at which the proposed merger with ATC was to be voted upon; that the proxy solicitation material so circulated was false and misleading in violation of § 14(a) of the Act and Rule 14a–9 which the Commission had promulgated thereunder,[4] that the merger was approved at the meeting by a small margin of votes and was thereafter consummated; that the merger would not have been approved but for the false and misleading statements in the proxy solicitation material; and that Case stockholders were damaged thereby. The respondent sought judgment holding the merger void and damages for himself and all other stockholders similarly situated, as well as such further relief "as equity shall require." The District Court ruled that the Wisconsin security for expenses statute did not apply to Count 2 since it arose under federal law. However, the court found that its jurisdiction was limited to declaratory relief in a private, as opposed to a government, suit alleging violation of § 14(a) of the Act. Since the additional equitable relief and damages prayed for by the respondent would, therefore, be available only under state law, it ruled those claims subject to the security for expenses statute. * * *

created by this title or the rules and regulations thereunder. Any criminal proceeding may be brought in the district wherein any act or transaction constituting the violation occurred. Any suit or action to enforce any liability or duty created by this title or rules and regulations thereunder, or to enjoin any violation of such title or rules and regulations, may be brought in any such district or in the district wherein the defendant is found or is an inhabitant or transacts business, and process in such cases may be served in any other district of which the defendant is an inhabitant or wherever the defendant may be found."

4. 17 CFR § 240.14a–9 provides: "*False or misleading statements.* No solicitation subject to §§ 240.14a–1 to 240.14a–10 shall be made by means of any proxy statement, form of proxy, notice of meeting, or other communication written or oral containing any statement which at the time and in the light of the circumstances under which it is made, is false or misleading with respect to any material fact, or which omits to state any material fact necessary in order to make the statements therein not false or misleading or necessary to correct any statement in any earlier communication with respect to the solicitation of a proxy for the same meeting or subject matter which has become false or misleading."

It appears clear that private parties have a right under § 27 to bring suit for violation of § 14(a) of the Act. Indeed, this section specifically grants the appropriate District Courts jurisdiction over "all suits in equity and actions at law brought to enforce any liability or duty created" under the Act. The petitioners make no concessions, however, emphasizing that Congress made no specific reference to a private right of action in § 14(a); that, in any event, the right would not extend to derivative suits and should be limited to prospective relief only. * * *

While the respondent contends that his Count 2 claim is not a derivative one, we need not embrace that view, for we believe that a right of action exists as to both derivative and direct causes.

The purpose of § 14(a) is to prevent management or others from obtaining authorization for corporate action by means of deceptive or inadequate disclosure in proxy solicitation. The section stemmed from the congressional belief that "[f]air corporate suffrage is an important right that should attach to every equity security bought on a public exchange." H.R.Rep.No. 1383, 73d Cong., 2d Sess. 13. It was intended to "control the conditions under which proxies may be solicited with a view to preventing the recurrence of abuses which frustrated the free exercise of the voting rights of stockholders." "Too often proxies are solicited without explanation to the stockholder of the real nature of the questions for which authority to cast his vote is sought." S.Rep.No. 792, 73d Cong., 2d Sess. 12. These broad remedial purposes are evidenced in the language of [§ 14(a)] * * *. While this language makes no specific reference to a private right of action, among its chief purposes is "the protection of investors," which certainly implies the availability of judicial relief where necessary to achieve that result.

The injury which a stockholder suffers from corporate action pursuant to a deceptive proxy solicitation ordinarily flows from the damage done the corporation, rather than from the damage inflicted directly upon the stockholder. The damage suffered results not from the deceit practiced on him alone but rather from the deceit practiced on the stockholders as a group. To hold that derivative actions are not within the sweep of the section would therefore be tantamount to a denial of private relief. Private enforcement of the proxy rules provides a necessary supplement to Commission action. As in antitrust treble damage litigation, the possibility of civil damages or injunctive relief serves as a most effective weapon in the enforcement of the proxy requirements. The Commission advises that it examines over 2,000 proxy statements annually and each of them must necessarily be expedited. Time does not permit an independent examination of the facts set out in the proxy material and this results in the Commission's acceptance of the representations contained therein at their face value, unless contrary to other material on file with it. Indeed, on the allegations of respondent's complaint, the proxy material failed to disclose alleged unlawful market manipulation of the stock of ATC, and this unlawful manipulation would not have been apparent to the Commission until after the merger.

We, therefore, believe that under the circumstances here it is the duty of the courts to be alert to provide such remedies as are necessary to make effective the congressional purpose. As was said in *Sola Electric Co. v. Jefferson Electric Co.*, 317 U.S. 173, 176 (1942):

> "When a federal statute condemns an act as unlawful, the extent and nature of the legal consequences of the condemnation, though left by the statute to judicial determination, are nevertheless federal questions, the answers to which are to be derived from the statute and the federal policy which it has adopted."

It is for the federal courts "to adjust their remedies so as to grant the necessary relief" where federally secured rights are invaded. "And it is also well settled that where legal rights have been invaded, and a federal statute provides for a general right to sue for such invasion, federal courts may use any available remedy to make good the wrong done." *Bell v. Hood*, 327 U.S. 678, 684 (1946). Section 27 grants the District Courts jurisdiction "of all suits in equity and actions at law brought to enforce any liability or duty created by this title. * * * "In passing on almost identical language found in the Securities Act of 1933, the Court found the words entirely sufficient to fashion a remedy to rescind a fraudulent sale, secure restitution and even to enforce the right to restitution against a third party holding assets of the vendor. *Deckert v. Independence Shares Corp.*, 311 U.S. 282 (1940). This significant language was used:

> "The power to *enforce* implies the power to make effective the right of recovery afforded by the Act. And the power to make the right of recovery effective implies the power to utilize any of the procedures or actions normally available to the litigant according to the exigencies of the particular case."

Nor do we find merit in the contention that such remedies are limited to prospective relief. * * * [W]e believe that the overriding federal law applicable here would, where the facts required, control the appropriateness of redress despite the provisions of state corporation law, for it "is not uncommon for federal courts to fashion federal law where federal rights are concerned." In addition, the fact that questions of state law must be decided does not change the character of the right; it remains federal. * * *

Moreover, if federal jurisdiction were limited to the granting of declaratory relief, victims of deceptive proxy statements would be obliged to go into state courts for remedial relief. And if the law of the State happened to attach no responsibility to the use of misleading proxy statements, the whole purpose of the section might be frustrated. Furthermore, the hurdles that the victim might face (such as separate suits, security for expenses statutes, bringing in all parties necessary for complete relief, etc.) might well prove insuperable to effective relief.

Our finding that federal courts have the power to grant all necessary remedial relief is not to be construed as any indication of what we believe to be necessary and appropriate relief in this case. We are concerned here only with a determination that federal jurisdiction for this purpose does exist. Whatever remedy is necessary must await the trial on the merits.

The other contentions of the petitioners are denied.

Affirmed.

Implication Analysis and Federal Common Law

Even though corporate losses cause economic harm to stockholders by diminishing the value of their holdings, stockholders ordinarily have no direct right of action for managerial misfeasance. In such a situation, however, an aggrieved stockholder may bring a derivative suit against the responsible corporate officer, asserting in effect the right of action the corporation itself has against officers or agents guilty of wrongful conduct that causes corporate losses. While any recovery in a derivative suit goes to the corporation, the fact that the plaintiff's attorneys fees, which may be considerable, are payable from the recovery provides a powerful incentive for bringing such suits.

Prior to the *Borak* case derivative suits were governed in almost all particulars by state law. The belief that such suits were subject to abuse by so-called "strike-suitors," holders of a few shares who instigated derivative litigation with the hope of forcing an extortionate settlement from corporate management, had led many states to enact security-for-expenses statutes like Wisconsin's. These statutes typically require that the plaintiff, as a condition to the filing of a derivative suit, post a bond sufficient to ensure that the defendants would have a fund out of which to recover their legal expenses should they prevail on the merits. Since corporations almost invariably reimburse the legal expenses of successful officer defendants, an unstated objective of these statutes was to discourage the filing of derivative suits altogether. One can readily infer, therefore, that count two of the plaintiff's complaint in *Borak*—the so-called "direct" action based on a violation of section 14(a) of the Securities Act—was calculated to get court "review" of the merger decision without posting the $75,000 bond required by the Wisconsin statute. To the extent that the plaintiff was seeking an end-run around the traditional practice of deciding stockholder's suits in accordance with state law, there thus were substantial federalism interests involved in the case.

Indeed, those interests go much beyond the obvious effect on security-for-expenses statutes. *Borak* unleashed a flood of private suits to enforce various sections of the Securities Act of 1933 and the Securities Exchange Act of 1934. This litigation provided alternative federal remedies for many state law causes of action relating to corporate managers' fiduciary duties and created new fiduciary responsibilities to shareholders where none previously existed. Federal securities law has thus become an integral part of the law governing corporations even though the latter is ostensibly a creature wholly of state law. But see *Burks v. Lasker*, 441 U.S. 471 (1979) (state law practice of allowing disinterested directors to terminate derivative suit could apply to action based on federal statute where practice is consistent with policy of federal legislation).

This federal law of corporations, however, is not "integrated" into state corporation law in the same sense that regulatory statutes are commonly incorporated into other aspects of state common law. Since *Erie Railroad Co. v. Tompkins*, 304 U.S. 64 (1938), there is no federal, general common law. Unlike a state court that adopts a legislative rule of conduct as defining the "duty owed" in a common-law tort action, the federal court that "implies" a private cause of action to effectuate a statute's purpose adds a remedy to the legislative scheme. In so doing the federal court is simultaneously more audacious and more constrained than its state counterpart would be: More audacious because it is assuming a creative remedial role which, since *Erie*, has been problematic outside special fields, such as admiralty law. See, e.g., *Moragne v. States Marine Lines, Inc.*, 398 U.S. 375 (1970). And more constrained because, in effectuating the legislature's purposes, the federal court draws upon a potentially narrower range of policies and principles than a state court, which has a general mandate to contribute to the evolution of the whole of a state's common law.

To put the matter somewhat differently, state and federal courts look at legislative intent from different perspectives when assessing the relevance of a statutory norm to a private claim for damages or injunction. State courts, following the famous English precedent of *Gorris v. Scott*, 9 L.R. 125 (Exch.1874), will be concerned not to extend a statutory duty to situations far beyond those risks of harm that inspired passage of the legislation. See, e.g., *De Haen v. Rockwood Sprinkler Co.*, 258 N.Y. 350, 179 N.E. 764 (1932). But state courts may feel free to treat violations of public regulatory provisions merely as evidence of negligence, or as establishing the defendant's fault only presumptively. Alternatively, they may "borrow" a standard of care from a statute that would be unenforceable by public prosecution because of some technical defect in its adoption. See *Clinkscales v. Carver*, 22 Cal.2d 72, 136 P.2d 777 (1943). The state courts' search is for an appropriate way to integrate statutes into the fabric of common law claims over which they have general jurisdiction, while likewise giving these general legislative norms an application that is sensible within the context of the facts of a particular case.

Federal court "implication" analysis is inevitably more oriented to statutory language and legislative intent. A private claim for relief in a federal district court based on the defendant's violation of a federal legislative rule of conduct presents a claim founded on the statute itself. It is not a common law claim that asks the court to redefine the defendant's duty in terms of the statutory command while providing a traditional common law remedy. For if the claim is not based on the federal statute (or the Constitution), it does not "arise under" federal law and, in the absence of some other basis for jurisdiction, the court cannot hear the case. See *Merrell Dow Pharmaceuticals v. Thompson*,

478 U.S. 804 (1986). Thus, when diversity is lacking, a defendant in federal court can frequently raise the issue of whether the plaintiff has stated a cause of action—whether the federal statute in question affords, or permits the court to afford, relief—through the device of a motion to dismiss for lack of jurisdiction. In recognizing a "claim" or a "cause of action" the court is thus defining its own jurisdiction and simultaneously raising the question whether—in a system of limited and legislatively conferred jurisdiction—the remedy was one that Congress "intended."

This focus on specific legislative intent can have the curious effect of broadening the reach of implied causes of action once recognized, while limiting the instances in which the courts are prepared to recognize private rights of enforcement in the first instance. For example, the enforcement rationale that pervades the *Borak* opinion has had significant effects on the willingness of courts in subsequent cases to allow various affirmative defenses or to otherwise limit the reach of the action. As one court noted:

> This policy of vigorous enforcement through private litigation has been the instrument for forging many salutary developments in the securities fraud area, including a broadening of standing to sue, and a relaxation of the elements of proof in a private action. * * * The scienter requirement * * * appears to have been reduced to a knowledge of falsity or reckless disregard for truth standard. * * * The reliance standard has also been relaxed. * * * These are merely examples of innovations that have been prompted in substantial part by a uniform policy of encouraging vigorous enforcement of the securities laws through private litigation.

Chris-Craft Industries, Inc. v. Piper Aircraft Corp., 480 F.2d 341, 356–57 (2d Cir.), *cert. denied*, 414 U.S. 910 (1973).

On the other hand, "jurisdictional" matters that raise both federalism and separation of powers concerns seem likely to induce a caution that *Borak* scarcely reflects. The post-*Borak* evolution of implied rights of action in the Supreme Court illustrates both preoccupations.

CORT v. ASH

Supreme Court of the United States, 1975.
422 U.S. 66, 95 S.Ct. 2080, 45 L.Ed.2d 26.

JUSTICE BRENNAN delivered the opinion of the Court.

There are other questions, but the principal issue presented for decision is whether a private cause of action for damages against corporate directors is to be implied in favor of a corporate stockholder under 18 U.S.C. § 610, a criminal statute prohibiting corporations from making "a contribution or expenditure in connection with any election at which Presidential and Vice Presidential electors * * * are to be voted for." We conclude that implication of such a federal cause of action is not suggested by the legislative context of § 610 or required to accomplish Congress' purposes in enacting the statute. * * *

* * *

We consider first the holding of the Court of Appeals that respondent has "a private cause of action * * * [as] a citizen [or as a stockholder] to secure injunctive relief." The 1972 Presidential election is history, and respondent as citizen or stockholder seeks injunctive relief only as to future elections. In that circumstance, a statute enacted after the decision of the Court of Appeals, the Federal Election Campaign Act Amendments of 1974, requires reversal of the holding of the Court of Appeals.

In terms, § 610 is only a criminal statute, providing a fine or imprisonment for its violation. At the time this suit was filed, there was no statutory provision for civil enforcement of § 610, whether by private parties or by a Government agency. But the Amendments created a Federal Election Commission; established an administrative procedure for processing complaints of alleged violations of § 610 after January 1, 1975, and provided that "[a]ny person who believes a violation * * * [of § 610] has occurred may file a complaint with the Commission." * * * The Statute expressly vests the Commission with "primary jurisdiction" over any claimed violation of § 610 within its purview.[9] Consequently, a complainant seeking as citizen or stockholder to enjoin alleged violations of § 610 in future elections must henceforth pursue the statutory remedy of a complaint to the Commission, and invoke its authority to request the Attorney General to seek the injunctive relief. Thus, the Amendments constitute an intervening law that relegates to the Commission's cognizance respondent's complaint as citizen or stockholder for injunctive relief against any alleged violations of § 610 in future elections. In that circumstance the holding of the Court of Appeals must be reversed. Our duty is to decide this case according to the law existing at the time of our decision.

* * *

* * * There is no "statutory direction or legislative history to the contrary" in or respecting the Amendments, nor is there any possible "manifest injustice" in requiring respondent to pursue with respect to alleged violations which have yet to occur the statutory remedy for injunctive relief created by the Amendments.

* * * [W]e turn next to the holding of the Court of Appeals that "a private cause of action * * * by a stockholder to secure * * * derivative

9. The parties disagree upon whether this reference to "primary jurisdiction" suggests that a complainant, after filing a complaint with the Commission, may file a civil suit for injunctive relief if the Commission fails to cause one to be filed. They also dispute whether the exhaustion requirement applies to a suit for damages. * * *

However, these issues are not here relevant; it suffices for the purposes of this case to hold that the statute requires that a private complainant, desiring injunctive relief against alleged future violations of § 610 must at least exhaust his statutory remedy under the Amendments when and if such violations occur. We note that the question of the availability of a private cause of action by respondent for injunctive relief may not arise at all if the Attorney General seeks and obtains injunctive relief for any claimed violations by Bethlehem.

damage relief [is] proper to remedy violation of § 610." We hold that such relief is not available with regard to a 1972 violation under § 610 itself, but rather is available, if at all, under Delaware law governing corporations.

In determining whether a private remedy is implicit in a statute not expressly providing one, several factors are relevant. First, is the plaintiff "one of the class for whose especial benefit the statute was enacted."—that is, does the statute create a federal right in favor of the plaintiff? Second, is there any indication of legislative intent, explicit or implicit, either to create such a remedy or to deny one? Third, is it consistent with the underlying purposes of the legislative scheme to imply such a remedy for the plaintiff? And finally, is the cause of action one traditionally relegated to state law, in an area basically the concern of the States, so that it would be inappropriate to infer a cause of action based solely on federal law? * * *

Clearly, provision of a criminal penalty does not necessarily preclude implication of a private cause of action for damages. However, in *Wyandotte [Wyandotte Transportation Co. v. United States*, 389 U.S. 191 (1967)], *Borak*, and *Rigsby [Texas & Pacific Railway Co. v. Rigsby*, 241 U.S. 33 (1916)], there was at least a statutory basis for inferring that a civil cause of action of some sort lay in favor of someone.[11] Here, there was nothing more than a bare criminal statute, with absolutely no indication that civil enforcement of any kind was available to anyone.

We need not, however, go so far as to say that in this circumstance a bare criminal statute can never be deemed sufficiently protective of some special group so as to give rise to a private cause of action by a member of that group. For the intent to protect corporate shareholders particularly was at best a subsidiary purpose of § 610, and the other relevant factors all either are not helpful or militate against implying a private cause of action.

First, § 610 is derived from the Act of January 26, 1907, which "seems to have been motivated by two considerations. First, the necessity for destroying the influence over elections which corporations exercised through financial contribution. Second, the feeling that corporate

11. In *Wyandotte*, it was conceded that the United States had a civil in rem action against the ship obstructing navigation under § 19 of the Rivers and Harbors Act of 1899, and could retain the proceeds of the sale of the vessel and its cargo. The only question was whether it also had other judicial remedies for violation of § 51 of the Act, aside from the criminal penalties provided in § 16.

In *Borak*, § 27 of the Securities Exchange Act of 1934 specifically granted jurisdiction to the district courts over civil actions to "enforce any liability or duty created by this title or the rules and regulations thereunder," and there seemed to be no dispute over the fact that at least a private suit for declaratory relief was authorized; the question was whether a derivative suit for rescission and damages was also available. Further it was clear that the Securities and Exchange Commission could sue to enjoy violations of § 41(a) of the Act, the section involved in *Borak*.

Finally, in *Rigsby*, the Court noted that the statutes involved included language pertinent only to a private right of action for damages, although such a right of action was not expressly provided, thus rendering "[t]he inference of a private right of action * * * irresistible."

officials had no moral right to use corporate funds for contributions to political parties without the consent of the stockholders." Respondent bases the derivative action on the second purpose, claiming that the intent to protect stockholders from use of their invested funds for political purposes demonstrates that the statute set up a federal right in shareholders not to have corporate funds used for this purpose.

However, the legislative history of the 1907 Act, * * * demonstrates that the protection of ordinary stockholders was at best a secondary concern. Rather, the primary purpose of the 1907 Act, and of the 1925 Federal Corrupt Practices Act, 43 Stat. 1070, which reenacted the 1907 provision with some changes as § 313 of that Act, was to assure that federal elections are "free from the power of money," to eliminate "the apparent hold on political parties which business interests * * * seek and sometimes obtain by reason of liberal campaign contributions." Thus, the legislation was primarily concerned with corporations as a source of aggregated wealth and therefore of possible corrupting influence, and not directly with the internal relations between the corporations and their stockholders. In contrast, in those situations in which we have inferred a federal private cause of action not expressly provided, there has generally been a clearly articulated federal right in the plaintiff, *e.g., Bivens v. Six Unknown Federal Narcotics Agents*, or a pervasive legislative scheme governing the relationship between the plaintiff class and the defendant class in a particular regard, *e.g., J.I. Case Co. v. Borak*.

Second, there is no indication whatever in the legislative history of § 610 which suggests a congressional intention to vest in corporate shareholders a federal right to damages for violation of § 610. True, in situations in which it is clear that federal law has granted a class of persons certain rights, it is not necessary to show an intention to create a private cause of action, although an explicit purpose to deny such cause of action would be controlling. But where, as here, it is at least dubious whether Congress intended to vest in the plaintiff class rights broader than those provided by state regulation of corporations, the fact that there is no suggestion at all that § 610 may give rise to a suit for damages or, indeed, to any civil cause of action, reinforces the conclusion that the expectation, if any, was that the relationship between corporations and their stockholders would continue to be entrusted entirely to state law.

Third, while "it is the duty of the courts to be alert to provide such remedies as are necessary to make effective the congressional purpose," in this instance the remedy sought would not aid the primary congressional goal. Recovery of derivative damages by the corporation for violation of § 610 would not cure the influence which the use of corporate funds in the first instance may have had on a federal election. Rather, such a remedy would only permit directors in effect to "borrow" corporate funds for a time; the later compelled repayment might well not deter the initial violation and would certainly not decrease the impact of the use of such funds upon an election already past.

Fourth, and finally, for reasons already intimated, it is entirely appropriate in this instance to relegate respondent and others in his situation to whatever remedy is created by state law. In addition to the ultra vires action pressed here, the use of corporate funds in violation of federal law may, under the law of some States, give rise to a cause of action for breach of fiduciary duty. Corporations are creatures of state law, and investors commit their funds to corporate directors on the understanding that, except where federal law expressly requires certain responsibilities of directors with respect to stockholders, state law will govern the internal affairs of the corporation. If, for example, state law permits corporations to use corporate funds as contributions in state elections, shareholders are on notice that their funds may be so used and have no recourse under any federal statute. We are necessarily reluctant to imply a federal right to recover funds used in violation of a federal statute where the laws governing the corporation may put a shareholder on notice that there may be no such recovery.

In *Borak*, we said: "[If] the law of the State happened to attach no responsibility to the use of misleading proxy statements, the whole purpose of [§ 14(a) of the Securities Exchange Act of 1934] might be frustrated." Here, committing respondent to state-provided remedies would have no such effect. In *Borak*, the statute involved was clearly an intrusion of federal law into the internal affairs of corporations; to the extent that state law differed or impeded suit, the congressional intent could be compromised in state-created causes of action. In this case, Congress was concerned, not with regulating corporations as such, but with dulling their impact upon federal elections. As we have seen, the existence or non-existence of a derivative cause of action for damages would not aid or hinder this primary goal.

Because injunctive relief is not presently available in light of the Amendments, and because implication of a federal right of damages on behalf of a corporation under § 610 would intrude into an area traditionally committed to state law without aiding the main purpose of § 610, we reverse. * * *

Cort's Four Factor Test

The test that Justice Brennan enunciated, and to which the whole Court subscribed, in *Cort* is a curious *pastiche* of prior doctrine which combines potentially incompatible concepts. The "especial benefit" idea is of common law origin and suggests a broad-gauged approach to determining whether the statute creates a "federal right" for which the Court then supplies a remedy. This factor resonates with Justice Harlan's description in *Bivens* that "[t]he notion of 'implying' a remedy * * * can only refer to a process whereby the federal judiciary exercises a choice among *traditionally available* judicial remedies according to reasons related to the substantive social policy embodied in an act of positive law."

The second factor, by contrast, focuses the Court on specific legislative intent (either express or implied) to create or deny a remedy. In most contexts where "implication" is necessary this search for intent must be conducted in the materials constituting the statute's legislative history. And if the statute is silent, the legislative history predictably will be either silent or inconclusive. The question then will be what to make of legislative intent. Should silence be construed as negating an intent to allow private suits, as it seems to have been in the *Cort* opinion? If so, what is the Court to do when the general "substantive social policy" of the statute might be furthered by granting the remedy requested?

The third factor then reintroduces a search for purpose, but in an ambiguous form. The question is apparently "consistency" with "underlying purposes" of the legislation, but it is unclear what a finding of "consistency" would add to the first factor. This puzzle suggests that the third factor serves primarily as a limitation; it cautions the court to beware of implying remedies even where the first two factors point in that direction without considering the consequences of implication for the coherence or efficacy of the overall statutory scheme.

The fourth factor similarly seems purely cautionary and is, in one sense, nonproblematic. It merely introduces the traditional "federalism" concern. Yet the suggestion that the question is whether the implication would be "in an area basically the concern of the states" introduces another unruly issue into the calculus. In most situations the "area" will not define itself, and *how* it is defined will determine whether it is basically of state concern. For example, is the question in *Cort* one of corporation law or of the law of federal elections?

Subsequent decisions have confirmed both the intellectual difficulty of applying the *Cort* formula and the message implied by the application in *Cort* itself—the Court was not inclined to carry the *Bivens-Borak* remedial approach over into the wide range of federal "rights" that might be found in the dense growth of statutes and regulations during and since the New Deal. *Cort*'s potential for both restrictive application and conceptual disagreement is well-illustrated by one of the few post-*Cort* Supreme Court decisions that has "implied" a private federal cause of action under a statute that provides no express remedy.

CANNON v. UNIVERSITY OF CHICAGO

Supreme Court of the United States, 1979.
441 U.S. 677, 99 S.Ct. 1946, 60 L.Ed.2d 560.

JUSTICE STEVENS delivered the opinion of the Court.

* * *

Only two facts alleged in the complaints are relevant to our decision. First, petitioner was excluded from participation in the respondents' medical education programs because of her sex. Second, these education programs were receiving federal financial assistance at the time of her exclusion. These facts, admitted *arguendo* by respondents' motion to dismiss the complaints, establish a violation of § 901(a) of Title IX of the Education Amendments of 1972 [20 U.S.C. § 1681] (hereinafter Title IX).

That section, in relevant part, provides:

> "No person in the United States shall, on the basis of sex, be excluded from participation in, be denied the benefits of, or be subjected to discrimination under any education program or activity receiving Federal financial assistance. * * * "

The statute does not, however, expressly authorize a private right of action by a person injured by a violation of § 901. For that reason, and because it concluded that no private remedy should be inferred, the District Court granted the respondents' motions to dismiss.

The Court of Appeals agreed * * *.

* * *

The Court of Appeals quite properly devoted careful attention to [the] question of statutory construction. As our recent cases—particularly *Cort v. Ash*—demonstrate, the fact that a federal statute has been violated and some person harmed does not automatically give rise to a private cause of action in favor of that person. Instead, before concluding that Congress intended to make a remedy available to a special class of litigants, a court must carefully analyze the four factors that *Cort* identifies as indicative of such an intent. Our review of those factors persuades us, however, that the Court of Appeals reached the wrong conclusion * * *.

First, the threshold question under *Cort* is whether the statute was enacted for the benefit of a special class of which the plaintiff is a member. That question is answered by looking to the language of the statute itself. * * *

[I]t was statutory language describing the special class to be benefited by § 5 of the Voting Rights Act of 1965 that persuaded the Court that private parties within that class were implicitly authorized to seek a declaratory judgment against a covered State. *Allen v. State Board of Elections*, 393 U.S. 544. The dispositive language in that statute—"no person shall be denied the right to vote for failure to comply with [a new state enactment covered by, but not approved under, § 5]"—is remarkably similar to the language used by Congress in Title IX.

The language in these statutes—which expressly identifies the class Congress intended to benefit—contrasts sharply with statutory language customarily found in criminal statutes, such as that construed in *Cort*, *supra*, and other laws enacted for the protection of the general public. There would be far less reason to infer a private remedy in favor of individual persons if Congress, instead of drafting Title IX with an unmistakable focus on the benefited class, had written it simply as a ban on discriminatory conduct by recipients of federal funds or as a prohibition against the disbursement of public funds to educational institutions engaged in discriminatory practices.

Unquestionably, therefore, the first of the four factors identified in *Cort* favors the implication of a private cause of action. * * *

Second, the *Cort* analysis requires consideration of legislative history. We must recognize, however, that the legislative history of a statute that does not expressly create or deny a private remedy will typically be equally silent or ambiguous on the question. * * * But this is not the typical case. Far from evidencing any purpose to *deny* a private cause of action, the history of the Title IX rather plainly indicates that Congress intended to create such a remedy.

Title IX was patterned after Title VI of the Civil Rights Act of 1964. Except for the substitution of the word "sex" in Title IX to replace the words "race, color, or nation origin" in Title VI, the two statutes use identical language to describe the benefited class. Both statutes provide the same administrative mechanism for terminating federal financial support for institutions engaged in prohibited discrimination. Neither statute expressly mentions a private remedy for the person excluded from participation in a federally funded program. The drafters of Title IX explicitly assumed that it would be interpreted and applied as Title VI had been during the preceding eight years.

In 1972 when Title IX was enacted, the critical language in Title VI had already been construed as creating a private remedy. * * *

* * * Indeed, during the period between the enactment of Title VI in 1964 and the enactment of Title IX in 1972, this Court had consistently found implied remedies—often in cases much less clear than this. It was *after* 1972 that this Court decided *Cort v. Ash* and the other cases cited by the Court of Appeals in support of its strict construction of the remedial aspect of the statute. We, of course, adhere to the strict approach followed in our recent cases, but our evaluation of congressional action in 1972 must take into account its contemporary legal context. In sum, it is not only appropriate but also realistic to presume that Congress was thoroughly familiar with these unusually important precedents from this and other federal courts and that it expected its enactment to be interpreted in conformity with them.

It is not, however, necessary to rely on these presumptions. The package of statutes of which Title IX is one part also contains a provision whose language and history demonstrate that Congress itself understood Title VI, and thus its companion, Title IX, as creating a private remedy. Section 718 of the Education Amendments authorizes federal courts to award attorney's fees to the prevailing parties, other than the United States, in private actions brought against public educational agencies to enforce Title VI in the context of elementary and secondary education. * * *

* * *

Third, under *Cort*, a private remedy should not be implied if it would frustrate the underlying purpose of the legislative scheme. On the other hand, when that remedy is necessary or at least helpful to the accomplishment of the statutory purpose, the Court is decidedly receptive to its implication under the statute.

Title IX, like its model Title VI, sought to accomplish two related, but nevertheless somewhat different, objectives. First, Congress wanted to avoid the use of federal resources to support discriminatory practices; second, it wanted to provide individual citizens effective protection against those practices. * * *

The first purpose is generally served by the statutory procedure for the termination of federal financial support for institutions engaged in discriminatory practices. That remedy is, however, severe and often may not provide an appropriate means of accomplishing the second purpose if merely an isolated violation has occurred. In that situation, the violation might be remedied more efficiently by an order requiring an institution to accept an applicant who had been improperly excluded. Moreover, in that kind of situation it makes little sense to impose on an individual, whose only interest is in obtaining a benefit for herself, or on HEW, the burden of demonstrating that an institution's practices are so pervasively discriminatory that a complete cutoff of federal funding is appropriate. The award of individual relief to a private litigant who has prosecuted her own suit is not only sensible but is also fully consistent with—and in some cases even necessary to—the orderly enforcement of the statute.

The Department of Health, Education, and Welfare, which is charged with the responsibility for administering Title IX, perceives no inconsistency between the private remedy and the public remedy. On the contrary, the agency takes the unequivocal position that the individual remedy will provide effective assistance in achieving the statutory purposes. * * *

Fourth, the final inquiry suggested by *Cort* is whether implying a federal remedy is inappropriate because the subject matter involves an area basically of concern to the States. No such problem is raised by a prohibition against invidious discrimination of any sort, including that on the basis of sex. Since the Civil War, the Federal Government and the federal courts have been the "*primary* and powerful reliances" in protecting citizens against such discrimination. Moreover, it is the expenditure of federal funds that provides the justification for this particular statutory prohibition. There can be no question but that this aspect of the *Cort* analysis supports the implication of a private federal remedy.

In sum, there is no need in this case to weigh the four *Cort* factors; all of them support the same result. Not only the words and history of Title IX, but also its subject matter and underlying purposes, counsel implication of a cause of action in favor of private victims of discrimination.

* * *

When Congress intends private litigants to have a cause of action to support their statutory rights, the far better course is for it to specify as much when it creates those rights. But the Court has long recognized that under certain limited circumstances the failure of Congress to do so is not inconsistent with an intent on its part to have such a remedy available to the persons benefited by its legislation. Title IX presents the atypical situation in which *all* of the circumstances that the Court has previously identified as supportive of an implied remedy are present. We therefore conclude that petitioner may maintain her lawsuit, despite the absence of any express authorization for it in the statute.

CHIEF JUSTICE BURGER concurs in the judgment.

JUSTICE REHNQUIST, with whom JUSTICE STEWART joins, concurring.

Having joined the Court's opinion in this case, my only purpose in writing separately is to make explicit what seems to me already implicit in that opinion. I think the approach of the Court, reflected in its analysis of the problem in this case * * * is quite different from the analysis in earlier cases such as *J.I. Case Co. v. Borak*, 377 U.S. 426 (1964). The question of the existence of a private right of action is basically one of statutory construction. And while state courts of general jurisdiction still enforcing the common law as well as statutory law may be less constrained than are federal courts enforcing laws enacted by Congress, the latter must surely look to those laws to determine whether there was an intent to create a private right of action under them.

We do not write on an entirely clean slate, however, and the Court's opinion demonstrates that Congress, at least during the period of the enactment of the several Titles of the Civil Rights Act, tended to rely to a large extent on the courts to *decide* whether there should be a private right of action, rather than determining this question for itself. Cases such as *J.I. Case Co. v. Borak*, *supra*, and numerous cases from other federal courts, gave Congress good reason to think that the federal judiciary would undertake this task.

I fully agree with the Court's statement that "[w]hen Congress intends private litigants to have a cause of action to support their statutory rights, the far better course is for it to specify as much when it creates those rights." It seems to me that the factors to which I have here briefly adverted apprise the lawmaking branch of the Federal Government that the ball, so to speak, may well now be in its court. Not only is it "far better" for Congress to so specify when it intends private litigants to have a cause of action, but for this very reason this Court in the future should be extremely reluctant to imply a cause of action absent such specificity on the part of the Legislative Branch.

JUSTICE WHITE, with whom JUSTICE BLACKMUN joins, dissenting.

[After an exhaustive analysis of the legislative history, Justices White and Blackmun concluded:]

The Court recognizes that because Title IX was explicitly patterned after Title VI of the Civil Rights Act of 1964, it is difficult to infer a private cause of action in the former but not in the latter. * * * [T]he legislative history, like the terms of Title VI itself, makes it abundantly clear that the Act was and is a mandate to federal agencies to eliminate discrimination in federally funded programs. Although there was no intention to cut back on private remedies existing under 42 U.S.C. § 1983 to challenge discrimination occurring under color of state law, there is no basis for concluding that Congress contemplated the creation of private remedies either against private parties who previously had been subject to no constitutional or statutory obligation not to discriminate, or against federal officials or agencies involved in funding allegedly discriminatory programs* * *.

Congress decided in Title IX, as it had in Title VI, to prohibit certain forms of discrimination by recipients of federal funds. Where those recipients were acting under color of state law, individuals could obtain redress in the federal courts for violation of these prohibitions. But, excepting post-Civil War enactments dealing with racial discrimination in specified situations, these forms of discrimination by private entities had not previously been subject to individual redress under federal law, and Congress decided to reach such discrimination not by creating a new remedy for individuals, but by relying on the authority of the Federal Government to enforce the terms under which federal assistance would be provided. Whatever may be the wisdom of this approach to the problem of private discrimination, it was Congress' choice, not to be overridden by this Court.

JUSTICE POWELL, dissenting.

* * * The time has come to reappraise our standards for the judicial implication of private causes of action.

Under Art. III, Congress alone has the responsibility for determining the jurisdiction of the lower federal courts. As the Legislative Branch, Congress also should determine when private parties are to be given causes of action under legislation it adopts. * * * When Congress chooses not to provide a private civil remedy, federal courts should not assume the legislative role of creating such a remedy and thereby enlarge their jurisdiction.

The facts of this case illustrate the undesirability of this assumption by the Judicial Branch of the legislative function. Whether every disappointed applicant for admission to a college or university receiving federal funds has the right to a civil-court remedy under Title IX is likely to be a matter of interest to many of the thousands of rejected applicants. It certainly is a question of vast importance to the entire higher educational community of this country. But quite apart from the interests of the persons and institutions affected, respect for our constitutional system dictates that the issue should have been resolved by the elected representatives in Congress after public hearings, debate, and legislative decision. It is not a question properly to be decided by relatively uninformed federal judges who are isolated from the political process.

In recent history, the Court has tended to stray from the Art. III and separation-of-powers principle of limited jurisdiction. This, I believe, is evident from a review of the more or less haphazard line of cases that led to our decision in *Cort v. Ash*. The "four factor" analysis of that case is an open invitation to federal courts to legislate causes of action not authorized by Congress. It is an analysis not faithful to constitutional principles and should be rejected. Absent the most compelling evidence of affirmative congressional intent, a federal court should not infer a private cause of action.

I

The implying of a private action from a federal regulatory statute has been an exceptional occurrence in the past history of this Court. A review of those few decisions where such a step has been taken reveals in almost every case special historical circumstances that explain the result, if not the Court's analysis. These decisions suggest that the doctrine of implication applied by the Court today not only represents judicial assumption of the legislative function, but also lacks a principled precedential basis.

The origin of implied private causes of actions in the federal courts is said to date back to *Texas & Pacific R. Co. v. Rigsby*, 241 U.S. 33 (1916). A close look at the facts of that case and the contemporary state of the law indicates, however, that *Rigsby's* reference to the "inference of a private right of action," carried a far different connotation than the isolated passage quoted by the Court might suggest. The narrow question presented for decision was whether the standards of care defined by the Federal Safety Appliance Act's penal provisions applied to a tort action brought against an interstate railroad by an employee not engaged in interstate commerce at the time of his injury. The jurisdiction of the federal courts was not in dispute, the action having been removed from state court on the ground that the defendant was a federal corporation. Under the regime of *Swift v. Tyson*, 16 Pet. 1 (1842), then in force, the Court was free to create the substantive standards of liability applicable to a common-law negligence claim brought in federal court. The practice of judicial reference to legislatively determined standards of care was a common expedient to establish the existence of negligence. See Thayer, *Public Wrong and Private Action*, 27 Harv. L.Rev. 317 (1914). *Rigsby* did nothing more than follow this practice, and cannot be taken as authority for the judicial creation of a cause of action not legislated by Congress.

For almost 50 years after *Rigsby*, this Court recognized an implied private cause of action in only one other statutory context. Four decisions held that various provisions of the Railway Labor Act of 1926 could be enforced in a federal court. * * * In each of these cases * * * the implication of some kind of remedial mechanism was necessary to provide the enforcement authority Congress clearly intended.

During this same period, the Court frequently turned back private plaintiffs seeking to imply causes of action from federal statutes. Even in cases where the statute might be said to have been enacted for the benefit of a special class comprising the plaintiff, the factor to which the Court today attaches so much importance, the court refused to create a private action if Congress had provided some other means of enforcing such duties. *See, e.g., Switchmen.s v. National Mediation Board* [320 U.S. 297 (1943)].

A break in this pattern occurred in *J.I. Case Co. v. Borak* * * *. I find this decision both unprecedented and incomprehensible as a matter of public policy. The decision's rationale * * * ignores the fact that Congress, in determining the degree of regulation to be imposed on companies covered by the Securities Exchange Act, already had decided that private enforcement was unnecessary. More significant for present purposes, however, is the fact that *Borak*, rather than signaling the start of a trend in this Court, constitutes a singular and, I believe, aberrant interpretation of a federal regulatory statute.

Since *Borak*, this Court has upheld the implication of private causes of actions derived from federal statutes in only three extremely limited sets of circumstances. First, the Court in *Jones v. Alfred H. Mayer Co.*, 392 U.S. 409 (1968); *Sullivan v. Little Hunting Park, Inc.*, 396 U.S. 229 (1969); and *Johnson v. Railway Express Agency, Inc.*, 421 U.S. 454 (1975), recognized the right of private parties to seek relief for violations of 42 U.S.C. §§ 1981 and 1982. But to say these cases "implied" rights of action is somewhat misleading, as Congress at the time these statutes were enacted expressly referred to private enforcement actions. * * *

Second, the Court in *Allen v. State Board of Elections* permitted private litigants to sue to enforce the preclearance provisions of § 5 of the Voting Rights Act of 1965. As the Court seems to concede, this decision was reached without substantial analysis, and in my view can be explained only in terms of this Court's special and traditional concern for safeguarding the electoral process. * * *

Finally, the Court in *Superintendent of Insurance v. Bankers Life & Cas. Co.*, 404 U.S. 6 (1971), ratified 25 years of lower-court precedent that had held a private cause of action available under the Securities and Exchange Commission's Rule 10b–5. As the Court concedes, this decision reflects the unique history of Rule 10b–5, and did not articulate any standards of general applicability. * * *

* * *

It was against this background of almost invariable refusal to imply private actions, absent a complete failure of alternative enforcement mechanisms and a clear expression of legislative intent to create such a remedy, that *Cort v. Ash* was decided. * * * [A]s the opinion of the Court today demonstrates, the *Cort* analysis too easily may be used to deflect inquiry away from the intent of Congress, and to permit a court instead to substitute its own views as to the desirability of private enforcement.

* * *

That the *Cort* analysis too readily permits courts to override the decision of Congress not to create a private action is demonstrated conclusively by the flood of lower-court decisions applying it. Although from the time *Cort* was decided until today this Court consistently has turned back attempts to create private actions, other federal courts have tended to proceed in exactly the opposite direction. In the four years since we decided *Cort*, no less than 20 decisions by the Courts of Appeals have implied private actions from federal statutes. It defies reason to believe that in each of these statutes Congress absentmindedly forgot to mention an intended private action. Indeed, the accelerating trend evidenced by these decisions attests to the need to re-examine the *Cort* analysis.

II

In my view, the implication doctrine articulated in *Cort* and applied by the Court today engenders incomparably greater problems than the possibility of occasionally failing to divine an unexpressed congressional intent. If only a matter of statutory construction were involved, our obligation might be to develop more refined criteria which more accurately reflect congressional intent. "But the unconstitutionality of the course pursued has now been made clear" and compels us to abandon the implication doctrine of *Cort. Erie R. Co. v. Tompkins*, 304 U.S. 64, 77–78 (1938).

As the * * * decisions of the Courts of Appeals illustrate, *Cort* allows the Judicial Branch to assume policymaking authority vested by the Constitution in the Legislative Branch. It also invites Congress to avoid resolution of the often controversial question whether a new regulatory statute should be enforced through private litigation. Rather than confronting the hard political choice involved, Congress is encouraged to shirk its constitutional obligation and leave the issue to the courts to decide.[14] When this happens, the legislative process with its public scrutiny and participation has been bypassed, with attendant prejudice to everyone concerned. Because the courts are free to reach a result different from that which the normal play of political forces would have produced, the intended beneficiaries of the legislation are unable to ensure the full measure of protection their needs may warrant. For the same reason, those subject to the legislative constraints are denied the opportunity to forestall through the political process potentially unneces-

14. Mr. Justice Rehnquist, perhaps considering himself temporarily bound by his position in *University of California Regents v. Bakke*, 438 U.S. 265, 418–421 (1978) (opinion of STEVENS, J.), concurs in the Court's decision today. But writing briefly, he correctly observes "that Congress, at least during the period of the enactment of the several Titles of the Civil Rights Act, tended to rely to a large extent on the courts to *decide* whether there should be a private right of action, rather than determining this question for itself." It does not follow, however, that this Court is obliged to indulge Congress in its refusal to confront these hard questions. In my view, the very reasons advanced by Mr. Justice Rehnquist why "this Court in the future should be extremely reluctant to imply a cause of action" absent specific direction by Congress, apply to this case with special force.

sary and disruptive litigation. Moreover, the public generally is denied the benefits that are derived from the making of important societal choices through the open debate of the democratic process.

The Court's implication doctrine encourages, as a corollary to the political default by Congress, an increase in the governmental power exercised by the federal judiciary. The dangers posed by judicial arrogation of the right to resolve general societal conflicts have been manifest to this Court throughout its history. * * *

It is true that the federal judiciary necessarily exercises substantial powers to construe legislation, including, when appropriate, the power to prescribe substantive standards of conduct that supplement federal legislation. But this power normally is exercised with respect to disputes over which a court already has jurisdiction, and in which the existence of the asserted cause of action is established. Implication of a private cause of action, in contrast, involves a significant additional step. By creating a private action, a court of limited jurisdiction necessarily extends its authority to embrace a dispute Congress has not assigned it to resolve. * * *

III

In sum, I believe the need both to restrain courts that too readily have created private causes of action, and to encourage Congress to confront its obligation to resolve crucial policy questions created by the legislation it enacts, has become compelling. Because the analysis suggested by *Cort* has proved inadequate to meet these problems, I would start afresh. Henceforth, we should not condone the implication of any private action from a federal statute absent the most compelling evidence that Congress in fact intended such an action to exist. Where a statutory scheme expressly provides for an alternative mechanism for enforcing the rights and duties created, I would be especially reluctant ever to permit a federal court to volunteer its services for enforcement purposes. Because the Court today is enlisting the federal judiciary in just such an enterprise, I dissent.

Notes

1. *What happened to* Cort v. Ash? Post-*Cannon* cases have not unified either the Court or the jurisprudence. Moreover, far from addressing each case in accordance with the *Cort v. Ash* four factors, analysis often focuses narrowly on precedent within a particular field. Thus, although the Court was unanimous in extending *Cannon* to find a damages remedy under Title IX, three Justices reached that conclusion solely on *stare decisis* grounds. *Franklin v. Gwinnett County Public Schools*, 503 U.S. 60 (1992).

The role of precedent has been particularly prominent in securities law cases. The Court has refused to overturn or substantially limit established causes of action in the securities area, see *Herman & MacLean v. Huddleston*, 459 U.S. 375 (1983), and has implied remedies under statutory provisions regulating commodities trading that were modeled on the securities laws. *Merrill Lynch, Pierce, Fenner & Smith v. Curran*, 456 U.S. 353 (1982). Yet it has refused to extend implied remedies to additional sections of the securities laws. *Touche Ross & Co. v. Redington*, 442 U.S. 560 (1979); *Transamerica Mortgage Advisors, Inc. (TAMA) v. Lewis*, 444 U.S. 11 (1979). Many opinions seem to convey the implicit message that *Cort v. Ash* does not adequately restrain implication analysis. Indeed, in its flight from judicial creativity, the Court unanimously refused to develop a federal rule of contribution among joint tortfeasors under a federal statute that explicitly provided a private remedy. *Northwest Airlines, Inc. v. Transport Workers Union of America, AFL–CIO*, 451 U.S. 77 (1981). Justice Stevens' majority opinion in *Northwest Airlines* hardly mentioned *Cort v. Ash* and seemed to emphasize only the "statutory construction" and separation of powers concerns featured by Justices Rehnquist and Powell in *Cannon*. Yet in the same term both he and Justice White described *Cort* as the fountainhead of implication analysis. See *California v. Sierra Club*, 451 U.S. 287, 292 (1981).

Congressional intent may have become the litmus test for finding an implied right of action under a federal statute; but, unlike litmus paper, legislative documents often seem to display more than two colors, which judges perceive in varying shades. To be sure, the tendency in recent years has been not to find the requisite congressional intent when focusing on intent as the "central inquiry." The eight-to-one opinion in *Touche Ross & Co. v. Redington, supra*, that gave voice to this notion is now recognized as having added a limiting gloss to *Cort v. Ash*:

> * * * [T]he court set forth four factors that it considered "relevant" in determining whether a private remedy is implicit in a statute not expressly providing one. But the court did not decide that each of these factors is entitled to equal weight. The central inquiry remains whether Congress intended to create, either expressly or by implication, a private cause of action. Indeed, the first three factors discussed in *Cort*—the language and focus of the statute, its legislative history, and its purpose—are ones traditionally relied upon in determining legislative intent.

The question is how much direction can be given to an inquiry into the intent of Congress under a vision of statutory construction that retains the general purpose of the statute as a central criterion. For it was, of course, the Court's perception of the general investor-protection purpose of the securities laws that gave critical support to the implication of a right of action in *Borak*, notwithstanding the absence of any evidence of specific legislative intent to provide a right of action for such plaintiffs.

2. *The Case for "Skeptical Textualism."* Building on Justice Powell's constitutional reasoning in *Cannon*, Justice Scalia has argued for a super-strong presumption against the implication of any private right of action for violation of a federal statute. His concurrence in *Thompson v. Thompson*, 484 U.S. 174, 188–92 (1988), articulates his views and recounts the Court's skeptical approach to implied rights from *Cort* forward:

> I agree that the Parental Kidnaping Prevention Act, 28 U.S.C. § 1738A, does not create a private right of action in federal court to determine which of two conflicting child custody decrees is valid. I

disagree, however, with the portion of the Court's analysis that flows from the following statement:

> "Our focus on congressional intent does not mean that we require evidence that Members of Congress, in enacting the statute, actually had in mind the creation of a private cause of action."

I am at a loss to imagine what congressional intent to create a private right of action might mean, if it does not mean that Congress had in mind the creation of a private right of action. Our precedents, moreover, give no indication of a secret meaning, but to the contrary seem to use "intent" to mean "intent." * * *

By 2001 Justice Scalia was writing for the majority.

ALEXANDER v. SANDOVAL

Supreme Court of the United States, 2001.
532 U.S. 275, 121 S.Ct. 1511, 149 L.Ed.2d 517.

JUSTICE SCALIA delivered the opinion of the Court.

This case presents the question whether private individuals may sue to enforce disparate-impact regulations promulgated under Title VI of the Civil Rights Act of 1964.

I.

The Alabama Department of Public Safety (Department), of which petitioner James Alexander is the Director, accepted grants of financial assistance from the United States Department of Justice (DOJ) and Department of Transportation (DOT) and so subjected itself to the restrictions of Title VI of the Civil Rights Act of 1964. Section 601 of that Title provides that no person shall, "on the ground of race, color, or national origin, be excluded from participation in, be denied the benefits of, or be subjected to discrimination under any program or activity" covered by Title VI. Section 602 authorizes federal agencies "to effectuate the provisions of [§ 601] * * * by issuing rules, regulations, or orders of general applicability," and the DOJ in an exercise of this authority promulgated a regulation forbidding funding recipients to "utilize criteria or methods of administration which have the effect of subjecting individuals to discrimination because of their race, color, or national origin* * *."

The State of Alabama amended its Constitution in 1990 to declare English "the official language of the state of Alabama." Pursuant to this provision and, petitioners have argued, to advance public safety, the Department decided to administer state driver's license examinations only in English. Respondent Sandoval, as representative of a class, brought suit in the United States District Court for the Middle District of Alabama to enjoin the English-only policy, arguing that it violated the DOJ regulation because it had the effect of subjecting non-English speakers to discrimination based on their national origin. The District Court agreed. * * * Petitioners appealed to the Court of Appeals for the

Eleventh Circuit, which affirmed. Both courts rejected petitioners' argument that Title VI did not provide respondents a cause of action to enforce the regulation.

II.

Although Title VI has often come to this Court, it is fair to say (indeed, perhaps an understatement) that our opinions have not eliminated all uncertainty regarding its commands. For purposes of the present case, however, it is clear from our decisions, from Congress's amendments of Title VI, and from the parties' concessions that three aspects of Title VI must be taken as given. First, private individuals may sue to enforce § 601 of Title VI and obtain both injunctive relief and damages. * * * Congress has since ratified [this position]. Section 1003 of the Rehabilitation Act Amendments of 1986, expressly abrogated States' sovereign immunity against suits brought in federal court to enforce Title VI. * * *

Second, it is similarly beyond dispute—and no party disagrees—that § 601 prohibits only intentional discrimination. [Citing *Regents of Univ. of Cal. v. Bakke*, 438 U.S. 265, 57 L.Ed. 2d 750, 98 S.Ct. 2733 (1978); *Guardians Assn. v. Civil Serv. Comm'n of New York City*, 463 U.S. 582, 77 L.Ed.2d 866, 103 S.Ct. 3221 (1983); and *Alexander v. Choate*, 469 U.S. 287, 293, 83 L.Ed.2d 661, 105 S.Ct. 712 (1985).]

Third, we must assume for purposes of deciding this case that regulations promulgated under § 602 of Title VI may validly proscribe activities that have a disparate impact on racial groups, even though such activities are permissible under § 601. Though no opinion of this Court has held that, five Justices in *Guardians* voiced that view of the law at least as alternative grounds for their decisions, and dictum in *Alexander v. Choate* is to the same effect. * * *

Respondents assert that the issue in this case, like the first two described above, has been resolved by our cases. To reject a private cause of action to enforce the disparate-impact regulations, they say, we would "[have] to ignore the actual language of *Guardians* and *Cannon*." * * * [T]his Court is bound by holdings, not language. *Cannon* was decided on the assumption that the University of Chicago had intentionally discriminated against petitioner. See 441 U.S. at 680 (noting that respondents "admitted *arguendo*" that petitioner's "application for admission to medical school was denied by the respondents because she is a woman"). It therefore *held* that Title IX created a private right of action to enforce its ban on intentional discrimination, but had no occasion to consider whether the right reached regulations barring disparate-impact discrimination. In *Guardians*, the Court *held* that private individuals could not recover compensatory damages under Title VI except for intentional discrimination. Five Justices in addition voted to uphold the disparate-impact regulations, but of those five, three expressly reserved the question of a direct private right of action to enforce the regulations. * * *

Thus, only two Justices had cause to reach the issue that respondents say the "actual language" of *Guardians* resolves * * *

* * * We do not doubt that regulations applying § 601's ban on intentional discrimination are covered by the cause of action to enforce that section. Such regulations, if valid and reasonable, authoritatively construe the statute itself, and it is therefore meaningless to talk about a separate cause of action to enforce the regulations apart from the statute. A Congress that intends the statute to be enforced through a private cause of action intends the authoritative interpretation of the statute to be so enforced as well. The many cases that respondents say have "assumed" that a cause of action to enforce a statute includes one to enforce its regulations illustrate (to the extent that cases in which an issue was not presented can illustrate anything) only this point; each involved regulations of the type we have just described, as respondents conceded at oral argument.

We must face now the question avoided by *Lau [v. Nichols*, 414 U.S. 563, 94 S.Ct. 786, 39 L.Ed.2d 1 (1974)], because we have since rejected *Lau's* interpretation of § 601 as reaching beyond intentional discrimination. It is clear now that the disparate impact regulations do not simply apply to § 601—since they indeed forbid conduct that § 601 permits—and therefore clear that the private right of action to enforce § 601 does not include a private right to enforce these regulations. That right must come, if at all, from the independent force of § 602. * * *

Implicit in our discussion thus far has been a particular understanding of the genesis of private causes of action. Like substantive federal law itself, private rights of action to enforce federal law must be created by Congress. The judicial task is to interpret the statute Congress has passed to determine whether it displays an intent to create not just a private right but also a private remedy. Statutory intent on this latter point is determinative. Without it, a cause of action does not exist and courts may not create one, no matter how desirable that might be as a policy matter, or how compatible with the statute. Raising up causes of action where a statute has not created them may be a proper function for common-law courts, but not for federal tribunals.

Respondents would have us revert in this case to the understanding of private causes of action that held sway 40 years ago when Title VI was enacted. That understanding is captured by the Court's statement in *J.I. Case Co. v. Borak*, that "it is the duty of the courts to be alert to provide such remedies as are necessary to make effective the congressional purpose" expressed by a statute. We abandoned that understanding in *Cort v. Ash*, which itself interpreted a statute enacted under the *ancien regime*—and have not returned to it since. Not even when interpreting the same Securities Exchange Act of 1934 that was at issue in *Borak* have we applied *Borak's* method for discerning and defining causes of action. Having sworn off the habit of venturing beyond Congress's intent, we will not accept respondents' invitation to have one last drink.

Nor do we agree with the Government that our cases interpreting statutes enacted prior to *Cort v. Ash* have given "dispositive weight" to the "expectations" that the enacting Congress has formed "in light of the 'contemporary legal context." Only three of our legion of implied-right-of-action cases have found this sort of "contemporary legal context" relevant, and two of those involved Congress's enactment (or reenactment) of the verbatim statutory text that courts had previously interpreted to create a private right of action. In the third case, this sort of "contemporary legal context" simply buttressed a conclusion independently supported by the text of the statute. We have never accorded dispositive weight to context shorn of text. In determining whether statutes create private rights of action, as in interpreting statutes generally, legal context matters only to the extent it clarifies text.

We therefore begin (and find that we can end) our search for Congress's intent with the text and structure of Title VI. Section 602 authorizes federal agencies "to effectuate the provisions of [§ 601] * * * by issuing rules, regulations, or orders of general applicability." It is immediately clear that the "rights-creating" language so critical to the Court's analysis in Cannon of § 601, is completely absent from § 602. Whereas § 601 decrees that "no person * * * shall * * * be subjected to discrimination," the text of § 602 provides that "each Federal department and agency * * * is authorized and directed to effectuate the provision of [§ 601]. Far from displaying congressional intent to create new rights, § 602 limits agencies to "effectuating" rights already created by § 601. § 602 is twice removed from the individuals who will ultimately benefit from Title VI's protection. Statutes that focus on the person regulated rather than the individuals protected create "no implication of an intent to confer rights on a particular class of persons." Section 602 is yet a step further removed: it focuses neither on the individuals protected nor even on the funding recipients being regulated, but on the agencies that will do the regulating. * * *

Nor do the methods that § 602 goes on to provide for enforcing its authorized regulations manifest an intent to create a private remedy; if anything, they suggest the opposite. Section 602 empowers agencies to enforce their regulations either by terminating funding to the "particular program, or part thereof," that has violated the regulation or "by any other means authorized by law." No enforcement action may be taken, however, "until the department or agency concerned has advised the appropriate person or persons of the failure to comply with the requirement and has determined that compliance cannot be secured by voluntary means." And every agency enforcement action is subject to judicial review. If an agency attempts to terminate program funding, still more restrictions apply. The agency head must "file with the committees of the House and Senate having legislative jurisdiction over the program or activity involved a full written report of the circumstances and the grounds for such action." And the termination of funding does not "become effective until thirty days have elapsed after the filing of such report." Whatever these elaborate restriction on agency enforcement may imply for the private enforcement of rights created *outside* of § 602, they tend to contradict a congressional intent to create private enforceable rights through § 602 itself. The express provision of one method of enforcing a substantive rule suggests that Congress intended to preclude others.

Both the Government and respondents argue that the regulations contain rights-creating language and so must be privately enforceable, but that argument skips an analytical step. Language in a regulation may invoke a private right of action that Congress through statutory text created, but it may not create a right that Congress has not. Thus, when a statute has provided a general authorization for private enforcement of regulations, it may perhaps be correct that the intent displayed in each regulation can determine whether or not it is private enforceable. But it is most certainly incorrect to say that language in a regulation can conjure up a private cause of action that has not been authorized by Congress. Agencies may play the sorcerer's apprentice but not the sorcerer himself. * * *

The judgment of the Court of Appeals is reversed.

JUSTICE STEVENS with whom JUSTICE SOUTER, JUSTICE GINSBURG, and JUSTICE BREYER join, dissenting.

* * *

Today, in a decision unfounded in our precedent and hostile to decades of settled expectations, a majority of this Court carves out an important exception to the right of private action long recognized under Title VI. In so doing, the Court makes three distinct, albeit interrelated, errors. First, the Court provides a muddled account of both the reasoning and the breadth of our prior decisions endorsing a private right of action under Title VI, thereby obscuring the conflict between those opinions and today's decision. Second, the Court offers a flawed and unconvincing analysis of the relationship between §§ 601 and 602 of the Civil Rights Act of 1964, ignoring more plausible and persuasive explanations detailed in our prior opinions. Finally, the Court badly misconstrues the theoretical linchpin of our decision in *Cannon v. University of Chicago*, mistaking that decisions' careful contextual analysis for judicial fiat.

I.

The majority is undoubtedly correct that this Court has never said in so many words that a private right of action exists to enforce the disparate-impact regulations promulgated under § 602. However, the failure of our cases to state this conclusion explicitly does not absolve the Court of the responsibility to canvass our prior opinions for guidance. Reviewing these opinions with the care they deserve, I reach the same conclusions as the Courts of Appeals: This Court has already considered the question presented today and concluded that a private right of action exists.

When this Court faced an identical case 27 years ago, all the Justices believed that private parties could bring lawsuits under Title VI and its implementing regulations to enjoin the provision of governmental services in a manner that discriminated against non-English speakers. See *Lau v. Nichols*. While five Justices saw no need to go beyond the command of § 601, Chief Justice Burger, Justice Stewart, and Justice Blackmun relied specifically and exclusively on the regulations to support the private action. There is nothing in the majority's opinion in *Lau*, or in earlier opinions of the Court, that is not fully consistent with the analysis of the concurring Justices. * * *

Five years later, we more explicitly considered whether a private right of action exists to enforce the guarantees of Title VI and its gender-based twin Title IX. See *Cannon v. University of Chicago*. * * * Our conclusion was unequivocal: "We have no doubt that Congress intended to create Title IX remedies comparable to those available under Title VI and that it understood Title VI as authorizing an implied private cause of action for victims of the prohibited discrimination."

The majority acknowledges that *Cannon* is binding precedent with regard to both Title VI and Title IX, but seeks to limit the scope of its holding to cases involving allegations of intentional discrimination. The distinction the majority attempts to impose is wholly foreign to *Cannon's* text and reasoning. * * *

Moreover, *Cannon* was itself a disparate-impact case. In that case, the plaintiff brought suit against two private universities challenging medical school admissions policies that set age limits for applicants. Plaintiff, a 39–year old woman, alleged that these rules had the effect of discriminating against women because the incidence of interrupted higher education is higher among women than among men. In providing a shorthand description of her claim in the text of the opinion, we ambiguously stated that she had alleged that she was denied admission "because she is a woman," but we appended a lengthy footnote setting forth the details of her disparate-impact claim. Other than the shorthand description of her claim, there is not a word in the text of the opinion even suggesting that she had made the improbable allegation that the University of Chicago and Northwestern University had intentionally discriminated against women. * * *

Our fractured decision in *Guardians Assn. v. Civil Serv. Comm'n of New York City*, reinforces the conclusion that this issue is effectively settled. While the various opinions in that case took different views as to the spectrum of relief available to plaintiffs in Title VI cases, a clear majority of the Court expressly stated that private parties may seek injunctive relief against governmental practices that have the effect of discriminating against racial and ethnic minorities. * * *

In summary, there is a clear precedent of this Court for the proposition that the plaintiffs in this case can seek injunctive relief * * * through an implied right of action. * * * Though the holding in *Guardians* does not compel the conclusion that a private right of action exists to enforce the Title VI regulations against private parties, the rationales of the relevant opinions strongly imply that result. When that fact is coupled with our holding in *Cannon* and our unanimous decision in *Lau*, the answer to the question presented in this case is overdetermined. * * *

II.

Underlying the majority's dismissive treatment of our prior cases is a flawed understanding of the structure of Title VI and, more particularly, of the relationship between §§ 601 and 602. * * *

On the surface, the relationship between §§ 601 and 602 is unproblematic—§ 601 states a basic principle, § 602 authorizes agencies to develop detailed plans for defining the contours of the principle and ensuring its enforcement. In the context of federal civil rights law, however, nothing is ever so simple. As actions to enforce § 601's antidiscrimination principle have worked their way through the courts, we have developed a body of law giving content to § 601's broadly worded commitment. As the majority emphasizes today, the Judiciary's understanding of what conduct may be remedied in actions brought directly under § 601 is, in certain ways, more circumscribed than the conduct prohibited by the regulations.

Given that seeming peculiarity, it is necessary to examine closely the relationship between §§ 601 and 602, in order to understand the purpose and import of the regulations at issue in this case. For the most part, however, the majority ignores this task, assuming that the judicial decisions interpreting § 601 provide an authoritative interpretation of its true meaning and treating the regulations promulgated by the agencies charged with administering the statute as poor step-cousins—either parroting the text of § 601 (in the case of regulations that prohibit intentional discrimination) or forwarding an agenda untethered to § 601's mandate (in the case of disparate-impact regulations).

The majority's statutory analysis does violence to both the text and the structure of Title VI. Section 601 does not stand in isolation, but rather as part of an integrated remedial scheme. Section 602 exists for the sole purpose of forwarding the antidiscrimination ideals laid out in § 601. * * *

This legislative design reflects a reasonable—indeed inspired—model for attacking the often-intractable problem of racial and ethnic discrimination. On its own terms, the statute supports an action challenging policies of federal grantees that explicitly or unambiguously violate antidiscrimination norms (such as policies that on their face limit benefits or services to certain races). With regard to more subtle forms of discrimination (such as schemes that limit benefits or services on ostensibly race-neutral grounds but have the predictable and perhaps intended consequence of materially benefitting some races at the expense of others), the statute does not establish a static approach but instead empowers the relevant agencies to evaluate social circumstances to determine whether there is a need for stronger measures. Such an approach builds into the law flexibility, an ability to make nuanced assessments of complex social realities, and an admirable willingness to credit the possibility of progress. * * *

To the extent that our prior cases mischaracterize the relationship between §§ 601 and 602, they err on the side of underestimating, not overestimating, the connection between the two provisions. While our cases have explicitly adopted an understanding of § 601's scope that is somewhat narrower than the reach of the regulations, they have done so in an unorthodox and somewhat haphazard fashion.

Our conclusion that the legislation only encompasses intentional discrimination was never the subject of thorough consideration by a Court focused on that question. In *Bakke*, five Members of this Court concluded that § 601 only prohibits race-based affirmative action programs in situations where the Equal Protection Clause would impose a similar ban. In *Guardians*, the majority of the Court held that the analysis of those five Justices in *Bakke* compelled *as a matter of stare decisis* the conclusion that § 601 does not on its own terms reach disparate impact cases. However, the opinions adopting that conclusion did not engage in any independent analysis of the reach of § 601. Indeed, the only writing on this subject came from two of the five Members of the *Bakke* "majority," each of whom wrote separately to reject the remaining Justices' understanding of their opinions in *Bakke* and to insist that § 601 does in fact reach some instances of unintentional discrimination. The Court's occasional rote invocation of this *Guardians* majority in later cases ought not obscure the fact that the question whether § 601 applies to disparate-impact claims has never been analyzed by this Court on the merits.

In addition, these Title VI cases seemingly ignore the well-established principle of administrative law that is now most often described as the "*Chevron* doctrine." In most other contexts when the agencies charged with administering a broadly-worded statute offer regulations interpreting that statute or giving concrete guidance as to its implementation, we treat their interpretation of the statute's breadth as controlling unless it presents an unreasonable construction of the statutory text. While there may be some dispute as to the boundaries of *Chevron* deference, it is paradigmatically appropriate when Congress has clearly delegated agencies the power to issue regulations with the force of law and established formal procedures for the promulgation of such regulations.

To resolve this case, however, it is unnecessary to answer the question whether our cases interpreting the reach of § 601 should be reinterpreted in light of *Chevron*. If one understands the relationship between §§ 601 and 602 through the prism of *either Chevron* or our prior Title VI cases, the questions presented all but answers itself. If the regulations promulgated pursuant to § 602 are either an authoritative construction of § 601's meaning or prophylactic rules necessary to actualize the goals enunciated in § 601, then it makes no sense to differentiate between private actions to enforce § 601 and private actions to enforce § 602. There is but one private action to enforce Title VI, and we already know that such an action exists.

III.

The majority couples its flawed analysis of the structure of Title VI with an uncharitable understanding of the substance of the divide between those on this Court who are reluctant to interpret statutes to allow for private rights of action and those who are willing to do so if the claim of right survives a rigorous application of the criteria set forth in *Cort v. Ash.* As the majority narrates our implied right of action jurisprudence, the Court's shift to a more skeptical approach represents the rejection of a common-law judicial activism in favor of a principled recognition of the limited role of a contemporary "federal tribunal." According to its analysis, the recognition of an implied right of action when the text and structure of the statute do not absolutely compel such a conclusion is an act of judicial self-indulgence. As much as we would like to help those disadvantaged by discrimination, we must resist the temptations to pour ourselves "one last drink." To do otherwise would be to "venture beyond Congress's intent."

Overwrought imagery aside, it is the majority's approach that blinds itself to congressional intent. While it remains true that, if Congress intends a private right of action to support statutory rights, "the far better course is for it to specify as much when it creates those rights," its failure to do so does not absolve us of the responsibility to endeavor to discern its intent. In a series of cases since *Cort v. Ash*, we have laid out rules and developed strategies for this task.

The very existence of these rules and strategies assumes that we will sometimes find manifestations of an implicit intent to create such a right. Our decision in *Cannon* represents one such occasion. * * *

Underlying today's opinion is the conviction that *Cannon* must be cabined because it exemplifies an "expansive rights-creating approach." But, as I have taken pains to explain, it was Congress, not the Court, that created the cause of action, and it was the Congress that later ratified the *Cannon* holding in 1986 and again in 1988. * * *

[I]f the majority is genuinely committed to deciphering congressional intent, its unwillingness to even consider evidence as to the context in which Congress legislated is perplexing. * * *

At the time Congress was considering Title VI, it was normal practice for the courts to infer that Congress intended a private right of action whenever it passed a statute designed to protect a particular class that did not contain enforcement mechanisms which would be thwarted by a private remedy. Indeed, the very year Congress adopted Title VI, this Court specifically stated that "it is the duty of the courts to be alert to provide such remedies as are necessary to make effective the congressional purpose." *J.I. Case Co. v. Borak*. Assuming, as we must, that

Congress was fully informed as to the state of the law, the contemporary context presents important evidence as to Congress' intent—evidence the majority declines to consider.

Ultimately, respect for Congress's prerogatives is measured in deeds, not words. Today, the Court coins a new rule, holding that a private cause of action to enforce a statute does not encompass a substantive regulation issued to effectuate that statute unless the regulation does nothing more than "authoritatively construe the statute itself." * * * [I]f we are faithful to the commitment to discerning congressional intent that all Members of this Court profess, the distinction is untenable. There is simply no reason to assume that Congress contemplated, desired, or adopted a distinction between regulations that merely parrot statutory text and broader regulations that are authorized by statutory text.

IV.

Beyond its flawed structural analysis of Title VI and an evident antipathy toward implied rights of action, the majority offers * * * two reasons for its position. First, it attaches significance to the fact that the "rights-creating" language in § 601 that defines the classes protected by the statute is not repeated in § 602. But, of course, there was no reason to put that language in § 602 because it is perfectly obvious that the regulations authorized by § 602 must be designed to protect precisely the same people protected by § 601. * * *

Second, the Court repeats the argument advanced and rejected in *Cannon* that the express provision of a fund cut-off remedy "suggests that Congress intended to preclude others." We carefully explained why the presence of an explicit mechanisms to achieve one of the statute's objectives (ensuring that federal funds are not used "to support discriminatory practices") does not preclude a conclusion that a private right of action was intended to achieve the statute's other principal objective ("to provide individual citizens effective protection against those practices). In support of our analysis, we offered policy arguments, cited evidence from the legislative history, and noted the active support of the relevant agencies. In today's decision, the Court does not grapple with—indeed, barely acknowledges—our rejection of this argument in *Cannon*.

Like much else in its opinion, the present majority's unwillingness to explain its refusal to find the reasoning in Cannon persuasive suggests that today's decision is the unconscious product of the majority's profound distaste for implied causes of action rather than an attempt to discern the intent of the Congress that enacted Title VI of the Civil Rights Act of 1964. Its colorful disclaimer of any interest in "venturing beyond Congress's intent," has a hollow ring. * * *

I respectfully dissent.

Notes

1. *Implication, Precedent, and Congressional Presuppositions.* Understanding what a silent Congress "intended" regarding private enforcement is a function, in part, of understanding the background law against which it legislated. As Justice Stevens argues in *Alexander v. Sandoval,* and he is surely correct, the adoption of Title IX against the backdrop of private remedies under Title VI obviously influenced the majority in *Cannon.* In relation to older legislation, adopted in an era more hospitable to the implication of private remedies, the Court has considered both what Congress would have assumed the law of implication to be at the time of enactment and how a decision based on the Court's contemporary skeptical view of implication fits into its earlier precedents. But, of course, finding new implied rights in old statutes runs the risk of creating a contemporary jurisprudence that fails to provide clear signals to Congress about how explicit it must be.

These problems have been pronounced in both the civil rights arena and in the securities and commodities regulation cases. For *Borak* remains good law under Rule 14, see *Herman & MacLean v. Huddleston, supra,* and has spawned analogous causes of action under other securities statutes. See *Merrill Lynch v. Curran, supra.* In one of his early opinions for the Court, *Virginia Bankshares Inc. v. Sandberg,* 501 U.S. 1083 (1991), Justice Souter demonstrated how a court might thread its his way cautiously through this minefield. The claim at issue sought to expand the right of action recognized in *Borak* to include shareholders whose votes, unlike the votes of the *Borak* plaintiffs, had not been necessary for the merger allegedly accomplished by a false and misleading proxy solicitation. The Court declined to recognize the claim but not before Justice Souter attempted to harmonize later cases with *Borak* itself:

> * * * The rule that has emerged * * * is that recognition of any private right of action for violating a federal statute must ultimately rest on congressional intent to provide a private remedy. From this the corollary follows that the breadth of the right once recognized should not, as a general matter, grow beyond the scope congressionally intended.
>
> This rule and corollary present respondents with a serious obstacle, for we can find no manifestation of intent to recognize a cause of action (or class of plaintiffs) as broad as respondents' theory of causation would entail. At first blush, it might seem otherwise, for the *Borak* Court certainly did not ignore the matter of intent. Its opinion adverted to the statutory object of "protection of investors" as animating Congress' intent to provide judicial relief where "necessary," and it quoted evidence for that intent from House and Senate Committee Reports. *Borak's* probe of the congressional mind, however, never focused squarely on private rights of action, as distinct from the substantive objects of the legislation, and one member of the *Borak* Court later characterized the "implication" of the private right of action as resting modestly on the Act's "exclusively procedural provision affording access to a federal forum." *Bivens v. Six Unknown Federal Narcotics Agents,* 403 U.S. 388

> (1971) (Harlan, J., concurring in judgment). In fact, the importance of enquiring specifically into intent to authorize a private cause of action became clear only later, see *Cort v. Ash*, and only later still, in *Touche Ross*, was this intent accorded primacy among the considerations that might be thought to bear on any decision to recognize a private remedy.
>
> * * * The congressional silence that is thus a serious obstacle to the expansion of cognizable *Borak* causation is not, however, a necessarily insurmountable barrier. This is not the first effort in recent years to expand the scope of an action originally inferred from the Act without "conclusive guidance" from Congress, see *Blue Chip Stamps v. Manor Drug Stores*, 421 U.S. at 737, and we may look to that earlier case for the proper response to such a plea for expansion. There, we accepted the proposition that where a legal structure of private statutory rights has developed without clear indications of congressional intent, the contours of that structure need not be frozen absolutely when the result would be demonstrably inequitable to a class of would-be plaintiffs with claims comparable to those previously recognized. Faced in that case with such a claim for equality in rounding out the scope of an implied private statutory right of action, we looked to policy reasons for deciding where the outer limits of the right should lie. We may do no less here, in the face of respondents' pleas for a private remedy to place them on the same footing as shareholders with votes necessary for initial corporate action.

While Justice Souter puts the matter primarily in terms of precedent and consistency, his analysis in the securities area might also have relied on general congressional intent. Presumably the *Borak* Court reflected pre-existing congressional expectations when it so non-problematically "implied" a cause of action from the 1934 Securities and Exchange Act. However, when addressing a pre-*Erie* statute, the 1899 Rivers and Harbors Act, which had previously supported an implied remedy in favor of the United States, see *United States v. Republic Steel Corp.*, 362 U.S. 482 (1960), and which had been enacted in part to overturn a Supreme Court decision denying a federal cause of action to abate navigational nuisances, *Willamette Iron Bridge Co. v. Hatch*, 125 U.S. 1 (1888), the Court balked at allowing a private remedy. A bemused Justice Stevens concurred in the following *non sequitur:*

> In these cases, I believe the Court correctly concludes that application of the *Cort v. Ash* analysis indicates that no private cause of action is available. I think it is more important to adhere to the analytical approach the Court has adopted than to base my vote on my own opinion about what Congress probably assumed in 1890. * * *

California v. Sierra Club, 451 U.S. 287, 298–301 (1981). This sentiment is, at the very least, in tension with Justice Stevens' opinion in *Alexander v. Sandoval*.

2. *Remedies v. Causes of Action*. Although reluctant to imply new causes of action from federal statutes, the Supreme Court has been less hesitant to provide a full range of remedies where the cause of action has been previously established. In *Franklin v. Gwinnett County Public Schools*, 503 U.S. 60 (1992), for example, the Court confronted the question whether the respondent could be held liable in damages under the right of action

confirmed in *Cannon*. The plaintiff alleged that a teacher had sexually harassed her and also that teachers and administrators who knew about the matter had taken no action to halt it—indeed, had discouraged her from pressing charges. Both the teacher and the responsible administrator had resigned and the petitioner was no longer in school. Hence, damages were the only remedy reasonably available to remedy the Title IX violation.

In a broadly worded majority opinion for six Justices, Justice White, reaffirmed the Court's traditional position enunciated in *Bell v. Hood*, 327 U.S. 678, 684 (1946), that "where legal rights have been invaded and a federal statute provides for a general right to sue for such invasion, federal courts may use any available remedy to make good the wrong done." The majority opinion was careful to distinguish the "remedy" question from the "cause of action" question. It strongly rejected the respondent's arguments, however, that the *Bell v. Hood* presumption in favor of all appropriate relief had been abandoned in later cases or was applicable only to actions claiming constitutional violations.

But it is unclear how much to read into this rights/remedies distinction. Justice Scalia, writing also for Chief Justice Rehnquist and Justice Thomas, concurred specially. The concurring Justices viewed subsequent legislation, the Civil Rights Remedies Equalization Amendment of 1986, 42 U.S.C. § 2000d–7(a)(2), as validating *Cannon*'s holding and as implicitly acknowledging that a damage action would lie when it explicitly withdrew the state's Eleventh Amendment immunity from Title IX suits.

The efforts of the concurring Justices to premise their decision on something other than the distinction between "right" and "remedy" is understandable. As Karl N. Llewellyn famously observed, "Absence of a remedy is absence of a right. Defect of remedy is defect of right. A right is as big, precisely, as what the courts will do." THE BRAMBLE BUSH 83–84 (1960). Nor need one be a legal realist to view right and remedy as deeply intertwined. See 4 ROSCOE POUND, JURISPRUDENCE 43 (1959) ("to enforce the duty [the law] allows an action, which has for its end a legal remedy.").

Moreover, the Supreme Court has often characterized the question in implied right of action cases as whether a cause of action or a "right" was conferred when that question might as easily have been put in remedial terms. *Transamerica Mortgage Advisors Inc. v. Lewis*, 444 U.S. 11 (1979) (one of the cases emphasizing congressional intent and refusing to imply a cause of action for damages under the Investment Advisors Act of 1940), for example, might just as easily have framed the question as whether a damages remedy should be available in addition to the remedies of rescission or injunction that the Court recognized Congress had assumed would be available. *Id.* at 16–17.

Similarly, in *Mertens v. Hewitt Associates*, 508 U.S. 248 (1993), the Court suggested in dicta that there was no private cause of action under the Employee Retirement Security Act of 1974 (ERISA) against non-fiduciaries who participate in a fiduciary breach. It then, to the surprise of every circuit in the country and the Securities and Exchange Commission, in *Central Bank v. First Interstate Bank of Denver*, 511 U.S. 164 (1994), followed *Mertens* by holding that there was no cause of action under § 10(b) of the Securities Exchange Act of 1934 against those who aid and abet violations of the Securities and Exchange Act. In both *Mertens* and *Central Bank*, there was no question that a cause of action existed under the respective statutes in favor of beneficiaries and against those upon whom fiduciary obligations were imposed. The Court might, therefore, have characterized the issue as whether a complete remedy under the statutes required the extension of the cause of action to a person who acted with, or aided or abetted, those fiduciaries in their breach of duty.

The point of this discussion is straightforward: Although the Court has clearly stated that its analysis shifts depending upon whether it is considering whether to extend a remedy rather than whether to imply a right, the distinction between remedies and rights is sufficiently elusive that it is unlikely to provide reliable guidance on how the Court will decide a case until after the Court has characterized the question as one of right or remedy.

3. *Implication Analysis and the Search for Baselines*. What the Congress intended, if anything, concerning unmentioned remedies (or "rights") will always be subject to doubt. The question then is whether those doubts should be resolved by some strong form of presumption, such as Justice Scalia's general negative implication from congressional silence, or by a more contextual analysis that shifts the presumption one way or another depending upon multiple factors, including: precedent, the need for a remedy to fulfill congressional purposes or to provide appropriate relief, the manageability of the cause of action as a judicial construct, the burden on the federal courts of recognizing new grounds for federal court litigation, the impact of a decision one way or another on state-federal responsibilities and the effect of a judicial remedy on the coherence of the overall enforcement regime established by the statute.

The establishment of a strong baseline presumption, that is, one that fits all or virtually all categories of cases is enticing given the potential "unruliness" of the balancing factors just enumerated. But justifying a particular baseline is not easy. Justice Powell tried to ground such a presumption in the Constitution in his *Cannon* dissent. Yet, as Justice Stevens argues in *Alexander v. Sandoval*, the Court just as clearly invades congressional prerogatives when it fails to provide remedies that would make congressional legislation effective and that Congress may have presumed to be available, as when it provides remedies that Congress did not intend. Separation of powers considerations seem merely to suggest that the courts should get the answer right. And, while Justice Scalia seems convinced that courts would get it right more often if they simply refused to imply causes of action not expressly provided by statute, he has not told us how he has gained access to Congress's "general intent" on this matter, when the Congress's "specific intent" in particular statutes seems so elusive.

A presumption might, of course, be premised simply on the need for a clear rule to which parties, including the Congress, might accommodate themselves. But, that tells us nothing about whether the clear rule should be one that more nearly approximates the position in *J.I. Case v. Borak* or in *Touche Ross*. If a bright line rule is all that is needed, either one should suffice. And, drawing an *arbitrary* bright line—and sticking to it—where the bright line inevitably ignores or deals cavalierly with the equitable, institutional, historical, precedential and other aspects of concrete cases is hard to square with deep-seated notions of the judicial role.

As Justice Scalia points out in *Alexander v. Sandoval*, the Supreme Court's behavior, whatever the language of its various members, now disfavors implying causes of action on federal statutes. That message seems to have been received by the lower courts. See, e.g., *Love v. Delta Air Lines*, 179 F.Supp.2d 1313, 1319 (M.D.Ala.2001). But, given the competing considerations in concrete cases, considerations that go beyond even the four-factor test of *Cort v. Ash*, it seems unlikely that the negative presumption to be implied from the Court's actions will ever be irrebuttable. See Susan J. Stabile, *The Role of Congressional Intent in Determining the Existence of Implied Rights of Action*, 71 Notre Dame L.Rev. 861 (1996), and authorities therein cited.

D. BENEFICIARY ENFORCEMENT UNDER 42 U.S.C. § 1983

MAINE v. THIBOUTOT

Supreme Court of the United States, 1980.
448 U.S. 1, 100 S.Ct. 2502, 65 L.Ed.2d 555.

JUSTICE BRENNAN delivered the opinion of the Court.

The case presents two related questions arising under 42 U.S.C. §§ 1983 and 1988. Respondents brought this suit in the Maine Superior Court alleging that petitioners, the State of Maine and its Commissioner of Human Services, violated § 1983 by depriving respondents of welfare benefits to which they were entitled under the federal Social Security Act, specifically 42 U.S.C. § 602(a)(7). The petitioners present two issues: (1) whether § 1983 encompasses claims based on purely statutory violations of federal law, and (2) if so, whether attorney's fees under § 1988 may be awarded to the prevailing party in such an action.

I

Respondents, Lionel and Joline Thiboutot, are married and have eight children, three of whom are Lionel's by a previous marriage. The Maine Department of Human Services notified Lionel that, in computing the Aid to Families with Dependent Children (AFDC) benefits to which he was entitled for the three children exclusively his, it would no longer make allowance for the money spent to support the other five children, even though Lionel is legally obligated to support them. Respondents, challenging the State's interpretation of 42 U.S.C. § 602(a)(7), exhausted their state administrative remedies and then sought judicial review of the administrative action in the State Superior Court. By amended complaint, respondents also claimed relief under § 1983 for themselves and others similarly situated. The Superior Court's judgment enjoined petitioners from enforcing the challenged rule and ordered them to adopt new regulations, to notify class members of the new regulations, and to pay the correct amounts retroactively to respondents and prospectively to eligible class members. The court, however, denied respondents' motion for attorney's fees. The Supreme Judicial Court of Maine, 405 A.2d 230 (1979), concluded that respondents had no entitlement to attorney's fees under state law, but were eligible for attorney's fees pursuant to the Civil Rights Attorney's Fees Awards Act of 1976, 42 U.S.C. § 1988. * * * We affirm.

II

Section 1983 provides:

> "Every person who, under color of any statute, ordinance, regulation, custom, or usage, of any State or Territory, subjects, or causes to be subjected, any citizen of the United States or other person within the jurisdiction thereof to the deprivation of any rights, privileges, or immunities secured by the Constitution *and laws*, shall be liable to the party injured in an action at law, suit in equity, or other proper proceeding for redress." (Emphasis added.)

The question before us is whether the phrase "and laws," as used in § 1983, means what it says, or whether it should be limited to some subset of laws. Given that Congress attached no modifiers to the phrase, the plain language of the statute undoubtedly embraces respondents' claim that petitioners violated the Social Security Act.

Even were the language ambiguous, however, any doubt as to its meaning has been resolved by our several cases suggesting, explicitly or implicitly, that the § 1983 remedy broadly encompasses violations of federal statutory as well as constitutional law. [*See, e.g.*] *Rosado v. Wyman*, 397 U.S. 397 (1970). * * *

While some might dismiss as dictum the foregoing statements, numerous and specific as they are, our analysis in several § 1983 cases involving Social Security Act (SSA) claims has relied on the availability of a § 1983 cause of action for statutory claims. Constitutional claims were also raised in these cases, providing a jurisdictional base, but the statutory claims were allowed to go forward, and were decided on the merits, under the court's pendent jurisdiction. * * *

In the face of the plain language of § 1983 and our consistent treatment of that provision, petitioners nevertheless persist in suggesting that the phrase "and laws" should be read as limited to civil rights or equal protection laws. Petitioners suggest that when § 1 of the Civil Rights Act of 1871, 17 Stat. 13, which accorded jurisdiction and a remedy for deprivations of rights secured by "the Constitution of the United States," was divided by the 1874 statutory revision into a remedial section, Rev.Stat. § 1979, and jurisdictional sections, Rev.Stat. §§ 563(12) and 629(16), Congress intended that the same change made in § 629(16) be made as to each of the new sections as well. Section 629(16), the jurisdictional provision for the circuit courts and the model for the current jurisdictional provision, 28 U.S.C. § 1343(3), applied to deprivations of rights secured by "the Constitution of the United States, or of any right secured by any law providing for equal rights." On the other hand, the remedial provision, the predecessor of § 1983, was expanded to apply to deprivations of rights secured by "the Constitution and laws," and § 563(12), the provision granting jurisdiction to the district courts, to deprivations of rights secured by "the Constitution of the United States, or of any right secured by any law of the United States."

We need not repeat at length the detailed debate over the meaning of the scanty legislative history concerning the addition of the phrase "and laws." * * * There is no express explanation offered for the insertion of the phrase "and laws." On the one hand, a principal purpose of the added language was to "ensure that federal legislation providing specifically for equality of rights would be brought within the ambit of the civil action authorized by that statute." On the other hand, there are no indications that that was the only purpose, and Congress' attention was specifically directed to this new language. Representative Lawrence, in a speech to the House of Representatives that began by observing that the revisers had very often changed the meaning of existing statutes, 2 Cong.Rec. 825 (1874), referred to the civil rights statutes as "possibly [showing] verbal modifications bordering on legislation." He went on to read to Congress the original and revised versions. In short, Congress was aware of what it was doing, and the legislative history does not demonstrate that the plain language was not intended. Petitioners' arguments amount to the claim that had Congress been more careful, and had it fully thought out the relationship among the various sections, it might have acted differently. That argument, however, can best be addressed to Congress, which, it is important to note, has remained quiet in the face of our many pronouncements on the scope of § 1983.

III

Petitioners next argue that, even if this claim is within § 1983, Congress did not intend statutory claims to be covered by the Civil Rights Attorney's Fees Awards Act of 1976, which added the following sentence to 42 U.S.C. § 1988 (emphasis added):

> "In *any action* or proceeding *to enforce* a provision of sections 1981, 1982, *1983*, 1985, and 1986 of this title, * * * the court, in its discretion, may allow the prevailing party, other than the United States, a reasonable attorney's fee as part of the costs."

Once again, given our holding in Part II, *supra*, the plain language provides an answer. The statute states that fees are available in *any* § 1983 action. Since we hold that this statutory action is properly brought under § 1983, and since § 1988 makes no exception for statutory § 1983 actions, § 1988 plainly applies to this suit.

The legislative history is entirely consistent with the plain language. * * *

* * *

Several States, participating as *amici curiae*, argue that even if § 1988 applies to § 1983 claims alleging deprivations of statutory rights, it does not apply in state courts. There is no merit to this argument. * * * *Martinez v. California*, 444 U.S. 277 (1980), held that § 1983 actions may be brought in state courts. Representative Drinan described the purpose of the Civil Rights Attorney's Fees Awards Act as "authoriz[ing] the award of a reasonable attorney's fee in actions brought in State or Federal courts." 122 Cong.Rec. 35122 (1976). And Congress viewed the fees authorized by § 1988 as "an integral part of the remedies necessary to obtain" compliance with § 1983. S.Rep.No. 94–1011, p. 5 (1976). It follows from this history and from the Supremacy Clause that the fee provision is part of the § 1983 remedy whether the action is brought in federal or state court.[12]

Affirmed.

JUSTICE POWELL, with whom THE CHIEF JUSTICE and JUSTICE REHNQUIST join, dissenting.

The Court holds today, almost casually, that 42 U.S.C. § 1983 creates a cause of action for deprivations under color of state law of any federal statutory right. Having transformed purely statutory claims into "civil rights" actions under § 1983, the Court concludes that 42 U.S.C. § 1988 permits the "prevailing party" to recover his attorney's fees. These two holdings dramatically expand the liability of state and local officials and may virtually eliminate the "American Rule" in suits against those officials.

The Court's opinion reflects little consideration of the consequences of its judgment. It relies upon the "plain" meaning of the phrase "and laws" in § 1983 and upon this Court's assertedly "consistent treatment" of that statute. But the reading adopted today is anything but "plain" when the statutory language is placed in historical context. * * *

* * *

Section 1983 derives from § 1 of the Civil Rights Act of 1871, which provided a cause of action for deprivations of constitutional rights only. "Laws" were not mentioned. The phrase "and laws" was added in 1874, when Congress consolidated the laws of the United States into a single volume under a new subject-matter arrangement. Consequently, the intent of Congress in 1874 is central to this case.

In addition to creating a cause of action, § 1 of the 1871 Act conferred concurrent jurisdiction upon "the district or circuit courts of the United States. * * * "In the 1874 revision, the remedial portion of § 1 was codified as § 1979 of the Revised Statutes, which provided for a cause of action in terms identical to the present § 1983. The jurisdiction-

12. If fees were not available in state courts, federalism concerns would be raised because most plaintiffs would have no choice but to bring their complaints concerning state actions to federal courts. Moreover, given that there is a class of cases stating causes of action under § 1983 but not cognizable in federal court absent the $10,000 jurisdictional amount of § 1331(a), some plaintiffs would be forced to go to state courts, but contrary to congressional intent, would still face financial disincentives to asserting their claimed deprivations of federal rights. [The jurisdictional amount requirement has subsequently been repealed. Eds.]

al portion of § 1 was divided into § 563(12), conferring district court jurisdiction, and § 629(16), conferring circuit court jurisdiction. Although §§ 1979, 563(12), and 629(16) came from the same source, each was worded differently. Section 1979 referred to deprivations of rights "secured by the Constitution and laws"; § 563(12) described rights secured "by the Constitution of the United States, or * * * by any law of the United States"; and § 629(16) encompassed rights secured "by the Constitution of the United States, or * * * by any law providing for equal rights of citizens of the United States." When Congress merged the jurisdiction of circuit and district courts in 1911, the narrower language of § 629(16) was adopted and ultimately became the present 28 U.S.C. § 1343(3).

In my view, the legislative history unmistakably shows that the variations in phrasing introduced in the 1874 revision were inadvertent, and that each section was intended to have precisely the same scope. * * *

* * * The Revision Commission, which worked for six years on the project, submitted to Congress a draft that did contain substantive changes. But a Joint Congressional Committee, which was appointed in early 1873 to transform the draft into a bill, concluded that it would be "utterly impossible to carry the measure through, if it was understood that it contained new legislation." Therefore, the Committee employed Thomas Jefferson Durant to "strike out * * * modifications of the existing law" "wherever the meaning of the law had been changed." On December 10, 1873, Durant's completed work was introduced in the House with the solemn assurance that the bill "embodies the law as it is."

The House met in a series of evening sessions to review the bill and to restore original meaning where necessary. During one of these sessions, Representative Lawrence delivered the speech upon which the Court now relies. Lawrence explained that the revisers often had separated existing statutes into substantive, remedial, and criminal sections to accord with the new organization of the statutes by topic. He read both the original and revised versions of the civil rights statutes to illustrate the arrangement, and "possibly [to] show verbal modifications bordering on legislation." 2 Cong.Rec. 827 (Jan. 21, 1874). * * *

In context, it is plain that Representative Lawrence did not mention changes "bordering on legislation" as a way of introducing substantive changes in § 1 of the 1871 Act. Rather, he was emphasizing that the revision was not intended to modify existing statutes, and that his reading might reveal errors that should be eliminated. No doubt Congress "was aware of what it was doing." It was meeting specially in one last attempt to detect and strike out legislative changes that may have remained in the proposed revision despite the best efforts of Durant and the Joint Committee. No Representative challenged those sections of the Revised Statutes that derived from § 1 of the Civil Rights Act of 1871.

That silence reflected the understanding of those present that "and laws" did not alter the original meaning of the statute.[6] * * *

The legislative history alone refutes the Court's assertion that the 43d Congress intended to alter the meaning of § 1983. But there are other compelling reasons to reject the Court's interpretation of the phrase "and laws." First, by reading those words to encompass every federal enactment, the Court extends § 1983 beyond the reach of its jurisdictional counterpart. Second, that reading creates a broad program for enforcing federal legislation that departs significantly from the purposes of § 1983. Such unexpected and plainly unintended consequences should be avoided whenever a statute reasonably may be given an interpretation that is consistent with the legislative purpose. * * *

* * * Nearly every commentator who has considered the question has concluded that § 1343(3) was intended to supply federal jurisdiction in all § 1983 actions. Since § 1343(3) covers statutory claims only when they arise under laws providing for the equal rights of citizens, the same limitation necessarily is implicit in § 1983. The Court's decision to apply that statute without regard to the scope of its jurisdictional counterpart is at war with the plainly expressed intent of Congress.

The Court's opinion does not consider the nature or scope of the litigation it has authorized. In practical effect, today's decision means that state and local governments, officers, and employees[10] now may face liability whenever a person believes he has been injured by the administration of *any* federal-state cooperative program, whether or not that program is related to equal or civil rights.

Even a cursory survey of the United States Code reveals that literally hundreds of cooperative regulatory and social welfare enactments may be affected.[12] The States now participate in the enforcement of federal laws governing migrant labor, noxious weeds, historic preservation, wildlife conservation, anadromous fisheries, scenic trails, and strip mining. Various statutes authorize federal-state cooperative agreements in most aspects of federal land management. In addition, federal grants administered by state and local governments now are available in virtually every area of public administration. Unemployment, Medicaid, school lunch subsidies, food stamps, and other welfare benefits may

6. The addition of "and laws" did not change the meaning of § 1 because Congress assumed that that phrase referred only to federal equal rights legislation. In 1874, the only such legislation was contained in the 1866 and 1870 Civil Rights Acts, which conferred rights also secured by the recently adopted Fourteenth Amendment.

10. Section 1983 actions may be brought against States, municipalities and other subdivisions, officers, and employees. Although I will refer to all such potential defendants as "state defendants" for purposes of this opinion, there may be a notable difference among them. States are protected against retroactive damages awards by the Eleventh Amendment, and individual defendants generally can claim immunity when they act in good faith. Municipalities, however, will be strictly liable for errors in the administration of complex federal statutes. See *Owen v. City of Independence*, 445 U.S. 622 (1980).

12. An incomplete sample of statutes requiring federal-state cooperation is collected in the Appendix to this opinion. * * *

provide particularly inviting subjects of litigation. Federal assistance also includes a variety of subsidies for education, housing, health care, transportation, public works, and law enforcement. Those who might benefit from these grants now will be potential § 1983 plaintiffs.

* * *

Moreover, state and local governments will bear the entire burden of liability for violations of statutory "civil rights" even when federal officials are involved equally in the administration of the affected program. Section 1983 grants no right of action against the United States, and few of the foregoing cooperative programs provide expressly for private actions to enforce their terms. Thus, private litigants may sue responsible federal officials only in the relatively rare case in which a cause of action may be implied from the governing substantive statute. It defies reason to believe that Congress intended—without discussion—to impose such a burden only upon state defendants.

Even when a cause of action against federal officials is available, litigants are likely to focus efforts upon state defendants in order to obtain attorney's fees under the liberal standard of 42 U.S.C. § 1988. There is some evidence that § 1983 claims already are being appended to complaints solely for the purpose of obtaining fees in actions where "civil rights" of any kind are at best an afterthought. In this case, for example, the respondents added a § 1983 count to their complaint some years after the action was initiated, apparently in response to the enactment of the Civil Rights Attorney's Fees Awards Act of 1976 * * *.

* * *

* * * If any Member of the 43d Congress had suggested legislation embodying these results, the proposal certainly would have been hotly debated. It is simply inconceivable that Congress, while professing a firm intention not to make substantive changes in the law, nevertheless intended to enact a major new remedial program by approving—without discussion—the addition of two words to a statute adopted only three years earlier.

The Court finally insists that its interpretation of § 1983 is foreordained by a line of precedent so strong that further analysis is unnecessary. * * *

* * * Yet, until last Term, neither this Court nor any Justice ever had undertaken—directly and thoroughly—a consideration of the question presented in this case. * * *

The Court quotes the statement in *Edelman v. Jordan*, 415 U.S. 651, 675 (1974), that *Rosado v. Wyman*, 397 U.S. 397 (1970), " 'held that suits in federal court under § 1983 are proper to secure compliance with the provisions of the Social Security Act on the part of participating States.' "If that statement is true, the confusion remaining after *Rosado* is simply inexplicable. In fact, of course, *Rosado* established no such proposition of law. The plaintiffs in that case challenged a state welfare provision on constitutional grounds, premising jurisdiction upon 28 U.S.C. § 1343(3), and added a pendent statutory claim. This Court held first that the District Court retained its power to adjudicate the statutory claim even after the constitutional claim, on which § 1343(3) jurisdiction was based, became moot. The opinion then considered the merits of the plaintiffs' argument that New York law did not comport with the Social Security Act. Although the Court had to assume the existence of a private right of action to enforce that Act, the opinion did not discuss or purport to decide whether § 1983 applies to statutory claims. * * *

To rest a landmark decision of this Court on two statements made in dictum without critical examination would be extraordinary in any case. In the context of § 1983, it is unprecedented. Our decisions construing the civil rights legislation of the Reconstruction era have repudiated "blind adherence to the principle of *stare decisis*. * * * "As Mr. Justice Frankfurter once observed, the issues raised under § 1983 concern "a basic problem of American federalism" that "has significance approximating constitutional dimension." *Monroe v. Pape*, 365 U.S., at 222 (dissenting opinion). Although Mr. Justice Frankfurter's view did not prevail in *Monroe*, we have heeded consistently his admonition that the ordinary concerns of *stare decisis* apply less forcefully in this than in other areas of the law. *E.g., Monell v. New York City Dept. of Social Services, supra.* Against this backdrop, there is no justification for the Court's reliance on unexamined dicta as the principal support for a major extension of liability under § 1983.

* * *

Some Perspectives on § 1983 Actions

Although section 1983 is couched in sweeping language, as Justice Powell notes, it was very rarely invoked during the 90 years following its passage. Section 1983's obscurity can partly be attributed to the Supreme Court's early narrow construction of the rights protected by the Fourteenth Amendment. In *The Slaughter–House Cases*, 83 U.S. (16 Wall.) 36 (1873), the Court held that the guarantee of section 1 against abridgements of "the privileges or immunities of citizens of the United States" embraced only those rights that arose immediately from an individual's relationship with the central government. These included the right to vote in federal elections, the right to travel from state to state, the right to be free from slavery, and the right to peaceably assemble and petition the federal government. But, the Court made clear, these "privileges or immunities" did not include such basic civil rights as the right to own or hold property, the right of free speech, the right to privacy, or rights relating to fair trial in state criminal proceedings. These were state creations and protected, if at all, by state law. See also *United States v. Williams*, 341 U.S. 70 (1951); *Twining v. New Jersey*, 211 U.S. 78 (1908).

At the time of *The Slaughter–House Cases*, the Fourteenth Amendment's due process guarantee had not yet been held to be a limitation on the substance of state legislation. Furthermore, as a guarantee of fair procedure in state proceedings its content was still narrowly, if dimly, viewed. The numerous Supreme Court decisions of the mid-Twentieth Century that interpreted due process as a constitutional shorthand for the procedural safeguards guaranteed against the federal government by the Bill of Rights (*e.g.*, right to jury trial, right to counsel) were several decades in the future. See, e.g., *Mapp v. Ohio*, 367 U.S. 643 (1961) (due process incorporates Fourth Amendment guarantee against unreasonable searches and seizures); *Gideon v. Wainwright*, 372 U.S. 335 (1963) (Sixth Amendment right to counsel). Moreover, the amendment's equal protection guarantee was for many decades viewed as prohibiting only discriminations based on race. In short, in the years immediately following the passage of section 1983, citizens had no basis for anticipating the expansive reading recent decisions have given the rights protected against state interference by the Fourteenth Amendment and, thus, by the language of the statute itself.

The Rise of Constitutional Torts: Interest in section 1983 was rekindled in 1961 when the Supreme Court decided *Monroe v. Pape*, 365 U.S. 167. In *Monroe* the complaint alleged:

> * * * that 13 Chicago police officers broke into petitioners' home in the early morning, routed them from bed, made them stand naked in the living room, and ransacked every room, emptying drawers and ripping mattress covers. * * * Mr. Monroe was then taken to the police station and detained on "open" charges for 10 hours, while he was interrogated about a two-day-old murder, that he was not taken before a magistrate, though one was accessible, that he was not permitted to call his family or attorney, that he was subsequently released without criminal charges being preferred against him. It is alleged that the officers had no search warrant and no arrest warrant and that they acted "under color of the statutes, ordinances, regulations, customs and usages" of Illinois and of the City of Chicago. * * *

Responding to this alleged outrage the Supreme Court, *per* Justice Douglas, held that section 1983 provided a damages remedy, notwithstanding the statute's rather special history and the possibility that it would provide federal "constitutional tort" remedies where conventional state law remedies already existed:

> Although the legislation was enacted because of the conditions that existed in the South at that time, it is cast in general language and is as applicable to Illinois as it is to the States whose names were mentioned over and again in the debates. It is no answer that the State has a law which if enforced would give relief. The federal remedy is supplementary to the state remedy, and the latter need not be first sought and refused before the federal one is invoked. Hence the fact that Illinois by its constitution and laws outlaws unreasonable searches and seizures is no barrier to the present suit in the federal court.

Justice Frankfurter, in dissent, agreed with the majority that the Fourth Amendment created rights cognizable under section 1983; that plaintiffs need not allege specific intent to deprive them of constitutional rights; and that the Court in earlier criminal cases had read "under color of state law" expansively in the context of the similar criminal provision of the Civil Rights Act. However, Frankfurter thought those decisions, in which he participated, ill-considered because the Court had not conducted a thorough analysis of the legislative history. Having made such an analysis he was convinced that Congress did not intend to substitute a federal remedy where state remedies were available:

> Rather, all the evidence converges to the conclusion that Congress by § [1983] created a civil liability enforceable in the federal courts only in instances of injury for which redress was barred in the state courts because some "statute, ordinance, regulation, custom, or usage" sanctioned the grievance complained of. This purpose * * * accords with the presuppositions of our federal system. The jurisdiction which Article III of the Constitution conferred on the national judiciary reflected the assumption that the state courts, not the federal courts, would remain the primary guardians of that fundamental security of person and property which the long evolution of the common law had secured to one individual as against other individuals. The Fourteenth Amendment did not alter this basic aspect of our federalism.

The rediscovery of section 1983 in *Monroe* generated the flood of litigation against state and local officials noted by Justice Powell in *Maine v. Thiboutot*, and called forth a substantial number of Supreme Court decisions developing both the contours of the section 1983 cause of action and the availability of various immunities, both official and governmental, from liability. These developments are summarized briefly in PETER SCHUCK, SUING GOVERNMENT, Appendix 2 (1983), and more extensively in Susan G. Kupfer, *Restructuring the* Monroe *Doctrine: Current Litigation Under Section 1983*, 9 Hastings Const.L.Q. 463 (1982).

Much of the ensuing litigation has involved Fourth, Fifth and Sixth Amendment claims against law enforcement personnel, although these are hardly the only constitutional provisions that have formed the basis for section 1983 suits. Indeed, the capacious language of the Fourteenth Amendment's Due Process and Equal Protection Clauses might, with modest creativity, cover virtually any offending act by a state or local official. See, e.g., *Parratt v. Taylor*, 451 U.S. 527 (1981); *Paul v. Davis*, 424 U.S. 693 (1976). These officials are protected by a range of immunities, see generally *Scheuer v. Rhodes*, 416 U.S. 232 (1974), "predicated upon a considered inquiry into the immunity historically accorded the relevant official at common law," *Imbler v. Pachtman*, 424 U.S. 409, 421 (1976) (public prosecutor absolutely immune), but tempered by the need to effectuate the policies of section 1983. See *Tower v. Glover*, 467 U.S. 914 (1984) (no immunity for a public defender accused of intentional misconduct). Many of the more important cases on official immunity are rehearsed in *Butz v. Economou*, excerpted in Chapter 8.

Much of the modern section 1983 jurisprudence from *Monroe v. Pape* to *Maine v. Thiboutot* focuses on the issues made relevant in *Monroe*. Actions are brought primarily as a means to enforce federal constitutional rights against state or local officials, and in most instances, the remedy sought is damages. From this perspective section 1983 is the analogue of *Bivens* actions, in which the defendants are state rather than federal officers—another brand of "constitutional tort" implicating issues of federalism, as Justice Frankfurter pointed out in *Monroe*. As such the section 1983 action has its own distinctive attributes. Because they enjoy explicit statutory recognition, "constitutional tort" claims against state officials under section 1983 have seldom invoked the hesitancy that appears in the post-*Bivens* cases discussed in Chapter 8. Nevertheless, section 1983 itself requires that there be some "right, privilege or immunity" for the violation of which it supplies an explicit remedy. Moreover, it imposes liability on institutions that are legal "persons" as well as on individual officers. Section 1983 liability thus implicates sovereign as well as official immunity. Where neither sovereign nor official immunity apply, as with municipalities, the effects of section 1983 exposure are both dramatic and controversial. For an excellent discussion, see Peter Schuck, *Municipal Liability Under § 1983: Some Lessons From Tort Law and Organization Theory*, 77 Geo.L.J. 1753 (1989).

Section 1983 and Judicial Review of Administrative Action. Maine v. Thiboutot suggests a quite different perspective on section 1983. There it functions as a means by which citizens claiming entitlements under a federal-state grant-in-aid scheme may obtain judicial review of the actions of state administrators—in particular, of their fidelity to the conditions or criteria contained in the federal legislation pursuant to which funding is made available to the state.

Indeed, this is the view of such beneficiary enforcement actions that the Court seems to have entertained when it decided *Rosado v. Wyman*, 397 U.S. 397 (1970), one of the cases upon which the majority principally relies. For while Justice Powell analogizes the action in *Thiboutot* to "implied rights of action," the *Rosado* Court cited *ADAPSO* as authority and characterized the question as one concerning the availability of judicial review. On the relationship between "standing," implied rights of action, and section 1983 actions, see generally Jerry L. Mashaw, *"Rights" in the Federal Administrative State*, 92 Yale L.J. 1129 (1983); Richard Stewart and Cass Sunstein, *Public Programs and Private Rights*, 95 Harv.L.Rev. 1193 (1982).

As Justice Powell suggests, Congress, for various reasons, increasingly implements federal policy through state and local agencies. Thus, as was discussed in Chapter One, the activities of the federal government have grown dramatically, and its budget has kept pace, but federal civilian employees constitute a smaller percentage of the population in

1998 than in 1958. In a service industry like government massive growth in activity with virtually no growth in staff generally involves some sleight-of-hand. Congress' trick has been to borrow someone else's employees, namely, those of states and localities. In THE TRUE SIZE OF GOVERNMENT (1999), Paul Light estimates that if contract, grant and "mandate" workers, the latter two categories being mostly state and local employees, were counted as federal employees, the federal civilian workforce would be about eight times the size of the official count. Thus many of the modern social programs of the American welfare state, as well as many of the safety and health regulatory programs that mark new federal initiatives since the 1970s, are programs planned in Washington but administered by officials whose primary allegiance is to Albany, Sacramento, or some other state capital. See generally Jerry L. Mashaw and Susan Rose–Ackerman, *Federalism and Regulation*, in GEORGE C. EADS AND MICHAEL FIX, EDS., THE REAGAN ADMINISTRATION'S REGULATORY RELIEF EFFORT (1984); Frederick Mosher, *The Changing Responsibilities and Tactics of the Federal Government*, in JAMES W. FESLER, ED. AMERICAN PUBLIC ADMINISTRATION: PATTERNS OF THE PAST 198 (1982).

This trend in American government puts stress on the remedial system for controlling official action. For in many of these programs the responsible administrators are not only state officials, they operate under state law, albeit statutes drafted to comply with federal criteria. These officials are not therefore subject to the Federal Administrative Procedure Act, and a citizen suing his or her own state for improper administration of a program authorized by state law raises no question over which a federal court would have jurisdiction. The possibility, then, is that programs ostensibly implementing national policies will be administered subject to remedial structures that vary from state to state and by administrators who might treat federal policies as no more than tangentially relevant. For example, a benefits program like that involved in *Thiboutot* might be excepted from most provisions of a state's administrative procedure act and perhaps from judicial review in state court as well. It is this perspective that suggests that a "standing" analysis might be the more suitable analogy for *Thiboutot*-style section 1983 suits than the "implied right of action" analysis suggested by Justice Powell. The plaintiffs in these lawsuits seek to control official illegality, not merely to obtain private compensation for harms. And again, by analogy to federal law, reviewability might be considered presumptively available.

Yet, respect for "cooperative federalism" forecloses these easy analogies. Before imposing obligations on states or state officials, courts are inclined to think carefully about whether Congress really intended to confer enforceable "rights, privileges or immunities" on program beneficiaries. A federal court order instructing state administrators how to carry out a federal-state program and requiring the expenditure of state funds raises not only issues of inter-governmental comity, but also may implicate a state's Eleventh Amendment immunity. Finally, in complex federal-state programs, the addition of a section 1983 action to other carefully crafted remedies may raise separation of powers concerns as well. A court facing a complicated and apparently carefully balanced remedial scheme might well wonder whether Congress meant implicitly to foreclose section 1983 actions in that particular context, or at least whether judicial intervention under the authority of the broad language of a more than 120–year-old statute, might not usurp Congress' prerogative to design remedial systems. The notion of an implied cause of action may therefore have a negative corollary—implied supersession. The post-*Thiboutot* jurisprudence has explored all of these issues.

PENNHURST STATE SCHOOL AND HOSPITAL v. HALDERMAN

Supreme Court of the United States, 1981.
451 U.S. 1, 101 S.Ct. 1531, 67 L.Ed.2d 694.

JUSTICE REHNQUIST delivered the opinion of the Court.

At issue in these cases is the scope and meaning of the Developmentally Disabled Assistance and Bill of Rights Act of 1975, 42 U.S.C. § 6000 *et seq.* The Court of Appeals for the Third Circuit held that the Act created substantive rights in favor of the mentally retarded, that those rights were judicially enforceable, and that conditions at the Pennhurst State School and Hospital (Pennhurst), a facility for the care and treatment of the mentally retarded, violated those rights. * * *

I

The Commonwealth of Pennsylvania owns and operates Pennhurst. Pennhurst is a large institution, housing approximately 1,200 residents. Seventy-five percent of the residents are either "severely" or "profoundly" retarded—that is, with an IQ of less than 35—and a number of the residents are also physically handicapped. About half of its residents were committed there by court order and half by a parent or other guardian.

* * *

The District Court['s] * * * findings of fact are undisputed: Conditions at Pennhurst are not only dangerous, with the residents often physically abused or drugged by staff members, but also inadequate for the "habilitation" of the retarded. Indeed, the court found that the physical, intellectual, and emotional skills of some residents have deteriorated at Pennhurst.

The District Court went on to hold that the mentally retarded have a federal constitutional right to be provided with "minimally adequate habilitation" in the "least restrictive environment," regardless of whether they were voluntarily or involuntarily committed. * * * In addition, it found that § 504 of the Rehabilitation Act of 1973, 29 U.S.C. § 794, and § 201 of the Pennsylvania Mental Health and Mental Retardation Act of 1966 provided a right to minimally adequate habilitation in the least restrictive environment.

Each of these rights was found to have been violated by the conditions existing at Pennhurst. * * *

The Court of Appeals for the Third Circuit substantially affirmed the District Court's remedial order. 612 F.2d 84 (1979) (en banc). Unlike the District Court, however, the Court of Appeals sought to avoid the constitutional claims raised by respondents and instead rested its order on a construction of the Developmentally Disabled Assistance and Bill of Rights Act, 42 U.S.C. § 6000 *et seq.* It found that §§ 6010(1) and (2) of the Act, the "bill of rights" provision, grant to mentally retarded persons a right to "appropriate treatment, services, and habilitation" in "the setting that is least restrictive of * * * personal liberty." * * * As an alternative ground, the court affirmed the District Court's holding that Pennhurst residents have a state statutory right to adequate "habilitation."

The court concluded that the conditions at Pennhurst violated these federal and state statutory rights. * * *

* * * Petitioners first contend that 42 U.S.C. § 6010 does not create in favor of the mentally retarded any substantive rights to "appropriate treatment" in the "least restrictive" environment. Assuming that Congress did intend to create such a right, petitioners question the authority of Congress to impose these affirmative obligations on the States under either its spending power or § 5 of the Fourteenth Amendment. Petitioners next assert that any rights created by the Act are enforceable in federal court only by the Federal Government, not by private parties. * * * Because we agree with petitioners' first contention—that § 6010 simply does not create substantive rights—we find it unnecessary to address the remaining issues.

II

We turn first to a brief review of the general structure of the Act. It is a federal-state grant program whereby the Federal Government provides financial assistance to participating States to aid them in creating programs to care for and treat the developmentally disabled. Like other federal-state cooperative programs, the Act is voluntary and the States are given the choice of complying with the conditions set forth in the Act or foregoing the benefits of federal funding. The Commonwealth of Pennsylvania has elected to participate in the program. The Secretary of the Department of Health and Human Services (HHS), the agency responsible for administering the Act, has approved Pennsylvania's state plan and in 1976 disbursed to Pennsylvania approximately $1.6 million. Pennhurst itself receives no federal funds from Pennsylvania's allotment under the Act, though it does receive approximately $6 million per year in Medicaid funds.

The Act begins with an exhaustive statement of purposes. 42 U.S.C. § 6000(b)(1). The "overall purpose" of the Act, as amended in 1978, is:

> "*[T]o assist* [the] states to assure that persons with developmental disabilities receive the care, treatment, and other services necessary

to enable them to achieve their maximum potential through a system which coordinates, monitors, plans, and evaluates those services and which ensures the protection of the legal and human rights of persons with developmental disabilities." (Emphasis supplied.)

As set forth in the margin, the "specific purposes" of the Act are to "assist" and financially "support" various activities necessary to the provision of comprehensive services to the developmentally disabled. § 6000(b)(2).[8]

The Act next lists a variety of conditions for the receipt of federal funds. Under § 6005, for example, the Secretary "as a condition of providing assistance" shall require that "each recipient of such assistance take affirmative action" to hire qualified handicapped individuals. Each State, in turn, shall "as a condition" of receiving assistance submit to the Secretary a plan to evaluate the services provided under the Act. § 6009. Each State shall also "as a condition" of receiving assistance "provide the Secretary satisfactory assurances that each program * * * which receives funds from the State's allotment * * * has in effect for each developmentally disabled person who receives services from or under the program a habilitation plan." § 6011(a). And § 6012(a) conditions aid on a State's promise to "have in effect a system to protect and advocate the rights of persons with developmental disabilities."

At issue here, of course, is § 6010, the "bill of rights" provision. It states in relevant part:

"Congress makes the following findings respecting the rights of persons with developmental disabilities:

"(1) Persons with developmental disabilities have a right to appropriate treatment, services, and habilitation for such disabilities.

"(2) The treatment, services, and habilitation for a person with developmental disabilities should be designed to maximize the devel-

8. Section 6000(b)(2) provides:

"The specific purposes of this chapter are—

"(A) to assist in the provision of comprehensive services to persons with developmental disabilities, with priority to those persons whose needs cannot be covered or otherwise met under the Education for All Handicapped Children Act, the Rehabilitation Act of 1973 * * *, or other health, education, or welfare programs;

"(B) to assist States in appropriate planning activities;

"(C) to make grants to States and public and private, nonprofit agencies to establish model programs, to demonstrate innovative habilitation techniques, and to train professional and paraprofessional personnel with respect to providing services to persons with developmental disabilities;

"(D) to make grants to university affiliated facilities to assist them in administering and operating demonstration facilities for the provision of services to persons with developmental disabilities, and interdisciplinary training programs for personnel needed to provide specialized services for these persons; and

"(E) to make grants to support a system in each State to protect the legal and human rights of all persons with developmental disabilities."

opmental potential of the person and should be provided in the setting that is least restrictive of the person's personal liberty.

"(3) The Federal Government and the States both have an obligation to assure that public funds are not provided to any institutio[n] * * * that—(A) does not provide treatment, services, and habilitation which is appropriate to the needs of such person; or (B) does not meet the following minimum standards * * *."

Noticeably absent from § 6010 is any language suggesting that § 6010 is a "condition" for the receipt of federal funding under the Act. Section 6010 thus stands in sharp contrast to §§ 6005, 6009, 6011, and 6012.

The enabling parts of the Act are the funding sections. Those sections describe how funds are to be allotted to the States, require that any State desiring financial assistance submit an overall plan satisfactory to the Secretary of HHS, and require that funds disbursed under the Act be used in accordance with the approved state plan. To be approved by the Secretary, the state plan must comply with several specific conditions set forth in § 6063. It, *inter alia*, must provide for the establishment of a State Planning Council, § 6063(b)(1), and set out specific objectives to be achieved under the plan, § 6063(b)(2)(A). Services furnished under the plan must be consistent with standards prescribed by the Secretary, § 6063(b)(5)(A)(I), and be provided in an individual manner consistent with § 6011, § 6063(b)(5)(B). The plan must also be supported by assurances that any program receiving assistance is protecting the human rights of the disabled consistent with § 6010, § 6063(b)(5)(C). Each State must also require its State Planning Council to serve as an advocate of persons with developmental disabilities. § 6067.

The Act further provides procedures and sanctions to ensure state compliance with its requirements. The Secretary may, of course, disapprove a state plan, § 6063(c). If a State fails to satisfy the requirements of § 6063, the Secretary may terminate or reduce the federal grant. § 6065. Any State dissatisfied with the Secretary's disapproval of the plan, or his decision to terminate funding, may appeal to the federal courts of appeals. § 6068. No other cause of action is recognized in the Act.

III

As support for its broad remedial order, the Court of Appeals found that 42 U.S.C. § 6010 created substantive rights in favor of the disabled and imposed an obligation on the States to provide, at their own expense, certain kinds of treatment. The initial question before us, then, is one of statutory construction: Did Congress intend in § 6010 to create enforceable rights and obligations?

In discerning congressional intent, we necessarily turn to the possible sources of Congress' power to legislate, namely, Congress' power to enforce the Fourteenth Amendment and its power under the Spending Clause to place conditions on the grant of federal funds. Although the court below held that Congress acted under both powers, the respondents themselves disagree on this point. The Halderman respondents argue that § 6010 was enacted pursuant to § 5 of the Fourteenth Amendment. Accordingly, they assert that § 6010 is mandatory on the States, regardless of their receipt of federal funds. The Solicitor General, in contrast, concedes that Congress acted pursuant to its spending power alone. Thus, in his view, § 6010 only applies to those States which accept federal funds.

Although this Court has previously addressed issues going to Congress' power to secure the guarantees of the Fourteenth Amendment, we have had little occasion to consider the appropriate test for determining when Congress intends to enforce those guarantees. Because such legislation imposes congressional policy on a State involuntarily, and because it often intrudes on traditional state authority, we should not quickly attribute to Congress an unstated intent to act under its authority to enforce the Fourteenth Amendment. * * * The case for inferring intent is at its weakest where, as here, the rights asserted impose *affirmative* obligations on the States to fund certain services, since we may assume that Congress will not implicitly attempt to impose massive financial obligations on the States.

Turning to Congress' power to legislate pursuant to the spending power, our cases have long recognized that Congress may fix the terms on which it shall disburse federal money to the States. Unlike legislation enacted under § 5, however, legislation enacted pursuant to the spending power is much in the nature of a contract: in return for federal funds, the States agree to comply with federally imposed conditions. The legitimacy of Congress' power to legislate under the spending power thus rests on whether the State voluntarily and knowingly accepts the terms of the "contract." There can, of course, be no knowing acceptance if a State is unaware of the conditions or is unable to ascertain what is expected of it. Accordingly, if Congress intends to impose a condition on the grant of federal moneys, it must do so unambiguously. By insisting that Congress speak with a clear voice, we enable the States to exercise their choice knowingly, cognizant of the consequences of their participation.

* * *

Applying those principles to these cases, we find nothing in the Act or its legislative history to suggest that Congress intended to require the States to assume the high cost of providing "appropriate treatment" in the "least restrictive environment" to their mentally retarded citizens.

There is virtually no support for the lower court's conclusion that Congress created rights and obligations pursuant to its power to enforce the Fourteenth Amendment. The Act nowhere states that that is its purpose. Quite the contrary, the Act's language and structure demonstrate that it is a mere federal-state funding statute. * * * Surely Congress would not have established such elaborate funding incentives had it simply intended to impose absolute obligations on the States.

Respondents nonetheless insist that the fact that § 6010 speaks in terms of "rights" supports their view. Their reliance is misplaced. * * * We are persuaded that § 6010, when read in the context of other more specific provisions of the Act, does no more than express a congressional preference for certain kinds of treatment. It is simply a general statement of "findings" and, as such, is too thin a reed to support the rights and obligations read into it by the court below. The closest one can come in giving § 6010 meaning is that it justifies and supports Congress' appropriation of money under the Act and guides the Secretary in his review of state applications for federal funds. As this Court recognized in *Rosado v. Wyman*, [397 U.S. 397 (1970)] "Congress sometimes legislates by innuendo, making declarations of policy and indicating a preference while requiring measures that, though falling short of legislating its goal, serve as a nudge in the preferred directions." This is such a case.

* * *

There remains the contention of the Solicitor General that Congress, acting pursuant to its spending power, conditioned the grant of federal money on the State's agreeing to underwrite the obligations the Court of Appeals read into § 6010. We find that contention wholly without merit. As amply demonstrated above, the "findings" in § 6010, when viewed in the context of the more specific provisions of the Act, represent general statements of federal policy, not newly created legal duties.

The "plain language" of § 6010 also refutes the Solicitor General's contention. When Congress intended to impose conditions on the grant of federal funds, as in §§ 6005, 6009, 6011, 6012, 6063, and 6067, it proved capable of doing so in clear terms. Section 6010, in marked contrast, in no way suggests that the grant of federal funds is "conditioned" on a state funding the rights described therein. * * *

Equally telling is the fact that the Secretary has specifically rejected the position of the Solicitor General. The purpose of the Act, according to the Secretary, is merely "to improve and coordinate the provision of services to persons with developmental disabilities." 45 C.F.R. § 1385.1 (1979). The Secretary acknowledges that "[n]o authority was included in [the 1975] Act to allow the Department to withhold funds from States on the basis of failure to meet the findings [of § 6010]." 45 Fed.Reg. 31,006 (1980). If funds cannot be terminated for a state's failure to comply with § 6010, § 6010 can hardly be considered a "condition" of the grant of federal funds. The Secretary's interpretation of § 6010, moreover, is well supported by the legislative history. In reaching the compromise on § 6010, the Conference Committee rejected the Senate's proposal to terminate federal funding of States which failed to comply with the standards enumerated in Title II of the Senate's bill. By eliminating that sanction, Congress made clear that the provisions of § 6010 were intended to be hortatory, not mandatory.

The fact that Congress granted to Pennsylvania only $1.6 million in 1976, a sum woefully inadequate to meet the enormous financial burden of providing "appropriate" treatment in the "least restrictive" setting, confirms that Congress must have had a limited purpose in enacting § 6010. When Congress does impose affirmative obligations on the States, it usually makes a far more substantial contribution to defray costs. It defies common sense, in short, to suppose that Congress implicitly imposed this massive obligation on participating States.

* * *

IV

Respondents also suggest that they may bring suit to compel compliance with those conditions which are contained in the Act. Of particular relevance to these cases are § 6011(a) and § 6063(b)(5)(C).*

That claim raises several issues. First, it must be determined whether respondents have a private cause of action to compel state compliance with those conditions. In legislation enacted pursuant to the spending power, the typical remedy for state noncompliance with federally imposed conditions is not a private cause of action for noncompliance but rather action by the Federal Government to terminate funds to the State. See § 6065. Just last Term, however, in *Maine v. Thiboutot*, we held that 42 U.S.C. § 1983 provides a cause of action for state deprivations of "rights secured" by "the laws" of the United States. Whether *Thiboutot* controls these cases depends on two factors. First, respondents here, unlike the plaintiffs in *Thiboutot*, who alleged that state law prevented them from receiving federal funds to which they were entitled, can only claim that the state plan has not provided adequate "assurances" to the Secretary. It is at least an open question whether an individual's interest in having a State provide those "assurances" is a "right secured" by the laws of the United States within the meaning of § 1983. Second, Justice Powell in dissent in *Thiboutot* suggested that § 1983 would not be available where the "governing statute provides an exclusive remedy for violations of its terms." It is unclear whether the express remedy contained in this Act is exclusive.

Second, it is not at all clear that the Pennhurst petitioners have violated § 6011 and § 6063(b)(5)(C). Those sections, by their terms, only refer to "programs assisted" under the Act. Because Pennhurst does not receive federal funds under the Act, it is arguably not a "program assisted." * * *

Third, there is the question of remedy. Respondents' relief may well be limited to enjoining the Federal Government from providing funds to the Commonwealth. As we stated in *Rosado v. Wyman*, welfare claimants were "entitled to declaratory relief and an appropriate injunction by the District Court against the payment of *federal* monies * * * should

* [Section 6063(b)(5)(C) requires each state plan to:

> contain or be supported by assurances satisfactory to the Secretary that the human rights of all persons with developmental disabilities * * * who are receiving treatment, services, or habilitation, under programs assisted under this chapter will be protected consistent with § 6010 of this Title (relating to rights of the developmentally disabled). Eds.]

the State not develop a conforming plan within a reasonable period of time." (Emphasis in original.) There, we rejected the suggestion that the courts could require the State to pay the additional sums demanded by compliance with federal standards. Relying on *King v. Smith*, 392 U.S. 309 (1968), we explained that "the State had alternative choices of assuming the additional cost" of complying with the federal standard "or not using federal funds." * * *

In other instances, however, we have implicitly departed from that rule and have affirmed lower court decisions enjoining a State from enforcing any provisions which conflict with federal law in violation of the Supremacy Clause, *e.g.*, *Carleson v. Remillard*, 406 U.S. 598 (1972). In still other cases, we have struck down state laws without addressing the form of relief, *e.g.*, *Townsend v. Swank*, 404 U.S. 282 (1971). In no case, however, have we required a State to provide money to plaintiffs, much less required a State to take on such open-ended and potentially burdensome obligations as providing "appropriate" treatment in the "least restrictive" environment. And because this is a suit in federal court, anything but prospective relief would pose serious questions under the Eleventh Amendment. *Edelman v. Jordan*, 415 U.S. 651 (1974).

These are all difficult questions. Because the Court of Appeals has not addressed these issues, however, we remand the issues for consideration in light of our decision here. * * *

[JUSTICE BLACKMUN'S concurring opinion is omitted.]

JUSTICE WHITE, with whom JUSTICE BRENNAN and JUSTICE MARSHALL join, dissenting in part.

* * *

In essence, the Court concludes that the so-called "Bill of Rights" section of the Act, 42 U.S.C. § 6010, merely serves to establish guidelines which States should endeavor to fulfill, but which have no real effect except to the extent that the Secretary of Health and Human Services chooses to use the criteria established by § 6010 in determining funding under the Act. In my view, this reading misconceives the important purposes Congress intended § 6010 to serve. That section, as confirmed by its legislative history, was intended by Congress to establish requirements which participating States had to meet in providing care to the developmentally disabled. The fact that Congress spoke in generalized terms rather than the language of regulatory minutia cannot make nugatory actions so carefully undertaken.

[After extensive analysis of the statute and its legislative and administrative history, Justice White continued:]

Given my view that Congress intended § 6010 to do more than suggest that the States act in a particular manner, I find it necessary to reach the question whether these rights can be enforced in federal courts in a suit brought by the developmentally disabled. * * *

As a general matter, it is clear that the fact that a federal administrative agency has the power to oversee a cooperative state-federal venture does not mean that Congress intended such oversight to be the exclusive remedy for enforcing statutory rights. This Court is "most reluctant to assume Congress has closed the avenue of effective judicial review to those individuals most directly affected by the administration of its program[s]" even if the agency has the statutory power to cut off federal funds for noncompliance. *Rosado v. Wyman*. In part, this reluctance is founded on the perception that a funds cutoff is a drastic remedy with injurious consequences to the supposed beneficiaries of the Act. Cf. *Cannon v. University of Chicago*. In this litigation, there is no indication that Congress intended the funds cutoff, which, as the Court notes, the Secretary believed was not within the power of the agency, to be the sole remedy for correcting violations of § 6010 * * *.

I would vacate the judgment of the Court of Appeals and remand the cases for further proceedings. This litigation does not involve the exercise of congressional power to enforce the Fourteenth Amendment as the Court of Appeals held, but is an exercise of the spending power. What an appropriate remedy might be where state officials fail to observe the limits of their power under the United States Constitution or fail to perform an ongoing statutory duty imposed by a federal statute enacted under the commerce power or the Fourteenth Amendment is not necessarily the measure of a federal court's authority where it is found that a State has failed to perform its obligations undertaken pursuant to a statute enacted under the spending power. * * * [T]he courts in such cases must take account of the State's privilege to withdraw and terminate its duties under the federal law. Although the court may enjoin the enforcement of a discrete state statutory provision or regulation or may order state officials prospectively to perform their duties incident to the receipt of federal funds, the prospective force of such injunctions cannot survive the State's decision to terminate its participation in the program. Furthermore, there are cases in which there is no identifiable statutory provision whose enforcement can be prohibited. *Rosado v. Wyman* was such a case, and there, after finding that the State was not complying with the provisions of the Social Security Act, we remanded the case to the District Court to "afford [the State] an opportunity to revise its program in accordance with [federal requirements]" as we have construed them to be, but to retain jurisdiction "to review * * * any revised program adopted by the State, or, should [the State] choose not to submit a revamped program by the determined date, issue its order restraining the further use of federal monies. * * * "

It is my view that the Court of Appeals should have adopted the *Rosado* approach in these cases. It found the State to be in noncompliance with the federal statute in major respects and proceeded to impose a far-reaching remedy, approving the appointment of a Special Master to decide which of the Pennhurst inmates should remain and which should be moved to community-based facilities. More properly, the court should have announced what it thought was necessary to comply with the Act and then permitted an appropriate period for the State to decide whether it preferred to give up federal funds and go its own route. If it did not, it should propose a plan for achieving compliance, in which event, if it satisfied the court, a decree incorporating the plan could be entered and if the plan was unsatisfactory, the further use of federal funds could be enjoined. In any event, however, the court should not have assumed the task of managing Pennhurst or deciding in the first instance which patients should remain and which should be removed. * * *

Finding Rights, Privileges and Immunities: From *Pennhurst* to *Gonzaga*

Whether Congress intended to create a "right, privilege, or immunity" is a question that can be raised in virtually any section 1983 case. It is not surprising, therefore, that the Supreme Court has revisited the question in several later cases. Given *Pennhurst*'s refusal to find a right under a statutory "bill of rights," one might be surprised to discover that these opinions are far from uniformly hostile to § 1983 claims.

In *Wright v. Roanoke Redevelopment and Housing Authority*, 479 U.S. 418 (1987), for example, petitioners were residents of low-income housing projects in Roanoke, Virginia. They claimed that their public housing authority had violated the so-called "Brooke Amendment" to the Housing Act of 1937 and the implementing regulations adopted by the Department of Housing and Urban Development (HUD). The Brooke Amendment imposed a ceiling for rents charged to low-income people living in federally supported public housing projects, fixed at a specified percentage of the client's income. The petitioners in *Wright* claimed that their local authority failed to include a reasonable amount for the use of utilities in the "rent," contrary to HUD's consistent interpretation of the Brooke Amendment. As a consequence, the total of rent and utilities that they paid exceeded the percentage of income that they could be charged.

The Authority claimed that the Brooke Amendment created no enforceable right within the meaning of section 1983. The Court's opinion gave this claim short shrift:

> The Brooke Amendment could not be clearer: As further amended in 1981, tenants could be charged as rent no more and no less than 30per cent of their income. This was a mandatory limitation focusing on the individual family and its income. The intent to benefit tenants is undeniable. Nor is there any question that HUD interim regulations, in effect when this suit began, expressly required that a "reasonable amount" for utilities be included in the rent that a PHA (Public Housing Authority) was allowed to charge, an interpretation to which HUD has adhered both before and after the adoption of the Brooke Amendment. HUD's view is entitled to deference as a

valid interpretation of the statute, and Congress in the course of amending that provision has not disagreed with it.

Although this analysis garnered only a bare majority of the Justices in *Wright*, subsequent majorities similarly found rights, privileges, or immunities enforceable through section 1983 in the National Labor Relations Act, *Golden State Transit Corp. v. Los Angeles*, 493 U.S. 103 (1989); the Boren Amendment to the Medicaid Act, *Wilder v. Virginia Hospital Ass'n*, 496 U.S. 498 (1990); and the Commerce Clause, *Dennis v. Higgins*, 498 U.S. 439 (1991).

Suter v. Artist M., 503 U.S. 347 (1992), might be thought to signal a shift in the Supreme Court's hospitality toward finding enforceable "rights, privileges and immunities" in federal grant-in-aid statutes. That case involved an attempt to enforce the provision in the Adoption Assistance and Child Welfare Act of 1980 that requires state social services programs that are assisted by federal grants in the administration of foster care and adoption services to use "reasonable efforts" to prevent the removal of children from their homes and to facilitate the reunification of families once removal has occurred. The respondents claimed that the State of Illinois was not making such "reasonable efforts" even though it had filed a "state plan" with the federal Department of Health and Human Services promising to do so. A seven-person majority of the Supreme Court believed that the "reasonable efforts" clause of the Adoption Act failed to "unambiguously confer an enforceable right upon the Act's beneficiaries." The *Wilder* case, in particular, was distinguished on the ground that, in *Wilder*, both the statute and departmental regulations had articulated objective standards by which it could be determined whether medical care providers were being reimbursed at rates that were "reasonable and adequate." Here there was no such articulation of standards in the statute; the HHS regulations were drafted in a form that might suggest to a state that its continued receipt of funds was contingent upon nothing more than a description in its state plan of what services the state offered to prevent removal of a child from its home and to reunify the family if removal from the home occurred.

Five years later, in *Blessing v. Freestone,* 520 U.S. 329 (1997), the Court tried again to specify how "rights" analysis under § 1983 should proceed. As described by the Court the facts were these:

> This controversy concerns an interlocking set of cooperative federal-state welfare programs. Arizona participates in the federal Aid to Families with Dependent Children (AFDC) program, which provides subsistence welfare benefits to needy families. To qualify for federal AFDC funds, the State must certify that it will operate a child support enforcement program that conforms with * * * Title IV–D * * * and will do so pursuant to a detailed plan that has been approved by the Secretary of Health and Human Services (Secretary). The Federal Government underwrites roughly two-thirds of the cost of the State's child support efforts. But the State must do

more than simply collect overdue support payments; it must also establish a comprehensive system to establish paternity, locate absent parents, and help families obtain support orders.

A State must provide these services free of charge to AFDC recipients and, when requested, for a nominal fee to children and custodial parents who are not receiving AFDC payments. AFDC recipients must assign their child support rights to the State and fully cooperate with the State's efforts to establish paternity and obtain support payments. Although the State may keep most of the support payment that it collects on behalf of AFDC families in order to offset the costs of providing welfare benefits, until recently it only had to distribute the first $50 pass-through with more generous distributions to families once they leave welfare. Non–AFDC recipients who request the State's aid are entitled to have all collected funds passed through. In all cases, the State must distribute the family's share of collected support payments within two business days after receipt. § 654(b)(c)(1).

The structure of each State's Title IV–D agency, like the services it provides, must conform to federal guidelines. * * *

To oversee this complex federal-state enterprise, Congress created the Office of Child Support Enforcement (OCSE) within the Department of Health and Human Services (HHS). * * * If a State does not "substantially comply" with the requirements of Title IV–D, the Secretary is authorized to penalize the State by reducing its AFDC grant by up to five percent. The Secretary has interpreted "substantial compliance" as (a) full compliance with requirements that services be offered statewide and that certain recipients be notified monthly of the support collected, as well as with reporting, recordkeeping, and accounting rules; (b) 90 percent compliance with case opening and case closure criteria; and (c) 75 percent compliance with most remaining program requirements. The Secretary may suspend a penalty if the State implements an adequate corrective action plan, and if the program achieves "substantial compliance," she may rescind the penalty entirely.

As Justice O'Connor's opinion noted, the Secretary had on numerous occasions found that Arizona had not substantially complied with significant program requirements and repeatedly penalized the State one percent of its AFDC grant. The State developed a corrective action plan after each failed audit, which prompted the Secretary to suspend and—in every instance but one—waive the one-percent reduction in Arizona's AFDC funding.

Respondents were five Arizona mothers whose children were eligible for Title IV–D child support services. As might be expected, given Arizona's record, respondents claimed that they had properly applied for child support services but that, despite their good faith efforts to cooperate, the agency never took adequate steps to obtain child support payments from the fathers of their children. These omissions, respondents contended, were largely attributable to structural defects in the State's child support efforts: staff shortages, high caseloads, unmanageable backlogs and deficiencies in the State's accounting methods and recordkeeping. With these facts in hand Justice O'Connor then tried to provide, based on the Court's prior decisions, a set of guidelines for determining whether persons in respondents' positions had a "right" under federal law sufficient to actuate § 1983's remedies:

> Section 1983 imposes liability on anyone who, under color of state law, deprives a person "of any rights, privileges, or immunities secured by the Constitution and laws." We have held that this provision safeguards certain rights conferred by federal statutes. *Maine v. Thiboutot*. In order to seek redress through § 1983, however, a plaintiff must assert the violation of a federal right, not merely a violation of federal law. *Golden State Transit Corp. v. Los Angeles*. We have traditionally looked at three factors when determining whether a particular statutory provision gives rise to a federal right. First, Congress must have intended that the provision in question benefit the plaintiff. Second, the plaintiff must demonstrate that the right assertedly protected by the statute is not so "vague and amorphous" that its enforcement would strain judicial competence. Third, the statute must unambiguously impose a binding obligation on the States. In other words, the provision giving rise to the asserted right must be couched in a mandatory rather than precatory terms.
>
> Even if a plaintiff demonstrates that a federal statute creates an individual right, there is only a rebuttable presumption that the right is enforceable under § 1983. Because our inquiry focuses on congressional intent, dismissal is proper if Congress "specifically foreclosed a remedy under § 1983." *Smith v. Robinson*, 468 U.S. 992, 1005, n. 9 (1984). Congress may do so expressly, by forbidding recourse to § 1983 in the statute itself, or impliedly, by creating a comprehensive enforcement scheme that is incompatible with individual enforcement under § 1983. *Livadas v. Bradshaw*, 512 U.S. 107 (1994).
>
> With these principles in mind, we turn first to the question whether respondents have established that Title IV–D gives them federal rights.
>
> In their complaint, respondents argued that federal law granted them "individual rights to all mandated services delivered in substantial compliance with Title IV–D and its implementing regulations." They sought a broad injunction requiring the director of Arizona's child support agency to achieve "substantial compliance * * * throughout all programmatic operations." Attributing the deficiencies in the State's program primarily to staff shortages and other structural defects, respondents essentially invited the District court to oversee every aspect of Arizona's Title IV–D program.

Without distinguishing among the numerous rights that might have been created by this federally funded welfare program, the Court of Appeals agreed in sweeping terms that "Title IV–D creates enforceable rights in families in need of Title IV–D services." The Court of Appeals did not specify exactly which "rights" it was purporting to recognize, but it apparently believed that federal law gave respondents the right to have the State substantially comply with Title IV–D in all respects. We disagree.

As an initial matter, the lower court's holding that Title IV–D "creates enforceable rights" paints with too broad a brush. It was incumbent upon respondents to identify with particularity the rights they claimed, since it is impossible to determine whether Title IV–D, as an undifferentiated whole, gives rise to undefined "rights." Only when the complaint is broken down into manageable analytic bites can a court ascertain whether each separate claim satisfies the various criteria we have set forth for determining whether a federal statute creates rights. * * *

* * * [T]he requirement that a State operate its child support program in "substantial compliance" with Title IV–D was not intended to benefit individual children and custodial parents, and therefore it does not constitute a federal right. Far from creating an individual entitlement to services, the standard is simply a yardstick for the Secretary to measure the systemwide performance of a State's Title IV–D program. Thus, the Secretary must look to the aggregate services provided by the State, not to whether the needs of any particular person have been satisfied. A State substantially complies with Title IV–D when it provides most mandated services (such as enforcement of support obligations) in only 75 percent of the cases reviewed during the federal audit period. States must aim to establish paternity in 90 percent of all eligible cases but may satisfy considerably lower targets so long as their efforts are steadily improving. It is clear, then, that even when a State is in "substantial compliance" with Title IV–D, any individual plaintiff might still be among the 10 or 25 percent of persons whose needs ultimately go unmet. Moreover, even upon a finding of substantial noncompliance, the Secretary can merely reduce the State's AFDC grant by up to five percent; she cannot, by force of her own authority, command the State to take any particular action or to provide any services to certain individuals. In short, the substantial compliance standard is designed simply to trigger penalty provisions that increase the frequency of audits and reduce the State's AFDC grant by a maximum of five percent. As such, it does not give rise to individual rights.

* * * It is readily apparent that many other provisions of that multifaceted statutory scheme do not fit our traditional three criteria for identifying statutory rights. To begin with, many provisions, like the "substantial compliance" standard, are designed only to guide the State in structuring its systemwide efforts at enforcing

support obligations. These provisions may ultimately benefit individuals who are eligible for Title IV–D services, but only indirectly. For example, Title IV–D lays out detailed requirements for the State's data processing system. * * * Obviously, these complex standards do not give rise to individualized rights to computer services. They are simply intended to improve the overall efficiency of the States' child support enforcement scheme.

The same reasoning applies to the staffing levels of the state agency, which respondents seem to claim are inadequate. Title IV–D generally requires each participating State to establish a separate child support enforcement unit "which meets such staffing and organizational requirements as the Secretary may by regulation prescribe." The regulations, in turn, simply provide that each level of the State's organization must have "sufficient staff" to fulfill specified functions. These mandates do not, however, give rise to federal rights. For one thing, the link between increased staffing and the services provided to any particular individual is far too tenuous to support the notion that Congress meant to give each and every Arizonan who is eligible for Title IV–D the right to have the State Department of Economic Security staffed at a "sufficient" level. Furthermore, neither the statute nor the regulation gives any guidance as to how large a staff would be "sufficient." Enforcement of such an undefined standard would certainly "strain judicial competence." *Livadas v. Bradshaw*, 512 U.S at 132.

We do not foreclose the possibility that some provisions of Title IV–D give rise to individual rights. * * * For example, respondent Madrid alleged that the sate agency managed to collect some support payments from her ex-husband but failed to pass through the first $50 of each payment, to which she was purportedly entitled under the pre–1996 version of § 657(b)(1). Although § 657 may give her a federal right to receive a specified portion of the money collected on her behalf by Arizona, she did not explicitly request such relief in the complaint.

GONZAGA UNIVERSITY v. JOHN DOE

Supreme Court of the United States, 2002.
536 U.S. 273, 122 S.Ct. 2268, 153 L.Ed.2d 309.

Chief Justice Rehnquist delivered the opinion of the court.

The question presented is whether a student may sue a private university for damages under 42 U.S.C. § 1983 to enforce provisions of the Family Educational Rights and Privacy Act of 1974 (FERPA or Act), which prohibit the federal funding of educational institutions that have a policy or practice of releasing education records to unauthorized persons. We hold such an action foreclosed because the relevant provisions of FERPA create no personal rights to enforce under 42 U.S.C. § 1983.

Respondent John Doe is a former undergraduate in the School of Education at Gonzaga University, a private university in Spokane,

Washington. He planned to graduate and teach at a Washington public elementary school. Washington at the time required all of its new teachers to obtain an affidavit of good moral character from a dean of their graduating college or university. In October 1993, Roberta League, Gonzaga's "teacher certification specialist," overheard one student tell another that respondent engaged in acts of sexual misconduct against Jane Doe, a female undergraduate. League launched an investigation and contacted the state agency responsible for teacher certification, identifying respondent by name and discussing the allegations against him. Respondent did not learn of the investigation, or that information about him had been disclosed, until March 1994, when he was told by League and others that he would not receive the affidavit required for certification as a Washington school teachers.

Respondent then sued Gonzaga and League (petitioners) in state court. He alleged violations of Washington tort and contract law, as well as a pendent violation of § 1983** for the release of personal information to an "unauthorized person" in violation of FERPA. A jury found for respondent on all counts, awarding him $1,155,000, including $150,000 in compensatory damages and $300,000 in punitive damages on the FERPA claim.

The Washington Court of Appeals reversed in relevant part, concluding that FERPA does not create individual rights and thus cannot be enforced under § 1983. The Washington Supreme Court reversed that decision, and ordered the FERPA damages reinstated. The court acknowledged that "FERPA itself does not give rise to a private cause of action," but reasoned that FERPA's nondisclosure provision "gives rise to a federal right enforceable under section 1983."

Like the Washington Supreme Court and the state court of appeals below, other state and federal courts have divided on the question of FERPA's enforceability under § 1983. The fact that al of these courts have relied on the same set of opinions from this Court suggests that our opinions in this area may not be models of clarity. We therefore granted certiorari to resolve the conflict among the lower courts and in the process resolve any ambiguity in our own opinions.

Congress enacted FERPA under its spending power to condition the receipt of federal funds on certain requirements relating to the access and disclosure of student educational records. The Act directs the Secretary of Education to withhold federal funds from any public or private "educational agency or institution" that fails to comply with these conditions. As relevant here, the Act provides:

** The Washington Court of Appeals and the Washington Supreme Court found petitioners to have acted "under color of state law" for purposes of ¶ 1983 when they disclosed respondent's personal information to state officials in connection with state-law teacher certification requirements. Although the petition for certiorari challenged this holding, we agreed to review only the question posed in the first paragraph of this opinion. * * * We therefore assume without deciding that the relevant disclosures occurred under color of state law.

"No funds shall be made available under any applicable program to any educational agency or institution which has a policy or practice of permitting the release of education records (or personally identifiable information contained therein * * *) of students without the written consent of their parents to any individual, agency, or organization." 20 U.S.C. § 1232g(b)(1).

The Act directs the Secretary of Education to enforce this and other of the Act's spending conditions. The Secretary is required to establish an office and review board within the Department of Education for "investigating, processing, reviewing, and adjudicating violations of [the Act]." Funds may be terminated only if the Secretary determines that a recipient institution "is failing to comply substantially with any requirement of [the Act]" and that such compliance "cannot be secured by voluntary means."

Respondents contends that this statutory regime confers upon any student enrolled at a covered school or institution a federal right, enforceable in suits for damages under § 1983, not to have "education records" disclosed to unauthorized persons without the student's express written consent. But we have never before held, and decline to do so here, that spending legislation drafted in terms resembling those of FERPA can confer enforceable rights.

Since Pennhurst, only twice have we found spending legislation to give rise to enforceable rights * * * [Justice Rehnquist here rehearses the jurisprudence from *Wright* through *Blessing*.]

Respondent reads this line of cases to establish a relatively loose standard for finding rights enforceable by § 1983. He claims that a federal statute confers such rights so long as Congress intended that the statute "benefit" putative plaintiffs. He further contends that a more "rigorous" inquiry would conflate the standard for inferring a private right of action under § 1983 with the standard for inferring a private right of action directly from the statute itself, which he admits would not exist under FERPA. * * *

Some language in our opinions might be read to suggest that something less than an unambiguously conferred right is enforceable by § 1983. *Blessing*, for example, set forth three "factors" to guide judicial inquiry into whether or not a statute confers a right: "Congress must have intended that the provision in question benefit the plaintiff," "the plaintiff must demonstrate that the right assertedly protected by the statute is not so 'vague and amorphous' that its enforcement would strain judicial resources," and "the provision giving rise to the asserted right must be couched in mandatory, rather than precatory, terms." In the same paragraph, however, *Blessing* emphasizes that it is only violations of *rights*, not *laws*, which give rise to § 1983 actions. This confusion has led some courts to interpret *Blessing* as allowing plaintiffs to enforce a statute under § 1983 so long as plaintiff falls within the general zone of interest that the statute is intended to protect; something less than what is required for a statute to create rights enforceable directly from the statute itself under an implied private right of action. Fueling this uncertainty is the notion that our implied private right of action cases have no bearing on the standards for discerning whether a statute creates rights enforceable by § 1983. *Wilder* appears to support this notion, while *Suter* and *Pennhurst* appear to disavow it.

We now reject the notion that our cases permit anything short of an unambiguously conferred right to support a cause of action brought under § 1983. Section 1983 provides a remedy only for the deprivation of "rights, privileges, or immunities secured by the Constitution and laws" of the United States. Accordingly, it is *rights*, not the broader or vaguer "benefits" or "interests," that may be enforced under the authority of that section. This being so, we further reject the notion that our implied rights of action cases are separate and distinct from our § 1983 cases. To the contrary, our implied rights of action cases should guide the determination of whether a statute confers rights enforceable under § 1983.

We have recognized that whether a statutory violation may be enforced through § 1983 "is a different inquiry than that involved in determining whether a private right of action can be implied from a particular statute." But the inquiries overlap in one meaningful respect—in either case we must first determine whether Congress intended to create a federal right. Thus we have held that "the question whether Congress * * * intended to create a private right of action [is] definitively answered in the negative" where "a statute by its terms grants no private rights to any identifiable class." *Touche Ross & Co. v. Redington*. For a statute to create such private rights, its text must be "phrased in terms of the persons benefitted." *Cannon v. University of Chicago*. We have recognized, for example, that Title VI of the Civil Rights Act of 1964 and Title IX of the Education Amendments of 1972 create individual rights because those statutes are phrased "with an *unmistakable focus* on the benefitted class." (Emphasis added). But even where a statute is phrased in such explicit rights-creating terms, a plaintiff suing under an implied right of action still must show that the statute manifests an intent "to create not just a private *right* but also a private *remedy*." *Alexander v. Sandoval* (emphases added).

Plaintiffs suing under § 1983 do not have the burden of showing an intent to create a private remedy because § 1983 generally supplies a remedy for the vindication of rights secured by federal statutes. Once a plaintiff demonstrates that a statute confers an individual right, the right is presumptively enforceable by § 1983. But the initial inquiry—determining whether a statute confers any right at all—is no different from the initial inquiry in an implied right of action case, the express purpose of which is to determine whether or not a statute "confers rights on a particular class of persons." * * *

With this principle in mind, there is no question that FERPA's nondisclosure provisions fail to confer enforceable rights. To begin with, the provisions entirely lack the sort of "rights-creating" language critical to showing the requisite congressional intent to create new rights.

Unlike the individually focused terminology of Titles VI and IX ("no person shall be subjected to discrimination"), FERPA's provisions speak only to the Secretary of Education, directing that "no funds shall be made available" to any "educational agency or institution" which has a prohibited" policy or practice." * * *

FERPA's nondisclosure provisions further speak only in terms of institutional policy and practice, not individual instances of disclosure. (Prohibiting the funding of "any educational agency or institution which has a *policy or practice* of permitting the release of education records" (emphasis added)). Therefore as in *Blessing*, they have an "aggregate" focus, they are not concerned with "whether the needs of any particular person have been satisfied," and they cannot "give rise to individual rights." Recipient institutions can further avoid termination of funding so long as they "comply substantially" with the Act's requirements. This, too, is not unlike *Blessing*, which found that Title IV–D failed to support a § 1983 suit in part because it only required "substantial compliance" with federal regulations. * * *

Our conclusion that FERPA's nondisclosure provisions fail to confer enforceable rights is buttressed by the mechanism that Congress chose to provide for enforcing those provisions. Congress expressly authorized the Secretary of Education to "*deal with violations*" of the Act, § 1232g(f) (emphasis added), and required the Secretary to "establish or designate [a] review board" for investigating and adjudicating such violations, § 1232g(g). Pursuant to these provisions, the Secretary created the Family Policy Compliance Office (FPCO) "to act as the Review Board required under the Act and to enforce the Act with respect to all applicable programs." The FPCO permits students and parents who suspect a violation of the Act to file individual written complaints. If a complaint is timely and contains required information, the FPCO will initiate an investigation, notify the educational institution of the charge, and request a written response. If a violation is found, the FPCO distributes a notice of factual findings and a "statement of the specific steps that the agency or institution must take to comply" with FERPA. These administrative procedures squarely distinguish this case from *Wright* and *Wilder*, where an aggrieved individual lacked any federal review mechanism, see supra, at 5, and further counsel against our finding a congressional intent to create individually enforceable private rights.

Congress finally provided that "except for the conduct of hearings, none of the functions of the Secretary under this section shall be carried out in any of the regional offices" of the Department of Education. This centralized review provision was added just four months after FERPA's enactment due to "concern that regionalizing the enforcement of [FERPA] may lead to multiple interpretations of it, and possibly work a hardship on parents, students, and institutions." 120 Cong. Rec. 39863 (1974) (joint statement). It is implausible to presume that the same Congress nonetheless intended private suits to be brought before thousands of federal-and state-court judges, which could only result in the sort of "multiple interpretations" the Act explicitly sought to avoid.

JUSTICE BREYER with whom JUSTICE SOUTER joins, concurring in the judgment.

The ultimate question, in respect to whether private individuals may bring a lawsuit to enforce a federal statute, through 42 U.S.C. § 1983 or otherwise, is a question of congressional intent. In my view, the factors set forth in this Court's § 1983 cases are helpful indications of that intent. But the statute books are too many, the laws too diverse, and their purposes too complex, for any single legal formula to offer more than general guidance. I would not, in effect, pre-determine an outcome through the use of a presumption—such as the majority's presumption that a right is conferred only if set forth "unambiguously" in the statute's "text and structure." * * * [For the reasons given in the majority opinion, Justices Breyer and Souter were nevertheless convinced that FERPA created no individual rights enforceable through an action under § 1983.]

JUSTICE STEVENS with whom JUSTICE GINSBURG joins, dissenting.

The Court's *ratio decidendi* in this case has a "now you see it, now you don't character." At times, the Court seems to hold that * * * FERPA simply does not create any federal rights, thereby disposing of the case with a negative answer to the question "whether Congress intended to *create a federal right*." This interpretation would explain the Court's studious avoidance of the rights-creating language in the title and the text of the Act. Alternatively, its opinion may be read as accepting the proposition that FERPA does indeed create both parental rights of access to student records and student rights of privacy in such records, but that those federal rights are of a lesser value because Congress did not intend them to be enforceable by their owners. I shall first explain why the statute does, indeed, create federal rights, and then explain why the Court's novel attempt to craft a new category of second-class statutory rights is misguided.

I.

Title 20 U.S.C. § 1232g, which embodies FERPA in its entirety, includes 10 subsections, which create rights for both students and their parents, and describe the procedures for enforcing and protecting those rights. Subsection (a)(1)(A) accords parents "the right to inspect and review the education records of their children." Subsection (a)(1)(D) provides that a "student or a person applying for admission" may waive "his right of access" to certain confidential statements. Two separate provisions protect students' privacy rights: subsection (a)(2) refers to "the privacy rights of students," and subsection (c) protects "the rights of privacy of students and their families." And subsection (d) provides that after a student has attained the age of 18, "the rights accorded to the parents of the student" shall thereafter be extended to the student. Given such explicit rights-creating language, the title of the statute, which describes "family educational rights," is appropriate. The entire statutory scheme was designed to protect such rights.

Of course, as we have stated previously, a "blanket approach" to determining whether a statute creates rights enforceable under 42 U.S.C. § 1983 is inappropriate. *Blessing v. Freestone*. The precise statutory provision at issue in this case is § 1232g(b). Although the rights-creating language in this subsection is not as explicit as it is in other parts of the statute, it is clear that, in substance, § 1232g(b) formulates an individual right: in respondent's words, the "right of parents to withhold consent and prevent the unauthorized release of education record information by an educational institution * * * that has a policy or practice of releasing such information." This provision plainly meets the standards we articulated in *Blessing* for establishing a federal right: It is directed to the benefit of individual students and parents; the provision is binding on States, as it is "couched in mandatory, rather than precatory, terms"; and the right is far from "vague and amorphous." Indeed, the right at issue is more specific and clear than rights previously found enforceable under § 1983. [citing *Wright*] * * *

The Court claims that § 1232g(b), because it references a "policy or practice," has an aggregate focus and thus cannot qualify as an individual right. But § 1232g(b) does not simply ban an institution from having a policy or practice—which would be a more systematic requirement. Rather, it permits a policy or practice of releasing information, *so long as* "there is written consent from the student's parents specifying records to be released, the reasons for such release, and to whom, and with a copy of the records to be released to the student's parents and the student if desired by the parents." The provision speaks of the individual "student," not students generally. In light of FERPA's stated purpose to "protect such individuals' rights to privacy by limiting the transferability of their records without their consent," 120 Cong. Rec. 39862 (1974) (statement of Sen. Buckley), the individual focus of § 1232g(b) is manifest. Moreover, simply because a "pattern or practice" is a precondition to individual relief does not mean that the right asserted is not an individually enforceable right.

* * * The Court also claims that "we have never before held * * * that spending legislation drafted in terms resembling those of FERPA can confer enforceable rights." In making this claim, the Court contrasts FERPA's "no funds shall be made available" language with "individually focused terminology" characteristic of federal antidiscrimination statutes, such as "no person shall be subjected to discrimination." But the sort of rights-creating language idealized by the Court has *never* been present in our § 1983 cases; rather, such language ordinarily gives rise to an implied cause of action. None of our four most recent cases involving whether a Spending Clause statute created rights enforceable under § 1983—*Wright*, *Wilder*, *Suter*, and *Blessing*—involved the sort of "no person shall" rights-creating language envisioned by the Court.

Although a "presumptively enforceable" right, has been created by § 1232g(b), one final question remains. As our cases recognize, Congress can rebut the presumption of enforcement under § 1983 either "expressly, by forbidding recourse to § 1983 in the statute itself, or impliedly, by creating a comprehensive enforcement scheme that is incompatible with individual enforcement [actions]." FERPA has not explicitly foreclosed enforcement under § 1983. The only question then is whether the administrative enforcement mechanisms provided by the statute are "comprehensive" and "incompatible" with § 1983 actions. * * * [FERPA's] administrative avenues fall far short of what is necessary to overcome the presumption of enforceability. We have only found a comprehensive administrative scheme precluding enforceability under § 1983 in two of our past cases—*Middlesex County Sewerage Authority v. National Sea Clammers Assn.*, 453 U.S. 1 (1981), and *Smith v. Robinson*, 468 U.S. 992 (1984). In *Sea Clammers*, the relevant statute not only had "unusually elaborate enforcement procedures," but it also permitted private citizens to bring enforcement actions in court. In *Smith*, the statute at issue provided for "carefully tailored" administrative proceedings followed by federal judicial review. In contrast, FERPA provides no guaranteed access to a formal administrative proceedings or to federal judicial review; rather, it leaves to administrative discretion the decision whether to follow up on individual complaints. As we said in *Blessing*, the enforcement scheme here is "far more limited than those in *Sea Clammers* and *Smith*," and thus does not preclude enforcement under § 1983.

II.

Since FERPA was enacted in 1974, all of the Federal Courts of Appeals expressly deciding the question have concluded that FERPA creates federal rights enforceable under § 1983. Nearly all other federal and state courts reaching the issue agree with these Circuits. Congress has not overruled these decisions by amending FERPA to expressly preclude recourse to § 1983. And yet, the Court departs from over a quarter century of settled law in concluding that FERPA creates no enforceable rights. Perhaps more pernicious than its disturbing of the settled status of FERPA rights, though, is the Court's novel use of our implied right of action cases in determining whether a federal right exists for § 1983 purposes.

In my analysis of whether § 1232g(b) creates a right for § 1983 purposes, I have assumed the Court's forthrightness in stating that the question presented is "whether Congress intended to create a federal right," and that "plaintiff's suing under § 1983 do not have the burden showing an intent to create a private remedy." Rather than proceeding with a straightforward analysis under these principles, however, the Court has undermined both of these assertions by needlessly borrowing from cases involving implied rights of action—cases which place a more exacting standard on plaintiffs. By using these cases, the Court now appears to require a heightened showing from § 1983 plaintiffs: "If

Congress wishes to create new rights enforceable under § 1983, it must do so in clear and unambiguous terms—no less and no more than what is required for Congress to create new rights enforceable under an implied private right of action."

A requirement that Congress intend a "right to support a cause of action," as opposed to simply the creation of an individual federal right, makes sense in the implied right of action context. As we have explained, our implied right of action cases "reflect a concern, grounded in separation of powers, that Congress rather than the courts controls the availability of remedies for violations of statutes." However, imposing the implied right of action framework upon the § 1983 inquiry, is not necessary: The separation-of-powers "concerns present in the implied right of action context" are not present in a § 1983 case, "because Congress expressly authorized private suits in § 1983 itself. * * * "

If it were true, as the Court claims, that the implied right of action and § 1983 inquiries neatly "overlap in one meaningful respect—in either case we must first determine whether Congress *intended to create a federal right*," then I would have less trouble referencing implied right of action precedent to determine whether a federal right exists. Contrary to the Court's suggestion, however, our implied right of action cases do not necessarily cleanly separate out the "right" question from the "cause of action" question. For example, in the discussion of rights-creating language in *Cannon*, which the Court characterizes as pertaining only to whether there is a right, *Cannon's* reasoning is explicitly based on whether there is "reason to infer a private remedy," and the "propriety of implication of a cause of action." Because *Cannon* and other implied right of action cases do not clearly distinguish the questions of "right" and "cause of action," it is inappropriate to use these cases to determine whether a statute creates rights enforceable under § 1983. * * *

By defining the § 1983 plaintiff's burden concerning "whether a statute confers any right at all," as whether "Congress nonetheless intended private suits to be brought before thousands of federal-and state-court judges," the Court has collapsed the ostensible two parts of the implied right of action test ("is there a right" and "is it enforceable") into one. As result, and despite its statement to the contrary, the Court seems to place the unwarranted "burden of showing an intent to create a private remedy," on § 1983 plaintiffs. Moreover, by circularly defining a right actionable under § 1983 as, in essence, "a right which Congress intended to make enforceable," the Court has eroded—if not eviscerated—the long-established principle of presumptive enforceability of rights under § 1983. Under this reading of the Court's opinion, a right under *Blessing* is second class compared to a right whose enforcement Congress has clearly intended. Creating such a hierarchy of rights is not only novel, but it blurs the long-recognized distinction between rights and remedies. And it does nothing to clarify our § 1983 jurisprudence.

Accordingly, I respectfully dissent.

Statutory Exclusion of § 1983 Claims

In *Blessing* the Supreme Court noted that plaintiffs may satisfy the three factor test for asserting a right under § 1983, yet fail to state a cause of action because Congress has expressly or impliedly denied them an action. But, the opinion further explained that such findings had been rare:

> "Because we leave open the possibility that Title IV–D may give rise to some individually enforceable rights, we pause to consider petitioner's final argument that no remand is warranted because the statute contains 'a remedial scheme that is' sufficiently comprehensive * * * to demonstrate congressional intent to preclude the remedy of suits under § 1983." Because petitioner does not claim that any provision of Title IV–D expressly curtails § 1983 actions, she must make the difficult showing that allowing § 1983 actions to go forward in these circumstances "would be inconsistent with Congress's carefully tailored scheme." *Golden State.*
>
> Only twice have we found a remedial scheme sufficiently comprehensive to supplant § 1983: in [*Middlesex County Sewerage Authority v. National Sea Clammers*, 453 U.S. 1 (1981)] and *Smith v. Robinson*, 468 U.S. 992 (1984). In *Sea Clammers*, we focused on the "unusually elaborate enforcement provisions" of the Federal Water Pollution Control Act, which placed at the disposal of the Environmental Protection Agency a panoply of enforcement options, including noncompliance orders, civil suits, and criminal penalties. We emphasized that several provisions of the Act authorized private persons to initiate enforcement actions. We found it "hard to believe that Congress intended to preserve the § 1983 right of action when it created so many specific statutory remedies, including the two citizen-suit provisions." Likewise, in *Smith*, the review scheme in the Education of the Handicapped Act permitted aggrieved individuals to invoke "carefully tailored" local administrative procedures followed by federal judicial review. We reasoned that Congress could not possibly have wanted parents to skip these procedures and go straight to court by way of § 1983, since that would have "rendered superfluous most of the detailed procedural protections outlined in the statute."
>
> We have also stressed that a plaintiff's ability to invoke § 1983 cannot be defeated simply by "the availability of administrative mechanisms to protect the plaintiff's interest." *Golden State.* Thus, in *Wright*, we rejected the argument that the Secretary of Housing and Urban Development's "generalized powers" to audit local public housing authorities, to enforce annual contributions contracts, and to cut off federal funding demonstrated a congressional intention to prevent public housing tenants from using § 1983 to enforce their rights under the federal Housing Act. We reached much the same

conclusion in *Wilder* where the Secretary of Health and Human Services had power to reject state Medicaid plans or to withhold federal funding to States whose plans did not comply with federal law. Even though in both cases these oversight powers were accompanied by limited state grievance procedures for individuals, we found that § 1983 was still available.

The enforcement scheme that Congress created in Title IV–D is far more limited than those in *Sea Clammers* and *Smith*. Unlike the federal programs at issue in those cases, Title IV–D contains no private remedy—either judicial or administrative—through which aggrieved persons can seek redress. The only way that Title IV–D assures that States live up to their child support plans is through the Secretary's oversight. The Secretary can audit only for "substantial compliance" on a programmatic basis. Furthermore, up to 25 percent of eligible children and custodial parents can go without most of the services enumerated in Title IV–D before the Secretary can trim a State's AFDC grant. These limited powers to audit and cut federal funding closely resemble those powers at issue in *Wilder* and *Wright*. Although counsel for the Secretary suggested at oral argument that the Secretary "has the same right under a contract as any other party to seek specific performance," this possibility was not developed in the briefs. Even assuming the Secretary's authority to sue for specific performance, Title VI–D's administrative enforcement arsenal would not compare to those in *Sea Clammers* and *Smith*, especially if, as the Government further contended, no private actor would have standing to force the Secretary to bring suit for specific performance. To the extent that Title VI–D may give rise to individual rights, therefore, we agree with the Court of Appeals that the Secretary's oversight powers are not comprehensive enough to close the door on § 1983 liability.

The *Gonzaga* opinions suggest that, *Blessing's* assurances notwithstanding, alternative remedies well short of those provided in *Sea Clammers* and *Smith v. Robinson* might be held to preclude finding a "right" susceptible of enforcement via § 1983. And, the trend toward more loosely coupled state-federal arrangements, such as "block grants," may (a) lessen the tendency to find that federal grant statutes create individual rights and (b) support an inference that Congress intends to preclude private enforcement. For example, the AFDC program established by Title IV of the Social Security Act and featured in many of the leading § 1983 cases has now been replaced by a block grant program of Temporary Assistance to Needy Families (TANF) under the Personal Responsibility and Work Improvement Act of 1996, 42 U.S.C. § 601 *et seq*. In TANF the Congress made clear that it intended to create no individual federal "entitlement" for program beneficiaries. See generally Jerry L. Mashaw and Dylan Calsyn, *Block Grants, Entitlements and Federalism: A Conceptual Map of Contested Terrain*, 14 Yale L. & Pol'y Rev. 297 (1996). This "rethinking" of federal-state relations under § 1983 has gained added impetus from the Court's parallel reconsideration of the reach of state sovereign immunity under the Tenth and Eleventh Amendments and of congressional power to enforce civil rights pursuant to any of the Civil War Amendments.

State Sovereign Immunity, Congressional Power and § 1983

Justice Rehnquist's cryptic reference in *Pennhurst* to *Edelman v. Jordan*, and to the "difficult questions" that Eleventh Amendment immunity might pose, was a harbinger of jurisprudential developments that now cast a long shadow over remedial actions brought pursuant to 42 U.S.C. § 1983. Adopted to overturn the Supreme Court's decision in *Chisholm v. Georgia*, 2 U.S. (2 Dall.) 419 (1793), the Eleventh Amendment imposes a special barrier to suits against state governments. The amendment provides: "The judicial power of the United States shall not be construed to extend to any suit in law or equity * * * against one of the United States by Citizens of another State. * * * "But the narrow language of the Eleventh Amendment's text is deceptive if taken as a guide to the reach of state sovereign immunity. For the Supreme Court has interpreted this language to bar unconsented suits against a state by its own citizens, see, e.g., *Employees v. Department of Public Health and Welfare*, 411 U.S. 279 (1973), and has extended state sovereign immunity to suits under federal law in state courts, *Alden v. Maine*, 527 U.S. 706 (1999), even where Congress attempts to foreclose state immunity pursuant to its Article 1 powers and the Supremacy Clause, *Florida Prepaid Postsecondary Educ. Expense Bd. v. College Sav. Bank*, 527 U.S. 627 (1999); *Seminole Tribe of Florida v. Florida*, 517 U.S. 44 (1996). Indeed, the locus of state sovereign immunity has been relocated to the Tenth Amendment and the constitution's basic federal structure. As a fundamental constitutional principle, state sovereign immunity now also sharply restricts congressional authority to eliminate state sovereign immunity when implementing the Civil War Amendments. *Board of Trustees v. Garrett*, 531 U.S. 356 (2001); *Kimel v. Florida*, 528 U.S. 62 (2000). Enacted as part of the Civil Rights Acts of 1866, § 1983 is, of course, just such an exercise of congressional power.

We cannot here plumb the depths of state immunity under the Eleventh Amendment or otherwise. Every term of the Supreme Court now seems to bring at least one new and ever-more complicated opinion on state sovereign immunity. The literature, most of it critical, grows apace. See generally John T. Noonan, Narrowing the Nation's Power: The Supreme Court Sides with the States (2002); *Symposium: Shifting the Balance of Power? The Supreme Court, Federalism, and State Sovereign Immunity*, 53 Stan. L. Rev. 1115 (2001); Carlos Manuel V'Azquez, *What is Eleventh Amendment Immunity?*, 106 Yale L.J. 1683 (1997). Our interest is in two more limited questions: (1) how has sovereign immunity doctrine affected the Supreme Court's construction of § 1983; and (2) to what extent does state sovereign immunity bar relief for plaintiffs pursuing § 1983 actions? The two questions are closely connected and speak to Justice Stevens' concern in *Sandoval* that the U.S. Code is now divided between first and second class rights.

Prior to the mid–1990s, one might have said that the difficulties facing § 1983 plaintiffs when confronted with a claim of state sovereign immunity were quite modest. Private plaintiffs could easily escape the sovereign immunity bar by naming state officials, rather than the state itself, as defendants. In *Ex Parte Young*, 209 U.S. 123 (1908), the Supreme Court held that the Eleventh Amendment did not bar a federal court injunction against a state officer who was acting unconstitutionally. In short, a plaintiff might claim not to be suing the state, even where, as in *Ex Parte Young*, the theory of the case required that "state action" be the basis for the law suit.

The *Ex Parte Young* dodge, the state sovereign immunity analogue of *Larson v. Domestic and Foreign Commerce Corp.*, *supra* p. 876, did not permit relief directly against the state, that is, where the remedy would necessarily come from the state treasury. As early as 1945, in *Ford Motor Co. v. Department of the Treasury*, 323 U.S. 459, the Court had said: "[W]hen the action is in essence for recovery of money from the state, the state is the real, substantial party in interest and is entitled to invoke its sovereign immunity from suit, even though individual officers are nominal defendants." *Ford Motor* involved a tax refund, but the same principles were applied to later cases where relief transparently involved a payment out of the state treasury. See, e.g., *Edelman v. Jordan*, 415 U.S. 651 (1974) (a case involving a suit for past due benefits under the grant-in-aid program of aid for the aged, blind and totally and permanently disabled, the predecessor of the current federal Supplemental Security Income (SSI) program.)

Yet, as the plaintiffs in *Thiboutot* clearly believed, the *Ford Motor* and *Edelman* rulings would not foreclose § 1983 suits, even those requiring relief form the state treasury, where those suits were brought in state rather than federal court. Cases such as *Howlett v. Rose*, 496 U.S. 356 (1990), and *Reich v. Collins*, 513 U.S. 106 (1994), seemed to confirm this understanding. In *Howlett* the Supreme Court held that Florida state courts could not exclude § 1983 suits against local governments from their courts under a state law provision extending state sovereign immunity to municipalities. The *Howlett* court relied on a long line of cases, including cases enunciating what is often called the "nondiscrimination principle," which states that state governments may not discriminate against federal law when deciding how widely to open the courthouse door.

To be sure there were some bumps in the road leading to effective enforcement of § 1983. In a confusing opinion, *Will v. Michigan Department of State Police*, 491 U.S. 58 (1989), the Supreme Court held that, not only states, but also state officials "acting in their official capacities" are outside the class of "persons" subject to liability under § 1983. Such a lawsuit would not lie, therefore, even in a state court. In some sense this is true of virtually all § 1983 suits. *Will*, therefore, seemed to undermine the longstanding fiction established by *Ex Parte Young*.

The Supreme Court sought to clear up this confusion, but may have only deepened it, in *Hafer v. Melo*, 502 U.S. 21 (1991). The *Hafer* opinion first makes clear that *Will* has no application to situations in which the official is sued in her "personal capacity." In rejecting the state officer's claim that she could only fire the state-employee plaintiff while acting in her "official capacity," the Court developed the exquisite distinction between "acting" in one's official capacity and being "sued" in it. According to the *Hafer* opinion, so long as plaintiffs sued defendants in their "personal capacity" their suit would not be barred.

It is hard to read the Supreme Court's language in *Hafer v. Melo* and not conclude that it was the state official who was taking *Will v. Michigan Department of State Police* seriously and the Court who was transforming *Will* into the "mere pleading device" that the *Hafer* opinion itself denies. Indeed, surveying all District Court cases for the period 1990–1995, John C. Jeffries, *In Praise of the Eleventh Amendment and § 1983*, 84 Va.L.Rev. 47 (1998), finds that those courts routinely interpreted § 1983 complaints as suing officials in their "personal capacity," even when plaintiffs' counsel were insufficiently attentive to include the talismanic verbiage. One might conclude, therefore, that *Will* places no more constraint on § 1983 actions for damages than *Ex Parte Young* places on suits for injunctions for violations of constitutional rights.

Nevertheless, Jeffries argues that this pleading convention has important substantive effects—it makes clear that § 1983 litigation must proceed, not against the state under a congressional waiver of state sovereign immunity, but against an official who can plead at least qualified immunity from suit. And, because the test for qualified immunity is very similar to a demand that the plaintiff show that the official was at fault—not just that he or she violated a constitutional or statutory provision—some variant of a fault requirement is thereby maintained in § 1983 actions. Jeffries goes on to argue that this is a good thing, although he recognizes that his position is controversial. Thus, although the Eleventh Amendment may change the criteria for the evaluation of official action under § 1983, it seldom bars pursuit of those actions. Jeffries' conclusion on this matter bears quotation:

> The Eleventh Amendment has survived not because it means so much but precisely because it means so little. If it were not possible to circumvent the Eleventh Amendment through § 1983, the Supreme Court would long ago have adopted * * * some * * * construction, such as that invented for prospective relief in *Ex Parte Young*. Put another way, *Monroe v. Pape* is the *Ex parte Young* of retrospective relief. Just as the fiction of *Ex Parte Young* routinely allows civil plaintiffs to evade the Eleventh Amendment when they seek injunctive relief, *Monroe v. Pape* (almost as) routinely allows civil rights plaintiffs to evade the Eleventh Amendment when they seek money damages.

Yet others saw trouble ahead for § 1983 plaintiffs, and indeed questioned the durability of *Ex Parte Young* in the wake of the Supreme Court's opinion in *Seminole Tribe of Florida v. Florida*, 517 U.S. 44 (1996). *See* Henry P. Monaghan, *Comment: The Sovereign Immunity "Exception,"* 110 Harv.L.Rev. 102 (1996). *Seminole Tribe* involved a suit under the Indian Gaming Regulatory Act (IGRA) which provided that certain gaming activities (including casino gambling) were lawful on Indian lands if those activities were authorized by tribal law, located in a state that permitted such gambling and conducted in conformance with a compact between the Tribe and the state. The IGRA also provides:

> United States District Courts shall have jurisdiction over—(i) any cause of action initiated by an Indian Tribe arising from the failure of the State to enter into negotiations with the Indian Tribe for the purpose of entering into a tribal-state compact * * * or to conduct such negotiations in good faith. * * *

Florida argued that this jurisdictional provision was unconstitutional under the Eleventh Amendment. The Supreme Court agreed. While dictum in *Seminole Tribe* confirms that Congress can abrogate state sovereign immunity when enforcing the provisions of the Fourteenth Amendment (as was held in *Fitzpatrick v. Bitzer*, 427 U.S. 445 (1976)) it overrules the decision in *Pennsylvania v. Union Gas Co.*, 491 U.S. 1 (1989), the only Supreme Court decision directly recognizing congressional power to abrogate Eleventh Amendment immunity pursuant to the Interstate Commerce Clause. Later cases, of course, confirmed that Congress had no power under any provision of Article 1 to override state sovereign immunity. *Florida Prepaid Postsecondary Educ. Expense Bd., supra.*

The decision in *Seminole Tribe* bears on *Ex Parte Young* and on § 1983 because the plaintiffs had also sued the Governor of Florida individually. The remedy sought was prospective in nature, and that alone would generally be sufficient to allow the suit to go forward. However, the Court held that the Governor could not be sued pursuant to *Ex Parte Young*. It premised that conclusion on its view that the remedial scheme developed in the IGRA was a carefully crafted and comprehensive congressional attempt to deal with the relationship between states and Indian tribes on the subject of reservation gambling. Because the remedy in *Ex Parte Young* is "constitutional common law," not constitutional law full stop, the Court concluded that the Congress could, adopting a comprehensive statutory remedial scheme, exclude an otherwise applicable constitutional-common-law remedy.

The implications of *Seminole Tribe* for § 1983 jurisprudence follow from the obvious fact that the suit against the Governor, in his personal capacity, could have been premised on § 1983. Should we then take *Seminole Tribe* to mean that the Congress can not provide § 1983 actions against officials where an action against the state would be barred by the Eleventh Amendment? Although confident assertions are treacherous wherever the Eleventh Amendment is implicated, one is tempted to answer, "Surely not." Section 1983 is, after all, part of a statute adopted precisely to enforce Section Five of the Fourteenth Amendment. Moreover, the limitation on *Ex Parte Young* litigation enunciated in *Seminole Tribe*, goes no further than similar limitations that have been placed on § 1983 actions where the Congress has adopted a "comprehensive remedial scheme." Yet, later cases suggest caution.

The plaintiffs in *Alden v. Maine*, 527 U.S. 706 (1999), were suing for back wages under the Federal Fair Labor Standards Act—a statute that contains an explicit congressional abrogation of state immunity. Having been thrown out of federal court on sovereign immunity grounds, plaintiffs repaired to state court where, presumably, the Eleventh Amendment did not apply.

Wrong, held the Supreme Court. A bare majority of the court engaged in a wide-ranging review of Eleventh Amendment jurisprudence and concluded that the Eleventh Amendment was not the major obstacle to the plaintiff's claim. According to the majority, the Eleventh Amendment had merely reestablished the fundamental principle of state sovereign immunity that *Chisholm v. Georgia* had ignored. That fundamental principle of state sovereign immunity, enshrined in the structure of the Constitution and particularly in the Tenth Amendment, preserves the essential "dignity" of the sovereign states. In the majority's view the framers could not have intended that these state sovereigns suffer the indignity of being hauled into their own courts without their consent pursuant to an exercise of the Congress's Article I powers. In the Court's words:

> The Eleventh Amendment makes explicit reference to the State's immunity from suits "commenced or prosecuted against one of the United States by Citizens of another State, or by Citizens or Subjects of any Foreign State." U.S. Const., Amdt. 11. We have, as a result, sometimes referred to the States' immunity from suit as "Eleventh Amendment immunity." The phrase is a convenient shorthand but something of a misnomer, for the sovereign immunity of the States neither derives from nor is limited by the terms of the Eleventh Amendment. Rather, as the Constitution's structure, and its history, and the authoritative interpretations by this Court make clear, the States' immunity from suit is a fundamental aspect of the sovereignty which the States enjoyed before the ratification of the Constitution, and which they retain today (either literally or by virtue of their admission into the Union upon an equal footing with the other States) except as altered by the plan of the Convention or certain constitutional Amendments.

Revisiting its earlier cases that seemed to preserve actions based on federal law brought in state court, the court reinterpreted *Reich v. Collins* as holding only "that, despite its immunity from suit in federal court, a State which holds out what plainly appears to be 'a clear and certain' post-deprivation remedy for taxes collected in violation of federal law may not declare, after disputed taxes have been paid in reliance on this remedy, that the remedy does not in fact exist." The Court went on to find that there was no evidence that Maine had manipulated its state immunity in a systematic fashion to discriminate against federal causes of action. Hence, the Court found no violation of the *Howlett v. Rose* nondiscrimination principle.

Alden can be read as having little impact on § 1983 actions. See, e.g., Stephen H. Steinglass, *Eleventh Amendment Federalism in State Sovereign Immunity Cases: Direct Effect on § 1983*, 16 Touro L. Rev. 769 (2000). *Alden* is, after all, not a § 1983 case. Moreover, the Supreme Court had held in *Will* that states were not "persons" within the meaning the § 1983. That principle applied in state as well as federal court, and on that view *Alden* adds little but federalism hyperbole to *Seminole Tribes'* determination that Article I does not permit Congress to abrogate state sovereign immunity.

Indeed, the Supreme Court's opinion in *Alden v. Maine* confirms that Congress retains power to eliminate state sovereign immunity when enforcing the Fourteenth Amendment, the presumed source of Congress' constitutional authority when enacting § 1983. As the *Alden v. Maine* opinion put the matter:

> We have held also that in adopting the Fourteenth Amendment, the people required the States to surrender a portion of the sovereignty that had been preserved to them by the original Constitution, so that Congress may authorize private suits against nonconsenting States pursuant to its § 5 enforcement power. *Fitzpatrick v. Bitzer*. By imposing explicit limits on the powers of the States and granting Congress the power to enforce them, the Amendment "fundamentally altered the balance of state and federal power struck by the Constitution." *Seminole Tribe*. When Congress enacts appropriate legislation to enforce this Amendment, see *City of Boerne v. Flores*, 521 U.S. 507 (1997), federal interests are paramount, and Congress may assert an authority over the States which would be otherwise unauthorized by the Constitution.

There are problems with this narrow reading. *Alden* confirms congressional power to enforce constitutional rights established by the Civil War Amendments free from the interposition of state sovereign immunity. But, congressional power to enforce those amendments has been narrowing. Under the Court's decisions in *Kimel v. Florida Bd. Of Regents*, 528 U.S. 62 (2000), and *Board of Trustees v. Garrett*, 531 U.S. 356 (2001), Congress is permitted to enforce Section 5 of the Fourteenth Amendment only in situations where it finds, as a court might, that there has been a history and pattern of state discrimination that violate the Equal Protection Clause. Moreover, Congress is required to craft remedies that are congruent with and proportional to the findings of discrimination. See *Kimel*, 528 U.S. at 81–91, and *Garrett*, 531 U.S. at 368–75.

Taken together these cases might suggest a substantial narrowing of the reach of § 1983 as an effective remedy. First, as Justice Powell pointed out in *Thiboutot*, one can read § 1983 in a way that is "congruent" and "proportional" to the power conferred in § 5 of the Fourteenth Amendment by reading § 1983 to cover only constitutional claims and claims based on laws enforcing "civil rights." "Federal law" in § 1983 would thus be understood to mean "federal civil rights law, if constitutional under the Supreme Court's reinterpretation of Congress' § 5 powers." This would not only eliminate enforcement of most federal statutes under § 1983, but presumably lead back into the dusty records of the 1866 Congress to determine what specific civil rights it had in mind, and made findings about, when it adopted the 1866 Civil Rights Acts. Only remedies for those sorts of violations could conceivably be "congruent and proportional" to violations of the Fourteenth Amendment present in 1866.

In addition, it is hard to see how the maintenance of the *Ex Parte Young* fiction, or its *Monroe v. Pape* damages counterpart, could be consistent with the Court's new dignitary theory of the position of the states in the federal union. As the Court's contortions concerning "personal" versus "official" capacity in *Hafer* reveal, suits against officers are very thin veils to pull across the real party in interest—state governments who virtually always pay any damages levied against state officials. Nor does it seem consistent with this dignitary theory to continue to find, as the Court did in *Owen v. City of Independence*, 445 U.S. 622 (1980), that municipalities, as creatures of the states, are both "persons" for purposes of § 1983 and are not protected by the states' sovereign immunity.

In short, the Court's recent jurisprudence on state sovereign immunity and congressional power under the Civil War Amendments creates a jurisprudential "magnetic field," or perhaps "black hole," into which most § 1983 claims might be swept. Indeed, in a portion of the *Gonzaga* opinion not reproduced above, Justice Rehnquist cited some of the Court's state sovereign immunity cases as representative of the federalism principles that might be violated by finding "rights" enforceable under § 1983 in federal statutes that did not unambiguously create them. And, as *Kimel* and *Garrett* attest, lack of ambiguity may be only a starting point for determining whether a federal statute can constitutionally invoke a § 1983 remedy.

Yet, it may be imprudent to read even broadly-worded opinions broadly. Where notions of federalism are implicated the only stable feature of the Supreme Court's recent jurisprudence may be the division between Chief Justice Rehnquist and Justices Kennedy, O'Connor, Scalia and Thomas on the one hand, and Justices Breyer, Ginsburg, Souter and Stevens on the other. Perhaps exasperated by the continuing necessity to write extended dissenting opinions, Justice Souter ends his dissent in *Alden v. Maine* with the prediction that only continuing instability lies ahead:

> The resemblance of today's state sovereign immunity to the *Lochner* era's industrial due process is striking. The Court began the century

by imputing immutable constitutional status to a conception of economic self-reliance that was never true to industrial life and grew instantly fictional with the years, and the Court has chosen to close this century by conferring like status on a conception of state sovereign immunity that is true neither to history nor to the structure of the Constitution. I expect the court's late essay into immunity doctrine will prove the equal of its early experiment in *laissez-faire,* one being as unrealistic as the other, as indefensible, and probably as fleeting.

In invoking the ghost of *Lochner*, Justice Souter may not have gone far enough back in American history. To read much of the Court's current jurisprudence, whether in majority opinions or in dissent, is to be cast back into the late Eighteenth Century and an apparent attempt to reconstruct the legal mind of 1787. These historical exegeses are often interesting, even instructive, and lure commentators to try to better the Court's "judicial chambers" history. See Caleb Nelson, *Sovereign Immunity as a Doctrine of Personal Jurisdiction*, 115 Harv. L. Rev. 1561 (2002) (suggesting that the Court has consistently confused ideas of personal jurisdiction and subject matter jurisdiction that Eighteenth Century lawyers understood to be distinct). The question remains, however, as Justice Souter's dissent in *Alden* also notes, what this quaint enterprise has to do with the appropriate structure of remedies for the peculiar federal-state division of responsibilities in the American administrative state of the Twenty–First Century.

Federalism, *Chevron*, and the Enforcement of Federal Regulations Under § 1983

The test enunciated in *Blessing v. Freestone* requires first that Congress intend that a statutory provision "benefit the plaintiff"; second, that the right asserted not be "vague and amorphous"; and finally, that the statute impose unambiguous obligations on the states. The *Gonzaga* majority makes clear its understanding that the first requirement must be distinguished from the sort of intent to benefit that might confer standing under the *ADAPSO* zone of interests test. The statute must instead indicate a congressional intent to confer a "right" that is individualized, that is, targeted on "a particular class of persons." And, as the dissenting Justices note, the majority opinion also seems to require that such rights be "unambiguously conferred."

This sort of language casts doubt on the use of § 1983 to enforce federal rights articulated in federal agencies' regulations, at least where the statute itself omits rights-conferring language. Yet, this position potentially conflicts with the Court's approach to agency rulemaking power under *Chevron*. For, if an agency's regulations particularize ambiguous statutory terms and thus confer rights on identifiable persons, *Chevron* deference would suggest that the agency interpretation embodied in the regulations should be respected, unless unreasonable. In this context, the Supreme Court's federalism jurisprudence seems to be on a collision course with *Chevron* deference.

The Court has never addressed directly the question of using § 1983 to enforce federal agency regulations. In *Wright,* and other § 1983 cases, the Court has seemed to assume that valid regulations would be given deference in situations in which the statute itself seemed to create rights. Justice Scalia says as much in his opinion in *Sandoval.* But remember that Justice Stevens' dissent in *Sandoval* is based, in part, on his belief that the majority has failed to give appropriate deference to the Justice Department's interpretation of § 602 of the Civil Rights Act. Hence, the Supreme Court's jurisprudence suggests little more than that agency regulations might, by particularizing a statute's requirements, help satisfy the *Blessing* demand that such requirements not be "vague or amorphous."

In the face of this uncertainty the courts of appeals have divided—or perhaps fractured would be the better term—concerning the role of § 1983 in enforcing agency regulations. Some seem to assume that regulations can be used to satisfy any of the prongs of the *Blessing* test, others use regulations only to clarify vague or ambiguous language. Yet others seem unwilling to consider regulations as a means of satisfying any of the *Blessing* factors. It remains to be seen whether the Supreme Court's commitment to a federalism-based textualism (that clearly dominates the Eleventh Amendment jurisprudence) will triumph over its commitment to *Chevron* deference, or vice versa. For an argument that *Chevron* should triumph because § 1983 review of state implementation serves both state and national interests, see Brian D. Galle, *Can Federal Agencies Authorize Private Suits Under § 1983?: A Theoretical Approach*, 68 Brook.L.Rev. ___ (forthcoming Sept. 2003).

E. SUBSTITUTION OF PUBLIC FOR PRIVATE RIGHTS

1. PRIMARY JURISDICTION

NADER v. ALLEGHENY AIRLINES, INC.

Supreme Court of the United States, 1976.
426 U.S. 290, 96 S.Ct. 1978, 48 L.Ed.2d 643.

JUSTICE POWELL delivered the opinion of the Court.

In this case we address the question whether a common-law tort action based on alleged fraudulent misrepresentation by an air carrier subject to regulation by the Civil Aeronautics Board (Board) must be stayed pending reference to the Board for determination whether the practice is "deceptive" within the meaning of § 411 of the Federal Aviation Act of 1958, 49 U.S.C. § 1381 (1970). We hold that under the circumstances of this case a stay pending reference is inappropriate.

I.

The facts are not contested. Petitioner agreed to make several appearances in Connecticut on April 28, 1972, in support of the fundraising efforts of the Connecticut Citizen Action Group (CCAG), a nonprofit public interest organization. * * * On April 25, petitioner reserved a seat on respondent's flight 864 for April 28. The flight was scheduled to leave Washington, D.C., at 10:15 a.m. and to arrive in Hartford at 11:15 a.m. * * *

Petitioner arrived at the boarding and check-in area approximately five minutes before the scheduled departure time. He was informed that all seats on the flight were occupied and that he, like several other passengers who had arrived shortly before him, could not be accommodated. * * *

Both parties agree that petitioner's reservation was not honored because respondent had accepted more reservations for flight 864 than it could in fact accommodate. One hour prior to the flight, 107 reservations had been confirmed for the 100 seats actually available. Such overbooking is a common industry practice, designed to ensure that each flight leaves with as few empty seats as possible despite the large number of "no-shows"—reservation-holding passengers who do not appear at flight time. * * * The chance that any particular passenger will be bumped is so negligible that few prospective passengers aware of the possibility would give it a second thought. * * * Nevertheless, the total number of confirmed ticket holders denied seats is quite substantial, numbering over 82,000 passengers in 1972 and about 76,000 in 1973.

Board regulations require each airline to establish priority rules for boarding passengers and to offer "denied boarding compensation" to bumped passengers. These "liquidated damages" are equal to the value of the passenger's ticket with a $25 minimum and a $200 maximum. Passengers are free to reject the compensation offered in favor of a common-law suit for damages suffered as a result of the bumping. Petitioner refused the tender of denied boarding compensation ($32.41 in his case) and, with CCAG, filed this suit for compensatory and punitive damages. His suit did not seek compensation for the bumping per se but asserted two other bases of liability: a common-law action based on fraudulent misrepresentation arising from respondent's alleged failure to inform petitioner in advance of its deliberate overbooking practices, and a statutory action under § 404(b) of the Act, 49 U.S.C. § 1374(b),[6] arising from respondent's alleged failure to afford petitioner the boarding priority specified in its rules filed with the Board under 14 CFR § 250.3 (1975).

The District Court entered a judgment for petitioner on both claims, awarding him a total of $10 in compensatory damages and $25,000 in punitive damages. Judgment also was entered for CCAG on its misrepre-

6. Section 404(b) provides:

"No air carrier or foreign air carrier shall make, give, or cause any undue or unreasonable preference or advantage to any particular person, port, locality, or description of traffic in air transportation in any respect whatsoever or subject any particular person, port, locality, or description of traffic in air transportation to any unjust discrimination or any undue or unreasonable prejudice or disadvantage in any respect whatsoever."

sentation claim, with an award of $51 in compensatory damages and $25,000 in punitive damages.

The Court of Appeals for the District of Columbia Circuit reversed. * * *

The only issue before us concerns the Court of Appeals' disposition of the merits of petitioner's claim of fraudulent misrepresentation. Although the court rejected respondent's argument that the existence of the Board's cease-and-desist power under § 411 of the Act eliminates all private remedies for common-law torts arising from unfair or deceptive practices by regulated carriers, it held that a determination by the Board that a practice is not deceptive within the meaning of § 411 would, as a matter of law, preclude a common-law tort action seeking damages for injuries caused by that practice.[7] Therefore, the court held that the Board must be allowed to determine in the first instance whether the challenged practice (in this case, the alleged failure to disclose the practice of overbooking) falls within the ambit of § 411. The court took judicial notice that a rulemaking proceeding concerning possible changes in reservation practices in response to the 1973–1974 fuel crisis was already underway and that a challenge to the carriers' overbooking practices had been raised by an intervenor in that proceeding.[8] The District Court was instructed to stay further action on petitioner's misrepresentation claim pending the outcome of the rulemaking proceeding. The Court of Appeals characterized its holding as "but another application of the principles of primary jurisdiction, a doctrine whose purpose is the coordination of the workings of agency and court."

II.

The question before us, then, is whether the Board must be given an opportunity to determine whether respondent's alleged failure to disclose its practice of deliberate overbooking is a deceptive practice under § 411 before petitioner's common-law action is allowed to proceed. * * *

Section 1106 of the Act, 49 U.S.C. § 1506 (1970), provides that "[n]othing contained in this chapter shall in any way abridge or alter the

7. Section 411 provides in full:

"The Board may, upon its own initiative or upon complaint by any air carrier, foreign air carrier, or ticket agent, if it considers that such action by it would be in the interest of the public, investigate and determine whether any air carrier, foreign air carrier, or ticket agent has been or is engaged in unfair or deceptive practices or unfair methods of competition in air transportation or the sale thereof. If the Board shall find, after notice and hearing, that such air carrier, foreign air carrier, or ticket agent is engaged in such unfair or deceptive practices or unfair methods of competition, it shall order such air carrier, foreign air carrier, or ticket agent to cease and desist from such practices or methods of competition."

8. * * *

In April of 1976 the Board announced a [second] proposed rulemaking proceeding with respect to deliberate overbooking and oversales. * * * The Board has decided to re-evaluate existing practices in light of a recent "trend toward a higher rate of oversales" and in light of the fact that oversales "continue to be a significant cause of [consumer] complaints." Among the options to be considered is a requirement that the practice of deliberate overbooking, if allowed to continue, be disclosed to customers.

remedies now existing at common law or by statute, but the provisions of this chapter are in addition to such remedies." The Court of Appeals found that "although the saving clause of section 1106 purports to speak in absolute terms it cannot be read so literally." In reaching this conclusion, it relied on *Texas & Pacific R. Co. v. Abilene Cotton Oil Co.*, 204 U.S. 426 (1907). * * *

In this case, unlike *Abilene*, we are not faced with an irreconcilable conflict between the statutory scheme and the persistence of common-law remedies. In *Abilene* the carrier, if subject to both agency and court sanctions, would be put in an untenable position when the agency and a court disagreed on the reasonableness of a rate. The carrier could not abide by the rate filed with the Commission, as required by statute, and also comply with a court's determination that the rate was excessive. The conflict between the court's common-law authority and the agency's ratemaking power was direct and unambiguous. The court in the present case, in contrast, is not called upon to substitute its judgment for the agency's on the reasonableness of a rate—or, indeed, on the reasonableness of any carrier practice. There is no Board requirement that air carriers engage in overbooking or that they fail to disclose that they do so. And any impact on rates that may result from the imposition of tort liability or from practices adopted by a carrier to avoid such liability would be merely incidental. Under the circumstances, the common-law action and the statute are not "absolutely inconsistent" and may coexist, as contemplated by § 1106.

Section 411 of the Act allows the Board, where "it considers that such action * * * would be in the interest of the public," "upon its own initiative or upon complaint by any air carrier, foreign air carrier, or ticket agent," to "investigate and determine whether any air carrier * * * has been or is engaged in unfair or deceptive practices or unfair methods of competition. * * * " Practices determined to be in violation of this section "shall" be the subject of a cease-and-desist order. The Court of Appeals concluded—and respondent does not challenge the conclusion here—that this section does not totally preclude petitioner's common-law tort action. But the Court of Appeals also held * * * that the Board has the power in a § 411 proceeding to approve practices that might otherwise be considered deceptive and thus to immunize carriers from common-law liability.

We cannot agree. No power to immunize can be derived from the language of § 411. And where Congress has sought to confer such power it has done so expressly, as in § 414 of the Act, 49 U.S.C. § 1384, which relieves those affected by certain designated orders (not including orders issued under § 411) "from the operations of the 'antitrust laws.' "When faced with an exemptive provision similar to § 414 in *United States Navigation Co. v. Cunard S.S. Co.*, 284 U.S. 474 (1932), this Court dismissed an antitrust action because initial consideration by the agency had not been sought. The Court pointed out that the Act in question was "restrictive in its operation upon some of the activities of common carriers * * *, and permissive in respect of others." Section 411, in contrast, is purely restrictive. It contemplates the elimination of "unfair or deceptive practices" that impair the public interest. Its role has been described in *American Airlines, Inc. v. North American Airlines, Inc.*, [351 U.S. 79 (1956)] at 85:

> " 'Unfair or deceptive practices or unfair methods of competition,' as used in § 411, are broader concepts than the common-law idea of unfair competition. * * * The section is concerned not with punishment of wrongdoing or protection of injured competitors, but rather with protection of the public interest."

As such, § 411 provides an injunctive remedy for vindication of the public interest to supplement the compensatory common-law remedies for private parties preserved by § 1106.

Thus, a violation of § 411, contrary to the Court of Appeals' conclusion, is not coextensive with a breach of duty under the common law. We note that the Board's jurisdiction to initiate an investigation under § 411 is expressly premised on a finding that the "public interest" is involved. * * * Indeed, individual consumers are not even entitled to initiate proceedings under § 411, a circumstance that indicates that Congress did not intend to require private litigants to obtain a § 411 determination before they could proceed with the common-law remedies preserved by § 1106.

Section 411 is both broader and narrower than the remedies available at common law. A cease-and-desist order may issue under § 411 merely on the Board's conclusion, after an investigation determined to be in the public interest, that a carrier is engaged in an "unfair or deceptive practice." No findings that the practice was intentionally deceptive or fraudulent or that it in fact has caused injury to an individual are necessary. On the other hand, a Board decision that a cease-and-desist order is inappropriate does not represent approval of the practice under investigation. It may merely represent the Board's conclusion that the serious prohibitory sanction of a cease-and-desist order is inappropriate, that a more flexible approach is necessary. A wrong may be of the sort that calls for compensation in an injured individual without requiring the extreme remedy of a cease-and-desist order. Indeed, the Board, in dealing with the problem of overbooking by air carriers, has declined to issue cease-and-desist orders, despite the determination by an examiner in one case that a § 411 violation had occurred. Instead, the Board has elected to establish boarding priorities and to ensure that passengers will be compensated for being bumped either by a liquidated sum under Board regulations or by resort to a suit for compensatory damages at common law.

In sum, § 411 confers upon the Board a new and powerful weapon against unfair and deceptive practices that injure the public. But it does not represent the only, or best, response to all challenged carrier actions that result in private wrongs.

The doctrine of primary jurisdiction "is concerned with promoting proper relationships between the courts and administrative agencies charged with particular regulatory duties." * * *

* * * In this case, however, considerations of uniformity in regulation and of technical expertise do not call for prior reference to the Board.

Petitioner seeks damages for respondent's failure to disclose its overbooking practices. He makes no challenge to any provision in the tariff, and indeed there is no tariff provision or Board regulation applicable to disclosure practices.[13] Petitioner also makes no challenge * * * to limitations on common-law damages imposed through exculpatory clauses included in a tariff.

Referral of the misrepresentation issue to the Board cannot be justified by the interest in informing the Court's ultimate decision with "the expert and specialized knowledge" * * * of the Board. The action brought by petitioner does not turn on a determination of the reasonableness of a challenged practice—a determination that could be facilitated by an informed evaluation of the economics or technology of the regulated industry. The standards to be applied in an action for fraudulent misrepresentation are within the conventional competence of the courts, and the judgment of a technically expert body is not likely to be helpful in the application of these standards to the facts of this case.[14]

We are particularly aware that, even where the wrong sought to be redressed is not misrepresentation but bumping itself, which has been the subject of Board consideration and for which compensation is provided in carrier tariffs, the Board has contemplated that there may be individual adjudications by courts in common-law suits brought at the option of the passenger. The present regulations dealing with the problems of overbooking and oversales were promulgated by the Board in 1967. They provide for denied boarding compensation to bumped passengers and require each carrier to establish priority rules for seating passengers and to file reports of passengers who could not be accommo-

13. In 1965, the Board proposed a rule requiring carriers to notify individual passengers of overbooked conditions 12 hours prior to the scheduled departure time. This proposal subsequently was abandoned after industry opposition on the ground that it was excessively rigid and unworkable.

The Board's abandonment of this proposal cannot be read as blanket approval of failure to make a public disclosure of overbooking practices. The cost of an individual notification program in terms of expense, public relations, and passenger confusion could be prohibitive. But alternative means of disclosure may be significantly less disruptive. Petitioner suggests, for example, that carrier overbooking practices be included in tariffs, which are required to be available for public inspection. And the Board has approved an innovative approach suggested by Eastern Air Lines, which provides for a system of limited overbooking in which passengers subject to possible denial of boarding are advised at the outset of their status.

14. For example, if respondent's overbooking practices were detailed in its tariff and therefore available to the public, a court presented with a claim of misrepresentation based on failure to disclose need not make prior reference to the Board, as it should if presented with a suit challenging the reasonableness of practices detailed in a tariff. Rather, the court could, applying settled principles of tort law, determine that the tariff provided sufficient notice to the party who brought the suit—as, indeed, petitioner suggests it would.

dated. The order instituting these regulations contemplates that the bumped passenger will have a choice between accepting denied boarding compensation as "liquidated damages for all damages incurred * * * as a result of the carrier's failure to provide the passenger with confirmed reserved space," or pursuing his or her common-law remedies. The Board specifically provided for a 30–day period before the specified compensation need be accepted so that the passenger will not be forced to make a decision before "the consequences of denied boarding have occurred and are known." After evaluating the consequences, passengers may choose as an alternative "to pursue their remedy under the common law."

III.

We conclude that petitioner's tort action should not be stayed pending reference to the Board and accordingly the decision of the Court of Appeals on this issue is reversed. The Court of Appeals did not address the question whether petitioner had introduced sufficient evidence to sustain his claim. We remand the case for consideration of that question and for further proceedings consistent with this opinion.[19] * * *

JUSTICE WHITE, concurring.

* * *

It may be that under its rulemaking authority the Board would have power to order airline overbooking and to pre-empt recoveries under state law for undisclosed overbooking or for overselling. But it has not done so, at least as yet. It is also unnecessary to stay proceedings on the present state-law claim pending Board action under § 411. Neither an order denying nor one granting relief under that section would foreclose claims based on state law; and there is not present here the additional consideration that a § 411 proceeding would be helpful in resolving, or affecting in some manner, the state-law claim for compensatory and punitive damages. I seriously doubt that any pending or future § 411 case would reveal anything relevant to this case about the Board's view of the propriety of overbooking and of overselling that is not already apparent from prior proceedings concerning those subjects.

Origin and Rationale of Primary Jurisdiction

In the absence of a clear legislative directive that public regulation is meant to abrogate private rights, courts have been reluctant to hold that

19. The Court of Appeals specifically remanded for reconsideration of the award of punitive damages on petitioner's claim of fraudulent misrepresentation. The propriety of that ruling was not challenged in this Court.

As the issues of ultimate liability and damages are not before us, we express no opinion as to their merits. We conclude above that mere compliance with agency regulations is not sufficient in itself under the Act to exempt a carrier from common-law liability. We make clear, however, that this conclusion is not intended to foreclose the courts on remand from considering, in relation to other issues in the case, evidence that the Board was fully advised of the practice complained of, and that the carrier had cooperated with the Board.

longstanding judicial remedies have been abolished. See generally Robert M. O'Neil, *Public Regulation and Private Rights of Action*, 52 Calif.L.Rev. 231 (1964). Instead, they have sought ways of accommodating the legislature's objective of placing primary responsibility for regulatory decisions in administrative hands without precluding the assertion of preexisting private rights in the courts. The doctrine of primary jurisdiction is the result of judicial attempts "to resolve both the procedural and substantive conflicts inevitably created when there is carved out for an agency an area of original jurisdiction which impinges on the congeries of original jurisdictions of the courts." LOUIS L. JAFFE, JUDICIAL CONTROL OF ADMINISTRATIVE ACTION 121 (1965). Yet, some cases make administrative jurisdiction effectively exclusive while suggesting that only "primary" jurisdiction is involved. See, e.g., *T.I.M.E. Inc. v. United States*, 359 U.S. 464 (1959).

Although the occasions for applying the doctrine of primary jurisdiction cannot be neatly defined, certain generalizations can be ventured. Generally, a court will focus on the issues raised by a litigant (not always the plaintiff) to determine whether they are of a kind that a particular regulatory agency should resolve. Factual issues, particularly if they require technical understanding or are likely to generate voluminous evidence, are more likely to be held within an agency's primary jurisdiction than are questions of law, unless the latter call for expert understanding. In *Far East Conference v. United States*, 342 U.S. 570 (1952), the Supreme Court declared:

> * * * [I]n cases raising issues of fact not within the conventional experiences of judges or cases requiring the exercise of administrative discretion, agencies created by Congress for regulating the subject matter should not be passed over. This is so even though the facts after they have been appraised by specialized competence serve as a premise for legal consequences to be judicially defined. Uniformity and consistency in the regulation of business entrusted to a particular agency are secured, and the limited functions of review by the judiciary are more rationally exercised, by preliminary resort for ascertaining and interpreting the circumstances underlying legal issues to agencies that are better equipped than courts by specialization, by insight gained through experience, and by more flexible procedure.

A series of well-known cases involving railroads subject to regulation by the ICC depicts the development of the doctrine in the Supreme Court. *Texas and Pacific Railway Co. v. Abilene Cotton Oil Co.*, 204 U.S. 426 (1907), is regularly cited as the foundation of the primary jurisdiction doctrine. The oil company, claiming that the carrier's published rate on file with the Interstate Commerce Commission was "unreasonable," sued in a state court to recover the excess. Section 22 of the Interstate Commerce Act provided that nothing in the Act "shall in any way abridge or alter the remedies now existing at common law or by statute," and it was undisputed that at common law a shipper had a right of action for any "unreasonable" charges exacted by a common carrier. Furthermore, section 9 provided that any person "claiming to be damaged by any common carrier * * * may either make complaint to the Commission * * * or may bring suit * * * for the recovery of the damages for which such common carrier may be liable under the provisions of this act. * * * "In the face of these provisions the Supreme Court held that the shipper's action would not lie. The central ground of its decision was that the congressional scheme for regulating railroad rates was incompatible with numerous and inconsistent judicial determinations of "reasonableness" that would result if shippers could bring suit "without previous action by the Commission."

This latter language, repeated several times in the Court's opinion, misleadingly suggests a qualification of its holding. The Court in substance held that the Act had extinguished the shipper's common law right to sue for unreasonable rates. It did not contemplate a situation in which a shipper might seek an initial ICC determination of reasonableness before proceeding to court to recover damages, for it construed section 9 as authorizing judicial redress only "of such wrongs as can, consistently with the content of the act, be redressed by courts without previous action by the Commission. * * * "The language in section 22 saving common law remedies was in effect repealed pro tanto, for the Act "cannot be held to destroy itself."

Several features of *Abilene Cotton* are noteworthy. While the Court did hold that the shipper's common law right had been extinguished (and, impliedly, that section 9 afforded no right to judicial relief), it did so realizing that the Interstate Commerce Act afforded a statutory reparations remedy before the ICC for rates the agency found unreasonable. Thus, the Court in substance concluded that the ICC's jurisdiction to remedy unreasonable rates was not simply "primary," but exclusive. There was obvious potential for inconsistent judicial rulings, as well as rulings contrary to ICC policy, if shippers could sue for damages. Moreover, a court determination that a railroad's rates were too high would confront the carrier with a serious dilemma, for under the Act no carrier could lawfully depart from rates on file with the ICC. The Court's reading of section 9 did not erase that provision, because later decisions made clear that shippers could still sue carriers in court for practices, such as charging more than the applicable rate, that ordinarily did not call for an initial ICC determination of legality.

In *Great Northern Railway Co. v. Merchants' Elevator Co.*, 259 U.S. 285 (1922), the Supreme Court added a new dimension to the "uniformity" rationale of *Abilene Cotton*. There a shipper brought suit, claiming that the railroad had improperly exacted a special charge for reconsignment of its goods. The Court held that *Abilene* did not preclude suit, because the construction of a written instrument, the carrier's published tariff, presented only a question of law when the words in the instrument "are used in their ordinary meaning." Uniformity of interpretation was assured by the availability of Supreme Court review. Moreover, Justice Brandeis for the Court observed: "Here no fact, evidential or ultimate, is in controversy; and there is no occasion for the exercise of administrative discretion." Since *Merchants' Elevator*, the federal courts have regularly cited the need for administrative expertise as a principal reason for deferring to an agency's primary jurisdiction.

Weinberger v. Bentex Pharmaceuticals, Inc., 412 U.S. 645 (1973), is a good modern example of the "expertise" rationale. (*Bentex* was a companion case to the *Hynson, Westcott & Dunning* opinion that validated the FDA's summary judgment process under the Federal Food, Drug and Cosmetic Act, which is discussed in Chapter 4.) The respondent in *Bentex* had begun a declaratory judgment action in federal district court seeking a determination that its pharmaceutical preparation was not a "new drug"—a classification that would subject it to the Act's exacting premarket approval requirements. The FDA interposed a defense of primary jurisdiction to decide the issue of "newness." In both the district court and the court of appeals, the manufacturer successfully argued that the issue of "newness" was separate from the question of whether a drug, if "new," was entitled to approval based on "substantial evidence" of its effectiveness. The company admitted that the FDA's jurisdiction to grant approval was primary, indeed exclusive. Under the statute, however, that licensing jurisdiction applied only to "new" drugs, and the agency had no routine administrative process for determining "newness." When a manufacturer applied for a license, the agency assumed that it was doing so because of regulatory necessity, that is, that it was intending to market a product that the manufacturer acknowledged to be a "new drug." If the agency believed that a drug marketed without approval was in fact "new," it traditionally brought suit in court seeking one of the remedies authorized by the Act—seizure, injunction, or criminal conviction. Given this statutory structure, the manufacturer argued and the lower courts agreed that the courts must of necessity determine whether a drug is "new" and could do so in a declaratory judgment action.

The Supreme Court disagreed. Justice Douglas noted that the statute's new drug definition required premarket approval of all drugs "not generally recognized, among experts qualified by scientific training and experience to evaluate the safety and effectiveness of drugs, as safe and effective for use." Thus, Douglas reasoned, the question of whether a drug is a "new drug" depends on precisely the sort of expert knowledge, experience, and scientific testing that would underlie an ultimate determination whether an admittedly new drug was entitled to approval. The overlap between the two types of decisions was so close that the Court believed it implicit in the regulatory scheme that Congress intended the FDA to have jurisdiction to make both. Justice Douglas' opinion also suggests that the Court was influenced by the burden that would be placed on the agency were manufacturers allowed to litigate first about the question of "newness," and then apply for a license if they lost. Thousands of drugs remained on the market in 1973 which, if "new," would be subject to the Act's requirement of effectiveness and for which manufacturers might seek de novo judicial determinations. FDA, on the other hand, explained to the Court that it was incapable of handling a caseload of more than 10 to 15 such proceedings per year. Recognizing the agency's "primary jurisdiction" may thus have been thought necessary to the continued operation of the regulatory scheme that Congress had enacted.

A court's deferral to a regulatory agency's primary jurisdiction may amount to a holding that the agency has exclusive authority to determine the merits of a litigant's claim and afford relief—as in *Abilene Cotton* and *Bentex*—or it may simply postpone judicial proceedings until the agency has had an opportunity to pass on one or more questions on which its expert judgment is sought. Moreover, the cases demonstrate that an agency need not have authority to afford the plaintiff complete, or indeed any, relief for a court to acknowledge its primary jurisdiction. Where the agency lacks authority to grant requested relief, such as money damages, a court may simply stay the case while the plaintiff seeks an administrative determination of issues within agency competence, remaining ready to afford full relief if warranted by the agency's determination and applicable legal principles. Indeed, as Justice Scalia explains in *Reiter v. Cooper*, 507 U.S. 258 (1993), dismissing a case over which a court has jurisdiction in order to get an agency opinion on one issue, is tantamount to confusing primary jurisdiction with the exhaustion doctrine:

> [R]espondents contend that the doctrine of primary jurisdiction requires petitioners initially to present their unreasonable-rate claims to the ICC, rather than to a court. That reflects a mistaken understanding of primary jurisdiction, which is a doctrine specifically applicable to claims properly cognizable in court that contain some issue within the special competence of an administrative agency. It requires the court to enable a "referral" to the agency, staying further proceedings so as to give the parties reasonable opportunity to seek an administrative ruling. * * * Referral of the issue to the administrative agency does not deprive the court of jurisdiction; it has discretion either to retain jurisdiction or, if the parties would not be unfairly disadvantaged, to dismiss the case without prejudice. * * *
>
> The result that respondents seek would be produced, not by the doctrine of primary jurisdiction, but by the doctrine of exhaustion of administrative remedies. Where relief is available from an administrative agency, the plaintiff is ordinarily required to pursue that avenue of redress before proceeding to the courts; and until that recourse is exhausted, suit is premature and must be dismissed. That doctrine is inapplicable to petitioners' reparations claims, however, because the ICC has long interpreted its statute as giving it no power to decree reparations relief. * * *

In the federal arena, generally speaking, any antitrust action against a regulated common carrier, whether brought by the Department of Justice or by a private plaintiff, will be referred to the responsible regulatory agency. E.g., *Far East Conference v. United States*, *supra*; *Pan*

American World Airways, Inc. v. United States, 371 U.S. 296 (1963); *Laveson v. Trans World Airlines*, 471 F.2d 76 (3d Cir.1972). Even in the absence of authority to immunize anticompetitive activity, courts find referral justified either because it is thought appropriate to afford the agency an opportunity initially to assess the competing policies of competition and regulation, or because the regulatory legislation is read as impliedly limiting the operation of the antitrust laws. See generally LOUIS L. JAFFE, JUDICIAL CONTROL OF ADMINISTRATIVE ACTION 141–51 (1965). Indeed, any antitrust suit against an enterprise whose activities are subject to broad federal regulation may founder initially on primary jurisdiction. See *Ricci v. Chicago Mercantile Exchange*, 409 U.S. 289 (1973) (suit by plaintiff claiming deprivation of seat on exchange violated exchange rules and antitrust laws held within primary jurisdiction of Commodity Exchange Commission). See also *Huron Valley Hospital, Inc. v. City of Pontiac*, 666 F.2d 1029 (6th Cir.1981); *Hansen v. Norfolk & Western Railway Co.*, 689 F.2d 707 (7th Cir.1982).

Primary jurisdiction has also been a recurrent issue in suits by unions or employers to enforce collective agreements falling generally within the ambit of the National Labor Relations Act and, thus, under the aegis of the NLRB. In most such cases, the Board's authority has not been held to preclude immediate resort to judicial enforcement. The numerous exceptions to this generalization, however, should caution against ready acceptance. See, e.g., Archibald Cox, *Labor Law Preemption Revisited*, 85 Harv.L.Rev. 1337 (1972); Note, *NLRB Primary Jurisdiction and Hot Cargo Issues Arising in Section 301(a) Actions*, 48 U.Chi.L.Rev. 992 (1981). The Supreme Court has also made clear that federal courts retain jurisdiction to hear suits pursuant to the judicially created duty of "fair representation," even though the determination of such a claim might involve issues that would be within the primary jurisdiction of the National Labor Relations Board when presented as a separate claim for relief. See *Communications Workers of America v. Beck*, 487 U.S. 735 (1988).

It is unclear whether litigants must have a *right* to an agency decision before a court will hold that they must first seek an administrative determination. In *Rosado v. Wyman*, 397 U.S. 397 (1970), welfare recipients challenged portions of New York's public assistance laws as inconsistent with the federal Social Security Act. The Department of HEW had already commenced an administrative review of the laws' compatibility, but had reached no decision. The Department declined the district court's invitation to make its views known by participating in the litigation. The Supreme Court rejected the defendants' suggestion that the matter fell within the Department's primary jurisdiction. In refusing to defer action, the Court emphasized that neither the Social Security Act nor HEW regulations authorized the Department to grant relief to recipients of assistance harmed by illegal state action, or, indeed, permitted them to trigger or participate in departmental proceedings to determine compliance. In *Ricci v. Chicago Mercantile Exchange*, *supra*, by contrast, the Court dismissed the plaintiff's suit in favor of the primary jurisdiction of the Commodity Exchange Commission, even though it acknowledged that the plaintiff could not force the Commission to institute proceedings to inquire into the propriety of the deprivation of his seat and that no statutory or regulatory provision guaranteed him the right to intervene in any proceedings that the Commission chose to initiate. All he could do was report to the Commission his belief that its rules had been violated. The Court's opinion, however, reflects an expectation that the Commission would institute appropriate proceedings if it found any basis for his charges.

The notion that an agency has "primary jurisdiction" to decide where its jurisdiction is discretionary seems odd. But the oddity may be more in the label, "primary jurisdiction," than in the doctrine. As Justice Scalia suggests in *Reiter*, the question usually is how to manage a case straddling judicial and administrative jurisdictions, and much lies within the discretion of the trial court judge. 570 U.S. at 270–71. Moreover, the "equities of the case" may make a strong argument for importing "excuses" from the exhaustion jurisprudence where agency processes are likely to be inadequate, dilatory or incomplete. See Bernard Schwartz, *Timing of Judicial Review: A Survey of Recent Cases*, 8 Admin.L.J.Am.U. 261 (1994).

2. SUPERSESSION OF FEDERAL COMMON LAW AND SECTION 1983 RIGHTS BY A COMPREHENSIVE STATUTORY SCHEME

As previously noted, *Middlesex County Sewerage Authority v. National Sea Clammers Assoc.* (*Sea Clammers*) ruled that a comprehensive federal remedial scheme could foreclose suits under § 1983. The *Sea Clammers* plaintiffs also sought relief pursuant to federal common law of interstate nuisance, but that claim too was rebuffed:

> The principal precedent on which these claims were based is *Illinois v. Milwaukee*, 406 U.S. 91 (1972), where the Court found that the federal courts have jurisdiction to consider the federal common-law issues raised by a suit for injunctive relief by the State of Illinois against various Wisconsin municipalities and public sewerage commission, involving the discharge of sewage into Lake Michigan. In these cases, we need not decide whether a cause of action may be brought under federal common law by a private plaintiff, seeking damages. The Court has now held that the federal common law of nuisance in the area of water pollution is entirely pre-empted by the more comprehensive scope of the FWPCA, which was completely revised soon after the decision in *Illinois v. Milwaukee*. See *Milwaukee v. Illinois*, 451 U.S. 304 (1981).
>
> This decision disposes entirely of respondents' federal common-law claims, since there is no reason to suppose that the pre-emptive effect of the FWPCA is any less when pollution of coastal waters is at issue. To the extent that this litigation involves ocean waters not

covered by the FWPCA, and regulated under the MPRSA, we see no cause for different treatment of the pre-emption question. The regulatory scheme of the MPRSA is no less comprehensive, with respect to ocean dumping, than are analogous provisions of the FWPCA.

Milwaukee v. Illinois, 451 U.S. 304 (1981), was an original proceeding brought by the State of Illinois, alleging that petitioners—the City of Milwaukee, its Sewerage Commission, Milwaukee County's Metropolitan Sewerage Commission, and other Wisconsin cities—were polluting Lake Michigan. That pollution resulted from overflows of untreated sewage from petitioners' sewer systems and discharges of inadequately treated sewage from their treatment plants. In *Illinois v. Milwaukee*, 406 U.S. 91 (1972), the Supreme Court recognized the existence of a federal "common law" which could give rise to a claim for abatement of a nuisance caused by interstate water pollution, but declined to exercise original jurisdiction because of the availability of a lower court action. Accordingly, Illinois filed suit in district court (in which respondent State of Michigan intervened) seeking abatement, under federal common law, of the public nuisance allegedly created by the petitioners' discharges. Five months later, Congress passed the Federal Water Pollution Control Act Amendments of 1972, which established a new system of regulation making it illegal to discharge pollutants into the nation's waters except pursuant to a permit that incorporated as conditions EPA regulations establishing specific effluent limitations. (Permits are issued either by the EPA or a qualifying state agency; the petitioners operated their sewer systems under permits issued by the Wisconsin Department of Natural Resources (DNR).)

While the federal court action was pending, DNR brought suits in a Wisconsin state court to compel compliance with the permits' requirements. The state court entered a judgment requiring discharges from the treatment plants to meet effluent limitations in the permits and establishing a timetable for additional construction to control sewage overflows. Thereafter, the district court, in the suit by Illinois, found that a federal common law nuisance had been proved and entered a judgment specifying effluent limitations for treated sewage and a construction timetable to eliminate overflows that went considerably beyond the terms of petitioners' permits and the state court's enforcement order. The court of appeals, ruling that the 1972 FWPCA Amendments had not preempted the federal common law of nuisance, upheld the district court's order as to elimination of overflows, but reversed insofar as the district court's effluent limitations on treated sewage were more stringent than those prescribed in the petitioners' permits and applicable EPA regulations. 599 F.2d 151 (7th Cir.1979).

The Supreme Court held that any federal common law right of action had been extinguished by the 1972 Amendments. In his opinion for the Court, Justice Rehnquist wrote:

Contrary to the suggestions of respondents, the appropriate analysis in determining if federal statutory law governs a question previously the subject of federal common law is not the same as that employed in deciding if federal law pre-empts state law. In considering the latter question " 'we start with the assumption that the historic police powers of the States were not to be superseded by the Federal Act unless that was the clear and manifest purpose of Congress.' "While we have not hesitated to find pre-emption of state law, whether express or implied, when Congress has so indicated, or when enforcement of state regulations would impair "federal superintendence of the field," our analysis has included "due regard for the presuppositions of our embracing federal system, including the principle of diffusion of power not as a matter of doctrinaire localism but as a promoter of democracy." Such concerns are not implicated in the same fashion when the question is whether federal statutory or federal common law governs, and accordingly the same sort of evidence of a clear and manifest purpose is not required. Indeed, as noted, in cases such as the present "we start with the assumption" that it is for Congress, not federal courts, to articulate the appropriate standards to be applied as a matter of federal law.

After calling attention to the self-consciously comprehensive nature of the 1972 FWPCA Amendments and to the DNR permits which addressed both the general effluent quality and overflow problems that had prompted the lawsuit, Justice Rehnquist's opinion continued:

The invocation of federal common law by the District Court and the Court of Appeals in the face of congressional legislation supplanting it is peculiarly inappropriate in areas as complex as water pollution control. * * * Not only are the technical problems difficult—doubtless the reason Congress vested authority to administer the Act in administrative agencies possessing the necessary expertise—but the general area is particularly unsuited to the approach inevitable under a regime of federal common law. Congress criticized past approaches to water pollution control as being "sporadic" and "ad hoc," apt characterizations of any judicial approach applying federal common law.

Nor was the Court impressed by arguments based on section 505(e)'s "savings clause":

Subsection 505(e) is virtually identical to subsections in the citizen-suit provisions of several environmental statutes. The subsection is common language accompanying citizen-suit provisions and we think that it means only that the provision of such suit does not revoke other remedies. It most assuredly cannot be read to mean that the Act as a whole does not supplant formerly available federal common-law actions but only that the particular section authorizing citizen suits does not do so. No one, however, maintains that the citizen-suit provision pre-empts federal common law.

Justice Blackmun, joined by Justices Marshall and Stevens, dissented both from the majority's holding and from its approach:

> The Court's analysis of federal common-law displacement rests, I am convinced, on a faulty assumption. In contrasting congressional displacement of the common law with federal pre-emption of state law, the Court assumes that as soon as Congress "addresses a question previously governed" by federal common law, "the need for such an unusual exercise of lawmaking by federal courts disappears." This "automatic displacement" approach is inadequate in two respects. It fails to reflect the unique role federal common law plays in resolving disputes between one State and the citizens or government of another. In addition, it ignores this Court's frequent recognition that federal common law may complement congressional action in the fulfillment of federal policies.
>
> It is well settled that a body of federal common law has survived the decision in *Erie R. Co. v. Tompkins. Erie* made clear that federal courts, as courts of limited jurisdiction, lack general power to formulate and impose their own rules of decision. The Court, however, did not there upset, nor has it since disturbed, a deeply rooted, more specialized federal common law that has arisen to effectuate federal interests embodied either in the Constitution or an Act of Congress. Chief among the federal interests served by this common law are the resolution of interstate disputes and the implementation of national statutory or regulatory policies. * * *

The dissenters believed that in the 1972 Amendments Congress had evinced an intent not to occupy fully the field of water pollution abatement:

> In my view, the language and structure of the Clean Water Act leave no doubt that Congress intended to preserve the federal common law of nuisance. Section 505(e) of the Act reads:
>
>> "Nothing in this section shall restrict any right which *any person* (or class of persons) may have under *any statute or common law* to seek enforcement of any effluent standard or limitation *or to seek any other relief* (including relief against the Administrator of a State agency)." (emphasis added).
>
> The Act specifically defines "person" to include States, and thus embraces respondents Illinois and Michigan. It preserves their right to bring an action against the governmental entities who are charged with enforcing the statute. Most important, as succinctly stated by the Court of Appeals in this case: "There is nothing in the phrase 'any statute or common law' that suggests that this provision is limited to state common law." * * *

3. CONGRESSIONAL SUPERSESSION OF STATE COMMON LAW RIGHTS

ALEXIS GEIER v. AMERICAN HONDA MOTOR COMPANY, INC.

Supreme Court of the United States, 2000.
529 U.S. 861, 120 S.Ct. 1913, 146 L.Ed.2d 914.

JUSTICE BREYER delivered the opinion of the Court.

In 1992, petitioner Alexis Geier, driving a 1987 Honda Accord, collided with a tree and was seriously injured. The car was equipped with manual shoulder and lap belts which Geier had buckled up at the time. The car was not equipped with airbags or other passive restraint devices.

Geier and her parents * * * sued the car's manufacturer, American Honda Motor Company, Inc., * * * [claiming] among other things, that American Honda had designed its car negligently and defectively because it lacked a driver's side airbag. The District Court dismissed the lawsuit. The court noted that FMVSS 208 gave car manufacturers a choice as to whether to install airbags. And the court concluded that petitioners' lawsuit, because it sought to establish a different safety standard—i.e., an airbag requirement—was expressly preempted by a provision of the Act which preempts "any safety standard" that is not identical to a federal safety standard applicable to the same aspect of performance.

The Court of Appeals agreed with the District Court's conclusion but on somewhat different reasoning. It had doubts, given the existence of the Act's "saving" clause that petitioners' lawsuit involved the potential creation of the kind of "safety standard" to which the Safety Act's express preemption provision refers. But it declined to resolve that question because it found that petitioners' state-law tort claims posed an obstacle to the accomplishment of FMVSS 208's objectives. For that reason, it found that those claims conflicted with FMVSS 208, and that, under ordinary preemption principles, the Act consequently preempted the lawsuit. * * *

We first ask whether the Safety Act's express preemption provision preempts this tort action. The provision reads as follows:

"Whenever a Federal motor vehicle safety standard established under this subchapter is in effect, no State or political subdivision of a State shall have any authority either to establish, or to continue in effect, with respect to any motor vehicle or item of motor vehicle equipment[,] any safety standard applicable to the same aspect of performance of such vehicle or item of equipment which is not identical to the Federal standard." 15 U.S.C. § 1392(d) (1988 ed).

American Honda points out that a majority of this Court has said that a somewhat similar statutory provision in a different federal statute—a provision that uses the word "requirements"—may well expressly preempt similar tort actions. See *e.g., Medtronic, Inc. v. Lohr*, 518 U.S. 470, 502–504 (1996) (plurality opinion). Petitioners reply that this statute speaks of preempting a state-law "safety standard," not a "requirement," and that a tort action does not involve a safety standard. Hence, they conclude, the express preemption provision does not apply.

We need not determine the precise significance of the use of the word "standard," rather than "requirement," however, for the Act contains another provision, which resolves the disagreement. That provision, a "saving" clause, says that "[c]ompliance with" a federal safety standard "does not exempt any person from any liability under common law." The saving clause assumes that there are some significant number of common-law liability cases to save. And a reading of the express preemption provision that excludes common-law tort actions gives actual meaning to the saving clause's literal language, while leaving adequate room for state tort law to operate—for example, where federal law creates only a floor, *i.e.*, a minimum safety standard. * * *

We have just said that the saving clause *at least* removes tort actions from the scope of the express preemption clause. Does it do more? In particular, does it foreclose or limit the operation of ordinary preemption principles insofar as those principles instruct us to read statutes as preempting state laws (including common-law rules) that "actually conflict" with the statute or federal standards promulgated thereunder? * * *

Nothing in the language of the saving clause suggests an intent to save state-law tort actions that conflict with federal regulations. The words "[c]ompliance" and "does not exempt," sound as if they simply bar a special kind of defense, namely, a defense that compliance with a federal standard automatically exempts a defendant from state law, whether the Federal Government meant that standard to be an absolute requirement or only a minimum one. See RESTATEMENT (THIRD) OF TORTS: PRODUCTS LIABILITY § 4(b), Comment *e* (1997) (distinguishing between state-law compliance defense and a federal claim of preemption). It is difficult to understand why Congress would have insisted on a compliance-with-federal-regulation precondition to the provision's applicability had it wished the Act to "save" all state-law tort actions, regardless of their potential threat to the objectives of federal safety standards promulgated under that Act. * * *

Moreover, this Court has repeatedly "decline[d] to give broad effect to saving clauses where doing so would upset the careful regulatory scheme established by federal law." We find this concern applicable in the present case. And we conclude that the saving clause foresees—it does not foreclose—the possibility that a federal safety standard will preempt a state common-law tort action with which it conflicts. * * *

Neither do we believe that the preemption provision, the saving provision, or both together, create some kind of "special burden" beyond that inherent in ordinary preemption principles—which "special burden" would specially disfavor preemption here. The two provisions, read together, reflect a neutral policy, not a specially favorable or unfavorable policy toward the application of ordinary conflict preemption principles. * * *

The basic question, then, is whether a common-law "no airbag" action like the one before us actually conflicts with FMVSS 208. We hold that it does.

In petitioners' and the dissent's view, FMVSS 208 sets a minimum airbag standard. As far as FMVSS 208 is concerned, the more airbags, and the sooner, the better. But that was not the Secretary's view. The Department of Transportation's (DOT's) comments, which accompanied the promulgation of FMVSS 208, make clear that the standard deliberately provided the manufacturer with a range of choices among different passive restraint devices. Those choices would bring about a mix of different devices introduced gradually over time; and FMVSS 208 would thereby lower costs, overcome technical safety problems, encourage technological development, and win widespread consumer acceptance—all of which would promote FMVSS 208's safety objectives. * * *

[After rehearsing the tortured history of FMVSS 208 as recounted in *State Farm, supra* p. ___, including DOT's many attempts to avoid prescribing a particular passive restraint technology, Justice Breyer concluded:] FMVSS 208 embodies the Secretary's policy judgment that safety would best be promoted if manufacturers installed *alternative* protection systems in their fleets rather than one particular system in every car. Petitioners' tort suit claims that the manufacturers of the 1987 Honda Accord had a duty to design, manufacture, distribute and sell a motor vehicle with an effective and safe passive restraint system, including, but not limited to, airbags.

In effect, petitioners' tort action depends upon its claim that manufacturers had a duty to install an airbag when they manufactured the 1987 Honda Accord. Such a state law—*i.e.*, a rule of state tort law imposing such a duty—by its terms would have required manufacturers of all similar cars to install airbags rather than other passive restraint systems, such as automatic belts or passive interiors. It thereby would have presented an obstacle to the variety and mix of devices that the federal regulation sought. It would have required all manufacturers to have installed airbags in respect to the entire District-of-Columbia-related portion of their 1987 new car fleet, even though FMVSS 208 at that time required only that 10per cent of a manufacturer's nationwide fleet be equipped with any passive restraint device at all. It thereby also would have stood as an obstacle to the gradual passive restraint phase-in that the federal regulation deliberately imposed. In addition, it could have made less likely the adoption of a state mandatory buckle-up law. Because the rule of law for which petitioners contend would have stood "as an obstacle to the accomplishment and execution of" the important means-related federal objectives that we have just discussed, it is preempted* * *.

One final point: We place some weight upon DOT's interpretation of FMVSS 208's objectives and its conclusion, as set forth in the Government's brief, that a tort suit such as this one would" 'stan[d] as an obstacle to the accomplishment and execution' " of those objectives. Congress has delegated to DOT authority to implement the statute; the subject matter is technical; and the relevant history and background are complex and extensive. The agency is likely to have a thorough understanding of its own regulation and its objectives and is "uniquely qualified" to comprehend the likely impact of state requirements. And DOT has explained FMVSS 208's objectives, and the interference that "no airbag" suits pose thereto, consistently over time. In these circumstances, the agency's own views should make a difference. * * *

The judgment of the Court of Appeals is affirmed.

JUSTICE STEVENS, with whom JUSTICE SOUTER, JUSTICE THOMAS, and JUSTICE GINSBURG join, dissenting.

[In Parts I and II the dissent provides its own history of FMVSS 208, a history emphasizing that rule's persistent efforts to encourage airbag use rather than require it. The dissent also argues that failure to preempt plaintiff's suit leads neither to the conclusion that they would prevail nor that success would change manufacturers' primary conduct.]

III

When a state statute, administrative rule, or common-law cause of action conflicts with a federal statute, it is axiomatic that the state law is without effect. *U.S. Const., Art. VI, cl. 2.* On the other hand, it is equally clear that the Supremacy Clause does not give unelected federal judges *carte blanche* to use federal law as a means of imposing their own ideas of tort reform on the States. Because of the role of States as separate sovereigns in our federal system, we have long presumed that state laws—particularly those, such as the provision of tort remedies to compensate for personal injuries, that are within the scope of the States' historic police powers—are not to be preempted by a federal statute unless it is the clear and manifest purpose of Congress to do so.

Regrettably, the Court has not always honored the latter proposition as scrupulously as the former * * *.

It is true that in three recent cases we concluded that broadly phrased preemptive commands encompassed common-law claims. In *Cipollone v. Liggett Group, Inc.*, while we thought it clear that the preemption provision in the 1965 Federal Cigarette Labeling and Advertising Act applied only to "rulemaking bodies," 505 U.S. at 518, 112 S.Ct. 2608, we concluded that the broad command in the subsequent 1969 amendment that "[n]o requirement or prohibition * * * shall be imposed under State law" did include certain common-law claims. SCALIA, J., concurring in judgment in part and dissenting in part). *CSX Transp., Inc. v. Easterwood*, where the preemption clause of the Federal Railroad Safety Act of 1970 expressly provided that federal railroad safety regulations would preempt any incompatible state" 'law, rule, regulation, order, or standard relating to railroad safety,' " we held that a federal regulation governing maximum train speed preempted a negligence claim that a speed under the federal maximum was excessive. [507 U.S. at 664, 113 S.Ct. at 1732] And in *Medtronic, Inc. v. Lohr*, we recognized that the statutory reference to "any requirement" imposed by a State or its political subdivisions may include common-law duties. 518 U.S. at 502–503 (plurality opinion).

The statutes construed in those cases differed from the Safety Act in two significant respects. First, the language in each of those preemption provisions was significantly broader than the text of § 1392(d). Unlike the broader language of those provisions, the ordinary meaning of the term "safety standard" includes positive enactments, but does not include judicial decisions in common-law tort cases.

Second, the statutes at issue in *Cipollone*, *CSX*, and *Medtronic* did not contain a saving clause expressly preserving common-law remedies. The saving clause in the Safety Act unambiguously expresses a decision by Congress that compliance with a federal safety standard does not exempt a manufacturer from *any* common-law liability. In light of this reference to common-law liability in the saving clause, Congress surely would have included a similar reference in § 1392(d) if it had intended to preempt such liability. * * *

Given the cumulative force of the fact that § 1392(d) does not expressly preempt common-law claims and the fact that § 1397(k) was obviously intended to limit the preemptive effect of the Secretary's safety standards, it is quite wrong for the Court to assume that a possible implicit conflict with the purposes to be achieved by such a standard should have the same preemptive effect " 'as an obstacle to the accomplishment and execution of the full purposes and objectives of Congress.' " Properly construed, the Safety Act imposes a special burden on a party relying on an arguable, implicit conflict with a temporary regulatory policy—rather than a conflict with congressional policy or with the text of any regulation—to demonstrate that a common-law claim has been preempted.

IV

Even though the Safety Act does not expressly preempt common-law claims, Honda contends that Standard 208–of its own force—implicitly preempts the claims in this case.

We have recognized that a federal statute implicitly overrides state law either when the scope of a statute indicates that Congress intended federal law to occupy a field exclusively, or when state law is in actual conflict with federal law. We have found implied conflict preemption where it is "impossible for a private party to comply with both state and federal requirements," or where state law "stands as an obstacle to the accomplishment and execution of the full purposes and objectives of Congress."

In addition, we have concluded that regulations "intended to preempt state law" that are promulgated by an agency acting nonarbitrarily and within its congressionally delegated authority may also have preemptive force. In this case, Honda relies on the last of the implied preemption principles * * * arguing that the imposition of common-law liability for failure to install an airbag would frustrate the purposes and objectives of Standard 208.

Both the text of the statute and the text of the standard provide persuasive reasons for rejecting this argument. The saving clause of the Safety Act arguably denies the Secretary the authority to promulgate standards that would preempt common-law remedies. Moreover, the text of Standard 208 says nothing about preemption, and I am not persuaded that Honda has overcome our traditional presumption that it lacks any implicit preemptive effect.

Honda argues, and the Court now agrees, that the risk of liability presented by common-law claims that vehicles without airbags are negligently and defectively designed would frustrate the policy decision that the Secretary made in promulgating Standard 208. This decision, in their view, was that safety—including a desire to encourage "public acceptance of the airbag technology and experimentation with better passive restraint systems"—would best be promoted through gradual implementation of a passive restraint requirement making airbags only one of a variety of systems that a manufacturer could install in order to comply, rather than through a requirement mandating the use of one particular system in every vehicle. In its brief supporting Honda, the United States agreed with this submission. It argued that if the manufacturers had known in 1984 that they might later be held liable for failure to install airbags that risk "would likely have led them to install airbags in all cars," thereby frustrating the Secretary's safety goals and interfering with the methods designed to achieve them.

There are at least three flaws in this argument that provide sufficient grounds for rejecting it. First, the entire argument is based on an unrealistic factual predicate. Whatever the risk of liability on a no-airbag claim may have been prior to the promulgation of the 1984 version of Standard 208, that risk did not lead any manufacturer to install airbags in even a substantial portion of its cars. If there had been a realistic likelihood that the risk of tort liability would have that consequence, there would have been no need for Standard 208. The promulgation of that standard certainly did not *increase* the pre-existing risk of liability. Even if the standard did not create a previously unavailable preemption defense, it likely *reduced* the manufacturers' risk of liability by enabling them to point to the regulation and their compliance therewith as evidence tending to negate charges of negligent and defective design. * * *

Second, even if the manufacturers' assessment of their risk of liability ultimately proved to be wrong, the purposes of Standard 208 would not be frustrated. In light of the inevitable time interval between the eventual filing of a tort action alleging that the failure to install an airbag is a design defect and the possible resolution of such a claim against a manufacturer, as well as the additional interval between such a resolution (if any) and manufacturers' compliance with the state-law duty in question, by modifying their designs to avoid such liability in the future, it is obvious that the phase-in period would have ended long before its purposes could have been frustrated by the specter of tort liability. * * *[18]

Third, despite its acknowledgment that the saving clause "preserves those actions that seek to establish greater safety than the minimum safety achieved by a federal regulation intended to provide a floor," the Court completely ignores the important fact that by definition all of the standards established under the Safety Act—like the British regulations that governed the number and capacity of lifeboats aboard the *Titanic*—impose minimum, rather than fixed or maximum, requirements. * * *

V

The Court apparently views the question of preemption in this case as a close one. Under "ordinary experience-proved principles of conflict preemption," therefore, the presumption against preemption should control. Instead, the Court simply ignores the presumption, preferring instead to put the burden on petitioners to show that their tort claim would not frustrate the Secretary's purposes. In view of the important principles upon which the presumption is founded, however, rejecting it in this manner is profoundly unwise. * * *

While the presumption is important in assessing the preemptive reach of federal statutes, it becomes crucial when the preemptive effect of an administrative regulation is at issue. Unlike Congress, administrative agencies are clearly not designed to represent the interests of States, yet with relative ease they can promulgate comprehensive and detailed regulations that have broad preemption ramifications for state law. We have addressed the heightened federalism and nondelegation concerns that agency preemption raises by using the presumption to build a procedural bridge across the political accountability gap between States and administrative agencies. Thus, even in cases where implied regulatory preemption is at issue, we generally "expect an administrative regulation to declare any intention to preempt state law with some specificity." * * *

18. The Court's failure to "understand [this point] correctly" is directly attributable to its fundamental misconception of the nature of duties imposed by tort law. A general verdict of liability in a case seeking damages for negligent and defective design of a vehicle that (like Ms. Geier's) lacked any passive restraints does not amount to an immutable, mandatory "rule of state tort law imposing * * * a duty [to install an airbag]." Rather, that verdict merely reflects the jury's judgment that the manufacturer of a vehicle without any passive restraint system breached its duty of due care by designing a product that was not reasonably safe because a reasonable alternative design—"including, but not limited to, airbags"—could have reduced the foreseeable risks of harm posed by the product. Such a verdict obviously does not foreclose the possibility that more than one alternative design exists the use of which would render the vehicle reasonably safe and satisfy the manufacturer's duty of due care. Thus, the Court is quite wrong to suggest that, as a consequence of such a verdict, only the installation of airbags would enable manufacturers to avoid liability in the future.

When the presumption and its underpinnings are properly understood, it is plain that Honda has not overcome the presumption in this case. Neither Standard 208 nor its accompanying commentary includes the slightest specific indication of an intent to preempt common-law no-airbag suits. Indeed, the only mention of such suits in the commentary tends to suggest that they would not be preempted. In the Court's view, however, "[t]he failure of the Federal Register to address preemption explicitly is * * * not determinate," because the Secretary's consistent litigating position since 1989, the history of airbag regulation, and the commentary accompanying the final version of Standard 208 reveal purposes and objectives of the Secretary that would be frustrated by no-airbag suits. Preempting on these three bases blatantly contradicts the presumption against preemption. When the 1984 version of Standard 208 was under consideration, the States obviously were not afforded any notice that purposes might someday be discerned in the history of airbag regulation that would support preemption. Nor does the Court claim that the notice of proposed rulemaking that led to Standard 208 provided the States with notice either that the final version of the standard might contain an express preemption provision or that the commentary accompanying it might contain a statement of purposes with arguably preemptive effect. Finally, the States plainly had no opportunity to comment upon either the commentary accompanying the final version of the standard or the Secretary's *ex post* litigating position that the standard had implicit preemptive effect. * * *

As to the Secretary's litigating position, it is clear that "an interpretation contained in a [legal brief], not one arrived at after, for example, a formal adjudication or notice-and-comment rulemaking[,] * * * do[es] not warrant. *Chevron*-style deference." Moreover, our preemption precedents and the APA establish that even if the Secretary's litigating position were coherent, the lesser deference paid to it by the Court today would be inappropriate. Given the Secretary's contention that he has the authority to promulgate safety standards that preempt state law and the fact that he could promulgate such a standard * * * with relative ease, we should be quite reluctant to find preemption based only on the Secretary's informal effort to recast the 1984 version of Standard 208 into a preemptive mold. Requiring the Secretary to put his preemptive position through formal notice-and-comment rulemaking—whether contemporaneously with the promulgation of the allegedly preemptive regulation or at any later time that the need for preemption becomes apparent—respects both the federalism and nondelegation principles that underlie the presumption against preemption in the regulatory context and the APA's requirement of rulemaking when an agency substantially modifies its interpretation of a regulation. * * *

The Perplexing World of Federal Preemption

Geier is typical of the Supreme Court's modern preemption cases along a number of dimensions: First, most federal statutes fail to address preemption and, even when they do, as with the "saving clause" in

Geier, their language seldom reaches a level of specificity that decides cases.

Second, the Supreme Court is hesitant to find what is sometimes termed "field" preemption, that is, that Congress has so "invaded the field" that there is no room left for state regulation through common law or otherwise. Because federal statutes now provide some regulatory requirements in most arenas of human conduct, giving a wide-scope to field preemption would lay waste much of state common law and perhaps even more state legislation. (Indeed, because states seldom leave any area of common law untouched by legislation, the difference between preempting legislative "police powers" and state common law is often blurred.) This hesitancy gives rise to the "presumption" that Congress does not normally intend to supplant state common law when it adopts federal regulatory legislation. As the dissenters in *Geier* are at pains to point out, this presumption is grounded in fundamental notions of federalism.

Third, given the absence of express statutory language and the narrow scope of field preemption, most cases fall into the domain of "obstacle" preemption, that is, where the Court asks whether state law "stands as an obstacle to the accomplishment and execution of the full purposes and objectives of Congress." The Supreme Court generally traces obstacle preemption to its opinion in *Hines v. Davidowitz*, 312 U.S. 52, 67 (1941). Obstacle preemption is actually a subpart of "conflict preemption" which includes, in addition, situations in which compliance with both state and federal law is "a physical impossibility." The physical impossibility test decides very few cases, leaving most to obstacle preemption analysis. Here, of course, different judges' understandings of the purposes of federal regulations combine with the variable weight accorded to agency statements of purpose and to the anti-preemption presumption, to yield a highly unpredictable jurisprudence. Litigation about preemption has become so ubiquitous that Steven Gardbaum claims that "preemption * * * is * * * the most frequently used doctrine of constitutional law in practice." Steven A. Gardbaum, *The Nature of Preemption*, 79 Corn. L. Rev. 767, 768 (1994).

It is but a short step from decrying legal uncertainty and predicting litigation explosions to the suggestion that Congress should itself pay more attention to resolving the question of preemption. See, e.g., Henry H. Drummonds, *The Sister Sovereign States: Preemption in the Second Twentieth Century Revolution in the Law of the American Work Place*, 62 Fordham L.Rev. 469 (1993). Nor has the importance of the issue escaped congressional notice. The Common Sense Legal Reforms Act of 1995, H.R. 10, 104th Cong., 1st Sess. § 106 (1995), a part of the Republican Party's "Contract with America," would have required that committee reports on legislation address certain issues, including preemption. Even without such a reporting requirement hundreds of federal recent statutes contain preemption clauses. The question is whether these clauses make the preemption inquiry any more tractable.

Two of the Supreme Court's best known modern preemption cases, *Cipollone v. Liggett Group Inc.*, 505 U.S. 504 (1992), and *Medtronic Inc. v. Lohr*, 518 U.S. 470 (1996), suggest that the answer is "no." Both cases produced plurality opinions in a fragmented Court notwithstanding explicit preemption clauses in the Cigarette Labeling and Advertising Act (*Cipollone*) and the Medical Device Amendments (*Medtronic*).

Section 360k of the Medical device Amendments (MDA) to the Federal Food, Drug, and Cosmetic Act provides:

> (a) General rule
>
> Except as provided in subsection (b) of this section, no State or political subdivision of a State may establish or continue in effect with respect to a device intended for human use any requirement—
>
> (1) which is different from, or in addition to, any requirement applicable under this chapter to the device, and
>
> (2) which relates to the safety or effectiveness of the device or to any other matter included in a requirement applicable to the device under this chapter.

The Lohrs sued Medtronic under state law, alleging that failure of the electrical leads in the pacemaker implanted in Mrs. Lohr caused her severe injuries. Medtronic contended that a tort verdict in favor of Mrs. Lohr would impose a "requirement" different from and in addition to the obligations imposed by the MDA—which contain no private remedy—and thus recovery on any theory was preempted. The company also argued that § 360k in any case precluded liability for failure to adopt any safety measures that FDA has not prescribed for its pacemakers.

The Supreme Court had no difficulty rejecting Medtronic's broad claim that the MDA had essentially erased state tort law. Characterizing this claim as "not only unpersuasive, [but] implausible," Justice Stevens' plurality opinion emphasized that "[t]hroughout our history the several States have exercised their policy powers to protect the health and safety of their citizens." It expressed skepticism that the statutory preemption clause was intended to apply to or limit state tort law—as well as "requirements" imposed by statute or administrative regulation—and concluded that it was at the very least "highly ambiguous." The plurality discussed, and found "helpful" but not decisive, an FDA regulation interpreting § 360k, in which the agency determined that it preempted only those state requirements that paralleled or went beyond requirements that the agency had specifically prescribed for the device in question. The plurality was ultimately convinced that the Lohrs' claims were not preempted after the Justices' careful examination of each proffered theory of liability revealed that none would impose obligations that duplicated or conflicted with any requirements that FDA had prescribed for pacemaker design, materials, or production.

The one concurring (Breyer) and four dissenting Justices found no ambiguity in § 360k; it prohibited additional or differing state "requirements" which could as easily be expressed as obligations of tort law as responsibilities imposed by statute or regulation. But in seeking to determine whether any of the Lohrs' common law theories would impose requirements "different from, or in addition to, *any requirement imposed under*" the MDA, even the dissenters (speaking through Justice O'Connor) found few conflicts between the Lohrs' allegations of negligence and defect and the existing MDA requirements for pacemakers. It was particularly important for Justice Breyer that the law allowed Medtronic to market its pacemaker without formal FDA review of either safety or effectiveness. Had the agency prescribed requirements specifically for pacemakers and approved Medtronic's particular device, a majority of the Justices made clear that they would have found most of the Lohrs' claims preempted.

Perhaps the only clear lesson that can be drawn from *Medtronic* and *Cipollone*, is that the Supreme Court is prepared to find that statutory language preempting state "requirements" may encompass, and displace, common law rules as well as statutory or administrative regulations. But, it is equally clear that each specific common law claim will be independently analyzed in light of the statute's language and overriding purpose—as interpreted by different Justices.

In *Preemption of State Law by Federal Law: A Task for Congress or the Courts?*, 40 Vill.L.Rev. 1 (1995), Professor Susan J. Stabile argues that preemption clauses, and the Court's reliance on express, rather than implied, preemption analysis, make matters worse. In her view the appropriate federalism goal, an attempt to pursue federal purposes without unduly interfering with legitimate state activities, has been undermined without any substantial gain in either predictable results or easily administered rules.

Professor Stabile's argument is detailed, but her main points can be easily summarized. First, Congress sometimes adopts sweeping preemption language that seems to resolve most cases. Primary examples are the Employee Retirement Income Security Act of 1974 and the Airline Deregulation Act of 1978. But, such provisions put courts in a double bind. On the one hand, they prevent the recognition of legitimate state interests in preserving certain common law actions. On the other hand, precisely because these draconian results often make little sense, they create interpretive tensions that lead courts into conflicting results.

The federalism issue is nicely illustrated by *Ingersoll–Rand Co. v. McClendon*, 498 U.S. 133 (1990). The respondent had sued for wrongful discharge, claiming that he was terminated in order to prevent his pension benefits from vesting. In fact, however, if the employer had been so motivated, it made a mistake. McClendon's pension benefits had actually vested under applicable regulations adopted pursuant to the Employee Retirement Income Security Act (ERISA). The suit therefore involved only a claim for lost wages, mental anguish and punitive damages for wrongful discharge.

Even so the employer defended on the ground that ERISA preempts any state common law action which (under ERISA's very broad preemption provision) "relates" to an ERISA regulated pension plan. And, even though McClendon's suit would have no effect on his employer's plan or his pension benefits, the Supreme Court held that the action was barred because it related to an employee benefit plan within the plain meaning of the ERISA preemption provision.

ERISA is, perhaps, the most prominent cause of the contemporary avalanche of preemption litigation, and that statute has been particularly prone to producing decisions, like *Ingersoll–Rand*, that are linguistically impeccable and purposively mystifying. See the cases collected in Stabile, *supra*, notes 77–79 and 102–104. These incursions on state interests in protecting their citizens against breach of contract, fraud, and a host of other torts could be a necessary price to pay for a clear rule on preemption. But clarity has not necessarily been achieved.

The Supreme Court has not been insensitive to ERISA's predilection for gobbling up state law, and it early on introduced a "rule of reason" into the ERISA preemption jurisprudence by recognizing that state law may affect plans in "too tenuous, remote, or peripheral a manner to warrant a finding that the law 'relates to' the plan." *Shaw v. Delta Air Lines Inc.*, 463 U.S. 85, 100 n. 21 (1983). Nor does state action "relate to" a protected plan if the effects are "indirect," unless such indirect effects are "acute." *New York State Conf. of Blue Cross and Blue Shield Plans v. Travelers Ins. Co.*, 514 U.S. 645 (1995). This purposive breach in the linguistic barricades of ERISA preemption was necessary to avoid preemption of virtually all state regulation, support or taxation of health insurance. The cost of "reasonableness" is, of course, a fractured and unpredictable jurisprudence.

Even so dedicated a "textualist" as Justice Scalia seems ready to throw ERISA's text overboard. Concurring specially in *Egelhoff v. Egelhoff*, 532 U.S. 141, 153 (2001), he opined: "I remain unsure (as I think the lower courts and everyone else will be) as to what else [besides the direct contradiction of ERISA by state law] triggers the 'relates to' provision, which—if it is interpreted to be anything other than a reference to our established jurisprudence concerning conflict and field preemption—has no discernible content that would not pick up every ripple in the pond, producing a result that no sensible person could have intended. I persist in the view that we can bring some coherence to this area, and can give the statute both a plausible and precise content, only by interpreting the 'relates to' clause as a reference to our ordinary preemption jurisprudence."

A similar fate has befallen the Airline Deregulation Act which, in language similar to ERISA's preemption provisions, bars the application of all state laws "relating to rates, routes, or services of any air carrier." Interpreting this language in *Morales v. Trans World Airlines, Inc.*, 504 U.S. 374 (1992), the Supreme Court found that it barred a suit by the Texas Attorney General under a general Texas consumer protection statute complaining of deceptive fare advertisements. Because fares are "rates" and the suit related to the advertising of them, the Court found the action clearly preempted.

The *Morales* result is textually defensible. But it is hard to see how a suit for false advertising interferes with federal deregulation of rates, routes, or services. Although the federal statute no longer imposes federal regulation on information dissemination by airlines, there is nothing in the statute to suggest that the Congress believed that airlines should be free from general strictures on fraud or misrepresentation.

Here again, clarity remains elusive. Courts have understandably attempted to read rule of reason interpretations into the "relate to" language of the Airline Deregulation Act as well. See cases cited at Stabile, *supra*, notes 189–201.

The Supreme Court has not clarified matters appreciably. In *American Airlines Inc. v. Wolens*, 513 U.S. 219 (1995), the respondent had sued American Airlines claiming that retroactive modifications to its frequent flyer program were both a breach of contract and a violation of the Illinois consumer fraud statute. The Supreme Court found that the consumer fraud claim, but not the contract claim, was barred by the Airline Deregulation Act. In reaching this result, the Court made a "nice" distinction between state attempts to impose their own public policies on airlines (the consumer fraud statute) and claims that merely seek to force an airline to maintain its own "self-imposed undertakings" (the contract claim).

This appears to be the traditional "distinction without a difference." The interpretation of American Airlines' contract with its customers can hardly be uninfluenced by the state's general policies concerning contractual fair dealing, particularly in adhesory contracts. State contract law requiring the airline to honor whatever a state court takes to be its implied contractual obligations "relates to" airline rates and services in the same fashion as a state statute imposing a duty not to defraud consumers. For a parallel ERISA holding, see *UNUM Life Ins. Co. v. Ward*, 526 U.S. 358 (1999).

Less sweeping preemption provisions have not fared much better. As previously mentioned, *Cipollone v. Liggett Group Inc.*, 505 U.S. 504 (1992), interpreted the preemption provision of the 1965 Cigarette Labeling Act. That statute provides that "no requirement or prohibition based on smoking and health shall be imposed under state law with respect to the advertising or promotion of any cigarettes, the packages of which are labeled in conformity with the provisions of this chapter." The question was whether state common law tort claims were preempted by this provision. Many lower courts had held that such claims were implicitly preempted because their underlying theory was "failure-to-warn." These courts reasoned that allowing failure-to-warn claims against tobacco companies would lead to further defensive labeling of cigarettes which would conflict with the congressional goal of uniformity in labeling. Other courts, construing the federal goal as primarily one of product information, not uniformity, held the claims were not barred by the Act. Both sets of courts agreed, of course, that claims were not expressly barred by the statute.

Agreeing with the circuit courts that the Cigarette Labeling Act did not expressly bar such suits, a divided Supreme Court declined to examine the provisions of the legislation further to attempt to discern implicit congressional intent. The plurality opinion thus appeared to establish a rule that when a statute expressly provides for preemption, its preemptive effect will not be extended beyond the statutory language. But, the line was not quite so bright. For, the Court also said that express language would control where that language was "a reliable indicium of congressional intent."

Whether a particular statute's express preemption provision provides a "reliable indicium" of congressional intent to limit preemption to those express provisions is certain to be controversial. The circuit courts have split over this issue when interpreting the preemption provisions of the Motor Vehicle Safety Act of 1966. And, when the Supreme Court returned to the fray, in *Freightliner Corp. v. Myrick*, 514 U.S. 280 (1995), it smudged *Cipollone's* bright line even further. It cited *Cipollone*'s "reliable indicium" language with no discussion of what such a legislative animal might look like. Moreover, it took the view that the presence of an express preemption provision merely supported a reasonable inference that Congress did not intend to preempt matters that were not within the scope of the express language. It thus left the lower courts pretty much at sea concerning when they should engage in a more purposive "implied preemption" analysis under statutes containing express preemption provisions. In *Medtronic* the whole idea of "reliable indicia" seemed to have evaporated.

Viewing the decidedly mixed results of congressional attempts to solve the preemption problem, Professor Stabile argues that contrary to received wisdom, congressional silence might be easier to "interpret" than explicit preemption language. She is skeptical that the Congress can predict the effects of its preemption language across the broad range of claims that might arise under state law or how time and change might affect the way in which preemption should be approached in particular contexts. Her somewhat paradoxical, but not unpersuasive, conclusion is that an implied preemption analysis, indulging the usual balancing of federal and state interests in the context of particular claims, is likely to be more satisfying substantively, and no less predictable, than congressional attempts to control the preemptive effect of federal regulatory statutes.

For a vigorous statement of the opposing view—that is, that the presumption against preemption should be made superstrong by the adoption of "clear statement" requirements—see Betsy J. Grey, *Make Congress Speak Clearly: Federal Preemption of State Tort Remedies*, 77 B.U.L.Rev. 559 (1997).

Confusion and uncertainty often produce calls for a complete rethinking of doctrine. Professor Caleb Nelson provides such a challenge in

Preemption, 86 Va. L. Rev. 225 (2000). In Professor Nelson's view preemption doctrine is doubly wrong-headed. It first enunciates a presumption against preemption that directly contradicts the *Non Obstante* Clause of the Supremacy Clause of the Constitution, which states: "Anything in the Constitution or laws of any state to the contrary notwithstanding." Relying on Eighteenth Century sources, Professor Nelson argues that although these clauses are not familiar to contemporary lawyers, they were well understood at the time of the Constitution's writing as instructions to courts not to apply traditional presumptions against implied repeal. The *Non Obstante* Clause thus instructs federal courts that they should not struggle to harmonize federal statutes with pre-existing state law but should give the statute whatever meaning seems most appropriate, thereby permitting it to displace whatever state law is contradicted.

Although many might believe, as Justice Stevens seemed to believe in *Geier*, that the presumption against preemption is all that stands between the states and hegemonic federal displacement of state decision rules, Professor Nelson argues that the elimination of the presumption would be counterbalanced if the Court would but correct another mistake in the preemption jurisprudence. For, in his view, there is no justification for the modern notion of "obstacle" preemption. The Supremacy Clause demands preemption if and only if state law contradicts a valid rule of federal law. For Nelson the conflation of "contradiction" and "serving as an obstacle to federal purposes" is both a semantic confusion and a misunderstanding of the balance between federal supremacy and reserved state powers that the Supremacy Clause establishes. Professor Nelson may be correct. But as a practical matter the "64,000-litigated-cases-question" is whether the state federal balance created by eliminating both the presumption against preemption and the category of obstacle preemption would be any easier to discern in particular cases than the balance the courts seek to strike employing current doctrine.

Although Congress may be poorly positioned to predict the effects of its preemption language on state law or, indeed, to anticipate the need for preemption in particular circumstances to preserve federal policies, agencies charged with implementing federal statutes can take a more informed and nuanced view. Moreover, much preemption litigation involves alleged conflicts, not with the language of a federal statute, but with agency policies that implement it. It is hardly surprising, therefore, that Justice Breyer's opinion in *Geier* analyzes the conflict between FMVSS 208 and state tort law largely in terms of the policy choices enunciated in the Statement of Basis and Purpose accompanying that regulation's promulgation. And the *Geier* majority gives weight to the Department of Transportation's determination that a suit like the one brought by the *Geier* plaintiffs would compromise the objectives of the agency's passive restraints rule, even though that view is enunciated in a brief for the government,

One solution to the uncertainties surrounding preemption might be to give agencies explicit authority to determine the preemptive effect of federal regulations. Indeed, Congress has done so in a number of statutes, including the Federal Boat Safety Act (FBSA), of 1971, which charges the Coast Guard with a responsibility for boat safety regulation that is quite similar to the authority granted the National Highway Traffic Safety Administration over motor vehicle safety. Section 10 of the FBSA provides:

> Unless permitted by the Secretary under § 4305 of this title, a state or political subdivision of a state may not establish, continue in effect, or enforce a law or regulation establishing a recreational vessel or associated equipment performance or other safety standard or imposing a requirement for associated equipment * * * that is not identical to a regulation prescribed under § 4302 of this title.

46 U.S.C. § 4306. Fearing that § 10 would preempt all existing state boat safety regulations before the Coast Guard issued any federal rules, the Secretary of Transportation (which until recently housed the Coast Guard) issued a regulation the day after the signing of the FBSA exempting all then-existing state laws from the preemption provisions of the Act. When the Coast Guard did issue regulations under the FBSA, it simultaneously limited the scope of its original blanket exemption to avoid preemption only of those state laws regulating matters not covered by the federal safety rules.

Unfortunately this orderly approach to the preemption problem may have scant effect on the troublesome and ubiquitous issue of the continued vitality of state common law. For, not only does the language of § 10 of the FSBA suggest that the Secretary's power to control preemptive effect covers only state statutes or administrative regulations, § 40 of the Act also provides that, "Compliance with this chapter or standards, regulations, or orders prescribed under this chapter does not relieve a person from liability at common law or under state law." 46 U.S.C. § 4311(g). Hence, in *Sprietsma v. Mercury Marine*, 537 U.S. 51 (2002), the Supreme Court was faced with deciding whether the failure of the Coast Guard to adopt a regulation requiring propeller guards on outboard motors foreclosed a state common law suit premised on the theory that the failure to provide a propeller guard rendered the defendant's outboard motors unreasonably dangerous. Once again the Court found that the language of the statute failed to solve the preemption problem. And, once again, although finding that this state common law claim was not preempted, the Supreme Court relied heavily on the agency's litigation submission that preemption was not necessary. Indeed, the opinion by Justice Stevens, for a unanimous court, highlighted the section of *Geier* (a section that Justice Breyer had labeled merely "a final note") that counseled deference to the agency's interpretation.

Perhaps Congress should broaden agency authority to determine the preemptive effect of federal policy by explicitly authorizing agencies to determine by regulation whether state common law is or is not preempted. And, of course, agencies might do so even in the absence of explicit authorization. Yet, notwithstanding the Supreme Court's deferential treatment of agency pronouncements in *Geier* and *Sprietsma*, the effect to be given agencies' determinations of their regulations' preemptive effect remains uncertain. Presumably such regulations, as interpretations of the agency's governing statute, should be accorded *Chevron* deference. Yet, as we noted in connection with § 1983, there is an obvious tension in this context between *Chevron* deference and the solicitude that the Supreme Court has showed for state prerogatives in its state sovereign immunity jurisprudence. A solicitude that seems to have been imported into the interpretation of § 1983 as well. If Congress has only sharply limited powers to abrogate state sovereign immunity, and must unambiguously (and presumably textually) establish rights that can be enforced through § 1983, one wonders why federal agency power to determine the continuing effectiveness of state legislation, state regulation and state common law should be viewed as constitutionally non-problematic.

Appendix A

THE CONSTITUTION OF THE UNITED STATES

ARTICLE I

Section 1. All legislative Powers herein granted shall be vested in a Congress of the United States, which shall consist of a Senate and House of Representatives. * * *

Section 7. All Bills for raising Revenue shall originate in the House of Representatives; but the Senate may propose or concur with Amendments as on other Bills.

Every Bill which shall have passed the House of Representatives and the Senate, shall, before it become a Law, be presented to the President of the United States; If he approve he shall sign it, but if not he shall return it, with his Objections to that House in which it shall have originated, who shall enter the Objections at large on their Journal, and proceed to reconsider it. If after such Reconsideration two thirds of that House shall agree to pass the Bill, it shall be sent, together with the Objections, to the other House, by which it shall likewise be reconsidered, and if approved by two thirds of that House, it shall become a Law. * * * If any Bill shall not be returned by the President within ten Days (Sunday excepted) after it shall have been presented to him, the Same shall be a Law, in like Manner as if he had signed it, unless the Congress by their Adjournment prevent its Return, in which Case it shall not be a Law.

Every Order, Resolution, or Vote to which the Concurrence of the Senate and House of Representatives may be necessary (except on a question of Adjournment) shall be presented to the President of the United States; and before the Same shall take Effect, shall be approved by him, or being disapproved by him, shall be repassed by two thirds of the Senate and House of Representatives, according to the Rules and Limitations prescribed in the Case of a Bill.

Section 8. The Congress shall have Power To lay and collect Taxes, Duties, Imposts and Excises, to pay the Debts and provide for the common Defense and general Welfare of the United States; * * *

To regulate Commerce with foreign Nations, and among the several States, and with the Indian Tribes;

To establish an uniform Rule of Naturalization, and uniform Laws on the subject of Bankruptcies throughout the United States; * * *

To constitute Tribunals inferior to the Supreme Court; * * *

To make all Laws which shall be necessary and proper for carrying into Execution the foregoing Powers, and all other Powers vested by this Constitution in the Government of the United States, or in any Department or Officer thereof. * * *

ARTICLE II

Section 1. The executive Power shall be vested in a President of the United States of America. * * *

Section 2. The President shall be commander in Chief of the Army and Navy of the United States * * *; he may require the Opinion, in writing, of the principal Officer in each of the executive Departments, upon any Subject relating to the Duties of their respective Offices * * *.

He shall have Power, by and with the Advice and Consent of the Senate, to make Treaties, provided two thirds of the Senators present concur; and he shall nominate, and by and with the Advice and Consent of the Senate, shall appoint Ambassadors, other public Ministers and Consuls, Judges of the Supreme Court, and all other Officers of the United States, whose Appointments are not herein otherwise provided for, and which shall be established by Law: but the Congress may by Law vest the Appointment of such inferior Officers, as they think proper, in the President alone, in the Courts of Law, or in the Heads of Departments.

The President shall have Power to fill up all Vacancies that may happen during the Recess of the Senate, by granting Commissions which shall expire at the End of their next Session.

Section 3. He shall from time to time give to the Congress Information of the State of the Union, and recommend to their Consideration such Measures as he shall judge necessary and expedient; * * * he shall take Care that the Laws be faithfully executed, and shall Commission all the Officers of the United States.

Section 4. The President, Vice President and all Civil Officers of the United States, shall be removed from Office on Impeachment for, and Conviction of, Treason, Bribery, or other high Crimes and Misdemeanors.

ARTICLE III

Section 1. The judicial Power of the United States, shall be vested in one Supreme Court, and in such inferior Courts as the Congress may from time to time ordain and establish. The Judges, both of the supreme and inferior Courts, shall hold their Offices during good Behaviour, and shall, at stated Times, receive for their Services, a Compensation, which shall not be diminished during their Continuance in Office.

Section 2. The judicial Power shall extend to all Cases, in Law and Equity, arising under this Constitution, the Laws of the United States, and Treaties made, or which shall be made, under their Authority;—to all Cases affecting Ambassadors, other public Ministers and Consuls;—to all Cases of admiralty and maritime Jurisdiction;—to Controversies to which the United States shall be a Party;—to Controversies between two or more States;—between a State and Citizens of another State;—between Citizens of different States;—between Citizens of the same State claiming Lands under Grants of different States, and between a State, or the Citizens thereof, and foreign States, Citizens or Subjects.

In all Cases affecting Ambassadors, other public Ministers and Consuls, and those in which a State shall be Party, the Supreme Court shall have original Jurisdiction. In all the other Cases before mentioned, the Supreme Court shall have appellate Jurisdiction, both as to Law and Fact, with such Exceptions, and under such Regulations as the congress shall make. * * *

ARTICLE V

The Congress, whenever two thirds of both Houses shall deem it necessary, shall propose Amendments to this Constitution, or, on the Application of the Legislatures of two thirds of the several States, shall call a Convention for proposing Amendments, which, in either Case, shall be valid to all Intents and Purposes, as Part of this Constitution, when ratified by the Legislatures of three fourths of the several States, or by Conventions in three fourths thereof, as the one or the other Mode of Ratification may be proposed by the Congress; Provided that no Amendment which may be made prior to the Year One thousand eight hundred and eight shall in any Manner affect the first and fourth Clauses in the Ninth Section of the first Article; and that no State, without its Consent, shall be deprived of its equal Suffrage in the Senate.

ARTICLE VI

* * *

This Constitution, and the Laws of the United States which shall be made in Pursuance thereof; and all Treaties made, or which shall be made, under the Authority of the United States, shall be the supreme Law of the Land; and the Judges in every State shall be bound thereby, any Thing in the Constitution or Laws of any State to the Contrary notwithstanding.

* * *

Amendment I [1791]

Congress shall make no law respecting an establishment of religion, or prohibiting the free exercise thereof; or abridging the freedom of speech, or of the press; or the right of the people peaceably to assemble, and to petition the Government for a redress of grievances.

* * *

Amendment IV [1791]

The right of the people to be secure in their persons, houses, papers, and effects, against unreasonable searches and seizures, shall not be violated, and no Warrants shall issue, but upon probable cause, supported by oath or affirmation, and particularly describing the place to be searched, and the persons or things to be seized.

Amendment V [1791]

No person shall be held to answer for a capital, or otherwise infamous crime, unless on a presentment or indictment of a Grand Jury, except in cases arising in the land or naval forces, or in the Militia, when in actual service in time of war or public danger; nor shall any person be subject for the same offence to be twice put in jeopardy of life or limb; nor shall be compelled in any criminal case to be a witness against himself, nor be deprived of life, liberty, or property, without due process of law; nor shall private property be taken for public use, without just compensation.

Amendment VI [1791]

In all criminal prosecutions, the accused shall enjoy the right to a speedy and public trial, by an impartial jury of the State and district wherein the crime shall have been committed, which district shall have been previously ascertained by law, and to be informed of the nature and cause of the accusation; to be confronted with the witnesses against him; to have compulsory process for obtaining Witnesses in his favor, and to have the Assistance of Counsel for his defense.

* * *

Amendment IX [1791]

The enumeration in the Constitution, of certain rights, shall not be construed to deny or disparage others retained by the people.

Amendment X [1791]

The powers not delegated to the United States by the Constitution, nor prohibited by it to the States, are reserved to the States respectively, or to the people.

Amendment XI [1798]

The Judicial power of the United States shall not be construed to extend to any suit in law or equity, commenced or prosecuted against one of the United States by Citizens of another State, or by Citizens or Subjects of any Foreign State.

* * *

Amendment XIV [1868]

Section 1. All persons born or naturalized in the United States, and subject to the jurisdiction thereof, are citizens of the United States and of the State wherein they reside. No State shall make or enforce any law which shall abridge the privileges or immunities of citizens of the United States; nor shall any State deprive any person of life, liberty, or property, without due process of law; nor deny to any person within its jurisdiction the equal protection of the laws.

* * *

Section 5. The Congress shall have power to enforce, by appropriate legislation, the provisions of this article.

Appendix B

SELECTED PROVISIONS OF TITLE 28, U.S.C.

---

§ 1331. Federal Question; Amount in Controversy; Costs

The district courts shall have original jurisdiction of all civil actions arising under the Constitution, laws, or treaties of the United States.

§ 1343. Civil Rights and Elective Franchise

(a) The district courts shall have original jurisdiction of any civil action authorized by law to be commenced by any person:

(1) To recover damages for injury to his person or property, or because of the deprivation of any right or privilege of a citizen of the United States, by any act done in furtherance of any conspiracy mentioned in section 1985 of Title 42;

(2) To recover damages from any person who fails to prevent or to aid in preventing any wrongs mentioned in section 1985 of Title 42 which he had knowledge were about to occur and power to prevent;

(3) To redress the deprivation, under color of any State law, statute, ordinance, regulation, custom or usage, of any right, privilege or immunity secured by the Constitution of the United States or by any Act of Congress providing for equal rights of citizens or of all persons within the jurisdiction of the United States;

(4) To recover damages or to secure equitable or other relief under Act of Congress providing for the protection of civil rights, including the right to vote.

* * *

§ 1346. United States as Defendant

(a) The district courts shall have original jurisdiction, concurrent with the United States Court of Federal Claims, of:

(1) Any civil action against the United States for the recovery of any internal-revenue tax alleged to have been erroneously or illegally assessed or collected, or any penalty claimed to have been collected without authority or any sum alleged to have been excessive or in any manner wrongfully collected under the internal-revenue laws;

(2) Any other civil action or claim against the United States, not exceeding $10,000 in amount, founded either upon the Constitution, or any Act of Congress, or any regulation of an executive department, or upon any express or implied contract with the United States, or for liquidated or unliquidated damages in cases not sounding in tort. * * *

(b)(1) Subject to the provisions of chapter 171 of this title, the district courts, together with the United States District Court for the District of the Canal Zone and the District Court of the Virgin Islands, shall have exclusive jurisdiction of civil actions on claims against the United States, for money damages, accruing on and after January 1, 1945, for injury or loss of property, or personal injury or death caused by the negligent or wrongful act or omission of any employee of the Government while acting within the scope of his office or employment, under circumstances where the United States, if a private person, would be liable to the claimant in accordance with the law of the place where the act or omission occurred.

(2) No person convicted of a felony who is incarcerated while awaiting sentencing or while serving a sentence may bring a civil action against the United States or an agency, officer, or employee of the Government, for mental or emotional injury suffered while in custody without a prior showing of physical injury.

(c) The jurisdiction conferred by this section includes jurisdiction of any set-off, counterclaim, or other claim or demand whatever on the part of the United States against any plaintiff commencing an action under this section.

* * *

(f) The district courts shall have exclusive original jurisdiction of civil actions under section 2409a to quiet title to an estate or interest in real property in which an interest is claimed by the United States. * * *

* * *

§ 1361. Action to Compel an Officer of the United States to Perform His Duty

The district courts shall have original jurisdiction of any action in the nature of mandamus to compel an officer or employee of the United States or any agency thereof to perform a duty owed to the plaintiff. * * *

* * *

§ 1391. Venue Generally

(a) A civil action wherein jurisdiction is founded only on diversity of citizenship may, except as otherwise provided by law, be brought only in (1) a judicial district where any defendant resides, if all defendants reside in the same State, (2) a judicial district in which a substantial part of the events or omissions giving rise to the claim occurred, or a substantial part of property that is the subject of the action is situated, or (3) a judicial district in which any defendant is subject to personal jurisdiction at the time the action is commenced, if there is no district in which the action may otherwise be brought.

(b) A civil action wherein jurisdiction is not founded solely on diversity of citizenship may, except as otherwise provided by law, be brought only in (1) a judicial district where any defendant resides, if all defendants reside in the same State, (2) a judicial district in which a substantial part of the events or omissions giving rise to the claim occurred, or a substantial part of property that is the subject of the action is situated, or (3) a judicial district in which any defendant may be found, if there is no district in which the action may otherwise be brought.

(c) For purposes of venue under this chapter, a defendant that is a corporation shall be deemed to reside in any judicial district in which it is subject to personal jurisdiction at the time the action is commenced. In a State which has more than one judicial district and in which a defendant that is a corporation is subject to personal jurisdiction at the time an action is commenced, such corporation shall be deemed to reside in any district in that State within which its contacts would be sufficient to subject it to personal jurisdiction if that district were a separate State, and, if there is no such district, the corporation shall be deemed to reside in the district within which it has the most significant contacts.

(d) An alien may be sued in any district.

(e) A civil action in which a defendant is an officer or employee of the United States or any agency thereof acting in his official capacity or under color of legal authority, or an agency of the United States, or the United States, may, except as otherwise provided by law, be brought in any judicial district in which (1) a defendant in the action resides, (2) a substantial part of the events or omissions giving rise to the claim occurred, or a substantial part of property that is the subject of the action is situated, or (3) the plaintiff resides if no real property is involved in the action. Additional persons may be joined as parties to any such action in accordance with the Federal Rules of Civil Procedure and with such other venue requirements as would be applicable if the United States or one of its officers, employees, or agencies were not a party. The summons and complaint in such an action shall be served as provided by the Federal Rules of Civil Procedure except that the delivery of the summons and complaint to the officer or agency as required by the rules may be made by certified mail beyond the territorial limits of the district in which the action is brought. * * *

§ 2674. Liability of United States

The United States shall be liable, respecting the provisions of this title relating to tort claims, in the same manner and to the same extent as a private individual under like circumstances, but shall not be liable for interest prior to judgment or for punitive damages. * * *

* * *

§ 2680. Exceptions

The provisions of this chapter and section 1346(b) of this title shall not apply to—

(a) Any claim based upon an act or omission of an employee of the Government, exercising due care, in the execution of a statute or regulation, whether or not such statute or regulation be valid, or based upon the exercise or performance or the failure to exercise or perform a discretionary function or duty on the part of a federal agency or an employee of the Government, whether or not the discretion involved be abused.

* * *

(h) Any claim arising out of assault, battery, false imprisonment, false arrest, malicious prosecution, abuse of process, libel, slander, misrepresentation, deceit, or interference with contract rights: Provided, That, with regard to acts or omissions of investigative or law enforcement officers of the United States Government, the provisions of this chapter and section 1346(b) of this title shall apply to any claim arising, on or after the date of the enactment of this proviso, out of assault, battery, false imprisonment, false arrest, abuse of process, or malicious prosecution. For the purpose of this subsection, "investigative or law enforcement officer" means any officer of the United States who is empowered by law to execute searches, to seize evidence, or to make arrests for violations of Federal law. * * *

Appendix C

ADMINISTRATIVE PROCEDURE ACT

5 U.S.C., Chapter 5.

§ 551. Definitions

For the purpose of this subchapter—

(1) "agency" means each authority of the Government of the United States, whether or not it is within or subject to review by another agency, but does not include—

(A) the Congress;

(B) the courts of the United States;

(C) the governments of the territories or possessions of the United States;

(D) the government of the District of Columbia, or except as to the requirements of section 552 of this title—

(E) agencies composed of representatives of the parties or of representatives of organizations of the parties to the disputes determined by them;

(F) courts martial and military commissions;

(G) military authority exercised in the field in time of war or in occupied territory; or

(H) functions conferred by sections 1738, 1739, 1743, and 1744 of title 12; chapter 2 of title 41; Subchapter II of chapter 471 of title 49 or sections 1884, 1891–1902, and former section 1641(b)(2), of title 50, appendix;

(2) "person" includes an individual, partnership, corporation, association, or public or private organization other than an agency;

(3) "party" includes a person or agency named or admitted as a party, or properly seeking and entitled as of right to be admitted as a party, in an agency proceeding, and a person or agency admitted by an agency as a party for limited purposes;

(4) "rule" means the whole or a part of an agency statement of general or particular applicability and future effect designed to implement, interpret, or prescribe law or policy or describing the organization, procedure, or practice requirements of an agency and includes the approval or prescription for the future of rates, wages, corporate or financial structures or reorganization thereof, prices, facilities, appliances, services or allowances therefor or of valuations, costs, or accounting, or practices bearing on any of the foregoing;

(5) "rule making" means agency process for formulating, amending, or repealing a rule;

(6) "order" means the whole or a part of a final disposition, whether affirmative, negative, injunctive, or declaratory in form, of an agency in a matter other than rule making but including licensing;

(7) "adjudication" means agency process for the formulation of an order;

(8) "license" includes the whole or a part of an agency permit, certificate, approval, registration, charter, membership, statutory exemption or other form of permission;

(9) "licensing" includes agency process respecting the grant, renewal, denial, revocation, suspension, annulment, withdrawal, limitation, amendment, modification, or conditioning of a license;

(10) "sanction" includes the whole or a part of an agency—

(A) prohibition, requirement, limitation, or other condition affecting the freedom of a person;

(B) withholding of relief;

(C) imposition of penalty or fine;

(D) destruction, taking, seizure, or withholding of property;

(E) assessment of damages, reimbursement, restitution, compensation, costs, charges, or fees;

(F) requirement, revocation, or suspension of a license; or

(G) taking other compulsory or restrictive action;

(11) "relief" includes the whole or a part of an agency—

(A) grant of money, assistance, license, authority, exemption, exception, privilege, or remedy;

(B) recognition of a claim, right, immunity, privilege, exemption, or exception; or

(C) taking of other action on the application or petition of, and beneficial to, a person;

(12) "agency proceeding" means an agency process as defined by paragraphs (5), (7), and (9) of this section;

(13) "agency action" includes the whole or a part of an agency rule, order, license, sanction, relief, or the equivalent or denial thereof, or failure to act; and

(14) "ex parte communication" means an oral or written communication not on the public record with respect to which reasonable prior notice to all parties is not given, but it shall not include requests for status reports on any matter or proceeding covered by this subchapter.

[5 U.S.C. §§ 552, 552a, and 552b now codify the Freedom of Information Act (including the earlier Federal Register Act), the Privacy Act, and the Government in the Sunshine Act, respectively. All but the Privacy Act are included in Appendix D, "Open Government Statutes."]

§ 553. Rule Making

(a) This section applies, accordingly to the provisions thereof, except to the extent that there is involved—

(1) a military or foreign affairs function of the United States; or

(2) a matter relating to agency management or personnel or to public property, loans, grants, benefits, or contracts.

(b) General notice of proposed rule making shall be published in the Federal Register, unless persons subject thereto are named and either personally served or otherwise have actual notice thereof in accordance with law. The notice shall include—

(1) a statement of the time, place, and nature of public rule making proceedings;

(2) reference to the legal authority under which the rule is proposed; and

(3) either the terms or substance of the proposed rule or a description of the subjects and issues involved.

Except when notice or hearing is required by statute, this subsection does not apply—

(A) to interpretative rules, general statements of policy, or rules of agency organization, procedure, or practice; or

(B) when the agency for good cause finds (and incorporates the finding and a brief statement of reasons therefor in the rules issued) that notice and public procedure thereon are impracticable, unnecessary, or contrary to the public interest.

(c) After notice required by this section, the agency shall give interested persons an opportunity to participate in the rule making through submission of written data, views, or arguments with or without opportunity for oral presentation. After consideration of the relevant matter presented, the agency shall incorporate in the rules adopted a concise general statement of their basis and purpose. When rules are required by statute to be made on the record after opportunity for an agency hearing, sections 556 and 557 of this title apply instead of this subsection.

(d) The required publication or service of a substantive rule shall be made not less than 30 days before its effective date, except—

(1) a substantive rule which grants or recognizes an exemption or relieves a restriction;

(2) interpretative rules and statements of policy; or

(3) as otherwise provided by the agency for good cause found and published with the rule.

(e) Each agency shall give an interested person the right to petition for the issuance, amendment, or repeal of a rule.

§ 554. Adjudications

(a) This section applies, according to the provisions thereof, in every case of adjudication required by statute to be determined on the record after opportunity for an agency hearing, except to the extent that there is involved—

(1) a matter subject to a subsequent trial of the law and the facts de novo in a court;

(2) the selection or tenure of an employee, except an administrative law judge appointed under section 3105 of this title;

(3) proceedings in which decisions rest solely on inspections, tests, or elections;

(4) the conduct of military or foreign affairs functions;

(5) cases in which an agency is acting as an agent for a court; or

(6) the certification of worker representatives.

(b) Persons entitled to notice of an agency hearing shall be timely informed of—

(1) the time, place, and nature of the hearing;

(2) the legal authority and jurisdiction under which the hearing is to be held; and

(3) the matters of fact and law asserted.

When private persons are the moving parties, other parties to the proceeding shall give prompt notice of issues controverted in fact or law; and in other instances agencies may by rule require responsive pleading. In fixing the time and place for hearings, due regard shall be had for the convenience and necessity of the parties or their representatives.

(c) The agency shall give all interested parties opportunity for—

(1) the submission and consideration of facts, arguments, offers of settlement, or proposals of adjustment when time, the nature of the proceeding, and the public interest permit; and

(2) to the extent that the parties are unable so to determine a controversy by consent, hearing and decision on notice and in accordance with sections 556 and 557 of this title.

(d) The employee who presides at the reception of evidence pursuant to section 556 of this title shall make the recommended decision or initial decision required by section 557 of this title, unless he becomes unavailable to the agency. Except to the extent required for the disposition of ex parte matters as authorized by law, such an employee may not—

(1) consult a person or party on a fact in issue, unless on notice and opportunity for all parties to participate; or

(2) be responsible to or subject to the supervision or direction of an employee or agent engaged in the performance of investigative or prosecuting functions for an agency.

An employee or agent engaged in the performance of investigative or prosecuting functions for an agency in a case may not, in that or a factually related case, participate or advise in the decision, recommended decision, or agency review pursuant to section 557 of this title, except as witness or counsel in public proceedings. This subsection does not apply—

(A) in determining applications for initial licenses;

(B) to proceedings involving the validity or application of rates, facilities, or practices of public utilities or carriers; or

(C) to the agency or a member or members of the body comprising the agency.

(e) The agency, with like effect as in the case of other orders, and in its sound discretion, may issue a declaratory order to terminate a controversy or remove uncertainty.

§ 555. Ancillary Matters

(a) This section applies, according to the provisions thereof, except as otherwise provided by this subchapter.

(b) A person compelled to appear in person before an agency or representative thereof is entitled to be accompanied, represented, and advised by counsel or, if permitted by the agency, by other qualified representative. A party is entitled to appear in person or by or with counsel or other duly qualified representative in an agency proceeding. So far as the orderly conduct of public business permits, an interested person may appear before an agency or its responsible employees for the presentation, adjustment, or determination of an issue, request, or controversy in a proceeding, whether interlocutory, summary, or otherwise, or in connection with an agency function. With due regard for the convenience and necessity of the parties or their representatives and within a reasonable time, each agency shall proceed to conclude a matter presented to it. This subsection does not grant or deny a person who is not a lawyer the right to appear for or represent others before an agency or in an agency proceeding.

(c) Process, requirement of a report, inspection, or other investigative act or demand may not be issued, made, or enforced except as authorized by law. A person compelled to submit data or evidence is entitled to retain or, on payment of lawfully prescribed costs, procure a copy or transcript thereof, except that in a non-public investigatory proceeding the witness may for good cause be limited to inspection of the official transcript of his testimony.

(d) Agency subpoenas authorized by law shall be issued to a party on request and, when required by rules of procedure, on a statement or showing of general relevance and reasonable scope of the evidence sought. On contest, the court shall sustain the subpoena or similar process or demand to the extent that it is found to be in accordance with law. In a proceeding for enforcement, the court shall issue an order requiring the appearance of the witness or the production of the evidence or data within a reasonable time under penalty of punishment for contempt in cases of contumacious failure to comply.

(e) Prompt notice shall be given of the denial in whole or in part of a written application, petition, or other request of an interested person made in connection with any agency proceeding. Except in affirming a prior denial or when the denial is self-explanatory, the notice shall be accompanied by a brief statement of the grounds for denial.

§ 556. Hearings; Presiding Employees; Powers and Duties; Burden of Proof; Evidence; Record as Basis of Decision

(a) This section applies, according to the provisions thereof, to hearings required by section 553 or 554 of this title to be conducted in accordance with this section.

(b) There shall preside at the taking of evidence—

(1) the agency;

(2) one or more members of the body which comprises the agency; or

(3) one or more administrative law judges appointed under section 3105 of this title.

This subchapter does not supersede the conduct of specified classes of proceedings, in whole or in part, by or before boards or other employees specially provided for by or designated under statute. The functions of presiding employees and of employees participating in decisions in accordance with section 557 of this title shall be conducted in an impartial manner. A presiding or participating employee may at any time disqualify himself. On the filing in good faith of a timely and sufficient affidavit of personal bias or other disqualification of a presiding or participating employee, the agency shall determine the matters as a part of the record and decision in the case.

(c) Subject to published rules of the agency and within its powers, employees presiding at hearings may—

(1) administer oaths and affirmations;

(2) issue subpoenas authorized by law;

(3) rule on offers of proof and receive relevant evidence;

(4) take depositions or have depositions taken when the ends of justice would be served;

(5) regulate the course of the hearing;

(6) hold conferences for the settlement or simplification of the issues by consent of the parties or by the use of alternative means of dispute resolution as provided in subchapter IV of this chapter;

(7) inform the parties as to the availability of one or more alternative means of dispute resolution, and encourage use of such methods;

(8) require the attendance at any conference held pursuant to paragraph (6) of at least one representative of each party who has authority to negotiate concerning resolution of issues in controversy;

(9) dispose of procedural requests or similar matters;

(10) make or recommend decisions in accordance with section 557 of this title; and

(11) take other action authorized by agency rule consistent with this subchapter.

(d) Except as otherwise provided by statute, the proponent of a rule or order has the burden of proof. Any oral or documentary evidence may be received, but the agency as a matter of policy shall provide for the exclusion of irrelevant, immaterial, or unduly repetitious evidence. A sanction may not be imposed or rule or order issued except on consideration of the whole record or those parts thereof cited by a party and supported by and in accordance with the reliable, probative, and substantial evidence. The agency may, to the extent consistent with the interests of justice and the policy of the underlying statutes administered by the agency, consider a violation of section 557(d) of this title sufficient grounds for a decision adverse to a party who has knowingly committed such violation or knowingly caused such violation to occur. A party is entitled to present his case or defense by oral or documentary evidence, to submit rebuttal evidence, and to conduct such cross-examination as may be required for a full and true disclosure of the facts. In rule making or determining claims for money or benefits or applications for initial licenses an agency may, when a party will not be prejudiced thereby, adopt procedures for the submission of all or part of the evidence in written form.

(e) The transcript of testimony and exhibits, together with all papers and requests filed in the proceeding, constitutes the exclusive record for decision in accordance with section 557 of this title and, on payment of lawfully prescribed costs, shall be made available to the parties. When an agency decision rests on official notice of a material fact not appearing in the evidence in the record, a party is entitled, on timely request, to an opportunity to show the contrary.

§ 557. Initial Decisions; Conclusiveness; Review by Agency; Submissions by Parties; Contents of Decisions; Record

(a) This section applies, according to the provisions thereof, when a hearing is required to be conducted in accordance with section 556 of this title.

(b) When the agency did not preside at the reception of the evidence, the presiding employee or, in cases not subject to section 554(d) of this title, an employee qualified to preside at hearings pursuant to section 556 of this title, shall initially decide the case unless the agency requires, either in specific cases or by general rule, the entire record to be certified to it for decision. When the presiding employee makes an initial decision, that decision then becomes the decision of the agency without further proceedings unless there is an appeal to, or review on motion of, the agency within time provided by rule. On appeal from or review of the initial decision, the agency has all the powers which it would have in making the initial decision except as it may limit the issues on notice or by rule. When the agency makes the decision without having presided at the reception of the evidence, the presiding employee or an employee qualified to preside at hearings pursuant to section 556 of this title shall first recommend a decision, except that in rule making or determining application for initial licenses—

(1) instead thereof the agency may issue a tentative decision or one of its responsible employees may recommend a decision; or

(2) this procedure may be omitted in a case in which the agency finds on the record that due and timely execution of its functions imperatively and unavoidably so requires.

(c) Before a recommended, initial, or tentative decision, or a decision on agency review of the decision of subordinate employees, the parties are entitled to a reasonable opportunity to submit for the consideration of the employees participating in the decisions—

(1) proposed finding and conclusions; or

(2) exceptions to the decisions or recommended decisions of subordinate employees or to tentative agency decisions; and

(3) supporting reasons for the exceptions or proposed findings or conclusions.

The record shall show the ruling on each finding, conclusion, or exception presented. All decisions, including initial, recommended, and tentative decisions, are a part of the record and shall include a statement of—

(A) findings and conclusions, and the reasons or basis therefor, on all the material issues of fact, law, or discretion presented on the record; and

(B) the appropriate rule, order, sanction, relief, or denial thereof.

(d)(1) In any agency proceeding which is subject to subsection (a) of this section, except to the extent required for the disposition of ex parte matters as authorized by law—

(A) no interested person outside the agency shall make or knowingly cause to be made to any member of the body comprising the agency, administrative law judge, or other employee who is or may reasonably be expected to be involved in the decisional process of the proceeding, an ex parte communication relevant to the merits of the proceeding;

(B) no member of the body comprising the agency, administrative law judge, or other employee who is or may reasonably be expected to be involved in the decisional process of the proceeding, shall make or knowingly cause to be made to any interested person outside the agency an ex parte communication relevant to the merits of the proceeding;

(C) a member of the body comprising the agency, administrative law judge, or other employee who is or may reasonably be expected to be involved in the decisional process of such proceeding who receives, or who makes or knowingly causes to be made, a communication prohibited by this subsection shall place on the public record of the proceeding:

(i) all such written communications;

(ii) memoranda stating the substance of all such oral communications; and

(iii) all written responses, and memoranda stating the substance of all oral responses, to the materials described in clauses (i) and (ii) of this subparagraph;

(D) upon receipt of a communication knowingly made or knowingly caused to be made by a party in violation of this subsection, the agency, administrative law judge, or other employee presiding at the hearing may, to the extent consistent with the interests of justice and the policy of the underlying statutes, require the party to show cause why his claim or interest in the proceeding should not be dismissed, denied, disregarded, or otherwise adversely affected on account of such violation; and

(E) the prohibitions of this subsection shall apply beginning at such time as the agency may designate, but in no case shall they begin to apply later than the time at which a proceeding is noticed for hearing unless the person responsible for the communication has knowledge that it will be noticed, in which case the prohibitions shall apply beginning at the time of his acquisition of such knowledge.

(2) This subsection does not constitute authority to withhold information from Congress.

§ 558. Imposition of Sanctions; Determination of Applications for Licenses; Suspension, Revocation, and Expiration of Licenses

(a) This section applies, according to the provisions thereof, to the exercise of a power or authority.

(b) A sanction may not be imposed or a substantive rule or order issued except within jurisdiction delegated to the agency and as authorized by law.

(c) When application is made for a license, required by law, the agency, with due regard for the rights and privileges of all the interested parties or adversely affected persons and within a reasonable time, shall set and complete proceedings required to be conducted in accordance with sections 556 and 557 of this title or other proceedings required by law and shall make its decision. Except in cases of willfulness or those in which public health, interest, or safety requires otherwise, the withdrawal, suspension, revocation, or annulment of a license is lawful only if, before the institution of agency proceedings therefor, the licensee has been given—

(1) notice by the agency in writing of the facts or conduct which may warrant the action; and

(2) opportunity to demonstrate or achieve compliance with all lawful requirements.

When the licensee has made timely and sufficient application for a renewal or a new license in accordance with agency rules, a license with reference to an activity of a continuing nature does not expire until the application has been finally determined by the agency.

§ 559. Effect on Other Laws; Effect of Subsequent Statute

This subchapter, chapter 7, and sections 1305, 3105, 3344, 4301(2)(E), 5372 and 7521 of this title, and the provisions of section 5335(a)(B) of this title that relate to administrative law judges, do not limit or repeal additional requirements imposed by statute or otherwise recognized by law. Except as otherwise required by law, requirements or privileges relating to evidence or procedure apply equally to agencies and persons. Each agency is granted the authority necessary to comply with the requirements of this subchapter through the issuance of rules or otherwise. Subsequent statute may not be held to supersede or modify this subchapter, chapter 7, sections 1305, 3105, 3344, 4301(2)(E), 5372 or 7521 of this title, or the provisions of section 5335(a)(B) of this title that relate to administrative law judges, except to the extent that it does so expressly.

Chapter 7—Judicial Review

§ 701. Application; Definitions

(a) This chapter applies, according to the provisions thereof, except to the extent that—

(1) statutes preclude judicial review; or

(2) agency action is committed to agency discretion by law.

(b) For the purpose of this chapter—

(1) "agency" means each authority of the Government of the United States, whether or not it is within or subject to review by another agency, but does not include—

(A) the Congress;

(B) the courts of the United States;

(C) the governments of the territories or possessions of the United States;

(D) the government of the District of Columbia;

(E) agencies composed of representatives of the parties or of representatives of organizations of the parties to the disputes determined by them;

(F) courts martial and military commissions;

(G) military authority exercised in the field in time of war or in occupied territory; or

(H) functions conferred by sections 1738, 1739, 1743, and 1744 of title 12; chapter 2 of title 41; subchapter II of chapter 471 of title 49; or sections 1884, 1891–1902, and former section 1641(b)(2), of title 50, appendix; and

(2) "person," "rule," "order," "license," "sanction," "relief," and "agency action" have the meanings given them by section 551 of this title.

§ 702. Right of Review

A person suffering legal wrong because of agency action, or adversely affected or aggrieved by agency action within the meaning of a relevant statute, is entitled to judicial review thereof. An action in a court of the United States seeking relief other than money damages and stating a claim that an agency or an officer or employee thereof acted or failed to act in an official capacity or under color of legal authority shall not be dismissed nor relief therein be denied on the ground that it is against the United States or that the United States is an indispensable party. The United States may be named as a defendant in any such action, and a judgment or decree may be entered against the United States: *Provided,* That any mandatory or injunctive decree shall specify the Federal officer or officers (by name or by title), and their successors in office, personally responsible for compliance. Nothing herein (1) affects other limitations on judicial review or the power or duty of the court to dismiss any action or deny relief on any other appropriate legal or equitable ground; or (2) confers authority to grant relief if any other statute that grants consent to suit expressly or impliedly forbids the relief which is sought.

§ 703. Form and Venue of Proceeding

The form of proceeding for judicial review is the special statutory review proceeding relevant to the subject matter in a court specified by statute or, in the absence or inadequacy thereof, any applicable form of legal action, including actions for declaratory judgments or writs of prohibitory or mandatory injunction or habeas corpus, in a court of competent jurisdiction. If no special statutory review proceeding is applicable, the action for judicial review may be brought against the United States, the agency by its official title, or the appropriate officer. Except to the extent that prior, adequate, and exclusive opportunity for judicial review is provided by law, agency action is subject to judicial review in civil or criminal proceedings for judicial enforcement.

§ 704. Actions Reviewable

Agency action made reviewable by statute and final agency action for which there is no other adequate remedy in a court are subject to judicial review. A preliminary, procedural, or intermediate agency action or ruling not directly reviewable is subject to review on the review of the final agency action. Except as otherwise expressly required by statute, agency action otherwise final is final for the purposes of this section whether or not there has been presented or determined an application for a declaratory order, for any form of reconsideration, or, unless the agency otherwise requires by rule and provides that the action meanwhile is inoperative, for an appeal to superior agency authority.

§ 705. Relief Pending Review

When an agency finds that justice so requires, it may postpone the effective date of action taken by it, pending judicial review. On such conditions as may be required and to the extent necessary to prevent irreparable injury, the reviewing court, including the court to which a case may be taken on appeal from or on application for certiorari or other writ to a reviewing court, may issue all necessary and appropriate process to postpone the effective date of an agency action or to preserve status or rights pending conclusion of the review proceedings.

§ 706. Scope of Review

To the extent necessary to decision and when presented, the reviewing court shall decide all relevant questions of law, interpret constitutional and statutory provisions, and determine the meaning or applicability of the terms of an agency action. The reviewing court shall—

(1) compel agency action unlawfully withheld or unreasonably delayed; and

(2) hold unlawful and set aside agency action, findings, and conclusions found to be—

(A) arbitrary, capricious, an abuse of discretion, or otherwise not in accordance with law;

(B) contrary to constitutional right, power, privilege, or immunity;

(C) in excess of statutory jurisdiction, authority, or limitations, or short of statutory right;

(D) without observance of procedure required by law;

(E) unsupported by substantial evidence in a case subject to section 556 and 557 of this title or otherwise reviewed on the record of an agency hearing provided by statute; or

(F) unwarranted by the facts to the extent that the facts are subject to trial de novo by the reviewing court.

In making the foregoing determinations, the court shall review the whole record or those parts of it cited by a party, and due account shall be taken of the rule of prejudicial error.

---

§ 1305. Administrative Law Judges

For the purpose of sections 3105, 3344, 4301(2)(D), and 5372 of this title and the provisions of section 5335(a)(B) of this title that relate to administrative law judges, the Office of Personnel Management may, and for the purpose of section 7521 of this title, the Merit Systems Protection Board may investigate, prescribe regulations, appoint advisory committees as necessary, recommend legislation, subpoena witnesses and records, and pay witness fees as established for the courts of the United States.

§ 3105. Appointment of Administrative Law Judges

Each agency shall appoint as many administrative law judges as are necessary for proceedings required to be conducted in accordance with sections 556 and 557 of this title. Administrative law judges shall be assigned to cases in rotation so far as practicable, and may not perform duties inconsistent with their duties and responsibilities as administrative law judges.

§ 3344. Details; Administrative Law Judges

An agency as defined by section 551 of this title which occasionally or temporarily is insufficiently staffed with administrative law judges appointed under section 3105 of this title may use administrative law judges selected by the Office of Personnel Management from and with the consent of other agencies.

§ 5372. Administrative Law Judges

(a) For the purposes of this section, the term "administrative law judge" means an administrative law judge appointed under section 3105.

(b)(1)(A)There shall be 3 levels of basic pay for administrative law judges (designated as AL–1, 2, and 3, respectively), and each such judge shall be paid at 1 of those levels, in accordance with the provisions of this section.

(B) Within level AL–3, there shall be 6 rates of basic pay, designated as AL–3, rates A through F, respectively. Level AL–2 and level AL–1 shall each have 1 rate of basic pay.

(C) The rate of basic pay for AL–3, rate A, may not be less than 65 percent of the rate of basic pay for level IV of the Executive Schedule, and the rate of basic pay for AL–1 may not exceed the rate for level IV of the Executive Schedule.

(2) The Office of Personnel Management shall determine, in accordance with procedures which the Office shall by regulation prescribe, the level in which each administrative-law-judge position shall be placed and the qualifications to be required for appointment to each level.

(3)(A) Upon appointment to a position in AL–3, an administrative law judge shall be paid at rate A of AL–3, and shall be advanced successively to rates B, C, and D of that level at the beginning of the next pay period following completion of 52 weeks of service in the next lower rate, and to rates E and F of that level at the beginning of the next pay period following completion of 104 weeks of service in the next lower rate.

(B) The Office of Personnel Management may provide for appointment of an administrative law judge in AL–3 at an advanced rate under such circumstances as the Office may determine appropriate.

(4) Subject to paragraph (1), effective at the beginning of the first applicable pay period commencing on or after the first day of the month in which an adjustment takes effect under section 5303 in the rates of basic pay under the General Schedule, each rate of basic pay for administrative law judges shall be adjusted by an amount determined by the President to be appropriate.

(c) The Office of Personnel Management shall prescribe regulations necessary to administer this section.

§ 7521. Actions Against Administrative Law Judges

(a) An action may be taken against an administrative law judge appointed under section 3105 of this title by the agency in which the administrative law judge is employed only for good cause established and determined by the Merit Systems Protection Board on the record after opportunity for hearing before the Board.

(b) The actions covered by this section are—

(1) a removal;

(2) a suspension;

(3) a reduction in grade;

(4) a reduction in pay; and

(5) a furlough of 30 days or less;

but do not include—

(A) a suspension or removal under section 7532 of this title;

(B) a reduction-in-force action under section 3502 of this title; or

(C) any action initiated under section 1215 of this title.

Appendix D

OPEN GOVERNMENT STATUTES

FREEDOM OF INFORMATION ACT

§ 552. Public information; agency rules, opinions, orders, records, and proceedings

(a) Each agency shall make available to the public information as follows:

(1) Each agency shall separately state and currently publish in the Federal Register for the guidance of the public—

(A) descriptions of its central and field organization and the established places at which, the employees (and in the case of a uniformed service, the members) from whom, and the methods whereby, the public may obtain information, make submittals or requests, or obtain decisions;

(B) statements of the general course and method by which its functions are channeled and determined, including the nature and requirements of all formal and informal procedures available;

(C) rules of procedure, descriptions of forms available or the places at which forms may be obtained, and instructions as to the scope and contents of all papers, reports, or examinations;

(D) substantive rules of general applicability adopted as authorized by law, and statements of general policy or interpretations of general applicability formulated and adopted by the agency; and

(E) each amendment, revision, or repeal of the foregoing.

Except to the extent that a person has actual and timely notice of the terms thereof, a person may not in any manner be required to resort to, or be adversely affected by, a matter required to be published in the Federal Register and not so published. For the purpose of this paragraph, matter reasonably available to the class of persons affected thereby is deemed published in the Federal Register when incorporated by reference therein with the approval of the Director of the Federal Register.

(2) Each agency, in accordance with published rules, shall make available for public inspection and copying—

(A) final opinions, including concurring and dissenting opinions, as well as orders, made in the adjudication of cases;

(B) those statements of policy and interpretations which have been adopted by the agency and are not published in the Federal Register;

(C) administrative staff manuals and instructions to staff that affect a member of the public;

(D) copies of all records, regardless of form or format, which have been released to any person under paragraph (3) and which, because of the nature of their subject matter, the agency determines have become or are likely to become the subject of subsequent requests for substantially the same records; and

(E) a general index of the records referred to under subparagraph (D);

unless the materials are promptly published and copies offered for sale. For records created on or after November 1, 1996, within one year after such date, each agency shall make such records available, including by computer telecommunications or, if computer telecommunications means have not been established by the agency, by other electronic means. To the extent required to prevent a clearly unwarranted invasion of personal privacy, an agency may delete identifying details when it makes available or publishes an opinion, statement of policy, interpretation, staff manual, instruction, or copies of records referred to in subparagraph (D). However, in each case the justification for the deletion shall be explained fully in writing, and the extent of such deletion shall be indicated on the portion of the record which is made available or published, unless including that indication would harm an interest protected by the exemption in subsection (b) under which the deletion is made. If technically feasible, the extent of the deletion shall be indicated at the place in the record where the deletion was made. Each agency shall also maintain and make available for public inspection and copying current indexes providing identifying information for the public as to any matter issued, adopted, or promulgated after July 4, 1967, and required by this paragraph to be made available or published. Each agency shall make the index referred to in subparagraph (E) available by computer telecommunications by December 31, 1999. Each agency shall promptly publish, quarterly or more frequently, and distribute (by sale or otherwise) copies of each index or supplements thereto unless it determines by order published in the Federal Register that the publication would be unnecessary and impracticable, in which case the agency shall nonetheless provide copies of such index on request at a cost not to exceed the direct cost of duplication. A final order, opinion, statement of policy, interpretation, or staff manual or instruction that affects a member of the public may be relied on, used, or cited as precedent by an agency against a party other than an agency only if—

(i) it has been indexed and either made available or published as provided by this paragraph; or

(ii) the party has actual and timely notice of the terms thereof.

(3)(A) Except with respect to the records made available under paragraphs (1) and (2) of this subsection, and except as provided in subparagraph (E), each agency, upon any request for records which (i) reasonably describes such records and (ii) is made in accordance with published rules stating the time, place, fees (if any), and procedures to be followed, shall make the records promptly available to any person.

(B) In making any record available to a person under this paragraph, an agency shall provide the record in any form or format requested by the person if the record is readily reproducible by the agency in that form or format. Each agency shall make reasonable efforts to maintain its records in forms or formats that are reproducible for purposes of this section.

(C) In responding under this paragraph to a request for records, an agency shall make reasonable efforts to search for the records in electronic form or format, except when such efforts would significantly interfere with the operation of the agency's automated information system.

(D) For purposes of this paragraph, the term "search" means to review, manually or by automated means, agency records for the purpose of locating those records which are responsive to a request.

(E) An agency, or part of an agency, that is an element of the intelligence community (as that term is defined in section 3(4) of the National Security Act of 1947 (50 U.S.C. 401a(4))) shall not make any record available under this paragraph to—

(i) any government entity, other than a State, territory, commonwealth, or district of the United States, or any subdivision thereof; or

(ii) a representative of a government entity described in clause (i).

(4)(A)(i) In order to carry out the provisions of this section, each agency shall promulgate regulations,

pursuant to notice and receipt of public comment, specifying the schedule of fees applicable to the processing of requests under this section and establishing procedures and guidelines for determining when such fees should be waived or reduced. Such schedule shall conform to the guidelines which shall be promulgated, pursuant to notice and receipt of public comment, by the Director of the Office of Management and

Budget and which shall provide for a uniform schedule of fees for all agencies.

(ii) Such agency regulations shall provide that—

(I) fees shall be limited to reasonable standard charges for document search, duplication, and review, when records are requested for commercial use;

(II) fees shall be limited to reasonable standard charges for document duplication when records are not sought for commercial use and the request is made by an educational or noncommercial scientific institution, whose purpose is scholarly or scientific research; or a representative of the news media; and

(III) for any request not described in (I) or (II), fees shall be limited to reasonable standard charges for document search and duplication.

(iii) Documents shall be furnished without any charge or at a charge reduced below the fees established under clause (ii) if disclosure of the information is in the public interest because it is likely to contribute significantly to public understanding of the operations or activities of the government and is not primarily in the commercial interest of the requester.

(iv) Fee schedules shall provide for the recovery of only the direct costs of search, duplication, or review. Review costs shall include only the direct costs incurred during the initial examination of a document for the purposes of determining whether the documents must be disclosed under this section and for the purposes of withholding any portions exempt from disclosure under this section. Review costs may not include any costs incurred in resolving issues of law or policy that may be raised in the course of processing a request under this section. No fee may be charged by any agency under this section—

(I) if the costs of routine collection and processing of the fee are likely to equal or exceed the amount of the fee; or

(II) for any request described in clause (ii)(II) or (III) of this subparagraph for the first two hours of search time or for the first one hundred pages of duplication.

(v) No agency may require advance payment of any fee unless the requester has previously failed to pay fees in a timely fashion, or the agency has determined that the fee will exceed $250.

(vi) Nothing in this subparagraph shall supersede fees chargeable under a statute specifically providing for setting the level of fees for particular types of records.

(vii) In any action by a requester regarding the waiver of fees under this section, the court shall determine the matter de novo: Provided, That the court's review of the matter shall be limited to the record before the agency.

(B) On complaint, the district court of the United States in the district in which the complainant resides, or has his principal place of business, or in which the agency records are situated, or in the District of Columbia, has jurisdiction to enjoin the agency from withholding agency records and to order the production of any agency records improperly withheld from the complainant. In such a case the court shall determine the matter de novo, and may examine the contents of such agency records in camera to determine whether such records or any part thereof shall be withheld under any of the exemptions set forth in subsection (b) of this section, and the burden is on the agency to sustain its action. In addition to any other matters to which a court accords substantial weight, a court shall accord substantial weight to an affidavit of an agency concerning the agency's determination as to technical feasibility under paragraph (2)(C) and subsection (b) and reproducibility under paragraph (3)(B).

(C) Notwithstanding any other provision of law, the defendant shall serve an answer or otherwise plead to any complaint made under this subsection within thirty days after service upon the defendant of the pleading in which such complaint is made, unless the court otherwise directs for good cause shown.

[(D) Repealed. Pub. L. 98–620, Title IV, § 402(2), Nov. 8, 1984, 98 Stat. 3357]

(E) The court may assess against the United States reasonable attorney fees and other litigation costs reasonably incurred in any case under this section in which the complainant has substantially prevailed.

(F) Whenever the court orders the production of any agency records improperly withheld from the complainant and assesses against the United States reasonable attorney fees and other litigation costs, and the court additionally issues a written finding that the circumstances surrounding the withholding raise questions whether agency personnel acted arbitrarily or capriciously with respect to the withholding, the Special Counsel shall promptly initiate a proceeding to determine whether disciplinary action is warranted against the officer or employee who was primarily responsible for the withholding. The Special Counsel, after investigation and consideration of the evidence submitted, shall submit his findings and recommendations to the administrative authority of the agency concerned and shall send copies of the findings and recommendations to the officer or employee or his representative. The administrative authority shall take the corrective action that the Special Counsel recommends.

(G) In the event of noncompliance with the order of the court, the district court may punish for contempt the responsible employee, and in the case of a uniformed service, the responsible member.

(5) Each agency having more than one member shall maintain and make available for public inspection a record of the final votes of each member in every agency proceeding.

(6)(A) Each agency, upon any request for records made under paragraph (1), (2), or (3) of this subsection, shall—

(i) determine within 20 days (excepting Saturdays, Sundays, and legal public holidays) after the receipt of any such request whether to comply with such request and shall immediately notify the person making such request of such determination and the reasons therefor, and of the right of such person to appeal to the head of the agency any adverse determination; and

(ii) make a determination with respect to any appeal within twenty days (excepting Saturdays, Sundays, and legal public holidays) after the receipt of such appeal. If on appeal the denial of the request for records is in whole or in part upheld, the agency shall notify the person making such request of the provisions for judicial review of that determination under paragraph (4) of this subsection.

(B)(i) In unusual circumstances as specified in this subparagraph, the time limits prescribed in either clause (i) or clause (ii) of subparagraph (A) may be extended by written notice to the person making such request setting forth the unusual circumstances for such extension and the date on which a determination is expected to be dispatched. No such notice shall specify a date that would result in an extension for more than ten working days, except as provided in clause (ii) of this subparagraph.

(ii) With respect to a request for which a written notice under clause (i) extends the time limits prescribed under clause (i) of subparagraph (A), the agency shall notify the person making the request if the request cannot be processed within the time limit specified in that clause and shall provide the person an opportunity to limit the scope of the request so that it may be processed within that time limit or an opportunity to arrange with the agency an alternative time frame for processing the request or a modified request. Refusal by the person to reasonably modify the request or arrange such an alternative time frame shall be considered as a factor in determining whether exceptional circumstances exist for purposes of subparagraph (C).

(iii) As used in this subparagraph, "unusual circumstances" means, but only to the extent reasonably necessary to the proper processing of the particular requests—

(I) the need to search for and collect the requested records from field facilities or other establishments that are separate from the office processing the request;

(II) the need to search for, collect, and appropriately examine a voluminous amount of separate and distinct records which are demanded in a single request; or

(III) the need for consultation, which shall be conducted with all practicable speed, with another agency having a substantial interest in the determination of the request or among two or more components of the agency having substantial subject-matter interest therein.

(iv) Each agency may promulgate regulations, pursuant to notice and receipt of public comment, providing for the aggregation of certain requests by the same requestor, or by a group of requestors acting in concert, if the agency reasonably believes that such requests actually constitute a single request, which would otherwise satisfy the unusual circumstances specified in this subparagraph, and the requests involve clearly related matters. Multiple requests involving unrelated matters shall not be aggregated.

(C)(i) Any person making a request to any agency for records under paragraph (1), (2), or (3) of this subsection shall be deemed to have exhausted his administrative remedies with respect to such request if the agency fails to comply with the applicable time limit provisions of this paragraph. If the Government can show exceptional circumstances exist and that the agency is exercising due diligence in responding to the request, the court may retain jurisdiction and allow the agency additional time to complete its review of the records. Upon any determination by an agency to comply with a request for records, the records shall be made promptly available to such person making such request. Any notification of denial of any request for records under this subsection shall set forth the names and titles or positions of each person responsible for the denial of such request.

(ii) For purposes of this subparagraph, the term "exceptional circumstances" does not include a delay that results from a predictable agency workload of requests under this section, unless the agency demonstrates reasonable progress in reducing its backlog of pending requests.

(iii) Refusal by a person to reasonably modify the scope of a request or arrange an alternative time frame for processing a request (or a modified request) under clause (ii) after being given an opportunity to do so by the agency to whom the person made the request shall be considered as a factor in determining whether exceptional circumstances exist for purposes of this subparagraph.

(D)(i) Each agency may promulgate regulations, pursuant to notice and receipt of public comment, providing for multitrack processing of requests for records based on the amount of work or time (or both) involved in processing requests.

(ii) Regulations under this subparagraph may provide a person making a request that does not qualify for the fastest multitrack processing an opportunity to limit the scope of the request in order to qualify for faster processing.

(iii) This subparagraph shall not be considered to affect the requirement under subparagraph (C) to exercise due diligence.

(E)(i) Each agency shall promulgate regulations, pursuant to notice and receipt of public comment, providing for expedited processing of requests for records—

(I) in cases in which the person requesting the records demonstrates a compelling need; and

(II) in other cases determined by the agency.

(ii) Notwithstanding clause (i), regulations under this subparagraph must ensure—

(I) that a determination of whether to provide expedited processing shall be made, and notice of the determination shall be provided to the person making the request, within 10 days after the date of the request; and

(II) expeditious consideration of administrative appeals of such determinations of whether to provide expedited processing.

(iii) An agency shall process as soon as practicable any request for records to which the agency has granted expedited processing under this subparagraph. Agency action to deny or affirm denial of a request for expedited processing pursuant to this subparagraph, and failure by an agency to respond in a timely manner to such a request shall be subject to judicial review under paragraph (4), except that the judicial review shall be based on the record before the agency at the time of the determination.

(iv) A district court of the United States shall not have jurisdiction to review an agency denial of expedited processing of a request for records after the agency has provided a complete response to the request.

(v) For purposes of this subparagraph, the term "compelling need" means—

(I) that a failure to obtain requested records on an expedited basis under this paragraph could reasonably be expected to pose an imminent threat to the life or physical safety of an individual; or

(II) with respect to a request made by a person primarily engaged in disseminating information, urgency to inform the public concerning actual or alleged Federal Government activity.

(vi) A demonstration of a compelling need by a person making a request for expedited processing shall be made by a statement certified by such person to be true and correct to the best of such person's knowledge and belief. (F) In denying a request for records, in whole or in part, an agency shall make a reasonable effort to estimate the volume of any requested matter the provision of which is denied, and shall provide any such estimate to the person making the request, unless providing such estimate would harm an interest protected by the exemption in subsection (b) pursuant to which the denial is made.

(b) This section does not apply to matters that are—

(1)(A) specifically authorized under criteria established by an Executive order to be kept secret in the interest of national defense or foreign policy and (B) are in fact properly classified pursuant to such Executive order;

(2) related solely to the internal personnel rules and practices of an agency;

(3) specifically exempted from disclosure by statute (other than section 552b of this title), provided that such statute (A) requires that the matters be withheld from the public in such a manner as to leave no discretion on the issue, or (B) establishes particular criteria for withholding or refers to particular types of matters to be withheld;

(4) trade secrets and commercial or financial information obtained from a person and privileged or confidential;

(5) inter-agency or intra-agency memorandums or letters which would not be available by law to a party other than an agency in litigation with the agency;

(6) personnel and medical files and similar files the disclosure of which would constitute a clearly unwarranted invasion of personal privacy;

(7) records or information compiled for law enforcement purposes, but only to the extent that the production of such law enforcement records or information (A) could reasonably be expected to interfere with enforcement proceedings, (B) would deprive a person of a right to a fair trial or an impartial adjudication, (C) could reasonably be expected to constitute an unwarranted invasion of personal privacy, (D) could reasonably be expected to disclose the identity of a confidential source, including a State, local, or foreign agency or authority or any private institution which furnished information on a confidential basis, and, in the case of a record or information compiled by criminal law enforcement authority in the course of a criminal investigation or by an agency conducting a lawful national security intelligence investigation, informa-

tion furnished by a confidential source, (E) would disclose techniques and procedures for law enforcement investigations or prosecutions, or would disclose guidelines for law enforcement investigations or prosecutions if such disclosure could reasonably be expected to risk circumvention of the law, or (F) could reasonably be expected to endanger the life or physical safety of any individual;

(8) contained in or related to examination, operating, or condition reports prepared by, on behalf of, or for the use of an agency responsible for the regulation or supervision of financial institutions; or

(9) geological and geophysical information and data, including maps, concerning wells.

Any reasonably segregable portion of a record shall be provided to any person requesting such record after deletion of the portions which are exempt under this subsection. The amount of information deleted shall be indicated on the released portion of the record, unless including that indication would harm an interest protected by the exemption in this subsection under which the deletion is made. If technically feasible, the amount of the information deleted shall be indicated at the place in the record where such deletion is made.

(c)(1) Whenever a request is made which involves access to records described in subsection (b)(7)(A) and—

(A) the investigation or proceeding involves a possible violation of criminal law; and

(B) there is reason to believe that (i) the subject of the investigation or proceeding is not aware of its pendency, and (ii) disclosure of the existence of the records could reasonably be expected to interfere with enforcement proceedings,

the agency may, during only such time as that circumstance continues, treat the records as not subject to the requirements of this section.

(2) Whenever informant records maintained by a criminal law enforcement agency under an informant's name or personal identifier are requested by a third party according to the informant's name or personal identifier, the agency may treat the records as not subject to the requirements of this section unless the informant's status as an informant has been officially confirmed.

(3) Whenever a request is made which involves access to records maintained by the Federal Bureau of Investigation pertaining to foreign intelligence or counterintelligence, or international terrorism, and the existence of the records is classified information as provided in subsection (b)(1), the Bureau may, as long as the existence of the records remains classified information, treat the records as not subject to the requirements of this section.

(d) This section does not authorize withholding of information or limit the availability of records to the public, except as specifically stated in this section. This section is not authority to withhold information from Congress.

(e)(1) On or before February 1 of each year, each agency shall submit to the Attorney General of the United States a report which shall cover the preceding fiscal year and which shall include—

(A) the number of determinations made by the agency not to comply with requests for records made to such agency under subsection (a) and the reasons for each such determination;

(B)(i) the number of appeals made by persons under subsection (a)(6), the result of such appeals, and the reason for the action upon each appeal that results in a denial of information; and

(ii) a complete list of all statutes that the agency relies upon to authorize the agency to withhold information under subsection (b)(3), a description of whether a court has upheld the decision of the agency to withhold information under each such statute, and a concise description of the scope of any information withheld;

(C) the number of requests for records pending before the agency as of September 30 of the preceding year, and the median number of days that such requests had been pending before the agency as of that date;

(D) the number of requests for records received by the agency and the number of requests which the agency processed;

(E) the median number of days taken by the agency to process different types of requests;

(F) the total amount of fees collected by the agency for processing requests; and

(G) the number of full-time staff of the agency devoted to processing requests for records under this section, and the total amount expended by the agency for processing such requests.

(2) Each agency shall make each such report available to the public including by computer telecommunications, or if computer telecommunications means have not been established by the agency, by other electronic means.

(3) The Attorney General of the United States shall make each report which has been made available by electronic means available at a single electronic access point. The Attorney General of the United States shall notify the Chairman and ranking minority member of the Committee on Government Reform and Oversight of the House of Representatives and the Chairman and ranking minority member of the Committees on Governmental Affairs and the Judiciary of the Senate, no later than April 1 of the year in which each such report is issued, that such reports are available by electronic means.

(4) The Attorney General of the United States, in consultation with the Director of the Office of Management and Budget, shall develop

reporting and performance guidelines in connection with reports required by this subsection by October 1, 1997, and may establish additional requirements for such reports as the Attorney General determines may be useful.

(5) The Attorney General of the United States shall submit an annual report on or before April 1 of each calendar year which shall include for the prior calendar year a listing of the number of cases arising under this section, the exemption involved in each case, the disposition of such case, and the cost, fees, and penalties assessed under subparagraphs (E), (F), and (G) of subsection (a)(4). Such report shall also include a description of the efforts undertaken by the Department of Justice to encourage agency compliance with this section.

(f) For purposes of this section, the term—

(1) "agency" as defined in section 551(1) of this title includes any executive department, military department, Government corporation, Government controlled corporation, or other establishment in the executive branch of the Government (including the Executive Office of the President), or any independent regulatory agency; and

(2) "record" and any other term used in this section in reference to information includes any information that would be an agency record subject to the requirements of this section when maintained by an agency in any format, including an electronic format.

(g) The head of each agency shall prepare and make publicly available upon request, reference material or a guide for requesting records or information from the agency, subject to the exemptions in subsection (b), including—

(1) an index of all major information systems of the agency;

(2) a description of major information and record locator systems maintained by the agency; and

(3) a handbook for obtaining various types and categories of public information from the agency pursuant to chapter 35 of title 44, and under this section.

GOVERNMENT IN THE SUNSHINE ACT

§ 552b. Open meetings

(a) For purposes of this section—

(1) the term "agency" means any agency, as defined in section 552(e) of this title, headed by a collegial body composed of two or more individual members, a majority of whom are appointed to such position by the President with the advice and consent of the Senate, and any subdivision thereof authorized to act on behalf of the agency;

(2) the term "meeting" means the deliberations of at least the number of individual agency members required to take action on behalf of the agency where such deliberations determine or result in the joint

conduct or disposition of official agency business, but does not include deliberations required or permitted by subsection (d) or (e); and

(3) the term "member" means an individual who belongs to a collegial body heading an agency.

(b) Members shall not jointly conduct or dispose of agency business other than in accordance with this section. Except as provided in subsection (c), every portion of every meeting of an agency shall be open to public observation.

(c) Except in a case where the agency finds that the public interest requires otherwise, the second sentence of subsection (b) shall not apply to any portion of an agency meeting, and the requirements of subsections (d) and (e) shall not apply to any information pertaining to such meeting otherwise required by this section to be disclosed to the public, where the agency properly determines that such portion or portions of its meeting or the disclosure of such information is likely to—

(1) disclose matters that are (A) specifically authorized under criteria established by an Executive order to be kept secret in the interests of national defense or foreign policy and (B) in fact properly classified pursuant to such Executive order;

(2) relate solely to the internal personnel rules and practices of an agency;

(3) disclose matters specifically exempted from disclosure by statute (other than section 552 of this title), provided that such statute (A) requires that the matters be withheld from the public in such a manner as to leave no discretion on the issue, or (B) establishes particular criteria for withholding or refers to particular types of matters to be withheld;

(4) disclose trade secrets and commercial or financial information obtained from a person and privileged or confidential;

(5) involve accusing any person of a crime, or formally censuring any person;

(6) disclose information of a personal nature where disclosure would constitute a clearly unwarranted invasion of personal privacy;

(7) disclose investigatory records compiled for law enforcement purposes, or information which if written would be contained in such records, but only to the extent that the production of such records or information would (A) interfere with enforcement proceedings, (B) deprive a person of a right to a fair trial or an impartial adjudication, (C) constitute an unwarranted invasion of personal privacy, (D) disclose the identity of a confidential source and, in the case of a record compiled by a criminal law enforcement authority in the course of a criminal investigation, or by an agency conducting a lawful national security intelligence investigation, confidential information furnished only by the confidential source, (E) disclose investigative techniques and procedures, or (F) endanger the life or physical safety of law enforcement personnel;

(8) disclose information contained in or related to examination, operating, or condition reports prepared by, on behalf of, or for the use of an agency responsible for the regulation or supervision of financial institutions;

(9) disclose information the premature disclosure of which would—

(A) in the case of an agency which regulates currencies, securities, commodities, or financial institutions, be likely to (i) lead to significant financial speculation in currencies, securities, or commodities, or (ii) significantly endanger the stability of any financial institution; or

(B) in the case of any agency, be likely to significantly frustrate implementation of a proposed agency action,

except that subparagraph (B) shall not apply in any instance where the agency has already disclosed to the public the content or nature of its proposed action, or where the agency is required by law to make such disclosure on its own initiative prior to taking final agency action on such proposal; or

(10) specifically concern the agency's issuance of a subpena, or the agency's participation in a civil action or proceeding, an action in a foreign court or international tribunal, or an arbitration, or the initiation, conduct, or disposition by the agency of a particular case of formal agency adjudication pursuant to the procedures in section 554 of this title or otherwise involving a determination on the record after opportunity for a hearing.

(d)(1) Action under subsection (c) shall be taken only when a majority of the entire membership of the agency (as defined in subsection (a)(1)) votes to take such action. A separate vote of the agency members shall be taken with respect to each agency meeting a portion or portions of which are proposed to be closed to the public pursuant to subsection (c), or with respect to any information which is proposed to be withheld under subsection (c). A single vote may be taken with respect to a series of meetings, a portion or portions of which are proposed to be closed to the public, or with respect to any information concerning such series of meetings, so long as each meeting in such series involves the same particular matters and is scheduled to be held no more than thirty days after the initial meeting in such series. The vote of each agency member participating in such vote shall be recorded and no proxies shall be allowed.

(2) Whenever any person whose interests may be directly affected by a portion of a meeting requests that the agency close such portion to the public for any of the reasons referred to in paragraph (5), (6), or (7) of subsection (c), the agency, upon request of any one of its members, shall vote by recorded vote whether to close such meeting.

(3) Within one day of any vote taken pursuant to paragraph (1) or (2), the agency shall make publicly available a written copy of such vote reflecting the vote of each member on the question. If a portion of a

meeting is to be closed to the public, the agency shall, within one day of the vote taken pursuant to paragraph (1) or (2) of this subsection, make publicly available a full written explanation of its action closing the portion together with a list of all persons expected to attend the meeting and their affiliation.

(4) Any agency, a majority of whose meetings may properly be closed to the public pursuant to paragraph (4), (8), (9)(A), or (10) of subsection (c), or any combination thereof, may provide by regulation for the closing of such meetings or portions thereof in the event that a majority of the members of the agency votes by recorded vote at the beginning of such meeting, or portion thereof, to close the exempt portion or portions of the meeting, and a copy of such vote, reflecting the vote of each member on the question, is made available to the public. The provisions of paragraphs (1), (2), and (3) of this subsection and subsection (e) shall not apply to any portion of a meeting to which such regulations apply: Provided, That the agency shall, except to the extent that such information is exempt from disclosure under the provisions of subsection (c), provide the public with public announcement of the time, place, and subject matter of the meeting and of each portion thereof at the earliest practicable time.

(e)(1) In the case of each meeting, the agency shall make public announcement, at least one week before the meeting, of the time, place, and subject matter of the meeting, whether it is to be open or closed to the public, and the name and phone number of the official designated by the agency to respond to requests for information about the meeting. Such announcement shall be made unless a majority of the members of the agency determines by a recorded vote that agency business requires that such meeting be called at an earlier date, in which case the agency shall make public announcement of the time, place, and subject matter of such meeting, and whether open or closed to the public, at the earliest practicable time.

(2) The time or place of a meeting may be changed following the public announcement required by paragraph (1) only if the agency publicly announces such change at the earliest practicable time. The subject matter of a meeting, or the determination of the agency to open or close a meeting, or portion of a meeting, to the public, may be changed following the public announcement required by this subsection only if (A) a majority of the entire membership of the agency determines by a recorded vote that agency business so requires and that no earlier announcement of the change was possible, and (B) the agency publicly announces such change and the vote of each member upon such change at the earliest practicable time.

(3) Immediately following each public announcement required by this subsection, notice of the time, place, and subject matter of a meeting, whether the meeting is open or closed, any change in one of the preceding, and the name and phone number of the official designated by

the agency to respond to requests for information about the meeting, shall also be submitted for publication in the Federal Register.

(f)(1) For every meeting closed pursuant to paragraphs (1) through (10) of subsection (c), the General Counsel or chief legal officer of the agency shall publicly certify that, in his or her opinion, the meeting may be closed to the public and shall state each relevant exemptive provision. A copy of such certification, together with a statement from the presiding officer of the meeting setting forth the time and place of the meeting, and the persons present, shall be retained by the agency. The agency shall maintain a complete transcript or electronic recording adequate to record fully the proceedings of each meeting, or portion of a meeting, closed to the public, except that in the case of a meeting, or portion of a meeting, closed to the public pursuant to paragraph (8), (9)(A), or (10) of subsection (c), the agency shall maintain either such a transcript or recording, or a set of minutes. Such minutes shall fully and clearly describe all matters discussed and shall provide a full and accurate summary of any actions taken, and the reasons therefor, including a description of each of the views expressed on any item and the record of any rollcall vote (reflecting the vote of each member on the question). All documents considered in connection with any action shall be identified in such minutes.

(2) The agency shall make promptly available to the public, in a place easily accessible to the public, the transcript, electronic recording, or minutes (as required by paragraph (1)) of the discussion of any item on the agenda, or of any item of the testimony of any witness received at the meeting, except for such item or items of such discussion or testimony as the agency determines to contain information which may be withheld under subsection (c). Copies of such transcript, or minutes, or a transcription of such recording disclosing the identity of each speaker, shall be furnished to any person at the actual cost of duplication or transcription. The agency shall maintain a complete verbatim copy of the transcript, a complete copy of the minutes, or a complete electronic recording of each meeting, or portion of a meeting, closed to the public, for a period of at least two years after such meeting, or until one year after the conclusion of any agency proceeding with respect to which the meeting or portion was held, whichever occurs later.

(g) Each agency subject to the requirements of this section shall, within 180 days after the date of enactment of this section, following consultation with the Office of the Chairman of the Administrative Conference of the United States and published notice in the Federal Register of at least thirty days and opportunity for written comment by any person, promulgate regulations to implement the requirements of subsections (b) through (f) of this section. Any person may bring a proceeding in the United States District Court for the District of Columbia to require an agency to promulgate such regulations if such agency has not promulgated such regulations within the time period specified herein. Subject to any limitations of time provided by law, any person may bring a proceeding in the United States Court of Appeals for the

District of Columbia to set aside agency regulations issued pursuant to this subsection that are not in accord with the requirements of subsections (b) through (f) of this section and to require the promulgation of regulations that are in accord with such subsections.

(h)(1) The district courts of the United States shall have jurisdiction to enforce the requirements of subsections (b) through (f) of this section by declaratory judgment, injunctive relief, or other relief as may be appropriate. Such actions may be brought by any person against an agency prior to, or within sixty days after, the meeting out of which the violation of this section arises, except that if public announcement of such meeting is not initially provided by the agency in accordance with the requirements of this section, such action may be instituted pursuant to this section at any time prior to sixty days after any public announcement of such meeting. Such actions may be brought in the district court of the United States for the district in which the agency meeting is held or in which the agency in question has its headquarters, or in the District Court for the District of Columbia. In such actions a defendant shall serve his answer within thirty days after the service of the complaint. The burden is on the defendant to sustain his action. In deciding such cases the court may examine in camera any portion of the transcript, electronic recording, or minutes of a meeting closed to the public, and may take such additional evidence as it deems necessary. The court, having due regard for orderly administration and the public interest, as well as the interests of the parties, may grant such equitable relief as it deems appropriate, including granting an injunction against future violations of this section or ordering the agency to make available to the public such portion of the transcript, recording, or minutes of a meeting as is not authorized to be withheld under subsection (c) of this section.

(2) Any Federal court otherwise authorized by law to review agency action may, at the application of any person properly participating in the proceeding pursuant to other applicable law, inquire into violations by the agency of the requirements of this section and afford such relief as it deems appropriate. Nothing in this section authorizes any Federal court having jurisdiction solely on the basis of paragraph (1) to set aside, enjoin, or invalidate any agency action (other than an action to close a meeting or to withhold information under this section) taken or discussed at any agency meeting out of which the violation of this section arose.

(i) The court may assess against any party reasonable attorney fees and other litigation costs reasonably incurred by any other party who substantially prevails in any action brought in accordance with the provisions of subsection (g) or (h) of this section, except that costs may be assessed against the plaintiff only where the court finds that the suit was initiated by the plaintiff primarily for frivolous or dilatory purposes. In the case of assessment of costs against an agency, the costs may be assessed by the court against the United States.

(j) Each agency subject to the requirements of this section shall annually report to the Congress regarding the following:

(1) The changes in the policies and procedures of the agency under this section that have occurred during the preceding 1-year period.

(2) A tabulation of the number of meetings held, the exemptions applied to close meetings, and the days of public notice provided to close meetings.

(3) A brief description of litigation or formal complaints concerning the implementation of this section by the agency.

(4) A brief explanation of any changes in law that have affected the responsibilities of the agency under this section.

(k) Nothing herein expands or limits the present rights of any person under section 552 of this title, except that the exemptions set forth in subsection (c) of this section shall govern in the case of any request made pursuant to section 552 to copy or inspect the transcripts, recordings, or minutes described in subsection (f) of this section. The requirements of chapter 33 of title 44, United States Code, shall not apply to the transcripts, recordings, and minutes described in subsection (f) of this section.

(*l*) This section does not constitute authority to withhold any information from Congress, and does not authorize the closing of any agency meeting or portion thereof required by any other provision of law to be open.

(m) Nothing in this section authorizes any agency to withhold from any individual any record, including transcripts, recordings, or minutes required by this section, which is otherwise accessible to such individual under section 552a of this title.

Appendix E

ALTERNATIVE ADMINISTRATIVE PROCEDURE PROVISIONS OF 1990, AS AMENDED

5 U.S.C., Chapter 5.

SUBCHAPTER III—NEGOTIATED RULEMAKING PROCEDURE

§ 561. Purpose

The purpose of this subchapter is to establish a framework for the conduct of negotiated rulemaking, consistent with section 553 of this title, to encourage agencies to use the process when it enhances the informal rulemaking process. Nothing in this subchapter should be construed as an attempt to limit innovation and experimentation with the negotiated rulemaking process or with other innovative rulemaking procedures otherwise authorized by law.

§ 562. Definitions

For the purposes of this subchapter, the term—

(1) "agency" has the same meaning as in section 551(1) of this title;

(2) "consensus" means unanimous concurrence among the interests represented on a negotiated rulemaking committee established under this subchapter, unless such committee—

(A) agrees to define such term to mean a general but not unanimous concurrence; or

(B) agrees upon another specified definition;

(3) "convener" means a person who impartially assists an agency in determining whether establishment of a negotiated rulemaking committee is feasible and appropriate in a particular rulemaking;

(4) "facilitator" means a person who impartially aids in the discussions and negotiations among the members of a negotiated rulemaking committee to develop a proposed rule;

(5) "interest" means, with respect to an issue or matter, multiple parties which have a similar point of view or which are likely to be affected in a similar manner;

(6) "negotiated rulemaking" means rulemaking through the use of a negotiated rulemaking committee;

(7) "negotiated rulemaking committee" or "committee" means an advisory committee established by an agency in accordance with this subchapter and the Federal Advisory Committee Act to consider and discuss issues for the purpose of reaching a consensus in the development of a proposed rule;

(8) "party" has the same meaning as in section 551(3) of this title;

(9) "person" has the same meaning as in section 551(2) of this title;

(10) "rule" has the same meaning as in section 551(4) of this title; and

(11) "rulemaking" means "rule making" as that term is defined in section 551(5) of this title.

§ 563. Determination of need for negotiated rulemaking committee

(a) Determination of need by the agency.—An agency may establish a negotiated rulemaking committee to negotiate and develop a proposed rule, if the head of the agency determines that the use of the negotiated rulemaking procedure is in the public interest. In making such a determination, the head of the agency shall consider whether—

(1) there is a need for a rule;

(2) there are a limited number of identifiable interests that will be significantly affected by the rule;

(3) there is a reasonable likelihood that a committee can be convened with a balanced representation of persons who—

(A) can adequately represent the interests identified under paragraph (2); and

(B) are willing to negotiate in good faith to reach a consensus on the proposed rule;

(4) there is a reasonable likelihood that a committee will reach a consensus on the proposed rule within a fixed period of time;

(5) the negotiated rulemaking procedure will not unreasonably delay the notice of proposed rulemaking and the issuance of the final rule;

(6) the agency has adequate resources and is willing to commit such resources, including technical assistance, to the committee; and

(7) the agency, to the maximum extent possible consistent with the legal obligations of the agency, will use the consensus of the committee with respect to the proposed rule as the basis for the rule proposed by the agency for notice and comment.

(b) Use of conveners.—

(1) Purposes of conveners.—An agency may use the services of a convener to assist the agency in—

(A) identifying persons who will be significantly affected by a proposed rule, including residents of rural areas; and

(B) conducting discussions with such persons to identify the issues of concern to such persons, and to ascertain whether the establishment of a negotiated rulemaking committee is feasible and appropriate in the particular rulemaking.

(2) Duties of conveners.—The convener shall report findings and may make recommendations to the agency. Upon request of the agency, the convener shall ascertain the names of persons who are willing and qualified to represent interests that will be significantly affected by the proposed rule, including residents of rural areas. The report and any recommendations of the convener shall be made available to the public upon request.

§ 564. Publication of notice; applications for membership on committees

(a) Publication of notice.—If, after considering the report of a convener or conducting its own assessment, an agency decides to establish a negotiated rulemaking committee, the agency shall publish in the Federal Register and, as appropriate, in trade or other specialized publications, a notice which shall include—

(1) an announcement that the agency intends to establish a negotiated rulemaking committee to negotiate and develop a proposed rule;

(2) a description of the subject and scope of the rule to be developed, and the issues to be considered;

(3) a list of the interests which are likely to be significantly affected by the rule;

(4) a list of the persons proposed to represent such interests and the person or persons proposed to represent the agency;

(5) a proposed agenda and schedule for completing the work of the committee, including a target date for publication by the agency of a proposed rule for notice and comment;

(6) a description of administrative support for the committee to be provided by the agency, including technical assistance;

(7) a solicitation for comments on the proposal to establish the committee, and the proposed membership of the negotiated rulemaking committee; and

(8) an explanation of how a person may apply or nominate another person for membership on the committee, as provided under subsection (b).

(b) Applications for membership on committee.—Persons who will be significantly affected by a proposed rule and who believe that their interests will not be adequately represented by any person specified in a notice under subsection (a)(4) may apply for, or nominate another person for, membership on the negotiated rulemaking committee to represent such interests with respect to the proposed rule. Each application or nomination shall include—

(1) the name of the applicant or nominee and a description of the interests such person shall represent;

(2) evidence that the applicant or nominee is authorized to represent parties related to the interests the person proposes to represent;

(3) a written commitment that the applicant or nominee shall actively participate in good faith in the development of the rule under consideration; and

(4) the reasons that the persons specified in the notice under subsection (a)(4) do not adequately represent the interests of the person submitting the application or nomination.

(c) Period for submission of comments and applications.—The agency shall provide for a period of at least 30 calendar days for the submission of comments and applications under this section.

§ 565. Establishment of committee

(a) Establishment.—

(1) Determination to establish committee.—If after considering comments and applications submitted under section 564, the agency determines that a negotiated rulemaking committee can adequately represent the interests that will be significantly affected by a proposed rule and that it is feasible and appropriate in the particular rulemaking, the agency may establish a negotiated rulemaking committee. In establishing and administering such a committee, the agency shall comply with the Federal Advisory Committee Act with respect to such committee, except as otherwise provided in this subchapter.

(2) Determination not to establish committee.—If after considering such comments and applications, the agency decides not to establish a negotiated rulemaking committee, the agency shall promptly publish notice of such decision and the reasons therefor in the Federal Register and, as appropriate, in trade or other specialized publications, a copy of which shall be sent to any person who applied for, or nominated another person for membership on the negotiating rulemaking committee to represent such interests with respect to the proposed rule.

(b) Membership.—The agency shall limit membership on a negotiated rulemaking committee to 25 members, unless the agency head determines that a greater number of members is necessary for the functioning of the committee or to achieve balanced membership. Each committee shall include at least one person representing the agency.

(c) Administrative support.—The agency shall provide appropriate administrative support to the negotiated rulemaking committee, including technical assistance.

§ 566. Conduct of committee activity

(a) Duties of committee.—Each negotiated rulemaking committee established under this subchapter shall consider the matter proposed by the agency for consideration and shall attempt to reach a consensus concerning a proposed rule with respect to such matter and any other matter the committee determines is relevant to the proposed rule.

(b) Representatives of agency on committee.—The person or persons representing the agency on a negotiated rulemaking committee shall participate in the deliberations and activities of the committee with the same rights and responsibilities as other members of the committee, and shall be authorized to fully represent the agency in the discussions and negotiations of the committee.

(c) Selecting facilitator.—Notwithstanding section 10(e) of the Federal Advisory Committee Act, an agency may nominate either a person from the Federal Government or a person from outside the Federal Government to serve as a facilitator for the negotiations of the committee, subject to the approval of the committee by consensus. If the committee does not approve the nominee of the agency for facilitator, the agency shall submit a substitute nomination. If a committee does not approve any nominee of the agency for facilitator, the committee shall select by consensus a person to serve as facilitator. A person designated to represent the agency in substantive issues may not serve as facilitator or otherwise chair the committee.

(d) Duties of facilitator.—A facilitator approved or selected by a negotiated rulemaking committee shall—

(1) chair the meetings of the committee in an impartial manner;

(2) impartially assist the members of the committee in conducting discussions and negotiations; and

(3) manage the keeping of minutes and records as required under section 10(b) and (c) of the Federal Advisory Committee Act, except that any personal notes and materials of the facilitator or of the members of a committee shall not be subject to section 552 of this title.

(e) Committee procedures.—A negotiated rulemaking committee established under this subchapter may adopt procedures for the operation of the committee. No provision of section 553 of this title shall apply to the procedures of a negotiated rulemaking committee.

(f) Report of committee.—If a committee reaches a consensus on a proposed rule, at the conclusion of negotiations the committee shall transmit to the agency that established the committee a report containing the proposed rule. If the committee does not reach a consensus on a proposed rule, the committee may transmit to the agency a report specifying any areas in which the committee reached a consensus. The committee may include in a report any other information, recommendations, or materials that the committee considers appropriate. Any committee member may include as an addendum to the report additional information, recommendations, or materials.

(g) Records of committee.—In addition to the report required by subsection (f), a committee shall submit to the agency the records required under section 10(b) and (c) of the Federal Advisory Committee Act.

§ 567. Termination of committee

A negotiated rulemaking committee shall terminate upon promulgation of the final rule under consideration, unless the committee's charter contains an earlier termination date or the agency, after consulting the committee, or the committee itself specifies an earlier termination date.

§ 568. Services, facilities, and payment of committee member expenses

(a) Services of conveners and facilitators.—

(1) In general.—An agency may employ or enter into contracts for the services of an individual or organization to serve as a convener or facilitator for a negotiated rulemaking committee under this subchapter, or may use the services of a Government employee to act as a convener or a facilitator for such a committee.

(2) Determination of conflicting interests.—An agency shall determine whether a person under consideration to serve as convener or facilitator of a committee under paragraph (1) has any financial or other interest that would preclude such person from serving in an impartial and independent manner.

(b) Services and facilities of other entities.—For purposes of this subchapter, an agency may use the services and facilities of other Federal agencies and public and private agencies and instrumentalities with the consent of such agencies and instrumentalities, and with or without reimbursement to such agencies and instrumentalities, and may accept voluntary and uncompensated services without regard to the provisions of section 1342 of title 31. The Federal Mediation and Conciliation Service may provide services and facilities, with or without reimbursement, to assist agencies under this subchapter, including furnishing conveners, facilitators, and training in negotiated rulemaking.

(c) Expenses of committee members.—Members of a negotiated rulemaking committee shall be responsible for their own expenses of participation in such committee, except that an agency may, in accordance with section 7(d) of the Federal Advisory Committee Act, pay for a member's reasonable travel and per diem expenses, expenses to obtain technical assistance, and a reasonable rate of compensation, if—

(1) such member certifies a lack of adequate financial resources to participate in the committee; and

(2) the agency determines that such member's participation in the committee is necessary to assure an adequate representation of the member's interest.

(d) Status of member as federal employee.—A member's receipt of funds under this section or section 569 shall not conclusively determine for purposes of sections 202 through 209 of title 18 whether that member is an employee of the United States Government.

§ 569. Encouraging negotiated rulemaking

(a) The President shall designate an agency or designate or establish an interagency committee to facilitate and encourage agency use of negotiated rulemaking. An agency that is considering, planning, or conducting a negotiated rulemaking may consult with such agency or committee for information and assistance.

(b) To carry out the purposes of this subchapter, an agency planning or conducting a negotiated rulemaking may accept, hold, administer, and utilize gifts, devises, and bequests of property, both real and personal if that agency's acceptance and use of such gifts, devises, or bequests do not create a conflict of interest. Gifts and bequests of money and proceeds from sales of other property received as gifts, devises, or bequests shall be deposited in the Treasury and shall be disbursed upon the order of the head of such agency. Property accepted pursuant to this section, and the proceeds thereof, shall be used as nearly as possible in accordance with the terms of the gifts, devises, or bequests.

§ 570. Judicial review

Any agency action relating to establishing, assisting, or terminating a negotiated rulemaking committee under this subchapter shall not be subject to judicial review. Nothing in this section shall bar judicial review of a rule if such judicial review is otherwise provided by law. A rule which is the product of negotiated rulemaking and is subject to judicial review shall not be accorded any greater deference by a court than a rule which is the product of other rulemaking procedures.

SUBCHAPTER IV—ALTERNATIVE MEANS OF DISPUTE RESOLUTION IN THE ADMINISTRATIVE PROCESS

§ 571. Definitions

For the purposes of this subchapter, the term—

(1) "agency" has the same meaning as in section 551(1) of this title;

(2) "administrative program" includes a Federal function which involves protection of the public interest and the determination of rights, privileges, and obligations of private persons through rule making, adjudication, licensing, or investigation, as those terms are used in subchapter II of this chapter;

(3) "alternative means of dispute resolution" means any procedure that is used to resolve issues in controversy, including, but not limited to, conciliation, facilitation, mediation, factfinding, minitrials, arbitration, and use of ombuds, or any combination thereof;

(4) "award" means any decision by an arbitrator resolving the issues in controversy;

(5) "dispute resolution communication" means any oral or written communication prepared for the purposes of a dispute resolution proceeding, including any memoranda, notes or work product of the neutral, parties or nonparty participant; except that a written agreement to enter into a dispute resolution proceeding, or final written agreement or arbitral award reached as a result of a dispute resolution proceeding, is not a dispute resolution communication;

(6) "dispute resolution proceeding" means any process in which an alternative means of dispute resolution is used to resolve an issue in controversy in which a neutral is appointed and specified parties participate;

(7) "in confidence" means, with respect to information, that the information is provided—

(A) with the expressed intent of the source that it not be disclosed; or

(B) under circumstances that would create the reasonable expectation on behalf of the source that the information will not be disclosed;

(8) "issue in controversy" means an issue which is material to a decision concerning an administrative program of an agency, and with which there is disagreement—

(A) between an agency and persons who would be substantially affected by the decision; or

(B) between persons who would be substantially affected by the decision;

(9) "neutral" means an individual who, with respect to an issue in controversy, functions specifically to aid the parties in resolving the controversy;

(10) "party" means—

(A) for a proceeding with named parties, the same as in section 551(3) of this title; and

(B) for a proceeding without named parties, a person who will be significantly affected by the decision in the proceeding and who participates in the proceeding;

(11) "person" has the same meaning as in section 551(2) of this title; and

(12) "roster" means a list of persons qualified to provide services as neutrals.

§ 572. General authority

(a) An agency may use a dispute resolution proceeding for the resolution of an issue in controversy that relates to an administrative program, if the parties agree to such proceeding.

(b) An agency shall consider not using a dispute resolution proceeding if—

(1) a definitive or authoritative resolution of the matter is required for precedential value, and such a proceeding is not likely to be accepted generally as an authoritative precedent;

(2) the matter involves or may bear upon significant questions of Government policy that require additional procedures before a final resolution may be made, and such a proceeding would not likely serve to develop a recommended policy for the agency;

(3) maintaining established policies is of special importance, so that variations among individual decisions are not increased and such a proceeding would not likely reach consistent results among individual decisions;

(4) the matter significantly affects persons or organizations who are not parties to the proceeding;

(5) a full public record of the proceeding is important, and a dispute resolution proceeding cannot provide such a record; and

(6) the agency must maintain continuing jurisdiction over the matter with authority to alter the disposition of the matter in the light of changed circumstances, and a dispute resolution proceeding would interfere with the agency's fulfilling that requirement.

(c) Alternative means of dispute resolution authorized under this subchapter are voluntary procedures which supplement rather than limit other available agency dispute resolution techniques.

§ 573. Neutrals

(a) A neutral may be a permanent or temporary officer or employee of the Federal Government or any other individual who is acceptable to the parties to a dispute resolution proceeding. A neutral shall have no official, financial, or personal conflict of interest with respect to the issues in controversy, unless such interest is fully disclosed in writing to all parties and all parties agree that the neutral may serve.

(b) A neutral who serves as a conciliator, facilitator, or mediator serves at the will of the parties.

(c) The President shall designate an agency or designate or establish an interagency committee to facilitate and encourage agency use of dispute resolution under this subchapter. Such agency or interagency committee, in consultation with other appropriate Federal agencies and professional organizations experienced in matters concerning dispute resolution, shall—

(1) encourage and facilitate agency use of alternative means of dispute resolution; and

(2) develop procedures that permit agencies to obtain the services of neutrals on an expedited basis.

(d) An agency may use the services of one or more employees of other agencies to serve as neutrals in dispute resolution proceedings. The agencies may enter into an interagency agreement that provides for the reimbursement by the user agency or the parties of the full or partial cost of the services of such an employee.

(e) Any agency may enter into a contract with any person for services as a neutral, or for training in connection with alternative means of dispute resolution. The parties in a dispute resolution proceeding shall agree on compensation for the neutral that is fair and reasonable to the Government.

§ 574. Confidentiality

(a) Except as provided in subsections (d) and (e), a neutral in a dispute resolution proceeding shall not voluntarily disclose or through discovery or compulsory process be required to disclose any dispute resolution communication or any communication provided in confidence to the neutral, unless—

(1) all parties to the dispute resolution proceeding and the neutral consent in writing, and, if the dispute resolution communication was provided by a nonparty participant, that participant also consents in writing;

(2) the dispute resolution communication has already been made public;

(3) the dispute resolution communication is required by statute to be made public, but a neutral should make such communication public only if no other person is reasonably available to disclose the communication; or

(4) a court determines that such testimony or disclosure is necessary to—

(A) prevent a manifest injustice;

(B) help establish a violation of law; or

(C) prevent harm to the public health or safety of sufficient magnitude in the particular case to outweigh the integrity of dispute resolution proceedings in general by reducing the confidence of parties in future cases that their communications will remain confidential.

(b) A party to a dispute resolution proceeding shall not voluntarily disclose or through discovery or compulsory process be required to disclose any dispute resolution communication, unless—

(1) the communication was prepared by the party seeking disclosure;

(2) all parties to the dispute resolution proceeding consent in writing;

(3) the dispute resolution communication has already been made public;

(4) the dispute resolution communication is required by statute to be made public;

(5) a court determines that such testimony or disclosure is necessary to—

(A) prevent a manifest injustice;

(B) help establish a violation of law; or

(C) prevent harm to the public health and safety, of sufficient magnitude in the particular case to outweigh the integrity of dispute resolution proceedings in general by reducing the confidence of parties in future cases that their communications will remain confidential;

(6) the dispute resolution communication is relevant to determining the existence or meaning of an agreement or award that resulted from the dispute resolution proceeding or to the enforcement of such an agreement or award; or

(7) except for dispute resolution communications generated by the neutral, the dispute resolution communication was provided to or was available to all parties to the dispute resolution proceeding.

(c) Any dispute resolution communication that is disclosed in violation of subsection (a) or (b), shall not be admissible in any proceeding relating to the issues in controversy with respect to which the communication was made.

(d)(1) The parties may agree to alternative confidential procedures for disclosures by a neutral. Upon such agreement the parties shall inform the neutral before the commencement of the dispute resolution proceeding of any modifications to the provisions of subsection (a) that will govern the confidentiality of the dispute resolution proceeding. If the parties do not so inform the neutral, subsection (a) shall apply.

(2) To qualify for the exemption established under subsection (j), an alternative confidential procedure under this subsection may not provide for less disclosure than the confidential procedures otherwise provided under this section.

(e) If a demand for disclosure, by way of discovery request or other legal process, is made upon a neutral regarding a dispute resolution communication, the neutral shall make reasonable efforts to notify the parties and any affected nonparty participants of the demand. Any party or affected nonparty participant who receives such notice and within 15 calendar days does not offer to defend a refusal of the neutral to disclose the requested information shall have waived any objection to such disclosure.

(f) Nothing in this section shall prevent the discovery or admissibility of any evidence that is otherwise discoverable, merely because the evidence was presented in the course of a dispute resolution proceeding.

(g) Subsections (a) and (b) shall have no effect on the information and data that are necessary to document an agreement reached or order issued pursuant to a dispute resolution proceeding.

(h) Subsections (a) and (b) shall not prevent the gathering of information for research or educational purposes, in cooperation with other agencies, governmental entities, or dispute resolution programs, so long as the parties and the specific issues in controversy are not identifiable.

(i) Subsections (a) and (b) shall not prevent use of a dispute resolution communication to resolve a dispute between the neutral in a dispute resolution proceeding and a party to or participant in such proceeding, so long as such dispute resolution communication is disclosed only to the extent necessary to resolve such dispute.

(j) A dispute resolution communication which is between a neutral and a party and which may not be disclosed under this section shall also be exempt from disclosure under section 552(b)(3).

§ 575. Authorization of arbitration

(a)(1) Arbitration may be used as an Alternative means of dispute resolution whenever all parties consent. Consent may be obtained either before or after an issue in controversy has arisen. A party may agree to—

(A) submit only certain issues in controversy to arbitration; or

(B) arbitration on the condition that the award must be within a range of possible outcomes.

(2) The arbitration agreement that sets forth the subject matter submitted to the arbitrator shall be in writing. Each such arbitration agreement shall specify a maximum award that may be issued by the arbitrator and may specify other conditions limiting the range of possible outcomes.

(3) An agency may not require any person to consent to arbitration as a condition of entering into a contract or obtaining a benefit.

(b) An officer or employee of an agency shall not offer to use arbitration for the resolution of issues in controversy unless such officer or employee—

(1) would otherwise have authority to enter into a settlement concerning the matter; or

(2) is otherwise specifically authorized by the agency to consent to the use of arbitration.

(c) Prior to using binding arbitration under this subchapter, the head of an agency, in consultation with the Attorney General and after taking into account the factors in section 572(b), shall issue guidance on the appropriate use of binding arbitration and when an officer or employee of the agency has authority to settle an issue in controversy through binding arbitration.

§ 576. Enforcement of arbitration agreements

An agreement to arbitrate a matter to which this subchapter applies is enforceable pursuant to section 4 of title 9, and no action brought to enforce such an agreement shall be dismissed nor shall relief therein be denied on the grounds that it is against the United States or that the United States is an indispensable party.

§ 577. Arbitrators

(a) The parties to an arbitration proceeding shall be entitled to participate in the selection of the arbitrator.

(b) The arbitrator shall be a neutral who meets the criteria of section 573 of this title.

§ 578. Authority of the arbitrator

An arbitrator to whom a dispute is referred under this subchapter may—

(1) regulate the course of and conduct arbitral hearings;

(2) administer oaths and affirmations;

(3) compel the attendance of witnesses and production of evidence at the hearing under the provisions of section 7 of title 9 only to the extent the agency involved is otherwise authorized by law to do so; and

(4) make awards.

§ 579. Arbitration proceedings

(a) The arbitrator shall set a time and place for the hearing on the dispute and shall notify the parties not less than 5 days before the hearing.

(b) Any party wishing a record of the hearing shall—

(1) be responsible for the preparation of such record;

(2) notify the other parties and the arbitrator of the preparation of such record;

(3) furnish copies to all identified parties and the arbitrator; and

(4) pay all costs for such record, unless the parties agree otherwise or the arbitrator determines that the costs should be apportioned.

(c)(1) The parties to the arbitration are entitled to be heard, to present evidence material to the controversy, and to cross-examine witnesses appearing at the hearing.

(2) The arbitrator may, with the consent of the parties, conduct all or part of the hearing by telephone, television, computer, or other electronic means, if each party has an opportunity to participate.

(3) The hearing shall be conducted expeditiously and in an informal manner.

(4) The arbitrator may receive any oral or documentary evidence, except that irrelevant, immaterial, unduly repetitious, or privileged evidence may be excluded by the arbitrator.

(5) The arbitrator shall interpret and apply relevant statutory and regulatory requirements, legal precedents, and policy directives.

(d) No interested person shall make or knowingly cause to be made to the arbitrator an unauthorized ex parte communication relevant to the merits of the proceeding, unless the parties agree otherwise. If a communication is made in violation of this subsection, the arbitrator shall ensure that a memorandum of the communication is prepared and made a part of the record, and that an opportunity for rebuttal is allowed. Upon receipt of a communication made in violation of this subsection, the arbitrator may, to the extent consistent with the interests of justice and the policies underlying this subchapter, require the offending party to show cause why the claim of such party should not be resolved against such party as a result of the improper conduct.

(e) The arbitrator shall make the award within 30 days after the close of the hearing, or the date of the filing of any briefs authorized by the arbitrator, whichever date is later, unless—

(1) the parties agree to some other time limit; or

(2) the agency provides by rule for some other time limit.

§ 580. Arbitration awards

(a)(1) Unless the agency provides otherwise by rule, the award in an arbitration proceeding under this subchapter shall include a brief, informal discussion of the factual and legal basis for the award, but formal findings of fact or conclusions of law shall not be required.

(2) The prevailing parties shall file the award with all relevant agencies, along with proof of service on all parties.

(b) The award in an arbitration proceeding shall become final 30 days after it is served on all parties. Any agency that is a party to the proceeding may extend this 30–day period for an additional 30–day period by serving a notice of such extension on all other parties before the end of the first 30–day period.

(c) A final award is binding on the parties to the arbitration proceeding, and may be enforced pursuant to sections 9 through 13 of title 9. No action brought to enforce such an award shall be dismissed nor shall relief therein be denied on the grounds that it is against the United States or that the United States is an indispensable party.

(d) An award entered under this subchapter in an arbitration proceeding may not serve as an estoppel in any other proceeding for any issue that was resolved in the proceeding. Such an award also may not be used as precedent or otherwise be considered in any factually unrelated proceeding, whether conducted under this subchapter, by an agency, or in a court, or in any other arbitration proceeding.

[(e) Redesignated (d)]

[(f) and (g) Repealed. Pub.L. 104–320, § 8(a)(1), Oct. 19, 1996, 110 Stat. 3872.]

§ 581. Judicial Review

(a) Notwithstanding any other provision of law, any person adversely affected or aggrieved by an award made in an arbitration proceeding conducted under this subchapter may bring an action for review of such award only pursuant to the provisions of sections 9 through 13 of title 9.

(b) A decision by an agency to use or not to use a dispute resolution proceeding under this subchapter shall be committed to the discretion of the agency and shall not be subject to judicial review, except that arbitration shall be subject to judicial review under section 10(b) of title 9.

[§ 582. Repealed. Pub.L. 104–320, § 4(b)(1), Oct. 19, 1996, 110 Stat. 3871.]

§ 583. Support services

For the purposes of this subchapter, an agency may use (with or without reimbursement) the services and facilities of other Federal agencies, State, local, and tribal governments, public and private organizations and agencies, and individuals, with the consent of such agencies, organizations, and individuals. An agency may accept voluntary and uncompensated services for purposes of this subchapter without regard to the provisions of section 1342 of title 31.

§ 584. Authorization of appropriations

There are authorized to be appropriated such sums as may be necessary to carry out the purposes of this subchapter.

Appendix F

EXECUTIVE ORDER 12866—REGULATORY PLANNING AND REVIEW*

3 C.F.R., 1993 Comp., at 638.

By the authority vested in me as President by the Constitution and the laws of the United States of America, it is hereby ordered that Executive Order 12866, of September 30, 1993, is amended as follows:

The American people deserve a regulatory system that works for them, not against them: a regulatory system that protects and improves their health, safety, environment, and well-being and improves the performance of the economy without imposing unacceptable or unreasonable costs on society; regulatory policies that recognize that the private sector and private markets are the best engine for economic growth; regulatory approaches that respect the role of State, local, and tribal governments; and regulations that are effective, consistent, sensible, and understandable. We do not have such a regulatory system today.

With this Executive order, the Federal Government begins a program to reform and make more efficient the regulatory process. The objectives of this Executive order are to enhance planning and coordination with respect to both new and existing regulations; to reaffirm the primacy of Federal agencies in the regulatory decision-making process; to restore the integrity and legitimacy of regulatory review and oversight; and to make the process more accessible and open to the public. In pursuing these objectives, the regulatory process shall be conducted so as to meet applicable statutory requirements and with due regard to the discretion that has been entrusted to the Federal agencies.

Accordingly, by the authority vested in me as President by the Constitution and the laws of the United States of America, it is hereby ordered as follows:

Sec. 1. Statement of Regulatory Philosophy and Principles.

* As amended by Executive Order 13258, 67 Fed. Reg. 9385 (Feb. 28, 2002).

(a) **The Regulatory Philosophy**. Federal agencies should promulgate only such regulations as are required by law, are necessary to interpret the law, or are made necessary by compelling public need, such as material failures of private markets to protect or improve the health and safety of the public, the environment, or the well-being of the American people. In deciding whether and how to regulate, agencies should assess all costs and benefits of available regulatory alternatives, including the alternative of not regulating. Costs and benefits shall be understood to include both quantifiable measures (to the fullest extent that these can be usefully estimated) and qualitative measures of costs and benefits that are difficult to quantify, but nevertheless essential to consider. Further, in choosing among alternative regulatory approaches, agencies should select those approaches that maximize net benefits (including potential economic, environmental, public health and safety, and other advantages; distributive impacts; and equity), unless a statute requires another regulatory approach.

(b) **The Principles of Regulation**. To ensure that the agencies' regulatory programs are consistent with the philosophy set forth above, agencies should adhere to the following principles, to the extent permitted by law and where applicable:

(1) Each agency shall identify the problem that it intends to address (including, where applicable, the failures of private markets or public institutions that warrant new agency action) as well as assess the significance of that problem.

(2) Each agency shall examine whether existing regulations (or other law) have created, or contributed to, the problem that a new regulation is intended to correct and whether those regulations (or other law) should be modified to achieve the intended goal of regulation more effectively.

(3) Each agency shall identify and assess available alternatives to direct regulation, including providing economic incentives to encourage the desired behavior, such as user fees or marketable permits, or providing information upon which choices can be made by the public.

(4) In setting regulatory priorities, each agency shall consider, to the extent reasonable, the degree and nature of the risks posed by various substances or activities within its jurisdiction.

(5) When an agency determines that a regulation is the best available method of achieving the regulatory objective, it shall design its regulations in the most cost-effective manner to achieve the regulatory objective. In doing so, each agency shall consider incentives for innovation, consistency, predictability, the costs of enforcement and compliance (to the government, regulated entities, and the public), flexibility, distributive impacts, and equity.

(6) Each agency shall assess both the costs and the benefits of the intended regulation and, recognizing that some costs and benefits are difficult to quantify, propose or adopt a regulation only upon a reasoned

determination that the benefits of the intended regulation justify its costs.

(7) Each agency shall base its decisions on the best reasonably obtainable scientific, technical, economic, and other information concerning the need for, and consequences of, the intended regulation.

(8) Each agency shall identify and assess alternative forms of regulation and shall, to the extent feasible, specify performance objectives, rather than specifying the behavior or manner of compliance that regulated entities must adopt.

(9) Wherever feasible, agencies shall seek views of appropriate State, local, and tribal officials before imposing regulatory requirements that might significantly or uniquely affect those governmental entities. Each agency shall assess the effects of Federal regulations on State, local, and tribal governments, including specifically the availability of resources to carry out those mandates, and seek to minimize those burdens that uniquely or significantly affect such governmental entities, consistent with achieving regulatory objectives. In addition, as appropriate, agencies shall seek to harmonize Federal regulatory actions with related State, local, and tribal regulatory and other governmental functions.

(10) Each agency shall avoid regulations that are inconsistent, incompatible, or duplicative with its other regulations or those of other Federal agencies.

(11) Each agency shall tailor its regulations to impose the least burden on society, including individuals, businesses of differing sizes, and other entities (including small communities and governmental entities), consistent with obtaining the regulatory objectives, taking into account, among other things, and to the extent practicable, the costs of cumulative regulations.

(12) Each agency shall draft its regulations to be simple and easy to understand, with the goal of minimizing the potential for uncertainty and litigation arising from such uncertainty.

Sec. 2. Organization. An efficient regulatory planning and review process is vital to ensure that the Federal Government's regulatory system best serves the American people.

(a) **The Agencies**. Because Federal agencies are the repositories of significant substantive expertise and experience, they are responsible for developing regulations and assuring that the regulations are consistent with applicable law, the President's priorities, and the principles set forth in this Executive order.

(b) **The Office of Management and Budget**. Coordinated review of agency rulemaking is necessary to ensure that regulations are consistent with applicable law, the President's priorities, and the principles set forth in this Executive order, and that decisions made by one agency do not conflict with the policies or actions taken or planned by another agency. The Office of Management and Budget (OMB) shall carry out that review function. Within OMB, the Office of Information and Regulatory Affairs (OIRA) is the repository of expertise concerning regulatory issues, including methodologies and procedures that affect more than one agency, this Executive order, and the President's regulatory policies. To the extent permitted by law, OMB shall provide guidance to agencies and assist the President and regulatory policy advisors to the President in regulatory planning and shall be the entity that reviews individual regulations, as provided by this Executive order.

(c) **Assistance.** In fulfilling his responsibilities under this Executive order, the President shall be assisted by the regulatory policy advisors within the Executive Office of the President and by such agency officials and personnel as the President may, from time to time, consult.

Sec. 3. Definitions. For purposes of this Executive order: (a) "Advisors" refers to such regulatory policy advisors to the President as the President may from time to time consult, including, among others: (1) the Director of OMB; (2) the Chair (or another member) of the Council of Economic Advisers; (3) the Assistant to the President for Economic Policy; (4) the Assistant to the President for Domestic Policy; (5) the Assistant to the President for National Security Affairs; (6) the Director of the Office of Science and Technology Policy; (7) the Deputy Assistant to the President and Director for Intergovernmental Affairs; (8) the Assistant to the President and Staff Secretary; (9) the Assistant to the President and Chief of Staff to the Vice President; (10) the Assistant to the President and Counsel to the President; (11) the Chairman of the Council on Environmental Quality and Director of the Office of Environmental Quality; (12) the Assistant to the President for Homeland Security; and (13) the Administrator of OIRA, who also shall coordinate communications relating to this Executive order among the agencies, OMB, the other Advisors, and the Office of the Vice President.

(b) "Agency," unless otherwise indicated, means any authority of the United States that is an "agency" under 44 U.S.C. 3502(1), other than those considered to be independent regulatory agencies, as defined in 44 U.S.C. 3502(10).

(c) "Director" means the Director of OMB.

(d) "Regulation" or "rule" means an agency statement of general applicability and future effect, which the agency intends to have the force and effect of law, that is designed to implement, interpret, or prescribe law or policy or to describe the procedure or practice requirements of an agency. It does not, however, include:

(1) Regulations or rules issued in accordance with the formal rulemaking provisions of 5 U.S.C. 556, 557;

(2) Regulations or rules that pertain to a military or foreign affairs function of the United States, other than procurement regulations and regulations involving the import or export of non-defense articles and services;

(3) Regulations or rules that are limited to agency organization, management, or personnel matters; or

(4) Any other category of regulations exempted by the Administrator of OIRA.

(e) "Regulatory action" means any substantive action by an agency (normally published in the Federal Register) that promulgates or is expected to lead to the promulgation of a final rule or regulation, including notices of inquiry, advance notices of proposed rulemaking, and notices of proposed rulemaking.

(f) "Significant regulatory action" means any regulatory action that is likely to result in a rule that may:

(1) Have an annual effect on the economy of $100 million or more or adversely affect in a material way the economy, a sector of the economy, productivity, competition, jobs, the environment, public health or safety, or State, local, or tribal governments or communities;

(2) Create a serious inconsistency or otherwise interfere with an action taken or planned by another agency;

(3) Materially alter the budgetary impact of entitlements, grants, user fees, or loan programs or the rights and obligations of recipients thereof; or

(4) Raise novel legal or policy issues arising out of legal mandates, the President's priorities, or the principles set forth in this Executive order.

Sec. 4. Planning Mechanism. In order to have an effective regulatory program, to provide for coordination of regulations, to maximize consultation and the resolution of potential conflicts at an early stage, to involve the public and its State, local, and tribal officials in regulatory planning, and to ensure that new or revised regulations promote the President's priorities and the principles set forth in this Executive order, these procedures shall be followed, to the extent permitted by law:

(a) **Agencies' Policy Meeting**. Early in each year's planning cycle, the Director shall convene a meeting of the Advisors and the heads of agencies to seek a common understanding of priorities and to coordinate regulatory efforts to be accomplished in the upcoming year.

(b) **Unified Regulatory Agenda**. For purposes of this subsection, the term "agency" or "agencies" shall also include those considered to be independent regulatory agencies, as defined in 44 U.S.C. 3502(10). Each agency shall prepare an agenda of all regulations under development or review, at a time and in a manner specified by the Administrator of OIRA. The description of each regulatory action shall contain, at a minimum, a regulation identifier number, a brief summary of the action, the legal authority for the action, any legal deadline for the action, and the name and telephone number of a knowledgeable agency official. Agencies may incorporate the information required under 5 U.S.C. 602 and 41 U.S.C. 402 into these agendas.

(c) **The Regulatory Plan**. For purposes of this subsection, the term "agency" or "agencies" shall also include those considered to be independent regulatory agencies, as defined in 44 U.S.C. 3502(10).

(1) As part of the Unified Regulatory Agenda, beginning in 1994, each agency shall prepare a Regulatory Plan (Plan) of the most important significant regulatory actions that the agency reasonably expects to issue in proposed or final form in that fiscal year or thereafter. The Plan shall be approved personally by the agency head and shall contain at a minimum:

(A) A statement of the agency's regulatory objectives and priorities and how they relate to the President's priorities;

(B) A summary of each planned significant regulatory action including, to the extent possible, alternatives to be considered and preliminary estimates of the anticipated costs and benefits;

(C) A summary of the legal basis for each such action, including whether any aspect of the action is required by statute or court order;

(D) A statement of the need for each such action and, if applicable, how the action will reduce risks to public health, safety, or the environment, as well as how the magnitude of the risk addressed by the action relates to other risks within the jurisdiction of the agency;

(E) The agency's schedule for action, including a statement of any applicable statutory or judicial deadlines; and

(F) The name, address, and telephone number of a person the public may contact for additional information about the planned regulatory action.

(2) Each agency shall forward its Plan to OIRA by June 1st of each year.

(3) Within 10 calendar days after OIRA has received an agency's Plan, OIRA shall circulate it to other affected agencies and the Advisors.

(4) An agency head who believes that a planned regulatory action of another agency may conflict with its own policy or action taken or planned shall promptly notify, in writing, the Administrator of OIRA, who shall forward that communication to the issuing agency and the Advisors.

(5) If the Administrator of OIRA believes that a planned regulatory action of an agency may be inconsistent with the President's priorities or the principles set forth in this Executive order or may be in conflict with any policy or action taken or planned by another agency, the Administrator of OIRA shall promptly notify, in writing, the affected agencies and the Advisors.

(6) The Director may consult with the heads of agencies with respect to their Plans and, in appropriate instances, request further consideration or inter-agency coordination.

(7) The Plans developed by the issuing agency shall be published annually in the October publication of the Unified Regulatory Agenda. This publication shall be made available to the Congress; State, local, and tribal governments; and the public. Any views on any aspect of any agency Plan, including whether any planned regulatory action might conflict with any other planned or existing regulation, impose any unintended consequences on the public, or confer any unclaimed benefits on the public, should be directed to the issuing agency, with a copy to OIRA.

(d) **Regulatory Working Group.** Within 30 days of the date of this Executive order, the Administrator of OIRA shall convene a Regulatory Working Group ("Working Group"), which shall consist of representatives of the heads of each agency that the Administrator determines to have significant domestic regulatory responsibility and the Advisors. The Administrator of OIRA shall chair the Working Group and shall periodically advise the Director on the activities of the Working Group. The Working Group shall serve as a forum to assist agencies in identifying and analyzing important regulatory issues (including, among others (1) the development of innovative regulatory techniques, (2) the methods, efficacy, and utility of comparative risk assessment in regulatory decision-making, and (3) the development of short forms and other streamlined regulatory approaches for small businesses and other entities). The Working Group shall meet at least quarterly and may meet as a whole or in subgroups of agencies with an interest in particular issues or subject areas. To inform its discussions, the Working Group may commission analytical studies and reports by OIRA, the Administrative Conference of the United States, or any other agency.

(e) Conferences. The Administrator of OIRA shall meet quarterly with representatives of State, local, and tribal governments to identify both existing and proposed regulations that may uniquely or significantly affect those governmental entities. The Administrator of OIRA shall also convene, from time to time, conferences with representatives of businesses, nongovernmental organizations, and the public to discuss regulatory issues of common concern.

Sec. 5. Existing Regulations. In order to reduce the regulatory burden on the American people, their families, their communities, their State, local, and tribal governments, and their industries; to determine whether regulations promulgated by the executive branch of the Federal Government have become unjustified or unnecessary as a result of changed circumstances; to confirm that regulations are both compatible with each other and not duplicative or inappropriately burdensome in the aggregate; to ensure that all regulations are consistent with the President's priorities and the principles set forth in this Executive order, within applicable law; and to otherwise improve the effectiveness of existing regulations:

(a) Within 90 days of the date of this Executive order, each agency shall submit to OIRA a program, consistent with its resources and regulatory priorities, under which the agency will periodically review its existing significant regulations to determine whether any such regulations should be modified or eliminated so as to make the agency's regulatory program more effective in achieving the regulatory objectives, less burdensome, or in greater alignment with the President's priorities and the principles set forth in this Executive order. Any significant regulations selected for review shall be included in the agency's annual Plan. The agency shall also identify any legislative mandates that require the agency to promulgate or continue to impose regulations that the agency believes are unnecessary or outdated by reason of changed circumstances.

(b) The Administrator of OIRA shall work with the Regulatory Working Group and other interested entities to pursue the objectives of this section. State, local, and tribal governments are specifically encouraged to assist in the identification of regulations that impose significant or unique burdens on those governmental entities and that appear to have outlived their justification or be otherwise inconsistent with the public interest.

(c) The Director, in consultation with the Advisors, may identify for review by the appropriate agency or agencies other existing regulations of an agency or groups of regulations of more than one agency that affect a particular group, industry, or sector of the economy, or may identify legislative mandates that may be appropriate for reconsideration by the Congress.

Sec. 6. Centralized Review of Regulations. The guidelines set forth below shall apply to all regulatory actions, for both new and existing regulations, by agencies other than those agencies specifically exempted by the Administrator of OIRA:

(a) Agency Responsibilities. (1) Each agency shall (consistent with its own rules, regulations, or procedures) provide the public with meaningful participation in the regulatory process. In particular, before issuing a notice of proposed rulemaking, each agency should, where appropriate, seek the involvement of those who are intended to benefit from and those expected to be burdened by any regulation (including, specifically, State, local, and tribal officials). In addition, each agency should afford the public a meaningful opportunity to comment on any proposed regulation, which in most cases should include a comment period of not less than 60 days. Each agency also is directed to explore and, where appropriate, use consensual mechanisms for developing regulations, including negotiated rulemaking.

(2) Within 60 days of the date of this Executive order, each agency head shall designate a Regulatory Policy Officer who shall report to the agency head. The Regulatory Policy Officer shall be involved at each stage of the regulatory process to foster the development of effective, innovative, and least burdensome regulations and to further the principles set forth in this Executive order.

(3) In addition to adhering to its own rules and procedures and to the requirements of the Administrative Procedure Act, the Regulatory Flexibility Act, the Paperwork Reduction Act, and other applicable law, each agency shall develop its regulatory actions in a timely fashion and adhere to the following procedures with respect to a regulatory action:

(A) Each agency shall provide OIRA, at such times and in the manner specified by the Administrator of OIRA, with a list of its planned regulatory actions, indicating those which the agency believes are significant regulatory actions within the meaning of this Executive order. Absent a material change in the development of the planned regulatory action, those not designated as significant will not be subject to review under this section unless, within 10 working days of receipt of the list, the Administrator of OIRA notifies the agency that OIRA has determined that a planned regulation is a significant regulatory action within the meaning of this Executive order. The Administrator of OIRA may waive review of any planned regulatory action designated by the agency as significant, in which case the agency need not further comply with subsection (a)(3)(B) or subsection (a)(3)(C) of this section.

(B) For each matter identified as, or determined by the Administrator of OIRA to be, a significant regulatory action, the issuing agency shall provide to OIRA:

(i) The text of the draft regulatory action, together with a reasonably detailed description of the need for the regulatory action and an explanation of how the regulatory action will meet that need; and

(ii) An assessment of the potential costs and benefits of the regulatory action, including an explanation of the manner in which the regulatory action is consistent with a statutory mandate and, to the extent permitted by law, promotes the President's priorities and avoids undue interference with State, local, and tribal governments in the exercise of their governmental functions.

(C) For those matters identified as, or determined by the Administrator of OIRA to be, a significant regulatory action within the scope of section 3(f)(1), the agency shall also provide to OIRA the following additional information developed as part of the agency's decision-making process (unless prohibited by law):

(i) An assessment, including the underlying analysis, of benefits anticipated from the regulatory action (such as, but not limited to, the promotion of the efficient functioning of the economy and private markets, the enhancement of health and safety, the protection of the natural environment, and the elimination or reduction of discrimination or bias) together with, to the extent feasible, a quantification of those benefits;

(ii) An assessment, including the underlying analysis, of costs anticipated from the regulatory action (such as, but not limited to, the direct cost both to the government in administering the regulation and to businesses and others in complying with the regulation, and any adverse effects on the efficient functioning of the economy, private markets (including productivity, employment, and competitiveness), health, safety, and the natural environment), together with, to the extent feasible, a quantification of those costs; and

(iii) An assessment, including the underlying analysis, of costs and benefits of potentially effective and reasonably feasible alternatives to the planned regulation, identified by the agencies or the public (including improving the current regulation and reasonably viable nonregulatory actions), and an explanation why the planned regulatory action is preferable to the identified potential alternatives.

(D) In emergency situations or when an agency is obligated by law to act more quickly than normal review procedures allow, the agency shall notify OIRA as soon as possible and, to the extent practicable, comply with subsections (a)(3)(B) and (C) of this section. For those regulatory actions that are governed by a statutory or court-imposed deadline, the agency shall, to the extent practicable, schedule rulemaking proceedings so as to permit sufficient time for OIRA to conduct its review, as set forth below in subsection (b)(2) through (4) of this section.

(E) After the regulatory action has been published in the Federal Register or otherwise issued to the public, the agency shall:

(i) Make available to the public the information set forth in subsections (a)(3)(B) and (C);

(ii) Identify for the public, in a complete, clear, and simple manner, the substantive changes between the draft submitted to OIRA for review and the action subsequently announced; and

(iii) Identify for the public those changes in the regulatory action that were made at the suggestion or recommendation of OIRA.

(F) All information provided to the public by the agency shall be in plain, understandable language.

(b) OIRA Responsibilities. The Administrator of OIRA shall provide meaningful guidance and oversight so that each agency's regulatory actions are consistent with applicable law, the President's priorities, and the principles set forth in this Executive order and do not conflict with the policies or actions of another agency. OIRA shall, to the extent permitted by law, adhere to the following guidelines:

(1) OIRA may review only actions identified by the agency or by OIRA as significant regulatory actions under subsection (a)(3)(A) of this section.

(2) OIRA shall waive review or notify the agency in writing of the results of its review within the following time periods:

(A) For any notices of inquiry, advance notices of proposed rulemaking, or other preliminary regulatory actions prior to a Notice of Proposed Rulemaking, within 10 working days after the date of submission of the draft action to OIRA;

(B) For all other regulatory actions, within 90 calendar days after the date of submission of the information set forth in subsections (a)(3)(B) and (C) of this section, unless OIRA has previously reviewed this information and, since that review, there has been no material change in the facts and circumstances upon which the regulatory action is based, in which case, OIRA shall complete its review within 45 days; and

(C) The review process may be extended (1) once by no more than 30 calendar days upon the written approval of the Director and (2) at the request of the agency head.

(3) For each regulatory action that the Administrator of OIRA returns to an agency for further consideration of some or all of its provisions, the Administrator of OIRA shall provide the issuing agency a written explanation for such return, setting forth the pertinent provision of this Executive order on which OIRA is relying. If the agency head disagrees with some or all of the bases for the return, the agency head shall so inform the Administrator of OIRA in writing.

(4) Except as otherwise provided by law or required by a Court, in order to ensure greater openness, accessibility, and accountability in the regulatory review process, OIRA shall be governed by the following disclosure requirements:

(A) Only the Administrator of OIRA (or a particular designee) shall receive oral communications initiated by persons not employed by the executive branch of the Federal Government regarding the substance of a regulatory action under OIRA review;

(B) All substantive communications between OIRA personnel and persons not employed by the executive branch of the Federal Government regarding a regulatory action under review shall be governed by the following guidelines: (i) A representative from the issuing agency shall be invited to any meeting between OIRA personnel and such person(s);

(ii) OIRA shall forward to the issuing agency, within 10 working days of receipt of the communication(s), all written communications, regardless of format, between OIRA personnel and any person who is not employed by the executive branch of the Federal Government, and the dates and names of individuals involved in all substantive oral communications (including meetings to which an agency representative was invited, but did not attend, and telephone conversations between OIRA personnel and any such persons); and

(iii) OIR shall publicly disclose relevant information about such communication(s), as set forth below in subsection (b)(4)(C) of this section.

(C) OIRA shall maintain a publicly available log that shall contain, at a minimum, the following information pertinent to regulatory actions under review:

(i) The status of all regulatory actions, including if (and if so, when and by whom) Presidential consideration was requested;

(ii) A notation of all written communications forwarded to an issuing agency under subsection (b)(4)(B)(ii) of this section; and

(iii) The dates and names of individuals involved in all substantive oral communications, including meetings and telephone conversations, between OIRA personnel and any person not employed by the executive branch of the Federal Government, and the subject matter discussed during such communications.

(D) After the regulatory action has been published in the Federal Register or otherwise issued to the public, or after the agency has announced its decision not to publish or issue the regulatory action, OIRA shall make available to the public all documents exchanged between OIRA and the agency during the review by OIRA under this section.

(5) All information provided to the public by OIRA shall be in plain, understandable language.

Sec. 7. Resolution of Conflicts.

(a) To the extent permitted by law, disagreements or conflicts between or among agency heads or between OMB and any agency that cannot be resolved by the Administrator of OIRA shall be resolved by the President, with the assistance of the Chief of Staff to the President ("Chief of Staff") with the relevant agency head (and, as appropriate, other interested government officials). Presidential consideration of such disagreements may be initiated only by the Director, by the head of the issuing agency, or by the head of an agency that has a significant interest in the regulatory action at issue. Such review will not be undertaken at the request of other persons, entities, or their agents.

(b) Resolution of such conflicts shall be informed by recommendations developed by the Chief of Staff, after consultation with the Advisors (and other executive branch officials or personnel whose responsibilities to the President include the subject matter at issue). The development of these recommendations shall be concluded within 60 days after review has been requested.

(c) During the Presidential review period, communications with any person not employed by the Federal Government relating to the substance of the regulatory action under review and directed to the Advisors or their staffs or to the staff of the Chief of Staff shall be in writing and shall be forwarded by the recipient to the affected agency(ies) for inclusion in the public docket(s). When the communication is not in writing, such Advisors or staff members shall inform the outside party that the matter is under review and that any comments should be submitted in writing.

(d) At the end of this review process, the President, or the Chief of Staff acting at the request of the President, shall notify the affected agency and the Administrator of OIRA of the President's decision with respect to the matter.

Sec. 8. Publication. Except to the extent required by law, an agency shall not publish in the Federal Register or otherwise issue to the public any regulatory action that is subject to review under section 6 of this Executive order until (1) the Administrator of OIRA notifies the agency that OIRA has waived its review of the action or has completed its review without any requests for further consideration, or (2) the applicable time period in section 6(b)(2) expires without OIRA having notified the agency that it is returning the regulatory action for further consideration under section 6(b)(3), whichever occurs first. If the terms of the preceding sentence have not been satisfied and an agency wants to publish or otherwise issue a regulatory action, the head of that agency may request Presidential consideration through the Director, as provided under section 7 of this order. Upon receipt of this request, the Director shall notify OIRA and the Advisors. The guidelines and time period set forth in section 7 shall apply to the publication of regulatory actions for which Presidential consideration has been sought.

Sec. 9. Agency Authority. Nothing in this order shall be construed as displacing the agencies' authority or responsibilities, as authorized by law.

Sec. 10. Judicial Review. Nothing in this Executive order shall affect any otherwise available judicial review of agency action. This Executive order is intended only to improve the internal management of the Federal Government and does not create any right or benefit, substantive or procedural, enforceable at law or equity by a party against the United States, its agencies or instrumentalities; its officers or employees, or any other person.

Sec. 11. Revocations. Executive Orders Nos. 12291 and 12498; all amendments to those Executive orders; all guidelines issued under those orders; and any exemptions from those orders heretofore granted for any category of rule are revoked.

WILLIAM J. CLINTON

THE WHITE HOUSE, September 30, 1993.

Appendix G

CONGRESSIONAL REVIEW OF AGENCY RULEMAKING

5 U.S.C., Chapter 8.

Sec. 801. Congressional review

(a)(1)(A) Before a rule can take effect, the Federal agency promulgating such rule shall submit to each House of the Congress and to the Comptroller General a report containing—

(i) a copy of the rule;

(ii) a concise general statement relating to the rule, including whether it is a major rule; and

(iii) the proposed effective date of the rule.

(B) On the date of the submission of the report under subparagraph (A), the Federal agency promulgating the rule shall submit to the Comptroller General and make available to each House of Congress—

(i) a complete copy of the cost-benefit analysis of the rule, if any;

(ii) the agency's actions relevant to sections 603, 604, 605, 607, and 609;

(iii) the agency's actions relevant to sections 202, 203, 204, and 205 of the Unfunded Mandates Reform Act of 1995; and

(iv) any other relevant information or requirements under any other Act and any relevant Executive orders.

(C) Upon receipt of a report submitted under subparagraph (A), each House shall provide copies of the report to the chairman and ranking member of each standing committee with jurisdiction under the rules of the House of Representatives or the Senate to report a bill to amend the provision of law under which the rule is issued.

(2)(A) The Comptroller General shall provide a report on each major rule to the committees of jurisdiction in each House of the Congress by the end of 15 calendar days after the submission or publication date as provided in section 802(b)(2). The report of the Comptroller General shall include an assessment of the agency's compliance with procedural steps required by paragraph (1)(B).

(B) Federal agencies shall cooperate with the Comptroller General by providing information relevant to the Comptroller General's report under subparagraph (A).

(3) A major rule relating to a report submitted under paragraph (1) shall take effect on the latest of—

(A) the later of the date occurring 60 days after the date on which—

(i) the Congress receives the report submitted under paragraph (1); or

(ii) the rule is published in the Federal Register, if so published;

(B) if the Congress passes a joint resolution of disapproval described in section 802 relating to the rule, and the President signs a veto of such resolution, the earlier date—

(i) on which either House of Congress votes and fails to override the veto of the President; or

(ii) occurring 30 session days after the date on which the Congress received the veto and objections of the President; or

(C) the date the rule would have otherwise taken effect, if not for this section (unless a joint resolution of disapproval under section 802 is enacted).

(4) Except for a major rule, a rule shall take effect as otherwise provided by law after submission to Congress under paragraph (1).

(5) Notwithstanding paragraph (3), the effective date of a rule shall not be delayed by operation of this chapter beyond the date on which either House of Congress votes to reject a joint resolution of disapproval under section 802.

(b)(1) A rule shall not take effect (or continue), if the Congress enacts a joint resolution of disapproval, described under section 802, of the rule.

(2) A rule that does not take effect (or does not continue) under paragraph (1) may not be reissued in substantially the same form, and a new rule that is substantially the same as such a rule may not be issued, unless the reissued or new rule is specifically authorized by a law enacted after the date of the joint resolution disapproving the original rule.

(c)(1) Notwithstanding any other provision of this section (except subject to paragraph (3)), a rule that would not take effect by reason of subsection (a)(3) may take effect, if the President makes a determination under paragraph (2) and submits written notice of such determination to the Congress.

(2) Paragraph (1) applies to a determination made by the President by Executive order that the rule should take effect because such rule is—

(A) necessary because of an imminent threat to health or safety or other emergency;

(B) necessary for the enforcement of criminal laws;

(C) necessary for national security; or

(D) issued pursuant to any statute implementing an international trade agreement.

(3) An exercise by the President of the authority under this subsection shall have no effect on the procedures under section 802 or the effect of a joint resolution of disapproval under this section.

(d)(1) In addition to the opportunity for review otherwise provided under this chapter, in the case of any rule for which a report was submitted in accordance with subsection (a)(1)(A) during the period beginning on the date occurring—

(A) in the case of the Senate, 60 session days, or

(B) in the case of the House of Representatives, 60 legislative days, before the date the Congress adjourns a session of Congress through the date on which the same or succeeding Congress first convenes its next session, section 802 shall apply to such rule in the succeeding session of Congress.

(2)(A) In applying section 802 for purposes of such additional review, a rule described under paragraph (1) shall be treated as though—

(i) such rule were published in the Federal Register (as a rule that shall take effect) on—(I) in the case of the Senate, the 15th session day, or (II) in the case of the House of Representatives, the 15th legislative day—after the succeeding session of Congress first convenes; and

(ii) a report on such rule were submitted to Congress under subsection (a)(1) on such date.

(B) Nothing in this paragraph shall be construed to affect the requirement under subsection (a)(1) that a report shall be submitted to Congress before a rule can take effect.

(3) A rule described under paragraph (1) shall take effect as otherwise provided by law (including other subsections of this section).

(e)(1) For purposes of this subsection, section 802 shall also apply to any major rule promulgated between March 1, 1996, and the date of the enactment of this chapter.

(2) In applying section 802 for purposes of Congressional review, a rule described under paragraph (1) shall be treated as though—

(A) such rule were published in the Federal Register on the date of enactment of this chapter; and

(B) a report on such rule were submitted to Congress under subsection (a)(1) on such date.

(3) The effectiveness of a rule described under paragraph (1) shall be as otherwise provided by law, unless the rule is made of no force or effect under section 802.

(f) Any rule that takes effect and later is made of no force or effect by enactment of a joint resolution under section 802 shall be treated as though such rule had never taken effect.

(g) If the Congress does not enact a joint resolution of disapproval under section 802 respecting a rule, no court or agency may infer any intent of the Congress from any action or inaction of the Congress with regard to such rule, related statute, or joint resolution of disapproval.

Sec. 802. Congressional disapproval procedure

(a) For purposes of this section, the term "joint resolution" means only a joint resolution introduced in the period beginning on the date on which the report referred to in section 801(a)(1)(A) is received by Congress and ending 60 days thereafter (excluding days either House of Congress is adjourned for more than 3 days during a session of Congress), the matter after the resolving clause of which is as follows: "That Congress disapproves the rule submitted by the ___ relating to ___, and such rule shall have no force or effect." (The blank spaces being appropriately filled in).

(b)(1) A joint resolution described in subsection (a) shall be referred to the committees in each House of Congress with jurisdiction.

(2) For purposes of this section, the term "submission or publication date" means the later of the date on which—

(A) the Congress receives the report submitted under section 801(a)(1); or

(B) the rule is published in the Federal Register, if so published.

(c) In the Senate, if the committee to which is referred a joint resolution described in subsection (a) has not reported such joint resolution (or an identical joint resolution) at the end of 20 calendar days after the submission or publication date defined under subsection (b)(2), such committee may be discharged from further consideration of such joint resolution upon a petition supported in writing by 30 Members of the Senate, and such joint resolution shall be placed on the calendar.

(d)(1) In the Senate, when the committee to which a joint resolution is referred has reported, or when a committee is discharged (under subsection (c)) from further consideration of a joint resolution described in subsection (a), it is at any time thereafter in order (even though a previous motion to the same effect has been disagreed to) for a motion to proceed to the consideration of the joint resolution, and all points of order against the joint resolution (and against consideration of the joint resolution) are waived. The motion is not subject to amendment, or to a motion to postpone, or to a motion to proceed to the consideration of other business. A motion to reconsider the vote by which the motion is agreed to or disagreed to shall not be in order. If a motion to proceed to the consideration of the joint resolution is agreed to, the joint resolution shall remain the unfinished business of the Senate until disposed of.

(2) In the Senate, debate on the joint resolution, and on all debatable motions and appeals in connection therewith, shall be limited to not more than 10 hours, which shall be divided equally between those favoring and those opposing the joint resolution. A motion further to limit debate is in order and not debatable. An amendment to, or a motion to postpone, or a motion to proceed to the consideration of other business, or a motion to recommit the joint resolution is not in order.

(3) In the Senate, immediately following the conclusion of the debate on a joint resolution described in subsection (a), and a single quorum call at the conclusion of the debate if requested in accordance with the rules of the Senate, the vote on final passage of the joint resolution shall occur.

(4) Appeals from the decisions of the Chair relating to the application of the rules of the Senate to the procedure relating to a joint resolution described in subsection (a) shall be decided without debate.

(e) In the Senate the procedure specified in subsection (c) or (d) shall not apply to the consideration of a joint resolution respecting a rule—

(1) after the expiration of the 60 session days beginning with the applicable submission or publication date, or

(2) if the report under section 801(a)(1)(A) was submitted during the period referred to in section 801(d)(1), after the expiration of the 60 session days beginning on the 15th session day after the succeeding session of Congress first convenes.

(f) If, before the passage by one House of a joint resolution of that House described in subsection (a), that House receives from the other House a joint resolution described in subsection (a), then the following procedures shall apply:

(1) The joint resolution of the other House shall not be referred to a committee.

(2) With respect to a joint resolution described in subsection (a) of the House receiving the joint resolution—

(A) the procedure in that House shall be the same as if no joint resolution had been received from the other House; but

(B) the vote on final passage shall be on the joint resolution of the other House.

(g) This section is enacted by Congress—

(1) as an exercise of the rulemaking power of the Senate and House of Representatives, respectively, and as such it is deemed a part of the rules of each House, respectively, but applicable only with respect to the procedure to be followed in that House in the case of a joint resolution described in subsection (a), and it supersedes other rules only to the extent that it is inconsistent with such rules; and

(2) with full recognition of the constitutional right of either House to change the rules (so far as relating to the procedure of that House) at any time, in the same manner, and to the same extent as in the case of any other rule of that House.

Sec. 803. Special rule on statutory, regulatory, and judicial deadlines

(a) In the case of any deadline for, relating to, or involving any rule which does not take effect (or the effectiveness of which is terminated) because of enactment of a joint resolution under section 802, that deadline is extended until the date 1 year after the date of enactment of the joint resolution. Nothing in this subsection shall be construed to affect a deadline merely by reason of the postponement of a rule's effective date under section 801(a).

(b) The term "deadline" means any date certain for fulfilling any obligation or exercising any authority established by or under any Federal statute or regulation, or by or under any court order implementing any Federal statute or regulation.

Sec. 804. Definitions

For purposes of this chapter—

(1) The term "Federal agency" means any agency as that term is defined in section 551(1).

(2) The term "major rule" means any rule that the Administrator of the Office of Information and Regulatory Affairs of the Office of Management and Budget finds has resulted in or is likely to result in—

(A) an annual effect on the economy of $100,000,000 or more;

(B) a major increase in costs or prices for consumers, individual industries, Federal, State, or local government agencies, or geographic regions; or

(C) significant adverse effects on competition, employment, investment, productivity, innovation, or on the ability of United States-based enterprises to compete with foreign-based enterprises in domestic and export markets.

The term does not include any rule promulgated under the Telecommunications Act of 1996 and the amendments made by that Act.

(3) The term "rule" has the meaning given such term in section 551, except that such term does not include—

(A) any rule of particular applicability, including a rule that approves or prescribes for the future rates, wages, prices, services, or allowances therefor, corporate or financial structures, reorganizations, mergers, or acquisitions thereof, or accounting practices or disclosures bearing on any of the foregoing;

(B) any rule relating to agency management or personnel; or

(C) any rule of agency organization, procedure, or practice that does not substantially affect the rights or obligations of non-agency parties.

Sec. 805. Judicial review

No determination, finding, action, or omission under this chapter shall be subject to judicial review.

Sec. 806. Applicability; severability

(a) This chapter shall apply notwithstanding any other provision of law.

(b) If any provision of this chapter or the application of any provision of this chapter to any person or circumstance, is held invalid, the application of such provision to other persons or circumstances, and the remainder of this chapter, shall not be affected thereby.

Sec. 807. Exemption for monetary policy

Nothing in this chapter shall apply to rules that concern monetary policy proposed or implemented by the Board of Governors of the Federal Reserve System or the Federal Open Market Committee.

Sec. 808. Effective date of certain rules

Notwithstanding section 801—

(1) any rule that establishes, modifies, opens, closes, or conducts a regulatory program for a commercial, recreational, or subsistence activity related to hunting, fishing, or camping, or

(2) any rule which an agency for good cause finds (and incorporates the finding and a brief statement of reasons therefor in the rule issued) that notice and public procedure thereon are impracticable, unnecessary, or contrary to the public interest, shall take effect at such time as the Federal agency promulgating the rule determines.

Index

References are to Pages

References are to Pages

†

0–314–14425–0
90000
9 780314 144256